THE DORLING KINDERSLEY

VISUAL
Encyclopedia

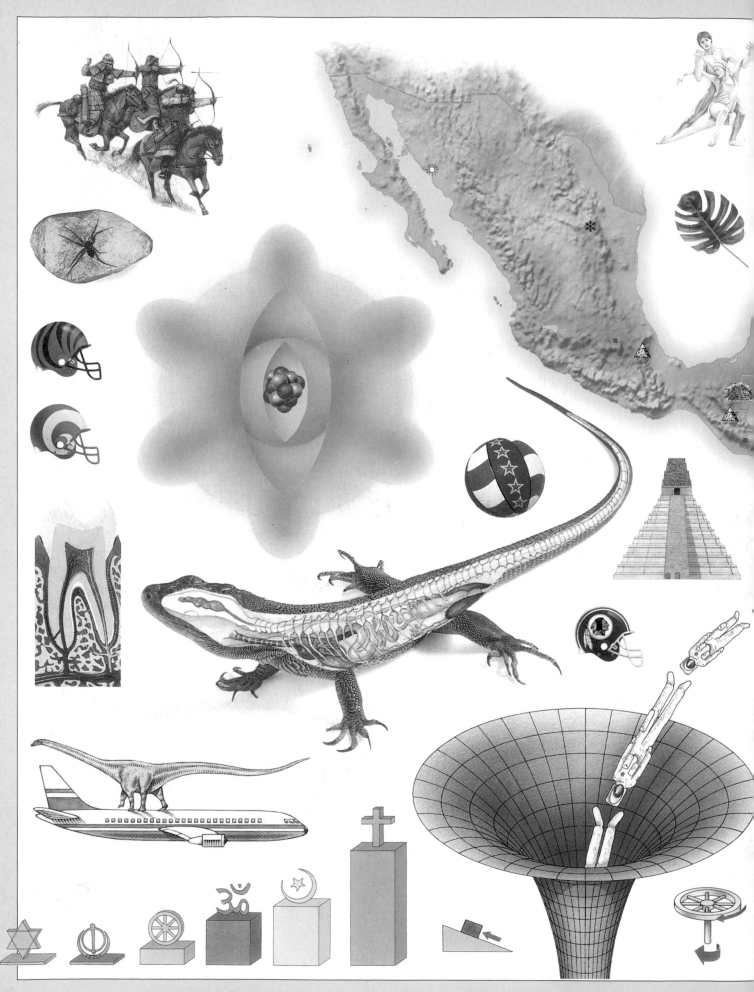

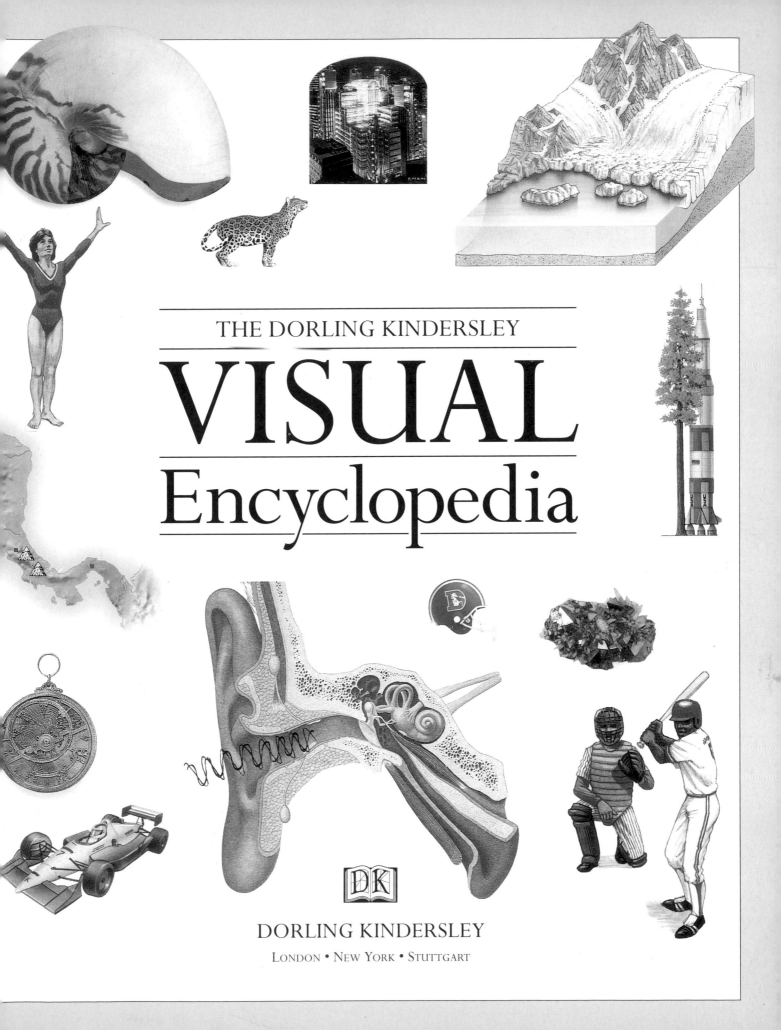

THE DORLING KINDERSLEY
VISUAL
Encyclopedia

DORLING KINDERSLEY

LONDON • NEW YORK • STUTTGART

A DORLING KINDERSLEY BOOK

Senior Editor Anna Kruger **Senior Art Editor** Gillian Shaw

Section Editors
Sue Copsey, Marie Greenwood, Fran K. Jones, James Pickford

Editors
Huw Clough, Carey Denton, Deborah Murrell

US Editor
Jill Hamilton

Art Editors
Shirley Gwillym, Rebecca Johns, Floyd Sayers, Dominic Zwemmer

Designers
Wayne Holder, Marcus James, Joanna Pocock, Wilfrid Wood

DTP Designers
Mathew Birch, Carol Titchener, Noel Barnes

Picture Manager
Lorna Ainger

Research and Editorial Assistance
Alex Tinley, Leo Vita-Finzi, Tim Hetherington, Giles Portman, Deslie Lawrence

Production
Catherine Semark, Samantha Larmour

Deputy Editorial Director Sophie Mitchell **Deputy Art Director** Miranda Kennedy

Models in Human Body section are original SOMSO models

First American Edition, 1995
2 4 6 8 10 9 7 5 3 1

Published in the United States by
Dorling Kindersley Publishing, Inc.,
95 Madison Avenue
New York, New York 10016

Library of Congress Cataloging-in-Publication Data
The Dorling Kindersley visual encyclopedia
p.   cm.
Includes index.
ISBN 1-56458-985-4
1. Children's encyclopedias and dictionaries.
AG5.D72   1994
031- - dc20   94-45785
                                                CIP

Reproduced by Colourscan, Singapore
Printed and bound in Italy by New Interlitho

CONSULTANTS

UNIVERSE
Professor Heather Couper
Television and radio broadcaster. Past president of the British Astronomical Assoociation. International author.
Nigel Henbest
International writer and science broadcaster. Past consultant, Royal Greenwich Observatory and the Science and Engineering Research Coucil.
Doug Millard
Associate curator, Space Technology, Science Museum, London.

EARTH
Maurice Crewe
Fellow, Royal Meteorological Society.
Cally Hall
Museum geologist, Mineralogy Department, Natural History Museum, London.
Donna Rispoli
Ecology and energy consultant.
Bob Symes
Associate keeper, Department of Mineralogy, Natural History Museum, London.
Barbara Taylor
Internationally acclaimed science and natural history writer.
Warren Yasso
Professor of Natural Sciences, Teachers College, Columbia University. Textbook author.

LIVING WORLD
Keith Banister
Government consultant on fisheries, broadcaster, writer.
David Burnie
Zoologist, biologist, and internationally acclaimed writer of science and nature books.
Barry Clarke
Curator, Amphibians, Natural History Museum, London.
Joseph DiCostanzo
Researcher, Great Gull Island Project, American Museum of Natural History. Past president, Linnaean Society of New York.
Theresa Greenaway
Botanist and natural history author.
Miranda Macquitty
Zoologist and best-selling natural history author.

Matthew Robertson
Professional entomologist. Former Head Keeper, Invertebrate House, London Zoo.
Ray Rogers
Horticulturist and gardening editor.

HUMAN BODY
Dr. Sarah Brewer
General practitioner and medical author.
Dr. Thaddeus M. Yablonsky
Physician and medical consultant.

BELIEFS, CUSTOMS, AND SOCIETY
W. Owen Cole
Lecturer and writer in religious studies.
John Gray
Fellow in Politics, Jesus College, University of Oxford.
John Keyworth
Curator, Museum of the Bank of England.
James Nicholson
Financial journalist, *Guardian* newspaper.
Helen Watson
Lecturer in Anthropology; Fellow St. John's College, University of Cambridge.

ARTS AND THE MEDIA
Christopher Cook
Documentary film maker and arts presenter for BBC Radio. Film advisor, National Gallery, London.
Alistair Niven
Literature Director, Arts Council of England
Brigid Pepin
Lecturer Art History and Architecture, University of North London.
Penelope Vita-Finzi
Former lecturer, English Literature and Theatre, Thames Valley University, England.
Rodney Wilson
Film, Video, and Broadcasting Director, Arts Council of England.
Ann Wingate
Independent film producer, including *Howards End*

SPORTS
Norman Barrett
Sports writer and consultant.
David Heidenstam
Sports writer and editor.

SCIENCE
Peter Bailes
Collections information manager Science Museum, London.
Marina Benjamin
Science writer and journalist.
Jack Challoner
Formerly with the Education Unit, Science Museum, London. Science author.
Eryl Davies
Science and technology writer and consultant.
Kimi Hosoume
Mathematics and science educator, Lawrence Hall, University of California at Berkeley.
Carole Stott
Former curator of Astronomy, Greenwich Royal Observatory, London. Science author.

TRANSPORTATION, COMMUNICATIONS, AND INDUSTRY
Christine Heap
Curator, National Railway Museum, York, England.
Eric Kentley
Curator, National Maritime Museum, London.
Bob McWilliam
Senior curator, Civil Engineering, Science Museum, London.
Andrew Nahum
Senior curator, Aeronautics, Science Museum, London.
Lynda Springate, Anice Collette, Marie Tieche
Curators, National Motor Museum, Beaulieu, England.

INTERNATIONAL WORLD
Dorling Kindersley Cartography in conjunction with leading cartographic consultants, embassies, and consulates.

HISTORY
Brian Dooley
Political journalist. Former Senate aide to Edward Kennedy.
Margaret Mulvihill
Historian and writer.
Philip Wilkinson
Historian and writer.
Charles S. Wills
US History consultant.

HOW TO USE THIS BOOK

EACH PAGE OR DOUBLE-PAGE spread in *The Visual Encyclopedia* is a self-contained unit, carefully designed to present the maximum number of facts about its subject in the most accessible manner. Information on each page follows a clear, logical order, beginning with the main feature and most important factual topics, then moving on to records, strange comparisons, and fascinating, collectible facts.

Main feature
Focuses on the subject and provides the most important facts.

Running head – thematic
Tells readers which thematic section they are in.

Introduction
A brief text introduction defines the subject and provides a number of key facts.

Topic headings
Easy-to-find topic headings draw the reader to subfeatures within the main subject. Each page contains an average of 10 subject-related topics.

Detailed artwork
Stunning, full-color cutaway artwork stimulates learning and provides maximum information.

Key facts
Bulleted key facts and figures give the reader the most essential facts at a glance.

Boxed types
To provide maximum information, an example of every major type of plant, animal, or object is illustrated.

Clear labels and annotation
Identify types and special features and clarify complex information.

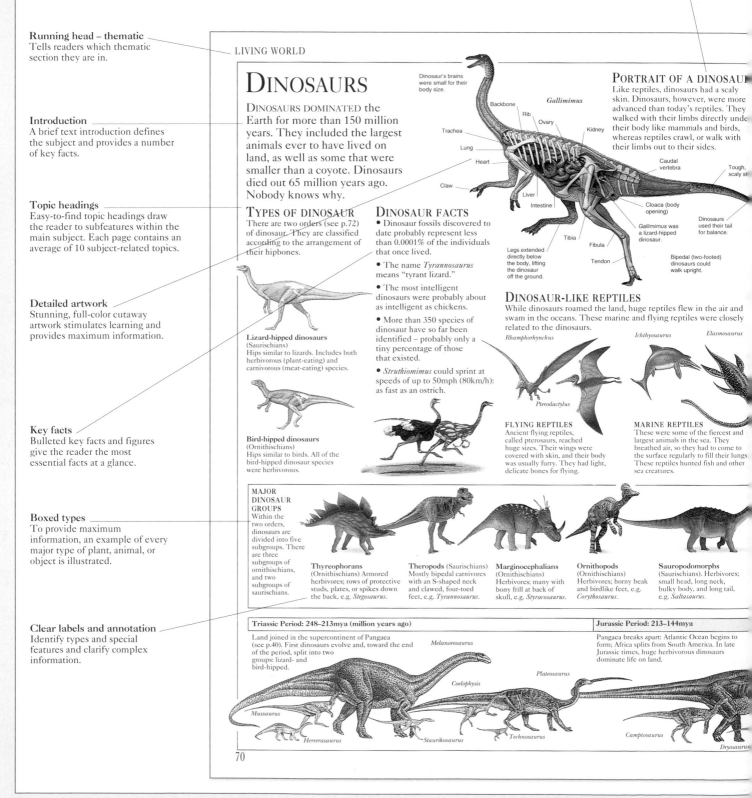

LIVING WORLD

DINOSAURS

DINOSAURS DOMINATED the Earth for more than 150 million years. They included the largest animals ever to have lived on land, as well as some that were smaller than a coyote. Dinosaurs died out 65 million years ago. Nobody knows why.

TYPES OF DINOSAUR
There are two orders (see p.72) of dinosaur. They are classified according to the arrangement of their hipbones.

Lizard-hipped dinosaurs (Saurischians)
Hips similar to lizards. Includes both herbivorous (plant-eating) and carnivorous (meat-eating) species.

Bird-hipped dinosaurs (Ornithischians)
Hips similar to birds. All of the bird-hipped dinosaur species were herbivorous.

DINOSAUR FACTS
• Dinosaur fossils discovered to date probably represent less than 0.0001% of the individuals that once lived.

• The name *Tyrannosaurus* means "tyrant lizard."

• The most intelligent dinosaurs were probably about as intelligent as chickens.

• More than 350 species of dinosaur have so far been identified – probably only a tiny percentage of those that existed.

• *Struthiomimus* could sprint at speeds of up to 50mph (80km/h): as fast as an ostrich.

PORTRAIT OF A DINOSAUR
Like reptiles, dinosaurs had a scaly skin. Dinosaurs, however, were more advanced than today's reptiles. They walked with their limbs directly under their body like mammals and birds, whereas reptiles crawl, or walk with their limbs out to their sides.

Dinosaur's brains were small for their body size.

Backbone
Gallimimus
Rib
Ovary
Trachea
Kidney
Lung
Heart
Caudal vertebra
Claw
Tough, scaly sk
Liver
Intestine
Cloaca (body opening)
Gallimimus was a lizard-hipped dinosaur.
Dinosaurs used their tail for balance.
Tibia
Fibula
Legs extended directly below the body, lifting the dinosaur off the ground.
Tendon
Bipedal (two-footed) dinosaurs could walk upright.

DINOSAUR-LIKE REPTILES
While dinosaurs roamed the land, huge reptiles flew in the air and swam in the oceans. These marine and flying reptiles were closely related to the dinosaurs.

Rhamphorhynchus
Ichthyosaurus
Elasmosaurus
Pterodactylus

FLYING REPTILES
Ancient flying reptiles, called pterosaurs, reached huge sizes. Their wings were covered with skin, and their body was usually furry. They had light, delicate bones for flying.

MARINE REPTILES
These were some of the fiercest and largest animals in the sea. They breathed air, so they had to come to the surface regularly to fill their lungs. These reptiles hunted fish and other sea creatures.

MAJOR DINOSAUR GROUPS
Within the two orders, dinosaurs are divided into five subgroups. There are three subgroups of ornithischians, and two subgroups of saurischians.

Thyreophorans (Ornithischians) Armored herbivores; rows of protective studs, plates, or spikes down the back, e.g. *Stegosaurus*.

Theropods (Saurischians) Mostly bipedal carnivores with an S-shaped neck and clawed, four-toed feet, e.g. *Tyrannosaurus*.

Marginocephalians (Ornithischians) Herbivores; many with bony frill at back of skull, e.g. *Styracosaurus*.

Ornithopods (Ornithischians) Herbivores; horny beak and birdlike feet, e.g. *Corythosaurus*.

Sauropodomorphs (Saurischians). Herbivores; small head, long neck, bulky body, and long tail, e.g. *Saltasaurus*.

Triassic Period: 248–213mya (million years ago)
Land joined in the supercontinent of Pangaea (see p.40). First dinosaurs evolve and, toward the end of the period, split into two groups: lizard- and bird-hipped.

Jurassic Period: 213–144mya
Pangaea breaks apart: Atlantic Ocean begins to form; Africa splits from South America. In late Jurassic times, huge herbivorous dinosaurs dominate life on land.

Melanorosaurus
Coelophysis
Plateosaurus
Mussaurus
Herrerasaurus
Staurikosaurus
Technosaurus
Camptosaurus
Dryosaurus

70

MEASUREMENTS AND ABBREVIATIONS

Some words and measurements are abbreviated, or shortened, in *The Visual Encyclopedia*. The following list explains what the abbreviations stand for:

°C = degrees Celsius
°F = degrees Fahrenheit
mm = millimeter
cm = centimeter
m = meter
km = kilometer
sq km = square kilometer
km/h = kilometers per hour
in = inch

ft = foot
yd = yard
sq mile = square mile
mph = miles per hour
g = gram
kg = kilogram
oz = ounce
lb = pound
c. before a date = about

B.C. = before Christ
A.D. = Anno Domini, after the birth of Christ
b. = born
r. = reigned
d. = died
CIS = Commonwealth of Independent States (formerly Russia)

DINOSAURS

DINOSAUR DISCOVERY

Pre-19th century: around the world, dinosaur fossils are believed to be various things, including dragon bones in China, and giant human bones in parts of Europe.

1800 Dinosaur footprints found in Massachusetts. Their discoverer claims they were made by the raven from Noah's Ark.

1820 *Iguanodon* teeth discovered in Tilgate Forest, Sussex, England, by doctor and fossil hunter Gideon Mantell (1790–1852) and his wife. He suspects they are the remains of ancient reptiles, but his theory is dismissed as heretical (antireligious).

1834 First glimpse of what dinosaurs looked like provided by find of a partial skeleton near Maidstone, England, known as the Maidstone *Iguanodon*.

1841 The term dinosaur, from the Greek words for "terrible" and "lizard," is coined by English anatomist Richard Owen (1804–92).

1800 · 1800 · 1820 · 1820 · 1830 · 1834 · 1840 · 1841

1851 First reconstruction of dinosaurs: *Iguanodon* and *Hylaeosaurus* models are made for the Great Exhibition at Crystal Palace, London, England. Results in huge public enthusiasm for dinosaurs. Before the *Iguanodon* is completed, the sculptor holds a dinner party inside it. *Dinner party in a model dinosaur*

1877 One of the greatest dinosaur collections found at Como Bluff, Wyoming, by O.C. Marsh (1831–99) of Yale.

1947 Largest number of dinosaurs ever found together: more than 100 *Coelophysis* skeletons.

1987 Evidence to support theory of warm-blooded dinosaurs found by paleontologists Tom Rich and Patricia Vickers-Rich of the Museum of Victoria, Australia. They discover dinosaur fossils in a part of South Australia that would have been inside the Antarctic Circle when these dinosaurs lived. The mean annual temperature in this region would have been near freezing at that time.

Leaellynasaura lived in polar regions.

1850 · 1851 · 1870 · 1877 · 1940 · 1947 · 1980 · 1987

DINOSAUR RECORDS

SMALLEST DINOSAUR was probably *Wannanosaurus*, a bipedal carnivore that measured 2ft (60cm) long. It was about the size of a chicken.

MOST PRIMITIVE KNOWN DINOSAUR is *Eoraptor*, a 228 million-year-old bipedal carnivore that was about the size of a large dog.

SMALLEST DINOSAUR BRAIN is believed to have been that of the *Stegosaurus*. It was less than 2in (5cm) long.

LARGEST DINOSAUR EGGS were probably those of *Hypselosaurus*. They measured about 12in (30cm) long and contained an estimated 7 pints (3.3 liters) of fluid: roughly the same as the fluid in 60 hens' eggs.

EARTH SHAKER
The name *Seismosaurus* means "earth-shaking lizard." This enormous plant-eating dinosaur was 131ft (40m) in length: longer than an Airbus A320.

LARGEST CARNIVORES

Dinosaur	Estimated length	
	m	ft
Acrocanthosaurus	12	39
Tyrannosaurus	12	39
Aliwalia	11	36
Allosaurus	11	36

LARGEST HERBIVORES

Dinosaur	Estimated length	
	m	ft
Seismosaurus	40	131
Barosaurus	27	89
Diplodocus	27	89
Brachiosaurus	25	82

WIDER GLIDER
The largest flying animal ever to have existed was *Quetzalcoatlus*, a flying reptile. Its wingspan measured about 39ft (12m) across: wider than the wingspan of a hang glider.

EXTINCTION THEORIES
About 65 million years ago the dinosaurs, together with many other animal species, became extinct. Other animal groups, including turtles, frogs, birds, and mammals, survived. There are many theories for this mass extinction: below are two of the most widely accepted.

GRADUAL EXTINCTION
Gradual changes in climate and vegetation caused by continental drift (see p.40) led to the dinosaurs' slow extinction over about 50,000 years. Warm, tropical conditions were replaced by cooler, more seasonal climates, and mammals slowly replaced dinosaurs as the dominant animal group.

CATASTROPHES
The period when dinosaurs were dying out coincided with many volcanic eruptions in India. At the same time, a huge meteorite hit the Earth. Dust thrown into the atmosphere blocked out sunlight, and dinosaurs could not survive the resulting climate changes.

Cretaceous Period: 144–65mya — 65mya

Continents split farther apart, eventually drifting into their present-day positions. Dinosaurs continue to flourish; those on different continents evolve separately, leading to great diversity.

Dinosaurs become extinct, together with many other animal species.

Diplodocus · *Stegosaurus* · *Allosaurus* · *Scelidosaurus* · *Deinonychus* · *Hypsilophodon* · *Iguanodon* · *Saltasaurus* · *Tyrannosaurus* · *Torosaurus*

71

Running head – by subject
Helps guide readers to the subject they want to find out about.

Timelines
Present and illustrate key historical dates, people, events, and developments for every subject.

Topic headings
Each main topic has its own look-up heading. There are 12 separate topics on this spread.

Exciting visual comparisons
Bring facts to life and make them memorable by placing them into interesting and unusual contexts.

Records
Provide the reader with all the record-breaking features: smallest, largest, fastest, slowest, earliest, and latest of every subject.

Data tables
Give the reader essential data in an immediately accessible form.

Detailed captions
Expand on the subject and reinforce the image.

Amazing facts
Words and pictures combine to present little-known or amazing and unusual facts.

Page size
The Dinosaurs spread is shown slightly smaller than actual size.

CONTENTS

Earth's tectonic plates

Jupiter

Vostok
119.5ft (36.4m)

Saturn V
363ft (110.6m)

67 LIVING WORLD

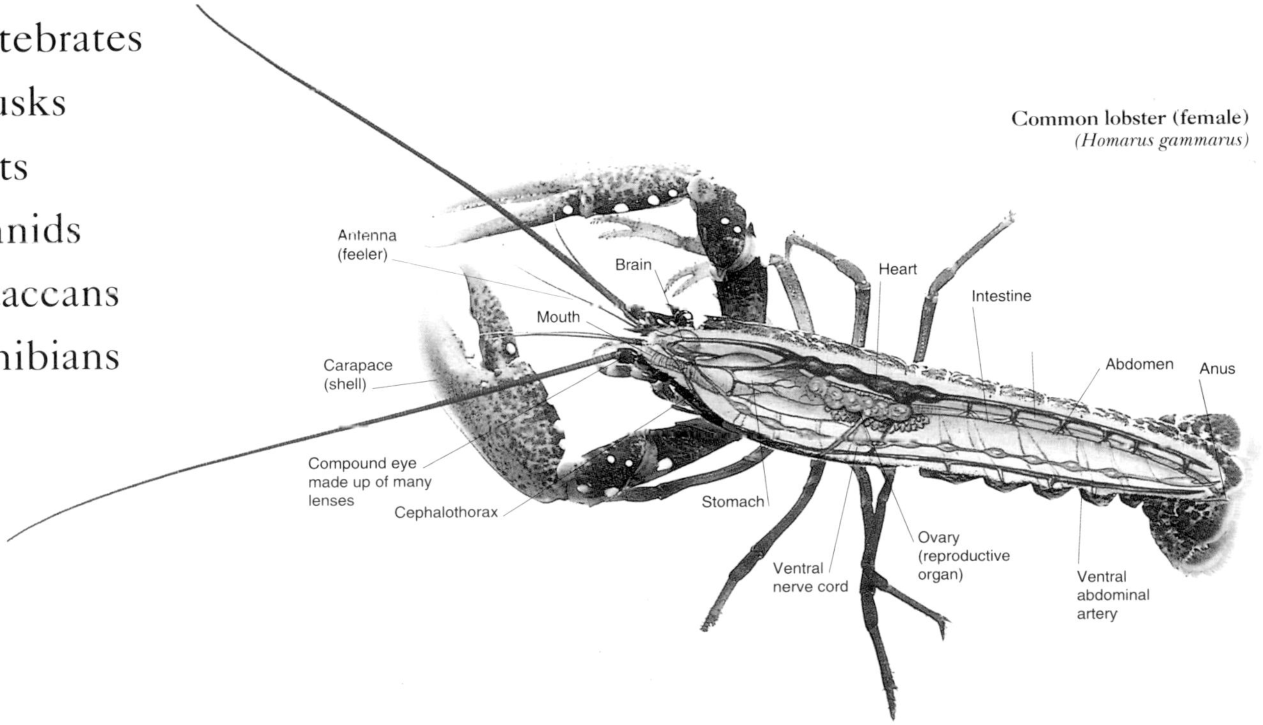

Common lobster (female)
(Homarus gammarus)

Antenna (feeler)

Brain

Heart

Intestine

Mouth

Abdomen

Anus

Carapace (shell)

Compound eye made up of many lenses

Cephalothorax

Stomach

Ventral nerve cord

Ovary (reproductive organ)

Ventral abdominal artery

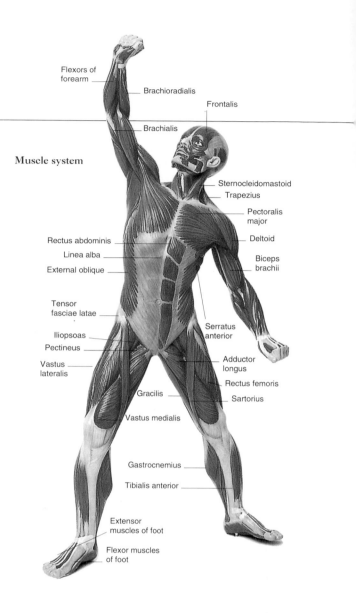

Muscle system

Flexors of forearm
Brachioradialis
Frontalis
Brachialis
Sternocleidomastoid
Trapezius
Pectoralis major
Rectus abdominis
Linea alba
External oblique
Deltoid
Biceps brachii
Tensor fasciae latae
Iliopsoas
Pectineus
Vastus lateralis
Serratus anterior
Adductor longus
Rectus femoris
Sartorius
Gracilis
Vastus medialis
Gastrocnemius
Tibialis anterior
Extensor muscles of foot
Flexor muscles of foot

113 HUMAN BODY

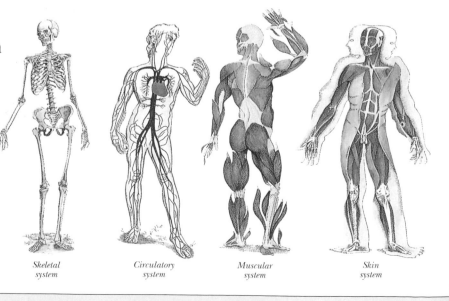

Body systems

Skeletal system   *Circulatory system*   *Muscular system*   *Skin system*

155 ARTS AND THE MEDIA

Welsh guard   *Nun*   *Bolivian dancer*   *Arab woman*

137 BELIEFS, CUSTOMS, AND SOCIETY

Phenakistoscope

11

Two-person dinghy

Vaulting over

Pole vault

219 Science and Technology

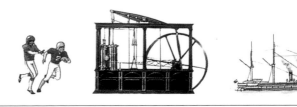

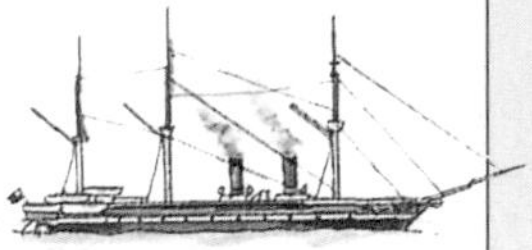

Isotopes

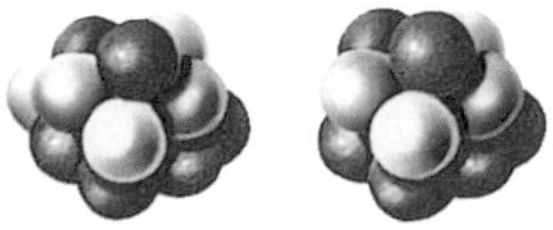

Fluorine–18 nucleus

Fluorine–19 nucleus

251 Transportation, Communications, and Industry

Nuclear-powered submarine

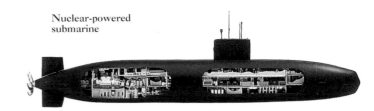

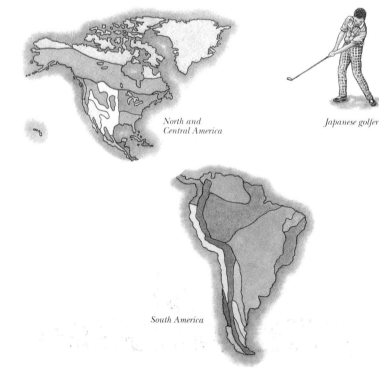

North and Central America

South America

Japanese golfer

Traditional Arab headdress

Bulgarians with rose petals

Decorative Islamic faceveil

West African children

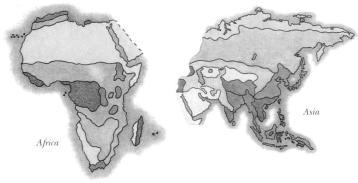

Africa

Asia

African elephants   Giraffe   Mountain gorilla

Kazakh yurts

UNIVERSE AND SPACE

Starting with the formation and scale of the known Universe, and including the latest theories about how it might end, this section provides facts and figures about every aspect of outer space. Vital statistics are given for planets, stars, the Moon, comets, meteors, and asteroids, as well as key dates in space exploration and great discoveries in astronomy.

Universe • Stars • Night Skies • Sun and Solar System
Planets • Moon • Comets, Meteors, and Asteroids • Astronomy
Space Exploration • Rockets

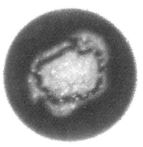

UNIVERSE

THE KNOWN UNIVERSE contains an estimated 100 billion galaxies. They are grouped in massive superclusters and separated by vast empty spaces.

EVOLUTION OF THE KNOWN UNIVERSE

The Universe is thought to have exploded into existence 15 billion years ago at the Big Bang. 300,000 years later ripples of matter began to form, followed 11.2 billion years later by the first known life forms.

15 billion years ago
At the time of the Big Bang, all matter and energy is concentrated into a single, tiny point.

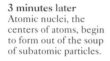

3 minutes later
Atomic nuclei, the centers of atoms, begin to form out of the soup of subatomic particles.

300,000 years after Big Bang
The first ripples of matter emerge.

14 billion years ago
One billion years after Big Bang, the first galaxies evolve. Light from their stars begins its journey across space.

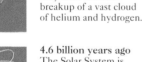

13 billion years ago
The stars of the Milky Way form from the breakup of a vast cloud of helium and hydrogen.

4.6 billion years ago
The Solar System is born out of a whirling cloud of gas studded with ice and rock.

3.8 billion years ago
Life evolves on Earth, the only planet known in the Universe to support living things.

FUTURE OF THE UNIVERSE

The empty spaces of the Universe may be full of dark matter, whose nature is not yet known. The strong gravitational pull of such vast amounts of matter may eventually reverse the expansion of the Universe and compress all of it in a Big Crunch.

AFTER BIG BANG
The Universe could follow different courses.

Big Bang
A huge explosion creates all existing matter.

Evolution
Stars and galaxies form.

The next Universe?
After Big Crunch the Universe may end or it may be reborn in an entirely new form.

Turning point
Dark matter begins to drag in all the galaxies.

Big Crunch
All matter is contracted into a single point of infinite density.

Present day
The Universe expands.

Eternal Expansion
The Universe could expand forever. Without dark matter, galaxies become enormous black holes. These eventually evaporate as subatomic particles.

Expansion or Contraction?
The Universe may grow forever or reach a maximum size.

COBE
In 1992, data from COBE (Cosmic Background Explorer satellite) found evidence for the first ripples of matter in the Universe. This suggests that the Universe is heading toward a Big Crunch.

FAMOUS COSMOLOGISTS

Cosmologists study the origin and structure of the Universe.

Sir Isaac Newton (1642–1727) laid the foundations of modern astronomy with his theory of Universal Gravity. He stated that it was gravity that held the planets in their orbits.

Max Planck (1858–1947) published his quantum theory concerning the nature of energy in 1900. It explained that light could take the form of waves or particles.

Albert Einstein (1879–1955) explained with his theories of relativity that light was the fastest thing in the Universe, and that matter and energy were the same thing.

Edwin Hubble (1889–1953) provided the first strong evidence that the Universe was expanding. In 1924 he discovered galaxies beyond the Milky Way.

Arno Penzias (born 1933) **Robert Wilson** (born 1936) discovered a constant level of background radiation in the Universe, said to be left over from the Big Bang.

Stephen Hawking (born 1942) made major discoveries about the nature of black holes and contributed greatly to our understanding of gravity.

UNIVERSE SCALE

The Universe spans more than 30 billion light-years. A light-year, the distance light travels in one year, is equal to 5,879 billion miles (9,461 billion km).

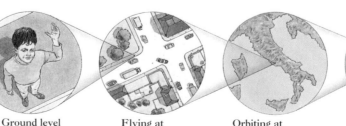
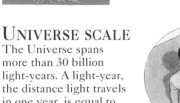

Ground level

Flying at low altitude
0.6 mile (1km)

Orbiting at high altitude
620 miles (1,000km)

Earth from space
62,000 miles (100,000km)

Earth and Moon
620,000 miles (1 million km)

GALAXY TYPES

Galaxies are huge families of stars held together by their own gravity. They take different forms. The Milky Way is a spiral galaxy. Other types include elliptical, barred spiral, and irregular galaxies.

SPIRAL
Spiral galaxies are shaped like disks. They have two or more curved arms of densely packed stars that rotate around a central bulge.

BARRED SPIRAL
Barred spiral galaxies have a rigid central bar with spiral arms beginning at the bar's ends. The central bar, made up of millions of stars, rotates.

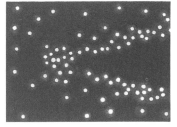

ELLIPTICAL
All the stars in elliptical galaxies formed at the same time. Elliptical galaxies range from the smallest to the largest galaxies of all.

CANNIBAL
Cannibal galaxies are a type of elliptical galaxy. They are so massive and exert such a powerful gravitational pull that they swallow up smaller galaxies.

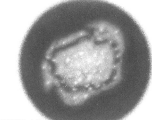

IRREGULAR
Irregular galaxies have no definite shape and are small in size. New stars continue to form inside them and they are rich in gas and dust.

MAJOR NEARBY GALAXIES

Galaxy	Type	Mass (billion solar masses)	Distance (light-years)
Andromeda (M 31)	Spiral	300	2,200,000
Milky Way galaxy	Spiral	150	0
Galaxy in Triangulum (M 33)	Spiral	10	2,400,000
Large Magellanic Cloud	Irregular	10	170,000
NGC 205	Elliptical	10	2,200,000
NGC 221	Elliptical	3	2,200,000
Small Magellanic Cloud	Irregular	2	190,000
NGC 185	Elliptical	1	2,200,000
NGC 147	Elliptical	1	2,200,000

COSMIC DUST AND THE ZONE OF AVOIDANCE

A cosmic dust grain is about ten billionths of an inch in diameter, smaller than a particle of smoke. Clouds of these grains dim our view of the Universe by scattering the light from stars. Until the invention of radio astronomy, parts of our galaxy were hidden.

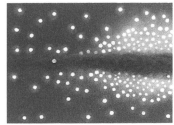

The Zone of Avoidance
Before the 1950s, astronomers were puzzled that a dark, empty zone appeared to stretch around the sky, avoided by stars and distant galaxies.

Exposing the Zone
New instruments were able to peer through the veil of dust. They revealed new stars and gas clouds at the galactic center, and many distant galaxies.

MILKY WAY DATA

Age	About 13 billion years
Number of stars	200 billion
Diameter	100,000 light-years
Maximum thickness	20,000 light-years
Thickness at Sun	700 light-years
Distance of Sun from galactic center	25,000 light-years
Time taken for Sun to orbit galactic center	240 million years

GALACTIC CENTER

This radio picture shows the center of the Milky Way galaxy. It is a hot region of stars, possibly containing a black hole.

QUASAR FACTS

• Quasars are exploding centers of remote, ancient galaxies.

• They are hundreds of times brighter than an average galaxy, yet fraction of the size.

• Remotest object in known Universe is quasar PC 1247 + 3406, 13.2 billion light-years away.

• In 1989, quasar PKS 0558-504 threw out as much energy in 3 minutes as the Sun throws out in 340,000 years.

• First discovered and nearest quasar is 3C–273, 2 billion light-years away. It is as bright as 200 galaxies combined.

X-ray photograph of quasar 3C-273

AMAZING JOURNEYS

A journey by jumbo jet to the nearest star, Proxima Centauri, would take 5 million years.

The flight time of a jumbo jet bound for the Sun would be 20 years.

A car driven at a steady speed of 55mph (88km/h) would reach space in 2-3 hours.

The Solar System
6.2 billion miles (10 billion km)

Interstellar space
620 billion miles (1 trillion km)

Nearest stars
100 light-years

Milky Way Galaxy
100,000 light-years

Local Group of galaxies
10 million light-years

Extent of the known Universe
20 billion light-years

STARS

A STAR IS an immense globe of fiery hydrogen gas powered by nuclear reactions at its core. Only gravity holds it together and keeps it from exploding. In the first stage of its life, a star generates energy by fusing hydrogen atoms to form helium.

STAR TYPES

Most stars are part of a system composed of two or more stars. Mintaka (in Orion) consists of three stars, while Castor (in Gemini) has six. Stars form in close-knit groups from a nebula. About 60% stay in groups, held together by one another's gravity. Our Sun is unusual in being a solitary star.

BINARY STARS
These stars of similar mass and size orbit a common center of gravity, or central balance point.

ECLIPSING BINARY
One star in a pair regularly moves in front of the other. First we see a reduction, then a recovery in the star's light.

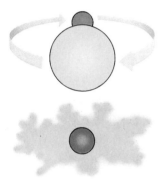

VARIABLE STAR
These stars vary in brightness. In some cases, explosions on the star's surface make it appear brighter than usual.

STAR RECORDS

FAINTEST KNOWN STAR
is brown star RG 0058.8-2807, with a visual brightness less than one-millionth of the Sun's.

BRIGHTEST KNOWN SUPERNOVA
was SN 1006, which flared in April 1006. It was easily visible during the day.

FASTEST KNOWN PULSAR
is PSR 1937+214, which spins 642 times a second.

FEATHERWEIGHT

On Earth, the average bird's feather weighs very little. On the surface of a neutron star, however, the intense gravity would cause a medium-sized feather to weigh as much as two Apollo lunar landing modules weigh on earth.

BIRTH AND LIFE OF A MASSIVE STAR

All stars begin life as enormous clouds of dust and gas. This cloud collapses in on itself and the star begins to shine. Death comes in two ways: average-sized stars such as the Sun simply swell and go out in a puff of smoke, leaving a small, fading core; massive stars end in a supernova.

1 A dark cloud of gas and dust – known as a molecular cloud – collapses under gravity and becomes more and more dense.

2 Parts of the cloud contract into clumps called protostars. These heat up, shrink, and become denser. Each protostar begins to spin and flattens into a disk.

3 Nuclear reactions begin. The remaining dust is either blown away by a violent stellar wind or forms planets orbiting the star.

4 On the main sequence, the star settles down into the major period of its life span. It shines steadily and radiates energy. Bigger and brighter stars burn hydrogen more quickly. They have shorter lifetimes.

STAR FACTS

• Red giant diameter: up to 100 times that of Sun. Red supergiant diameter: up to 1,000 times that of Sun.

• Energy released by a supernova in one minute is equivalent to total radiated by Sun in nine billion years.

• Average galaxy has 100 billion stars – it would take 1,000 years to count them all at rate of 3 per second.

MAIN SEQUENCE STARS

The main sequence is the central period of a star's lifetime. A star's brightness, color, temperature, size, and life span depend on its mass. Our Sun is a yellow star, a typical star of average size and temperature.

Brown dwarf 1,800°F (1,000°C)

Red dwarf 5,100°F (2,800°C)

Yellow star 9,900°F (5,500°C)

White star 18,000°F (10,000°C)

Blue/White star 28,800°F (16,000°C)

Blue star 43,200°F (24,000°C)

NEAREST STARS

Star	Star type	Distance (light-years)
Sun	Yellow main sequence	0
Proxima Centauri	Red dwarf	4.2
Alpha Centauri A	Yellow main sequence	4.3
Alpha Centauri B	Orange main sequence	4.3
Barnard's star	Red dwarf	5.9
Wolf 359	Red dwarf	7.6
Lalande 21185	Red dwarf	8.1
Sirius A	White main sequence	8.6
Sirius B	White dwarf	8.6
UV Ceti A	Red dwarf	8.9

SUPERNOVA REMAINS

One famous supernova was seen by Chinese astronomers in 1054. Its remains, a cloud of gas and dust particles called a nebula, can now be seen as the Crab nebula. This nebula is now expanding at a speed of 930 miles/sec (1,500km/sec): 130 times the top speed of the Saturn V Moon rocket.

Crab nebula

COLLAPSED STARS

A star's life on the main sequence ends either in a supernova explosion or a planetary nebula. Depending on its size, the remaining corpse collapses into one of three forms: white dwarf, neutron star, or black hole.

WHITE DWARF

When the planetary nebula of a typical star disperses into space, all that remains is a superdense core known as a white dwarf. Star corpses of less than 1.4 times the Sun's mass (i.e. typical star corpses) become white dwarfs.

Solid core

Gas

Radius = 3,700 miles (6,000km)

NEUTRON STAR

Neutron stars form when supernova corpses between 1.4 and 3 times the mass of our Sun collapse into the most solid state of matter possible. These neutron stars are so dense that a pinhead of their matter would weigh a million tons.

0.39in (1cm) thick atmosphere

Solid crust

Neutron fluid

Possible solid core

Radius = 10 miles (16km)

PULSAR

Rotating neutron stars are called pulsars. Their spin creates a massive magnetic field around them, a trillion times Earth's field. Like a lighthouse, a pulsar sends out beams of radiation from hot spots on or above its surface.

Axis of rotation

Beam of radiation from pulsar can be detected as it sweeps past Earth.

Hot spot

BLACK HOLE

A black hole is a region of powerful gravity surrounding a point of infinite density called a singularity. Nothing, not even light, can escape after falling past the event horizon (the "edge" of the black hole). Supernova corpses of more than three times the Sun's mass collapse into black holes.

Through the black hole
On approaching the event horizon, an astronaut would experience a pull on the head equal to the weight of 175 Saturn V rockets.

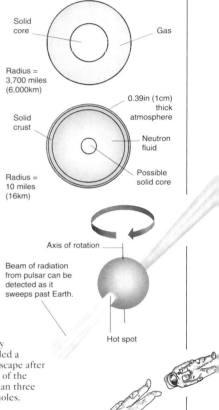

7 The core's contraction leads to a massive explosion called a supernova. The star shines as bright as a billion Suns as it blows apart. The core collapses in just one second.

6 Now a red supergiant, the swollen star swallows up its surrounding planets. Its core fuses carbon into iron, but lacks energy for further contraction.

5 The star begins to swell when its central supply of hydrogen is exhausted. The core fuses helium into carbon. Its outer layers swell and glow red.

Gravity weakens farther away from the hole. From here you can escape.

Event horizon: point of no return

BRIGHTEST STARS TO THE NAKED EYE

Star	Star type	Distance (light-years)
Sun	Yellow main sequence	0
Sirius A	White main sequence	8.6
Canopus	White supergiant	200
Alpha Centauri	Yellow main sequence	4.3
Arcturus	Red giant	36
Vega	White main sequence	26
Capella	Yellow giant	42
Rigel	Blue/white supergiant	910
Procyon	Yellow main sequence	11
Achernar	Blue/white main sequence	85

NIGHT SKIES

ANCIENT PEOPLES INVENTED names for different groups of stars, called constellations, to help them find their way about the skies. Stars in these constellations form patterns that have been observed over thousands of years.

CELESTIAL SPHERES

The celestial sphere is the huge, revolving, imaginary ball of stars enclosing Earth. In fact, it is Earth that rotates and the stars are scattered about in space; but the idea of a celestial sphere allows astronomers to plot the positions of stars and follow their movements.

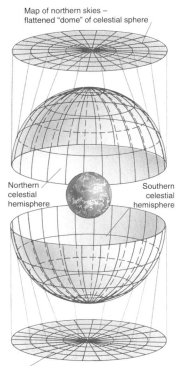

Map of northern skies – flattened "dome" of celestial sphere

Northern celestial hemisphere

Southern celestial hemisphere

Map of southern skies – flattened "bowl" of celestial sphere

OLDEST STAR MAP

The oldest example of a map of the heavens was discovered in 1987 on the ceiling of a tomb in Jiaotong University, Xian, China. It was painted in 25 B.C.

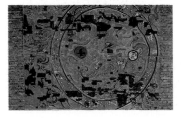

SKIES OF THE NORTHERN HEMISPHERE

The picture below shows the constellations an observer would see while standing at the North Pole and looking up into the night sky.

Pole position
In the Northern Hemisphere stars appear to revolve steadily about the star at the center: Polaris, the Pole Star. This star lies directly along Earth's axis of rotation.

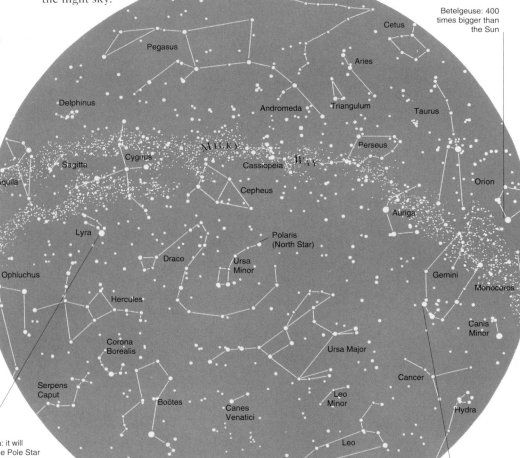

Betelgeuse: 400 times bigger than the Sun

Pisces

Cetus

Pegasus

Aries

Delphinus

Andromeda

Triangulum

Taurus

Sagitta

Cygnus

MILKY

WAY

Perseus

Cassiopeia

Aquila

Cepheus

Orion

Lyra

Polaris (North Star)

Auriga

Draco

Ophiuchus

Ursa Minor

Gemini

Hercules

Monoceros

Corona Borealis

Canis Minor

Serpens Caput

Ursa Major

Cancer

Boötes

Leo Minor

Hydra

Canes Venatici

Leo

Vega: it will be the Pole Star in 14,000 A.D.

Castor: in fact a family of six stars

Virgo

MONTHLY STARS

Stars that lie on the other side of the Sun from Earth cannot be seen at night – nighttime observers face the other way. Earth, however, revolves around the Sun once a year. So, the best time to see those stars is during the months when they lie on the opposite side of Earth from the Sun. This is why different constellations are visible at different times of the year.

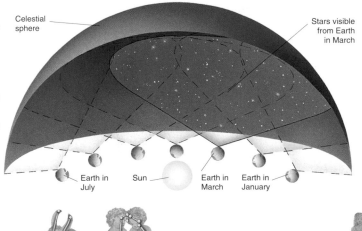

Celestial sphere

Stars visible from Earth in March

Earth in July

Sun

Earth in March

Earth in January

STARS OF THE ZODIAC

During the course of a year, the Sun appears in front of each constellation of the zodiac on the dates shown. These astronomical dates differ from astrological ones.

Aries the ram April 21– May 21

Taurus the bull May 22– June 21

Gemini the twins June 22– July 22

Cancer the crab July 23– August 23

Leo the lion August 24– September 22

Virgo the virgin September 23– October 23

SKIES OF THE SOUTHERN HEMISPHERE

In the South, no bright star lies along Earth's axis of rotation, so there is no Pole Star. Southern stars, however, are more spectacular.

Milky Way
The Solar System lies in the plane of the Milky Way Galaxy. So, when we look up in the sky, we see a band of bright stars, and none of the Galaxy's spiral details.

Orion Nebula: a region of star formation

Sirius: the brightest star in the sky

Canopus: used by space probes as a navigation aid.

Spica: 70,000 times brighter than the Sun

Alpha Centauri: a member of the closest star system to the Sun

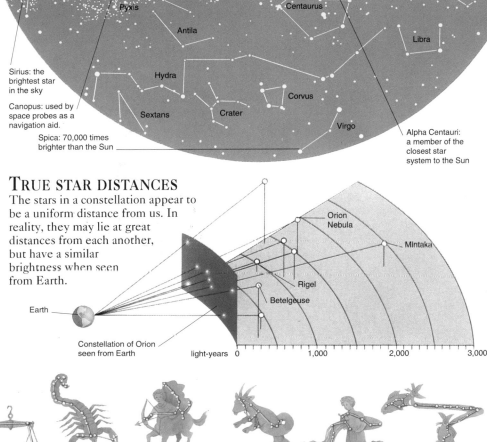

(Star map constellations: Cetus, Aquarius, Sculptor, Piscis Austrinus, Capricornus, Fornax, Phoenix, Grus, Microscopium, Aquila, Eridanus, Indus, Sagittarius, Tucana, Horologium, Pavo, Corona Australis, Caelum, Hydrus, Ophiuchus, Lepus, Dorado, Reticulum, Mensa, Apus, Ara, Scorpius, Columba, Volans, Chameleon, Triangulum Australe, Norma, Pictor, Musca, Canis Major, Carina, Crux, Lupus, Monoceros, Vela, Centaurus, Puppis, Libra, Pyxis, Antila, Hydra, Sextans, Corvus, Crater, Virgo, MILKY WAY)

TRUE STAR DISTANCES

The stars in a constellation appear to be a uniform distance from us. In reality, they may lie at great distances from each another, but have a similar brightness when seen from Earth.

Earth

Constellation of Orion seen from Earth

Orion Nebula

Mintaka

Rigel

Betelgeuse

light-years 0   1,000   2,000   3,000

Libra
the scales
October 24–
November 22

Scorpius
the scorpion
November 23–
December 21

Sagittarius
the archer
December 22–
January 20

Capricornus
the sea-goat
January 21–
February 18

Aquarius
the water-carrier
February 19–
March 20

Pisces
the fishes
March 21–
April 20

NIGHT SKY FACTS

• 2,000 years ago Sirius, the dog star, may have appeared red, and Romans used to sacrifice red dogs to it.

• Some "stars" seem to move very quickly across the night sky – these are in fact artificial satellites, reflecting the Sun's light at dawn or dusk.

• The Galaxy in Triangulum is the farthest object visible to the naked eye – it lies 2.4 million light-years away.

• The Ancient Chinese had constellations for every aspect of life – a celestial prison, a celestial stable, and a row of shops.

AURORA BOREALIS

The Northern Lights (Aurora Australis in the South) are colorful glowing lights that can be observed when near the Poles. They occur when the solar wind meets the Earth's heliosphere (see p.25).

CONSTELLATION CHANGES

The constellations seem fixed and eternal. Over hundreds of thousands of years, however, stars will change their positions, altering the overall shape.

1 The Big Dipper as ancient people saw it 100,000 years ago

2 The Big Dipper as it can be seen today

3 The Big Dipper as it will be seen in 100,000 years

LARGEST CONSTELLATIONS

Constellation	Meaning	Area (% of visible sky)
Hydra	The Watersnake	6.32
Virgo	The Virgin	6.28
Ursa Major	The Great Bear	6.20
Cetus	The Whale	5.97
Hercules	Hercules the Hero	5.94

SUN AND SOLAR SYSTEM

THE SUN IS THE STAR at the heart of the Solar System. Its huge gravitational pull anchors the nine planets, the asteroids, and comets in their orbits. The nuclear-reactor core at the Sun's center radiates light and heat throughout the entire Solar System.

ANATOMY OF THE SUN

Inside the core, nuclear fusion turns hydrogen into helium, creating energy that rises out into the photosphere, and from there into space.

Corona
The corona is a huge, thin halo of hot gas. It has a temperature of 1.8 million°F (1 million°C).

Corona seen at eclipse

Chromosphere
The chromosphere is a reddish outer layer of hydrogen that rises 620 miles (1,000 km) above the photosphere. It has a temperature of 7,200–14,400°F (4,000–8,000°C).

Photosphere
This is the surface layer of the Sun. Its white-hot hydrogen has a temperature of 9,900°F (5,500°C).

Convective zone
In the convective zone, rising and falling currents carry heat outward toward the photosphere. It has a temperature of 2.7 million°F (1.5 million °C).

Radiative zone
The core's energy radiates outwards through this hydrogen layer. It has a temperature of 2.7 million–25.2 million°F (1.5 million–14 million°C).

Core
The hydrogen core works as a massive nuclear reactor. It fuses hydrogen to create helium at a temperature of 25.2 million°F (14 million°C).

SUN DATA

Age	5 billion years
Diameter	865,000 miles (1,392,000km)
Mass (Earth = 1)	332,946
Density (water = 1)	1.41
Distance from Earth	92.9 million miles (149.6 million km)
Distance from nearest star	24,900 billion miles (40,000 billion km)
Core Temperature	25.2 million°F (14 million°C)
Surface Temperature	9,900°F (5,500°C)
Luminosity	390 billion billion megawatts
Life Expectancy	5 billion years
Speed	240 million years to orbit the galaxy

SUN FACTS

• One square yard (0.8sq m) of Sun's surface shines as brightly as 600,000 100-watt lightbulbs.

• Biggest observed solar prominence reached height of 435,000 miles (700,000km) in one hour in 1946.

• In one second, Sun gives out 35 million times average annual electricity supply for the entire United States.

• Solar flares can interrupt radio communications on Earth, cause magnetic storms, and confuse birds flying long distances.

• Rotation of Sun's surface varies from 25 days at equator to 35 days at poles. Radiative zone rotates regularly every 27 days.

• If Sun's cooler outer layers were peeled off, dangerous radiation from its core would destroy life on Earth.

SURFACE FEATURES OF THE SUN

SPICULES

Spicules are straight jets of gas that occur in the chromosphere. They rise as high as 6,200 miles (10,000km) at speeds of 16 miles/sec (25km/sec). After 5-10 minutes they dissolve into the surrounding corona. Spicules are thought to be caused by magnetic fields. There are 100,000 on the Sun's surface at any time.

GRANULES

The Sun's surface is made up of millions of upsurging granules. A granule is about 620 miles (1,000km) across: an area the size of France.

Granule

France

SUNSPOTS

These areas of darker cooler gas appear in pairs at a temperature of 7,200°F (4,000°C). They occur when the heat flow from the core is blocked by the Sun's magnetic field. Sunspot activity runs in 11.5-year cycles. It is due to peak next in 2001.

SOLAR FLARES

These enormous and unpredictable explosions occur in the Sun's atmosphere. Solar flares can throw billions of tons of the Sun's material out into space. These explosions release an amount of energy that is equivalent to a trillion times that of the first nuclear bomb.

SOLAR PROMINENCES

Solar prominences are arched plumes of flaming hydrogen gas that hang in the lower corona, supported by the force of the Sun's magnetic field. Some prominences erupt into space as great arches at speeds of 900mph (400m/sec).

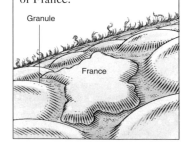

EVOLUTION OF THE SUN AND SOLAR SYSTEM

The Solar System began life 5 billion years ago as a massive cloud of gas with rocky and icy particles. When the cloud collapsed under its own gravity, the Sun formed, and the particles clumped together to form the planets.

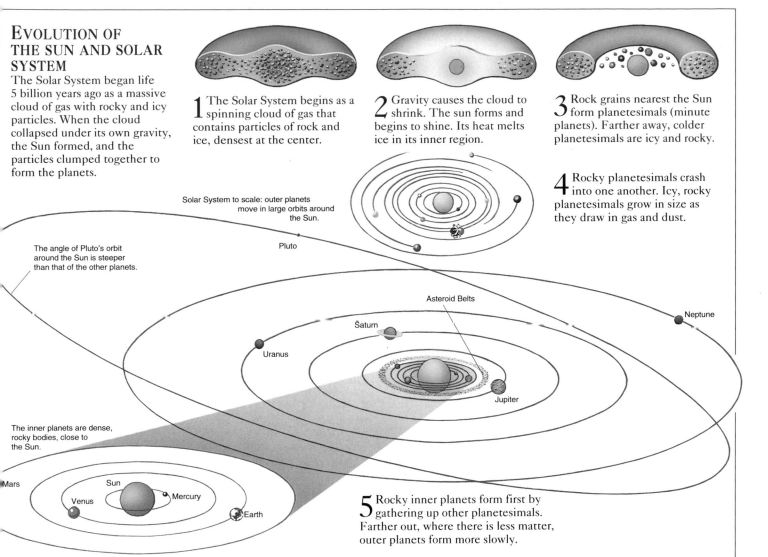

1 The Solar System begins as a spinning cloud of gas that contains particles of rock and ice, densest at the center.

2 Gravity causes the cloud to shrink. The sun forms and begins to shine. Its heat melts ice in its inner region.

3 Rock grains nearest the Sun form planetesimals (minute planets). Farther away, colder planetesimals are icy and rocky.

4 Rocky planetesimals crash into one another. Icy, rocky planetesimals grow in size as they draw in gas and dust.

Solar System to scale: outer planets move in large orbits around the Sun.

The angle of Pluto's orbit around the Sun is steeper than that of the other planets.

Pluto

Asteroid Belts

Saturn

Uranus

Neptune

The inner planets are dense, rocky bodies, close to the Sun.

Mars

Venus

Sun

Mercury

Earth

Jupiter

5 Rocky inner planets form first by gathering up other planetesimals. Farther out, where there is less matter, outer planets form more slowly.

AMAZING SCALES

If the Sun's diameter were the height of an average adult, then Jupiter would be the size of the head. Earth would be slightly bigger than the iris of the eyeball.

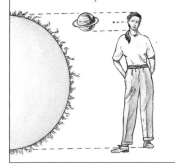

HELIOSPHERE

The Sun's magnetic field or heliosphere extends beyond the edge of the Solar System. It is generated by the gale of hot, charged particles known as the solar wind that streams in spirals off the corona. The Sun also generates a sheet of electrical current, smaller than the heliosphere.

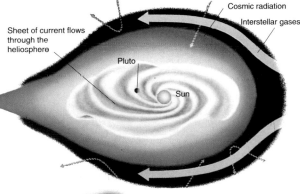

Cosmic radiation

Interstellar gases

Sheet of current flows through the heliosphere

Pluto

Sun

LARGEST BODIES IN THE SOLAR SYSTEM

Body	Maximum diameter	
	km	miles
Sun	1,392,000	865,000
Jupiter	142,984	88,846
Saturn	120,536	74,898
Uranus	51,118	31,763
Neptune	49,528	30,774
Earth	12,756	7,926
Venus	12,103	7,520
Mars	6,786	4,217
Ganymede (moon of Jupiter)	5,262	3,270
Titan (moon of Saturn)	5,150	3,200

DEATH OF THE SUN AND SOLAR SYSTEM

1 Five billion years from now, the Sun will swell to 100 times its present size, as its fuel begins to run low. Its outer layers will engulf Mercury, Venus, and possibly Earth.

2 After a further one million years, the Sun will have used up all its available hydrogen. Its gaseous outer layers will dissolve into space as a planetary nebula, a thin cloud of gas and dust particles.

3 The remaining core will finally become a white dwarf, a super-dense star about the size of Earth. It will slowly cool off and fade to a black dwarf. The outer planets of the present Solar System will still orbit this dwarf, but at a much greater distance.

PLANETS

A PLANET IS A BODY that orbits the Sun, or any other star. There are nine known planets and they can be divided into two groups: the dense, rocky inner planets, and the gassy or icy outer planets.

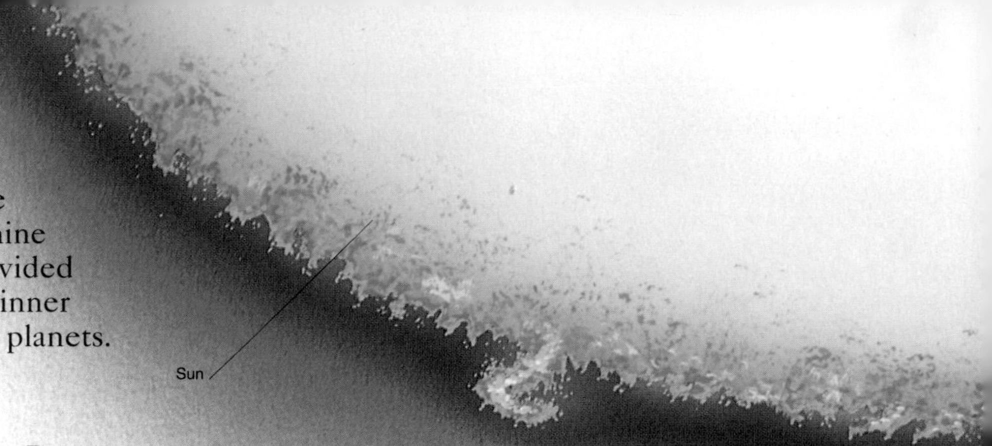

Sun

THE INNER PLANETS

Mercury, Venus, Earth, and Mars are known as the inner planets or terrestrials. They are made up of rocks and metals, are smaller than the outer planets, and their atmospheres contain very little of the gases hydrogen and helium. Earth, as far as we know, is the only planet where there is life.

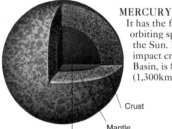

MERCURY
It has the fastest orbiting speed around the Sun. Its huge impact crater, Caloris Basin, is 800 miles (1,300km) across.

Crust
Mantle
Core

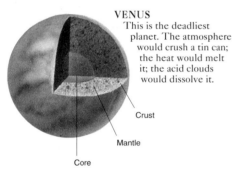

VENUS
This is the deadliest planet. The atmosphere would crush a tin can; the heat would melt it; the acid clouds would dissolve it.

Crust
Mantle
Core

EARTH
Earth is the only planet known to have any quantity of water and oxygen, and to support life. Its surface is constantly moving due to plate tectonics (see p.40).

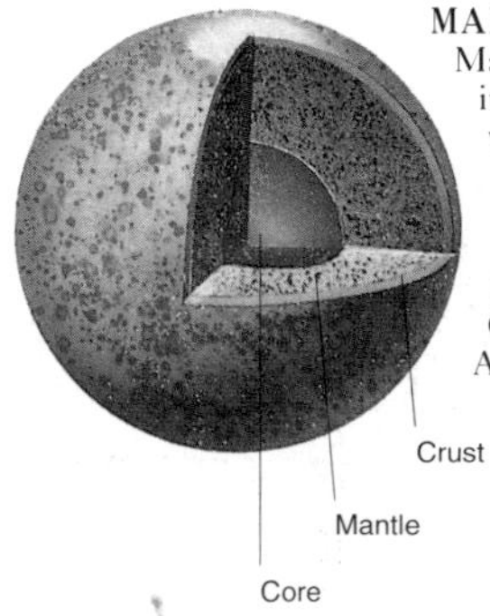

Crust
Mantle
Outer core
Inner core

MARS
Mars is the red planet: its plains are covered with reddish sediment. Its biggest canyon, Valles Marineris, is ten times longer than the Grand Canyon, Arizona.

Crust
Mantle
Core

RELATIVE SIZES
Pluto is the smallest planet and also the most distant. Jupiter is bigger than all the other planets put together.

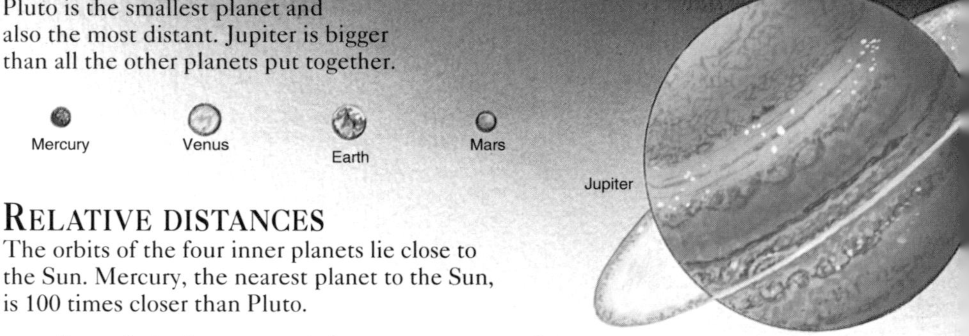

Mercury   Venus   Earth   Mars

Jupiter

RELATIVE DISTANCES
The orbits of the four inner planets lie close to the Sun. Mercury, the nearest planet to the Sun, is 100 times closer than Pluto.

Mercury   Venus Earth Mars   Jupiter   Saturn
Sun

INNER PLANETS

	Mercury	Venus	Earth	Mars
Distance from Sun million miles (million km)	36.0 (57.9)	67.2 (108.2)	93.0 (149.6)	141.6 (227.9)
Diameter miles (km)	3,031 (4,878)	12,103 (7,520)	7,926 (12,756)	4,217 (6,786)
Time taken to circle Sun	87.97 days	224.70 days	365.26 days	686.98 days
Orbital speed around Sun miles/sec (km/sec)	29.76 (47.89)	21.77 (35.03)	18.51 (29.79)	14.99 (24.13)
Time taken to turn on axis	58 days, 16 hours	243 days, 14 mins	23 hours, 56 mins	24 hours, 37 mins
Mass (Earth = 1)	0.055	0.81	1	0.11
Density (water = 1)	5.43	5.25	5.52	3.95
Temperature Fahrenheit (Celsius)	(on surface) -292 to +806°F (-180 to +430°C)	(on surface) 869°F (465°C)	(on surface) -94 to +131°F (-70 to +55°C)	(on surface) -184 to +77°F (-120 to +25°C)
Number of moons	-	-	1	2

MARS' GIANT MOUNTAIN
Olympus Mons is the biggest volcano (extinct) in the Solar System.

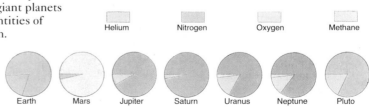

Olympus Mons 16 miles (26km) high

Everest 5.5 miles (8.8km) high

ATMOSPHERES
Scientists have identified various gases in the atmospheres of the planets. The giant planets all contain large quantities of helium and hydrogen.

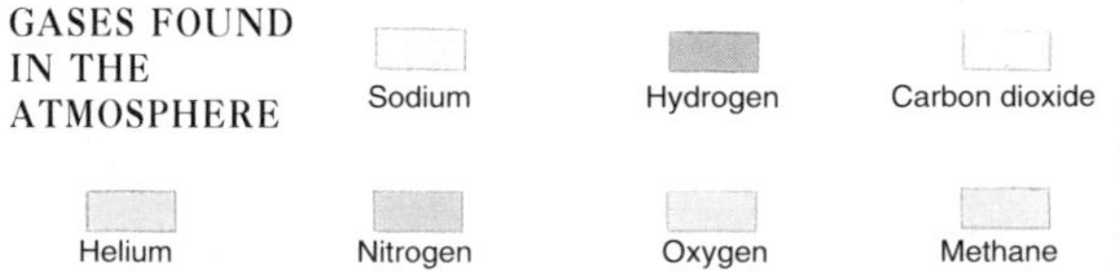

GASES FOUND IN THE ATMOSPHERE

Sodium   Hydrogen   Carbon dioxide

Helium   Nitrogen   Oxygen   Methane

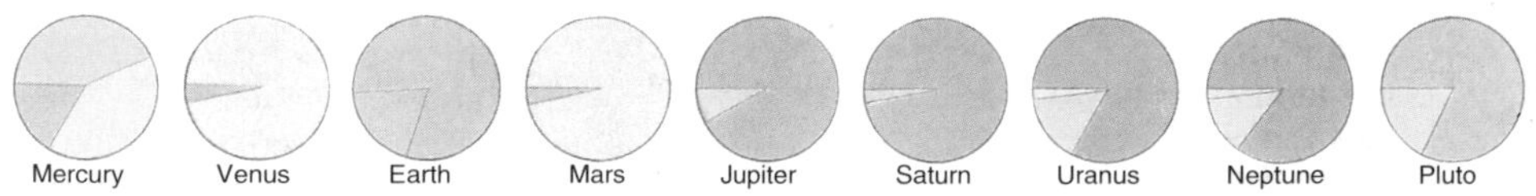

Mercury   Venus   Earth   Mars   Jupiter   Saturn   Uranus   Neptune   Pluto

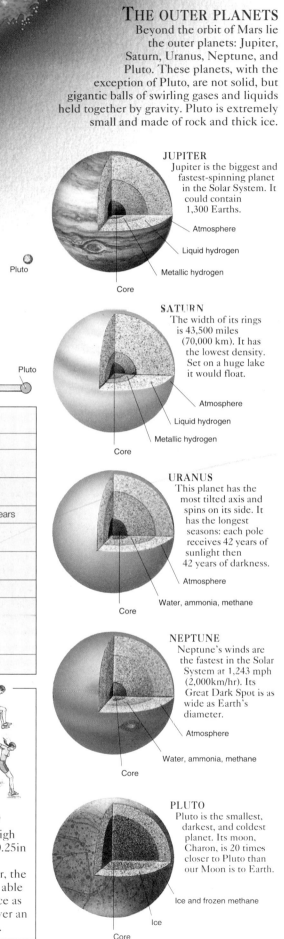

THE OUTER PLANETS

Beyond the orbit of Mars lie the outer planets: Jupiter, Saturn, Uranus, Neptune, and Pluto. These planets, with the exception of Pluto, are not solid, but gigantic balls of swirling gases and liquids held together by gravity. Pluto is extremely small and made of rock and thick ice.

JUPITER
Jupiter is the biggest and fastest-spinning planet in the Solar System. It could contain 1,300 Earths.

Atmosphere

Liquid hydrogen

Metallic hydrogen

Core

SATURN
The width of its rings is 43,500 miles (70,000 km). It has the lowest density. Set on a huge lake it would float.

Atmosphere

Liquid hydrogen

Metallic hydrogen

Core

URANUS
This planet has the most tilted axis and spins on its side. It has the longest seasons: each pole receives 42 years of sunlight then 42 years of darkness.

Atmosphere

Water, ammonia, methane

Core

NEPTUNE
Neptune's winds are the fastest in the Solar System at 1,243 mph (2,000km/hr). Its Great Dark Spot is as wide as Earth's diameter.

Atmosphere

Water, ammonia, methane

Core

PLUTO
Pluto is the smallest, darkest, and coldest planet. Its moon, Charon, is 20 times closer to Pluto than our Moon is to Earth.

Ice and frozen methane

Ice

Core

Saturn

Uranus

Neptune

Pluto

Uranus · Neptune · Pluto

OUTER PLANETS

	Jupiter	Saturn	Uranus	Neptune	Pluto
	483.6 (778.3)	887 (1,427)	1,784 (2,871)	2,794 (4,497)	3,675 (5,914)
	88,846 (142,984)	74,898 (120,536)	31,763 (51,118)	30,775 (49,528)	1,419 (2,284)
	11.86 years	29.46 years	84.01 years	164.79 years	248.54 years
	8.12 (13.06)	5.99 (9.64)	4.23 (6.81)	3.37 (5.43)	2.95 (4.74)
	9 hours, 55 mins	10 hours, 40 mins	17 hours, 14 mins	16 hours, 7 mins	6 days, 9 hours
	318	95.18	14.5	17.14	0.0022
	1.33	0.69	1.29	1.64	2.03
	(at cloud tops) -238°F -150°C	(at cloud tops) -292°F -180°C	(at cloud tops) -346°F -210°C	(at cloud tops) -346°F -210°C	-364°F -220°C
	16	18	15	8	1

PLANETARY MOON FACTS

• Saturn has the most moons of any planet in Solar System: 18. Jupiter comes in second with 16.

• Europa, Jupiter's moon, has a surface of ice 60 miles (97km) thick.

• Titan, Saturn's moon, is thought to have cliffs of solid methane and rivers of liquid methane.

• Phobos, Mars' moon, is being dragged closer to Mars. In 30 million years, it will be destroyed by crashing onto the surface.

• Miranda, Uranus' moon, has canyons ten times deeper than Earth's Grand Canyon. It has an ice cliff 3.23 miles (5.2km) high.

• Callisto, Jupiter's moon, has a more cratered surface than any other body in Solar System.

Callisto, a moon of Jupiter

MERCURY LEAP

The record women's high jump on Earth is 6ft 10.25in (2.09m). On Mercury, where gravity is weaker, the same athlete would be able to jump more than twice as high. She could leap over an elephant in one bound.

MOON

THE MOON IS EARTH'S constant companion in space. Held by our planet's gravity, it revolves around Earth in its orbit of the Sun, like a satellite. The Moon, like Earth, is 4.6 billion years old. Unlike Earth, the Moon is lifeless, waterless, and airless.

THEORY OF MOON'S ORIGIN

Astronomers have put forward several theories to explain the mystery of the Moon's origin. The most popular theory holds that a body the size of Mars collided with Earth in its early days. The impact threw vast amounts of matter into space, and these fragments of rock came together to form the Moon.

PHASES OF THE MOON

As the Moon orbits Earth, it receives light from the Sun, and a changing portion of its illuminated face is visible from Earth. These portions are the Moon's phases.

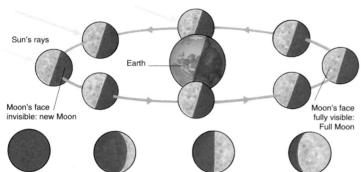

Sun's rays

Earth

Moon's face invisible: new Moon

Moon's face fully visible: Full Moon

MOON DATA

Age	4.6 billion years
Diameter	2,160 miles (3,476km)
Mass (Earth=1)	0.012
Surface gravity (Earth=1)	0.16
Average distance from Earth	238,900 miles (384,400km)
Time taken to orbit Earth	27.3 days
Time taken to rotate on axis	27.3 days
Surface temperature	-247°F to 221°F (-155°C to 105°C)

New Moon   Crescent   First quarter   Gibbous   Full Moon   Gibbous   Last quarter   Crescent

NEAR SIDE OF THE MOON

The near side of the Moon always faces Earth and is always at least partially visible in our night sky, except at a new Moon.

Plato: one of few craters with a dark floor of solidified lava

Mare Frigoris

Mare Imbrium

Maria

The dark areas, called maria, are seas of solidified lava. They are thought to have formed billions of years ago when lava, or molten rock, seeped out from beneath the crust to fill the craters, and then solidified into darker rock.

Oceanus Procellarum

Copernicus: a ray crater, about 800 million years old

Craters

The surface of the Moon is littered with craters formed billions of years ago by the impact of meteorites.

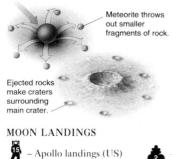

Meteorite throws out smaller fragments of rock.

Ejected rocks make craters surrounding main crater.

Ray craters

Some craters have bright "rays" extending from their rims. The rays are fragments of rock splashed from the meteoritic impact.

Site of Apollo 17 landing: the last manned Moon mission

Mare Serenitatis

Mare Crisium

Mare Tranquillitatis

Mare Fecunditatis

Mare Nectaris

Mare Nubium

Mare Humorum

Some of the Moon has yet to be mapped. An area around the South Pole still remains unseen.

Site of Apollo 11 Moon landing: first people on the Moon

Highland areas

The areas between the maria are higher, rougher, and brighter than the maria.

MOON LANDINGS

– Apollo landings (US)   – Luna landings (former USSR)

MOON AND EARTH: GRAVITY AND TIDES

The Moon is so close to Earth that it exerts a strong pull on Earth's waters. This gravitational pull produces a bulge on the side of Earth facing the Moon, and a corresponding bulge on the opposite side. So, the oceans have two daily high tides.

Neap tide
The position of the Sun also affects the strength of the tides. Here the Sun's gravity weakens the effect of the Moon's gravity, and Earth has weak or neap tides.

Spring tide
Here the Sun's gravity adds to the Moon's, and Earth has strong spring tides.

LUNAR AND SOLAR ECLIPSES

LUNAR ECLIPSE
When the Moon moves into the Earth's shadow, no sunlight is reflected off the Moon and it disappears from Earth's view. Normally the Moon passes above or below the shadow because its orbit is tilted at 5° from Earth's path.

SOLAR ECLIPSE
By chance, the Sun and Moon appear the same size in the sky. When, at a full Moon, the Moon lines up directly between Sun and Earth, its inner shadow creates a total eclipse. People in its outer shadow see a partial eclipse.

TOTAL LUNAR ECLIPSES

Date	Visible from
April 3-4, 1996	Europe, South America, Africa
Sept 27, 1996	Europe, Americas, West Africa
Sept 16, 1997	Europe, Africa, Australasia
Jan 21, 2000	Europe, Americas, Asia
July 16, 2000	Pacific, Australasia, Southwestern Asia

TOTAL SOLAR ECLIPSES

Date	Visible from
Mar 8-9, 1997	Japan, Philippines, Northwestern America
Feb 26, 1998	North America, Hawaii, Western Africa
Aug 11, 1999	Europe, North Africa, Arabia, Greenland
June 21, 2001	South Atlantic, Southern Africa
Dec 4, 2002	Southern Africa, Southern Indian Ocean

NEAR AND FAR SIDE

The Moon spins on its axis in exactly the same time that it takes to complete an orbit of Earth. The same side always faces us and the far side remains invisible. The Moon wobbles on its axis, and at some places on its orbit it surges forward or slows down. As a result, we can actually see 59% of its surface from Earth.

Near side always faces Earth

Far side never faces Earth

Earth

LASTING IMPRESSION

With no air, water, or volcanic activity to erode them, the footprints and tracks left by the Moon's astronauts could remain as they are for more than 100 million years

FAR SIDE OF THE MOON

The far side always faces away from Earth, and is more cratered and rugged than the near side.

Clearer view
For astronomers, who need a clear view of space, the far side would be an excellent place to build an observatory. It is totally shielded from the reflective glare and stray electrical signals of Earth, and it has no atmosphere to dim the stars' images.

Mare Moscoviense: one of the few far side maria

Mare Moscoviense

Mare Smithii

Tsiolovsky: a crater with terraced walls and a huge central mountain structure

Maria mystery
The far side has very few maria. Though we know that the crust is thicker on the far side (which made it more difficult for lava to seep out), no one knows why.

Mare Ingenii

Mare Orientalis: one of the biggest basins on the Moon, caused by the impact of a massive meteorite

Mare Australe

Schrödinger: a large rill or ridge, Rima Planck, extends from this crater

Montes Cordillera and Montes Rook: rings of mountains thrown up around Mare Orientalis

MOON FACTS

• Moon's first astronauts, Americans Neil Armstrong and Buzz Aldrin, landed in 1969 in Apollo XI.

• In 1970 Russian probe Luna 16 was the first unmanned spacecraft to bring back soil samples from the surface of the Moon.

• In 1950 the Moon appeared to turn blue after a forest fire in British Columbia, threw up clouds of smoke particles.

• A mistake of only 1 mph (1.6km/h) in Apollo XI's top speed would have led to it missing the Moon by 1,000 miles (1,600km).

COMETS, METEORS, AND ASTEROIDS

CHUNKS OF ROCK and metal, lumps of ice, and clouds of dust float far and wide in the Solar System. Scientists classify these wandering objects as comets, meteors, and asteroids. Rocky asteroids sometimes crash into planets or their moons, causing massive craters.

Dust tail

Gas tail

DEFINITIONS

Comet An icy object orbiting the Sun. It produces steam when it nears the Sun and develops a tail of dust and gas.

Meteor The streak of light seen in the sky when a particle of rock burns up in Earth's upper atmosphere.

Asteroid A small rocky object in the Solar System. Asteroids range in size from 578 miles (930km) across down to dust particles.

Meteorite A piece of rock that has survived passage through Earth's atmosphere: thought to be a fragment of an asteroid, not of a comet.

COMETS

Comets are chunks of ice and rock left over from the birth of the Solar System. Astronomers believe that these icy rocks are located in a zone called the Oort cloud, named after the Dutch astronomer Jan Oort (1900–92), that lies beyond the farthest planet in the Solar System.

Nucleus

Nucleus

MOST FREQUENTLY SEEN COMETS

Name	Period (years)
Encke	3.3
Grigg-Skjellerup	4.9
Honda-Mrkos-Pajdusakova	5.2
Tempel 2	5.3
Neujmin 2	5.4
Tuttle-Giacobini-Kresak	5.5
Tempel-Swift	5.7
Tempel 1	6.0
Pons-Winnecke	6.3
De Vico Swift	6.3

Jets of dust

Halley's comet photographed by the Schmidt telescope in 1986

HALLEY'S COMET

Every 76 years Halley's comet returns to the center of the Solar System. In 1705, English astronomer Edmund Halley (1658–1742) correctly predicted its return in the year 1758. On the last return in 1986, the space probe Giotto penetrated to within 370 miles (600km) of the comet's nucleus.

COMET NUCLEUS

The nucleus is a chunk of rock and ice that lies at the comet's core. As the comet nears the Sun, the heat melts the ice. Gas jets spring from the side facing the Sun. Fragments of rock break off to form the dust tail.

Ice

Gas and dust jets

Rock

COMET TAIL

Each comet has a dust tail and a gas tail. These are blown back by the solar wind, which forces the dust and gas away from the Sun.

Gas tail forced back by electrically charged particles of the solar wind

Dust tail follows curve of comet's path

Sun

Comet recedes from Sun, but tail always points away from Sun

SO LONG

The comet with the longest known tail was the Great Comet of 1843, which trailed for 205 million miles (330 million km). The tail could have wrapped around Earth 7,000 times. It will not return to the center of the Solar System until 2356.

COMET RECORDS

LONGEST KNOWN PERIOD of a comet is 24 million years. This comet, Delavan's comet, was last seen in 1914.

MOST FREQUENT COMET is Encke's comet, which returns every 3.3 years.

BRIGHTEST COMET this century was the Daylight Comet of 1910. It was as bright as the planet Venus.

METEORS

Meteors, or shooting stars, are streaks of light that appear briefly in the night sky. They occur when particles of rock or dust, left by comets, burn up in Earth's atmosphere at speeds of up to 44 miles/sec (70km/sec).

METEOR SHOWER

Comets leave trails of dust and debris along their orbits around the Sun. When Earth crosses one of these trails, the dust burns up in the atmosphere and we see a meteor shower in the sky.

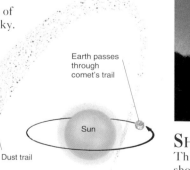

Earth passes through comet's trail

Sun

Dust trail

Comet

SHOOTING STAR

This long-exposure photograph shows a meteor from the Ursid meteor shower that occurs each year in December.

METEOR SHOWERS

Main showers (annual)	Date	Maximum number per hour
Quadrantids	Jan 3-4	50
Lyrids	April 22	10
Delta Aquarids	July 31	25
Perseids	Aug 12	50
Orionids	Oct 21	20
Taurids	Nov 8	10
Leonids	Nov 17	10
Geminids	Dec 14	50
Ursids	Dec 22	15

ASTEROIDS

Asteroids are pieces of rock smaller than planets that orbit the Sun. More than 4,000 have been found. They range in size from tiny fragments of rock to bodies hundreds of miles across.

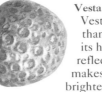

Ceres
Ceres, discovered in 1801, is the biggest known asteroid; it is 578 miles (930km) wide. If Ceres were placed on Earth it would cover France.

Vesta
Vesta is smaller than Ceres, but its highly reflective surface makes it the brightest asteroid.

Psyche
Psyche is irregularly shaped, made of iron, and about 160 miles (260km) long – the size of Jamaica.

Psyche

Jamaica

ASTEROID BELTS

Most asteroids lie in the Asteroid Belts between the orbits of Mars and Jupiter. The Trojan asteroids, though, follow Jupiter's orbit in two groups. Others orbit the Sun alone.

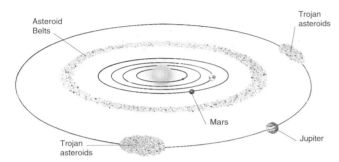

Asteroid Belts

Trojan asteroids

Mars

Jupiter

Trojan asteroids

ASTEROID FACTS

• An estimated 2,000 collisions have occurred between asteroids and Earth in the last 600 million years.

• If an asteroid of average size collided with Earth, it could destroy an entire country.

• In January 1991, an asteroid measuring about 33ft (10m) across passed between the Moon and Earth.

• In the future, asteroids could be mined for metals as resources on Earth grow scarce.

Captain James T. Kirk and Mr. Spock

• Asteroid 2309 is called Mr. Spock, after the character in the television series *Star Trek*.

• Ceres, the largest asteroid, contains a quarter of all the rock in the Asteroid Belts.

LARGEST ASTEROIDS

Name	First seen	Diameter km	Diameter miles
Ceres	1801	930	578
Pallas	1802	607	377
Vesta	1807	519	322
Hygeia	1849	450	280
Euphrosyne	1854	370	230
Interamnia	1910	349	217
Davida	1903	322	200
Cybele	1861	308	191
Europa	1858	288	179
Patienta	1899	275	171

METEOR CRATER

On Earth, the best example of an asteroid impact crater is Arizona's Meteor Crater which is 0.7 miles (1.2km) in diameter, 590ft (180m) deep, and 50,000 years old.

Walking on the Moon
In order to prepare for their work on the surface of the Moon, the Apollo astronauts trained on the slopes of the Meteor crater. Dressed in their spacesuits, they tested the Moon buggy and other equipment.

TUNGUSKA EVENT

In June 1908 a huge explosion occurred in the forested Tunguska region of Siberia, devastating an area of 1,500 sq miles (3,900 sq km). The shock wave was heard 600 miles (1,000km) away. The explosion is thought to have been caused by an asteroid.

METEORITES

A meteorite is a piece of rock from space that does not completely vaporize in Earth's atmosphere, and is able to reach the ground. There are three kinds of meteorites: stony, iron, and stony-iron.

Stony
Stony meteorites are the most common type. They consist mainly of the minerals olivine and pyroxene.

Iron
Iron meteorites come from small asteroids that broke up in space. They are rarer than stony meteorites.

Stony-iron
Stony-iron meteorites contain both rock and metal. The picture shows bright metal enclosing the mineral olivine.

METEORITE RECORDS

OLDEST METEORITES
called carbonaceous chondrites, are 4.55 billion years old.

LARGEST METEORITE
lies at Grootfontein, Namibia. It is called Hoba, is 9ft (2.75m) long, made of iron, and weighs 59 tons: as much as eight elephants.

ONLY PERSON INJURED
was Mrs. A. Hodges of Alabama. A 9lb (4kg) meteorite crashed through her roof in November 1954 and injured her arm.

ONLY FATAL METEORITE
killed a dog in Nakhla, Egypt in 1911.

FROM THE HAND OF GOD

The Black Stone of Mecca, housed in a shrine in Saudi Arabia, is the sacred stone of Islam. It is believed to be a meteorite that fell to Earth hundreds of years ago.

DUST COLLECTOR

Rock particles picked up from space add 10,000 tons to Earth's weight each year. This would be enough dust to give everyone on Earth 0.07oz (2g) per year.

ASTRONOMY

ASTRONOMY IS THE STUDY of the nature and movement of the heavenly objects in the Universe: planets, moons, comets, asteroids, stars, and galaxies.

335–323 B.C. Aristotle (384–322 B.C.), Greek physicist and philosopher, puts Earth at the center of the Universe. This central belief dominates until the 15th century.

Aristotle's Universe

A.D. 137–145 Ptolemy (c.120–180), Greek astronomer, records the positions of 1,080 stars and divides them into 48 constellations in his book, *Almagest*. His system uses Aristotle's beliefs as its basis and stands for 1,400 years.

Ptolemy

400 B.C. | 335 | 200 B.C. | A.D. | 137 | 200 A.D.

1543 Nicolas Copernicus (1473–1543), Polish monk, establishes the position of the Sun at the center of the Universe in his book, *De Revolutionibus Orbium Caelestium.*

Nicolas Copernicus

1596 Tycho Brahe (1546–1601), Danish nobleman, publishes his great star catalog, compiled from 1575 to 1595. His study fixes accurate positions for about 770 stars.

Tycho Brahe

1608 First telescope is thought to have been invented for military use by Dutch scientist Hans Lippershey (1570–1619).

1609 Elliptical motion of planets is established by German astronomer Johannes Kepler (1571–1630), overturning the theory of circular motion around the Sun.

1500 | 1543 | 1596 | 1600 | 1608 | 1609

1610 Galileo (1564–1642), Italian scientist and the first systematic user of the telescope, discovers the moons of Jupiter and identifies sunspots and craters on the Moon. He shows that Venus has phases like the Moon, adding support to the idea that the Sun is the center of the Universe.

Galileo

17th-century telescope

1667 Isaac Newton (1642–1727), English scientist, lays down the laws of gravitation governing celestial bodies, marking the beginning of modern astronomy. In 1668 he invents and builds the first reflecting telescope.

Isaac Newton

1705 Edmund Halley (1658–1742), English astronomer, correctly predicts the return of Halley's comet in 1758.

Edmund Halley

1610 | 1667 | 1700 | 1705

1781 Uranus is discovered by German-born musician William Herschel (1738–1822). Six years later, he finds four of its moons. He discovers binary stars, catalogs thousands of clusters and nebulae, and reasons the existence of other galaxies.

William Herschel

1846 Neptune is discovered by German astronomers Johann Galle (1812–1910) and Heinrich D'Arrest (1822–1875).

1849 First star photographs are taken at Harvard Observatory, Cambridge, Massachusetts.

Hydrogen — Deuterium — positron — gamma ray
proton
neutrino — Helium-3 — Helium-4

Fusion of hydrogen nuclei

1907 Albert Einstein (1879–1955), German-born physicist, discovers mass can turn into energy. This leads to the theory of how the Sun shines – by fusing hydrogen atoms to make helium (see p.223).

1781 | 1800 | 1846 | 1849 | 1900 | 1907

1919 Expanding Universe is suggested by American astronomer Vesto Slipher (1875–1969), who proves that most galaxies are red-shifted (see p.33).

1924–30 Big Bang theory (see p.18) is independently formulated by Belgian scientist Abbé Lemaitre (1894–1966) and Russian scientist A. Freidmann (1888–1925).

Edwin Hubble

1929 Edwin Hubble (1889–1953), American astronomer, finds strong evidence for an expanding Universe.

1930 Pluto is discovered by American astronomer Clyde Tombaugh (born 1906).

1932 Radio signals from outside Earth are discovered by American engineer Karl Jansky (1905–50). His improvised aerial accidentally picks up radio waves from the Milky Way.

Karl Jansky

1919 | 1920 | 1924 | 1929 | 1930 | 1932 | 1950

1965 3K cosmic background radiation (believed to be the remains of Big Bang's radiation) is discovered by Americans Arno Penzias (born 1933) and Robert Wilson (born 1936).

Cosmic radiation radio antenna at New Jersey.

1967 First pulsar (CP 1919) is identified by Belfast-born astronomer Jocelyn Bell (born 1943).

Jocelyn Bell

1986 Giotto space probe sends back the first pictures of a comet's nucleus (Halley's comet).

Giotto space probe (Europe)

1990 Hubble Space Telescope is launched, the first large optical telescope to be placed above Earth's atmosphere, where it has the clearest view of the Universe.

1992 COBE (Cosmic Background Explorer, see p.18) transmits evidence of a dense Universe.

1960 | 1965 | 1967 | 1970 | 1980 | 1986 | 1990 | 1992

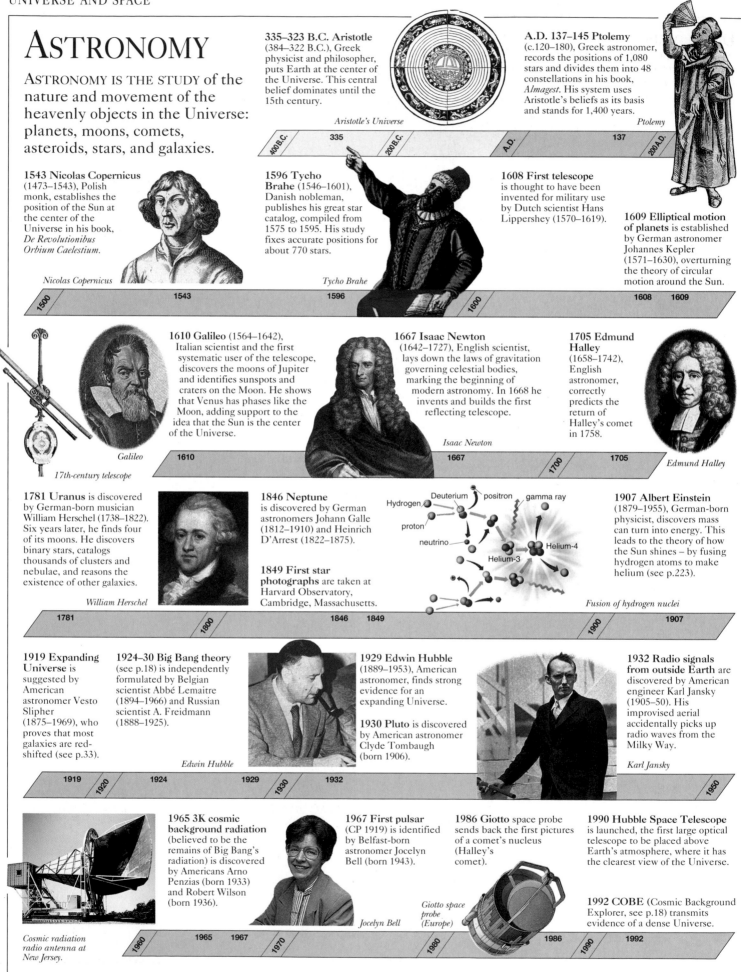

DEVELOPMENT OF THE OPTICAL TELESCOPE

Early telescopes produced images that were blurred, suffered color distortions, and showed only a small region of the sky. Better designs have produced more powerful telescopes.

REFRACTING TELESCOPE

The main glass lens focuses the starlight, while the eyepiece, a smaller lens, magnifies the image. It is called a refracting telescope because its main lens bends, or refracts, the light that enters. It can, however, introduce false colors and shows only a small region of the sky.

Refractor sees single bright galaxy

SCHMIDT CAMERA

Estonian optical worker Bernhard Schmidt (1879–1935) made a telescope with a specially shaped lens at its front. This directs light onto a spherical mirror. The image can then be photographed on a curved plate, providing a much wider view of the sky than is usually possible.

Schmidt camera shows many galaxies at once.

REFLECTING TELESCOPE

A reflecting telescope uses a curved mirror to focus light at the bottom of the tube. A second small mirror directs the light to the side of the tube or behind the main mirror. The largest and most powerful telescopes are reflectors, and they reveal the most distant objects in the Universe.

Reflector shows faint distant galaxies.

ASTRONOMY RECORDS

LOWEST OBSERVATORY

This observatory lies in the Homestake Mine, 0.9 miles (1.5km) below ground level in South Dakota. It detects minute particles from space, called neutrinos, that can pass straight through the Earth. An underground tank containing a special fluid shows when a neutrino passes through.

LARGEST SINGLE RADIO DISH

(1,000ft/305m diameter) is the Arecibo radio telescope. It is built into a natural valley in the hills of Puerto Rico.

OLDEST STANDING OBSERVATORY

is the Chomsung-Dae observatory, Kyongju, South Korea. It was built in A.D. 632.

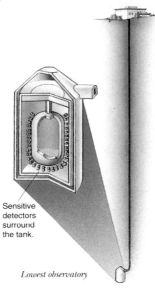

Sensitive detectors surround the tank.

Lowest observatory

INSTRUMENTS OF OBSERVATION

Telescopes that observe visible light waves can study only some of the wavelengths that come from space. Telescopes that detect other wavelengths from the electromagnetic spectrum (see p.231), such as radio waves, give astronomers a fuller picture of the Universe.

ASTRONOMICAL MEASUREMENT

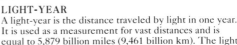

LIGHT-YEAR

A light-year is the distance traveled by light in one year. It is used as a measurement for vast distances and is equal to 5,879 billion miles (9,461 billion km). The light that we see today from the galaxy IC 4296 left its source 117 million years ago, when dinosaurs roamed Earth.

PARALLAX

A star appears to shift its position against the background of more distant stars if seen from opposite sides of Earth's orbit. Thus an astronomer can calculate the distance of a star from Earth from the size of this parallax shift, together with the diameter of Earth's orbit.

Star's image in July

Parallax shift

Star's image in January

The smaller the shift, the farther the star.

Earth in January

Sun

Earth in July

RED SHIFT

The speed at which a star moves can be calculated by analyzing its light. If a star is moving away from Earth, its light waves are stretched out, and this makes its analyzed spectrum of colors or wavelengths appear to be shifted to the red end of the spectrum. The size of this "red shift" gives the speed of the star.

Stationary star
If the star is not moving away from or toward Earth, an observer sees its light at its true wavelength.

Retreating star
If the star is moving away from Earth, its light waves are stretched and appear more red.

MAJOR WORLD OBSERVATORIES

Observatories	Height	
	meters	feet
Keck Observatory, Mauna Kea, Hawaii	4,205	13,796
Hale Observatory, Palomar, California	1,706	5,597
Whipple Observatory, Mt. Hopkins	2,600	8,530
Kitt Peak Observatory, Arizona	2,064	6,772
V.L.A., Socorro, New Mexico	2,124	6,969
Anglo-Australian Telescope, Siding Spring, Australia	1,165	3,822

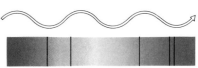

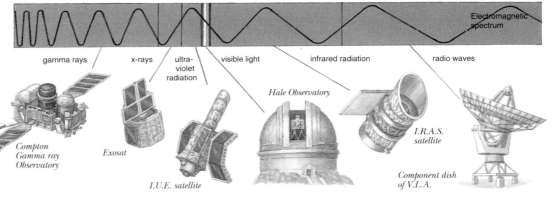

Electromagnetic spectrum

gamma rays   x-rays   ultra-violet radiation   visible light   infrared radiation   radio waves

Hale Observatory

Compton Gamma ray Observatory

Exosat

I.U.E. satellite

I.R.A.S. satellite

Component dish of V.L.A.

SPACE EXPLORATION

IN OCTOBER 1957, THE USSR put *Sputnik 1* into orbit around the Earth; the great achievements of the Space Age had begun.

c.1200 Chinese use gunpowder rockets in battle, with handheld launching baskets.

1926 Liquid fuel rocket launched by US pioneer Robert Goddard.

1934 Liquid oxygen and alcohol rocket launched by German pioneer rocket scientist Wernher Von Braun (1912–77).

1942 German V2 rocket, designed and built by Von Braun, used against Britain in World War II.

V2 rocket

1965 US Mars probe *Mariner 4* finds no water or life on Mars. First spacewalk by Soviet cosmonaut Leonov in *Voskhod 2*. US manned craft *Gemini 6* meets *Gemini 7* in space.

Leonov's spacewalk

1966 USSR's *Luna 9* probe lands on Moon . First panoramic photos of Moon surface by US *Lunar Orbiter 1*. US manned craft *Gemini 8* docks with *Agena* rocket stage.

Luna 9

1968 Space observatory launched to study UV rays. Three US astronauts orbit Moon in *Apollo 8*.

1969 First people on Moon. US *Apollo 11* astronauts take rock samples.

Edwin M. Aldrin steps onto Moon's surface

1974 Images of surface of Mercury sent by US *Mariner 10*.

1975 Images of surface of Venus sent by USSR's *Venera 9*. US and USSR craft, *Apollo 18* and *Soyuz 19*, meet in space.

Mariner 10

Venera 9

1976 US *Viking 1* lands on Mars. Surface tests confirm no life on Mars. Daily weather reports sent until Spring 1983.

1977 US *Voyagers 1* and *2* launched to outer planets and beyond.

Surface of Mars

Voyager probe

1982 Surface of Venus photographed in color by USSR's *Venera 13*.

Surface of Venus

1984 Manneuvering unit used by US astronaut Bruce McCandless to float untethered alongside Shuttle *Challenger*. First retrieval and repair of a satellite, *Solar Maximum* satellite, in space, using Canadian-designed *Canadarm*.

Bruce McCandless

Uranus

1986 *Voyager 2* finds ten moons and a ring system around Uranus. Shuttle *Challenger* explodes, killing crew of seven. Halley's comet returns, observed by four probes.

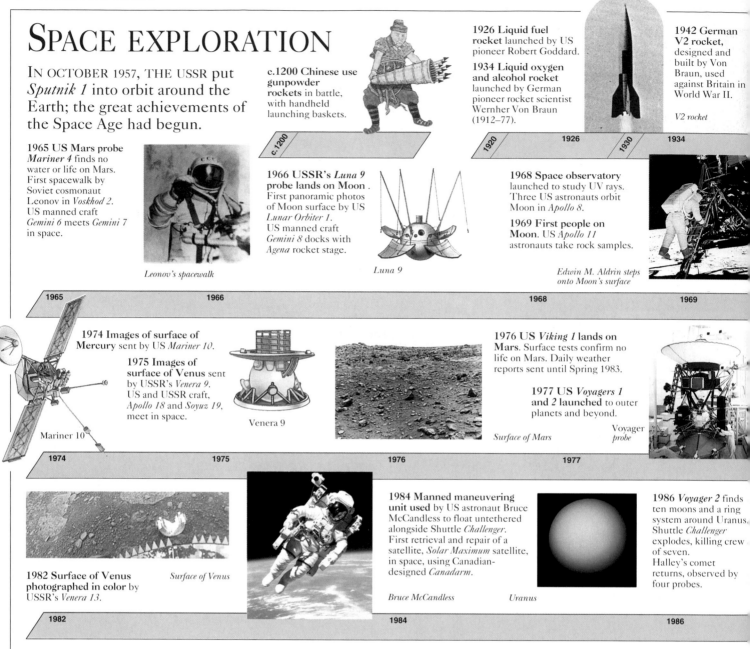

SPACE FACTS

• Rivalry between the two great powers after World War II, the US and USSR, resulted in the "Space Race." Each side tried to show its superiority in space and rocket technology.

• One-third of the world's population watched the *Apollo 11* Moon landing on television.

• More than 300 people in total have traveled into space.

• Everything becomes weightless when spacecraft leave Earth, so untethered objects float in midair. Liquid and food is stored in and eaten from sealed bags.

• Some spacesuits may have as many as 15 layers of different materials to protect and insulate.

• Inside a manned spacecraft, air is constantly being removed and purified. In a space station, this process has to continue for months or years at a time.

• The building in which *Saturn V* rockets were assembled was so large that small clouds sometimes formed in its roof.

• Cosmonauts aboard *Salyut 4* were not allowed to return to Earth when their air purifying system broke down, even when mold grew up the walls.

Salyut 4

Undersuit contains pipes for cool, flowing water to protect against Sun's heat.

Suit layers of nylon, dacron, and kevlar.

ASTRONAUT SUIT

Spacesuits have to be tough to protect the astronaut from small meteorites. Most have internal cooling systems to absorb the Sun's heat, and a dark, mirrored visor to shield the astronaut from the Sun's glare. Spacesuits are very heavy on Earth, but are weightless when in space.

SPACE RECORDS

LONGEST CONTINUOUS PERIOD IN SPACE was achieved by the Russian cosmonaut Musa Manarov (born 1951), who spent 365 days, 39 minutes, and 47 seconds on the space station *Mir*.

FIRST MARRIED COUPLE IN SPACE were Americans Mark Lee and Judy Davis, on shuttle *Endeavour* in September 1992.

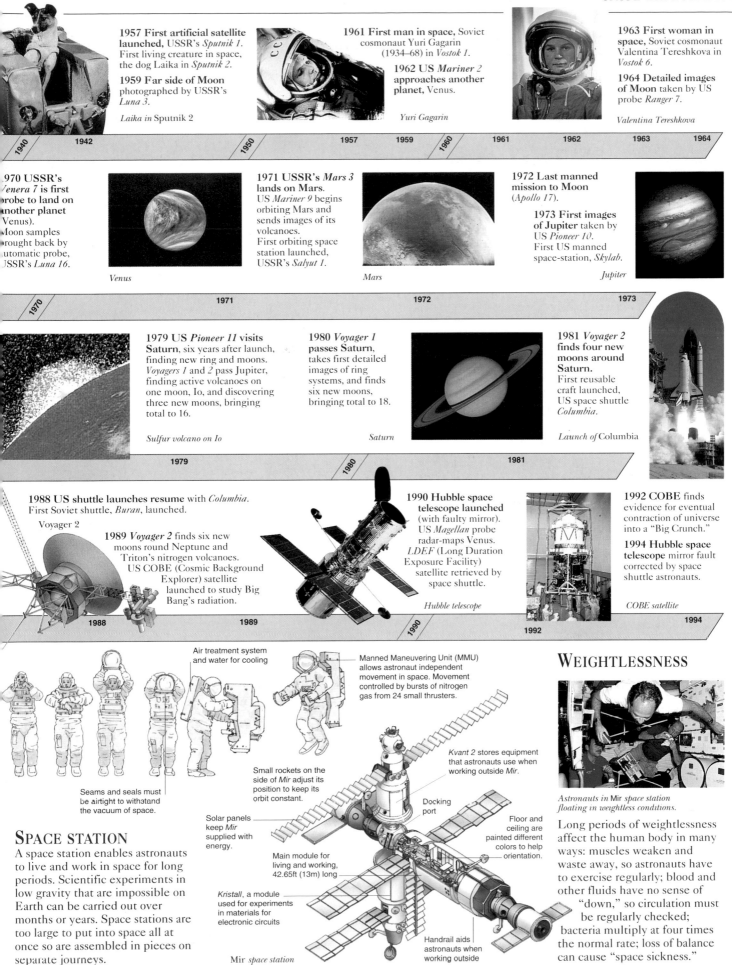

1957 First artificial satellite launched, USSR's *Sputnik 1*. First living creature in space, the dog Laika in *Sputnik 2*.

1959 Far side of Moon photographed by USSR's *Luna 3*.

Laika in Sputnik 2

1961 First man in space, Soviet cosmonaut Yuri Gagarin (1934–68) in *Vostok 1*.

1962 US *Mariner 2* approaches another planet, Venus.

Yuri Gagarin

1963 First woman in space, Soviet cosmonaut Valentina Tereshkova in *Vostok 6*.

1964 Detailed images of Moon taken by US probe *Ranger 7*.

Valentina Tereshkova

1940 · 1942 · 1950 · 1957 · 1959 · 1960 · 1961 · 1962 · 1963 · 1964

1970 USSR's *Venera 7* is first probe to land on another planet (Venus). Moon samples brought back by automatic probe, USSR's *Luna 16*.

1971 USSR's *Mars 3* lands on Mars. US *Mariner 9* begins orbiting Mars and sends images of its volcanoes. First orbiting space station launched, USSR's *Salyut 1*.

Venus

1972 Last manned mission to Moon (*Apollo 17*).

1973 First images of Jupiter taken by US *Pioneer 10*. First US manned space-station, *Skylab*.

Mars

Jupiter

1970 · 1971 · 1972 · 1973

1979 US *Pioneer 11* visits Saturn, six years after launch, finding new ring and moons. *Voyagers 1* and *2* pass Jupiter, finding active volcanoes on one moon, Io, and discovering three new moons, bringing total to 16.

Sulfur volcano on Io

1980 *Voyager 1* passes Saturn, takes first detailed images of ring systems, and finds six new moons, bringing total to 18.

Saturn

1981 *Voyager 2* finds four new moons around Saturn. First reusable craft launched, US space shuttle *Columbia*.

Launch of Columbia

1979 · 1980 · 1981

1988 US shuttle launches resume with *Columbia*. First Soviet shuttle, *Buran*, launched.

Voyager 2

1989 *Voyager 2* finds six new moons round Neptune and Triton's nitrogen volcanoes. US COBE (Cosmic Background Explorer) satellite launched to study Big Bang's radiation.

1990 Hubble space telescope launched (with faulty mirror). US *Magellan* probe radar-maps Venus. *LDEF* (Long Duration Exposure Facility) satellite retrieved by space shuttle.

Hubble telescope

1992 COBE finds evidence for eventual contraction of universe into a "Big Crunch."

1994 Hubble space telescope mirror fault corrected by space shuttle astronauts.

COBE satellite

1988 · 1989 · 1990 · 1992 · 1994

Air treatment system and water for cooling

Seams and seals must be airtight to withstand the vacuum of space.

Manned Maneuvering Unit (MMU) allows astronaut independent movement in space. Movement controlled by bursts of nitrogen gas from 24 small thrusters.

SPACE STATION

A space station enables astronauts to live and work in space for long periods. Scientific experiments in low gravity that are impossible on Earth can be carried out over months or years. Space stations are too large to put into space all at once so are assembled in pieces on separate journeys.

Small rockets on the side of *Mir* adjust its position to keep its orbit constant.

Solar panels keep *Mir* supplied with energy.

Main module for living and working, 42.65ft (13m) long

Kristall, a module used for experiments in materials for electronic circuits

Kvant 2 stores equipment that astronauts use when working outside *Mir*.

Docking port

Floor and ceiling are painted different colors to help orientation.

Handrail aids astronauts when working outside

Mir space station

WEIGHTLESSNESS

Astronauts in Mir *space station floating in weightless conditions.*

Long periods of weightlessness affect the human body in many ways: muscles weaken and waste away, so astronauts have to exercise regularly; blood and other fluids have no sense of "down," so circulation must be regularly checked; bacteria multiply at four times the normal rate; loss of balance can cause "space sickness."

ROCKETS

IN ORDER TO ESCAPE Earth's gravity, a rocket must reach 24,900mph (40,000km/h). Rockets burn fuel and liquid oxygen, ignited under pressure.

WHAT A BLAST!

The F1 engine of the *Saturn V* rocket (which carried the astronauts to the Moon) is the most powerful engine ever built. Each of its five nozzles is 12.5ft (3.81m) in diameter and 19ft (5.79m) high, as tall as a giraffe. At launch, each engine burns three tons of fuel every second.

SPACE MISSION FACTS

- Rockets are designed in separate stages, so that when all the fuel from a stage has been used up, that stage drops away, and the next takes over.

- The first 11 US unmanned missions to the Moon were unsuccessful: *Rangers 4* and *6* hit the Moon but failed to transmit any data. The rest missed the Moon, *Ranger 3* overshooting by 37,000 miles (59,500km).

- On January 28, 1986, the US space shuttle *Challenger* exploded 73 seconds after launch. The crew of seven was killed in the world's worst space disaster.

- A hyphen instead of a minus sign keyed into a computer caused *Mariner 1*'s launch vehicle to crash into the Atlantic in 1962.

- Each shuttle launch releases 75 tons of hydrogen chloride into the atmosphere, as well as tons of pollutant waste from the solid fuel burned during liftoff.

- The Moon's astronauts left behind them the remains of six lunar landers, three moon buggies, and more than 50 tons of litter.

JUNK ALERT

One great danger facing astronauts and satellites is fragments of old rockets and satellites. This crater in the *Solar Max* satellite was made by a paint fleck traveling at high speed.

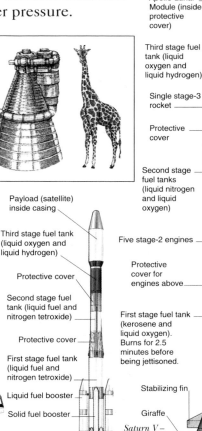

Launch escape tower
Apollo Command Module
Apollo Service Module
Apollo Lunar Module (inside protective cover)
Third stage fuel tank (liquid oxygen and liquid hydrogen)
Single stage-3 rocket
Protective cover
Second stage fuel tanks (liquid nitrogen and liquid oxygen)
Five stage-2 engines
Protective cover for engines above
First stage fuel tank (kerosene and liquid oxygen). Burns for 2.5 minutes before being jettisoned.
Stabilizing fin
Giraffe
Saturn V – 363ft (110.64m)

External fuel tank (liquid oxygen and liquid hydrogen)
Solid fuel rocket booster
O-ring (joint between booster sections)
Payload container (*Vostok* manned capsule)
Orbital stage
Central rocket
Payload bay 60ft (18.3m) long
Orbiter
Boosters
Vostok – 119.5ft (36.41m)
Space shuttle – 191.6ft (58.4m)

Payload (satellite) inside casing
Third stage fuel tank (liquid oxygen and liquid hydrogen)
Protective cover
Second stage fuel tank (liquid fuel and nitrogen tetroxide)
Protective cover
First stage fuel tank (liquid fuel and nitrogen tetroxide)
Liquid fuel booster
Solid fuel booster
Ariane 44LP – 186.2ft (56.76m)

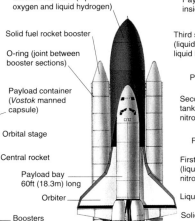

Solid fuel booster rockets, designed to be used 10 times, parachute back to Earth, and are later recovered from sea.

Solid fuel rocket boosters jettisoned 2 mins 5 secs after liftoff, at an altitude of 28 miles (45km). Shuttle now traveling at 4.5 times the speed of sound (Mach 4.5).

Liquid hydrogen from external fuel tank flows into orbiter engines at 820gal/sec (3,100 liters/sec).

Solid fuel (polybutadiene) burns for 2 mins. Each solid fuel rocket produces the thrust of 11 Boeing 747s at takeoff.

Rupture in O-rings (joints) of left solid fuel booster caused 1986 *Challenger* shuttle explosion.

External fuel tank
Orbiter
Solid fuel rocket boosters

Main engines on orbiter take fuel from external tank. Two solid fuel boosters fire for takeoff.

Shuttle reaches 81 miles (130km) at Mach 15. External tank released; burns up in Earth's atmosphere.

Shuttle engines put orbiter into circular orbit.

SATELLITE REPAIR JOB

In 1984, the shuttle *Challenger* retrieved and repaired the US *Solar Max* solar observatory while in space. One of the satellite's control systems had failed and it was falling toward Earth. The shuttle's robotic arm brought it into the cargo bay, where repairs were made. The satellite was then put back in orbit.

Orbiter remains in orbit for between 5 and 30 days. Mission can be carried out – new satellites put into orbit, old ones mended, experiments performed.

Cargo bay doors close. Engines rotate orbiter into reentry position.

Orbiter manoeuvres into precise angle for reentry. Begins 30-minute descent into atmosphere at Mach 22.4.

Parts of nose and wings reach 2,660°F (1,460°C) during reentry. They are covered with 32,000 carbon or silica insulating tiles, each glued on by hand.

Orbiter makes four "S-shaped" circuits to break its speed of Mach 2.5, before making a gliding landing.

SPACE CENTERS

Launch site	Launches	Type of launch
Pletsetsk cosmodrome, USSR	1,056	Secret military satellites
Baikonur cosmodrome, USSR	693	Manned craft, probes, and satellites
Cape Canaveral (USAF), US	1,045	Manned craft, probes, and satellites
Kennedy Space Center, US	66	Apollo missions and space shuttle

SPACE SHUTTLE MISSIONS

The US Space Shuttle is the first reusable spacecraft. During its missions, which usually last a week, the shuttle can put satellites into orbit, conduct experiments, and repair satellites in space. Thousands of heat-resistant tiles protect it on its reentry into Earth's atmosphere.

Orbiter lands at a speed of 214mph (345km/h). It is towed, or flown on the back of a Boeing 747 jet, to next launch site.

EARTH

From Earth's formation to the strongest earthquakes and the biggest volcanic eruptions, this section provides every essential fact and figure about our wonderful planet.

Earth • Continents • Volcanoes • Earthquakes • Rocks and Minerals
Ocean Floor • Oceans and Islands • Mountains • Valleys and Caves • Glaciation
Rivers and Lakes • Weather • Climates • Deserts • Forests • Earth's Biosphere
Earth in Danger • Saving the Earth

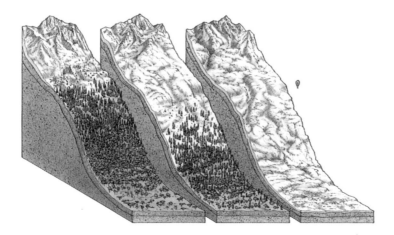

EARTH

THE EARTH IS ONE OF THE NINE planets in the Solar System. It is the fifth largest in size and is the only planet with plentiful oxygen and water: the necessary ingredients for life.

THEORY OF FORMATION

1 About 4.6 billion years ago a dense cloud of gas and dust contracted to form the Sun. Other matter in the cloud formed solid lumps of ice and rock, and these joined together to form the planets.

2 Radioactivity in the rocks caused the newborn Earth to melt. Iron and nickel sank to form the Earth's core, while oceans of molten rock floated on the surface.

3 About 4 billion years ago, the Earth's crust began to form. At first there may have been many small protocontinents floating on the molten rock beneath.

4 Over millions of years the crust thickened and volcanoes erupted. Gases pouring out of the volcanoes began to form the atmosphere, and water vapor condensed to fill the oceans.

ANATOMY OF THE EARTH

The Earth is made up of several layers of rock around a core of iron and nickel. The deeper the layer, the higher the temperature.

Atmosphere
Depth: approx.
400 miles (640km)

Crust
Depth: 4–44 miles
(6–70km)
Composition: rocks
similar to those on
the surface

Lithosphere
(Crust and upper mantle)
Depth: approx.124 miles
(200km)

Mantle
Depth: approx. 1,800 miles (2,900km)
Composition: mostly solid rock;
probably partly melted 50–93 miles
(80–150km) down

Outer core
Depth: approx. 1,240 miles (2,000km)
Composition: mostly liquid iron,
nickel, and oxygen

Inner core
Depth: 1,700 miles (2,740km) across
Composition: solid iron and nickel
The temperature of Earth's inner core is thought to be
about 8,100°F (4,500°C).

DEEPEST DRILLING INTO EARTH'S CRUST

The deepest mine in the world reaches 2.34 miles (3.7km) down into the Earth. A geological exploration has drilled more than 7.5 miles (12km) below the Earth's surface. Yet neither of these is anywhere near as deep as the bottom of the Earth's crust.

Depth (km)

8
6
4
2
Sea level

Mount Everest:
5.5 miles (8.85km)

A deep coal mine

Deepest mine: 2.34 miles (3.7km)

Deepest
ocean drilling:
1.05 miles
(1.7km)

Depth
(miles)
Sea level

2
4
6
8
10
12
14
16
18
20
22
24
26
28
30
32
34
36
38
40

Deepest drilled hole: 7.4 miles (12.1km)

Deepest hole projected to reach 9.3 miles (15km)

The Earth's crust is much thicker
beneath land than beneath the ocean.

CRUST

MANTLE

2
4
6
8
10
12
14
16
18
20
22
24

The atmosphere is the film of gases that surrounds the Earth. It is divided into four main layers – the troposphere, stratosphere, mesosphere, and thermosphere. The composition of the troposphere is 78% nitrogen, 21% oxygen, and 1% water vapor and other gases. The atmosphere is held in place by gravity. It stops the Earth from becoming too hot or too cold, and shields the planet from the Sun's harmful ultraviolet rays.

5 About 3.5 billion years ago most of the Earth's crust had formed, but the shapes of the continents looked very different from today. The oldest rocks on Earth date from just before this time.

6 Today the Earth is still changing. The lithosphere – the crust and upper mantle – is made up of huge plates that are constantly being created and destroyed at their edges. The plates are always on the move, powered by forces deep inside the Earth (see pp.40–41).

EARTH DATA

Age	4.6 billion years
Mass	5,854 billion billion tons
Volume	259,877,796,843cu miles (1,083,218,915,000cu km)
Diameter at equator	7,926 miles (12,756km)
Diameter at Poles	7,899 miles (12,713km)
Circumference at equator	24,901 miles (40,075km)
Circumference at Poles	24,819 miles (39,942km)
Distance from the Sun	93 million miles (150 million km)
Time for one spin	23 hours, 56 minutes, 4 seconds
Time to orbit Sun	365 days, 6 hours, 9 minutes, 9.5 seconds

EARTH FACTS

• Proportion of land and sea:
Area of land: 29.2%
Area of sea: 70.8%

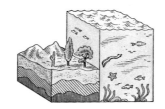

• If a car could travel nonstop around the equator at 62mph (100km/h), it would take 16 days, 16 hrs, 45 mins. A car driving from the N. Pole to the S. Pole and back would finish 80 mins earlier, because Earth is not a perfect sphere.

• An excavator digging a hole at 39in (1m) per min through the Earth would take 24 years to reach the other side.

EARTH'S MAGNETIC FIELD

Molten iron flowing in the Earth's outer core generates electric currents. These currents create the Earth's magnetic field. This field – the magnetosphere – stretches more than 37,000 miles (60,000km) into space. Sometimes Earth's magnetic field flips: north becomes south and vice versa. No one knows why this happens. The last pole reversal occurred about 700,000 years ago.

Geographical poles
The geographical North and South Poles lie on the Earth's axis (the imaginary line around which the Earth spins).

Magnetic poles
The magnetic north and south poles are a short distance away from geographical north and south.

Pattern of magnetic field
These lines show the pattern of the Earth's magnetic field. The field is strongest where the lines are close together.

JUST A PINPRICK

If the Earth were the size of an egg, the deepest hole ever drilled by humans would not even pierce its shell.

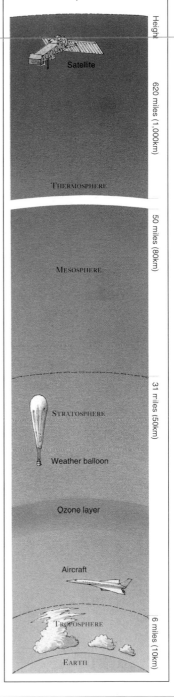

Satellite

Height

620 miles (1,000km)

THERMOSPHERE

50 miles (80km)

MESOSPHERE

31 miles (50km)

STRATOSPHERE

Weather balloon

Ozone layer

Aircraft

6 miles (10km)

TROPOSPHERE

EARTH

CONTINENTS

THE CONTINENTS ARE THE seven huge land masses that make up most of the Earth's land surface. They are always on the move, shifted around by forces deep inside the Earth. The concept of moving continents is known as continental drift.

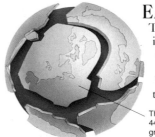

EARTH'S TECTONIC PLATES

The Earth's lithosphere is fragmented into slabs of crust and upper mantle, called tectonic plates. These slabs fit together like a huge jigsaw puzzle. Where the plates rise above sea level, they form continents and islands.

The Earth's crust is only 44 miles (70km) thick at its greatest depths.

CONTINENTAL DRIFT

1 Some 250 million years ago the continents were joined together in the giant supercontinent of Pangaea (from the Greek word meaning "all lands"). About 200 million years ago Pangaea slowly began to break up.

2 By 135 million years ago Pangaea had split into two main land masses, Gondwanaland and Laurasia. North America and Europe split apart, and about 120 million years ago India began to drift north toward Asia.

3 Over the next 120 million years the continents drifted into their present-day positions. The Americas moved away from Europe and Africa; India joined onto Asia; Australia and Antarctica split apart.

4 This is how the Earth might look 150 million years from now. Africa has split in two, and the larger section has drifted north to join Europe. Antarctica has joined Australia, and California has been crumpled against Alaska.

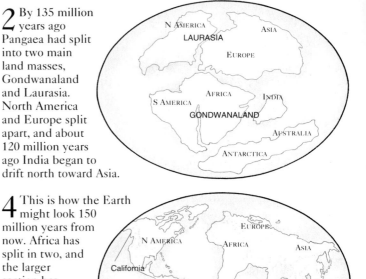

THE PLATES AND THEIR BOUNDARIES

The Earth's crust is made up of about 15 major plates. Plates that form the ocean floor are oceanic plates, and plates that form land are continental plates. Most plates are partly oceanic and partly continental. Scientists locate the boundaries by monitoring earthquakes and volcanoes.

KEY

◀▶ Pulling apart

▶◀ Colliding

········ Subduction zone

– – – Uncertain boundary

——— Mid-ocean ridge

Transform fault

Rift valley

SECTION THROUGH THE EARTH'S LITHOSPHERE

This illustration shows a cross-section of the Earth's lithosphere along the equator.

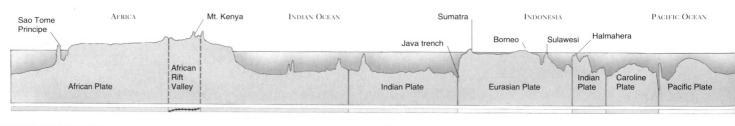

CONTINENT SIZES

Continent	Area	
	sq km	sq miles
Asia	44,485,900	17,176,090
Africa	30,269,680	11,687,180
North America	24,235,280	9,357,290
South America	17,820,770	6,880,630
Antarctica	13,209,000	5,100,020
Europe	10,530,750	4,065,940
Australasia	8,924,100	3,445,610

CONTINENT AND PLATE FACTS

- Europe and Africa would fit into Asia with room to spare.
- Europe and the Americas drift about 1.6in (4cm) further apart every year.
- The African Rift Valley grows about 0.04in (1mm) wider every year.
- Fossils of tropical plants are found as far north as Alaska, because North American land mass was once situated in tropics.
- Continental plates are up to 43 miles (70km) thick, but oceanic plates are only about 4 miles (6km) thick.

PROPORTION OF LAND PER CONTINENT

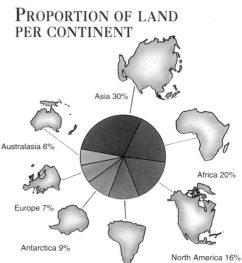

Asia 30%
Australasia 6%
Europe 7%
Antarctica 9%
South America 12%
North America 16%
Africa 20%

PLATE TECTONICS

Plate tectonics is the theory of how and why the Earth's plates move. At their boundaries, the plates may be colliding, pulling apart, or sliding past each other. These different types of motion build mountains, cause earthquakes and volcanoes, and create deep-sea trenches.

Chains of volcanoes often form at subduction zones.

Subduction zone

Mid-ocean ridge

Convergence

Transform fault

Rock melts when it is forced down into the mantle at a subduction zone.

TRANSFORM FAULT

Transform faults are boundaries where two plates are sliding past each other. Earthquakes often occur at this type of boundary, as the plates grind past each other (see p.44). The San Andreas Fault in California is a transform fault.

CONVERGENCE

When two continental plates collide, the Earth's crust often buckles and folds as they push against each other, forcing up great mountain ranges. The Himalayas and the Appalachians were formed by colliding plates.

SUBDUCTION ZONE

When two plates collide, one plate sometimes rides over the other, forcing it down into the mantle. This type of boundary, called a subduction zone, often occurs at the edges of oceans where the thicker continental plate rides over the thinner oceanic plate. Deep ocean trenches form at these boundaries.

PULLING APART

Where two plates are pulling apart, molten rock from the mantle rises to fill the gap, creating new crust. When this type of boundary occurs beneath the sea, ridges of mountains called mid-ocean ridges form. On land, these boundaries create steep-sided rift valleys.

THEORIES OF MOVEMENT

Scientists have not yet identified exactly what makes the Earth's tectonic plates shift around, but there are several theories to explain their movements. The three main theories involve convection, gravity, and the different weights of hot and cold rock.

CONVECTION

Heat generated deep inside the Earth creates convection currents in the mantle. These currents slowly push the overlying plates around.

DENSITY OF ROCK

Hot rock rising at mid-ocean ridges cools down as it moves farther away from the ridge. As it cools it becomes denser and sinks, pulling the rest of the plate down with it.

GRAVITY

The plates are about 1–2 miles (2–3km) higher at mid-ocean ridges than at ocean rims, so they could simply be sliding slowly downhill under the force of gravity.

AS FAST AS A FINGERNAIL GROWS

The tectonic plates move at different rates along their margins, and some plates move faster than others. The average rate of movement is approximately 1 inch (2.5cm) every year: about as fast as a finger-nail grows.

No land rises above the Pacific Ocean for thousands of miles.

PACIFIC OCEAN

Andes

SOUTH AMERICA

Amazon Basin

ATLANTIC OCEAN

Peru-Chile trench

Mid-Atlantic Ridge

Pacific Plate

Nazca Plate

American Plate

African Plate

VOLCANOES

VOLCANOES OCCUR where magma (molten rock) from deep inside the Earth forces its way to the surface. The magma may erupt as red-hot lava, or may explode into clouds of ash and volcanic bombs. Volcanic activity also produces strange landscapes of gushing geysers, steaming lakes, and bubbling mudpools.

VOLCANIC AREAS

There are around 1,300 active volcanoes in the world. Some of the major volcanoes are marked on this map. Most volcanoes are located on or close to the boundaries of the plates that make up the Earth's lithosphere (see pp.40–41).

Many of the Earth's volcanoes lie beneath the oceans.

MAJOR ERUPTIONS

The eruption of Mount St. Helens, Washington

MOUNT ST. HELENS
erupted in May 1980. The explosion was heard more than 217 miles (350km) away. Hot ash and gas rushed down the mountainside; 62 people died.

GREATEST VOLCANIC EXPLOSION
occurred when Krakatoa, Indonesia, blew up in 1883, hurling rocks 34 miles (55km) high. The explosion was heard in Australia, and generated a 131ft (40m) high seismic sea wave (see p.45); 36,000 people died.

GREATEST VOLCANIC ERUPTION
was Tambora on Sumbawa, Indonesia, in 1815, which threw up more than 24cu miles (100cu km) of ash. The island was lowered by 4,100ft (1,250m); 92,000 people died.

MAJOR ACTIVE VOLCANOES

The number of volcanoes active in historic times is shown in parentheses after each region.

Name	Height		Latest eruption
	meters	feet	
Africa and Indian Ocean (14)			
Mt. Cameroon, Cameroon	4,070	13,353	1982
Nyamuragira, Zaire	3,053	10,016	1989
Antarctica (9)			
Erebus, Ross Island	3,794	12,448	1989
Asia (210)			
Kliuchevskoi, Siberia	4,850	15,912	1990
Kerinci, Indonesia	3,805	12,484	1970
SW Pacific (54)			
Ruapehu, New Zealand	2,796	9,173	1989
Europe and Middle East (20)			
Stromboli, Italy	926	3,038	1990
Etna, Sicily, Italy	3,350	10,991	1992
North America and Hawaii (56)			
Mount St. Helens, Washington	2,549	8,363	1988
Mauna Loa, Hawaii	4,170	13,681	1984
Iceland and Atlantic (54)			
Pico de Teide, Canary Islands	3,713	12,182	1909
Central and South America (100)			
Sangay, Ecuador	5,230	17,159	1989
Llullaillaco, Chile	6,723	22,057	1877
Popocatepetl, Mexico	5,465	17,930	1943

ERUPTION SIZES

The amount of ash thrown out is a good indicator of the size of an eruption.

*Mount Vesuvius
Italy
A.D. 79*

*Tambora
Indonesia
1815*

*Krakatoa
Indonesia
1883*

*Katmai
Alaska
1912*

*Mount St. Helens
Washington
1980*

*El Chichón,
Mexico
1982*

VOLCANO TYPES AND SHAPES

A volcano's shape depends mainly on the type of lava that comes out of it. Thick, sticky lava forms tall, steep-sided cones; thin, runny lava forms gently sloping lava shields and plateaus.

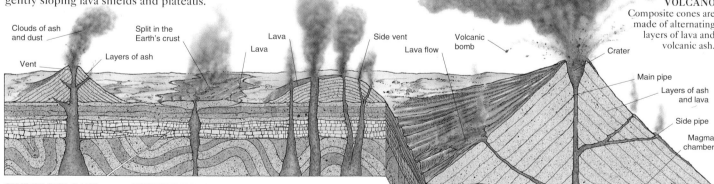

Clouds of ash and dust

Split in the Earth's crust

Lava

Side vent

Volcanic bomb

Lava flow

COMPOSITE VOLCANO
Composite cones are made of alternating layers of lava and volcanic ash.

Vent

Layers of ash

Lava

Crater

Main pipe

Layers of ash and lava

Side pipe

Magma chamber

CINDER VOLCANO
A cinder volcano is made up of layers of volcanic ash, and has a steep, conical shape. Each time the volcano erupts, another layer of ash is added.

FISSURE VOLCANO
Not all volcanoes form over a single hole. Sometimes a crack opens up in the Earth's crust, and runny lava flows out along its length, forming a plateau.

SHIELD VOLCANO
When the lava that erupts from a volcano is runny, it forms a gentle slope rather than a cone. These shield volcanoes often have many side vents.

TYPES OF LAVA

The type of lava that erupts from a volcano depends on several factors, such as the amount of gas it contains, and whether it is erupting onto land or into the sea. The two main types of lava flow, aa and pahoehoe, take their names from Hawaiian words.

PAHOEHOE LAVA
Pahoehoe lava is runny and moves fast. When it cools, it resembles coils of rope.

PILLOW LAVA
Lava erupting into the sea cools quickly in the water, forming pillow lava – round lumps of rock.

AA LAVA
Aa lava is thicker and stickier than pahoehoe lava. It cools to form sharp, chunky rock.

TALLEST GEYSER

In 1904, the Waimangu Geyser in New Zealand erupted to a height of around 1,500ft (457m). This is higher than the world's tallest building, the Sears Tower in Chicago, US, which is 1,460ft (445m) high. The Waimangu Geyser is no longer active.

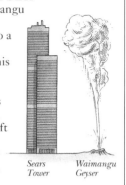

Sears Tower　　*Waimangu Geyser*

VOLCANIC PRODUCTS

The solid products of volcanic eruptions and explosions are called pyroclasts. These include cinders, volcanic ash, and large chunks of solidified lava. Cinders and ash may blanket a huge area after an eruption.

VOLCANIC BOMB
Blobs of molten lava erupting high into the air may fall as volcanic bombs.

LAPILLI
These cinder fragments are called lapilli, from the Latin for "little stones."

PUMICE
Pumice forms from lava containing bubbles of gas. It is often so light that it can float on water.

VOLCANIC DUST
Dust thrown high into the atmosphere during an eruption may fall hundreds of miles away.

VOLCANIC RECORDS

LARGEST ACTIVE VOLCANO
is Mauna Loa, Hawaii, which has a diameter of 62 miles (100km).

HIGHEST ACTIVE VOLCANO
is Guallatirir, Chile, which is 19,882ft (6,060m) high.

TALLEST ACTIVE GEYSER
is Steamboat Geyser, Wyoming. It erupts to a height of 195–380ft (60–115m).

VOLCANO PHASES

Most volcanoes have three phases: an active volcano has erupted in recent historic times or is still erupting; a dormant volcano has been quiet for a long time but may erupt again; an extinct volcano has stopped erupting and is not expected to erupt again.

Castle Rock, Edinburgh, Scotland: the remains of an extinct volcano.

LARGEST VOLCANIC EXPLOSIONS

Scientists measure the size of a volcanic explosion according to the Volcanic Explosivity Index (VEI). This grades explosions on a scale of 0 (a non-explosive eruption) to 7 or 8 for the largest eruptions. There have so far been no known eruptions with a VEI of 8.

Volcano and location	Date	VEI
Crater Lake, Oregon	c4895 B.C.	7
Kikai, Ryukyu Island, Japan	c4350 B.C.	7
Santorini (Thira), Greece	c1390 B.C.	6
Taupo, New Zealand	c130	7
Ilopango, El Salvador	c260	6
Oraefajokull, Iceland	1362	6
Long Island, New Guinea	c1660	6
Tambora, Indonesia	1815	7
Krakatoa, Indonesia	1883	6
Santa Maria, Guatemala	1902	6
Katmai (Novarupta), Alaska	1912	6

VOLCANOES ON OTHER PLANETS AND MOONS

Olympus Mons on Mars, which is the highest mountain in the Solar System, is an extinct volcano. The Moon also has extinct volcanoes, and there may be active volcanoes on Venus. Io, one of Jupiter's 16 moons, has active volcanoes that throw out plumes of gases up to 100 miles (160km) high.

Io's volcanoes throw out huge plumes of sulfurous gases.

VOLCANIC LANDSCAPE

Volcanic activity beneath the surface heats up water above and below the ground. This can create spectacular volcanic landscapes, called hydrothermal areas, where hot water, mud, and gases gush, bubble, and steam from vents in the ground.

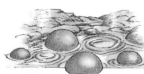

HOT SPRING
A steaming hot spring forms when underground water is heated by warm rocks. As it gets hotter, the water rises to the surface.

BUBBLING MUD POOL
A pool of hot, bubbling mud may form where hot water mixes with mineral particles. Acidic volcanic gases corrode these particles from the surrounding rocks.

FUMAROLE
A fumarole is a vent that releases jets of steam and hot volcanic gases. These gases often give off a smell of rotten eggs, because they contain sulfur.

GEYSER
A geyser is a tall jet of water that erupts when water trapped in underground chambers is heated to the boiling point by hot rocks.

SINTER TERRACE
Minerals deposited by a hot spring as it emerges onto the surface may build up into a beautiful, strangely colored sinter terrace.

EARTHQUAKES

EARTHQUAKES ARE caused by movements of the massive plates that make up the Earth's lithosphere. Each year scientists detect about 500,000 earthquakes and tremors (small earthquakes). Most are so small that they can hardly be felt, but about 1,000 cause damage. Severe earthquakes can reduce whole cities to rubble.

EARTHQUAKE BELTS

Most earthquakes occur on or near the edges of the Earth's tectonic plates (see pp.40–41). The ten earthquakes with the highest known death tolls are marked on this map.

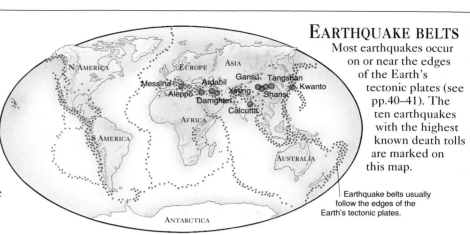

Earthquake belts usually follow the edges of the Earth's tectonic plates.

FOCUS AND EPICENTER

The exact point at which an earthquake occurs is the focus. The point on the Earth's surface directly above the focus is the epicenter.

The earthquake is strongest at the epicenter.

The focus is usually deep inside the Earth.

Shock waves can travel right through the Earth to the other side.

CLOSE-UP ON AN EARTHQUAKE

Many earthquakes occur at transform faults (see pp.40–41) where the jagged edges of two moving plates may occasionally lock together. Stress builds up within the plates, until they suddenly slip, making the ground shake violently.

The plates slip and lurch past each other, causing an earthquake.

This fault line marks the boundary of two plates.

MEASURING EARTHQUAKES

The study of earthquakes is called seismology. Scientists measure and record earthquakes using seismometers. The size of an earthquake is measured either according to its magnitude (the size of the shock waves and energy it produces) or according to its effects. Magnitude is usually measured by the Richter scale; effects are graded on the Modified Mercalli Intensity scale.

THE RICHTER SCALE
The Richter scale was devised by American Charles F. Richter in the 1930s.

Charles F. Richter (1900–1985)

Magnitude	Probable effects
1	Detectable only by instruments
2–3	Can just about be felt by people
4–5	Detectable within 20 miles (32km) of the epicenter. Possible slight damage within a small area
6	Fairly destructive
7	A major earthquake
8	A very destructive earthquake

THE MODIFIED MERCALLI INTENSITY SCALE
The Mercalli scale runs from I to XII. It grades earthquakes according to their effects, such as damage to buildings. The original scale was devised by Italian Giuseppe Mercalli (1850–1914) in 1902. It was later updated to create the Modified Mercalli Intensity scale.

 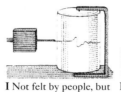 

I Not felt by people, but recorded by instruments. Animals may be uneasy. Doors may swing slowly.

II May be felt by a few people indoors, particularly those on upper floors.

III Felt indoors by several as a rapid vibration. Hanging objects may swing slightly.

IV Felt indoors by many, outdoors by a few. Standing cars rock. Dishes and windows rattle.

V Felt outdoors by most. Buildings tremble. Small objects are knocked over. Doors swing.

VI Felt by all; people afraid. Trees shake. Small bells ring. Dishes break. Pictures and books fall.

VII General alarm. Hard for people to stand. Chimneys crack. Plaster falls. Windows break.

VIII Difficult to drive. Considerable damage to buildings. Chimneys fall. Tree branches break.

IX General panic. Large cracks appear in the ground. Some buildings collapse.

X Water slops out of rivers. Underground pipes torn apart. Most buildings destroyed.

XI Few buildings remain standing. Bridges collapse. Railroad tracks buckle. Large landslides.

XII Almost all constructions destroyed. Waves seen on ground. Rivers change course.

EARTHQUAKE SIDE-EFFECTS

Earthquakes on land may flatten cities and towns, cause landslides and avalanches, and start fires. Earthquakes beneath the sea may cause giant waves called seismic sea waves or tsunamis. These can travel many miles across the ocean, building into a huge wall of water as they approach the coast.

FIRE
If an earthquake breaks gas mains, the slightest spark can cause huge fires.

LANDSLIDE
An earthquake may cause a huge chunk of mountainside to break away, burying all in its path.

SEISMIC SEA WAVE
A seismic sea wave can cause terrible devastation when it hits the coast.

WORST EARTHQUAKE DAMAGE ON RECORD

The most destructive earthquake happened in Kwanto, Japan in 1923. In nearby Tokyo, where many of the houses were built of wood and paper, the shaking ground overturned stoves, setting the houses on fire. A fire-storm then engulfed the city. Almost 144,000 people were killed, and 575,000 homes were destroyed.

Tokyo was devastated by the 1923 earthquake.

SAN ANDREAS FAULT

At the San Andreas Fault in California, two plates are sliding past each other at a rate of about 2in (5cm) every year. Earthquakes and tremors happen frequently and are sometimes severe. San Francisco is very close to the San Andreas Fault.

San Andreas Fault, California

SEISMIC SEA WAVE (TSUNAMI) RECORDS

HIGHEST SEISMIC SEA WAVE was estimated at 279ft (85m) high, almost as high as New York's Statue of Liberty. It appeared on April 24, 1971, off Ishigaki Island, Japan.

FASTEST SEISMIC SEA WAVES have been recorded traveling at approximately 560mph (900km/h), more than 186mph (300km/h) faster than the world water speed record of 345mph (556km/h), achieved by a hydroplane.

EARTHQUAKE-PROOF BUILDINGS

In earthquake-prone areas, specially designed buildings can lessen the effects of a serious earthquake. For example, a pyramidal or cone-shaped building is less likely to topple over than a building with vertical walls.

San Francisco's TransAmerica building

The central column of this Japanese pagoda helps to absorb earthquake shocks.

WORST EARTHQUAKE DEATH TOLLS

Location	Date	Estimated deaths
Shansi, China	1556	830,000
Calcutta, India	1737	300,000
Tangshan, China	1976	255,000
Aleppo, Syria	1138	230,000
Damghan, Iran	856	200,000
Gansu, China	1920	200,000
Nr. Xining, China	1927	200,000
Ardabil, Iran	893	150,000
Kwanto, Japan	1923	144,000
Messina, Italy	1908	70–100,000

STRONGEST KNOWN EARTHQUAKES

Location	Date	Magnitude Richter scale
Colombia	1906	8.9
Morioka, Japan	1933	8.9
Lisbon, Portugal	1755	8.75
Assam, India	1897	8.7

EARTHQUAKE FACTS

• Most earthquakes last less than a minute.

• Longest recorded earthquake lasted four minutes. Occurred on March 27, 1964, in Alaska. It was one of the strongest known earthquakes, but killed only 115 people due to low population density.

• First instrument for recording earthquakes was the seismoscope, invented in China in A.D. 132.

• Earthquake shock waves travel through rock at approx 16,000mph (25,000km/h): more than 20 times the speed of sound. They slow down in sand and mud.

• Some scientists believe animals can sense an earthquake's approach. Strange behavior includes: dogs howling; chickens fleeing roosts; rats and mice leaving holes; and fish thrashing about in ponds.

MOONQUAKES

Most moonquakes are caused by meteorites smashing into the Moon's surface. Moonquakes are monitored by seismometers left by American astronauts.

Seismometers on the Moon

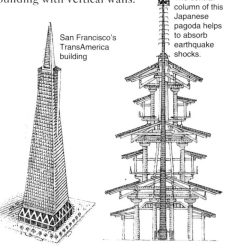

ROCKS AND MINERALS

AT ANY POINT ON THE EARTH'S SURFACE, if you dig down far enough, you will come to rock. Rocks are the building blocks of the Earth's crust. There are many different types of rock, and they are all composed of one or more minerals.

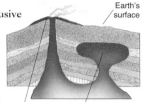

Limestone is a sedimentary rock (see below). About 75% of land is covered with sedimentary rocks.

ROCKS

The study of rocks is called petrology. All types of rock fall into one of three categories: igneous, sedimentary, or metamorphic.

IGNEOUS ROCK

Igneous rock starts off deep within the Earth as magma (molten rock). The magma rises toward the surface, where it may erupt from a volcano, or cool and solidify within the Earth's crust.

Basalt is an igneous rock.

Extrusive and intrusive igneous rock

Igneous rock that erupts from a volcano onto the Earth's surface is extrusive. Igneous rock that solidifies before it reaches the surface is intrusive.

Earth's surface

Extrusive igneous rock — Intrusive igneous rock

The Giant's Causeway in Northern Ireland is formed from basalt, an extrusive igneous rock.

Granite mountains in Yosemite, California: intrusive igneous rocks have been exposed by the erosion of overlying rocks.

SEDIMENTARY ROCK

Rocks are weathered into fragments that are carried away by water, wind, and ice. These sediments are laid down in lakes, rivers, sand dunes, and on the sea floor. Over millions of years they are compressed, forming layers of sedimentary rocks.

Sandstone is a sedimentary rock.

Ayers Rock (Uluru) in central Australia is composed of sandstone.

METAMORPHIC ROCK

Metamorphic rock is igneous or sedimentary rock that has been changed by heat and/or pressure. Heat may come from rising magma, and pressure may occur when rock is squeezed during mountain building.

Gneiss is a metamorphic rock.

This landscape in northwest Scotland is formed from gneiss.

GEOLOGICAL TIME CHART

Rocks are dated according to a geological timescale that divides the Earth's history into eras, periods, and epochs.

Era	Period	Million years ago
Cenozoic	Quaternary	
	Holocene (epoch)	0.01
	Pleistocene (epoch)	2
	Tertiary	
	Pliocene (epoch)	5
	Miocene (epoch)	25
	Oligocene (epoch)	38
	Eocene (epoch)	55
	Palaeocene (epoch)	65
Mesozoic	Cretaceous	144
	Jurassic	213
	Triassic	248
Paleozoic	Permian	286
	Pennsylvanian	320
	Mississippian	360
	Devonian	408
	Silurian	438
	Ordovician	505
	Cambrian	590
	Precambrian	4,600

THE ROCK CYCLE

All rocks are constantly passing through a recycling process.

Igneous rocks are weathered away and washed into the ocean.

Mineral particles sink to the sea floor where they are compacted into sedimentary rock.

Heat from molten rock changes surrounding sedimentary and igneous rock into metamorphic rock.

Rock may melt and rise to the surface where it cools to form igneous rock.

MINERALS

A mineral is a natural, non-living substance. Examples include gold, silver, gypsum, quartz, and sulfur.

ROCK-FORMING MINERALS

Different combinations of minerals form different types of rock.

Granite is composed of the minerals quartz, feldspar, and mica.

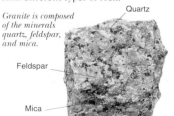

Quartz

Feldspar

Mica

ORE MINERALS

Ore minerals contain metals, and about 80 types of pure metal are extracted from them.

Titanium
A light, strong metal used in aircraft manufacture.

Rutile – titanium ore

Jet airliner

Aluminum
Used in construction, and the manufacture of consumer goods, e.g. saucepans.

Bauxite – aluminum ore

Aluminum can

Lead
The softest common metal, used in batteries and engineering.

Galena – lead ore

Battery

Iron
Used in construction, and in the manufacture of steel.

Hematite – iron ore

Stainless steel fork

Copper
A good conductor, widely used in the electricity industry.

Chalcopyrite – copper ore

Copper pipe

Mercury
Used in scientific instruments, and in the manufacture of drugs and pesticides.

Cinnabar – mercury ore

Mercury thermometer

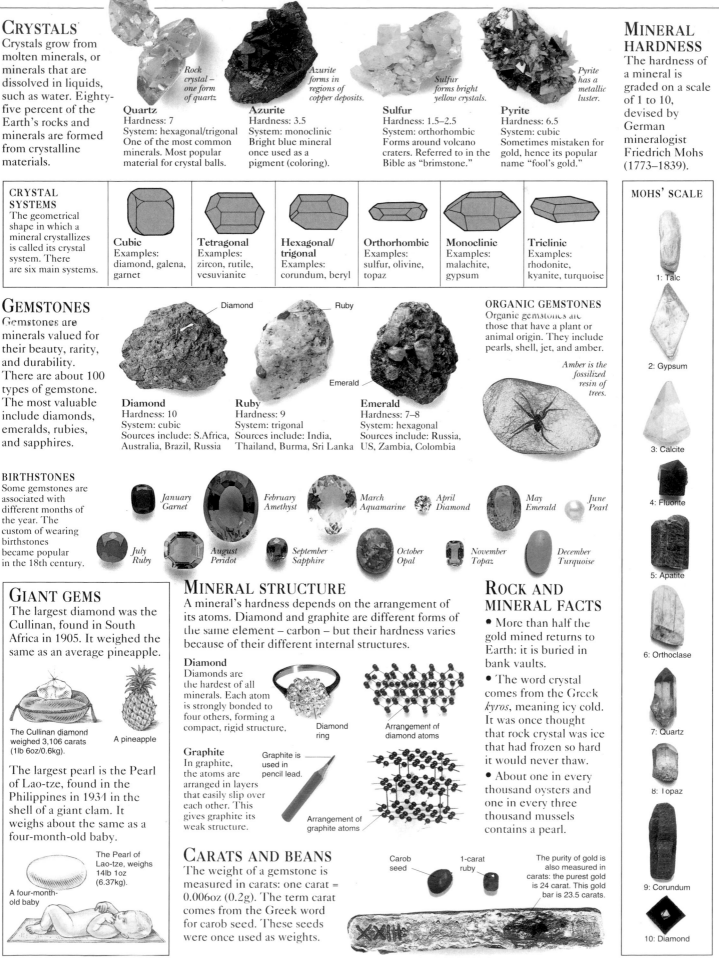

CRYSTALS
Crystals grow from molten minerals, or minerals that are dissolved in liquids, such as water. Eighty-five percent of the Earth's rocks and minerals are formed from crystalline materials.

Rock crystal – one form of quartz

Quartz
Hardness: 7
System: hexagonal/trigonal
One of the most common minerals. Most popular material for crystal balls.

Azurite forms in regions of copper deposits.

Azurite
Hardness: 3.5
System: monoclinic
Bright blue mineral once used as a pigment (coloring).

Sulfur forms bright yellow crystals.

Sulfur
Hardness: 1.5–2.5
System: orthorhombic
Forms around volcano craters. Referred to in the Bible as "brimstone."

Pyrite has a metallic luster.

Pyrite
Hardness: 6.5
System: cubic
Sometimes mistaken for gold, hence its popular name "fool's gold."

MINERAL HARDNESS
The hardness of a mineral is graded on a scale of 1 to 10, devised by German mineralogist Friedrich Mohs (1773–1839).

CRYSTAL SYSTEMS
The geometrical shape in which a mineral crystallizes is called its crystal system. There are six main systems.

Cubic
Examples: diamond, galena, garnet

Tetragonal
Examples: zircon, rutile, vesuvianite

Hexagonal/trigonal
Examples: corundum, beryl

Orthorhombic
Examples: sulfur, olivine, topaz

Monoclinic
Examples: malachite, gypsum

Triclinic
Examples: rhodonite, kyanite, turquoise

MOHS' SCALE
1: Talc
2: Gypsum
3: Calcite
4: Fluorite
5: Apatite
6: Orthoclase
7: Quartz
8: Topaz
9: Corundum
10: Diamond

GEMSTONES
Gemstones are minerals valued for their beauty, rarity, and durability. There are about 100 types of gemstone. The most valuable include diamonds, emeralds, rubies, and sapphires.

Diamond

Ruby

Emerald

Diamond
Hardness: 10
System: cubic
Sources include: S.Africa, Australia, Brazil, Russia

Ruby
Hardness: 9
System: trigonal
Sources include: India, Thailand, Burma, Sri Lanka

Emerald
Hardness: 7–8
System: hexagonal
Sources include: Russia, US, Zambia, Colombia

ORGANIC GEMSTONES
Organic gemstones are those that have a plant or animal origin. They include pearls, shell, jet, and amber.

Amber is the fossilized resin of trees.

BIRTHSTONES
Some gemstones are associated with different months of the year. The custom of wearing birthstones became popular in the 18th century.

January Garnet
February Amethyst
March Aquamarine
April Diamond
May Emerald
June Pearl
July Ruby
August Peridot
September Sapphire
October Opal
November Topaz
December Turquoise

GIANT GEMS
The largest diamond was the Cullinan, found in South Africa in 1905. It weighed the same as an average pineapple.

The Cullinan diamond weighed 3,106 carats (1lb 6oz/0.6kg).

A pineapple

The largest pearl is the Pearl of Lao-tze, found in the Philippines in 1934 in the shell of a giant clam. It weighs about the same as a four-month-old baby.

The Pearl of Lao-tze, weighs 14lb 1oz (6.37kg).

A four-month-old baby

MINERAL STRUCTURE
A mineral's hardness depends on the arrangement of its atoms. Diamond and graphite are different forms of the same element – carbon – but their hardness varies because of their different internal structures.

Diamond
Diamonds are the hardest of all minerals. Each atom is strongly bonded to four others, forming a compact, rigid structure.

Diamond ring

Arrangement of diamond atoms

Graphite
In graphite, the atoms are arranged in layers that easily slip over each other. This gives graphite its weak structure.

Graphite is used in pencil lead.

Arrangement of graphite atoms

CARATS AND BEANS
The weight of a gemstone is measured in carats: one carat = 0.006oz (0.2g). The term carat comes from the Greek word for carob seed. These seeds were once used as weights.

Carob seed

1-carat ruby

ROCK AND MINERAL FACTS
• More than half the gold mined returns to Earth: it is buried in bank vaults.

• The word crystal comes from the Greek *kyros*, meaning icy cold. It was once thought that rock crystal was ice that had frozen so hard it would never thaw.

• About one in every thousand oysters and one in every three thousand mussels contains a pearl.

The purity of gold is also measured in carats: the purest gold is 24 carat. This gold bar is 23.5 carats.

OCEAN FLOOR

THE OCEAN FLOOR IS the largest landscape on Earth. Beneath the oceans are mountains as high as the Himalayas, a rugged mountain range that circles the Earth, vast plains, deep canyons, and trenches plunging thousands of yards into the lithosphere. Most of this fascinating landscape is still unexplored.

SMOKERS

Smokers are tall, chimneylike vents on the ocean floor that belch out clouds of super-heated water. They occur at volcanically active spots on mid-ocean ridges.

Heated water erupts in tall jets

Temperature of heated water may be up to 662°F (350°C)

"Chimneys" up to 164ft (50m) high build up from minerals deposited by the hot water.

Smokers were discovered in 1977 by the American submersible "Alvin."

Heated water rises back to the surface of the ocean floor.

Clams

Tube worms

Life around smokers
Smokers support strange life forms that derive energy not from the Sun, like other life forms on Earth, but from volcanic activity.

Water seeps deep down into the sea floor where it is heated by volcanic activity.

MAJOR RIDGES AND TRENCHES

The major features of the ocean floor form at the boundaries of the plates that make up the Earth's crust (see pp.40–41). Mid-ocean ridges form where two plates are pulling apart, and trenches form at subduction zones, where one plate is plunging beneath another.

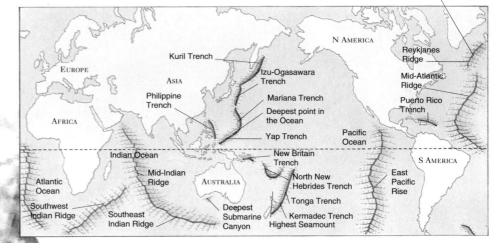

Vast undersea mountain ranges form where two tectonic plates are pulling apart.

N AMERICA
EUROPE
ASIA
AFRICA
Kuril Trench
Izu-Ogasawara Trench
Philippine Trench
Mariana Trench
Deepest point in the Ocean
Yap Trench
Reykjanes Ridge
Mid-Atlantic Ridge
Puerto Rico Trench
Pacific Ocean
Indian Ocean
New Britain Trench
S AMERICA
Atlantic Ocean
Mid-Indian Ridge
AUSTRALIA
North New Hebrides Trench
East Pacific Rise
Southwest Indian Ridge
Southeast Indian Ridge
Deepest Submarine Canyon
Tonga Trench
Kermadec Trench
Highest Seamount

DEEPEST TRENCHES

The depth of deep-sea trenches is measured from sea level.

Trench	Ocean	Depth meters	feet
Mariana Trench	West Pacific	10,920	35,827
Tonga Trench	South Pacific	10,800	35,433
Philippine Trench	West Pacific	10,057	32,995
Kermadec Trench	South Pacific	10,047	32,963
Izu-Ogasawara Trench	West Pacific	9,780	32,087
Kuril Trench	West Pacific	9,550	31,332
North New Hebrides Trench	South Pacific	9,175	30,102
New Britain Trench	South Pacific	8,940	29,331
Puerto Rico Trench	West Atlantic	8,605	28,232
Yap Trench	West Pacific	8,527	27,976

FEATURES OF THE OCEAN FLOOR

The ocean floor is where the lithosphere is created and destroyed. Volcanic activity associated with mid-ocean ridges and subduction zones (see pp.40–41) creates many ocean floor features.

SUBMARINE CANYON
Sediments deposited by a river flowing into the sea form a current that helps to erode a canyon in the ocean floor.

ABYSSAL PLAIN
Vast plains formed from a deep layer of sediment lie approximately 11,480–18,040ft (3,500–5,500m) below sea level.

SEAMOUNT
A seamount is an underwater volcano that rises 3,280ft (1,000m) or more above the surrounding plain.

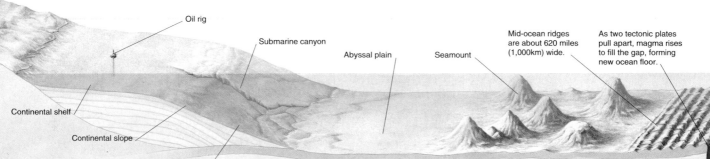

Oil rig
Submarine canyon
Abyssal plain
Seamount
Mid-ocean ridges are about 620 miles (1,000km) wide.
As two tectonic plates pull apart, magma rises to fill the gap, forming new ocean floor.
Continental shelf
Continental slope
Continental rise

CONTINENTAL SHELF
The continental shelf is the gently sloping rim of a continent.

CONTINENTAL SLOPE
The continental slope descends steeply from the continental shelf to the abyssal plain.

CONTINENTAL RISE
Beyond the steep continental slope there may be a gentler slope called the continental rise.

MID-OCEAN RIDGE
A long, undersea mountain range runs along the mid-ocean ridge, where two tectonic plates are pulling apart.

OCEAN FLOOR SEDIMENT

Close to the coast, sediment consists mainly of mud, sand, and silt washed off the land by rivers. The deep ocean floor is blanketed with ooze, the remains of dead marine plants and animals. The amount of sediment and ooze can help scientists calculate the age of the ocean floor.

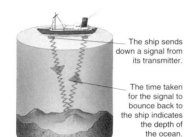

Newly formed rock
At the mid-ocean ridge, the new volcanic rock of the ocean floor is almost free of sediment.

5 million years later
The rock has moved 311 miles (500km) from the ridge. Sediment has started to gather in hollows.

10 million years later
The rock has moved 620 miles (1,000km) from the ridge. It is covered with a thick blanket of sediment.

MAPPING THE OCEAN FLOOR

Early explorations of the ocean floor were made from ships using a lead and line to estimate depth. Scientists today use echo-sounding techniques and special submarines – submersibles – that can descend to the very depths of the ocean.

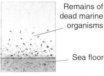

The ship sends down a signal from its transmitter.

The time taken for the signal to bounce back to the ship indicates the depth of the ocean.

OCEAN FLOOR FACTS

• A particle of ooze sinks 1–10ft (0.3–3m) per day. At this rate, it would take 25 years for the remains of a dead shrimp to sink from the ocean surface to the floor of a deep-sea trench.

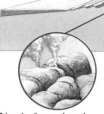

• The tube worm *Alvinella pompejana* can live on smoker walls where the temperature is 221°F (105°C) – higher than any land animal can tolerate.

• The Mariana trench could hold 28 Empire State Buildings standing on top of each other.

• Oldest parts of the ocean floor are about 200 million years old. Oldest rocks on land are about 3.5 billion years old.

• At a growth rate of about 0.08in (2mm) every million years, it takes 10 million years for a manganese nodule to reach the size of a grape.

FOUND ON THE OCEAN FLOOR

Many useful products are found on or under the ocean floor. They include diamonds, oil, gas, coal, sand, and metals from manganese nodules.

DIAMONDS
These are found in shallow waters off the coasts of Africa and Indonesia.

SAND, GRAVEL, AND LIMESTONE
These are found in coastal waters.

COAL
Coal is mined beneath the sea as well as on land.

OIL AND GAS
About 20% of oil comes from the ocean floor. Natural gas is found with oil deposits.

FORMATION OF OIL AND GAS

Under certain conditions, oil and gas form from the remains of dead plants and animals that accumulate on the floor of shallow seas.

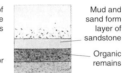 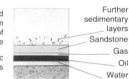

Remains of dead marine organisms — Sea floor

Mud and sand form layer of sandstone — Organic remains

Further sedimentary layers — Sandstone — Gas — Oil — Water

1 Dead plant and animal remains sink down to the floor of the continental shelf. Bacteria break the remains down into organic material.

2 Sediments of sand and mud washed off the land by rivers form layers of sandstone, covering the organic remains.

3 Increased pressure from further layers of sandstone and other sedimentary rock turns the organic remains into oil and gas.

HIGHEST SEAMOUNT AND DEEPEST SUBMARINE CANYON

The highest seamount is near the Tonga Trench between Samoa and New Zealand. The deepest submarine canyon is 25 miles (40km) south of Esperance, Australia.

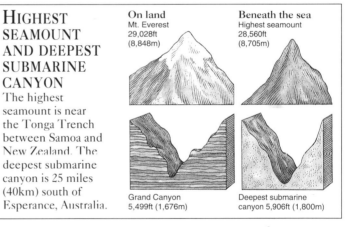

On land
Mt. Everest
29,028ft (8,848m)

Beneath the sea
Highest seamount
28,560ft (8,705m)

Grand Canyon
5,499ft (1,676m)

Deepest submarine
canyon 5,906ft (1,800m)

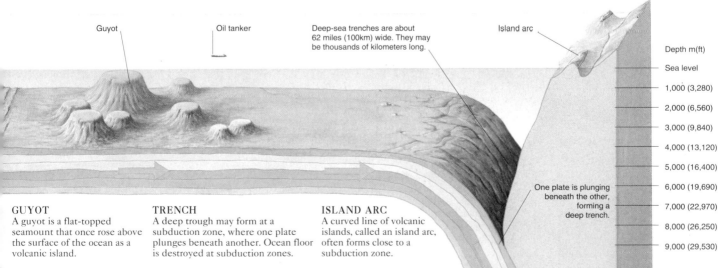

Guyot

Oil tanker

Deep-sea trenches are about 62 miles (100km) wide. They may be thousands of kilometers long.

Island arc

One plate is plunging beneath the other, forming a deep trench.

Depth m(ft)
Sea level
1,000 (3,280)
2,000 (6,560)
3,000 (9,840)
4,000 (13,120)
5,000 (16,400)
6,000 (19,690)
7,000 (22,970)
8,000 (26,250)
9,000 (29,530)

GUYOT
A guyot is a flat-topped seamount that once rose above the surface of the ocean as a volcanic island.

TRENCH
A deep trough may form at a subduction zone, where one plate plunges beneath another. Ocean floor is destroyed at subduction zones.

ISLAND ARC
A curved line of volcanic islands, called an island arc, often forms close to a subduction zone.

OCEANS AND ISLANDS

MORE THAN TWO-THIRDS of the Earth's surface lies beneath the oceans. Where the land rises above sea level it forms continents and islands. An island is a piece of land, smaller than a continent, that is surrounded by water.

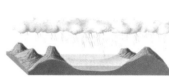

Baffin Island
Ellesmere Island
Victoria Island
Arctic Ocean
Greenland
N. AMERICA
EUROPE
ASIA
Honshu
Great Britain
Pacific Ocean
AFRICA
Sumatra
Borneo
Pacific Ocean
S. AMERICA
Indian Ocean
New Guinea
Atlantic Ocean
Madagascar
AUSTRALIA
ANTARCTICA

MAJOR OCEANS, ISLANDS, AND CURRENTS

This map shows the location of the world's major oceans, islands, and ocean currents. Currents are caused by winds blowing across the surface of the sea. The currents may be warm or cold.

→ warm current   → cold current

FORMATION OF THE OCEANS

The oceans began to form many millions of years ago when the Earth was still cooling and solidifying following its early molten state. Water vapor was thrown into the atmosphere by volcanoes.

Water vapor and carbon dioxide

1 As the young Earth cooled, volcanoes erupted, throwing out a mixture of gases that formed the early atmosphere.

2 When the atmosphere was saturated with water vapor, the vapor condensed, falling as rain. Rainwater began to collect in vast hollows.

3 The Earth cooled and volcanic eruptions became fewer. For the last 100 million years the water volume in the oceans has stayed about the same.

WAVE SEQUENCE

Waves are caused by wind blowing across the surface of the sea. The height and power of waves depends on the strength of the wind.

The water in a wave appears to be moving forward, but in fact it moves in a circle.

The base of the wave is held back by the shore. The crest of the wave moves faster, toppling over when it reaches land.

Water reaches the base of the circle in the trough of a wave.

Water reaches the top of the circle at the crest of the wave.

OCEAN DATA

Total surface area	139.8 million sq miles (362 million sq km)
Total volume	324 million cu miles (1.35 billion cu km)
Mean depth	2.2 miles (3.5km)
Weight of water	1.32×10^{18} tons
% of Earth's water	94%
Temperature range	29°F to 97°F (-1.9°C to 36°C)
Freezing temp. of sea water	29°F (-1.9°C)
Deepest known point	35,827ft (10,920m)

FORCE OF THE WAVES

When waves break on the shore, they exert a tremendous force. The weight of the sea hitting land can create pressures of more than 25 tons per square yard. This is 30 times as great as the pressure exerted on land by a human foot.

OCEAN FACTS

• More than 60% of the Earth's surface is covered by water deeper than 1 mile (1.6km).

• Average depth of Pacific Ocean: 2.4 miles (3.94km); average depth of Atlantic Ocean: 2.2 miles (3.57km).

• There is more gold dissolved in seawater than there is on land. The concentration is 0.000004 parts per million.

• The Gulf Stream ocean current contains about 100 times as much water as the combined volume of all the rivers in the world.

The Pacific Ocean covers more than a third of the Earth.

OCEAN AND SEA AREAS

Pacific Ocean
63,855,000sq miles (165,384,000sq km)
45.7% of sea area

Atlantic Ocean
31,744,000sq miles (82,217,000sq km)
22.7% of sea area

Indian Ocean
28,371,000sq miles (73,481,000sq km)
20.3% of sea area

Arctic Ocean
5,108,000sq miles (13,230,000sq km)
3.65% of sea area

Other seas
10,690,000sq miles (27,687,000sq km)
7.65 % of sea area

WHIRLPOOLS

Whirlpools are caused by a clash of tidal flows in places where the sea floor is uneven. Currents rush toward each other, and, if they hit a rocky shelf on the sea floor, water surges upward, turning the surface into a seething mass.

OCEAN ZONES

Depth
m(ft)
0

2,000
(6,560)

6,000
(19,690)

Bathal zone
surface – 6,560ft (2,000m)

Light disappears about
330ft (100m) down

Temperature declines
rapidly about
980ft (300m) down

Abyssal zone
6,560–19,690ft
(2,000–6,000m)

Hadal zone
below 19,690ft
(6,000m)

The temperature of
the deep ocean is
close to freezing.

Over half of
deep sea fish species
produce their own light.

MINERALS IN THE SEA

Minerals dissolved from rocks
by rivers are washed into the
oceans. The most abundant are
sodium and chlorine, which
together form salt. The average
salinity of the oceans is 33 to 38
parts salt per 1,000 parts water.

Potassium:
1.13%

Sulfate:
7.94%

Calcium: 1.19%

Magnesium:
3.66%

Salt (sodium
chloride)
molecule

Sodium:
30.79%

Chlorine: 55.27%

HEAPS OF SALT

The total amount of salt in
the world's oceans and seas
would cover Europe to a
depth of
3 miles
(5km).

ISLANDS

Islands are found in seas,
rivers, and lakes. They range
in size from small mud and
sand islands measuring only
a few square yards, to
the largest, Greenland, which
measures more than
three quarters of a million
square miles.

WORLD'S LARGEST ISLANDS

Madagascar
Indian Ocean
Area: 220,045sq miles
(587,009sq km)

Honshu
NW Pacific
Area: 87,800sq miles
(227,401sq km)

New Guinea
Western Pacific
Area: 305,983sq miles
(792,493sq km)

Baffin Island
Arctic Ocean
Area:
195,917 sq miles
(507,423sq km)

Victoria Island
Arctic Ocean
Area:
83,891sq miles
(217,278sq km)

Borneo
Indian Ocean
Area: 280,085sq miles
(725,416sq km)

Great Britain
North Atlantic
Area: 84,195sq miles
(218,065sq km)

Ellesmere Island
Arctic Ocean
Area:
75,763sq miles
(196,225sq km)

Sumatra
Indian Ocean
Area: 164,991sq miles
(427,325sq km)

Greenland
Arctic Ocean
Area: 839,856sq miles
(2,175,219sq km)

TYPES OF ISLAND

There are four main types
of island.

CORAL ISLAND

A coral island forms when corals (tiny
marine organisms) grow up toward the
surface of the ocean from a shallow
underwater platform, such as the peak
of a seamount (see p.48). The coral
skeletons build up over many years
until they reach the surface.

*The Maldives in the Indian Ocean
are coral islands.*

VOLCANIC ISLAND

Volcanoes that erupt beneath the
ocean may eventually grow to reach
the surface, where they emerge as
islands. Volcanic islands often form
close to plate boundaries
(see pp.40–41).

*The volcanic island of Surtsey
appeared south of Iceland in the
Atlantic Ocean in 1963.*

ISLAND FORMED BY A
CHANGE IN SEA LEVEL

A rise in sea level, for example at the
end of an ice age, may cut off an area
of land from a continent, forming an
island. Great Britain was formed in this
way. Some pieces of land become
islands at high tide.

*Mont St. Michel in France becomes an island
each time the tide comes in.*

ISLAND ARC

An island arc is a chain of volcanic
islands that usually forms landward of
a subduction zone (see pp.40–41).
Some island arcs contain many
thousands of islands. The Japanese
islands were formed in this way.

*Part of Indonesia, photographed from
the Space Shuttle in 1983. Indonesia is the
world's longest island arc.*

CORAL ATOLLS

An atoll is a ring-shaped coral island with
a lagoon in its center. Atolls form
when a coral reef builds up
around a volcanic island, and
the island subsequently
sinks below sea level. As
the island sinks, the
coral continues
to grow.

A coral reef builds up,
fringing the volcanic island.

As the island starts
to sink, coral continues
to grow upward.

Lagoon

The island has disappeared,
leaving a coral atoll.

OCEAN AND ISLAND RECORDS

GREATEST OCEAN CURRENT
is the Antarctic Circumpolar
Current (also known as the West
Wind Drift Current), which
flows at a rate of 4.6 billion cu ft
(130,000,000cu m) per second.

HIGHEST RECORDED WAVE
(excluding seismic sea waves)
was 112ft (34m) from trough to
crest, recorded in 1933 en route
from the Philippines to the US.

REMOTEST ISLAND
is Bouvet Island, about
1,056 miles (1,700km) from the
nearest land (Queen Maud
Land, eastern Antarctica).

LARGEST CORAL ATOLL
is Kwajalein in the Marshall
Islands, central Pacific Ocean.
Its reef is 176 miles (283km)
long, and encloses a lagoon of
1,100sq miles (2,850sq km).

MOUNTAINS

AS THE EARTH'S tectonic plates jostle and grind against each other, the crust may buckle and fold, throwing up lofty mountain ranges. Volcanoes also erupt at plate boundaries, and may build up into high mountains.

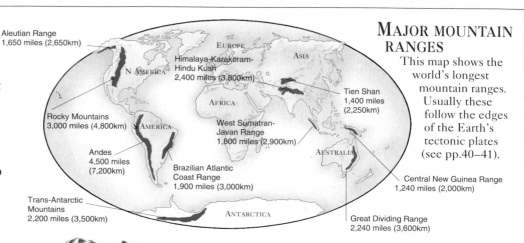

Aleutian Range 1,650 miles (2,650km)

Himalaya-Karakoram-Hindu Kush 2,400 miles (3,800km)

Tien Shan 1,400 miles (2,250km)

Rocky Mountains 3,000 miles (4,800km)

West Sumatran-Javan Range 1,800 miles (2,900km)

Andes 4,500 miles (7,200km)

Brazilian Atlantic Coast Range 1,900 miles (3,000km)

Central New Guinea Range 1,240 miles (2,000km)

Trans-Antarctic Mountains 2,200 miles (3,500km)

Great Dividing Range 2,240 miles (3,600km)

MAJOR MOUNTAIN RANGES

This map shows the world's longest mountain ranges. Usually these follow the edges of the Earth's tectonic plates (see pp.40–41).

TYPES OF MOUNTAIN

There are four main types of mountain.

FOLD MOUNTAINS

When two of the Earth's tectonic plates collide, the crust at the plate edges may crumple and fold under the strain, pushing up ranges of fold mountains.

Fold mountains form when the Earth's crust bends and buckles.

VOLCANOES

A volcano forms when magma (molten rock) from deep inside the Earth erupts onto the surface, building into a tall cone. Some of the highest mountains in the world are volcanoes.

Layers of lava build up into a mountain.

FAULT-BLOCK MOUNTAINS

Plate movements may squeeze layers of rock until they crack and snap. These cracks are faults. Mountains form when a slab or block of rock is squeezed upward.

Fault-block mountains form where one slab or rock is thrust above another.

DOME MOUNTAINS

A large upwelling of molten rock (an igneous intrusion) beneath the Earth's surface may force up the overlying layers of rock into a huge hump. Mountains formed in this way are dome mountains.

Rising molten rock forces up overlying layers of rock into mountains.

WORLD'S HIGHEST MOUNTAINS

The ten highest mountains in the world are all in the Himalayas.

Name	Location	Height meters	feet
Everest	Nepal/China	8,848	29,029
K2	Kashmir/China	8,611	28,251
Kanchenjunga	Nepal/Sikkim	8,598	28,209
Lhotse	Nepal/Tibet	8,511	27,923
Makalu	Nepal/Tibet	8,480	27,822
Cho Oyu	Nepal	8,201	26,906
Dhaulagiri	Nepal	8,172	26,811
Manaslu	Nepal	8,156	26,759
Nanga Parbat	Kashmir	8,126	26,660
Annapurna	Nepal	8,078	26,503

CLOSE-UP OF A MOUNTAIN

High mountains have several zones of vegetation, due to the drop in temperature at higher altitudes.

Nothing can survive

Specially adapted alpine species

Pine forest

Broadleaf forest

Wide range of vegetation

LIFE OF A MOUNTAIN

Young

YOUNG

Mountains that formed during the last few million years, or that are still growing, e.g. the Himalayas.

Mature

MATURE

Mountains several hundred million years old that have been eroded to a fraction of their former size, e.g. the Urals.

Ancient

ANCIENT

Mountains that have been eroded away until there are just a few hills on a low-lying peneplain.

The Eiffel Tower in Paris, France, is 984ft (300m) high.

Mt. Everest was first climbed on May 29, 1953 by New Zealander Edmund Hillary (born 1919) and Sherpa Tensing Norgay (1914–86) of Nepal.

Mt. Everest Nepal/China Asia 29,029ft (8,848m)

Aconcagua Argentina South America 22,835ft (6,960m)

Mt. McKinley Alaska, US North America 20,322ft (6,194m)

El'brus Russia Europe 18,510ft (5,642m)

Vinson Massif Antarctica 16,864ft (5,140m)

Kilimanjaro Tanzania Africa 19,341ft (5,895m)

Mt. Wilhelm Papua New Guinea Australasia 16,024ft (4,884m)

HIGHEST MOUNTAIN PER CONTINENT

This illustration shows the comparative size of the highest mountain on each continent.

VALLEYS AND CAVES

THE FORCES OF EROSION are constantly attacking the land, changing its appearance. Rain flows into rivers that cut valleys into the landscape. In limestone areas, rainwater may seep into the rock, eating it away to form caves.

The river valley begins high in the mountains as a narrow gully.

In the river's upper course, the valley is a characteristic V-shape.

Cross-section of a river valley's upper course

FEATURES OF A VALLEY
A river valley usually begins in the mountains as a steep-sided gully cut by a fast-flowing stream. As it flows down toward lower ground, the river slows down and the valley widens. As it nears the sea the river flows across a wide, level flood plain. Some rivers fan out into a delta at their estuary (see pp.56–57).

As the river reaches the gentler slopes of its middle course, its rate of flow slows down.

The river meanders back and forth, widening the valley.

The valley floor is covered in a thick carpet of sand and mud.

Estuary (see p.56)

Delta (see p.56)

Cross-section of a river valley's lower course

TYPES OF VALLEY

Milford Sound, New Zealand

FJORD
In glaciated areas of the world, deep valleys are scoured out by glaciers. When a glacier melts, for example at the end of an ice age, the sea level may rise, flooding the valley to form a fjord.

African Rift Valley

RIFT VALLEY
Rift valleys form when a long, narrow block of land sinks between two faults, at places where two tectonic plates are pulling apart (see pp.40–41).

Grand Canyon, Arizona

GORGE AND CANYON
A gorge is a deep ravine with walls that are almost vertical. A canyon is a gorge, usually with water flowing through it, found in the desert. The source of its river is often outside the desert.

Valley of Kings, Egyptian desert

WADI
A wadi is a narrow, steep-sided desert valley that is usually dry. A wadi's characteristic shape is carved out by the flash floods that occur after torrential desert rainfall.

CAVES
Caves are large, naturally occurring hollows in the ground, in cliffs, or in ice.

LIMESTONE CAVE
Most caves occur in limestone areas, because this type of rock is soluble (dissolves) in rainwater.

SEA CAVE
Waves crashing against cliffs erode away the rocks, forming sea caves.

ICE CAVE
A stream of meltwater running beneath a glacier may carve out an ice cave.

LAVA CAVE
When the crust of a lava flow hardens, the molten lava beneath may flow out, leaving a lava cave.

CROSS-SECTION OF A LIMESTONE CAVE
Limestone dissolves in rainwater.

Rainwater eats away at the rock, forming a cave.

A stream plunges underground at a sink hole.

Water enlarges cracks and joints.

Waterfall

Stalactites grow down from the roof.

Stalagmites build up on the cave floor.

A stalactite and stalagmite have joined, forming a column.

LIMESTONE CAVE FEATURES
Water dripping in limestone caves leaves behind tiny amounts of calcite. These mineral deposits build up to form distinctive limestone cave features. It can take from four to four thousand years for a stalactite or stalagmite to grow one inch (2.5cm).

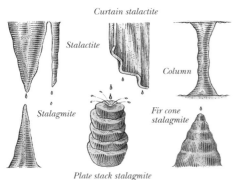
Curtain stalactite
Stalactite
Column
Stalagmite
Fir cone stalagmite
Plate stack stalagmite

VALLEY AND CAVE RECORDS
LONGEST FJORD is Nordvest Fjord, Greenland, which extends 194 miles (313km) inland.

LARGEST GORGE is the Grand Canyon in Arizona, at 217 miles (349km) long and up to 5,499ft (1,676m) deep.

LARGEST CAVE CHAMBER is the Sarawak Chamber in Sarawak, Malaysia, which has an area of 1,751,300sq ft (162,700sq m). The cave chamber is 2,300ft (700m) long, and has an average width of 980ft (300m). The lowest part of the roof is 230ft (70m) high.

LONGEST CAVE SYSTEM is the Mammoth Cave system, Kentucky, which is 348 miles (560km) long.

LONGEST STALACTITE is 20ft 4in (6.2m) long. It is in the Poll an Ionana, a cave in Co. Clare, Ireland.

TALLEST STALAGMITE is 105ft (32m) tall, in the Krásnohorska cave in the Czech Republic.

Size of tallest stalagmite compared to an adult

GLACIATION

MORE THAN A TENTH of the Earth's surface is covered with ice throughout the year. Ice sheets and sea ice blanket the polar areas, and glaciers flow down the slopes of high mountain ranges. Glaciers are found even on mountains at the equator.

GLACIATED REGIONS

This map shows the areas of the world with permanent snow cover. The total area of snow and ice is about 6,020,000sq miles (15,600,000sq km): one-and-a-half times the size of Europe.

NORTH AMERICA (including Greenland) 784,810sq miles (2,032,649sq km)

EUROPE 30,682sq miles (79,465sq km)

ASIA 65,900sq miles (170,679sq km)

AFRICA 5sq miles (12sq km)

SOUTH AMERICA 10,232sq miles (26,500sq km)

AUSTRALASIA 392sq miles (1,015sq km)

ANTARCTICA 4,860,252sq miles (12,588,000sq km)

The Antarctic ice sheet contains 90% of the world's ice.

FORMATION OF AN ICE CAP

1 Heavy winter snowfall blankets the land. Fresh layers compress the older snow beneath, turning it into an icy mass called firn.

2 The temperature rises in summer, but on high ground it is not warm enough to melt the ice. Over successive winters, the blanket of firn becomes thicker.

3 Eventually the firn forms an ice cap. Gravity causes it to flow down from colder or higher ground. Tongues of ice fill the valleys, forming glaciers.

FEATURES OF A GLACIER

Glaciers usually begin high in the mountains. Most flow at a rate of up to 7ft (2m) per day, although glaciers on steeper slopes may flow much more quickly. It may take thousands of years for ice to reach the end of a slow-moving glacier.

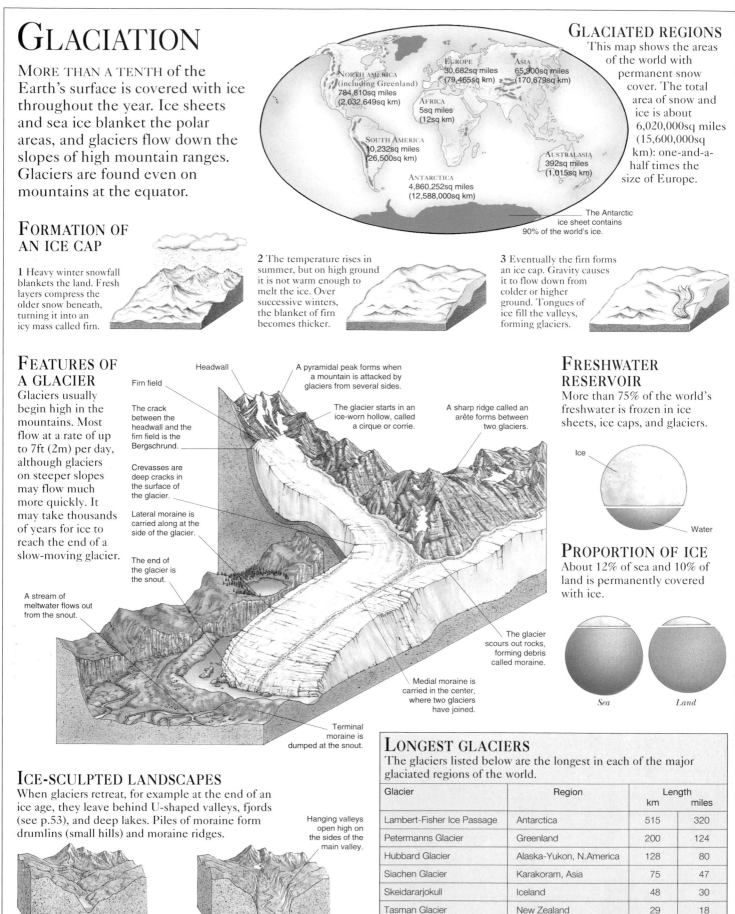

Headwall

Firn field

A pyramidal peak forms when a mountain is attacked by glaciers from several sides.

The crack between the headwall and the firn field is the Bergschrund.

The glacier starts in an ice-worn hollow, called a cirque or corrie.

A sharp ridge called an arête forms between two glaciers.

Crevasses are deep cracks in the surface of the glacier.

Lateral moraine is carried along at the side of the glacier.

The end of the glacier is the snout.

A stream of meltwater flows out from the snout.

The glacier scours out rocks, forming debris called moraine.

Medial moraine is carried in the center, where two glaciers have joined.

Terminal moraine is dumped at the snout.

FRESHWATER RESERVOIR

More than 75% of the world's freshwater is frozen in ice sheets, ice caps, and glaciers.

Ice

Water

PROPORTION OF ICE

About 12% of sea and 10% of land is permanently covered with ice.

Sea

Land

ICE-SCULPTED LANDSCAPES

When glaciers retreat, for example at the end of an ice age, they leave behind U-shaped valleys, fjords (see p.53), and deep lakes. Piles of moraine form drumlins (small hills) and moraine ridges.

Hanging valleys open high on the sides of the main valley.

Before glaciation: a V-shaped river valley

After glaciation: a U-shaped river valley

LONGEST GLACIERS

The glaciers listed below are the longest in each of the major glaciated regions of the world.

Glacier	Region	Length	
		km	miles
Lambert-Fisher Ice Passage	Antarctica	515	320
Petermanns Glacier	Greenland	200	124
Hubbard Glacier	Alaska-Yukon, N.America	128	80
Siachen Glacier	Karakoram, Asia	75	47
Skeidararjokull	Iceland	48	30
Tasman Glacier	New Zealand	29	18
Aletsch Gletscher	European Alps	24	15
Gyabrag Glacier	Himalayas	21	13

SNOWLINE

The snowline is the level that divides year-round snow from snow that melts during warmer weather. The closer a mountain area is to the equator, the higher the snowline.

Mt. Kenya, which is close to the equator, has glaciers on its summit.

Mt. Vinson, Antarctica, is covered in snow and ice from foot to summit.

On the equator
the snowline lies about 16,000ft (4,900m) high.

In the European Alps
the snowline lies about 9,000ft (2,700m) high.

In polar regions
the snowline lies at sea level.

ICE AGES

Ice ages occur when the Earth's average temperature becomes slightly cooler and the amount of ice increases. Scientists believe that four major ice ages and many smaller ice advances occurred during the last two million years.

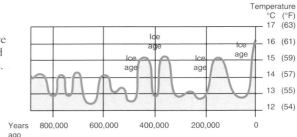

MOST RECENT ICE AGE

The last ice age began about 72,000 years ago, and ended about 10,000 years ago. This map shows the areas of the world that were covered with ice. The sea level was about 490ft (150m) lower than today, because so much water was locked up in ice.

Huge ice sheets covered much of North America, Europe, and Asia.

The land where New York now stands was covered with ice.

Southern Argentina was covered by an ice sheet.

Up to 30% of the Earth's surface was glaciated.

New Zealand was covered by an ice cap.

AVALANCHES

An avalanche is a mass of snow and ice that suddenly crashes down a mountainside. It may be up to 0.6 miles (1km) across, and can move at up to 200mph (320km/h). If a town or village lies in the path of an avalanche, houses may be flattened and people killed.

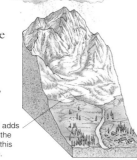

Heavy snowfall adds extra weight to the snow cover on this mountain slope.

The extra weight of snow, combined with a sudden rise in temperature, triggers an avalanche.

AVALANCHE FACTS

• An avalanche can generate winds of up to 186mph (300km/h).

• About 18,000 Austrian and Italian soldiers are thought to have been killed in a single day in 1916 by more than 100 avalanches in the Dolomites, northern Italy. Many of these avalanches were started by gunfire.

• The biggest avalanches usually occur on slopes with an angle of 30° or more.

SEA ICE

The sea freezes over when its temperature falls below 29°F (-1.9°C). Sea ice is never more than about 16ft (5m) thick.

Sea ice off the western Antarctic coast

TALLEST ICEBERG

The tallest iceberg ever reported was 550ft (167m) high – taller than St. Paul's Cathedral, London. It was sighted off Greenland in 1958.

ICEBERGS

Icebergs are large chunks of ice that break off the end of ice sheets, ice caps, and glaciers, and float out to sea. The process of icebergs breaking off a body of ice is called calving.

The rising and falling tide, together with buffeting from the waves, breaks the iceberg off the end of the glacier.

Once an iceberg has broken away, its movements are controlled by ocean currents and the wind.

ICY RECORDS

FASTEST-MOVING GLACIER is the Quarayaq, Greenland, which can flow 66–79ft (20–24m) per day.
THICKEST ICE ever recorded is 3 miles (5km) deep, in Wilkes Land, Antarctica. This would reach over halfway up Mt. Everest.

LARGEST ICEBERG
The largest iceberg ever recorded was more than 208 miles (335km) long and 60 miles (97km) wide – an area about the size of Maryland.
GREATEST NUMBER OF DEATHS FROM AN AVALANCHE was 5,000 at Huaras, Peru, on December 13 1941.

Only a small proportion of an iceberg – about 12% – is visible above the surface of the ocean. The remainder is hidden beneath the water.

ICEBERG FACTS

• About 10,000 icebergs a year break away from the glaciers of western Greenland.

• Scientists estimate that the average age of the ice in icebergs is 5,000 years.

RIVERS AND LAKES

MOST OF THE freshwater on Earth is frozen in ice, or is held in rocks below the surface as groundwater. Less than 1% is contained in rivers and lakes, yet these features have a significant effect on the landscape.

MAJOR RIVERS AND LAKES

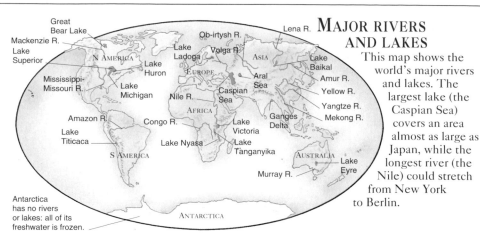

This map shows the world's major rivers and lakes. The largest lake (the Caspian Sea) covers an area almost as large as Japan, while the longest river (the Nile) could stretch from New York to Berlin.

Great Bear Lake · Mackenzie R. · Lake Superior · N AMERICA · Mississippi-Missouri R. · Lake Huron · Lake Michigan · EUROPE · Lake Ladoga · Volga R. · Ob-irtysh R. · ASIA · Lena R. · Lake Baikal · Amur R. · Yellow R. · Aral Sea · Caspian Sea · Yangtze R. · Mekong R. · Nile R. · AFRICA · Congo R. · Ganges Delta · Amazon R. · Lake Titicaca · S AMERICA · Lake Victoria · Lake Nyasa · Lake Tanganyika · AUSTRALIA · Lake Eyre · Murray R. · ANTARCTICA

Antarctica has no rivers or lakes: all of its freshwater is frozen.

TYPES OF RIVER

PERENNIAL RIVER
Perennial rivers flow all year round. They are usually found in temperate and tropical areas (see pp.60–61), where rain falls throughout the year.

The Nile: a perennial river

SEASONAL RIVER
Seasonal rivers flow only during wet seasons. California and Mediterranean countries have seasonal rivers that flow in the winter season, but are dry in summer.

Seasonal river in Crete during summer.

EPHEMERAL RIVER
Ephemeral rivers are usually dry. Many desert rivers are ephemeral; for example, the Todd River in central Australia hardly ever has water in it.

The Todd River in central Australia.

RIVER RECORDS

LONGEST EUROPEAN RIVER is the Volga, Russia, which is 2,194 miles (3,531km) long.

LONGEST AUSTRALASIAN RIVER is the Murray, Australia, which is 1,609 miles (2,589km) long.

LARGEST DELTA is the Ganges and Brahmaputra delta, which covers about 30,000sq miles (75,000sq km). South Carolina would fit into it with room to spare.

HIGHEST WATERFALL

The Angel Falls in Venezuela have a total drop of 3,212ft (979m): almost three times as high as the Empire State Building.

FEATURES OF A RIVER

A river is a body of water that flows downhill in a channel, usually toward the ocean. Rivers have three sections: the upper course, middle course, and lower course.

Upper course
The young, fast-flowing river rushes down a steep gradient, cutting a V-shaped gully.

The river plunges over a shelf of hard rock, forming a waterfall.

Many rivers begin in mountain ranges.

The waterfall wears away the rock and moves slowly upstream, cutting a deep gorge.

Where the river flows down a steep slope of hard rock, it forms swirling rapids.

In its upper course, the river flows over obstacles.

The river cuts farther into the bank, widening the meander (loop).

A meander cut off after flooding forms an oxbow lake.

Middle course
The mature river's gradient is more gentle, and its rate of flow slower. It snakes over the floodplain, forming meanders.

Lower course
In its old age segment, with almost no gradient, the river flows sluggishly and drops its sediment load. It frequently floods and changes course.

The river estuary is where fresh river water meets salty seawater.

The wide, flat floodplain is submerged when the river floods.

The river may block its own route with sediment, forcing it to split into separate streams. These fan out, forming a delta.

RIVER WATER SOURCES

All rivers receive their water, either directly or indirectly, from precipitation (see pp.60–61).

Rainfall runs off the mountain slopes into the river system.

Tributary streams feed the main river.

OVERLAND FLOW
Rainfall runs down slopes into small streams. These tributaries eventually flow into the main river.

SPRING
Rain soaks into the ground and is absorbed into the aquifer – a layer of rock that can hold water. Where the water table (the upper surface of the groundwater) meets the ground surface, a spring may occur.

MELTWATER
Many rivers rise (begin) in glaciated regions of the world, where they are fed by melting snow and ice.

LONGEST RIVERS

River	Location	Length km	Length miles
Nile	Africa	6,695	4,160
Amazon	South America	6,439	4,001
Yangtze	Asia	6,379	3,964
Ob-Irtysh	Asia	5,410	3,362
Yellow	Asia	4,672	2,903
Amur	Asia	4,464	2,774
Lena	Asia	4,400	2,734
Congo	Africa	4,374	2,718
Mackenzie	North America	4,270	2,653
Mekong	Asia	4,184	2,600

TYPES OF LAKE

A lake is an inland body of water that collects in a large depression. Most lakes are fed by rivers (plus a small amount of rainfall), and most lose water into an outlet river. Some lakes, however, have no outlet and only lose water by evaporation. These lakes, such as Australia's Lake Eyre, or Utah's Great Salt Lake, are often salty.

EARTH MOVEMENT

When the Earth's crust is uplifted (see p.52), a body of water may be cut off from the sea, forming a lake. Similarly, when a rift valley forms (see p.53), water collects in the trough forming long, narrow lakes, e.g. Lake Nyasa, Africa.

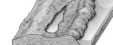

Lake formed by crustal uplift

Rift valley lake

VOLCANIC ACTIVITY

Rainwater often collects in volcano craters, forming lakes such as Crater Lake in Oregon. Some lakes, such as the Sea of Galilee in Israel, form when a river is dammed by a lava flow (see p.42).

Crater lake

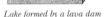

Lake formed by a lava dam

EROSION

Lakes fill hollows scoured out by glaciers during ice ages, e.g. the lakeland plateau of Kuopio, Finland. When desert winds erode a deflation hollow (see p.62) to below the water table, groundwater may fill the depression, forming a lake.

Lakes in ice-worn hollows

Lake in a deflation hollow

DEPOSITION

An oxbow lake forms when a meander is cut off from a river by the deposition of sediment. Deposition lakes also form when a landslide dams a river, and when sandbars and dunes cut off coastal waters from the sea.

Oxbow lake

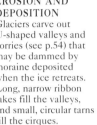
Lake formed by a landslide

EROSION AND DEPOSITION

Glaciers carve out U-shaped valleys and corries (see p.54) that may be dammed by moraine deposited when the ice retreats. Long, narrow ribbon lakes fill the valleys, and small, circular tarns fill the cirques.

Ribbon lake

Tarn

DEEPEST LAKE

Lake Baikal in Siberia has a maximum depth of 5,315ft (1,620m). Its deepest point could swallow five Eiffel Towers standing on top of each other.

USES OF RIVERS AND LAKES

SOURCE OF FRESHWATER

Lakes and rivers supply water for factories and industry. They also provide freshwater for towns and cities.

TRANSPORTATION

Lakes and rivers have been used for centuries to transport goods, animals, and people.

ELECTRICITY

Hydroelectric power is produced at dammed rivers by water flowing through turbines.

FISHING

Some of the world's larger lakes and rivers support important fishing industries.

SPORT

Sports such as sailing and windsurfing are enjoyed on lakes. Canoeing and rafting are popular on rivers.

IRRIGATION

Rivers are an important source of water for irrigating crops in many arid regions.

LARGEST LAKES

Lake	Location	Area sq km	Area sq miles
Caspian Sea	Asia	370,980	143,236
Lake Superior	North America	82,098	31,698
Lake Victoria	Africa	69,480	26,826
Lake Huron	North America	59,566	22,999
Lake Michigan	North America	57,754	22,299
Aral Sea	Asia	37,056	14,307
Lake Tanganyika	Africa	32,891	12,699
Lake Baikal	Russia	31,498	12,161
Great Bear Lake	Canada	31,327	12,095
Lake Nyasa	Africa	28,877	11,149

VANISHING LAKES

Most lakes are geologically short-lived, lasting less than a million years. Most are filled in by sediment dumped by rivers; others disappear when rainfall dwindles. The remnants of lakes form swamps, marshes, and bogs.

RIVER AND LAKE FACTS

• About 6.4 million cu ft (180,000cu m) of water flows out of the Amazon into the ocean every second: it would take just over a second to fill London's St. Paul's Cathedral.

• Each year rivers dump about 20 billion tons of sediment in the sea, removing an average of 1.23in (3.13cm) of soil from the land every thousand years.

• Lake Geneva will be filled in by the River Rhône within approximately 40,000 years.

LAKE RECORDS

LARGEST EUROPEAN LAKE is Lake Ladoga, Russia, which has an area of 6,835sq miles (17,702sq km).

LARGEST AUSTRALASIAN LAKE is Lake Eyre, Australia, which has an area of 3,600sq miles (9,323sq km). This salt lake is usually dry.

LARGEST SOUTH AMERICAN LAKE is Lake Titicaca in Peru and Bolivia, which has an area of 3,200sq miles (8,288sq km).

1 The river dumps its load of mud and gravel when it reaches the lake.

2 The sediment builds up, forming a sediment fan at one end of the lake.

3 Additional sediment extends the fan out into the lake which shrinks, forming a shallow swamp.

4 The lake is completely filled in with sediment. Plants eventually cover the old lake site.

WEATHER

THE WEATHER CHANGES that affect us directly – sunshine, clouds, rain, snow, and storms – occur in the bottom layer of the Earth's atmosphere. This churning layer of gas is being heated and cooled constantly by wind, water, and the Sun.

WATER CYCLE

Water moves in a never-ending cycle. The Sun's heat evaporates water from seas, lakes, and rivers. As it rises into the atmosphere, the vapor cools and condenses into clouds. Eventually the droplets fall back to Earth as rain.

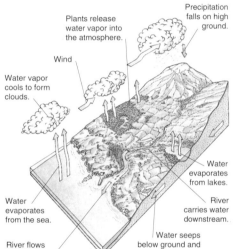

Plants release water vapor into the atmosphere.

Precipitation falls on high ground.

Wind

Water vapor cools to form clouds.

Water evaporates from the sea.

Water evaporates from lakes.

River carries water downstream.

Water seeps below ground and flows to the sea.

River flows into the sea.

TYPES OF CLOUD

Clouds are classified according to their shape and their height above the ground.

Cirrostratus
16,000–40,000ft (5,000–13,000m)
Semitransparent layer; causes halo around the Sun.

Cirrocumulus
16,000–40,000ft (5,000–13,000m)
Made of icy particles; resemble fish scales. Often called "mackerel sky."

Cumulonimbus
Massive, flat-topped storm clouds that may stretch up to 49,000ft (15,000m) above the ground. Can bring heavy showers, thunderstorms, hail, or tornadoes.

Altostratus
6,500–23,000ft (2,000–7,000m)
Thin, watery layer; forms colored ring (corona) around Sun and Moon.

Cirrus
16,000–40,000ft (5,000–13,000m)
Highest clouds; wispy

Altocumulus
6,500–23,000ft (2,000–7,000m)
Lumpy globules of white and gray cloud.

Stratocumulus
0–6,500ft (0–2,000m)
Low sheet of gray or white, lumpy clouds.

Cumulus
0–6,500ft (0–2,000m)
Puffy clouds; gray at the bottom, brilliant white at the top.

Nimbostratus
0–6,500ft (0–2,000m)
Thick multilayered clouds covering the sky; bring continuous rain or snow.

Stratus
0–6,500ft (0–2,000m)
Lowest clouds; hide hills in fog.

FORMATION OF CLOUDS

Clouds form when warm air rises, cools, and its water vapor condenses. The highest clouds usually consist of tiny ice crystals; lower clouds are made up mostly of water droplets.

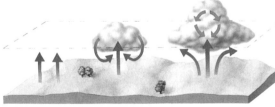

1 Warm air containing invisible water vapor rises from the ground.

2 As water vapor cools it condenses into droplets, forming a cloud.

3 Cloud goes on forming as long as warm, moist air continues to rise.

WEATHER FACTS

• The first thermometer was made in about 1600 by Italian scientist Galileo Galilei (1564–1642).

• There is enough water in the troposphere (see p.39) to flood the world to a depth of 3.3ft (1m).

• On any one day there may be 44,000 storms over the Earth.

• In 1888, 246 people died because of a hailstorm in Moredabad, India.

• Over a 30-year period in the US, there was an average of 730 tornadoes a year, causing more than 100 deaths annually.

• During a tornado, one house can be destroyed, but another 66ft (20m) away can remain intact.

THE WORLD'S WINDS

Wind is air moving from one place to another. Winds always blow from areas of high pressure to areas of low pressure.

Prevailing winds are winds that blow almost all the time in the same parts of the world.

Over the equator is a region of calm winds and sudden storms, called the doldrums.

Earth's rotation deflects the prevailing winds, causing them to blow from northeast north of the equator, and southeast south of the equator.

Westerlies

Trade winds

Trade winds

Westerlies

At the equator the Sun is almost directly overhead. Its concentrated heat causes air to expand, rise, and billow out at high altitudes.

As it cools, the air sinks back to the surface just beyond the tropics, creating regions of high pressure. Winds blow from there back into the low-pressure zone around the equator.

AIR PRESSURE

Cold air sinks, creating areas of high pressure called anticyclones, or highs. Warm air rises, creating areas of low pressure called depressions, lows, or cyclones.

Air rises, forming clouds.

In the Southern Hemisphere, air in highs and lows circulates in the opposite direction.

Air sinks to the ground and spreads, absorbing moisture.

Anticyclone
An anticyclone has descending air and light winds, and brings clear skies.

Depression
A depression often has rising air, strong winds, and may bring clouds, rain, or snow.

AIR MASSES AND FRONTS

Air masses are huge bodies of air that form over continents and oceans. They can be warm, cold, moist, or dry, depending on where they form. The boundary between two air masses is a front. As a front sweeps across the land, it usually brings a change in the weather.

Cold front
Cold air mass
Cold air moves in under warm air, bringing heavy rain followed by showers.
Warm air mass

Warm front
Warm, moist air mass
Long spells of rain occur as warm air rises above cold air, before the front arrives on the ground.
Cold, moist air mass

Occluded front
An occluded front forms when a cold front overtakes a warm front, lifting warm air above it.
Cold air mass
Cold air mass
Warm air mass
Rain falls along the occluded front.

WEATHER WORDS

Blizzard A severe snowstorm with strong winds.

Dew Tiny drops of water that condense on cold objects near to the ground.

Fog Ground-level cloud: visibility less than 0.6 miles (1km).

Frost Ice crystals or frozen particles of moisture that form on cold surfaces.

Hail Pellets of ice that fall during storms.

Mist Thin fog: visibility 0.6–1.25 miles (1–2km).

Precipitation Rain, drizzle, hail, or snow.

Rainbow A seven-colored arc that forms in the sky when sunlight shines through raindrops.

Squall A sudden increase in wind, accompanied by rain.

Waterspout A tornado that forms over an ocean or lake, sucking up water.

LIGHTNING

Lightning is the visible flash that occurs when electric energy is released from a cloud. It is often accompanied by thunder – a loud bang caused by rapidly expanding air.

Positive charge

Negative charges are attracted to positive charges in the ground below.

Negative charge

Positive charges

TORNADO

A tornado is a violently whirling column of wind averaging 300ft (100m) across. It forms a funnel of cloud that can suck up objects lying in its path. Tornadoes last from a few minutes to two hours.

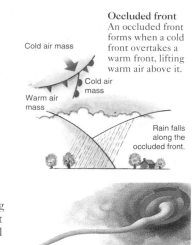

Tornadoes move at an average speed of 35mph (55km/h).

Base of tornado measures less than 0.6 miles (1km) across.

Rising air sucks up dirt, and objects as large as vehicles.

SHOCKING FACTS

• Twenty-one people died when a single bolt of lightning hit a hut near Umtali, Zimbabwe, on December 23, 1975.

• The CN Tower is struck about 10 times during each thunderstorm in Toronto, Ontario.

• Every minute, there are about 6,000 flashes of lightning around the world.

• The longest lightning flashes measure up to 20 miles (32km). They occur in flat areas with very high clouds.

UNLUCKY STRIKES

Ex-US park ranger Roy Sullivan was struck by lightning seven times in 35 years.

BEAUFORT SCALE

In 1805, British Admiral Francis Beaufort (1774–1857) devised a scale of 12 wind forces for use in sailing. For many years this scale has been used on land as well as at sea, although winds of force 10, 11, and 12 rarely occur over land.

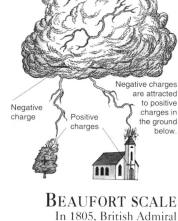

0 Calm. Chimney smoke rises straight up.

1 Light air. Smoke drifts gently. Wind speed 2mph (3km/h).

2 Light breeze. Leaves rustle. Wind speed 6mph (9km/h).

3 Gentle breeze. Flags flutter. Wind speed 9mph (15km/h).

4 Moderate wind. Small branches move. Wind speed 16mph (25km/h).

5 Fresh wind. Small trees sway. Wind speed 22mph (35km/h).

6 Strong wind. Difficult to control umbrellas. Wind speed 28mph (45km/h).

7 Near-gale. Large trees sway. Wind speed 35mph (56km/h).

8 Gale. Twigs break off trees. Wind speed 43mph (68km/h).

9 Severe gale. Slates and chimney pots blow off. Wind speed 51mph (81km/h).

10 Storm. Houses damaged; trees blow down. Wind speed 59mph (94km/h).

11 Severe storm. Serious damage to buildings. Wind speed 69mph (110km/h).

12 Hurricane. Widespread damage. Wind speed 73mph (117km/h).

HURRICANE

A hurricane is a violent tropical storm with winds of at least 73mph (117km/h) spiraling inward toward the eye: a center of low pressure. Some hurricanes remain over the ocean and last only a few days; others last from three to five weeks and devastate islands and coastal regions with high winds, torrential rain, and huge waves.

Hurricanes range in size from 200 miles (300km) to 2,000 miles (3,000km) across.

Air spreads out from the top of the storm, forming a huge circle of cloud.

Many hurricanes move westward at 12–18mph (19–28km/h).

The eye may be 31 miles (50km) across, with light winds and little cloud and rain.

A young storm may cross 1,200 miles (2,000km) of ocean on its way to becoming a hurricane.

Air spirals counterclockwise in the Northern Hemisphere, and clockwise in the Southern Hemisphere.

Deep cumulus clouds.

Winds of more than 73mph (117km/h) whirl around the eye, gusting to 220mph (360km/h).

WEATHER RECORDS

WETTEST DAY ON RECORD occurred when 73.63in (1,870mm) fell at Cilaos, Reunion Island, in March 1952.

WIND SPEED RECORD is 231mph (371km/h), recorded on Mt. Washington, New Hampshire, in 1934.

HIGHEST RECORDED TEMPERATURE is 136°F (58°C), at Azizia, Libya, in 1922. (Temperature readings are always taken in the shade.)

LOWEST RECORDED TEMPERATURE is -128°F (-89°C), at Vostok, Antarctica, in 1983.

CLIMATES

A REGION'S CLIMATE is its characteristic weather over a long period of time. The climate type is determined by its latitude, topography, and distance from large bodies of water.

CLIMATIC ZONES

The world's climates run in broad zones each side of the equator. There are many ways to classify climate: most use a combination of temperature and rainfall. A region's climate, together with the physical landscape, determines its characteristic vegetation.

CLIMATE MAP

This map shows the major climatic zones of the world. Also marked are places featured on the page opposite: those holding climate records; cities featured in the city climate graphs; and the locations of some of the places listed in the temperature variations table.

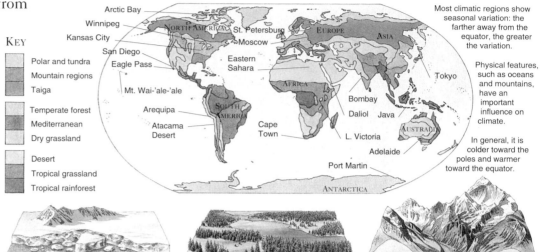

KEY
- Polar and tundra
- Mountain regions
- Taiga
- Temperate forest
- Mediterranean
- Dry grassland
- Desert
- Tropical grassland
- Tropical rainforest

Most climatic regions show seasonal variation: the farther away from the equator, the greater the variation.

Physical features, such as oceans and mountains, have an important influence on climate.

In general, it is colder toward the poles and warmer toward the equator.

DRY GRASSLAND
Vast expanses of dry grassland occur in the middle of some continents, where temperatures are extreme and there is not enough rainfall for forests to grow. These areas have very hot summers and very cold winters.

DESERT
Deserts are the hottest and driest climates in the world, receiving less than 10in (250mm) of rain per year. They are often found in areas of continents that are far from the sea, or in rainshadow areas (see p.62). Only a few specially adapted plants can survive in the harsh desert climate.

POLAR AND TUNDRA REGIONS
In polar regions all freshwater is frozen solid, so land plants cannot grow. The sea's surface is frozen, but underneath is a rich diversity of life. The land bordering the ice caps is the tundra. The temperature in this treeless land rises above freezing for at least one month each year.

TAIGA
Taiga is a Russian word meaning "cold forest." The taiga is a huge area of coniferous forest that lies south of the tundra, stretching across northern Canada, Scandinavia, and the Russian Federation. Four to six months of the year are dark, with the temperature falling well below 32°F (0°C).

MOUNTAIN REGIONS
On mountain ranges, temperature decreases with altitude. Although mountain climates vary according to how close a region is to the equator, most have distinct vegetation zones that change with altitude. At the highest points, temperatures are often too low for vegetation to survive.

TROPICAL GRASSLANDS
Tropical grasslands, such as the African savanna, occur between the equatorial forests and the hot, dry deserts. The climate is always hot, but the year is divided into a dry and a wet season. Vegetation consists of grasses that grow up to 6ft (2m) tall during the wet season, and low trees and bushes.

MEDITERRANEAN
The type of climate around the Mediterranean Sea is found in several other parts of the world, including California. Summers are hot and dry, and winters are cool and wet. Plants in these regions, such as olive trees, have adapted to the dry summer conditions.

MOIST TEMPERATE FOREST
Temperate climates are rarely very hot or very cold: the average temperature is usually 50°F (10°C) or more for four months of the year, and below 41°F (5°C) for at least one month. In temperate regions, many types of plant, e.g. deciduous trees (see p.78), are dormant during winter.

MOIST TROPICAL RAINFOREST
In equatorial regions the climate is hot and wet throughout the year. The average monthly temperature is about 80–82°F (27–28°C), and it rains almost every day. This climate results in the most abundant plant and animal growth in the world: equatorial forests contain 40% of all species.

PINK PEAKS
Winds sometimes pick up dust and sand that may eventually fall as colored rain or snow. Pink snow has fallen on the European Alps, caused by seasonal winds from the Sahara desert picking up red sand.

CLIMATE PROPORTIONS
This table shows the percentage of the Earth that has each basic climate type.

Climate	Continent %	Ocean %	Total Earth %
Polar	17	19.5	18.8
Taiga	21.3	1.7	7.3
Moist temperate	15.5	31.9	27.2
Moist tropical	19.9	42.7	36.1
Dry	26.3	4.2	10.6

MICROCLIMATES
Microclimates are small areas that have their own climate. They include cities, where the air temperature may be 11°F (6°C) higher than the surrounding area. On this special satellite photograph of Paris, the hottest areas are blue, and the coolest areas are green.

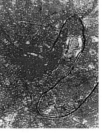

CLIMATE FACTS
- In parts of the Atacama Desert, Chile, it has not rained for 400 years.
- In India, during the summer monsoon (see opposite page), up to 75% of annual rainfall may fall in just three months.
- In the tropics, the difference between the highest annual noon temperature and the lowest may be only 3.6°F (2°C).

SEASONS

Summer occurs because one hemisphere receives more direct rays of sunlight and has more daylight hours.

In the tropics there are often just two seasons a year: wet and dry.

SUN'S RAYS

Equatorial regions always receive the Sun's full heat.

Summer in the Southern Hemisphere

Regions between the poles and the tropics have four seasons. They change slowly from spring to summer to autumn to winter.

In midwinter, when the Southern Hemisphere is at its farthest from the Sun, the South Pole is in darkness all day.

The poles have only two seasons: six months of winter and six months of summer.

Winter in the Northern Hemisphere

Seasons in the Northern Hemisphere are opposite to those in the Southern Hemisphere.

The hemisphere tilted toward the Sun receives more sunlight and heat, bringing summer.

SUN'S RAYS

Winter in the Southern Hemisphere

MONSOONS

Monsoons are seasonal winds that affect large areas of the tropics and subtropics. In southern Asia, monsoons blow from southwest in summer, and northeast in winter.

Areas of the world that experience monsoons are marked in pink.

Himalayas
Rain cloud
Warm sea
Moist, southwest monsoon brings rain
Indian Ocean

Dry northeast monsoon
Cool sea

Southwest monsoon
In early summer, the hot dry lands of Asia draw in warm, moisture-laden air from the Indian Ocean.

Northeast monsoon
In winter, cold dry air spreads out from central Asia, bringing chilly weather.

CLIMATE CHANGE

Factors that influence the world's climate include changes in the Earth's orbit, volcanic dust, ocean heat, polar ice caps, plants of the biosphere (see p.64), and human activity. A change in one of these factors may affect the others.

Large volcanic eruptions throw dust and sulfur dioxide gas high into the atmosphere, where it forms a fine haze, blocking some of the Sun's heat.

Human activities such as deforestation, large-scale changes in land use, and the release of various chemicals into the air can affect the world's climate.

SOGGIEST SPOT

Hawaii's Mt. Wai-'ale-'ale receives an average of about 460.6in (11,700mm) of rain a year, making it the rainiest place in the world. If it did not drain away, this volume of rain would almost submerge a two-story house.

TEMPERATURE VARIATIONS

This table illustrates how a region's temperatures depend on its closeness to the equator. These North American locations are situated at similar longitudes; some are marked on the map opposite.

Location/ Maximum Temp.	Minimum Temp.
Arctic Bay 52°F (11°C)	-50°F (-28°C)
Churchill 64°F (18°C)	-11°F (-24°C)
Winnipeg 79°F (26°C)	7°F (-14°C)
Minneapolis 82°F (28°C)	22°F (-6°C)
Kansas City 92°F (00°C)	37°F (3°C)
Dallas 95°F (35°C)	56°F (13°C)
Eagle Pass 100°F (38°C)	66°F (19°C)

CLIMATE FACTS

• At the equator, the temperature is about 77–86°F (25–30°C) every day.

• The average temperature close to the South Pole is -58°F (-50°C). This is much colder than a deep freeze, which is about 0°F (-18°C).

• Tundra regions are sometimes described as cold deserts, because their climate is so dry.

CITY CLIMATES

These graphs show the average temperature and rainfall for various cities around the world. Locations are marked on the map opposite.

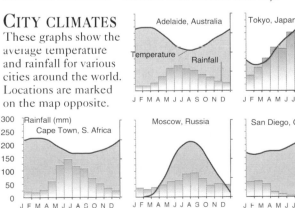

Adelaide, Australia
Temperature
Rainfall
J F M A M J J A S O N D

Tokyo, Japan
J F M A M J J A S O N D

Bombay, India
Temp. (°C)
30 25 20 15 10 5 0 -5 -11
J F M A M J J A S O N D

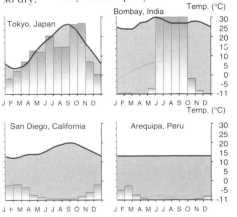

300 250 200 150 100 50 0
Rainfall (mm)
Cape Town, S. Africa
J F M A M J J A S O N D

Moscow, Russia
J F M A M J J A S O N D

San Diego, California
J F M A M J J A S O N D

Arequipa, Peru
Temp. (°C)
30 25 20 15 10 5 0 -5 -11
J F M A M J J A S O N D

CLIMATE RECORDS

Most of the climate records listed below are based on annual averages.

MOST THUNDER
is experienced in parts of Java, and around Africa's Lake Victoria: thunderstorms occur 200–250 days per year.

DRIEST PLACE
is the Atacama Desert, Chile, with an average of only 0.02in (0.51mm) of rain per year.

SUNNIEST PLACE
is the Eastern Sahara, which has sunshine for more than 90% of daylight hours.

HOTTEST PLACE
is Daliol, Ethiopia, where the average temperature over a six-year period was 94°F (34.4°C).

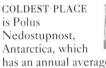

COLDEST PLACE
is Polus Nedostupnost, Antarctica, which has an annual average temperature of -72°F (-57.8°C).

WINDIEST PLACE
is Port Martin, Antarctica, which had a mean wind speed of 65mph (105km/h) over a one-month period.

MOST RAINY DAYS
are experienced by Mount Wai-'ale-'ale (altitude 5,148ft/ 1,569m) on the Hawaiian island of Kauai, which has up to 350 days of rain per year.

DESERTS

DESERTS ARE areas of land that receive less than 10in (250mm) of rain per year. They are barren regions of rugged hills, clifflike canyons, and pebble or dune-covered plains. Low rainfall and high temperatures make life in the desert hard: only a few plant and animal species can survive.

Existing deserts

Areas at risk of desertification

Average rainfall in Death Valley, California, is 1.5in (38mm) per year.

NORTH AMERICA
EUROPE
ASIA
Great Basin
Kara Kum
Chihuahuan
Gobi
Sahara
AFRICA
Sonoran
SOUTH AMERICA
Arabian
Atacama
Great Sandy
Namib
AUSTRALIA
Great Victoria
Patagonian

Hot deserts, such as the Namib, have hot days and cold nights.

ANTARCTICA

MAJOR DESERTS
About 12% of land is covered with desert, and another third is thought to be at risk of desertification (see p.65).

Cold deserts, such as the Gobi, have hot summers and very cold winters.

Desert covers nearly 80% of Australia.

DESERT FEATURES
Weathering caused by fierce winds, huge temperature variations between day and night, and occasional fast-flowing water forms distinctive desert features.

Mesas are steep-sided, tablelike hills that form where layers of resistant rock protect softer rock beneath.

Deep canyons are usually fed by rain that falls outside the desert area.

Desert water courses, called arroyos, are steep-sided with a flat floor. They are usually dry.

Buttes are isolated, flat-topped hills. They are similar to mesas, but smaller.

Mushroom-shaped pedestal rocks form where sand, blown by the wind, cuts into the rock close to the ground.

Zeugen are parallel, flat-topped ridges with caps of hard, resistant rock perched on softer rock below.

Hamada, or reg (gravel covered surface)

Barcans

Alluvial fans form where water flowing down wadis meets the desert plain and dumps its sediment.

Dry salt lake (playa)

Most oases form at deflation hollows where the water table (see p.56) is near the surface.

A shallow depression, called a deflation hollow, has been scooped out by the wind.

Hard sandstone

Seif dunes

Transverse dunes

SAND DUNES
Dunes develop in flat areas. They range from a few feet to 700ft (200m) high, and can be 3,000ft (900m) wide. There are many types of sand dune, including the four shown below.

BARCANS
These crescent-shaped dunes may grow up to 100ft (30m) high. Barcans move in the direction of the horns.

Wind direction

Crescent-shaped dune

Horn

SEIFS
These sand ridges occur where there is little sand and powerful winds blowing through mountain passes.

Wind direction

Parallel dunes up to 700ft (215m) high.

TRANSVERSE DUNES
These long ridges of sand are separated by deep troughs. Transverse dunes form at right angles to the wind direction.

Wind direction

Dune at right angles to wind

STAR DUNES
These dunes form where several ridges of sand meet, and the wind comes from different directions.

Point where ridges meet

Wind direction

TYPES OF DESERT

CONTINENTAL DESERTS
Continental deserts, such as the Sahara (right), form because they are too far from the sea for winds to bring them much rain. Winds travel over thousands of miles of land before they reach these deserts, losing moisture as they do so.

RAIN-SHADOW DESERTS
Rain-shadow deserts, such as the Atacama desert in Chile (right), form next to mountain ranges. As winds rise up over the mountains, the moisture they carry falls as rain, so the winds are dry as they flow down the other side.

DEAD HOT
If a person spent a day in the Sahara with no shade, food, water, or clothes, their temperature would be about 115°F (46°C) by sunset, and they would have lost 15–19 pints (7–9 liters) of water. By nightfall they would be dead.

MIRAGES
Mirages are often seen in hot deserts. They occur when a layer of warm air next to the ground is trapped by cooler air above. Light bends toward the horizontal line of vision, and eventually travels upward: the mirage is an upside-down "virtual" image.

Cool air

Warm air

Light rays travel straight through cool air.

Observer

Virtual image seen by observer

Light rays traveling through cool and warm air are bent.

LARGEST DESERTS

Desert	Area	
	sq km	sq miles
Sahara	8,600,000	3,320,000
Arabian	2,330,000	900,000
Gobi	1,200,000	463,000
Patagonian	673,000	260,000
Great Victoria	647,000	250,000
Great Basin	492,000	190,000
Chihuahuan	450,000	174,000
Kara Kum	350,000	135,000
Sonoran	310,000	120,000
Great Sandy	258,000	92,000

FORESTS

A THIRD OF THE Earth's land surface is covered by forest: areas of land with dense tree cover. Forests range from the vast, cold taiga of the Northern Hemisphere, to the steamy tropical rainforest of the Amazon Basin, which contains half of all known plant and animal species.

RAINFOREST DIVERSITY

About 750 species of tree grow in a single 25-acre patch of rainforest in Malaysia. There are only 700 species of tree in the whole of North America.

FOREST FACTS

- An area of rainforest the size of a soccer field disappears every second, and more than 50 species of rainforest plants and animals become extinct every day.

- A single tree in Amazonia may be home to 43 species of ant – about the same number found in the whole of the British Isles.

- Forest destruction contributes to the loss of about 55 billion tons of topsoil every year.

- During the monsoon (see p.61), deforested areas of Nepal may experience up to 20,000 landslides in a single day.

- One in five of all birds lives in the Amazon rainforest.

Scarlet macaw (Ara macao)

RAINFOREST REGENERATION

When large gaps occur in a forest, through natural causes or human activity, it takes at least 100 years to return to its natural state. If the thin topsoil is lost, the forest may be replaced by scrubby vegetation only.

Emergent layer
The crowns of giant, scattered, emergent trees spread out above the canopy to form this layer.

Canopy layer
The canopy layer forms the dense forest roof about 100–130ft (30–40m) above the ground.

Most rainforest animals live in the canopy, where there is plenty of light, warmth, rainfall, and food.

Rainforest trees have long, slim trunks.

Understory
The understory layer of the rainforest consists of plants that thrive in shady places, such as palm trees, and young trees growing toward the canopy.

On the forest floor, dead organisms and leaf litter are quickly broken down in the warm, humid climate.

CROSS-SECTION OF A FOREST

Forests consist of several layers of vegetation. This illustration shows the layers of a rainforest. Rainforests grow in parts of the world that receive more than 80in (2,000mm) of rainfall per year. They consist of broadleaved evergreen trees (see p.78), and cover about 6% of the Earth's land surface.

In the understory, lianas and other climbing plants twine around the trees.

Forest floor
The shady rainforest floor has poor soil covered by a thin blanket of leaves. Many of the plants are fungi or parasites, which do not need light to make food.

DESTRUCTION OF EARTH'S FORESTS

Ten thousand years ago, about half of the world's land surface was covered with trees. Today about 33% of those forests have been destroyed, and about 65% of what remains has been greatly changed. Half of the world's tropical rainforests have been felled this century.

Northwest America has lost much of its forest: 60% of the Canadian part and 90% of the US part has been felled.

90% of Central America's rainforest is gone.

The Amazon rainforest originally covered an area nearly two-thirds the size of the US. An area of the size of Europe has been felled.

Trees originally covered about 95% of western and central Europe. By the late Middle Ages, only 20% of the forest was left.

Since 1950, at least 40% of the Himalayan forest has been cut down.

The Ethiopian highlands have lost 90% of their trees in this century.

NORTH AMERICA
SOUTH AMERICA
EUROPE
ASIA
AFRICA
AUSTRALIA

Present-day forest cover

RAINFOREST PRODUCTS

Perfumes
Rainforest plants are used in the manufacture of perfumes and incense.

Rubber
Rubber was originally used by South American Indians to make toys. Rubber tapping is now an important forest industry around the world.

Rattan
Rattan, a woody, climbing rainforest plant, is used to make furniture.

Drugs
One in four types of drug contains chemicals developed from rainforest species.

Insects
A weevil from the Cameroon forests is used to pollinate oil palms in Malaysia: a huge task that was once done by hand.

FOREST RECORDS

LARGEST FOREST
is the taiga (see p.60), which stretches in a wide band across the north of Europe, Asia, and North America.

LARGEST RAINFOREST
is the Amazon rainforest, which covers an area of 2.7 million sq miles (7 million sq km).

Natural, uncut forest

Forest is cut down and burned to enrich the soil.

Land can be used for farming for about two years.

Two years after farming stopped, specialized pioneer species are established.

After 15 years, more typical forest species appear.

After 60 years, typical forest species become dominant.

More than 100 years later, the forest has returned to its natural state.

EARTH'S BIOSPHERE

THE BIOSPHERE is the area of the Earth's surface and its immediate atmosphere that supports life. It stretches from the depths of the oceans to about 9 miles (15km) up into the atmosphere.

BIOSPHERE UNITS

Ecologists (scientists who study the relationship between living things and their environment) break down the biosphere into progressively smaller units, to make it simpler to study.

Earth
The only planet in the Universe known to support life.

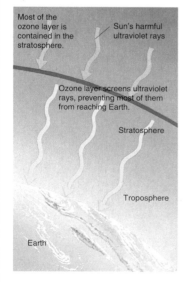

OZONE LAYER

The ozone layer encircles the Earth at a height of 9–30 miles (15–50km). Ozone is the only gas in the atmosphere that can screen out ultraviolet rays from the Sun. Without this protective layer, all life on Earth would die.

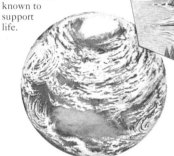

Most of the ozone layer is contained in the stratosphere.

Sun's harmful ultraviolet rays

Ozone layer screens ultraviolet rays, preventing most of them from reaching Earth.

Stratosphere

Troposphere

Earth

Niche
The position of a plant or animal within an ecosystem (see below), including how it relates to other species.

Habitat
The natural home of a plant or animal. A habitat often contains a number of niches.

Ecosystem
The combination of a plant and animal community and its nonliving environment.

Biosphere
The living part of the Earth, including the atmosphere close to the ground. It contains many different ecosystems.

OXYGEN CYCLE

Living things take in oxygen from the air and use it to obtain energy from the food they eat. Plants and animals take in oxygen during respiration, and green plants release oxygen back into the atmosphere during photosynthesis.

Oxygen in the atmosphere

At night, plants take in oxygen and give out carbon dioxide.

In the daytime, plants take in carbon dioxide and give out oxygen during photosynthesis.

Animals inhale oxygen and exhale carbon dioxide.

Night

Day

BODIES OF WATER

Water circulates through the biosphere in a continuous cycle, in oceans, rivers, clouds, and as rain and snow. Living things also form part of this water cycle: the composition of almost all plants and animals, including humans, is nearly 75% water.

BIOSPHERE FACTS

• Ozone is spread so finely that, collected together, it would form a ring around the Earth no thicker than the sole of a shoe.

• Without life, the composition of the Earth's atmosphere would probably be very similar to that of the planet Mars.

• Humans are the first and only species to produce things that cannot be reabsorbed into the Earth's natural systems (nonbiodegradable products). Most plastics are nonbiodegradable.

• If life disappeared from Earth, oxygen would escape from the atmosphere and not be replaced.

EARTH'S CYCLES

Everything in nature is constantly being recycled. Living things take in water, carbon, nitrogen, and oxygen, and use them to live and grow. When they die, they decompose (break down), and the substances they are made of are recycled back into the biosphere and used again for new life. (See p.58 for the water cycle.)

CARBON CYCLE

All living things are based on the element carbon, which originates from carbon dioxide in the Earth's atmosphere. Green plants and some bacteria take in carbon dioxide and use it to make food. When animals eat plants they take in some of this carbon. Carbon dioxide returns to the atmosphere when animals breathe out, produce waste, and finally die and decompose.

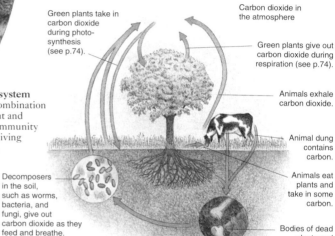

Green plants take in carbon dioxide during photosynthesis (see p.74).

Carbon dioxide in the atmosphere

Green plants give out carbon dioxide during respiration (see p.74).

Animals exhale carbon dioxide.

Animal dung contains carbon.

Animals eat plants and take in some carbon.

Decomposers in the soil, such as worms, bacteria, and fungi, give out carbon dioxide as they feed and breathe.

Bodies of dead plants and animals decay.

NITROGEN CYCLE

All living things need nitrogen, but most cannot use nitrogen in the atmosphere directly: it has to be fixed (combined with other elements) by bacteria, algae, and some lichens, to form nitrates. Plants can take in nitrates, and animals obtain nitrogen by eating plants.

Nitrogen in the atmosphere

Decaying animal waste and dead organisms release nitrogen compounds into the soil.

Animals eat plants containing nitrates.

Other types of bacteria take in nitrates and release nitrogen back into the atmosphere.

Bacteria in roots and soil convert nitrogen compounds to nitrates.

GAIA THEORY

The Gaia theory was developed in 1979 by British scientist James Lovelock (born 1919) (below) and American biologist Lynn Margulis (born 1938). The basis of the theory is that the Earth acts as a single living, self-sustaining organism that can regulate and organize itself. The hypothesis was named after Gaia, the Greek goddess of the Earth.

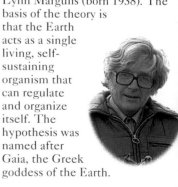

EARTH IN DANGER

THE ACTIVITIES OF the rapidly expanding human population create environmental problems that can upset the balance of the biosphere. Pollution and the destruction of the rainforests, for example, seriously threaten the future of life on Earth.

GLOBAL WARMING

Greenhouse effect
Carbon dioxide and certain other gases in the atmosphere act like glass in a greenhouse. They let the Sun's rays through, but trap some of the heat which would otherwise be reflected back into space. The greenhouse effect has always existed.

Sun's heat
Balanced conditions
Troposphere
Trapped heat is reflected back to Earth.
Excess heat escapes into space.

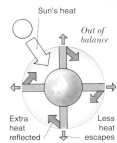

Sun's heat
Out of balance
Extra heat reflected
Less heat escapes

Raising the temperature
Burning fossil fuels (see p.272) increases the amount of carbon dioxide in the atmosphere, which traps extra heat. If we continue to release heat-trapping gases, the Earth's temperature will rise, creating many problems.

OZONE HOLE

A hole in the ozone layer opens over Antarctica every spring. The main cause of the hole is the release of chemicals that destroy the ozone layer, such as chlorofluorocarbons (CFCs), into the atmosphere. The thinning of the ozone layer means that more of the Sun's ultraviolet rays can reach Earth, leading to an increase in skin cancers and damage to crops.

ACID RAIN

Acid rain is caused mainly by sulfur and nitrogen oxides given off by power stations, industry, and vehicle engines. When these pollutants combine with water vapor, sunlight, and oxygen in the atmosphere, they create weak sulfuric and nitric acids. This mixture falls as rain, increasing the acidity of lakes and rivers. These unfavorable conditions often cause a decline in the numbers of animals and plants.

UPSETTING THE BALANCE

The use of chemicals, such as those in pesticides and fertilizers, can interfere with Earth's natural cycles. For example, the large amount of nitrogen used in farming can lead to pollution of the water supply.

DEFORESTATION

Forests are being felled for timber and to create land for agriculture. This reduces biodiversity (range and number of species), leads to soil erosion, upsets cycles, and contributes to global warming.

Chemicals released by factories pollute the air, rivers, lakes, and oceans.

More than a million tons of oil a year are deliberately discharged from tankers.

12% of marine pollution is caused by shipping.

Litter is unsightly and unhygienic, and can harm animals that eat it.

URBAN AIR POLLUTION

In many large cities, air pollution caused by vehicles and industry has become a serious problem. It causes human health problems such as eye irritation, coughs, and asthma, and damages plants and buildings.

MARINE POLLUTION

The sea has always been a dumping ground for human wastes, but in the last century the amount of pollutants being discharged into the oceans increased dramatically. This pollution causes problems such as toxic algae, health risks to bathers, and danger to aquatic life.

Toxic algae

One of the most serious effects of marine pollution is toxic (poisonous) algae. Chemicals from sewage discharges, fertilizers, and industrial wastes nourish these algae, causing a huge increase in their numbers and, consequently, the death of marine animals.

Toxic algae

POLLUTION FACTS

• Some scientists believe that global warming will cause the average world temperature to rise by 1.8°F (1°C) by the year 2030, and by 7.2°F (4°C) by the end of the 21st century.

• In January 1989, Mexico City's smog (urban pollution) was so bad that schoolchildren were given the whole month off.

• About 50 outbreaks of toxic algae occur in Japanese waters every year.

• 2,200 Swedish lakes are nearly lifeless because of acid rain, and 80% of Norway's lakes are biologically dead or threatened.

POLLUTED CITIES

The table below shows the average number of days in recent years that the suspended particulate matter (soot and smoke) for some of the world's most polluted cities was above the World Health Organization's recommended standard.

City	Number of days above standard
New Delhi, India	294
Beijing, China	272
Tehran, Iran	174
Bangkok, Thailand	97
Madrid, Spain	60

A FOREST A WEEK

It takes an entire forest – more than half a million trees – to supply North Americans with their Sunday newspapers every week.

POPULATION GROWTH

Population growth creates huge pressure on the Earth's resources. This graph shows population growth over the last 1,000 years.

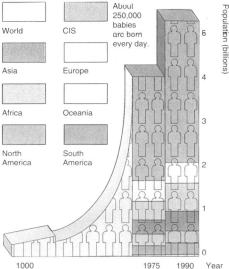

World
CIS
Asia
Europe
Africa
Oceania
North America
South America

About 250,000 babies are born every day.

Population (billions)

1000   1975   1990   Year

WASTING EARTH'S RESOURCES

The world's industrialized nations use a far greater proportion of the Earth's resources than the developing nations, even though their combined population is small. The richest 20% of the world's population consumes 70% of the world's energy, 75% of its metals, 85% of its wood, and 60% of its food. Many resources are unnecessarily wasted: much of what people consume ends up on garbage dumps.

SAVING THE EARTH

PEOPLE ARE beginning to accept responsibility for Earth's future. The main environmental problems have been recognized, and ways of reducing their impact are being explored. Positive steps toward the long-term survival of our planet are shown here, but there is still much work to be done.

LIMITING POPULATION GROWTH

Slowing down population growth is one of the most important factors in saving the Earth's diminishing resources. Ways include family planning and improving standards of living. (In many countries, a large family is seen as a secure source of income.) Family planning measures that were introduced in Kerala, India, led to a 66% decline in the birthrate between 1983 and 1993.

PROMOTING ECOTOURISM

Tourism that benefits the environment is known as ecotourism. For example, money earned from tourism can be spent on the creation and management of national parks. A report by the US Forest Service showed that the potential earnings from forest recreational activities such as camping and canoeing are twice what could be made by selling the timber.

WAYS TO HELP THE ENVIRONMENT

• Use recycled paper and cardboard.

• Recycle plastics, glass, metal, and wastepaper.

• Avoid buying tropical hardwoods, such as mahogany.

REDUCING URBAN POLLUTION

Car pooling, using public transportation, bicycling, and walking all reduce vehicle use in urban areas. Catalytic converters can help reduce pollution from cars. Working at home using computer technology ("telecommuting"), instead of traveling to an office, also reduces the number of vehicles on the roads.

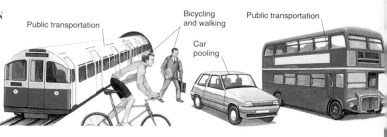
Public transportation | Bicycling and walking | Car pooling | Public transportation

HALTING DESERTIFICATION

Farming methods such as terracing (right) can reduce desertification and the loss of topsoil. In China, a "great green wall" of trees (the San Bei Forest Belt) has been planted to hold back the advancing desert. Somalia has begun a major anti-desertification program that includes a ban on cutting trees for fuel.

Trees planted to hold back the desert

CONSERVING HABITATS AND SPECIES

Projects have been set up worldwide to conserve habitats and the species they contain. These include the establishment of national parks and other conservation areas – more than 5% of the world's total land area is now protected. The Convention on International Trade in Endangered Species (CITES) is an international treaty signed by 122 countries. It aims to prevent trade in endangered plant and animal species and in products such as animal skins and ivory.

The tiger is endangered.

REDUCING POLLUTION

Many countries are reducing sulfur dioxide emissions to prevent acid rain and global warming. The EC has ruled that large fossil-fuel power plants must cut emissions of sulfur dioxide by 60% by 2003. Ways of improving toxic waste treatment and disposal are also being explored. International treaties have been developed to regulate the dumping of waste at sea and to control the discharge of other pollutants into the the oceans.

USING RENEWABLE ENERGY

Fossil fuels (see p.272) will eventually run out. Meanwhile, their use creates pollution and contributes to global warming. Cleaner, renewable methods of generating energy are being developed, such as wind, wave, solar, and tidal power. Some countries, including Norway and Brazil, already obtain more than half their energy from renewable sources.

Hydroelectric power (right) is a clean, renewable energy source.

Wind turbines

Solar collectors trap sunlight to generate power.

REDUCING FIREWOOD USE

Tree cover is being lost where large amounts of wood are chopped for fire. Alternative, more efficient cooking methods are being introduced in some countries affected by this deforestation. In Kenya, where wood energy accounts for more than 75% of energy consumption, 180,000 jikos (charcoal-burning stoves) have been distributed (right).

SAVING THE RAIN FORESTS

Many initiatives have been introduced to try and save the remaining areas of rain forest. Debt-swap deals, in which a country protects an area of forest in return for a reduction in their foreign debt, have been negotiated. Practices that do not damage the forest, such as rubber tapping, are being encouraged, together with trade in forest products such as spices, rattan, nuts, and medicinal plants. These products may be worth as much as timber.

Brazil nuts

Rubber tapping

• Walk, bicycle, or use public transportation instead of the car whenever possible.

• Turn off lights and other appliances when not in use.

• When getting rid of an old refrigerator, make sure that its CFCs are safely removed.

• Start a compost heap for vegetable peels and garden waste, such as leaves and grass cuttings.

• When ordinary lightbulbs are spent, replace them with energy-efficient, compact fluorescent lightbulbs.

PROTECTED AREAS OF THE WORLD

This table shows the percentage of land area on each continent (except Antarctica) that is protected in national parks or other conservation areas. It also shows the country with the most protected land.

Continent	% land protected	Country with most protected land (%)
North & Central America	10.4	Panama 17.2
Europe	7.5	Austria 19
South America	5.7	Ecuador 37.7
Oceania	5.7	New Zealand 10.5
Africa	3.9	Bostwana 17.2
Asia	2.1	Bhutan 19.7

LIVING WORLD

In this fascinating survey of the natural world, all living things are classified, and every major plant and animal group is illustrated. Stunning cutaway artworks show anatomical details, and there is a wealth of factual information about attack and defense, movement, and reproduction. Tables list record breakers from the heaviest to the most deadly.

Evolution • Fossils • Dinosaurs • Classifying Living Things
Plants • Flowers • Leaves • Trees • Food Plants • Fungi and Lichens
Microorganisms • Animals • Invertebrates • Mollusks • Insects
Arachnids • Crustaceans • Amphibians • Reptiles • Fish
Birds • Domestic Birds • Mammals • Domestic Mammals
Animal Senses and Behavior • Migration and Homes
Food Chains and Webs • Endangered Species
Animal Records and Comparisons

EVOLUTION

LIFE ON EARTH probably originated from chemicals dissolved in the oceans. From these simple beginnings, life has gradually developed into many different forms. All living things change as one generation succeeds another. This process is called evolution.

EVOLUTION TERMS

Variation Almost all living things vary in size, shape, color, and strength from others in the same species.

Adaptations These are certain features, such as color, that may give one individual or species a better chance of survival than another.

Inheritance Characteristics are passed on, or inherited, when living things reproduce. Most living things have a unique combination of characteristics.

Natural selection Through natural selection, inherited characteristics that help a living thing survive are passed on; those that do not gradually die out.

Competition/survival of the fittest More individuals are born than can survive. Strong, well-adapted individuals are more likely to survive than weak, poorly adapted individuals.

SLOTH GROWTH

During the Tertiary Period, South America was cut off from other landmasses, and there were few predators. Several types of mammal became gigantic; for example *Megatherium*, the giant ground sloth, grew to more than 20ft (6m) long.

EVOLUTION OF THE ELEPHANT

Fossils reveal that several elephant-like species have existed and become extinct over the last 40 million years. It is likely that they were related, and that today's elephants evolved from them.

Platybelodon lived from 12 to 7 million years ago.

Trilophodon lived from 26 to 3 million years ago.

Woolly mammoth lived about 2 million years ago.

African elephant

Moenitherium lived about 38 million years ago.

ADAPTATION EXAMPLE

The 28 species of honeycreeper in the Hawaiian islands probably all evolved from one species. Each has a beak adapted for a particular way of feeding. Some are now extinct.

The iiwi's beak and tongue are adapted for sipping nectar.

The Kona grosbeak (now extinct) had a strong bill for crushing seeds.

The Kauai akialoa uses its long beak to probe for insects.

EVOLUTION FACTS

• Ninety-five percent of all animals and plants that have ever existed on Earth have become extinct.

• Between 35 and 20 million years ago, giant rhinoceroses, such as *Paraceatherium*, roamed America. This animal measured up to 26ft (8m) long and was as tall as a giraffe.

• Moas – the giant, flightless birds of New Zealand (now extinct) – show what could have happened in a world without mammals: birds would have become dominant. (New Zealand has no native mammals except for a few bats.)

• The earliest horse, *Hyracotherium*, was about the size of a modern fox terrier.

CHARLES DARWIN (1809–1882) The theory of natural selection was developed by English naturalist Charles Darwin, and published in 1859 in his book *The Origin of Species*. Darwin developed his theory after studying the animals of the Galapagos Islands, which were unique, but similar to those on the South American mainland.

• Australia's largest ever marsupial was *Diprotodon optatum*, which was as big as a rhinoceros and weighed up to 3,300lb (1,500kg).

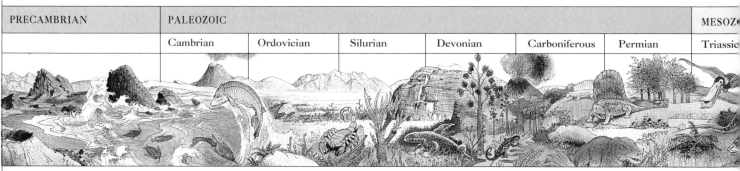

PRECAMBRIAN	PALEOZOIC							MESOZOIC
	Cambrian	Ordovician	Silurian	Devonian	Carboniferous	Permian	Triassic

4,600–590mya (million years ago) Earth forms and gradually cools; atmosphere has no oxygen. First bacteria appear. Blue-green algae evolve and produce oxygen-rich atmosphere. Protists (single-celled organisms) develop. Nonflowering plants evolve and become abundant. First animals, including worms and jellyfish, appear.

590–505mya Invertebrates (see p.84) become widespread in the oceans. Trilobites are common. First mollusks evolve.

505–438mya First crustaceans evolve. First fishlike vertebrates (see p.84) appear: they have no fins or jaws.

438–408mya First fish with jaws evolve. Coral reefs flourish in the oceans. Huge sea scorpions hunt. On land, the first small plants appear.

408–360 mya "Age of Fish." Fish dominate life in the seas. First insects evolve. First amphibians appear on land.

360–286mya (Mississippian and Pennsylvanian) Warm, damp climate; huge forests lay down remains that will turn into coal. First reptiles evolve from amphibians. Insects abundant.

286–248mya Earth cooler. Amphibians decline; reptiles diversify. Ferns and conifers widespread. Many species vanish in greatest mass extinction known.

248–213 Climate to warm conifers ferns for forests. First din evolve. mar ev

FOSSILS

FOSSILS PROVIDE a history book of life on Earth. They are the remains of dead animals and plants that have been preserved naturally for thousands or millions of years. The study of fossils is called paleontology.

FORMS OF FOSSILIZATION

Fossils are preserved in several different ways. Most are found in rocks, but fossils also occur in ice, tar, peat, and amber.

MINERALIZATION
This is the most common form of preservation. It occurs when the organic matter of a fossil is replaced by durable (long lasting) minerals. Petrified wood is formed by mineralization.

Petrified wood

FREEZING
Low temperatures can preserve animal and plant remains. Well-preserved mammoths have been found in Siberian permafrost (permanently frozen ground). Flesh and skin, as well as bones, are preserved by freezing.

Fossilized mammoth

AMBER
Tree resin (sap) can trap and surround small animals such as insects and spiders. The resin, with the animal still intact inside, is fossilized, turning into amber.

Spider in amber

PEAT AND TAR
Animals and plants can be preserved in peat and tar. Human bodies more than 2,000 years old have been found in peat bogs, and animal remains up to 20,000 years old have been found in tar.

Human preserved in peat

TYPES OF FOSSIL

Any organism can be mineralized, provided it is buried by mud or sand before it rots away. Most fossils form on the seabed, so the most common are those of sea creatures. Fossils of land animals and plants are much rarer.

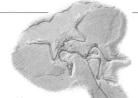

Ammonites
Ammonites were marine (sea-dwelling) mollusks that became extinct about 65 million years ago. Their shells were often fossilized.

Archaeopteryx
Prehistoric flying animal believed to be the evolutionary link between reptiles and birds. Seven fossilized *Archaeopteryx* have been found.

Trilobites
Marine arthropods (see p.85) distantly related to the sowbug. They died out about 286 million years ago.

Soft-bodied animals
Most fossils are the remains of bones or shells. Fossils of soft-bodied animals, such as this dragonfly, are rare.

Coprolites
These are fossilized animal droppings. Dinosaur coprolites can measure more than 2ft (60cm) long.

Plant fossils
This fossilized poplar leaf is about 25 million years old. Modern poplar leaves are almost identical: these trees have hardly changed.

FOSSIL FACTS

• Fossils are found only in sedimentary rocks (see p.46). Marine limestones, shales, and some sandstones contain the most fossils.

• Some ammonites measured up to 6.6ft (2m) in diameter.

FORMATION OF FOSSILS

This sequence shows how the remains of sea creatures may be fossilized and brought to the land surface.

MAMMOTH MISTAKE

For centuries, fossils were associated with myths and legends. Fossilized mammoth tusks discovered in about 1600 were believed at the time to be the horns of unicorns.

FOSSIL RECORDS

EARLIEST FOSSILS are prokaryotes (cells without nuclei) found in Western Australia, which are an estimated 3.5 billion years old.

LARGEST FOSSIL is a *Brachiosaurus* skeleton (see p.71), which is 72ft (22m) long.

1 Dead animals, such as fish, sink to the seabed. Their remains are slowly buried by layers of sediment.

2 The lower layers of sediment turn to rock, and the animal remains are mineralized, becoming fossils.

3 Over many years the rock is folded, and the upper layers are eroded.

4 The rock is eroded further, and the fossils are eventually exposed on the surface.

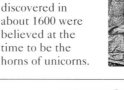

CENOZOIC								
Cretaceous	Tertiary						Quaternary	
	Paleocene	Eocene	Oligocene	Miocene	Pliocene	Pleistocene	Holocene

4mya
much than Dinosaurs re life on rst bird, oteryx, from

144–65mya
First flowering plants evolve. Dinosaurs flourish. Period ends with mass extinction: sweeps away many species including all dinosaurs and ammonites.

65–55mya
Climate warm and damp. Flowering plants continue to evolve and, together with insect pollinators, become widespread.

55–38mya
Mammals continue to diversify, becoming larger and more numerous. Primates (apes, monkeys, and lemurs) evolve into many forms.

38–25mya
First humanlike primates appear. Many early mammals become extinct. Giant flightless hunting birds flourish.

25–5mya
Climate cools; forests begin to decrease worldwide. Hoofed mammals, such as deer, flourish. Toward the end of the epoch, the first hominids evolve.

5–2mya
Climate cold and dry. Mammals reach peak of their diversity. Many land creatures similar to today's. Bony fish dominate life in the sea.

2m–10,000 years ago
Time of ice ages. Many mammal species, including mammoths and saber-toothed tigers, become extinct. *Homo sapiens* evolves.

10,000 years ago – today
Humans develop agriculture and technology; population expands.

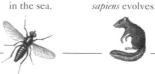

DINOSAURS

DINOSAURS DOMINATED the Earth for more than 150 million years. They included the largest animals ever to have lived on land, as well as some that were smaller than a coyote. Dinosaurs died out 65 million years ago. Nobody knows why.

Dinosaur's brains were small for their body size.

PORTRAIT OF A DINOSAUR

Like reptiles, dinosaurs had a scaly skin. Dinosaurs, however, were more advanced than today's reptiles. They walked with their limbs directly under their body like mammals and birds, whereas reptiles crawl, or walk with their limbs out to their sides.

Gallimimus

Backbone
Rib
Ovary
Kidney
Trachea
Lung
Heart
Claw
Liver
Intestine
Caudal vertebra
Tough, scaly skin
Cloaca (body opening)
Dinosaurs used their tail for balance.
Gallimimus was a lizard-hipped dinosaur.
Tibia
Fibula
Tendon
Legs extended directly below the body, lifting the dinosaur off the ground.
Bipedal (two-footed) dinosaurs could walk upright.

TYPES OF DINOSAUR

There are two orders (see p.72) of dinosaur. They are classified according to the arrangement of their hipbones.

Lizard-hipped dinosaurs (Saurischians) Hips similar to lizards. Includes both herbivorous (plant-eating) and carnivorous (meat-eating) species.

Bird-hipped dinosaurs (Ornithischians) Hips similar to birds. All of the bird-hipped dinosaur species were herbivorous.

DINOSAUR FACTS

• Dinosaur fossils discovered to date probably represent less than 0.0001% of the individuals that once lived.

• The name *Tyrannosaurus* means "tyrant lizard."

• The most intelligent dinosaurs were probably about as intelligent as chickens.

• More than 350 species of dinosaur have so far been identified: probably only a tiny percentage of those that existed.

• *Struthiomimus* could sprint at speeds of up to 50mph (80km/h): as fast as an ostrich.

DINOSAUR-LIKE REPTILES

While dinosaurs roamed the land, huge reptiles flew in the air and swam in the oceans. These marine and flying reptiles were closely related to the dinosaurs.

Rhamphorhynchus
Ichthyosaurus
Elasmosaurus
Pterodactylus

FLYING REPTILES
Ancient flying reptiles, called pterosaurs, reached huge sizes. Their wings were made of skin, and their body was usually furry. They had light, delicate bones for flying.

MARINE REPTILES
These were some of the fiercest and largest animals in the sea. They breathed air, so they had to come to the surface regularly to fill their lungs. These reptiles hunted fish and other sea creatures.

MAJOR DINOSAUR GROUPS

Within the two orders, dinosaurs are divided into five subgroups. There are three subgroups of ornithischians, and two subgroups of saurischians.

Thyreophorans (Ornithischians) Armored herbivores; rows of protective studs, plates, or spikes down the back, e.g. *Stegosaurus*.

Theropods (Saurischians) Mostly bipedal carnivores with an S-shaped neck and clawed, four-toed feet, e.g. *Tyrannosaurus*.

Marginocephalians (Ornithischians) Herbivores; many with bony frill at back of skull, e.g. *Styracosaurus*.

Ornithopods (Ornithischians) Herbivores; horny beak and birdlike feet, e.g. *Corythosaurus*.

Sauropodomorphs (Saurischians). Herbivores; small head, long neck, bulky body, and long tail, e.g. *Saltasaurus*.

Triassic Period: 248–213 mya (million years ago)	Jurassic Period: 213–144 mya
Land joined in the supercontinent of Pangaea (see p.40). First dinosaurs evolve and, toward the end of the period, split into two groups: lizard- and bird-hipped.	Pangaea breaks apart: Atlantic Ocean begins to form; Africa splits from South America. In late Jurassic times, huge herbivorous dinosaurs dominate life on land.

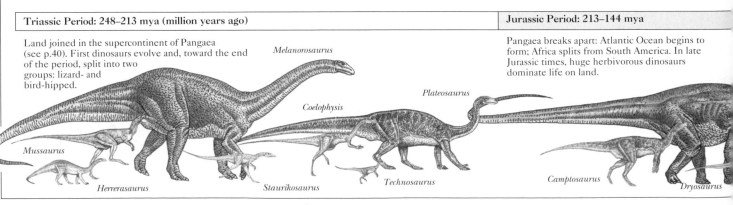

Melanorosaurus
Coelophysis
Plateosaurus
Mussaurus
Herrerasaurus
Staurikosaurus
Technosaurus
Camptosaurus
Dryosaurus

DINOSAUR DISCOVERY

Pre-19th century: around the world, dinosaur fossils are believed to be various things, including dragon bones in China, and giant human bones in parts of Europe.

1800 Dinosaur footprints found in Massachusetts. Their discoverer claims they were made by the raven from Noah's Ark.

1820 Iguanodon teeth discovered in Tilgate Forest, Sussex, England, by doctor and fossil hunter Gideon Mantell (1790–1852) and his wife. He suspects they are the remains of ancient reptiles, but his theory is dismissed as heretical (antireligious).

1834 First glimpse of what dinosaurs looked like provided by find of a partial skeleton near Maidstone, England, known as the Maidstone *Iguanodon*.

1841 The term dinosaur, from the Greek words for "terrible" and "lizard," is coined by English anatomist Richard Owen (1804–1892).

1800	**1800**	1820	**1820**	1830	**1834**	1840	**1841**

1851 First reconstruction of dinosaurs: *Iguanodon* and *Hylaeosaurus* models are made for the Great Exhibition at Crystal Palace, London, England. Results in huge public enthusiasm for dinosaurs. Before the *Iguanodon* is completed, the sculptor holds a dinner party inside it.

Dinner party in a model dinosaur

1877 One of the greatest dinosaur collections found at Como Bluff, Wyoming, by O.C. Marsh (1831–99) of Yale.

1947 Largest number of dinosaurs ever found together: more than 100 *Coelophysis* skeletons.

1987 Evidence to support theory of warm-blooded dinosaurs found by paleontologists Tom Rich and Patricia Vickers-Rich of the Museum of Victoria, Australia. They discover dinosaur fossils in a part of South Australia that would have been inside the Antarctic Circle when these dinosaurs lived. The mean annual temperature in this region would have been near freezing at that time.

Leaellynasaura lived in polar regions.

1850	**1851**	1870	**1877**	1940	**1947**	1980	**1987**	

DINOSAUR RECORDS

SMALLEST DINOSAUR
was probably *Wannanosaurus*, a bipedal carnivore that measured 2ft (60cm) long. It was about the size of a chicken.

MOST PRIMITIVE KNOWN DINOSAUR
is *Eoraptor*, a 228 million-year-old bipedal carnivore that was about the size of a large dog.

SMALLEST DINOSAUR BRAIN
is believed to have been that of the *Stegosaurus*. It was less than 2in (5cm) long.

LARGEST DINOSAUR EGGS
were probably those of *Hypselosaurus*. They measured about 12in (30cm) long and contained an estimated 7 pints (3.3 liters) of fluid: roughly the same as the fluid in 60 hens' eggs.

WIDER GLIDER

The largest flying animal ever to have existed was *Quetzalcoatlus*, a flying reptile. Its wingspan measured about 39ft (12m) across: wider than the wingspan of a hang glider.

EARTH SHAKER

The name *Seismosaurus* means "earth-shaking lizard." This enormous plant-eating dinosaur was 131ft (40m) in length: longer than an Airbus A320.

LARGEST CARNIVORES

Dinosaur	Estimated length	
	m	ft
Acrocanthosaurus	12	39
Tyrannosaurus	12	39
Aliwalia	11	36
Allosaurus	11	36

LARGEST HERBIVORES

Dinosaur	Estimated length	
	m	ft
Seismosaurus	40	131
Barosaurus	27	80
Diplodocus	27	89
Brachiosaurus	25	82

EXTINCTION THEORIES

About 65 million years ago the dinosaurs, together with many other animal species, became extinct. Other animal groups, including turtles, frogs, birds, and mammals, survived. There are many theories for this mass extinction: below are two of the most widely accepted.

GRADUAL EXTINCTION
Gradual changes in climate and vegetation caused by continental drift (see p.40) led to the dinosaurs' slow extinction over about 50,000 years. Warm, tropical conditions were replaced by cooler, more seasonal climates, and mammals slowly replaced dinosaurs as the dominant animal group.

CATASTROPHES
The period when dinosaurs were dying out coincided with many volcanic eruptions in India. At the same time, a huge meteorite hit the Earth. Dust thrown into the atmosphere blocked out sunlight, and dinosaurs could not survive the resulting climate changes.

Cretaceous Period: 144–65mya	65 mya

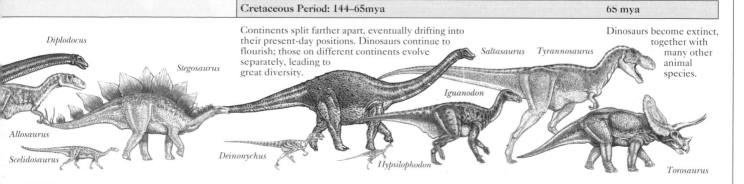

Continents split farther apart, eventually drifting into their present-day positions. Dinosaurs continue to flourish; those on different continents evolve separately, leading to great diversity.

Dinosaurs become extinct, together with many other animal species.

Diplodocus
Stegosaurus
Saltasaurus
Tyrannosaurus
Iguanodon
Allosaurus
Scelidosaurus
Deinonychus
Hypsilophodon
Torosaurus

CLASSIFYING LIVING THINGS

LIVING THINGS ARE classified in groups according to the features they have in common. The largest groups are the five kingdoms: animals, plants, fungi, protists, and monerans. Each kingdom is then subdivided into smaller and smaller groups.

KEY

These colors show the classification groupings used in the chart. All numbers of species are approximate. A division is the plant equivalent of a phylum.

- Kingdom
- Phylum
- Sub-phylum
- Class
- Order
- Division

SCIENTIFIC NAMES

Many living things have different common names around the world. To avoid confusion, every species also has a two-part scientific name which is the same worldwide. The first part of the name gives the genus; the second part the species. This system was devised by Swedish botanist Carolus Linnaeus (1707–1778). Larger groups, such as orders, also have a scientific name. Throughout the *Living World* section, scientific names are given wherever possible for genera and species.

CLASSIFYING A TIGER

This illustration shows how a biologist would classify a tiger.

Kingdom Animal (Animalia) Many-celled organisms with no cell walls; cannot make their own food.

Phylum Chordate (Chordata) Animals that have a single nerve cord at some time in their life.

Class Mammal (Mammalia) Animals that suckle their young on milk and have fur or hair.

Order Carnivores (Carnivora) Land mammals specialized for hunting.

Family Cats (Felidae) Carnivores with sharp front claws that can be retracted (drawn in).

Genus Big cats (*Panthera*) The five species of big cats: lion, tiger, leopard, snow leopard, and jaguar.

Species Tiger (*Panthera tigris*)

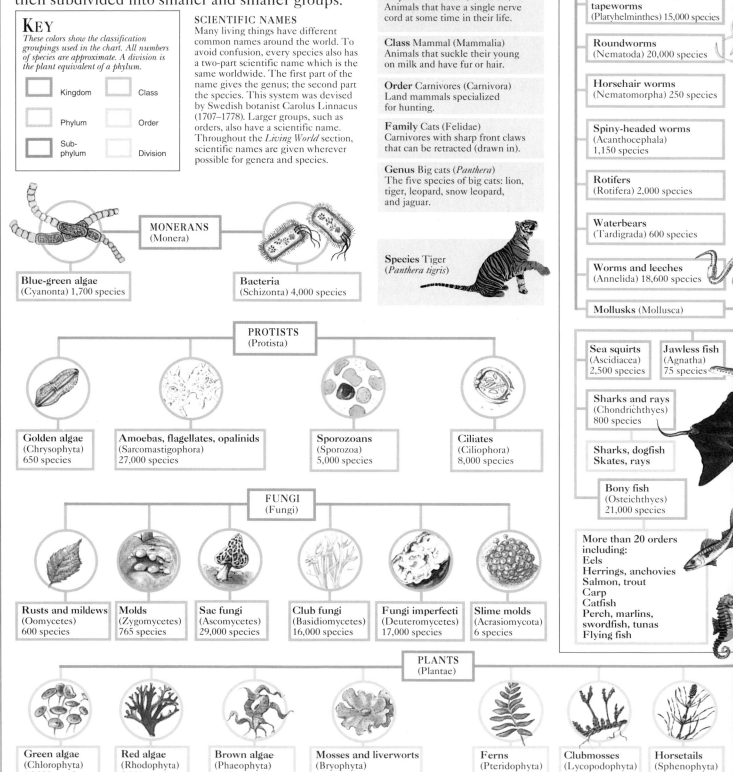

MONERANS (Monera)

Blue-green algae (Cyanonta) 1,700 species

Bacteria (Schizonta) 4,000 species

Sponges (Porifera) 9,000 species

Sea anemones, hydras, corals, jellyfish (Cnidaria) 9,500 species

Comb jellies (Ctenophora) 90 species

Flatworms, flukes, tapeworms (Platyhelminthes) 15,000 species

Roundworms (Nematoda) 20,000 species

Horsehair worms (Nematomorpha) 250 species

Spiny-headed worms (Acanthocephala) 1,150 species

Rotifers (Rotifera) 2,000 species

Waterbears (Tardigrada) 600 species

Worms and leeches (Annelida) 18,600 species

Mollusks (Mollusca)

PROTISTS (Protista)

Golden algae (Chrysophyta) 650 species

Amoebas, flagellates, opalinids (Sarcomastigophora) 27,000 species

Sporozoans (Sporozoa) 5,000 species

Ciliates (Ciliophora) 8,000 species

Sea squirts (Ascidiacea) 2,500 species

Jawless fish (Agnatha) 75 species

Sharks and rays (Chondrichthyes) 800 species

Sharks, dogfish Skates, rays

Bony fish (Osteichthyes) 21,000 species

FUNGI (Fungi)

Rusts and mildews (Oomycetes) 600 species

Molds (Zygomycetes) 765 species

Sac fungi (Ascomycetes) 29,000 species

Club fungi (Basidiomycetes) 16,000 species

Fungi imperfecti (Deuteromycetes) 17,000 species

Slime molds (Acrasiomycota) 6 species

More than 20 orders including:
Eels
Herrings, anchovies
Salmon, trout
Carp
Catfish
Perch, marlins, swordfish, tunas
Flying fish

PLANTS (Plantae)

Green algae (Chlorophyta) 14,000 species

Red algae (Rhodophyta) 5,000 species

Brown algae (Phaeophyta) 1,500 species

Mosses and liverworts (Bryophyta) 14,000 species

Ferns (Pteridophyta) 12,000 species

Clubmosses (Lycopodophyta) 1,000 species

Horsetails (Sphenophyta) 40 species

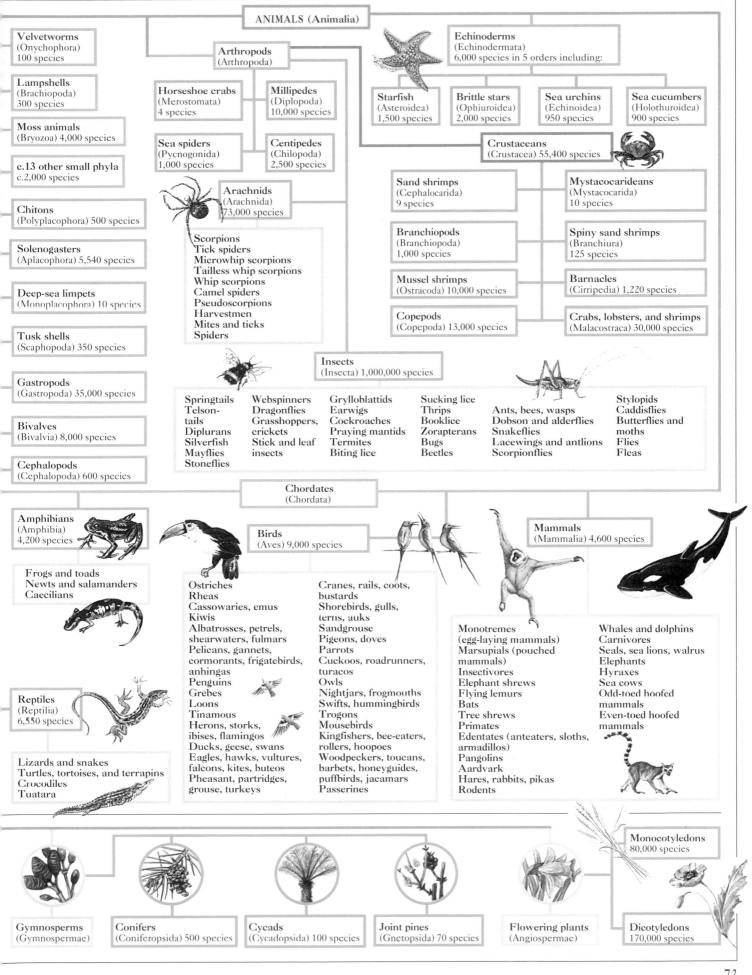

ANIMALS (Animalia)

Velvetworms
(Onychophora)
100 species

Lampshells
(Brachiopoda)
300 species

Moss animals
(Bryozoa) 4,000 species

c.13 other small phyla
c.2,000 species

Chitons
(Polyplacophora) 500 species

Solenogasters
(Aplacophora) 5,540 species

Deep-sea limpets
(Monoplacophora) 10 species

Tusk shells
(Scaphopoda) 350 species

Gastropods
(Gastropoda) 35,000 species

Bivalves
(Bivalvia) 8,000 species

Cephalopods
(Cephalopoda) 600 species

Arthropods
(Arthropoda)

Horseshoe crabs
(Merostomata)
4 species

Millipedes
(Diplopoda)
10,000 species

Sea spiders
(Pycnogonida)
1,000 species

Centipedes
(Chilopoda)
2,500 species

Arachnids
(Arachnida)
73,000 species

Scorpions
Tick spiders
Microwhip scorpions
Tailless whip scorpions
Whip scorpions
Camel spiders
Pseudoscorpions
Harvestmen
Mites and ticks
Spiders

Echinoderms
(Echinodermata)
6,000 species in 5 orders including:

Starfish
(Asteroidea)
1,500 species

Brittle stars
(Ophiuroidea)
2,000 species

Sea urchins
(Echinoidea)
950 species

Sea cucumbers
(Holothuroidea)
900 species

Crustaceans
(Crustacea) 55,400 species

Sand shrimps
(Cephalocarida)
9 species

Mystacocarideans
(Mystacocarida)
10 species

Branchiopods
(Branchiopoda)
1,000 species

Spiny sand shrimps
(Branchiura)
125 species

Mussel shrimps
(Ostracoda) 10,000 species

Barnacles
(Cirripedia) 1,220 species

Copepods
(Copepoda) 13,000 species

Crabs, lobsters, and shrimps
(Malacostraca) 30,000 species

Insects
(Insecta) 1,000,000 species

Springtails	Webspinners	Grylloblattids	Sucking lice		Stylopids
Telson-tails	Dragonflies	Earwigs	Thrips	Ants, bees, wasps	Caddisflies
Diplurans	Grasshoppers, crickets	Cockroaches	Booklice	Dobson and alderflies	Butterflies and moths
Silverfish	Stick and leaf insects	Praying mantids	Zorapterans	Snakeflies	Flies
Mayflies		Termites	Bugs	Lacewings and antlions	Fleas
Stoneflies		Biting lice	Beetles	Scorpionflies	

Chordates
(Chordata)

Amphibians
(Amphibia)
4,200 species

Frogs and toads
Newts and salamanders
Caecilians

Reptiles
(Reptilia)
6,550 species

Lizards and snakes
Turtles, tortoises, and terrapins
Crocodiles
Tuatara

Birds
(Aves) 9,000 species

Ostriches
Rheas
Cassowaries, emus
Kiwis
Albatrosses, petrels, shearwaters, fulmars
Pelicans, gannets, cormorants, frigatebirds, anhingas
Penguins
Grebes
Loons
Tinamous
Herons, storks, ibises, flamingos
Ducks, geese, swans
Eagles, hawks, vultures, falcons, kites, buteos
Pheasant, partridges, grouse, turkeys

Cranes, rails, coots, bustards
Shorebirds, gulls, terns, auks
Sandgrouse
Pigeons, doves
Parrots
Cuckoos, roadrunners, turacos
Owls
Nightjars, frogmouths
Swifts, hummingbirds
Trogons
Mousebirds
Kingfishers, bee-eaters, rollers, hoopoes
Woodpeckers, toucans, barbets, honeyguides, puffbirds, jacamars
Passerines

Mammals
(Mammalia) 4,600 species

Monotremes
(egg-laying mammals)
Marsupials (pouched mammals)
Insectivores
Elephant shrews
Flying lemurs
Bats
Tree shrews
Primates
Edentates (anteaters, sloths, armadillos)
Pangolins
Aardvark
Hares, rabbits, pikas
Rodents

Whales and dolphins
Carnivores
Seals, sea lions, walrus
Elephants
Hyraxes
Sea cows
Odd-toed hoofed mammals
Even-toed hoofed mammals

Gymnosperms
(Gymnospermae)

Conifers
(Coniferopsida) 500 species

Cycads
(Cycadopsida) 100 species

Joint pines
(Gnetopsida) 70 species

Flowering plants
(Angiospermae)

Monocotyledons
80,000 species

Dicotyledons
170,000 species

PLANTS

PLANTS, UNLIKE ANIMALS, can manufacture their own food. This makes them the starting point of most food chains, and almost all other living organisms depend on them for food.

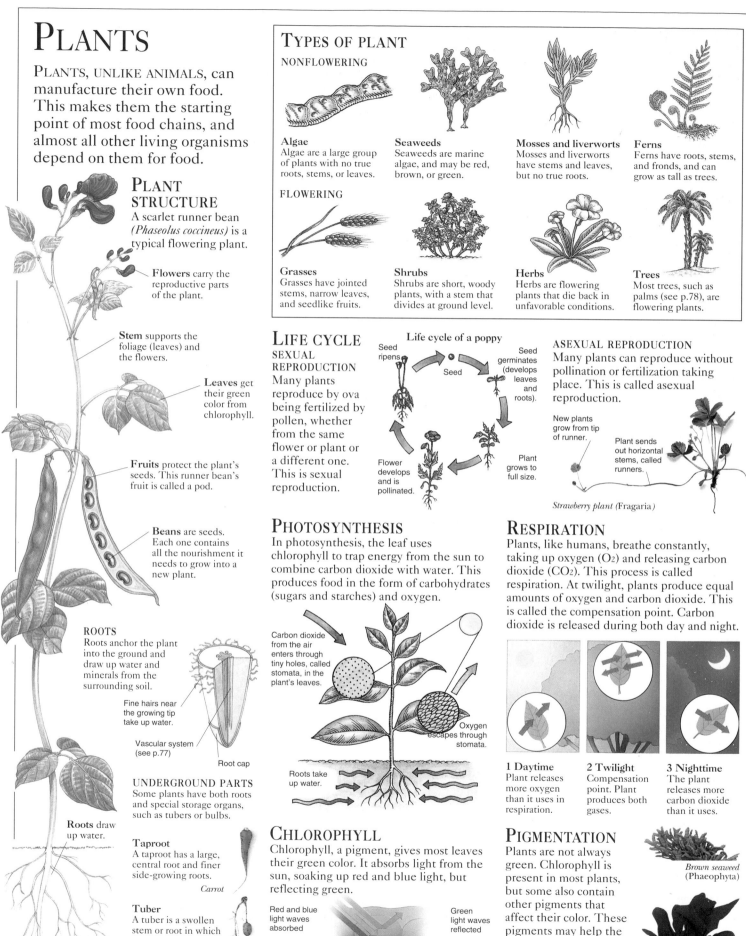

TYPES OF PLANT

NONFLOWERING

Algae
Algae are a large group of plants with no true roots, stems, or leaves.

Seaweeds
Seaweeds are marine algae, and may be red, brown, or green.

Mosses and liverworts
Mosses and liverworts have stems and leaves, but no true roots.

Ferns
Ferns have roots, stems, and fronds, and can grow as tall as trees.

FLOWERING

Grasses
Grasses have jointed stems, narrow leaves, and seedlike fruits.

Shrubs
Shrubs are short, woody plants, with a stem that divides at ground level.

Herbs
Herbs are flowering plants that die back in unfavorable conditions.

Trees
Most trees, such as palms (see p.78), are flowering plants.

PLANT STRUCTURE

A scarlet runner bean (*Phaseolus coccineus*) is a typical flowering plant.

Flowers carry the reproductive parts of the plant.

Stem supports the foliage (leaves) and the flowers.

Leaves get their green color from chlorophyll.

Fruits protect the plant's seeds. This runner bean's fruit is called a pod.

Beans are seeds. Each one contains all the nourishment it needs to grow into a new plant.

ROOTS
Roots anchor the plant into the ground and draw up water and minerals from the surrounding soil.

Fine hairs near the growing tip take up water.

Vascular system (see p.77)

Root cap

UNDERGROUND PARTS
Some plants have both roots and special storage organs, such as tubers or bulbs.

Roots draw up water.

Taproot
A taproot has a large, central root and finer side-growing roots.
Carrot

Tuber
A tuber is a swollen stem or root in which the plant stores food.
Potato

LIFE CYCLE

SEXUAL REPRODUCTION
Many plants reproduce by ova being fertilized by pollen, whether from the same flower or plant or a different one. This is sexual reproduction.

Life cycle of a poppy

Seed ripens

Seed germinates (develops leaves and roots).

Seed

Flower develops and is pollinated.

Plant grows to full size.

ASEXUAL REPRODUCTION
Many plants can reproduce without pollination or fertilization taking place. This is called asexual reproduction.

New plants grow from tip of runner.

Plant sends out horizontal stems, called runners.

Strawberry plant (Fragaria)

PHOTOSYNTHESIS

In photosynthesis, the leaf uses chlorophyll to trap energy from the sun to combine carbon dioxide with water. This produces food in the form of carbohydrates (sugars and starches) and oxygen.

Carbon dioxide from the air enters through tiny holes, called stomata, in the plant's leaves.

Oxygen escapes through stomata.

Roots take up water.

CHLOROPHYLL

Chlorophyll, a pigment, gives most leaves their green color. It absorbs light from the sun, soaking up red and blue light, but reflecting green.

Red and blue light waves absorbed

Green light waves reflected

RESPIRATION

Plants, like humans, breathe constantly, taking up oxygen (O_2) and releasing carbon dioxide (CO_2). This process is called respiration. At twilight, plants produce equal amounts of oxygen and carbon dioxide. This is called the compensation point. Carbon dioxide is released during both day and night.

1 Daytime
Plant releases more oxygen than it uses in respiration.

2 Twilight
Compensation point. Plant produces both gases.

3 Nighttime
The plant releases more carbon dioxide than it uses.

PIGMENTATION

Plants are not always green. Chlorophyll is present in most plants, but some also contain other pigments that affect their color. These pigments may help the plant to photosynthesize in difficult conditions.

Brown seaweed (Phaeophyta)

Red seaweed (Rhodophyta)

PLANT HABITATS

Plants will grow wherever there is enough moisture, light, warmth, and nourishment in the soil. Some plants have developed particular ways of coping with extreme conditions.

Tropical
Many bromeliads (*Bromeliaceae* family) in tropical rainforests live on tall trees where sunlight can reach their leaves.

Brackish and salt water
Mangroves (*Rhizophora*) have special pores in their roots to take in oxygen from the air.

Desert
Saguaro cactus (*Carnegiea gigantea*) lacks leaves, reducing water loss. Its spines protect it from animals.

Aquatic
Water lilies (*Nymphaea*) have a waxy outer layer, so the leaves float; stomata are on the upper surface only.

Sand and gravel
Sand couch grass (*Elymus farctus*) has very long roots that can reach water below ground.

Alpine
Alpine anemone (*Pulsatilla alpina*) has white hairs on its leaves to reflect the heat of the alpine summer sun.

HORMONES

Plants, like humans, have hormones. These control whether a plant makes a leaf or a flower. They also ensure that its stem grows up toward the sun, and its roots grow down toward underground water.

If a plant is turned on its side, its stem and roots soon change direction.

PLANT FACTS

- Air plants have no roots. They grow on tree branches in tropical and sub-tropical Americas, absorbing all the moisture they need from the air.
- Resurrection plants shrivel up in dry weather. As soon as it rains, they become green and begin to photosynthesize again.
- Ant plants have ants living in spaces, called domatia, in their stems. The ants protect the plants from attacks by other insects.

WEEDS

Weeds are simply plants that grow in places where they are a nuisance to people, such as in gardens or crop fields. Some are as colorful and sweet-smelling as garden flowers.

English Daisy (*Bellis perennis*)

PLANT GROWTH RATES

Giant bamboo (*Dendrocalamus giganteus*) grows 3ft (90cm) in a day

Giant kelp (*Macrocystis pyrifera*) grows 12in (30cm) in a day.

Bermuda grass (*Cynodon dactylon*) grows 6in (15cm) in a day.

Albizzia falcataria grows 1in (2cm) in a day.

Eucalyptus regnans grows 0.5in (1cm) in a day.

PARASITES AND EPIPHYTES

Some plants cannot photosynthesize. Instead, they live and feed on the stems or roots of other plants. These plants are called parasites. Epiphytes also live on other plants, but they can photosynthesize, so do not feed on the host plant.

This epiphytic bromeliad (*Aechmea miniata*) grows on the bark of trees.

The plant traps water in the spaces formed by its overlapping leaf bases.

CARNIVOROUS PLANTS

Carnivorous (meat-eating) plants feed on small animals, such as insects, as well as producing their own food by photosynthesis. Insects provide minerals and other nutrients that help these plants survive.

1 The Venus flytrap (*Dionaea muscipula*) attracts insects with its unusual leaf tips.

2 The insect touches sensory hairs, which trigger the two halves of the leaf to snap shut.

3 Comblike teeth trap the insect, and the plant slowly digests it.

GIANT FRONDS

The Pacific giant kelp (*Macrocystis pyrifera*) has the longest fronds of any plant. Each frond can grow up to 394ft (120m), taller than the Statue of Liberty.

COMMON USES OF PLANTS

LEAVES

Panama hats, from the leaves of the jipijapa tree (*Carludovica palmata*).

Skin cream, including juice from the leaves of *Aloe vera*.

Ice cream, thickened with agar-agar from seaweeds (*Gelidium*).

SAP

Rubber, from the latex of the rubber tree (*Hevea brasiliensis*).

FIBER

Rope, from the fibers of the hemp plant (*Cannabis sativa*).

Linen, from the fibers of the flax plant (*Linum usitatissimum*).

ENDANGERED PLANTS

Scientific name	Common name	Location
Phragmipedium exstaminodium	Chiapas slipper orchid	Mexico
Sarracenia oreophila	Green pitcher plant	US
Marojejya darianii	Big-leaf palm	Madagascar
Euphorbia handiensis	(succulent)	Canary Islands
Kerriodoxa elegans	(palm)	Thailand
Swainsona recta	(pea)	Australia
Dicliptera dodsonii	(vine)	Ecuador
Punica protopunica	Socotran pomegranate	Socotra

FLOWERS

FLOWERS HELP ENSURE that a plant is pollinated, and protect its seeds until they are shed. Flowers are often scented, and may be brightly colored. They consist of sepals, petals, stamens, and carpels.

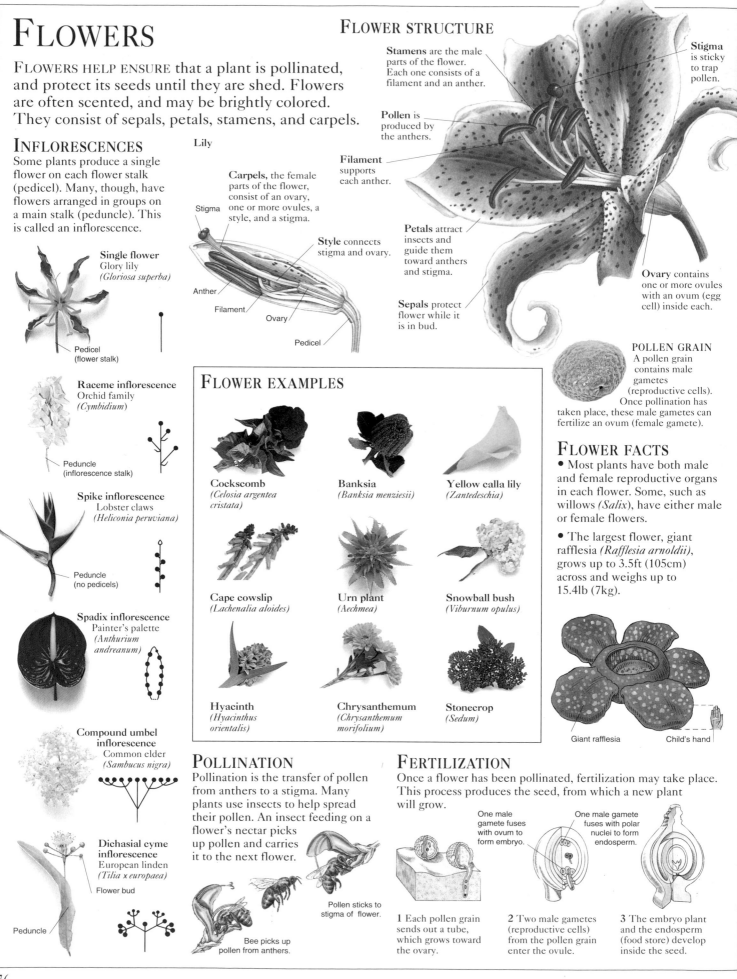

INFLORESCENCES

Some plants produce a single flower on each flower stalk (pedicel). Many, though, have flowers arranged in groups on a main stalk (peduncle). This is called an inflorescence.

Single flower
Glory lily
(*Gloriosa superba*)

Pedicel
(flower stalk)

Raceme inflorescence
Orchid family
(*Cymbidium*)

Peduncle
(inflorescence stalk)

Spike inflorescence
Lobster claws
(*Heliconia peruviana*)

Peduncle
(no pedicels)

Spadix inflorescence
Painter's palette
(*Anthurium andreanum*)

Compound umbel inflorescence
Common elder
(*Sambucus nigra*)

Dichasial cyme inflorescence
European linden
(*Tilia x europaea*)

Flower bud

Peduncle

Lily

Carpels, the female parts of the flower, consist of an ovary, one or more ovules, a style, and a stigma.

Stigma

Style connects stigma and ovary.

Anther

Filament

Ovary

Pedicel

FLOWER STRUCTURE

Stamens are the male parts of the flower. Each one consists of a filament and an anther.

Stigma is sticky to trap pollen.

Pollen is produced by the anthers.

Filament supports each anther.

Petals attract insects and guide them toward anthers and stigma.

Sepals protect flower while it is in bud.

Ovary contains one or more ovules with an ovum (egg cell) inside each.

POLLEN GRAIN
A pollen grain contains male gametes (reproductive cells). Once pollination has taken place, these male gametes can fertilize an ovum (female gamete).

FLOWER FACTS
• Most plants have both male and female reproductive organs in each flower. Some, such as willows (*Salix*), have either male or female flowers.

• The largest flower, giant rafflesia (*Rafflesia arnoldii*), grows up to 3.5ft (105cm) across and weighs up to 15.4lb (7kg).

Giant rafflesia   Child's hand

FLOWER EXAMPLES

Cockscomb
(*Celosia argentea cristata*)

Banksia
(*Banksia menziesii*)

Yellow calla lily
(*Zantedeschia*)

Cape cowslip
(*Lachenalia aloides*)

Urn plant
(*Aechmea*)

Snowball bush
(*Viburnum opulus*)

Hyacinth
(*Hyacinthus orientalis*)

Chrysanthemum
(*Chrysanthemum morifolium*)

Stonecrop
(*Sedum*)

POLLINATION
Pollination is the transfer of pollen from anthers to a stigma. Many plants use insects to help spread their pollen. An insect feeding on a flower's nectar picks up pollen and carries it to the next flower.

Pollen sticks to stigma of flower.

Bee picks up pollen from anthers.

FERTILIZATION
Once a flower has been pollinated, fertilization may take place. This process produces the seed, from which a new plant will grow.

One male gamete fuses with ovum to form embryo.

One male gamete fuses with polar nuclei to form endosperm.

1 Each pollen grain sends out a tube, which grows toward the ovary.

2 Two male gametes (reproductive cells) from the pollen grain enter the ovule.

3 The embryo plant and the endosperm (food store) develop inside the seed.

LEAVES

MOST LEAVES HAVE a stalk, called a petiole, and a blade, or lamina. Chlorophyll, a pigment that the leaves use in photosynthesis (see p.74), makes them green.

VASCULAR SYSTEM
The vascular system, made up of phloem and xylem, carries nutrients around the leaf.

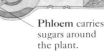

Phloem carries sugars around the plant.

Xylem carries water and minerals around the plant.

LEAF STRUCTURE

Midrib

Lamina

Vein

Phlox

Petiole

Stoma (pore through which gases flow in and out)

HEAVY SWEATER

Trees lose water through their leaves. An average birch tree with 200,000 leaves can lose up to 106 gallons (400 liters) on a hot day – enough to fill about 1,200 soft drink cans.

LEAF TEXTURES

Smooth, waxy leaves allow water to flow off, so they do not become waterlogged.

Rhododendron

Hard, spiky leaves help prevent the flower and leaf buds from being eaten by animals.

Holly

Hairy leaves trap a layer of air, so they do not burn in sun, or freeze in cold weather.

Tanacetum

Needle-shaped leaves offer little resistance to wind, preventing it from damaging the plant.

Cypress

LEAF EXAMPLES

Hornbeam maple
(Acer carpinifolium)

Conifer *(Taiwania cryptomerioides)*

Castor aralia *(Kalopanax pictus)*

Asparagus *(Asparagus)*

Bur oak *(Quercus macrocarpa)*

Swiss cheese plant *(Monstera deliciosa)*

Lily family *(Lilium)*

Lungwort *(Pulmonaria officinalis)*

Black locust *(Robinia x holdtii)*

Sassafras *(Sassafras albidum)*

Blue echeveria *(Echeveria)*

Black wattle acacia *(Acacia mearnsii)*

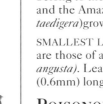

LEAF RECORDS

LARGEST LEAVES belong to the raffia palm (*Raphia farinifera*) and the Amazonian bamboo palm (*Raphia taedigera*) growing up to 64ft (20m) long.

SMALLEST LEAVES (flowering plants) are those of a floating duckweed (*Wolffia angusta*). Leaves grow to about 0.2in (0.6mm) long and 0.1in (0.3mm) wide.

POISONOUS LEAVES

The leaves of many plants contain poisons. Rhubarb leaves contain high concentrations of oxalic acid, which is particularly dangerous for people suffering from rheumatism or arthritis. Jimson weed and aconite leaves can also cause sickness in humans.

Rhubarb *(Rheum rhaponticum)* leaves contain oxalic acid.

Jimson weed *(Datura stramonium)* leaves contain atropine.

Aconite *(Aconitum napellus)* leaves contain aconitine and ephedrine.

LEAF MOLD

When dead plants and leaves decay and are broken down they form topsoil, which contains nutrients essential for plant growth.

Leaf litter

Centipede

Ant

Earthworm

Plants, such as this bluebell, thrive in the fertile topsoil.

1 Fallen leaves and dead plants lie on the surface. They slowly decompose, forming a layer of leaf mold.

2 Tiny animals, such as earthworms, eat the leaf mold, grinding it, breaking it down, and mixing it with the soil.

3 Valuable nutrients are released in the process, forming a rich layer of topsoil in which new plants grow.

LEAF RAFT

The leaves of the giant water lily *(Victoria amazonica)* can grow up to 8ft (2.4m) across. They can support the weight of a young child.

TREES

TREES ARE GENERALLY tall plants, usually with a single trunk (main stem). They are all perennial (live for many years), and most are broadleaved plants, which bear flowers.

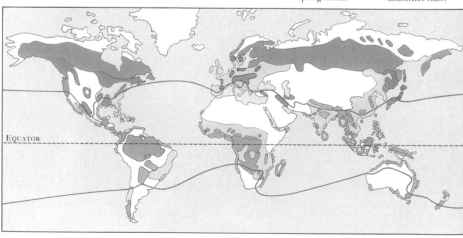

English oak (*Quercus robur*) in spring and autumn

Buds appear in early spring. They will soon grow into flowers called catkins.

Leaves

Fruit of the oak tree is a nut, called an acorn. Nuts are hard, dry fruits with only one seed.

Bark

Trunk

Roots

LIFE CYCLE

Once a tree is mature, it can produce flowers, fruits, and seeds each year.

Seed grows into sapling (young tree).

Seed falls on fertile ground.

Fruit protects seed.

Fertilized flowers produce fruits.

Flower buds appear on mature tree.

ROOTS

A tree's roots take up water from the soil. The vascular system (see p.77) transports the water around the tree.

TREE STRUCTURE

Broadleaved trees, like most flowering plants, have a main stem, or trunk, leaves, flowers, fruits, and seeds.

INSIDE THE TRUNK

A tree trunk grows new layers of cells outside the old layers. Trees grow quickly in favorable conditions, and slower in less favorable ones, forming visible rings in the trunk. Heartwood consists of dead cells, containing chemicals such as tannins or resins, which produce rich, deep colors.

Heartwood

Sapwood

One year's growth ring

Waterproof layer of cork

Bark

TYPES OF TREE

BROADLEAVED TREES
There are many thousands of species of broadleaved trees. Most are deciduous (shed their leaves seasonally).

Most broadleaved trees, as their name suggests, have broad, flat leaves.

All the trees in this group are angiosperms (flowering plants).

NEEDLE-LEAVED TREES
The group called needle-leaved trees includes pines, firs, and yews. There are over 500 species of needle-leaved trees, most of which are evergreen.

Many conifers have needle-shaped leaves, but some are strap-shaped, or even oval.

Most needle-leaved trees bear seeds in woody cones.

PALM TREES
The palm family contains about 2,800 species. Palms have only one growing point, called the apical bud. If this is damaged, the tree dies.

Palm trees have this name because the leaves are often shaped like a hand.

Palm trees, like broadleaved trees, are flowering plants.

HARDWOODS AND SOFTWOODS

Broadleaved trees are sometimes referred to as hardwoods, and conifers as softwoods. However, some conifers, such as Douglas fir and yew, produce harder wood than many broadleaved trees. Balsa, the softest of all, is a broadleaf.

Pine is a softwood. Its timber is soft and open-grained.

Walnut is a hardwood with a distinctive color.

TREES AROUND THE WORLD

Trees grow wherever there are at least 8in (200mm) of rain each year, and a temperature of at least 50°F (10°C) in summer. These conditions are not met in the white areas on the map. In the Arctic tundra, in Antarctica, or on very high mountaintops, no trees grow.

MAP KEY

Boreal forest (conifers)

Tropical rainforest (broadleaved)

Mangroves

Temperate forest (mixed)

Limited forest cover

Tropical dry forest (deciduous)

Limit of palm trees

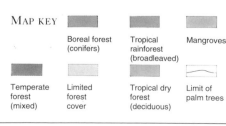

EQUATOR

BARK

A tree's bark consists of dead cells, which protect the living cells of the sapwood. As the tree grows, the outer layer of bark splits and is replaced by a new layer. Sometimes many layers are visible at the same time.

Younger, pinkish layer shows beneath peeling outer layer.

Lenticels (cell areas) allow the tree to breathe.

The paper birch (*Betula papyrifera*) has a very pale bark.

This cherry tree (*Prunus serrula*) has a dark, glossy bark.

River birch (*Betula nigra*) has bark that peels in flaky layers.

TREE FACTS

• The Bishop pine (*Pinus muricata*) can reproduce only after a forest fire. It needs the heat of the fire to crack open its cones.

• 1.3 cubic yards (1 cubic meter) of dried ebony weighs 2,271lb (1,030kg). The same volume of balsa weighs only 234lb (160kg).

• Mangroves are the only trees that can grow in salty water. They have special roots that help them take in oxygen.

TRUNK ROAD

Californian redwoods (*Sequoia sempervirens*) grow up to 25ft (7.6m) across. It is sometimes easier to cut through the trunk than to remove the tree.

COMMON USES OF TREES

WOOD

Oak (*Quercus*) for furniture.

Maple (*Acer pseudoplatanus*) for violins.

Poplar (*Populus*) for buildings (some countries).

Ebony (*Diospyros*) for carving work.

PULP PRODUCTS

Paper is made from the pulp of many kinds of trees. Pulp is used for paper products such as paper towels, tissues, and books.

FIBER PRODUCTS

Rayon fabric is made from cellulose using wood fibers from many species of trees.

SEED PRODUCTS

Kapok stuffing is made from the hairs that cover the seeds of the kapok or silk-cotton tree (*Ceiba pentandra*).

TREE RECORDS

TALLEST LIVING TREE is a coast redwood (*Sequoia sempervirens*) in Redwood National Park, California. It is 365ft (111.25m) tall, about the same as an Apollo space rocket.

OLDEST KNOWN TREE, a bristlecone pine (*Pinus longaeva*) in Nevada, was over 5,100 years old.

MOST DROUGHT-RESISTANT TREE, the baobab (*Adansonia digitata*) of Africa, can store up to 35,900 gallons (136,000 liters) of water in its swollen trunk.

Height ft(m)
365 (111.25)
300 (90)
200 (60)
100 (30)
0

GROWTH RATES

Trees grow at different rates. Below and right are the heights of some trees after 15 years.

Adult human, 6ft (1.8m)

Juniper (Juniperus), 10ft (3m)

Oak (Quercus), 25ft (7.5m)

Birch (Betula), 30ft (9m)

Douglas fir (Pseudotsuga), 40ft (12.2m)

BARK

Cinnamon from the bark of the cinnamon (*Cinnamomum zeylanicum*).

Cork from the bark of the cork oak (*Quercus suber*)

SAP

Maple syrup from the sap of the sugar maple (*Acer saccharum*).

Chewing gum from the sap of the sapodilla tree (*Manilkara zapota*).

Turpentine from the sap of the longleaf pine (*Pinus palustris*).

Amber fossilized resin from conifer trees that are now extinct.

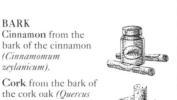

LEAF FALL

In harsh conditions, leaves do not photosynthesize properly, and water lost from them cannot be replaced if the ground is dry or frozen. So a tree withdraws the useful substances from its leaves, and then sheds them.

Deciduous forest in autumn, New England

AUTUMN COLORS

Chlorophyll is the first leaf pigment to break down when autumn arrives. Other color pigments, such as carotenoids, now show through. Carotenoids darken as they age, turning from yellow through orange to red. Both carotenoids and anthocyanins, from sugars in the leaves, give them their wide range of color. Many leaves are brown because they are dead. They may remain on the tree for many months. A layer of cells, called the abscission layer, develops as the leaf changes color, forming at the base of the leaf stalk. This layer causes the leaf to fall.

A maple leaf, as it dies, changes color dramatically.

ENDANGERED TIMBER TREES

Scientific name	Common name	Location
Abies guatemalensis	(Fir)	North and Central America
Aniba duckei	Bois de rose	South America
Dalbergia nigra	Bahia rosewood	South America
Hopea erosa	(Dipterocarp family)	Southeast India
Rousselia erratica	(Nettle family)	Central America
Vatica soepadmoi	(Dipterocarp family)	Sumatra

FOOD PLANTS

MANY TYPES OF PLANT ARE important food sources for humans. They include fruits, vegetables, herbs, spices, and cereals.

FRUIT EXAMPLES

Fruits form an important part of the human diet. There is a huge variety of wild and cultivated fruits, some of which are shown below.

TEMPERATE

Apple
(*Malus domestica*)

Strawberry
(*Fragaria*)

Cherry
(*Prunus avium*)

TROPICAL

Papaya
(*Carica papaya*)

Durian
(*Durio zibethinus*)

Star fruit
(*Averrhoa carambola*)

NUTS

Walnut
(*Juglans regia*)

Brazil nut
(*Bertholletia excelsa*)

Hazelnut
(*Corylus avellana*)

GRAPE SCOTT!

One year's worldwide grape harvest would bury Manhattan, New York, to a depth of 407ft (124m).

TOP FIVE FRUIT

Fruit	Annual worldwide consumption (tons)
Bananas (*Musa*)	44,750,700
Apples (*Malus domestica*)	37,943,874
Oranges (*Citrus sinensis*)	34,010,585
Watermelons (*Citrullus lanatus*)	21,308,658
Plantains (*Musa*)	19,985,304

FRUIT RECORDS

LARGEST SEED
is the "double coconut" of the coco de mer palm (*Lodoicea maldivica*), which can weigh up to 55lb (25kg).

LARGEST TREE FRUIT
comes from the jackfruit tree (*Artocarpus heterophyllus*): it can weigh up to 110lb (50kg).

FOOD PLANT ANCESTORS

The size, shape, and flavor, of many food plants have been altered by selective breeding.

Wild tomatoes (Lycopersicon esculentum) are about the size of grapes and sweeter than cultivated tomatoes.

The primitive form of a corn plant (Zea mays) with its cob is much smaller than a modern corncob.

FRUIT

The fruit is the part of a flower that develops to contain the seed or seeds. Fruits can be succulent or dry. Succulent fruits, such as lemons, are fleshy and brightly colored.

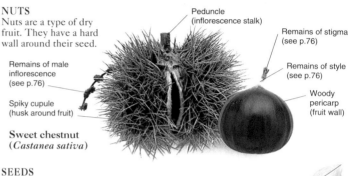

Pedicel (flower stalk)

Carpel (section of fruit containing vesicles)

Seed

Endocarp (inner layer of pericarp)

Exocarp (outer layer of pericarp)

Mesocarp (middle layer of pericarp)

Remains of style (see p.76)

Pericarp (fruit wall)

Vesicle (juice sac)

Lemon (*Citrus limon*)

NUTS

Nuts are a type of dry fruit. They have a hard wall around their seed.

Peduncle (inflorescence stalk)

Remains of stigma (see p.76)

Remains of male inflorescence (see p.76)

Remains of style (see p.76)

Spiky cupule (husk around fruit)

Woody pericarp (fruit wall)

Sweet chestnut (*Castanea sativa*)

SEEDS

Each fruit contains one or more seeds that will germinate and grow into new plants if conditions are suitable. Some types of fruit, such as cherries and peaches, contain just one seed. Other fruits, such as strawberries and apples, contain several seeds.

Hilum (point of attachment to ovary)

Testa (seed coat)

Lemon seed

DEVELOPMENT OF A FRUIT

A plant's fruit begins to form after fertilization has taken place (see p.76).

Development of a blackberry (*Rubus fruticosus*)

Ovaries begin to swell; stamens wither.

Carpels expand and become more fleshy.

Carpels continue to expand and begin to change color.

Carpels mature into drupelets: small fleshy fruit with a single seed in each.

Drupelets ripen fully. Fruit is ready to eat.

FRUIT ORIGINS

This map shows the origins of several fruits now found worldwide.

KEY

Cherries (Egypt)

Peaches (China)

Lemons (India)

Watermelons (Africa)

Strawberries (North and South America)

Passionfruit (Brazil)

VEGETABLE EXAMPLES
Vegetables can be leaves, stalks, flowers, tubers, or shoots.

LEAVES

Cabbage
(*Brassica oleracea*)

Spinach
(*Spinacia oleracea*)

Lettuce
(*Lactuca sativa*)

STALKS

Asparagus
(*Asparagus officinalis*)

Celery
(*Apium graveolens*)

Bean sprout
(*Vigna radiata*)

FLOWERS

Globe artichoke
(*Cynara scolymus*)

Cauliflower
(*Brassica oleracea*)

Broccoli
(*Brassica oleracea*)

ROOTS

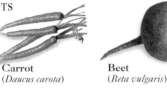

Carrot
(*Daucus carota*)

Beet
(*Beta vulgaris*)

Turnip
(*Brassica rapa*)

VEGETABLES
The term vegetable describes an edible plant, or part of a plant. Some fruits, such as tomatoes and eggplants, are also commonly called vegetables.

VEGETABLE RECORDS
All of the following records are held by Mr. Bernard Lavery (born 1938) of Llanharry, Wales, UK. Mr. Lavery also holds three other world records for growing large vegetables.

LARGEST CABBAGE
weighed 124lb (56.24kg).

LARGEST SQUASH
(*Cucurbita pepo*) weighed 108.1lb (49.05kg).

LONGEST PARSNIP
(*Pastinaca sativa*) was 14.3ft (4.36m) long.

LONGEST CARROT
was 16.9ft (5.14m) long.

LARGEST CELERY
weighed 46lb (20.89kg).

LARGEST BRUSSELS SPROUT
weighed 18.2lb (8.25kg).

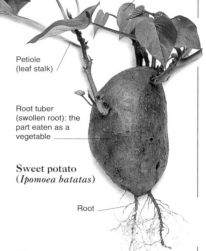

Leaf

Petiole
(leaf stalk)

Root tuber
(swollen root): the part eaten as a vegetable

Sweet potato
(*Ipomoea batatas*)

Root

KNOW YOUR ONIONS
Onions, chives, garlic, and leeks all belong to the lily family. Different parts of each plant are eaten as vegetables: the bulbs of onion and garlic, the stems of leeks, and the leaves of chives.

Onion
(*Allium cepa*)

Chives
(*Allium schoenoprasum*)

Garlic
(*Allium sativum*)

Leeks
(*Allium porrum*)

FRUIT AND VEGETABLE FACTS
• For 2,000 years the Chinese have considered lychees (*Litchi chinensis*) to be the finest fruits. Relays of horsemen took them to court, and in some districts, tax collectors demanded them as payment.

• Even the hottest chili pepper (*Capsicum annuum*) derives all its heat from no more than 0.1% of the fruit.

• There are 6,000 varieties of potato in Peru.

TOP FIVE VEGETABLES

Vegetable	Annual worldwide consumption (tons)
Tomatoes (*Lycopersicon esculentum*)	63,410,656
Cabbages (*Brassica oleracea*)	37,939,923
Onions (*Allium cepa*)	28,597,608
Cucumbers/gherkins (*Cucumis sativus*)	17,473,076
Carrots (*Daucus carota*)	12,912,025

FRUIT EATEN AS VEGETABLES
Some foods usually regarded as vegetables are in fact fruits. Familiar examples are shown below.

Tomato
(*Lycopersicon esculentum*)

Peppers
(*Capsicum*)

Eggplant
(*Solanum melongena*)

Pumpkin
(*Cucurbita pepo*)

SPICE EXAMPLES
Spices are strongly flavored plants used in cooking.

Cinnamon
(*Cinnamomum*)

Chili peppers
(*Capsicum annuum*)

Cloves
(*Syzygium aromaticum*)

HERB EXAMPLES
Herbs are used to flavor food, and in medicine.

Basil
(*Ocimum basilicum*)

Coriander
(*Coriandrum sativum*)

Spearmint
(*Mentha spicata*)

FRUIT AND VEGETABLE PRODUCTS
Many products in daily use come from fruits and vegetables.

Vegetable dyes
Dyes are made from plants such as indigo (*Indigofera*) and henna (*Lawsonia inermis*).

Cooking oil
Cooking oils are extracted from several fruit and seeds, including olives (*Olea europaea*).

Face powder
Finely ground walnut (*Juglans regia*) shells are used to make cosmetic face powder.

Loofahs
People use dried loofahs (*Luffa cylindrica*), a tropical fruit, to wash in the bath.

Chocolate
Chocolate comes from the beans of the cacao tree (*Theobroma*).

Coffee
Coffee is produced from the ground beans of the *Coffea* tree.

COLOSSAL CUCUMBER
The largest cucumber ever grown weighed 20lb (9.1kg). This would have provided enough slices to make 1,137 cucumber sandwiches.

FUNGI AND LICHENS

FUNGI WERE ONCE CLASSIFIED as plants, but since about 1969 botanists have treated them as a separate kingdom. Most fungi are immobile, like plants, but cannot make their own food. Instead, they feed on living or dead plants or animals, dung, and other organic materials.

FUNGUS EXAMPLES

There are about 65,000 known species of fungus and 20,000 lichens. Many more may be discovered.

Orange peel fungus
(*Aleuria aurantia*)

Oak maze-gill
(*Daedalea quercina*)

Water-measure Earthstar (*Astraeus hygrometricus*)

Fly agaric
(*Amanita muscaria*)

Green wood-cup
(*Chlorociboria aeruginascens*)

Clavulinopsis helvola

Scarlet hood
(*Hygrocybe coccinea*)

Chanterelle
(*Cantharellus cibarius*)

Common stinkhorn
(*Phallus impudicus*)

TYPES OF LICHEN

The many species of lichen grow in five distinct ways. Three of these are shown below.

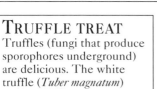
Fruticose
(*Cladonia portentosa*)

Foliose
(*Hypogymnia physodes*)

Squamulose
(*Cladonia floerkeana*)

Gills produce and store spores.

Cap

Cap curls upward to release the spores.

Stem

Cortinarius armillatus

Hyphae form the mycelium (main body) and anchor the sporophore (fruiting body).

FUNGUS STRUCTURE

Mushrooms and toadstools are the fruiting bodies of fungi. They grow up out of the soil to spread their spores (reproductive bodies).

LICHEN STRUCTURE

Lichens consist of fungi living in association with algae (simple plants) or cyanobacteria, the only organisms apart from plants that can photosynthesize.

Soredium may develop into a new lichen

Algal layer

Fungal mycelium

Hypogymnia physodes

LIFE CYCLE

Fungi reproduce through spores, which are the equivalent of a plant's seeds. The fungal mycelium spreads underground until it meets another mycelium of the same species. They bond together and, given the right conditions, produce a fruiting body that generally grows above ground.

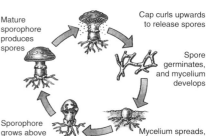
Mature sporophore produces spores

Cap curls upwards to release spores

Spore germinates, and mycelium develops

Sporophore grows above ground level

Mycelium spreads, meets another one, and bonds; forms sporophore

SYMBIOTIC RELATIONSHIPS

Many fungi live in close association, or symbiotic relationships, with plants and animals. The three main kinds of symbiotic relationships are parasitic, mutualistic, and saprophytic.

PARASITIC
Some parasitic fungi cause galls and can even kill the plant they live on.

MUTUALISTIC
Many orchids need the presence of a fungus for their seeds to germinate.

SAPROPHYTIC
Some fungi live on dead wood, animals, and other organic matter in the soil.

FUNGUS RECORDS

LONGEST LIVING MUSHROOM, *Ganoderma applanatum*, can live for as long as fifty years.

MOST IMPORTANT FUNGI belong to *Penicillium* genus. They are used in blue cheeses, and the antibiotic penicillin.

BIGGEST FRUITING BODY is giant puffball (*Lycoperdon gigantea*), which can measure up to 6.6ft (2m) in circumference.

TRUFFLE TREAT

Truffles (fungi that produce sporophores underground) are delicious. The white truffle (*Tuber magnatum*) from Italy costs about $3,308 per lb ($1,500 per kg).

FUNGUS AND LICHEN FACTS

• Fungus cells contain a light, strong substance called chitin. Chitin is also found in the cuticle, or outer layer, of some animals, such as insects.

• Lichen extracts produce orchil, the dye used for litmus paper, as well as the dyes once used to color Scottish tartans.

Fairy ring

• Fairy rings are formed when a mycelium spreads outward. Mushrooms grow from the youngest part of the mycelium.

• Lichens are very sensitive to air pollution, and several kinds are used to indicate pollution levels.

POISONOUS FUNGI

Name	Poison	Symptoms
Fly agaric (*Amanita muscaria*)	muscarine	Stomach pain, hallucinations, delirium, convulsions; rarely fatal
Death cap (*Amanita phalloides*)	amanitine, phalloidine	Nausea, liver and kidney failure, abdominal pain; can be fatal
False morel (*Gyromitra esculenta*)	gyromitrin	Stomach pain, nausea, jaundice; can be fatal
Never eat wild mushrooms unless they have been identified by an expert as edible.		

MICROORGANISMS

A MICROORGANISM IS a life-form that is usually too small for the human eye to see. The most familiar types are protozoa, bacteria, and viruses. Some microorganisms are harmful, but many are vital: without them, life as we know it could not continue.

TYPES OF PROTOZOA

There are more than 40,000 species of protozoa, in seven phyla (see p.72). Two phyla are shown below.

Ciliates
(Ciliophora)
8,000 species

Flagellates, amoebae, opalinids
(Sarcomastigophora)
27,000 species

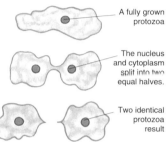

Cytoplasm

Nucleus

Food vacuole

Cell wall

Pseudopodia: extensions that flow out from the body

Portrait of an amoeba
Amoebas are irregularly shaped protozoa that crawl about on the bottom of ponds.

REPRODUCTION

Most protozoa reproduce by splitting themselves in two. Each of the two halves then becomes a single cell. This process is called binary fission. Many types of bacteria also reproduce in this way.

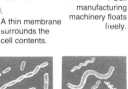

A fully grown protozoa

The nucleus and cytoplasm split into two equal halves.

Two identical protozoa result

PROTOZOA

Protozoa are neither animals nor plants. They belong to a separate kingdom (see p.72). Protozoa have just one cell, which carries out all the functions necessary for them to live and reproduce. They live in watery environments, from damp soil and puddles, to lakes and oceans.

FEEDING

Many protozoa trap their food, which includes algae and other protozoa, by engulfing it with part of their jellylike body.

The amoeba's pseudopodia surround its prey.

Food is trapped, forming a food vacuole.

BACTERIA

Bacteria, together with blue-green algae, belong to the Moneran kingdom. Monerans are the simplest, and probably the most ancient, forms of life on Earth. Bacteria are found everywhere, from the depths of the oceans to the upper atmosphere.

Some bacteria have flagella.

Some types of bacteria look hairy.

A rigid wall protects the bacteria.

The cell wall may be surrounded by a slimy capsule.

Material stored in granules

Bacteria do not have a nucleus: their genetic material floats freely.

A thin membrane surrounds the cell contents.

Cell manufacturing machinery floats freely.

BACTERIA SHAPES

Bacteria are often classified according to their shape, which is spherical, rod-shaped, or curved.

Coccus

Bacillus

Spirillum

VIRUSES

A virus is a tiny package of chemicals surrounded by a protein coat. The many virus shapes include rod-shaped, round, and many-sided forms. They are all so small (the largest are about 0.0003mm) that they can be seen only with an electron microscope.

Influenza virus particles seen through an electron microscope. Viruses cause many diseases, from the common cold to yellow fever.

HOW A BACTERIOPHAGE VIRUS MULTIPLIES

A virus shows no signs of life until it invades the cell of a living organism. The bacteriophage is a complex virus that reproduces by invading bacteria cells. It is replicated at a rate of 300 every half-hour.

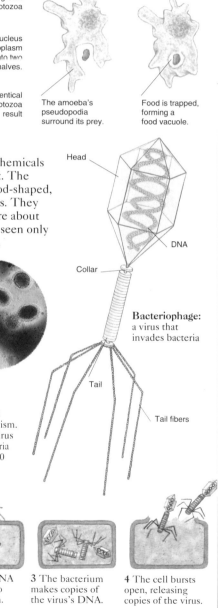

Head

DNA

Collar

Bacteriophage: a virus that invades bacteria

Tail

Tail fibers

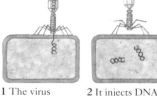

1 The virus lands on the wall of the bacterium.

2 It injects DNA (see p.68) into the bacterium.

3 The bacterium makes copies of the virus's DNA.

4 The cell bursts open, releasing copies of the virus.

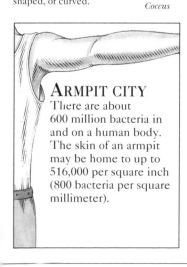

ARMPIT CITY

There are about 600 million bacteria in and on a human body. The skin of an armpit may be home to up to 516,000 per square inch (800 bacteria per square millimeter).

USEFUL BACTERIA

Bacteria are nature's most important recycling agents. They break down dead plants and animals, and return the materials to the ecosystem. Most bacteria are harmless to humans. Some are vital: without them we could not digest our food.

Bacteria are important in the production of many foods.

Vinegar

Cheese

Yogurt

MICROORGANISM FACTS

• It would take a ciliate (protozoa) about five minutes to swim the length of this page.
• One gram of soil may contain over 150,000 protozoa.

• The largest species of protozoa ever to have lived grew to over 8in (20cm) in diameter: the width of this page. It has now become extinct.

ANIMALS

MORE THAN A million animal species have been discovered. They have adapted to just about every habitat: some even spend their entire life inside the body of another animal.

ANIMAL CHARACTERISTICS

Animals, unlike plants, cannot manufacture their own food, so they have to eat other organisms. They have many cells, can reproduce, and can sense and respond to their surroundings. Most animals move around at some stage in their lives.

Most animals have eyes.

Most animals take in food through the mouth.

Land-dwelling vertebrates breathe air through their nostrils.

All animals have an excretory system that gets rid of waste products.

Vertebrates have an internal bony skeleton to support the body.

Skin may be covered in scales, feathers, or fur, to protect the animal and keep it warm.

Muscles enable animals to move in search of food.

Many animals have legs to help them move efficiently.

Gray crowned crane (*Balearica regulorum*)

TYPES OF ANIMAL

INVERTEBRATES
About 97% of animal species are invertebrates (have no backbone). Some of the most important phyla (see p.72) are shown here.

Sea anemones, corals, jellyfish, hydras (Cnidaria)
Ring of tentacles armed with stinging cells surrounds the mouth.

Worms
At least ten phyla, including segmented worms (Annelida) and roundworms (Nematoda).

Mollusks (Mollusca)
Most have a hard shell to protect their soft body. Includes snails and slugs, squid and octopuses, clams, mussels, and scallops.

Arthropods (Arthropoda)
Jointed limbs and a tough external skeleton. Includes insects, arachnids, and crustaceans.

Starfish, sea urchins, and sea cucumbers (Echinodermata)
Marine; body usually made up of five identical parts.

VERTEBRATES
Only about 3% of animal species are vertebrates (animals with a backbone). There are more than 40,000 species, in seven classes (see p.72). Three of these classes are fish.

Fish (Agnatha, Chondrichthyes, Osteichthyes). Three classes: jawless fish, sharks and rays, and bony fish.

Amphibians (Amphibia)
Can live both on land and in water. Includes frogs, toads, newts, and salamanders.

Reptiles (Reptilia)
Scaly skin; most species lay eggs. Includes snakes, lizards, crocodiles, and turtles.

Birds (Aves)
Covered with feathers. Have wings, a beak, and no teeth. Most species can fly.

Mammals (Mammalia)
Feed young on milk produced in female's body. Most have fur or hair.

ANIMAL REPRODUCTION

The main function of an animal's life is to continue its species. Some animals reproduce without mating (asexual reproduction), but most mate with a partner to produce offspring (sexual reproduction).

Asexual reproduction
Some organisms, e.g. hydras, reproduce by budding: part of the parent becomes detached and forms a new individual.

Sexual reproduction
Most animals reproduce sexually: a cell from a male (a sperm) joins with a cell from a female (an ovum). The egg grows into a new individual.

ANIMAL LIFESPANS

Lifespans range from a few days for some insects, to more than 200 years for a giant clam (*Tridacna*). Most mammals have about the same number of heartbeats in their lifetime.

Elephants and shrews have a similar number of heartbeats during their lives, but the shrew's heart beats much faster during its short life.

LARVA'S LARDER
The female tarantula wasp (*Pepsis*) paralyzes a tarantula with her sting. She then bites off its legs to make it easier to carry, puts it in a burrow, and lays an egg on it. When the larva hatches, it feeds off the still-living spider.

ANIMAL FACTS
• Only about 0.3% of animal species are mammals, and only about 0.7% are birds. Most creatures on Earth are insects or worms.

• A large locust swarm can eat 90,000 tons of food in a day: equivalent to the amount of food eaten by 35,000 American families in a year.

FEEDING
Some animals have specialized diets, while others eat almost anything. Animals have evolved different teeth to suit their diet.

Mongoose skull

Gazelle skull

Moonrat skull

Monkey skull

Carnivore
Meat-eater: sharp canine teeth

Herbivore
Plant-eater: flat molars

Insectivore
Insect-eater: sharp, pointed teeth

Omnivore
Meat- and plant-eater: sharp and flat teeth

ANIMAL GROUPS

A cast of hawks
A covert of coots
A bazaar of guillemots
A pride of lions
A clowder of cats
A leap of leopards
A sloth of bears
A skulk of foxes
A labor of moles
A crash of rhinoceroses
A shrewdness of apes
A pod of dolphins

INVERTEBRATES

THE VAST MAJORITY of creatures are invertebrates – animals without a backbone. They include insects, spiders, crabs, worms, jellyfish, and corals. Many invertebrates are tiny, but others, such as the giant squid and the Japanese spider crab, can grow to be larger than humans.

TYPES OF INVERTEBRATE

There are more than a million known species of invertebrate, in about 30 phyla (see p.72). Some of the largest and most important phyla are shown below; the number of species in each is approximate.

Sponges (Porifera) 9,000 species

Sea anemones, corals, jellyfish, hydras (Cnidaria) 9,500 species

Flatworms, flukes, and tapeworms (Platyhelminthes) 15,000 species

Roundworms (Nematoda) 20,000 species

Mollusks (Mollusca) 51,000 species

Worms and leeches (Annelida) 18,600 species

Arthropods (Arthropoda) 1,092,000 species

Starfish, sea urchins, and sea cucumbers (Echinodermata) 6,000 species

PORTRAIT OF AN INVERTEBRATE

Invertebrates range from simple microscopic animals to complex, intelligent mollusks, such as octopuses. Invertebrates do not have an internal skeleton: their body shape is maintained either by a tough, external coat, called an exoskeleton, or by body fluid pressing out against the skin.

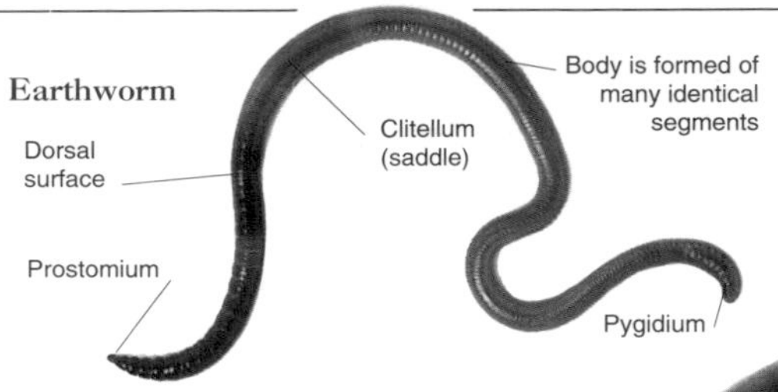

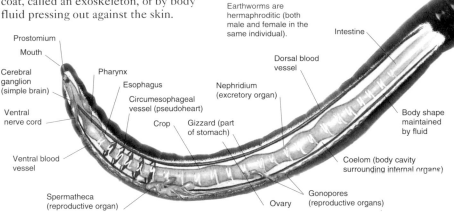

Earthworm

Dorsal surface

Clitellum (saddle)

Body is formed of many identical segments

Prostomium

Pygidium

Earthworms are hermaphroditic (both male and female in the same individual).

Intestine

Prostomium

Mouth

Cerebral ganglion (simple brain)

Pharynx

Esophagus

Circumesophageal vessel (pseudoheart)

Dorsal blood vessel

Nephridium (excretory organ)

Ventral nerve cord

Crop

Gizzard (part of stomach)

Body shape maintained by fluid

Ventral blood vessel

Coelom (body cavity surrounding internal organs)

Spermatheca (reproductive organ)

Ovary

Gonopores (reproductive organs)

LIFE CYCLE

There is a huge diversity of invertebrate life cycles. Most species lay eggs, then many pass through several larval stages that may look very different to the adult stage. Other species hatch as miniature adults. Some invertebrates, such as houseflies, live for just a few weeks, but others may live for many years: the giant clam *(Tridacna)* can live to be more than 200 years old.

Life cycle of a jellyfish

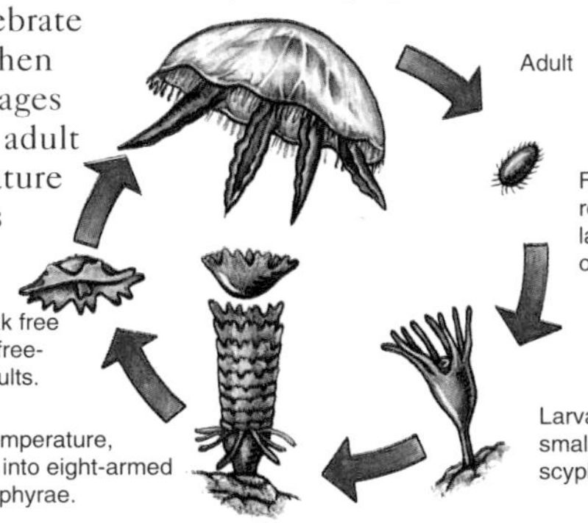

Adult

Female jellyfish releases fertilized larvae which settle on the sea bed.

Ephyrae break free and become free-swimming adults.

At the right temperature, polyps divide into eight-armed buds called ephyrae.

Larvae grow into small polyps called scyphistoma.

TAPE MEASURE

The pork tapeworm *(Taenia solium)* can grow to over 23ft (7m) long inside the human body: as long as four adult humans. It has as many as 1,500 segments, each containing 80,000 tapeworm embryos. Tapeworms can cause death if they enter the bloodstream.

WORM FACTS

• Roundworms are probably the most numerous animals on Earth. 20,000 species have been discovered, but scientists believe there are at least 500,000 species.

• Up to 500 million hookworms may be found in a single human.

ECHINODERMS

Echinoderms include starfish, sea urchins, and sea cucumbers. An echinoderm's body is divided into five parts radiating out from a central point, and it moves using tiny, water-filled tube feet. All echinoderms live in the sea.

Starfish are among the strongest animals for their size: they can prize apart the shells of bivalve mollusks, such as scallops.

ARTHROPODS

This huge phylum contains the largest variety of creatures in the animal kingdom, including insects, crustaceans, spiders, centipedes, millipedes, and horseshoe crabs. All arthropods have a tough exoskeleton, jointed limbs, and a nerve cord running the length of the body.

The tiger centipede (Scolopendra hardwickii) is the largest species of centipede. It grows to just under 12in (30cm) long.

ZOOPLANKTON

Plankton is made up of small invertebrates (zooplankton) and plants (phytoplankton) that drift along in water currents. Zooplankton includes jellyfish and the larvae of sea creatures such as starfish and crabs.

Zooplankton

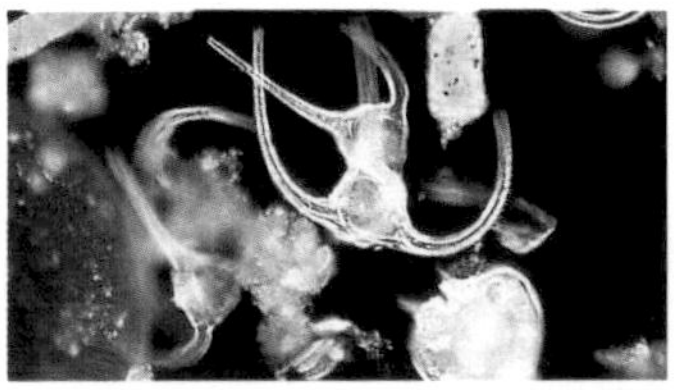

INVERTEBRATE RECORDS

LARGEST JELLYFISH is the giant North Atlantic jellyfish *(Cyanea capillata)*, which grows to more than 6.6ft (2m) in diameter, and may have tentacles nearly 121.4ft (37m) long.

LONGEST EARTHWORM is the *Mirochaetus* earthworm from South Africa, which grows up to 19.7ft (6m) long.

MOLLUSKS

MOLLUSKS FORM the second largest group of animals on Earth. They range from tiny snails to the giant squid, which grows as long as a sperm whale. Mollusks are found all over the world. They live in oceans and seas, in fresh water, and on land.

TYPES OF MOLLUSK

There are more than 50,000 species of mollusk. They are divided into seven classes (see p.72).

Chitons
(Polyplacophora)
coat-of-mail shells
500 species

Solenogasters
(Aplacophora)
wormlike marine mollusks
5,540 species

Monoplacophorans
(Monoplacophora)
deep-sea limpets
10 species

Tusk shells
(Scaphopoda)
350 species

Gastropods
(Gastropoda)
e.g. slug, snail, whelk
35,000 species

Bivalves
(Bivalvia)
two-shelled mollusks
e.g. oyster, clam
8,000 species

Cephalopods
(Cephalopoda)
squid, octopuses,
nautiluses, cuttlefish
600 species

PORTRAIT OF A MOLLUSK

A typical mollusk has a soft body divided into the head, the foot, and a hump containing the main organs. This hump is covered by a fold of skin called the mantle. The body is usually protected by a hard shell.

Eye · Shell · Tentacle · Heart · Kidney · Collar · Foot · Lung · Mantle · Crop (digestive tract) · Brain · Mucus gland · Mouth · Ovotestis (reproductive organ) · Hermaphrodite duct · Snails have both male and female reproductive organs · Stomach · Oviduct · Radula (toothed tongue) · Reproductive organs · Salivary gland · Anus · Excretory gland · Sperm duct

Giant African land snail (Achatina)

LIFE CYCLE

Most mollusks lay eggs. Many marine (sea-dwelling) species hatch into tiny larvae. Other mollusks, such as some snails, hatch into miniature adults.

Life cycle of an oyster

Egg

Egg hatches into free-swimming larva, called a trochophore

Larva grows larger, shell develops. This stage called a veliger larva

Young adult sinks to sea bed and settles in suitable place

MOLLUSK FACTS

• The giant clam (*Tridacna*) is the longest-lived animal in the world: it can live more than 200 years.

• Larger species of octopus can measure up to 30ft (9m) across with their tentacles spread out.

• The mucus secreted by snails is so effective that they can crawl along the edge of a razor without cutting themselves.

• Limpets have such strong teeth on their radula that they leave scratch marks on rocks when they browse.

FEEDING

Bivalve mollusks are filter feeders, sifting tiny organisms from the water. Most other mollusks have a toothed tongue, called a radula, which they use to scratch food into their mouth.

Close-up of a snail's radula showing rows of rasping teeth

The giant clam's gills sift food from the water. The gills are also used for breathing.

MOLLUSK MOVEMENT

Some mollusks, such as mussels, anchor themselves to one place. Most mollusks, however, move around in search of food and to escape from predators.

BIVALVES

Some bivalves, e.g. scallops, suck in water and then expel it rapidly by clapping their two shells together. This propels them through the water in a series of jerks.

GASTROPODS

Gastropods create a wave of muscle contractions that runs from the rear of the foot to the front. This wave slowly drags them along.

CEPHALOPODS

Cephalopods, such as squid, take in water and then force it out again, pushing themselves rapidly backward. They also have fins which they use to pull themselves forward.

Squid can swim at speeds of up to 25mph (40km/h).

Slugs and snails secrete a slimy mucus that helps them to slide along.

This *Euglandina* snail is the fastest mollusk on land.

TOP OF THE CLASS

Octopuses are intelligent animals and have the ability to learn. An octopus at London Zoo in England learned how to twist the lid off a jar to reach the crab inside.

Cross-section of a squid's mantle

Expanded mantle cavity takes in water

Contracted mantle cavity shoots out jet of water, propelling squid along

DEFENSE AND ATTACK

Mollusks have evolved several unique ways of protecting themselves from enemies. Many carnivorous (meat-eating) mollusks are also efficient predators.

STINGING
Some sea slugs eat jellyfish, and can swallow the stinging cells without being stung. The cells are then carried to the slug's back, where they protect it from enemies.

POISONOUS HARPOONS
Cone shells have long, barbed teeth on their radula. They thrust one of these into their prey like a harpoon, deliver a venomous sting, then pull the impaled victim back into their mouth.

SQUIRTING INK
Octopuses, squid, and cuttlefish squirt a cloud of ink at their enemies. This allows them to escape behind a dark screen. *Heteroteuthis*, a type of deep-sea squid, squirts a cloud of luminous bacteria to dazzle its enemy.

Squid squirting ink from its siphon

SAFETY IN SHELLS
Many mollusks, including gastropods and bivalves, retreat into their shell if danger threatens.

MOLLUSK FACTS
- The ink squirted by cuttlefish was the original sepia coloring used by artists.
- Several species of cone shell can kill a human with their sting.
- The Mediterranean fan mussel (*Pinna nobilis*) anchors itself to the sea bed with strong, golden brown threads. These threads were once used to make "cloth of gold."

CHANGING COLOR
Squid, octopuses, and cuttlefish can change color in less than a second to blend in with their surroundings. They also change color to indicate their mood. Male cuttlefish turn black with anger; octopuses turn white with fear, and blue with rage.

Cuttlefish with mottled brown and white coloring

The same cuttlefish has turned red. It is probably signaling to another cuttlefish.

MOLLUSK SHELLS
Mollusk shells are made of layers of calcium carbonate secreted from the mantle. They form in a huge variety of shapes, sizes, patterns, and colors.

Pacific thorny oyster

West African margin shells

Cockle shells

Royal cloak scallop

Marlinspike auger

Nautilus: the only cephalopod with a true external shell

Rose-branch murex

Limpet

Elephant tusk shell

Cuban land snail

Lammellose ormer

HOW PEARLS FORM
Some mollusks form pearls in their shells. Oyster pearls are highly valued.

1 A tiny piece of grit or a parasite lodges in the oyster's shell, causing irritation.

2 The oyster secretes mother-of-pearl (nacre) around the cause of irritation.

3 The pearl breaks free of the shell, removing the source of irritation.

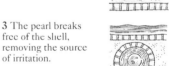

Oyster shell

Pearl

PRIZE EYES
The giant Atlantic squid has the largest eyes of any animal in the world, each with a diameter of more than 16in (40cm).

MOLLUSK RECORDS

LARGEST MOLLUSK and largest invertebrate (see p.83), is the giant Atlantic squid (*Archteuthis*), which can grow up to 66ft (20m) long.

LARGEST BIVALVE MOLLUSK is the giant clam, which can weigh over 661lb (300kg): the same as three large humans.

SMALLEST MOLLUSK is the gastropod *Ammonicera*, which is only 0.04in (1mm) long.

LONGEST SHELL was over 16.4ft (5m) long. It belonged to a prehistoric cephalopod.

LARGEST LAND SNAIL is the giant African land snail, which can grow up to 15.4in (39cm) from snout to tail.

It has taken just over one minute for this *Euglandina* snail to crawl along the bottom of these two pages.

INSECTS

THERE ARE MORE species of insect than of any other animal phylum. For every human, there are about 200 million insects. They live just about everywhere, including rainforests, polar lands, deserts, and pools of gasoline.

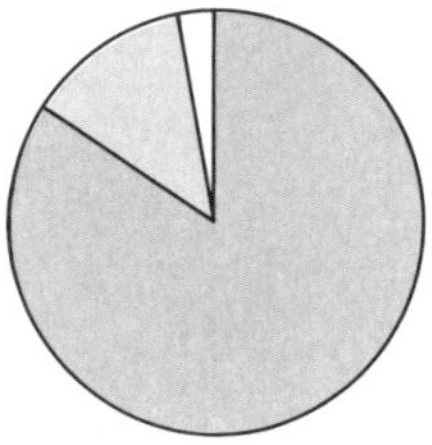

PORTRAIT OF AN INSECT

Insects have three distinct body regions: the head, the thorax, and the abdomen. They have six jointed legs, and a tough outer skeleton called an exoskeleton. Most insects have wings at some stage during their life.

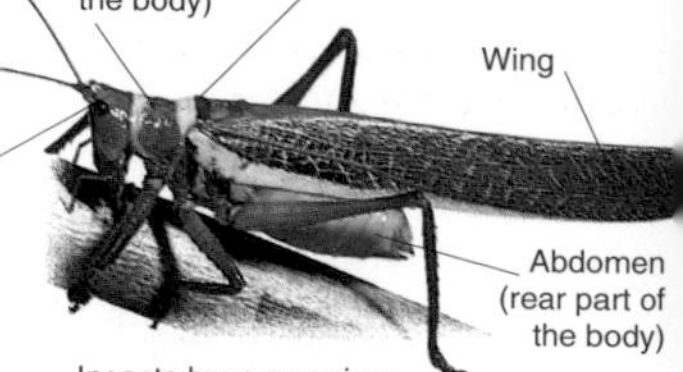

Antenna (feeler)
Thorax (middle section of the body)
Exoskeleton
Wing
Compound eye
Abdomen (rear part of the body)

Insects have no veins: blood flows freely around the body.

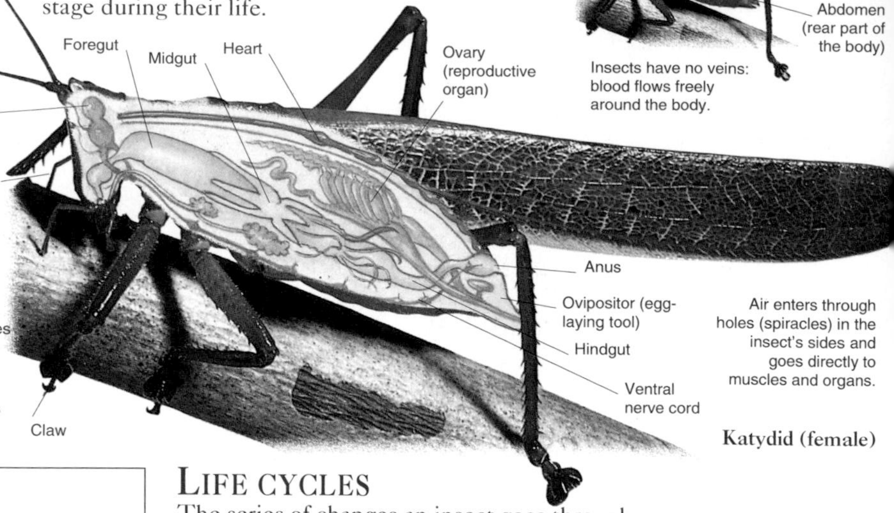

Foregut
Midgut
Heart
Ovary (reproductive organ)
Brain
Mandibles (mouthparts)
Anus
Ovipositor (egg-laying tool)
Hindgut
Ventral nerve cord
Claw

Air enters through holes (spiracles) in the insect's sides and goes directly to muscles and organs.

Katydid (female)

PROPORTION OF INSECTS

Insects make up about 85% of all the animal species on Earth.

Insects 85%
Other invertebrates 12.5%
Vertebrates 2.5%

TYPES OF INSECT

There are over a million known species of insect, with perhaps 30 million still to be discovered. They are grouped into 32 orders (see p.72), including those illustrated below.

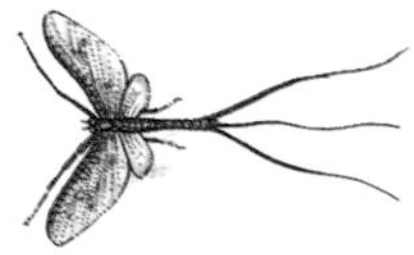

Mayflies
(Ephemeroptera)
2,000 species

Dragonflies
(Odonata)
5,000 species

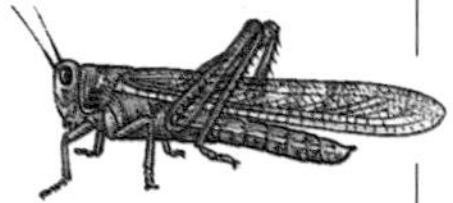

Grasshoppers, crickets
(Orthoptera)
20,000 species

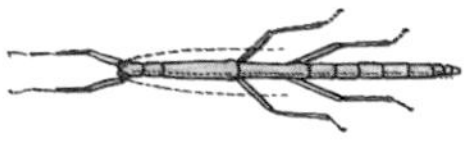

Stick and leaf insects
(Phasmida)
2,500 species

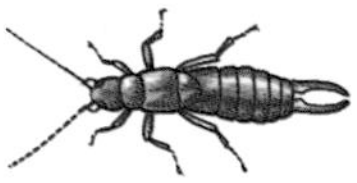

Earwigs
(Dermaptera)
1,500 species

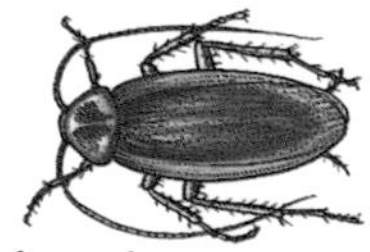

Cockroaches
(Blattodea)
3,700 species

Praying mantids
(Mantodea)
1,800 species

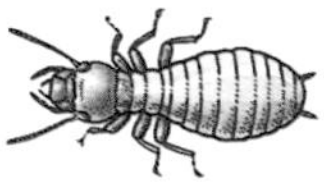

Termites
(Isoptera)
2,300 species

Biting lice
(Mallogaphaga)
2,700 species

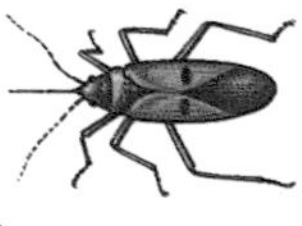

Bugs
(Hemiptera)
82,000 species

Beetles
(Coleoptera)
300,000 species

Ants, bees, and wasps
(Hymenoptera)
110,000 species

Butterflies and moths
(Lepidoptera)
136,800 species

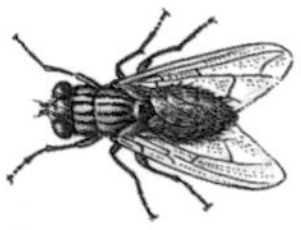

Flies
(Diptera)
98,500 species

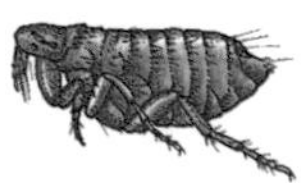

Fleas
(Siphonaptera)
1,800 species

LIFE CYCLES

The series of changes an insect goes through during its life is called its metamorphosis.

Complete metamorphosis: butterfly

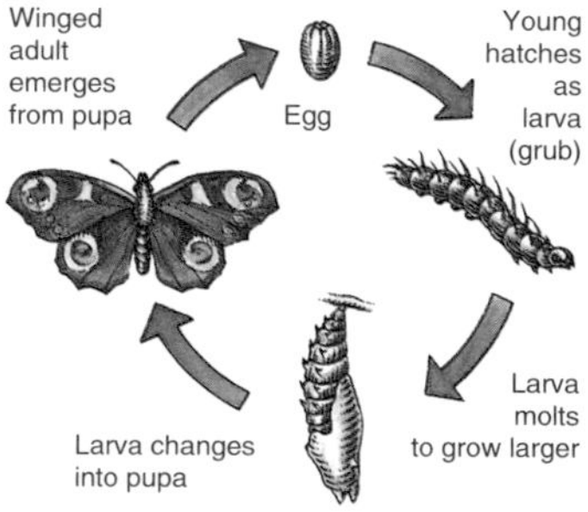

Winged adult emerges from pupa
Egg
Young hatches as larva (grub)
Larva changes into pupa
Larva molts to grow larger

Incomplete metamorphosis: grasshopper

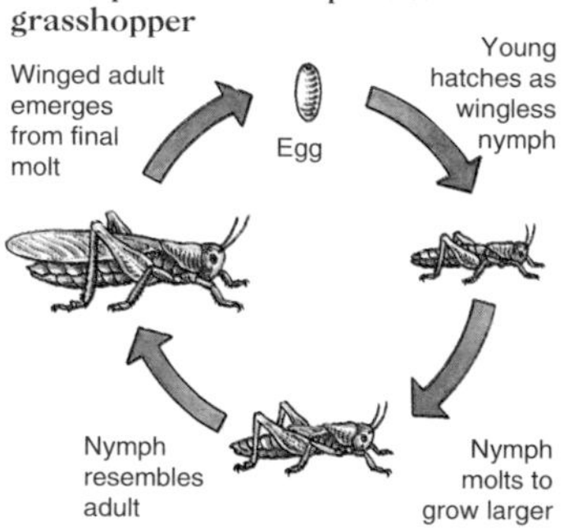

Winged adult emerges from final molt
Egg
Young hatches as wingless nymph
Nymph resembles adult
Nymph molts to grow larger

MOLTING

A young insect's tough exoskeleton cannot stretch, so the insect has to molt (shed its skin) several times in order to grow. The sequence below shows the final molt of a damselfly, as it changes from nymph to adult.

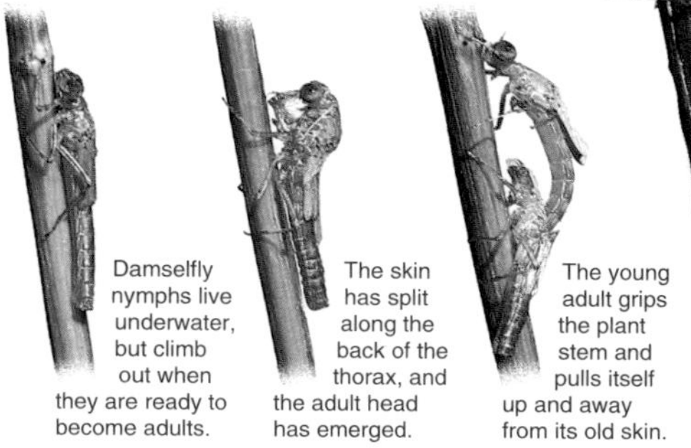

Two hours after leaving the water, the nymph has become an adult damselfly. Its old skin is left behind on the stalk.

Damselfly nymphs live underwater, but climb out when they are ready to become adults.

The skin has split along the back of the thorax, and the adult head has emerged.

The young adult grips the plant stem and pulls itself up and away from its old skin.

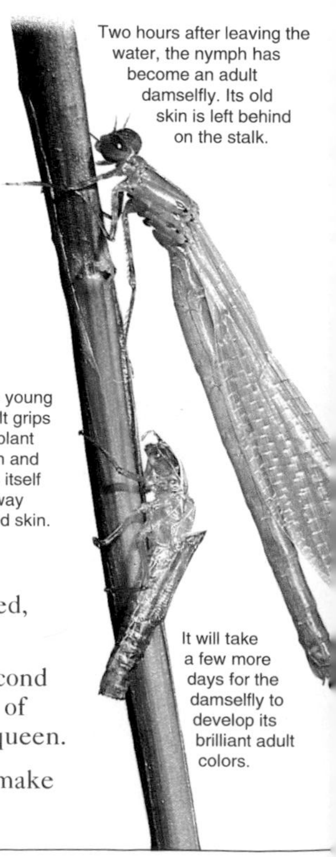

It will take a few more days for the damselfly to develop its brilliant adult colors.

INSECT FACTS

• If all the animals on Earth were weighed, ants would make up 10% of the total.

• Queen termites can lay one egg per second for more than 14 years. This gives a total of more than 440,000,000 babies from one queen.

• A bee must visit over 4,000 flowers to make one tablespoon of honey.

INSECT WINGS

Wings enable an insect to escape from predators, and to fly to new areas in search of food.

Moth wing

Dragonfly wing

Beetle forewing (elytron)

INSECT VISION

An insect's compound eyes are made up of hundreds of individual lenses.

Dragonflies have the largest eyes of any insect.

INSECT RECORDS

LOUDEST INSECTS
are cicadas, which can be heard up to 1,312ft (400m) away.

FASTEST FLYING INSECTS
are dragonflies, which have been recorded flying at speeds of over 31mph (50km/h).

FASTEST RUNNING INSECT
is the American cockroach (*Periplaneta americana*), which can run at speeds of almost 3mph (5km/h).

GIANT DRAGONFLY
The biggest insect ever to have lived was a prehistoric dragonfly. It had a wingspan of 29.5in (75cm): about the same as a Eurasian kestrel's.

DEFENSE AND ATTACK

Insects have developed many ways of defending themselves against enemies. These include camouflage, stinging, and squirting noxious chemicals. In several cases these methods are also useful for attacking prey.

The insect curls its body, completing its leafy disguise.

CAMOUFLAGE

Many insects are so well-camouflaged that they are almost impossible for predators to spot. The green markings of this Javanese leaf insect (*Phyllium bioculatum*), complete with holes and brown edges, make it look just like a dying leaf.

Real leaf

Imitation leaf midrib

Imitation leaf vein

When the Javanese leaf insect sits on a twig or branch, it blends in completely with its leafy surroundings.

INSECT HOMES

Bees, wasps, termites, and ants are the only insects that build permanent homes. These range from a simple hole in the ground to complex termite mounds up to 39ft (12m) high.

This umbrella-shaped mound is home to the African termites Cubitermes.

Common wasps (Vespula vulgaris) *build their nests from chewed-up wood fibers.*

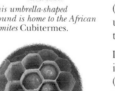

Inside wasps' and bees' nests are combs of cells. A single larva develops in each cell.

HELPFUL INSECTS

BEES
Bees pollinate many types of crops, and produce honey (the first sweetener used by humans) and beeswax.

SILK MOTHS
Silk is produced from the cocoon (pupa) of the silk moth *Bombyx mori*. Each cocoon produces a thread of silk that may be over 0.6 miles (1km) long.

DUNG BEETLES
Dung beetles were introduced to Australia to eat the large amounts of dung produced by cattle.

HARMFUL INSECTS

FLEAS AND FLIES
Diseases carried by fleas and flies have caused more than half of all human deaths since the Stone Age.

BODY LICE
More than 3,800 body lice can live on one person. In unhygienic situations they can transmit disease.

KILLER BEES
An aggressive type of African honey bee (*Apis mellifera adansonii*) attacks humans without provocation. More than 300 people have been killed.

The orchid mantis (*Hymenopus coronatus*) is camouflaged as an orchid flower.

CHEMICALS
Ants squirt stinging formic acid from their abdomen at enemies.

STINGING
Wasps and bees defend themselves by delivering a painful sting.

MIMICRY
The hover fly's colors resemble the warning stripes of wasps. This may put off predators.

INSECT SIZES

Insects range from tiny wasps smaller than a period, to beetles as big as a human hand. (The insects below are not shown actual size.)

SMALLEST INSECTS
are fairyfly wasps, which measure only 0.2mm long.

HEAVIEST INSECTS
are the goliath beetles (*Goliathus*), which weigh up to 3.9oz (110g): about the same as an apple.

LONGEST INSECT
is the giant stick insect (*Pharnacia serratipes*), which measures up to 17.7in (45cm) from leg tip to leg tip.

Giant stick insect's leg, actual size

LARGEST WING-SPAN
is that of the owlet moth (*Thysania agripina*), which measures up to 12in (30cm) across.

ARACHNIDS

SOME OF THE world's least loved animals are arachnids. They include spiders, scorpions, ticks, and mites. Most arachnids live on land. They are found all over the world in almost every habitat: there is even a species of spider that lives high on Mount Everest.

PORTRAIT OF AN ARACHNID

Arachnids have eight legs, and their body is divided into the cephalothorax (front and middle), and the abdomen (rear). They have a pair of leglike or pincerlike pedipalps for feeling and feeding.

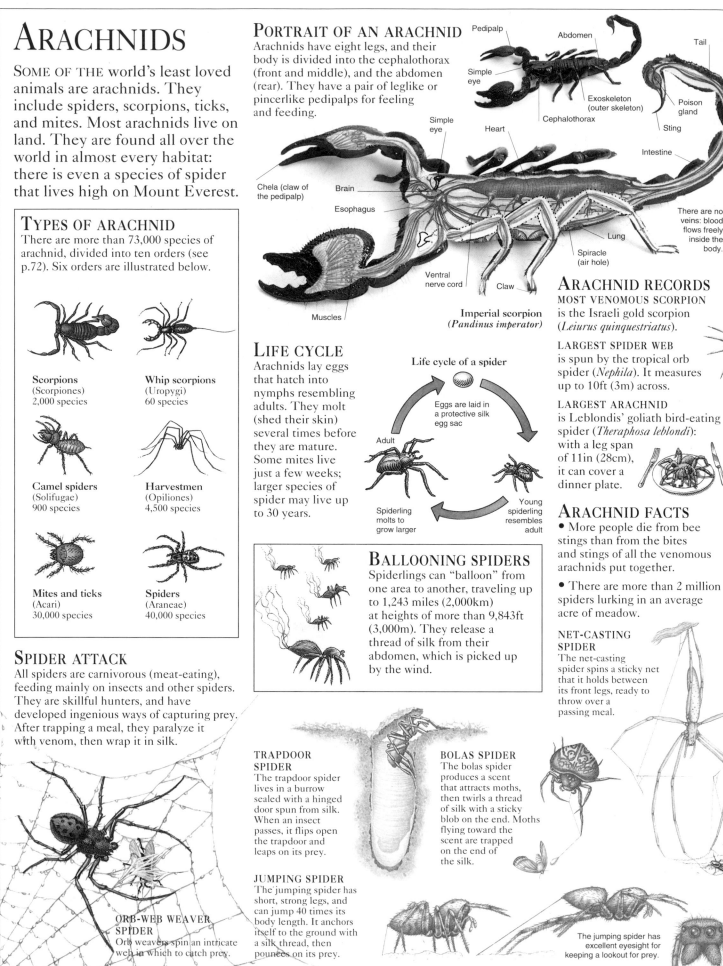

Imperial scorpion (*Pandinus imperator*)

TYPES OF ARACHNID

There are more than 73,000 species of arachnid, divided into ten orders (see p.72). Six orders are illustrated below.

Scorpions
(Scorpiones)
2,000 species

Whip scorpions
(Uropygi)
60 species

Camel spiders
(Solifugae)
900 species

Harvestmen
(Opiliones)
4,500 species

Mites and ticks
(Acari)
30,000 species

Spiders
(Araneae)
40,000 species

LIFE CYCLE

Arachnids lay eggs that hatch into nymphs resembling adults. They molt (shed their skin) several times before they are mature. Some mites live just a few weeks; larger species of spider may live up to 30 years.

Life cycle of a spider

Eggs are laid in a protective silk egg sac

Adult

Young spiderling resembles adult

Spiderling molts to grow larger

BALLOONING SPIDERS

Spiderlings can "balloon" from one area to another, traveling up to 1,243 miles (2,000km) at heights of more than 9,843ft (3,000m). They release a thread of silk from their abdomen, which is picked up by the wind.

ARACHNID RECORDS

MOST VENOMOUS SCORPION is the Israeli gold scorpion (*Leiurus quinquestriatus*).

LARGEST SPIDER WEB is spun by the tropical orb spider (*Nephila*). It measures up to 10ft (3m) across.

LARGEST ARACHNID is Leblondis' goliath bird-eating spider (*Theraphosa leblondi*): with a leg span of 11in (28cm), it can cover a dinner plate.

ARACHNID FACTS

• More people die from bee stings than from the bites and stings of all the venomous arachnids put together.

• There are more than 2 million spiders lurking in an average acre of meadow.

NET-CASTING SPIDER

The net-casting spider spins a sticky net that it holds between its front legs, ready to throw over a passing meal.

SPIDER ATTACK

All spiders are carnivorous (meat-eating), feeding mainly on insects and other spiders. They are skillful hunters, and have developed ingenious ways of capturing prey. After trapping a meal, they paralyze it with venom, then wrap it in silk.

ORB-WEB WEAVER SPIDER

Orb weavers spin an intricate web in which to catch prey.

TRAPDOOR SPIDER

The trapdoor spider lives in a burrow sealed with a hinged door spun from silk. When an insect passes, it flips open the trapdoor and leaps on its prey.

JUMPING SPIDER

The jumping spider has short, strong legs, and can jump 40 times its body length. It anchors itself to the ground with a silk thread, then pounces on its prey.

BOLAS SPIDER

The bolas spider produces a scent that attracts moths, then twirls a thread of silk with a sticky blob on the end. Moths flying toward the scent are trapped on the end of the silk.

The jumping spider has excellent eyesight for keeping a lookout for prey.

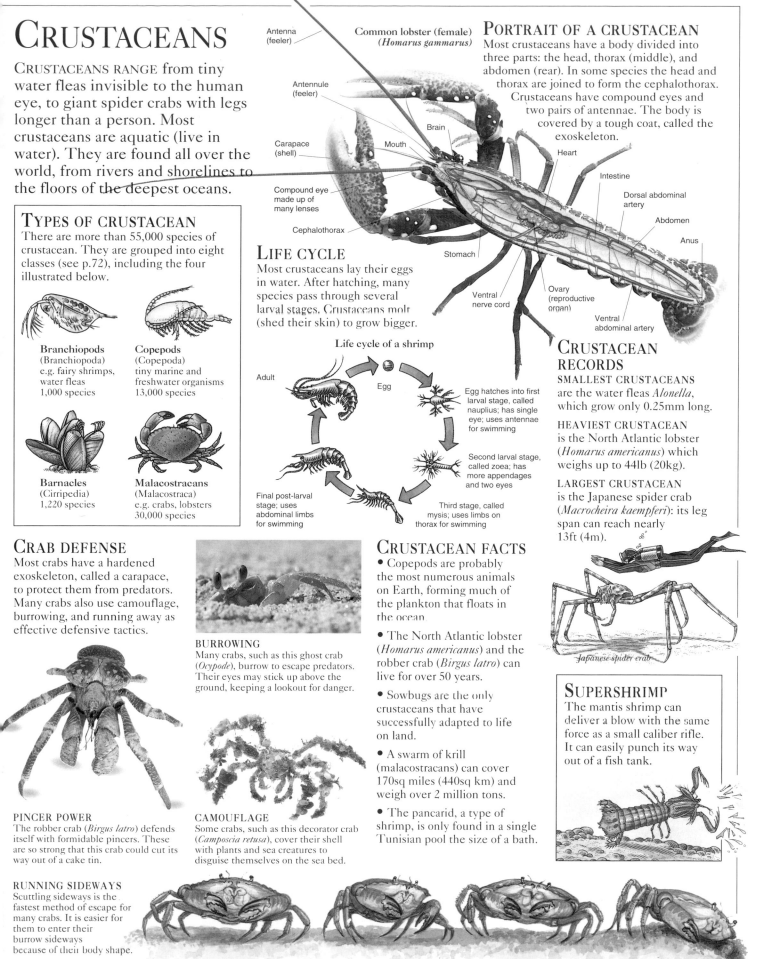

CRUSTACEANS

CRUSTACEANS RANGE from tiny water fleas invisible to the human eye, to giant spider crabs with legs longer than a person. Most crustaceans are aquatic (live in water). They are found all over the world, from rivers and shorelines to the floors of the deepest oceans.

Antenna (feeler)

Antennule (feeler)

Carapace (shell)

Compound eye made up of many lenses

Cephalothorax

Common lobster (female) (*Homarus gammarus*)

Brain

Mouth

Heart

Intestine

Dorsal abdominal artery

Abdomen

Anus

Stomach

Ventral nerve cord

Ovary (reproductive organ)

Ventral abdominal artery

TYPES OF CRUSTACEAN
There are more than 55,000 species of crustacean. They are grouped into eight classes (see p.72), including the four illustrated below.

Branchiopods (Branchiopoda) e.g. fairy shrimps, water fleas 1,000 species

Copepods (Copepoda) tiny marine and freshwater organisms 13,000 species

Barnacles (Cirripedia) 1,220 species

Malacostracans (Malacostraca) e.g. crabs, lobsters 30,000 species

LIFE CYCLE
Most crustaceans lay their eggs in water. After hatching, many species pass through several larval stages. Crustaceans molt (shed their skin) to grow bigger.

Life cycle of a shrimp

Adult

Egg

Egg hatches into first larval stage, called nauplius; has single eye; uses antennae for swimming

Second larval stage, called zoea; has more appendages and two eyes

Third stage, called mysis; uses limbs on thorax for swimming

Final post-larval stage; uses abdominal limbs for swimming

PORTRAIT OF A CRUSTACEAN
Most crustaceans have a body divided into three parts: the head, thorax (middle), and abdomen (rear). In some species the head and thorax are joined to form the cephalothorax. Crustaceans have compound eyes and two pairs of antennae. The body is covered by a tough coat, called the exoskeleton.

CRUSTACEAN RECORDS
SMALLEST CRUSTACEANS are the water fleas *Alonella*, which grow only 0.25mm long.

HEAVIEST CRUSTACEAN is the North Atlantic lobster (*Homarus americanus*) which weighs up to 44lb (20kg).

LARGEST CRUSTACEAN is the Japanese spider crab (*Macrocheira kaempferi*): its leg span can reach nearly 13ft (4m).

Japanese spider crab

CRAB DEFENSE
Most crabs have a hardened exoskeleton, called a carapace, to protect them from predators. Many crabs also use camouflage, burrowing, and running away as effective defensive tactics.

BURROWING
Many crabs, such as this ghost crab (*Ocypode*), burrow to escape predators. Their eyes may stick up above the ground, keeping a lookout for danger.

PINCER POWER
The robber crab (*Birgus latro*) defends itself with formidable pincers. These are so strong that this crab could cut its way out of a cake tin.

CAMOUFLAGE
Some crabs, such as this decorator crab (*Camposcia retusa*), cover their shell with plants and sea creatures to disguise themselves on the sea bed.

RUNNING SIDEWAYS
Scuttling sideways is the fastest method of escape for many crabs. It is easier for them to enter their burrow sideways because of their body shape.

CRUSTACEAN FACTS
• Copepods are probably the most numerous animals on Earth, forming much of the plankton that floats in the ocean.

• The North Atlantic lobster (*Homarus americanus*) and the robber crab (*Birgus latro*) can live for over 50 years.

• Sowbugs are the only crustaceans that have successfully adapted to life on land.

• A swarm of krill (malacostracans) can cover 170sq miles (440sq km) and weigh over 2 million tons.

• The pancarid, a type of shrimp, is only found in a single Tunisian pool the size of a bath.

SUPERSHRIMP
The mantis shrimp can deliver a blow with the same force as a small caliber rifle. It can easily punch its way out of a fish tank.

AMPHIBIANS

MOST AMPHIBIANS CAN live both on land and in water. They need a moist environment because their skin is not waterproof and they rapidly lose body water in dry conditions. Amphibians have, nevertheless, adapted to a wide range of habitats, even deserts. They are found on every continent except Antarctica.

TYPES OF AMPHIBIAN

There are more than 4,200 species of amphibian, divided into three orders (see p.72).

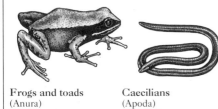

Frogs and toads
(Anura)
3,700 species

Caecilians
(Apoda)
170 species

Newts and salamanders
(Urodela)
350 species

AMPHIBIAN FEET

Amphibians' feet are adapted for their particular way of life. Many species have webbed feet for swimming, while others are adapted to burrow or climb.

*The palmate newt
(Triturus helveticus)
has webbed feet for
swimming.*

*The tiger salamander
(Ambystoma tigrinum)
has flattened feet for
burrowing.*

*The White's treefrog
(Litoria caerulea) has
sticky disks on its toes for
gripping leaves.*

*The African clawed toad
(Xenopus) has webbed feet
for swimming and claws for
gripping slippery surfaces.*

PORTRAIT OF AN AMPHIBIAN

Amphibians are vertebrates (see p.83). Their skin has no hair or scales, and is important for keeping the correct balance of water in the body. Most adult amphibians have lungs, but can also breathe through their skin.

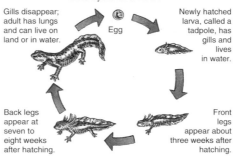

Brain
Vocal sac
Shoulder blade (outline)
Spinal cord
Backbone
Heart
Stomach
Kidney
Lungs
Intestine
Liver

Large bulging eyes
Eardrum

Adults can breathe through their skin.

European common toad
(*Bufo bufo*)

Frogs and toads have no tail.

LIFE CYCLE

Most amphibians lay their eggs in water. The young pass through a series of changes, called metamorphosis, before becoming adults. Life spans range from a brief breeding season to more than 50 years for the Japanese giant salamander (*Andrias japonicus*).

Life cycle of a newt

Gills disappear; adult has lungs and can live on land or in water.

Egg

Newly hatched larva, called a tadpole, has gills and lives in water.

Back legs appear at seven to eight weeks after hatching.

Front legs appear about three weeks after hatching.

AMPHIBIAN FACTS

• Young frogs are called froglets, and young toads are toadlets.

• Amphibian comes from the Greek words *amphi* and *bios*, meaning "double life," because amphibians can live both on land and in water.

• The smallest frog in the world, *Psyllophryne didactyla*, is smaller than a fingernail at just 0.41in (10.4mm) long.

• Poison-dart frogs are so named because the indigenous (native) people of South America tip their arrows with their poison.

LARGEST FROGS AND TOADS

Length is measured from the snout to the end of the body.

Common name	Scientific name	Size (approx) mm	in
Goliath frog	*Conraua goliath*	358	14
American bullfrog	*Pyxicephalus adspersus*	230	9
Cane toad	*Bufo marinus*	230	9
Rococo toad	*Bufo paracnemis*	230	9

CARING FOR EGGS AND YOUNG

Many amphibians lay their eggs and then leave the young to fend for themselves. Others protect them in a variety of ways.

VOCAL SAC BROODER
The male Darwin's frog (*Rhinoderma*) swallows his tadpoles into his vocal sac for protection. When they become froglets, he spits them out one at a time.

CARRYING TO WATER
The poison-dart frog (*Dendrobates*) carries its newly hatched tadpoles on its back to a nearby pool or stream.

EGGS ON LEGS
The male midwife toad (*Alytes obstetricans*) wraps his string of eggs around his back legs and carries them until they are ready to hatch.

UNDER THE SKIN
The Surinam toad's (*Pipa pipa*) eggs are placed on the female's back. Her skin swells around them until they are almost covered. The young develop into toadlets under her skin, then hatch out of her back.

Eggs embedded in female toad's skin

BIG TADPOLE, LITTLE FROG

The South American paradoxical frog (*Pseudis paradoxa*) is larger when it is a tadpole than when it turns into an adult frog.

AMPHIBIAN COLORS AND SHAPES

Amphibians have evolved a wide range of shapes and colors to suit their habitat and lifestyle. Many poisonous species are brightly colored to warn predators to keep away, while others have colors and shapes that help them blend in with their surroundings.

Mottled coloring helps disguise this South American horned toad (Ceratophrys).

This brightly colored golden mantella (Mantella aurantiaca) is a poisonous frog from Madagascar.

This South African shovel-nosed frog (Hemisus guttatus) uses its shovel-shaped snout for burrowing.

The shape and colors of this Asian leaf frog (Megophrys nasuta) resemble a dead leaf.

The tiger salamander's (Ambystoma tigrinum) spots are a signal to predators that it may make an unpleasant meal.

Poison-dart frogs are the most poisonous of all amphibians. Their startling colors make them easier for enemies to spot and avoid.

The colors and shape of this Malaysian narrow-mouthed toad (Kaloula pulchra) may fool predators into thinking it is a wet stone.

The flattened shape of this burrowing frog (Rhinophrynus dorsalis) helps it to slip easily through the soil.

DEFENSE AND ATTACK

Amphibians are carnivorous (meat-eating), and many species rely on camouflage to stay hidden from prey as well as from predators. Other defensive tactics include oozing poison, looking fierce, and startling enemies.

SURPRISE
The fire-bellied toad (*Bombina bombina*) relies on its camouflage to stay hidden from enemies. But if it is attacked, the toad displays the bright warning colors on its belly, hoping that the startled predator will leave it alone.

SCARING TACTICS
If this Budgett's frog (*Lepidobatrachus asper*) is attacked, it puts on a fearsome display. It opens its mouth, screams, and makes loud grunting noises. If this performance fails to scare away the enemy, the frog may bite it.

STICKY TONGUE
Frogs have a long, sticky tongue for flicking out at prey, such as insects.

The tongue is attached to the front of the mouth.

European common frog (Rana temporaria) attacking prey

LEAPING AND SWIMMING
If a frog is attacked, for example by a bird, it quickly leaps out of danger using its powerful back legs. If the frog is close to a pond or stream, it will dive into the water and swim out of the predator's reach.

LEAP FROG
The African sharp-nosed frog (*Ptychadena oxyrhynchus*) holds the frog long jump record. One individual leaped 17.5ft (5.35m) at the Calaveras County Frog Jubilee, California, in 1975.

CAMOUFLAGE
This European yellow-bellied toad (*Bombina variegata*) is almost completely hidden when it sits on a piece of bark.

Patches of green complete the toad's disguise.

Sharp rib

PRICKLY RIBS
The ribs of the Spanish sharp-ribbed salamander (*Pleurodeles waltl*) have needlelike tips. If a predator tries to eat it, the ribs pass through its skin giving the predator a sharp surprise.

Toad tries to make itself look bigger

LOOKING FIERCE
This European common toad is confronting an enemy. It has puffed up its body, and is standing on its toes to make itself appear larger.

AMPHIBIAN RECORDS

LARGEST SALAMANDER is the Japanese giant salamander, which grows up to 5ft (1.5m) long.

SMALLEST SALAMANDERS are the Mexican lungless salamanders (*Thorius*), which grow only 0.55in (14mm) long.

MOST POISONOUS AMPHIBIAN is the golden yellow poison-dart frog (*Phyllobates terribilis*). The poison from the skin of a single frog could kill up to 20,000 mice.

MOST EGGS are laid by the female cane toad (*Bufo marinus*): she can produce up to 35,000 eggs in one year.

POISON If a predator tries to eat them, many amphibians ooze a nasty tasting poison from their skin. This should make the attacker spit them out.

If attacked, the red eft, the young form of the eastern newt (Notophthalmus viridescens), secretes poison from special glands in its skin.

An oriental fire-bellied toad (Bombina orientalis) swimming away from danger.

REPTILES

REPTILES RANGE from tiny lizards to snakes up to 33ft (10m) long. They live in oceans, lakes, rivers, and on land. All reptiles have a scaly skin. They depend on their surroundings for warmth, so they are more numerous in hot countries.

PORTRAIT OF A REPTILE

Most reptiles (excluding snakes) have four legs and a tail. Their scaly skin retains water inside the body, enabling them to live in dry, barren regions.

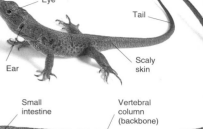

Nostril
Mouth
Brain
Esophagus
Trachea (windpipe)
Heart
Lung
Liver
Spinal cord
Small intestine
Stomach
Bladder
Claw
Five toes
Kidney
Eye
Tail
Scaly skin
Vertebral column (backbone)

Eyed lizard (female) (*Lacerta lepida*)

TYPES OF REPTILE

There are nearly 6,000 species of reptile, grouped into four orders (see p.72).

Lizards and snakes (Squamata) 5,700 species

Crocodilians (Crocodylia) 23 species

Tuatara (Rhynochocephalia) 2 species

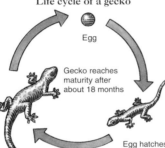

Turtles, tortoises, and terrapins (Chelonia) 200 species

LIFE CYCLE

Most reptiles lay leathery-shelled eggs, although some give birth to fully developed young. Reptiles continue to grow after reaching maturity, so older individuals may reach a huge size.

Life cycle of a gecko

Egg

Gecko reaches maturity after about 18 months

Egg hatches into young that resembles adult

REPTILE SHELLS

Turtles, tortoises, and terrapins have a bony shell covered with horny plates or leathery skin. The shell is for protection, and often acts as a camouflage.

Tortoise
Tortoises usually have a strong, high-domed shell to protect the body from predators' jaws.

SLOUGHING

Snakes and lizards slough (shed) their skin from time to time, either in large flakes or in one piece. This allows them to grow, and replaces worn-out skin.

Turtle and terrapin
A turtle's shell is lighter and flatter than a tortoise's shell. The streamlined shape enables the turtle to glide through the water.

Soft-shelled turtle
These turtles have a light, flat, shell for bouyancy (floating), and for hiding in the sand and mud of the riverbed.

REPTILE SKINS

The outer layer of a reptile's skin is thickened, forming waterproof scales. These scales are composed of keratin: the same substance that hoofs, hair, and fingernails are made of.

Crocodilians
Crocodilians have a tough, armorlike skin made of rough, horny scales (scutes).

Caiman skin

Snakes
Most snakes have a smooth skin. The scales overlap so that the snake can bend easily.

Snake skin

Lizards
Lizard skins range from smooth and slippery, to rough and spiky.

Gecko skin

REPTILE COLORS

CAMOUFLAGE

Many reptiles have skin colors and patterns that enable them to blend in with their surroundings, from bright green forest lizards, to dull brown desert snakes.

WARNING COLORS

Many venomous snakes, such as the Eastern coral snake (*Micrurus fulvius*), have bright colors to warn predators to keep away. Some harmless species have also developed these colors, to fool enemies into thinking they are dangerous; this is called Batesian mimicry.

The colors of this diadem snake (*Spalerosophis diadema cliffordi*) make it difficult to spot in its desert habitat.

The emerald tree skink (*Dasia smaragdina*) blends in with its leafy surroundings.

LONGEST SNAKE

The longest and heaviest snake in the world is the anaconda (*Eunectes murinus*). The longest anaconda on record measured 33ft 8in (10.26m): longer than a bus.

REPTILES ON THE ATTACK

Most reptiles are carnivorous (meat-eating). From deadly venom to sticky tongues and snapping jaws, they have evolved some of the most efficient methods of attack in the animal kingdom.

VENOM
Poisonous snakes, such as this green mamba (*Dendroaspis angusticeps*), kill prey by biting it and injecting venom through their fangs.

CONSTRICTION
Pythons and boas, such as this anaconda, coil their body around their prey, slowly squeezing the animal until it suffocates.

STICKY TONGUE
Chameleons have a long tongue with a sticky tip that they shoot out at prey. The chameleon's tongue is as long as its body and tail combined.

SNAPPING BEAKS
Tortoises and turtles do not have teeth: instead, they have a sharp, horny beak. Carnivorous turtles, such as snapping turtles, have strong jaws for grabbing and chopping up a passing meal.

This alligator snapping turtle (*Macroclemys*) has a pink, worm-like tongue for luring fish into its mouth.

Alligators can grow up to 50 new sets of teeth in a lifetime.

TERRIBLE TEETH
Crocodiles and their relatives have formidable sharp, pointed teeth for grabbing prey and tearing off chunks of flesh.

REPTILE RECORDS

LARGEST CROCODILIAN is the saltwater crocodile (*Crocodylus porosus*), which can grow up to 20ft (6m) long.

LARGEST LIZARD is the Komodo dragon (*Varanus komodoensis*), which grows up to 10ft (3m) long.

SMALLEST REPTILE is the British Virgin Island gecko (*Sphaerodactylus parthenopion*), with a body just 0.7in (18mm) in length.

DEFENSIVE TACTICS

Many reptiles have developed effective ways of putting off their enemies. A predator attacking a reptile may receive an unpleasant surprise.

HISSING AND SPITTING
Cobras rear up off the ground and hiss to scare off an enemy. Most cobras inject deadly venom by biting, but spitting cobras squirt jets of venom into their attacker's eyes.

When they are alarmed, cobras spread the skin of their neck into a hood.

NASTY SMELLS
The stinkpot turtle (*Sternotherus odoratus*) emits a foul-smelling yellow liquid to put off attackers.

SQUIRTING BLOOD
Some horned lizards (*Phrynosoma*) squirt drops of blood from their eyes at enemies. The blood may contain irritants.

Monocled cobra (*Naja naja kaouthia*)

LOOKING FIERCE
When startled, the Australian frilled lizard (*Chlamydosaurus kingi*) erects a large, ruff-like flap of loose skin on its neck. This usually scares away the attacker.

REPTILE FACTS

• Some snakes push their windpipe out of their mouth to avoid being suffocated when swallowing a large animal.

• When a snake charmer's snake weaves to and fro, it is not dancing to the music, but following the snake charmer's movements.

• A chameleon's eyes can move independently. One eye can look up while the other looks down.

• Spitting cobras can squirt their venom up to 9ft (2.7m).

WALKING ON WATER
Basilisk lizards (*Basiliscus*) drop onto water and run across the surface on their back legs to escape from a predator.

"FLYING"
Some lizards, such as this flying dragon (*Draco volans*), escape attack by leaping and gliding from tree to tree.

DEADLIEST SNAKES
Some 50,000–100,000 people die each year from snake bites. These are some of the worst culprits.

Common name and distribution	Scientific name	No. of deaths per year (approx.)
Asian cobras (Asia)	*Naja*	15,000
Saw-scaled vipers (Asia and Africa)	*Echis*	10,000
Russell's viper (Asia)	*Daboia russelii*	5,000
Kraits (Asia)	*Bungarus*	3,000
Lance-headed vipers (Central and South America)	*Bothrops*	3,000

LOSING THE TAIL
Many lizards can shed their tail if an attacker grabs hold of it; this allows them to escape. A new tail eventually grows in its place.

This lizard has recently lost part of its tail while escaping from a predator.

Two months later the tail is growing back.

After eight months the tail has almost reached its original length.

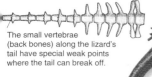

The small vertebrae (back bones) along the lizard's tail have special weak points where the tail can break off.

FISH

THERE IS NO SUCH thing as a typical fish: the three groups are as different from each other as a camel is from a crow. All fish live in water, although some species can spend time on land. Their habitats range from the cold, inky depths of the deepest oceans, to warm, sluggish, tropical rivers.

TYPES OF FISH
There are more than 20,000 species of fish, the vast majority of which are bony fish. Fish are divided into three classes (see p.72).

Jawless fish
(Agnatha)
hagfish and lampreys
75 species

Cartilaginous fish
(Chondrichthyes)
sharks, rays, and chimaeras
800 species

Bony fish
(Osteichthyes)
e.g. plaice, carp, cod
20,000–22,000 species

FISH RECORDS
LARGEST FISH
is the whale shark (*Rhincodon typus*), which grows to more than 50ft (15m) long.

SMALLEST FISH
is the goby (*Pandaka pygmaea*), which grows just 0.3in (7.6mm) long: smaller than a housefly.

FASTEST SWIMMER
is the tunny (*Thunnus*), which has been recorded swimming at 44mph (71km/h).

SWIMMING
Fish swim by creating a series of S-shaped waves that travel along the body from head to tail.

PORTRAIT OF A FISH
Fish are vertebrates (see p.83). The most familiar and numerous are the bony fish, which have a skeleton made of bone, a swim bladder for buoyancy, and a gill cover, called the operculum. Most fish are covered with scales.

Lateral line (sense organ)
Operculum (gill cover)
Dorsal fin
Backbone
Stomach
Scales
Kidney
Spinal cord
Dorsal artery
Brain
Gill arch
Gill slits
Eye
Mouth
Pharynx
Heart
Pectoral fin
Caudal fin
Swim bladder
Anal fin
Cloaca (anus and urinogenital opening)
Pelvic fin
Ovary
Intestine
Liver

Crucian carp (female)
(*Carassius carassius*)

LIFE CYCLES
Most fish release eggs, although some give birth to fully formed young. Many fish produce thousands of eggs at a time, because so few survive to become adults. Life spans range from a few months, to over 100 years for the giant sturgeon (*Huso huso*).

Life cycle of a trout
Egg
Adult
Trout takes from 8 months to 3 years to mature, depending on species.

Life cycle of a hammerhead shark
Adult gives birth to up to 40 live young.
Tiny young, called a fry, resembles adult trout.
Shark takes from 5 to 15 years to mature, depending on species.
Young, called a pup, resembles adult, but its head projectiles are bent back.

HOW FISH BREATHE
Fish "breathe" using their gills. As water flows over the gills, oxygen passes through thin membranes into the blood.

Gill rakers sieve the water.
The fish takes in water through its mouth.
Pharynx (connects mouth with esophagus).
Water flows out through the gill cover (operculum).
Water flows past the gills.

SMALL BEGINNINGS
An adult ocean sunfish (*Mola mola*) is about 60 million times bigger than its young: newly hatched sunfish are about 0.25in (6mm) long, while adults measure about 10ft (3m).

FISH MOVEMENT
Fish move in three dimensions: forward and backward; up and down; and left and right. They use different fins to control these movements.

ROLL
The fish uses its dorsal, pectoral, and pelvic fins to roll.

YAW
A combination of fin movements steers the fish to the left and right.

PITCH
The fish swivels its pectoral and pelvic fins to rise, stay level, and dive.

Dogfish
The S-shaped wave begins when the fish swings its head to the right.

First dorsal fin
Pelvic fin
The peak of the wave has traveled to the region of the pelvic and first dorsal fins.

Peak
The peak is now between the two dorsal fins, and the tail begins to thrust to the right.

Peak
The peak reaches the tail, and the head swings for the next wave.

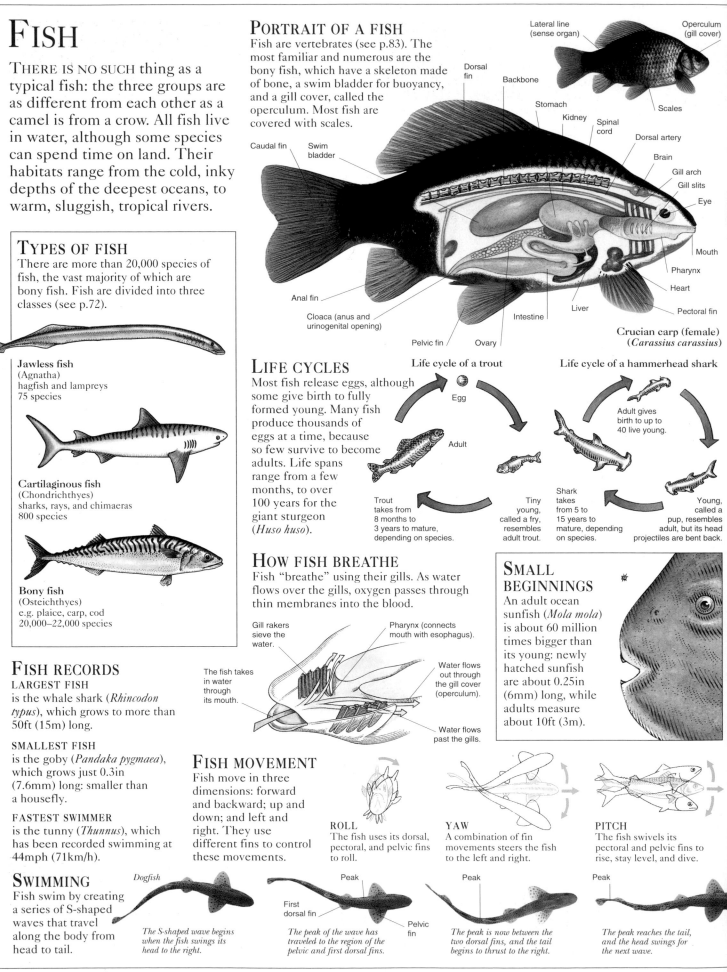

CARING FOR YOUNG

Many fish do not look after their eggs and young, leaving them to fend for themselves. Others are caring parents, fiercely protecting their offspring from predators.

PROTECTIVE POUCH
The female seahorse lays her eggs into a special pouch on the male seahorse's body. The eggs grow inside the pouch, and are "born" when the young are developed.

MOUTH BROODING
Many cichlids keep their eggs in their mouth while they develop. After hatching, the young usually stay in the mouth for safety, finally leaving it when they are large enough.

PARENT NIBBLING
The common brown discus fish (*Symphysodon*) secretes a special nourishing substance from its skin for the young to nibble. They feed on their parents for about four weeks.

FEEDING AND DIET

Fish feed in a variety of ways, depending on their diet. There are plant-eaters, meat-eaters, scavengers (feed on dead plants and animals), and parasites (see below).

FILTER FEEDING
Filter feeders, such as this paddlefish (*Polyodon spathula*), sift food from the water with their gill rakers.

TEARING TEETH
Many fish, such as this great white shark (*Carcharodan carcharias*), have razor-sharp teeth for biting chunks out of their prey.

SUCKING BLOOD
The lamprey is a parasitic fish (feeds on living things). It attaches itself to prey with a sucker, rasps at the flesh with its teeth, then sucks its blood.

DEFENSIVE TACTICS

Many fish rely on camouflage to stay hidden from predators. Several species are poisonous, while the electric eel (*Electrophorus electricus*) can deliver a 500-volt shock.

Poison is delivered through sharp spines.

PUFFING UP
When attacked, the porcupine fish inflates its body and erects its spines in the hope that it will be too large and prickly to be eaten.

POISON
More than 50 species of fish are poisonous. This lion fish (*Pterois volitans*) is one of the deadliest in the world.

CAMOUFLAGE
Some fish, such as these pipefish, look exactly like the vegetation where they make their homes.

The pipefish resembles a piece of seaweed.

ON THE ATTACK

Most fish rely on speed and surprise to catch prey. Some species have developed other methods of attack.

SQUIRTING
The archer fish squirts water at its prey, knocking it into the water.

LURES
Some fish use lures to catch prey. Deep sea angler fish have a luminous organ on the end of a long, polelike fin ray. Prey are attracted by the light, and are snapped up by the waiting fish.

FISH SHAPES

Fish have evolved many different shapes to suit their particular way of life, from streamlined sharks shaped for fast swimming, to flatfish that lie motionless on the sea floor.

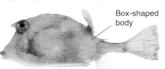

The John Dory (Zeus) approaches prey head-on. Its slim shape makes it difficult for the victim to spot.

Box-shaped body

Protective bony plates beneath the cowfish's skin give it a distinctive boxy shape.

Deep body

The freshwater hatchetfish "flies" for short distances above the water. Its deep body shape keeps it steady.

The plaice's (Pleuronectes) flat shape allows it to remain almost invisible on the seabed.

Plaice seen from above

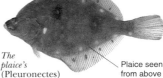

The long-nosed gar (Lepisosteus osseus) has a long, thin shape for quick dashes.

FISH FACTS

• The basking shark (*Cetorhinus maximus*) filters about 396,000 gallons (1,500cu m) of water per hour: enough to fill 66,000 baths.

• Needlefish are the only fish that have green bones.

• It would take 2,000 gobies (smallest fish) to equal the length of a whale shark (largest fish).

• Some sharks give birth to just one live young: the first to develop inside the mother eats all the other eggs and embryos.

• In times of drought, the African lungfish (*Protopterus*) buries itself in mud. It can survive for at least three years by digesting its own muscles.

FISH HABITATS

Mountain lakes and streams
Fish live at altitudes of up to 16,000ft (4,900m).

Loach: probably the highest living species

Lakes and rivers
Carp, characins, and catfish are some of the most common freshwater fish.

Upside-down catfish

Shoreline
Some species that live on the shoreline can survive for long periods out of the water.

Mudskipper

Coastal waters
In tropical coastal waters, coral reefs are home to many brightly colored fish

Mandarin fish

Open ocean
Many species of fish that live in the open ocean grow to a huge size.

Caves
Several species of cave fish have no eyes: they do not need them since they spend their lives in darkness.

Blind cave characin

Deep-ocean
Food is scarce here. Many fish have large jaws to make the most of feeding opportunities.

Gulper eel

Middle ocean depths
Light disappears and fish are fewer in deeper ocean waters.

Pacific manta ray

Oarfish

BIRDS

THERE ARE MORE than 9,000 species of bird – about two for every species of mammal. All birds have feathers, and most can fly. They range in size from tiny hummingbirds to the ostrich, which can grow one and a half times as tall as a human. Birds are found in almost all habitats.

PORTRAIT OF A BIRD

The body of a typical bird is superbly adapted for flight. The front limbs are modified to form wings, and the body is a streamlined shape. Birds have some hollow bones to keep them light.

Speckled pigeon (*Columba guinea*)

Beak
Brain
Esophagus
Trachea
Spinal cord
Backbone
Lung
Heart
Kidney
Gizzard (muscular bag for grinding food)
Duodenum
Secondary flight feathers
Primary flight feathers
Crop
Liver
Claw
Rectum
Stomach
Cloaca
Ureter
Tail feathers

TYPES OF BIRD

The 9,000 or so known species of bird are divided into 28 orders (see p.72).

Ostrich
(Struthioniformes)
1 species

Rheas
(Rheiformes)
2 species

Emu, cassowaries
(Casuariiformes)
4 species

Tinamous
(Tinamiformes)
46 species

Kiwis
(Apterygiformes)
3 species

Penguins
(Sphenisciformes)
18 species

Loons
(Gaviiformes)
5 species

Albatrosses, petrels
(Procellariiformes)
110 species

Owls
(Strigiformes)
174 species

Waterfowl
(Anseriformes)
150 species

Birds of prey
(Falconiformes)
290 species

Game birds
(Galliformes)
274 species

Cranes, rails, bustards
(Gruiformes)
190 species

Shorebirds, gulls, terns, auks
(Charadriiformes)
337 species

Parrots, lories, cockatoos
(Psittaciformes)
342 species

Herons, storks, ibises
(Ciconiiformes)
117 species

Nightjars, frogmouths
(Caprimulgiformes)
109 species

Mousebirds
(Coliiformes)
6 species

Kingfishers, bee-eaters, hoopoes
(Coraciiformes)
204 species

Passerines
(Passeriformes)
5,414 species

Sandgrouse
(Pteroclidiformes)
16 species

Pelicans, gannets, cormorants
(Pelecaniformes)
55 species

Cuckoos, turacos
(Cuculiformes)
159 species

Swifts, hummingbirds
(Apodiformes)
429 species

Trogons
(Trogoniformes)
39 species

Woodpeckers, toucans, barbets
(Piciformes)
381 species

Pigeons
(Columbiformes)
300 species

Grebes
(Podicipediformes)
21 species

LIFE CYCLE

Birds lay hard-shelled eggs which one or both parents usually incubate. The hatchlings of some species are blind and helpless, and have to be looked after for many weeks. Other species are able to leave the nest just one day after hatching. Lifespans range from five years for some species of hummingbird, to more than 72 years for the Andean condor (*Vultur gryphus*).

HATCHING

Most types of chick are ready to hatch out of their egg a few weeks after it was laid. This sequence shows a duckling chipping its way out of its shell.

1 The duckling chips a hole in the blunt end of the shell with its special egg tooth. This tooth falls off after hatching.

2 The duckling turns as it chips, cutting a circle in its shell. It takes long rests between bursts of pecking.

3 When the circle is complete, the duckling straightens its neck to push the top of the egg away.

4 After a further push with its feet and shoulders, the duckling breaks off the end of the shell.

5 The duckling finally falls out of the egg. Its feathers are still wet.

6 Within two or three hours the duckling's soft, fluffy down feathers have dried. It will soon take to the water.

Life cycle of a moorhen (*Gallinula chloropus*)

Egg

Chick chips its way out of the egg using a special egg tooth.

Young chick is covered in soft, fluffy down feathers.

After six to seven weeks the moorhen has its adult plumage and can fly.

CLOSE-UP OF A FEATHER

Feathers are strong and flexible. They are made from keratin: the same protein that hair, fingernails, and hooves contain.

Tip

Outer vane (windward edge)

Downcurved edge

Inner vane (leeward edge)

Upcurved edge

Shaft of feather is hollow.

Macaw feather

Barbs are locked tightly together to form a smooth surface.

Quill

TYPES OF FEATHER

There are four main types of feather, each with a different function.

Down feathers
These soft, fluffy feathers keep the bird warm.

Body feathers
Sleek body feathers emphasise the bird's streamlined shape.

Wing feathers
Strong wing feathers provide the surface the bird needs for flight.

Tail feathers
The bird uses its long tail feathers for steering, balance, and braking.

FEET SHAPES

Birds' feet come in many different shapes and sizes, to suit their various habitats and lifestyles.

The moorhen's long toes are widely spread, enabling the bird to walk across mud and floating vegetation.

Waterbirds, such as Canada geese (Branta canadensis), have webbed feet to paddle through the water.

Woodpeckers have two toes pointing forward and two pointing backward, to anchor them as they chip away at tree trunks.

Perching birds, such as crows, have a single hind toe that enables them to hold tightly onto branches.

Owls' legs and feet are covered in feathers to silence their approach as they swoop on prey.

The feet of birds of prey, such as hawks, are equipped with long, sharp talons for gripping prey.

POISONOUS BIRD

The only known poisonous bird is the hooded pitohui (*Pitohui dichrous*) from New Guinea. Its skin, feathers, and internal organs contain a poison similar to that secreted by poison arrow frogs (see p.93).

WING SHAPES

Birds' wings are shaped to suit their lifestyles. They may be broad or slender; long or short.

Gulls have slender, pointed wings for gliding.

Woodpeckers have broad, rounded wings for maneuverability.

Geese have long, broad wings to lift their heavy body and keep it airborne.

Swifts have slender, curved wings for rapid and powerful flight.

The wings of flightless birds, such as rheas, are useless for flight.

Penguins have paddle-shaped wings for swimming.

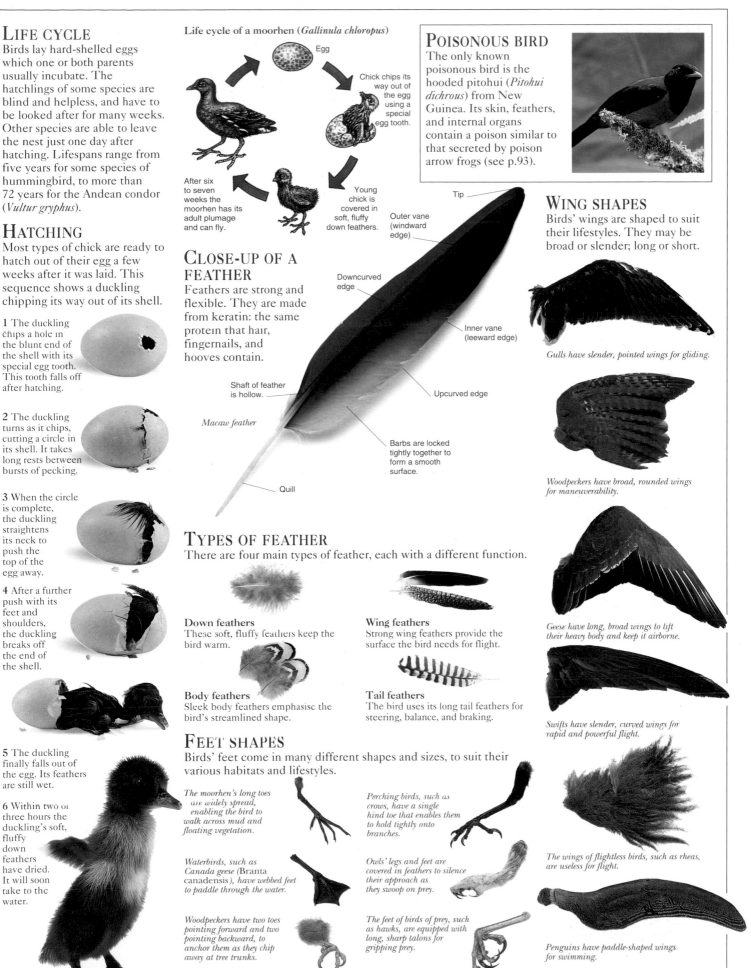

ATTRACTING A MATE

Birds go to great lengths to attract a mate. Usually, the males court the females: they may sing, dance, strut, or show off their colors to attract attention.

Display
Many birds display brightly colored parts of the body to attract a female. The male raggiana bird of paradise (*Paradisaea raggiana*) may hang upside down as part of his display.

Presenting gifts
Some birds attract a female by presenting a gift. The male greater roadrunner (*Geococcyx californianus*) offers his mate a lizard, while the male sandwich tern (*Sterna sandvicensis*) (left) presents his with a fish.

Building a bower
Male bowerbirds build a bower to attract a mate. The male vogelkop gardener's (*Amblyornis inornatus*) bower is a complex shelter of twigs. The bower is only for attraction; after mating, the female builds her own nest in which to lay her eggs.

EGGS

The type and number of eggs a bird lays depends on its lifestyle and habitat. Some species lay just one egg; others lay several. Eggs vary widely in size and shape. Many are colored and patterned for camouflage, making them difficult for predators, such as foxes, to spot.

The eggs of the bee hummingbird (Mellisuga helenae) are the smallest in the world, weighing only 0.009oz (0.25g).

Ostrich (Struthio camelus) eggs are the largest in the world, weighing up to 3.64lb (1.65kg), and measuring up to 8in (20cm) long.

BIRD FACTS

- Hummingbirds need to eat half their body weight every day to stay alive.

- Pelican chicks can attract their parents' attention while still inside the egg: they call when they are too hot or too cold.

- Starlings are some of the best mimics in the bird world: they can mimic other birds, and even ringing telephones.

- Ostrich eggs are the largest single cells in the world.

- Once a young sooty tern (*Sterna fuscata*) takes to the wing, it may stay airborne for four years before returning to the ground to breed.

- Large birds, e.g. swans, may have more than 25,000 feathers.

- The peregrine falcon (*Falco peregrinus*) can reach speeds of 112mph (180km/h) during a stoop (dive).

WIDEST WINGSPAN

The wandering albatross (*Diomedea exulans*) has the largest wingspan of any bird, measuring 12ft (3.6m) from wingtip to wingtip: greater than the length of a small car.

DIETS AND BEAKS

Birds eat a huge variety of food, including meat, fish, seeds, insects, and fruit. Their beaks are adapted to suit their particular diets.

Serrated beaks
Birds do not have teeth, but some, such as mergansers (*Mergus*), have teethlike structures on the sides of their beak. These serrations help them to catch fish.

Avocet beak
Avocets (*Recurvirostra*) have an upturned beak which they sweep from side to side to catch worms and other invertebrates in shallow estuary waters.

Fruit and nut eaters
Parrots' beaks are shaped for cracking nuts and eating fruit. The hook at the front of the beak is for tearing at fruit, and the strong base of the beak cracks open seeds.

Flamingo beak
Flamingos have a "bent" beak for sifting food from water. The tongue pumps water through fringes on either side of the bill, trapping small animals and plants.

Predators
Birds of prey, such as falcons (*Falco*), are carnivorous (meat-eating). They have a strong, hooked beak for tearing apart prey too large to be swallowed whole.

BIRDS' NESTS

Most birds build a nest in which to lay their eggs and rear their chicks. They range from simple scrapes to intricately woven nests.

Simple nests
Some birds lay their eggs in a scrape in the ground. Others have no nest at all: murres (right) lay eggs on rocky ledges.

Burrows
Some birds, including puffins (*Fratercula arctica*) (right), nest inside a burrow.

Nests of mud
Flamingos build conical pots of sand and mud to lay their eggs in.

Woven nests
Many birds weave nests of grass, leaves, or twigs. Weaverbirds build elaborate grass nests (right): the long entrance stops snakes from getting inside.

Nests of sticks
The hamerkop (*Scopus umbretta*) builds a huge, roofed nest of sticks, grass, and mud. The nest measures up to 5ft (1.5m) across.

Nests of saliva
Edible-nest swiftlets (*Collocalia fuciphaga*) build their nests from saliva. These nests are used to make bird's nest soup: a food delicacy in China.

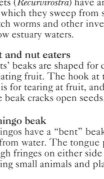

HIGH FLIER

Rüppell's griffons (*Gyps rueppelli*) are the highest-flying birds. They can reach heights of 37,000ft (11,278m): as high as airplanes fly.

BIRD RECORDS

LARGEST BIRD is the ostrich (*Struthio camelus*), which weighs up to 344lb (156kg), and grows up to 8.9ft (2.7m) tall.

SMALLEST BIRD is the bee hummingbird (*Mellisuga helenae*), which weighs about 0.056oz (1.6g) and grows just 2.24in (5.7cm) long.

FASTEST SWIMMER is the gentoo penguin (*Pygoscelis papua*), which can reach speeds of 17mph (27.4km/h).

MOST ABUNDANT BIRD is the red-billed quelea (*Quelea quelea*), with an adult population of about 1.5 billion. There may be up to 10 million birds in a single colony.

FASTEST-FLYING BIRDS

Bird	Scientific name	Speed km/h	Speed mph
White-throated needletail	*Hirundapus caudacutus*	171	106
Alpine swift	*Apus melba*	160	99.4
Magnificent frigatebird	*Fregata magnificens*	159	99
Spurwing goose	*Plectropterus gambensis*	142	88
Red-breasted merganser	*Mergus serrator*	129	80

DOMESTIC BIRDS

DOMESTIC BIRDS ARE birds that are kept and bred by humans. They include chickens, ducks, and geese. Domestic birds are kept for various purposes: some are bred for their meat, eggs, or feathers; others for sports such as pigeon racing and falconry.

CHICKEN BREEDS
All chickens are descended from the red jungle fowl (*Gallus gallus*) of southeast Asia, which is a member of the pheasant family. Chicken breeds are generally classified into American, Mediterranean, English, and Asian. Eight of the 150 breeds are illustrated here.

Salmon faverolle

Barred Plymouth Rock

Bantam Orpington Blue

Japanese yokohama

White silky

Silver braekel fowl

Red jungle fowl (Gallus gallus)

Turken

Mille fleur bantam

TURKEY FACTS
• Turkeys were first domesticated by the Aztec and Zuni Indians for food and sacrifice. They also used the feathers for decoration.

• Turkeys were first taken to Europe by the Spanish in about 1511.

• There are about 124 million domestic turkeys in the world.

CHICKEN FACTS
• Chickens were domesticated about 8,000 years ago.

• In the Middle Ages, chicken was eaten only by royalty and the aristocracy. The poor kept chickens for eggs and new chicks, and killed a hen only when it became too old to lay. Today, chicken is probably the most widely eaten meat in the world.

• Hens can lay about 250 eggs a year.

EGGSTRAORDINARY!
About 160 billion hens' eggs are laid every year in China: enough to make an omelette that would give every person in the world a piece measuring 3.28ft (1m) across.

DUCK FACT
• The Muscovy duck was first domesticated in South America by pre-Columbian Indians. The mallard (right) was domesticated in China at least 3,000 years ago.

DOMESTIC BIRD RECORDS
FASTEST EGG-LAYING CHICKEN was a white leghorn that laid 371 eggs in 364 days.

LARGEST CHICKEN'S EGG weighed 16oz (454g). It was laid by a white leghorn in Vineland, New Jersey, in 1956.

MOST YOLKS in a chicken's egg was nine, laid by a hen in Mount Morris, New York, in 1971.

LARGEST CHICKEN PRODUCER is the US, which produces about 13 million tons of chicken meat a year.

LARGEST GOOSE EGG weighed 24oz (680g). It was laid by "Speckle" in Goshen, Ohio.

GOOSE FACTS
• Geese were first domesticated more than 3,000 years ago.

• Goose was considered the finest poultry for festive occasions until the turkey became more popular in the 16th and 17th centuries.

• In the Middle Ages, gooseherds in Britain would drive flocks of up to 20,000 geese to be sold at goose fairs.

TYPES OF DOMESTIC BIRD

Domestic bird	Uses	Number of breeds (approx)	Descended from
Chicken	Meat, eggs	150	Red jungle fowl (*Gallus gallus*)
Duck	Meat, eggs, down	97	Muscovy duck (*Cairina moschata*) and wild mallard (*Anas platyrhyncos*)
Goose	Meat, eggs, down	43	Most breeds from the greylag (*Anser anser*)
Turkey	Meat	33	Common turkey (*Meleagris gallopavo*)

OTHER DOMESTIC BIRDS

Racing pigeons (Columba livia) are kept for sport.

Racing pigeons are descended from the rock dove.

Guinea fowl (Numida), native to Africa and Madagascar, are now raised for their meat in many countries.

Long, tapering breast feathers

Swans are reared for their down, and as ornamental birds.

Hooked beak for tearing at prey.

Falcons are used in the sport of falconry.

Ostriches (Struthio camelus) are reared for their meat and their decorative feathers.

Many types of bird are kept as pets. The budgerigar (Melopsittacus undulatus) is particularly popular.

The budgerigar is native to Australia.

Canaries (Serinus canaria) are kept as pets for their beautiful song.

Pheasants, native to Asia, are reared as game birds.

Pheasants have been introduced into Europe and North America.

The partridge is native to Europe and Asia.

Partridges are reared as game birds.

MAMMALS

MAMMALS RANGE IN size from tiny shrews to the blue whale – the largest animal that has ever lived on Earth. Mammals are found all over the world: on land, in oceans and rivers, and even, in the case of bats, in the air.

PORTRAIT OF A MAMMAL
Mammals usually have fur or hair. Almost all species give birth to live young which they feed with milk produced in the female's body.

Male rabbit (*Oryctolagus cuniculus*)

Eye

Furry skin

Tail

Pinna (ear flap) directs sounds toward inner ear.

Brain

Nasal cavity

Mouth

Esophagus

Trachea

Lung

Heart

Diaphragm

Gall bladder

Liver

Stomach

Kidney

Spinal cord

Backbone

Colon

Ureter

Bladder

Reproductive organs

Anus

ARMADILLO SHELL-TER
Some ancient mammals grew to huge sizes. The ancestors of modern armadillos measured up to 10ft (3m) long. South American Indians used their shells as roofs.

TYPES OF MAMMAL
There are more than 4,600 known species of mammal, divided into 21 orders (see p.72).

Monotremes (Monotremata) 3 species

Marsupials (Marsupialia) 272 species

Insectivores (Insectivora) 428 species

Elephant shrews (Macroscelidia) 15 species

Flying lemurs (Dermoptera) 2 species

Bats (Chiroptera) 925 species

Tree shrews (Scandentia) 19 species

Apes, monkeys, and lemurs (Primates) 233 species

Edentates (Edentata) 29 species

Pangolins (Pholidota) 7 species

Aardvark (Tubulidentata) 1 species

Hares, rabbits, pikas (Lagomorpha) 80 species

Rodents (Rodentia) 2,021 species

Whales and dolphins (Cetacea) 78 species

Carnivores (Carnivora) 237 species

Seals, sea lions, walrus (Pinnipedia) 34 species

Elephants (Proboscidea) 2 species

Hyraxes (Hyracoidea) 6 species

Sea cows (Sirenia) 5 species

Odd-toed hoofed mammals (Perissodactyla) 18 species

Even-toed hoofed mammals (Artiodactyla) 220 species

MAMMAL REPRODUCTION

EGG-LAYING MAMMALS
Monotremes are the only mammals that lay eggs. Female duck-billed platypuses (*Ornithorhynchus anatinus*) (right) incubate their eggs in a nest inside their burrow; female echidnas incubate their eggs in a pouch .

MARSUPIAL MAMMALS
Marsupials, such as kangaroos, give birth when the young are at a very early stage of development. The tiny baby crawls across its mother's belly to reach the pouch, where it latches on to a teat and feeds on milk. The baby remains in the pouch for many weeks, leaving it for longer periods as it grows older.

Newborn joey (baby kangaroo) in the pouch.

PLACENTAL MAMMALS
Most mammals are placental: the young grow inside the female and receive nutrients via the placenta (a connection between the mother's and baby's blood systems). At birth, the young are physically well developed.

Newborn kittens feeding on their mother's milk.

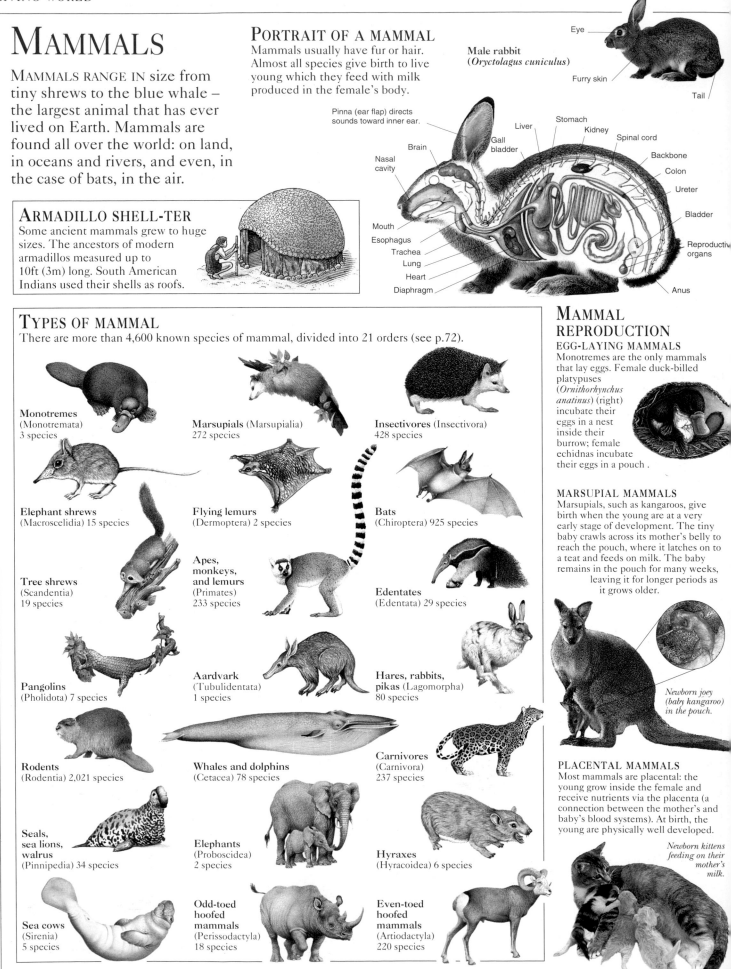

MAMMAL HIDES

Arctic fox fur

FURRY HIDE
Fur and hair enable mammals to live in almost every climate. By trapping air, a furry coat, such as the Arctic fox's (*Alopex lagopus*), keeps out the cold, stops body heat from escaping, and protects the skin from wind, rain, and strong sunlight.

Jaguar fur

CAMOUFLAGE PATTERNS
Many mammals have hides that are colored and patterned for camouflage. This enables them to blend in with their background, hidden from enemies and prey. A jaguar's (*Panthera onca*) spots blend in with the dappled sunlight of the forest floor where it stalks its prey.

Armadillo skin

ARMOR PLATING
Pangolins and armadillos are covered with bony plates and scales that provide a tough, armored coat to protect them from predators. Some, such as the three-banded armadillo (*Tolypeutes*), can roll themselves up into a ball to defend their body completely.

Zebra fur

CONFUSING PATTERNS
A zebra's (*Equus*) stripes break up its outline, making it more difficult for predators, such as lions (*Panthera leo*), to pick out one individual from the herd. This black and white pattern is particularly effective at night, protecting the herd from nocturnal hunters.

Dolphin skin

NAKED SKIN
Hair or fur would slow down whales and dolphins in the water, so they have lost all but a few tufts. Naked mole rats (*Heterocephalus glaber*) have also lost their hair: it is easier for them to move forward and backward along a tunnel with a smooth, hairless skin.

Hedgehog spines

SPINY FUR
The hairs of hedgehogs and porcupines have developed into stiff, sharp spines that form an effective defense against predators. The European hedgehog (*Erinaceus europaeus*) has up to 5,000 spines. When it senses danger, it rolls itself up into a ball.

MAMMAL HANDS AND FEET

All early mammals probably had five fingers and toes on each hand and foot. Over time, these basic digits evolved to suit different lifestyles and habitats. Humans (*Homo sapiens*) have the five fingers and toes typical of many mammals. The colors of the various parts of a human hand (right) are repeated in the illustrations that follow, to show how those parts have developed to suit different animals' lifestyles.

Human hand

Finger bones (toe bones)

Wrist bones (ankle bones)

Palm bones (sole bones)

Lower arm bones (lower leg bones)

Cats walk on the tips of their toes. Each toe is armed with a sharp claw for catching prey.

Elephants have five toes on each foot, and a big fleshy pad to support their immense weight.

*Tapirs' (*Tapirus*) front feet have four toes, while their back feet have three.*

Gazelles have light, dainty, two-toed feet that enable them to run very fast.

Badgers' hands and feet are adapted for digging. They are broad and strong with wide claws.

*Horses (*Equus*) have one long, strong toe on each foot, protected by a hoof.*

Seals' hands and feet have evolved into large, paddle-shaped flippers for swimming.

MAMMAL RECORDS

LARGEST MAMMAL
is the blue whale (*Balaenoptera musculus*), which weighs up to 150 tons and grows up to 111.5ft (34m) long.

SMALLEST MAMMAL
is the Kitti's hog-nosed bat (*Craseonycteris thonglongyai*), which weighs only 0.05oz (1.5g) and is about the size of a large bumblebee.

Kitti's hog-nosed bat and bumblebee, shown actual size.

TALLEST MAMMAL
is the giraffe (*Giraffa camelopardalis*), which grows up to 19.4ft (5.9m) tall: more than three times the height of an adult human.

FASTEST SWIMMER
is the sei whale (*Balaenoptera borealis*), which can swim at speeds of up to 30mph (48km/h).

MAMMAL FACTS

• Some types of traditional Chinese warrior armor were based on the protective overlapping scales of the pangolin's skin.

• There are only two types of poisonous mammal: the duck-billed platypus, which injects poison through a sharp spur on its ankle; and some shrews, which paralyze the earthworms they feed on with poisonous saliva.

BIG HOUSE ON THE PRAIRIE
Black-tailed prairie dog (*Cynomys ludovicianus*) colonies can cover huge areas. A colony in Texas had an area of about 24,000sq miles (62,160 sq km): twice the size of Belgium.

LONGEST GESTATION PERIODS
The gestation period is the amount of time the young take to develop inside the mother. (Humans have a gestation period of nine months.)

Mammal	Scientific name	Gestation period
African elephant	*Loxodonta africana*	22 months
Asian elephant	*Elephas maximus*	22 months
Baird's beaked whale	*Berardius bairdii*	17 months
White rhinoceros	*Ceratotherium simum*	16 months

TUSKS, HORNS, AND ANTLERS
Some mammals have antlers, horns, or tusks that are used mainly for fighting and establishing dominance within their social group. Antlers are shed and regrown each year; horns grow steadily throughout an animal's life. Tusks are elongated, pointed teeth.

*Black rhino (*Diceros bicornis*) horn*

Elephant tusks grow about 7in (17cm) per year.

*Red deer (*Cervus elephus*) antlers*

*Indian blackbuck (*Antilope cervicapra*) horn*

MAMMAL TAILS

Most mammals have a tail. Tails have a variety of uses, including swatting flies, communication, and providing warmth.

The flying squirrel uses its flattened tail as a rudder for steering as it leaps from tree to tree. The tail also acts as a brake in the air.

A horse's (Equus) tail is made of many long, thick hairs. It is used mainly to keep flies and other pests away.

Some animals, for example spider monkeys (Ateles), have a prehensile tail that can grip branches like a fifth limb. This prehensile opossum tail has scaly skin at the tip to give the animal a firm grip.

The fallow deer's (Dama dama) tail is dark on top and white underneath. If danger threatens, the deer holds up its tail to flash a warning to the other deer in the herd.

Elephants have wiry hair at the end of their tail. They sometimes hold onto each other's tails when walking along in single file.

Beavers use their flat, scaly tail as a rudder when swimming. They also slap it down on the water as a warning signal to other beavers when danger threatens.

Ring-tailed lemurs (Lemur catta) use their striped tail for signaling, and for spreading around their scent to establish dominance over other lemurs.

Foxes wrap their bushy tail around their body to keep warm. They also use their tail to signal to others in their family group.

Rats have a long, hairless, and scaly tail that they use for balance.

MAMMAL RECORDS

SHORTEST GESTATION PERIOD is that of the brindled bandicoot (*Isoodon macrourus*). The young of this marsupial are born into the pouch after an average of just 12.5 days.

MOST TEATS are found on the common tenrec (*Tenrec ecaudatus*), which has 29.

DEEPEST DIVER is the sperm whale (*Physeter macrocephalus*), which can dive to depths of 3,900ft (1,200m) or more.

LONGEST LIFE-SPANS are those of the Asian elephant (*Elephas maximus*), at up to 90 years, and humans (*Homo sapiens*), at up to 120 years.

LARGEST ELEPHANT TUSK was 11.3ft (3.45m) long, and weighed 258lb (117kg).

LARGEST PRIMATE is the gorilla (*Gorilla gorilla*), which weighs up to 485lb (220kg).

MAMMAL FACT

• The vampire bat (*Desmodus rotundus*) is the only mammal that lives on nothing but blood. In the 10 minutes or so it spends feeding on its victim, it can drink more than its own body weight in blood. The bat becomes so heavy that it is unable to fly for a while afterward.

MAMMAL MOVEMENT

Most mammals walk and run on all fours. Some species have developed other ways of moving more suited to their habitat.

FLYING
Bats are the only mammals that can fly, although some, such as flying squirrels, can glide for long distances when leaping between trees.

SWIMMING
Many mammals can swim. Some, for example whales and dolphins, spend their entire life in the water.

BRACHIATION
Apes and monkeys swing through trees using their long arms. This method of movement is called brachiation. Gibbons (*Hylobytes*) can cover more than 10ft (3m) in a single swing.

BOUNDING
Kangaroos bound along when they need to move quickly. Their tails help them to balance. Some small rodents, for example jerboas, also move around by bounding.

BURROWING
Some mammals, such as moles, spend all their time underground. Moles have broad front paws for burrowing, and strong hind legs for bracing themselves against tunnel walls.

FASTEST MAMMALS

Common name	Scientific name	Maximum speed	
		km/h	mph
Cheetah	*Acinonyx jubatus*	105	65
Pronghorn antelope	*Antilocapra americana*	86	53
Mongolian gazelle	*Procapra gutturosa*	80	50
Springbok	*Antidorcas marsupialis*	80	50
Grant's gazelle	*Gazella granti*	76	47
Thomson's gazelle	*Gazella thomsoni*	76	47
European hare	*Lepus capensis*	72	45
Horse	*Equus*	70	43

FELINE PECKISH

A man-eating tiger (*Panthera tigris*) in Champawat district, India, was reputed to have killed 436 people. It was shot in 1907.

DOMESTIC MAMMALS

DOMESTIC MAMMALS are mammals that are kept and bred by humans. They include sheep, cattle, dogs, and cats. Many domestic mammals have been selectively bred over hundreds of years: today some breeds look and behave very differently from their wild counterparts.

DOMESTIC MAMMAL RECORDS

LARGEST DOG BREED
is the St. Bernard, which can weigh up to 170lb (77kg).

SMALLEST DOG BREED
is the chihuahua, which weighs as little as 1lb (0.45kg).

COUNTRY WITH THE MOST SHEEP
is Australia, which has about 167,781,000 individuals.

COUNTRY WITH THE MOST CATTLE
is India, which has about 197,300,000.

COUNTRY WITH THE MOST CAMELS
is Somalia, which has about 6,855,000 individuals.

SMALLEST CAT BREED
is the Singapura, which weighs as little as 4lb (1.81kg).

Chihuahua *St. Bernard*

Singapura

Ragdoll

LARGEST CAT BREEDS
include the ragdoll: males can weigh up to 20lb (9.07kg).

TYPES OF DOMESTIC MAMMAL

Domestic mammal	Uses	Number of breeds (approx)
Sheep (*Ovis aries*)	Meat, wool	300
Llama (*Llama glama*)	Pack animal, meat, wool, hides, dried dung for fuel, tallow for candles	2
Goat (*Capra*)	Milk, meat, cheese, hair, leather	300
Pig	Meat, leather	180
Cattle	Meat, milk and dairy products, leather, transportation	280
Cat (*Felis catus*)	Pets, pest control	110
Dog (*Canis familiaris*)	Pets, working dogs, sports dogs	186
Buffalo	Milk, butter, transportation	32
Bactrian camel (*Camelus bactrianus*)	Transportation, wool, milk, hides, meat, dried dung for fuel (as for Bactrian camel)	3
Arabian camel (*Camelus dromedarius*)		4
Horse, donkey, mule (*Equus*)	Sport and leisure, transportation, meat	100 (horse)

EVOLUTION OF THE DOMESTIC DOG

Dogs were the first mammals to be domesticated. They were tamed by humans about 12,000 years ago. Every breed of dog is descended from the wolf (*Canis lupus*). This illustration shows the possible wolf ancestors of various dog breeds.

Gun dogs
Spaniels
Guard dogs
Hounds
Greyhounds
Herding dogs
Feral dogs
Terriers
Indian wolf
European wolf
Canis lupus
Chinese wolf
Oriental spaniels
European toy dogs
North American wolf
Oriental toy dogs
European spitz dogs
Oriental spitz dogs
Eskimo spitz dogs

CAT FACTS

• Cats were sacred to the ancient Egyptians. Many dead cats were mummified, and the Egyptians shaved off their eyebrows to mourn the loss of a cat.

• In 1951, a cat named Sugar traveled 1,500 miles (2,414km) to Oklahoma to rejoin the Woods family who had left him behind in California.

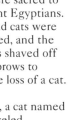

PIG FACTS

• Pigs are the most common provider of meat in China.

• In parts of Melanesia (see p.355), pigs are treated as members of the family.

• Pigs are often thought of as dirty animals, but in fact they keep themselves cleaner than most other domestic animals.

• Many Oceanic (see p.352–53) peoples measure their wealth in terms of the number of pigs they own.

HORSES FOR COURSES

Every Thoroughbred racehorse is said to have descended from three desert stallions: the Darley Arabian, the Godolphin Barb, and the Byerly Turk. These stallions were taken to England between 1689 and 1724.

SHEEP FACTS

• The finest sheep's wool comes from the merino sheep.

• Astrakhan fur comes from the karakul sheep of central Asia.

• Parchment, an early type of writing paper, was made from untanned sheep hide.

MULE FACTS

• Mules are produced by crossing a donkey (*Equus asinus*) with a female horse. Mules are surer-footed and more intelligent than horses, but cannot reproduce.

• At one time there were many different types of mules, including draft mules, farm mules, sugar mules, cotton mules, and mining mules.

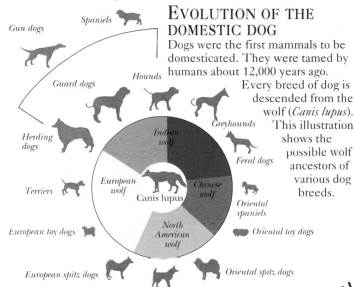

Mule: a cross between a donkey and a mare (female horse)

CATTLE FACTS

• There are about 1.21 billion cattle worldwide: more than the human population of China.

• Cattle are descended from the auroch, which once roamed across Asia and Europe. The last auroch died in 1627.

• Kenyan Masai warriors live almost entirely on blood and milk from their cattle.

ANIMAL SENSES AND BEHAVIOR

ANIMALS HAVE EVOLVED senses and patterns of behavior that ensure the survival of their species. Many animals have senses that are more highly developed than a human's.

COURTSHIP BEHAVIOR

Female animals select the best available mate in order to produce strong and healthy offspring. To attract a female, male animals have evolved a fascinating range of courtship behavior, including strutting, singing, and presenting gifts to the female.

To court a female, the common peafowl, or peacock (Pavo cristatus), fans out and shakes his colorful tail.

ANIMAL SENSES

Many animals have excellent sight and hearing. Some have "sixth" senses that can detect magnetism, electricity, and even infrared.

An eagle's eyes see a magnified picture at the center of its field of vision.

Many animals, e.g. foxes, can hear higher frequency sounds than humans.

Many mammals, e.g. dogs, have a highly developed sense of smell.

Sensitive whiskers help animals such as cats to find their way in the dark.

An invertebrate's antennae touch, taste, and smell its surroundings.

Spiders and scorpions have sensitive hairs that can detect the slightest air movements.

Fish have a lateral line: a row of sensitive pits that detect movements in the water.

Bats navigate by echolocation: they emit squeaks, and judge distances by how long the squeaks take to bounce back.

Sharks have sensors around their head that pick up electrical fields produced by prey.

Some migratory animals may navigate by sensing the Earth's magnetic field.

Pit vipers "see" an infra-red picture of their prey by detecting heat radiation given off by its body.

ATTACK AND DEFENSE BEHAVIOR

Animals use a wide variety of attack and defense tactics. Attack strategies include stalking and pouncing; defensive tactics include stinging and oozing poison.

The caracal (Lynx caracal) leaps into the air to catch birds.

Bombardier beetles (Brachinus) spray their attackers with hot, unpleasant chemicals.

SENSES AND BEHAVIOR FACTS

• Net-casting spiders' eyes are 19 times more sensitive than a human's.

• The blue whale's (Balaenoptera musculus) call is the loudest noise made by any animal. It can travel up to 1,000 miles (1,600km).

FAKE SNAKE

Some animals mimic others to defend themselves. This Costa Rican moth caterpillar fools predators into thinking it is a poisonous snake.

TERRITORIAL BEHAVIOR

Animals may fiercely defend their territory so that others cannot steal their food or harm their young. To let other animals know where their territorial boundaries lie, animals call, mark trees and bushes with scent, or leave piles of droppings.

A cheetah (Acinonyx jubatus) marking its territory.

• The malleefowl's (Leipoa ocellata) beak acts as a thermometer. The bird incubates its eggs in a heap of rotting vegetation, checking the temperature with its beak.

• A hibernating mammal's body can be up to 90°F (32°C) below its normal temperature.

SOCIAL BEHAVIOR

Animals that live in communities, such as chimpanzees (Pan troglodytes) and lions (Panthera leo), have a social hierarchy ("pecking order"). This is reinforced in various ways.

Herds of elephants are dominated by an elderly female, the matriarch. She keeps order and decides where the herd will go.

Wolves use facial expressions to establish hierarchy, and cower in front of dominant members of the pack.

Matriarch

Herd is made up of adult females and young.

Young male

Six-year-old female

SURVIVING HEAT AND COLD

HIBERNATION

Many animals in cold climates hibernate to survive the harsh conditions and lack of food that winter brings. Their body temperature drops, their heartbeat slows down, and they go into a deep sleep, surviving on food reserves stored in the body.

ESTIVATION

Some animals estivate to survive hot and dry periods, becoming sluggish or dormant until favorable conditions return. Many desert animals estivate.

Dormice in cold countries hibernate for up to nine months of the year.

These snails are collecting together on grass stems, ready to estivate.

USING TOOLS

Some animals use tools to obtain food, e.g. chimpanzees poke twigs into termite mounds, and Egyptian vultures (Neophron percnopterus) throw stones at eggs to break them.

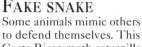

Sea otters (Enhydra lutris) smash sea urchins and shellfish on a stone which they place on their stomach.

MIGRATION AND HOMES

WHEN WINTER approaches, many animals migrate to warmer climates. Others rely on their homes to protect them from harsh conditions. Some animals live alone, while others live in pairs or in large, complex communities.

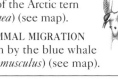

MIGRATION

Many animals migrate to avoid the cold weather and lack of food that winter brings. Some species migrate a few miles from high ground to low; others travel vast distances across continents and oceans.

NAVIGATION

It is still a mystery how some migrating animals find their way. Most species probably use a combination of methods, including navigation by the Sun and stars, and using an inherited mental map.

Sight
Many birds can recognize physical features such as coastlines, mountain ranges, and deserts.

Using Earth's magnetic field
Some animals, e.g. monarch butterflies (*Danaus plexippus*), may navigate using a magnetic sense.

Smell
Atlantic salmon (*Salmo salar*) return to the river in which they hatched. They navigate by smell.

ANIMAL HOMES

Some animals do not build homes: they simply find a tree hole, perch on a branch, or hide under a stone for protection. Others construct intricate nests or burrows.

KEY

← Blue whale 12,500 miles (20,000km)
← Arctic tern 24,855 miles (40,000km)
← Caribou 1,400 miles (2,250 km)
← Monarch butterfly 3,500 miles (5,600km)
← Green turtle over 1,240 miles (2,000km)
← Atlantic salmon over 1,240 miles (2,000km)

MIGRATION RECORDS

FARTHEST BIRD MIGRATION and the longest migration of any animal, is that of the Arctic tern (*Sterna paradisaea*) (see map).

FARTHEST MAMMAL MIGRATION is undertaken by the blue whale (*Balaenoptera musculus*) (see map).

LOADS OF LEMMINGS

Norway lemmings (*Lemmus lemmus*) migrate when population explosions occur. Their huge numbers stop traffic and trains. When they reach the coast, some swim out to sea and drown, hence the tales of lemming "mass suicides."

FARTHEST INSECT MIGRATION is undertaken by the painted lady butterfly (*Vanessa cardui*), which flies up to 5,280 miles (8,500km) a year. (This is not marked on the map, since it does not follow a set route).

ANIMAL RELATIONSHIPS

SOLITARY ANIMALS
The giant panda (*Ailuropoda melanoleuca*) spends most of its life alone, only meeting up for mating.

PAIRS AND FAMILIES
Golden eagles (*Aquila chrysaetos*) spend their life with the same mate, raising a family each year.

LARGE GROUPS
Meerkats (*Suricata suricatta*), a type of mongoose, live in large colonies with a complex social structure.

MUTUALISM
Some different species live together for mutual benefit: oxpeckers are picking ticks off this warthog.

COMMENSALISM
Two species may live together but only one benefits: this crab carries stinging anemones for protection.

PARASITISM
Parasites live in or on another species, causing it harm: this flea is sucking its host's blood.

ANIMAL HOME NAMES

Animal	Description of home	Name of home
Squirrel	Nest of twigs	Drey
Badger	Underground chambers	Sett
Eagle	Nest of twigs	Eyrie
Rabbit	Burrow	Warren
River otter	Burrow in river bank	Holt

TYPES OF ANIMAL HOME

Nests
Many animals, including birds, mice, and ants, build nests. They use various materials such as twigs, mud, leaves, and hair.

Burrows
A burrow is a hole or tunnel dug by one or more animals. It may be a simple hole in the ground, or a complex network of tunnels and chambers, such as a rabbit warren.

Mounds
Termite colonies build complex mounds from mud. These structures have galleries, turrets, and towers, and even built-in air conditioning.

Termite mound

Rabbit warren

Pots
Potter wasps build tiny pots of mud to lay their eggs in. They build one pot for each egg.

Potter wasp's pot

Tree holes and caves
Many animals take advantage of ready-made homes, e.g. owls use tree holes, and bears often use caves.

Reed-warbler's nest

ANIMAL COLONY FACT
• Australia's Great Barrier Reef is the largest structure in the world made by living things. It is more than 1,429 miles (2,300km) long, and has taken about 800 million years to build.

BEAVER DAM
Beavers dam a river, then construct their lodge on the shore, or on an island in the middle of the lake.

Upstream side of the dam is plastered with mud to make it watertight. Winter food store. The only way into the lodge is through a tunnel that opens under water. Lodge is a dome of branches, reeds and mud. The living chamber is inside.

FOOD CHAINS AND WEBS

A FOOD CHAIN shows how energy, in the form of food, passes from one living thing to another. At each chain's base is a primary producer – an organism that can make its own food. Most primary producers are plants.

ENERGY PYRAMID

About 90% of the energy a living thing takes in as food is used to make its body work. Only the remaining 10% is built into the body itself, and is therefore passed on to the next organism along the food chain. This means there is very little energy left toward the top of the food chain.

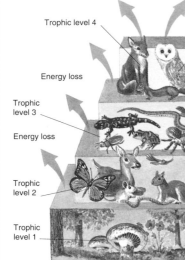

Trophic level 4

Energy loss

Trophic level 3

Energy loss

Trophic level 2

Trophic level 1

Only about 10% of energy is passed on to the next trophic level.

The amount of energy received by each successive link in the food chain decreases toward the top.

The various levels of an energy pyramid are called trophic levels.

Primary producers

FOOD CHAIN

Plant plankton is the primary producer at the bottom of this chain. When it is eaten, the plankton's energy is passed on to the next organism in the chain.

FOOD WEB

This illustration shows how the above food chain links with others to form the food web of a North American lake community. The arrows link each living thing to the organism that eats it, beginning with plankton at the bottom, and ending with carnivores (meat-eaters) at the top.

Plant plankton (microscopic water plants) use sunlight to produce energy.

Animal plankton eat plant plankton.

Insect larvae eat animal plankton.

Bears eat fish.

Fish eat insect larvae.

Bears

Otters

Beavers

Frogs

Beetles

Birds

Water plants

Insect larvae

Animal plankton

Plant plankton

Fish

Freshwater mollusks

Freshwater shrimps

POISONS IN THE FOOD CHAIN

Poisons, such as pesticides, are taken in by organisms at the lower end of a food chain. These poisons pass up the chain, and may eventually build into high concentrations in animals at the top of the chain. The process of poison building up in a food chain is called bioaccumulation.

Pesticides are sprayed on to crops to kill insect pests.

Small amounts of poison on each seed build up into larger amounts inside the bodies of seed-eating birds.

A bird of prey eats several seed-eating birds. Poison from all these birds collects in the bird of prey's body.

PRIMARY PRODUCTIVITY

The longest food chains occur where the amount of organic matter made by primary producers (primary productivity) is high. This table shows the primary productivity of various habitats.

Habitat	Primary productivity (grams of dry plant material per sq meter per year)
Coral reef	2,500
Tropical rainforest	2,200
Temperate forest	1,250
Savanna	900
Cultivated land	650
Open sea	125
Semidesert	90

FOOD CHAIN FACTS

• The majority of food chains have three or four links.

• The only food chains that do not obtain energy from sunlight are those at deep sea vents, which derive energy from volcanic activity (see p.48).

TOXIC WHALES

Over the last 40 years, pollutants in Canada's St. Lawrence River have built up in the food chain, at the top of which is the beluga whale (*Delphinapterus leucas*). Chemicals are now so concentrated in these whales that, when they die, they are disposed of as toxic waste.

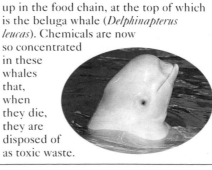

FOOD CHAIN RECORDS

SHORTEST FOOD CHAINS consist of only two organisms, for example the giant panda (*Ailuropoda melanoleuca*) and its major food source, bamboo.

Giant panda eating bamboo

LONGEST FOOD CHAINS often involve both land and water organisms, e.g. diatom (microscopic plant) to *Daphnia* (water flea), to newly hatched fish, to dragonfly larva, to adult fish, to heron.

ENDANGERED SPECIES

AN ENDANGERED SPECIES is a species that may become extinct in the near future. Throughout evolutionary history, millions of species have died out due to natural processes. Over the past 300 years, however, humans have speeded up the extinction rate more than 1,000 times: it is now estimated that one species dies out every 15 minutes.

THREATS TO WILDLIFE

Humans are responsible for almost all recent animal and plant extinctions. Threats to wildlife are caused by various human activities.

As the human population expands, more and more land is needed for planting crops, and for building settlements and roads. Natural vegetation and wildlife are destroyed.

Many animals are killed for their skins, bones, or horns. The jaguar (Panthera onca) and ocelot (Felis pardalis) are among the many species of cat that have become endangered through poaching for skins.

Pollution from industry and farming can poison wildlife. Chemical spills and acid rain (see p.65) can kill river life, and fertilizers and pesticides used in farming can upset natural systems and cycles.

When non-native animals are introduced to a country, they may have a disastrous impact on native wildlife, preying on animals and competing for food. The cane toad (Bufo marinus), introduced into Australia, has now overrun native species in some areas.

THREATENED ANIMALS

This table shows the number of threatened species in each animal group. Endangered species are monitored by the International Union for the Conservation of Nature, and recorded in their Red Data Book.

Animal group	Species at risk
Mammals	500
Birds	880
Reptiles	170
Amphibians	60
Fish	270
Insects	875
Other invertebrates	510

SAVING ENDANGERED SPECIES

Various measures are being used around the world in an effort to save endangered species from extinction.

Antipoaching squads have been set up to protect animals such as rhinoceroses, elephants, and gorillas. Some countries, including Kenya, shoot poachers on sight.

The Arabian oryx (Oryx leucoryx) was hunted to extinction in the wild. After a captive breeding program in zoos, it was returned to its natural habitat.

DECLINING TIGER HABITAT

Tiger numbers have dropped dramatically in the last 100 years because of the destruction of their habitat and poaching. Tiger reserves have been established, but poaching is still a serious problem. This map shows the declining range of the tiger, and gives the estimated numbers of tigers left today.

RATES OF EXTINCTION

A species is considered to be extinct if it has not been found in the wild for 50 years. This graph illustrates the dramatic increase in the rate of extinction over the past 300 years.

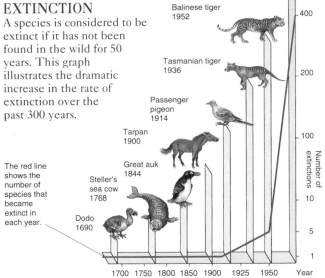

The red line shows the number of species that became extinct in each year.

Balinese tiger 1952
Tasmanian tiger 1936
Passenger pigeon 1914
Tarpan 1900
Great auk 1844
Steller's sea cow 1768
Dodo 1690

Number of extinctions

400
200
100
10
5
1

1700 1750 1800 1850 1900 1925 1950 Year

MOST ENDANGERED ANIMALS

This table lists some of the rarest animal species in the world. Some endangered species are now extinct in the wild but are being bred in captivity. They will eventually be released into the wild if conditions are safe.

Common name	Scientific name	Distribution
Queen Alexandra's birdwing butterfly	Ornithoptera alexandrae	Papua New Guinea
Devil's Hole pupfish	Cyprinodon diabolis	Nevada, US
Kemp's Ridley sea turtle	Lepidochelys kempii	Mexico
Spix's macaw	Cyanopsitta spixii	Brazil
Seychelles magpie robin	Copsychus sechellarum	Fregate Island, Seychelles
California condor	Gymnogyps californianus	California, US
Black-footed ferret	Mustela nigripes	North America
Giant panda	Ailuropoda melanoleuca	China
Javan rhinoceros	Rhinoceros sondaicus	Southeast Asia
Woolly spider monkey	Brachyteles arachnoides	Brazil
Mediterranean monk seal	Monachus monachus	Mediterranean coasts
Yangtze River dolphin	Lipotes vexillifer	Yangtze River, China

KEY

Previous tiger range

Current, fragmented tiger range

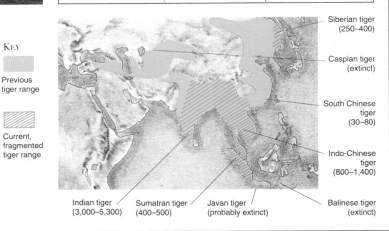

Siberian tiger (250–400)
Caspian tiger (extinct)
South Chinese tiger (30–80)
Indo-Chinese tiger (800–1,400)
Balinese tiger (extinct)
Indian tiger (3,000–5,300)
Sumatran tiger (400–500)
Javan tiger (probably extinct)

ANIMAL RECORDS AND COMPARISONS

THERE IS A REMARKABLE DIVERSITY within the animal kingdom, from wasps no bigger than a period to crabs that grow larger than people, and from tiny, deadly cone shells to the blue whale – the gentle giant of the oceans.

LARGEST WINGSPANS

BIRD
The wandering albatross (*Diomedea exulans*) has a wingspan measuring about 12ft (3.6m) across.

BAT
Flying foxes of the *Pteropus* genus are the largest bats in the world, with wingspans up to 6.6ft (2m) across.

Wandering albatross

Flying fox (Pteropus)

LARGEST ANIMALS

Largest mollusk
Giant Atlantic squid (*Archteuthis*) 66ft (20m) long North Atlantic Ocean

Largest insect
Goliath beetle (*Goliathus*) 3.9oz (110g) Equatorial Africa

Largest arachnid
Leblondis' goliath bird-eating spider (*Theraphosa leblondi*); leg span 11in (28cm); Brazil, Venezuela, Guyana, French Guiana

Largest crustacean
Japanese spider crab (*Macrocheira kaempferi*) Leg span nearly 13ft (4m) Japan

Largest amphibian
Japanese giant salamander (*Andrias japonicus*) 5ft (1.5m) long Japan

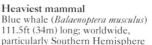

Heaviest reptile
Saltwater crocodile (*Crocodylus porosus*); 20ft (6m) long Southeast Asia, Indonesia, Philippines, New Guinea, Australia

Largest fish
Whale shark (*Rhincodon typus*) 50ft (15m) long; Atlantic, Pacific, and Indian Oceans

Largest bird
Ostrich (*Struthio camelus*) 8.9ft (2.7m) tall Mainly eastern and southern Africa

Heaviest mammal
Blue whale (*Balaenoptera musculus*) 111.5ft (34m) long; worldwide, particularly Southern Hemisphere

LOUDEST ANIMALS

MARINE ANIMAL
The blue whale's (*Balaenoptera musculus*) call is the loudest noise made by any animal. It registers up to 188 decibels, and can be heard by other whales up to 1,000 miles (1,600km) away.

LAND ANIMAL
The howler monkey (*Alouatta*) can be heard up to 2 miles (3km) away.

Howler monkey

INSECT
Cicadas can be heard up to 1,312ft (400m) away.

Cicada

SMALLEST ANIMALS

Smallest insect
Fairyfly wasps 0.2mm long Worldwide

Smallest amphibian
Psyllophryne didactyla; 0.41in (10.4mm) long Brazil

Smallest fish
Dwarf goby (*Pandaka pygmaea*) 0.3in (7.6mm) long Philippines

Smallest reptile
British Virgin Island gecko (*Sphaerodactylus parthenopion*) 0.7in (18mm) long Virgin Islands

Smallest bird
Bee hummingbird (*Mellisuga helenae*) 2.2in (5.7cm) long Cuba

Smallest mammal
Kitti's hog-nosed bat (*Craseonycteris thonglongyai*) 1.3in (3.3cm) long Thailand

ANIMAL REPRODUCTION FACTS

• After spending a year or more as a nymph, the adult mayfly (*Ephemera danica*) has only a day in which to mate and lay eggs before it dies.

• A tapeworm may release a million eggs a day for several years. Hardly any eggs survive.

• Many fish lay millions of eggs at a time, since so few young survive. The ocean sunfish (*Mola mola*) lays about 30 million eggs.

ANIMAL LIFESPANS

Animals live from a few days to more than 200 years. The lifespans shown here are approximate maximum ages.

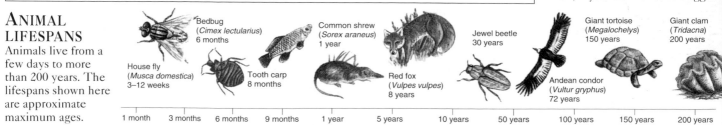

Bedbug (*Cimex lectularius*) 6 months

House fly (*Musca domestica*) 3–12 weeks

Tooth carp 8 months

Common shrew (*Sorex araneus*) 1 year

Red fox (*Vulpes vulpes*) 8 years

Jewel beetle 30 years

Andean condor (*Vultur gryphus*) 72 years

Giant tortoise (*Megalochelys*) 150 years

Giant clam (*Tridacna*) 200 years

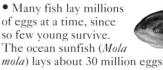

| 1 month | 3 months | 6 months | 9 months | 1 year | 5 years | 10 years | 50 years | 100 years | 150 years | 200 years |

POISONOUS ANIMALS

MOST POISONOUS MOLLUSKS
A sting from a blue-ringed octopus (*Hapalochlaena*) can kill a human. Three species of cone shell (*Conus*) (right) also have a deadly sting.

MOST POISONOUS JELLYFISH
A human stung more than six times by a chironex (*Chironex fleckeri*) can die within two to three minutes. This jellyfish occurs in huge swarms off the northern coast of Australia.

MOST POISONOUS FISH
When stepped on, the stonefish (*Synanceja*), which lurks in shallow waters in the Pacific and Indian Oceans, injects venom through spines in its dorsal fin, causing intense pain and sometimes death.

MOST POISONOUS SPIDER
The Brazilian wandering spider (*Phoneutria*), which has a leg span of 4in (10cm), has the most poisonous of all spider bites. This spider has difficulty injecting venom into humans, so it causes few deaths.

MOST POISONOUS FROG
The golden yellow poison dart frog (*Phyllobates terribilis*), which lives in Colombia, South America, oozes the strongest animal poison in the world from its skin. Toxin from a single frog could kill nearly 1,500 people.

MOST POISONOUS SNAKES
Sea snakes of the genus *Hydrophis* have extremely poisonous venom. The toxin of *Hydrophis belcheri*, which lives in the Timor Sea off northwestern Australia, is about 100 times as strong as that of the taipan (see below).

MOST POISONOUS MAMMAL
The duck-billed platypus (*Ornithorhynchus anatinus*) injects venom through a spur on one of its hind legs. Its sting causes intense pain in humans. The platypus is one of only two species of poisonous mammal (see p.103).

ONLY POISONOUS BIRD
The only bird known to be poisonous is the hooded pitohui (*Pitohui dichrous*), from New Guinea. This brightly colored bird secretes a poison similar to that produced by poison dart frogs, although far less toxic.

TERRIBLE TAIPAN
The taipan (*Oxyuranus*) of northeastern Australia and New Guinea is one of the most poisonous snakes in the world. The venom from just one of these snakes could kill 125,000 mice.

LARGEST INSECT HOMES
Mounds built by termites can reach up to 39ft (12m) tall: more than six times the height of an adult human.

ANIMALS OF THE DEEP

The deepest-diving bird is the emperor penguin (*Aptenodytes forsteri*), which reaches depths of up to 870ft (265m).

The deepest-diving turtle is the leatherback turtle (*Dermochelys coriacea*), which dives to 3,937ft (1,200m).

The deepest-diving mammal is the sperm whale (*Physeter macrocephalus*), which dives down to 3,937ft (1,200m).

Rat-tails are some of the deepest-living fish in the oceans.

TALLEST ANIMALS

MAMMAL
The giraffe (*Giraffa camelopardalis*) measures up to 19.4ft (5.9m) tall.

BIRDS
The tallest bird is the ostrich. The tallest flying birds are cranes: some species, e.g. the Japanese crane (*Grus japonensis*) (above), stand nearly 6.6ft (2m) high.

HEAVIEST ANIMALS

Animal	Scientific name	Weight kg	lb
Blue whale	*Balaenoptera musculus*	190,000	418,878
African elephant	*Loxodonta africanus*	5,000	11,023
Asian elephant	*Elephas maximas*	4,000	8,818
White rhinoceros	*Ceratotherium simum*	2,200	4,850
Hippopotamus	*Hippopotamus amphibius*	2,000	4,409
Giraffe	*Giraffa camelopardalis*	1,200	2,646
Saltwater crocodile	*Crocodylus porosus*	1,100	2,425
Asian gaur	*Bos frontalis*	900	1,984
American bison	*Bison bison*	800	1,764
Kodiak bear	*Ursus arctos middendorffi*	800	1,764
Yak	*Bos grunniens*	800	1,764

ANIMAL SPEEDS

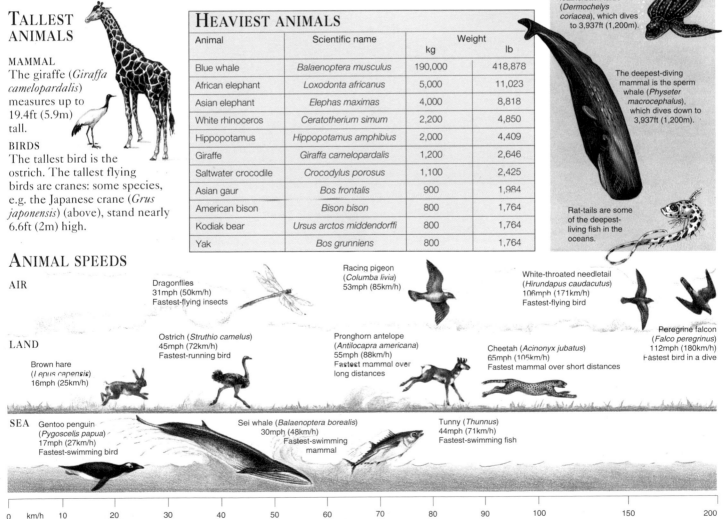

AIR

Dragonflies 31mph (50km/h) Fastest-flying insects

Racing pigeon (*Columba livia*) 53mph (85km/h)

White-throated needletail (*Hirundapus caudacutus*) 106mph (171km/h) Fastest-flying bird

Peregrine falcon (*Falco peregrinus*) 112mph (180km/h) Fastest bird in a dive

LAND

Brown hare (*Lepus capensis*) 16mph (25km/h)

Ostrich (*Struthio camelus*) 45mph (72km/h) Fastest-running bird

Pronghorn antelope (*Antilocapra americana*) 55mph (88km/h) Fastest mammal over long distances

Cheetah (*Acinonyx jubatus*) 65mph (105km/h) Fastest mammal over short distances

SEA

Gentoo penguin (*Pygoscelis papua*) 17mph (27km/h) Fastest-swimming bird

Sei whale (*Balaenoptera borealis*) 30mph (48km/h) Fastest-swimming mammal

Tunny (*Thunnus*) 44mph (71km/h) Fastest-swimming fish

| 0 | km/h | 10 | 20 | 30 | 40 | 50 | 60 | 70 | 80 | 90 | 100 | 150 | 200 |

LEAPS AND BOUNDS

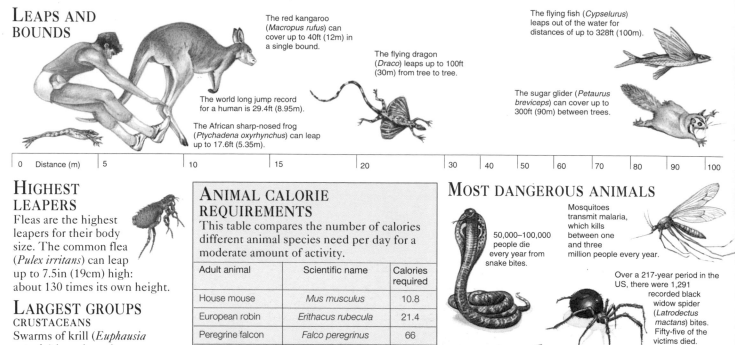

The red kangaroo (*Macropus rufus*) can cover up to 40ft (12m) in a single bound.

The flying dragon (*Draco*) leaps up to 100ft (30m) from tree to tree.

The flying fish (*Cypselurus*) leaps out of the water for distances of up to 328ft (100m).

The world long jump record for a human is 29.4ft (8.95m).

The sugar glider (*Petaurus breviceps*) can cover up to 300ft (90m) between trees.

The African sharp-nosed frog (*Ptychadena oxyrhynchus*) can leap up to 17.6ft (5.35m).

| 0 | Distance (m) | 5 | 10 | 15 | 20 | 30 | 40 | 50 | 60 | 70 | 80 | 90 | 100 |

HIGHEST LEAPERS

Fleas are the highest leapers for their body size. The common flea (*Pulex irritans*) can leap up to 7.5in (19cm) high: about 130 times its own height.

LARGEST GROUPS

CRUSTACEANS

Swarms of krill (*Euphausia superba*) have been known to cover areas of ocean measuring up to 170sq miles (440sq km). These large swarms may contain up to 80 billion individuals: about 16 times the world's human population.

BIRDS

The red-billed quelea (*Quelea quelea*) gathers in roosts of up to 10 million birds.

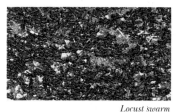

Locust swarm

INSECTS

Locusts gather in enormous numbers. In 1873, a swarm of Rocky Mountain locusts estimated to contain 10 trillion insects crossed the US.

BEEFY BEETLE

One of the strongest insects is the Atlas beetle (*Chalcosoma atlas*). It can lift more than 800 times its own body weight – equivalent to a man lifting a *Leopard 2* tank.

ANIMAL CALORIE REQUIREMENTS

This table compares the number of calories different animal species need per day for a moderate amount of activity.

Adult animal	Scientific name	Calories required
House mouse	*Mus musculus*	10.8
European robin	*Erithacus rubecula*	21.4
Peregrine falcon	*Falco peregrinus*	66
Gray squirrel	*Sciurus carolinensis*	92
Fennec fox	*Vulpes zerda*	254
Domestic cat	*Felis catus*	370
Baboon	*Papio hamadryas*	1,610
Giant anteater	*Myrmecophaga tridactyla*	1,760
Female human	*Homo sapiens*	2,400
Male human	*Homo sapiens*	3,265
Llama	*Lama glama*	3,840
Tiger	*Panthera tigris*	8,000
Gorilla	*Gorilla gorilla*	8,100
American black bear	*Ursus americanus*	9,180
Giraffe	*Giraffa camelopardalis*	36,370
Walrus	*Odobenus rosmarus*	38,060
Male Asian elephant	*Elephas maximus*	61,160

MOST DANGEROUS ANIMALS

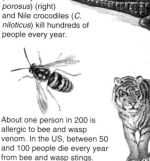

50,000–100,000 people die every year from snake bites.

Mosquitoes transmit malaria, which kills between one and three million people every year.

Over a 217-year period in the US, there were 1,291 recorded black widow spider (*Latrodectus mactans*) bites. Fifty-five of the victims died.

Sharks attack about 100 people per year: about 25 attacks result in death.

Saltwater crocodiles (*Crocodylus porosus*) (right) and Nile crocodiles (*C. niloticus*) kill hundreds of people every year.

In the Sunderbans region of India, 521 people were killed by tigers between 1975 and mid-1989.

About one person in 200 is allergic to bee and wasp venom. In the US, between 50 and 100 people die every year from bee and wasp stings.

GESTATION PERIODS

The gestation period is the length of time an animal takes to develop inside its mother before it is born.

Virginia opossum (Didelphis virginiana) *12 days; 8–14 young*

Golden hamster (Mesocricetus auratus) *15 days; 6–8 young*

House mouse (Mus musculus) *20 days; 6–8 young*

Red kangaroo (Macropus rufus) *33 days 1 young*

Lion (Panthera leo) *105–108 days 3–4 young*

Goat (Capra) *150 days 1–2 young*

Orangutan (Pongo pygmaeus) *250 days 1 young*

Human (Homo sapiens) *267 days; 1 young*

Cow *278 days; 1 young*

Dolphin *360 days 1 young*

Asian elephant (Elephas maximus) *660 days; 1 young*

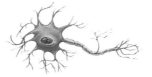

HUMAN BODY

Stunning detailed illustrations, supported by a wealth of facts and figures, show the amazing workings of the human body. Other topics include evolution, reproduction and growth, the history of medicine, traditional medicine, nutrition, and first aid.

Humankind • Human Body • The Brain • Nervous System • Eyes • Ears
Skin, Hair, and Nails • Smell, Taste, and Throat • Skeleton and Teeth • Muscles
Heart • Circulation and Blood • Respiratory System • Digestion • Urinary System
Endocrine System • Reproduction and Growth • Medicine • Nutrition
Traditional Medicine • First Aid

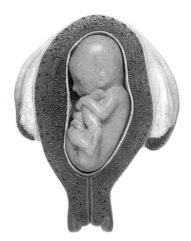

HUMANKIND

SCIENTISTS BELIEVE the first living thing on Earth was a single-celled organism that developed almost four billion years ago. From that organism, plant and animal life evolved. Finally, just five million years ago, hominids appeared.

**Aegyptopithecus
30 million years ago**
Ancestor of monkeys, apes, and humans

HUMAN FAMILY TREE

**Sivapithecus
7–13 million years ago**
Early ancestor of the orangutan

Orangutan
Differences in skull shape put them in a separate family from humans and gorillas.

**Australopithecus
1.5–5 million years ago**
Earliest ape people to walk upright

Chimpanzee/gorilla
Skull shape links them to human family, but they do not walk upright and brain is smaller.

**Homo habilis
1.5–2 million years ago**
Made tools to assist with hunter-scavenger lifestyle.

**Homo sapiens sapiens
40,000 years ago**
Modern humans were the first artists. Emerged in Africa and spread to all continents by 11,000 years ago.

**Homo erectus
0.5–1.5 million years ago**
Used fire and dwellings to survive in cooler climates.

**Homo sapiens neanderthalensis
40,000–100,000 years ago**
Subspecies of modern humans with overhanging brow. First burial ceremonies

BRAIN POWER

Homo habilis had a larger brain than the first ape people, but it was only half the size of a modern human brain. As the brain grew in size, people developed greater powers of reasoning and survival.

Australopithecus

Homo habilis

Homo sapiens

HUMAN FOSSILS

The structure of human remains and where they are found tell us a great deal about the growth and development of the human race.

- **Lucy**
A three million-year-old *Australopithecus* skeleton, found in Ethiopia.
- **Homo habilis skull**
Fossils and tools found in same area in East Africa.
- **Beijing man**
Homo erectus skull found. Evidence of fire in area.
- **Neanderthals**
Fossils found in Europe.

SKELETON SHAPES

Gorilla foot

Human

The human skeleton is designed for upright walking. Human toes point forward, whereas a gorilla's big toe is at an angle for grasping. The *Homo sapiens* hip bone is shorter than a gorilla's for easy striding. The human head is more centrally balanced on the backbone than a gorilla's.

Gorilla

Human foot

EVOLUTION FACTS

- Early humans used wisdom teeth to eat roots and berries. Today, some people do not even develop them.

- Neanderthals had a slightly bigger brain than humans today. It may have signified a stronger body, not high intelligence.

THE ICEMAN

In 1991 the oldest complete *Homo sapiens* corpse was found in a glacier in the European Alps. His internal organs, skin, and even his eyes were intact.

The Iceman had been frozen for 5,300 years.

HUMAN FAMILY

As humans spread across the world, they gradually evolved different features, such as dark and light hair, that were suited, for example, to a particular climate.

East Indian

Native American

Australian Aboriginal

Caucasoid

Black African

Mongoloid

EVOLUTIONARY CLOCK

Dinosaurs 200 million years ago

Humans

Earth formed 4.6 billion years ago.

Apes

Reptiles

Land plants

Marine life 1.5 billion years ago

Bacteria 3.8 billion years ago

The clock starts running as the Earth is formed. It takes 20 minutes for the most basic life-form to appear. It is over 55 minutes before the dinosaurs evolve. Apes arrive at 40 seconds to the hour, and humans evolve just as the hour strikes.

If this clock face represents the time the Earth has existed, human life began only a few seconds ago. Our five-million-year history is short compared to other life-forms.

PILTDOWN HOAX

Remains found in Piltdown, England, were first thought to show a missing link between apes and humans. But in 1953, tests showed them to be the skull of a 14th-century man and the jaw of a 15th-century orangutan.

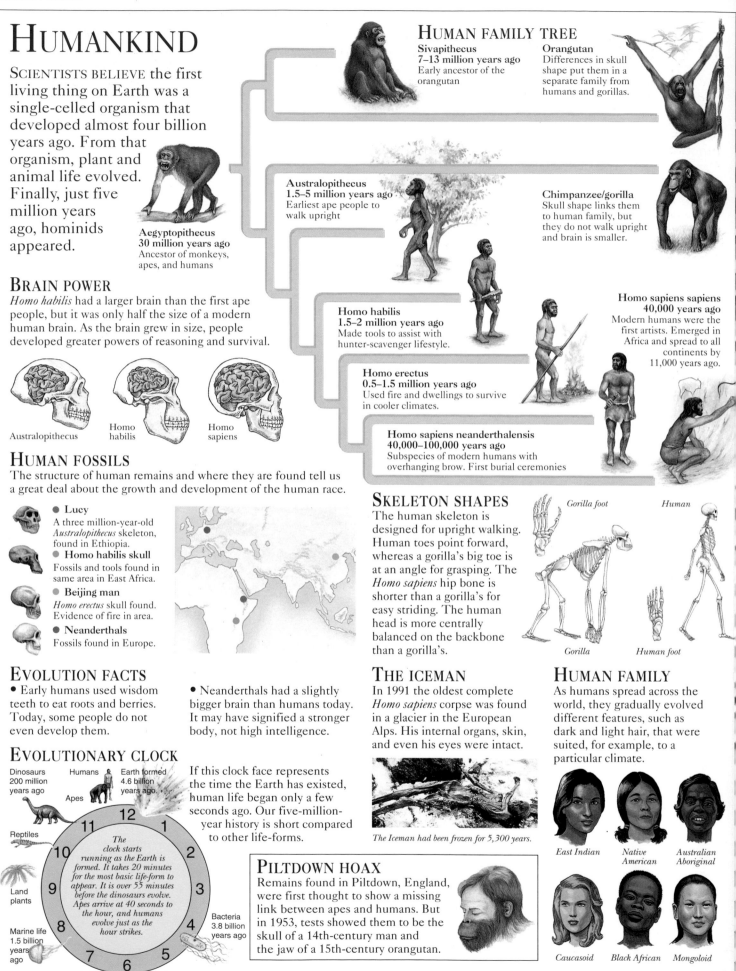

HUMAN BODY

EACH BODY SYSTEM is composed of organs made from different types of tissue. Tissue is made from cells all performing a similar function. There are roughly 50 billion cells in the body.

CELL GROWTH

As cells divide and multiply, children and young people grow. In later life, some cells still multiply, but this is to replace the millions of cells that die every second.

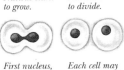

Nucleus starts to grow.

Nucleus starts to divide.

First nucleus, then cell divides in two.

Each cell may grow to size of parent cell.

THE BODY AT WORK

Each body system combines cells, tissue, and organs.

There are many millions of nerve cells in the human body.

Individual cells combine to make cell tissue, such as major nerves.

Cells, tissue, and nerves make up the brain and spinal cord: the major organs of the human nervous system.

INSIDE A CELL

Nearly all human cells are too small to see without a microscope: the average diameter is 0.02mm. Inside each there are organelles that control and run the cell.

Pores are dents in the cell membrane.

Ribosomes manufacture proteins.

Lysosomes store chemicals to break down nutrients for the cell to use.

Endoplasmic reticulum consists of channels to carry chemicals around the cell.

Nucleus controls the cell.

Membrane holds cell together and filters materials passing in and out.

Cytoplasm is mostly water and protein and makes up body of cell.

Mitochondria make energy to power the cell.

Golgi apparatus stores proteins for use outside cell.

Nucleus contains genetic material.

CELL DISCOVERY

In 1838, German botanist Matthias Schleiden recognized that plants are made up of cells. In 1839, German physiologist Theodor Schwann extended this theory to animal life. Schwann cells are so named because of his research on the nervous system.

Matthias Schleiden (1804–81)

Theodor Schwann (1810–82)

TYPES OF CELL

More than 200 cell types each perform specialized functions.

Duodenal cells use mucus to protect against stomach acid.

Secretory thyroid gland cells control the metabolism.

Sperm cells can live in the female tract for up to seven days.

Red blood cells carry oxygen and live for about 120 days.

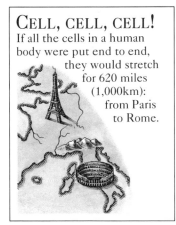

Brain cell: after 18 years we lose more than 1,000 a day.

Bone-maintaining cells develop from bone-forming cells.

CELL, CELL, CELL!

If all the cells in a human body were put end to end, they would stretch for 620 miles (1,000km): from Paris to Rome.

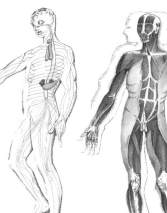

CELL FACTS

• Some gut cells have a life expectancy of only three days. A brain cell can last for life.

• An egg cell (ovum) is the largest human cell and can just be seen without a microscope.

• Red blood cells are the only cells without a nucleus.

• Cancer causes cells in many body systems to multiply uncontrollably, form tumors, and invade neighboring tissue.

• All humans develop from just two cells: an ovum and a sperm.

• Neurons, the message carriers of the nervous system, are the longest cells in the human body. Some are up to 4ft (1.2m) long.

BODY SYSTEMS

The major systems shown here work together to help the body function efficiently. Each system consists of organs that carry out a similar task.

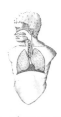

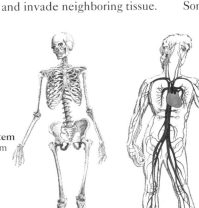

Respiratory system draws oxygen into the body and expels carbon dioxide.

Excretory system filters waste from the blood.

Digestive system processes food, absorbs nutrients, and expels waste.

Skeletal system is usually made up of 206 individual bones.

Circulatory system consists of the heart, blood, and blood vessels.

Muscular system has 650 muscles that exert pulling power on bones.

Nervous system carries messages to and from the brain. Endocrine system carries hormones.

Skin system consists of the skin, nails, and hair covering the body.

THE BRAIN

THE BRAIN IS THE major organ of the nervous system. It is the control center of the body, responsible for thought, memory, language, and emotion. The brain is protected by the skull, which encases it, and the cerebrospinal fluid, which cushions it.

SENSORY AREAS

Different parts of the brain carry out specialized functions. For example, the occipital lobe deals with vision, an area in the frontal lobe controls speech, and the temporal lobe receives and interprets information from the ears.

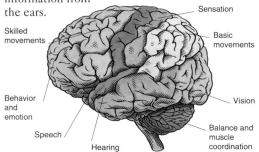

Skilled movements
Sensation
Basic movements
Behavior and emotion
Vision
Speech
Balance and muscle coordination
Hearing

BRAIN FUNCTIONS

The brain stem controls digestion, breathing, and heartbeat, and the cerebellum controls muscle coordination. These are all involuntary activities (see p.117). Conscious functions, such as memory, learning, speech, and the conscious control of movement, take place in the cerebrum. Thoughts also occur here.

BRAIN COMPARISONS

Animals have brains of varying shapes and sizes. Some have larger brains than humans, including dolphins, elephants, and whales. An elephant's brain is four times as heavy as a human's. However, the human brain is much heavier in relation to body weight than the brain of any other animal.

STRUCTURE OF THE BRAIN

The brain has three main regions: the brain stem, which merges with the spinal cord; the cerebellum; and the cerebrum, which contains the two cerebral hemispheres. The cerebrum makes up 90% of the brain.

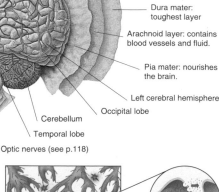

Hemispheres have a cortex of nerve cells (gray matter), and inner areas of nerve fibers (white matter).
Occipitofrontalis (muscle sheet)
Skull
Fat
Skin
Frontal sinus
Nasal cavity
Hypothalamus controls part of the nervous system
Right cerebral hemisphere
Corpus callosum
Periosteum (skull membrane)
Frontal lobe
Pituitary gland (see p.129)
Brain stem
Spinal cord
Optic nerves (see p.118)
Parietal lobe
Three layers, called meninges, cover the brain.
Dura mater: toughest layer
Arachnoid layer: contains blood vessels and fluid.
Pia mater: nourishes the brain.
Left cerebral hemisphere
Occipital lobe
Cerebellum
Temporal lobe

BRAIN POWER

The brain sends and receives messages as impulses of electrical energy. The energy travels via nerve cells, called neurons, that run down the spinal cord to the rest of the body. Each neuron ends in a network of fine branches.

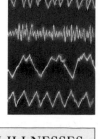

Information passes between nerve cells at the synapses: the points where the tips of axons and dendrites meet.

Close-up of a synapse transferring information from one nerve cell to another.

CEREBRAL HEMISPHERES

The cerebrum is divided into two halves, called cerebral hemispheres. The left half is usually dominant and controls speech and thought; the right half manages artistic and imaginative activity. The corpus callosum joins the two hemispheres.

The left side of the brain is responsible for logical activities such as language and numeracy.

The right side mainly controls the imagination, and artistic activities such as music and painting.

Human brain: the size of a cauliflower

Bird brain

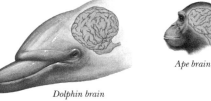

Dolphin brain

Snake brain

Ape brain

Fish brain

MEMORY

Memory works in three ways: iconic memory briefly remembers things seen for a split-second; short-term memory stores things for about five minutes; and long-term memory can store things for a lifetime.

BRAIN WAVES

An electroencephalogram (EEG) records tiny electrical impulses produced by brain activity.

Alpha waves
Awake and relaxed

Beta waves
Concentrating

Delta waves
Asleep

Theta waves
Meditation and creative thought

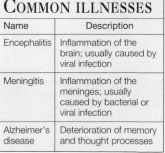

MEGAMEMORY

In 1974, a man named Bhandanta Vicitsara recited 16,000 pages of Buddhist text from memory: enough to fill books equaling the height of a six-year-old.

MEMORY FACTS

• Short-term memory can hold about seven unrelated facts at any one time.

• As a person gets older, it becomes easier for them to remember past events than to remember recent events.

• The brain has to forget certain things in order to make room for new memories.

BRAIN FACTS

• A typical adult brain weighs about 3lb (1.3kg).

• About 1.8 pints (0.85 liters) of blood travel through the brain every minute.

• A human brain contains about fifteen billion cells.

• The gray matter of a brain's cortex, laid out flat, would cover an office desk.

COMMON ILLNESSES

Name	Description
Encephalitis	Inflammation of the brain; usually caused by viral infection
Meningitis	Inflammation of the meninges; usually caused by bacterial or viral infection
Alzheimer's disease	Deterioration of memory and thought processes

NERVOUS SYSTEM

THE NERVOUS SYSTEM is a huge communications network of nerves. This network allows us to feel, see, and hear the world, and to detect and respond quickly to changes inside and outside the body.

NEURONS (NERVE CELLS)

Neurons are the building blocks of the nervous system. Each consists of a cell body containing the nucleus, and a long, threadlike nerve fiber called the axon.

The axon carries impulses away from the cell.

An insulating layer of myelin (a fatty material) protects the axon and speeds up the electrical impulses.

Nerve fibers consist of the axon and dendrites of a neuron.

The cell body contains the nucleus.

Synapses are gaps where the axon of one neuron meets the dendrites of the next.

Dendrites are nerve fibers that carry impulses toward a cell body.

INVOLUNTARY ACTIONS

Automatic actions that the brain does not consciously decide on, such as heartbeat, are called involuntary actions. They include the actions of internal organs (autonomic actions), and reflex actions. This sequence shows how the nervous system produces an involuntary reflex action in response to touching a flame.

1 When the hand touches a hot object, sensory neurons produce a signal.

2 The signal passes along the neuron's axon to an association neuron in the spinal cord.

3 The signal passes across a synapse to a motor neuron.

4 A motor neuron makes the muscles contract, pulling the hand away from the source of pain.

5 Signals also travel up to the brain. When they reach the cerebral cortex, the person feels pain.

SPINAL CORD

The spinal cord is a bundle of nerves that runs down from the brain inside the backbone (see p.122). Spinal nerves branch out from the spinal cord through the gaps between the vertebrae.

Spinal cord
Vertebra
Nerve roots
Spinal nerve
Disk
Vertebra
Vertebral canal

NERVE FACTS

- Electric signals travel through some nerve fibers at more than 250mph (400km/h). Small axons conduct impulses more slowly.

- All the nerves in the body laid end to end would stretch for about 47 miles (75km).

- The tip of the index finger is one of the most sensitive parts of the body, with many thousands of sense receptors.

- The longest nerve is the sciatic nerve, stretching from base of the spine to the knee.

STRUCTURE OF THE NERVOUS SYSTEM

The nervous system is made up of the central nervous system (CNS), which consists of the brain and spinal cord, and the peripheral nervous system, which consists of the nerves extending from the CNS to the rest of the body.

NERVES

There are millions of nerves and billions of nerve cells in the body. This close-up shows nerve cells in the brain.

NEURON FUNCTIONS

There are three types of neuron: sensory neurons send signals triggered by sensations to the CNS; motor neurons carry signals from the CNS to muscles to make them contract; and association neurons transfer signals between other neurons.

NERVE ENDINGS

There are several types of nerve ending. Each detects a different type of feeling.

Pressure
Touch
Cold
Heat
Pain

ACUPUNCTURE

This is an ancient Chinese method of treating illness by inserting fine needles into energy points on the body. These points are found along a system of channels, called meridians, that runs the length of the body, rather like the nervous system.

19th-century woodcut showing acupuncture points on the face, neck, shoulder, and hand.

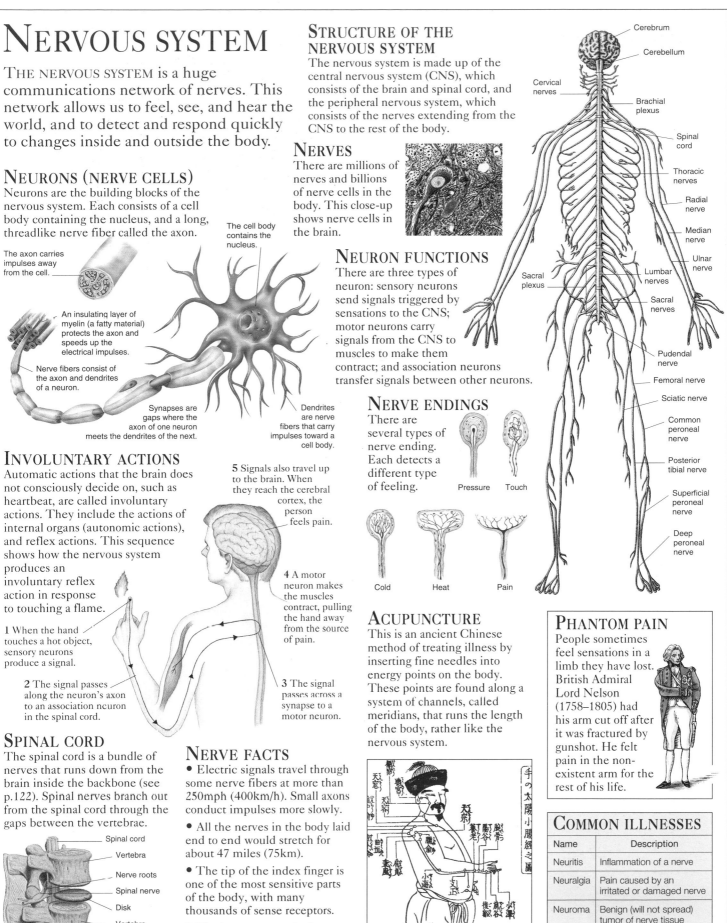

Cerebrum
Cerebellum
Cervical nerves
Brachial plexus
Spinal cord
Thoracic nerves
Radial nerve
Median nerve
Ulnar nerve
Lumbar nerves
Sacral nerves
Sacral plexus
Pudendal nerve
Femoral nerve
Sciatic nerve
Common peroneal nerve
Posterior tibial nerve
Superficial peroneal nerve
Deep peroneal nerve

PHANTOM PAIN

People sometimes feel sensations in a limb they have lost. British Admiral Lord Nelson (1758–1805) had his arm cut off after it was fractured by gunshot. He felt pain in the non-existent arm for the rest of his life.

COMMON ILLNESSES

Name	Description
Neuritis	Inflammation of a nerve
Neuralgia	Pain caused by an irritated or damaged nerve
Neuroma	Benign (will not spread) tumor of nerve tissue
Multiple sclerosis	Progressive disease of the central nervous system

EYES

THE EYES ARE probably the most important of the sense organs, enabling us to see and react to the world around us. They are positioned in protective bony sockets in the skull. Eyes work in pairs to transmit images to the brain via the optic nerves.

EYE FUNCTION

Light rays enter the eye through the pupil, and are focused by the cornea and the lens to form an image on the retina. Light-sensitive cells in the retina convert the image into nerve impulses that travel along the optic nerve to the brain.

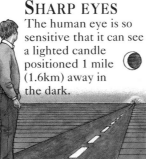

Light rays reflected off the image travel to the eye.

Cornea partly focuses the rays.

Lens fine-focuses the image.

Image is reflected onto the retina.

Image is upside down, because light rays cross over behind the lens.

Image flashes along the optic nerve to the brain, where it is turned the right way up.

RODS AND CONES
Millions of light-sensitive cells, called rods and cones, pick up the image. Rods see black and white, and cones see color.

Close-up of rods and cones

STEREOSCOPIC VISION

Two eyes give a wide range of vision, and enable us to judge depth, distance, and speed effectively. Each eye receives a slightly different view of the same object. The brain combines the two images to give a three-dimensional interpretation of the object.

Visual region of the brain

Right eye receives this image.

Left eye receives this image.

Combined, three-dimensional image

SIGHT PROBLEMS
COLOR BLINDNESS
Color-blind people are unable to tell the difference between certain colors: normally red and green. The problem is normally caused by a defect in some of the retina's cone cells. True color blindness, where people can only see shades of black and white, is very rare.

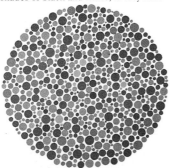

This is a test for color blindness. If you have normal vision you can see the number 29. If you are color blind you see the number 70.

EYE STRUCTURE

The eye is a round bag of clear, jellylike fluid called vitreous humor, surrounded by a tough outer covering called the sclera. Each eyeball measures about 1in (2.5cm) across.

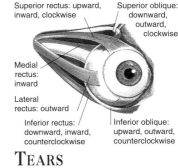

Area of optic disc (forms blind spot)

Optic nerve to brain

Retina: detects light

Retinal blood vessel

Choroid: contains nourishing blood vessels.

Medial rectus muscle

Lateral rectus muscle

Vitreous humor: allows light through to retina

Conjunctiva: thin membrane skin; keeps eye moist

Iris: muscular body; controls pupil size

Cornea bends light

Pupil: hole through which light enters the eye. Widens (dilates) in dim light and shrinks in bright light.

Aqueous humor: watery fluid; fills chamber behind cornea

Pigments in iris give eye its color

Lens focuses light.

Sclera forms white of eye

Ciliary body: muscular ring; controls shape of lens

BLIND SPOT

This is a tiny, oval-shaped area on the retina where the optic nerve joins the eye. There are no rods or cones here, so this area of the retina cannot see.

Retina

Blind spot

Optic nerve

Light rays

EYE FACTS

• Most people blink about 15 times a minute.

• About one person in thirty is color blind. More men are affected than women.

• The best photographic film is at least 1,000 times less sensitive than the human eye.

• Male eyes are about 0.5 mm bigger than female eyes.

• Carrots help you to see in the dark: they contain vitamin A, from which the light-sensitive chemical in the rods is made.

• The body produces excess tears in times of strong emotion. No one knows why humans cry.

MUSCLES

Each eye has six muscles to move the eyeball around. Movements are coordinated, so it is impossible to look in two different directions at once.

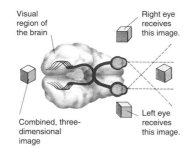

Superior rectus: upward, inward, clockwise

Superior oblique: downward, outward, clockwise

Medial rectus: inward

Lateral rectus: outward

Inferior rectus: downward, inward, counterclockwise

Inferior oblique: upward, outward, counterclockwise

TEARS

Tears are necessary to keep the eyes moist and clean.

Eyelid washes tears across the eye.

Tear gland continually produces tears.

Surplus tear fluid drains down the tear ducts to the nose.

SHARP EYES
The human eye is so sensitive that it can see a lighted candle positioned 1 mile (1.6km) away in the dark.

FAR- AND NEAR-SIGHTEDNESS
Near-sighted people cannot see distant objects clearly, and far-sighted people cannot see near objects clearly. These problems are caused by irregularly shaped eyeballs.

Far-sightedness: rays focused behind the retina. Convex lens corrects focus.

Near-sightedness: rays focused in front of the retina. Concave lens corrects focus.

COMMON PROBLEMS

Name	Description
Cataracts	Loss of transparency of the lens. Causes near-sightedness and distorted vision or blindness
Conjunctivitis	Inflammation of the conjunctiva. Causes redness, discomfort, and discharge
Glaucoma	Abnormally high pressure of fluid in the eye. Causes severe pain, and partial or complete loss of vision

EARS

EARS ARE THE organs of hearing and balance. Set on either side of the head, only part of each ear is visible; the rest is protected by the bones of the skull. Ears work in pairs to collect sound vibrations and turn them into signals, which are then passed to the brain, enabling us to hear.

EAR BONES

The three tiny ossicles in the middle ear are named the hammer, the anvil, and the stirrup because of their shapes.

- Stirrup
- Anvil
- Hammer
- Eardrum

BALANCE

Every time the body moves, fluid, called perilymph, flows around the three semicircular canals. Tiny hair cells sense the movement and send signals to the brain to communicate the body's position. This helps the body to keep its balance.

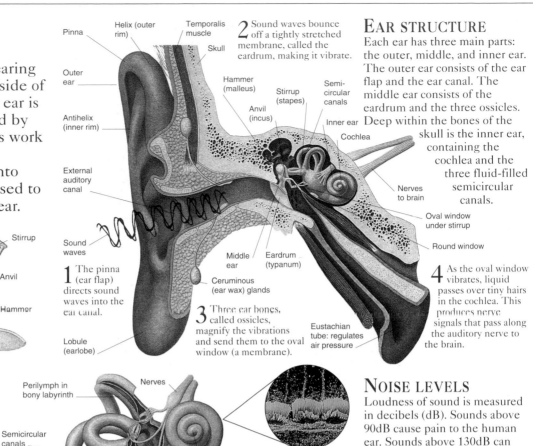

- Pinna
- Helix (outer rim)
- Temporalis muscle
- Skull
- Outer ear
- Hammer (malleus)
- Stirrup (stapes)
- Semi-circular canals
- Anvil (incus)
- Antihelix (inner rim)
- Inner ear
- Cochlea
- External auditory canal
- Nerves to brain
- Oval window under stirrup
- Round window
- Sound waves
- Middle ear
- Eardrum (typanum)
- Ceruminous (ear wax) glands
- Eustachian tube: regulates air pressure
- Lobule (earlobe)

2 Sound waves bounce off a tightly stretched membrane, called the eardrum, making it vibrate.

1 The pinna (ear flap) directs sound waves into the ear canal.

3 Three ear bones, called ossicles, magnify the vibrations and send them to the oval window (a membrane).

EAR STRUCTURE

Each ear has three main parts: the outer, middle, and inner ear. The outer ear consists of the ear flap and the ear canal. The middle ear consists of the eardrum and the three ossicles. Deep within the bones of the skull is the inner ear, containing the cochlea and the three fluid-filled semicircular canals.

4 As the oval window vibrates, liquid passes over tiny hairs in the cochlea. This produces nerve signals that pass along the auditory nerve to the brain.

- Perilymph in bony labyrinth
- Nerves
- Semicircular canals
- Cochlea

Fluid flows over more than 20,000 fine hairs inside the cochlea.

NOISE LEVELS

Loudness of sound is measured in decibels (dB). Sounds above 90dB cause pain to the human ear. Sounds above 130dB can damage the ear, and may cause deafness. This diagram compares some noise levels.

HEARING RANGES

Animals hear different levels of sound frequency (see p.233). This diagram compares the hearing ranges of some animals.

- 100,000 Hz
- 10,000 Hz
- 1,000 Hz
- 100 Hz
- 10 Hz
- Bat
- Dolphin
- Dog
- Human

EAR FACTS

- Stirrup is the smallest bone in the human body, at only 0.12in (3mm) long.
- Sensation of ears "popping" is caused by the eustachian tube opening to equalize air pressure in the middle ear.
- Ear canal is about 1in (2.5cm) in length.
- Ears can detect the direction of a sound within three degrees.
- Children usually have more sensitive ears than adults.
- Ears can detect 1,500 different tones, and 350 degrees of loudness.

DIZZINESS

If you spin around and around and then stop, the fluid in the semicircular canals continues to move for a while. This confuses the brain, causing dizziness.

EAR WAX

Glands in the skin lining the ear canal produce ear wax. This wax protects the eardrum from dirt and dust, and its unpleasant smell discourages insects from entering the ear.

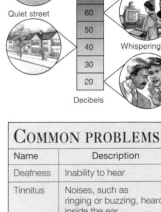

- Airplane at 300ft
- Heavy traffic
- Quiet street
- Pneumatic drill
- Office
- Whispering
- Decibels
- 120, 110, 100, 90, 80, 70, 60, 50, 40, 30, 20

PERFECT BALANCE

In 1973, Frenchman Henri Rochatain (b. 1926) spent 185 days on a tightrope 82ft (25m) above a supermarket in St. Etienne, France.

HEARING AIDS

In the past, people with hearing difficulties used large ear trumpets. Modern hearing aids are smaller and less noticeable.

Ear trumpets were held against the ear to amplify (increase) sound.

This hearing aid is worn on the head.

- Volume control
- Earphone (receiver)

This ear trumpet is 12in (30cm) long.

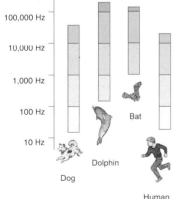

Modern hearing aid consisting of a microphone, amplifier, and battery; worn behind the ear.

This tiny hearing aid fits inside the ear where it is almost completely hidden.

COMMON PROBLEMS

Name	Description
Deafness	Inability to hear
Tinnitus	Noises, such as ringing or buzzing, heard inside the ear
Ménière's disease	Inner ear disorder. May cause tinnitus, deafness, and vertigo (illusion of spinning)
Earache	Pain often caused by infection of the middle ear

SKIN, HAIR, AND NAILS

THE SKIN IS THE largest organ of the body. It is waterproof, bacteria-proof, and repairs itself. Hair and nails are extensions of the skin and are mainly composed of keratin, a protein that also protects the skin. The skin has nerve cells that respond to touch, heat, and pain. Hair and nails, however, lack nerve cells.

HAIR STRUCTURE

A tube of the protein keratin is pushed up from the hair follicle to form the hair shaft. Each hair is attached to a tiny muscle that allows it to move independently.

Medulla
Cortex
Melanin granule
Cell nucleus residue
Macrofibril
Cuticle

HAIR TYPES

The shape of the hair follicle determines whether the hair grows straight, wavy, or curly.

Curly hair grows from an oval follicle.

Wavy hair grows from a flat follicle.

Straight hair grows from a round follicle.

HAIR FACTS

• There are about 100,000 hairs on the head; 80 fall out every day.

• Hair grows about 0.08–0.1in (2–3mm) in a week.

RARE HAIR

These two boys have a rare medical condition known as "werewolf syndrome." Their faces are covered in hair.

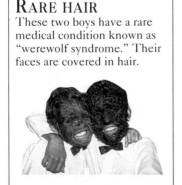

Movement of hairs creates the sensation of touch

Outer layers consist of dead skin cells containing a hard protein called keratin.

Sebaceous glands coat hair and skin in waterproof oil.

Hair follicles are surrounded by touch-sensitive nerve endings.

Hair-erector muscle tightens in the cold, causing hairs to stand on end and trap warmth.

Sweat gland produces sweat to cool down body temperature.

Sense receptor cells

SKIN STRUCTURE

The skin has two main layers: the outer epidermis and the inner dermis. The surface of the epidermis consists of dead skin cells. These are worn away and replaced by new skin cells from deep in the epidermis. The dermis is living and contains vital nerves, glands, hairs, and blood vessels.

Epidermis contains layers of new and dead skin cells.

Basal cell layer produces new cells which continually move toward the surface.

Blood vessels expand when body is hot. The skin flushes and heat is rapidly lost.

Beneath the skin is an insulating layer of fat.

The dermis is about four times thicker than the epidermis.

SKIN FACTS

• Protects internal organs from injury and infection.

• Sweat glands control body temperature by pushing water and salt to the surface.

• Contains thousands of nerve cells that can detect pressure, temperature, and pain.

• Contains the pigment melanin that gives the skin its color and protects against the Sun's rays. Dark skin contains more melanin than fair.

• In most places skin is about 0.08in (2mm) thick.

• Freckles are due to an uneven production of melanin.

• Household dust is mostly made up of dead skin cells.

NAIL STRUCTURE

Nails are made of a tough protein called keratin. The half-moon at the base of each nail – the lunula – is covered by a flap of skin called the cuticle.

Lunula
Nail
Dermis
Nail root: a flap of skin from which the nail grows.
Bone
Fatty pad cushions the sensitive skin of the fingertip.

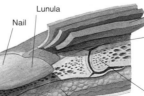

NAIL FACTS

• Fingernails take six months to grow from the base to the tip.

• Nails grow at a rate of 0.02in (0.5mm) per week. They can grow up to 12in (30cm) long.

BLOOD CLOTTING

Red blood cells help cuts to heal quickly by binding together and forming a clot.

1 A cut in the skin triggers the release by platelets of substances to make blood cells sticky.

Red blood cells

2 White blood cells fight infection in the cut. Fibrin threads are made from blood-clotting factors.

White blood cell

3 Fibrin threads contract and bind red blood cells into a clot. This hardens to a scab which protects the cut as it heals.

Fibrin threads stop blood flow

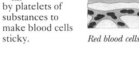

FINGERPRINTS

The patterns made by the ridges on your fingertips are called fingerprints. The patterns are formed months before birth, and no two fingerprint patterns are the same.

SKIN LOSS

The body sheds about 40lb (18kg) of dead skin in a lifetime: about the weight of a six- to seven-year-old child.

SKIN'S SURFACE

These magnified images show details of the skin's surface.

Sweat pores allow fluid to escape. This cools the skin.

Hair grows out of pits called hair follicles.

COMMON PROBLEMS

Name	Description
Acne	Skin disorder: raised red spots that may scar
Eczema	Itchy skin inflammation: may cause blisters and scaling
Psoriasis	Skin disorder: patches of red skin often covered with silvery scales
Alopecia	Patchy loss of hair, usually on scalp

SMELL, TASTE, AND THROAT

TASTE AND smell are closely linked. The flavor sensation combines messages from taste buds and smell receptors, as well as heat and texture. An increase or decrease of 30 percent in the strength of a smell or taste is needed for the brain to detect a change. Humans can distinguish 2,000 to 4,000 different smells.

SENSE OF SMELL

There are specialized nerve endings at the back of the nose called smell receptors. These are sensitive to chemicals in the airstream deposited in mucus.

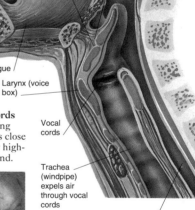

Air passes over smell receptors attached to the olfactory bulb. These are made up of thousands of cells bearing microscopic hairs that are sensitive to chemicals in the mucus.

Olfactory bulb

The smell receptors send a message to the brain through the olfactory nerve.

Olfactory nerve

Nasal cavity

Chemicals from the airstream are deposited in the mucus.

The nasal cavity is lined with a very thin skin called the mucus membrane, which secretes mucus.

Nasal hairs filter particles as they are breathed in.

Mucus moves back toward the throat. Harmful microorganisms are swallowed and made harmless by acids in the stomach.

TONGUE AND TASTE

The human tongue measures about 4in (10cm) in length, and is covered with taste buds. These microscopic nerve endings are the main organs of taste. Different areas detect different tastes. There are four basic tastes: sweet, sour, salt, and bitter.

Tongue surface magnified to show sensory nerve endings.

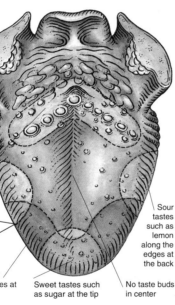

Bitter tastes such as coffee are tasted at the back of the tongue.

Salt is tasted along the sides at the front.

Sweet tastes such as sugar at the tip

No taste buds in center

Sour tastes such as lemon along the edges at the back

THE VOICE

Sounds are made by forcing air from the lungs up the trachea and through the vocal cords, causing them to vibrate. The tongue, throat, mouth, and lips change the sounds into words.

Nasal cavity and mouth passage join at the throat (pharynx)

Epiglottis flap

Tongue

Larynx (voice box)

Vocal cords

Trachea (windpipe) expels air through vocal cords

Esophagus carries food down to the stomach

Relaxed chords
Vocal chords are far apart for low-pitched noise and breathing.

Active chords
Muscles bring vocal chords close together for high-pitched sound.

VOICE RECORDS

LOUDEST RECORDED shout measured 119 decibels – louder than a loud rock concert.

FASTEST SPEAKERS can say more than 300 words per minute and still be understood.

SNEEZING RECORD

An Englishwoman sneezed about 2.7 million times over 2.7 years. With each sneeze she expelled about 0.2 cu ft of air. During her world record sneezing fit, she blew out enough air to fill eight hot air balloons.

LOSS OF SMELL

Immediately after birth the efficiency of our smell receptors begins to decline. This graph shows how the sense of smell deteriorates as we age.

82%
38%
28%
Age 20   Age 60   Age 80

SMELL FACTS

• You can smell better if you sniff hard because more chemicals reach the receptors in your nose.

• The brain can become used to smells, even the most horrible ones. It simply switches off and you stop detecting them.

VOICE BOX

The vocal cords are two rubbery ligaments in the larynx.

The harder air is forced through the vocal cords, the louder the sound they make

Thyroid cartilage (Adam's apple)

Rings of cartilage hold trachea open to allow air through

Epiglottis flap closes when we swallow to stop food from going the wrong way

Trachea (windpipe) shown sliced open and laid flat

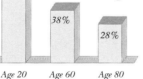

TASTE FACTS

• Taste buds work only when saliva dissolves chemicals in food and washes over the buds.

• Babies are born with taste buds all over their mouth. They gradually disappear, remaining only on the tongue. Adults have about 1,000 taste buds.

VOICE FACTS

• The larynx is larger in men, which is why they can produce deeper sounds.

• A boy's voice changes when the larynx enlarges at puberty.

• If the larynx lining is tickled by a food particle, a reflex contraction causes coughing, which ejects the foreign body.

COMMON PROBLEMS

Name	Description
Allergic rhinitis (hay fever)	Inflammation of mucus membrane caused by allergy to pollen or dust
Common cold	Viral infection causing stuffed-up or runny nose and sneezing
Laryngitis	Inflammation of the larynx caused by infection, resulting in loss of voice

SKELETON AND TEETH

THE FRAMEWORK OF bones in the human body, including the teeth, is called the skeleton, and it supports and protects delicate internal organs, such as the brain, lungs, and heart. The skeleton also provides strong fixed points of attachment for muscles. Bones contain marrow, which generates red and white blood cells.

BONE STRUCTURE

Bones contain calcium and phosphorus, which make them hard. The strongest part of a bone is its compact outer layer. Inside longer bones, softer living tissue, called marrow, produces red and white blood cells and stores fat.

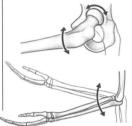

Compact bone
Spongy bone
Fatty bone-marrow
Micrograph of marrow

Cross-section of a humerus (upper arm bone)

JOINTS

Where bones meet, a joint forms. In a mobile joint, the bone surface is coated with slippery cartilage and lubricated with synovial fluid. Most joints are held together by cords or bands called ligaments. Below are several types of joints.

Ball-and-socket
Ball-and-socket joints (e.g. shoulder, hip) allow the most movement of any joint.

Hinge
Hinge joints (e.g. elbow, knee) allow movement in just one plane.

Fixed
Some bones lock together, allowing no movement at all (e.g. cranial joints).

Pivot
Pivot joints consist of a bony projection that pivots within a ring (e.g. neck).

Ellipsoidal
An ellipsoidal joint (e.g. wrist) is one where an oval bone fits into an oval cavity.

A BONE TO PICK

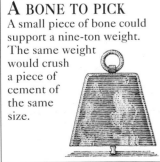

A small piece of bone could support a nine-ton weight. The same weight would crush a piece of cement of the same size.

BONE RECORDS

LARGEST BONE in the body is the thigh bone (femur): average male length 18.1in (46cm).

SMALLEST BONE is the stirrup (stapes) bone in the middle ear, 0.1–0.13in (2.6–3.4mm) long.

TEETH

Teeth are covered with enamel, the hardest substance made by animals. They are connected to the jaw by strong fibers that allow slight movement when chewing or biting. Humans have two sets of teeth: the first, of 20, called "milk" teeth, starts to fall out at about age 6; the second, of 32, replaces the first and is permanent.

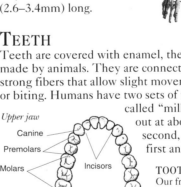

Upper jaw
Canine
Premolars
Molars
Incisors

Lower jaw
Molars
Incisors
Premolars
Canine

TOOTH TYPES

Our front 12 teeth (incisors and canines) are sharp; they grip and tear off pieces of food. Our back 20 teeth (premolars and molars) grind and crush food for later digestion. The third molars, or wisdom teeth, sometimes remain embedded beneath gum in the jawbone.

TOOTH STRUCTURE

Enamel forms the hard, nonliving, surface of the tooth. The pulp contains vessels that bring blood to the tooth, enabling it to live and grow.

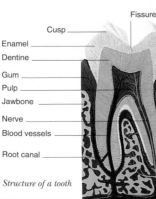

Fissure
Cusp
Enamel
Dentine
Gum
Pulp
Jawbone
Nerve
Blood vessels
Root canal

Structure of a tooth

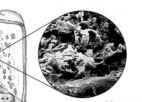

Cranium (skull)
Mandible (jawbone)
Clavicle
Ribs
Humerus (upper arm bone)
Vertebrae (spine)
Radius
Ulna
Carpals (wrist bones)
Sacrum
Pelvis (hipbone)
Metacarpals (finger bones)
Femur (thighbone)
Patella
Tibia (shinbone)
Fibula (calfbone)
Tarsals and metatarsals (footbones)

Cervical
Thoracic
Vertebral disk
Lumbar
Sacrum
Coccyx

SKELETON

The average person has 206 bones. Some people have extra bones in their thumbs or big toes, called sesamoid bones. Women have shallower and wider pelvic bones than men, to help with childbirth.

BONE FACTS

- Some people have an extra (thirteenth) pair of ribs.

- A giraffe's neck contains the same number of bones as the human neck.

- The bones in a baby's head are not fused – they can overlap slightly to ease birth.

- Babies have more than 300 bones – they fuse together later.

SPINAL COLUMN

The spinal column has four curves: cervical, thoracic, lumbar, and sacral. Each bone in the spine is called a vertebra and most are separated from their neighbors by shock-absorbing vertebral disks. Vertebrae interlock with each other by cartilaginous joints.

TOOTH FACTS

- Teeth decay more easily during the first 25 years of life; mature enamel is more resistant to attack.

- Some babies are born with a full set of teeth – King Louis XIV of France, for instance.

- Some adults' four back molars (wisdom teeth) never fully grow.

CARING FOR TEETH

Tooth decay can be reduced by cutting down on the sugar and starch we eat and by brushing (with a fluoride-based toothpaste) and flossing after meals.

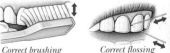

Correct brushing   *Correct flossing*

COMMON PROBLEMS

Name	Description
Osteoarthritis	Degeneration of cartilage or bone ends in the joints
Osteoporosis	Thinning of bone, with aging. Bone fractures easily
Caries	Patches of decay and erosion of tooth enamel and dentine by plaque (bacteria, saliva, and food remains)
Gingivitis	Inflammation of the gums, due to infection

MUSCLES

MUSCLES CARRY OUT all the body's movements. They number more than 600, accounting for about half the body's weight. Muscles are arranged in groups of fibers that contract when triggered by nerves. Regular, vigorous exercise increases a muscle's size and improves its circulation of blood.

TYPES OF MUSCLE

Voluntary muscles (e.g. bicep) can be consciously controlled; involuntary ones do internal jobs, such as the muscles of the intestine, which move food through the digestive system.

Voluntary muscle
Voluntary (skeletal) muscle cells appear striped close up. The muscle fibers are bundled together for quick contraction.

Involuntary muscle
Involuntary (smooth) muscle cells are tapered and loosely woven, and contract more slowly than other muscle types.

Cardiac muscle
Cardiac (heart) muscle has short, branching cells; these help spread the nerve signals that cause contraction.

CONTRACTION

Muscle fiber contains tiny strands called myofibrils. A myofibril contains overlapping layers of two proteins: actin and myosin. When triggered by an electrical nerve signal, the actin and myosin attract each other, and their layers slide closer together. The myofibril shortens; the muscle contracts.

Structure of a muscle

Myofibril
Muscle fibre
Actin
Myosin
Bundle of muscle fibres
Relaxed myofibril
Contracted myofibril
Overlapping and interlocking myosin and actin proteins
Tough membrane protects muscle.

MULTI-MUSCLE MOVER

Humans have more than 600 muscles, but an average-sized caterpillar has over 2,000.

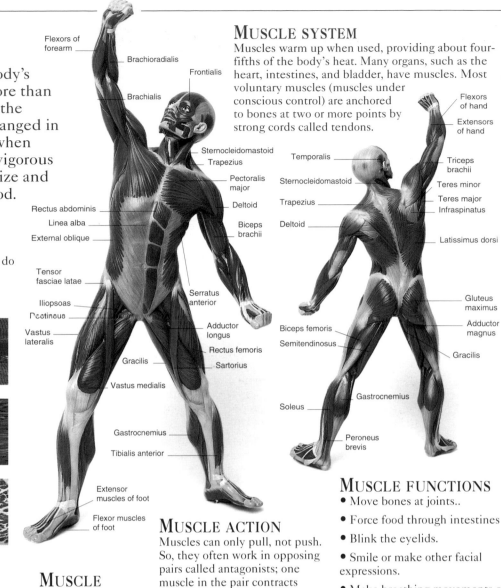

Flexors of forearm
Brachioradialis
Brachialis
Frontalis
Sternocleidomastoid
Trapezius
Pectoralis major
Deltoid
Biceps brachii
Rectus abdominis
Linea alba
External oblique
Tensor fasciae latae
Iliopsoas
Pectineus
Vastus lateralis
Serratus anterior
Adductor longus
Rectus femoris
Sartorius
Gracilis
Vastus medialis
Gastrocnemius
Tibialis anterior
Extensor muscles of foot
Flexor muscles of foot

Flexors of hand
Extensors of hand
Temporalis
Sternocleidomastoid
Trapezius
Deltoid
Triceps brachii
Teres minor
Teres major
Infraspinatus
Latissimus dorsi
Biceps femoris
Semitendinosus
Gluteus maximus
Adductor magnus
Gracilis
Soleus
Gastrocnemius
Peroneus brevis

MUSCLE SYSTEM

Muscles warm up when used, providing about four-fifths of the body's heat. Many organs, such as the heart, intestines, and bladder, have muscles. Most voluntary muscles (muscles under conscious control) are anchored to bones at two or more points by strong cords called tendons.

MUSCLE RECORDS

LONGEST MUSCLE is the sartorius, which runs from the pelvis to just below the knee.

BIGGEST MUSCLE is the gluteus maximus (buttock).

SMALLEST MUSCLE is the stapedius in the middle ear – less than 0.05in (1.27mm) long.

FASTEST MUSCLE blinks the eyelids up to five times every second.

MUSCLE ACTION

Muscles can only pull, not push. So, they often work in opposing pairs called antagonists; one muscle in the pair contracts while the other relaxes.

Biceps contracts.
Biceps relaxes.
Triceps contracts.
Triceps relaxes.
Muscles lift the forearm.
Tendon attaches muscle to bone
Muscles straighten the forearm.

TYPES OF EXERCISE

Muscles normally use glucose and oxygen for day-to-day (aerobic) exercise. If glucose or oxygen are in short supply, muscles use their own energy stores. This anaerobic exercise generates lactic acid, which causes muscles to tire and ache, and makes us gasp for replacement oxygen.

Aerobic exercise
Anaerobic exercise

MUSCLE FUNCTIONS

• Move bones at joints..

• Force food through intestines

• Blink the eyelids.

• Smile or make other facial expressions.

• Make breathing movements of chest and diaphragm.

• Contract walls of blood vessels.

MUSCLE FACTS

• Muscle cells can contract by up to one-third of their length.

• The muscles working a gnat's wings can make them beat over 1,000 times a second.

• When we walk, we use more than 200 different muscles.

COMMON PROBLEMS

Name	Description
Cramp	Painful spasms from acid buildup in muscles
Strain	Tear in muscle, causing bleeding and swelling
Tetanus	Toxin makes muscle contract continuously
Muscular dystrophy	Gradual wasting of muscle fibers, an inherited illness
Tendinitis	Inflammation of tendon, usually caused by injury

HEART

THE HEART IS a fist-sized muscular pump that pushes blood around the body. It has two sides, and each side has two chambers. These chambers contract and relax about once every four-fifths of a second, ensuring blood continually flows in the right direction.

Heart lies in middle of chest; it feels farther left since left side beats stronger.

HEARTBEAT CYCLE

The heart is a special kind of muscle, a cardiac muscle, that works automatically. A heartbeat has four phases, or stages, and lasts for about four-fifths of a second.

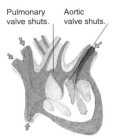

Pulmonary valve shuts. Aortic valve shuts. Tricuspid valve opens. Mitral valve opens.

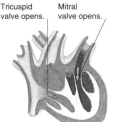

1 The left and right atria relax. Blood fills them through pulmonary veins and vena cava.

2 Blood passes through tricuspid and mitral valves from atria into right and left ventricles.

Tricuspid valve shuts. Mitral valve shuts. Pulmonary valve shuts. Aortic valve shuts.

3 Ventricles contract and force blood through aortic and pulmonary valves into main arteries.

4 Pulmonary and aortic valves close as ventricles relax. Cycle restarts at phase one.

HEART STRUCTURE

The septum divides the two sides of the heart. Each side has two chambers: an atrium and a ventricle, separated by valves. The stronger left side pumps oxygenated blood from the lungs to the rest of the body; the right brings deoxygenated (used) blood back to the lungs.

Right pulmonary artery

Location of sinoatrial node

Right pulmonary vein

In this diagram, arteries are colored red and veins are colored blue.

Myocardium
Pericardium
Right ventricle

Inferior vena cava

Superior vena cava
Aorta
Artery to head
Coronary nerves
Right atrium
Pulmonary valve
Tricuspid valve

Coronary nerves stimulate the heart muscle, passing electrical signals from the brain to tell the heart how fast it should beat.

Valves stop blood from going the wrong way when the heart muscle contracts.

Left pulmonary artery
Aortic valve
Left pulmonary vein
Mitral valve
Tendon supporting valve
Septum
Coronary vein
Coronary artery

Fat
Left ventricle
Muscular column supporting valve tendons
Aorta

HEART FACTS

• Heart sounds are caused by the valves snapping shut, and the whoosh of blood leaving the heart.

• Bicuspid valves have two flaps; tricuspid have three.

• A heart beats more than 30 million times a year, and about 3 billion times in a lifetime.

• Our heart rate increases when we exercise, to supply our muscles with extra oxygen.

• The heart rests between beats. In an average lifetime of 70 years, the heart will be at rest for about 40 years.

HEART RECORDS

LONGEST CARDIAC ARREST lasted four hours – Norwegian fisherman Egil Refsdahl (b.1936), later revived.

FIRST HUMAN HEART TRANSPLANT was performed on December 3, 1967 by South African surgeon Christiaan Barnard, on grocer Louis Washkansky.

LONGEST-SURVIVING TRANSPLANTEE survived for 22 years, 10 months, 24 days.

HEARTBEAT PACEMAKER

The heart has a built-in pacemaker that keeps it beating rhythmically. It lies at the top of the heart, at the sinoatrial node, and sends an electrical signal around the heart just before every beat. An electrocardiograph machine can record these impulses painlessly.

Electrocardiogram of electrical impulse just before a heartbeat

ECG (electrocardiogram) of a normal heartbeat

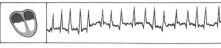

ECG of complete heart block (chambers beat independently)

BLOOD WAGON

The heart ejects about 0.17 pints (80ml) of blood with every beat. If an adult heart was connected to an 2,000-gallon (7,600-liter) container truck, it could fill it in a day, with blood to spare.

HOLE IN THE HEART

Sometimes the right and left sides of the heart connect through a hole in the septum. Holes are closed by surgery; otherwise, fresh blood from the lungs returns there directly, without going around the body.

Septum
Surgical seal

Ventricular septal defect (hole in the septum)

ARTIFICIAL VALVES

Caged-ball valve
Closed   Open

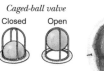

Tilting disk valve
Closed   Open

Modified pig's valve

Sometimes valves do not work properly, and blood flows the wrong way. Surgeons replace them with real valves from pigs or artificial, mechanical ones.

COMMON PROBLEMS

Name	Description
Angina	Tight heart pain caused by lack of oxygen, often from narrowed arteries
Coronary heart disease	Reduced blood supply from narrowed arteries
Cardiac arrest	Part or all of heart muscle stops beating
Endocarditis	Infection of the heart valves.
Arrhythmia	Disturbance in heartbeat

CIRCULATION AND BLOOD

THE CIRCULATORY SYSTEM supplies each body cell with life-giving blood. Blood flows round the body in a continuous circuit, through a network of vessels that is thousands of miles long. The heart acts as a pump, keeping the entire system moving.

THE CIRCULATORY SYSTEM

Veins bring deoxygenated blood from the body to the right-hand side of the heart. The right ventricle pumps it to the lungs, where it becomes saturated with oxygen. This blood returns to the left atrium of the heart and enters the left ventricle. The ventricle then pumps it into the network of arteries, keeping the body constantly supplied with oxygen.

Head
Aorta
Arm
Superior vena cava
Lung
Arm
Lung
Liver
Kidney
Inferior vena cava
Digestive tract
Kidney
Legs

BLOOD

White blood cell (lymphocyte)
Platelet
Red blood cell (erythrocyte)

Blood consists of red blood cells, white blood cells, and cell fragments called platelets, floating in a fluid called plasma. Proteins, hormones, and minerals are dissolved in the plasma. Red blood cells contain hemoglobin, which stores oxygen and releases it to the body. White blood cells fight infection. Platelets help blood to clot when we cut our skin.

VESSEL RECORDS

LARGEST ARTERY
is the aorta. It has an internal diameter of 1in (2.5cm).

LARGEST VEIN
is the vena cava. It has an internal diameter of 1in (2.5cm).

BLOOD VESSELS

Muscular-walled arteries divide into smaller arterioles, then into capillaries, which have thin walls through which oxygen can pass. Deoxygenated blood returns via venules, which join up into wider, thin-walled veins.

Vein
Endothelium
Fatty deposits
Muscle fibers
Artery
Arteriole
Venule
Single cell layer
Valve action in vein
Capillary
Valve open   Valve shut

BLOOD FACTS

• There are four main types, or groups, of blood: A, B, AB, and O. Blood transfusions (transfers) must use compatible groups.

• Red blood cells last about four months and make about 172,000 circuits around the body.

LEECH LUNCH

Leeches attach themselves with suckers to animals and feed off their blood. They can drink up to ten times their own bodyweight of blood – enough to last them for nine months.

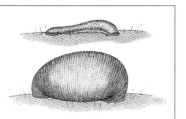

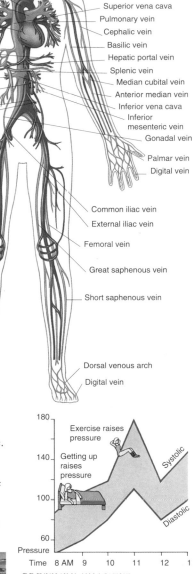

ARTERIES

Common carotid artery
Subclavian artery
Aortic arch
Pulmonary artery
Axillary artery
Coronary artery
Brachial artery
Gastric artery
Hepatic artery
Renal artery
Superior mesenteric artery
Inferior mesenteric artery
Gonadal artery
Palmar arch
Digital artery
Ulnar artery
Radial artery
Common iliac artery
External iliac artery
Femoral artery
Popliteal artery
Peroneal artery
Anterior tibial artery
Posterior tibial artery
Lateral plantar artery
Dorsal metatarsal artery

VEINS

Internal jugular vein
Brachiocephalic vein
Subclavian vein
Axillary vein
Superior vena cava
Pulmonary vein
Cephalic vein
Basilic vein
Hepatic portal vein
Splenic vein
Median cubital vein
Anterior median vein
Inferior vena cava
Inferior mesenteric vein
Gonadal vein
Palmar vein
Digital vein
Common iliac vein
External iliac vein
Femoral vein
Great saphenous vein
Short saphenous vein
Dorsal venous arch
Digital vein

BLOOD PRESSURE

Blood circulates under pressure. This is measured using two figures: the systole, or first figure, gives the pressure as the heart pumps blood into the system; the diastole, or second figure, gives the pressure when the heart rests between beats.

A nurse or doctor measures blood pressure.

180
140
100
60
Pressure

Exercise raises pressure
Getting up raises pressure
Systolic
Diastolic

Time   8 AM   9   10   11   12   1

PRESSURE CHANGES

Blood pressure is low when we sleep, and rises during exercise. Also, it may rise as we grow older. A 20-year-old might have a pressure of 110/70mm mercury; a 60-year-old of 160/90mm.

HIV AND AIDS

The HIV virus that causes AIDS disables the immune system. One way it achieves this is by destroying the T4-lymphocytes (white blood cells) that help "killer" lymphocytes attack invaders.

Micrograph of an HIV virus bursting from a T4 lymphocyte

COMMON PROBLEMS

Name	Description
Hemophilia	Deficiency of a blood-clotting factor
Anemia	Hemoglobin deficiency causing lack of oxygen
Arterio-sclerosis	Thickening of artery wall due to deposits of fat
Varicose vein	Swelling, twisting, and distortion of a vein
Aneurysm	Thinning and dilation (widening) of artery wall

RESPIRATORY SYSTEM

WHEN WE BREATHE IN, we supply our bodies with oxygen from the air, and when we breathe out, we expel a waste gas, carbon dioxide. We breathe about 10.56 pints (6 liters) of air every minute, and adult lungs hold about 5.28 pints (3 liters) of air.

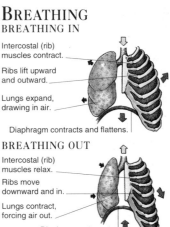

Location of respiratory system

RESPIRATORY SYSTEM

Air enters the body at the upper respiratory tract (nose, mouth, and trachea). The trachea splits into two bronchi (tubes), which divide into narrower bronchi, leading to tiny, hollow capsules called alveoli. Air is drawn in and out of this system by the action of the diaphragm muscle.

ALVEOLI

The lungs' 700 million microscopic alveoli are hollow and covered in a network of capillary arteries and veins. Their moist walls are so thin that blood passing by can release its waste carbon dioxide and take up oxygen. The capillaries then join up to form the pulmonary vein.

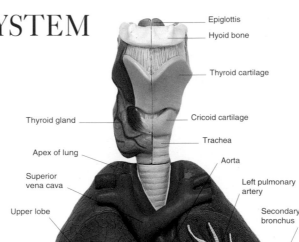

Labels: Epiglottis, Hyoid bone, Thyroid cartilage, Cricoid cartilage, Trachea, Aorta, Left pulmonary artery, Secondary bronchus, Thyroid gland, Apex of lung, Superior vena cava, Upper lobe

Labels: Lower lobe, Middle lobe of right lung, Esophagus, Heart, Muscular wall of diaphragm, Tertiary bronchus

Labels: Mucous membrane, Smooth muscles, Cartilage, Capillary network, Elastic fibers, Alveolus

Alveoli

ACE AIRWAYS

If the inner surfaces of the lungs were laid out flat, their total area would be 1,938sq ft (180sq m). This would cover more than two-thirds of a tennis court.

BREATHING

BREATHING IN

Intercostal (rib) muscles contract.

Ribs lift upward and outward.

Lungs expand, drawing in air.

Diaphragm contracts and flattens.

BREATHING OUT

Intercostal (rib) muscles relax.

Ribs move downward and in.

Lungs contract, forcing air out.

Diaphragm returns to natural arch shape.

The bases of our lungs rest on the diaphragm, a dome-shaped muscle. When we inhale, it pulls the bases down, and chest (intercostal) muscles expand the ribcage. Air rushes into the lungs through the trachea.

RESPIRATION FACTS

• The left lung has two lobes, or sections, and the right has three. Each lung is encased in a lubricated skin called a pleural membrane. It allows the lungs to slide easily during breathing.

X-ray of lungs

• Rings of cartilage reinforce the trachea and bronchi to prevent them from collapsing.

• Thousands of tiny hairs, called cilia, line the walls of the airways. They carry dust and bacteria away from the lungs. A mucous lining also catches dust.

• We can survive with just one fully working lung.

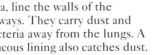

Oxygen: 21%
Nitrogen: 75%
Carbon dioxide: 4%

Composition of inhaled air

Oxygen: 16%
Nitrogen: 75%
Carbon dioxide: 9%

Composition of exhaled air

• Nitrogen dissolves in blood plasma, but is not used in any of the body's processes.

• Hiccups are caused by the rapid contraction of the diaphragm. Air is drawn in very rapidly and the vocal cords snap shut quickly, causing the noise we hear as a hiccup.

• Between the trachea and the alveoli the airways divide 23 times, totaling 1,491 miles (2,400km) of airways.

HIC HIC

American farmer Charles Osborne (1894–1991) began hiccuping in 1922. He continued until 1990, after 68 years of constant hiccups.

Healthy lung *Smoker's lung*

LUNGS AND SMOKING

More than 4,000 chemicals have been identified in cigarette smoke, and many of these irritate the lungs and cause cancer. Many people die each year from the effects of smoking.

COMMON PROBLEMS

Name	Description
Asthma	Causes wheezing and difficulty of breathing out
Bronchitis	Inflammation of the bronchi
Pneumonia	Inflammation of lungs caused by infection
Lung cancer	Malignant tumors of the lung
Emphysema	Damage to alveoli, causes breathlessness

SMOKING HEALTH RISK

Cigarettes per day	Lung cancer deaths per year per 100,000 males
0	10
1–14	78
15–24	127

DIGESTION

FOOD HAS TO BE broken down into small particles before the body can make use of its energy and nutrients. This process is called digestion and happens in the digestive tract, a tube 29.5ft (9m) long.

DIGESTIVE TRACT

The digestive tract runs from the mouth to the anus. Organs such as the liver, pancreas, and gall bladder connect with the tract and help it to break down and absorb food.

THE LIVER

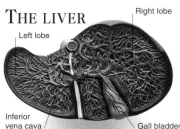

Right lobe

Left lobe

Inferior vena cava

Gall bladder

The liver receives blood from the hepatic and portal (intestinal) arteries, and has a great many functions, including:
• Makes bile for digesting food.
• Helps maintain blood sugar levels.
• Makes blood proteins.
• Helps blood to clot.
• Controls blood cell formation and destruction.
• Stores vitamins.
• Removes poisons from body.
• Stores energy.
• Makes heat.
• Destroys microorganisms.

ABSORBING FOOD

The lining of the small intestine has millions of microscopic, fingerlike projections called villi. They are packed with blood and lymph vessels and have thin walls through which nutrients from the partly digested food can easily pass.

1 MOUTH AND THROAT

Digestion begins as soon as you take a bite of food: chewing breaks down food into smaller lumps; enzymes (proteins that speed up chemical reactions) in saliva begin to break down complex carbohydrates into simpler sugars. The tongue rolls food into a bolus (lump) and pushes it to the back of the throat, where a swallowing reflex is activated. The bolus passes down the esophagus (food pipe) toward the stomach.

Esophagus

2 STOMACH

The lining of the stomach gives out highly acidic juices and enzymes that break down food. Acid helps the enzymes work and kills bacteria. The resulting soupy liquid is called chyme.

Stomach

3 DUODENUM

The duodenum receives bile (green, watery fluid) from the liver and juices from the pancreas. Pancreatic juice continues to break down food, but also neutralizes stomach acids so that other enzymes can act. Bile emulsifies (splits up) fats for later digestion.

Duodenum

4 ILEUM (SMALL INTESTINE)

Food is absorbed in the ileum, and some substances, such as fats, lactose, and sucrose, are finally digested here. Nutrients absorbed into the blood are sent to the liver for processing.

Colon

Villus: 0.04in (1mm) long

Capillaries

Lacteal

Epithelium

Muscles contract and relax to squeeze food along.

Mucosa layer contains venules, arterioles, and thin muscle sheets.

5 COLON AND RECTUM (LARGE INTESTINE)

Water and fiber from food pass into the colon, where much of the water is absorbed into the body. The large intestine does not secrete enzymes, but contains bacteria which break down the fibrous, undigested leftovers. This semisolid waste, called feces, then passes into the rectum, and is later expelled through the anus.

Tongue

Maxilla (upper jaw)

Mandible (lower jaw)

Trachea

Epiglottis

Esophagus

Fold of mucous membrane

Stomach

Liver

Pancreas | Spleen

Appendix

Colon

Small intestine

Rectum

Anal sphincter muscle

Ileum

Anus

IRON AND FIBER

Since 1966, Frenchman Michel Lolito, "Monsieur Mangetout," has eaten and digested ten bicycles, seven TVs, six chandeliers, and a Cessna light aircraft.

DIGESTION FACTS

• Food spends 3 to 5 hours in the stomach, and 6 to 20 hours in the large intestine.

• The stomach wall is protected by a mucus lining; otherwise, it would start to digest itself.

• When we swallow, a lid called the epiglottis covers the trachea to stop food from entering.

PERISTALSIS

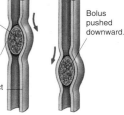

Bolus

Circular muscle contracts.

Muscular wall of tract

Bolus pushed downward.

A muscular, wavelike movement called peristalsis pushes food through the digestive tract. The walls of the tract contain rings and lengths of muscle. These contract and relax alternately to propel food through the system.

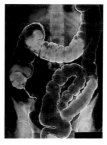

X-ray of feces passing through the colon

KEY ENZYMES

Region	Enzymes produced	Foods acted on by enzymes
Mouth	Salivary amylase	Starch (carbohydrate)
Stomach	Pepsin and rennin	Proteins and milk protein
Duodenum	Trypsin, amylase, lipase	Proteins, peptides, starch, and fats
Ileum	Trypsin, amylase, lipase	Peptides, fats, maltose, sucrose, lactose
Colon	Bacterial enzymes	Undigested food and fiber

COMMON PROBLEMS

Name	Description
Indigestion	Stomach pain, when stomach stretches with gas or acid buildup
Diarrhea	Liquid or semiliquid feces caused by poisoned food or infection
Constipation	Slow bowel actions; can be caused by lack of fiber in diet
Cirrhosis	Scarring and breakdown of liver commonly caused by alcohol abuse
Hepatitis	Inflammation of liver caused by viral infection, drugs, or poisons

URINARY SYSTEM

THE KIDNEYS CONTROL the amount of water and minerals in our blood by getting rid of unwanted substances in the form of urine. Urine is expelled from the body via a muscular reservoir called the bladder. This system is known as the urinary or excretory system. The kidneys filter all the blood in the body every five minutes.

Location of urinary system

THE KIDNEYS

The two kidneys contain about 1.3 million tiny tubes, called nephrons, that cleanse the blood. As blood passes through the tubes into a network of tiny blood vessels, called the glomerulus, wastes and water are filtered out into a cup-shaped organ called a Bowman's capsule. Some of this filtrate is reabsorbed into the blood. The rest, now concentrated, travels down the ureter toward the bladder.

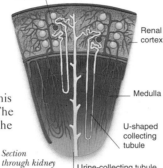

Glomerulus and Bowman's capsule

Renal cortex

Medulla

U-shaped collecting tubule

Section through kidney

Urine-collecting tubule

URINARY FACTS

- Up to about two years of age, the bladder is emptied by a reflex action. After this age, a child learns to control the bladder.

- ADH (antidiuretic hormone), made in the pituitary gland, controls the uptake of water in the kidneys.

- We can survive with only one kidney. If one stops working the other enlarges in order to do the work for both.

KIDNEY FILTRATES

This table shows percentages of major substances in the blood serum (plasma), and how much is then filtered out by the kidneys as urine.

Compounds	Blood %	Urine %
Proteins	7–9	0
Urea	0.03	2
Uric Acid	0.005	0.05
Ammonium	0.0001	0.04
Water	90–93	95

KIDNEY STONES

Sometimes, minerals from urine solidify and block the tubes inside the kidneys, forming kidney stones. Some are smooth, like pebbles, while others, called staghorn stones, are spiked. Passing a small stone causes intense pain. Larger stones can be broken up by ultrasound waves, or removed by surgery.

Dissected kidney with stones

1 KIDNEYS
Blood enters the kidneys and flows into the nephrons. Each nephron contains a filtering unit called a glomerulus. Water and salts pass from the blood into collecting tubules.

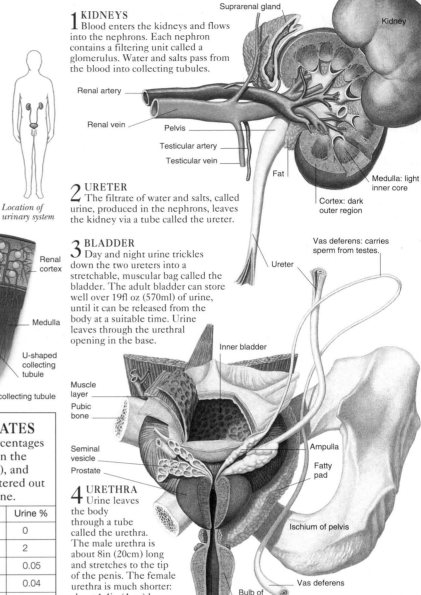

Suprarenal gland

Kidney

Renal artery

Renal vein

Pelvis

Testicular artery

Testicular vein

Fat

Medulla: light inner core

Cortex: dark outer region

2 URETER
The filtrate of water and salts, called urine, produced in the nephrons, leaves the kidney via a tube called the ureter.

3 BLADDER
Day and night urine trickles down the two ureters into a stretchable, muscular bag called the bladder. The adult bladder can store well over 19fl oz (570ml) of urine, until it can be released from the body at a suitable time. Urine leaves through the urethral opening in the base.

Vas deferens: carries sperm from testes.

Ureter

Inner bladder

Muscle layer

Pubic bone

Seminal vesicle

Prostate

Ampulla

Fatty pad

Ischium of pelvis

4 URETHRA
Urine leaves the body through a tube called the urethra. The male urethra is about 8in (20cm) long and stretches to the tip of the penis. The female urethra is much shorter: about 1.4in (4cm) long.

Vas deferens

Bulb of penis

Urethra

PROSTATE GLAND
This gland, found only in males, surrounds the part of the urethra nearest the bladder. It secretes a milky fluid into the urethra, which forms about 30% of the seminal fluid in which sperm are ejaculated. After the age of about 50, this gland naturally enlarges. However, sometimes it may squash the urethra and make urination difficult. Treatment usually involves removal of all or part of the gland.

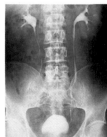

X-ray showing enlarged prostate gland

WASTE NOT
Our word "lotion" comes from the Latin word for urine, *lotium*. Romans used stale urine as a hair lotion because it prevented dandruff and killed lice. It was also used to help dye clothes.

KIDNEY DIALYSIS AND TRANSPLANT
If the kidneys fail completely, a dialysis machine can be used to filter blood. Blood passes through the machine 20 times before it is properly cleansed, and the patient must have two to three of these filtering sessions every week. More often, kidney failure is treated by transplanting a healthy organ. Drugs then prevent the body from rejecting the new kidney. Kidneys are the most commonly transplanted organ.

Patient connected to a kidney dialysis machine

COMMON PROBLEMS

Name	Description
Cystitis	Inflammation of inside of bladder caused by bacterial infection; more common in women than in men
Pyelonephritis	Infection of the kidney caused by bacteria
Kidney stones	Stones formed from salts in urine
Polycystic kidneys	Multiple fluid sacs that grow in kidneys
Bladder stones	Stones formed in bladder resulting from solidified salts in urine; can block urethral opening

ENDOCRINE SYSTEM

ENDOCRINE GLANDS produce chemicals that the body needs in order to grow properly and work smoothly. The chemicals that these glands (e.g. pituitary, thyroid gland) produce are called hormones and are released directly into the bloodstream. Tiny amounts can have great effects on the body's systems.

MAJOR ENDOCRINE GLANDS

Endocrine glands have no ducts or openings, but the hormones they produce enter the bloodstream as it passes through the gland. Hormones released by endocrine glands tend to have profound effects.

THE PITUITARY GLAND

The pituitary gland, situated in the brain, is often called the master gland; it secretes more than 10 hormones that act on other glands (e.g. thyroid, adrenals, ovaries, testes, mammary glands) to help them produce hormones of their own. Some of the functions of the pituitary gland are controlled by an area of the brain that lies just above it, called the hypothalamus. It also produces ADH (antidiuretic hormone), which controls the level of water in the body.

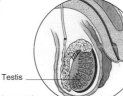

Micrograph showing cross-section of pituitary gland

The liver controls the duration of some hormones' action. When hormones pass through the liver, they are made inactive and pass, via the kidneys, into urine. (So, doctors test for pregnancy by analyzing urine for hormone changes).

- Pituitary gland
- Thyroid gland
- Parathyroid glands
- Adrenal gland
- Pancreas
- Ovaries

In women, the ovaries produce estrogen and progesterone, which control the development of sexual characteristics at puberty, such as breast growth and pubic hair, and aspects of menstruation.

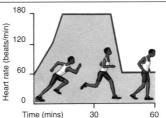

Testis

In men, the testes produce testosterone, a hormone that controls the development of sexual characteristics at puberty, such as pubic and body hair, and voice pitch.

FIGHT AND FLIGHT

In situations of fear, anger, or shock, adrenal glands produce adrenaline, which mobilizes the body in preparation for strong physical exertion. Levels return to normal after exercise.

HORMONE IMBALANCE

One of the hormones produced by the pituitary controls our rate of growth. Too much can cause gigantism (excessive growth). Too little causes short stature.

Tallest person: 8ft 11in (2.7m) tall

Smallest person: 24 in (61cm) tall

NERVOUS ENERGY

When Mrs. Maxwell Rogers of Florida found her son pinned underneath their car, fear and adrenaline gave her the strength to lift the 1.6-ton vehicle. She cracked several vertebrae.

ENDOCRINE GLANDS AND THEIR HORMONES

Gland	Hormones produced	Function	Effect of deficiency	Effect of excess
Thyroid	Thyroxine, triiodothyronine	Regulate chemical activity in cells. Essential for normal physical growth and mental development in children	In children, retards growth and mental development (cretinism)	Thyrotoxicosis: overactivity, anxiety, weight loss, diarrhea, rapid pulse
Pituitary	Growth hormone TSH Prolactin ACTH LH and FSH MSH ADH Oxytocin	Stimulates cell growth in bone, cartilage, and soft tissue Stimulates thyroid gland to secrete hormones Stimulates breast growth and milk production Stimulates adrenal glands to secrete hormones Controls functioning of sexual organs Controls skin darkening Acts on kidneys to decrease water loss Stimulates uterus contraction during birth	Short stature Slow metabolism, bloating Reduced sex drive Can cause infertility Increases water loss Prolonged labor	Gigantism Overproduction of eggs Causes fluid retention, bloating
Parathyroid	Parathyroid hormone (PTH)	Regulates blood calcium levels; important for nerves and muscle functioning	Tetany: spasm and twitching of the muscles	May cause thinning of bones (osteoporosis), or kidney stones
Adrenal	Epinephrine Cortisone Aldosterone	Mobilizes body in response to fear, anger, shock Controls metabolism, body shape Controls level of salts in body	Addison's disease: salt imbalance, low blood pressure, weakness, weight loss, intestinal upsets	Cushing's Disease: obesity, moon face, high blood pressure, high blood sugar levels, hairiness
Pancreas	Insulin Glucagon	Control level of sugar in blood	Diabetes: excess sugar in blood	Rare: Coma, due to reduced sugar in blood
Kidneys	Erythropoietin 1,25 dihydroxychole-calciferol Renin	Acts on bone marrow to produce red blood cells Raises amount of calcium absorbed in gut, formed from Vitamin D Helps control blood pressure	Anemia Rickets, osteomalacia	High blood pressure
Ovaries	Estrogen Progesterone	Stimulates breast growth and egg production, pubic and body hair, changes distribution of body fat at puberty. Thickens uterus walls after ovulation	Infertility	Levels naturally high during pregnancy: at other times, can cause blood clots
Testes	Testosterone	Stimulates sperm production, muscle and bone enlargement, deepening of voice, pubic and body hair. Small amounts present in females	In males, low sperm count and sex drive. Hair thinning	Excessive muscular development and body hair. In males, can cause painful, persistent erection (priapism)

REPRODUCTION AND GROWTH

PLANTS AND ANIMALS produce young like themselves. This creation of life is called reproduction. Humans reproduce sexually: men and women mate to produce their young. A new human life begins when a sperm cell from the father joins an egg cell from the mother. This cell divides into many cells, until it begins to look like a baby.

REPRODUCTION SYSTEMS

FEMALE SEX ORGANS
Eggs are stored in both ovaries. Each month, during the menstrual cycle, one egg ripens, leaves the ovary, and enters the fallopian tube. If it is then fertilized by sperm, it becomes implanted in the uterus. If the egg is not fertilized, the uterus lining breaks up and is shed from the body (menstruation).

The woman's main sex organs, the two ovaries, are inside the abdomen.

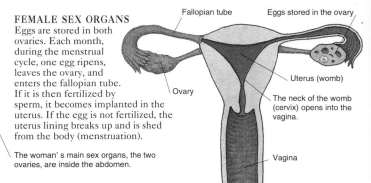

Fallopian tube
Eggs stored in the ovary
Uterus (womb)
Ovary
The neck of the womb (cervix) opens into the vagina.
Vagina

MALE SEX ORGANS
The two testes produce fresh sperm cells every day. The cells are stored in the testes and epididymides. If the sperm are not released, the cells break down and are reabsorbed into the bloodstream.

The man's main sex organs, the testes and penis, are outside the abdomen.

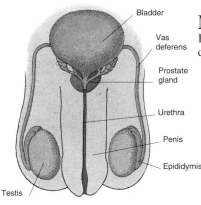

Bladder
Vas deferens
Prostate gland
Urethra
Penis
Epididymis
Testis

MENSTRUAL CYCLE

From puberty until menopause, a woman has monthly menstrual cycles (menstruation), during which she loses blood.

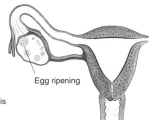

Egg ripening

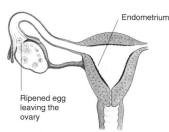

Endometrium
Ripened egg leaving the ovary

1 An egg starts to ripen in one of the ovaries. The lining of the uterus, called the endometrium, swells with blood in preparation for the egg.

2 About two weeks later, the ripe egg enters the fallopian tube. It is now ready to be fertilized.

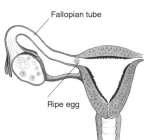

Fallopian tube
Ripe egg

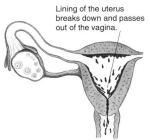

Lining of the uterus breaks down and passes out of the vagina.

3 The egg reaches the uterus. If the egg is not fertilized, it is expelled.

4 The lining of the uterus breaks down and passes out of the vagina as menstrual blood flow.

REPRODUCTION FACTS

• The sperm cell is about 0.002in (0.05mm) long and can be seen only with a microscope. It can swim at about 7in (18cm) per hour and takes, on average, 2 hours to reach the egg.

• The testes are kept outside the body in the scrotum, since they need to be 7°F (4°C) cooler than the body temperature. If they heat up, sperm production slows down and infertility may result.

• The biggest human cell is the egg cell; it measures 0.004–0.008in (0.1–0.2mm) in diameter and is just visible to the naked eye.

Types of contraceptive

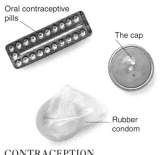

Oral contraceptive pills
The cap
Rubber condom

CONTRACEPTION
Contraceptives are used to prevent conception (pregnancy). A rubber sheath, or condom, fits over the penis to catch semen. Hormones in the oral contraceptive pill prevent eggs from being released. The cap is placed over the cervix to stop sperm from entering the uterus.

SEXUAL INTERCOURSE

For the egg to be fertilized by sperm, a man and woman must have sexual intercourse. The man's penis becomes erect and enters the woman's vagina. When the man climaxes, he ejaculates a fluid, semen, which contains sperm cells. The cells swim into the fallopian tube. One of these cells may reach the egg and fertilize it.

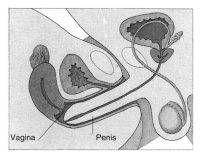

Vagina
Penis

SPERM RACE

More than 300 million sperm are ejaculated into the vagina; 50–150 sperm reach the egg in the fallopian tube, but only one may fertilize the egg.

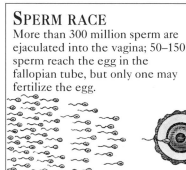

FERTILIZATION

After sexual intercourse, sperm cells enter the uterus and travel along the fallopian tube. Only one sperm cell may break through the outer layer of the egg cell. Once the egg is fertilized, it divides into two cells, then into four, and so on.

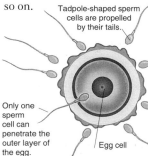

Tadpole-shaped sperm cells are propelled by their tails.

Only one sperm cell can penetrate the outer layer of the egg.

Egg cell

IMPLANTATION

Once an egg has been fertilized, it divides into a ball of cells, called the morula, as it travels down the fallopian tube. After five days, the cells form a hollow ball, or blastocyst. About a week after fertilization, the blastocyst becomes implanted in the rich lining of the uterus.

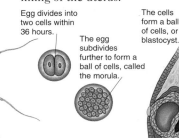

Egg divides into two cells within 36 hours.

The egg subdivides further to form a ball of cells, called the morula.

The cells form a ball of cells, or blastocyst.

Uterus

STAGES OF GROWTH

FOUR-WEEK EMBRYO
The blastocyst quickly develops to form the placenta, umbilical cord, and the developing baby, or embryo. The embryo is protected by amniotic fluid. About now, its heart begins to beat.

Formation of the eye begins.

Leg bud

Arm bud

Vertebra, or backbone

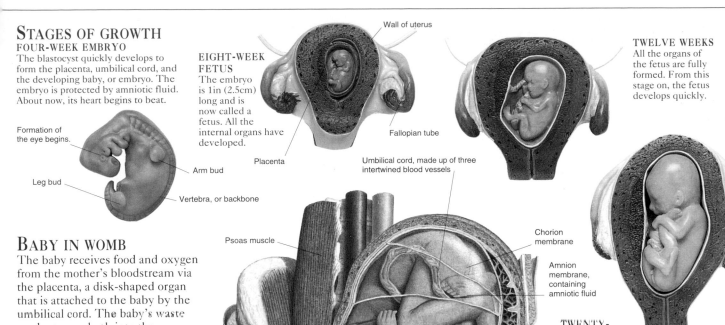

Wall of uterus

EIGHT-WEEK FETUS
The embryo is 1in (2.5cm) long and is now called a fetus. All the internal organs have developed.

Placenta

Fallopian tube

Umbilical cord, made up of three intertwined blood vessels

TWELVE WEEKS
All the organs of the fetus are fully formed. From this stage on, the fetus develops quickly.

Psoas muscle

Chorion membrane

Amnion membrane, containing amniotic fluid

BABY IN WOMB

The baby receives food and oxygen from the mother's bloodstream via the placenta, a disk-shaped organ that is attached to the baby by the umbilical cord. The baby's waste products pass back into the mother's bloodstream for excretion. The baby is surrounded by amniotic fluid, which cushions it from knocks and bumps.

CHILD DEVELOPMENT

SIX-MONTH BABY
Most babies sit propped up and can support the weight of their heads. They will start to make word sounds such as "Da-Da" or "Ma-Ma." The first teeth start to show.

NINE- TO TWELVE-MONTH BABY
Most babies learn to crawl, can pull themselves upright on furniture, and can stand unsupported for a second or two. By 12 months, they may have up to eight teeth and weigh three times their birthweight.

During the last few weeks of pregnancy, the baby turns around so its head is facing downward, ready to be born.

Vagina

Placenta

TWENTY-WEEK FETUS
During the last 6 months of growth, the baby develops fine details like fingernails and hair. From 16 to 20 weeks, it starts to move and kick. This is called quickening. The baby can now hear, tell light from dark, swallow, and suck its thumb.

NEWBORN BABY
After about 40 weeks, or 9 months, of development, the baby is ready to be born. The muscles of the uterus contract and the cervix dilates, pushing the baby out, usually headfirst. The baby soon takes its first breath of fresh air. The newborn baby can hear well but cannot focus its eyes properly.

Newborn baby

EIGHTEEN-MONTH CHILD
Most children can walk unaided. They will know at least six words, usually many more, and can put words together to make simple phrases. They can climb stairs and make towers of blocks.

TWO- TO THREE-YEAR-OLD CHILD
Children can hold a pencil and draw. By age 3, they can talk in simple sentences and copy basic shapes.

PUBERTY FACTS

- When children reach puberty, they undergo physical and psychological changes that prepare them for sexual maturity.

- A girl's ovaries produce the hormones progesterone and estrogen. These cause breasts to develop, hips to broaden, and pubic hair to grow. At this time menstruation begins.

- A boy's testes produce the hormone testosterone. This causes muscles to develop, hair to grow on the face and body, the voice to deepen, and sperm to be produced.

GENETICS

Egg and sperm cells each contain 23 chromosomes. When an egg and a sperm cell join, the new cell has 46 chromosomes – the same as all other types of cell in the human body. A baby's sex is determined by one chromosome, X or Y. The egg carries only X, but the sperm can carry either X or Y. If the egg is fertilized by a sperm carrying an X, the sex will be female (XX); if the sperm carries a Y, the sex will be male (XY).

Father (XY)   *Mother (XX)*

Girl (XX) *Boy (XY)*   *Girl (XX)* *Boy (XY)*

GROWTH FACTS

- The proportions of our bodies change as we grow. A baby's head accounts for about one-fourth of its body length. By adulthood, the proportion has reduced to one-eighth.

- Girls grow faster than boys during the early stages of growth. A girl is about three-quarters of her adult height by the age of 7½; a boy reaches this height by the age of 9.

- A person is about 0.4in (1cm) taller in the morning than in the evening. This is because the pads of cartilage in the spine become more compressed during the day.

COMMON PROBLEMS

Ectopic pregnancy	Fetus implanted outside the womb.
Infertility	Inability to conceive a child.
Miscarriage	Premature ending of pregnancy on or before 24 weeks.
Preeclampsia	High blood pressure developed during pregnancy.

MEDICINE

THROUGHOUT THE AGES, people have tried to find ways to cure illness. In early times, it was believed that disease was a punishment from the gods. Today, scientists are constantly searching for new ways of treating and preventing illness.

c.10,000 B.C. Trepanning is practiced in Europe and America. Holes are drilled into a person's skull to cure illness. People believed that evil spirits left through these holes.

Trepanning

2700 B.C. First named doctor is Imhotep of Egypt. He acquired a great reputation for healing. He later became known as the Egyptian god of medicine.

Imhotep

c.A.D. 130 Galen, a Greek physician, introduces the idea that a person's mood depends on the balancing of four fluids, or humors, in the body: black bile (melancholy), yellow bile (choleric), blood (sanguine), and phlegm (phlegmatic).

The four humors: choleric (with lion), sanguine (with ape), phlegmatic (with sheep), and melancholic (with hog).

1300s Leeches are used to suck blood from the body, since it was believed that too much blood was the cause of some illnesses. Blood-letting is used to treat a variety of illnesses, such as tumors, fevers, and gout.

Leech

1543 First accurate anatomical drawings of the human body are drawn by Flemish doctor Andreas Vesalius (1514–64). Stolen corpses are used for his studies.

First anatomical drawings

c.1590 Compound microscope invented. Dutchman, Zacharias Janssen (1580–c.1638) makes lenses held in two iron tubes, one inside the other.

Early microscope

1683 Bacteria first seen under a microscope by Antonie van Leeuwenhoek (1632–1723), a Dutch scientist.

Antonie van Leeuwenhoek

1796 Vaccination against smallpox is discovered by English doctor Edward Jenner (1749–1823). He innoculates an eight-year-old boy with cowpox taken from a sore on the hand of a dairymaid.

Coin issued c.1800 to celebrate Edward Jenner's discovery of vaccination.

1800 Effects of electricity on muscles described by Italian physicist Volta (1745–1827).

1805 Morphine, a painkiller, is separated from opium.

1810 Homeopathy is introduced by German physician Samuel Hahnemann (1755–1843). This new system is based on the principle of curing like with like.

Samuel Hahnemann

1854 Florence Nightingale (1820–1910), born in Florence, Italy, nurses soldiers during the Crimean War (1854–56) in the hospital at Scutari, Turkey. She becomes known as "the lady with the lamp." Four years later, she opens the Nightingale Training School for nurses in London, which greatly improves nursing standards.

Florence Nightingale

1860 Antiseptic, in the form of weak carbolic acid, is used to prevent infections during operations by English surgeon Joseph Lister (1827–1912).

Joseph Lister

1864 Red Cross Society founded in Geneva, Switzerland, by Swiss businessman Henri Dunant (1829–1910), after helping casualties at the Battle of Solferino (1859).

Henri Dunant

1895 X-rays discovered by German physicist Wilhelm Roentgen (1845–1923). He uses his wife's hand for the first pictures.

One of the first X-rays

1895 Psychoanalysis founded by Austrian doctor Sigmund Freud (1856–1939). He treats people with mental disorders by talking to them about their dreams and childhood experiences.

Sigmund Freud

1902 Radium and polonium discovered by Polish-born Marie Curie (1867–1934) and her husband, Pierre Curie (1859–1906), of France. These elements are now used in radiation therapy to treat cancer.

Marie and Pierre Curie

1910 Four blood groups, A, B, AB, O, discovered by Austrian pathologist Dr. Karl Landsteiner (1868–1943).

1912 Vitamins discovered by British biochemist Sir Frederick Gowland Hopkins (1861–1947).

1920 First EEG machine is developed to record electrical brain waves.

1921 First birth control clinic founded by Marie Stopes (1880–195?) in London.

1952 Vaccine against polio produced by American scientist Jonas Salk (born 1914).

Jonas Salk

1953 Structure of genetic material (DNA) discovered by American biologist James Watson (born 1928) and English biochemist Francis Crick (born 1916).

Watson and Crick

1954 Heart–lung machine developed for use during heart surgery.

1954 First internal heart pacemaker fitted in Stockholm, Sweden.

1958 Endoscope, a flexible telescope that looks inside the body, is developed.

1967 First heart transplant, performed by South African surgeon Christiaan Barnard (born 1922). The patient survives 18 days.

1970 Heart pacemakers in general use.

Christiaan Barnard

B.C. *The Canons of [Med]icine* is written in China. [In]cludes an account of blood [circu]lation.

B.C. **Surgery** practiced [in In]dia. Surgeons perform [amp]utations and skin grafts and [remo]ve cataracts from eyes.

400 B.C. Greek physician Hippocrates (c.460–377 B.C.) teaches that the first duty of a doctor is to do what is best for his patients and makes rules for his pupils to follow. They form the basis of the Hippocratic Oath, which doctors still follow today.

Hippocrates

2 B.C. Acupuncture, puncturing the skin with needles to cure illness, is practiced in China.

Acupuncture chart

B.C. | 1000 B.C. | 1000 B.C. | 400 B.C. | 400 B.C. | 2 B.C.

[16..]s **Quinine** is used to [treat] malaria in South [Ame]rica.

[161]5 **First thermometer** [for ta]king human [temp]erature invented by [Italia]n physician Sanctorius [(1561]–1636).

Sanctorius' thermometer

1628 First description of the circulation of the blood by Englishman William Harvey (1578–1657), physician to King James I and King Charles I of England.

William Harvey with Charles I

1600 | 1615 | 1628

First stethoscope [mad]e from a roll of paper [by F]rench doctor René [Laën]nec (1781–1826).

[184]4 **Laughing gas** [(nitro]us oxide) is first used [as a g]eneral anesthetic by [Hora]ce Wells (1815–48).

René Laënnec

1846 Ether used as an anesthetic by William Morton (1819–68), an American dentist.

1847 Chloroform is used as an anesthetic by Sir James Young Simpson (1811–70).

1849 First female medical graduate in the US is Elizabeth Blackwell (1821–1910).

Elizabeth Blackwell

1844 | 1846 | 1847 | 1849

[18..] **Elizabeth [Ga]rrett Anderson** is [first] woman to practice [medi]cine in Britain.

[Past]eurization invented [by F]renchman Louis [Paste]ur (1822–95) to [help] treat food and kill [bact]eria.

Louis Pasteur

1883 Bacteria that cause tuberculosis and cholera discovered by German scientist Robert Koch (1843–1910).

1883 Cocaine used as a local anesthetic during an eye operation.

1886 Surgical instruments are sterilized by steam. Masks, gowns, and capes are used by surgeons in operations.

Operation, 1880s

1880 | 1883 | 1886

[19..] **Insulin** discovered by Canadian scientists Banting [(1891]–1941) and Best (1899–1978).

[1928] **Penicillin** [discov]ered by Scottish [bacte]riologist Alexander [Flemi]ng (1881–1955), in a [green] mold growing on a

Alexander Fleming

1936 First mobile blood-transfusion service organized by Canadian doctor Norman Bethune.

1950 First kidney transplant performed in Chicago, Illinois.

1950s Birth control pill developed for women. By the early 1960s, it is widely used.

Birth control pill

1928 | 1950 | 1950

[19..] **CT (computerized [tomo]graphy) scan** introduced. [Produ]ces more detailed picture of [intern]al organs than an X-ray.

[MRI] (magnetic resonance [imagi]ng) scan uses radio waves [to pro]duce pictures of the inside [of the] body.

MRI scan

1976 Bionic, transistorized arm is fitted to the victim of a road accident in Australia.

1978 First test tube baby, Louise Brown, is born in Britain.

1980s–1990s Laser surgery used in eye operations and to remove cancer cells.
Keyhole surgery is practiced: operations are performed through small incisions in the body.
Gene transplants performed: defective or missing genes are replaced with artificial copies.

1976 | 1978 | 1980 | 1990

BRANCHES OF MEDICINE

Name	What it deals with
Cardiology	Heart and arteries
Chiropody	Feet
Dermatology	Skin
Endocrinology	Hormones
Gastroenterology	Stomach, intestines
Geriatrics	Elderly people
Gynecology	Female reproductive organs
Hematology	Blood
Neurology	Brain and nerves
Ophthalmology	Eyes
Osteopathy	Manipulation of back and limbs to ease pain
Pediatrics	Children
Pharmacology	Drugs
Physical therapy	Exercise and massage of the body
Psychiatry	Mental illness
Obstetrics	Pregnancy
Oncology	Growths and tumors
Orthopedics	Bones, joints, muscles
Pathology	Body tissues and fluids
Radiology	X-rays
Renal medicine	Kidneys
Surgery	Operations

DRUG TYPES

Name	Use
Analgesic	Provides relief from pain, such as headache and stomachache.
Antacid	Counteracts acid in the stomach to relieve heartburn, indigestion, etc.
Antibiotic	Treats infections by killing bacteria.
Antihistamine	Counteracts allergies such as hay fever.
Antipyretic	Reduces fevers, such as those caused by influenza.
Bronchodilator	Eases breathing in diseases such as asthma.
Decongestant	Common cold treatment; works by unblocking nasal passages.

RETURN OF THE LEECH

Leeches are being used again in modern medicine. After certain operations, they are used to restore blood circulation and to prevent the blood from clotting.

NUTRITION

A GOOD DIET is an essential part of a healthy lifestyle for children and adults. Rich in vitamins, minerals, and other nutrients, a balanced diet will assist growth and help fight disease.

VITAL COMPONENTS OF FOOD

Nutrients are the essential elements for healthy eating and include:

Vitamins
These aid the release of energy from glucose, and assist the body's growth and repair.

Minerals
These help growth and repair processes, the release of energy from nutrients, and help form new tissues.

Fiber
The indigestible part of fruit, vegetables, bread, and cereals, fiber aids normal bowel function.

Carbohydrates
These are compounds of carbon, hydrogen, and oxygen, such as starch and sugar, that provide the body with energy.

Fats
These supply concentrated energy. They also help form chemical "messengers," such as hormones.

Protein
This is a substance the body needs for growth and repair. It is found in foods such as meat, fish, cheese, and beans.

A BALANCED DIET

The food pyramid was developed by American nutritionists in the early 1990s. It represents the proportions in which the five food groups should be eaten each day for a balanced diet.

Sugars, fats, and oils (use sparingly)

Dairy products (2–3 servings)

Meat, poultry, seafood, eggs, beans, nuts (2–3 servings)

Vegetables (3–5 servings)

Fruit (2–4 servings)

Grains and grain products (5–12 servings)

FOOD FACTS

• Surprisingly, frozen vegetables are just as good for you as fresh vegetables.
• In India, many people are vegetarian, following the Hindu belief that all life is sacred.
• All vegetables contain some protein, but dried peas and beans have large amounts.

FOOD WORDS

Acid A substance produced by the stomach that helps digest food.
Antibodies Proteins in the blood that protect the body by fighting bacteria and viruses.
Antioxidant A substance added to foods to prevent them from oxidizing and going stale.
Calorie A unit used to measure the energy content of foods.
Carnivore Person who eats meat.
Cholesterol A chemical found in certain foods, such as eggs, and produced in the liver from saturated fats.
Digestion The breaking down of food in the stomach so that nutrients may be absorbed into the body.
Glucose A sugar, released from the digestion of starch and sucrose, that is the body's main energy source.
Hormone Chemical "messenger" that moves in the bloodstream and controls the functions of the body.
Kilojoule A unit of measurement showing energy content in food. One kilojoule equals 1,000 joules.
Metabolism The chemical processes occurring in the body that result in growth, production of energy, and elimination of waste.
Nutrient An essential dietary factor – carbohydrate, fat, protein, vitamin, and mineral.
Saturated fat Fat that tends to increase the amount of unwanted cholesterol in the blood. Mostly found in animal fats.
Starch A polymer found in plants that is an important part of the human diet.
Unsaturated fat Fat that helps decrease unwanted types of cholesterol in the blood. Most vegetable fats are unsaturated.
Vegan Person who does not eat or use any products or by-products from animals.
Vegetarian Person who does not eat animal products, sometimes with the exception of fish and eggs.

MAIN VITAMIN SOURCES AND REQUIREMENTS

Type of vitamin	Where found	Required for
Vitamin A	Liver, fish-liver oils, egg yolk, and yellow-orange-colored fruit and vegetables.	Growth, healthy eyes and skin. Fights infection.
Vitamin B$_1$ (Thiamine)	Whole grains (whole-grain bread and pasta), brown rice, liver, beans, peas, and nuts.	Healthy functioning of nervous and digestive systems
Vitamin B$_2$ (Riboflavin)	Milk, liver, cheese, eggs, green vegetables, brewer's yeast, lean meat, and wheat germ.	Metabolism of protein, fat, and carbohydrates. Keeps tissues healthy.
Vitamin B$_3$ (Niacin)	Liver, lean meats, poultry, fish, nuts, whole-grain cereals, and dried beans.	Production of energy and a healthy skin.
Vitamin B$_6$ (Pyridoxine)	Liver, poultry, pork, fish, bananas, potatoes, dried beans, and most fruit and vegetables.	Metabolism of protein and production of red blood cells.
Vitamin C	Citrus fruit, strawberries, tomatoes, and potatoes.	Healthy skin, teeth, bones, and tissues, and for fighting disease.
Vitamin D	Oily fish (such as salmon), liver, eggs, cod-liver oil, and sunlight.	The absorption of calcium and phosphorus.
Vitamin E	Margarine, lettuce, leafy green vegetables, whole-grain cereals, and nuts.	The formation of new red blood cells. Protection of cell linings in the lungs.

BURNING CALORIES

The energy from food is measured in calories. But if your calorie intake exceeds your energy and body maintenance requirements, you will put on weight. Physical activity helps you avoid putting on weight by burning off calories. Different activities will burn off calories at different rates.

Judo
Male: 815 calories per hour
Female: 702 calories per hour

Running
Male: 810 calories per hour
Female: 695 calories per hour

Basketball
Male: 580 calories per hour
Female: 497 calories per hour

TRADITIONAL MEDICINE

MORE AND MORE people are now turning to traditional, or alternative, forms of medicine to improve their health or simply to stay well. Many of these therapies treat the whole person and aim to restore the body's natural state of balance, or harmony.

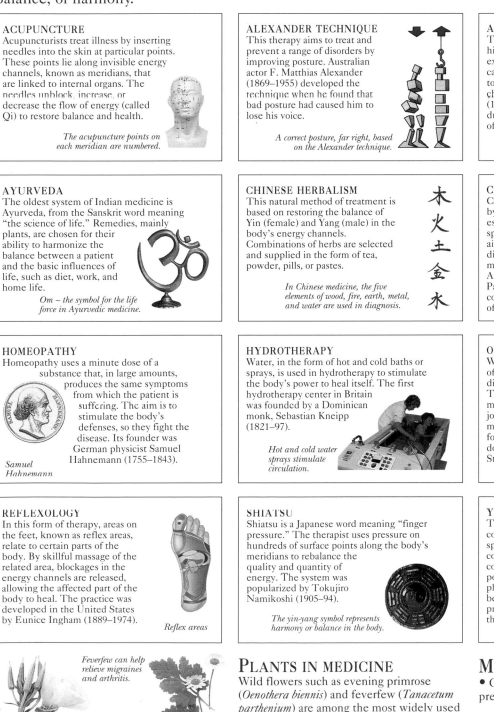

EARLY HEALING

For thousands of years, people have used plants and minerals to ease pain, heal wounds, and relieve the symptoms of illness. In ancient Egypt, records from about 1600 B.C. list plant remedies, such as gentian, senna, and thyme, that are still used today. Archaeologists have also found in China lists of herbs carved on oracle bones dated about the same time.

This detail from the 12th-century Persian Book of Antidotes shows the growing of plants for medicinal purposes.

ACUPUNCTURE
Acupuncturists treat illness by inserting needles into the skin at particular points. These points lie along invisible energy channels, known as meridians, that are linked to internal organs. The needles unblock, increase, or decrease the flow of energy (called Qi) to restore balance and health.

The acupuncture points on each meridian are numbered.

ALEXANDER TECHNIQUE
This therapy aims to treat and prevent a range of disorders by improving posture. Australian actor F. Matthias Alexander (1869–1955) developed the technique when he found that bad posture had caused him to lose his voice.

A correct posture, far right, based on the Alexander technique.

AROMATHERAPY
This form of treatment uses highly concentrated oils extracted from plants. The oils can be used in massage, added to baths, or inhaled. French chemist Réné Gattefossé (1881–1950), who treated soldiers during World War I, was a pioneer of modern aromatherapy.

Rose oil has a soothing effect.

AYURVEDA
The oldest system of Indian medicine is Ayurveda, from the Sanskrit word meaning "the science of life." Remedies, mainly plants, are chosen for their ability to harmonize the balance between a patient and the basic influences of life, such as diet, work, and home life.

Om – the symbol for the life force in Ayurvedic medicine.

CHINESE HERBALISM
This natural method of treatment is based on restoring the balance of Yin (female) and Yang (male) in the body's energy channels. Combinations of herbs are selected and supplied in the form of tea, powder, pills, or pastes.

In Chinese medicine, the five elements of wood, fire, earth, metal, and water are used in diagnosis.

CHIROPRACTIC
Chiropractic relieves pain by manipulating the joints, especially those of the spine. It can be used to aid people with disorders of the joints, muscles, and spine. American David Daniel Palmer (1845–1913) is considered the founder of modern chiropractic.

A chiropractor checks the spine.

HOMEOPATHY
Homeopathy uses a minute dose of a substance that, in large amounts, produces the same symptoms from which the patient is suffering. The aim is to stimulate the body's defenses, so they fight the disease. Its founder was German physicist Samuel Hahnemann (1755–1843).

Samuel Hahnemann

HYDROTHERAPY
Water, in the form of hot and cold baths or sprays, is used in hydrotherapy to stimulate the body's power to heal itself. The first hydrotherapy center in Britain was founded by a Dominican monk, Sebastian Kneipp (1821–97).

Hot and cold water sprays stimulate circulation.

OSTEOPATHY
When the body's framework is out of alignment, osteopaths can diagnose and treat disorders. They use their hands to massage and manipulate the joints to restore normal movement. Osteopathy was founded by American doctor Andrew Taylor Still (1828–1917).

Shoulders and spine out of alignment

REFLEXOLOGY
In this form of therapy, areas on the feet, known as reflex areas, relate to certain parts of the body. By skillful massage of the related area, blockages in the energy channels are released, allowing the affected part of the body to heal. The practice was developed in the United States by Eunice Ingham (1889–1974).

Reflex areas

SHIATSU
Shiatsu is a Japanese word meaning "finger pressure." The therapist uses pressure on hundreds of surface points along the body's meridians to rebalance the quality and quantity of energy. The system was popularized by Tokujiro Namikoshi (1905–94).

The yin-yang symbol represents harmony or balance in the body.

YOGA
This well-known Hindu system combines physical, mental, and spiritual health. The most common form is Hatha yoga, a course of exercises and postures designed to promote physical and mental well-being. Yoga has been practiced in India for thousands of years.

The lotus position

Feverfew can help relieve migraines and arthritis.

Evening primrose is used for skin problems.

PLANTS IN MEDICINE
Wild flowers such as evening primrose (*Oenothera biennis*) and feverfew (*Tanacetum parthenium*) are among the most widely used medicinal herbs. Research has confirmed their power to heal.

MEDICINE FACTS
• Chinese medicine uses dried seahorse in preparations to treat kidney problems.

• In Ayurvedic medicine, the flesh from a pit viper is given to relieve muscular pain.

FIRST AID

FIRST AID IS the first assistance or treatment given to a person for any injury or sudden illness, before the arrival of an ambulance, doctor, or other qualified help. The main aim of first aid is to prevent the injury from becoming worse.

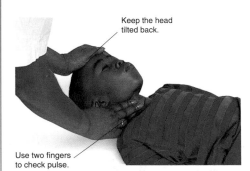

Keep the head tilted back.

Use two fingers to check pulse.

CHECK FOR A PULSE

If the heart is beating, there will be a pulse in the neck. Tilt the head back and feel for the Adam's apple with the pads of two fingers. Slide your fingers back into the gap between the windpipe and the muscle that runs beside it. Feel for five seconds before deciding that the pulse is absent.

CALL AN AMBULANCE OR DOCTOR FOR:

• Unexplained drowsiness or loss of consciousness
• Severe bleeding
• Unexplained convulsions of any sort
• Difficulty in breathing
• Severe abdominal pain
• Sudden blurred vision or seeing colored halos around lights

FIRST-AID KIT

Every home and car should have a first-aid kit containing items needed for emergency treatment. Keep the box clean and clearly labeled, and out of reach of children. Replace items as soon as you use them.

LEARNING THE A, B, AND C

The A (Airway), B (Breathing), and C (Circulation) of any unconscious person must be established within three minutes in order to prevent permanent injury.

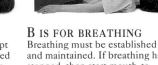

A IS FOR AIRWAY

Airway must be opened and kept open. Tilt the head of the injured person (victim) back and lift the chin forward to open the airway.

B IS FOR BREATHING

Breathing must be established and maintained. If breathing has stopped, then start mouth-to-mouth resuscitation by blowing your own expelled air into the victim's lungs.

C IS FOR CIRCULATION

Circulation of blood must be maintained. Be sure the heart is beating by feeling for a pulse. If the heart has stopped, chest compressions can be applied, together with artificial respiration. In the US and Canada, the hand nearest the victim's feet should be used for compressions.

RECOVERY POSITION

If an injured child is unconscious but still breathing and has a pulse, place her or him in the recovery position.

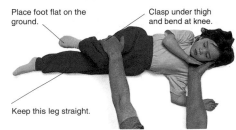

Place foot flat on the ground.

Clasp under thigh and bend at knee.

Keep this leg straight.

First, lay the child on her back and straighten her legs. Bend the arm nearest to you and lay it on the ground with the palm up. Bring the other arm across her chest and hold the palm of your hand against her cheek. Use your free hand to pull her knee up.

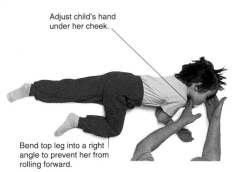

Adjust child's hand under her cheek.

Bend top leg into a right angle to prevent her from rolling forward.

Gently pull on the thigh of the bent leg, and roll the patient toward you and onto her side. Bend this same leg into a right angle to prevent her from rolling forward. Tilt her head back to make sure the airway is still open. Call an ambulance.

ADVICE NOTE

This page supplies some basic information on first aid. It does not offer complete procedures, and readers are advised to refer to a first-aid manual for full guidance.

Scissors for cutting bandages

Different injuries require a variety of dressings and bandages.

Tweezers for removing splinters

Cotton is useful for cleaning wounds.

Adhesive bandages protect minor cuts and scrapes while they heal.

Safety pins to hold dressings in place.

Eye bath is useful for washing the eye clean of chemicals such as bleach.

Elastic bandages stretch to provide support for sprained ankles.

Antiseptic cream protects minor cuts against infection.

HOME SAFETY FACTS

Although most people think of home as the safest place, you are more likely to have an accident in the home than at work or school. To make the home a safer place:

• Do not use electrical equipment in the bathroom or near water.

• Keep saucepan handles turned inward so they do not hang over the work surface, and use back burners of a stove first.

• Store dangerous items on a high shelf, out of the reach of children.

• Do not put toxic substances in a familiar food or drink container.

• Run the cold water into the bath first, and keep testing the temperature as you add the hot water.

• Do not hold a hot drink when you have a baby on your lap.

• Do not put an iron on the floor to cool; put it out of reach.

BELIEFS, CUSTOMS, AND SOCIETY

Focusing on the way we live, this section provides detailed facts and figures on religion, politics, philosophy, and money around the world, as well as describing all kinds of strange customs and rituals.

Myths and Legends • Faith Systems • Other Faiths
Great Thinkers • Patterns of Family and Society • Customs and Rituals
Celebration and Decoration • Money • Politics • Law and Order

On pages 139 to 143, B.C.E. (Before the Common Era)
and C.E. (Common Era) stand for the same dates
as B.C. and A.D.

MYTHS AND LEGENDS

FROM ANCIENT TIMES people have invented stories to explain the world around them. Myths help explain events such as how the world was created and why people die, as well as natural phenomena such as the weather. Legends are closely related to myths but may be based on actual events.

AN AZTEC MYTH

Quetzalcoatl, the chief god of the Aztecs, who lived in Central Mexico, took the form of a feathered serpent. He created humans and gave them knowledge, but then he sailed away on a raft of serpents. The Aztecs believed that their world would end upon his return.

This mask, representing the god Quetzalcoatl, is made of turquoise mosaic.

FIGURE OF VENUS
This clay figure from Austria shows the Venus of Willendorf, dated 25,000 B.C. Her full figure represents the fertility of the goddess.

EARTH GODDESS

For thousands of years, people in different parts of the world worshipped images of the Earth Goddess, or Great Mother. As the "mother of the world," she was believed to give life to plants, animals, and humans. Because the power of fertility ensures the future of humanity, earth goddesses have always played an important role in mythology.

KING ARTHUR

A famous British legend tells how the magic sword Excalibur was given to King Arthur by the Lady of the Lake. Another version tells how he proved himself king by pulling the sword from a stone. It is thought that Arthur may have been a real king or chieftain in 5th-century Britain.

Arthur watches the sword Excalibur rise from the lake.

CREATION MYTHS

Stories that try to answer the mystery of how the world began are called creation myths.

IZANAGI AND IZANAMI
The Japanese thought the Earth was once a shapeless mass. A god and goddess, Izanagi and Izanami, stirred the mass with a long spear. Gradually the mixture thickened and dropped off the spear to form an island. The god and goddess married and had children who became the eight islands of Japan.

THE RAVEN
A Native American myth tells how a raven, flying over water, could find nowhere to land. He dropped pebbles to make islands and then created trees. Beasts lived in the forests and fish in the sea. When the raven had made the first man and woman out of wood and clay, the world was complete.

SACRED SITES

Mount Shasta, California, is a Native American site where the power of the Earth Spirit is strong.

Glastonbury Tor, England, is one of the reputed resting places of the Holy Grail, the cup Christ drank from at the Last Supper.

Uluru, Australia, is a special place to the Aboriginals. Paintings in rock shelters show the journeys of the ancestral beings who formed its features.

Cape Reinga, New Zealand, is where spirits of the dead depart for Hawaiki, far away in the mystical beginnings of Polynesia.

THE WORLD EGG
In Egyptian mythology, life began from water. The first dry land – a primeval mound – rose above the water. A large bird called the Great Cackler alighted on the land and laid the world egg, which brought the first life.

Uluru (Ayers Rock)

EGYPTIAN MYTHOLOGY

Gods in Egypt often had a human body and the head of an animal or bird to represent their power.

Name	Form
Ra (Amun-Ra)	Universal god, takes many forms
Anubis	Jackal or dog
Apis	Bull
Bastet	Cat
Hathor	Cow
Isis	Woman with throne on her head
Khepri	Scarab
Mut	Vulture
Nut	Woman with long body, or cow
Osiris	Mummified man
Set, or Seth	Fantastic beast
Sobek	Crocodile
Tefnut	Lioness
Thoth	Ibis or baboon

MYTHICAL BEASTS

There are some frightening creatures in mythology that may have been created to represent evil. Some appear as half-human, half-animal; others take on shapes they can change at will.

DEMONS
Demons, or evil spirits, are often shown as grotesque beings who haunt cemeteries and force people to commit violent acts. They appear in various forms in the religions of the world, sometimes with cloven feet, horns, and a long tail.

MONSTERS
This figure shows a gorgon, a female monster from Greek mythology, who had snakes for hair. Medusa is the most famous of the three gorgons. Even after she was beheaded by Perseus, her head still had the power to turn anyone who looked at it into stone.

GREEK AND ROMAN MYTHOLOGY

The Greeks had 12 main gods and goddesses who cared for different aspects of their life. The Romans later adopted many Greek gods as their own, but with new names.

Greek	Roman	Role
Zeus	Jupiter	King of the gods, god of thunder
Hera	Juno	Queen of the gods, protector of women
Aphrodite	Venus	Goddess of beauty and love
Apollo	Apollo	Sun god, and god of prophecy
Ares	Mars	God of war
Artemis	Diana	Goddess of hunting, protector of animals and children
Athena	Minerva	Goddess of wisdom and war
Demeter	Ceres	Goddess of fertility and of fruit and crops
Hephaestus	Vulcan	God of fire
Hermes	Mercury	Messenger god, god of travelers
Hestia	Vesta	Goddess of the hearth and home
Poseidon	Neptune	God of the sea

FAITH SYSTEMS

FAITH SYSTEMS ARE sets of beliefs that help to explain some of the mysteries of life and death. Most people who have a faith believe in either one god or several gods.

TOP SIX FAITHS

Faith	Number of followers
Christianity	1,833 million
Islam	971 million
Hinduism	733 million
Buddhism	315 million
Sikhism	13.5–16 million
Judaism	13–14.3 million

DIVISION OF MAJOR FAITHS BY GEOGRAPHIC AREA

Figures are given in percentages. (L.A. = Latin America. N.A. = North America)

Faith	Africa	Asia	Europe	L.A.	N.A.	Oceania	Eurasia	Total
Christianity	17.9	15.6	22.55	23.75	13.0	1.2	6.0	(100%)
Islam	28.66	65.56	1.30	0.14	0.29	0.01	4.04	(100%)
Hinduism	0.2	99.37	0.1	0.1	0.17	0.059	0.001	(100%)
Buddhism	0.01	99.42	0.08	0.17	0.18	0.01	0.13	(100%)
Sikhism	0.14	97.2	1.2	0.05	1.36	0.05	0.00	(100%)
Judaism	1.89	31.35	8.24	6.13	39.29	0.55	12.55	(100%)

WORLD PERCENTAGES

This bar chart shows the percentage distribution of the major world faiths. The figure for "Others" includes those who do not follow a faith system.

Judaism 0.3%
Sikhism 0.3%
Buddhism 5.7%
Hinduism 13.4%
Islam 17.7%
Others 29.2%
Christianity 33.4%

HISTORY OF RELIGIONS

B.C.E. (Before the Common Era) and C.E. (Common Era) stand for the same dates as B.C. and A.D.

✡ JUDAISM

c.2000 B.C.E.

c.2000 B.C.E. Abraham, patriarch of Judaism, Christianity, and Islam, is born in Ur, in present-day Iraq.

c.1200 B.C.E.

c.1200 B.C.E. Hebrews settle in Canaan, mainly present-day Israel, after the Exodus from Egypt.

c.900 B.C.E.

931 B.C.E. Hebrew kingdom divides into Israel and Judah.
c.900 B.C.E. Torah, the first five books of the Bible, is written.

587 B.C.E.

587 B.C.E. Jerusalem, in present-day Israel, is captured by the Babylonians and the Jews sent into exile.

C.E. 70

Herod's Temple

C.E. 70 Herod's Temple, Jerusalem, is destroyed by the Romans. Today, only the Western Wall remains.

☪ ISLAM

c.2000 B.C.E.

c.2000 B.C.E. Abraham and his son, Ishmael, build Ka'ba, an Islamic shrine, in Mecca (Makkah), in present-day Saudi Arabia.

C.E. 570

C.E. 570–632 Muhammad, the last and most important Islamic prophet, is born in Mecca.

Mecca, Saudi Arabia

c.C.E. 610–632 Koran (Qur'an), the Islamic scriptures, is revealed to Muhammad by the angel Gabriel.

c.C.E. 622

c.C.E. 622 Muhammad goes to Medina, in present-day Saudi Arabia. This marks the beginning of the Islamic calendar.

ॐ HINDUISM

c.1750 B.C.E.

c.1750 B.C.E. Beginning of Hinduism in India is influenced by the Aryan people, who worship many gods.

c.1700 B.C.E.

c.1700 B.C.E. Hindu beliefs are revealed to the *rishis*, or holy men, and passed on by word of mouth. *The rishis*

c.1400 B.C.E.

c.1400 B.C.E. Rig Veda, the earliest and most important book of the *Vedas*, which contain Hindu beliefs, is written.

c.800 B.C.E.

c.800 B.C.E The Upanishads, the final books of the *Vedas*, are written. They develop the idea of Brahman, the soul of the Universe.

Brahma, the creator god, the masculine form of Brahman

☸ BUDDHISM

c.563 B.C.E.

c.563–483 B.C.E. Siddharta Gautama, later known as Buddha, founder of Buddhism, lives in northeast India.

c.100 B.C.E.

c.100 B.C.E. The Pali Canon, or *Tripitaka* (three baskets), the holy book of Theravada Buddhists, is written. *The Buddhist wheel of life*

c.C.E 20

c.C.E. 20–200 The Sutras (collections of sayings), the earliest holy books of Mahayana Buddhists, is written. *Shwe Dagon Pagoda*

c.1300 Shwe Dagon Pagoda, major Buddhist temple, is built in Rangoon in Burma. It is said to contain the hairs of Buddha.

✝ CHRISTIANITY

c.4 B.C.E.

c.4 B.C.E. Jesus Christ, founder of Christianity, is born in Bethlehem, in present-day Israel.

c.C.E. 30 Jesus is crucified on a cross. Three days later he is raised from the dead (the Resurrection). *The Crucifixion*

c.C.E. 40

c.C.E. 40–100 New Testament of the Christian Bible is written. Christianity spreads throughout the Roman empire

c.1506 St. Peter's Basilica, a major Christian church, is built in Rome. (Original built in c.C.E. 330.)

St. Peter's, Rome

☬ SIKHISM

c.1469

1469–1539 Guru Nanak, leader and founder of Sikhism, lives in the Punjab region of north India and Pakistan.

Guru Nanak and the other nine Gurus who developed Sikhism

c.1600

c.1600 Golden Temple of Amritsar, major Sikh temple, is built in the Punjab by Guru Arjan (1563–1606), the fifth Guru.

c.1604 Adi Granth, Sikh holy book, is compiled by Guru Arjan. This was later added to and called the *Guru Granth Sahib*.

A Sikh reading the Guru Granth.

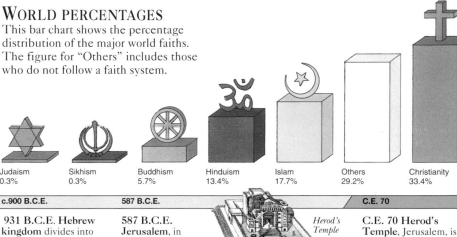

CHRISTIANITY

CHRISTIANS BELIEVE THAT Jesus Christ is the Son of God. Their symbol is a cross, which stands for the cross on which Jesus was crucified.

LEBANON / JORDAN / ISRAEL / Jerusalem

ORIGIN
Christianity originated in about C.E. 30 in Jerusalem, in present-day Israel. Today, it is practiced throughout the world.

JESUS CHRIST

Jesus was born in Bethlehem, Israel, in c.4 B.C.E. From the age of 30, he began to preach and heal the sick. A few years later he was tried and executed for having beliefs against Hebrew law.

TEN COMMANDMENTS
Christians obey these ten rules adapted from the Jewish scriptures (which Christians call the Old Testament).
1 Worship only one God.
2 Make no image of God.
3 Respect God's name.
4 Keep Sunday holy.
5 Honor your parents.
6 Do not kill.
7 Do not commit adultery.
8 Do not steal.
9 Do not tell lies.
10 Do not be envious.

KEY POINTS
• Jesus rose from the dead.

• The Holy Trinity is God as the Father, Son, and Holy Spirit.

• Jesus taught that people must love God, and love their neighbor as God loves them.

BAPTISM
The ceremony of being dipped in water is called baptism. It is practiced by Christians throughout the world, upon entering the faith. This practice dates from when Jesus was baptized by John the Baptist.

John the Baptist baptized Jesus in the River Jordan.

BIBLE
This holy book is made up of two parts, the Old and the New Testaments. The Old Testament contains the sacred writings of the Jews. The New Testament is about the life of Jesus and the growth of the early Church.

First printed Bible, 1455, by Johannes Gutenberg.

TYPES OF CHRISTIAN

9.3%	10.2%	24.5%	56%
Eastern Orthodox	Others	Protestants	Roman Catholics

CHRISTIAN HOLY DAYS

Name	Event
Christmas	The birthday of Jesus Christ
Good Friday	Jesus is crucified on a cross
Easter	Jesus is resurrected from the dead
Pentecost	Coming of the Holy Spirit

ST PETER'S BASILICA
This Roman Catholic church in the Vatican City, Rome, Italy, took more than 100 years to build. Ten architects worked on it, including Michelangelo, who designed the dome.

CHRISTIAN WORDS
Advent Preparation for the coming of Jesus.
Ascension Raising of Jesus to Heaven.
Eucharist Bread and wine taken in memory of Jesus.
Evangelist One of the four Gospel writers.
Gospel One of four accounts of Jesus' life in the New Testament.
Lent Forty days of preparation for Easter.

ISLAM

THE ISLAMIC FAITH is based on belief in one God, Allah. Followers of Islam are called Muslims. Their symbol is a star and a crescent moon.

SAUDI ARABIA / Red Sea / Mecca

ORIGIN
Islam originated in about C.E. 600 in Mecca (Makkah), in present-day Saudi Arabia. It is now practiced throughout the world.

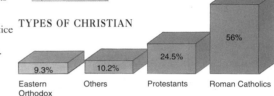

Shahada

MUHAMMAD
The last and greatest of the 26 Islamic prophets was Muhammad, born in Mecca in c.C.E. 570. The *shahada* states that Muhammad is Allah's messenger.

PILLARS OF ISLAM
Muslims must obey these five rules:
1 **Shahadah** Allah is the only god, and Muhammad is his messenger.
2 **Salah** Pray five times a day.
3 **Zakah** Give aid to charity.
4 **Sawm** Fast during month of Ramadan.
5 **Hajj** Make at least one pilgrimage to Mecca in a lifetime.

KEY POINTS
• Muslims promise to obey the will of Allah.

• Islam is Allah's chosen faith for the human race.

• Muhammad is Allah's main messenger.

• The Islamic calendar has no leap years.

MECCA (MAKKAH)
This city in Saudi Arabia is the most sacred place in the Muslim world. It contains a cube-shaped shrine, the Ka'ba, believed to have been built by Abraham and Ishmael over 3,000 years ago. Every year, especially during their month of pilgrimage, Muslims flock to Mecca and gather around the Ka'ba.

KORAN (QUR'AN)
In this sacred book of Islam, Allah revealed to Muhammad how humankind should live on earth. Muslims treat the book with great respect. They keep it in a clean place and wash before touching it.

TYPES OF MUSLIM

1%	16%	83%
Others	Shi'ites	Sunnis

ISLAMIC FESTIVALS

Name	Event
Mawlid al-Nabi	Birthday of Muhammad
Layl'at al-Qadr	Koran revealed to Muhammad
Id al-Fitr	Celebration of end of Ramadan
Id al-Adha	End of pilgrimage to Mecca

AT PRAYER
Muslims often pray together in groups. They kneel, facing Mecca, on clean ground, or on fabric; this may be a woven carpet, straw mat, or even a handkerchief.

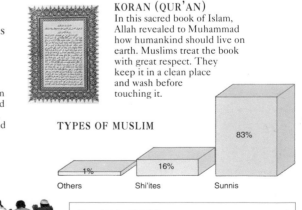

ISLAMIC WORDS
Ayatollah Shi'ite leader.
Hadith Stories about Muhammad.
Hafiz Muslim who has memorized the Koran.
Hajji One who has fulfilled the *Hajj*.
Jihad Striving to spread the Islamic way of life.
Shari'ah Islamic law.
Masjid Place of worship.
Mulla Scholar.

HINDUISM

MOST HINDUS BELIEVE in many gods, but in one underlying Reality, and that when a person dies the soul is reborn again in another body. Their symbol is a sacred sound, OM.

ORIGIN
Hinduism originated in India, in about 1750 B.C.E. Today it has spread throughout much of southeast Asia.

FOUNDERS
Hinduism has no single founder. Its early gods were brought by the Aryan people who invaded India. Shiva is one of the main Hindu gods.

Shiva

HINDU GODS
These are some of the most important gods:
Brahman Divine, absolute reality.
Vishnu Life-giver.
Shiva God of good and evil.
Sarasvati Goddess of truth.
Indra God of war.
Lakshmi Goddess of beauty.
Kali Goddess of death.
Krishna Hero and lover.

KEY POINTS
• People living good lives are born again in a higher life; bad lives lead to a lower life.

• Hindus aim to be free from the cycle of rebirth to become one with Brahman.

HOLY CITY
Varanasi, or Benares, in India, is one of the oldest cities in the world and the chief place of Hindu pilgrimage. Every year millions come to bathe in its sacred river, the Ganges. The waters are believed to wash away sin. People's ashes are often scattered on the river.

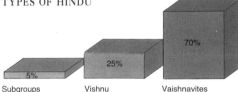
Rig Veda

VEDAS
The earliest Hindu beliefs were written down as the *Vedas* in c.1400 B.C.E., which consists of hymns and chants. The *Rig Veda* is the most important book of the *Vedas*.

TYPES OF HINDU

Subgroups 5%
Vishnu 25%
Vaishnavites 70%

HINDU HOLY DAYS

Name	Event
Divali	New Year Festival of Lights
Holi	Spring Festival
Janmashtami	Birthday of Krishna
Shiva Ratri	Main festival of Shiva

SACRED COW
Hindus respect all animals, especially cows, as sacred beings. Most Hindus are vegetarians. The cow is a symbol of the Earth and feeding a cow is considered an act of worship.

HINDU WORDS
Atman Individual soul.
Avatar Appearance of Vishnu on Earth.
Guru Religious teacher.
Karma Moral law.
Mantra Sacred chant, hymn, or poem.
Moksha Release from the life cycle.
Nirvana Total peace.
Puja Worship.
Sanskrit Hindu language.
Yogi Holy man.

BUDDHISM

THE BUDDHIST faith is based on the teachings of the Buddha. Its symbol is an eight-spoked wheel.

ORIGIN
Buddhism originated in northern India in about 500 B.C.E. Today it has spread throughout most of southeast Asia.

BUDDHA
Siddharta Gautama was born in India c.563 B.C.E. Brought up as a prince, he left his home at age 29 to lead a life of meditation and preaching. He was named Buddha, "the enlightened one."

FOUR TRUTHS
These holy principles are contained in the scripture, the *Dhammapada*.
1 Dukkha To live is to suffer.
2 Samudaya Desire or craving causes suffering.
3 Nirodha Freedom from desire leads to the end of suffering.
4 Magga Freedom can be found by following the eight-fold path of Buddhism.

KEY POINTS
• Spiritual fulfillment comes from right actions and thoughts.

• Life is a sequence of birth, death, and rebirth.

GOLDEN PAGODA
The Shwedagon pagoda in Rangoon, Myanmar, is one of the earliest and most important Buddhist temples of worship. It is covered with gold and is topped by an "umbrella" of more than 4,000 diamonds.

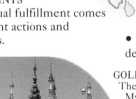

Shwedagon pagoda

MONKS
Buddhist monks live a simple life, giving up most of their possessions. They pray, teach, meditate, and beg for their food.

Monks wear saffron-yellow robes.

Begging bowl

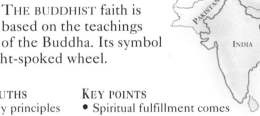
Extracts from the Pali Canon

HOLY TEXT
The *Dhammapada* is the best-known part of the *Pali Canon*, the collected teachings of Buddha. It contains the Four Truths and the Eightfold Path: rightness of views, intention, speech, action, way of life, effort, awareness, and concentration.

TYPES OF BUDDHIST

Other 6%
Theravada 38%
Mahayana 56%

BUDDHIST HOLY DAYS

Name	Event
Sakyamuni (or Wesak)	Birth of Siddharta Gautama
Bodhi Day	Buddha's enlightenment
Parinirvana	Buddha's ascent from Earth
Phagguna	Origin of life cycle

BUDDHIST WORDS
Anatta No such thing as self.
Anicca Self is impermanent.
Arahat Worthy, used to describe Buddha.
Bhikkhu Monk.
Jataka Accounts of Buddha's lives.
Nibbana State of peace.
Sangha Order of monks.
Vihaia Monastery.

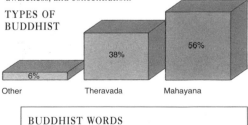

SIKHISM

THE SIKH faith is based on the worship of one God and on the cycle of rebirth. God is the eternal Guru who inspires all religious teachers. The Sikh symbol is the Khanda, a design of weapons.

Punjab
Pakistan
India

ORIGIN

Sikhism began in the Punjab region of northern India and Pakistan in about 1500 C.E. Today, it has spread to Britain and North America.

GURU NANAK

Guru Nanak was born in the Punjab region in 1469. At the age of 30, he underwent a religious experience and founded the Sikh religion. He was succeeded by nine other Gurus.

KEY POINTS

- God is found in all things.
- All humans will be reborn.
- All people are equal in the eyes of God.

FIVE K'S

The Khalsa (Pure Ones) are deeply committed to Sikhism. They must wear five items:
1 **Kesh** Uncut hair, worn in a turban if a man.
2 **Kara** Steel bracelet.
3 **Kangha** Hair comb.
4 **Kirpan** Sword.
5 **Kaccha** Short trousers often worn as an undergarment.

Turban
Sword
Steel bracelet

Guru Granth Sahib

GURU GRANTH

The *Guru Granth Sahib* contains hymns and poems written by the Gurus, especially Guru Arjan, the fifth Guru. The book is central to Sikh ritual and is treated with great respect. Sikhs bow down before the book, which is placed under a special canopy.

AMRITSAR

This town in the Punjab is sacred to Sikhs. They make pilgrimages to its Golden Temple, which is situated in the middle of a lake.

MEDITATION

Sikhs believe that God is inside everybody. Guru Nanak taught the importance of meditation to strengthen a person's sense of God. Sikhs often use beads *(Mala)* during meditation.

A Sikh meditating.

SIKH HOLY DAYS	
Name	Event
Baisakhi	New Year and formation of Khalsa
Divali	Release from prison of Guru Hargobind, the sixth Guru
Guru Nanak	Birthday of the Founder

SIKH WORDS
Darbar Sahib Name for Golden Temple.
Diwan Group worship.
Gurdwara Place of worship.
Guru Name for leader, scripture, and God.
Japji Morning prayer.
Kaur Female surname.
Mool Mantra Statement of belief.
Mukti Freedom of the spirit from cycle.
Singh Male surname.

JUDAISM

FOLLOWERS OF Judaism are called Jews. They believe in one God, who revealed the Law to his people. Their symbol is the Star of David.

Lebanon
Israel
Jordan
Egypt

ORIGIN

Judaism originated in about 2000 B.C.E. in Canaan, the Promised Land, mainly present-day Israel. Today, it has spread throughout the world.

ABRAHAM

Abraham, the first leader of the Hebrews, was born in Ur, in present-day Iraq, in about 2000 B.C.E. At God's command, he later settled in Canaan.

RULES AND RITUALS

These are some of the traditions of Jewish life:

- Baby boys are circumcised eight days after birth.
- The Sabbath day (Saturday) is the holy day of rest.
- Pork and shellfish must not be eaten.
- A Jewish boy becomes a *Bar-Mitzvah*, an adult member of Jewish life, when he is 13.

KEY POINTS

- God created the world and all its history.
- The Jews are descendants of the Hebrew people.
- The Jews are God's chosen people, "a light to all nations."

WESTERN WALL

This wall in Jerusalem, also known as the Wailing Wall, is the only remaining part of Herod's Temple, which was destroyed in C.E. 70. Today, Jews come here to pray and to tuck written prayers and requests in between the huge blocks of stone.

TENAKH

The Jewish Bible is called the *Tenakh*. It tells the history of the Jewish people. The most important part is the *Torah*, the first five books of the Bible. It contains the laws, including the Ten Commandments, that God revealed to Moses.

Tenakh scroll

TYPES OF JEW

5% Sephardis
10% Orientals
85% Ashkenazi

JEWISH HOLY DAYS	
Name	Event
Hannukah	Festival of Lights
Pesach/Passover	Deliverance from slavery in Egypt
Yom Kippur	Day of Atonement

Taliith, or prayer shawl

Menorah, or branched candlestick
Yarmulke, or skull cap
The Tenakh

JEWISH WORDS
Diaspora Dispersion, or spread, of Jews.
Exodus Israelites' escape from Egypt.
Gentiles Non-Jewish people.
Kaddish Synagogue prayer.
Rabbi Teacher and leader.
Synagogue Place of worship.
Tephillin Prayer box containing words from the Torah worn strapped to forehead and arm.

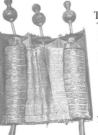

OTHER FAITHS

THERE ARE thousands of faith systems, with millions of followers all around the world. Apart from the six major faiths already discussed, the faiths below are among the best-known. Each has an organized structure and established beliefs.

ORIGIN OF OTHER FAITHS

- Baha'ism (Iran)
- Confucianism (China)
- Jainism (India)
- Shintoism (Japan)
- Taoism (China)
- Zoroastrianism (Iran)

BAHA'I FAITH

The Baha'i faith is based on the worship of one God, who is at the root of all religions. The Baha'i symbol is a nine-pointed star that stands for this combination of faiths.

WORLD CENTER
Baha'is worship in private homes and Houses of Worship. The most famous is the World Center in Haifa, Israel, which is also the center of administration.

FACTS
- Founded in Persia (present-day Iran) in the 19th century.
- The founder was Baha'u'llah (1817–1892).
- *Al-Kitab al-Aqdas* is the most important scripture.
- There are about 6 million followers; many of them are in India and South America.

CONFUCIANISM

Confucianism is not based on the worship of a god, but on following *The Tao* (The Way). It teaches the wisdom of living a balanced life that is in harmony with nature.

CONFUCIUS
Confucius, or K'ung Fu Tze, (551–479 B.C.E.) was the founder of Confucianism. Born in China, he worked as a government administrator, and became a respected teacher and moral philosopher. He was known for his wise sayings, such as "A good man is never alone."

FACTS
- Confucianism originated in the Shantung province of China c.6th century B.C.E.
- The *Analects* are the major scriptures.
- Confucianism is practiced throughout China.
- Its main teaching is "Never do to others what you would not like them to do to you."

JAINISM

Jains do not believe in a god. Their faith is based on nonviolence to all living things, or *ahimsa*. Jains believe in the cycle of rebirth. A good person is born again into a higher life.

JAIN NUN
Jain nuns and monks lead a life of poverty, obedience, and chastity. They must protect all forms of life. They use a brush to sweep the ground in front of them, for fear of treading on any insects, and wear masks to prevent insects from entering their mouths.

FACTS
- Founded in India, in the 6th century B.C.E.
- The founder was Mahavira (c.540–468 B.C.E.).
- Jains worship in temples, or in shrines in the home.
- There are approximately 4 million Jains; most of them live in India.

SHINTOISM

This faith is based on the worship of the gods of nature. Its symbol is the outline of a temple gateway.

MOUNT FUJI
Shintoists love nature. Many Shinto shrines are in parks, gardens, and on mountains. Mount Fuji, in Japan, is a Shinto god. People come to pray at a shrine on its summit.

FACTS
- Shintoism started in Japan in the 8th century B.C.E.
- The *Chronicles of Japan* and the *Record of Ancient Things* contain Shinto stories.
- Shintoists worship alone, not in groups.
- One of the chief Shinto deities is Amaterasu, the Sun Goddess.
- Most followers live in Japan.

TAOISM

Taoists believe in many gods. They aim to live in harmony with nature. Their symbol, *Yin Yang*, stands for balance and harmony.

LAO TZU
Lao Tzu, the founder of Taoism, was born in about the 4th century B.C.E. His name means "Old Master." According to legend, he was born with white hair.

FACTS
- Taoism originated in China in about the 4th century B.C.E.
- The *Tao Te Ching* is the most important scripture.
- Most Taoists live in China and the Far East.
- Taoists aim to balance the calm, feminine side of the body (*Yin*), with the active, male side (*Yang*).

ZOROASTRIANISM

This faith is based on two gods: Ahura Mazda, a good spirit; and Angra Mainyu, an evil spirit. Its symbol is a winged image of Ahura.

FIRE TEMPLE
Sacred fires, symbolizing Ahura Mazda, burn continually in Zoroastrian fire temples. Priests cover their mouths when tending the sacrificial fires.

FACTS
- Founded in Persia (present-day Iran), c.1000 B.C.E.
- Zoroaster, or Zarathustra, was the major prophet.
- The scripture is the *Avesta*, which explains the struggle between good and evil.
- There are about 140,000 followers; most of them are in India and Iran.

GREAT THINKERS

FROM EARLY TIMES, philosophers have used argument and reason to try to understand the world and our place in it. They question the meaning of ideas such as reality, right and wrong, and art.

624 B.C. Thales (624–550 B.C.) is born in Miletus, Greece. He is interested in astronomy and politics, as well as philosophy. He became known as the first Western philosopher.

Thales

Pythagoras (c.580–500 B.C.), Greek philosopher, explores the importance of numbers. He discovers the mathematical relationship between sound vibrations and the length of a string or pipe.

Pythagoras

650 B.C.   **624 B.C.**   600 B.C.   **580 B.C.**   500 B.C.

Aristotle (384–322 B.C.) is the last and most influential of the Greek philosophers. He stresses the importance of logic, or reasoning, in philosophy.

Aristotle tutoring Alexander the Great (356-323 B.C.).

St. Augustine (A.D. 354–430), North African philosopher, uses Plato's philosophy to express Christian ideas.

1225–74 St. Thomas Aquinas, Italian friar, aims to make Christian teaching consistent with Aristotle's philosophy.

St. Thomas Aquinas

Thomas Hobbes (1588–1679), English political philosopher, says that giving all power to the state is the only way to avoid chaos and endless war. He writes the *Leviathan* in 1651.

400 B.C.   **384 B.C.**   A.D 300   **A.D. 354**   1200   **1225**   1500   **1588**

George Berkeley (1685–1753), Irish bishop and idealist philosopher, believes that objects, such as tables and chairs, are collections of ideas, and exist only if a person perceives (is aware of) them.

David Hume (1711–76), Scottish empiricist and skeptic, states that all knowledge is taken from ideas and experience, but denies that this knowledge can ever be proved.

David Hume

Jean-Jacques Rousseau (1712–78), French political philosopher, is against the limitations of civilized society and advises a return to nature.

Rousseau

Immanuel Kant (1724–1804), German thinker, says that we gain knowledge through both experience and understanding.

Immanuel Kant

1650   **1685**   1700   **1711**   **1712**   **1724**

John Stuart Mill (1806–73), English utilitarian, emphasizes that some pleasures are worthier than others. He writes *On Liberty* in 1859.

John Stuart Mill

Søren Kierkegaard (1813–55), Danish founder of existentialism and religious writer, claims that the only real thing is individual existence.

Karl Marx (1818–83), German revolutionary thinker, founds Communism, adapting ideas from Hegel's philosophy. He writes *Das Kapital* in 1867.

William James (1842–1910), American psychologist and pragmatist, sees the truthfulness of any idea in terms of the usefulness of its results.

Karl Marx

1800   **1806**   1810   **1813**   **1818**   1840   **1842**

Bertrand Russell (1872–1970), English thinker and political activist, tries to provide firm foundations in philosophy for mathematics.

Bertrand Russell

Martin Heidegger (1889–1976), German existentialist, writes *Being and Time* in 1927.

Ludwig Wittgenstein (1889–1951), Austrian analytic philosopher, explores the relationship between language and the world. He argues that everything that can be thought can also be said.

Ludwig Wittgenstein

Jean-Paul Sartre (1905–80), French existentialist, says there is no fixed human nature or destiny, and that people are free to choose their actions without following society's rules.

Sartre

1870   **1872**   1880   **1889**   **1889**   1900   **1905**

FAMOUS PHILOSOPHICAL SAYINGS

Philosopher	Dates	Nationality	Quotation
Protagoras	c.485-410 B.C.	Greek	*Man is the measure of all things.*
Socrates	470-399 B.C.	Greek	*The unexamined life is not worth living.*
Francis Bacon	1561-1626	English	*Knowledge is power.*
René Descartes	1596-1650	French	*I think, therefore I am.*
George Berkeley	1685-1753	Irish	*To be is to be perceived.*
David Hume	1711-76	Scottish	*Beauty in things exists in the mind which contemplates them.*
Jean-Jacques Rousseau	1712-78	French	*Man is born free, and everywhere he is in chains.*
G.W.F. Hegel	1770-1831	German	*History teaches us that people have never learnt anything from history.*
John Stuart Mill	1806-73	English	*Ask yourself whether you are happy, and you cease to be so.*
Karl Marx	1818-83	German	*Philosophers have only interpreted the world, the point is to change it.*
Friedrich Nietzsche	1844-1900	German	*God is dead.*
Ludwig Wittgenstein	1889-1951	Austrian	*The limits of my language are the limits of my world.*

WARM THOUGHTS

In 1620, René Descartes thought up his most famous statement, "I think, therefore I am," as he kept warm by a stove while on military service in Bavaria, Germany.

470–399 B.C. Socrates, Greek philosopher, and Plato's teacher, uses question and answer method of inquiry. His main concern is morality (right and wrong). He is accused by the state of corrupting young people and is sentenced to death.

Socrates is forced to drink hemlock, a poison.

Plato (c.428–347 B.C.), of Athens, Greece, founds the Academy (a university) in Athens and teaches Aristotle there. He outlines his ideal city-state in *The Republic*.

Plato's Academy

470 B.C.   470 B.C.   428 B.C.

René Descartes (1596–1650), French dualist, rationalist philosopher, and mathematician, is considered the first modern philosopher. He bases all knowledge on one truth: that we cannot doubt the existence of our own thoughts.

Descartes

John Locke (1632–1704), English philosopher and political writer, founds classical British empiricism. His political writings form the foundations of modern democracy. He wrote *Two Treatises of Government* in 1690.

John Locke

1596   1600   1632

Jeremy Bentham (1748–1832), English utilitarian, judges an action to be right by the extent to which it promotes happiness or minimizes pain.

G.W.F. Hegel (1770–1831), German idealist, says that the history of events and thoughts is a process of conflict, which will lead to an inevitable conclusion.

Hegel

Arthur Schopenhauer (1788–1860), German idealist, saw art as the only escape from a world without reason.

Schopenhauer

1740   1748   1770   1788

Friedrich Wilhelm Nietzsche (1844–1900), German philosopher, argues that people are driven in life by the "will to power," and that society will evolve into a race of "supermen." He rejects Christianity, and influences the Nazi party.

Nietzsche's "Übermenschen" ("supermen")

Edmund Husserl (1859–1938), German philosopher, develops the basic ideas of phenomenology (descriptions of human experience).

1844   1850   1859

Simone de Beauvoir (1908–86), French existentialist and founder of modern feminist philosophy.

Willard van Orme Quine (born 1908), American pragmatist, points out inconsistencies in early analytic philosophy.

Simone de Beauvoir

Michel Foucault (1926–84), French philosopher, looks at ways in which the individual is controlled by society's rules.

Jacques Derrida (born 1930), French founder of deconstructionism, which rejects the idea of any fixed truths in language and philosophy.

Michel Foucault

1906   1908   1920   1926   1930   1930

PHILOSOPHY FACTS

● Pythagoras refused to eat beans, since he believed they had souls.

● English philosopher Francis Bacon (1561–1626) died of pneumonia, caught while stuffing a dead chicken with snow on Hampstead Heath, London, in an early attempt to preserve it by refrigeration.

● The most influential philosopher of the 20th century, Ludwig Wittgenstein, published one work in his lifetime. Parts of his *Tractatus Logico-philosophicus* were written in the trenches during World War I (1914–18), while he was on sentry duty.

● In his will, Jeremy Bentham left his body to University College, London. His corpse was preserved and dressed, and crowned with a wax head. The corpse was kept in a glass case, along with his real head, which

Jeremy Bentham

was mummified. Bentham's dressed corpse is still on display at the university.

● René Descartes was tutor to the Swedish monarch Queen Christina (1626–89). She made him give her philosophy lessons at dawn, even though she knew of his preference for lying in bed and meditating until 11 o'clock in the morning.

● Until the 18th and 19th centuries, the term "philosophy" included many branches that have since become areas of study in their own right: physics, biology, mathematics, and engineering.

PHILOSOPHY WORDS

Analytic Movement that considers philosophy to be based essentially on logic.

A priori Knowledge based on reasoning rather than experience.

Determinism Idea that all things, including "free will," are already fixed, or predetermined.

Dualism Belief that there are two distinct types of substance in the world: the physical and the mental.

Empiricism Belief that all knowledge is based on experience. At birth, the mind is a blank sheet, on which experience then makes its mark.

Epistemology Study of the theory of knowledge: what knowledge is, how we come to know things, how much we can hope to know, etc.

Ethics Study of moral systems, or ideas about how people ought to live and behave.

Existentialism Belief that the individual has free will and must take responsibility for his or her actions in a world where there are no definite rights or wrongs.

Idealism Belief that the world is in some way created by the mind. Idealists do not deny that the world exists, but deny that it can be separated from a person's perception of it.

Logic Series of statements that necessarily follow from each other. Also called a chain of reasoning.

Materialism Belief that everything that exists is either matter (substance), or is dependent on matter for its existence.

Metaphysics Study of principles of nature, such as being, identity, substance, time, and space.

Objectivity Existence outside a person's mind; the opposite of subjectivity.

Pragmatism A practical view of philosophy: the truthfulness of an idea is seen in terms of the usefulness of its results.

Rationalism Belief that reason alone, without any reliance on experience, can reveal the basic truths of the Universe, and that everything can be explained by a single system.

Realism Belief, usually contrasted with idealism, that physical objects exist independently of the mind.

Relativism Belief that there are no universal standards or truths; usually a rejection of absolute rights and wrongs.

Skepticism Belief that nothing can be known for certain.

Subjectivity Existence inside a person's mind; the opposite of objectivity.

Solipsism Belief that the only reality is inside your own mind.

Utilitarianism Belief that actions are right if they result in happiness, wrong if they result in unhappiness.

PATTERNS OF FAMILY AND SOCIETY

EVERY HUMAN SOCIETY (community of people) in the world is based on the family. Types of family and marriage arrangements, however, vary from one society to the next. Organization and living habits can also be very different, according to how and where people live and work.

Aboriginal Rainbow Snake Dreaming

DREAMING
Aboriginal Australians believe the land and all the living creatures were formed by spirit ancestors in the dawn of time called the Dreaming.

KINSHIP

Kinship is a way of describing bonds between people of the same family. A family may be defined as just parents and children, or it may include other types of relatives.

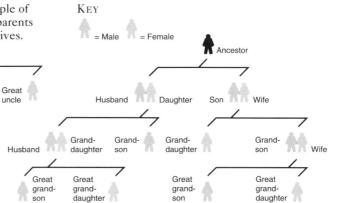

KEY

= Male   = Female

FAMILY WORDS

Ancestor An earlier member of the family.

Clan A family group descended from a common ancestor.

Dowry A wedding payment from the bride to the groom.

Lineage A line of family relations.

Marriage A legal bond between two people.

Tribe A group of people linked to an ancestor.

Western society People living in industrialized areas.

EGO-FOCUSED KINSHIP
People can use themselves as the starting point from which to construct a family tree. They trace their roots back as far as they can through both their fathers' and mothers' families. This is called ego-focused kinship.

ANCESTOR-FOCUSED KINSHIP
People can trace their roots to a known ancestor who starts off the family tree. This is called ancestor-focused kinship and is found, for example, in Scottish clans where everyone shares the same last name.

DESCENT

The system linking families to their ancestors is called descent. Inheritance of family property and titles is based on rules of descent.

Duke of Westminster, a British aristocrat

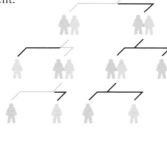
Green line shows patrilineal line of descent

PATRILINEAL DESCENT
Descent traced through the male line is called patrilineal descent. The Duke of Westminster inherited his title as the first-born son – a feature of a type of European patrilineal descent.

Trobriand Island mother and child

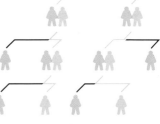
Orange line shows matrilineal line of descent

MATRILINEAL DESCENT
Matrilineal families trace their descent through female relatives. Many tribal societies, such as that of the Trobriand Islanders of the southwestern Pacific, are matrilineal.

HOUSEHOLDS

A household is a group of people who live together as a family. The number of people in a family household can vary widely around the world; so can the way in which members of a household organize family life and bring up their children.

Kibbutzim
In communities in Israel called kibbutzim families live and work together, helping to bring up each others' children.

Extended family
In many tribal societies several generations of the same family live together and share the responsibility for domestic duties.

Nuclear family
Anthropologists use the term nuclear family to mean a household consisting of two parents who bring up their own children.

MARRIAGE TYPES

Endogamy Marriage between members of the same family or clan.

Exogamy Marriage between members of a different family or clan.

Monogamy Marriage of one man to one wife.

Bigamy Marriage of one man to two wives or one woman to two husbands.

Polygamy Marriage of one man or one woman to several wives or several husbands at the same time.

Polyandry Marriage of one woman to several husbands at the same time.

Polygyny Marriage of one man to several wives at the same time.

Levirate Remarriage of a woman to her dead husband's brother.

Sororate Remarriage of a man to his dead wife's sister.

TAKING THE PLUNGE

On September 13, 1991, Dustin and Becca Webster of California completed their wedding by diving 70ft (21.30m) into a swimming pool.

MARRIAGE RECORDS

LARGEST GROUP WEDDING was between 60,000 members of the Unificationist Church on August 25, 1992, in the Seoul Olympic Stadium, Korea.

MOST EXPENSIVE WEDDING was 20 million dollars for Mohammed, son of Sheik Rashid Bin Saeed Al Maktoum, and Princess Salama, in Dubai, in May 1981.

MOST MARRIED MAN was Giovanni Vigliotto from New York, who married 104 times in 15 different countries, from 1949 to 1981.

TRADITIONAL BRIDES

Brides who want a traditional wedding can choose from many different styles of outfit.

Chinese brides may wear a traditional head-dress of pierced metal strips, often silver, with a veil made from feathers and pearls.

Western brides wear a long dress and veil in white, symbolizing purity and innocence. This custom dates from the 19th century.

Japanese brides may dress in a brightly colored traditional kimono. This contrasts with the black costumes of the brides' attendants.

Hindu brides wear a red dress and both bride and groom wear colorful garlands of flowers around their necks.

MARRIAGE AND DIVORCE STATISTICS

Country	Marriages per year 1979	Marriages per year 1991	Divorces per year 1979	Divorces per year 1991
US	9.9	9.4	5.0	4.73
Japan	8.5	6.0	1.1	1.27
New Zealand	8.0	6.8	1.6	2.7
Australia	7.8	6.8	1.3	2.49
France	7.1	5.0	1.0	1.87
Cuba	7.0	15.0	2.4	4.05
Italy	6.7	5.4	0.3	0.48
Sweden	5.5	4.7	2.7	2.20
Guatemala	4.1	5.3	0.1	0.18
UK	7.7	-	2.0	-
(figures given per thousand people)				

WEDDING CUSTOMS

- Greek Orthodox couples wear wedding crowns linked by a red ribbon.

- Indian couples tie their clothes together and walk seven times around a fire.

- In Egypt the bride's father signs her wedding contract while she sits alone in a separate room.

- Japanese couples take three sips of sake (rice wine) to complete their wedding ceremony.

- Jewish couples do not eat or drink on their wedding day until the ceremony is over.

- Ancient Romans first gave pieces of wedding cake to guests.

SYMBOLS

A symbol is something, such as an object, a sign, or a mark, that stands for something else. All the symbols shown below have a clear meaning.

Wedding ring A wedding ring is worn by both the bride and the groom to show their bond to each other.

The Scout Association The symbol of the Scout Association stands for this worldwide movement for boys and girls, which started in 1908.

US Navy Commander Three equal lace stripes on the sleeve are worn by US Navy commanders.

Olympic rings Five colored rings are the symbol that stands for the International Olympic Committee.

SOCIETY TYPES

Work and home life influence how people live.

City dwellers Many city dwellers live in apartment buildings or housing developments.

Hunter-gatherers Hunters and gatherers live in small groups of several families. They move home from one place to another in search of wild animals and plants to eat.

Pastoral nomads Nomads are groups of people who have no fixed home, but who move with their animals from one grazing ground to another.

SOCIETY WORDS

Rural People who live and work in the countryside.

Urban People who live and work in towns or cities.

Suburban People who live on the edges of a large city.

Migrant People who have moved from one region to another, or one country to another.

ONE WORLD

Different societies' customs can travel all over the world via film and television. A Campa Indian boy from Peru now enjoys a game with a frisbee.

CUSTOMS AND RITUALS

THROUGHOUT THE WORLD, different societies have their own traditions for marking important events such as the birth of a child, or the harvesting of crops. These traditions are called customs and rituals, and many are based around the cycles of nature, and the mystery of life and death.

THE JAPANESE TEA CEREMONY
In Japan, drinking tea is a long-established ritual that is based on the teachings of Zen Buddhism. Tea is prepared and served in a special tea room or tea house.

BIRTH RITES
The Azande people of the Sudan gently wave newborn babies through smoke to protect them against witchcraft and to help them grow up strong and healthy.

Azande birth rites

DEATH RITES
Traditional Taoist (see p.143) funerals involve the burning of imitation money. The smoke will carry it to the dead to spend in a future life.

Taoist funeral

BIRTH AND DEATH FACTS
• Many Christian babies are baptised in holy water in a church font.

• Jewish baby boys are circumcised eight days after birth.

• Romany gypsies press a gold ring against their baby's hand to bring it wealth.

• Pregnant women in New Guinea live alone until their baby is born.

• Death rites in Melanesia last for several years, until the deceased becomes an ancestor.

• Chinese coffins are painted white to give the dead a happy future life.

GREETINGS
A greeting is a means of friendly communication. between two or more people.

Handshake
The gripping and shaking of hands is a formal greeting around the world.

Bow
Bowing is a greeting in the Far East, showing politeness by lowering the head.

Nose rub
This Maori greeting is called a *hongi*. It is usually made on ceremonial occasions.

Wave
A friendly waving of the hand and arm means hello or goodbye, all around the world.

GESTURES
A gesture is an action that sends a visual signal to an onlooker.

Thumbs up
Raising the thumb is a friendly gesture. It is a sign of approval, or that all is going well.

V for victory
This victory gesture was made famous by Sir Winston Churchill during World War II.

Ssshh!
A finger pressed to the lips is a worldwide sign meaning "keep quiet" or "keep this a secret."

Beautiful!
This Native American gesture means beauty. It combines the signs for "good" and "looking."

INITIATION RITES
Initiation is a rite to welcome adolescents into adulthood in many traditional societies. The White Mountain Apache from North America perform a ritual for teenage girls, called the Sunrise Dance.

1 Ground-up plants and colored rocks are daubed over the girl's head with a brush made from plant stalks.

2 The girl kneels facing the sun, acting out the legend of the creation of the First Woman. Finally, as a woman, she is given the powers of a goddess for four days.

CHARMS
People keep or carry certain objects to bring them good luck or to ward off evil.

Pocket-sized Buddhas are popular good-luck charms worldwide.

Horseshoe
Hanging a horseshoe over the doorway brings good luck to the household.

4-leaf clover
Finding a rare four-leaf clover is said to bring good luck.

Cork & coin
A coin wedged into a champagne cork acts as a lucky charm.

Charm bracelet
This chain holds a variety of tiny lucky charms.

Garlic
A clove of garlic has many powers: it cures warts and keeps vampires away!

Sugar skull
This lucky candy is eaten during the Mexican Day of the Dead Festival.

CELEBRATION AND DECORATION

CELEBRATIONS that involve the whole community mark events such as the passing of the seasons and holy days. These events contain a mixture of customs, using music, dance, and costume.

Mexican Day of the Dead Festival

CELEBRATION FACTS

- Dragon Boat Festival of China is held to give thanks for food and water in the dry season, with races of decorated boats.

- On Thanksgiving Day in the US and Canada, families sit down to a special meal in celebration of the harvest.

- Diwali Festival in India celebrates the harvest with decorative lights and offerings to Lakshmi, Hindu goddess of prosperity.

- Inti Raymi is the Peruvian Festival of the Sun god, Inti, held in an Inca fortress.

- The Rio de Janeiro Carnival is a mass parade of costume and dance, based on the Christian celebration of the end of Lent.

Rio de Janeiro Carnival

DRESS CODES

Wearing certain items of clothing helps to identify what a person is or does.

Graduate's gown
College students wear a black gown and a hat called a mortarboard at their graduation ceremony.
Mortarboard

Nun's habit
Nuns wear a plain robe called a habit. Their head is covered by a hood called a wimple.
Wimple

Arab burka
The burka is a single length of cloth worn by Arab women. It covers the body, except for the eyes.
Eye-slits

Bolivian dancer's mask
This Devil mask is worn as part of the colorful costume at the annual Diablada Festival in Bolivia.
Devil mask

Welsh Guard
Various army regiments, such as the Welsh Guards, wear ceremonial uniforms topped by hats made of bear fur.
Bearskin

Chef's whites
Chefs wear starched white clothing they call their whites, and a tall white cloth hat called a toque.
Toque

DANCING FOR JOY

Dancing is one of the earliest known activities of humankind. Some dances are purely for fun; others are important rituals.

A ritual tribal dance from Kenya. *The jitterbug, popular in the US in the 1940's.*

BODY DECORATION

Decorative jewelry and body scars are part of a person's appearance. Each society, however, has different ideas about what makes the body beautiful.

Forehead spot
Hindu women paint a red spot on their forehead called a *tilak*, as a symbol of wisdom.

Earring
A ring through the ear draws attention to the eyes and adds to the beauty of the face.

Lip plug
Kaiapo men from the Brazilian Amazon wear a wooden lip plug to decorate their mouths.

MOST TATTOOS

Tom Leppard, a Scotsman, has leopard skin tattoos covering 99.2% of his body.

Scarification
Many African tribal people decorate their face and body with scars to add to their beauty.

Samoan tattoo
Men from the Pacific islands of Samoa are tattooed all over the body as a sign of manliness.

Punk jewelry
Safety pins and other unusual objects are worn as jewelry for their startling effect.

Sikh hand-painting
Sikh brides paint decorative patterns on their hands with dye from the henna plant.

COSMETIC SURGERY

The three most popular cosmetic surgery operations in the US in 1990 were:

Women (87% of all operations)	Men (13% of all operations)
Liposuction	Nose reshaping
Breast enlargement	Eyelid surgery
Collagen injection	Liposuction

MONEY

MONEY COMES IN the form of cash, which consists of coins and banknotes. Anything that represents cash, such as the computer records of a bank account, a check, or a credit card, is also money. Today, many people prefer to pay for things with cards rather than carry around cash.

EARLY MONEY

The oldest recorded use of money was in ancient Mesopotamia (Iraq), about 4,500 years ago. Inscribed tablets describe payments made with weighed amounts of silver. Other early forms of money include cowrie shells, used in ancient Egypt, and feather money on Santa Cruz island, Pacific Ocean.

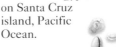

THE FIRST COINS

The first known coins were made 2,700 years ago in Lydia, Turkey, from a mixture of gold and silver called electrum. They were stamped at mints to confirm their weight and value. Today, most coins are made out of cheaper metals.

BANKNOTES

Banknotes have extremely complicated designs with special security features, to make it as difficult as possible for forgers to copy them. The four main stages of making a banknote are design, papermaking, ink-mixing, and printing. When the notes are printed, three separate processes are used.

SKETCHES

An artist makes two preliminary sketches for the note: the first one shows the main features; the second shows the background details.

Position of main features

Colored background

PAPER MONEY

Paper money – banknotes – was invented by the Chinese in the 10th century. People tired of carrying coins around and left them with merchants instead. Merchants provided vouchers (receipts) for the money and people exchanged the vouchers among themselves, rather than turn them back into cash.

BACKGROUND DESIGN

This design uses eight different colored inks. First, these are printed on three sheets in groups of colors: blues, yellows, and reds.

Inks for each color group are combined on a single sheet.

FINISHED NOTE

This type of specimen banknote is produced by the company, Thomas de La Rue, to show to its customers all over the world.

Sharp burins

Burnisher for smoothing

INTAGLIO ENGRAVING

The features of the note are engraved onto a steel plate by hand, using special sharp tools, called burins. The engraved area is then inked.

SECURITY THREAD

Banknote paper is made with a plastic thread sealed inside it. This feature is extremely difficult for forgers to copy.

NUMBERING

Numbering barrels print a different serial number on each banknote.

MONEY RECORDS

BIGGEST MINT in the world is in Philadelphia, US, where 15 billion coins are made each year.

FIRST CREDIT CARD was the Diners Club card, issued in the US in 1950. The card enabled the first 200 members to eat on credit at 27 New York restaurants.

GREATEST GOLD RESERVES are held by the United States at Fort Knox, Kentucky. The gold bars are stored in bomb-proof vaults, surrounded by armed guards.

AMAZING MONEY

The people of Yap, a Pacific island, used large stone disks for money. The largest was about 12ft (3.7m) across – as big as two adults standing on each other's shoulders.

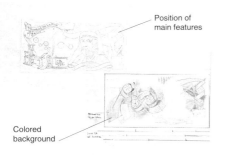

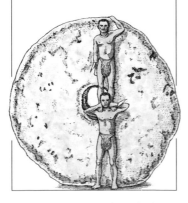

WORLD'S RICHEST PEOPLE
(excluding heads of state)

Name	Country	Business
Walton family	US	Discount store chain
Mars family	US	Confectionery (sweets)
Du Pont family	US	Nylon and Lycra
Rausing Brothers	Sweden	Packaging
Yoshiaki Tsutsumi	Japan	Land, railroads, leisure
Bill Gates	US	Computer software

MONEY FACTS

• The ancient Greeks put a silver coin into the mouths of corpses. The purpose was to pay the ferryman, Charon, to carry their souls across the River Styx.

• Numismatists are people who collect coins. Gold coins are the oldest and most precious.

• Forgers try to make copies of notes and pass them off as genuine. Forgers are highly skilled professional criminals.

• "Piggy banks" have been used for saving money since the 14th century. The first pigs were made of clay and had to be smashed to extract the money.

Fort Knox

BANKS

Most people find it convenient to keep their money in a bank. The bank keeps a record of how much each person takes out or puts into their account. This information is printed out in the form of a bank statement.

Automatic teller machine

STOCKS AND SHARES

People can invest in a company by buying shares (stocks) in it. If the company makes a profit, the shareholders are entitled to some of it. Share prices can rise or fall according to the company's performance. Share prices are displayed in the financial sections of newspapers.

THE STOCK MARKET

The stock market is a place where shares are bought and sold. People who want to invest in a company employ a stockbroker who buys and sells the shares for them. The activity of a stock market reflects the economic performance and prospects of a country.

Tokyo Stock Exchange

Company	Price	Weekly change +/-
Birch Interiors	69	-1
Gunzi Properties	44	-2
Kennedy Holdings PLC	46	+2
Kruger Corporation	162	+7
Shaw Associates	121	+5

Shares listing (imaginary) as shown in many newspapers

KEY STOCK EXCHANGES

Country	City	Index
Japan	Tokyo	Nikkei Average
United States	New York	Dow-Jones
United Kingdom	London	FTSE-100*
Germany	Frankfurt	DAX**
* Financial Times Stock Exchange 100		
** Deutsche Aktien Index		

BANKING FACTS

• Automatic teller machines allow people to withdraw money from their bank accounts 24 hours a day.

• Banks today arrange insurance, pensions, and mortgages (loans to buy houses), as well as keeping money safe.

• Checks, written instructions to make payments, can be written on anything, even a cow.

• Banking began in the 14th century, in Lombardy, northern Italy.

FINANCIAL WORDS

Accountant A person who keeps and checks financial records for a person or business

Credit An amount of money made available to make purchases on the basis that they will be paid for later.

Crash A very quick and huge drop in the price of shares, causing people to lose a great deal of money.

Dividend Share of a company's profits that is paid out to shareholders.

Exchange rate The amount of one country's currency needed to buy a fixed amount of another country's currency.

Merchant bank A bank that deals in finance and loans for businesses.

Share index Shows the price of selected shares being traded.

Stockbroker/Broker A member of a stock exchange who buys and sells shares.

Takeover When one company buys another.

FOREIGN CURRENCY

Every country has its own money, or currency. Some currencies hold their value longer than others because they reflect the economic strength of the country. Stable, widely traded currencies are known as hard currency. Dealers buy and sell them on foreign currency markets.

KEY HARD CURRENCIES

Country	Currency
France	Franc
Germany	Deutschmark
Japan	Yen
Switzerland	Swiss franc
United Kingdom	Pound sterling
United States	US dollar

GALLOPING INFLATION

Inflation results when prices increase and the purchasing power of money decreases. Very rapid price rises, called "hyperinflation," took place in Germany between 1921 and 1923. At this time, money was worth so little that children used banknotes for building blocks.

German inflation, 1923

CURRENCY VALUES (1994)

Nearly every country has its own money, or currency. Usually each currency can be broken down into 100 smaller units. Currencies are worth different amounts, as you can see from the cost of an ounce (28.35g) of gold in each currency in this table.

Country	Currency	Value	Cost for an ounce of gold
Chile	Peso	100 centavos	164,800
China	Yuan	100 fen, 10 jiao	3,480
Ethiopia	Birr	100 cents	2,400
Germany	Deutschmark	100 pfennigs	640
India	Rupee	100 paise	12,400
Japan	Yen	100 sen	40,000
Papua New Guinea	Kina	100 toea	380
Poland	Zloty	100 groszy	8,960,000
United Kingdom	Pound	100 pence	267
US	Dollar	100 cents	400

TODAY'S MONEY

Increasingly, plastic cards are taking the place of cash and checks as a form of payment. Banks, credit companies, and stores issue credit, or charge, cards. These allow people to buy things and pay for them later. The latest cards, smart cards, use microchips to store information.

SMART CARDS

Money from a bank account can be transferred onto a smart card. This card can then be used to pay for many things, from goods in stores to electricity bills.

CHARGE CARDS

You can pay for something with a charge card at a store or pay for goods over the phone. The credit company records all transactions and sends a bill each month.

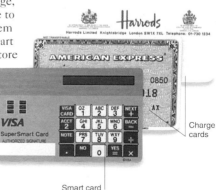

Charge cards

Smart card

POLITICS

POLITICS IS CONCERNED with the organization of society. Political parties are groups of people who agree about the way in which a country should be run and who seek to gain power in government.

POLITICAL SYSTEMS

Every political system has a central authority called a government that is responsible for organizing the duties of the state. The most common form of government in the world today is the presidential system. This system has three branches.

Pericles, leader of Athens at the height of its power

THE BIRTH OF DEMOCRACY

Democracy means "rule by the people." Democratic traditions of debate and voting first appeared 2,500 years ago in the ancient Greek city-state of Athens. A regular general assembly was held where every male citizen was free to speak and vote. Daily running of the city was in the hands of an elected "Council of Five Hundred." Women and slaves, however, were not allowed to vote.

Bill Clinton is sworn in as US President.

PRESIDENT

In a presidential system, an elected president is the head of state and chief executive. He or she proposes new laws and sends them to the legislature, which may or may not pass them, and can also refuse to pass laws proposed by the legislature. The president is Commander-in-Chief of the army and controls foreign policy.

US Congress, Washington D.C.

LEGISLATURE

The legislature is an assembly of elected representatives. Every new law must be passed by this assembly. It may propose laws itself and votes on those proposed by the president. In most presidential systems, the legislature is composed of two assemblies, or houses. In the US, the legislature is called Congress.

US Supreme Court, Washington D.C.

JUDICIARY

The judiciary is a legal body that reviews the laws passed by the legislature and ensures that they are in line with the country's written Constitution. In the US, the highest legal body is the Supreme Court. It can judge the activities of the executive and legislative branches, and reverse judicial decisions made by lower courts.

EXECUTIVE

US State Department

The president, as chief executive, is responsible for the administration of the state and for putting into practice new acts of law. He or she appoints the heads of the many administrative departments such as Defense, Trade, Education, Agriculture, and State.

PARLIAMENTARY SYSTEM

In a parliamentary system, political activity focuses on an assembly where matters are debated and laws are passed. Citizens elect members to act as their representatives. In Britain, the political party with the largest number of members elected to the House of Commons forms the government. The leader of that party becomes the Prime Minister, or chief executive. All executive power is held by the Prime Minister and his or her cabinet.

House of Commons – the political focus of Parliament and of British democracy

POLITICAL FACTS

• The word "government" comes from the latin word *gubernare*, meaning "to steer."

• In Switzerland, voting in elections is compulsory – it is regarded as every citizen's duty.

• Until the 1980s, Soviet leaders were able to rule Communist USSR as virtual dictators – with more power than US presidents.

• The terms right and left wing come from France's Assembly of the 1790s: conservatives sat on the right of the speaker's chair, and reformers sat on its left.

French Assembly, c.1865

POLITICAL RECORDS

OLDEST RECORDED LAW-MAKING BODY is the Althing in Iceland. It was formed in about A.D. 930 and consisted of 40 local priest-chieftains. It was abolished in 1800 but then restored in 1843.

OLDEST CONSTITUTION still in use is that of the US, which was written in 1787.

LARGEST LAW-MAKING BODY is the National People's Congress of the People's Republic of China.

PEACEFUL PARLIAMENT

During debates in the British House of Commons, the leaders of the government and opposition stand at two swords' lengths from each other. This is a symbol of the parliamentary rule that members should never use violence to solve political problems.

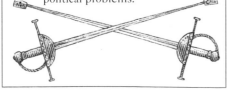

COMMUNISM

German thinker Karl Marx (1818–83) devised a new political and economic system, which he called Communism, in which all property is owned by the community and everyone shares in the country's wealth. In 1917, the USSR became the first communist state. Wealth was shared more or less equally but, unlike Marx's ideal communist state, a single party, the Soviet Communist party, wielded total power and was able to use it unfairly.

Communist magazine, showing a worker smashing the chains of capitalism.

COMMUNISM

Under Communism, workers own the factories and share their profits equally.

CAPITALISM

Under capitalism, a few people own all the factories, but do not share profits with the workers.

Members of Greenpeace protest against plans for a nuclear power station.

POLITICAL ORGANIZATIONS AND PRESSURE GROUPS

Throughout the world, people and countries with shared interests form organizations to promote and defend their interests. Some, such as the United Nations, the Arab League, and the European Community, are concerned with the common interests of member states. Others, such as the environmental group Greenpeace and the human rights group Amnesty International, devote themselves to a particular cause.

VOTING

People hold elections to choose people to represent them. Each person usually casts one vote, and the candidate who receives the most votes is elected to office. This system is used in electing one representative for each constituency. An alternative system, proportional representation, allocates the seats in numbers proportional to the total number of votes given for each party.

South African citizen casts her vote in 1994 elections for president and parliament.

WOMEN'S VOTING RIGHTS

Women have not always shared in decisions about the way they were governed.

Country	First vote
New Zealand	1893
Australia	1902
Finland	1906
Norway	1913
Denmark	1915
Former USSR	1917
Britain	1918
US	1920
Japan	1945

Emmeline Pankhurst, a British supporter of women's voting rights, arrested during a protest.

POLITICAL WORDS

Anarchism Movement in favor of the abolition of the state.

Cabinet Group of advisors to a head of state.

Capitalism Economic system where invested capital (accumulated wealth) and profit-making drives industry.

Coalition Temporary alliance between different parties for combined action.

Communism Political and economic system in which all property is commonly owned and each person is paid according to their needs and abilities.

Congress US legislature composed of two houses – the Senate and the House of Representatives.

Constituency The residents in an electoral district.

Constitution Basic set of laws that set out the institutions through which political power is exercised.

Constitutional monarchy System of government authorized by a constitution with a monarch as the head of state.

Coup d'Etat Violent overthrow of government by a small group.

Democracy System of government by the whole population or its representatives.

Dictatorship Government by a ruler who holds unrestricted authority.

Electorate Body of people entitled to vote in an election.

Executive Branch of government that carries out laws and performs general administration.

Fascism Extreme right-wing nationalist movement.

House of Commons In Britain, the elected chamber of Parliament.

Judiciary All the nation's judges.

Legislature Assembly or group that passes laws.

Lobby Group of people seeking to influence law-makers.

Prime minister Chief executive of government in countries with a parliamentary system.

Republic State in which power is held by the people or their elected representatives.

Revolution Forcible overthrow of a government or social order.

Socialism System in which the means of production (factories, etc.) and distribution are owned by the community as a whole.

Suffrage Right to vote in a political election.

Suffragette A woman who protests for her right to vote.

Trade union Group of workers or professionals united to protect and promote their rights and interests.

Totalitarianism Dictatorial system of government that extends its control to all social institutions.

GOVERNMENT EXAMPLES AROUND THE WORLD

Power may be held by groups or individuals. Democracies may differ in structure.

Monarchies
Saudi Arabia is an absolute monarchy with no political parties.

Totalitarian regimes
China is ruled by one party, the Communist Party, and other parties are forbidden.

Facade democracies
Iran holds elections for its presidency, but candidates are chosen by those in power.

Military dictatorships
Myanmar (Burma) is ruled by a 19-member military council.

Presidential republics
France's democracy has both a president and prime minister.

KEY POLITICAL THINKERS

Thinker	Dates	Biographical details
Plato	429–347 B.C.	Greek philosopher, rejected democracy in *The Republic* and insisted that government was a science, requiring experts.
Niccolo Machiavelli	1469–1527	Italian political thinker and diplomat, wrote a book, *The Prince*, that described methods of achieving political unity.
Thomas Hobbes	1588–1679	English philosopher, argued in *Leviathan* that human nature made absolute monarchy desirable and inevitable.
Jean-Jacques Rousseau	1712–78	French philosopher. His *Social Contract* argued that people sacrifice their rights in return for protection by a head of state.
Comte de Saint-Simon	1760–1825	French social scientist, believed that society should be organized along industrial lines.
John Stuart Mill	1806–73	English philosopher and political activist, argued for truly representative democracy.
Karl Marx	1818–83	German philosopher and economist, founder of Communism. Wrote *Das Kapital*.
Emile Durkheim	1858–1917	French founder of sociology.
Max Weber	1864–1920	German economist. Described the relationship between economy and society.

FALSE STARTER

Bolivia's political system has experienced great turmoil. In the 156 years from its independence from Spain (1825) to 1981, Bolivia has had 192 changes of government. This is an average of a new government every ten months.

LAW AND ORDER

EVERY COUNTRY HAS a set of rules or laws designed to protect the rights of its citizens. Laws are usually enforced by government through the police and the courts. In most countries, legal systems are the result of years of development and reform.

EARLY LAW

About 4,000 years ago, King Hammurabi of Babylon set out some of the first recorded codes of behavior. He devised laws, as well as penalties, covering family, property, slaves, and wages. These laws were engraved on a stone pillar.

Hammurabi meets the god of justice.

SCALES OF JUSTICE

The Statue of Justice at the Old Bailey, London (above), holds scales to show that justice weighs opposing evidence the way a balance weighs goods. The sword represents punishment. Some countries abuse their legal powers and remove freedoms instead of upholding them.

THE FIRST COURTS

In about 450 B.C., the Romans formed a system of courts in which trials were held; judges decided whether a person had broken the law. In serious cases, the accused paid a lawyer, called an *advocatus*, to speak for him. Most European law is based on Roman law.

TYPES OF LAW

There are several branches of the law, each devised to meet the different problems of society.

CRIMINAL LAW

This branch of the law covers acts such as murder, arson, rape, and robbery. In the US, these are broken down into first, second, third, and fourth degrees, depending on the state of mind of the accused.

TRIAL BY JURY

Anyone accused of a serious crime has the right to a trial by a jury, usually 12 men and women, chosen at random.

The judge helps the jury on points of the law, listens to the evidence, and passes sentence if there is a guilty verdict.

Prisoner on trial (the accused)

Prosecuting lawyer

CIVIL LAW

This law deals with cases in which no crime has taken place, but someone's rights have been infringed. It covers day-to-day events such as buying a house or making a will, as well as resolving disputes between companies.

RELIGIOUS LAW

This law deals with cases in which religious code determines the law. For example, Islamic Law is based on the Koran and the teachings of Muhammad and is the basis for the law in North Africa and the Middle East.

COURT PROCEDURE

A prosecuting lawyer tries to convince the jury that the accused is guilty, while a defense lawyer sets out to prove the person's innocence. After listening to evidence from various witnesses, the jury has to decide whether the prosecution has proved guilt.

Prosecution tries to prove guilt.

Defense tries to convince the jury that the prisoner is not guilty.

Jury of 12 men and women chosen from members of the public aged over 18

PRISON POPULATION WESTERN EUROPE (1994)

Country	Prisoners per 100,000 population
UK	92.1
Spain	91.8
Austria	87.5
Switzerland	84.9
France	83.9
Portugal	82.0
Germany	78.8
Denmark	63.0
Finland	62.6
Belgium	60.5

PRISON FACTS

- Early prisons were filthy, and people often died of a kind of typhus known as "jail fever."

- The longest prison sentence was 141,078 years, passed on a woman in Thailand, for fraud.

- The world's most secure prison was Alcatraz, on an island off the California coast. Although 24 convicts tried to break free, no one ever managed to escape.

THE DEATH PENALTY

The death penalty is still legal in 105 countries, although many of them never carry out the sentence. Offenses range from murder to drug trafficking or counterfeiting banknotes. The first country to abolish the death penalty was Austria, in 1787.

LEGAL WORDS

Accused Person charged with committing a crime.
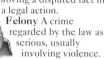
Arson Criminal damage caused by fire. *Arson*
Assault Threat or attempt to physically harm a person.
Bail Money given to gain temporary release of a prisoner facing trial.
Bankruptcy Situation in which a person is unable to pay their debts.
Barrister In Britain, a lawyer who practices in the higher courts.
Damages Money claimed or awarded as compensation for loss or injury.
Defendant Person prosecuted in a criminal action.
Defense Defendant's case in a law suit.
Evidence The means used for proving a disputed fact in a legal action.

Felony A crime regarded by the law as serious, usually involving violence.

English judge

Fraud Deliberate trickery to gain an advantage, often financial.
Insolvent Situation in which a company is unable to pay its debts.
Judge Official who hears and tries cases in a court of law.
Jury Group of people who give a verdict in criminal cases on the basis of evidence given in court.
Kidnap To carry off a person against their will.
Libel Words published about people that may harm their good reputation.
Murder To kill a person.
Oath Formal declaration as to the truth of something.
Perjury To willfully tell an untruth when under oath.
Probation An alternative to a prison sentence whereby an offender must report regularly to a probation officer.
Prosecution The carrying on of legal proceedings.
Rape To force a person to have sexual intercourse against her will.
Sentence The judgment and punishment passed on a person in criminal proceedings.
Slander Words spoken about people that may harm their good reputation.
Subpoena A written demand that a person appear in court.
Sue To begin legal proceedings.
Summons A call to appear before a judge or magistrate.
Theft To take another's property without their consent. *Subpoena*
Trial Legal proceedings to determine issues between parties.
Verdict Decision made in a criminal case.
Warrant Written authorization allowing police to search property and make arrests.

ARTS AND THE MEDIA

All the major art forms, from architecture to music, are given detailed treatment in this section. Timelines present key developments in the arts, and tables list famous painters, composers, architects, and writers. The media pages feature the latest in modern technology, including virtual reality.

Architecture • Fine Arts • Artists and Materials • Photography
Theater • Dance • Ballet and Modern Dance • Traditional World Dance
Music • Classical Music • Popular Music • Musical Instruments
Writing • Printing • Radio • Television • Movies • Animation
Video • Newspapers

ARCHITECTURE

ARCHITECTURE IS the art and science of designing and constructing buildings. Modern steel-and-glass structures are now a feature of cities worldwide.

Step Pyramid

c.6500 B.C. Çatal Hüyük in Turkey, one of the first known towns, has rectangular houses built from mud bricks.

c.2650–2150 B.C. Pyramids are constructed in the lower Nile Valley, Egypt. The famous Step Pyramid at Saqqara is designed by Imhotep, a doctor and the first recorded architect.

c.2200 B.C. Stonehenge, a massive stone circle that is one of prehistoric Europe's most complex stone monuments, is erected for religious purposes.

Ston

6500 B.C.   2600 B.C.   2200 B.C.

700–400 B.C. Ancient Greece. Architects of Greek temples develop three architectural "orders": Doric, Ionic, and Corinthian. Each order has its own style and proportions, based on mathematics and geometry, that are thought to be pleasing to the Greek gods.

Parthenon, Athens

Indian stupa

c.300 B.C. Buddhist stupas appear in India and Southeast Asia. These solid mounds symbolize the dome of heaven and contain sacred Buddhist relics.

c.200 B.C.–A.D. 500 Roman architectur takes over the Greek orders and the Etruscan arch. The Romans develop concrete and use i construct huge vaults an domes. Their public buildings include cou bathhouses, temples, amphitheaters.

Colosseum, Rome

700 B.C.   300 B.C.   200 B.C.

607–670 Japan's temple of the Horyuji Buddhist monastery, Nara, is the world's oldest surviving wooden building.

618–782 China. Nanchan Buddhist temple, Shaanxi province, built on a holy mountain, is the earliest surviving traditional Chinese timber-framed building.

Horyuji Temple

690–850 Early Islamic mosques, palaces, and houses are designed around courtyards. Mosques have minarets (prayer towers), arcades, and vaulted porches. Surface decoration is often mosaic – patterns of glass, stone, or marble pieces.

778–850 Borobudur Buddhist temple, Indonesia, has 8 stone terraces and 72 bell-shaped stupas.

Great Mosque, Samarra

c.900–1150 Romanes style of architecture develops in western Europe. Romanesque churches have massive rubble-filled walls with small windows. Arches semicircular in shape a stand on top of huge cylindrical columns.

Pisa Cathedral, Italy

600   607   618   700   778   900

c.1420 Renaissance begins in Florence, Italy. Key figures are Brunelleschi (1377–1446) and Alberti (1404–72). This study of and adaptation of classical Roman styles and building techniques soon spreads through western Europe.

The Duomo, Florence, Italy

c.1650 Baroque style in Europe reinterprets Roman and Renaissance styles. Architects are commissioned by the Catholic Church and the royalty to build large-scale, grand, and very ornate churches and palaces.

Church of St. Nicholas, Prague

1750–1840 Neo-Classicism. Architects rediscover the proportions and details of Roman and then Greek classical architecture. A fine example is the church of Sainte Geneviève, Paris, later renamed the "Panthéon."

Pant

1400   c.1420   1600   c.1650   1700   1750

1900–40s American architect Frank Lloyd Wright (1867–1959) promotes "organic" architecture – buildings that blend in with nature, such as Falling Water, Pennsylvania.

Falling Water

1919–33 Bauhaus, Germany, an influential design school led by Walter Gropius (1883–1969), teaches design based on modern industrial technologies.

Bauhaus, Dessau

1920s International Modernism. Leading Swiss-born architect, Le Corbusier (1887–1965) defines a house as "a machine for living in."

Le Corbusier

1970s High-Tech styl In the steel-and-glass buildings of Richard Rogers (born 1933) and Norman Foster (born 1935), parts of the structure and services (pipes) are left expose A typical example is th Lloyds Building, Lond

1900   1919   1920   1970

ORDERS

In classical Greek architecture, an order consists of an upright column supporting a horizontal entablature. A cornice, a frieze, and an architrave make up the entablature itself. The three Greek orders are Doric, Ionic, and Corinthian.

entablature
- cornice
- frieze
- architrave

column

Doric
The Greeks used this order from about 700 B.C.

Ionic
From 600 B.C., this order appeared in western Asia.

Corinthian
This decorative order originated in Athens in 500 B.C.

Caryatids
These female statues are used as supporting columns.

Atlas (male caryatid)

Pedestal

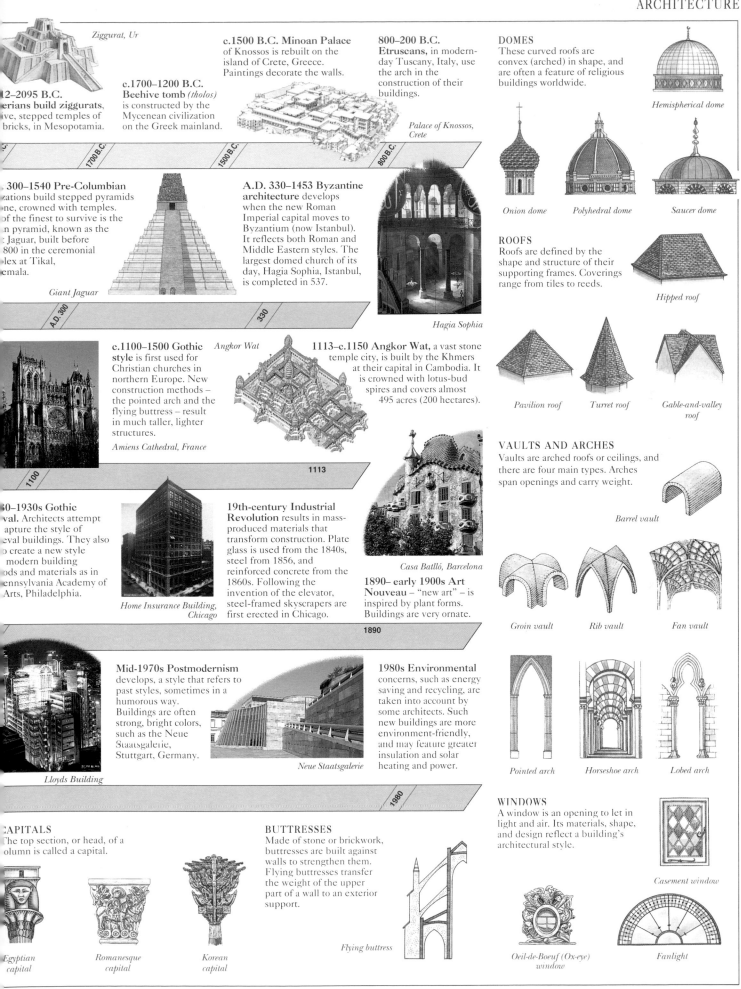

Ziggurat, Ur

12–2095 B.C. ...erians build ziggurats, ...ive, stepped temples of ...bricks, in Mesopotamia.

c.1700–1200 B.C. Beehive tomb *(tholos)* is constructed by the Mycenean civilization on the Greek mainland.

c.1500 B.C. Minoan Palace of Knossos is rebuilt on the island of Crete, Greece. Paintings decorate the walls.

800–200 B.C. Etruscans, in modern-day Tuscany, Italy, use the arch in the construction of their buildings.

Palace of Knossos, Crete

...300–1540 Pre-Columbian ...ations build stepped pyramids ...ne, crowned with temples. ...of the finest to survive is the ...n pyramid, known as the ... Jaguar, built before ...800 in the ceremonial ...lex at Tikal, ...emala.

Giant Jaguar

A.D. 330–1453 Byzantine architecture develops when the new Roman Imperial capital moves to Byzantium (now Istanbul). It reflects both Roman and Middle Eastern styles. The largest domed church of its day, Hagia Sophia, Istanbul, is completed in 537.

Hagia Sophia

c.1100–1500 Gothic style is first used for Christian churches in northern Europe. New construction methods – the pointed arch and the flying buttress – result in much taller, lighter structures.

Amiens Cathedral, France

Angkor Wat

1113–c.1150 Angkor Wat, a vast stone temple city, is built by the Khmers at their capital in Cambodia. It is crowned with lotus-bud spires and covers almost 495 acres (200 hectares).

...0–1930s Gothic ...val. Architects attempt ...apture the style of ...eval buildings. They also ...o create a new style ...modern building ...ods and materials as in ...ennsylvania Academy of ...Arts, Philadelphia.

Home Insurance Building, Chicago

19th-century Industrial Revolution results in mass-produced materials that transform construction. Plate glass is used from the 1840s, steel from 1856, and reinforced concrete from the 1860s. Following the invention of the elevator, steel-framed skyscrapers are first erected in Chicago.

Casa Batlló, Barcelona

1890– early 1900s Art Nouveau – "new art" – is inspired by plant forms. Buildings are very ornate.

Mid-1970s Postmodernism develops, a style that refers to past styles, sometimes in a humorous way. Buildings are often strong, bright colors, such as the Neue Staatsgalerie, Stuttgart, Germany.

Neue Staatsgalerie

Lloyds Building

1980s Environmental concerns, such as energy saving and recycling, are taken into account by some architects. Such new buildings are more environment-friendly, and may feature greater insulation and solar heating and power.

CAPITALS
The top section, or head, of a column is called a capital.

Egyptian capital

Romanesque capital

Korean capital

BUTTRESSES
Made of stone or brickwork, buttresses are built against walls to strengthen them. Flying buttresses transfer the weight of the upper part of a wall to an exterior support.

Flying buttress

DOMES
These curved roofs are convex (arched) in shape, and are often a feature of religious buildings worldwide.

Hemispherical dome

Onion dome

Polyhedral dome

Saucer dome

ROOFS
Roofs are defined by the shape and structure of their supporting frames. Coverings range from tiles to reeds.

Hipped roof

Pavilion roof

Turret roof

Gable-and-valley roof

VAULTS AND ARCHES
Vaults are arched roofs or ceilings, and there are four main types. Arches span openings and carry weight.

Barrel vault

Groin vault

Rib vault

Fan vault

Pointed arch

Horseshoe arch

Lobed arch

WINDOWS
A window is an opening to let in light and air. Its materials, shape, and design reflect a building's architectural style.

Casement window

Oeil-de-Boeuf (Ox-eye) window

Fanlight

SEVEN WONDERS OF THE WORLD

Temple of Artemis
Originally erected in about 550 B.C., this marble temple was burned down and later rebuilt. The gold statue of Artemis was destroyed, and only one of the original 127 Ionic columns remains.

Mausoleum at Halicarnassus
This vast marble tomb of Turkish ruler Mausolos was built in about 350 B.C. On site, only the foundations remain, but some statues are in London's British Museum.

Pharos of Alexandria
Built in about 297 B.C., this lighthouse stood on the island of Pharos, Alexandria, Egypt. At night a fire burned, reflected by bronze mirrors. Three earthquakes reduced the building to rubble.

Pyramids of Giza
These pyramids were built at Giza, Egypt, between about 2575 and 2465 B.C. The Great Pyramid of Cheops is said to have taken 100,000 men 20 years to build.

Statue of Zeus, Olympia
This huge statue of the king of the gods was made from ivory and gold. The head alone measured 43ft (13m) in height.

Colossus of Rhodes
This bronze statue of the Sun god, Helios, stood more than 110ft (35m) high at the entrance to Rhodes harbor, Greece. An earthquake toppled it.

Hanging Gardens of Babylon
Nebuchadnezzar II (c.605–562 B.C.), King of Babylon, built these magnificent terraced gardens for one of his wives. Although descriptions exist, archaeologists are still looking for the site.

ARCHITECTURE FACTS

• Ancient Greeks painted the inside and outside of their temples in brilliant colors. The present whitened marble is due to weathering and bleaching by the hot sun.

• There is about 100 times more stone and brick in the Great Pyramid of Cheops than there is in the Empire State Building.

• Our ancestors' homes were dark caves. Today, in the mining community of Coober Pedy, Australia, people live in well-equipped dugouts with TVs and showers.

RECORDS

BIGGEST CASTLE
in the world is Prague Castle in the Czech Republic. Founded in about 850, the castle now covers about 20 acres (8 hectares).

TALLEST RESIDENTIAL BLOCK OF FLATS
is Lake Point Tower, Chicago, Illinois. It has 70 floors and is 639ft (195m) high.

BIGGEST SHOPPING CENTER
in the world is West Edmonton Mall, Alberta, Canada, which is as big as 90 American football fields.

TRADITIONAL HOMES AROUND THE WORLD

AFRICA

Zulu kraal, South Africa
Kraals are traditional dome-shaped, grass-covered houses with low openings at the front.

Masai house, Kenya
The Masai people build their rounded houses from bent branches covered with cow dung.

Algerian desert village
Houses are packed tightly together, so that as little of the house as possible is exposed to the blistering heat of the sun.

Dogon village, Mali
In these West African villages, houses are built of mud-brick, and storehouse roofs are thatched.

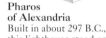

OCEANIA
Longhouse
These communal houses are raised on wooden stilts to keep animals out.

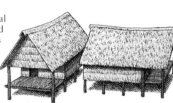

EUROPE

Swiss mountain chalet
These traditional wooden chalets have sloping roofs to stop too much snow from collecting.

Scandinavian house
Roofs of traditionally built houses in such cold climates are turf covered to keep in the heat.

Mediterranean village house
The whitewashed stone houses of this region reflect the sun's heat, keeping the interior cool.

ASIA

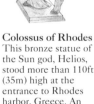  

Yurt
Nomads from Iran to Mongolia live in these willow-framed tents covered in felt and canvas.

Japanese house
Traditional timber-framed houses have sliding walls and doors that can be opened to the outside.

Chinese house
In China, traditional houses are arranged around a courtyard. The main part is on the north side.

AMERICAS

Amyara Indian house
On Lake Titicaca, Bolivia, Amyara Indians live in houses constructed from woven reeds.

Adobe houses
In New Mexico, traditional houses are built with adobe – bricks of sun-baked mud.

New England house
The walls of these North American houses have overlapping wooden boards (clapboards).

158

CROSS-SECTION OF A SKYSCRAPER, HONG KONG AND SHANGHAI BANK, HONG KONG

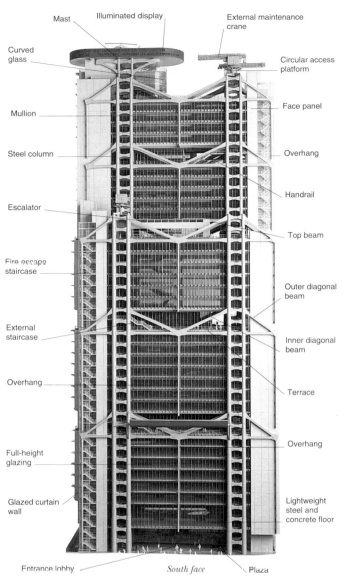

Mast
Illuminated display
External maintenance crane
Curved glass
Circular access platform
Mullion
Face panel
Steel column
Overhang
Handrail
Escalator
Top beam
Fire escape staircase
Outer diagonal beam
External staircase
Inner diagonal beam
Overhang
Terrace
Overhang
Full-height glazing
Glazed curtain wall
Lightweight steel and concrete floor
Entrance lobby
South face
Plaza

KEY ARCHITECTS

Name	Dates	Nationality	Building
Filippo Brunelleschi	1377–1446	Italian	Santa Maria del Fiore, Florence, Italy
Michelangelo Buonarroti	1475–1564	Italian	Dome of St. Peter's, Vatican City
Andrea Palladio	1508–80	Italian	Villa Rotonda, Vicenza, Italy
Inigo Jones	1573–1652	British	Banqueting House, London, England
François Mansart	1598–1666	French	Chateau de Maisons, Paris, France
Christopher Wren	1632–1723	British	St. Paul's, London, England
Jacques-Germain Soufflot	1713–80	French	The Panthéon, Paris, France
Andreyan Zakharov	1761–1811	Russian	The Admiralty, St. Petersburg, Russia
Karl Friedrich Schinkel	1781–1841	German	Altes Museum, Berlin, Germany
Antonio Gaudi	1852–1926	Spanish	La Sagrada Familia, Barcelona, Spain
Frank Lloyd Wright	1867–1959	American	Falling Water, Pennsylvania
Edwin Lutyens	1869–1944	British	Viceroy's House, New Delhi, India
Adolf Loos	1870–1933	Czech	Scheu House, Vienna, Austria
Walter Gropius	1883–1969	German	Bauhaus, Dessau, Germany
Mies van der Rohe	1886–1969	German	Seagram Building, New York, US
Erich Mendelsohn	1887–1953	German	Einstein Tower, Potsdam, Germany
Le Corbusier	1887–1965	Swiss	Notre Dame du Haut, Ronchamp, France
R. Buckminster Fuller	1895–1983	American	USA Pavilion, Expo 67, Montreal, Canada
Philip Johnson	b.1906	American	The Glass House, Connecticut
Oscar Niemeyer	b.1907	Brazilian	Government Buildings, Brasilia, Brazil
Ieoh Ming Pei	b.1917	American	Louvre Pyramid, Paris, France
Arthur Erikson	b. 1924	Canadian	Canadian Embassy, Washington D.C., US
Richard Rogers	b.1933	British	Lloyds Building, London, England
Norman Foster	b.1935	British	Hong Kong and Shanghai Bank, Hong Kong

ON A HIGH

When the Manhattan skyscrapers were erected, red-hot rivets were driven into holes in narrow steel beams hundreds of feet up in the air with nothing beneath. Iroquois and Mohawk Indians show no fear of heights and have put up many of these skyscrapers.

TALLEST BUILDINGS

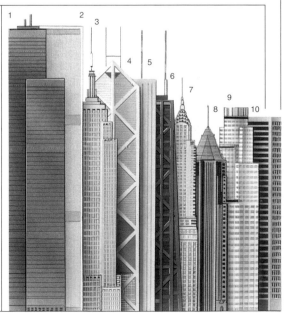

Towers (not illustrated)	Height m	ft
KTHI-TV Mast, North Dakota, US	629	2,064
KSLA-TV Mast, Louisiana, US	579	1,900
CN Tower, Toronto, Canada	555	1,821
Building and location		
1 Sears Tower, Chicago, US	443	1,453
2 World Trade Center, New York, US	417	1,368
3 Empire State Building, New York, US	381	1,250
4 Bank of China, Hong Kong	368	1,207
5 Amoco Building, Chicago, US	346	1,135
6 John Hancock Center, Chicago, US	344	1,129
7 Chrysler Building, New York, US	319	1,047
8 Nations Bank Plaza, Atlanta, US	312	1,024
9 First Interstate, Los Angeles, US	310	1,018
10 Texas Commerce Tower, Houston, US	305	1,001

FINE ARTS

EVERY CULTURE HAS its own works of art. In some cultures, artistic styles have changed significantly; others have remained more or less the same over thousands of years. Movements in Western art have been given names and dates by specialists called art historians.

c.27,000 B.C. "Venus" figurines, small clay statues of pregnant women, appear across Europe.

Figurine, Lespugue, France

Horse, Lascaux

c.500–323 B.C. Greek Classical sculptors study the form of the human body and explore its movement, making detailed figures of gods and athletes in marble, bronze, and clay. Phidias, a famous sculptor, makes a huge statue of Athena for the Parthenon, Athens, between 445 and 432 B.C.

Bronze charioteer, Greece

323–31 B.C. Greek Hellenistic sculptors make statues that emphasize the body's gracefulness. The portrait is developed and profiles of Greek rulers appear on coins.

Detail, Trajan's column

c.100 B.C.–A.D. 400 Roman decorative art flourishes. Relief carvings (standing out from the surface), often depicting Roman military victories, adorn arches and columns.

A.D. 100–400 Gandharan sculpture, influenced by Greek art, develops in the Indus Valley region (Pakistan). Sculptures show scenes from the Buddha's life.

Gandhara Buddha teaching

1000–1200 Romanesque style in Europe is displayed in church sculpture and mural painting and in embroideries such as the Bayeux Tapestry, showing the Norman conquest of England.

Detail, Bayeux Tapestry, 1066

1000–1600 Easter Island (Polynesia). Gigantic, half-length figures up to 33ft (10m) in height are carved from volcanic rock and erected facing the sea.

Statue, Easter Island

1368–1644 Ming Dynasty in China is famous for its glazed blue and white porcelain bowls and vases.

1450s Printing process develops in Germany. Illustrations are first printed using carved woodblocks; images are then engraved onto copper for greater detail.

1600s Dutch Golden Age painters represent scenes from everyday life, portraits and still-life subjects (such as fruit and flowers), and landscapes. Key artists are Rembrandt van Rijn (1606–69) and Jan Vermeer (1632–75).

Saskia as Flora, Rembrandt, c.1635

1600s Baroque style develops in Europe. Paintings feature energetic movement and strong contrasts of light and shadow to create dramatic effects. Michelangelo da Caravaggio (1573–1610) is one of the most influential artists.

Late 1700s to mid-1800s. Romantic school of painting reflects the power of human emotions and nature. Key painters include J.M.W. Turner (1775–1851) and Caspar David Friedrich (1774–1840).

Norham Castle, Turner, 1824

1880–1905 Post-Impressionist artists Paul Cézanne (1839–1906), Vincent Van Gogh (1853–90), and Paul Gauguin (1848–1903), develop in their own different directions.

White Horse, Gauguin, 1898

1880s–90s Expressionism develops in Europe. Intense color and free brushstrokes communicate artists' feelings. Ernst Ludwig Kirchner (1880–1938) is a key figure in Germany.

Drawing, Kirchner

1880s–90s Symbolist artists create images that portray inner feelings and suggest what may lie beneath the surface of things. Key painters include Gustave Moreau (1826–98).

1905–7 Fauves, a group of French painters that includes Henri Matisse (1869–1954), represent the world in brilliant color harmonies.

1920s Surrealism develops from Dada and Freud's theories of psychoanalysis (see p.132). Artists such as Salvador Dali (1904–89) and Max Ernst (1891–1976) use dreams to explore their hidden feelings.

Salvador Dali, 1971

1940s Abstract Expressionism appears in New York. Artists create abstract images, while experimenting with the physical properties of paint and different ways of applying it to the canvas. Jackson Pollock (1912–56) develops his paint-dripping technique as a way of expressing his feelings more directly.

Mid-1950s Pop Art develops in the US and Britain. Artists use consumer goods and images from the media in their work. A key figure is Andy Warhol (1928–87).

Andy Warhol, 1971

Late 1950s Performance artists combine different art forms – painting, music, theater, film, video – in their work. Key figures are Gilbert (born 1943) and George (born 1942), and Joseph Beuys (1921–86).

Planted, Gilbert and George, 19...

c.15,000 B.C. Lascaux caves, France, are decorated with images of animals. Artists use natural mineral colors, applying them with fingers, brushes, and by blowing through hollow reeds.

c.4000–1000 B.C. Egyptian art includes painted statues sculpted from limestone, wall and scroll paintings, and fine gold jewelry, set with precious stones.

Nefertiti, Queen of Egypt

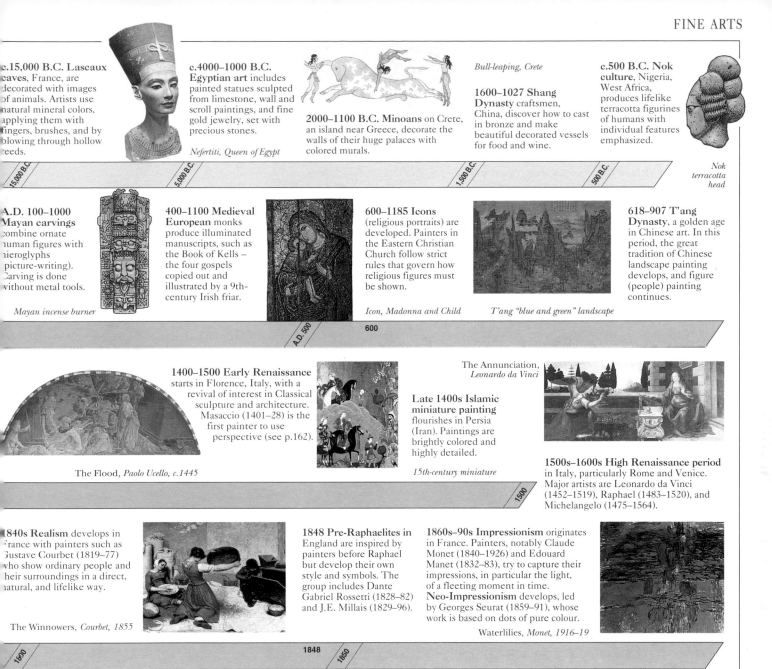

Bull-leaping, Crete

2000–1100 B.C. Minoans on Crete, an island near Greece, decorate the walls of their huge palaces with colored murals.

1600–1027 Shang Dynasty craftsmen, China, discover how to cast in bronze and make beautiful decorated vessels for food and wine.

c.500 B.C. Nok culture, Nigeria, West Africa, produces lifelike terracotta figurines of humans with individual features emphasized.

Nok terracotta head

A.D. 100–1000 Mayan carvings combine ornate human figures with hieroglyphs (picture-writing). Carving is done without metal tools.

Mayan incense burner

400–1100 Medieval European monks produce illuminated manuscripts, such as the Book of Kells – the four gospels copied out and illustrated by a 9th-century Irish friar.

600–1185 Icons (religious portraits) are developed. Painters in the Eastern Christian Church follow strict rules that govern how religious figures must be shown.

Icon, Madonna and Child

T'ang "blue and green" landscape

618–907 T'ang Dynasty, a golden age in Chinese art. In this period, the great tradition of Chinese landscape painting develops, and figure (people) painting continues.

1400–1500 Early Renaissance starts in Florence, Italy, with a revival of interest in Classical sculpture and architecture. Masaccio (1401–28) is the first painter to use perspective (see p.162).

The Flood, Paolo Ucello, c.1445

Late 1400s Islamic miniature painting flourishes in Persia (Iran). Paintings are brightly colored and highly detailed.

15th-century miniature

The Annunciation, Leonardo da Vinci

1500s–1600s High Renaissance period in Italy, particularly Rome and Venice. Major artists are Leonardo da Vinci (1452–1519), Raphael (1483–1520), and Michelangelo (1475–1564).

1840s Realism develops in France with painters such as Gustave Courbet (1819–77) who show ordinary people and their surroundings in a direct, natural, and lifelike way.

The Winnowers, Courbet, 1855

1848 Pre-Raphaelites in England are inspired by painters before Raphael but develop their own style and symbols. The group includes Dante Gabriel Rossetti (1828–82) and J.E. Millais (1829–96).

1860s–90s Impressionism originates in France. Painters, notably Claude Monet (1840–1926) and Edouard Manet (1832–83), try to capture their impressions, in particular the light, of a fleeting moment in time. **Neo-Impressionism** develops, led by Georges Seurat (1859–91), whose work is based on dots of pure colour.

Waterlilies, Monet, 1916–19

1907–1920s Cubism develops in Paris, France, with Pablo Picasso (1881–1973) and Georges Braque (1882–1963), who use geometric shapes to portray what they see.

Picasso, 1955

1910–50 Abstract movement appears, in which artists' paintings and sculptures do not directly resemble people or things in everyday life. The first abstract painting may be a work (c.1910) by Wassily Kandinsky (1866–1944).

Hornform, Kandinsky, 1924

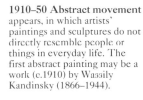

1916 Dada movement, originally a protest against World War I, rejects traditional forms of art. Marcel Duchamp (1887–1968), selects and displays everyday objects, which he calls "ready-mades."

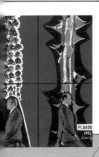

From 1970s Video Artists use video and computer technology. Their installations (exhibitions) feature video projection. A key figure is Korean-born Nam Jun Paik (born 1932).

1980s Art in Nature. Artists such as Richard Long (born 1945) and Andy Goldsworthy (born 1956) create outdoor works of art that are in harmony with the landscape. Materials – stones, leaves, etc. – are found on-site.

Flower, Andy Goldsworthy, 1992

MOST EXPENSIVE PAINTINGS SOLD AT AUCTION

Title, artist, date sold	Price in US$
Portrait of Dr. Gachet, Van Gogh, 1990	82,500,000
Au Moulin de la Galette, Renoir, 1990	78,100,000
Irises, Van Gogh, 1987	53,900,000
Les Noces de Pierette, Picasso, 1989	51,895,000
Self Portrait: Yo Picasso, Picasso, 1989	47,850,000
Au Lapin Agile, Picasso, 1989	40,700,000
Sunflowers, Van Gogh, 1987	40,342,500
Portrait of Cosimo I de Medici, Pontormo, 1989	35,200,000

Source: Sotheby's, London

ARTISTS AND MATERIALS

ARTISTS USE PAINT to create images of the world as they see it. Originally they painted on cave walls, using the most basic materials. Today, an artist can choose different materials and techniques to express his or her ideas and feelings.

MATERIALS

Artists paint on many surfaces using a range of materials. One person may spread thick blobs of oil paint on a canvas with a knife, while another will apply delicate brushstrokes of watercolor onto a sheet of paper. Some artists paint with their fingers, or employ traditional methods such as egg tempera.

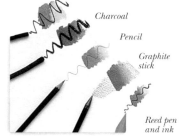

Varnish
Paint layers
Drawing layer
Imprimatura
Priming
Size
Ground

LAYERS OF A PAINTING

There are several layers to an oil painting. These can help modern historians to date a picture accurately, and also to spot whether it is a fake. This artwork, showing a section of Caravaggio's *Youth with a Ram*, reveals the layers through a typical 17th-century oil painting.

ARTIST FACTS

• Architect and artist Leon Battista Alberti (1404–72) wrote a key book about perspective in 1436. His methods enabled artists to create a geometrically controlled space on a two-dimensional surface.

• Making copies of paintings by Old Masters was considered an essential part of a young painter's training. Edouard Manet made copies of both Delacroix and Titian while working as a student.

• Pablo Picasso's famous work *Guernica* (1937) depicts scenes from the Spanish Civil War. Picasso refused to let the painting hang in Spain until the country was free. It remained in New York until 1981, when democracy was restored.

• Katsushika Hokusai (1760–1849) was a master of the Japanese ukiyo-e (pictures of the floating world) school. He made beautiful woodblock color prints showing views of Mt. Fuji.

PIGMENTS

Paint is made from pigments (powdered colors). Pigments were first found in natural substances such as carbon (black), chalk (white), and red and yellow earths. The ancient Egyptians added mineral colors such as malachite (green) from copper, and ultramarine (blue) from lapis lazuli.

Malachite

Lapis lazuli

DRAWING TOOLS

Artists often make sketches (quick drawings) to record what they see, or to prepare for a finished work. Many drawings are sold as finished works of art. A variety of tools is available.

Conté crayon
Charcoal
Pencil
Graphite stick
Reed pen and ink

BRUSHES

Paintbrushes fall into two main groups, soft-hair brushes, mostly used for watercolors, and bristle brushes, used in oil painting and acrylics. Within these groups there are three main types (round, flat, and filbert) defined by the length and shape of the hairs.

Round
Flat
Filbert

MATERIAL FACTS

• The pigment Indian yellow used to be made by boiling the urine of cows fed only on mango leaves. The urine was mixed with earth, heated, and dried.

• Brushes were once made by tying white hog bristles to a stick. The brush was then used to whitewash a wall until the bristles became supple.

• Thousands of years ago, artists in Australia mixed paint, such as red ocher or charcoal, in their mouths and spat the color into paintings on the cave walls.

PAINTS
Oil paints
These are a mixture of dry pigment and an oil – usually linseed oil. They were first used by 15th-century painters, such as Jan van Eyck.

Watercolor paints
These are pigments bound with gum arabic and diluted with water. They became popular with 18th-century landscape artists, such as J.M.W. Turner.

Acrylic paints
These were developed in the US during the 1920s. Acrylic is applied with a knife, or diluted and used with a brush. Acrylic was used by Andy Warhol.

Oil paint

Watercolor paint

Acrylic paint

FAKE FACTS

• Paint can be dated by analyzing its content. Cobalt blue, for example, was not produced before 1802, but is used by forgers when they need a cheap substitute for ultramarine.

• Many signed drawings and paintings, supposedly by Rembrandt, were actually done by artists of his school.

• Leonardo da Vinci's *Mona Lisa* was stolen from the Louvre in 1912. It took three years to find, during which time six forgeries turned up in the US, each selling for a very high price.

POPULAR EUROPEAN GALLERIES (1993)

Art Gallery	Visitors
Louvre, Paris	5,000,000
Prado, Madrid	1,828,058
Uffizi Gallery, Florence	1,020,972
Van Gogh Museum, Amsterdam	850,952
National Gallery, London	575,880
Alte Pinakothek, Munich	325,84

SCULPTOR FACTS

• When Rodin exhibited his first major work, *The Age of Bronze* (1878), it caused a sensation. The figure was so lifelike he was accused of casting it from a living model.

• Henry Moore's work was influenced by the carvings of the Aztecs. A sculpture of their ancient rain god, Tlaloc, gave him the idea for his statues of *Reclining Women*.

LABOR OF LOVE

Michelangelo painted the ceiling of the Sistine Chapel in Rome. The fresco covers more than 9,688sq ft (900sq m), and took four and a half years to complete.

ARTISTS' WORDS

Airbrushing Spraying on color under pressure with an airbrush.

Alla prima A direct form of painting made in one session. Used by artists when they want to paint spontaneously.

Casting To make an object, often a sculpture, by pouring metal into a mold and letting it harden.

Chiaroscuro The treatment of light and shade in drawing and painting.

Chroma The intensity or saturation of a color.

Collage A pictorial technique in which various materials are arranged and fixed to a backing.

Craquelure The network of small cracks that appears on a painting when, in the course of time, the pigment's varnish has become brittle.

Craquelure

Engraving The various processes of cutting a design into a plate or block of metal or wood, and the prints taken from these plates or blocks.

Etching A method of engraving in which a corrosive acid "eats" a design into a metal plate.

Ferrule The metal part of a brush that surrounds and retains the hairs.

Fresco Powdered pigments mixed in water and applied to wet lime-plaster. Fresco means "fresh" in Italian.

Gesso A traditional surface for tempera and oil painting on a panel made of glue and plaster of paris.

Glaze Film of transparent color laid over a painting once it has dried.

Gouache Similar technique to watercolor but glue is used to bind the color together. Used since the 18th century.

Ground The surface on which color is applied.

Gum arabic Gum from the acacia tree, which is used as a binding material in the manufacture of watercolor paints.

Impasto Paint put on so thickly that it stands up from the surface.

Imprimatura A thin overall film or stain of translucent color over a white priming.

Pigment The coloring matter, usually powder, which forms the basis of all paint.

S'graffito

Priming The preliminary coating that is put onto the support before painting.

S'graffito A technique using a scalpel or sharp knife in which dried paint is scraped off the painted surface. Used to create texture.

Size Material such as glue or gelatin used to prepare canvas prior to priming or to reduce the absorbency of paper.

Support The material on which a painting is made, such as paper, canvas, or a wooden panel.

Tempera Usually refers to egg tempera, a pigment bound with egg white instead of glue. Most important technique for panel painting (wood) in Europe from 13th to 15th centuries before oil. Layers of paint are built up slowly.

Tone The degree of darkness or lightness of a color.

Trompe-l'oeil A still-life painting designed to give an illusion of reality.

Varnish Protective surface over a finished painting that gives a glossy or matt appearance.

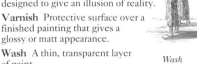

Wash A thin, transparent layer of paint.

Wash

KEY ARTISTS

Name	Dates	Nationality	Key work
Donatello	c.1386–1466	Italian	*David*
Jan van Eyck	c.1390–1441	Flemish	*Arnolfini and his Wife*
Piero della Francesca	c.1420–92	Italian	*Dream of Constantine*
Sandro Botticelli	c.1445–1510	Italian	*Birth of Venus*
Albrecht Dürer	1471–1528	German	*Melancholia*
Michelangelo Buonarroti	1475–1564	Italian	*David, The Creation of Adam*
Raphael	1483–1520	Italian	*The Sistine Madonna*
Titian	c.1487–1576	Italian	*Assumption of the Madonna*
Leonardo da Vinci	1452–1519	Italian	*Mona Lisa*
Pieter Bruegel the Elder	c.1525–69	Flemish	*A Country Wedding*
Michelangelo da Caravaggio	1573–1610	Italian	*The Supper at Emmaus*
Peter Paul Rubens	1577–1640	Flemish	*Peace and War*
Frans Hals	1580–1666	Flemish	*Laughing Cavalier*
Artemisia Gentileschi	1593–1651	Italian	*Judith and Holofernes*
Nicholas Poussin	1594–1665	French	*Et in Arcadia Ego*
Diego do Velázquez	1599–1660	Spanish	*Las Meninas*
Claude Lorrain	1600–82	French	*Landscape with Sacrifice to Apollo*
Rembrandt van Rijn	1606–69	Dutch	*The Night Watch*
Jan Vermeer	1632–75	Dutch	*Young Woman with a Water Jug*
Antoine Watteau	1684–1721	French	*Embarcation for the Isle of Cythera*
Antonio Canaletto	1697–1768	Italian	*The Stonemason's Yard*
Thomas Gainsborough	1727–88	English	*The Blue Boy*
Francisco de Goya y Lucientes	1746–1828	Spanish	*The Second of May*
Jacques-Louis David	1748–1825	French	*The Death of Marat*
Caspar David Friedrich	1774–1840	German	*Solitary Tree*
Joseph Mallord William Turner	1775–1851	English	*The Fighting Temeraire*
John Constable	1776–1837	English	*The Hay Wain*
Eugène Delacroix	1798–1863	French	*The Massacre at Chios*
Gustave Courbet	1819–77	French	*The Peasants of Flagey*
Edouard Manet	1832–83	French	*Dejeuner sur l'herbe*
Paul Cézanne	1839–1906	French	*Mont Ste. Victoire*
Auguste Rodin	1840–1917	French	*The Kiss*
Claude Monet	1840–1926	French	*The Water Lilies*
Auguste Renoir	1841–1919	French	*Le Moulin de la Galette*
Mary Cassatt	1844–1926	American	*La Loge*
Paul Gauguin	1848–1903	French	*Te Rereioa (Rest)*
Vincent van Gogh	1853–90	Dutch	*Sunflowers*
Georges Seurat	1859–91	French	*A Summer Sunday at La Grande Jatte*
Gustave Klimt	1862–1918	Austrian	*The Kiss*
Edvard Munch	1863–1944	Norwegian	*The Scream*
Henri de Toulouse-Lautrec	1864–1901	French	*Le Moulin Rouge*
Wassily Kandinsky	1866–1944	Russian	*Shrill-Peaceful Pink*
Käthe Kollwitz	1867–1945	German	*Bread*
Pierre Bonnard	1867–1947	French	*At the Table*
Henri Matisse	1869–1954	French	*La Danse*
Piet Mondrian	1872–1944	Dutch	*New York City I*
Constantin Brancusi	1876–1957	Romanian	*Endless Column*
Paul Klee	1879–1940	Swiss	*Ambassador of Autumn*
Fernand Léger	1881–1955	French	*The Outing*
Pablo Picasso	1881–1973	Spanish	*Les Demoiselles d'Avignon*
Georges Braque	1882–1963	French	*Man with a Pipe*
Marcel Duchamp	1887–1968	French	*The Large Glass*
Georgia O'Keeffe	1887–1986	American	*Lilies*
Egon Schiele	1890–1918	Austrian	*Death and the Maiden*
Max Ernst	1891–1976	German	*On the Threshold of Liberty*
Joan Miró	1893–1983	Spanish	*The Birth of the World*
René Magritte	1898–1967	Belgian	*The Use of Words*
Henry Moore	1898–1986	English	*Reclining Figure*
Alberto Giacometti	1901–66	Swiss	*The Forest*
Mark Rothko	1903–70	American	*Blue, Orange, and Red*
Barbara Hepworth	1903–75	English	*Wave*
Salvador Dali	1904–89	Spanish	*Premonition of a Civil War*
Francis Bacon	1909–92	English	*The Screaming Pope*
Jackson Pollock	1912–56	American	*Lavender Mist*
Joseph Beuys	1921–86	German	*The Pack*
Jean Tinguely	b.1925–	Swiss	*Homage to New York*
Robert Rauschenberg	b.1925–	American	*Bed*
Andy Warhol	1928–87	American	*Marilyn Monroe*
Jasper Johns	b.1930–	American	*Three Flags*
Bridget Riley	b.1931–	English	*Late Morning*
David Hockney	b.1937–	English	*A Bigger Splash*
Gilbert and George	b.1943–, 1942–	English	*Underneath the Arches*
Anselm Kiefer	b.1945–	German	*Scorched Earth*

PHOTOGRAPHY

PHOTOGRAPHY IS a way of recording images using a lens and some light-sensitive material. Taking a good photograph depends more on the photographer's visual skills than on the equipment used.

11th century Camera obscura ("dark room") is invented in Arabia for observing solar eclipses. It later forms the basis of photography.

18th-century camera obscura includes a mirror.

1727 Johann Schulze (1687–1744), a German doctor, discovers that silver nitrate darkens when exposed to light.

1827 First photographic image is produced by Joseph Nicéphore Niepce (1765–1833). It takes eight hours of exposure time.

First photographic image

1100		1700	1727	1800	1827

1839 Daguerrotype process is developed by Frenchman Louis Daguerre (1757–1851).

Daguerrotype camera

1839 Calotype process is invented by Englishman William Fox Talbot (1800–77). This negative-positive process allows photographs to be copied.

William Fox Talbot

1851 Collodion process is developed by English sculptor Frederick Archer (1813–57). His glass-plate negatives allow paper prints to be made.

Frederick Archer

1907 First practical color photographic process is introduced by French brothers Auguste (1862–1954) and Louis (1864–1948) Lumière.

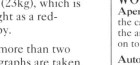
First Kodak color film

1913 35mm film is used for the first time.

Auguste and Louis Lumière

1800	1839	1851	1900	1913

1924 The Leica I, the first 35mm camera, is launched commercially. Its frame counter runs to 36 exposures, setting the standard for later cameras.

Leica I

1935 Kodachrome film is invented, allowing color transparencies to be both projected and reproduced.

1939 First important negative color film is produced by Agfa.

Edwin Land

1947 First instant picture camera, invented by American Edwin Land (1909–90), is marketed by Polaroid Corporation.

1975 Using special cameras and lights, an American scientist photographs a bullet passing through an apple at one three-millionth of a second exposure.

1976 First compact camera with automatic focusing is produced in Japan by Konica. It is called the Konica C35AF.

1990 First "Eye-Start" system is introduced. The camera lens automatically zooms in on the subject when you look through the viewfinder.

1994 First integral 35mm still and video camera is launched.

1900	1924	1935	1939	1947	1975	1976	1990	1994

TYPES OF CAMERA

Automatic SLR camera

Manual SLR camera

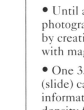
Basic compact camera

Advanced compact camera

6cm x 4.5cm roll film camera

6cm x 6cm roll film camera

Direct vision camera

6cm x 7cm roll film camera

6cm x 9cm roll film camera

Instant camera

Waterproof camera

Wide-view camera

Panoramic camera

Large-format camera

Single-use camera

PHOTOGRAPHY FACTS

• The first successful camera weighed 51lb (23kg), which is the same weight as a red-necked wallaby.

• Every day, more than two million photographs are taken around the world.

• Until about 1930, photographers made flash lights by creating small explosions with magnesium powder.

• One 35mm transparency (slide) can hold as much information as a single high-density floppy disk for a personal computer.

STIFF SHOT

The first cameras required long exposure times, so people had to stand still for long periods in order to avoid a blurred image. The photographer also attached a clamp to the subject's head and body.

PHOTOGRAPHY WORDS

Aperture The opening in the camera lens that controls the amount of light passing on to the film.

Auto-focus A system in the camera which adjusts the focus automatically.

Darkroom A lightproof room used for developing photographic film.

Electronic flash The light source on a camera that is needed for taking pictures after dark, indoors, or in dim light.

Enlargement A photographic print that is larger than the negative from which it was developed.

Motor-drive The device on a camera that enables you to take a rapid sequence of photographs.

SLR (single-lens reflex) A type of camera where the view through the viewfinder is what will actually be recorded on the film.

Transparency A positive image, in black and white or color, that is produced on a transparent film.

Tripod A stand that supports a camera to keep it steady and avoid blurred images.

Viewfinder The device on a camera that shows what will be in the photograph.

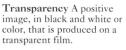

INSIDE A CAMERA

A camera is basically a lightproof box that has a hole, or lens, at one end. An open lens allows light to enter and shine on a piece of film (light-sensitive paper) inside the camera, forming an image. The most important parts of a camera are the lens, shutter, and diaphragm.

Rear viewfinder camera
Flash-ready indicator
Frame counter
Shutter speed dial
Shutter release button
Strap attachment
Film
Film take-up spool
Internal lens elements
Lens housing
Aperture control ring
Light path through the camera
Front lens element

THE LIGHT PATH INSIDE THE CAMERA

This diagram shows how light is adjusted when it travels through the camera to form an image on the light-sensitive film.

Light source The light illuminating the subject is reflected through the camera lens.

Lens A piece of curved glass that reflects the light rays.

Diaphragm A device for controlling the amount of light entering the camera, made of metal plates. It forms an adjustable aperture (hole).

Shutter The shutter can be set to open and close at different speeds, which determines for how long the film is exposed to the light.

Focal plane and film The focal plane is where the light from the lens is brought into focus, coinciding with the position of the film.

TYPES OF LENSES

Lenses can be fitted onto the basic camera lens of certain types of cameras to create different effects in a photograph or to help take a better picture of difficult subjects.

Fisheye lens is a wide-angle lens which covers up to 210° of vision.

Fisheye lens

Filters are flat, colored disks that are attached to the front of a camera lens to alter or distort the subject.

Green

Wide-angle lens allows 50% more of the subject to appear on the film than a standard lens.

Wide-angle lens

Standard lens shows the scene almost as it appears to the naked eye.

Standard lens

Purple

Orange

Telephoto lens is used to take close-ups of subjects from a distance and to make them appear bigger.

Telephoto lens

Super telephoto lens is a specialized lens that needs a tripod to support its weight.

Super telephoto lens

Red

Yellow

FILM SPEED

Film comes in various speeds, which are shown on the package as ISO (International Standards Organization) numbers. This table shows their uses for different situations and subjects.

ISO	Speed	Situations and subjects
32	Slow	Well lit, still life
200	Medium	General subjects and lighting levels
400	Moderate-fast	Dimly lit, moving subjects

FAMOUS PHOTOGRAPHERS

Julia Margaret Cameron (1815–79) British-born portrait photographer.

Robert Capa (1913–54) Hungarian-born war photographer. In 1947 Capa and Cartier-Bresson founded Magnum Studios.

Henri Cartier-Bresson (born 1908) French photographer who did much to establish photo-journalism as an art form.

Richard Avedon (born 1923) American photographer famous for portraits and fashion pictures.

DEVELOPING

A photograph is developed by fixing the image onto special photographic paper using chemicals. This process is done in the dark.

1 Each grain of silver on the film changes when it is exposed to light. The film must be processed before the image can be seen.

2 Developing and fixing chemicals imprint the image onto the film.

Equipment

3 The pictures on the film are called negatives because the light and dark areas are reversed.

Negatives

4 The negative is printed onto white paper using an enlarger.

Enlarger

5 The exposed white paper is developed and set with chemicals.

Developing tray

6 After the print has been developed, it is washed and dried.

Finished print

Color film has three layers of light-sensitive emulsion. Each reacts to a color – either blue, green, or red. The emulsion layers record how much of each color there is in the image.

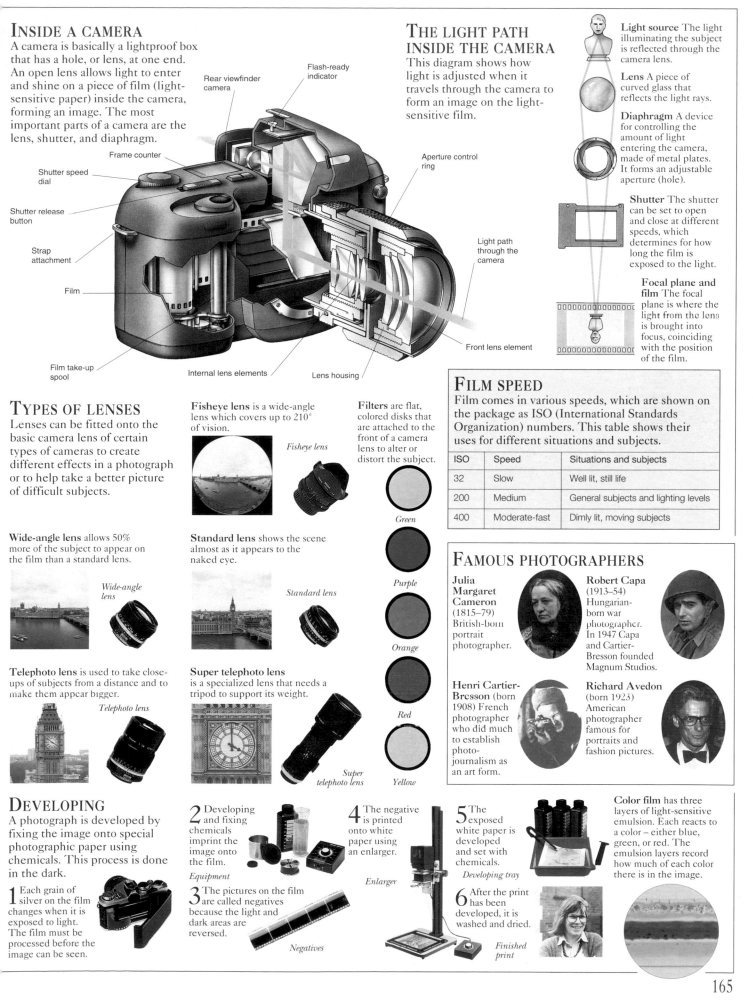

THEATER

MODERN WESTERN THEATER has its origins in ancient Greece. The word itself comes from the ancient Greek word *theatron*, meaning "place for viewing."

c. 3000 B.C. Religious ceremonies all over the world include music, dance, and elements of drama.

c. 1000 B.C. Chinese and Indian dance-dramas develop and become more formalized in style.

Egyptian hunters

Thespis's cart

534 B.C. Thespis, the first actor to step outside the chorus of singers and dancers, arrives in Athens.

c. 500 B.C. Tragedy, and soon comedy, develops in Greece.

384–322 B.C. Aristotle, Greek philosopher, explains his theories of tragedy in *The Poetics*.

Timeline: 3000 B.C. | 3000 B.C. | 1000 B.C. | 1000 B.C. | 600 B.C. | 534 B.C. | 500 B.C. | 400 B.C. | 320 B.C.

c. 200 B.C. Romans adapt Greek comedies. Plautus (254–184) and Terence (190–159) are among the most popular playwrights.

c. A.D. 1 Sanskrit theater quickly flourishes in India.

c. A.D. 1–100 Pantomimus, a form of theater in which actors used gesture and movement to act out tragic stories, was popular in Rome throughout the first century.

Pantomimus

c. 1200 Traveling story-tellers in Middle Eastern countries use mime to break through language barriers.

c. 1300 Indian folk theater develops, following the decline of Sanskrit theater. Noh theater becomes the dominant form in Japan.

1453 The Renaissance begins in Italy, and soon spreads to the rest of Europe. Roman plays are revived, and buildings reflect the style of classical architecture.

c. 1500 Commedia dell'Arte companies from Italy travel widely in Europe, greatly influencing theatrical styles.

Harlequin

Timeline: 200 B.C. | 200 B.C. | A.D. | A.D. 1 | A.D. 1–100 | 1200 | 1200 | 1300 | 1300 | 1450 | 1453 | 1500 | 1500

1564 William Shakespeare, an English dramatist, is born.

c. 1600 Kathakali (meaning story-play) is created in India. Actors use body language and mime to tell popular Hindu epic stories.

Kathakali

1603 Okuni, a young Japanese woman, creates a new dance called **Kabuki**.

1653 Japanese authorities allow only adult males to perform Kabuki, and it begins to develop a more theatrical style.

1678 Aphra Behn (1640–1689), an English dramatist, stages *The Rover*, a Restoration comedy. Behn is the first British woman to write plays for a living. She is also a spy.

Aphra Behn

1782 Friedrich von Schiller (1759–1805), a German dramatist, stages *The Robbers*. This play is among those that inspire the German Romantic movement of the late 18th and early 19th centuries (see p.161).

Friedrich von Schiller

Timeline: 1560 | 1564 | 1600 | 1600 | 1603 | 1650 | 1653 | 1670 | 1678 | 1780 | 1782

c. 1800 Peking Opera begins in China. The performances are a mixture of mime, song, dance, dialogue, and acrobatics. In Vietnam, **Hat Boi** uses a similar theatrical style to dramatize tales of war and suffering.

Peking Opera

1877 Henrik Ibsen (1828–1906), a Norwegian dramatist, stages *The Pillars of Society*.

c. 1890 Symbolism (see p.160) begins in the German theater.

1894 George Bernard Shaw (1856–1950), an Irish dramatist, stages *Arms and the Man*.

1894 The Olympia Theater is the first to open on Broadway, New York.

1896 Alfred Jarry (1873–1907), a French dramatist, stages *Ubu Roi* in Paris. The play later influences the movement called *Theater of the Absurd*.

Poster for Ubu Roi

c. 1905 Expressionism (see p.161) emerges in Germany. Georg Kaiser (1878–1945) and Ernst Toller (1893–1939) are popular playwrights.

Timeline: 1800 | 1800 | 1870 | 1877 | 1890 | 1890 | 1894 | 1896 | 1910 | 1905

1905 The Russian Revolution creates a need for *Agit-prop* (agitational propaganda) theater. Actors act out political events, replacing newspapers for the many people who cannot read.

Agit-prop

1935 Antonin Artaud (1896–1948), a French dramatist, stages *Les Cenci*, the first play to represent *Theater of Cruelty*. This style of theater is intended to horrify the audience.

Bertolt Brecht

1949 Bertolt Brecht (1898–1956), a German dramatist, founds the Berliner Ensemble. The company stages plays in Brecht's "epic" style, always reminding the audience that it is watching a play, and not real events.

1950 Eugène Ionesco (1912–1994), a French dramatist, stages *The Bald Primadonna*, the first example of his *Theater of the Absurd*.

1955 Tennessee Williams (1911–1983), an American dramatist, stages *Cat on a Hot Tin Roof*.

Timeline: 1900 | 1905 | 1930 | 1935 | 1940 | 1949 | 1950 | 1950 | 1955

1956 John Osborne (born 1929), an English dramatist, stages *Look Back in Anger*. The term "kitchen sink drama" is used to describe its realistic coverage of everyday life.

Look Back in Anger

1959 Jerzy Grotowski (born 1933), a Polish actor, founds the Polish Laboratory Theater.

1970s The Women's Liberation Movement produces many women's theater groups.

1986 Wole Soyinka (born 1934), a Nigerian dramatist, becomes the first black African to win the Nobel Prize for literature. He was imprisoned from 1967 to 1969 for criticizing the Nigerian government.

Wole Soyinka

1990s Musicals, especially revivals such as *Crazy for You*, are the most popular form in most commercial western theaters.

Crazy For You

Timeline: 1950 | 1956 | 1959 | 1970 | 1980 | 1986 | 1990

A MODERN THEATER

Many modern theaters are designed like this one, with a proscenium arch separating the real world of the audience from the pretend world of the actors. The word "proscenium" comes from the ancient Greek *pro skene*, meaning "in front of the stage."

Upstage (farthest from the audience) actors are well lit, and draw the audience's attention. Actors are sometimes accused of "upstaging" each other.

Props (properties) are objects that the actors carry on stage. They are kept on a table in the wings.

Wings at each side of the stage provide space for scenery and costumes that will be used later.

Scenery is suspended by ropes from a grid above the stage. This area is called the "flies."

Curtain is usually lowered while stagehands change the set (scenery).

Iron, or safety curtain, separates stage and auditorium so that a fire cannot spread too quickly.

FOLLOW SPOT OPERATOR

The follow spot operator controls a heavy spotlight, directing the beam of light so that a moving actor is always lit. The follow spot is usually either in the lighting box, or high up at one side of the auditorium.

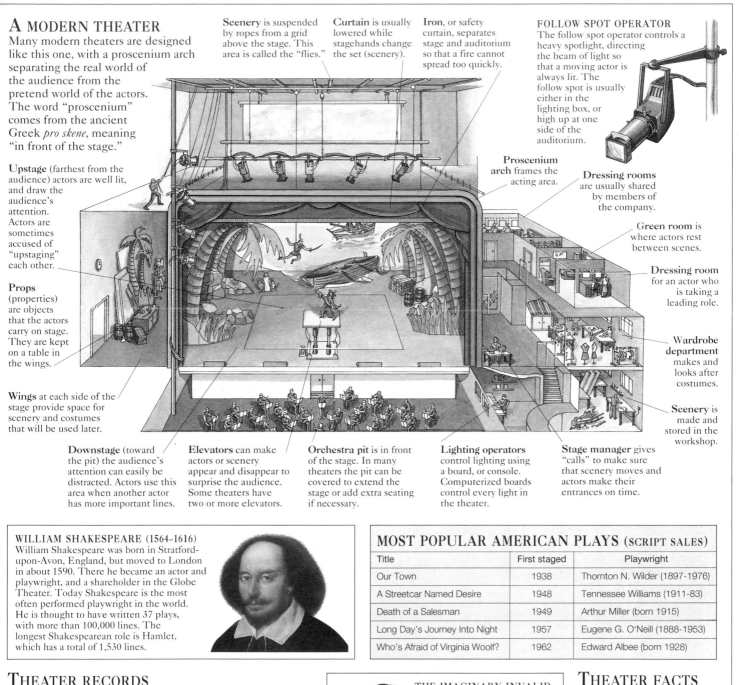

Proscenium arch frames the acting area.

Dressing rooms are usually shared by members of the company.

Green room is where actors rest between scenes.

Dressing room for an actor who is taking a leading role.

Wardrobe department makes and looks after costumes.

Scenery is made and stored in the workshop.

Downstage (toward the pit) the audience's attention can easily be distracted. Actors use this area when another actor has more important lines.

Elevators can make actors or scenery appear and disappear to surprise the audience. Some theaters have two or more elevators.

Orchestra pit is in front of the stage. In many theaters the pit can be covered to extend the stage or add extra seating if necessary.

Lighting operators control lighting using a board, or console. Computerized boards control every light in the theater.

Stage manager gives "calls" to make sure that scenery moves and actors make their entrances on time.

WILLIAM SHAKESPEARE (1564–1616)

William Shakespeare was born in Stratford-upon-Avon, England, but moved to London in about 1590. There he became an actor and playwright, and a shareholder in the Globe Theater. Today Shakespeare is the most often performed playwright in the world. He is thought to have written 37 plays, with more than 100,000 lines. The longest Shakespearean role is Hamlet, which has a total of 1,530 lines.

MOST POPULAR AMERICAN PLAYS (SCRIPT SALES)

Title	First staged	Playwright
Our Town	1938	Thornton N. Wilder (1897-1976)
A Streetcar Named Desire	1948	Tennessee Williams (1911-83)
Death of a Salesman	1949	Arthur Miller (born 1915)
Long Day's Journey Into Night	1957	Eugene G. O'Neill (1888-1953)
Who's Afraid of Virginia Woolf?	1962	Edward Albee (born 1928)

THEATER RECORDS

SMALLEST PROFESSIONAL THEATER is the Piccolo in Hamburg, Germany. It can seat no more than 30 people.

LONGEST RUNNING PLAY is *The Mousetrap*, which has been running in London since 1952.

EARLIEST KNOWN STONE AMPHITHEATER was built in Rome in about 54 B.C. It held approximately 40,000 people.

SHORTEST RECORDED PLAY, *Breath*, by Samuel Beckett, consists of 35 seconds of human cries and breaths.

THE IMAGINARY INVALID

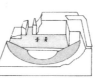

Molière (1622–1673), France's most famous dramatist, acted and managed a theatrical company as well as writing plays. He died within hours of collapsing on stage in a production of his own play, *Le Malade Imaginaire (The Imaginary Invalid).*

THEATER FACTS

• Until the invention of greasepaint in the 1860s, stage make up contained lead. Many actors died from lead poisoning.

• The title of *Macbeth* is considered unlucky in the theater. Instead, the play is called "the Scottish play."

BUILDING THEATERS

Since the ancient Greeks built the first theaters in the 5th century B.C. the style of theatrical buildings has altered constantly to suit the demands of the plays performed in them. In many modern theaters, the shape and size of the stage can be changed for each production.

Ancient Greek theaters had seats built into the sides of a natural bowl. The center was used for singing and dancing, and the small stage for acting.

Roman theaters were built of wood or stone in a semicircular shape. A permanent roof sheltered the actors on stage.

Renaissance theaters were loosely based on those of ancient Rome, with the audience on one side only.

Elizabethan English theaters had several entrances and exits, used for acting out complex plots.

Modern stages take many forms. One is theater-in-the-round, where the audience surrounds the stage.

JAPANESE THEATER

The two traditional forms of Japanese theater are *Noh* and *Kabuki*. The actors are male, and usually trained by their fathers to act a particular role. *Noh* actors wear masks, and *Kabuki* actors use make-up.

KABUKI CHARACTERS

A Noh actor

Noble male　　*Crab*　　*Wicked male*

CABARET

Cabaret may be pure entertainment, or it can contain political statements. Writers and performers often use cabaret to comment on society or to challenge fixed ideas.

Au und aus, performed at the Admirals Palace, Berlin, 1926

PUPPETS AND PUPPETRY

There have been puppet shows in Europe since at least 500 B.C., and probably even earlier than this in other parts of the world.

ANIMATRONICS
The term *animatronics* is used to describe a puppet that is partly controlled by electronics. Operators control the facial movements from a distance by sending electronic signals through a cable.

SHADOW PUPPETS
Shadow puppets are one of the most versatile kinds of puppet. They are controlled by sticks joined to their arms and legs. In Indonesia shadow puppetry is called *Wayang Kulit*.

STRING PUPPETS
In some parts of the world string puppets perform complete operas or tragedies. The puppeteers move the puppets' limbs from above using strings.

FINGER PUPPETS
Finger puppets are easy to make and operate, but limited in movement. Glove puppets fit over the whole hand, and each finger moves a different part of the puppet.

The operator inside moves the puppet's body and limbs.

MIME

Mime, or the art of gesture and movement, has always been part of acting. But modern mime, which developed mainly in France, does not use the spoken word at all. One of the most famous mime artists is the Frenchman Marcel Marceau (born 1923).

Tying a love knot means marriage.

COSTUMES

Costumes play an important part in any production. They can change an actor's appearance by altering shape or height, indicate the period and country in which a play is set, or completely transform an actor into an animal, an object, or a fantasy figure.

Ancient Greek actors wore masks, and often platform shoes, to make them appear godlike.

Animal costumes are usually padded and heavy, and can be difficult to move in.

Modern costumes tell us about the period as well as the character.

PUPPET FACTS

• *Wayang Kulit* plays may last a whole week, and some use as many as 200 puppets.

• Punch and Judy (British) and Petrushka (Russian) grew out of characters in *Commedia dell'Arte* (see p.166).

• It takes three puppeteers to control each of the *Bunraku* doll puppets of Japan.

THEATERGOING AROUND THE WORLD

Country	Theater visits in a year (per 100 people)
Cuba	255
Mongolia	170
Vietnam	100
UK	72
Iceland	65
Bulgaria	65
Luxembourg	62
Romania	58
Netherlands	58
US	17

THEATER WORDS

Angel Someone who provides the financial backing for a production.

Apron The part of the stage in front of the proscenium arch (see p.167).

Arena A stage that is surrounded by seating for the audience.

Block To set the actors' movements around the stage.

Chorus Actors in ancient Greek drama who sang and commented on the action.

Corpse To burst into laughter on stage.

Deus ex machina (God from the machine) A god brought in to resolve the plot in ancient Greek drama.

Deus ex machina

Director The person who has artistic control of a production, interpreting the script and rehearsing the actors.

Dress rehearsal The last rehearsal before the opening night, with costumes, lights, and scenery.

Dry To forget one's lines.

Flats Screens painted with scenery, often on both sides, which can be moved around the stage for different effects.

Footlights Lights at the front of the stage, near the auditorium.

Fringe theater Alternative theater, including unconventional plays, venues, or theatrical styles.

Gallery Seats at the top rear of the auditorium. Also called "the gods."

Ham A bad actor, usually one who overacts.

House The audience.

Limelight Powerful light, like that once produced by burning lime.

Open stage A stage without a proscenium arch, with the audience seated on three sides.

Ham

Producer The person responsible for financial and practical aspects of a production. A theatrical producer is not usually involved in artistic direction.

Prompt To whisper lines to an actor who has forgotten them. A "prompt" is someone employed for this purpose.

Rake The angle of the stage. In modern theaters the rake can be altered for different productions.

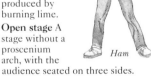

Rake

Trap A trapdoor opening into the area below the stage. Often used together with an elevator for surprise entrances (see p.167).

Walk-on A nonspeaking part.

DANCE

PEOPLE HAVE been dancing since prehistoric times. Over thousands of years, many different styles of dance have developed all over the world.

c.15,000 B.C. Stone Age rock paintings in Europe and Africa show people in dancelike ritual formation.

Tanzanian Stone Age rock painting

3000–1000 B.C. Ancient Egyptians use ritual and ceremonial dance in the worship of gods and goddesses such as Isis.

Fresco (wall painting) from Thebes, showing dancers at a banquet, 1425 B.C.

15,000 B.C. — 3000 B.C.

c.1400 B.C. Bull dancing is a popular entertainment in Crete. People dance around a bull, springing on and off its back or leaping between its horns.

Bronze sculpture of boy leaping over a bull

c.1000 B.C. Chinese shamans (healers and spirit guides) use dance to bring spirits down to Earth.

c.500–400 B.C. Spartan warriors in Greece use dance as part of their training. Socrates (470–399 B.C.), Greek philosopher, states "The best dancer is also the best warrior."

Spartan warriors

c.150 B.C. Romans close all dance schools. Cicero (106–43 B.C.), Roman consul, states that no man dances unless he is insane.

c.A.D. 400 Kagura dances performed to religious chants at Shinto shrines in Japan. Dancers accompanied by drums, brass, gongs, and flutes.

Kagura dancer

c.800 Early Christians include traditional pagan dances in Christian ceremonies. Charlemagne (742–814), the Holy Roman Emperor, bans dancing, but the ban is ignored.

1400 B.C. — 1000 B.C. — 500 B.C. — 500–400 B.C. — 150 B.C. — A.D. 400 — 400 — 800 — 800

1300s Ballroom dancing emerges in the royal palaces of Europe.

1300–1500 Mass dances in Europe cause frenzy and often trances. In Italy the *tarantella* is devised to sweat the poison from a spider's bite out of the victim's body.

Medieval German peasants

1416 First European dancing manual, *On the Art of Dancing and Directing Choruses*, is published.

Late 1400s Ballo, Italian dance performance with a story line, is the earliest form of ballet.

c.1600 Kathakali (see p.171) emerges in India.

Louis XIV in Le Ballet de la Nuit

1653 Louis XIV (1638–1715), 14-year-old French king, appears in *Le Ballet de la Nuit* (Ballet of the Night).

1681 Women are now allowed to dance in ballets, although their long, bulky skirts get in the way.

1700s The waltz develops from German folk dances, and will become popular in European courts.

Waltzers in The Court Ball

1300 — 1400 — 1416 — 1600 — 1653 — 1681 — 1700

Late 1700s French ballet masters, frustrated by lack of opportunity, travel to Russia and develop the full-length story-ballet.

1830–1840s Romantic ballet develops and flourishes. The ballerina is the most important dancer in the performance.

Cancan dancer

1832 Marie Taglioni (1804–84), Italian, is the first ballerina to go *en pointe* (on points) in *La Sylphide*.

1870s The cancan, a high-kicking dance, becomes very fashionable in France.

Marie Taglioni

1880s–1890s Classical ballet (see p.170) reaches its peak in Russia.

1892 Loie Fuller (1862–1928), American dancer, uses fabric and lighting in her *Serpentine Dance* to create a dreamlike effect.

Loie Fuller, 1897

c.1900 American Isadora Duncan (1877–1927), the first modern dancer, develops freer forms of dance.

1909 Serge Diaghilev (1872–1929), Russian arts promoter, presents his Ballets Russes company in Paris. Dancers include Vaslav Nijinsky (1889–1950) and Anna Pavlova (1881–1931).

1700 — 1830 — 1832 — 1880 — 1892 — 1900 — 1909

1913 Nijinsky uses turned-in feet in his ballet, *The Rite of Spring*.

1920s Tap, charleston, jazz, and many other dance forms influenced by African-American dancing, are increasingly popular.

Nijinsky in Giselle

1927 Rudolf von Laban (1879–1958), Hungarian dancer and choreographer, invents a method of recording ballet movements using geometric sketches, called Labanotation.

1927 Martha Graham, (1894–1991), American modern dancer and choreographer, founds her own company.

Martha Graham

1930s Jitterbug and jive are two lively, popular jazz dances.

1933 Ted Shawn (1891–1972), American dancer, forms an all-male company to show men as dancers in their own right, not just as supports for women.

1933 Fred Astaire (1899–1987) and **Ginger Rogers** (born 1911), American dancers, appear in the film *Flying Down to Rio.* More films follow, including *The Gay Divorcée* and *Top Hat.*

Fred Astaire

1910 — 1913 — 1920 — 1927 — 1930 — 1933

1945 Latin American rumba, samba, calypso, and cha-cha are added to the established ballroom dances.

1950s Rock and roll develops as a social dance, mainly for teenagers.

1952 Merce Cunningham (born 1919), American dancer and choreographer, forms his own company. He uses natural movement to create a free-flowing effect.

Rock-and-roll dancers, 1956

1960s Post-modern dance develops in New York. It is experimental, and often improvised.

1970s Disco dancing is popular in Europe and the US.

1976 Twyla Tharp (born 1942), American dancer, choreographs *Push Comes to Shove.* Tharp uses elements of many other styles in her dances.

1980s Break dancing and body-popping are born. Dancers spin around on their backs and heads, and imitate robotic movements. These styles appear in other media, such as film.

Break dancing

1990s DV8 and other companies design dances for television as well as stage.

DV8 Physical Theatre

1940 — 1945 — 1950 — 1952 — 1960 — 1970 — 1976 — 1980 — 1990

BALLET AND MODERN DANCE

BALLET IS A combination of music, dance, and mime, with set steps and techniques. Modern dance developed from it as a freer, more natural form.

BALLET STYLES

The three main styles of ballet are Romantic, Classical, and modern. The style of ballet is usually reflected in the type of costume that the dancers wear.

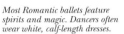

Most Romantic ballets feature spirits and magic. Dancers often wear white, calf-length dresses.

In Classical ballets, dancers wear short dresses, called tutus, to show off their footwork.

In modern ballets, dancers usually wear simple costumes.

THE FIVE POSITIONS

In ballet there are five basic positions for the arms, and five for the feet.

Positions of the arms
Second, fourth, and fifth positions have variations, e.g. in *demi-seconde*, the arms are raised half-way between first and second positions.

First position

Second position

Third position

Fourth position

Fifth position

Positions of the feet
Almost every movement danced in a ballet begins and ends with one of the five positions of the feet.

First position

Second position

Third position

Fourth position

Fifth position

CHOREOGRAPHY

Choreography is the art of designing and devising the steps of a ballet or dance routine. The term comes from the ancient Greek words *khoreia* (dancing) and *graphos* (writing). Choreographers – the people who devise dance routines – work with dancers to compose a dance sequence, then record it using notation.

MODERN DANCE

In the late 1800s, Isadora Duncan and Loie Fuller (see p.169) felt ballet movements were unnatural, and developed a new, freer style. Martha Graham and Merce Cunningham (see p.169) are the two most famous dancer-choreographers of the modern dance movement.

Isadora Duncan pioneered modern dance.

Twyla Tharp (see p.169) was a later modern dance innovator.

Today, new modern dance techniques are still being developed.

FAMOUS 20TH CENTURY DANCERS

Many dancers have become choreographers and teachers, passing their style and skills on to others.

Marie Rambert (1888–1982) Polish teacher and dancer, founded the Ballet Rambert (now the Rambert Dance Company).

Margot Fonteyn (1919–91) British, and **Rudolf Nureyev** (1938–93), Russian, formed the world's most famous and most popular partnership.

Vaslav Nijinsky (1890–1950) Russian Classical dancer, was famous for his athletic style and innovative choreography. He was the star of the Ballets Russes.

Arthur Mitchell (born 1934) American dancer. In 1969 he founded the Dance Theater of Harlem, the first dance company with only black dancers.

BALLET RECORDS

MOST CURTAIN CALLS was 89, taken by Margot Fonteyn and Rudolf Nureyev after a performance of *Swan Lake* in Austria in 1964.

MOST EXPENSIVE COSTUME was made for the part of the Chinese conjurer in *Parade*, premièred in Paris in 1917. Designed by Pablo Picasso (see p.161), the costume fetched $42,000 at auction in 1984.

DANCE NOTATION

Like music, dance is written down using a system of symbols. There are two forms of dance notation: Benesh and Laban. The Benesh method, which is usually used for ballet, was devised by Rudolf (1916–75) and Joan Benesh (born 1920). Labanotation, named after Rudolf von Laban (see p.169), is mainly used to record modern dance.

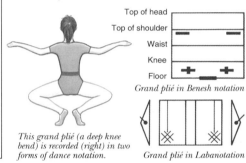

Top of head
Top of shoulder
Waist
Knee
Floor

Grand plié in Benesh notation

This grand plié (a deep knee bend) is recorded (right) in two forms of dance notation.

Grand plié in Labanotation

FAMOUS BALLETS

Title	Choreographer	First danced
La Sylphide	Filippo Taglioni (1777–1871), Italian	1832
Nutcracker	Lev Ivanov (1834–1901), Russian	1892
Swan Lake	Lev Ivanov and Marius Petipa (1818–1910), French	1895
Manon	Kenneth MacMillan (1929–93), British	1974

BALLET FACTS

• A ballerina who dances regularly wears out about ten pairs of *pointe* shoes each month.

• During the average-length career, dancers practise for eight hours a day, six days a week: in total, about five-and-a-half years.

BALLET TERMS

Barre The bar that dancers use to help them balance during exercises

Battement A beating movement of the leg (many forms)

Corps de ballet The chorus of dancers (those not dancing solo roles)

Jeté A jump from one leg to the other

Pas de chat A jumping step

Pas de deux A dance for two people (male and female), usually the principals

Pirouette A complete 360° turn on one leg

Pas de deux

Plié A knee-bending movement

Pointe On the points or the tips of the toes (female dancers)

FEET FEAT

British dancer Wayne Sleep (born 1948) achieved six *entrechats* in 1973, crossing and uncrossing his legs six times while still in the air.

TRADITIONAL WORLD DANCE

MOST COUNTRIES OF the world have a traditional form of dance that has evolved over many years. These dances have often developed from simple religious or tribal rituals into complex dance forms with set movements.

Thai classical dancer

SOUTHEAST ASIA
Classical dance is performed by highly trained artists. Dancing is slow, with complex hand movements.

POLYNESIAN DANCE
Dance plays an important role in traditional Polynesian culture. Women often swing and rotate their hips rapidly, e.g. in the Hawaiian hula.

Polynesian dancer

AMERICAN DANCE
Native Americans dance at special ceremonies to win the goodwill of spirits, ancestors, and gods.

Native American dancer

European folk dancers

Japanese gagaku dancer

African tribal dancer

Indian temple dancer

EUROPEAN DANCE
Many traditional European folk dances have their roots in religious rituals. For example, dancing in a circle probably originated from circling around an object of worship.

EAST ASIA
Most East Asian dance forms part of theatrical dance drama, e.g. Chinese opera. Japanese *gagaku* and *bugaka* are the world's oldest forms of traditional court dance.

AFRICAN DANCE
Most African dance has its roots in tribal rituals. It includes Sun- and Moon- worshipping, weapon, fertility, and hunting dances.

INDIA
Indian classical dance developed from religious rituals in which dancers told stories about the lives of the gods. There are six styles of dance, including *kathakali* and *bharata natyam*.

TRANCE DANCES
In many cultures, people dance themselves into a trance as a way of communicating with spirits and gods. They may perform acts that would normally be dangerous, but which leave them unharmed.

Barong dancers in Bali strike themselves with daggers while in a trance.

DANCE PROPS
Props (items in addition to costume that a dancer may use) are important in many traditional dances.

Prop	Country	Significance
Maypole	England	The maypole is a fertility object symbolizing a tree. People dance around it, holding ribbons that represent branches.
Weapons	Worldwide	The use of weapons, e.g. swords, clubs, and shields, dates back to religious ceremonies in which the gods were asked for help in battle.
Snakes	N. America	The Hopi people use snakes in their rain dances. Snakes are believed to be brothers of the spirits that control clouds and rain.
Instruments	Worldwide	Dancers often wear or use instruments to accentuate the rhythm of a dance, e.g. castanets in Spanish flamenco; bells worn by classical Indian dancers.

LOW-DOWN LIMBO
Caribbean limbo dancers can pass underneath bars as low as 6in (15cm) off the ground.

DANCE FACTS
• In North Africa, belly dancers are judged by how well they move their shoulders.

• Judges at Irish jigging contests sit under the stage to assess the speed and precision of the dancers' steps.

• The cakewalk was the first African-American dance to be taken up by white Americans. It developed from dance competitions where the prize was usually a cake.

• Between 1910 and 1920, animal dances such as the chicken scratch and the grizzly bear were popular in the US. Not everyone approved: a woman was jailed for 50 days for doing the turkey trot, a dance that was officially denounced by the Vatican.

• Flamenco dancers can tap their heels at a rate of up to 16 taps per second.

FACE FACTS
Kathakali dancers take up to four hours to apply their makeup. They have such control over their facial muscles that they can laugh with one side of their face and cry with the other.

DANCE RECORDS
FASTEST TAP DANCE
was 32 taps per second by Englishman Stephen Gare (born 1967), in 1990.

LONGEST CONGA
was the Miami Super Conga in 1988, which consisted of 119,986 people.

MUSIC

FROM A PRIMITIVE war cry to the complex sound of a symphony orchestra, music has been created by every known society. Vibrations are the source of all musical sound.

MUSICAL SOUNDS AND NOTATION

Most Western music is based on major and minor scales – traditional patterns of pitches that sound pleasing to the ear. Composers write down these pitches using notation – a code of signs and symbols that enables a musician to interpret and play a musical composition.

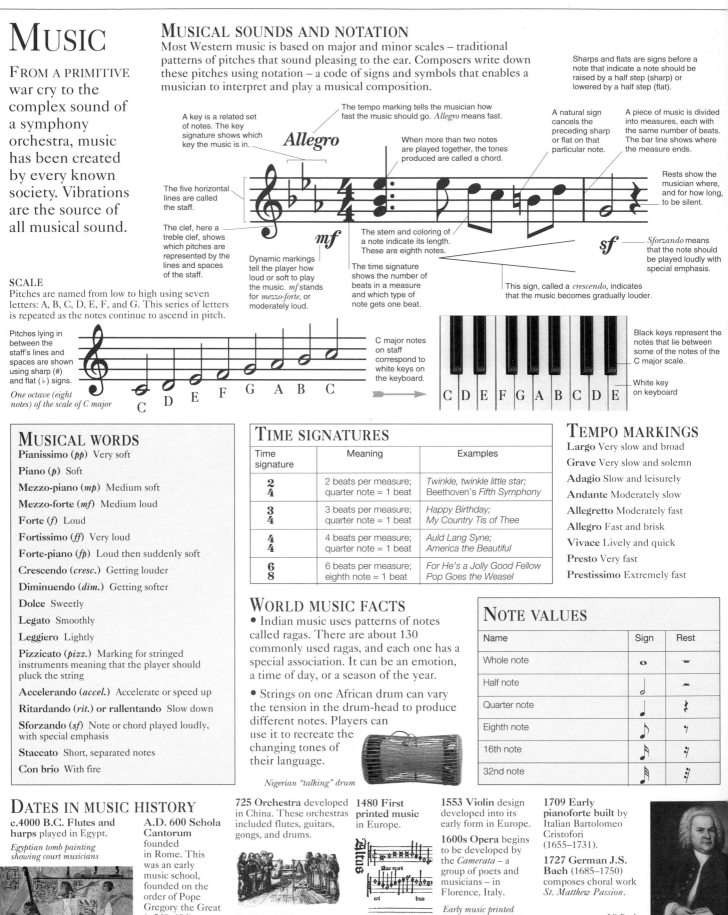

A key is a related set of notes. The key signature shows which key the music is in.

The tempo marking tells the musician how fast the music should go. *Allegro* means fast.

When more than two notes are played together, the tones produced are called a chord.

A natural sign cancels the preceding sharp or flat on that particular note.

Sharps and flats are signs before a note that indicate a note should be raised by a half step (sharp) or lowered by a half step (flat).

A piece of music is divided into measures, each with the same number of beats. The bar line shows where the measure ends.

The five horizontal lines are called the staff.

The clef, here a treble clef, shows which pitches are represented by the lines and spaces of the staff.

Dynamic markings tell the player how loud or soft to play the music. *mf* stands for *mezzo-forte*, or moderately loud.

The stem and coloring of a note indicate its length. These are eighth notes.

The time signature shows the number of beats in a measure and which type of note gets one beat.

Rests show the musician where, and for how long, to be silent.

Sforzando means that the note should be played loudly with special emphasis.

This sign, called a *crescendo*, indicates that the music becomes gradually louder.

SCALE

Pitches are named from low to high using seven letters: A, B, C, D, E, F, and G. This series of letters is repeated as the notes continue to ascend in pitch.

Pitches lying in between the staff's lines and spaces are shown using sharp (#) and flat (♭) signs.

One octave (eight notes) of the scale of C major

C D E F G A B C

C major notes on staff correspond to white keys on the keyboard.

Black keys represent the notes that lie between some of the notes of the C major scale.

White key on keyboard

C D E F G A B C D E

MUSICAL WORDS

Pianissimo (*pp*) Very soft

Piano (*p*) Soft

Mezzo-piano (*mp*) Medium soft

Mezzo-forte (*mf*) Medium loud

Forte (*f*) Loud

Fortissimo (*ff*) Very loud

Forte-piano (*fp*) Loud then suddenly soft

Crescendo (*cresc.*) Getting louder

Diminuendo (*dim.*) Getting softer

Dolce Sweetly

Legato Smoothly

Leggiero Lightly

Pizzicato (*pizz.*) Marking for stringed instruments meaning that the player should pluck the string

Accelerando (*accel.*) Accelerate or speed up

Ritardando (*rit.*) or rallentando Slow down

Sforzando (*sf*) Note or chord played loudly, with special emphasis

Staccato Short, separated notes

Con brio With fire

TIME SIGNATURES

Time signature	Meaning	Examples
2/4	2 beats per measure; quarter note = 1 beat	*Twinkle, twinkle little star*; Beethoven's *Fifth Symphony*
3/4	3 beats per measure; quarter note = 1 beat	*Happy Birthday*; *My Country Tis of Thee*
4/4	4 beats per measure; quarter note = 1 beat	*Auld Lang Syne*; *America the Beautiful*
6/8	6 beats per measure; eighth note = 1 beat	*For He's a Jolly Good Fellow*; *Pop Goes the Weasel*

WORLD MUSIC FACTS

• Indian music uses patterns of notes called ragas. There are about 130 commonly used ragas, and each one has a special association. It can be an emotion, a time of day, or a season of the year.

• Strings on one African drum can vary the tension in the drum-head to produce different notes. Players can use it to recreate the changing tones of their language.

Nigerian "talking" drum

TEMPO MARKINGS

Largo Very slow and broad

Grave Very slow and solemn

Adagio Slow and leisurely

Andante Moderately slow

Allegretto Moderately fast

Allegro Fast and brisk

Vivace Lively and quick

Presto Very fast

Prestissimo Extremely fast

NOTE VALUES

Name	Sign	Rest
Whole note	𝅝	▬
Half note	𝅗𝅥	▬
Quarter note	𝅘𝅥	𝄽
Eighth note	𝅘𝅥𝅮	𝄾
16th note	𝅘𝅥𝅯	𝄿
32nd note	𝅘𝅥𝅰	𝅀

DATES IN MUSIC HISTORY

c.4000 B.C. Flutes and harps played in Egypt.

Egyptian tomb painting showing court musicians

A.D. 600 Schola Cantorum founded in Rome. This was an early music school, founded on the order of Pope Gregory the Great (c.540–604).

Traditional Chinese orchestra

725 Orchestra developed in China. These orchestras included flutes, guitars, gongs, and drums.

1480 First printed music in Europe.

Early music printed from carved woodblocks.

1553 Violin design developed into its early form in Europe.

1600s Opera begins to be developed by the *Camerata* – a group of poets and musicians – in Florence, Italy.

1709 Early pianoforte built by Italian Bartolomeo Cristofori (1655–1731).

1727 German J.S. Bach (1685–1750) composes choral work *St. Matthew Passion*.

J.S.Bach

4000 B.C.	A.D.600	725	1480	1553	1600	1709	1727

MUSICAL GROUPS

Groups range from duos, which have two performers, to symphony orchestras, which contain up to 120 (see p.174). Most classical music groups play written music. Jazz groups take a theme and invent variations on it as they play.

Duo

In a duo, one player usually plays a brass, string, or wind instrument and the other a piano. Pieces for two players are called duets.

Cello and piano duo

Trio

Trios have three players. A string trio uses a violin, viola, and cello. Piano trios are written for violin, cello, and piano.

String trio

Quartet

Jazz groups often use quartets (groups of four players). String quartets contain two violins, a viola, and a cello.

Jazz quartet

Quintet

Quintets use five players and usually contain wind or brass instruments or instruments from different families.

Mixed quintet

Choir

A choir is a group of singers. A mixed voice choir contains men and women, who sing four parts. Most choirs sing religious music.

Small church choir

LARGER GROUPS

• Large groups of wind, brass, and percussion players, called bands, play for outdoor concerts and military ceremonies.

• A medium-sized string group, often including a few wind instruments, is called a chamber orchestra. Many composers have written for this group.

MAJOR COMPOSERS IN WESTERN MUSIC

Composer	Nationality, dates	Major work(s), date(s) composed
Renaissance (1450–1600) Guillaume Dufay	Flemish, c.1400–74	Church music and secular pieces
Josquin des Prés	Flemish, c.1445–1521	Choral church and secular music
Giovanni Palestrina	Italian, c.1525–94	Choral church and secular music
William Byrd	English, 1543–1623	Church music, string music, keyboard music, and madrigals
Baroque (1600–1750) Claudio Monteverdi	Italian, 1567–1643	*Orfeo* (1607), *Vespers* (1610)
Heinrich Schütz	German, 1585–1672	*Symphoniae Sacrae* (1650)
Jean Baptiste Lully	French, 1632–87	Operas, church compositions
Henry Purcell	English, 1659–95	*Dido and Aeneas* (1689)
Antonio Vivaldi	Italian, 1678–1741	*Four Seasons* (1725)
Jean Phillippe Rameau	French, 1683–1764	*Castor and Pollux* (1737)
Johann Sebastian Bach	German, 1685–1750	*Brandenburg Concertos* (1721), *St. Matthew Passion* (1727)
George Frederic Handel	German, 1685–1759	*The Messiah* (1741), *Music for the Royal Fireworks* (1749)
Classical (1750–1820) Joseph Haydn	Austrian 1732–1809	*London Symphonies*: 1st set (1791–92) *London Symphonies*: 2nd set (1793–95),
Wolfgang Amadeus Mozart	Austrian, 1756–91	*Piano Concertos in C Major and D Minor* (1785), *The Marriage of Figaro* (1786), *Don Giovanni* (1787)
Ludwig van Beethoven	German, 1770–1827	*Symphonies No. 3* (1802), *No. 5* (1809), and *No. 9* (1823)
Romantic 1820–1900 Franz Schubert	Austrian, 1797–1828	*Piano Quintet in A* (1819), *"Unfinished" Symphony No. 8* (1822)
Hector Berlioz	French, 1803–69	*Symphonie Fantastique* (1830), *The Trojans* (1859)
Frederic Chopin	Polish, 1810–49	Piano compositions, *Preludes* (1839)
Franz Liszt	Hungarian, 1811–86	*Piano Sonata in B Min* (1853), *Hungarian Rhapsodies* (1839–85)
Richard Wagner	German, 1813–83	*The Flying Dutchman* (1841), *The Ring of the Nibelung* (1848–74)
Giuseppe Verdi	Italian, 1813–1901	*Aida* (1871), *Requiem Mass* (1873), *Otello* (1887)
Johannes Brahms	German, 1833–97	*Violin Concerto in D Major* (1878), *Symphony No. 4* (1884)
Peter Ilyich Tchaikovsky	Russian, 1840–93	*Piano Concerto No 1* (1874–5), *Swan Lake* (1876)
Edvard Grieg	Norwegian, 1843–1907	*Piano Concerto in A Minor* (1869), *Peer Gynt* (1876)
Edward Elgar	English, 1857–1934	*Enigma Variations* (1899), *Violin Concerto* (1910)
Modern 1900 to present Claude Debussy	French, 1862–1918	*Pelléas and Mélisande* (1892–1902), *Images* (1905-07)
Arnold Schoenberg	Austrian, 1874–1951	*First String Quartet* (1897), *Pierrot Lunaire* (1912)
Béla Bartók	Hungarian, 1881–1945	*Six String Quartets* (1939), *Concerto for Orchestra* (1944)
Igor Stravinsky	Russian, 1882–1971	*The Firebird* (1910), *The Rite of Spring* (1913)
Sergei Prokofiev	Russian, 1891–1953	*Romeo and Juliet* (1935), *Peter and the Wolf* (1936)
Lili Boulanger	French, 1893–1918	*Faust and Helène* (1913)
George Gershwin	American, 1898–1937	*Rhapsody in Blue* (1924), *Porgy and Bess* (1935)
Dmitry Shostakovich	Russian, 1906–75	*Symphonies No.5* (1937) and *No.10* (1953)
John Cage	American, 1912–92	*Music of changes* (1951), *4' 33"* (1954)
Pierre Boulez	French, born 1925	*Le Marteau sans Maître* (1954), *Memoriales* (1975)
Karlheinz Stockhausen	German, born 1928	*Groups* (1955–57)
Philip Glass	American, born 1937	*Einstein on the Beach* (1976)

Austrian composer
ang A. Mozart (1756–91)
oses opera, *Don Giovanni*.

1808 German composer **Ludwig van Beethoven** (1770–1827) composes Symphonies No.5 and No.6.

Ludwig van Beethoven

1874 German composer Richard Wagner (1813–83) finishes *The Ring of the Nibelung*.

c.1900 Jazz music appears in New Orleans, US. It combines African rhythms with Western harmony.

Early jazz music

1940 Synthesizers appear, giving composers new electronic sounds.

1955 Rock music appears in US.

Rock singer Chuck Berry

OFF BEAT

Jean Baptiste Lully (1632–87), court musician to Louis XIV of France, stabbed his foot with the long staff that he banged on the floor in order to keep his orchestra in time. He later died from an abscess caused by this injury.

ng Mozart
the piano

787   1808   1874   1900   1950

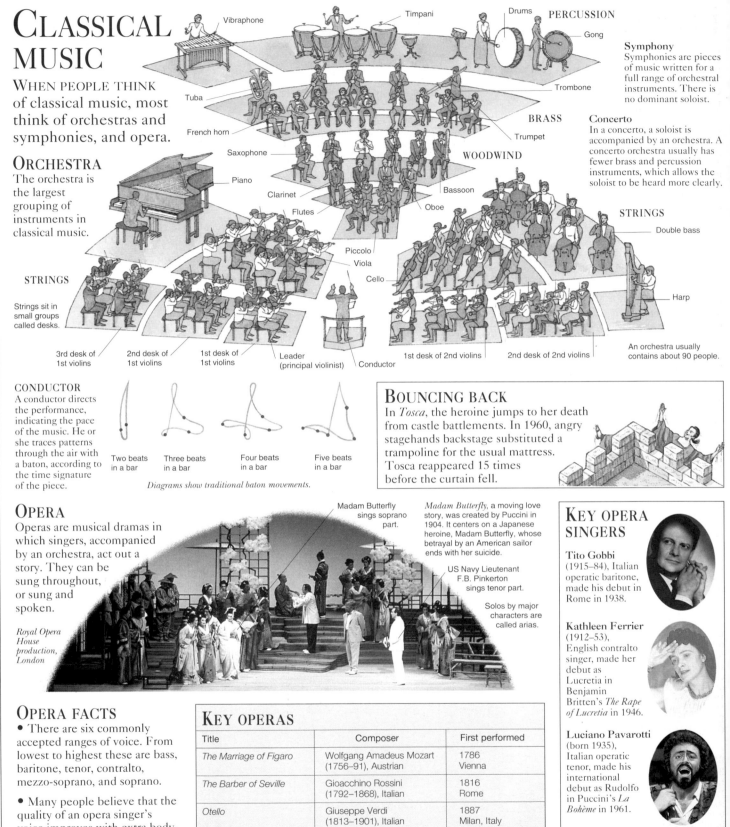

CLASSICAL MUSIC

WHEN PEOPLE THINK of classical music, most think of orchestras and symphonies, and opera.

ORCHESTRA

The orchestra is the largest grouping of instruments in classical music.

Vibraphone

Timpani

Drums

PERCUSSION

Gong

Trombone

BRASS

Trumpet

Tuba

French horn

Saxophone

WOODWIND

Bassoon

Oboe

Piano

Clarinet

Flutes

Piccolo

Viola

Cello

STRINGS

Double bass

Harp

STRINGS

Strings sit in small groups called desks.

3rd desk of 1st violins

2nd desk of 1st violins

1st desk of 1st violins

Leader (principal violinist)

Conductor

1st desk of 2nd violins

2nd desk of 2nd violins

An orchestra usually contains about 90 people.

Symphony
Symphonies are pieces of music written for a full range of orchestral instruments. There is no dominant soloist.

Concerto
In a concerto, a soloist is accompanied by an orchestra. A concerto orchestra usually has fewer brass and percussion instruments, which allows the soloist to be heard more clearly.

CONDUCTOR
A conductor directs the performance, indicating the pace of the music. He or she traces patterns through the air with a baton, according to the time signature of the piece.

Two beats in a bar

Three beats in a bar

Four beats in a bar

Five beats in a bar

Diagrams show traditional baton movements.

BOUNCING BACK
In *Tosca*, the heroine jumps to her death from castle battlements. In 1960, angry stagehands backstage substituted a trampoline for the usual mattress. Tosca reappeared 15 times before the curtain fell.

OPERA
Operas are musical dramas in which singers, accompanied by an orchestra, act out a story. They can be sung throughout, or sung and spoken.

Royal Opera House production, London

Madam Butterfly sings soprano part.

Madam Butterfly, a moving love story, was created by Puccini in 1904. It centers on a Japanese heroine, Madam Butterfly, whose betrayal by an American sailor ends with her suicide.

US Navy Lieutenant F.B. Pinkerton sings tenor part.

Solos by major characters are called arias.

KEY OPERA SINGERS

Tito Gobbi (1915–84), Italian operatic baritone, made his debut in Rome in 1938.

Kathleen Ferrier (1912–53), English contralto singer, made her debut as Lucretia in Benjamin Britten's *The Rape of Lucretia* in 1946.

Luciano Pavarotti (born 1935), Italian operatic tenor, made his international debut as Rudolfo in Puccini's *La Bohème* in 1961.

Kiri Te Kanawa (born 1944), New Zealand operatic soprano, made her international debut in 1971, as the Countess in Mozart's *The Marriage of Figaro*.

OPERA FACTS
• There are six commonly accepted ranges of voice. From lowest to highest these are bass, baritone, tenor, contralto, mezzo-soprano, and soprano.

• Many people believe that the quality of an opera singer's voice improves with extra body-weight. In fact, a person's weight is irrelevant: thin people may possess the finest voices.

• Some people can identify the pitch of any note that they hear, without needing to refer to an instrument. This ability is called "perfect pitch."

KEY OPERAS

Title	Composer	First performed
The Marriage of Figaro	Wolfgang Amadeus Mozart (1756–91), Austrian	1786 Vienna
The Barber of Seville	Gioacchino Rossini (1792–1868), Italian	1816 Rome
Otello	Giuseppe Verdi (1813–1901), Italian	1887 Milan, Italy
The Ring of the Nibelung	Richard Wagner (1813–83), German	1876 Bayreuth, Germany
Carmen	Georges Bizet (1838–75), French	1875 Paris
La Bohème	Giacomo Puccini (1858–1924), Italian	1896 Turin, Italy
Peter Grimes	Benjamin Britten (1913–76), British	1945 London

POPULAR MUSIC

MANY DIFFERENT styles of music have evolved in the twentieth century. Here the most popular Western styles are described.

FOLK MUSIC

In the 19th century, America's southern black population, including transport workers on the railroads and riverboats, as well as cotton workers, sang and listened to folk songs at work, or at the end of the day. They created a new kind of folk song in which they mixed the complex, overlapping rhythms

Album of early African-American songs

and free melodies of West African music with the harmonics of Western music. This combination formed the foundation for music that would dominate popular tastes during the 20th century.

BLUES

The blues express the troubles and emotions of the performer in a simple but strict form. The performer sets three lines of poetry to 12 bars of music. The blues use a basic, set pattern of harmonies (chords), over which the performer invents variations.

Leadbelly
Leadbelly's Last Sessions

JAZZ

Jazz emerged in the early 1900s in New Orleans, US, as a mixture of blues, religious gospel singing, and European influences. Driven by the urgent rhythms of West African music and using the melodic style of the Blues, jazz musicians improvise – they recreate the

Louis Armstrong
Laughing Louis

melody of a piece each time it is performed. This allows each player to express their emotions through their special version of the music. Major artists of the "jazz age" of the 1920s included American trumpeters Louis "Satchmo" Armstrong (c.1898–1971) and Bix Beiderbecke (1903–31), and the orchestral composer George Gershwin (1898–1937).

BIG BANDS AND BE-BOP

In the 1930s and early 1940s, swing, a form of jazz, was played by "big bands," under great bandleaders such as Duke Ellington (1899–1974). Later, a new style emerged, called be-bop. It was pioneered by trumpeter Dizzy Gillespie (born 1917) and saxophonist Charlie Parker (1920–55). Be-bop led to more complex schemes of harmony. Major artists included trumpeter Miles Davis (1926–91) and saxophonist John Coltrane (1926–67).

Charlie Parker Bird Lives

COUNTRY AND WESTERN

Country and Western music takes its inspiration from the country life of the American West. Its performers, often dressed as cowboys of the Old West, sing with the accent of southern US and are accompanied by instruments such

Johnny Cash
The Johnny Cash Collection

as the banjo, fiddle, and guitar. Performers include Hank Williams (born 1923), Johnny Cash (born 1932), and Tammy Wynette (born 1942).

ROCK AND ROLL

Rock and roll began in the 1950s as a mix of rhythm-and-blues and country music and was played loudly on newly invented electric guitars. Though this style arose in black communities, white singer and guitarist Elvis Presley (1935–77) greatly increased its popularity.

Elvis Presley Elvis Presley

ROCK

In the 1960s, rock and roll was abbreviated to "rock" music. Rock music has a heavy, driving rhythm, with eight eighth notes to the bar and accents on the second and fourth beats. Early rock bands included The Beatles, The Rolling Stones, Pink Floyd, The Who, and The Jimi Hendrix Experience.

The Rolling Stones
Their Satanic Majesties Request

REGGAE

West Indian reggae music was spread abroad by West Indian communities overseas. It is closely associated with the Rastafarian religion. Its most famous artist was Bob Marley (1945–81), whose music calls for an end to racism and political repression.

Bob Marley and The Wailers

DISCO

In the 1970s, new music centered around the disco movement. It was promoted by films such as *Saturday Night Fever* and by a revival of interest in 1950s music by black artists such as James Brown (born 1933). Disco artists include The Bee Gees and Donna Summer.

The Bee Gees
Saturday Night Fever

PUNK

Punk music exploded onto the scene at the close of the 1970s, led by the British groups The Sex Pistols and The Clash. It had a savage character, and appealed to young people whose dress, language, and behavior were designed to outrage traditional tastes.

The Damned
Damned, Damned, Damned

1980s POP MUSIC

Pop music in the 1980s became lighter and more concerned with dance rhythms. Major pop artists and groups included Michael Jackson, The Pet Shop Boys, Madonna, and Bryan Ferry. Pop videos, in which the music was accompanied by images, made it possible for a performer to be seen on television by millions at the same time as the release of their record.

Michael Jackson Thriller

1990s POPULAR MUSIC

A specialized form of dance music, called house music, emerged in the 1980s, based on very rapid rhythms and electronic sounds. The technology for making and mixing these sounds is now widely available to musicians, and their music has since developed into the related styles of acid house, techno, trance, ambient, and jungle music.

The Orb Blue Room

BEST-SELLING SINGLES WORLDWIDE

Single	Performer/group	Copies sold (approx.)
White Christmas	Bing Crosby	30,000,000
Rock Around the Clock	Bill Haley and His Comets	17,000,000
I Want to Hold Your Hand	The Beatles	12,000,000
It's Now or Never	Elvis Presley	10,000,000
Hound Dog/Don't Be Cruel	Elvis Presley	9,000,000
Diana	Paul Anka	9,000,000
Hey Jude	The Beatles	8,000,000
I'm a Believer	The Monkees	8,000,000
Can't Buy Me Love	The Beatles	7,000,000
Do They Know It's Christmas?	Band Aid	7,000,000

POP MUSIC RECORDS

MOST EXPENSIVE GUITAR was a Fender Stratocaster belonging to Jimi Hendrix (1942–70). It was sold for £180,000 (US $275,940) at Sotheby's, London, in 1990.

MOST SUCCESSFUL SONGWRITERS are Paul McCartney (born 1942), who has had 32 number one singles in the US and 28 in the UK, and John Lennon (1940–80), with 26 number one singles in the US and 29 in the UK.

MUSICAL INSTRUMENTS

MUSICAL INSTRUMENTS are designed to make vibrations that our ears and brain recognize as musical sounds. They are usually classified into percussion, stringed, woodwind, brass, and keyboard. Archaeologists excavating the sites of ancient Mesopotamian cities (see p.375) have found evidence for every basic instrument type.

VIOLIN
The violin is the smallest stringed instrument. It also produces the highest sound. The player holds the violin between the chin and the shoulder, drawing the bow across the strings to produce a clear tone.

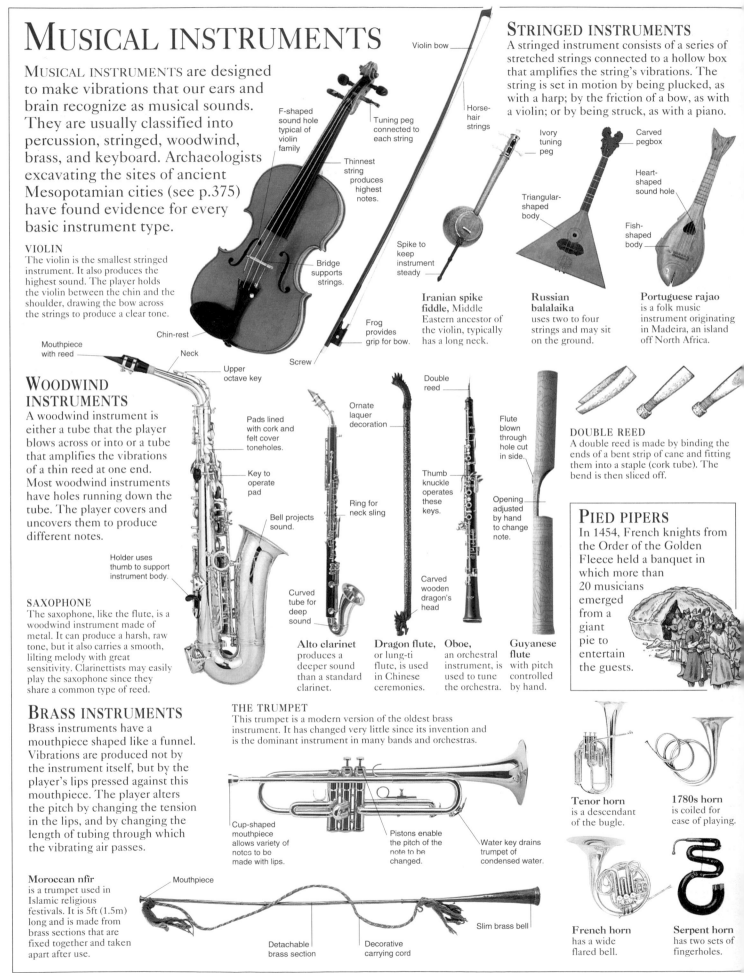

Violin bow

F-shaped sound hole typical of violin family

Tuning peg connected to each string

Horse-hair strings

Thinnest string produces highest notes.

Bridge supports strings.

Spike to keep instrument steady

Frog provides grip for bow.

Chin-rest

Screw

STRINGED INSTRUMENTS
A stringed instrument consists of a series of stretched strings connected to a hollow box that amplifies the string's vibrations. The string is set in motion by being plucked, as with a harp; by the friction of a bow, as with a violin; or by being struck, as with a piano.

Ivory tuning peg

Carved pegbox

Heart-shaped sound hole

Triangular-shaped body

Fish-shaped body

Iranian spike fiddle, Middle Eastern ancestor of the violin, typically has a long neck.

Russian balalaika uses two to four strings and may sit on the ground.

Portuguese rajao is a folk music instrument originating in Madeira, an island off North Africa.

WOODWIND INSTRUMENTS
A woodwind instrument is either a tube that the player blows across or into or a tube that amplifies the vibrations of a thin reed at one end. Most woodwind instruments have holes running down the tube. The player covers and uncovers them to produce different notes.

Mouthpiece with reed

Neck

Upper octave key

Pads lined with cork and felt cover toneholes.

Key to operate pad

Bell projects sound.

Holder uses thumb to support instrument body.

SAXOPHONE
The saxophone, like the flute, is a woodwind instrument made of metal. It can produce a harsh, raw tone, but it also carries a smooth, lilting melody with great sensitivity. Clarinettists may easily play the saxophone since they share a common type of reed.

Ornate laquer decoration

Ring for neck sling

Curved tube for deep sound

Alto clarinet produces a deeper sound than a standard clarinet.

Double reed

Thumb knuckle operates these keys.

Carved wooden dragon's head

Dragon flute, or lung-ti flute, is used in Chinese ceremonies.

Oboe, an orchestral instrument, is used to tune the orchestra.

Flute blown through hole cut in side.

Opening adjusted by hand to change note.

Guyanese flute with pitch controlled by hand.

DOUBLE REED
A double reed is made by binding the ends of a bent strip of cane and fitting them into a staple (cork tube). The bend is then sliced off.

PIED PIPERS
In 1454, French knights from the Order of the Golden Fleece held a banquet in which more than 20 musicians emerged from a giant pie to entertain the guests.

BRASS INSTRUMENTS
Brass instruments have a mouthpiece shaped like a funnel. Vibrations are produced not by the instrument itself, but by the player's lips pressed against this mouthpiece. The player alters the pitch by changing the tension in the lips, and by changing the length of tubing through which the vibrating air passes.

THE TRUMPET
This trumpet is a modern version of the oldest brass instrument. It has changed very little since its invention and is the dominant instrument in many bands and orchestras.

Cup-shaped mouthpiece allows variety of notes to be made with lips.

Pistons enable the pitch of the note to be changed.

Water key drains trumpet of condensed water.

Tenor horn is a descendant of the bugle.

1780s horn is coiled for ease of playing.

Moroccan nfir is a trumpet used in Islamic religious festivals. It is 5ft (1.5m) long and is made from brass sections that are fixed together and taken apart after use.

Mouthpiece

Detachable brass section

Decorative carrying cord

Slim brass bell

French horn has a wide flared bell.

Serpent horn has two sets of fingerholes.

PERCUSSION INSTRUMENTS

Percussion instruments are played by being struck, rubbed, or shaken; they usually provide the rhythmic beat in an instrumental group. They include snare drums, bass drums, tambourines, cymbals, gongs, castanets, maracas, tom-toms, timpani, bells, the xylophone, celesta, marimba, vibraphone, and chimes.

DRUM KIT
A drum kit consists of different types of drums and cymbals. The player uses both hands and feet to operate it.

Crash cymbal loosely fitted to allow vibrations

High-hat uses two cymbals.

Tom-tom drums

Snare drum

Ride cymbal

Key to adjust height

Floor tom-tom

Bass drum pedal

Felt-covered beater

Bass drum gives deep thud.

Egyptian darabuka is an example of the goblet drum popular in many Arab countries.

Oriental gong is struck in the center to cause the greatest vibrations.

Nigerian gourd rattle

Chinese rattle drum

Gourd

Brazilian berimbau with resonating gourd.

Tambourine has cymbals set into frame, which sound when shaken.

KEYBOARD INSTRUMENTS

Keyboard instruments have an arrangement of levers or keys that activate the source of sound. Their popularity arose from a capacity to play melody and accompaniment at the same time. The three major keyboard instruments are the pianoforte or piano, the harpsichord, and the organ.

PIANOFORTE

The keys of a pianoforte manipulate felt-covered hammers. These strike wire strings, causing them to resonate. The player can sound many notes at once and can vary the loudness of individual notes.

Strings

Heavy iron frame

Hammers

Raised lid gives fuller sound.

Left or soft pedal moves hammer nearer to strings, allowing softer tone.

Right or sustaining pedal controls duration of sound.

Tuning pins

88-note keyboard

Square pianoforte made in England in 1773.

Italian spinet of 1550s used a four-octave keyboard.

Strings plucked by wooden jacks.

Wooden soundboard

MOST EXPENSIVE INSTRUMENTS

Instrument	Date made	Value $
"Mendelssohn" violin by Stradivari	1720	1,382,766
"Cholmondeley" cello by Stradivari	1698	950,460
"Bonjour" cello by Stradivari	1690	927,465
Violin by Joseph del Gesu	1743	797,160
"Marie Hall" violin by Stradivari	1709	659,190
"Schreiber" violin by Stradivari	1712	539,616
Violin by Pietro Guarneri	1715	339,560
"Ex-Kosman" violin by G. Guadagnini	c.1750	339,560
"Montagnana" violin by D. Montagnana	1741	314,265
Jimi Hendrix's *Stratocaster* guitar	1968	275,940

ELECTRONIC INSTRUMENTS

The electronic synthesizer creates sound by artificial means. It changes electric impulses into sound, and every aspect of the sound can be controlled. The synthesizer player can generate virtually any sound imaginable, from those of the natural world or of traditional instruments, to new, unique, "space-age" sounds.

Electronic keyboard can change a sound wave to produce a great variety of sounds.

Drum pad emits electric signal when struck, to produce electronic drum sound.

1950s electric guitar pioneered rock as musical form. Most bands have three guitars, a lead, rhythm, and bass.

Futuristic V-shaped wooden body

Output socket

Pickups that convert string vibrations into electrical impulses.

MUSIC FACTS

• Italian violinist Niccolò Paganini (1782–1840) was the most skilled violin virtuoso of the 19th century. He was the fastest violinist in the world, playing his own *Mouvement Perpetuel* in three minutes, three seconds. This translates as 12 notes per second.

• In 1846, Belgian instrument maker Adolphe Sax invented the saxophone.

• The harmonica is the world's most popular instrument. In 1965, more than 28 million were sold in the US.

• The drum used on British explorer Sir Francis Drake's ship hangs in Buckland Abbey, England. It is believed to roll by itself when England faces danger. It was last heard in World War I (1914–18).

• In 1709, the first piano was built by Italian Bartolomeo Cristofori (1655-1731) . The first iron-framed piano appeared in 1859.

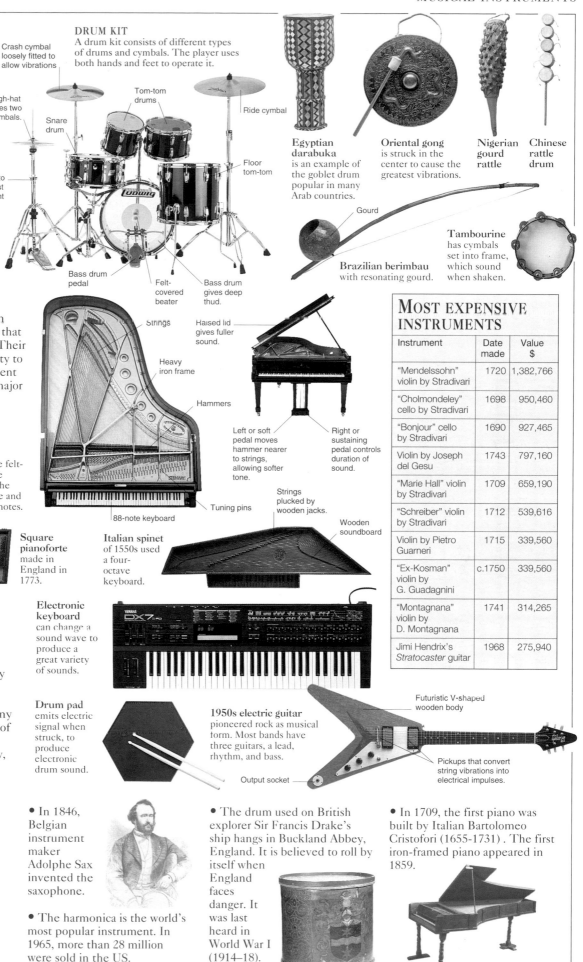

WRITING

THE FIRST WRITING began as a way to keep accounts and to record details of history. Today people read books for pleasure and to learn about the world.

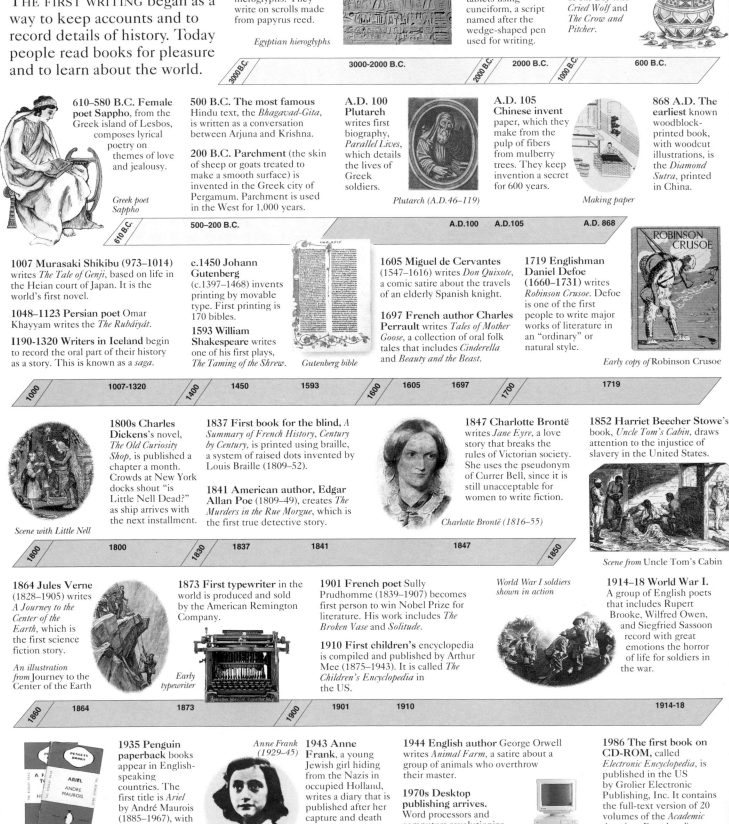

3000 B.C. The Egyptians invent a form of writing using picture signs called hieroglyphs. They write on scrolls made from papyrus reed.

Egyptian hieroglyphs

2000 B.C. Sumerian epic poem *Gilgamesh* is recorded on 12 clay tablets using cuneiform, a script named after the wedge-shaped pen used for writing.

600 B.C. Greek writer Aesop composes his fables, including the story of *The Boy Who Cried Wolf* and *The Crow and Pitcher*.

3000 B.C. — *3000-2000 B.C.* — *2000 B.C.* — *2000 B.C.* — *1000 B.C.* — *600 B.C.*

610–580 B.C. Female poet Sappho, from the Greek island of Lesbos, composes lyrical poetry on themes of love and jealousy.

Greek poet Sappho

500 B.C. The most famous Hindu text, the *Bhagavad-Gita*, is written as a conversation between Arjuna and Krishna.

200 B.C. Parchment (the skin of sheep or goats treated to make a smooth surface) is invented in the Greek city of Pergamum. Parchment is used in the West for 1,000 years.

A.D. 100 Plutarch writes first biography, *Parallel Lives*, which details the lives of Greek soldiers.

Plutarch (A.D.46–119)

A.D. 105 Chinese invent paper, which they make from the pulp of fibers from mulberry trees. They keep invention a secret for 600 years.

Making paper

868 A.D. The earliest known woodblock-printed book, with woodcut illustrations, is the *Diamond Sutra*, printed in China.

610 B.C. — *500–200 B.C.* — *A.D.100* — *A.D.105* — *A.D. 868*

1007 Murasaki Shikibu (973–1014) writes *The Tale of Genji*, based on life in the Heian court of Japan. It is the world's first novel.

1048–1123 Persian poet Omar Khayyam writes the *The Rubáiyát*.

1190-1320 Writers in Iceland begin to record the oral part of their history as a story. This is known as a *saga*.

c.1450 Johann Gutenberg (c.1397–1468) invents printing by movable type. First printing is 170 bibles.

1593 William Shakespeare writes one of his first plays, *The Taming of the Shrew.*

Gutenberg bible

1605 Miguel de Cervantes (1547–1616) writes *Don Quixote*, a comic satire about the travels of an elderly Spanish knight.

1697 French author Charles Perrault writes *Tales of Mother Goose*, a collection of oral folk tales that includes *Cinderella* and *Beauty and the Beast.*

1719 Englishman Daniel Defoe (1660–1731) writes *Robinson Crusoe*. Defoe is one of the first people to write major works of literature in an "ordinary" or natural style.

Early copy of Robinson Crusoe

1000 — *1007-1320* — *1400* — *1450* — *1593* — *1600* — *1605* — *1697* — *1700* — *1719*

1800s Charles Dickens's novel, *The Old Curiosity Shop*, is published a chapter a month. Crowds at New York docks shout "is Little Nell Dead?" as ship arrives with the next installment.

Scene with Little Nell

1837 First book for the blind, *A Summary of French History, Century by Century*, is printed using braille, a system of raised dots invented by Louis Braille (1809–52).

1841 American author, Edgar Allan Poe (1809–49), creates *The Murders in the Rue Morgue*, which is the first true detective story.

1847 Charlotte Brontë writes *Jane Eyre*, a love story that breaks the rules of Victorian society. She uses the pseudonym of Currer Bell, since it is still unacceptable for women to write fiction.

Charlotte Brontë (1816–55)

1852 Harriet Beecher Stowe's book, *Uncle Tom's Cabin*, draws attention to the injustice of slavery in the United States.

Scene from Uncle Tom's Cabin

1800 — *1800* — *1830* — *1837* — *1841* — *1847* — *1850*

1864 Jules Verne (1828–1905) writes *A Journey to the Center of the Earth*, which is the first science fiction story.

An illustration from Journey to the Center of the Earth

1873 First typewriter in the world is produced and sold by the American Remington Company.

Early typewriter

1901 French poet Sully Prudhomme (1839–1907) becomes first person to win Nobel Prize for literature. His work includes *The Broken Vase* and *Solitude.*

1910 First children's encyclopedia is compiled and published by Arthur Mee (1875–1943). It is called *The Children's Encyclopedia* in the US.

World War I soldiers shown in action

1914–18 World War I. A group of English poets that includes Rupert Brooke, Wilfred Owen, and Siegfried Sassoon record with great emotions the horror of life for soldiers in the war.

1860 — *1864* — *1873* — *1900* — *1901* — *1910* — *1914-18*

1935 Penguin paperback books appear in English-speaking countries. The first title is *Ariel* by André Maurois (1885–1967), with a printing of 25,000 copies.

Penguin paperbacks

Anne Frank (1929–45)

1943 Anne Frank, a young Jewish girl hiding from the Nazis in occupied Holland, writes a diary that is published after her capture and death in a concentration camp.

1944 English author George Orwell writes *Animal Farm*, a satire about a group of animals who overthrow their master.

1970s Desktop publishing arrives. Word processors and computers revolutionize book printing. *Word processor*

1986 The first book on CD-ROM, called *Electronic Encyclopedia*, is published in the US by Grolier Electronic Publishing, Inc. It contains the full-text version of 20 volumes of the *Academic American Encyclopedia.*

1995 Production and marketing of CD-ROM titles increases significantly.

1930 — *1935* — *1940* — *1943* — *1944* — *1970s* — *1986* — *1990*

LITERARY WORDS

Allegory A story with a second meaning hidden beneath its obvious meaning.

Alliteration The repetition of the same sounds (usually consonants of words or stressed syllables) e.g., "landscape-lover, lord of language" (Alfred Lord Tennyson).

Allusion An indirect reference to some event, person, place, or work of art; its nature or relevance is not explained by the writer but relies on the reader's familiarity with what is mentioned.

Autobiography An account of a person's life that is written or recorded by that person.

Biography An account of a person's life written by another.

Character A person in a story or drama, or a sketch describing some recognizable type of person.

The character Huckleberry Finn

Cliché A phrase or saying made commonplace by overuse.

Couplet A pair of rhyming verse lines.

Criticism The reasoned discussion of literary works.

Drama A story written in dialogue, or conversational, form so that it can be spoken and acted.

Elegy A poem lamenting the death of a friend or public figure, or reflecting seriously on a solemn subject.

Epic A long narrative poem celebrating, in a grand style, the great deeds of one or more legendary heroes.

Fable A short story, often about animals who behave and talk as humans, that teaches about right and wrong.

Fiction Something that is not true. A category used to describe a novel.

Genre French term for a type, species, or class of composition.

Gothic novel A story of terror and suspense, usually set in a gloomy castle or monastery.

Lyric Expressing the writer's personal feelings and thoughts. Used to describe poetry.

Metaphor A word or phrase used about a thing or an action that is not literally true, but describes it imaginatively.

A Gothic castle

Nonfiction A written work that is based on fact.

Novel An invented, or fictitious, story that usually deals with human relationships, often in a specified setting.

Onomatopoeia The use of words that seem to imitate the sounds they refer to (e.g., buzz, crackle, hiss, snap, splash).

Oral Anything that is spoken or verbal.

Plot The pattern of events in a story or a play.

Rhetoric Eloquence in public speaking or writing for the most persuasive effect.

Satire A kind of writing that makes fun of the failings of individuals, or societies, such as William Golding's *Lord of the Flies*.

Sonnet A lyric poem of 14 rhyming lines of equal length.

Tragedy A serious work representing the unhappy downfall of a central character, such as William Shakespeare's *Hamlet*.

KEY WRITERS

Name	Dates	Nationality	Key work
Homer	c.800 B.C.	Greek	*The Iliad*
Virgil	70–1 B.C.	Roman	*The Aeneid*
Dante Alighieri	1265–1321	Italian	*Divine Comedy*
Giovanni Boccaccio	1313–75	Italian	*The Decameron*
Geoffrey Chaucer	c.1340–1400	English	*The Canterbury Tales*
Miguel de Cervantes	1547–1616	Spanish	*Don Quixote*
Edmund Spenser	1552–99	English	*The Faerie Queene*
John Milton	1608–74	English	*Paradise Lost*
John Bunyan	1628–88	English	*The Pilgrim's Progress*
Henry Fielding	1707–54	English	*Tom Jones*
Laurence Sterne	1713–68	Irish	*Tristram Shandy*
J. W. Von Goethe	1748–1832	German	*Faust*
William Wordsworth	1770–1850	English	*Lyrical Ballads*
Jane Austen	1775–1817	English	*Pride and Prejudice*
Mary Shelley	1797–1851	English	*Frankenstein*
Honoré de Balzac	1799–1850	French	*Old Goriot*
Victor Hugo	1802–85	French	*Les Misérables*
Charles Dickens	1812–70	English	*Oliver Twist*
Charlotte Brontë	1816–55	English	*Jane Eyre*
Emily Brontë	1818–48	English	*Wuthering Heights*
George Eliot	1819–80	English	*Middlemarch*
Herman Melville	1819–91	American	*Moby Dick*
Walt Whitman	1819–92	American	*Leaves of Grass*
Gustave Flaubert	1821–80	French	*Madame Bovary*
Feodor Dostoyevsky	1821–81	Russian	*Crime and Punishment*
Leo Tolstoy	1828–1910	Russian	*War and Peace*
Émile Zola	1840–1902	French	*Germinal*
Thomas Hardy	1840–1928	English	*Tess of the d'Urbervilles*
Henry James	1843–1916	American	*Portrait of a Lady*
Joseph Conrad	1857–1924	British	*Heart of Darkness*
Rabindranath Tagore	1861–1941	Indian	*Gitanjali*
W.B. Yeats	1865–1939	Irish	*The Tower*
Marcel Proust	1871–1922	French	*Remembrance of Things Past*
Thomas Mann	1875–1955	German	*The Magic Mountain*
E.M. Forster	1879–1970	English	*Passage to India*
James Joyce	1882–1941	Irish	*Ulysses*
Virginia Woolf	1882–1941	English	*To the Lighthouse*
Franz Kafka	1883–1924	Czechoslovakian	*The Trial*
D.H. Lawrence	1885–1930	English	*Sons and Lovers*
Ezra Pound	1885–1972	American	*The Cantos*
T.S. Eliot	1888–1965	American	*The Waste Land*
Boris Pasternak	1890–1960	Russian	*Dr. Zhivago*
Aldous Huxley	1894–1963	English	*Brave New World*
F. Scott Fitzgerald	1896–1940	American	*The Great Gatsby*
Ernest Hemingway	1899–1961	American	*A Farewell to Arms*
Vladimir Nabokov	1899–1977	Russian	*Lolita*
Jorge Luis Borges	1899–1986	Argentinian	*Labyrinths*
John Steinbeck	1902–68	American	*The Grapes of Wrath*
George Orwell	1903–50	English	*Animal Farm*
Evelyn Waugh	1903–66	English	*Brideshead Revisited*
Pablo Neruda	1904–73	Chilean	*Great Song*
Graham Greene	1904–91	English	*The Power and the Glory*
William Golding	1911–93	English	*Lord of the Flies*
Patrick White	1912–90	Australian	*Voss*
Albert Camus	1913–60	French	*The Stranger*
Dylan Thomas	1914–53	Welsh	*Under Milk Wood*
Anthony Burgess	b.1917–	English	*A Clockwork Orange*
Doris Lessing	b.1919–	English	*The Golden Notebook*
Iris Murdoch	b.1919–	English	*Bruno's Dream*
Italo Calvino	1923–85	Italian	*The Path to the Nest of Spiders*
Yukio Mishima	1925–1970	Japanese	*The Sound of Waves*
Günter Grass	b.1927–	German	*The Tin Drum*
Gabriel García Márquez	b.1928–	Colombian	*One Hundred Years of Solitude*
Toni Morrison	b.1931–	American	*Beloved*

PRINTING

BEFORE PRINTING WAS invented, information was written by hand. The introduction of printing with movable type (one block for each character or letter) allowed many copies of an original work to be made quickly and cheaply. Today, many stages of printing are done by computer.

Virtually any color can be created from a combination of the four colors shown.

Yellow

Magenta

Cyan

Black

COLOR SEPARATION

Color illustrations are separated into four colors (magenta, cyan, yellow, and black) by an electronic scanner before printing. A laser scans the pictures four times, once for each separation. This process results in four pieces of film, one for each color.

The illustration is placed on a revolving drum and is scanned by a laser.

Paper is fed through the press, and comes into contact with each of the color plates in turn.

The final full-color printed sheets appear at the far end of the press.

PRINTING PRESS

After color separation, the details on each of the colored films is transferred onto a plate. Each plate is treated with chemicals, then fitted to rollers on a press. The paper feeds through, and as it comes into contact with each plate, the four colors are added one by one.

TYPOGRAPHY

Typography is the design of letters and words printed on a page. Typographers create a page of print using different type styles which, when put together, make the page look appealing and easy to read. Typefaces can be divided into two main groups:

SERIF

Serif faces have little strokes (serifs) at the end of many letters. The serifs form a link between the letters, which helps bind them together as words.

SANS SERIF

Sans serif typefaces do not have serifs. They are harder to read than serif faces.

TYPESETTING

Today, this is mainly done by computer. The typeface and text width is set, and corrections can be made on screen. A laser printer, which is connected to the computer, prints the words onto a sheet of light-sensitive film, or type film.

TYPEFACES

There are thousands of different typefaces. Some of the most common are shown on the right. A typeface comes in a range of styles (such as italics) and sizes, which are measured in points. This book is set in the Caslon typeface.

Typeface
Caslon Roman, 30 point

Typeface
Caslon italic, 30 point

Typeface
Caslon bold, 30 point

Helvetica ABCDEFGHIJKLMNOPQR STUVWXYZ

Times ABCDEFGHIJKLMNOPQ RSTUVWXYZ

Futura ABCDEFGHIJKLMNOPQRST UVWXYZ

Baskerville ABCDEFGHIJKLMNOPQRSTUVWXYZ

PRINTING WORDS

Ascender Part of a lower-case letter that is above the x-height.
Bromide Photosensitive paper on which an image is created.
Cold type Modern method of printing that produces a photographic image.
Color correction Changing the strength of colors in an illustration before going to print.
Cropping Trimming and shaping illustrations.
Descender Part of a lower-case letter that is below the x-height.
Em Unit of measurement.
Flat color Area of printed color without variations in tone.
Flop Reversal of an illustration.
Font Set of typed characters of the same style.
Format Size of a book or a page.
Gutter Margin that runs down the center of a spread.
Hot metal Traditional method of printing in which type is cast from molten lead.
Kerning Adjusting the space between letters.
Leading Space between lines of type.
Lower case Letters that are not capitals.
Measure Length of a line of type.
Mechanical Illustrations and text drawn up for reproduction.
Orphan The start of a paragraph at the foot of the page.
Ozalid Reproduction of printed material onto chemically treated, usually blue, paper.
Phototypesetting Setting of type on film or photographic paper.
Pica Unit of type measurement equal to 12 points.
Point A measurement of type equal to 0.013837in (0.351457mm).
Proof A reproduction of illustrations or text before the printing stage.
Range Lining up of type either vertically or horizontally.
Reproduction Process by which artwork is reproduced, through color separation, before printing.
Upper case Letters that are capitals.
Widow A short line.
X-height The height of a letter that does not include its ascender or descender.

h
ascender

flat color

X
x-height

p
descender

PRINTING FACTS

• First printers were the Chinese, who printed scrolls and books using wooden blocks in about A.D. 770.

Chinese wooden block

• Today, there are more than 11,000 Western typefaces.

RADIO

RADIO WAVES WERE first used for communication some 30 years before television appeared. The invention of radio also made possible television broadcasting.

1888 Heinrich Hertz (1857–1894), German physicist, discovers radio waves.

Heinrich Hertz

1894 Guglielmo Marconi (1874–1937), Italian-born physicist, sends radio waves across a room, making a bell ring.

1901 Morse code (see p.269) is transmitted across the Atlantic by Marconi.

Guglielmo Marconi

1800 | 1888 | 1890 | 1894 | 1900 | 1901

1912 Titanic sends an emergency signal by radio after hitting an iceberg.

1920 First commercial radio station, KDKA of Pittsburgh, starts broadcasting with a transmission of the presidential election results.

RMS Titanic

1927 BBC (British Broadcasting Corporation) is granted its first charter, or license.

1932 Frequency Modulation, which reduces interference, is invented by American inventor Edwin Armstrong (1890–1954).

BBC Radio microphone

1954 First transistor radio appears in the US. Transistors replace tubes.

Early transistor radio

1960 First VHF-FM stereo broadcasts, from KDKA-FM.

1988 Radio Data System (automatic station identification and traffic news for car radios) is introduced in the UK and Sweden.

1910 | 1912 | 1920 | 1920 | 1927 | 1930 | 1932 | 1950 | 1954 | 1960 | 1960 | 1980 | 1988

RADIO FACTS

• Australian RPH radio stations broadcast only programs for the vision impaired.

• During the five days in 1991 that Cyclone Val pounded Samoa, the island's only link with the outside world was ham-operated radio.

• Digital Audio Broadcasting (DAB) is a new radio system that produces CD-quality digital sound.

• The distance radio waves travel around the Earth depends partly on the number of sunspots at the time.

TOP RADIO OWNERS

Country	Radios per person
US	2.1
Bermuda	1.4
Australia	1.3
Gibraltar	1.2
United Kingdom	1.1

RADIO FREQUENCIES

Radio waves are waves of electromagnetic energy that have varying lengths and that vibrate at varying speeds. The rate of vibration is called frequency. Radio stations use long, medium, or short waves. TV satellite link-ups and microwave ovens also use radio waves.

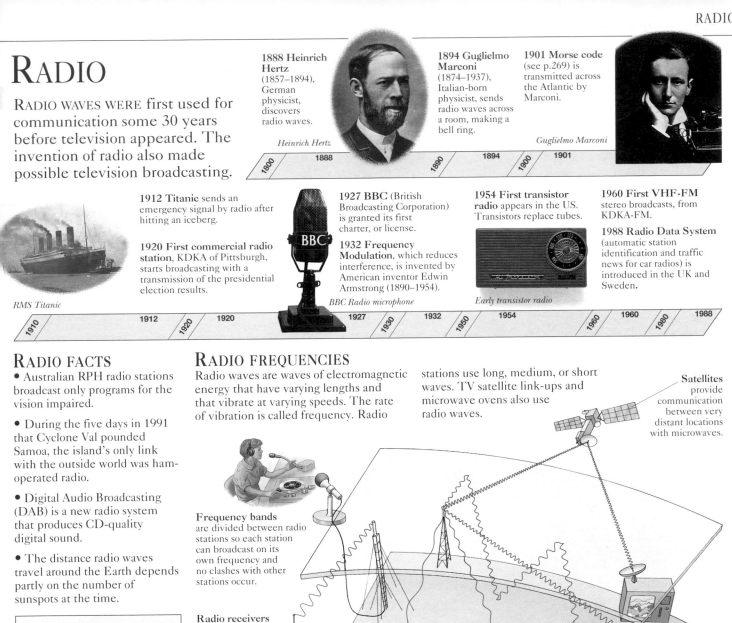

Frequency bands are divided between radio stations so each station can broadcast on its own frequency and no clashes with other stations occur.

Radio receivers select a single radio channel and convert the waves back into sound.

Satellites provide communication between very distant locations with microwaves.

Long waves (LW) can travel almost 1,240 miles (2,000km). They are used for some national broadcasts.

Medium waves (MW) travel for a few hundred miles. National and local radio stations often transmit in MW.

Short waves (SW) travel thousands of miles. International radio stations use SW.

Very high frequency waves (VHF) travel short distances.

RADIOS OLD AND NEW

1930s This 1936 set was 16in (41cm) tall, 13in (33cm) wide, and used tubes.

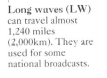

TODAY Radios can now be fitted inside wristwatches.

RADIO RECORDS

LARGEST AUDIENCE is for the BBC's World Service, with at least 120 million regular listeners around the world.

LONGEST-RUNNING SHOW is *Rambling with Gambling* on WOR-NY (New York), first broadcast in 1925.

LONGEST-RUNNING SOAP is *The Archers*, first broadcast by the BBC in 1950.

ALIEN ATTACK!

In 1938 American actor and director Orson Welles (1915-85) dramatized H.G. Wells' *War of the Worlds*, in which Earth is invaded by aliens. Thousands of people panicked, believing the program to be a news bulletin.

TELEVISION

TELEVISION SETS convert radio waves into pictures and sound. A single event can be watched live by billions of people all over the world.

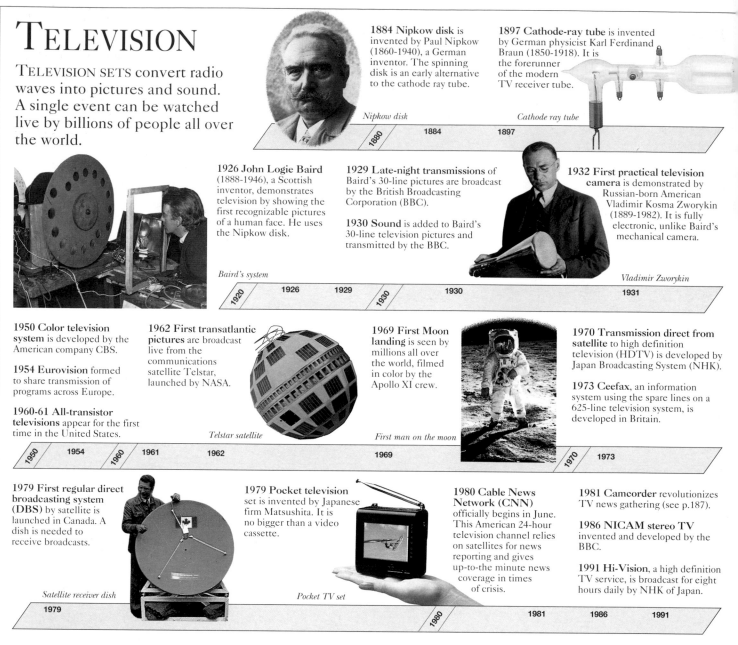

1884 Nipkow disk is invented by Paul Nipkow (1860-1940), a German inventor. The spinning disk is an early alternative to the cathode ray tube.

Nipkow disk

1897 Cathode-ray tube is invented by German physicist Karl Ferdinand Braun (1850-1918). It is the forerunner of the modern TV receiver tube.

Cathode ray tube

1880 | 1884 | 1897

1926 John Logie Baird (1888-1946), a Scottish inventor, demonstrates television by showing the first recognizable pictures of a human face. He uses the Nipkow disk.

1929 Late-night transmissions of Baird's 30-line pictures are broadcast by the British Broadcasting Corporation (BBC).

1930 Sound is added to Baird's 30-line television pictures and transmitted by the BBC.

1932 First practical television camera is demonstrated by Russian-born American Vladimir Kosma Zworykin (1889-1982). It is fully electronic, unlike Baird's mechanical camera.

Baird's system

Vladimir Zworykin

1920 | 1926 | 1929 | 1930 | 1930 | 1931

1950 Color television system is developed by the American company CBS.

1954 Eurovision formed to share transmission of programs across Europe.

1960-61 All-transistor televisions appear for the first time in the United States.

1962 First transatlantic pictures are broadcast live from the communications satellite Telstar, launched by NASA.

Telstar satellite

1969 First Moon landing is seen by millions all over the world, filmed in color by the Apollo XI crew.

First man on the moon

1970 Transmission direct from satellite to high definition television (HDTV) is developed by Japan Broadcasting System (NHK).

1973 Ceefax, an information system using the spare lines on a 625-line television system, is developed in Britain.

1950 | 1954 | 1960 | 1961 | 1962 | 1969 | 1970 | 1973

1979 First regular direct broadcasting system (DBS) by satellite is launched in Canada. A dish is needed to receive broadcasts.

Satellite receiver dish

1979 Pocket television set is invented by Japanese firm Matsushita. It is no bigger than a video cassette.

Pocket TV set

1980 Cable News Network (CNN) officially begins in June. This American 24-hour television channel relies on satellites for news reporting and gives up-to-the minute news coverage in times of crisis.

1981 Camcorder revolutionizes TV news gathering (see p.187).

1986 NICAM stereo TV invented and developed by the BBC.

1991 Hi-Vision, a high definition TV service, is broadcast for eight hours daily by NHK of Japan.

1979 | 1980 | 1981 | 1986 | 1991

TV SETS OLD AND NEW
TV technology has advanced rapidly over its brief history.

1930s
Early sets had small black-and-white screens but contained so much electronic equipment that they were housed in large boxes.

1960s
In the 1960s smaller, color TVs became common. Transistors replaced tubes.

TODAY
Pocket-sized TVs are now widely available. Very small sets often use liquid crystal screens.

TELEVISION RECORDS
WORLD'S LONGEST-RUNNING TV SHOW
is NBC's *Meet the Press*, first shown in 1947.

WORLD'S SMALLEST TV SET
is Seiko's TV-Wrist Watch, launched in 1982. It has a 1.2inch (30.5mm) screen.

LONGEST CONTINUOUS BROADCAST
was by GTV 9, Australia, lasting 163 hrs 18 mins, of Apollo XI's Moon mission (July 19-26, 1969).

FIRST DAILY BROADCASTS
were made by the BBC, broadcasting from London, starting November 10, 1936.

TV GENERATION
Americans watch more television than any other nationality. In an average household the TV set is turned on for seven hours a day. By the time they are 65 years old, most Americans have watched more than nine years' worth of television.

POPULAR TELEVISION

SOAP OPERAS ('SOAPS')

Soaps are dramas with continuous storylines shown in regular episodes. The world's longest-running soap is *Coronation Street*, first shown on British TV in 1960. The earliest American soaps of the 1950s were sponsored by soap-powder companies.

SPORTS PROGRAMS

The biggest ever TV audience was estimated at 26.5 billion for the 1990 World Cup finals.

World Cup finals, 1990

SITUATION COMEDIES (SITCOMS)

Sitcoms are comedies showing the humorous side of supposedly real-life situations. NBC's *The Cosby Show* was the highest-rated sitcom in American history (1984), and Bill Cosby was the highest-paid performer in the world (1991).

CHILDREN'S PROGRAMS

Children's programs show a wide range of material suitable for a younger audience. *Sesame Street*, first shown in the US in 1969, is seen in 80 countries.

MAKING A DOCUMENTARY

This diagram shows one way of making a documentary. The two main players are the production company, which makes the film, and the TV station, which broadcasts it. The three main stages of the process are preproduction (organization of the shoot), production (filming) and postproduction (editing).

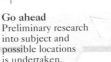

Idea is taken to the production company that will make the program and arrange for it to be shown on TV.

Go ahead
Preliminary research into subject and possible locations is undertaken.

Finance committee
Committee, which includes accountants, commissioning editor, and controller, approves project and budget.

Treatment
This written outline is taken to a TV station.

Commissioning editor
Commissioning editor, a TV executive, receives and approves treatment .

Rushes
If shot on videotape, material can be checked instantly on playback. If film has been used, previous day's work, developed overnight, is viewed daily.

Production
Shooting begins. Crew go on location.

Preproduction
Equipment and crew hired, interviews set up, locations found, filming permissions obtained.

Contract
After signing, preparation and shooting of documentary can begin.

Viewing
Documentary is seen on television.

Postproduction
Editor and director put the program together in its finished version, adding sound and titles.

Delivery
Completed film is delivered to TV station.

Transmission
Program is broadcast by TV station.

INSIDE A TELEVISION SET

The TV set's aerial picks up radio waves and converts them into electronic signals. These signals in turn are converted into pictures by the picture tube.

Electron guns fire streams of electrons (see p.226) that sweep across the inside of the screen, building up the image.

Picture tube is the most important single component of a TV set. All the air has been pumped out of the tube to allow free flow of electrons.

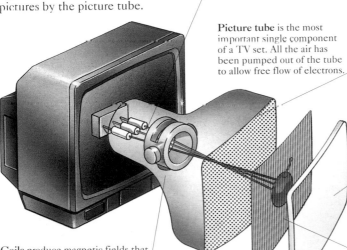

Coils produce magnetic fields that deflect the electron beams, creating a new picture 25 times a second.

Phosphor strips coat the inside of the screen. Three different types of phosphor are used: one which glows red when struck by electrons; one green; and one blue.

Shadow mask has slots which ensure that the electrons light phosphor of the correct color.

WORLD TV VIEWING

Country	Hours per week
United States	49.35
Italy	28.93
Hong Kong	28.70
Colombia	23.80
United Kingdom	23.80
Canada	23.30
Australia	21.98
Chile	17.50
China	10.59
World average	19.67

TELEVISION FACTS

- By 1993 there were 746,829,000 homes worldwide with a TV set. By 2005 there will be an estimated billion.

- In 1977 hundreds of bald men invaded an English farm after a BBC April fool joke suggested that water there had hair-restoring properties.

- High definition TV uses twice as many lines to build up each frame as ordinary TV; therefore the picture is much sharper.

- Virtual Vision Sport is a TV system in which the viewer wears a pair of special glasses. They create a color picture that appears to be 5ft (1.5m) wide floating in space about 10ft (3m) away.

Virtual vision glasses

MOVIES

FILM-MAKING IS A million-dollar industry that makes, sells, and shows movies worldwide. Film stars attract publicity and often become household names.

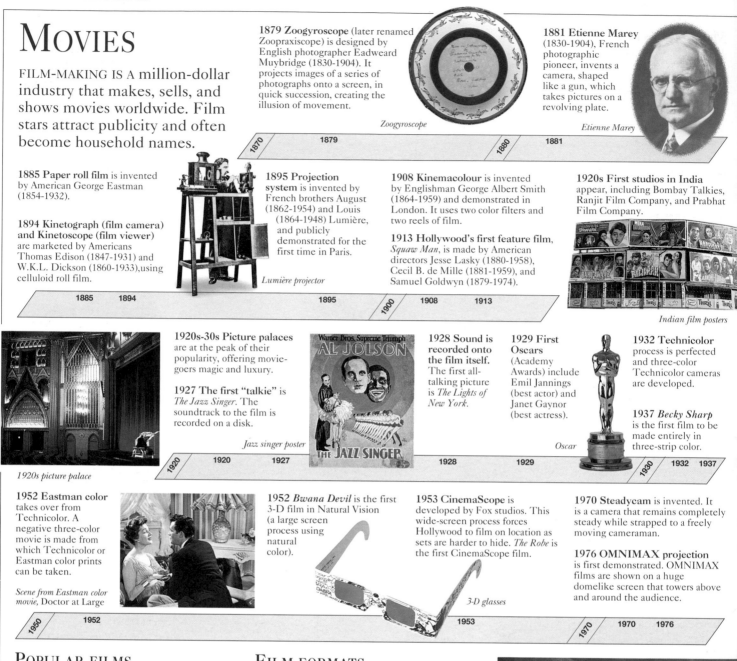

1879 Zoogyroscope (later renamed Zoopraxiscope) is designed by English photographer Eadweard Muybridge (1830-1904). It projects images of a series of photographs onto a screen, in quick succession, creating the illusion of movement.

Zoogyroscope

1881 Etienne Marey (1830-1904), French photographic pioneer, invents a camera, shaped like a gun, which takes pictures on a revolving plate.

Etienne Marey

1885 Paper roll film is invented by American George Eastman (1854-1932).

1894 Kinetograph (film camera) and Kinetoscope (film viewer) are marketed by Americans Thomas Edison (1847-1931) and W.K.L. Dickson (1860-1933),using celluloid roll film.

1895 Projection system is invented by French brothers August (1862-1954) and Louis (1864-1948) Lumière, and publicly demonstrated for the first time in Paris.

Lumière projector

1908 Kinemacolour is invented by Englishman George Albert Smith (1864-1959) and demonstrated in London. It uses two color filters and two reels of film.

1913 Hollywood's first feature film, *Squaw Man*, is made by American directors Jesse Lasky (1880-1958), Cecil B. de Mille (1881-1959), and Samuel Goldwyn (1879-1974).

1920s First studios in India appear, including Bombay Talkies, Ranjit Film Company, and Prabhat Film Company.

Indian film posters

1920s-30s Picture palaces are at the peak of their popularity, offering movie-goers magic and luxury.

1927 The first "talkie" is *The Jazz Singer*. The soundtrack to the film is recorded on a disk.

1920s picture palace

Jazz singer poster

1928 Sound is recorded onto the film itself. The first all-talking picture is *The Lights of New York*.

1929 First Oscars (Academy Awards) include Emil Jannings (best actor) and Janet Gaynor (best actress).

Oscar

1932 Technicolor process is perfected and three-color Technicolor cameras are developed.

1937 *Becky Sharp* is the first film to be made entirely in three-strip color.

1952 Eastman color takes over from Technicolor. A negative three-color movie is made from which Technicolor or Eastman color prints can be taken.

Scene from Eastman color movie, Doctor at Large

1952 *Bwana Devil* is the first 3-D film in Natural Vision (a large screen process using natural color).

1953 CinemaScope is developed by Fox studios. This wide-screen process forces Hollywood to film on location as sets are harder to hide. *The Robe* is the first CinemaScope film.

3-D glasses

1970 Steadycam is invented. It is a camera that remains completely steady while strapped to a freely moving cameraman.

1976 OMNIMAX projection is first demonstrated. OMNIMAX films are shown on a huge domelike screen that towers above and around the audience.

POPULAR FILMS

Three of the most popular types of film at the movies are science fiction (sci-fi), action, and horror.

SCIENCE FICTION
The most expensive film ever made was American sci-fi thriller *Terminator 2*, starring Arnold Schwarzenegger. The film cost $95 million.

ACTION
The three *Indiana Jones* films were all in the top ten most successful films of the 1980s, earning at least $100 million each.

HORROR
Count Dracula, the vampire, is the most frequently filmed horror character. Since his screen debut in 1931, he has appeared on film more than 160 times.

Terminator 2

FILM FORMATS

One minute of a movie uses over 90ft (27m) of film, and a full-length feature about 1.5 miles (2.5km). The standard size used now is 35mm (standard gauge).

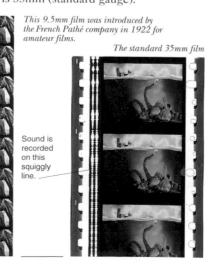

This 9.5mm film was introduced by the French Pathé company in 1922 for amateur films.

The standard 35mm film

Sound is recorded on this squiggly line.

Scene from an IMAX film

IMAX

The IMAX projection system was first demonstrated in Japan in 1970. The films are shown on giant screens with a full range of digital sound. 70mm film is used with special cameras and projectors to create very clear, vivid pictures on screen.

MOVIE MAKERS

This diagram shows many of the most important people involved in making a movie. The producer has overall financial responsibility and the director has overall creative control.

PREPRODUCTION
All the necessary arrangements are made to ensure that filming runs smoothly.

Producer
The producer raises money for the film and puts together the creative package: director, script, and actors. Once funds has been raised, filming begins.

Scriptwriter
Works on story to make it attractive to stars as well as to financial backers.

Production manager
Controls the budget and expenditure; oversees practicalities of the shoot such as scheduling, travel, and accommodation.

Director
Liaises with producer over script, hiring of stars, and key crew.

Financing
Once enough money has been raised, filming can begin.

Stars
Popular actors are important for the success of the film.

Casting director
Works with the director, selecting actors.

Location manager
Finds suitable locations and arranges for their use.

Production coordinator
Runs production office and makes sure information is circulated to crew and cast.

Production assistant
Performs a variety of tasks including liaising between office and set, and administration.

Cast
Actors for each part in the script.

PRODUCTION

Filming begins. The story is shot out of sequence in an order decided by the director and other department heads. Each take (uninterrupted sequence of filming) is logged by the script supervisor. Then sound and film are turned over to editors for synchronization and editing.

Director
The director is the creative force behind the film, controlling the action and bringing the script to life.

Director of photography
Responsible for lighting, composition, and choice of camera, lens, and film.

Production designer
Responsible for the overall design of the film, including sets and costumes.

First assitant director
Controls day-to-day filming on the set. Ensures schedule of film is on target.

Sound engineer
In charge of the sound quality of the film. Also supervises placing of microphones.

Camera operator works camera during shooting.

Focus puller adjusts focus on lens.

Clapper loader checks, cleans and loads the camera, operates the clapperboard, and sends film to the laboratory.

Grip lays tracks for dolly (support for camera that moves in any direction); moves dolly, as well as camera and camera equipment.

Gaffer is in charge of rigging and setting the lights.

Best boy assists the gaffer.

Art director draws up the designs for the sets on the film, supervises their construction, and orders the dressing of the set.

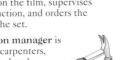

Construction manager is in charge of carpenters, painters, stagehands.

Set dresser places the many objects around the set that give it the appearance of reality.

Second assistant director helps First assistant director and coordinates cast, crew, and background action.

OTHER SERVICES
Costume design and costume department (buys and maintains costumes); make-up department (applies general and special effect make-up); transport; catering; stills photography (for publicity shots).

Boom operator positions and operates the microphone known as the boom.

POSTPRODUCTION
After all the film has been shot, the editor cuts up the individual film sequences and links them together. Working closely with the director, the editor then adds the sound. The finished version is sold for distribution to theaters.

FAMOUS DIRECTORS

Fritz Lang (1890-1976), Austrian director of *Metropolis* (1926) and *Fury* (1936).

Sergei Eisenstein (1898-1948), Russian, directed *Battleship Potemkin* (1925) and *October (Ten Days That Shook the World)* 1928.

Alfred Hitchcock (1899-1980), British director of *The Lady Vanishes* (1938), *Dial M for Murder* (1954), and *Psycho* (1960).

Contemporary poster advertising the film Metropolis

Akira Kurosawa (born 1910), Japanese director of *Rashomon* (1950) and *Hakuchi* (*The Idiot*) 1951.

Ingmar Bergman (born 1918), Swedish director of *Smultronstallet* (*Wild Strawberries*) 1957.

Frederico Fellini (1920-1993), Italian, directed *Il Bidone* (*The Swindle*) 1955.

Satyajit Ray (born 1921), Indian director of *The Apu Trilogy* (1955-1959).

Orson Welles (1915-1985), American who directed *Citizen Kane* (1940).

MOVIE FACTS

• Movie screens are coated with minute plastic prisms that make the screen as bright as possible. Before their introduction, large screens were sprayed with water to improve reflection.

• First feature film was *The Story of the Kelly Gang*, made in Australia in 1906.

• Longest film ever made is *The Cure for Insomnia* (1987), directed by American J.H. Timmis. Lasts 85 hours.

MOST OSCARS WON

Name of film	Oscars
Ben Hur (1959)	11
Gone with the Wind (1939)	10
West Side Story (1961)	10
Gandhi (1982)	9
The Last Emperor (1987)	9
From Here to Eternity (1953)	8
On the Waterfront (1954)	8
Gigi (1958)	8
Cabaret (1972)	8
Amadeus (1984)	8

ANIMATION

ANIMATORS BRING TO life, on film, drawings (cartoons), or objects (animation). Computers can now create many effects similar to traditional animation.

1832 Phenakistoscope is invented by Belgian Joseph Plateau (1801–83). Images painted in sequence on the disk seem to move when it is spun.

Phenakistoscope

1908 Emile Cohl (1857–1938), French animator, draws cartoons. His technique requires 16 pictures to make one second of screen time.

1914 Earl Hurd (1880–1950) and **J.R. Bray** (1879–1978), American animators, draw cartoons on clear celluloid sheets. The background does not have to be redrawn for every frame (shot) of an animated sequence, only the moving parts.

1919 Walt Disney (1901–66) meets Ub Iwerks (1901–71). These American animators refine and develop the celluloid-sheet technique. Disney Studios' Multiplane technique adds realism and depth to their cartoons.

WALT DISNEY'S **MICKEY MOUSE** in **STEAMBOAT WILLIE**

1928 Mickey Mouse stars in Disney's *Steamboat Willie*, the first animated cartoon with synchronized sound. Disney himself provides Mickey's voice. The cartoon causes a sensation.

Mickey Mouse

1930s Len Lye (born 1901), New Zealand animator, makes short films by drawing abstract images directly onto the film itself, thus skipping the photographic process.

Len Lye

1939 Tom and Jerry, created by Americans Bill Hanna (born 1910) and Joe Barbera (born 1911), appear in their first cartoon, *Puss Gets the Boot*. They receive the first of their seven Oscars in 1943 for *Yankee Doodle Mouse*.

1952 Norman McLaren (1914–87), Canadian animator, photographs real people frame by frame in his short film *Neighbours*, to make them look like animated robots.

Norman McLaren

1991 *Creature Comforts*, created by Aardman Animation (UK) and featuring clay zoo animals, wins an Oscar.

A gorilla from Creature Comforts

1990s Computer graphics may be used to enhance or manipulate hand-drawn images, as in *Aladdin* (1992). Some animators save time by using them to draw the intermediate images between the key, hand-drawn positions.

Aladdin

ANIMATION TYPES

ANIMATION
The twin Brothers Quay, born in Philadelphia in 1947, bring strange, dead objects to life in their animated films. *Street of Crocodiles*, made in 1986, features eyeless dolls. The brothers were influenced by Czech animator, Jan Svankmajer (born 1934).

CARTOONS
Walt Disney achieved huge popularity and won a special Oscar for the first feature-length cartoon, *Snow White and the Seven Dwarfs* (1937).

© Walt Disney

ANIMATION FACTS
• First ever motion-picture cartoon film was *Humorous Phases of Funny Faces* (1906), made by American J. Stuart Blackton (1875–1941) for Vitagraph. The cartoon required 3,000 drawings.

• First animated film nominated for an Oscar for best picture was the Disney production of *Beauty and the Beast* (1991).

• Since the 1930s cartoon characters have been drawn with only three fingers instead of four. This looks just as realistic and is much quicker for the animators.

TOP BOX OFFICE HITS

Film	Production company and date
Who Framed Roger Rabbit?	Disney, 1988
Snow White and The Seven Dwarfs	Disney, 1937
The Jungle Book	Disney, 1967
Bambi	Disney, 1942
Fantasia	Disney, 1940
Cinderella	Disney, 1950
Lady and the Tramp	Disney, 1955
The Little Mermaid	Disney, 1989

MORPHING
This computer technique is used either to transform a person or object into something different, or to create animation in a live-action film. The illustration shows part of a morphing sequence.

The points of both objects, hand and spider, are plotted on the computer. When the two sets of points coincide the transformation is complete.

VIRTUAL REALITY
Virtual reality is a three-dimensional computer-generated world. The special headset contains miniature TV screens that provide stereo vision. If you wear the headset and move around, the virtual-reality world moves with you. The data glove allows you to operate tools in the virtual world.

The outline of the spider is just visible.

The mid-point of the morphing process.

The spider is almost complete.

VIDEO

THE TERM VIDEO refers to video cassettes, video recorders, and video cameras. Many TV programs, advertisements, and music videos are shot on video.

1929 Phonovision is introduced by John Logie Baird (1888–1946), Scottish inventor. This video system uses 12 inch disks with pictures recorded onto them.

Phonovision disk

1956 First working video recorder, the VR1000, is introduced by Ampex Corporation of California.

1965 First portable video camera introduced by Japanese company Sony. It has a bulky separate unit containing the recording equipment, and records in black and white.

1970 First video cassette is part of the U-Matic system, made by Sony.

Sony 1970 U-Matic video cassette

1972 First domestic video recorder is the N1500, brought out by Philips of Holland. It is the first video recorder to have its own tuner and timer.

1975 Laser Video Disk introduced by Sony/Philips.

1976 VHS system, launched by Japanese company JVC, proves more commercially successful than its rival Betamax.

An early camcorder

1981 Camcorder is invented. It is a camera with a built-in recorder, which records onto videotape instead of film.

1990s CDTV uses pre-recorded video disks similar to music CDs, instead of video tapes.

CDTV disc

VIDEO FACTS
• Approximately 25% of all video sales in the world are of animated films.

• Japanese companies account for over 80% of worldwide video recorder (VCR) production.

TOP VIDEO SPENDERS

Country	US $ Billions
US	11.0
Japan	2.6
UK	1.4
Canada	1.2
France	0.7
Germany	0.7
Australia	0.7

• A basic VCR contains over 2,500 components, compared to about 360 that make up a color TV set.

• Laser video disks spin approximately fifty times faster than a long-playing record. European models revolve 1,500 times a minute, and American and Japanese disks 1,800 times a minute.

• US has the most video rental outlets in the world (55,000 in 1992). Japan is second with 11,500 stores.

• There are 230 million homes around the world with at least one VCR. The US has the most, with 65 million.

ELECTRONIC NEWS GATHERING
Electronic news gathering (ENG) teams use professional video cameras to record onto video cassettes. Unlike film, videos do not need to be processed before broadcasting.

On location abroad
ENG crew films news story.

Customized van
Cassette taken to van containing microwave transmitter. Pictures beamed home via nearby transmitting station.

Transmitting station
Signals received from van sent on to satellite.

Satellite
Signals beamed down to studio receiver dish.

Studio
TV station can broadcast immediately or tape pictures for later use.

At home
Viewer watches the news footage taken by the ENG team.

VIDEO CAMERAS
Early video cameras were carried on the shoulder and were connected by cables to separate recording equipment (called a portapak).

Portable video camera

Tripod

Video recorder

This camcorder films and records in one unit. It is small enough to be held in the palm of the hand.

VIDEO RECORDERS
The VR 1000 was 3.7 ft (1.1m) high

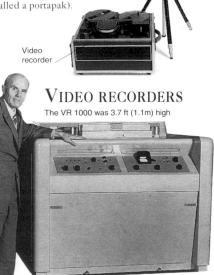

The 1956 Ampex VR1000 video recorder weighed 1,465lb (665kg), the same as a small car, and used tape which was 4 times wider than that of today's VCRs.

Modern recorders like this one are only slightly larger than the cassette inside.

VIDEO RECORDS
FASTEST VIDEOTAPE ON SALE was the wedding of HRH Prince Andrew to Sarah Ferguson on July 23, 1986. The fully edited and packaged tapes were available in Virgin Megastore, London, 5 hours 41 minutes after the event.

THE FIRST MUSIC VIDEO was for *Bohemian Rhapsody* by Queen, in 1975.

BEST-SELLING VIDEO is Disney's animated feature film *Beauty and the Beast* (1992): 20 million copies sold, earning $135 million in the first six months after going on sale.

NEWSPAPERS

NEWSPAPERS KEEP everyone in touch with local, national, and world events for a small price. They give more information on a wider range of topics and more detail than TV news.

59 B.C. Romans produce the *Acta diurna* (daily acts). They report on the social and political events of the day.

Roman reading a scroll.

A.D. 618 Newsletter reporting on court affairs is circulated by civil servants in Peking, China.

1440–50 Printing by movable type is invented by Johannes Gutenberg (c.1398–1468) of Germany. This leads to more printed material being produced and a growth in readership.

Johannes Gutenberg

Timeline: 59 B.C. | A.D.600 | 618 | 1440

1513 Newsbooks, forerunners of newspapers, produced. One surviving copy from England, *The Trew Encountre*, dated September 1513, gives a four-page eyewitness account of the Battle of Flodden Field.

1620 One of the first papers to be printed from movable type is a Dutch newspaper, called *Corantos* (currents of news). It contains extracts from foreign journals.

Corantos

1600s–1800s In Japan, people pay a small fee for the news to be read aloud to them. It is known as *yomiuri* (sell and read). *Kawara-ban* (tile-block printing) broadsheets are also produced.

In Japan, the news is read out loud for a fee.

1645 Oldest continuously published weekly newspaper, the *Post- och inrikes tidningar*, is published in Sweden.

Timeline: 1500 | 1513 | 1600 | 1620 | 1645

1703 Oldest surviving daily newspaper in the world is the *Wiener Zeitung* (Viennese newspaper), Austria.

Wiener Zeitung

1704 *The Boston News-letter*, first official newspaper in the US, appears. It replaces newsletters that had previously been sent from London.

The Boston News-letter

The Boston News-Letter.

1766 Sweden becomes the first country to guarantee freedom of the press.

1833 First successful penny paper, the *Sun*, appears in New York.

1842 *The Illustrated London News*, containing sketches by artists from all over the world, is established.

THE ILLUSTRATED LONDON NEWS.

The Illustrated London News

1858 P. J. Reuter (1816–99), of Germany, starts a foreign news agency. It is now one of the biggest in the world.

P.J. Reuter

Timeline: 1700 | 1703 | 1704 | 1760 | 1766 | 1800 | 1833 | 1842 | 1858

1878 *The Hindu* is one of the first Indian newspapers to be established.

THE HINDU.

The Hindu

1903 First tabloid, the *Mirror*, is launched in Britain. The paper was half the size of other newspapers, had shortened articles, and was reasonably priced. Later, it became the *Daily Mirror*.

The Mirror

1910–20s American publisher, Edward Scripps (1854–1926), pioneers the collection and ownership of popular working-class newspapers. By the 1920s, there are about 6,000 newspapers in the US.

Edward Scripps

1955 The *Village Voice* is published in New York. This, along with other alternative newspapers, brings a new, radical approach to news reporting.

1970s Computers and advanced technology replace typesetters and printers. This leads newspaper owners to lay off large numbers of employees.

Timeline: 1870 | 1878 | 1900 | 1903 | 1910 | 1920 | 1955 | 1970

NEWSPAPER FACTS

- Sweden sells 574 newspapers for every 1,000 people: the highest sales in the world.
- First newspaper to achieve a circulation of one million was the French paper *Le Petit Journal*, in 1886.

COUNTRIES WITH THE MOST DAILY NEWSPAPERS

Country	Number
US	1,657
India	1,423
Germany	766
CIS	726
Turkey	364
Brazil	364
Argentina	227
China	222
Sweden	169
Greece	124
Japan	124
UK	112

BEST-SELLING NEWSPAPERS IN THE WORLD

Newspaper	Country	Average daily circulation
Yomissi Shimbun	Japan	8,700,000
Asahi Shimbun	Japan	7,400,000
People's Daily	China	6,000,000
Bild Zeitung	Germany	5,900,000
The Wall Street Journal	US	1,818,562
USA Today	US	1,494,929
New York Times	US	1,141,366
Los Angeles Times	US	1,089,690
Washington Times	US	813,908
New York Daily News	US	764,070

NEWSPAPER WORDS

Broadsheet Newspaper with a large format, usually 24in x 15in (61cm x 38cm).
Circulation Number of newspapers sold each issue.
Editor Person with complete control over the contents of a newspaper.
Feature A non-news article.
Hard news Up-to-the-minute news.
Editorial Article giving newspaper's own opinion.
Popular press, or tabloids. Newspapers aiming to provide lively news and entertainment for a mass readership. Also called tabloids, since they usually have a smaller format than broadsheets.
Quality press Newspapers aiming to provide serious news, information, and analysis. Also called broadsheets, since they usually have a large format.
Soft news Background news or news that is not up-to-the-minute.
Syndication Group of publishers who sell the reprint rights to articles or comics all around the world.
Tabloid Newspaper with a smaller format, about half the size of broadsheets.

SPORTS

This factual survey covers every major sport from baseball to weight lifting, identifying Olympic sports and giving tables of Olympic events. For each sport, special clothing, and equipment are clearly illustrated, and all dimensions, weights, and distances are included. The section features rules and record breakers, glossaries to explain specialized terms, and amazing facts and comparisons.

Sports • Olympic Games • Track Events • Field Events • Weight lifting
Gymnastics • Combat Sports • Court Games • Basketball • Rugby • Football
Cricket • Baseball • Stick Games • Golf • Water Sports • Swimming
Equestrian • Winter Sports • Wheeled Sports • Target Sports

In this section the official measurements, whether
in metric or imperial, are given for each sport.

SPORTS

THE FIRST SPORTS, such as hunting and running, grew out of a need for survival. Today, people take part in sports for fitness and enjoyment.

c.3000–1500 B.C. Wrestling and boxing are practiced by the early Mediterranean civilizations. **Bull sports** feature in Minoan festivals in Crete. Acrobats leap over the backs of running bulls.

Bull-leaping is practiced in Crete.

c.1500 B.C. Hunting, archery, wrestling, fighting, and organized running are practiced in ancient Egypt.

An Egyptian nobleman hunts for birds with a curved stick.

3000 B.C. | 3000–1500 B.C. | 1500 B.C. | 1500 B.C.

c.776 B.C. First Olympic Games held at Olympia, Greece. They last one day, with sacrifices to the gods followed by a single race, a sprint of 630ft (192m), the length of the stadium. Coroebus, a cook, wins the race.

c.200 B.C. Chariot racing is popular in Rome, where the Circus Maximus arena holds 200,000 people. Gladiators fight to the death in amphitheaters such as the Colosseum, Rome.

Chariot racing, Rome

c.20 B.C. Sumo wrestling develops in Japan from Chiao-Li, a form of wrestling used by the Chinese army in training.

Sumo wrestler, Japan

c.A.D. 400 Religious ball game, *tlachtli,* is played by the Aztec Indians of Central America. Players use their elbows, knees, and hips to hit a rubber ball.

Aztec ball court

800 B.C. | 776 B.C. | 200 B.C. | 200 B.C. | 20 B.C. | 20 B.C. | A.D. 400 | A.D. 400

c.1100 Knights take part in jousting tournaments in England and France to practice for warfare.

Knights jousting

1200s Tennis played by the clergy and royalty in France. **Skating** on frozen canals popular in Holland. **Bowls** played in English gardens.

Skating, Holland

1400s Calcio (kick), a form of football, is played in Florence, Italy. Each side has 27 players.

1636 Lacrosse develops from baggataway, played by the American Indian Huron tribe in present-day Ontario, Canada. The word *crosse* describes the stick used.

Early lacrosse

1777 People surfing off the islands of Tahiti and Oahu are seen by Captain James Cook (1728–79), British explorer. Surfing was later banned by missionaries who thought it immoral.

1811 First outdoor gymnasium is opened by German teacher Friedrich Jahn (1778–1852), inventor of rings and parallel bars.

Friedrich Jahn

1200 | 1200 | 1400 | 1630 | 1636 | 1770 | 1777 | 1810 | 1811

1823 Rugby is born when William Webb Ellis, a pupil at Rugby School, England, picks up the ball and runs with it during a game of soccer.
William Webb Ellis

c.1829 Baseball, derived from the English game of rounders, is first played in the US.

Early baseball

1839 First Grand National steeplechase is held at Aintree, England.

Jumping the Brook at the Grand National, 1839

1843 First cross-country ski race held in Tromso, Norway.

1846 Soccer rules drawn up at Cambridge University, England.

1847 Tenpin bowling is born in Connecticut. Ninepins had been banned, so a pin is added.

1860 First British Open Golf Championship held at Prestwick, Scotland.

1861 First hockey club formed in London.

1865 Gloved boxing develops from bare-knuckle fighting using the Marquess of Queensberry's rules.

Bare-knuckle fighter

1820 | 1823 | 1829 | 1830 | 1840 | 1843 | 1846 | 1847 | 1860 | 1860 1861 1865

1866 First show-jumping event is held in Paris.

1874 American football is born when teams from McGill University, Canada, and Harvard, US, play a game that is half soccer, half rugby.

1876 Modern badminton rules are drawn up in Poona, India.

1877 First cricket Test Match held between England and Australia in Melbourne.

England cricket team, 1886

1877 First Wimbledon lawn tennis championships held in England.

Wimbledon

1882 Judo developed by Jigoro Kano (1860–1938) in Japan.

1891 Basketball invented in Massachusetts, by Canadian Dr. James Naismith, who hangs two peach baskets on a veranda for goals.

Dr. James Naismith (1861-1939)

1866 | 1870 | 1874 | 1876 | 1877 | 1880 | 1882 | 1890 | 1891

1895 Volleyball devised by William G. Morgan in Massachusetts. **First motor race** held, Paris–Bordeaux–Paris.

1896 First modern Olympic Games held in Athens, inspired by Baron Pierre de Coubertin (1863-1937) of France.

1903 First Tour de France multistage bicycle race.
1924 First Winter Olympics staged at Chamonix, France.

1930 Soccer's first World Cup is held in Uruguay.

1960 First Paralympics is held for handicapped people in Rome, Italy.

Canadian ice hockey team, winners at the first Winter Olympics, 1924.

1970 South Africa is expelled from the Olympic movement because of apartheid policy.

1972 At the Munich Olympics, Germany, Palestinian terrorists kill 11 members of the Israeli team.

1980–1990s Commercial sponsorship becomes increasingly important in sport. Satellites bring live international sports to worldwide TV audiences.

Regular mass marathons, with more than 15,000 entrants, are staged. Some marathons include wheelchair events.

The London marathon

1895 1896 | 1900 | 1903 | 1924 | 1930 | 1960 | 1970 | 1970 1972 | 1980 | 1980-1990 | 1990

OLYMPIC GAMES

EVERY FOUR YEARS, athletes from all over the world meet to compete in the Summer Olympic Games. About 7,000 competitors take part in more than 20 different sports.

OLYMPIC SYMBOL
The Olympic symbol is made up of five interlocking rings, standing for Europe, Asia, Africa, Australia, and America.

CROWNING GLORY
In the ancient Olympic Games, winners were crowned with a sacred olive wreath.

MEDALS
Individuals and teams compete for gold (first), silver (second), and bronze (third) medals in the modern Games.

Gold medal from the 1984 Games

SUMMER OLYMPIC VENUES

Date	Place	Country
1896	Athens	Greece
1900	Paris	France
1904	St. Louis, Missouri	US
1908	London	Britain
1912	Stockholm	Sweden
1920	Antwerp	Belgium
1924	Paris	France
1928	Amsterdam	Netherlands
1932	Los Angeles, California	US
1936	Berlin	Germany
1948	London	Britain
1952	Helsinki	Finland
1956	Melbourne	Australia
1960	Rome	Italy
1964	Tokyo	Japan
1968	Mexico City	Mexico
1972	Munich	Germany
1976	Montreal	Canada
1980	Moscow	USSR
1984	Los Angeles, California	US
1988	Seoul	South Korea
1992	Barcelona	Spain
1996	Atlanta, Georgia	US
2000	Sydney	Australia

OLYMPIC FLAME
This flame symbolizes the athlete's strive for perfection. A torch is carried by a series of runners from the site of the ancient Olympics in Greece to the stadium where the current Games are to be held.

PARALYMPIC VENUES

Date	Place	Country
1960	Rome	Italy
1964	Tokyo	Japan
1968	Tel Aviv	Israel
1972	Heidelberg	Germany
1976	Toronto	Canada
1980	Arnhem	Netherlands
1984	New York	US
1988	Seoul	South Korea
1992	Barcelona	Spain
1996	Atlanta, Georgia	US
2000	Sydney	Australia

PARALYMPICS
Disabled people compete in the Paralympic Games, which are held every four years. Events include cycling and judo. The Winter Paralympics have been held since 1976.

WINTER OLYMPIC VENUES

Date	Place	Country
1924	Chamonix	France
1928	St. Moritz	Switzerland
1932	Lake Placid, New York	US
1936	Garmisch-Partenkirchen	Germany
1948	St. Moritz	Switzerland
1952	Oslo	Norway
1956	Cortina d'Ampezzo	Italy
1960	Squaw Valley, California	US
1964	Innsbruck	Austria
1968	Grenoble	France
1972	Sapporo	Japan
1976	Innsbruck	Austria
1980	Lake Placid, New York	US
1984	Sarajevo	Yugoslavia
1988	Calgary, Alberta	Canada
1992	Albertville	France
1994	Lillehammer	Norway
1998	Nagano	Japan

WINTER OLYMPICS
Until 1994, the Winter Games were held in the same year as the Summer Olympics. Events include skiing, figure and speed skating, and ice hockey.

CLASSIFICATION OF SPORTS
One way of classifying the many different types of sports is to put them into three basic groups, which can then be subdivided further.

This symbol is shown next to all Olympic sports featured on the pages following.

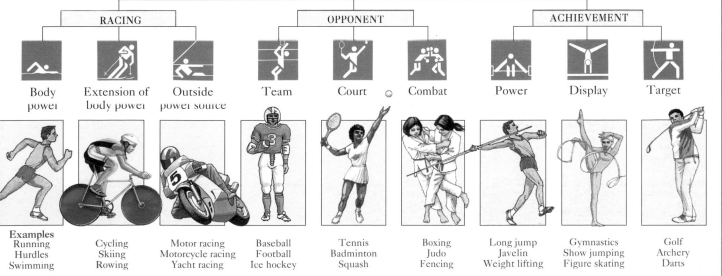

CLASSIFICATION

RACING			OPPONENT			ACHIEVEMENT		
Body power	Extension of body power	Outside power source	Team	Court	Combat	Power	Display	Target

Examples

Running Hurdles Swimming	Cycling Skiing Rowing	Motor racing Motorcycle racing Yacht racing	Baseball Football Ice hockey	Tennis Badminton Squash	Boxing Judo Fencing	Long jump Javelin Weight lifting	Gymnastics Show jumping Figure skating	Golf Archery Darts

TRACK EVENTS

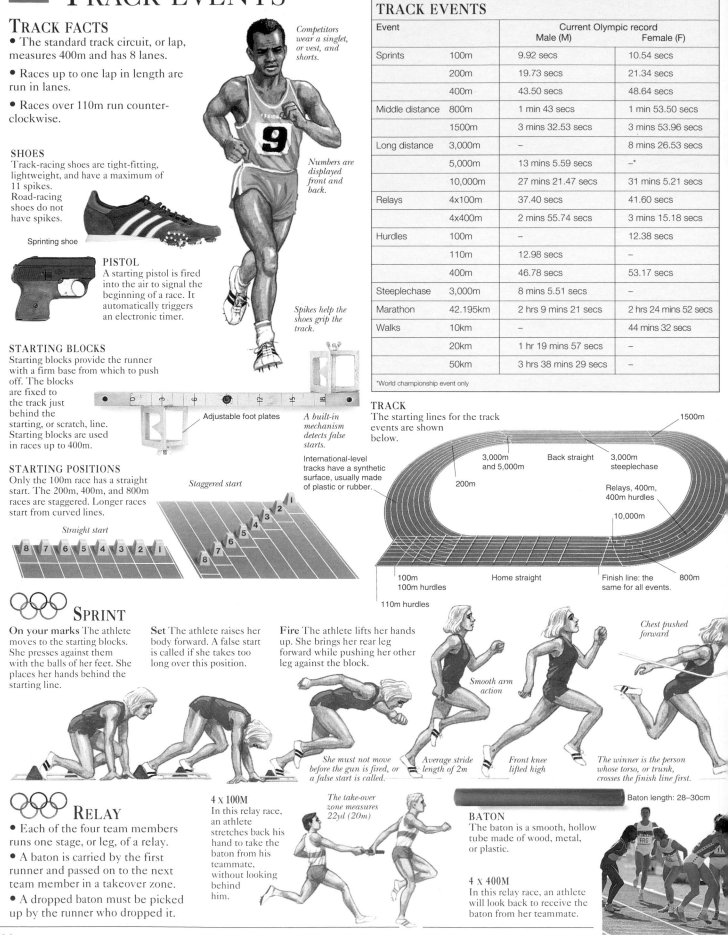

TRACK FACTS

- The standard track circuit, or lap, measures 400m and has 8 lanes.

- Races up to one lap in length are run in lanes.

- Races over 110m run counter-clockwise.

SHOES

Track-racing shoes are tight-fitting, lightweight, and have a maximum of 11 spikes.
Road-racing shoes do not have spikes.

Sprinting shoe

PISTOL

A starting pistol is fired into the air to signal the beginning of a race. It automatically triggers an electronic timer.

STARTING BLOCKS

Starting blocks provide the runner with a firm base from which to push off. The blocks are fixed to the track just behind the starting, or scratch, line. Starting blocks are used in races up to 400m.

Adjustable foot plates

A built-in mechanism detects false starts.

STARTING POSITIONS

Only the 100m race has a straight start. The 200m, 400m, and 800m races are staggered. Longer races start from curved lines.

Staggered start

Straight start

Competitors wear a singlet, or vest, and shorts.

Numbers are displayed front and back.

Spikes help the shoes grip the track.

OLYMPIC AND WORLD CHAMPIONSHIP TRACK EVENTS

Event		Current Olympic record	
		Male (M)	Female (F)
Sprints	100m	9.92 secs	10.54 secs
	200m	19.73 secs	21.34 secs
	400m	43.50 secs	48.64 secs
Middle distance	800m	1 min 43 secs	1 min 53.50 secs
	1500m	3 mins 32.53 secs	3 mins 53.96 secs
Long distance	3,000m	–	8 mins 26.53 secs
	5,000m	13 mins 5.59 secs	–*
	10,000m	27 mins 21.47 secs	31 mins 5.21 secs
Relays	4x100m	37.40 secs	41.60 secs
	4x400m	2 mins 55.74 secs	3 mins 15.18 secs
Hurdles	100m	–	12.38 secs
	110m	12.98 secs	–
	400m	46.78 secs	53.17 secs
Steeplechase	3,000m	8 mins 5.51 secs	–
Marathon	42.195km	2 hrs 9 mins 21 secs	2 hrs 24 mins 52 secs
Walks	10km	–	44 mins 32 secs
	20km	1 hr 19 mins 57 secs	–
	50km	3 hrs 38 mins 29 secs	–

*World championship event only

TRACK

The starting lines for the track events are shown below.

International-level tracks have a synthetic surface, usually made of plastic or rubber.

1500m

3,000m and 5,000m

Back straight

3,000m steeplechase

200m

Relays, 400m, 400m hurdles

10,000m

100m
100m hurdles

Home straight

Finish line: the same for all events.

800m

110m hurdles

SPRINT

On your marks The athlete moves to the starting blocks. She presses against them with the balls of her feet. She places her hands behind the starting line.

Set The athlete raises her body forward. A false start is called if she takes too long over this position.

Fire The athlete lifts her hands up. She brings her rear leg forward while pushing her other leg against the block.

Chest pushed forward

Smooth arm action

She must not move before the gun is fired, or a false start is called.

Average stride length of 2m

Front knee lifted high

The winner is the person whose torso, or trunk, crosses the finish line first.

RELAY

- Each of the four team members runs one stage, or leg, of a relay.

- A baton is carried by the first runner and passed on to the next team member in a takeover zone.

- A dropped baton must be picked up by the runner who dropped it.

4 x 100M

In this relay race, an athlete stretches back his hand to take the baton from his teammate, without looking behind him.

The take-over zone measures 22yd (20m)

Baton length: 28–30cm

BATON

The baton is a smooth, hollow tube made of wood, metal, or plastic.

4 x 400M

In this relay race, an athlete will look back to receive the baton from her teammate.

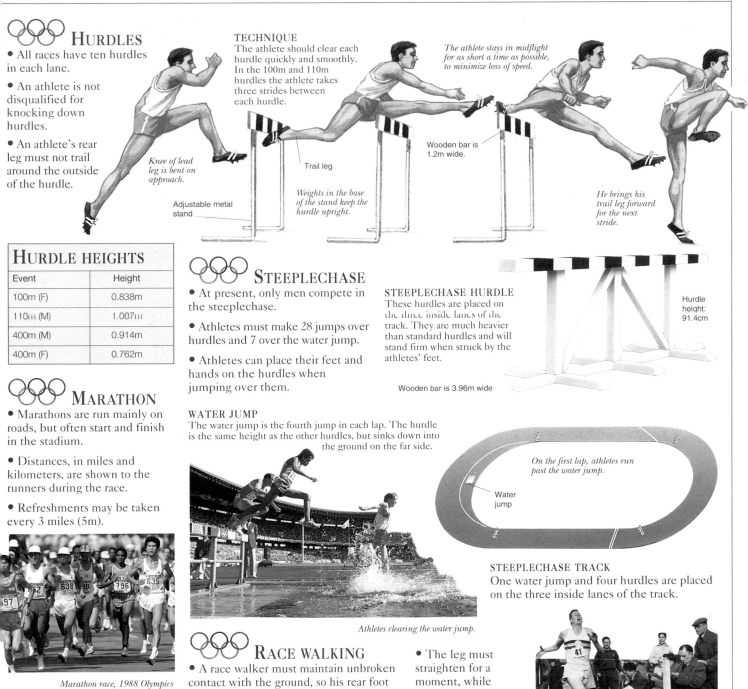

HURDLES

- All races have ten hurdles in each lane.

- An athlete is not disqualified for knocking down hurdles.

- An athlete's rear leg must not trail around the outside of the hurdle.

Knee of lead leg is bent on approach.

Adjustable metal stand

TECHNIQUE

The athlete should clear each hurdle quickly and smoothly. In the 100m and 110m hurdles the athlete takes three strides between each hurdle.

Trail leg

Weights in the base of the stand keep the hurdle upright.

The athlete stays in midflight for as short a time as possible, to minimize loss of speed.

Wooden bar is 1.2m wide.

He brings his trail leg forward for the next stride.

HURDLE HEIGHTS

Event	Height
100m (F)	0.838m
110m (M)	1.007m
400m (M)	0.914m
400m (F)	0.762m

STEEPLECHASE

- At present, only men compete in the steeplechase.

- Athletes must make 28 jumps over hurdles and 7 over the water jump.

- Athletes can place their feet and hands on the hurdles when jumping over them.

STEEPLECHASE HURDLE
These hurdles are placed on the three inside lanes of the track. They are much heavier than standard hurdles and will stand firm when struck by the athletes' feet.

Wooden bar is 3.96m wide

Hurdle height: 91.4cm

WATER JUMP
The water jump is the fourth jump in each lap. The hurdle is the same height as the other hurdles, but sinks down into the ground on the far side.

On the first lap, athletes run past the water jump.

Water jump

STEEPLECHASE TRACK
One water jump and four hurdles are placed on the three inside lanes of the track.

Athletes clearing the water jump.

MARATHON

- Marathons are run mainly on roads, but often start and finish in the stadium.

- Distances, in miles and kilometers, are shown to the runners during the race.

- Refreshments may be taken every 3 miles (5m).

Marathon race, 1988 Olympics

MARATHON ORIGIN
The marathon originated in 490 B.C. when a Greek messenger, Pheidippides, ran 24 miles (39km) to report the Athenian victory over the Persians at the Battle of Marathon.

RACE WALKING

- A race walker must maintain unbroken contact with the ground, so his rear foot must not leave the ground until the front one has made contact.

- The leg must straighten for a moment, while the foot is on the ground.

By rotating his hips, the walker can increase the length of his stride.

Leg kept straight

RECORD BREAKERS
FOUR-MINUTE MILE
was first broken in 1954 by Roger Bannister (born 1929), of Britain.

TEN-SECOND 100M
was first broken in 1968 by Jim Hines (born 1946), of the US.

YOUNGEST INDIVIDUAL
world record breaker in track events is Wang Yan (born 1971), of China. The 14-year-old girl set a women's 5,000m walk record at Jian, China, in 1986.

FIELD EVENTS

FIELD FACTS

- Field events include all the major athletic jumping and throwing sports.

- At the Olympic Games, men and women compete in all field events apart from the hammer and pole vault, which are for men only.

THROWING EVENTS

- Athletes must not touch any point outside the throwing area until their throw has landed.

- A white flag is shown for a correct attempt, a red flag signals a foul.

INFIELD
The positioning of the field areas varies from stadium to stadium, but, generally, events are held inside the track (the infield).

Shot put

Hammer and discus

Pole vault

Javelin

29° arc

40° arc

45° arc

Long jump

Triple jump

High jump

OLYMPIC THROWING EVENTS

Event	Weight	Current Olympic record
Javelin (F)	0.6kg	74.68m
Javelin (M)	0.8kg	89.66m
Discus (F)	1kg	72.30m
Discus (M)	2kg	68.82m
Shot put (F)	4kg	22.41m
Shot put (M)	7.26kg	22.47m
Hammer (M)	7.26kg	84.80m

JAVELIN

- The javelin is thrown from behind a curved line at the end of a run-up track, and must land within a 29° arc.

JAVELIN
The javelin looks like a spear. It has a long shaft, a cord grip, and a metal tip.

The length of the men's javelin is 260–270cm; the women's javelin measures 220–230cm.

Sharply-pointed metal tip

THROWING THE JAVELIN
The athlete stretches his throwing arm behind him, to give him extra power. The javelin must land tip first, but it does not need to dig into the ground.

Cord grip

DISCUS

- The discus is thrown from a circle and must land within a 40° arc.

- Though any holding and throwing techniques are allowed, the discus is usually held and thrown with one hand.

DISCUS
The discus has a metal rim, with a metal weight at the center.

The width of the men's discus is 219–221mm; the width of the women's discus is 180–182mm.

THROWING THE DISCUS
The athlete stands with her back to the throwing area and turns one and a half times before releasing the discus.

The athlete usually takes one or two swings before starting to turn.

Her throwing arm is fully extended.

She turns one and a half times before release.

SHOT PUT

- The shot is thrown, or put, from a circle and must land within a 45° arc.

- Only one hand is used, and the put must not start from behind the line of the shoulders.

SHOT
The shot is a smooth metal ball. The men's shot is slightly larger than the women's.

PUTTING THE SHOT
The athlete puts the shot with a single pushing action. She must not let the hand holding the shot fall below its starting position.

Jesse Owens

She raises one leg and hops backward.

Her body straightens on facing the throwing area.

She pushes the shot up and away from her.

The athlete nestles the shot under her chin.

RECORD BREAKERS

SIX WORLD RECORDS, including a long jump record of 8.13m that lasted 25 years, were set in 45 minutes by Jesse Owens (1913–80) of the US in 1935 in Michigan.

OLDEST FEMALE ATHLETE ever to win an Olympic title is Lia Manoliu (born 1932) of Romania, who was 36 years old when she won the discus at the 1968 Olympics in Mexico City.

HAMMER
The hammer is a metal ball that is attached to a handle by a length of steel wire. Although the hammer weighs the same as the men's shot, the different throwing technique means that it can travel much farther.

HAMMER

- The hammer is thrown from a circle surrounded by a safety cage and must land within a 40° arc.

The hammer weighs the same as the men's shot.

THROWING THE HAMMER
The athlete throws the hammer using both hands. The head of the hammer may touch the ground during the first few swings.

The athlete turns two or three times before releasing the hammer.

OLYMPIC JUMPING EVENTS

Event	Current Olympic record
High jump (M)	2.38m
High jump (F)	2.02m
Pole vault (M)	5.90m
Long jump (M)	8.90m
Long jump (F)	7.40m
Triple jump (M)	18.17m
Triple jump (F)	new event in 1996

COMBINED EVENTS

DECATHLON
• Men compete in the Decathlon, which covers ten events.

EVENTS

First day	Second day
100m race	110m hurdles
Long jump	Discus
Shot put	Pole vault
High jump	Javelin
400m race	1500m race

HEPTATHLON
• Women compete in the Heptathlon; it covers seven events.

EVENTS

First day	Second day
100m hurdles	Long jump
High jump	Javelin
Shot put	800m race
200m race	

MODERN PENTATHLON
• Men and women compete in the Modern Pentathlon, though only men in the Olympics; it covers five events.

EVENTS

Fencing (Épée)
Freestyle swimming – 300m (M) and 200m (F)
Pistol shooting
Cross-country running – 4,000m (M) and 2,000m (F)
Riding

TRIATHLON
• Men and women compete in the Triathlon; it covers three events.

EVENTS

Course	Events		
	Swimming	Cycling	Running
Short Course	1.5km	40km	10km
Long Course	3.8km	180km	42.2km

JUMPING EVENTS
• In all jumping events, athletes may take any length of run and may place markers to help judge their approach.

The athlete jumps backward over the bar.

FOSBURY FLOP
Most high-jumpers use a technique called the "Fosbury flop," in which the athlete jumps backward over the bar.

HIGH JUMP
• The crossbar is raised for each round by a minimum of 2cm.

• The high jump has a fan shaped run-up area.

POLE VAULT
• The crossbar is raised for each round by a minimum of 5cm.

• The pole vault has a straight run-up with a sunken box at the end.

• Poles may be of any size or material, but are usually made of fiberglass.

The pole vaulter tucks himself under the pole until it straightens, and then rotates to come down facing the bar.

VAULTING OVER
The athlete must make an accurate run-up, to ensure that the pole is placed in the correct position for takeoff. As he pushes off from the ground, the pole bends with the weight of his body. He levers himself over the bar, feet first.

On leaving the ground, athletes may not climb the pole (by moving the lower hand above the upper hand).

LONG JUMP
• The athlete makes a straight run-up to a wooden takeoff board which is sunk into the runway.

• Just beyond the takeoff line is a soft substance that records foot faults.

• Jumps are measured to the nearest mark in the sand made by any part of the body.

TECHNIQUE
The athlete leaves the take-off board in an upright position. She increases the distance she travels by leaning back in midair before landing.

The athlete throws her legs forward as she lands.

TRIPLE JUMP
• This event uses the same run-up and landing area as the long jump.

• The athlete must use a hop, step, and jump action.

THREE STAGES

Hop The athlete must land on the same foot that was used for takeoff.

Step The athlete must land on the other foot.

Jump The athlete throws his arms and legs forward, ready for landing.

Hop   *Step*   *Jump*

WEIGHT LIFTING

- Weight lifters compete in different classes according to their body weight.

- There are two types of lifts: the snatch, and the clean and jerk.

- Men and women compete in weight lifting, but only men take part in Olympic events.

GEAR
The weight lifter must wear a one-piece costume. He may wear a T-shirt underneath if he wishes. A wide belt may be worn to support the back.

BAR
The weight lifting bar is made progressively heavier during each round of a competition. Disks of varying weights are loaded onto the bar, with the heaviest on the inside.

The rubber- or plastic-covered disks are color-coded according to weight.

Red (25kg)   Yellow (15kg)

DISK WEIGHTS
The cast-iron disk weights range from 0.25kg to 25kg. By adding a combination of disks, any weight can be added to the bar.

10kg

7.5kg (Not a current official weight)

5kg

2.5kg

1.5kg (Not a current official weight)

Length of bar: 2m

Boots must give firm support and have a maximum height above the sole of 130mm.

CLASSES OF WEIGHT LIFTING

Category	Weight (in kg) Male	Female
1	54	46
2	59	50
3	64	54
4	70	59
5	76	64
6	83	70
7	91	76
8	99	83
9	108	Over 83
10	Over108	–

POWER LIFTING
Power lifters can lift much heavier weights than weight lifters because they do not have to raise the bar above their heads.

TYPES OF POWER LIFTING
Squat The bar rests on a stand and the lifter squats below it. He must stand up and lift the bar across the shoulders.

Bench press The lifter lies on a bench with the bar resting on a stand above his chest. On the instruction "press," the lifter must push the bar up until both arms are straight.

Deadlift The competitor lifts the bar from the floor and rises to a standing position with the bar resting across the front of his thighs.

In the bench press, the athlete lifts the bar out of a stand.

The height of the bench is adjustable.

SNATCH
- The weight lifter must lift the bar in a single movement until the bar is above the head and the arms are fully extended.

- Once the bar is above his head, the weight lifter can take as much time as he needs to straighten his position (the recovery).

The weight lifter uses chalk to help him grip the bar.

- On completing a lift, the weight lifter must hold the position until the referee signals to replace the bar.

He must be completely still, and his arms and legs fully stretched, for the lift to be counted.

He can take unlimited time over the recovery.

He may bend or split his legs during the lift.

He must not turn his wrists over until the bar is past head height.

CLEAN AND JERK
- In the clean and jerk, the bar is lifted to the shoulders (the clean) and then to full arm's length overhead (the jerk).

- At the end of the clean, the lifter may rest the bar on the collarbones, chest, or fully bent arms, and may change his grip.

Knees may be split or bent.

As in the snatch, the lifter can take any length of time over the recovery position.

The lifter must not let the bar touch his body until it has reached his shoulders.

During the clean the lifter must not let his elbows or upper arms touch his knees or thighs.

WEIGHTY MATTERS
Weight lifters can lift more than 2.5 times their own body weight in the snatch, and more than 3 times their own body weight in the clean and jerk. Power lifters can lift more than 5 times their own body weight.

Snatch

Clean and jerk

Power lifting

RECORD BREAKERS
FIRST MAN TO CLEAN AND JERK more than three times his own body weight was Stefan Topurov (born 1964), of Bulgaria, who lifted 180kg in Moscow, USSR, in 1983.

GYMNASTICS

- The gymnast must combine acrobatic agility and muscle power with grace of movement.
- There are two Olympic events: artistic gymnastics, and rhythmic gymnastics, which is for women only.

ARTISTIC GYMNASTICS

- Gymnasts are awarded marks out of ten for their performances on various pieces of equipment.
- Women perform four types of exercise, men perform six.

GEAR

Men wear vests and long pants. They may wear shorts for the floor and vault exercises. Women wear leotards, and may wear gymnastic slippers or go barefoot. Handguards may be worn for the ring and bar exercises.

Gymnasts use a chalky powder to keep their hands dry while using the apparatus.

BEAM

This event is for women only. The whole routine should flow smoothly, and take between 70 and 90 seconds to complete.

Length: 5m   Height: 120cm (maximum)   Width: 10cm

The beam is made of wood and is covered with suede, which helps give the gymnast a good grip.

The gymnast walks, runs, leaps, and rolls along the beam, while keeping her balance throughout.

She will perform movements such as forward and backward somersaults, splits, and handstands.

VAULT

Both men and women perform exercises on the vault. Women jump over the width of the vaulting horse, men jump over the length.

The horse is covered in smooth leather; it is set at different heights for male and female events.

Men's horse height: 135cm length: 160cm

Women's horse height: 120cm length: 160cm

The gymnast pushes off from the horse and performs twists or somersaults.

Barcelona'92   Barcelona'92

ASYMMETRIC BARS

This event is for women only. The gymnast must move from bar to bar using swinging and circular movements.

The whole routine should be rhythmic and continuous.

Height of higher bar: 235–240cm

Width between bars: 43cm

Height of lower bar: 140–160cm

Bars are made of wood or fiberglass.

The gymnast must change handholds and direction constantly.

FLOOR

This event is for men and women. The women's routine is set to music and must last between 110 and 130 seconds. The men's exercise takes from 50 to 70 seconds to complete.

The gymnast performs a series of tumbling, leaping, and balancing movements, using the entire floor area.

RINGS

The rings are for men only. The gymnast demonstrates swinging movements, and holds positions for at least two seconds. He should not allow the rings to swing during the routine.

Steel wires

Canvas straps

Wooden rings

Height of frame: 575cm

The gymnast displays great strength in his arms and shoulders as he swings through his routine.

He holds positions such as the crucifix, or cross position.

POMMEL HORSE

This event is for men only. The gymnast supports himself above the pommel horse with his hands. He must make sure he does not touch the horse with any other part of his body.

The pommel horse is the same as the vaulting horse, but has wooden handles, or pommels, attached.

The gymnast makes continuous swinging movements with his legs.

HORIZONTAL BAR

This event is for men only. The gymnast performs continuous swings and circular movements on a steel bar which is 240cm wide and 275cm high. At least one release from the bar must be made.

PARALLEL BARS

This event is for men only. The gymnast performs swinging and balancing movements on the parallel bars. He will sometimes let go of the bars with both hands.

Adjustable wooden bars provide plenty of spring.

Length of bars: 350cm

Height: 195cm

Width between bars: 42cm

Weighted metal frame

RHYTHMIC GYMNASTICS

- Gymnasts perform routines set to music, using small, hand-held pieces of equipment, which must be kept moving at all times.
- Balletic, rather than acrobatic, movements are performed.

Ribbon The gymnast makes the ribbon form moving patterns in the air and on the floor.

Hoop The gymnast rotates the hoop around her, and throws and catches it.

Ball The gymnast bounces, throws, and catches the ball.

Clubs The gymnast throws, rolls, and juggles with two clubs.

Rope The gymnast jumps and skips while throwing and catching the rope.

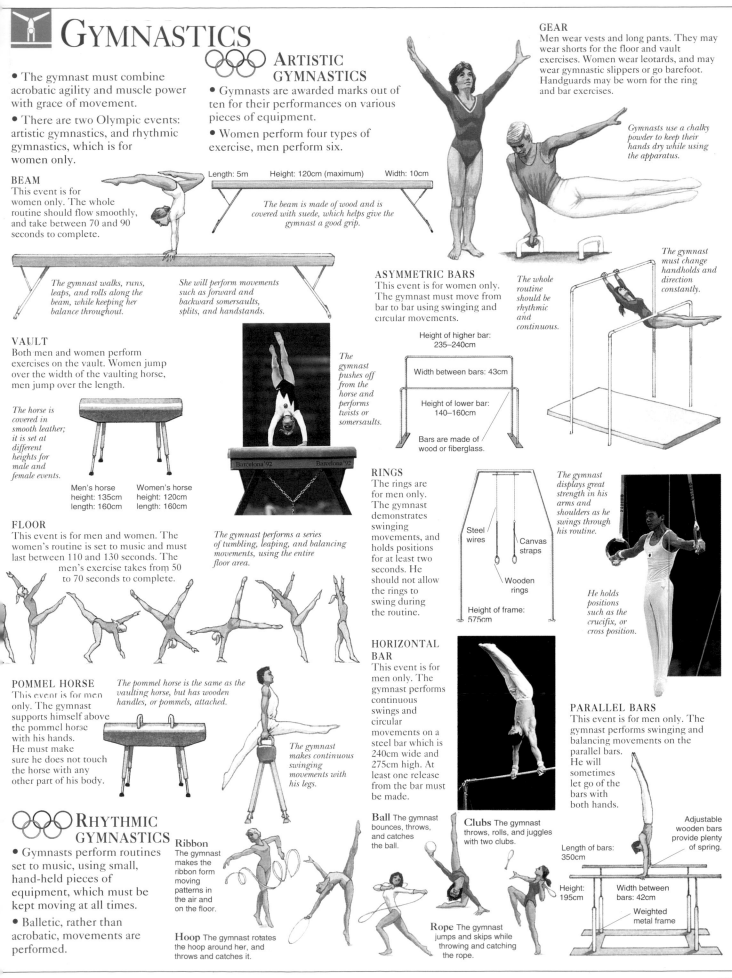

COMBAT SPORTS

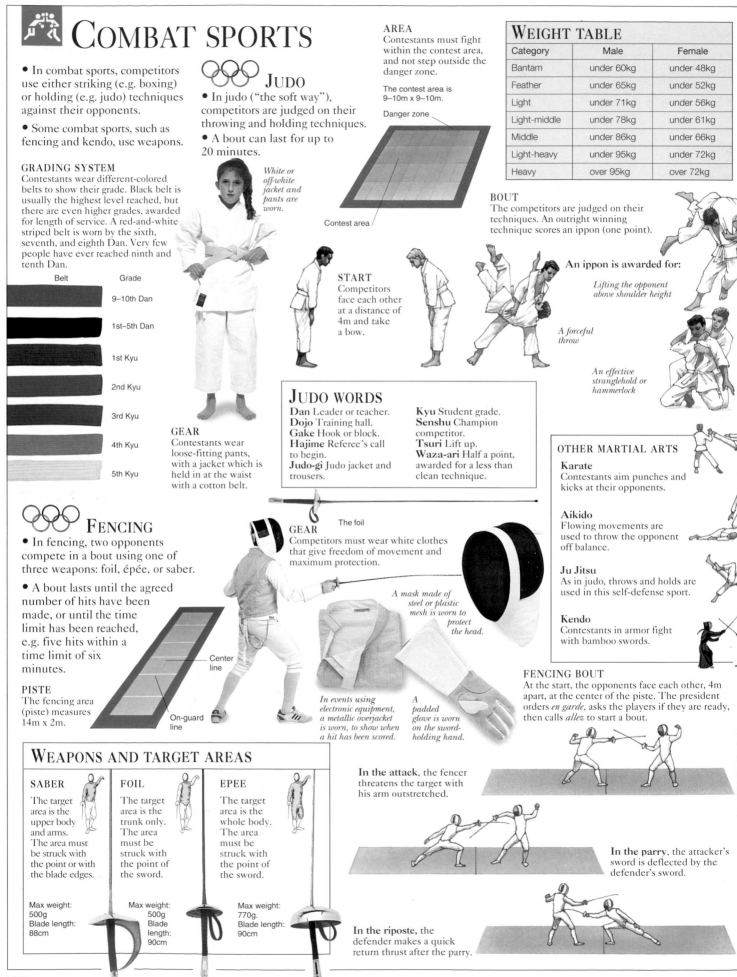

- In combat sports, competitors use either striking (e.g. boxing) or holding (e.g. judo) techniques against their opponents.

- Some combat sports, such as fencing and kendo, use weapons.

GRADING SYSTEM

Contestants wear different-colored belts to show their grade. Black belt is usually the highest level reached, but there are even higher grades, awarded for length of service. A red-and-white striped belt is worn by the sixth, seventh, and eighth Dan. Very few people have ever reached ninth and tenth Dan.

Belt	Grade
	9–10th Dan
	1st–5th Dan
	1st Kyu
	2nd Kyu
	3rd Kyu
	4th Kyu
	5th Kyu

GEAR
Contestants wear loose-fitting pants, with a jacket which is held in at the waist with a cotton belt.

JUDO

- In judo ("the soft way"), competitors are judged on their throwing and holding techniques.

- A bout can last for up to 20 minutes.

White or off-white jacket and pants are worn.

JUDO WORDS
Dan Leader or teacher.
Dojo Training hall.
Gake Hook or block.
Hajime Referee's call to begin.
Judo-gi Judo jacket and trousers.
Kyu Student grade.
Senshu Champion competitor.
Tsuri Lift up.
Waza-ari Half a point, awarded for a less than clean technique.

AREA
Contestants must fight within the contest area, and not step outside the danger zone.

The contest area is 9–10m x 9–10m.

Danger zone

Contest area

START
Competitors face each other at a distance of 4m and take a bow.

BOUT
The competitors are judged on their techniques. An outright winning technique scores an ippon (one point).

An ippon is awarded for:

Lifting the opponent above shoulder height

A forceful throw

An effective stranglehold or hammerlock

WEIGHT TABLE

Category	Male	Female
Bantam	under 60kg	under 48kg
Feather	under 65kg	under 52kg
Light	under 71kg	under 56kg
Light-middle	under 78kg	under 61kg
Middle	under 86kg	under 66kg
Light-heavy	under 95kg	under 72kg
Heavy	over 95kg	over 72kg

OTHER MARTIAL ARTS

Karate
Contestants aim punches and kicks at their opponents.

Aikido
Flowing movements are used to throw the opponent off balance.

Ju Jitsu
As in judo, throws and holds are used in this self-defense sport.

Kendo
Contestants in armor fight with bamboo swords.

FENCING

- In fencing, two opponents compete in a bout using one of three weapons: foil, épée, or saber.

- A bout lasts until the agreed number of hits have been made, or until the time limit has been reached, e.g. five hits within a time limit of six minutes.

PISTE
The fencing area (piste) measures 14m x 2m.

Center line

On-guard line

GEAR
Competitors must wear white clothes that give freedom of movement and maximum protection.

The foil

A mask made of steel or plastic mesh is worn to protect the head.

In events using electronic equipment, a metallic overjacket is worn, to show when a hit has been scored.

A padded glove is worn on the sword-holding hand.

FENCING BOUT
At the start, the opponents face each other, 4m apart, at the center of the piste. The president orders *en garde*, asks the players if they are ready, then calls *allez* to start a bout.

In the attack, the fencer threatens the target with his arm outstretched.

In the parry, the attacker's sword is deflected by the defender's sword.

In the riposte, the defender makes a quick return thrust after the parry.

WEAPONS AND TARGET AREAS

SABER
The target area is the upper body and arms. The area must be struck with the point or with the blade edges.

Max weight: 500g
Blade length: 88cm

FOIL
The target area is the trunk only. The area must be struck with the point of the sword.

Max weight: 500g
Blade length: 90cm

EPEE
The target area is the whole body. The area must be struck with the point of the sword.

Max weight: 770g.
Blade length: 90cm

BOXING

- In boxing, competitors use their gloved hands to punch each other in specific areas of the body.

- Fights can be won on points, or because the opponent is counted out, retires, or is judged unfit to continue.

RING

Contests are held in a square "ring" surrounded by ropes.

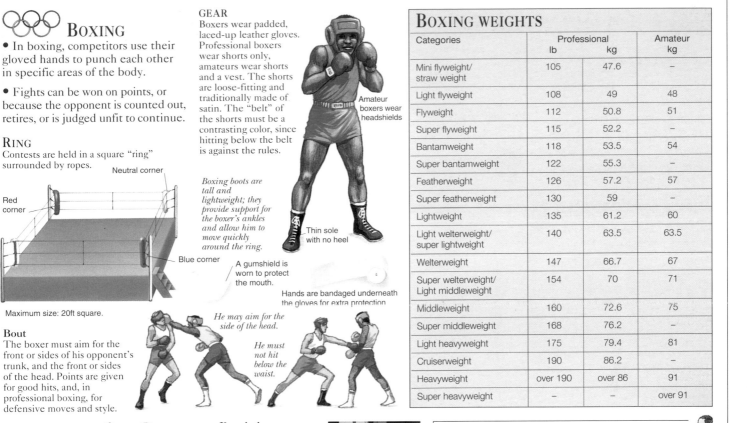

Neutral corner

Red corner

Blue corner

Maximum size: 20ft square.

Bout

The boxer must aim for the front or sides of his opponent's trunk, and the front or sides of the head. Points are given for good hits, and, in professional boxing, for defensive moves and style.

The boxer must strike a blow using the knuckle part of the glove.

GEAR

Boxers wear padded, laced-up leather gloves. Professional boxers wear shorts only, amateurs wear shorts and a vest. The shorts are loose-fitting and traditionally made of satin. The "belt" of the shorts must be a contrasting color, since hitting below the belt is against the rules.

Amateur boxers wear headshields

Boxing boots are tall and lightweight; they provide support for the boxer's ankles and allow him to move quickly around the ring.

Thin sole with no heel

A gumshield is worn to protect the mouth.

Hands are bandaged underneath the gloves for extra protection

He may aim for the side of the head.

He must not hit below the waist.

Knock-down

In a knock-down, a count of ten begins. If the fallen boxer cannot rise before the count ends, he loses the fight. If he rises, and is judged by the referee to be fit to continue, the fight goes on.

BOXING WEIGHTS

Categories	Professional		Amateur
	lb	kg	kg
Mini flyweight/ straw weight	105	47.6	–
Light flyweight	108	49	48
Flyweight	112	50.8	51
Super flyweight	115	52.2	–
Bantamweight	118	53.5	54
Super bantamweight	122	55.3	–
Featherweight	126	57.2	57
Super featherweight	130	59	–
Lightweight	135	61.2	60
Light welterweight/ super lightweight	140	63.5	63.5
Welterweight	147	66.7	67
Super welterweight/ Light middleweight	154	70	71
Middleweight	160	72.6	75
Super middleweight	168	76.2	–
Light heavyweight	175	79.4	81
Cruiserweight	190	86.2	–
Heavyweight	over 190	over 86	91
Super heavyweight	–	–	over 91

FIGHTING FIT

The longest boxing fight on record lasted 7 hours, 19 minutes and was held in New Orleans, US, in 1893. Andy Bowen fought Jack Burke over 110 rounds, and the match was finally declared a draw.

WRESTLING

- There are two Olympic wrestling events: freestyle and Greco-Roman.

- Points are awarded for successful moves and holds.

GEAR

Wrestlers wear one-piece leotards that leave upper chest and shoulders bare. One competitor wears red, and the other blue. Wrestlers must not oil or grease their bodies.

Wrestling boots are tall and lightweight, have no heels, rings, or buckles.

Fall

The main aim in wrestling is to achieve a "fall," by forcing the opponent's shoulder blades onto the mat for one second, or for as long as it takes the referee to say to himself *tomber* (French for fall).

- In Greco-Roman contests, wrestlers must not use their legs or grip an opponent below the hips.

MAT

The contest circle, which includes the red band, is 9m in diameter.

Red corner

Wrestling surface

Blue corner

WRESTLING WEIGHTS

Category	Weight limits in kg
1	48
2	52
3	57
4	62
5	68
6	74
7	82
8	90
9	100
10	130

SUMO WRESTLING

- Ritual and tradition play an important part in Sumo wrestling.

- Bouts are won by pushing an opponent out of the ring, or by making him touch the ground with any part of his body other than the soles of his feet.

- Pushes, slaps, and holds are the main techniques.

Rice is thrown up at the beginning of the bout.

A loincloth is worn wrapped around the waist and between the legs.

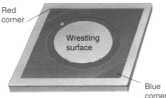

SUMO GRADINGS

Sumo wrestlers are graded according to skill, not weight. There are ten grades:

Jonokuchi Novice
Jonidan Qualified
Sandamne Lower junior
Makushita Leading junior
Juryo Contender
Maegashira Senior
Komusubi Second grade junior champion
Sekiwake Junior champion
Ozeki Champion
Yokozuna Grand champion

HEAVY WEIGHTS

The heaviest Sumo wrestler weighs 551lb (250kg): equal to the total average weight of four teenage boys. This is about twice the weight of the heaviest world champion boxer, and almost twice the maximum weight permitted for an Olympic wrestler.

Boxer

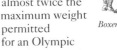

Wrestler

Sumo wrestler

COURT GAMES

TENNIS

• The aim is to hit a ball over the net with a racket so that it lands inside the court, and cannot be returned.

• A match is divided into sets and ends when one player has won three sets (for men) or two sets (for women).

• Each set is divided into games, and a player must win at least six games, and have a two-game lead, to win a set.

• A tie-breaker is used if the set reaches six-all: the first player to score seven or more points, with a two-point lead, wins.

• A match lasts for a maximum of five sets for men and three sets for women.

SCORING A GAME

After scoring 4 points a player wins a game. But, if the players tie at 3 points each (that is, 40-all, or *deuce*), play continues until one player has a 2-point lead.

SCORING A GAME

Points	Score
0	love
1	15
2	30
3	40

Martina Navratilova

RECORD BREAKERS

RECORD NUMBER OF WIMBLEDON SINGLES TITLES held is nine, by Martina Navratilova, US (born in the former Czechoslovakia in 1956). MOST SINGLES CHAMPIONSHIPS won in grand slam tournaments is 24, by Margaret Court, Australia (born 1942). YOUNGEST MALE CHAMPION at Wimbledon is Boris Becker, Germany (born 1967), who won the singles title in 1985, aged 17.

GEAR

Traditionally, clothing is white, though today the only professional tournament that insists on white is Wimbledon, England. The gear, which is similar in all court sports, is a shirt and shorts for men, and a shirt and skirt, or a dress, for women.

Wristbands are worn for wiping the forehead and keeping palms dry.

Socks are cushioned to protect soles and heels.

Rubber-soled shoes

COURT

Tennis can be played indoors and outdoors. The court surface may be grass, wood, clay, or artificial.

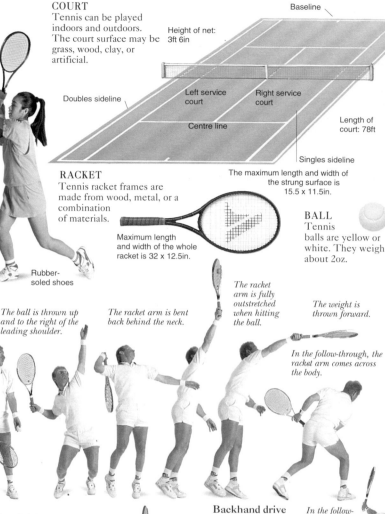

Height of net: 3ft 6in

Baseline

Doubles sideline

Left service court

Right service court

Centre line

Singles sideline

Length of court: 78ft

The maximum length and width of the strung surface is 15.5 x 11.5in.

RACKET

Tennis racket frames are made from wood, metal, or a combination of materials.

Maximum length and width of the whole racket is 32 x 12.5in.

BALL

Tennis balls are yellow or white. They weigh about 2oz.

SERVING

The player serves behind the baseline. He throws the ball in the air and hits it before it touches the ground. The ball must clear the net without bouncing and touch ground in the opposing service court.

The ball is thrown up and to the right of the leading shoulder.

The racket arm is bent back behind the neck.

The racket arm is fully outstretched when hitting the ball.

The weight is thrown forward.

In the follow-through, the racket arm comes across the body.

PLAYING

The player receiving the serve must let the ball bounce once before returning it. A return is still good if the ball touches the net or passes outside the net post, as long as it lands in the opposing player's side of the court.

Forehand drive

This is the most natural basic groundstroke in the game. A right-handed player plays it on his right side.

The shoulders turn as the racket swings back.

Knees are bent.

The racket is swung forward to meet the ball.

Backhand drive

This basic stroke is less instinctive than the forehand drive. A right-handed player plays it on his left side.

In the follow-through, the racket arm is fully extended.

The leading shoulder is turned away from the ball.

The ball is hit once it is to the front of the right foot.

The weight is put onto the front foot.

GRAND SLAM

Players who achieve the "grand slam" hold, all in the same year, the singles titles at these four major tournaments.

Tournament	Place	Surface
Wimbledon	London, UK	Grass
United States Open	Flushing Meadows, New York, US	Artificial material
Australian Open	Kooyong stadium, Melbourne, Australia	Synthetic grass
French Open	Roland Garros stadium, Paris, France	Clay

TENNIS WORDS

Ace A service beyond the reach of the receiver.
Advantage The first point scored after deuce.
Let A serve that scrapes the top of the net before landing in the correct court; it is played again.
Rally A long series of hits.
Seedings List showing where a player is expected to finish in a tournament.
Straight-sets Winning the match without losing a set.

BADMINTON

- In badminton, players hit a shuttlecock over a high net.

- In doubles and men's singles, the first side to score 15 points is the winner; in women's singles, it is the first player to score 11 points.

- Usually, a match is decided by the winner of two games.

COURT

Short service line

Left service court

Right service court

Long service line for singles

Long service line for doubles

Length of court: 44ft

Height of net: 5ft

Width of court: 20ft

SHUTTLECOCK
At top-class level, the shuttlecock is made of a "skirt" of 14–16 goose feathers fixed in a cork base.

RACKET
These are usually made of metal or carbon fiber, and strung with gut.

TABLE TENNIS

- In this indoor game, the players use rackets, or bats, to hit a hollow ball across a table over a low net.

- The first side to score 21 points wins the game, but if the score reaches 20-all, the game continues until one side has a 2-point lead.

- A match is decided by the best of five games (for men), or three games (for women).

BAT
Originally, bats were made of wood only. The pimpled rubber face was added in the 1920s to allow players to give the ball spin.

Pimpled rubber

TABLE
The chipboard top is usually dark green.

Width: 1.52m

Height of net: 15.25cm

Length: 2.74m

Height: 76cm

BALL
The lightweight plastic ball is either white or yellow.

SQUASH

- Squash is played using all four walls of an enclosed court.

- The ball is hit against the front wall first and must be returned before it has bounced twice on the floor.

- A match consists of the best of five games; the winner of a game is the first to score nine points.

BALL
There are four varieties of squash ball: the slower balls are used in hot conditions, and the faster balls are used in cold conditions.

Yellow dot: very slow

White dot: slow

Red dot: fast

Blue dot: very fast

RACKET
The head of a squash racket is smaller and rounder than that of a badminton or tennis racket.

JAI ALAI

- In the fast court game of Jai alai, or Pelota, players use wicker baskets, called *cestas*, in place of rackets. The court is long and narrow and has three playing walls.

The player wears a rubber glove, which is sewn onto the cesta.

RACQUETBALL

In racquetball, players use a short-handled racquet and a hollow rubber ball. The ball can be hit against the ceiling, as well as all four walls of the court.

The fast game of racquetball is similar in many ways to squash.

SERVING
The player serves underhand and must hit the shuttlecock below waist level. If it is not returned, it must land within the service court diagonally opposite. Only the server can score points.

Arm is bent, and the racket held behind the shoulder.

Grip should be relaxed, not too tight, but not too loose.

Racket is angled downward.

Racket is raised directly upward, and the arm straightens on making contact with the shuttlecock.

PLAYING
The receiver must return the shuttle over the net before it touches the ground in the serving court. Most badminton shots are played overhead.

SERVING
The ball must be thrown vertically at least 16cm from the flat palm of the hand, and the ball must not spin. At the moment of striking, the racket must be behind the end of the table. The ball must bounce on the server's side first.

The ball is hit as it begins to fall.

GRIPS
There are two main grips used in table tennis.

Handshake grip
The bat is held as though the player is shaking hands.

Penholder grip
The bat is held as though the player is holding a pen.

Out-of-court line

Cut line

Length: 32ft

Service box

Width: 21ft

COURT
The white, concrete walls of a squash court must be completely smooth. In tournaments, courts are often made of glass and Perspex, so that spectators can watch the match from all sides of the court. In the US, squash is played on a narrower court with a harder ball.

SERVING
The player must stand with at least one foot in the service box, throw the ball into the air, and hit it at the first attempt. The ball must hit the front wall above the cut line, but below the out-of-court line, without bouncing elsewhere first.

The server can use any kind of stroke.

TOP BALL SPEEDS

Jai alai	188mph (302km/h)
Squash	144mph (232km/h)
Tennis	138mph (222km/h)
Badminton	124mph (200km/h)
Table tennis	106mph (170km/h)

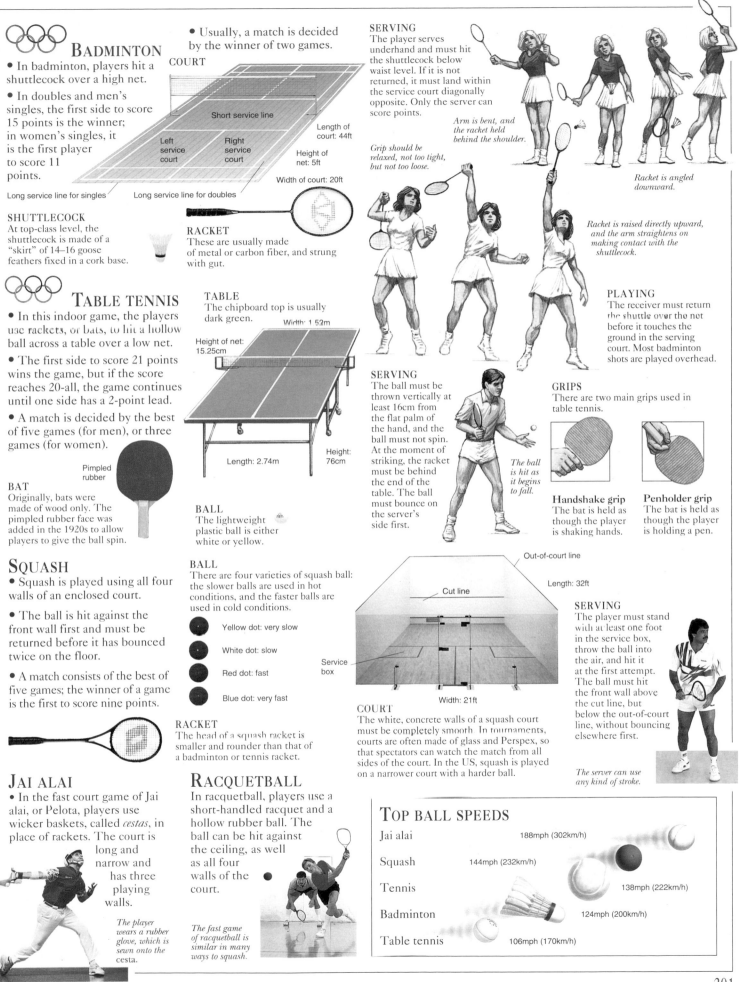

BASKETBALL

FACTS

- The aim of basketball is to throw the ball into a basket at the opponent's end of the court.

- There are ten players in each team; only five are on the court at any one time.

- Players may throw and bounce the ball, but must not carry or kick it.

- A game consists of two halves of 20 minutes each.

GEAR
Players wear brightly colored singlets and shorts. Singlets have large numbers on the front and back.

The rim of the net is 3.05m off the ground.

BALL
The ball is made of rubber encased in leather, rubber, or synthetic material.

The high, padded sides of basketball boots give firm support.

COURT
The dimensions given for this court are based on international rules. In the US, the courts are slightly bigger.

Free-throw line.

Backboard   Length: 28m

Three points are awarded for baskets scored from outside the semicircle.

Two points are awarded for baskets scored from inside the semicircle.

End line   Width: 15m

TIME RULES

Time limit	Action
3 seconds	A player may remain in the restricted area between his opponent's end line and the free-throw line.
5 seconds	A player may hold onto the ball.
10 seconds	The team with the ball must move from the back court to the front court.
30 seconds	The team with the ball must try for a goal.

BASKETBALL WORLD CHAMPIONS

Year	Men	Year	Women
1950	Argentina	1953	US
1954	US	1957	US
1959	Brazil	1959	USSR
1963	Brazil	1964	USSR
1967	USSR	1967	USSR
1970	Yugoslavia	1971	USSR
1974	USSR	1975	USSR
1978	Yugoslavia	1979	US
1982	USSR	1983	USSR
1986	US	1986	US
1990	Yugoslavia	1990	US
1994	US	1994	Brazil

STARTING JUMP
At the beginning of a match, the referee throws the ball up and two opponents jump to hit it. A player may tap the ball twice after it has reached its highest point.

The player stands near the center line, in his own half of the court.

SHOOTING
When attempting to score a basket, a player holds the ball high above his head and throws it toward the net.

MOVING WITH THE BALL
A player who has stopped while holding the ball may pivot on one foot, at the same time stepping in any direction with the other foot. A moving player may take one stride with the ball.

DRIBBLING
A player can progress with the ball by dribbling. He can take as many steps as he wishes while bouncing the ball.

VOLLEYBALL

- Volleyball is a ball game played between two teams of six players each.

- The aim of volleyball is to use any part of the body above the waist to send a ball over a net, so that the opposing team is unable to return it.

- A team may touch the ball up to three times before returning it over the net.

Length of court: 18m

Height of net: 1m

Width of court: 9m

UP AND OVER
Because of the height of the net, players have to jump up high in the air to hit the ball. Players must not touch or reach over the net. The ball is smaller than a basketball or netball.

NETBALL

- The aim in netball is to throw the ball into the opponent's net.

- The game is played between two teams of seven players each.

- Each player must keep to a particular area of the court.

NETBALL POSITIONS
Players wear letters to indicate their positions, and to show which zone they should stay in.

WA — Wing attack
GS — Goal shooter
GA — Goal attack
C — Center
WD — Wing defense
GK — Goalkeeper
GD — Goal defense

HANDBALL

- The aim is to pass or dribble the ball with the hands until a goal is scored.

- It is played between two teams of seven players each.

- Players may take three steps when holding the ball.

The player must not hold onto the ball for longer than three seconds.

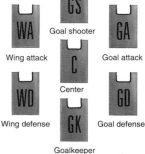

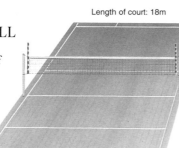

RUGBY

FACTS

• The aim of rugby is to score points by placing an oval-shaped ball on or over the opponent's goal line (a try), or by kicking it over the opponent's crossbar.

• Players may carry, pass, or kick the ball, but they cannot throw the ball in front of them.

• A game consists of two halves of 40 minutes each.

• There are two types of rugby: Rugby Union (R.U.), and Rugby League (R.L.).

SCORING

Type of goal	Points		Action
	R.U.	R.L.	
Try	5	4	Placing the ball by hand on or over the goal line.
Dropped goal	3	1	Ball is dropped and kicked over the crossbar.
Penalty goal	3	2	A penalty kick awarded for a foul.
Conversion	2	2	A goal kick awarded after a try.

PASSING THE BALL

A player can run while holding the ball, but must not pass forward. He should, however, pass to the front of the receiving player, to enable the player to run on to the ball.

Correct throw

Foul throw

LINE-OUT

A line-out is used to restart play after a ball crosses the touchline, or is "in-touch." At least two players from each team form separate lines at right angles to the touchline. The ball must be thrown straight between the two lines of players.

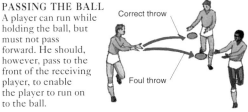

RUGBY LEAGUE

• This game developed from Rugby Union, and is played by professionals and amateurs.

• It is played by two teams of 13 players each.

• Rugby League, although very similar, follows slightly different rules from those of Rugby Union.

• One difference is that in Rugby League, players can restart the game after a tackle with the "play the ball" rule.

RUGBY UNION

• Rugby Union is the earliest and most widely played form of rugby.

• The game is played by amateurs only.

• There are two teams of 15 players each.

BALL

The oval-shaped ball is usually made of leather.

Length: 28cm

GEAR

Although rugby is a tough game, players are not allowed to wear protective clothing, apart from a scrum cap made of soft leather, shin guards, and a gum shield. Sweat bands are also often worn.

SHOES

Players may wear shoes similar to those worn by soccer players, or high-sided shoes to support the ankles.

FIELD

The field usually has a grass surface, but may be made of clay or sand.

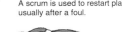

22m line
6m line
10m line
Halfway line

Length of field between the goal lines: 100m

Goal line

Dead ball line

Width of field: 69m

The goal is 5.6m wide; the height of the crossbar is 3m.

A scrum is used to restart play, usually after a foul.

SCRUM

Players from both teams close up around the ball and link arms. The front row must be made up of three players: a "hooker" and two "props" who stand on each side of him. The ball is thrown into the scrum and the hooker will try to hook the ball to his teammates behind him.

The scrum must not break up until the ball is cleared.

PLAY THE BALL RULE

A tackled player is allowed to drop the ball before kicking it in any direction, usually to a teammate behind him. This may be done for five consecutive tackles. After the sixth tackle, the team must give up possession.

Two members of the opposing team may stand directly in front of the player with the ball.

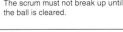
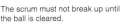

OLYMPIC RUGBY

Rugby was last staged at the Olympics in 1924, in Paris. There were three entrants: Romania, US, and France. US won the gold medal.

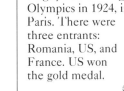

INTERNATIONAL RUGBY TEAMS

Each major international rugby team has its own symbol.

Australia

England

France

Ireland

New Zealand

Scotland

South Africa

Wales

RUGBY WORDS

Backs Players who position themselves behind a scrum.
Dummy Pretending to pass the ball to another player, while keeping possession.
Goal Combination of a try and conversion, worth seven points.
Knock-on The ball bouncing forward off the hand or arm of a player.
Loose-head prop The prop who is nearest to where the ball is put into the scrum.
Mark Place at which a free-kick or penalty kick is given.
Maul A scrum around a player carrying the ball.
Punt Dropping the ball and kicking it before it touches the ground.
Ruck A scrum around a player who has dropped the ball.
Touchdown A player grounding the ball in his own in-goal area.
Up-and-under A ball kicked high in the air, while players run upfield to catch it.

FOOTBALL

SOCCER

• Soccer, or Association football, is a ball game played by two teams of 11 players each.

• The aim is to hit the ball into the opponent's goal, and the team that scores the most goals wins.

• Players use their feet, head, thighs, and chest to hit or control the ball; only the goalkeeper may touch the ball with his hands or arms.

• A game consists of two periods, or halves, of 45 minutes each.

FORMATIONS
Soccer is a flexible game, but most teams start with players in a particular formation. The one shown below is 4–3–3. It uses four defenders, three midfielders, and three in attack.

The 4–3–3 formation

GEAR
Players wear jerseys with numbers on the back. The soles of the boots may be fitted with studs or bars.

Soccer boot

Fat rubber studs for hard ground.

Aluminum for wet, slippery ground.

Nylon for soft ground.

Shin pads must be worn under socks.

Soccer balls used in professional play are made of rubber encased in leather.

DRIBBLING
When dribbling, the player keeps the ball close to his feet, to prevent an opposing player taking the ball from him.

The player keeps close control of the ball while approaching his opponent.

In order to get round him, the player may pretend to go one way.

He then confuses his opponent by turning to go in the opposite direction.

FIELD

Width: 50-100yd

Center circle

Penalty spot

Length: 100-130yd

Penalty area

Goal area

Goal line

Goalpost length: 8yd; height: 8ft

WORLD CUP COMPETITIONS

Date	Host country	Winner
1930	Uruguay	Uruguay
1934	Italy	Italy
1938	France	Italy
1950	Brazil	Uruguay
1954	Switzerland	West Germany
1958	Sweden	Brazil
1962	Chile	Brazil
1966	England	England
1970	Mexico	Brazil
1974	West Germany	West Germany
1978	Argentina	Argentina
1982	Spain	Italy
1986	Mexico	Argentina
1990	Italy	West Germany
1994	US	Brazil

DEFENDING
A defender will often mark, or guard, one opponent throughout the game. Defenders must make strong tackles in order to take possession of the ball from their opponents.

Good timing is essential for a clean sliding tackle.

The defender must be careful not to foul his opponent.

GOALKEEPING
The goalkeeper can touch the ball with his hands, but only within his own penalty area. He is not allowed to pick up a back pass from a teammate.

He slides down in front of his opponent and wins the ball.

For a short pass, a goalkeeper will throw or roll the ball underarm.

Ideally, the ball is rolled along the ground for an accurate pass.

GOAL SCORING
Any player in a team may score a goal, but the main goal-scorers are called strikers, who must be able to shoot and head the ball accurately.

Opportunist sliding shot into goal.

MAJOR TEAMS
These are the basic colors worn by some of the top international teams. The flags are not part of the uniform.

Argentina Belgium Brazil Bulgaria Cameroon Colombia Denmark England France Germany Republic of Ireland

Italy Mexico Netherlands Nigeria Norway Poland Spain Sweden Switzerland Romania Uruguay US

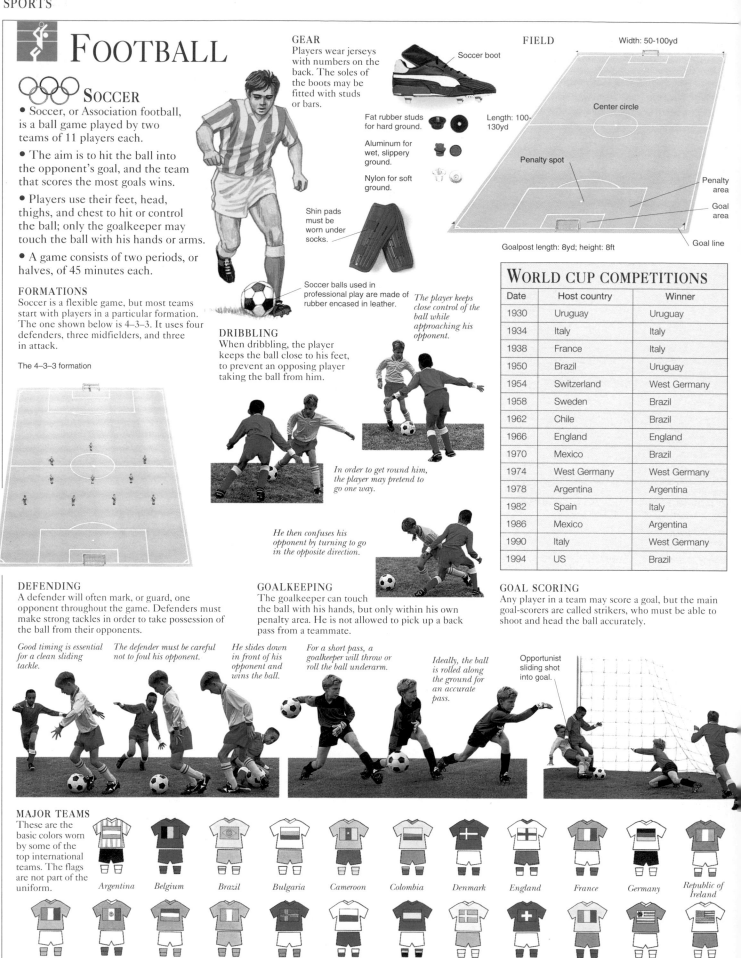

AMERICAN FOOTBALL

- American football is played by two teams of 11 players each, though frequent substitution is allowed and up to 40 people can play for each team.

- A team earns points by making a touchdown (putting the ball behind the opposing team's goal line), or by kicking the ball between the goal posts.

- A game consists of four quarters, of 15 minutes each.

GRIDIRON
The field is commonly called the gridiron, because the lines make it look like a cooking grill. The field is marked out in yards to show how far a team has advanced.

End line

End zone

Yardline every 5 yds

Length: 360ft

Height of crossbar: 10ft

Width of goal: 18ft 6in

Goal line

Width: 160ft

GEAR
There is a lot of physical contact in American football, so players wear several layers of protective clothing.

Chest protector

Groin protector

Shoulder pads

Leg pads

Helmets are made of tough plastic.

Face mask

Tight, knee-length pants lace up at the front.

BALL
The oval-shaped ball is made of leather, and has laces and a pebbled finish to provide a good grip.

SHIRT NUMBERS
NFL players are numbered according to their positions.

Number	Position
1-19	Quarterbacks, punters, kickers
20-49	Running and defensive backs
50-59	Centers and linebackers
60-79	Defensive linemen, offensive guards, and tackles
80-89	Wide receivers and tight ends
90-99	Defensive linemen

OFFENSE
The team that is in possession of the ball is the offense, or attacking team. They are allowed four attempts, or downs, at advancing with the ball by at least 10yd. If they fail to do this, their opponents gain possession of the ball.

The snap is the start of the down.

BLOCKING
A blocker may use the upper part of his body to obstruct an opponent who does not have the ball. He may use his arms to push, but not grab hold of, him. Blocking is used by offensive and defensive players.

DEFENSE
The team that does not have the ball uses its defense players, usually the biggest men, to try to prevent the offense from advancing and scoring. A defender needs to be a good tackler. He is allowed to push, pull, or grab the person in possession of the ball, who is called the runner. If the defense manages to get hold of the ball, it is called a turnover, and possession changes to the other team.

SCORING

Score	Points	Action
Touchdown	6	Taking the ball across the opponent's goal line, or gaining possession within the opponents' end zone.
Field goal	3	Place-kicking the ball through the goal posts.
Safety	2	Tackling an opponent who is carrying the ball behind his own goal line.
Extra point (conversion)	1	Kicking the ball through the goal posts from a scrimmage, after scoring a touchdown.

AUSTRALIAN FOOTBALL

- The game is played by two teams of 18 players. The aim is to score goals by kicking an oval-shaped ball between two tall posts.

- A player can kick, punch, and run with the ball, but he must not throw it.

- A game consists of 4 quarters, lasting 25 minutes each.

FIELD
The game is played on an oval-shaped field. Six points are scored for kicking the ball between the two central "goal" posts.

One point is given for scoring between the outer, or "behind" posts.

FOOTBALL LEAGUE
American football is the major national sport in the US. There are 28 teams in the National Football League (NFL), each with its own distinctive helmet design.

Atlanta Falcons

Buffalo Bills

Chicago Bears

Cincinnati Bengals

Cleveland Browns

Dallas Cowboys

Denver Broncos

Detroit Lions

Green Bay Packers

Houston Oilers

Indianapolis Colts

Kansas City Chiefs

Los Angeles Raiders

Los Angeles Rams

Miami Dolphins

Minnesota Vikings

New England Patriots

New Orleans Saints

New York Giants

New York Jets

Pittsburgh Steelers

Philadelphia Eagles

St. Louis Cardinals

San Diego Chargers

San Francisco Forty-niners

Seattle Seahawks

Tampa Bay Buccaneers

Washington Redskins

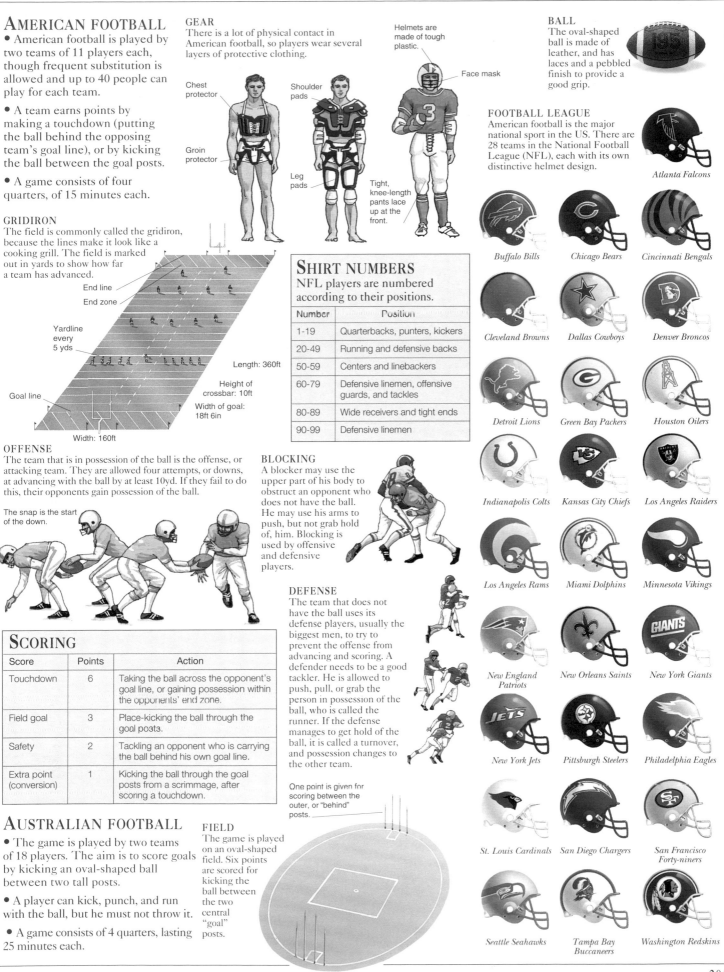

CRICKET

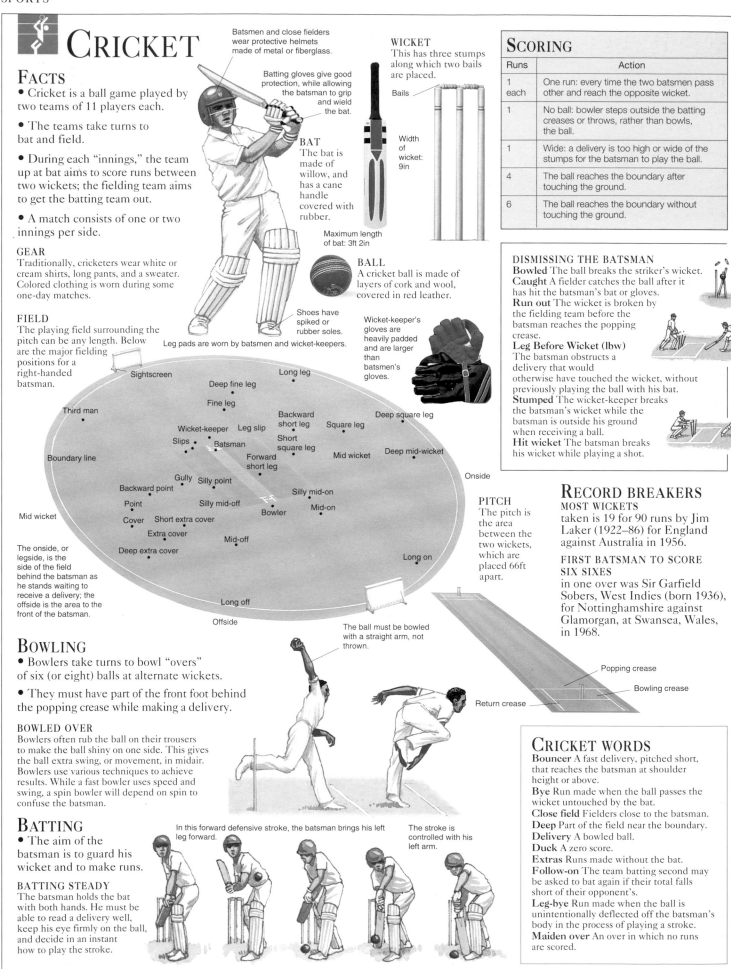

FACTS

- Cricket is a ball game played by two teams of 11 players each.

- The teams take turns to bat and field.

- During each "innings," the team up at bat aims to score runs between two wickets; the fielding team aims to get the batting team out.

- A match consists of one or two innings per side.

GEAR

Traditionally, cricketers wear white or cream shirts, long pants, and a sweater. Colored clothing is worn during some one-day matches.

FIELD

The playing field surrounding the pitch can be any length. Below are the major fielding positions for a right-handed batsman.

The onside, or legside, is the side of the field behind the batsman as he stands waiting to receive a delivery; the offside is the area to the front of the batsman.

Batsmen and close fielders wear protective helmets made of metal or fiberglass.

Batting gloves give good protection, while allowing the batsman to grip and wield the bat.

BAT
The bat is made of willow, and has a cane handle covered with rubber.

Maximum length of bat: 3ft 2in

WICKET
This has three stumps along which two bails are placed.

Bails

Width of wicket: 9in

BALL
A cricket ball is made of layers of cork and wool, covered in red leather.

Shoes have spiked or rubber soles.

Leg pads are worn by batsmen and wicket-keepers.

Wicket-keeper's gloves are heavily padded and are larger than batsmen's gloves.

Field positions: Sightscreen, Deep fine leg, Long leg, Fine leg, Backward short leg, Square leg, Deep square leg, Wicket-keeper, Leg slip, Short square leg, Deep mid-wicket, Slips, Batsman, Mid wicket, Forward short leg, Third man, Boundary line, Gully, Silly point, Silly mid-on, Backward point, Point, Silly mid-off, Mid-on, Cover, Short extra cover, Bowler, Extra cover, Mid-off, Deep extra cover, Mid wicket, Long on, Long off, Onside, Offside

BOWLING

- Bowlers take turns to bowl "overs" of six (or eight) balls at alternate wickets.

- They must have part of the front foot behind the popping crease while making a delivery.

BOWLED OVER

Bowlers often rub the ball on their trousers to make the ball shiny on one side. This gives the ball extra swing, or movement, in midair. Bowlers use various techniques to achieve results. While a fast bowler uses speed and swing, a spin bowler will depend on spin to confuse the batsman.

The ball must be bowled with a straight arm, not thrown.

BATTING

- The aim of the batsman is to guard his wicket and to make runs.

BATTING STEADY

The batsman holds the bat with both hands. He must be able to read a delivery well, keep his eye firmly on the ball, and decide in an instant how to play the stroke.

In this forward defensive stroke, the batsman brings his left leg forward.

The stroke is controlled with his left arm.

SCORING

Runs	Action
1 each	One run: every time the two batsmen pass other and reach the opposite wicket.
1	No ball: bowler steps outside the batting creases or throws, rather than bowls, the ball.
1	Wide: a delivery is too high or wide of the stumps for the batsman to play the ball.
4	The ball reaches the boundary after touching the ground.
6	The ball reaches the boundary without touching the ground.

DISMISSING THE BATSMAN
Bowled The ball breaks the striker's wicket.
Caught A fielder catches the ball after it has hit the batsman's bat or gloves.
Run out The wicket is broken by the fielding team before the batsman reaches the popping crease.
Leg Before Wicket (lbw) The batsman obstructs a delivery that would otherwise have touched the wicket, without previously playing the ball with his bat.
Stumped The wicket-keeper breaks the batsman's wicket while the batsman is outside his ground when receiving a ball.
Hit wicket The batsman breaks his wicket while playing a shot.

PITCH
The pitch is the area between the two wickets, which are placed 66ft apart.

RECORD BREAKERS
MOST WICKETS
taken is 19 for 90 runs by Jim Laker (1922–86) for England against Australia in 1956.

FIRST BATSMAN TO SCORE SIX SIXES
in one over was Sir Garfield Sobers, West Indies (born 1936), for Nottinghamshire against Glamorgan, at Swansea, Wales, in 1968.

Popping crease
Bowling crease
Return crease

CRICKET WORDS
Bouncer A fast delivery, pitched short, that reaches the batsman at shoulder height or above.
Bye Run made when the ball passes the wicket untouched by the bat.
Close field Fielders close to the batsman.
Deep Part of the field near the boundary.
Delivery A bowled ball.
Duck A zero score.
Extras Runs made without the bat.
Follow-on The team batting second may be asked to bat again if their total falls short of their opponent's.
Leg-bye Run made when the ball is unintentionally deflected off the batsman's body in the process of playing a stroke.
Maiden over An over in which no runs are scored.

BASEBALL

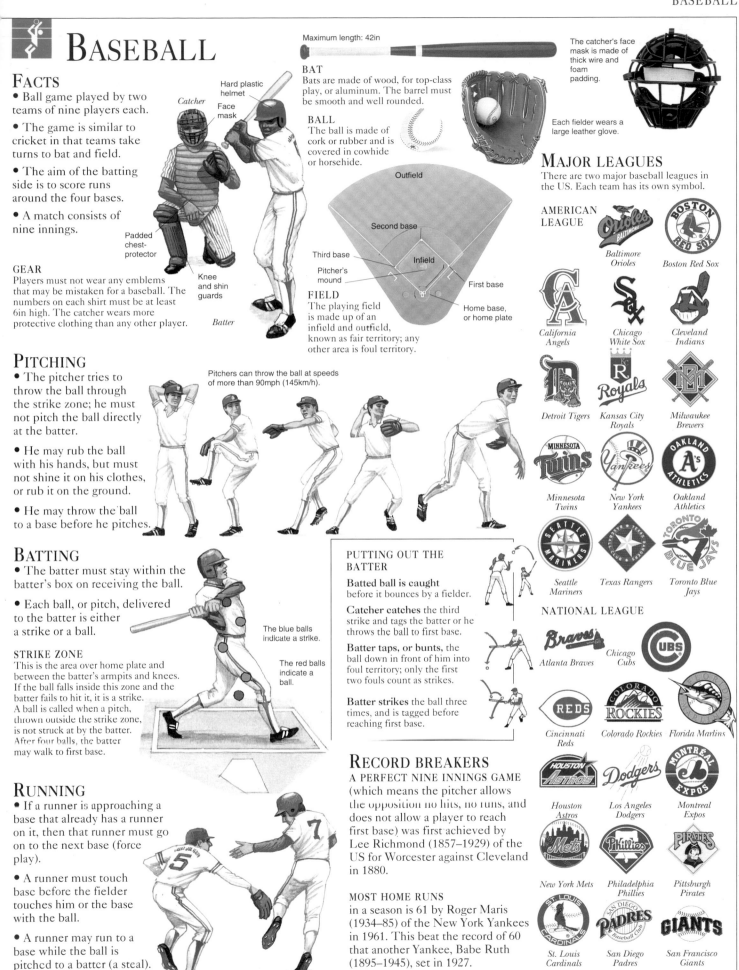

Maximum length: 42in

BAT
Bats are made of wood, for top-class play, or aluminum. The barrel must be smooth and well rounded.

The catcher's face mask is made of thick wire and foam padding.

FACTS

• Ball game played by two teams of nine players each.

• The game is similar to cricket in that teams take turns to bat and field.

• The aim of the batting side is to score runs around the four bases.

• A match consists of nine innings.

Catcher

Hard plastic helmet

Face mask

Padded chest-protector

Knee and shin guards

Batter

BALL
The ball is made of cork or rubber and is covered in cowhide or horsehide.

Each fielder wears a large leather glove.

Outfield

Second base

Third base

Pitcher's mound

Infield

First base

Home base, or home plate

FIELD
The playing field is made up of an infield and outfield, known as fair territory; any other area is foul territory.

GEAR
Players must not wear any emblems that may be mistaken for a baseball. The numbers on each shirt must be at least 6in high. The catcher wears more protective clothing than any other player.

MAJOR LEAGUES
There are two major baseball leagues in the US. Each team has its own symbol.

AMERICAN LEAGUE

Baltimore Orioles | *Boston Red Sox*

California Angels | *Chicago White Sox* | *Cleveland Indians*

Detroit Tigers | *Kansas City Royals* | *Milwaukee Brewers*

Minnesota Twins | *New York Yankees* | *Oakland Athletics*

Seattle Mariners | *Texas Rangers* | *Toronto Blue Jays*

PITCHING

• The pitcher tries to throw the ball through the strike zone; he must not pitch the ball directly at the batter.

• He may rub the ball with his hands, but must not shine it on his clothes, or rub it on the ground.

• He may throw the ball to a base before he pitches.

Pitchers can throw the ball at speeds of more than 90mph (145km/h).

NATIONAL LEAGUE

Atlanta Braves | *Chicago Cubs*

Cincinnati Reds | *Colorado Rockies* | *Florida Marlins*

BATTING

• The batter must stay within the batter's box on receiving the ball.

• Each ball, or pitch, delivered to the batter is either a strike or a ball.

STRIKE ZONE
This is the area over home plate and between the batter's armpits and knees. If the ball falls inside this zone and the batter fails to hit it, it is a strike. A ball is called when a pitch, thrown outside the strike zone, is not struck at by the batter. After four balls, the batter may walk to first base.

The blue balls indicate a strike.

The red balls indicate a ball.

PUTTING OUT THE BATTER

Batted ball is caught before it bounces by a fielder.

Catcher catches the third strike and tags the batter or he throws the ball to first base.

Batter taps, or bunts, the ball down in front of him into foul territory; only the first two fouls count as strikes.

Batter strikes the ball three times, and is tagged before reaching first base.

RUNNING

• If a runner is approaching a base that already has a runner on it, then that runner must go on to the next base (force play).

• A runner must touch base before the fielder touches him or the base with the ball.

• A runner may run to a base while the ball is pitched to a batter (a steal).

RECORD BREAKERS
A PERFECT NINE INNINGS GAME (which means the pitcher allows the opposition no hits, no runs, and does not allow a player to reach first base) was first achieved by Lee Richmond (1857–1929) of the US for Worcester against Cleveland in 1880.

MOST HOME RUNS in a season is 61 by Roger Maris (1934–85) of the New York Yankees in 1961. This beat the record of 60 that another Yankee, Babe Ruth (1895–1945), set in 1927.

Houston Astros | *Los Angeles Dodgers* | *Montreal Expos*

New York Mets | *Philadelphia Phillies* | *Pittsburgh Pirates*

St. Louis Cardinals | *San Diego Padres* | *San Francisco Giants*

STICK GAMES

HOCKEY

- Hockey has 11 players on each team; the aim is to shoot a ball with hooked sticks into the opposing team's goal.

- Goals may be scored only from within the striking, or shooting, circle.

- A game consists of two 35-minute halves.

STICK
Hockey sticks are steam bent, so that the grain of the wood follows the bend. This helps strengthen the stick. The ball may be struck with the flat face of the stick only.

The stick weighs between 12oz and 28oz for men, and up to 23oz for women.

BALL
The ball is traditionally white and is made of cork and twine, with a leather casing.

BULLY
The bully is a distinctive feature of hockey. It is used to restart the game after certain stoppages. A player from each side stands over the ball. They tap the ground and each other's sticks alternately three times before attempting to play the ball.

GEAR
Players wear a shirt and skirt, or shorts, and guards on their shins and ankles. The goalkeeper wears extra protective clothing.

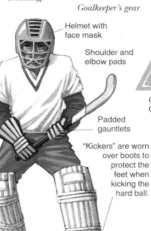

Goalkeeper's gear

Helmet with face mask

Shoulder and elbow pads

Padded gauntlets

"Kickers" are worn over boots to protect the feet when kicking the hard ball.

Light-weight leg guards

PITCH
Hockey is usually played outdoors, on grass or on artificial surfaces.

Width: 60yd

Length: 100yd

Goal height: 7ft
Goal width: 12ft

Shooting circle; goals can only be scored from inside here.

OLYMPIC HOCKEY CHAMPIONS (MEN)

Year	Country
1908	Britain
1920	Britain
1928	India
1932	India
1936	India
1948	India
1952	India
1956	India
1960	Pakistan
1964	India
1968	Pakistan
1972	West Germany
1976	New Zealand
1980	India
1984	Pakistan
1988	Britain
1992	Germany

OLYMPIC HOCKEY CHAMPIONS (WOMEN)

Year	Country
1980	Zimbabwe
1984	Netherlands
1988	Australia
1992	Spain

ICE HOCKEY

- Ice hockey has six players, with up to 14 substitutes.

- The aim is to send a disk, called a puck, into the opponent's goal.

- There are three periods, of 20 minutes each.

ICE HOCKEY PENALTIES

Type	Minutes in "Sin Bin"
Minor	2
Major	5
Misconduct	10*
Match	Rest of game**

*Substitute may replace immediately.
**Substitute may replace after 5 minutes.

Goalkeeper's stick

Outfielder's stick

Puck is traditionally black and made from vulcanized rubber.

Width: 29–30m

ICE HOCKEY STICKS
The outfielder's stick has a shaft with an angled blade. The goalkeeper's stick is heavier and has a wider blade.

There are four face-off circles.

Goal width: 2.53m
Goal height: 1.22m

Length: 60–61m

RINK
The rink is an iced surface surrounded by wooden boards.

OLYMPIC ICE-HOCKEY CHAMPIONS

Year	Country
1920	Canada
1924	Canada
1928	Canada
1932	Canada
1936	Britain
1948	Canada
1952	Canada
1956	USSR
1960	US
1964	USSR
1968	USSR
1972	USSR
1976	USSR
1980	US
1984	USSR
1988	USSR
1992	CIS
1994	Sweden

LACROSSE

- Players use a net on the end of their stick (crosse) to carry and pass a ball and try to send it into the opposing team's goal.

- The men's and women's games are played under different rules. One of the main differences is that physical contact is allowed in the men's game, but not in the women's.

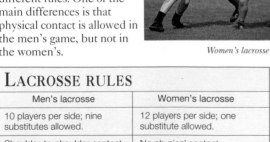

Women's lacrosse

LACROSSE RULES

Men's lacrosse	Women's lacrosse
10 players per side; nine substitutes allowed.	12 players per side; one substitute allowed.
Shoulder-to-shoulder contact and body-checking allowed.	No physical contact allowed.
Time: four 15-min periods.	Time: two 25-min periods.
Playing field usually measures 100m x 55m.	No measured boundaries.
Crosse measures: 1–1.8m.	Crosse measures: 0.9–1.1m.

HOCKEY SPEEDS
Ice hockey is the fastest team game in the world. The puck is hit at speeds of up to 118mph (190km/h). A hockey ball is hit at speeds of up to 100mph (160km/h).

GOLF

FACTS

• A standard golf course has 18 holes of various lengths (a round).

• There are two main types of competition: stroke play and match play.

• In stroke play, the player who completes a round in the fewest strokes wins the match; in match play the winner is the one who wins the most holes in a round.

Wood
Woods, or drivers, are used for long shots. They are numbered 1–9. Their large heads may be made from wood, plastic, or light metal.

Iron
Irons are used for a variety of shots. The steel heads are numbered 1–10. The lower numbers hit the ball farthest and lowest.

Putter
Putters are used mainly on the putting green. Unlike the other clubs, they have two striking faces. They are the lightest of the clubs.

CLUBS
Players may not start or play a round of golf with more than 14 clubs. Most players use three or four woods, nine or ten irons, and one putter.

BALL
Golf balls are covered in more than 400 dimples. They help the ball travel farther and straighter through the air.

Golf bag and trolley

TEES
Tees are small, usually plastic, pegs on which the ball is placed for the first shot to a hole.

COURSE
Courses vary in length from 100 to 600yd (90–550m). The length determines the "par" of each hole: the average number of strokes needed to get the ball into the hole.

The teeing ground, from which the first stroke is made, is a smooth, level area.

SWING TECHNIQUE
The swing is one continuous, smooth action.

The upper body turns as the arms swing up and back (the backswing).

As the club is brought down, the weight is moved from the back foot to the front foot.

Weight is fully on the left foot as the swing is followed through.

The rough is uneven land surrounding the fairway.

The head is kept down as the club makes contact with the ball.

The body faces the target as the club is brought past the left shoulder.

The fairway is a closely mown strip of ground which stretches from tee to green, along which the players attempt to play the ball.

Hazards may include ponds, streams, and sand bunkers.

Sand bunker

Flagstick

Diameter of hole: 4.25in (10.8cm)

The apron is the short grass surrounding the green.

The putting green is the smooth, grassy area that surrounds the hole.

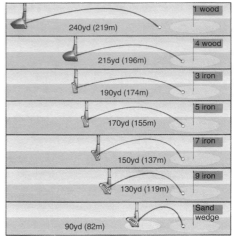

STRIKING DISTANCES

240yd (219m)	1 wood
215yd (196m)	4 wood
190yd (174m)	3 iron
170yd (155m)	5 iron
150yd (137m)	7 iron
130yd (119m)	9 iron
90yd (82m)	Sand wedge

MAJOR GOLF TOURNAMENTS

Tournament	First held
British Open	1860
US Open	1895
US PGA	1916
US Masters	1934
Ryder Cup (male team event)	1927
Curtis Cup (female team event)	1932

LONG SHOT
In a qualifying match in Pennsylvania, in the early 1900s, one entrant drove her ball into a river at the 16th hole. She set out in a boat to reach it, and finally completed the hole in 166 shots.

GOLF WORDS

Approach Shot played to the green from the fairway or rough.

Birdie A score of one stroke under par for a hole.

Bogey A score of one stroke over par for a hole.

Eagle A score of two strokes under par for a hole.

Fourball Two play against two, each player having one ball, the lower score of each pair being their score at a hole.

Foursome Two play against two, each side having one ball and taking alternate strokes at each hole.

Handicap Number of strokes a player may subtract from his or her score for a round; enables players of different abilities to compete on equal terms.

Hole A complete section, from tee to putting green; the round hole into which the ball is played.

Par The standard score for a hole or round (18 holes) on a course, based on what a top player would be expected to shoot, and allowing for two putts.

Tee The ground that marks the start of a hole; a peg on which the ball is put for the first stroke of a hole.

WATER SPORTS

ROWING

- Rowing is a racing sport for boats containing one, two, four, or eight rowers, sometimes with a cox to steer.

- In sculling, each rower uses two oars instead of one.

- Races in major championships, or regattas, take place in lanes over a distance of 2,000m.

- In head-of-the-river, or processional, races, crews start at intervals and race against the clock.

BOAT
Rowing boats used in racing vary in length depending on the event, but the basic design remains the same.

Boats are made from wood or reinforced plastic.

ROWING TECHNIQUE
The rowers lean forward, legs are bent and arms are straight.

Safety helmets are worn by canoeists on rough or rocky courses.

Light, padded buoyancy aids are worn by canoeists.

Wetsuits give protection in wet weather and in cold water; they are worn by sailors and windsurfers.

Rowers wear singlets or T-shirts, and shorts.

WATER SPORT GEAR
Competitors must wear safety equipment for most water sports. Lifejackets are worn for yachting, water skiing, and powerboat racing. Buoyancy aids are less bulky than lifejackets and are worn in canoeing.

OLYMPIC ROWING EVENTS

Event	Approximate length of boat	
Sculls		26ft (8m)
Double sculls		33ft (10m)
Quadruple sculls		43ft (13m)
Coxless pairs		33ft (10m)
Coxed pairs (men only)		36ft (11m)
Coxless fours		43ft (13m)
Coxed fours (men only)		46ft (14m)
Eights		56ft (17m)

SCULLING TECHNIQUE
The rower holds the blades just above the water.

He leans forward and bends his knees as he pulls the oars through the water.

He straightens his legs, and then his back when the oars are at right angles to the boat.

He leans back, arms bent, and pulls the oars up out of the water.

Their backs straighten as they pull the blades through the water.

They lean back, arms bent, as they pull the oars out of the water.

CANOEING

- There are two main types of competition boats: the kayak and the Canadian canoe.

- The kayak has a closed deck. The paddler sits inside, with legs outstretched underneath the deck. The paddle has a blade at each end.

- Most Canadian canoes have an open deck. The paddler sits or kneels in the canoe and uses a single-bladed paddle.

Kayak — Stern — Cockpit — Bow — Double-bladed paddle

Canoe — Bow — Stern — Thwart — Single-bladed paddle

SPRINT RACING
Sprint races take place on water that is as still as possible. Kayaks race in lanes, usually over distances of 500m or 1,000m. Some courses have windbreaks to limit the effect of crosswinds.

Men's K2 race

OLYMPIC CANOEING EVENTS

Type of boat	Length (max.)	Event	
		Male	Female
K1	5.20m	500m, 1,000m, slalom	500m, slalom
K2	6.50m	500m, 1,000m	500m
K4	11m	1,000m	500m
C1	5.20m	500m, 1,000m, slalom	—
C2	6.50m	500m, 1,000m, slalom	—

K=Kayak, C=Canadian, 1=singles, 2=twos, 4=fours

LONG-DISTANCE RACING
In 5,000m and 10,000m races, canoeists paddle around buoys at each end of the course. Marathons range from 5km to 200km and more in length. Competitors avoid obstacles, such as locks or waterfalls, by carrying their canoes along the bank (portage).

Canoe marathon

WHITEWATER RACING
There are two types of whitewater racing. In wildwater racing, paddlers are timed over a course that includes obstacles such as rocks and rapids. In slalom, paddlers negotiate multiple gates.

Slalom

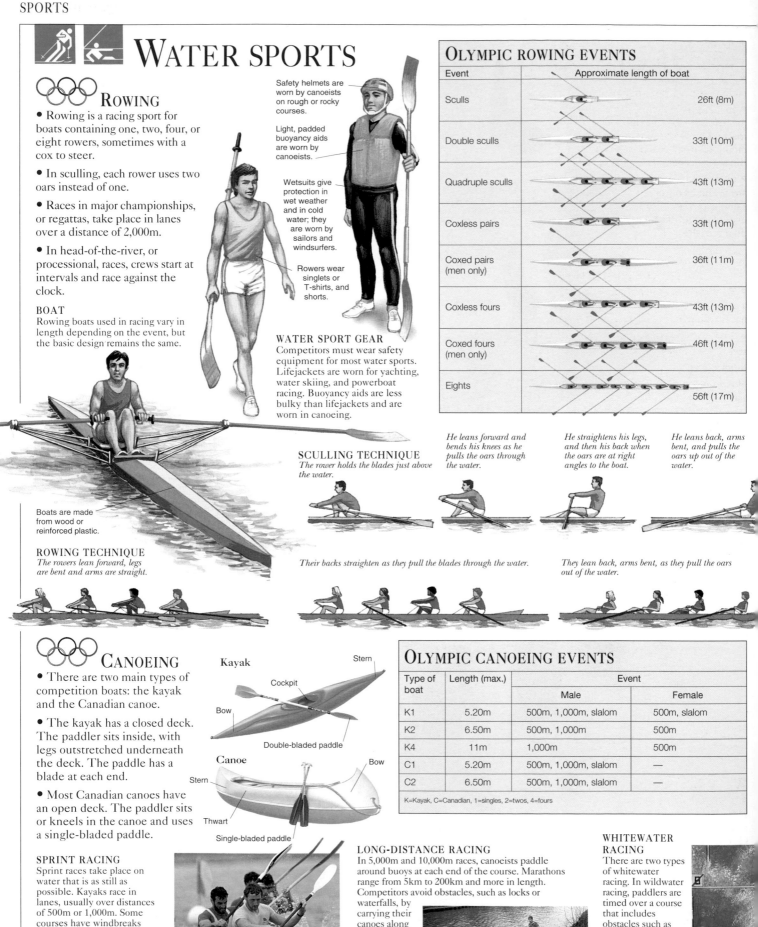

SAILING

- There are two types of yacht racing: inshore and offshore.

- Inshore racing takes place just off the coast on courses marked by buoys. Offshore racing takes place across the sea or ocean.

- One-design events are for boats of the same class. Handicap events are for boats of different designs.

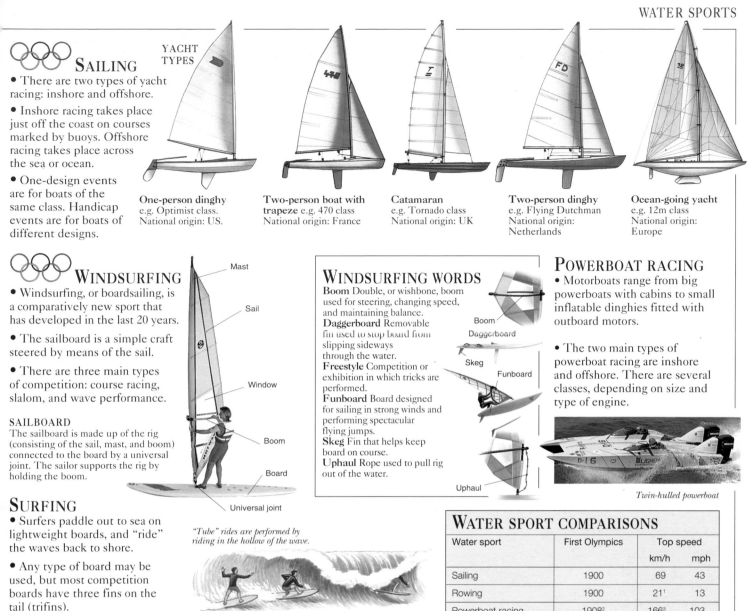

YACHT TYPES

One-person dinghy
e.g. Optimist class.
National origin: US.

Two-person boat with trapeze e.g. 470 class
National origin: France

Catamaran
e.g. Tornado class
National origin: UK

Two-person dinghy
e.g. Flying Dutchman
National origin:
Netherlands

Ocean-going yacht
e.g. 12m class
National origin:
Europe

WINDSURFING

- Windsurfing, or boardsailing, is a comparatively new sport that has developed in the last 20 years.

- The sailboard is a simple craft steered by means of the sail.

- There are three main types of competition: course racing, slalom, and wave performance.

SAILBOARD
The sailboard is made up of the rig (consisting of the sail, mast, and boom) connected to the board by a universal joint. The sailor supports the rig by holding the boom.

Labels: Mast, Sail, Window, Boom, Board, Universal joint

WINDSURFING WORDS
Boom Double, or wishbone, boom used for steering, changing speed, and maintaining balance.
Daggerboard Removable fin used to stop board from slipping sideways through the water.
Freestyle Competition or exhibition in which tricks are performed.
Funboard Board designed for sailing in strong winds and performing spectacular flying jumps.
Skeg Fin that helps keep board on course.
Uphaul Rope used to pull rig out of the water.

Labels: Boom, Daggerboard, Skeg, Funboard, Uphaul

POWERBOAT RACING
- Motorboats range from big powerboats with cabins to small inflatable dinghies fitted with outboard motors.

- The two main types of powerboat racing are inshore and offshore. There are several classes, depending on size and type of engine.

Twin-hulled powerboat

SURFING

- Surfers paddle out to sea on lightweight boards, and "ride" the waves back to shore.

- Any type of board may be used, but most competition boards have three fins on the tail (trifins).

GEAR
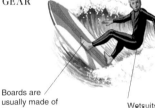
Boards are usually made of fiberglass.

Wetsuits are worn in cold conditions.

"Tube" rides are performed by riding in the hollow of the wave.

SURFING MOVES
Surfers perform a variety of moves. Judges assess surfers for style, grace, and timing, and award points, depending on the difficulty of the wave, for various aspects of the ride.

In a "turn," the surfer turns and cuts back through the wave.

WATER SPORT COMPARISONS

Water sport	First Olympics	Top speed	
		km/h	mph
Sailing	1900	69	43
Rowing	1900	21[1]	13
Powerboat racing	1908[2]	166[3]	103
Canoeing	1936	20[4]	12
Whitewater canoeing	1972	–	–
Windsurfing	1984	82	51
Water-skiing	–	230	143

(1) Average Olympic record speed for an eight over 2km. (2) Only inclusion. (3) Much higher speeds have been reached by boats specially designed for record breaking. (4) Average Olympic record speed for a K4 over 1km.

WATER-SKIING

- The water-skier is towed behind a motorboat, which needs a speed of at least 19mph (30km/h) to keep the skier upright. Competitions are divided into three sections.

Labels: Lifejacket, Ramp

SLALOM
Skiers negotiate a series of buoys while crossing the boat's wake. There are six buoys on each run, or pass, with a gate at each end. Each successive pass is made with a faster boat speed to a maximum of 36mph (58km/h) for men or 34mph (55km/h) for women.

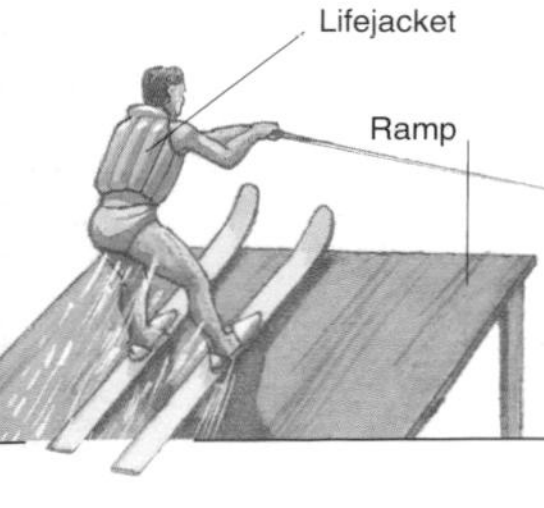

JUMPING
This is performed from a ramp and is judged on distance.

TRICKS
Points are awarded for a variety of moves, such as a backward turn, performed while being towed.

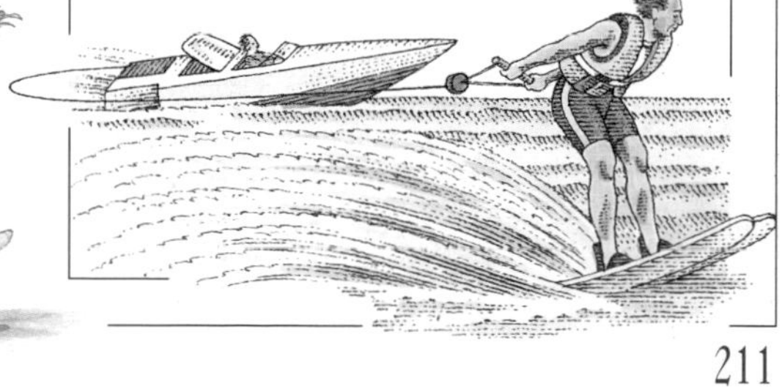

SPEEDY SKIS
The world water-skiing speed record is more than 124mph (200km/h), which is more than three times the speed of the boat. A skier will cross from side to side behind the towing motorboat, and so can travel much faster.

SWIMMING AND DIVING

SWIMMING

- There are four strokes in competitive swimming: freestyle (swimmers always use the front crawl), backstroke, breaststroke, and butterfly.

- Competitors dive from starting blocks in all events (except for backstroke), and race in lanes.

- They are timed to one-thousandth of a second by touching sensitive pads at the end of the race.

RACING FACTS

- Swimmers must not leave their starting blocks until the starter fires the gun or, as in relay races, until the previous swimmer in their team has touched the electronic pad.

- Rules govern the style of each stroke (except for freestyle), including the turns made at the ends of the pool.

- In the individual medley race, competitors swim each quarter with a different stroke in the following order: butterfly, backstroke, breaststroke, and freestyle.

DIVING

- Competitive diving is a sport in which contestants are awarded points by judges.

- There are two divisions of diving: springboard and platform, or highboard, diving.

Forward dive

Forward dives may be performed from a run-up or standing position.

In the layout position, the body should not be bent at the hips or knees.

The diver must keep his feet together and his toes pointed.

He must keep his body as straight as possible when entering the water.

GEAR

Swim cap

Goggles are worn to protect the eyes from chemicals in the water.

Women and men wear light, tight-fitting nylon racing suits.

POOL

Length: 50m

Starting block

Width of each lane: 2.5m

STROKES

Front crawl
This is the fastest stroke and is used in freestyle races.

The swimmer moves his legs up and down from the hips.

His arms and legs move alternately.

He keeps his body as straight and flat as possible.

Breaststroke
This is the slowest stroke. Arms and legs stay underwater.

Her arms move together, circling from an outstretched position around and under the chin.

Her legs move together with a froglike kick.

Backstroke
This is the only racing stroke in which the swimmers start in the water.

Her arms pull alternately in a "windmill" motion.

Her body is kept as straight as possible.

Butterfly
Like the breaststroke, this is a symmetrical stroke.

The swimmer uses a strong, double-arm pull to propel himself through the water.

He uses an up-and-down "dolphin kick" of the legs.

TYPES OF DIVE

The six types of dive are: forward, backward, twist, inward, reverse, and armstand. Within these six groups, there are many different starting positions and varieties of moves in the air, making a total of more than 100 recognized dives.

Backward dive

In the starting position, the diver must keep his body straight and his head up; his arms swing upward just before leaving the platform or springboard.

Armstand dive

Armstand dives are made from the platform only.

Reverse dive

A reverse dive (body facing away from board or platform) in the pike position

Twist dive

The diver performs a twist in midair.

Inward dive

An inward dive in the tuck position

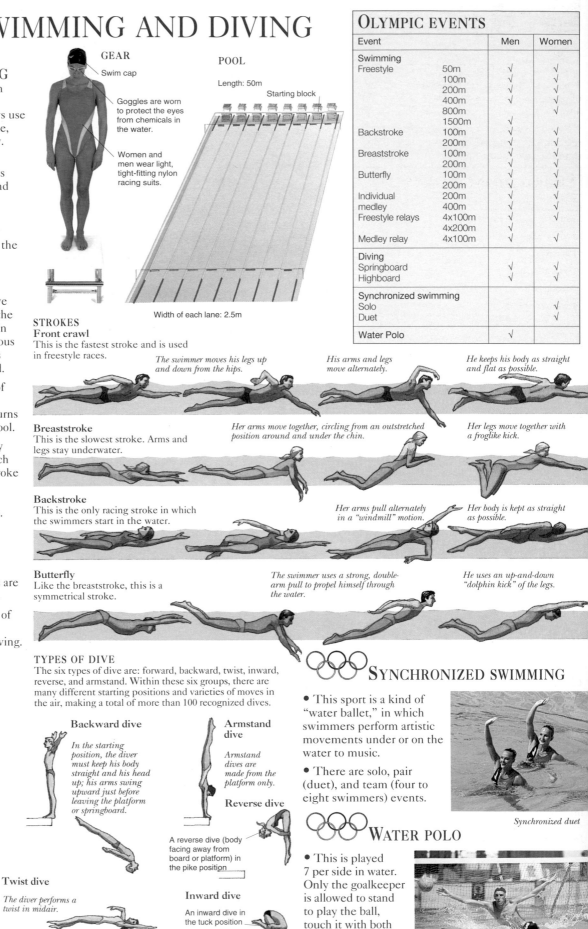

OLYMPIC EVENTS

Event		Men	Women
Swimming			
Freestyle	50m	√	√
	100m	√	√
	200m	√	√
	400m	√	√
	800m		√
	1500m	√	
Backstroke	100m	√	√
	200m	√	√
Breaststroke	100m	√	√
	200m	√	√
Butterfly	100m	√	√
	200m	√	√
Individual medley	200m	√	√
	400m	√	√
Freestyle relays	4x100m	√	√
	4x200m	√	√
Medley relay	4x100m	√	√
Diving			
Springboard		√	√
Highboard		√	√
Synchronized swimming			
Solo			√
Duet			√
Water Polo		√	

SYNCHRONIZED SWIMMING

- This sport is a kind of "water ballet," in which swimmers perform artistic movements under or on the water to music.

- There are solo, pair (duet), and team (four to eight swimmers) events.

Synchronized duet

WATER POLO

- This is played 7 per side in water. Only the goalkeeper is allowed to stand to play the ball, touch it with both hands, or punch it.

EQUESTRIAN

SHOW JUMPING

- Riders take their mounts around a course of obstacles such as gates, walls, fences, and a water jump.

- Penalty faults are given for errors such as a refusal, knocking off a pole, or taking longer than the specified time.

SHOW-JUMPING FAULTS

Error	Faults
Fence (or part of fence) down	4
Foot in water	4
Refusal	3
2nd refusal	6
3rd refusal	Elimination
Fall (horse or rider)	8
Exceeding time allowance	1/4 per second
Taking jumps out of sequence	Elimination

COMPETITION APPAREL
Riders must wear a hard hat or crash helmet, and formal dress for show jumping and dressage competitions.

Riding hat

Jacket

Bridle, made of adjustable lengths of leather

Gloves

Whip

Jodhpurs

Boots

Saddle

SHOW-JUMPING COURSE

Gate

Triple bars

Start

Wall

Finish

JUMPING TECHNIQUE
When jumping, the rider should bend forward from the hips and look up. On landing, the body must straighten up to take weight off the horse's front legs.

Takeoff

Flight

Landing

DRESSAGE

- Riders take their mounts through an official test made up of a variety of paces, movements, and figures.

- Marks are awarded for the quality of the test performance.

Walk

Canter

Trot

THREE-DAY EVENT

- Riders take their mounts through three different disciplines over three days: day one, dressage; day two, speed and endurance; day three, show jumping.

- Speed and endurance is made up of four phases (see table).

Clearing a water jump in the three-day event.

SPEED AND ENDURANCE

Phase	Distance	Details
A Roads and tracks	16-20km	Trot or slow canter
B Steeplechase	approx. 3.5-4km	9 or 10 fences
C Roads and tracks	16-20km	Trot or slow canter
D Cross-country	up to 8km	28-32 obstacles

POLO

- Polo is a game played by two teams of four players. The aim is to hit a ball between the opposition's goalposts with a long stick called a mallet.

Polo

HARNESS RACING

- The horses pull their drivers around an oval track on light, two-wheeled "sulkies." Most races are 1 mile long.

Harness racing

HORSE RACING

- Flat races are for horses of 2 years old and over, most are from 5 furlongs to 1.5 miles long, with no jumps.

- Hurdle races are for 3-year-olds and over; they are from 2 to 3.25 miles long.

- Steeplechases have fences instead of hurdles. They are for 4-year-olds and over, and are from 2 to about 4.5 miles long.

MAJOR HORSE RACES

Race	Course	Distance	Type
Preakness	Pimlico Park, US	1 mile, 1f	Flat
Belmont	Belmont Park, US	1 mile, 4f	Flat
Derby	Epsom, England	1 mile, 4f*	Flat
Breeder's Cup	Location varies, US	1 mile, 2f	Flat
St. Leger	Doncaster, England	1 mile, 6f, 132yd	Flat
Irish Derby	The Curragh, Ireland	1 mile, 4f	Flat
Arc de Triomphe	Longchamp, France	2,400m	Flat
Kentucky Derby	Churchill Downs, US	1 mile, 2f	Flat
Melbourne Cup	Melbourne, Australia	3,200m	Flat
Grand National	Aintree, England	4 mile, 4f	Steeplechase
Cheltenham Gold Cup	Cheltenham, England	3 miles, 2f	Steeplechase
Champion Hurdle	Cheltenham, England	2 miles	Hurdle

*f = furlong (220yd); 8 furlongs = one miile

RECORD BREAKERS

ONLY THREE-TIME WINNER of the Grand National horse race in England is Red Rum, who won it in 1973, 1974, and 1977.

MOST WINS IN HORSE RACING is 8,833 in 40,350 races by US jockey Bill Shoemaker (born 1931), who rode his first winner in March 1949 and retired in 1990.

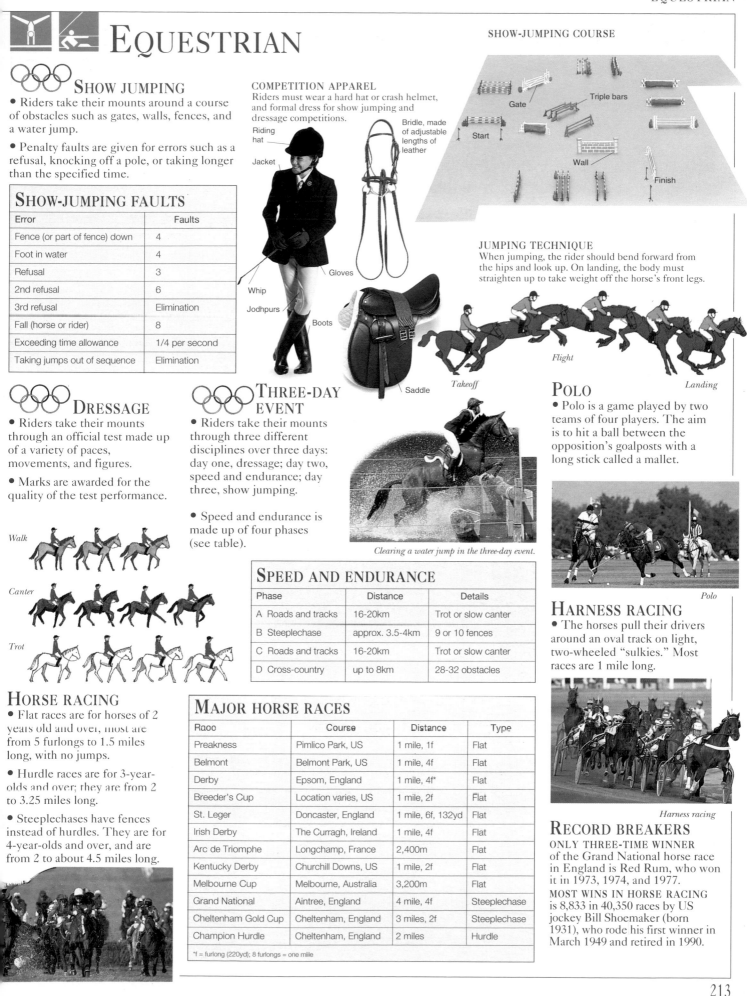

WINTER SPORTS

SKIING

- There are two basic groups: alpine, which includes downhill and slalom racing, and nordic, which includes cross-country and ski jumping.

- Alpine skiing comes from the Alps; nordic skiing comes from northern Europe.

GEAR
Ski racers wear one-piece outfits made of spandex, which give little wind resistance.

SKI POLES
Poles should be made of a strong, light material such as aluminum. The basket stops the pole from sinking too deep into the snow. Nordic ski poles are longer than alpine poles.

ALPINE SKIING

RACING
There are four main types:
Downhill This is the fastest race, in which skiers follow a set route down the mountain.
Slalom A short race downhill with quick turns through a series of "gates," 55–75 for men and 40–60 for women.
Giant slalom This race has fewer, wider gates than a slalom, and it takes place over a longer course.
Super giant slalom This is like a downhill race with gates; it contains up to two jumps.

FREESTYLE
There are three main types:
Aerials Acrobatics performed in midair after taking off from a ramp, judged on style and technique.
Mogul racing Skiing down a course of large round bumps, judged on skill as well as time.
Ballet Performed to music on smooth slopes, judged on grace and skill.

Aerials

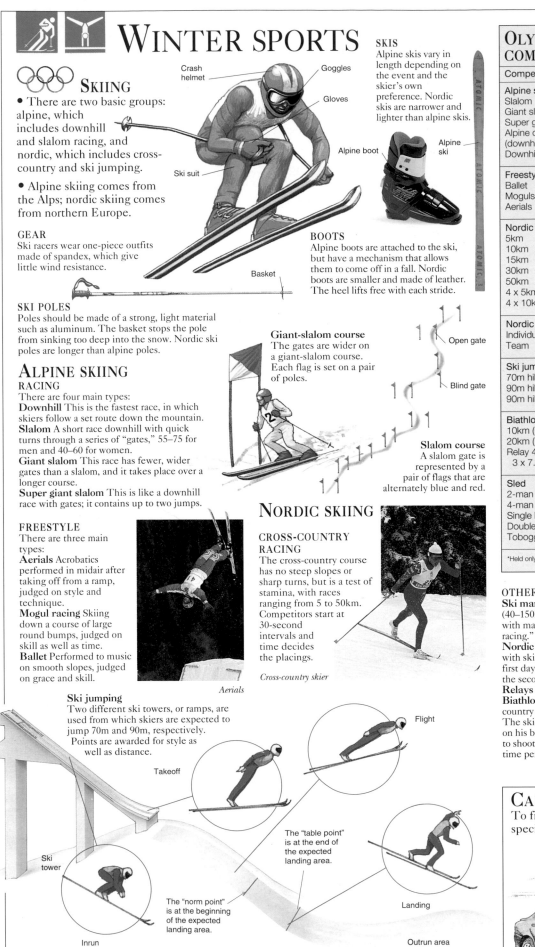

Crash helmet
Goggles
Gloves

Ski suit

Basket

SKIS
Alpine skis vary in length depending on the event and the skier's own preference. Nordic skis are narrower and lighter than alpine skis.

Alpine boot
Alpine ski

BOOTS
Alpine boots are attached to the ski, but have a mechanism that allows them to come off in a fall. Nordic boots are smaller and made of leather. The heel lifts free with each stride.

Giant-slalom course
The gates are wider on a giant-slalom course. Each flag is set on a pair of poles.

Open gate
Blind gate

Slalom course
A slalom gate is represented by a pair of flags that are alternately blue and red.

NORDIC SKIING

CROSS-COUNTRY RACING
The cross-country course has no steep slopes or sharp turns, but is a test of stamina, with races ranging from 5 to 50km. Competitors start at 30-second intervals and time decides the placings.

Cross-country skier

Ski jumping
Two different ski towers, or ramps, are used from which skiers are expected to jump 70m and 90m, respectively. Points are awarded for style as well as distance.

Takeoff
Flight

The "table point" is at the end of the expected landing area.

The "norm point" is at the beginning of the expected landing area.

Ski tower
Landing

Inrun
Outrun area

OLYMPIC SKI AND SLED COMPETITIONS

Competition	Men	Women
Alpine ski racing		
Slalom	√	√
Giant slalom	√	√
Super giant slalom	√	√
Alpine combined (downhill and slalom)	√	√
Downhill	√	√
Freestyle		
Ballet	√	√
Moguls	√	√
Aerials	√	√
Nordic		
5km		√
10km	√	√
15km	√	√
30km	√	√
50km	√	
4 x 5km relay		√
4 x 10km relay	√	
Nordic combined		
Individual	√	
Team	√	
Ski jumping		
70m hill	√	
90m hill	√	
90m hill team	√	
Biathlon		
10km (M) / 7.5km (W)	√	√
20km (M) / 15km (W)	√	√
Relay 4 x 7.5km	√	
3 x 7.5km		√
Sled		
2-man bob	√	
4-man bob	√	
Single luge	√	√
Double luge	√	
Toboggan*	√	

*Held only on Cresta Run at St.. Moritz, Switzerland (1928 and 1948).

OTHER NORDIC COMPETITIONS
Ski marathons Long-distance (40–150km) cross-country events with mass starts, also called "citizen racing."
Nordic combined Two-day event with ski jumping (70m hill) on the first day and cross-country (15km) on the second day.
Relays Races between teams of four.
Biathlon Combination of cross-country skiing and rifle shooting. The skier carries his weapon on his back and stops regularly to shoot at targets, incurring time penalties for missing.

Rifle shooting at a biathlon

CAR SKIING
To find the best position for skiing in special high-speed events on smooth slopes, a skier practices on top of a fast-moving car.

SLED RACING

LUGE TOBOGGANING
A luge is a one- or two-person toboggan with no steering or brakes. It is ridden face-up in a sitting or lying position.

BOBSLED RACING
Bobsleds, for two or four men, have metal runners, steering, and brakes.

SKELETON TOBOGGANING
Competitors ride face-down on an open toboggan. There is only one major competition, the Cresta Run at St. Moritz, Switzerland.

FIGURE SKATING

• Competitors perform routines to music containing both compulsory movements and moves they choose themselves.

• A maximum of nine judges give marks for technical merit and artistic impression; 6.0 is the perfect score.

Top male skaters often wear all-in-one bodysuits made of stretch material.

SINGLES
Solo competitions, for men and women, have two parts: a short program with compulsory moves and a long program (freestyle).

Camel spin

The skater lifts one leg behind him, and holds it parallel to the ice.

Lutz jump

The skater increases her speed before attempting the jump.

She makes one turn, or two for a double lutz, in the air before landing.

ICE DANCE
Ice-dance competitions have three parts: compulsory dances, original set pattern dance, and free dance. Couples choose their own music and movements in the free dance. During their routine, they must not separate more than five times, or for longer than five seconds. Lifts must not be made above shoulder-height.

Expressiveness is important in ice dancing.

PAIRS
Pair competitions are made up of two parts: a short program and a free-skating program.

A skating pair perform a high lift.

SPEED SKATING

• Competitors race in pairs against the clock around an oval two-lane track, 400m in length.

• Competitors switch lanes each lap in a changeover zone.

• In short-track speed skating, a maximum of six competitors race around a 110-meter oval track. The first to finish is the winner.

Competitors wear body-hugging spandex suits to cut down air resistance.

Speed skates have a thin aluminum blade attached to a lightweight boot.

GEAR
Top female skaters wear short fitted skirts or dresses.

RINK
Maximum length: 60m
Maximum width: 30m

Figure skating usually takes place on adapted ice-hockey rinks.

Toe-rake helps in spinning and in certain jumps.

Figure skate
A figure skate has a steel blade about 3mm wide. The bottom of the blade is concave to make two edges. Figures are skated on one of these two edges.

TRACK

Width of lane: 4–5m

Length of track: 400m

CURLING

• In curling, two teams with four players each slide curling stones across the ice, aiming to get them as close as possible to the center (tee) of a target area (house).

• Teammates with brooms sweep the ice in front of the stones to change their speed and direction.

Curling

RECORD BREAKER
THREE CONSECUTIVE OLYMPIC GOLD MEDALS (1928–36) and ten consecutive world championships (1927–36) were won by Sonja Henie, a Norwegian figure skater. She then turned professional and made several Hollywood films featuring her grace and skills on ice.

OLYMPIC SKATING EVENTS

	Men	Women
Figure skating	√	√
Pairs	Together	
Ice dancing	Together	
Speed skating		
500m	√	√
1,000m	√	√
1500m	√	√
3,000m		√
5,000m	√	√
10,000m	√	
Short-track		
500m	√	√
1,000m	√	√
3,000m		√
5,000m	√	

WHEELED SPORTS

MOTOR RACING

- Competitions are held for different types of car on a variety of tracks. Races are held around circuits, on roads, and on grass and dirt tracks.

FORMULA 1

- Grand Prix races take place on circuits.

- Drivers and car-makers attempt to win points for the world championships.

FLAG SIGNALS

Flags are held out during the race. Each color has its own meaning.

- Checkered: end of race
- Yellow: danger
- Red and yellow stripes: oil on course
- White: service car on track
- Black: car must stop in pits
- Red: all cars must stop

INDY CAR RACING

- Most races take place in the US, mainly on oval circuits.

- The annual championships are decided on points. The cars are similar to Formula One cars.

Turns bank at 9°

INDY 500
The most famous circuit is the Indianapolis, which is 4km long. The Indy 500 race is held over 200 laps of the circuit.

Pits area
Start/Finish

GO-CARTING

- The simplest go-carts have a 100cc engine and no gearbox. The most powerful go-carts are like small racing cars and can reach speeds of 150mph (240km/h).

RACE CIRCUIT
A Grand Prix circuit has corners and straights to test the drivers' car-handling skills. Above is a plan of the Suzuka circuit in Japan.

Straight
Spoon curve
S-curve
Start/Finish

GEAR
Motor racing drivers wear a crash helmet and a thick, often fire-resistant suit for protection in case of an accident.

Crash helmet
Face shield
Driving gloves
Heavy-duty racing suit
Driving shoes
Airfoil pushes the car down on the track.

GRAND PRIX CIRCUITS			
Grand Prix	Circuit	Length (km)	Laps
Belgium	Spa-Francorchamps	6.94	44
Germany	Hockenheim	6.81	45
Japan	Suzuka	5.86	53
Italy	Monza	5.80	53
Great Britain	Silverstone	5.23	59
San Marino	Imola (Italy)	5.04	61
Spain	Catalunya	4.75	65
Canada	Gilles Villeneuve	4.43	69
Portugal	Estoril	4.35	71
Brazil	Interlagos	4.32	71
South Africa	Kyalami	4.26	72
France	Magny-Cours	4.25	72
Hungary	Hungaroring	3.97	77
Australia	Adelaide	3.78	81
Pacific	TI AIDA (Japan)	3.70	83
Monaco	Monte Carlo	3.33	78

Smooth tires called slicks for use in dry weather.
Body shell
Detachable steering wheel
Roll bar

FORMULA 1 RACING CAR
These streamlined cars are made of lightweight materials to make them go as fast as possible.

RALLY DRIVING

- In rally driving, strengthened sedan cars race against the clock, rather than each other. The route is divided into sections called "stages," with time-control points between them. Points are lost for exceeding time.

Rally cars are faster and stronger than ordinary cars.

RECENT FORMULA 1 WORLD CHAMPION DRIVERS		
Year	Driver	Country of origin
1984	Niki Lauda	Austria
1985	Alain Prost	France
1986	Alain Prost	France
1987	Nelson Piquet	Brazil
1988	Ayrton Senna	Brazil
1989	Alain Prost	France
1990	Ayrton Senna	Brazil
1991	Ayrton Senna	Brazil
1992	Nigel Mansell	UK
1993	Alain Prost	France
1994	Michael Schumacher	Germany

DRAG RACING

- Races are held along straight 0.25 mile (400m) tracks called drag strips.

- Cars race in pairs. They reach speeds of 300mph (485km/h), and need parachutes to slow down.

DRAGSTER
A dragster has a lightweight body, with big wheels that give good grip at the back, and smaller, lighter front wheels. The fastest dragsters are called top-fuelers.

Airfoil
Powerful, supercharged engine
Rear slicks
Lightweight front wheels

RECORD BREAKERS

MOST FORMULA 1 WORLD DRIVERS' CHAMPIONSHIP WINS is five by Juan Manuel Fangio (born 1911) of Argentina.

CLOSEST FINISH TO A WORLD CHAMPIONSHIP GRAND PRIX RACE is 0.014 seconds, when Ayrton Senna (1960-94) of Brazil, beat Nigel Mansell (born 1953) of UK.

LONGEST ANNUALLY HELD RALLY RACE is the Safari Rally, Kenya. The race has covered up to 3,874 miles (6,234km).

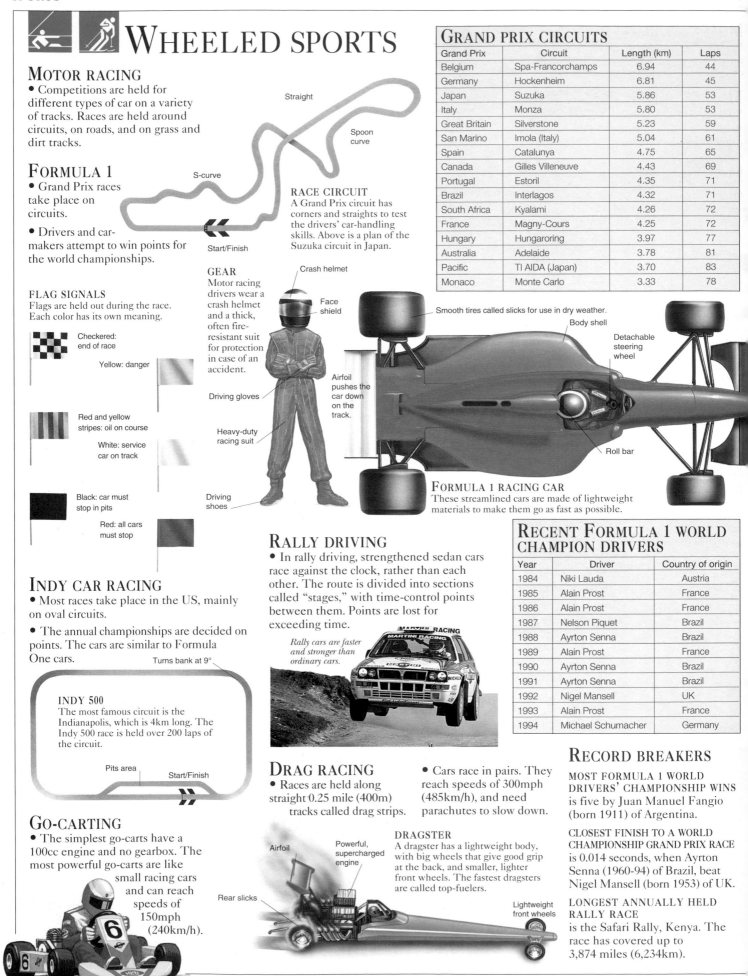

MOTORCYCLE SPORT

- There are a variety of competitions for different types of bike. They take place on circuits or cross-country tracks.

MOTORCYCLE RACING

- Grand Prix races take place on circuits.
- There are different classes for bikes of different engine sizes, and a class for sidecars.

RACING MOTORBIKE
The bikes are powerful machines designed for speed.

Streamlined plastic body

Light aluminum frame

CYCLE SPORTS

- Races range from track sprints held over 1,094yd (1,000m) to multistage road races lasting several weeks.
- The bicycles differ according to the type of race.

OLYMPIC CYCLING EVENTS

	Men	Women
Track:		
Sprint	√	√
Time trial	√	
Pursuit	√	√
Team pursuit	√	
Points race	√	
Road:		
Individual	√	√

ROAD-RACING BICYCLE
The best bicycles are made of carbon tubing to save weight and are designed to be as streamlined as possible yet reliable and stable.

TOUR DE FRANCE
This famous race covers 3,400km in 24 one-day stages. Each year the route changes. The tour can even leave France and stretch over the border into neighboring countries.

WORLD CHAMPIONSHIP MOTORCYCLE CLASSES

Motorcycle	Racing	Motocross
500cc	√	√
250cc	√	√
125cc	√	√
80cc	√	
Sidecar	√	√

RACING SIDECAR
A racing sidecar is a bike and sidecar molded together to make one piece. The driver and passenger work together as a team. The passenger leans over behind the driver to help with cornering. The passenger platform may be attached to either side of the bike.

Racing sidecar

◯◯◯◯◯ ROAD RACING

- Races are run on courses set along ordinary roads.
- In stage races, such as the Tour de France, each stage is a race in itself, and the overall winner is the one with the lowest aggregate time.

GEAR
Bicycle riders wear long close-fitting shorts to prevent thighs from chafing against the saddle, and a top that allows the body to breathe and soaks up sweat.

A helmet is compulsory.

◯◯◯ TRACK RACING

- Races take place on hard tracks including tightly banked wooden indoor tracks and almost flat asphalt outdoor tracks. Some races are held on closed circuits (roads that have been closed to the public).

MOTOCROSS

- Motocross, also known as scrambling, is the "cross-country" branch of motorcycle racing.
- Races take place on tracks that include muddy slopes, grass, and bumps.

MOTOCROSS BIKE
These bikes are adapted to cope with rough ground.

Swinging arm allows vertical movement of wheel.

Mudguard

Chunky-tread tires for gripping loose surfaces

OTHER MOTORCYCLE SPORT

Speedway Riders race over four laps of a dirt track. The bikes have no brakes or gearbox so riders slow down by sliding their machines through turns.

Trials Riders negotiate a natural course with obstacles such as boulders, fast-flowing water, loose rocks, and deep mud, and lose points for putting a foot down or stopping.

TYPES OF TRACK RACING

Points race Points are scored on each lap for crossing the line first, with double points on the last lap.

Sprint Riders spend most of the race jockeying for position before making a final dash for the line.

Individual pursuit Two riders start on opposite sides of the track, and the race is decided on time, or if one rider catches the other.

Team pursuit Similar to individual pursuit, but there are two teams of four riders. Only the times of the first three riders in each team are counted.

Italian pursuit For teams of up to five riders. The leading cyclist in each team drops out after each lap. The finishing time of the last rider of each team decides the race.

Devil-take-the-hindmost Last rider over the line at the end of each lap is eliminated.

Time trial Competitors ride on their own over a set distance from a standing start, and the rider with the fastest time wins.

OFF-ROAD RACING

- Cyclocross takes place on cross-country courses, and competitors may carry their bikes across obstacles.
- Mountain-bike racing includes several different styles, including trials and cross-country racing.

A cyclist carrying his bike across a river during a cyclocross race.

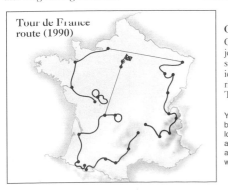

Tour de France route (1990)

Color codes
Color-coded jerseys help spectators identify leading riders in the Tour de France.

Yellow top is worn by the rider with the lowest overall time after each stage and by the ultimate winner of the Tour.

Polkadot top is worn by the rider with most points from the climbing stages.

Green top worn by the rider with most points from sprints.

TARGET SPORTS

BOWLS

- Bowls (woods) are rolled along a flat, smooth green, aiming at a target ball (jack). It is similar to the Italian game, *Bocci*.

- A point is scored for each bowl that is nearer to the jack than any opponent's wood.

WOOD
Woods can be made of wood, rubber, or a composition material.

They are weighted, or biased, on one side so they curve when rolled.

Jack

ARCHERY

- Competitors use a bow to fire a certain number of arrows at targets set at different distances.

- The closer to the center of the target an arrow lands, the higher the score.

BOW AND ARROWS
The bow is usually made of fiberglass. The arrow shafts are made of aluminum or carbon.

DARTS

- Opponents take turns to throw three darts at a board from a distance of 2.4m.

- Each player usually starts with a score of 501 and must reduce it to the exact score of zero by finishing with a double or an inner bull.

DARTBOARD
The board is divided into different scoring sections, indicated by the numbers on the outer ring. Certain areas count double or treble.

Bull

Dart Treble ring Double ring

SNOOKER

- Players score points by pocketing balls. A cue is used to hit a cue ball against one of 15 red or 6 colored balls, causing it to fall into a pocket.

TABLE

Pocket

Cushion

BOULES

- In boules, which is similar to bowls, metal balls are thrown at a small wooden target ball.

- The game can be played on any bare stretch of land, but it is usually played on sandy ground.

Boule

TENPIN BOWLING

- This is an indoor sport in which players roll a ball down an alley to knock down pins.

- Points are scored for each pin knocked down. Bonuses are given for knocking down all ten pins in one roll (a strike) or two rolls (a spare).

Plastic fletches

Aluminum or carbon shaft

Stabilizers keep the bow steady while shooting.

Quiver for carrying arrows

SHOOTING

- Rifles, pistols, and shotguns are used in shooting sports. The size of the target varies with the weapon and distance.

- Pistol shooting includes rapid-fire pistol shooting, in which 5 targets are exposed for only 4–8 seconds, and free pistol shooting in which competitors fire at a fixed target.

- Shotgun is firing with a double-barreled gun at saucer-shaped targets released randomly from a spring-catapult.

Black ball (7 points)

Fifteen red balls (1 point each)

Pink ball (6 points)

Blue ball (5 points)

Green ball (3 points)

Cue ball

Brown ball (4 points)

Yellow ball (2 points)

CUE
The cue, used in both snooker and pool, is a tapered stick with a leather tip.

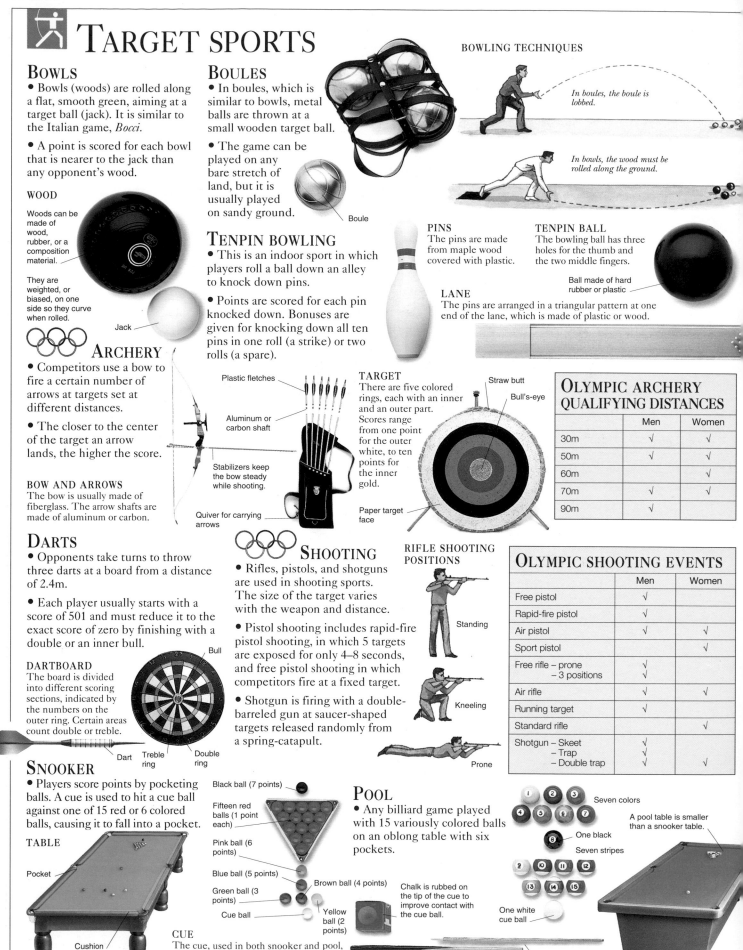

BOWLING TECHNIQUES

In boules, the boule is lobbed.

In bowls, the wood must be rolled along the ground.

PINS
The pins are made from maple wood covered with plastic.

TENPIN BALL
The bowling ball has three holes for the thumb and the two middle fingers.

Ball made of hard rubber or plastic

LANE
The pins are arranged in a triangular pattern at one end of the lane, which is made of plastic or wood.

TARGET
There are five colored rings, each with an inner and an outer part. Scores range from one point for the outer white, to ten points for the inner gold.

Straw butt

Bull's-eye

Paper target face

RIFLE SHOOTING POSITIONS

Standing

Kneeling

Prone

OLYMPIC ARCHERY QUALIFYING DISTANCES

	Men	Women
30m	√	√
50m	√	√
60m		√
70m	√	√
90m	√	

OLYMPIC SHOOTING EVENTS

	Men	Women
Free pistol	√	
Rapid-fire pistol	√	
Air pistol	√	√
Sport pistol		√
Free rifle – prone – 3 positions	√ √	
Air rifle	√	√
Running target	√	
Standard rifle		√
Shotgun – Skeet – Trap – Double trap	√ √ √	 √

POOL

- Any billiard game played with 15 variously colored balls on an oblong table with six pockets.

Seven colors

One black

Seven stripes

A pool table is smaller than a snooker table.

Chalk is rubbed on the tip of the cue to improve contact with the cue ball.

One white cue ball

Two-piece cue

SCIENCE AND TECHNOLOGY

From the atom to the latest in information technology, this section offers a wealth of scientific facts and figures.

Matter • Atoms • Periodic Table • Energy
Forces and Machines • Electricity and Magnetism • Light and Color
Sound • Electronics • Computers • Mathematics • Weights and Measures
Time • Engines • Space and Time • Natural Science
Physical Science • Weapons

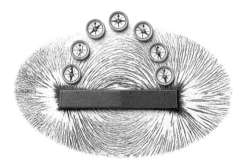

MATTER

EVERYTHING IS MADE up of matter. It can be a solid, such as wood or iron, a liquid, such as water or oil, or a gas, such as air. Heat or pressure can change matter from one state into another.

Lead: solid

Glass: transparent solid

Terrarium, containing many types of matter

Droplets of water condensed from vapor

STATES OF MATTER

Matter exists in three basic forms, called states, depending on how their atoms and molecules (see p.222) are arranged.

GAS

A gas is a substance that does not have a fixed volume but fills all the space it occupies. Gas particles are not bound together and move rapidly and freely in all directions.

Gas particles, free to move around

LIQUID

A liquid has a fixed volume but can change shape to fit the space it occupies. Its particles are in contact with each other but can move around with some freedom.

Liquid particles, able to move short distances

SOLID

A solid is a substance with a definite size and shape. A solid's particles are tightly linked by strong bonds, making a firm structure.

Solid particles, held in a rigid pattern

THREE IN ONE

Water is one substance we often find in its different states.

ICE
Water is solid when its temperature is below 32°F (0°C) – what we know as ice.

Ice forms solid blocks with definite shapes.

WATER
Water is liquid when it has a temperature of between 32°F (0°C) and 212°F (100°C).

Liquid fills up its container to a horizontal surface.

STEAM
Water turns to steam, a gas, when it has a temperature of more than 212°F (100°C).

Liquid turns to gas.

CHANGING STATES

Evaporation and condensation
Particles can free themselves from the body of a liquid (evaporation). Above the boiling point, all of the liquid becomes gas. When the gas cools, it becomes a liquid (condenses) again.

Freezing and melting
A liquid becomes a solid (freezes) below a temperature called its freezing point. It becomes a liquid again (melts) if the temperature rises above the freezing point.

Sublimation
Some substances, such as carbon dioxide, will change from a solid to a gas when heated, without becoming liquid in between. This is sublimation. The reverse process, from a gas to a solid, is also called sublimation.

Changes of state

evaporating

subliming

condensing

subliming

freezing

melting

TYPES OF MIXTURE

There are two main types of mixture: colloids and solutions. In a solution, two or more substances are broken down into individual atoms or molecules. A colloid is a mixture of larger particles of one substance, distributed in another.

Emulsion
Paint is an emulsion of oil particles dispersed in another liquid, water.

Gel
Hair gel is composed of particles of oil suspended in a solid.

Foam
Shaving foam is composed of bubbles of gas suspended in liquid.

Mist
Steam from a kettle is a mist of liquid particles suspended in a gas.

Smoke
A bonfire gives off a cloud of smoke composed of solid matter suspended in air.

Solution
A solvent, such as water, makes a solution by dissolving another substance, the solute.

WEB FEAT
Some of the threads in a spider's web are stronger than a steel wire of the same width.

LIQUID GLASS
Over long periods of time and pressure, glass behaves like a liquid. Ancient Roman glassware has been found slightly flattened.

AIR SPEED
Each of the billions of air molecules that fill a balloon travels at the average speed of a jet plane.

COMPOUNDS

Elements that exist on their own are rare in the natural world. Most substances are made up of two or more elements bonded together by chemical reaction to form a compound. When iron and sulfur are heated together, a chemical reaction bonds their atoms into a solid structure.

MIXTURE

Iron filings and sulfur

Iron filings and sulfur can be mixed up together, but their atoms will not be chemically bound unless a chemical reaction takes place.

COMPOUND

A new substance, iron sulfide

When iron and sulfur are heated together, their atoms bind to form a new compound of iron sulfide. It is a completely new substance.

PHYSICAL PROPERTIES

There is a wide variety of matter, with a range of different properties. These properties help identify the substance, and also determine to what use it can be put.

Viscosity
Viscous matter is liquid that does not flow easily. Friction between molecules makes a liquid viscous. Honey is highly viscous, whereas water is not.

Ductility and malleability
Ductile matter can be drawn out into a wire. Malleable matter can be molded or beaten into other shapes.

Elasticity
Elastic matter can be stretched or squeezed and returns to its original size and shape.

Density
Two objects of the same size may not have the same mass, so they will not weigh the same. The denser of the two will weigh more, because it has more matter packed into the same space.

Dense tip

Conductivity
Matter that transfers heat and electricity is conductive. Many solids have a close-knit molecular structure that causes them to be cold to the touch, because it conducts heat away quickly.

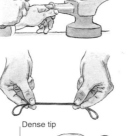

Warm stone retains heat.

ANTIMATTER

For every type of particle that exists, such as the electron (see p.222), there is a corresponding antiparticle. Just as matter consists of particles, antimatter consists of antiparticles. If matter and antimatter are brought together, they will violently destroy each other, to become energy.

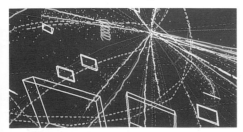

False-color image of subatomic particles

COMBUSTION (BURNING)

A substance burns when it reacts with oxygen, releasing heat. A candle is made from carbon and hydrogen. These elements burn to form carbon dioxide and water.

Candle flame
A candle flame contains tiny particles of carbon. As they burn, they become so hot that they glow bright yellow.

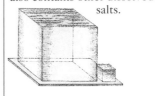

Burning food
Food dissolved in your blood "burns" as it reacts with oxygen. The heat released provides you with the energy you need to live.

PLASTIC

Most synthetic plastics are made from chemicals in oil in a chemical process called polymerization. To make PVC, small molecules of chlorethene polymerize to form a long chain, or polymer.

Inflatable snake made of PVC (polyvinyl chloride).

Molecule of chlorethene (vinyl chloride)

Long chain molecule of PVC (polyvinyl chloride)

Polyvinyl chloride has a chain of molecules, from 70 to a million long.

KEY PLASTICS

Name	Uses
Polystyrene	Packaging, cups, bowls, ceiling tiles
Polyester	Artificial fibers, fiberglass
Polyethylene	Carrier bags, bottles, food wrapping
Nylon	Artificial fibers, carpets, fishnets
PVC (Polyvinyl chloride)	Raincoats, garden hoses, gutters
Polyurethane	Plastic packaging foam, adhesives
Polymethyl methacrylate (perspex)	Substitute for glass

DEGRADABILITY

In time, most matter will degrade naturally, breaking down into simpler substances. Nondegradable pollution will remain in rivers, seas, and in the atmosphere.

An apple core takes 20 days to decompose.

Plastic can take more than 100 years to decompose.

Glass takes more than 4,000 years to decompose.

SAVORY SEA

220 gallons (1cu meter) of typical seawater contains 1.4cu inches (23cu cm) of salt (sodium chloride). Seawater also contains other dissolved salts.

ACIDS AND ALKALIS

Acids are substances that dissolve in water to form sour-tasting solutions. Alkalis dissolve in water to form soapy solutions. Both acids and alkalis can be corrosive. The strength of an acid or alkali is measured by its pH.

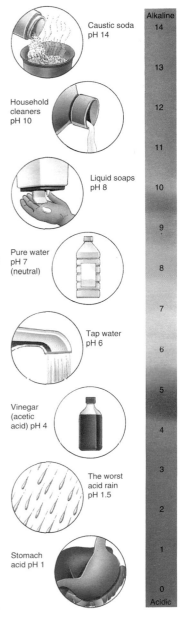

Alkaline

Caustic soda pH 14

Household cleaners pH 10

Liquid soaps pH 8

Pure water pH 7 (neutral)

Tap water pH 6

Vinegar (acetic acid) pH 4

The worst acid rain pH 1.5

Stomach acid pH 1

Acidic

ATOMS

EVERYTHING AROUND YOU is made up of tiny particles called atoms. Different atoms make up different kinds of matter.

ELEMENTS

Elements are substances made up of one kind of atom only. One element is fluorine.

INSIDE THE FLUORINE ATOM

If a fluorine atom could be cut open, it might look like this.

The illustration below distorts the real sizes of the atomic components – the nucleus is very large compared to electrons, and electrons orbit at a great distance from the nucleus.

Nucleus
The central core of the atom is called the nucleus. It consists of protons and neutrons. The nucleus makes up 99.9% of an atom's mass, but only a tiny part of its volume.

Inner electron shell

Electrons
Electrons are negatively charged particles. They surround the nucleus in regions called orbitals.

Ions
When an atom loses or gains an electron, it becomes an ion. If it loses an electron, it becomes positively charged and is called a cation. If it gains an electron, it becomes negatively charged and is called an anion.

Neutrons
Neutrons are particles in a nucleus. They have no electric charge. They cling to the protons and to each other, keeping the nucleus together.

Protons
Protons are particles in a nucleus that carry a positive electric charge. The number of protons in an atom is called its atomic number. Fluorine has nine.

Quarks
Protons and neutrons are made up of even smaller particles, called quarks. There are two main types of quark. Up quarks have a positive charge. Down quarks have a negative one. Neutrons have one Up and two Down quarks. Protons have two Up and one Down.

Proton, with two Up quarks and one Down

ATOM FACTS
• Quarks are named after a word that appears in the novel *Finnegan's Wake* by Irish writer James Joyce (1882–1941).

• Some atomic isotopes are highly dangerous – if stored in large enough quantities, a nuclear reaction can result.

• Scientists have discovered many particles that are smaller than atoms. They have weird names, such as gluons, leptons, and taus, and properties such as charm, strangeness, and flavor. They appear briefly when larger particles are smashed in massive "particle accelerators."

ISOTOPES
Some atoms of the same element may have different numbers of neutrons. These different kinds of atoms are called isotopes. These two nuclei are from isotopes of fluorine. Fluorine–19 has 10 neutrons, while fluorine–18 has 9 neutrons.

Fluorine–19 nucleus

Extra neutron

Fluorine–18 nucleus

INTO THE ATOM
What would happen if you could tear this book in half, and then in half again and again – until you broke it down into the tiniest particles possible?

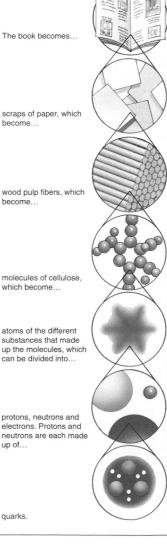

The book becomes…

scraps of paper, which become…

wood pulp fibers, which become…

molecules of cellulose, which become…

atoms of the different substances that made up the molecules, which can be divided into…

protons, neutrons and electrons. Protons and neutrons are each made up of…

quarks.

MOLECULES
There are only about 100 kinds of atoms, but millions of different substances called compounds. Most substances are made of particular combinations of atoms, called molecules.

Double bond

Carbon nucleus

Hydrogen atom

Molecule of ethylene (C_2H_4)

FORCES OF ATTRACTION
If an atom's nucleus were the size of a sport stadium, some of its electrons would revolve at the distance of a low-orbiting satellite.

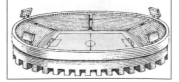

ATOMIC BONDING
Atoms join to form molecules. They do this by bonding (sticking together). There are two main types of bonding: ionic and covalent. In each case, the electrons form the bond.

IONIC BOND
In an ionic bond, atoms lose or gain electrons to form ions of opposite charge. These opposite charges attract each other, and bond the two ions together.

Fluorine atom

Electron

Lithium atom loses electron to become a positive ion, or cation.

Fluorine atom gains electron to become a negative ion, or anion.

Molecule of lithium fluoride

Ions attract each other to form a molecule of lithium fluoride.

COVALENT BOND
A covalent bond occurs where electrons are shared between atoms. This sharing keeps the atoms together. One or two, or occasionally three, nuclei are attracted to the same electrons at once. Water and nitrogen gas are substances with covalent bonds.

Hydrogen atom

Fluorine atom

Both fluorine and hydrogen atoms need one electron to become stable.

Shared electron

Atoms form a covalent bond, becoming stable as they do so.

RADIOACTIVITY

Large nuclei can be unstable, and they can decay. When they do, charged particles are lost from them. This process is called radioactivity. Most elements have unstable forms, called radioisotopes. Some occur naturally, others are made in nuclear reactors. The most radioactive substances have the highest number of particles in their nuclei. Uranium has 238.

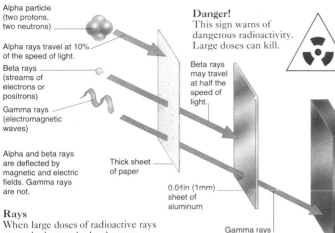

Alpha particle (two protons, two neutrons)

Alpha rays travel at 10% of the speed of light.

Beta rays (streams of electrons or positrons)

Gamma rays (electromagnetic waves)

Alpha and beta rays are deflected by magnetic and electric fields. Gamma rays are not.

Danger!
This sign warns of dangerous radioactivity. Large doses can kill.

Beta rays may travel at half the speed of light.

Thick sheet of paper

0.04in (1mm) sheet of aluminum

Gamma rays travel at speed of light.

0.59in (1.5cm) sheet of lead

Rays
When large doses of radioactive rays enter the human body, they can damage tissues and nerve cells.

RADIATION FACTS

• Levels of radiation can be measured with a device called a Geiger counter. A probe filled with gas at low pressure triggers an electric pulse, heard as a click, when radiation is near.

• About 200 million gamma rays pass through the body every hour from soil and buildings.

• All-out nuclear war would force people to live underground for months, and possibly years.

• Exposure to gamma rays can kill bacteria in food. This process, called irradiation, keeps the food fresh for longer, but many people are afraid of its possible long-term health risks.

NUCLEAR REACTIONS

There are two kinds of nuclear reaction – fission and fusion. Both are a release of the "binding energy" that keeps the nucleus of an atom together. Atoms are called "stable" if they have a lot of binding energy, "unstable" if they have little.

NUCLEAR FISSION

If a neutron hits the nucleus of the unstable element uranium 235, the nucleus splits into two lighter nuclei. More neutrons shoot off to bombard other nuclei in a chain reaction. Energy is released. In nuclear power stations, this energy is used to generate electricity.

Neutron

Uranium–235 nucleus

Nuclear fission reaction

Barium atom

Krypton atom

Neutron

Neutron

Energy released

MAJOR RADIATION LEAKS

Location	Date	Effects
Windscale, UK (now Sellafield)	1957	39 radiation-related deaths by 1979. Area of 309sq miles (800sq km) contaminated
Three Mile Island, US	1979	Numbers of deaths not released – significant contamination
Kyshtym, Russia (former USSR)	1985	Area of 460sq miles (1,191sq km) contaminated
Chernobyl, Ukraine (former USSR)	1986	35 died within two weeks, and 135,000 were permanently evacuated

USES OF RADIATION

ALPHA RADIATION
Alpha rays are charged particles of two protons and two neutrons. Nuclear batteries, which give off harmless alpha rays, power heart pacemakers, because they last much longer than normal ones.

Alpha rays from the radio-isotope plutonium power heart pacemakers.

Heart pacemaker

BETA RADIATION
During radioactive decay, a neutron can change into a proton, and vice versa. Streams of electrons or positrons are given off in this process – these are beta rays. The isotope carbon–14, found in all living things, produces beta radiation as it decays. Scientists can date once-living things by seeing how much carbon–14 has decayed. This is called carbon dating.

Once thought to be the 2,000-year-old death shroud of Jesus Christ, the cloth was carbon dated and found to be only 600 years old.

The Turin shroud

GAMMA RADIATION
Gamma radiation, an electromagnetic wave, travels at the speed of light, but with much more energy. These waves, like light or radio waves, are given off when a nucleus has too much energy. Not often found on their own, they are given off with alpha and beta particles.

Person undergoes chemotherapy (cancer treatment)

Cobalt–60 produces gamma radiation. Here, it is being used to kill cancerous body cells. It can also be used to sterilize medical instruments.

KEY HALF-LIVES
The half-life of an element is the time it takes for half its atoms to decay into other materials. A strongly radioactive substance has a short half-life – it decays quickly.

Isotope	Half-life	Type of decay	Use
Radium–221	30 sec	Alpha and gamma	Cancer therapy
Iron (Fe–59)	45 days	Beta and gamma	Testing car parts
Carbon–14	5,570 yr	Beta and gamma	Carbon dating
Uranium–238	500 million yr	Alpha and gamma	Nuclear energy

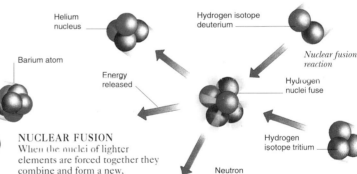

Helium nucleus

Hydrogen isotope deuterium

Nuclear fusion reaction

Energy released

Hydrogen nuclei fuse

Hydrogen isotope tritium

Neutron released

NUCLEAR FUSION
When the nuclei of lighter elements are forced together they combine and form a new, heavier nucleus, releasing energy. In the Sun, hydrogen atoms fuse together to make helium, and produce the Sun's heat. Scientists hope to find a safe way of creating fusion on Earth.

MARIE CURIE
French scientist Marie Curie (1867–1934) pioneered the study of radiation. A flask that she used in her experiments turned blue after constant exposure to radioactive ores.

COLD ENERGY
In 1989, Stanley Pons and Martin Fleischmann claimed to have succeeded in making fusion reactions at room temperature. This claim has since been shown to be false.

PERIODIC TABLE

THE ELEMENTS THAT MAKE UP all of the matter around us can be arranged into a table. The table is arranged in vertical columns, called groups, and in horizontal rows, called periods. The complete table includes elements that do not occur naturally but that have been made artificially.

6   12
C
Carbon

Atomic number
The number of protons in the nucleus defines what element a particular atom is. This is the atomic number.

Atomic mass
Carbon occurs with 6, 7, 8, and 9 neutrons in its nucleus, in addition to its 6 protons, giving it a mass of between 12 and 15.

Chemical symbol
Each element has a symbol; it is used for identification in chemical equations.

Carbon–12 nucleus

Proton – total number is atomic number

Neutron – with protons, makes atomic mass

TABLE PATTERNS
We can tell a lot about an element from its position on the periodic table. Elements situated in the same area behave in the same way.

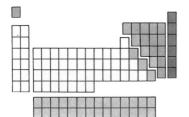

Metals
Metals are mostly solids, and are all good conductors of heat and electricity.

Nonmetals
Nonmetals are not good conductors of heat or electricity, and can be solid, liquid, or gas.

Metalloids
Metalloids, also called semi-metals, are nonmetals that behave like metals in some ways, or in some conditions.

Noble gases
Noble gases are also called inert gases because they are not reactive. They are all gas at room temperature.

Lanthanides and actinides
These elements are separated out from the table to give it a regular shape.

 GROUPS AND PERIODS

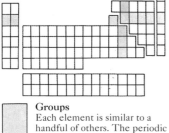

Groups
Each element is similar to a handful of others. The periodic table is arranged so that similar elements are put together in vertical columns, or groups.

Periods
Elements are arranged into horizontal rows, or periods. The electron arrangement around the nucleus (see p.222) determines the period's length.

PERIODIC PIONEER
The first person to arrange the elements into the shape of a table was Russian chemist, Dmitri Mendeleyev (1834–1907). In 1869, he made cards for each element, and laid them out according to the property of each element. The cards formed the periodic table.

SODIUM
There are about 19,800,000,000,000 tons of this element in the world's oceans; most of it is in a solution of sodium chloride.

RUBIDIUM
Rubidium is typical of elements in its group. It reacts violently with water or even air, catching fire immediately. Its salts give a red flame when heated.

CESIUM
The nucleus of this element can be made to vibrate at an extremely reliable rate – 9,192,631,770 times every second. Cesium is used in atomic clocks, which are accurate to one second in thousands of years.

URANIUM
There are two main types, or isotopes, of uranium. Uranium–238 (with 92 protons and 146 neutrons) accounts for 99% of all uranium. The isotope that is useful in nuclear reactors, uranium–235 (with 92 protons and 143 neutrons), accounts for only about 1%.

TUNGSTEN
Tungsten has the highest boiling point of all the elements. It boils at a temperature of 11,190°F (6,200°C), which makes it useful for filaments in electric light bulbs. Their temperatures would melt most of the other elements.

1 1 *H* Hydrogen	Elements on handwritten cards occur naturally. Others have been artificially produced by scientists.

3 7 *Li* Lithium	4 9 *Be* Beryllium
11 23 *Na* Sodium	12 24 *Mg* Magnesium

The periodic table elements:

19 39 K Potassium	20 40 Ca Calcium	21 45 Sc Scandium	22 48 Ti Titanium	23 51 V Vanadium	24 52 Cr Chromium	25 55 Mn Manganese	26 56 Fe Iron	27 59 Co Cobalt
37 85 Rb Rubidium	38 88 Sr Strontium	39 89 Y Yttrium	40 91 Zr Zirconium	41 93 Nb Niobium	42 96 Mo Molybdenum	43 97 Tc Technetium	44 101 Ru Ruthenium	45 103 Rh Rhodium
55 133 Cs Cesium	56 137 Ba Barium	57 139 La Lanthanum	72 180 Hf Hafnium	73 181 Ta Tantalum	74 184 W Tungsten	75 187 Re Rhenium	76 190 Os Osmium	77 192 Ir Iridium
87 223 Fr Francium	88 226 Ra Radium	89 227 Ac Actinium	104 260 Db Dubnium	105 262 Jl Joliotium	106 263 Rf Rutherfordium	107 262 Bh Bohrium	108 265 Hn Hahnium	109 266 Mt Meitnerium

Lanthanides:

58 140 Ce Cerium	59 141 Pr Praseodymium	60 142 Nd Neodymium	61 145 Pm Promethium	62 152 Sm Samarium	63 153 Eu Europium	64 158 Gd Gadolinium

Actinides:

90 232 Th Thorium	91 231 Pa Protactinium	92 238 U Uranium	93 237 Np Neptunium	94 244 Pu Plutonium	95 243 Am Americium	96 247 Cm Curium

ABUNDANT ELEMENTS

The most abundant elements in the Earth's crust (by mass), in elemental or compound form

Element	Abundance (%)
Oxygen	49
Silicon	26
Aluminum	7
Iron	4
Calcium	3

FLUORINE
Fluorine is very reactive – a typical property of the elements in its group. It is often added to water supplies and to toothpaste in the form of fluoride ions (fluorine atoms with an extra electron).

MERCURY
Used in thermometers, mercury is the only metal that is liquid at room temperature. It is very poisonous, and affects mental health. The phrase "mad as a hatter" arose because hatters, who used mercury, often went mad.

ELEMENT RECORDS

RAREST METAL
is rhodium. Just 3 tons are produced each year, compared with 1,700 tons of gold.

MOST COMMON ELEMENT
in the Universe is hydrogen; the next is helium.

NITROGEN
Nitrogen accounts for over 75% of the Earth's atmosphere and is essential to plants and animals. It is an ingredient in fertilizers, and plants need it to help them grow.

ELEMENT FACTS
• In 1994, elements 104–109 were renamed by an international commission. Disputes over who had discovered them first had led to a temporary system of naming by their atomic number.

HELIUM
The lowest possible temperature is 0K (-459.69°F/-273.16°C). Helium has the lowest boiling point of any element: 4.23K (-452.07°F/-268.93°C).

• The element dysprosium is named after the Greek word *dysprositos*, which means "difficult to obtain."

• Helium was discovered by analysing light from the Sun. Its name comes from *helios*, the Greek word for Sun.

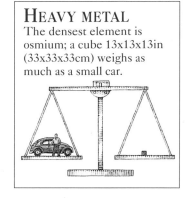

HEAVY METAL
The densest element is osmium; a cube 13x13x13in (33x33x33cm) weighs as much as a small car.

BODY ELEMENTS
Many elements are essential to the human body. Minute amounts of certain elements, called trace elements, are important for health.

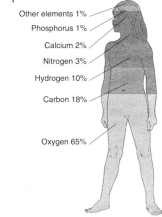

- Other elements 1%
- Phosphorus 1%
- Calcium 2%
- Nitrogen 3%
- Hydrogen 10%
- Carbon 18%
- Oxygen 65%

PLUTONIUM
If the artificial element plutonium–239 is not produced and stored in quantities of less than 0.66lb (300g), a spontaneous nuclear reaction begins, and dangerous amounts of energy are released.

SILICON
Pure silicon, a semiconductor, is used in electronic devices to provide a base for minute integrated circuits.

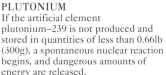

TECHNETIUM
This element does not occur naturally; it was the first of many elements to be made artificially, in nuclear reactions. It is used to some extent in medical diagnosis.

IODINE
Once prepared from seaweed, iodine is essential to the human diet. It turns into a violet vapor when heated.

ARTIFICIAL ELEMENTS

Element	Year produced	Maker
Technetium	1937	C. Porrior and E.G. Sogró
Astatine	1940	D.R. Corson
Neptunium	1940	E.M. McMillan and P. Abelson
Plutonium	1940	Glenn Seaborg
Americium	1944	Glenn Seaborg
Curium	1944	Glenn Seaborg
Promethium	1945	J.A. Marinsky
Berkelium	1949	S.G. Thompson
Californium	1950	S.G. Thompson, Glenn Seaborg K. Street, and Albert Ghiorso
Einsteinium	1952	Gregory R. Choppin
Fermium	1952	Gregory R. Choppin
Mendelevium	1955	Albert Ghiorso
Nobelium	1958	Albert Ghiorso
Lawrencium	1961	Albert Ghiorso

ENERGY

ENERGY AND FORCES constantly change the world. Energy takes many forms – the only visible one is light energy – and people have built many types of machine to convert and control all its forms.

The car has a certain mass, which gives it a certain weight.

The tension in the rope is a force, which pulls the car up the slope.

The total energy expended is the same as if the car were lifted vertically.

The person is using energy to produce a force on the handle of the winch.

Friction is a force that acts in the opposite direction to the movement of the car.

Gears magnify the force produced by the person, but the rope moves much more slowly than the winch handle.

Weight is a force.

The ramp is a machine.

ENERGY AND FORCE

How can one person lift a heavy car? He or she can use a force, applied through a machine such as a winch, but must still provide the total amount of energy required to lift the car. Twice as much energy is needed to lift the car twice as high, or if the car is twice as heavy.

ENERGY CONVERSION

Energy can be neither destroyed, nor can it be created from nothing. Whenever anything happens, one form of energy is simply changed into another.

TEMPERATURE SCALE

Temperature is measured in degrees of Fahrenheit or Celsius, but also in kelvins (K).

Burning point of wood: 523K; 250°C; 482°F

Explosion point of nitroglycerin: 491K; 218°C; 424°F

Sauna bath: 413K; 140°C; 284°F

Boiling point of water: 373K; 100°C; 212°F

Midday heat in Death Valley, California: 329.7K; 56.7°C; 134°F

Human body temperature: 310K; 37°C; 98.6°F

Body temperature of spiny anteater: 295K; 22°C; 71.6°F

Freezing point of pure water: 273K; 0°C; 32°F

Freezing point of mercury: 234K; -39°C; -38°F

Absolute zero: 0K; -273°C; -459°F

ENERGY CONVERSION IN A CAR JOURNEY

Chemical energy
Gasoline releases lots of energy when ignited under pressure.

Sound energy
Radio and loudspeakers convert electrical energy into sound.

Kinetic energy
Any moving object possesses kinetic energy. The faster it moves and the greater its mass, the greater its kinetic energy.

Electrical energy
Movement of car's wheels recharges battery.

Light energy
Car headlights are powered by battery.

Potential energy
Energy that is "stored" is potential energy. When released, it is converted into other forms.

Heat energy
Movement of engine parts generates heat.

Heat energy (brakes)
When brakes are applied, friction between car tires and ground generates heat.

ENERGY MEASURE

All forms of energy – potential, kinetic, sound, chemical, light, heat, etc. – can be measured in units called joules.

Energy of a thunderstorm
About 1 quadrillion joules of heat and potential (stored) energy.

Energy released by a lightning strike
100 million joules of electrical energy becoming 100 million joules of heat energy.

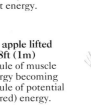

An apple lifted 3.28ft (1m)
1 joule of muscle energy becoming 1 joule of potential (stored) energy.

1 second of a 100-watt light bulb
100 joules of electrical energy becoming 15 joules of light energy and 85 joules of heat energy.

1 second of Itaipu Dam, Brazil
Potential energy becoming 12.6 million joules of electrical energy.

EVER READY

The amount of atomic energy in a kilogram of radioactive uranium–235 would keep a 100-watt light bulb alight for 27,400 years.

TEMPERATURE

The particles that make up all matter, such as atoms, are constantly in motion, vibrating back and forth or speeding through space. The temperature of matter is the average energy of its particles. Matter with more energy can raise the temperature of other matter around it.

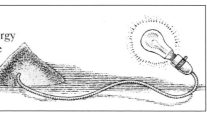

Ice molecules have low energy.

Hot water molecules transfer kinetic energy to ice molecules – ice melts.

Hot water

Hot water molecules have more energy.

ENERGY UNITS
Other energy units can be converted into joules

Unit	Joule equivalent
Joule (J)	
Watts (W)	1J per second
Horsepower (Hp)	2,600,000 J
Calories (Kcal)	4,184 J
Kilowatt hour (kWh)	3,600,000 J

FORCES

A FORCE IS a push or a pull. A force can start an object moving, slow it down, or change its direction. Forces can also change the shape of an object.

GRAVITY

One of the most familiar forces is a force of attraction between objects, called gravity. Gravity keeps us on the Earth and gives us weight. Anything with mass exerts gravity, and the size of this force depends on the masses of the objects and the distance between them. It becomes weaker as bodies move farther apart or lose mass.

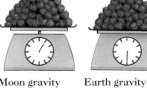

Moon gravity
The Moon exerts less gravitational force than Earth because it has less mass.

Earth gravity
Earth's large mass makes things on its surface weigh six times more than on the Moon.

ADDING FORCES TOGETHER

If more than one force acts on an object, the overall effect will be the same as one force acting in one direction. This force is called the resultant.

BOW AND ARROW
The force of an arrow fired from a bow is the resultant of the two forces that act along the upper and lower halves of the bowstring.

TUG OF WAR
In a tug of war, the resultant force is almost zero, because the two forces on the rope act in exactly opposite directions.

Opposing forces

TURNING FORCES

Forces can turn objects. The greater the force, and the greater its distance from the turning point, the greater the turning force.

TURNING NUTS
The spanner is useful for turning a nut because its long handle means that you can apply a force far away from the nut. This produces a stronger turning force (moment).

NEWTON'S LAWS OF MOTION

In 1687, English mathematician Isaac Newton (1642–1725) identified three laws that describe the motion of objects under the influence of forces.

NEWTON'S FIRST LAW

An object will not change its motion unless a force acts upon it.

A frog will stay still unless a force makes it move. If the frog was drifting along at a constant speed, it would continue to do so until a force stopped it, slowed it down, or made it speed up.

NEWTON'S SECOND LAW

A change in an object's motion depends upon the force acting on it and on the mass of the object.

The frog needs twice as much force to change its motion twice as much.

NEWTON'S THIRD LAW

For every force there is an equal force acting in the other direction.

Forces come in pairs. The frog and the lilypad push against each other.

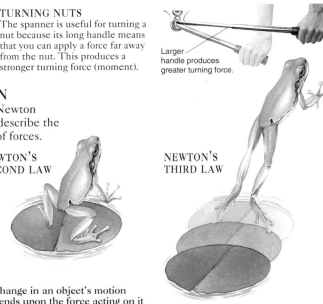

CIRCULAR MOTION

A moving object will travel in a straight line, unless a force changes its direction.

Hammer thrower
To make a hammer go in a circle, an athlete must supply a force, called centripetal force, that constantly pulls it around in a circle. As soon as the athlete lets go, the hammer flies off in a straight line.

Athlete uses centripetal force to throw hammer.

PRESSURE

Pressure is a measure of how "concentrated" a force is. A force applied over a small area exerts more pressure than the same force applied over a large area.

PRESSURE AND AREA
If a watering can and trowel are pushed into sand with about the same force, the trowel sinks farther into the sand. This is because the force is exerted over a smaller area – the trowel's thin blade.

Larger handle produces greater turning force.

FORCES WORDS

Acceleration Rate of change of velocity.

Center of gravity The point on an object at which it balances.

Equilibrium State produced when forces acting on an object balance, so that there is no resultant.

Momentum Mass of an object multiplied by its velocity.

Newton Unit of force. One newton (1N) causes a mass of one kilogram to move with an acceleration of one meter (3.28ft) per second per second.

Resultant Force produced by combining two or more forces.

Velocity Speed and direction of an object.

BRAIN POWER

The ancient Greek scientist Archimedes was said to have constructed a pulley mechanism that enabled a ship that had run aground to be dragged into open water by just one man.

MACHINES

A machine is a device that can change the size and direction of a force. With a block and tackle, for example, a person can lift a very heavy load. This is because the arrangement of ropes in the block and tackle means that the person needs to pull a long length of rope to lift the load a small distance.

PULLEY
Effort is magnified by the rope and the wheels in order to lift the load.

WEDGE
The slope requires less effort to lift the load than by picking it up vertically.

SCREW
Effort is magnified by the thread, acting as a long slope wrapped around the screw.

WHEEL AND AXLE
Effort applied to the wheel is magnified by the axle, turning it with greater force.

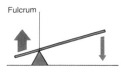

Fulcrum

LEVER
Effort applied at one end of a bar is magnified by the fulcrum to lift the load at the other end.

ELECTRICITY AND MAGNETISM

PUT A PIN CLOSE to a magnet, and it will cling to the magnet. Rub a balloon on a sweater and the balloon will cling to a wall. These things happen because invisible forces are at work – magnetism and electricity. These forces are important, since they hold almost everything together.

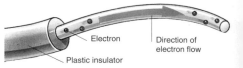

Electron — An electron carries negative electric charge. When millions of electrons flow in a conductor, an electric current is produced.

Proton — A proton carries a positive charge. Protons lie in the nucleus of the atom.

Atom — Nucleus

Normally, atoms have no electrical charge – the charges from the protons in the nucleus and electrons orbiting around the nucleus cancel each other out.

Location of one of atom's electrons

CURRENT ELECTRICITY

The unit of charge is the coulomb. One coulomb is equal to the charge of 6 billion billion electrons. An electric current is a flow of electrons. A current of one ampere (see below) means that a charge of one coulomb is flowing per second.

Electron — Direction of electron flow
Plastic insulator

STATIC ELECTRICITY

When you rub a balloon on a sweater, some electrons get separated from their atoms. This creates an electrical charge. Charges of the same type repel (push each other away). Opposite charges attract. The balloon gains a negative charge. This gives the wall a positive charge, and the balloon clings to it.

Positive charge
Negative charge

Comb negatively charged by being run through hair.

Negatively charged leaves repel each other.

ELECTROSCOPE

An electroscope is an instrument for detecting electric charge. It has two pieces of gold leaf fixed to a brass rod. The leaves separate when an electric charge is brought near to the rod.

ELECTRICITY WORDS

Ampere The unit of current. If a wire carries one ampere (1A), one coulomb (1C) of charge is flowing along the wire each second.

Volt The unit of voltage or electromotive force. This is a measure of how much energy charges have. One volt (1V) means that each coulomb (1C) has one joule (1J) of energy.

Ohm The unit of resistance. If a wire has a one ohm (1Ω) resistance, a voltage of one volt will produce a current of one ampere.

Watt The unit used to measure power. An electric current of one ampere (1A) at one volt (1V) will have a power of one watt (1W).

SHOCKING CURE

The bite of the South American Bushmaster snake can be treated by a series of short electric shocks at around 20,000–25,000V. In remote areas, car or outboard motors are sometimes used to deliver the voltage.

ELECTRIC FACTS

• The word "electricity" comes from the Greek word for amber, *elektron*. The ancient Greeks noticed that when amber was rubbed with a cloth, small objects would cling to it.

• A television on "standby" uses one-third as much electrical power as a television that is switched on.

• The body's nerves carry electric currents to and from the brain at speeds of up to 249mph (400km/h).

Small, positively charged particles move to top of cloud.

Large, negatively charged particles move to bottom of cloud.

Negative cloud charge induces positive ground charge.

Lightning conductor

LIGHTNING

Lightning is a tremendous spark of electricity, caused by a buildup of electric charge in clouds. The spark passes between clouds, or from the cloud to the ground. Many buildings are fitted with lightning conductors, which reduce the risk of lightning striking by draining electric charge away from clouds.

BATTERY

Inside a battery, chemical reactions separate electrons from atoms of the chemicals present. These electrons move around a circuit from the negative to the positive terminal.

Positive terminal
Carbon rod
Ammonium chloride paste
Negative terminal
Electron flow

SERIES AND PARALLEL CIRCUITS

Two bulbs one after the other in a circuit are said to be "in series." Each bulb only gets half the energy (voltage), so they shine dimly. In parallel, the bulbs would shine more brightly, since each bulb gets the full voltage – but the current will be doubled.

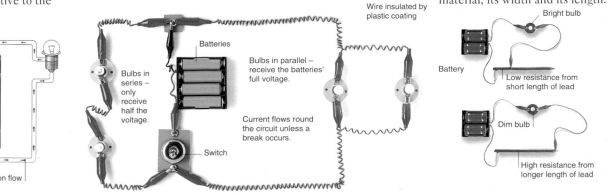

Wire insulated by plastic coating

Batteries

Bulbs in series – only receive half the voltage.

Bulbs in parallel – receive the batteries' full voltage.

Current flows round the circuit unless a break occurs.

Switch

RESISTANCE

The resistance of a material is a measure of how easily electric current will flow through it. Resistance depends upon the material, its width and its length.

Bright bulb
Battery
Low resistance from short length of lead
Dim bulb
High resistance from longer length of lead

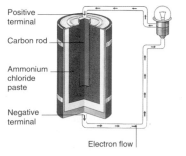

MAGNETISM

Certain materials exert invisible forces, similar to electric forces. A magnet will attract objects made of iron, and a few other metals. Also magnets will attract or repel other magnets. Every magnet has two ends, called poles, where the forces it exerts are strongest. One is called the north pole and the other is called the south pole.

Magnet exerts force around it in an area called a magnetic field.

Iron filings and compasses show magnetic lines of force.

North pole

South pole

Lines of force loop around magnet and splay out from poles.

Unlike poles attract
If unlike poles – one north and one south – are placed together, they attract each other.

Fields of attracting magnets

Like poles repel
If like poles – both north or both south – are put together they repel each other.

Fields of repeling magnets

Iron filings show distortion of normal lines of force when two magnets meet.

Magnet
When a magnet attracts objects, the objects become magnetized and can attract other objects.

Each steel ball acts as a magnet.

LODESTONE

Metal objects, such as pins, are attracted to the lodestone.

Lodestone is a magnetic rock of iron oxide that occurs naturally. In ancient times people used lodestones as compasses and later to make magnetic compass needles.

EARTH MAGNET

The Earth's metallic core is a giant magnet, which lines up near to the true North Pole and South Pole, moving slightly every year. A compass contains a magnetized needle, which always points toward the magnetic north and south poles, enabling navigators to find their way.

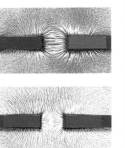

Magnetic north

True North

Lines of magnetic force

Earth's magnetic field

DOMAINS

Magnetic objects contain small regions, between 0.1 and 1mm across, called domains. Each domain has two poles, and most of a magnet's domains are oriented in the same direction. If the domains are made to point in different directions the magnet will lose its magnetism.

Domain poles not in line

Poles line up.

Domains are jumbled up In unmagnetized iron or steel.

Domains may be aligned by stroking with another magnet.

Magnets also demagnetized by heating

Striking with a hammer jumbles up domains, demagnetizing the bar.

BARKING MAD

Scottish physicist James Clerk Maxwell, who first explained the relationship between electricity and magnetism, used to talk through his theories with his dog, often at noisy parties.

MAGNETISM FACTS

• A wire carrying an electric current straight into this page would have a magnetic field going clockwise around it.

• Keepers are pieces of iron that help a magnet keep its power.

• Near the North and South Poles, the Earth's magnetic field traps charged particles emitted by the Sun. These particles react with the Earth's field to produce layers of colored lights in the night sky, called Northern Lights or aurora borealis in the North, and Southern Lights or aurora australis in the south.

ELECTROMAGNETISM

Magnetic forces are not only produced by magnets. Magnetism is also produced by an electric current flowing through a wire. This magnetism can be made stronger by wrapping the wire around an iron core, such as a nail.

Insulated copper wire wrapped around iron nail

Wire connected to a battery

Metal objects are attracted to electromagnet.

ELECTRIC MAGNET

The magnetism produced by an electric current is exactly the same as magnetism produced by a magnet – it has a magnetic field, and a north and south pole. It can be switched on and off, however, with the electric current.

Magnetic field

North pole

South pole

Flow of current

MAGNETIC FIELDS

Field	Strength in tesla (unit of field measurement)
Weakest measured field	0.000000000008T
Earth's field	0.00003T
Powerful magnet	1T
Highest field on record	30.1T

ELECTRIC MOTOR

An electric motor contains magnets and coils of wire. When current passes through the coil, it produces magnetism, which makes the coil turn in the magnetic field of the magnets.

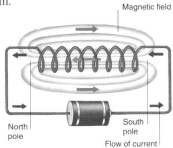

Magnetic field

Direction of rotation

Permanent magnet

Direction of current

In an electric motor, the magnetic fields of the coil and magnet interact and force the coil to rotate. This rotational motion can be harnessed to provide power for machines.

Coil

Brush

Commutator – reverses flow of current at each half-turn, reversing the coil's magnetic field and keeping coil moving.

Battery

Simple direct current motor

GENERATOR

A generator is like a motor in reverse. Turning the coil inside the magnet's field produces an electric current. Power stations use huge generators to produce electricity for homes, schools, and factories.

Handle turns coil inside magnet and commutator

Commutator

Direction of current flow

Simple direct current generator

Current is generated in coil when it cuts through lines of force of magnet.

Coil

Permanent magnet

Magnetic field of magnet

Bulb lights up when handle is turned.

Direction of current reverses at every half-turn of the handle – one brush is always negative, the other positive, producing direct current in the circuit.

LIGHT AND COLOR

WITHOUT LIGHT, WE WOULD not be able to see. Nature provides our most important light source – the Sun – and its light, either directly, or by bouncing off our surroundings, enters our eyes and enables us to recognize our world.

LIGHT ACTION

Light travels in straight lines at 980 million ft/sec (300 million m/sec). It creates shadows, bounces or reflects off smooth surfaces, and bends when it passes through different transparent materials.

LIGHT SPEED

Knowing the speed of light, astronomers have measured the distance to the Moon very accurately by bouncing a laser beam off a mirror left there by astronauts, and timing its return journey.

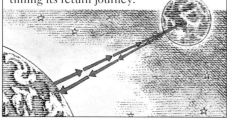

BRIGHTNESS

Light is given off by many different light sources, such as candles and light bulbs. Some light sources are brighter than others, and will provide better illumination.

Brightness in candela
The luminous intensity (brightness) of a light source is measured in candela (cd). One candela is approximately equal to the brightness of a candle.

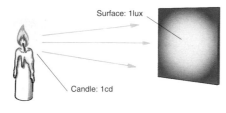

Surface: 1lux

Candle: 1cd

Illumination in lux
Light from a source illuminates a surface placed in its path. This illumination is measured in lux (lx). From a distance of 1m (3.28ft) away, a source of light intensity one candela (1cd) will illuminate a 1sq m (10.8sq ft) surface with an illumination of 1lux.

EYE SEE
When comparing areas of different color, in good light and using both eyes, the human eye can distinguish surfaces of 10 million different colors. No machine yet invented can distinguish as many colors.

LIGHT LAWS

Law of reflection
The angle at which light hits a mirror is equal to the angle that light leaves the mirror.

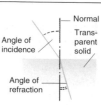

Incident light ray (ray approaching mirror)

Reflected light ray

Law of refraction
Light changes speed when it passes from one material to another. The more it slows down, the more it bends.

Angle of incidence

Normal

Transparent solid

Angle of refraction

Ray of light passes from less dense medium (air) to a more dense one (glass).

REFLECTION
When light bounces off a surface, we say it is reflected. Few things we see give off their own light – we see them only because of reflection. Flat and shiny surfaces, such as mirrors, reflect light evenly to form an image, or picture.

Surface reflection
Most surfaces are not flat, even if they seem to be. When light reflects from an irregular surface, the reflected rays return at many different angles.

Shadow

Opaque object

Mirror – flat and shiny surface

Image appears "behind" mirror.

SHADOW
Light travels through transparent substances, such as water or glass, in straight lines. Nontransparent (opaque) materials, such as wood or metal, do not allow light to pass through them. They cause a shadow to be cast on the opposite side from the light source.

REFRACTION
Light changes direction when it passes from one transparent material to another. This happens because light travels at different speeds through different materials. The change in direction is called refraction.

Glass – denser substance than air

Angle of light ray changes.

Emerging light ray is parallel to original ray but shifted to left.

LENSES
Lenses are specially shaped pieces of glass, or other transparent substances, that focus or disperse light evenly.

Convex lens
A block of glass that curves outward is called a convex lens. Its shape focuses light on a point. It is used in cameras, magnifying glasses, and microscopes.

Lens

Focus

Focal length

Parallel light

Concave lens
A block of glass that curves inward is called a concave lens. Its shape causes light to diverge (spread out). It is used in wide-angle and telephoto lenses.

Lens

Rays diverge.

MIRROR
If the light falls on a completely smooth surface, all the rays are reflected regularly, at the same angle. An image forms, and the object looks as if it is behind the mirror.

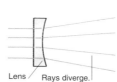

Eye of observer

Mirror

Image of cup and saucer forms behind mirror.

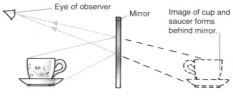

HOW LIGHT IS MADE
There are two ways of making light – incandescence and luminescence. Incandescence happens when something gets very hot. Luminescence happens in four major ways.

Incandescence
In a light bulb, the fine filament heats up and gives out incandescent light. Other forms of incandescent light are candle flames, or the red glow from an electric element.

Phosphorescence
Phophorescent paint makes the numbers on clock faces glow in the dark. The paint stores energy when light falls on it. The energy is slowly released, as light, so the paint can be seen at night.

Fluorescence
Fluorescent chemicals in some washing powders make clothes look brighter in sunlight. Ultraviolet light energy is briefly stored, then released as visible light.

Bioluminescence
Some animals, such as the firefly, produce chemicals that release light energy when combined in their bodies.

Triboluminescence
Some substances, such as sugar, give out light when suddenly broken apart or crushed.

ELECTROMAGNETIC SPECTRUM

Light is part of a range of radiation called the electromagnetic spectrum. Different parts of the spectrum have different energy – from low-energy radio waves to high-energy gamma rays. Wavelengths can be as short as one nanometer (1nm – one billionth of a meter).

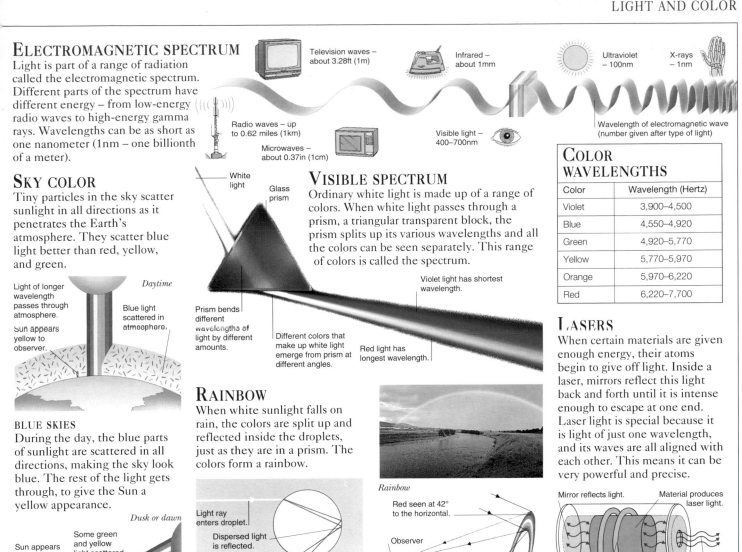

Television waves – about 3.28ft (1m)

Infrared – about 1mm

Ultraviolet – 100nm

X-rays – 1nm

Radio waves – up to 0.62 miles (1km)

Microwaves – about 0.37in (1cm)

Visible light – 400–700nm

Wavelength of electromagnetic wave (number given after type of light)

White light

Glass prism

SKY COLOR

Tiny particles in the sky scatter sunlight in all directions as it penetrates the Earth's atmosphere. They scatter blue light better than red, yellow, and green.

Daytime

Light of longer wavelength passes through atmosphere.

Sun appears yellow to observer.

Blue light scattered in atmosphere.

BLUE SKIES

During the day, the blue parts of sunlight are scattered in all directions, making the sky look blue. The rest of the light gets through, to give the Sun a yellow appearance.

Dusk or dawn

Sun appears red-orange to observer.

Some green and yellow light scattered.

SUNSET RED

In the evening, sunlight passes through a longer distance in the atmosphere. This means that some green and yellow light also gets scattered. Only orange and red light gets through, so the Sun looks orange-red.

MIRAGES

Light is refracted as it passes through layers of air at different temperatures. This can make objects seem nearer than they are and can make hot air layers look like water. When hot air lies above cool air, objects far away, such as ships, can seem to loom upside down. This occurs because light rays traveling from cool to hot air bend down and form an inverted image.

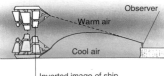

Observer

Warm air

Cool air

Inverted image of ship seen by observer.

VISIBLE SPECTRUM

Ordinary white light is made up of a range of colors. When white light passes through a prism, a triangular transparent block, the prism splits up its various wavelengths and all the colors can be seen separately. This range of colors is called the spectrum.

Violet light has shortest wavelength.

Prism bends different wavelengths of light by different amounts.

Different colors that make up white light emerge from prism at different angles.

Red light has longest wavelength.

RAINBOW

When white sunlight falls on rain, the colors are split up and reflected inside the droplets, just as they are in a prism. The colors form a rainbow.

Light ray enters droplet.

Dispersed light is reflected.

Reflected light leaves droplet.

Rainbow

Red seen at 42° to the horizontal.

Observer

Violet seen at 40° to the horizontal.

MIXING COLORS

Magenta

Blue

Black

Red

Yellow

Cyan

Green

PIGMENTS

Any color of paint, ink, or dye can be formed from the three colors of magenta, cyan, and yellow. Together they produce black.

INTERFERENCE

When light strikes a bubble, it is reflected off both the inside and outside surfaces. The two rays combine in a process called interference and create beautiful colors on the thin surface.

Colors vary with thickness of bubble.

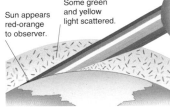

Colors on bubble surface

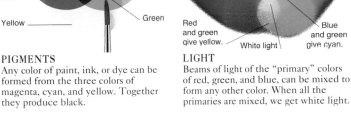

Red light

Red and blue give magenta.

Blue light

Green light

Red and green give yellow.

White light

Blue and green give cyan.

LIGHT

Beams of light of the "primary" colors of red, green, and blue, can be mixed to form any other color. When all the primaries are mixed, we get white light.

LIGHT AND ATMOSPHERE

Not every wavelength of light from space reaches the ground. Some infrared waves (1,100–2,300nm) are absorbed by carbon dioxide, water vapor, and ozone. "Hard" ultraviolet waves (about 220nm) are filtered out by ozone.

COLOR WAVELENGTHS

Color	Wavelength (Hertz)
Violet	3,900–4,500
Blue	4,550–4,920
Green	4,920–5,770
Yellow	5,770–5,970
Orange	5,970–6,220
Red	6,220–7,700

LASERS

When certain materials are given enough energy, their atoms begin to give off light. Inside a laser, mirrors reflect this light back and forth until it is intense enough to escape at one end. Laser light is special because it is light of just one wavelength, and its waves are all aligned with each other. This means it can be very powerful and precise.

Mirror reflects light.

Material produces laser light.

Power supply excites light-producing material.

Laser light emerges from hole in mirror.

LIGHT FACTS

• Electromagnetic radiation can be thought of as waves. The higher the energy, the shorter the wavelength.

• Bees' eyes can detect ultraviolet light. A flower looks bright to a bee because the petals reflect a lot of ultraviolet.

• The word laser stands for Light Amplification by Stimulated Emission of Radiation.

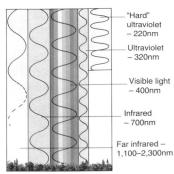

"Hard" ultraviolet – 220nm

Ultraviolet – 320nm

Visible light – 400nm

Infrared – 700nm

Far infrared – 1,100–2,300nm

Effects of atmosphere on wavelengths of light

SOUND

SOUND IS PRODUCED BY objects vibrating. This vibration first pushes the air forward, compressing (squashing) it, then it pulls it back, causing it to expand. These contractions and expansions travel through the air as vibrations, called sound waves.

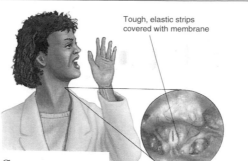

Tough, elastic strips covered with membrane

SOUND WAVE

When people shout, they use the vocal cords in their throat to make a sound. Vocal cords vibrate as air passes through them.

Vocal cords
Larynx muscles stretch vocal cords loosely for low sounds, tightly for high sounds.

Rarefaction
When air expands, the molecules are spread out. This is called rarefraction. The air exerts less pressure than normal.

Compression
When air is compressed, all its molecules are pushed together. The air exerts more pressure than normal.

THE DECIBEL SCALE

The loudness of sound is measured in decibels (db). A 10-db sound increase corresponds to a ten*fold* increase in loudness.

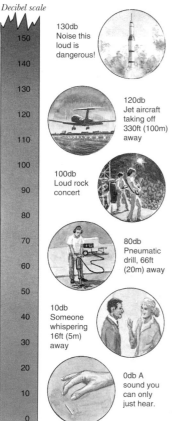

Decibel scale

130db Noise this loud is dangerous!

120db Jet aircraft taking off 330ft (100m) away

100db Loud rock concert

80db Pneumatic drill, 66ft (20m) away

10db Someone whispering 16ft (5m) away

0db A sound you can only just hear.

SOUND FACTS

• Sometimes, a sound and its echo are so close together they seem to be one long sound. This is called reverberation.

• You can hear the sound of a horse's hooves a long time before it arrives, by putting your ear to the ground. Sound waves travel much faster through the ground than through air.

• Sound travels quickly, but light travels much more quickly. You can work out how far away a storm is from the time between the lightning flash and the thunder. Sound travels at about 1,096ft/sec (334m/s). So a storm is about 0.62 miles (1km) away for every three seconds elapsed.

SOUND SPEEDS

Sound travels at different speeds through different materials.

Material	Speed m/sec	ft/sec
Rubber	54	177
Air at 32°F	334	1,096
Air at 212°F	366	1,201
Water	1,284	4,213
Mercury	1,452	4,764
Wood (Oak)	3,850	12,631
Iron	5,000	16,404
Glass	5,000	16,404

ECHOES

An echo is heard when a sound wave bounces off a hard surface. The length of time between the original sound and the echo depends on how far the sound travels before it bounces back. The farther it travels, the longer it is before the echo is heard. Most sounds we hear arrive at our ears as a mixture of direct waves and echoes bouncing off surrounding surfaces.

ULTRASOUND

Ultrasound is sound at a frequency too high for humans to hear. Some animals can hear ultrasounds by echolocation and some make ultrasounds. Bats use ultrasound to catch their food. Depending on their frequency, the sounds they make bounce off flying insects, which the bat can locate and catch.

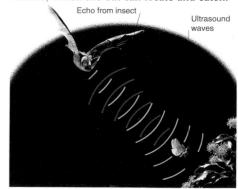

Echo from insect

Ultrasound waves

Echo

Listener hears one sound only, because sound wave travels quickly from hands to wall and back.

Clapping hands compress air, creating sound wave.

Outgoing wave

Wall acts as barrier to sound wave. Distant barriers, such as cliffs or hills, will create separate echo, heard slightly later.

SOUND MAN

One of the most important contributors to our understanding of how we hear sounds was Georg von Békésy. In his research into hearing, he examined the ears of a dead zoo elephant that he had rescued from a glue factory.

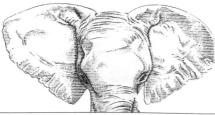

SONIC BOOM

A sonic boom happens when the source of a sound, such as a jet aircraft, travels faster than the sound it produces (at about 745mph, or 1,200km/h). At such times, many wave fronts reach the ears of people standing directly below at the same time, making a very loud noise like a huge clap of thunder.

Subsonic flight

When flying below speed of sound, jet aircraft compresses air in front of it. Near to speed of sound, a wall or barrier of compressed air forms.

Supersonic flight

When aircraft reaches speed of sound, air pressure wave at nose produces massive shock wave. This causes sonic boom.

FREQUENCY

Frequency is the number of sound waves per second. The higher the number, the higher the pitch of the sound. Frequency is measured in hertz (Hz).

Sound wave The loudness of a sound depends on its amplitude. This is the difference between the point in a sound wave where the air is exerting the least pressure, and the point where it exerts the most.

Peak
Trough
Amplitude
Wavelength

Soft sound
There is not much difference between the low-pressure area of the sound wave and the high-pressure area.

Loud sound
As a sound gets louder, there is a greater difference between areas of high and low pressure.

Low sound
Low-pitched sounds have low frequency – fewer waves per second.

High sound
The sound waves are closer together – there are more of them per second.

SHATTERED

If a sound makes an object vibrate at its natural frequency, the vibrations will build to a greater and greater amplitude. This effect is called resonance, and it can even make an object break.

DOPPLER EFFECT

A police car's siren becomes more high-pitched as it approaches, and less high-pitched as it moves away. This is called the Doppler effect, and is caused by sound waves being pushed together in front of a moving source of sound, and spaced out behind it.

Waves spread out behind car as it moves forward.

Waves compressed as car moves

Pitch of note lowers for listener when car passes.

1 As the sound gets nearer, the waves are pushed closer together and are heard at a higher frequency.

2 As the sound moves away, the waves are farther apart and the sound is heard at a lower frequency.

KEY FREQUENCY RANGES
Various animals and machines make or detect sounds over different ranges of frequency. The human voice creates sound over a relatively narrow range of frequencies.

Bat
Hears: 1,000–120,000Hz
Makes: 10,000–120,000Hz

Human
Hears: 20–20,000Hz
Makes: 85–1,100Hz

Ultrasound scanner
Makes and receives: 3,500,000–7,500,000Hz

Frequency scale   Audible sounds   *Ultrasounds*

Infrasound

Elephant
Hears: 1–20,000Hz
Makes: 12Hz–unknown

Nuclear explosion: as low as 0.01Hz

Dog
Hears: 15–50,000Hz
Makes: 450–1,080Hz

Porpoise
Hears: 150–150,000Hz
Makes: 7,000–120,000Hz

SONAR ECHO

SONAR (Sound Navigation and Ranging) is a way of using echoes from ultrasound to detect the presence of objects. The echoes are used to form a picture on a screen.

Pictures from sound
Waves of ultrasound can be directed into the human body – to an unborn child, for example. The ultrasound echoes off the unborn child, then the ultrasound equipment picks up the echo and turns it into electrical impulses. These form a picture of the baby on a screen.

Ultrasound scan of fetus in womb

MUSIC

Musical instruments may make the same notes (sounds of different pitch) but they sound different because each one has its own quality. Although the main frequency is the same for each, they also produce overtones of other frequencies. These vary for each instrument.

Ranges
Some instruments produce a greater range of frequency than others.

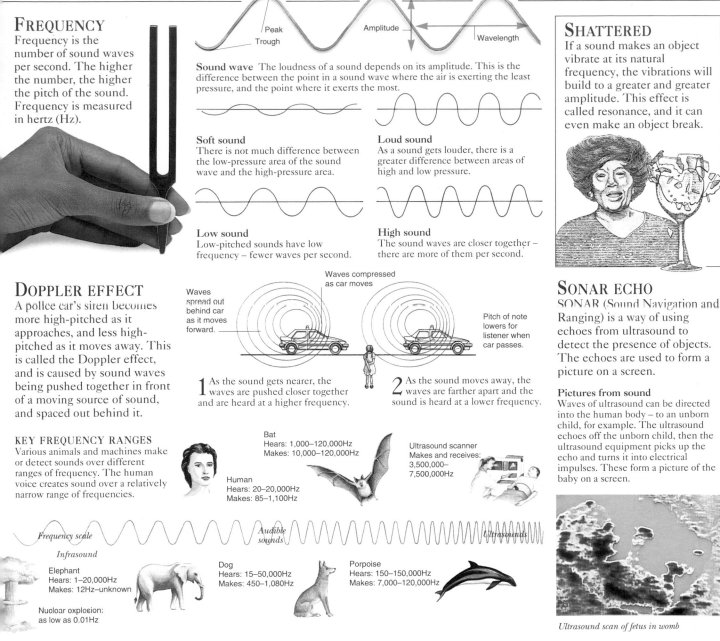

Pipe organ
10–8,000Hz

Violin
200–2,650Hz

Trumpet
190–990Hz

Clarinet 75–1,800Hz

Comparison of instrument ranges

Piano
30–4,100Hz

RECORDING SOUND

There are several different ways of recording sound. All recorders work by turning the sound into some sort of electrical signal, which can be turned back into a sound later.

Vinyl records
These record signals appear as a wavy groove. They make the stylus vibrate, which in turn creates electrical signals that can be turned into sound.

Cassette tapes
Sounds are recorded as signals on a magnetic tape. A pattern of strong or weak magnetic signals forms on the tape. This can be played back, making electrical signals later used to make a sound.

Compact discs
Sounds are recorded in the CD's surface as tiny pits, which pass under a laser beam. Reflections from the beam are turned into electrical signals and used to make sound.

Vinyl record

Cassette tape

Compact disc

Record player's stylus fits into spiral groove.

Contours in groove wall record loudness and frequency of sound.

Magnetic alignment of particles on tape records sound.

Track is thinner than a hair and several miles long.

Sequence of microscopic pits records sound.

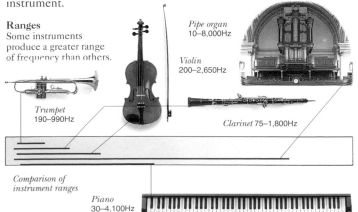

ELECTRONICS

ELECTRONICS, WHICH IS concerned with the movement and control of electrons, plays a crucial role in the efficient operation of modern technology.

1879 Cathode rays observed by English physicist William Crookes (1832–1919), using a specially designed vacuum tube. He finds that the rays, which he calls cathode rays, are deflected by magnetic fields.

Crookes tube

1880 American inventor Thomas Edison (1847–1931) observes tiny currents flowing from a lamp filament. This becomes known as the Edison effect.

1882 Edison effect investigated by Englishman John Ambrose Fleming (1849–1945).

Thomas Edison

| 1850 | 1879 | | 1880 | 1882 |

1906 Use of crystals as radio wave detectors discovered independently by Americans H.H.C. Dunwoody and G.W. Pickard.

Early crystal radio set (c.1920)

1917 First crystal grown by artificial means by German J. Czochralski (1885–1953).

1918/19 Switching circuits devised by British scientists W.H. Eccles and F.W. Jordan.

1933 Electron microscope invented by German scientists Ernst Ruska (1906–88) and Max Knoll (1897–1969).

1934 Liquid-crystal effect investigated in detail by John Dreyer at Marconi laboratories, UK.

1938 Mathematical rules for computing with electronic circuits formulated.

1940 Electronic computers (using valves) developed. These first computers are as big as buildings.

Image from modern electron microscope

| 1917 | 1918 | 1930 | 1933 | 1934 | 1938 | 1940 |

TRANSISTOR

The transistor, the most important component in electronics, replaced the valve (below). It can turn a current on and off, and it can alter its strength. If enough transistors are connected together, their particular state at any time (on or off) can be used by computers to store and manipulate numbers, words, and pictures.

Audion valve of 1907, invented by Lee de Forest

Plate (anode)

Grid gives off weak signal.

Filament (cathode) gives off electrons.

VALVE
Valves control the strength and direction of a current. A red-hot filament (cathode) in a vacuum tube gives off streams of electrons. These are attracted toward a positively charged plate (anode), but a grid placed in the flow's path and given its own current will copy any variations in its current onto the larger current.

MINIATURIZED TRANSISTOR
A transistor can permit or prevent a current from flowing using a small charge.

1 A small, positive electric charge is given to a layer of conductive polysilicon that is embedded in nonconductive silicon dioxide.

2 The positive charge in the polysilicon attracts electrons from the base layer of P-type silicon (see below).

3 The flow of electrons toward the polysilicon makes current flow from the N-type silicon point, called the source, to another, the drain.

4 When current flows between source and drain in this way, the transistor is switched on. If the polysilicon is negatively charged, current stops, and the transistor switches off.

Semiconductors
Silicon is used for microchips because it is a semiconductor – it varies in conductivity. Different types of silicon – N-type and P-type – placed side-by-side, allow current flow to be directed. This property directs current in miniature transistors.

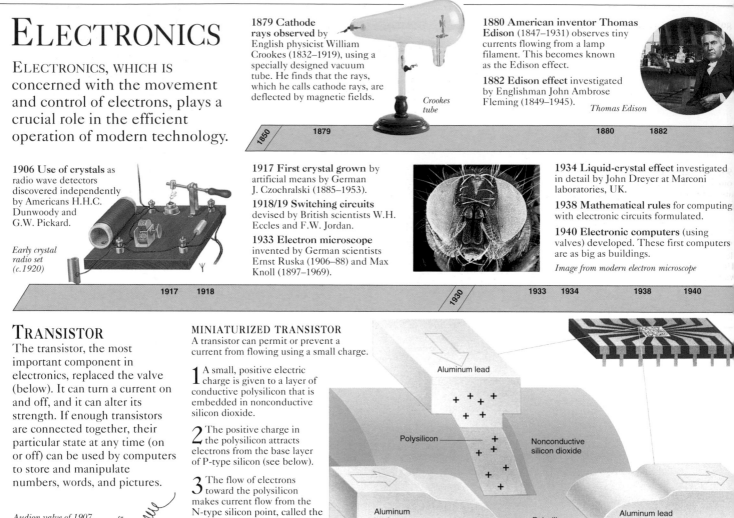

Aluminum lead

Polysilicon

Nonconductive silicon dioxide

Aluminum lead

Polysilicon

Aluminum lead

Source **Drain**

N-type silicon

N-type silicon

P-type silicon

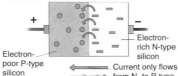

+

Electron-poor P-type silicon

–

Electron-rich N-type silicon

Current only flows from N- to P-type

CIRCUIT SYMBOLS

Diode		Resistor	
Light-emitting diode		Speaker	
Photodiode		Bulb	
N-P-N transistor		Transformer	
P-N-P transistor		Battery	

CHIP RESULT
A single microchip produced in 1994 contained 9 million transistors. A similar number of transistors in 1950 would cover an area larger than eight soccer fields.

MAKING A MICROCHIP
Thousands of tiny transistors (above) and other components can be put on one tiny slice of silicon to make a complete electronic circuit – an integrated circuit, or microchip. Most electronic devices contain one or more of these silicon chips.

Design
The first stage in making a microchip is to plan and map the thousands of transistors and other components that the chip needs to perform its tasks. Modern chips are so complicated that most of this work is done by computers, not people.

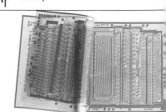

Photography and checking
Once the circuit has been planned, computers check the proposed chip for possible design weaknesses. Microchips contain layers of different materials, and transparent, enlarged plans are used to check that each layer fits precisely with all the others.

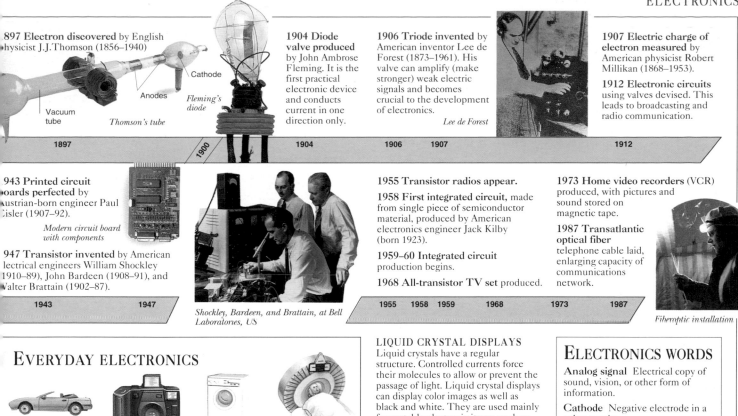

1897 Electron discovered by English physicist J.J.Thomson (1856–1940)

Cathode
Anodes
Vacuum tube
Thomson's tube

Fleming's diode

1904 Diode valve produced by John Ambrose Fleming. It is the first practical electronic device and conducts current in one direction only.

1906 Triode invented by American inventor Lee de Forest (1873–1961). His valve can amplify (make stronger) weak electric signals and becomes crucial to the development of electronics.

Lee de Forest

1907 Electric charge of electron measured by American physicist Robert Millikan (1868–1953).

1912 Electronic circuits using valves devised. This leads to broadcasting and radio communication.

| 1897 | 1900 | 1904 | 1906 | 1907 | 1912 |

1943 Printed circuit boards perfected by Austrian-born engineer Paul Eisler (1907–92).

Modern circuit board with components

1947 Transistor invented by American electrical engineers William Shockley (1910–89), John Bardeen (1908–91), and Walter Brattain (1902–87).

Shockley, Bardeen, and Brattain, at Bell Laboratories, US

1955 Transistor radios appear.

1958 First integrated circuit, made from single piece of semiconductor material, produced by American electronics engineer Jack Kilby (born 1923).

1959–60 Integrated circuit production begins.

1968 All-transistor TV set produced.

1973 Home video recorders (VCR) produced, with pictures and sound stored on magnetic tape.

1987 Transatlantic optical fiber telephone cable laid, enlarging capacity of communications network.

Fiberoptic installation

| 1943 | 1947 | 1955 | 1958 | 1959 | 1968 | 1973 | 1987 |

EVERYDAY ELECTRONICS

Modern car control systems

Automatic camera

Washing machine

Medical scanner

Mobile telephone

Radar system

Factory robot

Electronic shaver

LIQUID CRYSTAL DISPLAYS

Liquid crystals have a regular structure. Controlled currents force their molecules to allow or prevent the passage of light. Liquid crystal displays can display color images as well as black and white. They are used mainly for portable electronic items, such as computers and hand-held games.

ELECTRONICS WORDS

Analog signal Electrical copy of sound, vision, or other form of information.

Cathode Negative electrode in a valve or tube.

Digital signal Electrical stream of information in the form of on or off pulses.

Diode Permits electric current in circuit to travel in one direction only.

LED Light-emitting diode.

Semiconductor Substance that conducts slightly; it can be combined with other substances to control conductivity.

Solid-state Using the electronic properties of solids, especially semiconductors, to act as valves.

Resistor Controls amount of current flowing in a circuit.

Microprocessor Integrated circuit that can decode instructions and manipulate information.

Transistor Miniature electronic device that can amplify electric current and turn it on or off.

ELECTRONICS RECORDS

DENSEST MICROCHIP (1994) is a microprocessor measuring 0.03sq in (17sq mm), which contains 9 millon transistors.

LARGEST VALVES are about 6.6ft (2m) long and handle about 10 million watts. They are used in military radars and particle accelerators.

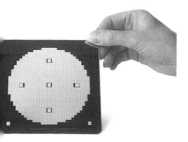

Silicon slice
Silicon metal, which is cheap and strong, needs to be highly refined before it can be used in chips. A pure enough piece, sliced and polished into thin wafers, is treated in a chemical process that etches the grid of components and tracks onto its surface.

ELECTRONICS FACTS

• Microchips are the size of a fingernail, and yet a drawing showing all their workings in detail would be bigger than a detailed map of a major city.

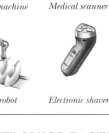

Chemical and heat treatment
The potential microchip is now heated to a high temperature at which the chemicals that will form its several layers can attach to the etched silicon surface. The delicacy of this process requires extreme cleanliness. All workers wear gowns and gloves.

• Fiberoptic cables, made of fine strands of glass, transmit information in the form of pulses of light. They are able to carry much more data than traditional copper cables.

• Filmmakers use electronics to generate astonishing special effects in their films. Animation, once produced by hand, can now be done by computers

Electronics in special effects – scene from Disney film Tron

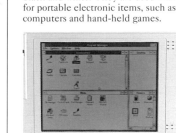

Integrated circuit (chip)

Protective plastic casing

Chip with connections
When the silicon slice has been fully treated, it is placed on a plastic base and connected to metal leads that expand and connect to other parts of a circuit. These conductive leads send out the chip's signals and receive signals from other components.

Pocket calculators – covered and uncovered

Liquid crystal display

Microchip

Uncovered keyboard

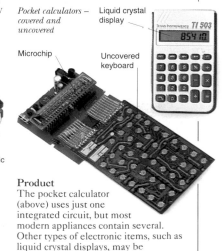

Product
The pocket calculator (above) uses just one integrated circuit, but most modern appliances contain several. Other types of electronic items, such as liquid crystal displays, may be included in a final product.

COMPUTERS

COMPUTERS ARE AUTOMATIC electronic devices that can perform complex tasks by breaking them down into many simple calculations and doing them extremely quickly. Their ability to store, manipulate, and communicate information has had a massive impact on our lives.

1945 First electronic general-purpose calculator, ENIAC (Electronic Numerical Integrator and Calculator), built in US. Using valves, it weighs 33 tons, consumes 150kW, and averages 5,000 operations per second. The US Army uses it to calculate tables for aiming artillery.

ENIAC

1964 BASIC (Beginners All-Purpose Symbolic Instruction Code) programming language is created by professors at Dartmouth College, US. BASIC later becomes popular among users of personal computers.

1965 First commercially successful minicomputer, DEC PDP–8, is produced in US. It sits on a desktop.

1971 First microprocessor chip, the Intel 4004, produced in US. It performs 60,000 operations per second.

1975 Microsoft founded by American businessmen Bill Gates (born 1955) and Paul Allen (born 1953). They develop DOS, which later becomes the dominant operating system for computers.

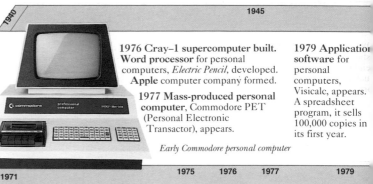

1976 Cray–1 supercomputer built. Word processor for personal computers, *Electric Pencil*, developed. **Apple** computer company formed.

1977 Mass-produced personal computer, Commodore PET (Personal Electronic Transactor), appears.

1979 Application software for personal computers, Visicalc, appears. A spreadsheet program, it sells 100,000 copies in its first year.

Early Commodore personal computer

Timeline: 1960 | 1964 | 1965 | 1971 | 1975 | 1976 | 1977 | 1979 | 1945

ANATOMY OF A COMPUTER

Every computer has four basic parts, or units: an input unit, such as a keyboard, that feeds information into the computer; a central processing unit (CPU) that performs the computer's tasks; an output unit, such as a monitor, that displays the results; a memory unit for storing information and instructions.

Input and output devices
These allow the computer to communicate with people and other computers. The keyboard and mouse are input devices. The monitor and printer are output devices.

Microprocessor
The microprocessor is the central control unit. It carries out a program's instructions and controls the information flowing around the computer on the Bus and the input and output devices.

Bus
The Bus links the microprocessor, memory, and input and output devices.

RAM (Random-Access Memory)
RAM is used to store programs that are being run. When a computer is switched off the information in the RAM is lost.

ROM (Read-Only Memory)
When you switch on a computer, a program that is permanently stored in the ROM checks the computer and makes it ready for use. The ROM's program cannot be changed.

Monitor

Cards for different systems can be added, e.g. modem, sound card, video card.

Power supply

CD–ROM drive

Floppy disk drive

Compact disc

Hard disk

Floppy disk

Mouse pad

Mouse

Keyboard

COMPUTER WORDS

Applications software Software used for specific tasks, e.g. word processors, databases.

Bit Binary digit (a 1 or a 0).

Bug Error in a program.

Byte Piece of information. One byte contains eight bits.

Database Set of data on computer accessible in various ways.

Hardware Machinery and components of the computer.

Internet Worldwide network of computer networks.

Megabyte One million bytes.

Modem Device that allows computers to exchange information using the telephone network.

Operating system The program that enables the computer to perform general operations.

Software The variety of programs used by a computer.

CD–ROM drive
Compact discs, read using lasers, store more data than floppy disks.

Hard disk
The hard disk stores data when the computer is switched off. It is usually used to store larger amounts of data than the RAM.

Floppy disks
These can be used to transfer data between computers.

GENERATIONS OF COMPUTER

Generation	Dates	Characteristic
1st	1944–59	Use valves (vacuum tubes)
2nd	1959–64	Use transistors
3rd	1964–75	Large Scale Integrated Circuits (LSI)
4th	1975–	Very Large Scale Integrated Circuits (VLSI)
5th	Under development	"Artificial Intelligence"-based computers

COMPUTER RECORDS

BIGGEST COMPUTER is the CM–5 "Thinking Machine" at the Los Alamos National Laboratories, US. It can perform 131 billion operations in a second. With a normal calculator, the same number would take 41,000 years.

LARGEST COMPUTER COMPANY is American company IBM, which employs 220,000 people. In 1992, its turnover was $62.7 billion.

LARGEST SOFTWARE COMPANY is American company Microsoft, which employs 16,140 people.

1947 Transistor, ...sential storage device ...r computers, invented ...y American engineers ...illiam Shockley ...910–89), John Bardeen ...908–91), and Walter ...rattain (1902–87).

1948 First stored-program computer, Manchester Mark 1, built in UK. Using valves, it can perform about 500 operations per second and has the first RAM (see ...opposite). It fills a room the size of a small office.

Visible portion of Manchester Mark 1 computer

1951 Early computer game, *Nim*, played by Ferranti Nimrod Computer at the Festival of Britain.

1957 FORTRAN (Formula Translator) programming language invented at IBM.

1958 Integrated circuit (microchip) produced by American engineer Jack Kilby (born 1923). His circuit is made on a single piece of semiconductor.

Jack Kilby

1947   1948   1950

1951   1957   1958

...981 First portable computer, ...sborne 1, produced. At the size and ...eight of a sewing machine, however, it is ...uch less convenient than current ...ortable computers.

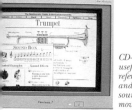

Osborne 1 portable computer

1981 IBM launches IBM PC on the personal computer market. IBM makes the first massive sales in the personal computer market.

1984 Apple Macintosh computer (or Apple Mac) becomes first successful personal computer with a mouse (see opposite) and easy-to-use Graphical User Interface (GUI).

Microsoft Windows title screen

1985 Microsoft launches Windows for the PC. Windows is a Graphical User Interface similar to the Apple Mac's, making personal computers much easier to use.

1990 IBM Pentium PC produced. It holds up to 4,000 megabytes of RAM and can perform up to 112 million instructions per second. The microprocessor chip at the heart of the computer measures 16mm by 17mm and contains 3.1 million transistors. It is designed using a system called VLSI (Very Large Scale Integration).

1980   1981   1984   1985   1990

...OMPUTER FACTS

All the data that computers use is ...binary code: a signal of electrical ...lses that is either on (1) or off ...). Words, numbers, and pictures ...n be expressed as sequences of ...nary code.

Computer viruses may multiply in a computer's memory like bacteria.

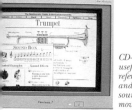

CD-ROM is useful for reference books and can use sound and moving images.

...CD–ROM is a form of compact ...sc player modified for computers. ...Ds for CD–ROM can store 450 ...mes as much data as can be held ...a floppy disk.

- Computer viruses are programs that destroy stored information. A virus may enter the computer's memory and copy itself so many times that it uses up all the memory, or it may make the computer destroy all the data in its memory.

- Computers can communicate with each other over a telephone line, using a machine called a modem.

- Computer performance increased by a factor of about a million between 1950 and 1990.

PROGRAMS

A program is the set of instructions that a computer needs to carry out a particular task, such as word processing. Instructions may be written in "machine code," or other computer languages, such as BASIC or FORTRAN.

A computer's program may be printed out.

SUPERCOMPUTERS

Computers designed to operate at the highest possible speeds are called supercomputers. By performing several processes at once and by being cooled – which causes their components to conduct electricity more efficiently – they can calculate at a very fast rate.

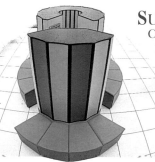

Cray X–MP/48 supercomputer, used in study of particle physics at CERN, Switzerland.

...OW A FLOPPY DISK WORKS

...omputer users can store data on floppy disks ...d transfer it to other computers.

Electromagnet inside computer

Surface of floppy disk

Electrical pulses pass down wire.

Iron core becomes magnetized.

Band pair represents one bit.

1 The surface of a floppy disk is coated with iron particles. Small bands of these particles can be made to line up in one direction or another by an electromagnet inside the computer.

2 Current is passed down a coil, magnetizing an iron core and forcing the iron particles to line up. If current is reversed, the particles line up in the other direction.

3 One pair of particle bands makes up a bit of data. If the bands in the pair lie in the same direction, they represent the binary number 0. If not, the pair represents 1.

IMAGES ON SCREEN

A computer screen consists of a grid of small picture cells called pixels. Each pixel has a horizontal and vertical position code and a color code. The computer's microprocessor generates the picture as a series of these codes, lighting up each pixel in a certain color.

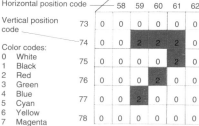

Example of screen image, showing enlarged area with individual pixels.

Horizontal position code

Vertical position code

Color codes:
0   White
1   Black
2   Red
3   Green
4   Blue
5   Cyan
6   Yellow
7   Magenta

	58	59	60	61	62		
73	0	0	0	0	0	0	0
74	0	0	2	2	2	0	0
75	0	0	0	0	2	0	0
76	0	0	0	2	0	0	0
77	0	0	2	0	0	0	0
78	0	0	0	0	0	0	0

COMPUTER-AIDED DESIGN

Computers allow engineers to test new designs without having to build prototype models. They can also be used to help model complex systems, such as weather systems.

Computer model of airflow over airplane

BRAIN DRAIN

The first all-purpose computer, ENIAC, required so much electricity to process information that the lights in a nearby town dimmed each time it was used.

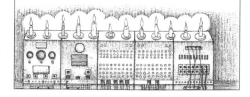

MATHEMATICS

MATHEMATICS IS THE STUDY of numbers and shapes. It is a vital tool, not only for scientists and engineers, but for everyone. Algebra is the branch of mathematics that uses abstract symbols in place of numbers, while geometry deals with shapes and lines.

MATH TOOLS

Set squares and compasses enable us to draw shapes precisely, such as circles and squares. Electronic tools, such as the calculator, save time.

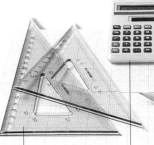

Compasses

Protractor for measuring angles

Set square

Calculator

ONE TO TEN: SYMBOL SYSTEMS

Different civilizations have used different symbols for numbers, and some do not include a zero symbol.

Number	Babylonian	Roman	Mayan	Arabic
Zero				0
One		I	•	1
Two		II	••	2
Three		III	•••	3
Four		IV	••••	4
Five		V	—	5
Six		VI	•	6
Seven		VII	••	7
Eight		VIII	•••	8
Nine		IX	••••	9
Ten		X		10

NEGATIVE NUMBERS

Sometimes it is useful to use numbers less than zero – negative numbers. For example, if the temperature on a winter's day falls below zero, it is referred to as a negative number, such as -3.

-5 -4 -3 -2 -1 0 1 2 3 4 5 6

Number line

SQUARE NUMBERS

9-dot matrix, 3-by-3 square

When a number is multiplied by itself, it is said to be squared. This is usually written as the number, with a small 2 next to and above it. So, three squared is $3^2 = 3 \times 3 = 9$.

BINARY SYSTEM

We use a number system based on the number ten, but a number system can be based on any number. Computers use binary numbers, based on the number two. Binary uses only two digits: 0 and 1.

Base 10 number	Binary number
1	1
2	10
3	11
4	100
5	101
6	110
7	111

PRIME NUMBERS

Prime numbers are those that can be divided only by themselves and one, e.g., 17. 12 is not a prime, since it can be divided by 2, 3, 4, and 6, as well as by itself and 1.

2	3	5	7
11	13	17	19
23	29	31	37
41	43	47	53
59	61	67	71
73	79	83	89
97	101	103	107
109	113	127	131

FRACTIONS

When a cake is halved, each piece is equivalent to the whole divided by two. This is written $^1/_2$, the line meaning "divided by." So, $^3/_4$ (three-quarters) means three divided by four.

PERCENTAGES

It is sometimes useful to write fractions as percentages. Percent means "for each hundred." Written as a percentage, $^1/_2$ becomes 50%, since half of 100 is 50.

DECIMALS

Numbers less than one can be written as decimals. A decimal point is used. The number after the decimal point represents a number of tenths. So, one-half is written as 0.5 ($^5/_{10}$).

STYLE TABLE

Fractions	Decimals	Percentages
$^1/_2$	0.5	50%
$^1/_4$	0.25	25%
$^1/_{10}$	0.1	10%
$^1/_{100}$	0.01	1%

MATHEMATICAL SYMBOLS

Symbol	Meaning	Symbol	Meaning	Symbol	Meaning
+	Add (plus)	=	Equal to	√	Square root of
−	Subtract (minus)	≠	Not equal to	%	Percent
×	Multiply (times)	<	Less than	≤	Less than or equal to
÷	Divided by	>	Greater than	≥	Greater than or equal to

CHAOS THEORY

The intricate pattern (below) was created using a simple mathematical equation. These equations are a product of a recent field of mathematics called chaos theory.

Fractal (computer-generated image)

SCIENTIFIC NOTATION

Very large or small numbers are often written using a system called scientific notation.

Number	Number between 1 and 10	Power of ten	Scientific notation
10	1	10	1×10
150	1.5	10^2 (= 100)	1.5×10^2
274,000,000	2.74	10^8 (= 100,000,000)	2.74×10^8
0.0023	2.3	10^{-3} (= 0.001)	2.3×10^{-3}

DEAD RIGHT

At 20 years of age, Pierre Galois wrote his most important mathematical ideas in a letter to a friend, the night before he was killed in a duel. His results are still used today.

GEOMETRY

Geometry is the study of lines, angles, solid shapes, and surfaces.

PLANE FIGURES

Any two-dimensional (flat) shape, such as a circle, is a plane figure. A polygon is a plane figure with three or more straight sides.

Area

The area of a shape or surface is a measure of the size of the surface. For example, the area of a soccer field is greater than the area of a tennis court.

SOLIDS

Solids are not flat, but three-dimensional (they take up space). A polyhedron is a solid that has plane (flat) faces.

Volume

The volume of a solid is the amount of space it takes up. For example, a football has a greater volume than that of a golf ball.

Square *Polygon with four equal sides, all meeting at right angles* Area = length^2

Circle *Curve on which all points are equidistant from the center* Area = π x radius^2

Equilateral triangle *Has three equal sides* Area (of any triangle) = ½ x base x height

Isoceles triangle *Triangle with two equal sides* Area = ½ x base x height

Quadrilateral *Polygon with four sides*

Rhombus *Quadrilateral with sides of equal length* Area = ½ x (a x b)

Rectangle *Quadrilateral with opposite sides of equal length that meet at right angles* Area = base x height

Parallelogram *Quadrilateral with opposite sides that are parallel and of equal length* Area = a x b

Trapezium *Quadrilateral with only two sides parallel* Area = ½ x sum of parallel sides x distance between them

Pentagon *Polygon with five sides*

Hexagon *Polygon with six sides*

Octagon *Polygon with eight sides*

Tetrahedron *Polyhedron with four triangles as faces*

Cube *Six squares of equal sides as faces* Volume = length^3

Octahedron *Tetrahedron with eight flat sides*

Square pyramid *Tetrahedron with square base and four triangular sides*

Triangular prism *Solid figure with two triangular ends* Volume = area of triangular ends x distance between them

Rectangular block Volume = length x breadth x height

Sphere *Globe-shaped figure with every point on its surface equidistant from its center* Volume = ⁴/₃ x π x radius^3 Surface area = 4 x π x radius^2

Hemisphere *Half-sphere*

Apex

Spheroid *Egg-shaped figure*

Cone *Circular base, narrowing to a point, or apex* Volume = ⅓ x π x radius^2 x height

Cylinder *Two circular faces, connected by a tube* Surface area = π x diameter x length Volume = π x radius^2 x length

CIRCLE TERMS

Arc Part of curve.

Circumference Distance around edge of circle.

Chord Straight line joining any two points on edge.

Diameter Line from one side of circle to other, passing through center.

Pi (π) Ratio of circumference to diameter (approx. 3.14159, same for all circles).

Radius Distance from center of circle to edge.

Sector Slice of circle between two radii.

Segment Part of circle between chord and edge.

PYTHAGORAS' THEOREM

For any right-angled triangle, the squares of the two sides adjacent to the right angle (B and C, below) add up to the square of the longest side, or hypotenuse (A).

$$A^2 = B^2 + C^2$$

B — A

Right angle — C

MATH FACTS

• Perfect numbers are those that are equal to the sum of their factors (a number that divides equally into another number). The first perfect number is six, since 1 + 2 + 3 = 6.

ANGLE

An angle is a measure of the space between two lines, formed when one line is rotated (turned). The hands of a clock form an angle between each other as they turn. Angles are measured in degrees (°), or radians.

Obtuse angle
90°
130°
45°
Reflex angle
0°
360°
Right angle
Acute angle
Round angle
240°

TRIGONOMETRY

Trigonometry is the study of the relationships between the sides of a right-angle triangle.

TRIGONOMETRIC RATIOS

Three simple relationships, or ratios, are commonly used in trigonometry: sine (sin), cosine (cos), and tangent (tan). The sine of an angle in a right-angled triangle is given by dividing the length of the side opposite the angle by the length of the hypotenuse.

Right-angled triangle

Opposite

Hypotenuse

Adjacent

$$\sin = \frac{\text{length of opposite}}{\text{length of hypotenuse}}$$

$$\cos = \frac{\text{length of adjacent}}{\text{length of hypotenuse}}$$

$$\tan = \frac{\text{length of opposite}}{\text{length of adjacent}}$$

Trigonometry calculation
To find the height of the tower, multiply the tangent (tan) of the angle from the ground to the top of the tower by the distance from the building – 2,162ft (659m). This gives a height of 1,814ft (553m).

659m (2,162ft)

40°

Position of observer

KEY MATHEMATICIANS

Euclid (c.300 B.C.), Greek mathematician, whose geometric proofs in *The Elements* were taught in schools for 2,000 years. He studied irrational numbers (numbers, such as √2, that cannot be written as fractions or decimals).

Gottfried Wilhelm Leibniz (1646–1716), German mathematician and philosopher, independently invented the theory of calculus, at the same time as Isaac Newton. He built a mechanical multiplying machine.

Karl Friedrich Gauss (1777–1855), German mathematician and astronomer. He wrote first major book on number theory, which included a theory of complex numbers. He contributed to many areas.

Baron Augustin-Louis Cauchy (1789–1857), French mathematician, modernized calculus, contributed to an area of mathematics called group theory. He is said to have more theorems named after him than any other mathematician.

• The theorem that Greek mathematician Pythagoras discovered and that bears his name was known by Babylonian and Egyptian mathematicians hundreds of years earlier.

• The Maya in South America were the first people to invent a symbol for the number zero.

• There is an infinite number of prime numbers.

• The mathematical term "algorithm" is derived from the name of the 9th-century Arabic mathematician al-Khwarizmi. The term "algebra" comes from the title of his book.

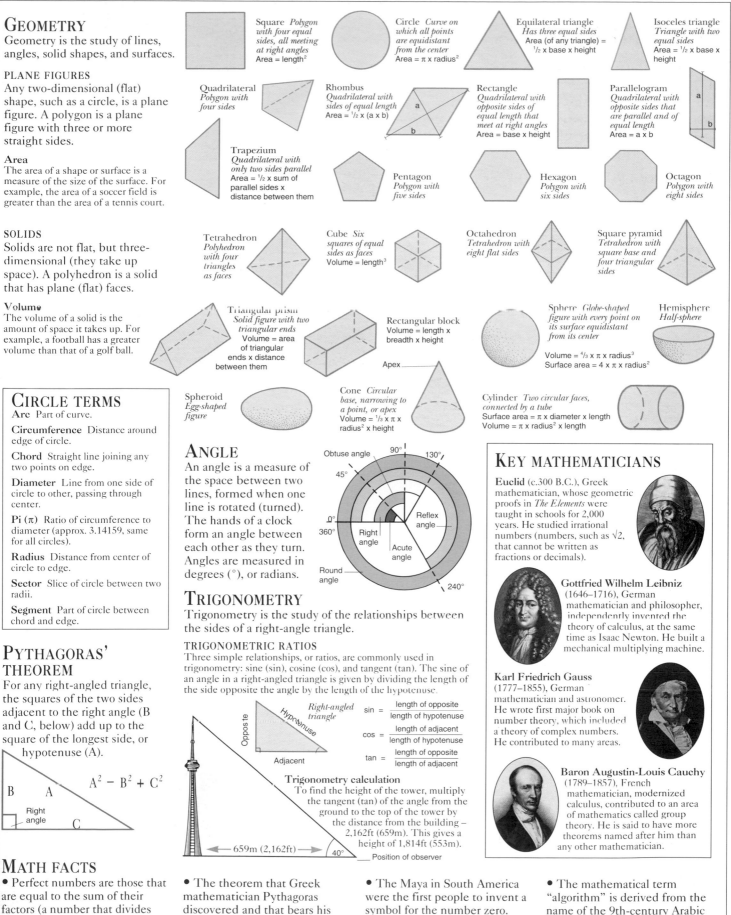

WEIGHTS AND MEASURES

THERE ARE TWO MAJOR systems of measurement. The metric system, based on the number ten, is the most common and is used by scientists worldwide. Certain countries, such as the US, use the older imperial system. You can convert between systems using conversion tables (right).

5 kite

4 deben
2 kite

EGYPTIAN WEIGHTS
Ancient Egyptians used a weight called a deben, made of copper. The value of the standard deben was later increased, and divided into ten "kite."

1 kite

ANCIENT MEASURES

MAYAN NUMBER KNOTS
The ancient Maya of Central America used an arrangement of knotted strings, called a quipu, to record numerical information. The type and position of knot and the length and color of string were all significant.

ASSYRIAN WEIGHTS
The first standard system of weights arose when traders needed to measure quantities of goods. Assyrian weights (right) were made for King Shalmaneser III.

Mayan quipu

Assyrian ingot weights

INDUS VALLEY WEIGHTS
The people of Mohenjo-Daro, a city of the Indus valley civilization (c. 2500 B.C.), used cubic weights made of a stone called chert. The largest of these weights could not be lifted by one person alone.

Indus valley chert weights

THE SEVEN BASE SI UNITS

SI (Système Internationale d'Unités) is the standard system of units for scientists throughout the world. There are seven base units, from which the other units are derived (shown below).

Quantity	Unit	Symbol
Mass	Kilogram	kg
Length	Meter	m
Time	Second	s
Electric current	Ampere	A
Temperature	Kelvin	K
Luminous intensity	Candela	cd
Amount of substance	Mole	mole

MEASUREMENT FACTS
• The metric system was first adopted in France in 1791. King Louis XVI approved it the day before he attempted to flee the revolution that was unfolding.

• China was the first country to use a decimal system. Wooden rulers divided into units of ten that date back to the 6th century B.C. have been found.

• Units used today in the imperial system have evolved over centuries, mainly by custom. The origins of some of these units can be found in the earliest civilizations of the Near and Middle East. The metric system commonly used today – the SI system – was devised by scientists and adopted in a single period by many nations.

STANDARDS
To ensure that everyone means the same thing when stating measurements, several units have very precisely defined out standards. A few are explained below.

THE STANDARD SECOND
One second is defined as "the duration of 9,192,631,770 periods of the radiation corresponding to the transition between the two hyperfine levels of the ground state of the cesium–133 atom."
Cesium clock

THE STANDARD KILOGRAM
A kilogram of the metal platinum was made as a worldwide standard for the kilogram. It is kept under carefully controlled conditions at the International Bureau of Weights and Measures at Sèvres, France.
Standard kilogram

THE STANDARD METER
One meter is defined as "the length equal to 1,650,763.73 wavelengths, in a vacuum, of the radiation corresponding to the transition between the levels 2p10 and 5d5 of the krypton–86 atom."
Krypton gas

DERIVED UNITS
This table shows a selection of the derived units in the SI (Système Internationale d'Unités).

Quantity	Unit	Symbol
Frequency	Hertz	Hz
Energy	Joule	J
Force	Newton	N
Power	Watt	W
Pressure	Pascal	Pa
Electric charge	Coulomb	C
Electrical resistance	Ohm	Ω
Electric potential difference	Volt	V
Radiation activity	Becquerel	Bq

MUSICAL MEASURE
In ancient China, a vessel that was used to measure out grain or wine was known to contain the correct volume of goods if it made the right sound when struck.

NUMBER TERMS: GREAT AND SMALL
Prefixes inserted before a unit signify multiples or fractions of that unit.

Prefix	Symbol	Meaning	Prefix	Symbol	Meaning
tera	T	One trillion	deci	d	One-tenth
giga	G	One billion	centi	c	One-hundredth
mega	M	One million	milli	m	One-thousandth
kilo	k	One thousand	micro	µ	One-millionth
hecto	h	One hundred	nano	n	One-billionth

LENGTH

1 inch (in)	
1 foot (ft)	12 in
1 yard (yd)	3 ft
1 mile	1,760 yd
1 millimeter (mm)	
1 centimeter (cm)	10 mm
1 meter (m)	100 cm
1 kilometer (km)	1,000 m

AREA

1 square inch (in^2)	
1 sq foot (ft^2)	144 in^2
1 sq yard (yd^2)	9 ft^2
1 acre	4,840 yd^2
1 sq mile	640 acres
1 sq millimeter (mm^2)	
1 sq centimeter (cm^2)	100 mm^2
1 sq meter (m^2)	10,000 cm^2
1 hectare (ha)	10,000 m^2
1 sq kilometer (km^2)	1,000,000 m^2

VOLUME

1 cubic inch (in^3)	
1 cubic foot (ft^3)	1,728 in^3
1 cubic yard (yd^3)	27 ft^3
1 fluid ounce (fl oz)	
1 pint (pt)	20 fl oz
1 gallon (gal)	8 pt
1 cubic mm (mm^3)	
1 cubic cm (cm^3)	1,000 mm^3
1 cubic meter (m^3)	1,000,000 cm^3
1 liter (l)	1,000 cm^3

MASS AND WEIGHT

1 ounce (oz)	
1 pound (lb)	16 oz
1 stone	14 lb
1 hundredweight (cwt)	8 stones
1 ton	20 cwt
1 gram (g)	
1 kilogram (kg)	1,000 g
1 tonne (t)	1,000 kg

BODY MEASURE

Ancient civilizations used proportions of the body as units of measurement because of their convenience. Since the unit varied slightly according to the size of the person making the measurement, a master unit, or standard was often made.

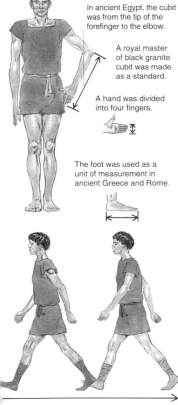

In ancient Egypt, the cubit was from the tip of the forefinger to the elbow.

A royal master of black granite cubit was made as a standard.

A hand was divided into four fingers.

The foot was used as a unit of measurement in ancient Greece and Rome.

Two steps = one pace

The mile originated in Rome – it consisted of 1,000 paces, each of which was two steps.

LENGTH CONVERSION

To convert:	Into:	Multiply by:
Inches	Centimeters	2.54
Feet	Meters	0.3048
Yards	Meters	0.9144
Miles	Kilometers	1.6093
Centimeters	Inches	0.3937
Meters	Feet	3.2808
Meters	Yards	1.0936
Kilometers	Miles	0.6214

VOLUME CONVERSION

To convert:	Into:	Multiply by:
Cubic inches	Cubic centimeters (milliliters)	16.3871
Cubic feet	Liters	28.3169
Cubic yards	Cubic meters	0.7646
US fluid ounces	Cubic centimeters (milliliters)	29.5735
US pints	Liters	0.4732
US gallons	Liters	3.7854
Cubic centimeters (milliliters)	Cubic inches	0.0610
	US fluid ounces	0.0338
Liters	Cubic feet	0.0353
Cubic meters	Cubic yards	1.3080
Cubic centimeters (millilitres)	US fluid ounces	0.0338
Liters	US pints	2.1138
	US gallons	0.2642

AREA CONVERSION

To convert:	Into:	Multiply by:
Sq inches	Sq centimeters	6.4516
Sq foot	Sq meters	0.0929
Sq yards	Sq meters	0.8361
Acres	Hectares	0.4047
Sq miles	Sq kilometers	2.5900
Sq centimeters	Sq inches	0.155
Sq meters	Sq feet	10.7639
Sq meters	Sq yards	1.1960
Hectares	Acres	2.4711
Sq kilometers	Sq miles	0.3861

MASS AND WEIGHT CONVERSIONS

To convert:	Into:	Multiply by:
Ounces	Grams	28.3495
Pounds	Kilograms	0.4536
Stones	Kilograms	6.3503
Hundredweights	Kilograms	50.802
US tons	Tonnes	0.9072
Grams	Ounces	0.0352
Kilograms	Pounds	2.2046
	Stones	0.1575
	Hundredweights	0.0197
Tonnes	US Tons	1.1023

TEMPERATURE CONVERSION

To convert Fahrenheit (°F) into Celsius (°C), use the following formula:
$$°C = (°F - 32) \div 1.8$$

To convert Celsius (°C) into Fahrenheit (°F), use the following formula:
$$°F = (°C \times 1.8) + 32$$

SPEED CONVERSION

To convert:	Into:	Multiply by:
Miles per hour	Kilometers per hour Meters per second	1.6093 0.4470
Kilometers per hour	Miles per hour	0.6214
Meters per second	Miles per hour	2.2370
Feet per second	Miles per hour	0.6818

MEASURING MARATHON

An acre was originally defined as the area of land that a pair of oxen could plow in one day.

TIME

TIME IS THE INTERVAL between one instant and another. People measure time by recording the movements of the Earth traveling in space: one Earth spin is a day and one orbit of the Earth around the Sun is a year. People keep time with mechanical timekeepers such as clocks and watches.

NATURAL TIME

DAYS AND YEARS

The Earth orbits the Sun in one year. At the same time, the Earth spins on its own axis. It completes one spin in a single day and 365 ¼ spins in a year. The quarter day is impractical, so after four years they are added together. Every fourth year has 366 days and is known as a leap year.

Day

The Earth completes one spin on its axis in one day.

STANDARD TIME

The time measured at Greenwich, London, is the standard time for the whole world. For every 15 degrees of longitude east or west of Greenwich, the time is one hour ahead of or behind Greenwich time.

Moscow, Russia: 3:00 p.m.

London, England: 12:00 noon

New York, US: 7:00 a.m.

Tokyo, Japan: 9:00 p.m.

Rio de Janeiro, Brazil: 9:00 a.m.

There are 24 time zones around the globe.

Year

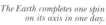

Sun

Earth

The Earth takes a year to travel round the Sun.

MONTH

While the Earth orbits the Sun, the Moon orbits the Earth. The phases of the moon add up to 29.5 days. This cycle is the lunar month and is the basis of our present-day months.

Earth

Moon

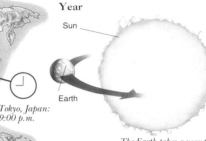

TIME FACTS

• The Earth is slowing down: a few million years from now leap years will not be needed.

• The Sumerians of Mesopotamia (present-day Iraq) first divided hours into 60 minutes, and minutes into 60 seconds in about 3000 B.C. They used 60, because it was easily divisible by 2, 3, and 4.

TIME WORDS

a.m. Before noon (ante meridiem)

Equinox The two times in a year when the Sun crosses the equator and day and night are of equal length.

Local time The time at points that

are on the same meridian.

Meridian Line of longitude

p.m. After noon (post meridiem)

Solstice The two times in the year when the Sun is farthest from the equator. These are the shortest and the longest days.

HISTORY OF TIMEKEEPING

People originally measured time by the position of the Sun in the sky. Later, they began to rely on machines for timekeeping, with mechanical motions that were repeated over and over again. Today, people use clocks and watches that can measure time in fractions of a second.

c.2200 B.C. Stonehenge stone circles, England, may have been used by Neolithic people to tell the time. The position of the circles allows the Sun to shine through or rise above certain stones.

Stonehenge

c.1500 B.C. Sundials are used by the Egyptians. A shadow cast by the Sun's rays indicates the time on a marked surface.

Position of the stars is used by the peoples of Babylon, Egypt, and China to tell the time.

Sund

2200 B.C.

1500 B.C. 1500 B.C.

1335 First mechanical clock is erected in Milan, Italy. The turret, or tower, clock, has no face, but simply strikes the hours. Turret clocks are later built throughout Europe.

1364 First known domestic clocks made by Giovanni Dondi (1318–89) of Italy. These early clocks are small versions of turret clocks, with the addition of an hour hand.

1386 Oldest mechanical clock still working is built at Salisbury Cathedral, England.

The clock in Salisbury Cathedral is driven by a revolving drum.

1510 First portable clocks made by Peter Henlein (1479–1542), a German locksmith. These small clocks are driven by a spring. The open face has an hour hand only.

Early portable clock

| 1330 | 1335 | 1360 | 1364 | 1380 | 1386 | 1500 | 1510 |

c.1730 Cuckoo clocks first introduced in the Black Forest, Germany.

1754 Lever escapement, combined with the balance spring, gives an accuracy to within ten seconds a day.

Cuckoo clock

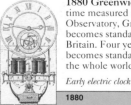

1759 An accurate marine timekeeper, Harrison 4, is introduced by Englishman John Harrison (1693-1776). It can withstand the changing movement and temperatures on board ship and has less than one minute of error after five months at sea.

1800s Cheaper clocks are developed in US by American Eli Tery (1772–1852).

1840 Electricity is used to drive clocks that in turn control distant, subsidiary clocks. These clocks are known as the master and its slaves.

1880 Greenwich time, time measured at the Ro Observatory, Greenwich, becomes standard time i Britain. Four years later i becomes standard time fo the whole world.

Early electric clock

| 1730 | 1730 | 1754 | 1759 | 1800 | 1800 | 1840 | 1880 |

GREGORIAN CALENDAR

Most Western countries use the Gregorian calendar, which is based on the time it takes for the Earth to circle the Sun. At first, the Romans began their year in March, which is why September to December are named after the Latin numbers seven to ten. Later, in about 150 B.C., January became the first month of the year.

NAMES OF THE MONTHS

January Janus, god of gateways

February Februa, festival of purification

March Mars, god of war

April Aperire, to open

May Maia, goddess of fertility

June Juno, goddess of the Moon

July Julius Caesar

August Augustus, the first Roman emperor

September Septem, seven
October Octo, eight
November Novem, nine
December Decem, ten

LONGEST YEAR

The longest year ever was 46 B.C., which lasted for 445 days. Lengthened by 90 days to bring it in line with the solar year, it became known as the Year of Confusion.

HEBREW AND MUSLIM CALENDARS

These are based on the Moon's cycle.

Hebrew months	Muslim months	Gregorian date
Tishri	Muharram	Sept. to Oct.
Heshvan	Safar	Oct. to Nov.
Kislev	Rabi I	Nov. to Dec.
Tevet	Rabi II	Dec. to Jan.
Shevat	Jumada I	Jan. to Feb.
Adar	Jumada II	Feb. to Mar.
Nisan	Rajab	Mar. to Apr.
Iyar	Sha'ban	Apr. to May
Sivan	Ramadan	May to June
Tammuz	Shawwal	June to July
Av	Dhu al-Qa'dah	July to Aug.
Elul	Dhu al-Hijjah	Aug. to Sept.

ANCIENT CHINESE CALENDAR

This calendar, based on the Sun and the Moon, is no longer used in China, but is still in use in some Asian countries. It is divided into 24 seasons.

Season	Meaning	Gregorian date
Li Chun	Spring begins	Feb. 5 to Feb. 19
Yu Shui	Rain water	Feb. 19 to Mar. 5
Jing Zhe	Excited insects	Mar. 5 to Mar. 20
Chun Fen	Vernal equinox	Mar. 20 to Apr. 5
Qing Ming	Clear and bright	Apr. 5 to Apr. 20
Gu Yu	Grain rains	Apr. 20 to May 5
Li Xia	Summer begins	May 5 to May 21
Xiao Man	Grain fills	May 21 to June 5
Mang Zhong	Grain in ear	June 5 to June 21
Xia Zhi	Summer solstice	June 21 to July 7
Xiao Shu	Slight heat	July 7 to July 23
Da Shu	Great heat	July 23 to Aug. 7
Li Qiu	Autumn begins	Aug. 7 to Aug. 23
Chu Shu	Limit of heat	Aug. 23 to Sept. 7
Bai Lu	White dew	Sept. 7 to Sept. 23
Qui Fen	Autumn equinox	Sept. 23 to Oct. 8
Han Lu	Cold dew	Oct. 8 to Oct. 23
Shuang Jiang	Frost descends	Oct. 23 to Nov. 7
Li Dong	Winter begins	Nov. 7 to Nov. 22
Xiao Xue	Little snow	Nov. 22 to Dec. 7
Da Xue	Heavy snow	Dec. 7 to Dec. 22
Dong Zhi	Winter solstice	Dec. 22 to Jan. 6
Xiao Han	Little cold	Jan. 6 to Jan. 21
Da Han	Severe cold	Jan. 21 to Feb. 5

1400 B.C. Water clocks are used by the Egyptians. A bowl with a hole in the bottom is filled with water. The passing of time is shown by a drop in the level of water, which lines up with one of the marks carved into the bowl. *Water clock*

c.A.D. 890 Clock candles are used by the English king, Alfred the Great (849–899). When a candle, which has hours marked down its length, has burned down to a mark, it indicates that an hour has passed by.

1100s Hourglasses used in navigation, by physicians to time a pulse, and by teachers and preachers to time lessons and sermons. Sand drains from the top glass bulb to the bottom. Some glasses measure 15 or 30 minutes as well as up to one or two hours. *Hourglass*

1300s Monasteries use simple machinery that sounds bells at regular intervals to call worshippers to prayer. A person called a clock jack rings the bells.

1400 B.C.	A.D. 500	A.D. 890	1100	1100	1300	1300

1582 Regularity of pendulum's swing shown by Italian scientist Galileo (1564–1642). *Galileo's design for a pendulum*

1657 First pendulum clock is made by Dutch astronomer Christiaan Huygens (1629–95). The pendulum controls the rotation of the wheels of the clock.

1670 Long, or seconds, pendulum is introduced by William Clement (c.1638–1704), an English clockmaker.

1675 Spiral balance spring, giving clocks an accuracy to within two minutes a day, is invented by Huygens. *Huygens' balance spring*

c.1690s Astronomers at the Royal Observatory, Greenwich, London, measure the stars to determine time.

Royal Observatory

1582	1650	1657	1670	1670	1675	1690	1690

1900 First wristwatches introduced. At first only women wear them, until World War I (1914–18), when they become popular with men in the trenches. *Early wristwatch*

1939 First quartz crystal clock is installed at Greenwich. The quartz crystals vibrate 100,000 times per second. These vibrations are controlled, counted, recorded, and used to establish precise time. The maximum error is two-thousandths of a second per day.

1948 First atomic clock developed in the US. It works by counting the natural vibrations of cesium atoms, which vibrate 9,192,631,770 times per second. Time for the whole world is now established by using 80 atomic clocks from 24 countries. *Early atomic clock*

1970 Atomic clock is accurate to one second in 30,000 years.

1970s–1990s Digital watches are increasingly popular. A microchip changes the numbers every second, so that the time kept is very precise.

1900	1900	1930	1939	1940	1948	1970	1970	1990

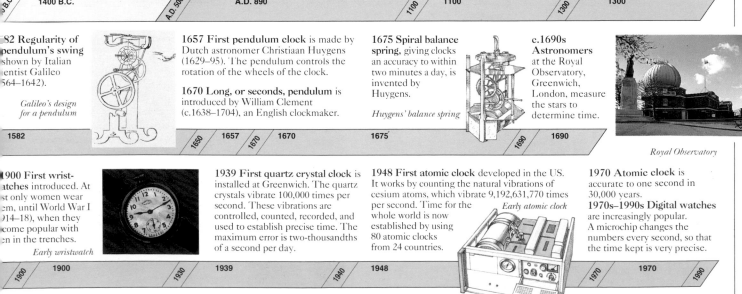

ENGINES

AN ENGINE TURNS different forms of energy into motion, or kinetic energy. In the last two centuries, engine efficiency has substantially improved.

50 B.C. Chinese engineers build water wheels that use the energy of moving water.

A.D. c.600 Early windmills appear, converting wind energy into mechanical motion.

1712 Practical steam engine using piston and cylinder built by English inventor Thomas Newcomen (1663–1729).

1769 Steam carriage built by French military engineer Nicolas Joseph Cugnot (1725–1804).

Watt's rotative engine

1783 Steam-powered paddleboat, *Pyroscaphe,* sailed up Saône River, France, by French engineer Jouffroy d'Abbans (1751–1832).

1782 Rotative steam engine built by Scottish engineer James Watt (1736–1819). Watt's engine is much more efficient and practical than Newcomen's engine.

| 50 B.C. | A.D. 1 | 600 | 1700 | 1712 | 1769 | 1782 | 1783 |

1892 German Rudolf Diesel (1858–1913) invents engine (later named diesel engine) with fuel that ignites on compression. When later built, the engine is more efficient than existing internal combustion engines.

1897 Ship powered by new steam turbine launched by British engineer Charles Parsons (1854–1931), revolutionizing marine engineering. His ship, *Turbinia,* unexpectedly appears at a British naval review and, at 34.5 knots, easily outruns the launch sent to stop it.

Queen (1904), fitted with marine turbine

1903 Powered flight by American brothers, Orville (1871–1948) and Wilbur (1867–1912) Wright, using internal combustion engine.

First sustained powered flight of Kitty Hawk

1907 Supercharger used on a car by American engineer Lee S. Chadwick.

1926 Liquid-fuel rocket launched by American Robert Goddard (1882–1945).

Robert Goddard

| 1892 | 1897 | 1900 | 1903 | 1907 | 1926 |

INTERNAL COMBUSTION ENGINE

The internal combustion engine, developed in the 19th century, has several advantages over earlier types of engine. It does not require stoking, like a steam engine; it is portable, unlike windmills or water wheels; and its fuel is highly efficient.

FOUR-STROKE ENGINE CYCLE

1 Inlet valve opens. Piston slides down cylinder, sucking in a mixture of fuel and air, called the charge.

Induction stroke

2 Inlet valve snaps shut and piston rises, squeezing charge into small space, under pressure.

Compression stroke

3 Spark ignites compressed charge. Expanding gases force piston down cylinder. Piston spins crankshaft.

Power stroke

4 Exhaust valve opens. Hot gases escape, pushed out by rising piston. Cycle restarts.

Exhaust stroke

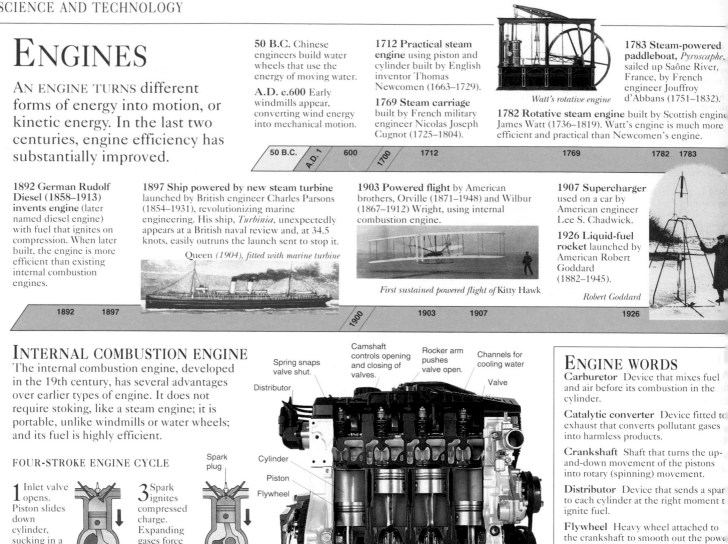

Camshaft controls opening and closing of valves.

Spring snaps valve shut.

Distributor

Rocker arm pushes valve open.

Channels for cooling water

Valve

Spark plug

Cylinder

Piston

Flywheel

Clutch disconnects engine while driver changes gear.

Crankshaft drives wheels via gearbox and clutch.

Oilpan contains reservoir of oil for lubricating engine parts.

Crankshaft bearing where crankshaft runs through engine block.

Dipstick for checking level of lubricating oil

Fanbelt drives a cooling fan.

ENGINE WORDS

Carburetor Device that mixes fuel and air before its combustion in the cylinder.

Catalytic converter Device fitted to exhaust that converts pollutant gases into harmless products.

Crankshaft Shaft that turns the up-and-down movement of the pistons into rotary (spinning) movement.

Distributor Device that sends a spark to each cylinder at the right moment to ignite fuel.

Flywheel Heavy wheel attached to the crankshaft to smooth out the power from individual cylinders.

Horsepower Measure of the power of an engine; one horsepower is equal to 746 watts.

Internal combustion engine Engine in which fuel is burned (combusted) inside the cylinder of the engine, e.g., gasoline engine.

Throttle Flap controlling flow of air and fuel through carburetor.

r.p.m. Revolutions (of the crankshaft) per minute.

TYPES OF ENGINE

The first engines harnessed natural forces to produce motive force. In this century, several new types have appeared.

WINDMILL
The force of the wind across the sails produces a stronger driving force at the central shaft.

STEAM ENGINE
Water, heated by a furnace, produces steam. Expanding steam drives a piston back and forth.

GASOLINE ENGINE
Hot gases from an ignited gasoline and air mixture push a piston, moving a crankshaft.

TURBO JET
Jet engines, used mainly in planes, draw in, compress, and throw out air at high speeds.

LINEAR ENGINE
Magnetic fields lift the train from the track, and shifting fields then propel it along the track.

ROCKET
Rocket fuel burns in a combustion chamber and the resultant hot gases drive the rocket forward.

ION MOTOR
Ionized molecules (see p.222) are made to rush out by an electrical process in the motor.

STEAM ENGINE

Water in a boiler is heated by a coal fire and turns to steam. The expanding steam, fed into a cylinder, moves a piston back and forth, and the piston turns the train's wheels via a connecting rod and crank. Ships were also powered by steam engines.

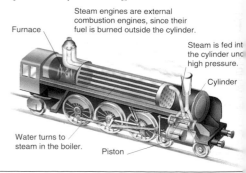

Steam engines are external combustion engines, since their fuel is burned outside the cylinder.

Furnace

Steam is fed into the cylinder under high pressure.

Cylinder

Water turns to steam in the boiler.

Piston

1800 First engine to use high pressure steam built by English engineer Richard Trevithick (1771–1833).

1852 Steam-powered airship built by French engineer Henri Giffard (1825–82).

1859 Internal combustion engine built by Belgian-French inventor Etienne Lenoir (1822–1900).

1877 Four-stroke internal combustion engine built by German Nikolaus Otto (1832–91).

Etienne Lenoir's internal combustion engine

1883 High-speed internal combustion engine built by German Gottlieb W. Daimler (1834–1900).

1884 Steam turbine generator for electricity is built by English engineer Charles Parsons (1854–1931).

1885 Motorbike engine built by Daimler. **Three-wheeled automobile,** built by German Karl Benz (1844–1929), is the first gasoline driven motor vehicle.

| 1800 | 1852 | 1859 | 1877 | 1883 | 1884 | 1885 |

1934 Liquid-fuel rocket reaches a height of 1.5 miles (2.4km), launched by German engineer Wernher von Braun (1912–77).

1937 First working jet engine built by British engineer Frank Whittle (born 1907).

Frank Whittle (right) with early jet engine

1939 First plane with a jet engine, Heinkel *He 178*, built and flown by German engineer Hans von Ohain.

1948 First turboprop airliner.

1962 First nuclear-powered ship, *USS Savannah*, begins sea trials.

1970 Bypass ("turbofan") jet engine used, now the most common type of jet engine; *Boeing 747* "Jumbo Jet" goes into service.

USS Savannah

1979 Catalytic converter developed by British firm, Ricardo Consulting Engineers, to remove harmful gases from exhaust fumes.

| 1934 | 1937 | 1939 | 1948 | 1950 | 1962 | 1970 | 1979 |

JET ENGINE

A jet engine sucks in and compresses air using fan blades. When this air is ignited with kerosene, the hot gases produced thrust the engine forward. Before leaving the exhaust nozzle, these gases pass over and drive turbines that are connected to the initial compressor blades. In a turbofan jet engine, air flows around the engine, cooling and quieting it.

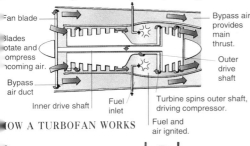

Fan blade / **Blades rotate and compress incoming air.** / **Bypass air duct** / **Inner drive shaft** / **Fuel inlet** / **Fuel and air ignited.** / **Turbine spins outer shaft, driving compressor.** / **Outer drive shaft** / **Bypass air provides main thrust.**

HOW A TURBOFAN WORKS

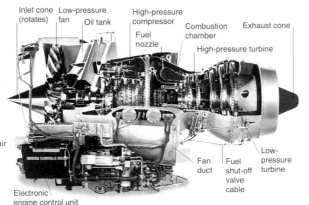

Inlet cone (rotates) / Low-pressure fan / Oil tank / High-pressure compressor / Fuel nozzle / Combustion chamber / High-pressure turbine / Exhaust cone / Fan duct / Fuel shut-off valve cable / Low-pressure turbine / Electronic engine control unit

MODERN TURBOFAN JET ENGINE – CANADA PW 305
Most jet aircraft, including passenger airliners, use turbofan engines. Their main thrust comes from the air that bypasses the engine itself. Fuel and fan adjustments are controlled electronically.

ROCKET ENGINE

Rockets, the simplest and most powerful type of engine, are powered by solid or liquid fuel. The fuel burns in a combustion chamber with one open end, and the escaping hot gases thrust the rocket upward.

Saturn V rocket at take-off

Most liquid-fuel rockets use liquid hydrogen and liquid oxygen.

Casing of rocket

Combustion chamber

Escaping gases provide thrust for rocket.

ENGINE EFFICIENCY

An engine with 100 percent efficiency converts all its fuel's energy into useful work.

Engine Type		Efficiency
Steam		7%
Internal combustion	Gasoline	25–35%
	Diesel	30–40%
Power station (oil or coal-burning)		35%
Hydroelectric plant		80%

HOT ROD
The temperature inside the cylinders of an internal combustion engine can reach 3,100°F (1,700°C) – as hot as molten lava.

EXTRA POWER
There are several ways of getting more power from an engine.

SUPERCHARGERS AND TURBOCHARGERS
Gasoline and diesel engines can be fitted with pumps that force the fuel and air mixture into the cylinders. This increases the strength of the explosion on the power stroke. Two types of pump are used – supercharger and turbocharger.

Supercharged 1935 Auburn Speedster

Supercharger
A supercharger is driven by a belt or gears from the engine itself.

AFTERBURNERS
Afterburners inject extra fuel into the hot jet exhaust, giving the engine extra thrust, almost like a rocket. Jet aircraft such as Concorde use afterburners for takeoff, or for sudden, fast maneuvers. They use much more fuel and are extremely loud.

Afterburners on a jet-fighter aircraft

LINEAR ENGINE
A linear engine uses powerful magnetism to lift a train off its track and propel it forward. These trains are called maglev (magnetic levitation) trains, because they glide along just above their tracks.

Maglev train, Birmingham airport, UK

ENGINE RECORDS
SMALLEST INTERNAL COMBUSTION ENGINE is the 0.1cc model aircraft.

LARGEST INTERNAL COMBUSTION ENGINES are Sulzer ship engines, providing up to 60,000 horsepower, at 100 r.p.m.

Turbocharger

Inlet duct / Inlet rotor squeezes extra fuel and air into cylinder.

Turbocharger
Turbochargers are more common today; they are driven directly by the engine's exhaust gases.

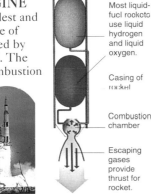

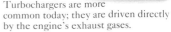

SPACE AND TIME

THE UNIVERSE IN WHICH we live is vast, and it has existed for a very long time. Everything we see or do takes place in space and time. Objects in space have physical dimensions and mass. Time runs from the past into the future, never the other way around.

TIME SLOWED DOWN

The Theory of Relativity (below) describes how space and time are related. It shows that, since the speed of light is always the same, time may speed up or slow down, and space may stretch or shrink.

Two rockets fly past Earth at a speed close to that of light. To the astronauts aboard, a flash of light sent from one to the other seems to travel in a straight line between them. To an observer on Earth, the flash follows a diagonal line. Since light travels at a constant speed, its crossing time for those on Earth must be longer than for those on board. Time passes at different rates for different observers.

To observers on Earth, a light flash between rockets appears to follow a long path, and take a longer time to cross space.

To astronauts on rocket, same light flash follows shorter route straight between rockets, taking a short time to cross.

Rockets travel at speed close to speed of light.

JET SET

Relativity states that clocks run faster in weaker gravity. In 1975, this was proved using two atomic clocks. One, carried in a plane at high altitude, ran faster.

TIME AND SPACE FACTS

- The smallest unit of time that scientists believe we can measure is called the "Planck time." One second contains 600,000,000,000, 000,000,000,000,000,000,000, 000,000,000 Planck times.

- Gravity has an effect on the passage of time. Time runs more quickly at the top of a mountain, where gravity is weaker, than at sea level.

Time, like length, can be divided only a finite number of times.

- In a famous experiment during a solar eclipse in 1919, it was shown that light from a distant star was "bent." The strong gravity of the Sun has a tiny effect on time and space nearby, not normally visible.

Solar eclipse of 1919 showed bending of light – the first evidence in support of Einstein's Theory of Relativity.

TIME PERIODS

Time is usually measured in seconds, or hours and minutes.

Time period		Example
0.000 000 000 001	second	A gas molecule to spin around once
0.000 000 001	second	The time it takes light to travel 12in (31cm) in air
0.000 001	second	The duration of a flash of lightning
0.001	second	The time it takes sound to travel 12in (31cm) in air
0.1	second	Olympic sprinter to run 1yd (0.9m)
1	second	Quartz in a watch to vibrate 32,768 times
1 000	seconds	Time for a snail to move 40ft (12m)
1 000 000	seconds	11.5 days
1 000 000 000	seconds	Time for Saturn to orbit the Sun once
1 000 000 000 000	seconds	Age of the earliest cave paintings

RELATIVITY

In 1905, German scientist Albert Einstein (1879–1955) published the *Special Theory of Relativity*. It shocked the scientific world because it showed that time and space are not fixed things. His *General Theory of Relativity* (1915) later suggested that space is distorted by matter. In this theory, space and time coexist as spacetime. Space-time can be visualized as a rubber sheet, which stretches as objects are placed upon it. Objects with mass deform real space-time in a similar way. The larger the mass, the more space-time deforms.

Albert Einstein

DISTANCES: SMALL AND GREAT

The range of distances in the Universe is vast. The table below gives a scale of distances in meters.

Distance		Example
0.000 000 000 000 001	m	The diameter of an atomic nucleus
0.000 000 000 001	m	The wavelength of high energy X-rays
0.000 000 001	m	The diameter of an oil molecule
0.000 001	m	The diameter of a single-celled organism
0.001	m	The wavelength of microwave radiation
0.1	m	The diameter of a croquet ball
1	m	Height of a child
1 000	m	One kilometer
1 000 000	m	The width of Egypt
1 000 000 000	m	The diameter of the Sun
1 000 000 000 000	m	The distance from Saturn to the Sun
1 000 000 000 000 000	m	1/40 the distance to the nearest star

NATURAL SCIENCE

THE STUDY OF the origins and processes of life is called natural science. Scientific discoveries have helped us to understand and influence these processes.

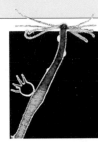

Aristotle

c.350–340 B.C. Greek thinker Aristotle (384–322B.C.) attempts system of animal classification, distinguishing between animals with blood and animals without.

1543 Science of anatomy developed by Flemish doctor Andreas Vesalius (1514–64). His accurate illustrations of dissected bodies appear in *The Fabric of the Human Body* (1543).

Andreas Vesalius

400 B.C. | 350 | A.D. 1 | 1500 | 1543

1665 English scientist Robert Hooke (1653–1703) publishes *Micrographia*, showing detailed microscopic drawings. He introduced the term "cell" to biology and helped improve the design of the compound microscope.

Drawing of magnified slice of cork

1677 Protozoa discovered by Dutch naturalist Antonie van Leeuwenhoek (1632–1723), using a simple microscope. He later becomes first person to observe bacteria.

1701 Asexual reproduction first observed by Antonie van Leeuwenhoek, while watching hydra under a microscope (see p.83).

Hydra

1735 System of classification of living organisms invented by Swedish botanist Carolus Linnaeus (1707–78). His binomial (two-part) system identifies each species and shows its relation to others.

Carolus Linnaeus

1600 | 1665 | 1677 | 1700 | 1701 | 1735

1749 French naturalist Georges-Louis Buffon (1707–88) suggests that some species of plants or animals give rise to others.

1771 Connection between muscle movements and electrical impulses discovered by Italian anatomist Luigi Galvani (1737–98), while experimenting on the leg muscles of a dissected frog.

Galvani demonstrates nerve impulses.

1779 Process of photosynthesis discovered by Dutch-born scientist Jan Ingenhousz (1730–99).

1805 Term "biology" coined by Jean-Baptiste Lamarck (1744–1829) and Gottfried Treviranus (1776–1837). Science of anthropology founded by German Johann Blumenbach (1750–1840).

1812 Science of paleontology (fossil studies) developed by pioneer French zoologist Georges Cuvier (1769–1832). He showed the connection between patterns of rock layers and patterns of fossil remains.

Fossil jawbone of a paleotherium

Diagram of typical cell

1749 | 1771 | 1779 | 1800 | 1805 | 1812

1839 Cell theory founded by German scientists Theodor Schwann (1810–82) and Matthias Schleiden (1804–81), which holds that all living things are made from cells. Also observed that single egg-cells grow into organisms.

1855 Theory of homeostasis proposed by French physiologist Claude Bernard (1813–78), describing how organs interact to maintain steady internal conditions.

1856 French chemist Louis Pasteur (1822–95) disproves long-held idea that living organisms could grow from non-living matter (spontaneous generation).

Louis Pasteur

1859 Charles Darwin (1809–82) publishes the *Origin of Species*, which explains his principle of natural selection and theory of evolution (see p.68).

Cartoon of Charles Darwin, mocking idea that humans are descended from apes

1839 | 1855 | 1856 | 1859

1860s Science of heredity (how characteristics are inherited) pioneered by Austrian monk and botanist Gregor Mendel (1822–84), after long experimentation on pea plants.

Gregor Mendel

1889 Important role of acids in food digestion discovered by German researchers. **Russian scientist Ivan Pavlov (1849–1936) shows** that reflex actions can be conditioned (learned), and are not just built-in. His proof involves teaching dogs to salivate at the ring of a bell.

1937 Chemistry of respiration, the way that food is converted into energy in cells, discovered by German-born biochemist Hans Krebs (1900–81). The series of chemical reactions that he identifies is central to nearly all metabolic reactions (reactions in living organisms).

Spiral of DNA

1953 Double-helix structure of DNA, the substance responsible for heredity, discovered by American and British biologists James Watson (born 1928) and Francis Crick (born 1916).

1860 | 1889 | 1900 | 1937 | 1953

1963 Mechanism by which nerves convey messages explained by Australian John Eccles (born 1903) and British doctors Andrew Huxley (born 1917) and A. Hodgkin (born 1914).

Eccles receives Nobel prize

1974 Oldest and most complete skeleton of early upright-walking hominid discovered by American anthropologists in Ethiopia. This hominid, *Lucy*, is estimated to be 3–3.5 million years old.

Bone fragments from Lucy

1979 "Gaia" theory of the living planet proposed by British scientist James Lovelock (born 1919). He suggests that the Earth is a living, self-regulating organism that adjusts itself so that life will continue, with or without humans.

James Lovelock

1984 Genetic fingerprinting, a way of identifying genetic material, developed by British scientist Alec Jeffreys at Leicester University, UK.

1990 Human genome project begins in several countries. It aims to map the position of all the genetic material in human chromosomes. This will enable scientists to eradicate inherited diseases.

1963 | 1974 | 1979 | 1984 | 1990

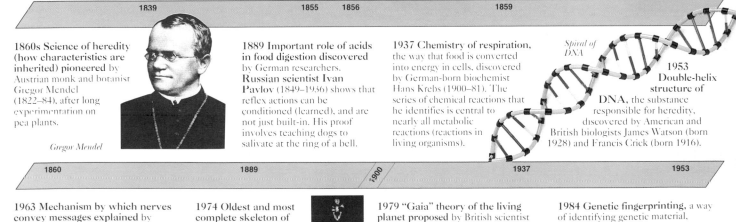

PHYSICAL SCIENCE

EVEN BEFORE THE TERM science was coined, people devised experiments to test their ideas about the physical universe.

Democritus

c.400 B.C. Greek thinker Democritus (c.460–361 B.C.) teaches that matter consists of small, hard, indivisible particles, called atoms.

c.260 B.C. Flotation principle discovered by Greek scientist Archimedes (c.287–212 B.C.). He also studied principles of levers and invented many machines.

Archimedes realizes that the volume of his body is equal to the volume of water spilled from full bath.

400 B.C.   260   200 B.C.

1643 Air pressure discovered and measured by Italian scientist and pupil of Galileo, Evangelista Torricelli (1608–47). He measures it using mercury barometer, his invention.

Mercury barometer

1665 Laws of motion and law of gravitation formulated by English mathematician Isaac Newton (1643–1727) in *Principia Mathematica*. Also discovers that white light is made up of a spectrum of colors.

Isaac Newton

1701 French scientist Joseph Sauveur (1653–1716) studies relationship between sound waves and vibrations and suggests term "acoustics" for the science of sound.

1706 Friction machine to generate electrical sparks made by English scientist Francis Hauksbee (1666–1713).

1712 Successful steam engine, with piston and cylinder, built by English engineer Thomas Newcomen (1663–1729).

Newcomen's engine, used for draining mines.

1643   1665   1700   1701   1706   1712

1800 Infrared waves discovered by German-born astronomer William Herschel (1738–1822). Infrared is an invisible form of electromagnetic wave (see p.231). Herschel discovered Uranus and hundreds of stars and nebulae.

William Herschel

Dalton's atomic models

1803 Atomic theory of matter proposed by Englishman John Dalton (1766–1844), introducing modern ideas about elements and compounds made of atoms and molecules.

1807–8 Potassium, sodium, magnesium, barium, calcium, and strontium discovered by British chemist Humphrey Davy (1778–1829).

Davy performs a public experiment.

1811 Avogadro's Law formulated by Italian physicist Amedeo Avogadro (1776–1856). This law states that the same volume of any gas contains the same number of molecules.

1800   1803   1807   1811

1843 Relationship between heat, power, and work investigated and formulated by English scientist James Joule (1818–89).

Joule's machine for measuring energy conversion

1846 Laws of thermodynamics developed by British physicist William Thomson (1824–1907), later Lord Kelvin. In 1862 he uses them to estimate Earth's age.

1865 Relationship between electricity and magnetism formulated by Scottish physicist James Clerk Maxwell (1831–79).

1869 Periodic Table devised by Russian schoolteacher Dmitri Mendeleyev (1834–1907). It classifies elements into family groups by atomic weight.

James Clark Maxwell

1876 Telephone invented in Canada by Scottish-born inventor Alexander Graham Bell (1847–1922). His device uses a thin diaphragm to convert the vibrations of the human voice into electrical signals, then reconvert them into sound waves.

Alexander Graham Bell's telephone

1840   1843   1846   1865   1869

1900 Quantum theory proposed by German physicist Max Planck (1858–1947), stating that energy consists of small units, called "quanta." This leads to theory that light acts as both a wave and particles.

1905 *Special Theory of Relativity* published by German physicist Albert Einstein (1879–1955). Together with *General Theory* (1915), it revolutionizes the foundations of physics.

Albert Einstein

1909 First stable plastic, "Bakelite," developed by American chemist Leo Henrick Backeland (1863–1944). This helped found plastics industry.

Telephone receiver made of early plastic

1911 Atomic nucleus discovered by New Zealand-born physicist Ernest Rutherford (1871–1937).

1913 Electron shells around nuclei discovered by Danish physicist Niels Bohr (1885–1962).

Electron shells

1900   1905   1909   1911   1913

1938 Nuclear fission, splitting of nuclei to release energy, discovered by German physicists Otto Hahn (1879–1968) and Fritz Strassmann (born 1902).

Uranium fission reaction

1939 Nature of the chemical bond between atoms and molecules explained by American chemist Linus Pauling (1901–94).

1942 First nuclear reactor built by Italian physicist Enrico Fermi (1901–54).

Fermi's reactor, built on a squash court at Chicago University

1945 Heating effect of microwaves discovered by American engineer Percy Le Baron Spencer (1894–1970), when a candy melts in his pocket during experiments with microwaves.

1946 Carbon dating invented by American scientist Willard Frank Libby (1908–80).

1947 Transistor invented by American physicists John Bardeen (1908–91), Walter Brattain (1902–87), and William Shockley (1910–89).

Replica of early transistor

1938   1939   1942   1945   1946   1947

A.D. 1100s Compass used by Italian and Chinese navigators. They independently discover that a free or floating magnetic needle always indicates north.

1600 English doctor William Gilbert (1544–1603), in his book *De Magnete*, claims that the core of the Earth is a great magnet with poles at its north and south points.

Diagram showing dip of compass at different latitudes.

1620s Modern scientific method developed by English philosopher Francis Bacon (1561–1626). He advocates experiment as the best basis for knowledge.

1638 Science of mechanics founded by Italian scientist Galileo Galilei (1564–1642) in *Dialogue Concerning Two New Sciences*. He investigated how force causes acceleration and discovered the properties of the pendulum.

Apparatus to demonstrate Galileo's work on the paths of projectiles (objects thrown up and along)

1000 | 1100 | 1600 | 1620 | 1638

1755 Carbon dioxide discovered by Scottish chemist Joseph Black (1728–99), who calls it "fixed air."

1765 First efficient steam engine built by Scottish engineer James Watt (1736–1819).

1766 Hydrogen discovered by English chemist Henry Cavendish (1731–1810), who calls the gas "inflammable air."

Henry Cavendish

1779 Oxygen named by French chemist Antoine Lavoisier (1743–94), who demonstrates its role in combustion. Also shows air to be a mixture of gases, and that water is a compound of oxygen and hydrogen.

Antoine Lavoisier with wife and coworker Marie-Anne

1799 Battery invented by Italian chemist Alessandro Volta (1745–1827), using different metals separated by salt solutions.

Cell

Voltaic pile or battery (collection of cells)

1755 | 1765 | 1766 | 1779 | 1799

1830s German chemists focus on carbon as the basis of the organic chemistry of living things. Carbon takes many forms, from coal to diamonds.

1831 English scientist Michael Faraday (1791–1867) uses magnetism to make electricity, a process called electromagnetic induction. American Joseph Henry (1797–1878) makes same discovery independently.

Faraday's induction ring

1836 Catalysts discovered by Swedish scientist Jöns Berzelius (1779–1848). Catalysts speed up certain chemical reactions without themselves being used in the reactions.

1839 Practical photographic processes invented independently by Englishman William Fox Talbot (1800–77) and Frenchman Louis Daguerre (1789–1851).

Daguerrotype image on copper plate

1831 | 1836 | 1839

1888 Existence of radio waves demonstrated by German physicist Heinrich Hertz (1857–94). **Induction motor** invented by Croatian-born physicist Nikolai Tesla (1856–1943).

Heinrich Hertz

Marconi

1894 Radio communication invented by 20-year-old Italian Guglielmo Marconi (1874–1937).

1895 X-rays discovered by German physicist Wilhelm Roentgen (1845–1925).

1896 Effects of radioactivity discovered by French physicist Antoine-Henri Becquerel (1852–1908).

1897 Electron discovered by British physicist Joseph John Thompson (1856–1940).

1898 Elements radium and polonium isolated by Polish-born chemist Marie Curie (1867–1934) and Pierre Curie (1859–1906). She calls the powerful emissions of radiation "radioactivity."

Marie and Pierre Curie

1876 | 1888 | 1894 | 1895 | 1896 | 1897 | 1898

1915 X-ray crystallography, a way of finding out the structure of crystals, invented by British father and son physicists, William H. Bragg (1862–1942) and Lawrence Bragg (1890–1971).

Mineral with crystalline atomic structure

1919 New Zealand-born physicist Ernest Rutherford (1871–1937) changes one element into another. He converts nitrogen nuclei into oxygen nuclei.

Ernest Rutherford

1931 Neutron (particle in nucleus) discovered by British physicist James Chadwick (1891–1974).

1932 First subatomic particle accelerator built by British physicists J. Cockcroft (1897–1967) and Ernest Walton (born 1903), **Positron**, a particle of antimatter, discovered by American physicist Carl David Anderson (born 1905).

1935 Nylon developed by American chemist Wallace H. Carothers (1896–1937).

First particle accelerator, built at Manchester University, UK

1915 | 1919 | 1920 | 1931 | 1932 | 1935

1960 First laser built by American physicist Theodore Maiman (born 1927), based on ideas developed by American physicist Gordon Gould in 1957.

1964 Existence of quarks, the constituent parts of neutrons and protons, proposed by Murray Gell-Mann, American physicist (born 1929).

Atomic nucleus, showing quarks

1980s Chaos theory developed by American mathematicians, based on the unpredictability of nature. Chaos theory is used to try to predict complex systems.

Fractal: computer-generated pattern derived from chaos theory

1983 Existence of two important subatomic particles (W±, Z°) confirmed at CERN laboratories in Switzerland.

1986 Superconductors, substances with extremely low resistance to electricity, are developed.

1990 COBE (Cosmic Background Explorer) satellite discovers ripples in background radiation – evidence in support of Big Bang theory of the origin of the Universe.

1960 | 1964 | 1983 | 1986 | 1990

WEAPONS

WEAPONS ARE TOOLS for attacking people and animals. Technology has made weapons increasingly efficient in their ability to wound and kill.

c.100,000 B.C. Neanderthal people use sharpened wooden spear point and simple stone ax.

c.2800–2000 B.C. Composite bow, first effective military bow, developed in Middle East. Made of strips of wood, animal horn, and sinew, glued together.

Flint hand-ax

Egyptian battle chariot

c.2000–1500 B.C. Two-wheeled fighting chariot introduced. Provides fast and stable platform for archers and spearmen.

c.1000 B.C. Iron sword developed in southern and central Europe. Far superior to weapons made from bronze, iron is hard and sharp.

| 100,000 B.C. | 2800 | 2000 B.C. | 1000 | *Viking sword, c.1000* |

200 B.C.–A.D. 400 Siege weapons used by Roman soldiers to batter down walls of enemies.

Ballista (giant crossbow)

Bolt

1100 Mace becomes a common weapon of war. It can smash human bones protected by plate armor or chain mail.
Crossbow developed and used for 400 years, a powerful weapon that can be used with little

Bronze mace on modern haft

1340–1400 Cannons introduced into warfare. Powered by gunpowder, they fire small stone balls or large crossbow-type arrows. Large cannons, called bombards, lay open castles to attack.

Replica of small early cannon   Muzzle

1500 Harquebus developed, a hand-held firearm capable of being operated by a single infantryman.

1550 Naval warfare revolutionized as ships are fitted with cannons.

1680 Flintlock musket is dominant weapon for infantry soldiers for next 140 years. A piece of flint ignites gunpowder in musket's barrel.

| A.D. 1 | 1000 | 1100 | 1340 | 1500 | 1550 | 1680 |

1836 First effective revolver developed by American gunsmith Samuel Colt (1814–62). Revolvers can fire several shots in a row before they need reloading.

Five-shot Colt police revolver from 1862

1837 Bolt-action, breech-loading rifle developed by Prussian gunsmith J. N. Dreyse (1787–1867), with increased accuracy and firing rate. Soon all armies are armed with this type of rifle. It remains in use today.

1890s Belt-fed machine guns introduced. Allows two people to fire at great speed. Fires 600 bullets per minute, over 0.62 mile (1km).

RAF No.1 Squadron of 1918

1915 Aircraft first used as weapons when armed with machine guns.

1916 First tank used in war during Battle of the Somme. Although slow and unreliable, the lumbering British tanks cause panic among German troops.

Early British tank

| 1800 | 1836 | 1837 | 1890 | 1900 | 1915 | 1916 |

1940s Submarines, with torpedoes, become a decisive weapon of war. German U-boats almost defeat Allies in Battle of the Atlantic (1939–44).

German U-boat submarine

1945 Dropping of atomic bomb on Japan changes nature of warfare. Now a single bomb can destroy a whole city.

1950s Missiles become effective weapons delivery system. Inter-Continental Ballistic Missiles (ICBMs) carry nuclear warheads thousands of miles; smaller missiles are used to knock out aircraft and tanks.

1960s Assault rifle introduced in large numbers. It provides infantrymen with a light weapon capable of full automatic fire.

US M16A1 assault rifle fitted with 40mm grenade launcher

1980s Attack helicopter, armed with laser-guided missiles and machine guns, proves highly effective in battle. It becomes a key element in rapid reaction forces.

Tiger antitank attack helicopter

| 1940 | 1945 | 1950 | 1960 | 1980 |

AUTOMATIC PISTOL

A pistol is loaded with cartridges, each containing a lead bullet and a casing packed with explosive. When the trigger is pulled, the hammer forces the firing pin into the back of the cartridge, igniting the explosive. The force of this explosion drives the bullet down the barrel and it leaves the pistol at high speed.

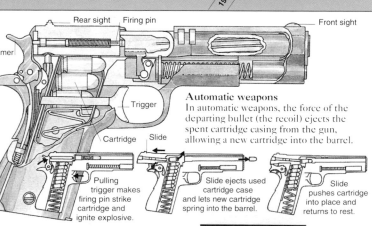

Rear sight   Firing pin   Front sight

Hammer

Trigger

Cartridge   Slide

Automatic weapons
In automatic weapons, the force of the departing bullet (the recoil) ejects the spent cartridge casing from the gun, allowing a new cartridge into the barrel.

Pulling trigger makes firing pin strike cartridge and ignite explosive.

Slide ejects used cartridge case and lets new cartridge spring into the barrel.

Slide pushes cartridge into place and returns to rest.

WEAPONS FACTS

• Powered by their own nuclear reactors, nuclear submarines can remain underwater for months on end, and can fire nuclear missiles over thousands of miles without being detected. They are the deadliest of modern weapons systems.

• "Smart" weapons allow a warhead to be guided directly onto its target. Some "smart" missiles have television cameras in their nose, while others use radar or infrared homing to reach their targets.

Tomahawk Cruise missile, with 1,000lb (454kg) warhead, locates and destroys target below in pre-programmed attack.

READY... AIM...

In 1830, a musket could fire a maximum of four bullets every minute. A modern M61 cannon will fire up to 100 bullets every second.

• In the 19th century, the development of rifled barrels (with spiral grooves running inside the barrel) made guns much more accurate. They made the bullet spin in flight, allowing it to travel farther and straighter.

TRANSPORTATION, COMMUNICATIONS, AND INDUSTRY

Factual coverage of every major transportation group and major world industries, plus global communications, including alphabets and major languages.

Cars • Bicycles • Motorcyles • Trains • Boats • Warships and Submarines
Aircraft • Airline Insignia • Communications • Language • Alphabets and Scripts
Energy • Major Industries • Roads • Construction

CARS

THE FIRST mass-produced car, the Oldsmobile, appeared less than a hundred years ago. Since then, car ownership around the world has grown dramatically: there will probably be a billion cars on the road by the year 2025.

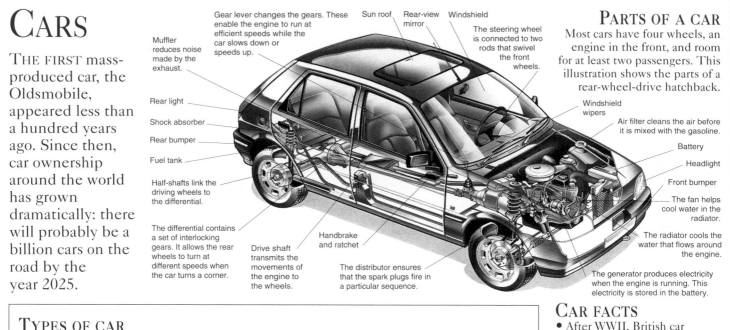

Muffler reduces noise made by the exhaust.

Gear lever changes the gears. These enable the engine to run at efficient speeds while the car slows down or speeds up.

Sun roof

Rear-view mirror

Windshield

The steering wheel is connected to two rods that swivel the front wheels.

Rear light

Shock absorber

Rear bumper

Fuel tank

Half-shafts link the driving wheels to the differential.

The differential contains a set of interlocking gears. It allows the rear wheels to turn at different speeds when the car turns a corner.

Drive shaft transmits the movements of the engine to the wheels.

Handbrake and ratchet

The distributor ensures that the spark plugs fire in a particular sequence.

PARTS OF A CAR

Most cars have four wheels, an engine in the front, and room for at least two passengers. This illustration shows the parts of a rear-wheel-drive hatchback.

Windshield wipers

Air filter cleans the air before it is mixed with the gasoline.

Battery

Headlight

Front bumper

The fan helps cool water in the radiator.

The radiator cools the water that flows around the engine.

The generator produces electricity when the engine is running. This electricity is stored in the battery.

TYPES OF CAR

Veteran car
Veteran cars are the oldest surviving cars. They were built between 1896 and 1903.

Vintage car
Vintage cars are those that were built between 1904 and 1930.

Classic car
Classic cars are outstanding examples of design and engineering.

Sedan
Sedans can usually carry four passengers and have a trunk for luggage.

Station wagon
Station wagons are similar to sedans, with a large loading space at the rear.

Hatchback
Hatchbacks have a rear door that lifts upward for easy access to the loading space.

Convertible
These are open-topped cars. The roof folds back or can be lifted off.

Coupe
Coupes have a sloping roof. They are usually two-seater cars.

Limousine
These extended cars are designed for comfort and luxury. Some have a television and cocktail cabinet.

Sports car
Sports cars display high performance and good road handling. Most have two seats.

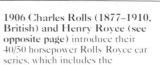

Racing car
Racing cars are custom-built for racing on a track. There are several types (see p.255).

Tourer
Tourers were designed for touring, with room for several passengers and plenty of luggage.

Custom car
Custom cars are adapted by their owners to their personal preferences.

Off-road car
Off-road cars are designed for driving on rough terrain. They have four-wheel drive.

Gull-wing car
These cars have upswinging doors that, when open, resemble the wings of a gull.

CAR FACTS

• After WWII, British car manufacturers turned down the chance to make the German Beetle on the grounds that it was too ugly and would not sell. It has since become the best-selling car of all time, with more than 20 million produced.

Volkswagen Beetle

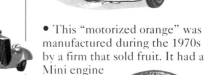

• This "motorized orange" was manufactured during the 1970s by a firm that sold fruit. It had a Mini engine with a specially built chassis and fiberglass skin.

• The most widely traveled car is the Moon Buggy, which the US astronauts drove on the Moon in 1971/72. It also has one of the lowest recorded mileages, at only 18 miles (29km).

HISTORY OF CARS

1886 Gottlieb Daimler (1834–1900, German) fixes an engine to a horse-drawn carriage.

1891 Frenchmen René Panhard (1841–1908) and Emile Levassor (1844–97) produce a car that establishes the classic layout.

1901 First mass-produced car, the Oldsmobile, is produced by Ransom Eli Olds (1864–1950, American).

Oldsmobile

1906 Charles Rolls (1877–1910, British) and Henry Royce (see opposite page) introduce their 40/50 horsepower Rolls Royce car series, which includes the *Silver Ghost*.

1910 First car to be assembled on a moving production line. Henry Ford (see opposite page) introduces the Model T.

Model T

1913 Mass produc[tion] begins in Britain w[ith] William Morris's (se[e] opposite page) Morr[is] Oxford.

Morris Oxford

| 1880 | 1886 | 1890 | 1891 | 1900 | 1901 | 1906 | 1910 | 1910 | 1913 |

FASTEST LUXURY SEDAN CARS

Car	Top speed km/h	mph
Aston Martin Vantage	285	177
Lotus Carlton	282	175
BMW 850I	256	159
Mercedes-Benz 600 SEL	256	159
Mercedes-Benz 600 SL	256	159
BMW M5	254	158
Aston Martin Virage 5.3	253	157
Mercedes-Benz 500 SL	253	157
Mercedes-Benz 500 E	251	156
Mercedes-Benz 500 SE	249	155

TOP CAR-OWNING COUNTRIES

Country	Total cars registered
US	141,251,695
Japan	30,776,243
Germany	29,190,322
Italy	23,500,000
France	22,370,000
UK	20,923,423
CIS	15,874,700
Canada	11,900,000
Brazil	11,760,459
Spain	10,787,424

CAR FACTS
• The luxurious interior of a 1927 Rolls Royce Phantom 1 was upholstered in Aubusson silk tapestry.

• William Morris hated the popular Morris Minor, which was built for 31 years. He called it the "poached egg."

WORLD'S TOP CAR MANUFACTURERS

Company	Total annual car production
General Motors	5,662,843
Ford Motor Company	4,234,583
Toyota	3,093,692
Volkswagen	2,748,152
Peugeot-Citroën	2,227,528
Nissan	2,016,626
Fiat	1,790,631
Renault	1,767,516

FAMOUS MOTOR MEN

Henry Royce (1863–1933, British) was the engineering partner of Rolls Royce. He once said: "There is no such thing as good enough."

Henry Ford (1863–1947) was a talented American mechanic. He introduced mass-production into car manufacturing.

Herbert Austin (1866–1941) set up his own firm in Britain after working for Wolseley car manufacturers.

Frederick Lanchester (1868–1946) designed cars in Britain from 1896. His key inventions included a semi-automatic gearbox.

William Morris (1877–1963) produced the "Bullnose" Morris and played an important role in the British motor industry.

Ettore Bugatti (1882–1947) was an Italian engineer who built the Classic type 35 racing car, as well as beautiful touring models.

Kiichiro Toyoda (1895–1952) founded Toyota cars in Japan. His dream was to see as many cars on the streets of Japan as on those of America.

Alexander Issigonis (1904–88) was a Turkish car designer who went to the UK in 1922. He designed the Morris Minor and the Mini.

HELPING HAND
Before indicators were invented, drivers used hand signals. This false hand clipped onto the car door. It mimicked each signal.

TOP CAR-PRODUCING COUNTRIES

Country	Total annual production
Japan	9,052,406
US	6,823,097
Germany	4,563,673
France	3,409,017
Italy	1,971,969

CAR RECORDS
WORLD LAND SPEED RECORD is 633mph (1,019km/h), achieved by American Richard Noble (born 1946) in *Thrust II*. At this speed, it would take less than 40 hours to drive round the equator.

Thrust II

LONGEST PRODUCTION CAR was the Bugatti Royale (below) with a length of more than 22ft (6.7m). The first was produced in 1927, but only six were made.

MOST ECONOMICAL PRODUCTION CAR is the Daihatsu Charade Diesel Turbo (below), which can achieve 65.9mpg (28km/l) at a steady 56mph (90km/h).

HIGHEST PRICE PAID FOR A CAR THROUGH PRIVATE SALE was over $15,330,000 for a 1962 Ferrari 250 GTO (below) in 1989. The vendor had bought the car for $7,665 in 1971.

Frenchman André ën (1878–1935) duces front-wheel (*traction avant*). This opment bankrupts ën, who dies a year

1935 World's first parking meter is installed, in Oklahoma, US.
1936 Austrian Dr. Ferdinand Porsche (1875–1951) is instructed by Hitler (see p.404) to make a "people's car" and develops the Beetle.

1949 The Citroën 2CV, the people's car of France, is launched.

1958 The Austin Mini is launched. It can seat four people despite its small size.

1979 The catalytic converter is introduced. It reduces pollution from car exhausts.
1988 Fastest speed by a solar-powered vehicle is achieved by the General Motors *Sunraycer* (see p.254), which reaches 48.71mph (78.4km/h).

1990s New safety features, such as air bags, are developed. Other safety options are researched; the experimental *Venus* has two cameras to help the driver see the road in bad conditions.

1930s Citroën   *Beetle*   *Citroën 2CV*   *Austin Mini*   *Venus*

| 1930 | 1934 | 1935 | 1936 | 1940 | 1949 | 1950 | 1958 | 1970 | 1979 | 1980 | 1988 | 1990 |

MARQUES AND MAKES

Automobile manufacturers each have a badge, called a marque, to identify their vehicles. Some well-known marques are shown below.

MOTORING WORDS

Air bag A safety device that fills with air on impact to protect the driver in a collision.

Antilock braking system (ABS) A system that prevents skidding by detecting if a wheel is about to lock during braking.

Brake horsepower (BHP) The power of an engine calculated in terms of the force needed to stop it.

Catalytic converter A filter that absorbs many exhaust pollutants.

Fuel injection (FI) The direct introduction of fuel under pressure into the engine.

Ignition The mechanism that starts a car's engine.

Power steering A steering system that reduces the effort needed to park and maneuver at low speeds.

Roll bar An overhead bar that strengthens the car, protecting passengers if the vehicle overturns.

Spoiler An extension that improves a car's road-holding at high speeds.

Supercharger A mechanism that supplies air or fuel to the engine at above-normal pressure to increase efficiency.

Turbo charger A supercharger driven by a turbine powered by the engine's exhaust gases.

CAR FACTS

• André Citroën (see p.253) used many attention-grabbing forms of publicity. He once hired the Eiffel Tower in Paris, and had his name illuminated in lights down the side. More than 250,000 light bulbs were used.

• The car that reached a production of one million in the shortest time was the Volkswagen Golf. Introduced in 1974, it passed the million mark in 31 months.

MANY IN A MINI

Since the Austin Mini was first produced (see p.253), records have been set and broken for how many people can squeeze inside one. The record currently stands at 24.

• A Lincoln Continental presidential limousine built in the US in 1968 weighed 5.9 tons (5.35 tonnes), more than one-half of which was protective armor plating.

• In the early days of driving, Italians drove on the right-hand side of the road in the country, and on the left in towns. One of the last towns to end this practice was Milan, in 1926.

• From 1865 to 1896, British law stated that every car on the road had to have a person running along in front of it waving a red flag.

AMAZING CARS

Car designers have produced some unusual models over the years. Some have been built purely to break records, others as experiments in car design.

Honda's *Genius E* holds the record for lowest gasoline consumption. It achieved 6,409mpg (2,279km/l).

The *Peel* is one of the smallest cars ever built, at only 4.4ft (1.34m) long. It has no reverse gear.

The *Sunraycer* runs on solar energy. It has special panels that convert sunlight into electrical energy.

A limousine built in the US had 26 wheels and was more than 98ft (30m) long. It had a swimming pool and a helicopter landing pad.

MOST EXPENSIVE CARS SOLD AT AUCTION

Make	Car	Price $
Any car	1962 Ferrari 250 Gran Turismo Berlinetta Competition GTO	8,853,690
Bugatti	1931 Bugatti Type 41 Royale Sports Coupé	7,665,000
Rolls Royce	1907 Rolls Royce Silver Ghost 40/50hp tourer	2,386,706
Mercedes-Benz	1936 Mercedes-Benz 500 K Special Roadster	2,222,850

DASHBOARD AND CONTROLS

Pedals to control the car's acceleration, clutch, and brakes are situated on the car floor. Instruments to indicate speed, fuel levels, temperature, and so on are usually found on the dashboard.

Signaling lights are flicked on and off with this lever.

The driver slows down and stops the car with the brake pedal.

The driver pushes down the clutch pedal when changing gear.

Accelerator controls the car's speed.

Speedometer indicates the car's speed.

Steering wheel

Small items are stored in the glove compartment.

Gear lever

Handbrake stops the car from moving when it is parked.

RACING CARS

RACING CARS ARE designed to compete on a race track. They range from simple stock cars to high technology Formula 1 racing cars, which can achieve speeds of more than 190mph (300km/h).

MOTOR RACING FACTS

- Ferrari is the only motor-racing team to have competed in the Formula 1 world championship every year since it started in 1950.

- The youngest world champion racing driver was Brazilian Emerson Fittipaldi (born 1946), who won his first world championship in 1972, at the age of 25 years and 9 months.

Emerson Fittipaldi

- The oldest world champion racing driver was Argentinian Juan Manuel Fangio (born 1911). When Fangio won his last world championship race in 1957, he was 46 years and 41 days old.

WINNING FORMULA

It takes 150 Renault-Sport staff to produce one of their Formula 1 engines, including 35 mechanics and 25 engineers.

TYPES OF RACING CAR

Formula 1
These are the fastest racing cars. They compete in races called Grand Prix.

Formula 2
These are the second most powerful class of racing car after Formula 1.

Formula 3
These racing cars have engines of up to 2,000cc.

Rally cars
Rally cars are usually ordinary cars with specially strengthened bodies.

Indycars
Indycars are similar to Formula 1 cars, but are larger. They are named after the Indianapolis 500, the most famous race in which they compete.

Le Mans
These racing cars are specially adapted sports cars that race at the 24-hour Le Mans circuit in France.

US stock cars
These are simple cars that are raced around oval dirt tracks.

Dragsters
Dragsters race a short distance along a straight track, at speeds of more than 300mph (485km/h).

RACING RECORDS

FASTEST PIT STOP
(break in a race for refueling or servicing) was four seconds, made by American Robert William "Bobby" Unser (born 1934) in the 1976 Indianapolis 500.

COUNTRY WITH MOST FORMULA 1 DRIVERS
from 1950 to 1993 was Great Britain, which had 131 drivers (21% of total drivers).

WORST CRASH
in a motor race occurred at Le Mans in 1955: 83 spectators were killed and more than 100 were injured when a car somersaulted over the safety barrier, burst into flames, and disintegrated. The driver also died.

LONGEST RALLY
was from Covent Garden, London, UK, to the Sydney Opera House, Australia: a distance of 19,329 miles (31,107km).

HISTORY OF MOTOR RACING

1895 First motor race with gasoline engine vehicles takes place, from Paris to Bordeaux, France, and back. The first car past the finishing line averages 15mph (24km/h) for the race.

1906 First Grand Prix in Le Mans, France, is won by Austro-Hungarian Ferenc Szisz (1873–1970).

Ferenc Szisz

1907 First track constructed for motor car racing opens: the Brooklands Motor Course, UK.

1911 First Indianapolis 500 race takes place in Indianapolis, US.

1929 Bentley cars take first, second, third, and fourth places at Le Mans.

| 1895 | 1900 | 1906 | 1907 | 1910 | 1911 | 1920 | 1929 |

1950 First international Formula 1 race, the Pau Grand Prix, is held in France. It is won by Juan Manuel Fangio (see above). Formula 1 cars are cigar-shaped with front-mounted engines. The driver sits in an upright position.

1951 Fangio wins the first of five World Drivers' Championships.
1958 First rear-mounted engines appear in Formula 1 cars.

Cooper 45, 1958

1960s Formula 1 drivers wear helmets and fireproof overalls, and sit in a more reclined position.

1968 Airfoil wings are introduced by Ferrari and Brabham to produce downforce (holds the car flat on the track).

1970s Formula 1 cars take on a more wedgelike shape.
1988 Raised noses are introduced on Formula 1 cars. They improve airflow past the chassis.

| 1950 | 1951 | 1958 | 1960 | 1968 | 1970 | 1980 | 1988 |

BICYCLES

BICYCLES ARE RIDDEN by millions of people around the world. They range from simple models with no gears, to sophisticated, multigeared mountain bicycles and racers. Bicycles are the most energy-efficient of all forms of transport.

PARTS OF A BICYCLE

The basic design of all bicycles (bikes) is the same. They are made up of a frame, wheels, transmission (cogs, chains, and gears), brakes, stem, handlebars, and saddle. This photograph shows the parts of a racing bike.

TYPES OF BICYCLE

Racing bicycle
Racing bicycles are fast, lightweight, and multigeared, with drop handlebars.

Mountain bicycle
These bicycles are built for off-road cycling. They have thick tires, a lightweight frame, and a wide range of gears.

BMX (Bicycle Motocross)
The BMX bike is designed for rough-terrain cycling, and is often used for acrobatics and tricks.

Tandem
Tandems are bicycles for two riders, with two saddles, two handlebars, and two wheels.

Bicycle rickshaw
Rickshaws are bicycles adapted to carry two passengers behind or in front, in a wheeled chair.

BICYCLE OWNERSHIP AROUND THE WORLD

This table shows the number of bicycles owned in various different countries.

Country	Bicycles (millions)
China	300
US	103
Japan	60
India	45
Mexico	12
Netherlands	11
Australia	6.8
South Korea	6
Argentina	4.5
Egypt	1.5
Tanzania	0.5

GEAR SYSTEMS

Many bicycles have gear systems that enable the cyclist to travel quickly or slowly while pedaling at a comfortable rate. By moving the gear lever, the cyclist lifts the chain from one cog to another.

A small cog turns the wheel slowly, producing extra force for climbing uphill.

A large cog turns the wheel quickly, allowing the bicycle to travel fast downhill or on flat ground.

BICYCLE RECORDS

LONGEST BICYCLE is 72.96ft (22.24m) long. Built in 1988, it was ridden by four riders for a distance of 807ft (246m).

LARGEST BICYCLE (front-wheel diameter) is the *Frankencycle*, with a diameter of 10ft (3.05m).

BICYCLE FACTS

• There are 800 million bicycles in the world: they outnumber cars two to one.

• The Belgian army added elbow rests to the bicycles ridden by their regimental bands, so that they could play their instruments while cycling.

HISTORY OF BICYCLES

1790 The *célérifère*, a wooden, hobbyhorse-like machine, is built by a Frenchman, the Compte de Sivrac.

1813 The *Draisienne* is built by Carl Von Drais (1785–1851, German). It has a steerable front wheel and a saddle.

1839 First bicycle with pedals turning the rear wheel is built. It is nicknamed the "Boneshaker."

1790	1800	1813	1830	1839
1790		1813		1839

PEDAL POWER

The fastest speed on a bicycle was 152.29mph (245.08km/h), achieved by American John Howard in 1985. He was helped by the slipstreaming effect of the leading vehicle.

1861 First bicycle with pedals on the front wheel is built. The saddle is mounted on a spring for comfort, and there is a braking system for the front wheel.

c.1870 The Penny Farthing, named after two British coins, is developed. It proves unsafe.

1879 First commercial bicycle, the Bicyclette, is patented.

1959 First new bicycle design for 50 years – the Moulton – is produced.

1970s BMX bikes are launched. They appeal particularly to children.

1990s Human-powered vehicles (HPVs), such as this *Windcheetah SL*, are developed. They can reach greater speeds than ordinary bicycles.

1990s Lightweight composite materials, such as carbon fiber, and new aerodynamic shapes revolutionize bicycle design.

1860	1861	1870	1879	1950	1959	1990
	1861		1879		1959	

MOTORCYCLES

THE BASIC DESIGN of a motorcycle consists of a bicycle powered by an engine. Motorcycles range from small-engined mopeds to racing motorcycles that can reach speeds of more than 311mph (500km/h).

PARTS OF A MOTORCYCLE

The largest to the smallest machines are all built in a similar way, with a piston engine and telescopic forks. Motorcycle engine sizes range from 50cc (cubic capacity) to more than 1,000cc. This Yamaha motorcycle has a 1,002cc engine.

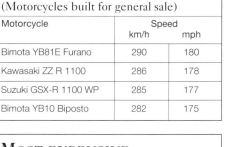

- Mirror
- Windshield
- The throttle is on the handlebars.
- Air scoops feed the air box to supply the carburetors.
- Twin spar chassis
- Saddle
- Four-cylinder engine
- Signaling light
- This motorcycle has upside-down telescopic forks; the lower section of the fork slides into the upper.
- This motorcycle can reach a speed of 167mph (269km/h).
- Exhaust
- Three-spoke wheels
- Radiator
- The fairing (front enclosure) has been removed to show the engine.
- Chain

1992 Yamaha FZR 1000 Exup

TYPES OF MOTORCYCLE

Motorcycle rickshaw These three-wheeled taxis are adapted motorcycles.

Trail bike Lightweight trail motorcycles are designed for rough terrain.

Custom motorcycle These motorcycles are adapted by their owners to individual specifications.

Moped Mopeds are 50cc motorcycles restricted by law to 30mph (48km/h).

Scooter Scooters are small-wheeled motorcycles.

Combination Combination or outfit motorcycles are those with a sidecar attached.

MOTORCYCLE RECORDS

LONGEST JUMP FROM A RAMP was 251ft (76.5m), by American Doug Danger on a 991 Honda CR 500.

LONGEST WHEELIE (traveling nonstop on the rear wheel) was 206 miles (331km), by Yasuyuki Kudoh of Japan.

LARGEST MOTORCYCLE PYRAMID consisted of 45 riders of the Indian Army motorcycle display team. They rode eight motorcycles a distance of 2,625ft (800m).

LONGEST STREET-LEGAL MOTORCYCLE was 15ft (4.57m) long, built by American Gregg Reid.

SMALLEST MOTORCYCLE had a wheelbase of 4.25in (10.79cm), a seat height of 3.75in (9.5cm), a front wheel diameter of 0.75in (1.9cm), and a back wheel diameter of 0.95in (2.41cm). It was ridden over a distance of 3.3ft (1m).

Smallest motorcycle

FASTEST PRODUCTION MOTORCYCLES

(Motorcycles built for general sale)

Motorcycle	Speed	
	km/h	mph
Bimota YB81E Furano	290	180
Kawasaki ZZ R 1100	286	178
Suzuki GSX-R 1100 WP	285	177
Bimota YB10 Biposto	282	175

MOST EXPENSIVE PRODUCTION MOTORCYCLES

Motorcycle	Price US$
Bimota Tesi 1D ES	35,300
Bimota Tesi 1D SR	33,300
Bimota YB10 Furano	32,200

HISTORY OF MOTORCYCLES

1818 First idea for a motorcycle, a steam-driven motorcycle, *Velocipedraisiavaporianna*, appears in a cartoon in Paris, France.

1884 Britain's first motorcycle, the *Petrolcycle*, is patented. It is not built until 1888.

1885 Germans Wilhelm Maybach (1846–1929) and Gottlieb Daimler (1834–1900) build a motorcycle with a wooden frame and wheels, powered by Daimler's four-stroke internal combustion engine. Daimler's son rides 6 miles (10km) before the saddle catches fire.

| 1818 | 1818 | 1884 | 1885 |

MOTORCYCLE MADNESS

The most people to ride one motorcycle was 16, in 1987. All the members of the Illawarra Mini Bike Training Club, Australia, rode a motorcycle for 1 mile (1.6km).

1892 First commercially produced motorcycle is launched.

1901 One of the first practical motorcycles, the new Werner, is produced.

1904 Harley Davidson begin motorcycle production with their *Silent Gray Fellow*.

1907 First TT (Tourist Trophy) race is held in the Isle of Man, UK.

1910 Sidecars become popular.

1959 Triumph introduce their most famous motorcycle, the high performance Bonneville.

1972 First superbike produced by Honda.

1978 New motorcycle speed record set by Donald Vesco (born 1939), who reaches 318mph (512km/h) (below).

1990s The R1100, with computerized engine management, is launched by German company BMW.

| 1890 | 1892 | 1900 | 1901 | 1904 | 1907 | 1910 | 1950 | 1959 | 1970 | 1972 | 1978 | 1990 |

TRAINS

A TRAIN IS A SERIES of vehicles pushed or pulled along a track (a railroad) by a locomotive. Trains are an efficient method of transportation: they use less fuel than cars and trucks require.

TYPES OF TRAIN

Electric locomotive

Diesel locomotive

Steam locomotive

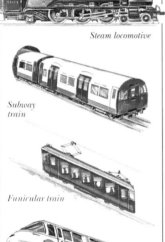

Subway train

Funicular train

Monorail

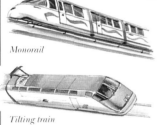

Tilting train

PARTS OF A TRAIN

This illustration shows the *Train à Grande Vitesse* (TGV) – the French high-speed train. It runs on specially built tracks with gentle grades and curves. The TGV was introduced in 1983.

The pantograph picks up an electric current from overhead cables.

Air-conditioned carriages

An air-powered suspension system and large shock absorbers enable the train to run smoothly.

The power cars pull and push the train.

Trains run on "trucks," which have four or more wheels. The trucks swivel to enable the train to go around curves.

The wheels under the power cars and the leading carriage are driven by electric motors.

The driver's cab has a computer that checks for faults on the train, and a radio that keeps the driver in touch with the signaling center and other trains.

The TGV's streamlined shape reduces air resistance, enabling it to travel at high speeds.

BRING YOUR OWN CARRIAGE

On some of the earliest trains, passengers' own carriages were attached to wagons pulled behind the locomotive. Passengers sat in them during the journey.

TRAIN FACTS

• Steam trains are still used in several countries, including Zimbabwe, India, and China.

• The first toilets on trains appeared in the 1850s, in the US and Europe.

RAILS AND SWITCHES

Rails are usually welded into one continuous track as they are laid, allowing trains to run smoothly. Switches, or points, are intersections in the rails that move trains onto a new section of track.

When a switch takes place, one rail of the track onto which the train will pass slides up against the far rail of the track on which it has been traveling.

A small gap opens in the near rail of the old track, and the train moves onto the new track.

The track rests on beams of wood or concrete called ties or sleepers.

RAILROAD GAUGES

The gauge of a railroad is the distance between the two running rails. Railroads are laid to different gauges in different parts of the world. This table shows some of the countries that have the various gauges.

Gauge metric	imperial	Countries
1,676mm	5ft 6in	Argentina, Chile, India, Pakistan, Portugal, Spain
1,600mm	5ft 3in	Brazil, Ireland, South Australia, Victoria (Australia)
1,520mm	5ft	Finland, former USSR
1,435mm	4ft 8.5in	Canada, China, France, Germany, Great Britain, Italy, New South Wales (Australia), Scandinavia (except Finland), US
1,067mm	3ft 6in	Japan, Queensland, Tasmania, Western Australia (Australia), South Africa, Zimbabwe
1m	3ft 3in	Argentina, Brazil, Myanmar, Chile, East Africa, Thailand

HISTORY OF TRAINS

Pre-19th century
Wagons are pulled along tracks by horses and humans.

Stones being hauled along a track

1804 First successful steam railroad locomotive built by Richard Trevithick (1771–1833, English) for the Pen-y-darren ironworks in South Wales, UK.

1829 *Rocket* **built by Robert Stephenson** (see opposite page). It is the first locomotive to incorporate modern features.

1830 First public steam railroad for goods and passengers, the Liverpool and Manchester railroad, UK, opens.

1881 World's first public electric railroad opens, in Germany.

1890 World's first electric underground railroad, the City and South London Line, UK opens (below).

B.C. | 1800 | 1804 | 1829 | 1830 | 1881 | 1890

TRAIN RECORDS

MOST POWERFUL SINGLE-UNIT DIESEL-ELECTRIC LOCOMOTIVES
are 6,600 horsepower, owned by the US Union Pacific Railroad.

LONGEST AND HEAVIEST FREIGHT TRAIN
was a 500-car coal train that stretched for 4 miles (6.4km) and weighed 46,300 tons. It ran on the Norfolk and Western Railroad, Ohio, in 1967, and was hauled by six diesels.

Grand Central Terminal, New York

LARGEST STATION
is the Grand Central Terminal in New York, US, which has 44 platforms.

HIGHEST STATION
is at Condor, Bolivia. It is situated at an altitude of 15,705ft (4,787m).

OLDEST SURVIVING STATION
is Liverpool Road, Manchester, UK, which opened in 1830. It is now part of the Museum of Science and Industry.

MAJOR PASSENGER RAILROAD USERS

This table shows the countries with the highest passenger railroad usage.

Country	Distance traveled (in billions)	
	km	miles
Russia	410.7	255.2
Japan	390	242
Germany	65.9	40.9
France	64.3	40.0
Italy	44.4	27.6
UK	33.2	20.6

FAMOUS TRAINS

ROCKET
This early steam engine was designed by English engineers Robert Stephenson (1803–59) and Henry Booth in 1829. It reached speeds of 29mph (47km/h) and heralded the age of the passenger train.

THE GENERAL
This train was built for the Western and Atlantic Railroad in 1855. It was typical of the steam engines that opened up the American West, with a cowcatcher on the front, and a large funnel for catching sparks.

ORIENT EXPRESS
The luxurious *Orient Express* was introduced in 1883. It ran between London, Paris, Vienna, Budapest, and Constantinople (Istanbul). So many secret agents used this train that it became known as the "Spies Express."

TWENTIETH CENTURY LTD.
This luxury train was run by the New York Central and Hudson River Railroad. It ran between New York and Chicago from 1902 to 1967, and had a rear observation car and an onboard barber shop.

TRAIN FACTS
• A high-speed diesel railcar introduced in Germany in 1933 ran at speeds of 100mph (161km/h) between Berlin and Hamburg. It was widely known as the *Flying Hamburger*.

TRANS-SIBERIAN EXPRESS
This service runs from Moscow to Vladivostock, taking almost eight days to cover 5,777 miles (9,297km) – the longest regular train journey in the world. The first through Trans-Siberian train ran in 1914.

FLYING SCOTSMAN
Flying Scotsman – London and North Eastern Railway locomotive No. 4472 – was built in 1923. It hauled express passenger trains between London, England, and Edinburgh, Scotland, until 1963.

HIAWATHA
Hiawatha was a steam-powered train built to provide a high-speed passenger service in the US. It began in 1935, and traveled between Chicago and Minneapolis–St. Paul, taking just five hours and five minutes.

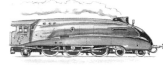

MALLARD
This steam locomotive – London and North Eastern Railway locomotive No. 4468 – holds the world speed record for steam traction. In 1938 it reached a speed of 126mph (203km/h), pulling a seven-coach train.

Steam locomotive works, Newcastle, UK, 1864

BLUE TRAIN
The *Blue Train* is probably the most luxurious train in the world: it has been described as a "five-star hotel on wheels." Introduced in 1939, it runs between the South African cities of Pretoria and Cape Town.

"BIG BOYS"
These locomotives were built from 1941 to 1944 by the American Locomotive Company, for the Union Pacific Railroad. They were among the largest conventional steam locomotives ever built.

ETR450 TILTING TRAIN
This Italian train was introduced in 1988. It provides fast passenger service on routes between Rome and other cities in Italy. It can tilt at an angle of up to 10° and has a maximum speed of 155mph (250km/h).

BULLET TRAIN
This is the nickname of Japan's high-speed train, which began running between Tokyo and Osaka in 1965. The Bullet Train's aerodynamic shape enables it to travel at speeds of up to 130mph (210km/h).

• Between 1804 and 1968, more than 130,000 steam locomotives were built in Britain.

• The first railway to serve meals on a train was the US Baltimore and Ohio Railroad, in 1853.

1895 Electric traction is introduced in the US, on a 3.7-mile (6km) stretch of track in Baltimore.

1913 First diesel-powered railcar, built in Sweden, enters service.
1923 Flying Scotsman (see above) enters service.

1934 Pioneer Zephyr, a streamlined diesel-electric train, is introduced in the US. It sets the long-distance nonstop speed record.

1968 Last scheduled passenger steam train runs on British Railways: the 21.15 Preston to Liverpool.

1987 World speed record for diesel traction is set by British Railways' High-Speed Train, which achieves 176.4mph (283.9km/h).

1990 World speed record for an electric locomotive is set by the French TGV. It achieves a speed of 320mph (515km/h).

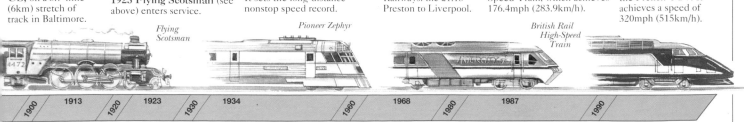
Flying Scotsman   *Pioneer Zephyr*   *British Rail High-Speed Train*

| 1900 | 1913 | 1920 | 1923 | 1930 | 1934 | 1960 | 1968 | 1980 | 1987 | 1990 |

BOATS

FROM HUGE OIL tankers to simple dugout canoes, boats play a vital role in the transportation of people and goods. For many centuries, much of the world's trade has depended on shipping.

SAILS

Sails catch the wind to provide power for boats.

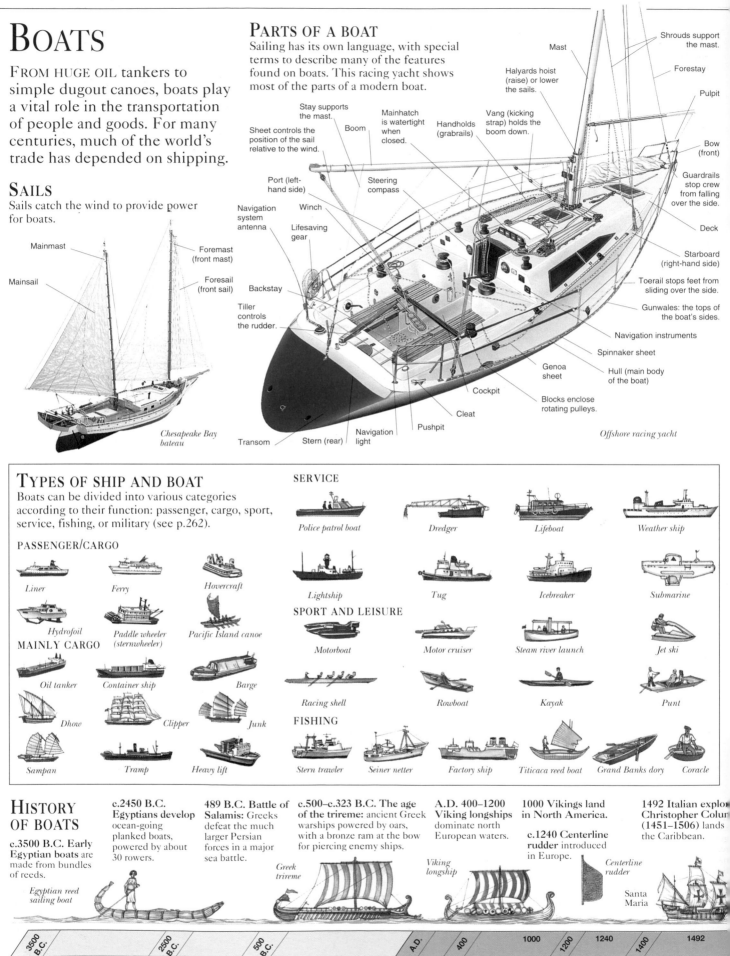

Mainmast

Foremast (front mast)

Mainsail

Foresail (front sail)

Chesapeake Bay bateau

PARTS OF A BOAT

Sailing has its own language, with special terms to describe many of the features found on boats. This racing yacht shows most of the parts of a modern boat.

Stay supports the mast.

Sheet controls the position of the sail relative to the wind.

Port (left-hand side)

Navigation system antenna

Backstay

Tiller controls the rudder.

Boom

Mainhatch is watertight when closed.

Handholds (grabrails)

Steering compass

Winch

Lifesaving gear

Transom

Stern (rear)

Navigation light

Pushpit

Cleat

Cockpit

Genoa sheet

Blocks enclose rotating pulleys.

Mast

Halyards hoist (raise) or lower the sails.

Vang (kicking strap) holds the boom down.

Shrouds support the mast.

Forestay

Pulpit

Bow (front)

Guardrails stop crew from falling over the side.

Deck

Starboard (right-hand side)

Toerail stops feet from sliding over the side.

Gunwales: the tops of the boat's sides.

Navigation instruments

Spinnaker sheet

Hull (main body of the boat)

Offshore racing yacht

TYPES OF SHIP AND BOAT

Boats can be divided into various categories according to their function: passenger, cargo, sport, service, fishing, or military (see p.262).

PASSENGER/CARGO

Liner

Ferry

Hovercraft

Hydrofoil

Paddle wheeler (sternwheeler)

Pacific Island canoe

MAINLY CARGO

Oil tanker

Container ship

Barge

Dhow

Clipper

Junk

Sampan

Tramp

Heavy lift

SERVICE

Police patrol boat

Dredger

Lifeboat

Weather ship

Lightship

Tug

Icebreaker

Submarine

SPORT AND LEISURE

Motorboat

Motor cruiser

Steam river launch

Jet ski

Racing shell

Rowboat

Kayak

Punt

FISHING

Stern trawler

Seiner netter

Factory ship

Titicaca reed boat

Grand Banks dory

Coracle

HISTORY OF BOATS

c.3500 B.C. Early Egyptian boats are made from bundles of reeds.

Egyptian reed sailing boat

c.2450 B.C. Egyptians develop ocean-going planked boats, powered by about 30 rowers.

489 B.C. Battle of Salamis: Greeks defeat the much larger Persian forces in a major sea battle.

Greek trireme

c.500–c.323 B.C. The age of the trireme: ancient Greek warships powered by oars, with a bronze ram at the bow for piercing enemy ships.

A.D. 400–1200 Viking longships dominate north European waters.

Viking longship

1000 Vikings land in North America.

c.1240 Centerline rudder introduced in Europe.

Centerline rudder

1492 Italian explor[er] Christopher Colun[bus] (1451–1506) lands the Caribbean.

Santa Maria

3500 B.C.	2500 B.C.	500 B.C.	A.D.	400	1000	1200	1240	1400	1492

SAILING WORDS

Aft At or near the stern.

Beating Sailing into the wind; wind coming from the bow.

Forward At or toward the bow.

Gangplank Portable bridge for boarding or leaving the boat.

Heave-to To slow or stop a boat using the sails and rudder.

Jibing Turning the stern of a boat through the wind.

Knot Unit of speed used by ships and aircraft: one knot = one nautical mph.

Log The record of a ship's voyage.

Nautical mile Unit of length used in sailing: one nautical mile = 6,076ft (1,852m). (One land mile = 5,280ft/1,609m.)

Reaching Sailing across the wind; wind coming from the beam (side).

Running Sailing with the wind coming from astern.

Tacking Turning the bow of a boat through the wind.

Wind

Destination

Second tack

First tack

SHIP RECORDS

LARGEST SAILING SHIP was the *France*, which measured 418.8ft (127.7m) long.

LARGEST CONTAINER SHIPS are owned by American President Lines. Five of their ships are 902ft (275m) long. These ships are too large for the Panama Canal, and are known as *Post-Panamax* ships.

Queen Elizabeth

LARGEST PASSENGER LINER is the *Norway*, which is 1,035ft (315.5m) long. The *Queen Elizabeth*, launched in 1938, was 1,031ft (314m) long.

FAMOUS SHIPS

SANTA MARIA
This was the flagship of Italian explorer Christopher Columbus (1451–1506) on his voyage of discovery to the West Indies in 1492. *Santa Maria* was wrecked, and Columbus continued on the *Nina*.

MAYFLOWER
This square-rigged sailing ship took 100 Puritans from Southampton, England, in 1620, to form the first permanent European colony in New England. Plymouth, Massachussets is now located on the site.

ENDEAVOUR
Captain James Cook (1728–1779) undertook his first scientific and exploratory voyage in this ship, in 1768. During this three-year voyage, Cook mapped 5,000 miles (8,000km) of coastline.

BOUNTY
In 1788, a famous mutiny took place on the *Bounty*. Lieutenant Fletcher Christian (1764–c.1790) led a revolt against commanding officer William Bligh (1754–1817) after the ship had collected breadfruit from Tahiti.

CUTTY SARK
This was the most famous of the clippers. By the time the *Cutty Sark* was launched in 1869, the Suez Canal was open and steamships could travel east economically. The era of the sailing ship was drawing to an end.

KON TIKI
Norwegian Thor Heyerdahl (born 1914) built the raft *Kon Tiki* in 1947 to prove that the Polynesian islands could have been populated from South America. He sailed 3,800 miles (6,115km) from Peru to Raroia.

VIKING VERY LONG SHIP
The world's largest ship is the Norwegian oil tanker *Jahre Viking*, which is 1,503ft (458m) long. It takes five minutes to walk from one end to the other.

SHIPWRECKS AND DISASTERS

Ship	Date	Shipwreck/disaster
Armada	1588	Spanish fleet of 130 ships sent to invade England. After losing the battle, the surviving ships fled north around Scotland and Ireland where many were wrecked by storms. Only 60 ships returned to Spain; about 15,000 sailors died.
Marie Celeste	1872	Found abandoned and empty, with no trace of the ten people originally on board.
Titanic	1912	Struck an iceberg and sank, with the loss of about 1,500 lives.
Lusitania	1915	Torpedoed with the loss of 1,198 lives.
Wilhelm Gustloff	1945	Torpedoed with the loss of more than 7,000 lives.
Dona Paz	1963	Collided with tanker *Vector*: 4,386 people died.
Queen Elizabeth	1972	Burned and sank in Hong Kong Harbor while being refitted.
Amoco Cadiz	1978	Spilled 223,000 tons of oil, with drastic environmental consequences.

SHIP FACTS

• Japanese companies own 3,041 large- and medium-sized ships (those with more than 1,000 gross tons); Greek companies own 2,773, and US companies own 1,654.

• A large oil tanker carries about 29,240,000 gallons (132,925,040 liters) of gasoline: this is enough to enable a car to drive around the Earth nearly 47,000 times.

• About 92% of the world's trading goods are carried by ships.

SUPERSTORER
Large container ships can carry about 2,700 containers. Stacked, they would stand almost twice as high as Mt. Everest.

-22 First ~~cir~~mnavigation ~~of the~~ world by ~~Portu~~guese ~~explo~~rer ~~Ferd~~nand ~~Mage~~lan ~~1480~~–1521).

c.1700 Introduction of the steering wheel.

Ship's steering wheel

1838 First crossing of the Atlantic entirely under steam, by *Sirius*.

Sirius

1850–1859 Heyday of the clipper: fast sailing ship that transports tea from China to Europe and North America.

Clipper

1968–69 First nonstop solo circumnavigation of the world from west to east, by English yachtsman Robin Knox-Johnston (born 1939), in *Suhaili*.

Suhaili

1994 Englishman Mike Golding (born 1960) breaks east-west (against the prevailing wind), single-handed, non-stop round-the-world record, in *Group 4 Securitas*, completing his voyage in 167 days.

| 1519 | 1700 | 1800 | 1838 | 1850 | 1900 | 1968 | 1994 |

WARSHIPS AND SUBMARINES

THERE ARE MANY types of fighting vessel, from light, speedy frigates to massive aircraft carriers and nuclear-powered submarines. A country or state's fighting force of ships and submarines is called its navy.

TYPES OF WARSHIP

The main function of a warship is to defend its country, sea-lanes, and shipping from enemy attack.

Aircraft carrier
The aircraft carrier is the largest of all warships. It acts as a floating airfield for up to 100 aircraft. It may have a crew of more than 2,000, plus a flying crew of more than 1,000.

Cruiser
The cruiser's speed and endurance are considered more important than its protection (self-defense) and weapons. Cruiser functions vary from navy to navy.

Battleship
Before aircraft carriers were built, the battleship was the most heavily armed and armored ship. There are now very few battleships remaining in service.

Destroyer
The destroyer was originally intended to defend fleets against attack from torpedo boats. Today's destroyers are armed with guided missiles.

Frigate
The frigate was developed during World War II to escort convoys and protect them from submarines. Today's frigates perform a variety of functions.

Minesweeper
Minesweepers have special equipment for locating and destroying mines. They are usually small craft of 440–880 tons (400–800 tonnes).

PARTS OF A WARSHIP

Modern warships are armed with guns and guided missiles for attack and defense. Most are also equipped with advanced electronic equipment for detecting targets.

Frigate

Ensign staff · Sonar torpedo decoy · Lynx helicopter · Seacat missile launcher · Funnel · Mast · Surveillance radar · Navigation/helicopter control radar antenna · Radar for gunnery and missile control · Signaling lamp · Exocet missile launcher · Gun tower · 4.4in (11cm) gun

Rudder · Variable-pitch propeller · Antisubmarine torpedo tube · Liferaft cylinder · Rocket launcher · Pennant number · Porthole · Sonar bulge · Anchor

F174

SUBMARINES

There are two main types of military submarine: patrol submarines, which seek and destroy ships, and missile-carrying submarines. Today's nuclear missile-carrying submarines are the most powerful weapons carriers of all time.

Stabilized fin · Aft hydroplane · Main turbine · Snort mast · Conning tower · Control room · Periscope · Senior ratings' mess · Galley · Officers' mess

Propeller · Lower rudder · Diesel motor compartment · Reactor space · Junior ratings' mess · Torpedo compartment · Torpedo tube

Nuclear-powered submarine

WARSHIP AND SUBMARINE RECORDS

LARGEST SUBMARINE is the Russian Typhoon class, which measures about 558ft (170m) long.

Russian Typhoon class submarine

FASTEST SUBMARINE is the Russian *Alpha*, which can probably exceed 42 knots (see p.261) when submerged.

WARSHIP WITH THE LARGEST NUMBER OF HEAVY GUNS was the battleship *Agincourt*, built in 1914, which had fourteen 12in (30.5cm) guns.

WARSHIP HARDSHIP

During the late 18th century, only about 9% of deaths on British Royal Navy warships were due to enemy action. About 50% were caused by disease, 31% by accidents, and about 10% by fires and wrecks.

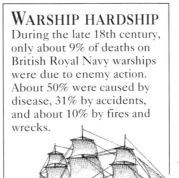

FAMOUS FIGHTING SHIPS

VICTORY
The *Victory*, built in 1765, was British Admiral Lord Nelson's (1758–1805) flagship. It had 100 guns and a crew of 850.

WARRIOR
The *Warrior*, built in 1860, was the first iron battleship. This British ship was protected by a 4.5in (114mm) iron belt.

MONITOR
In 1862, during the American Civil War, the US *Monitor* took part in the first battle between ironclad warships.

DREADNOUGHT
This British ship, built in 1906, was the first modern battleship. It was armed with heavy guns and protected by thick steel.

BISMARCK
This German WWII battleship, launched in 1939 and sunk in May 1941, had eight 15in (38cm) guns.

YAMATO
This Japanese battleship, launched in 1940, was the largest battleship of all time. It was sunk in 1945.

ESSEX
The US aircraft carrier *Essex*, launched in 1942, could carry 91 aircraft and achieve a speed of 32 knots.

NIMITZ
The US nuclear-powered aircraft carrier *Nimitz* was completed in 1975. It carries 90 aircraft.

AIRCRAFT

THE TERM AIRCRAFT refers to all flying machines, including airplanes, helicopters, and hot-air balloons. Aircraft range from simple hang-gliders to the enormous Boeing 747, which can carry more than 550 people.

The fin stops the back of the plane from swinging from side to side.

The elevators control the plane's ascent and descent.

Piper Cherokee

Wings are covered with thin aluminum sheeting.

Fuselage

Pilot's seat

The rudder steers the plane.

Strong metal cables run from the pilot's control stick and rudder pedals to the control surfaces.

Fuel tanks in the wings and wing tips hold up to 85 gallons (320 liters) of fuel.

Engine

Ailerons control the plane's balance and, together with the rudder, steer the plane.

Flap

Spinner

Propeller

Nose landing gear

Undercarriage (main landing gear)

Wings are made from spars. These long, strong rods stretch from the fuselage to the wing tip.

PARTS OF AN AIRCRAFT

This small, propellered light aircraft shows the features of a typical airplane. Its main structures are the fuselage, wings, stabilizer (or tail plane), rudder, one or more engines, and the landing gear.

TYPES OF AIRPLANE

Airplanes (planes) are powered, heavier-than-air aircraft with fixed wings. There are many different types of airplane; their uses include warfare, sport, and transportation.

Jet aircraft
Jet aircraft are powered by jet engines (see p.247). Most civil airliners (large passenger aircraft) and military planes have jet engines.

Propellered plane
Propellered planes are cheaper to run than jet aircraft, and can take off easily from short runways. Many airlines use turboprop aircraft for regional air services. The propellers of these planes are driven by gas turbines.

Biplane
Biplanes have two sets of wings, one above the other, braced with wires. Early planes were built in this style because two wings were stronger than one long, single wing. Today's biplanes are strong enough to withstand aerobatic displays.

Light aircraft
Light aircraft are powered by piston engines similar to those found in cars. These small airplanes are used mainly for leisure and short business trips.

Observation plane
Observation planes are used by police, rescue services, and armies. They are usually standard light aircraft, although the *Edgeley Optica* (above) is a custom-built model.

Supersonic plane
Supersonic planes are jet aircraft that can fly faster than the speed of sound (see p.236). Their shape is different from that of conventional airplanes, because air flows in a different way at such high speeds.

Seaplane
Seaplanes can take off from and land on water. They are used mainly in remote areas with few airfields, such as northern Canada and Alaska, where the country is undeveloped and lakes abound.

FLIGHT DECK

The flight deck contains the controls and data-display instruments. Today's flight decks, such as this 1980s airliner cockpit, have cathode-ray tubes (CRTs). These display computerized information on screens that can be changed at the touch of a button.

Primary flight display CRT: includes artificial horizon, altimeter, and airspeed indicator.

Landing and taxi light switches

Warning lights

Second CRT displays navigational information; it functions as a simple compass, radar screen, or map display.

Engine throttles

Navigation computer equipment

Independent weather radar

Wing flap control

FLYING A PLANE

Airplanes have three main controls: the throttle, which controls the speed; the rudder pedals; and the control column.

Rolling
To roll, the pilot moves the control column to the left or right, raising the ailerons on one wing and lowering them on the other.

The plane rolls when the ailerons are raised and lowered.

Control column

Aileron

Elevator

Pitching
To pitch the plane up or down, the pilot pushes or pulls the control column, raising or lowering the elevator flaps on the tail wing.

Yawing
To make the plane yaw (swerve) to the left or right, the pilot swivels the rudder bar with the feet. This turns the upright rudder on the tail.

Rudder pedals steer the plane to the left and right.

Rudder

The control column tilts the aircraft to either side (rolling), and up and down (pitching).

Plane banks in order to turn.

Banking
Airplanes have to bank in order to turn. The pilot uses the control column and the rudder pedals together, so that the aircraft rolls and yaws at the same time.

HISTORY OF FLIGHT

For centuries, people tried to fly. They made elaborate wings, launching themselves from high places, often with fatal results. Only during the last 100 years have humans learned to fly, advancing from simple machines to jet airplanes.

Daedalus

c.2000 B.C. According to legend, Daedalus, a craftsman working on the labyrinth for King Minos of Crete, makes wings for himself and his son to escape the island.

1010 Oliver of Malmesbury (c.980–1066), a Benedictine monk, attaches wings to his arms and jumps from a tower. He travels for a short distance but breaks his legs.

1486–1500 Italian artist Leonardo da Vinci (1452–1519) sketches designs for flapping wing craft (ornithopters), as well as parachutes and helicopters.

2000 B.C. — A.D. — 1000 — 1010 — 1400 — 1486

1853 Sir George Cayley builds a full-size glider, which, it is claimed, carries his coachman across a small valley.

1891–96 The world's first aviator, German Otto Lilienthal (1848–96), invents a practical hang-glider and becomes the first person to make repeated controlled flights.

Otto Lilienthal, 1896

1896 American scientist Samuel Langley (1834–1906) builds a tandem-winged, steam-powered model, the *Aerodrome.*

Samuel Langley flew 0.6 miles (1km) in the Aerodrome.

1903 The world's first power-driven airplane flight is made by the Wright brothers, Orville (1871–1948) and Wilbur (1867–1912), who fly 853 (260m) at Kitty Hawk, US.

1853 — 1891 — 1896 — 1900 — 1903

1919 First nonstop flight across the Atlantic is made by British aviators John Alcock (1892–1919) and Arthur Whitten-Brown (1886–1948), in a Vickers Vimy with Rolls-Royce engines. It takes 16 hours.

Alcock and Brown

1920s Vast airships fly people across the Atlantic in ocean-liner style.

1924 Hugo Junkers (1859–1935, German) produces a pioneering all-metal three-engined monoplane airliner.

All-metal Junkers airliner

1927 First solo flight across the Atlantic is made by American Charles Lindbergh (1902–74) in a Ryan monoplane, *Spirit of St. Louis.*

Spirit of St. Louis

1928 First flight a the mid-Pacific is by Australian Charl Kingsford Smith (1897–1935).

1928 World's first modern airport is at Croydon, near London, UK.

1919 — 1920 — 1924 — 1927 — 1928

1939 First jet-propelled flight is made by a Heinkel He178, powered by an engine designed by German Hans von Ohain (born 1911).

1937 First experimental jet engine is designed by British engineer Frank Whittle (born 1907) (above right).

Heinkel He178

1940 Battle of Britain: the victory of the British Royal Air Force over the German Luftwaffe ensures that Britain is not invaded.

1941 Frank Whittle's jet engine is used in the Gloster E28/39.

Gloster E28/39

1947 The Bell X-1 experimental rocket plane, piloted by American Chuck Yeager (born 1923), breaks the sound barrier.

Bell X-1

Hav

1952 The world's first jetlin the De Havilland Comet, com into service, halving internatio flight times. Two years later it withdrawn following crashes d to metal fatigue.

1939 — 1940 — 1940 — 1941 — 1947 — 1950 — 1952

OTHER AIRCRAFT TYPES

HOT-AIR BALLOON
Hot-air balloons are used mainly for recreation. Modern hot-air balloons use propane burners carried above the balloon's basket to heat up the air.

AIRSHIP
Modern airships are filled with helium or hot air. Their long, thin shape keeps them stable. Airships can be steered, and many have swiveling propellers to assist with takeoff and landing. Airships are sometimes used for advertising, with messages displayed on their sides.

GLIDER
Gliders are unpowered planes with a wide wingspan measuring up to 82ft (25m). They use currents of hot, rising air (thermals) to stay aloft, and are controlled with a rudder, elevators, and ailerons (see p.263).

HANG GLIDER
Hang gliders are made of material stretched across a simple frame, forming wings. The pilot hangs beneath the wings in a harness or body-bag and steers by shifting weight from side to side. Hang gliders are not powered: the pilot relies on thermals for lift.

MICROLIGHT
A microlight is basically a powered hang glider. It has a small engine and an open fiberglass car, called a trike, that can hold a crew of two. The trike is suspended on a strong frame. Pilots steer by shifting their weight against the frame. Microlights can reach speeds of up to 100mph (160km/h).

HELICOPTER
Helicopters are powered, lifted, and steered by rotating blades. They take off vertically, fly slowly and hover, and move in any direction. This maneuverability makes them ideal for functions such as crop-spraying, traffic surveillance, and rescue.

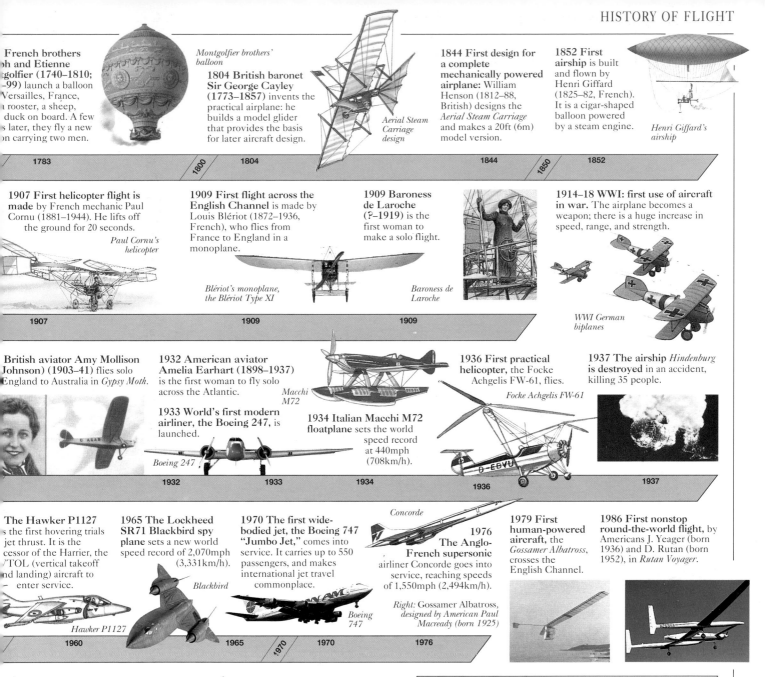

French brothers
[Josep]h and Etienne
[Mont]golfier (1740–1810;
[17–]99) launch a balloon
[at] Versailles, France,
[with] a rooster, a sheep,
[and] duck on board. A few
[month]s later, they fly a new
[balloo]n carrying two men.

Montgolfier brothers' balloon

1804 British baronet Sir George Cayley (1773–1857) invents the practical airplane: he builds a model glider that provides the basis for later aircraft design.

Aerial Steam Carriage design

1844 First design for a complete mechanically powered airplane: William Henson (1812–88, British) designs the *Aerial Steam Carriage* and makes a 20ft (6m) model version.

1852 First airship is built and flown by Henri Giffard (1825–82, French). It is a cigar-shaped balloon powered by a steam engine.

Henri Giffard's airship

| 1783 | 1800 | 1804 | 1844 | 1850 | 1852 |

1907 First helicopter flight is made by French mechanic Paul Cornu (1881–1944). He lifts off the ground for 20 seconds.

Paul Cornu's helicopter

1909 First flight across the English Channel is made by Louis Blériot (1872–1936, French), who flies from France to England in a monoplane.

Blériot's monoplane, the Blériot Type XI

1909 Baroness de Laroche (?–1919) is the first woman to make a solo flight.

Baroness de Laroche

1914–18 WWI: first use of aircraft in war. The airplane becomes a weapon; there is a huge increase in speed, range, and strength.

WWI German biplanes

| 1907 | 1909 | 1909 |

British aviator Amy Mollison [née Johnson) (1903–41) flies solo [from] England to Australia in *Gypsy Moth*.

1932 American aviator Amelia Earhart (1898–1937) is the first woman to fly solo across the Atlantic.

1933 World's first modern airliner, the Boeing 247, is launched.

Boeing 247

Macchi M72

1934 Italian Macchi M72 floatplane sets the world speed record at 440mph (708km/h).

1936 First practical helicopter, the Focke Achgelis FW-61, flies.

Focke Achgelis FW-61

1937 The airship *Hindenburg* is destroyed in an accident, killing 35 people.

| 1932 | 1933 | 1934 | 1936 | 1937 |

The Hawker P1127 [i]s the first hovering trials [using] jet thrust. It is the [prede]cessor of the Harrier, the [V/S]TOL (vertical takeoff [and] landing) aircraft to [—] enter service.

Hawker P1127

1965 The Lockheed SR71 Blackbird spy plane sets a new world speed record of 2,070mph (3,331km/h).

Blackbird

1970 The first wide-bodied jet, the Boeing 747 "Jumbo Jet," comes into service. It carries up to 550 passengers, and makes international jet travel commonplace.

Boeing 747

Concorde

1976 The Anglo-French supersonic airliner Concorde goes into service, reaching speeds of 1,550mph (2,494km/h).

Right: Gossamer Albatross, designed by American Paul Macready (born 1925)

1979 First human-powered aircraft, the *Gossamer Albatross*, crosses the English Channel.

1986 First nonstop round-the-world flight, by Americans J. Yeager (born 1936) and D. Rutan (born 1952), in *Rutan Voyager*.

| 1960 | 1965 | 1970 | 1970 | 1976 |

AIRCRAFT FACTS

• One of first airline services was provided by German Zeppelin airships. They carried a total of 35,000 passengers between Lake Constance, Berlin, and other cities.

• The world's first electrically powered aircraft, the MB–E1, flew in 1973, in Germany.

WINGED THING

In the 1890s, Horatio Phillips (1845–1926, British) built a plane with 20 sets of wings. It looked like a venetian blind.

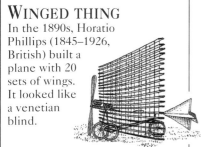

AIRCRAFT RECORDS

LARGEST AIRCRAFT WINGSPAN is that of the Hughes H4 Hercules flying boat *Spruce Goose*, which measures 319.9ft (97.51m) across.

Hughes H4 Hercules flying boat Spruce Goose

SMALLEST BIPLANE is *Bumble Bee Two*, which is just 8.7ft (2.64m) long, and weighs 396lb (179.6kg).

HEAVIEST AIRCRAFT is the Antonov An-225 Mriya (*Dream*), which weighs 661 tons (600 tonnes).

WORST AIR DISASTERS

Year	Incident	Number of people killed
1977	Two Boeing 747s (KLM and Pan Am) collided on the runway at Tenerife, Canary Islands.	583
1985	A Japan Airlines Boeing 747 crashed en route from Tokyo to Osaka.	520
1974	A Turkish Airlines DC-10 crashed at Ermenonville, France, immediately after take-off from Paris.	346
1985	An Air India Boeing 747 exploded in mid-air off the Irish coast, en route from Vancouver to Delhi.	329
1980	A Saudi Arabian Airlines Lockheed Tristar caught fire during an emergency landing.	301

LARGEST AIRLINER is the Boeing 747-400, which has a wingspan of 211ft (64.4m). It can carry up to 567 passengers.

TYPES OF WARPLANE

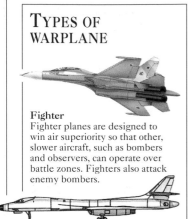

Fighter
Fighter planes are designed to win air superiority so that other, slower aircraft, such as bombers and observers, can operate over battle zones. Fighters also attack enemy bombers.

Bomber
Bombers can carry a wide range of weapons and bombs, including nuclear weapons, and special bombs for destroying runways.

Transport aircraft
Modern armies rely on transport planes and helicopters to move troops and equipment rapidly into battle zones.

Helicopter gunship
Helicopter gunships are heavily armed helicopters, with rapid-fire machine guns that fire from the doorways. They were widely used by US forces in Vietnam (see p.409).

Aerial reconnaissance plane
Army commanders rely on airborne observers to report on the movements of enemy forces. Observation planes are a prime target for enemy fighters, so pilotless remote-controlled aircraft (RPVs) are often used.

VTOL aircraft
VTOL (vertical takeoff and landing) aircraft use the immense power of the jet engine to rise vertically, or after a short run. VTOL craft do not need a long runway and can therefore be hidden near the battlefront.

PARTS OF A FIGHTER
Modern fighter planes are equipped with sophisticated electronic instruments for detecting and attacking enemy aircraft and ground targets. This fighter can fly at more than 1,852mph (2,980km/h), at a height of 60,000ft (18,288m).

Two turbofan (jet) engines
F-15E Eagle

This fighter carries a crew of two: the pilot, and the weapon systems operator.

The crew can escape from ejector seats if the aircraft is in danger of crashing.

The large, transparent canopy gives the crew a good range of vision.

An infrared heat-sensitive camera enables the crew to fly in the dark.

Radar antennae detect other aircraft.

The rotary cannon can fire more than 6,000 rounds of ammunition per minute.

Four air-to-air missiles for shooting down enemy aircraft.

The plane's fuselage is made of composite plastic materials and light metal alloys.

Terrain-following radar enables the plane to fly at high speeds close to the ground.

AIRCREW
Aircrew consists of flying crew, who fly in the planes, and ground crew. Armorers ensure that the planes are adequately equipped with ammunition and bombs.

The pilot flies the aircraft. He or she carries flight plans in knee pads.

Women flying crew do not usually fly aircraft in battles.

Aircraft engineers check the planes after every flight.

The ground crew carry out maintenance and repair of the aircraft.

FAMOUS WAR PLANES

FOKKER TRIPLANE
German WWI flying ace Manfred von Richthofen (1892–1918), the "Red Baron," flew many aircraft. The best-known was the Fokker Triplane.

SPITFIRE
The Spitfire was the fastest and most effective British fighter plane of WWII. It had a Rolls-Royce Merlin engine and could reach a speed of 425mph (684km/h).

MESSERSCHMITT-109
During WWII, this fighter plane was the German Luftwaffe's equivalent of the Spitfire.

FLYING FORTRESS
These heavily armed US WWII bombers were designed for daylight raids. Fortresses were meant to fly in formation and protect each other, but this strategy failed. They were only safe when escorted by fighters.

AVRO LANCASTER
This was the main British bomber used by the RAF during WWII. It flew mainly at night to avoid detection by enemy fighters.

VULCAN
The Vulcan was the main British nuclear attack aircraft in the 1950s and 1960s. Although it was not supersonic, its large delta wing allowed it to fly higher than Soviet fighters.

TORNADO
The Tornado is NATO's (see p.406) most powerful fighting plane. It is built in two forms: one carries bombs and guided weapons for ground attack; the other attacks enemy fighters.

MIG 25
The Russian MIG 25 is one of the fastest aircraft in service, reaching speeds of Mach 2.8 (see p.236). It was developed to counter the threat of American supersonic nuclear bombers.

NORTHROP B-2 "STEALTH" BOMBER
This US bomber is designed to absorb or deflect enemy radar, so that it can remain undetected when approaching its targets. It is made of composite plastics.

MIRAGE
This plane is used by airforces around the world. Different models are used as fighters, as fighter-bombers, and for reconnaissance.

KING OF THE ACES
During WWII, German Major Erich Hartmann (1922–93) shot down 352 planes, making him the war's top air ace.

AIR FORCE RECORDS

LARGEST AIR FORCE
ever was the US Army Air Corps (now the US Air Force), which in 1944 numbered 79,908 aircraft and 2,411,294 personnel.

HEAVIEST BOMBER
is the Boeing B-52H Stratofortress (below). It has a max. takeoff weight of 488,000lb (221,353kg) and can carry 12 SRAM thermonuclear short-range missiles or 24 750lb (340kg) bombs under its wings, and 8 SRAMS or 84 500lb (227kg) bombs in the fuselage.

TOP WOMAN ACE
was Junior Lieutenant Lydia Litvak (1921–43) of the USSR, who shot down 12 planes between 1941 and 1943.

TOP JET ACE
was Captain Joseph McConnell Jr. (1922–54), of the US Air Force, who shot down 16 planes in the Korean War.

AIRLINE INSIGNIA

MOST COUNTRIES have a national airline. Each airline has its own distinctive insignia (emblem) and colors, which make its aircraft easy to identify. A selection of airline insignia is shown here.

Aer Lingus
Irish airlines

AEROLINEAS ARGENTINAS

الخطوط الجوية الجزائرية
AIR ALGERIE

AIR FRANCE

Air Namibia

air new zealand

AIRLANKA

AUSTRIAN AIRLINES

Avianca
The Airline of Colombia

Bahamasair

BALKAN
BULGARIAN AIRLINES

BRITISH AIRWAYS

BWIA
WE ARE THE CARIBBEAN

CAMEROON AIRLINES

Canadian
Canadian Airlines International

CROATIA AIRLINES

CYPRUS AIRWAYS

EgyptAir مصر للطيران

EL AL
Israel airlines

ETHIOPIAN AIRLINES

FINNAIR

Garuda Indonesia

GHANA AIRWAYS

GULF AIR

IBERIA
Spanish airline

ICELANDAIR

İstanbul Airlines
Ihre türkischen Ferienflieger

JAL
Japan Airlines

JERSEY EUROPEAN

Kenya Airways
The Pride of Africa

KLM
KLM Royal Dutch Airlines

KOREAN AIR

Lauda-air
Independent airline

POLISH AIRLINES
LOT

Lufthansa
German airlines

LUXAIR
Luxembourg airlines

malaysia
AIRLINES

MEA
Middle East Airlines

NIGERIA AIRWAYS LIMITED

NORTHWEST AIRLINES
American airline

OLYMPIC AIRWAYS
Greek airlines

Philippine Airlines

PIA
Pakistan International Airlines

QANTAS
Australian airlines

sabena
Belgian airlines

SAS
Scandinavian Airlines System

saudia
SAUDI ARABIAN AIRLINES
السعودية
الخطوط الجوية العربية السعودية

SINGAPORE AIRLINES

SAA
SOUTH AFRICAN AIRWAYS

swissair

Thai
Thai Airways International Limited

TURKISH AIRLINES

UZBEKISTAN
airways

VARIG
Brazilian Airlines

virgin atlantic
Virgin

COMMUNICATIONS

DEVELOPMENTS IN COMMUNICATION systems have changed people's lives. Today, a person can make instant contact, whether by phone or fax, with someone on the other side of the world. People can travel to distant countries in a matter of hours. Advances in computer technology have transformed many workplaces.

TELECOMMUNICATIONS

Telecommunications covers communication by telephone, fax, television, and radio. All these forms of communication need a transmitter to send out the information, something to carry the signal, and a receiver to convert the signal back into an understandable message.

FIBEROPTICS

Today, most international calls are routed through fiberoptic cables, which lie on the seabed. A telephone call is carried as a pulse of light along a cable that is made up of a few fine strands of pure glass, called optical fibers.

Fiberoptic cable

POSTAL COMMUNICATIONS

One of the earliest, cheapest, and most reliable forms of communication is the postal service. Letters and packages can be sent by air from one part of the world to another in a matter of days.

POSTAL PROCESSING

1 Letters and small packages are dropped in a mailbox.

2 They are collected by mail carriers and taken to the local post office.

3 Letters and packages are sorted and put in a sack with others going to the same area.

4 They are transported by road, rail, or air to their destination.

5 The mail is taken to a main post office and is sorted into districts.

6 It is taken to a local post office.

7 The letters are sorted by street.

8 They are then delivered by foot or truck.

MAIL SORTING

Most letter sorting in post offices is done by machine. An operator reads the address on a letter and punches a keyboard that prints a code of dots or bars. Other sorting machines "read" the codes and sort the letters further.

Letter sorting

FIBEROPTIC SUBMARINE SYSTEMS

This map shows the fiberoptic routes existing today; many more are in the process of being built.

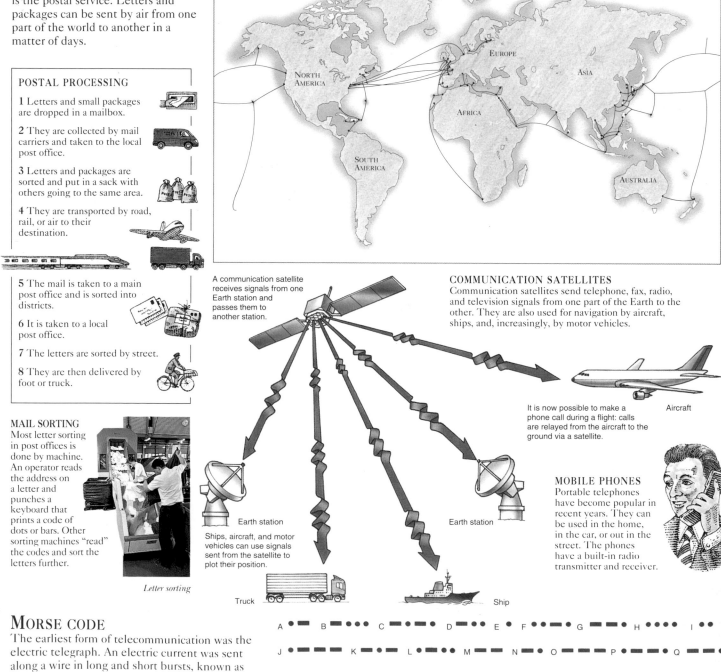

A communication satellite receives signals from one Earth station and passes them to another station.

COMMUNICATION SATELLITES

Communication satellites send telephone, fax, radio, and television signals from one part of the Earth to the other. They are also used for navigation by aircraft, ships, and, increasingly, by motor vehicles.

It is now possible to make a phone call during a flight: calls are relayed from the aircraft to the ground via a satellite.

Aircraft

Earth station

Earth station

Ships, aircraft, and motor vehicles can use signals sent from the satellite to plot their position.

Truck

Ship

MOBILE PHONES

Portable telephones have become popular in recent years. They can be used in the home, in the car, or out in the street. The phones have a built-in radio transmitter and receiver.

MORSE CODE

The earliest form of telecommunication was the electric telegraph. An electric current was sent along a wire in long and short bursts, known as Morse code.

AIR TRAVEL

There are hundreds of airline companies operating throughout the world, offering safe, affordable travel to billions of people.

AIR TRAVEL FACTS

- Chicago International Airport in the US is the busiest airport in the world. Aircraft take off or land about every 40 seconds.
- London's Heathrow Airport handles the most international flights in the world.

AIR TRAFFIC CONTROL

Airplanes carry a device, called a transponder, that sends out a signal when it receives a pulse of radio energy from the secondary scanner. This signal tells air traffic control the aircraft's identity, height, and speed.

A MAJOR AIRLINE'S WORLD ROUTES

NORTH AMERICA
ASIA
EUROPE
AFRICA
SOUTH AMERICA
AUSTRALIA

The aircraft reflects the pulses back to the scanner.

The aircraft replies with a signal only when it receives a pulse from the secondary scanner.

The radar sends out pulses to the aircraft.

Secondary radar system sends out pulses to the aircraft, and receives signals from the aircraft's transponder.

Radar antenna spins slowly, scanning for aircraft coming in different directions.

BUSINESS COMMUNICATIONS

The development of communications technology in the workplace has changed the way many people do their work. Because of the speed of communication possible with the use of fax machines, electronic mail, and telephone systems, it is likely that in the future more people will be able to work from home.

VIDEO CONFERENCE

Instead of spending time and money traveling to meetings, people can now communicate with each other by going to video conference centers. People speak through microphones and are able to see each other on screens. Although not yet widespread, video conferences are expected to become more common in the future.

At video conference centers, people can see each other on screen.

Computer screen

Keyboard

FAX MACHINE

Text and illustrations can be sent through a facsimile (fax) machine. Whatever is written or drawn on the page is transmitted in the same way as a telephone message.

Fax machine

COMMUNICATION WORDS

Cable television Television programs delivered by a metal or fiberoptic cable.

CD-ROM Compact Disc Read-Only Memory: a laser disc used to store computer data. The data cannot be removed, and new data cannot be recorded.

Database Information stored on a computer.

Navigation Finding a route between two places.

Network A system of interconnected pieces of equipment that communicate with each other.

Satellite An object held in orbit around a planet.

COMPUTERS

Information can be collected, stored, processed, and transmitted very quickly on computer.

INTERNET

The world's largest computer network is called the Internet. It enables all types of computer to share services and communicate directly.

INTERNET SERVICES

Some of the services available on Internet include:
Electronic mail (E-mail) This allows messages to be sent from one computer to another.
CU SeeMe This enables up to eight people to see and hear each other on their computer screens.
Usernet A collection of electronic bulletin boards (called Newsgroups) set up by subject matter. It is used for news and information.

COMMUNICATION FACTS

- A post office sorting machine can sort about 36,000 letters an hour.
- A pair of optical fibers can hold up to 61,440 telephone conversations at any one time.
- First country to introduce car navigation systems was Japan, in 1990.
- More than 4,000,000,000 messages are sent by E-mail in North America each year.

SEMAPHORE

Semaphore flag signals were used for signaling between ships until the early 1900s and by the army. It remains a quick method of visual signaling and is still used for passing messages between ships sailing close to each other.

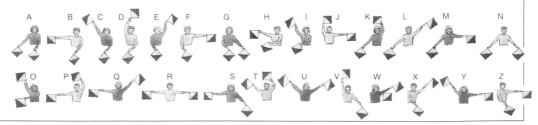

A B C D E F G H I J K L M N
O P Q R S T U V W X Y Z

LANGUAGE

LANGUAGE is a system of sounds and signs that people use to express their thoughts and communicate with others. There are thousands of languages throughout the world.

There are 845 languages in India, more than any other country in the world.

COMMON WORLD LANGUAGES

This map shows the distribution of the major world languages. It shows how European nations, when they explored the world, brought their languages to other countries; for example, English settlers brought their language to North America and Australia.

Mandarin Chinese
English
Russian
Spanish
French
Portuguese
Arabic
Other

MOST COMMON LANGUAGES

Language	Number of speakers
Chinese (Mandarin)	1,093 million
English	450 million
Hindi	367 million
Spanish	352 million
Russian	204 million
Arabic	202 million
Bengali	187 million
Portuguese	175 million
Malay-Indonesian	145 million
Japanese	126 million

HOW TO SAY "YES" AND "NO" IN DIFFERENT LANGUAGES AROUND THE WORLD

Words in brackets are a guide to pronunciation.

Language	Yes	No	Language	Yes	No	Language	Yes	No
Arabic	نَعَم (Na'am)	لاَ (La'a)	German	Ja	Nein	Polish	Tak	Nie
Bengali	হাঁ (Haa)	না (Naa)	Greek	Ne	Óhee	Portuguese	Sim	Não
Bulgarian	Da	He	Hebrew	כֵּן (Ken)	לֹא (Lo)	Punjabi	ਹਾਂ (Haan)	ਨਹੀਂ (Nahi)
Chinese (Cantonese)	係 (Hai)	唔係 (M hai)	Hindi	हां (Haan)	नहीं (Nahl)	Romanian	Da	Nu
Chinese (Mandarin)	是 (Shi)	不是 (Bu shi)	Hungarian	Igen	Nem	Russian	Да (Dah)	Нет (Nyet)
Czech	Ano	Ne	Icelandic	Já	Nei	Serbo-Croat	Da	Ne
Danish	Ja	Nej	Indonesian	Ja	Tidak	Slovak	Áno	Nie
Dutch	Ja	Nee	Italian	Sì	No	Spanish	Si	No
English	Yes	No	Japanese	はい (Hai)	いいえ (Lie)	Swedish	Ja	Nej
Finnish	Kyllä	Ei	Korean	네 (Nye)	아니오 (A-ni-o)	Thai	ค่ะ (Kha [female])	ไม่ค่ะ (Mai kha [female])
Flemish	Ja	Nee	Malay	Ya	Tidak	Thai	ครับ (Khrap [male])	ไม่ครับ (Mai khrap [male])
French	Oui	Non	Norwegian	Ya	Nej	Turkish	Evet	Hayir

SIGN LANGUAGE

People who cannot hear or speak can communicate through sign language. Signs may stand for whole words as well as individual letters. There are many different sign language systems. The example shown is used in Britain.

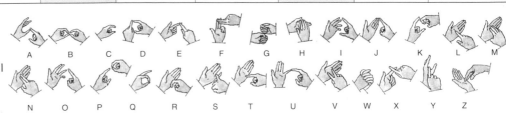

A B C D E F G H I J K L M
N O P Q R S T U V W X Y Z

SCRIPTS

SCRIPTS ARE SETS of symbols that we use to write things down. One script can be used to form words in different languages; for example, the Roman alphabet is used in many European languages, such as English and French.

PICTOGRAMS

The first scripts were pictograms. Pictures were drawn of an object or idea. These pictures were gradually simplified, to make them quicker and easier to write.

CUNEIFORM

The first successful pictogram script was cuneiform, which means "wedge-shaped." It was invented by the Sumerians of Mesopotamia (present-day Iraq) in about 3000 B.C. The script was written on damp clay with a wedge-shaped stylus. After a while, the pictograms were written sideways and developed into simple, stylized symbols.

Bird
Ox

HIEROGLYPHS

The ancient Egyptians had a system of picture writing called hieroglyphs, meaning "sacred carvings." They were carved and painted on temple walls and tombs.

Eagle
Owl
Reed
Snail
Arm
Shutter
Double reed
Water
Chick
Mouth
Leg
Lion

PRESENT-DAY SCRIPTS

CYRILLIC (RUSSIAN)

The Cyrillic alphabet is named after St. Cyril, who spread the Christian faith to the Slavonic peoples in A.D. 800.

А Б В Г Д Е Ж З И І Й К Л М Н О П Р С
Т У Ф Х Ц Ч Ш Щ Ъ Ы Ь Ѣ Э Ю Я Ѳ Ѵ

HINDI

There are about 200 Indian scripts in use today. The most widely known is Hindi.

अ आ इ ई उ ऊ
ऋ ए ऐ ओ औ क ख ग घ ङ च छ ज
झ ञ ट ठ ड ढ ण त थ द ध न प फ ब
भ म य र ल व श ष स ह

BRAILLE

People who are blind or have poor eyesight can read by using braille, invented by Frenchman Louis Braille (1809–1852). People read texts by touching a raised pattern of dots with their fingertips.

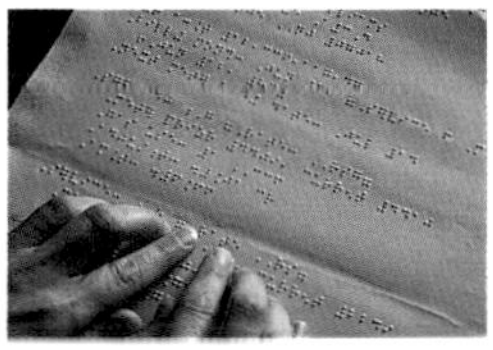
Braille

CHINESE

The Chinese use more than 50,000 signs, but only a few thousand are commonly used. A character is made up of a combination of up to 26 different strokes, which must be made in a particular order.

This character, "Yong," is made up of the five basic strokes.

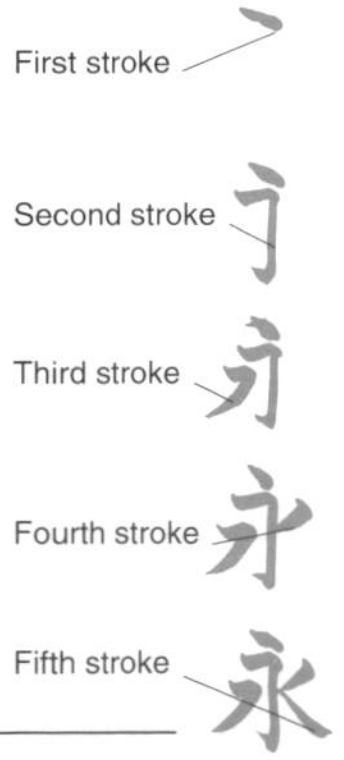
First stroke
Second stroke
Third stroke
Fourth stroke
Fifth stroke

JAPANESE

The Japanese adapted Chinese characters so that they could write down their spoken language, which in fact belongs to a different family from Chinese. Japanese, like Chinese, is written and read in vertical columns from right to left.

Japanese book

ALPHABETS

The letters of an alphabet are signs that represent sounds. This way of writing was quicker and easier to remember than pictogram writing.

GREEK WORDS

The ancient Greeks based their own alphabet on the Phoenician one. To begin with, they wrote in almost any direction, even in a spiral.

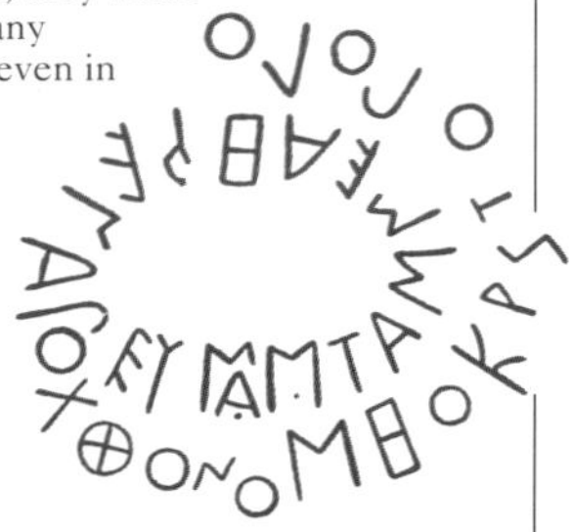
Greek inscription

DEVELOPMENT OF ALPHABETS

The Phoenicians developed the first alphabet around 1600 B.C. The Greek alphabet was adapted by the Etruscans in about 700 B.C. The Romans based their alphabet on the Etruscans'. The modern Hebrew alphabet has changed little from the original biblical Hebrew, and has similarities to the Phoenician alphabet.

Phoenician	Modern Hebrew	Early Greek	Classical Greek	Etruscan	Classical Roman	Modern Roman
𐤀	א	Α	Α	𐌀	A	A
𐤁	ב	Β	Β	𐌁	B	B
𐤂	ג	Γ	Γ	𐌂	C	C
𐤃	ד	Δ	Δ	𐌃	D	D
𐤄	ה	Ε	Ε	𐌄	E	E
𐤅	ו	Ϝ		𐌅	F	F
					G	G
𐤆	ז	Ζ	Ζ	𐌆		
𐤇	ח	Η	Η	𐌇	H	H
𐤈	ט	Θ	Θ	𐌈		
𐤉	י	Ι	Ι	𐌉	I	I
						J
𐤊	כ	Κ	Κ	𐌊	K	K
𐤋	ל	Λ	Λ	𐌋	L	L
𐤌	מ	Μ	Μ	𐌌	M	M
𐤍	נ	Ν	Ν	𐌍	N	N
𐤎	ס		Ξ	𐌎		
𐤏	ע	Ο	Ο	𐌏	O	O
𐤐	פ	Π	Π	𐌐	P	P
𐤑	צ	Ϻ		𐌑		
𐤒	ק	Ϙ		𐌒	Q	Q
𐤓	ר	Ρ	Ρ	𐌓	R	R
𐤔	ש	Σ	Σ	𐌔	S	S
𐤕	ת	X	Τ	𐌕	T	T
						U
			Υ		V	V
						W
			Φ			
			Χ		X	X
			Ψ			
			Ω			
					Y	Y
					Z	Z

SCRIPT FACTS

- The oldest letter still in use is "O," which has not changed its shape since it was part of the Phoenician alphabet in about 1600 B.C.
- Children in Japan are taught 881 characters in their first six years at school.
- The longest alphabet is Cambodian (Khmer), with 74 letters.

ENERGY

INDUSTRY, TRANSPORTATION, and homes require energy to power everything from furnaces to televisions. Much of this energy is produced by burning fossil fuels, such as oil. Renewable energy sources, such as wind and solar power, are also playing an increasing role in energy generation.

FOSSIL FUELS

Oil, coal, and natural gas are called fossil fuels because they are made of the remains of long-dead plants and animals. When burned they release energy, which is used to generate power. Fossil fuels are nonrenewable energy sources, because they will eventually run out.

COAL
About 20% of the world's energy is generated from coal, and its use is increasing.

OIL AND NATURAL GAS
About 60% of the world's energy comes from oil and natural gas. Oil is the main fuel used in transportation, and both oil and gas are burned to produce heat.

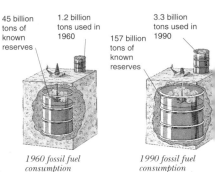

Some heat escapes through the chimney.

Cooling tower

Coal is crushed in a mill, and the powder is blown to the furnace.

Water from the condenser flows to cooling towers. Here it is sprayed into the air for cooling.

GENERATING ELECTRICITY
This illustration shows a coal-fired power station. Coal is burned in a furnace to heat water and produce steam. The steam drives a turbine attached to an electricity generator, which sends electricity down a network of cables called a grid.

Steam turns the turbines.

Electricity generator

Transformer changes the voltage before it is supplied to homes and factories.

Furnace   Condenser

MAJOR OIL PRODUCERS

Country	Million tons per year
CIS	628
US	460.3
Saudi Arabia	360.6
Iran	171.2
Mexico	160.2
China	153
Venezuela	131.6

FOSSIL FUELS IN RESERVE
In 1960, it was estimated that existing underground fossil fuels would last for about 40 years. By 1990, more reserves had been found, but the rate at which they were being used had increased. In 1990, the reserves were still estimated to last about 40 years.

45 billion tons of known reserves

1.2 billion tons used in 1960

157 billion tons of known reserves

3.3 billion tons used in 1990

1960 fossil fuel consumption

1990 fossil fuel consumption

RENEWABLE ENERGY SOURCES
Renewable energy sources are those that will not run out in the foreseeable future. Most "renewables" are cleaner and less harmful to the environment than fossil fuels.

WIND POWER
Wind turbines generate electricity at "wind farms," such as the one at Altmont Pass, California (right). During the 1980s more than 20,000 wind turbines were erected worldwide. Scientists estimate that by 2030, wind power could provide more than 10% of the world's electricity.

SOLAR POWER
The Sun is a nonpolluting source of renewable energy. Solar energy is converted into electricity in photovoltaic (solar) cells, which are used to power various devices, including calculators, space satellites, and telephone links in remote areas. The Sun's heat is also used to heat water in many hot countries.

TIDAL POWER
Tidal power is generated at barrages (barriers) built across estuaries. As the tide rises or falls, water is kept at high or low tide level inside the barrage. When the water level differs by about 10ft (3m), water flows through huge turbines.

HYDROELECTRIC POWER
Hydroelectric power is generated at dams and waterfalls. Falling water drives turbines, which in turn drive electricity generators. About 7% of the world's energy is provided by hydroelectricity.

GEOTHERMAL ENERGY
Geothermal energy is generated by heat energy in the Earth's crust. At present, most geothermal energy is generated in volcanically active regions, such as Iceland and New Zealand. Approximately 20 countries use geothermal energy for heating, or for generating electricity.

WAVE POWER
Wave power is still being researched and developed. Several experimental generators have been built. Some are sited on the seashore. Others are designed for the deep sea, where the energy content per meter of wave can be equivalent to the power source for 50 single-bar electric fires.

BIOMASS ENERGY
Biomass energy is derived from organic matter, such as wood and agricultural waste. Biomass power plants are being built in many countries. They produce little air pollution and do not usually contribute to global warming.

ENERGY FACTS
• Watching color television accounts for 20% of the average British person's energy consumption.

• Worldwide, lighting accounts for about 17% of electricity use.

• The average person in the UK uses 10 times more energy each year than the average person in India.

MAJOR WOOD USERS
Many developing countries depend on wood for fuel and energy production.

Country	Wood as % of total energy consumption
Mali	97
Rwanda	96
Tanzania	94
Burkina	94
Ethiopia	93
Central African Republic	91
Somalia	90

NUCLEAR ENERGY

Nuclear energy is generated by the breakdown of uranium and plutonium atoms. There are about 350 nuclear power stations around the world, and they supply more than 5% of the world's electricity. Nuclear power stations do not emit polluting gases or contribute to global warming, but accidents and the disposal of fuel rods pose serious risks.

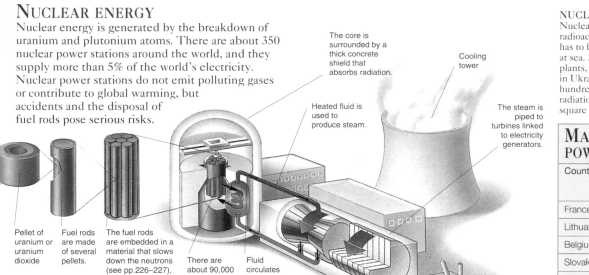

The core is surrounded by a thick concrete shield that absorbs radiation.

Cooling tower

Heated fluid is used to produce steam.

The steam is piped to turbines linked to electricity generators.

Pellet of uranium or uranium dioxide

Fuel rods are made of several pellets.

The fuel rods are embedded in a material that slows down the neutrons (see pp.226–227), called a moderator.

There are about 90,000 fuel rods in the nuclear reactor core

Fluid circulates through the core to carry away heat produced by nuclear fission.

NUCLEAR ENERGY RISKS

Nuclear waste remains dangerously radioactive for thousands of years, and has to be buried deep underground or at sea. Accidents at nuclear power plants, such as the Chernobyl disaster in Ukraine in 1986, can expose hundreds of thousands of people to radiation and contaminate millions of square miles of land.

MAJOR NUCLEAR POWER USERS

Country	% of total electricity generated by nuclear power
France	72.9
Lithuania	60
Belgium	59.9
Slovakia	49.5
Hungary	46.4
South Korea	43.2
Sweden	43.2
Switzerland	39.6
Spain	36.4
Taiwan	35.4

MAJOR ENERGY CONSUMERS

This table includes commercially traded fuels (oil, coal, gas, etc.) only. Fuels such as wood and animal waste are excluded, as figures are unreliable.

Country	Consumption as % of world total
US	24.6
CIS	16.8
China	8.4
Japan	5.4
Germany	4.3
Central Europe	4.2
Canada	3
France	2.6

ENERGY CONSUMPTION OF VARIOUS HOUSEHOLD PRODUCTS IN THE US

Household product	% of homes with product	Typical energy consumption (kilowatts per year)
Freezer (frost-free)	11.7	1,820
Refrigerator (frost-free)	67.3	1,591
Aquarium/terrarium	5–15	200–1,000
Color television	96–99	75–1,000
Electric stove or oven	56.8	650
Computer	10–20	25–400
Dishwasher	43.1	165
Iron	20–40	20–150
Clock	100	17–50
Video recorder	60–70	10–70

RENEWABLE ENERGY FACTS

• The amount of sunshine that falls on roads in the US in one year contains twice as much energy as all the coal and oil used worldwide in a year.

• Owing to strict energy efficiency standards, new houses in Sweden use at least three times less energy than the average British home to keep warm in winter .

Energy-efficient Swedish village

• Tokyo, Japan, has more than 1.5 million solar collectors for domestic water heating.

• About 90% of Israel's domestic hot water is supplied by solar heating.

GREAT LENGTHS

The world's largest wind turbines have blades up to 164ft (50m) long. One hundred people could stand side by side on a single blade.

ALTERNATIVE VEHICLE ENERGY

Oil will eventually run out, and in the meantime vehicle exhaust fumes are polluting the atmosphere. It is therefore important that clean, renewable energy sources are developed. Those being researched include compressed natural gas, electricity, hydrogen, ethanol (grain alcohol), and methanol (wood alcohol).

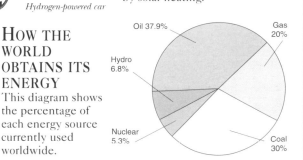

Hydrogen-powered car

OIL FACTS

• About 500,000 different materials can be made from crude oil. The products on the right are all made from materials derived from crude oil. They include wax, plastics, fertilizers, and detergents.

• One day's world oil supply took 110,000 years to fossilize.

• More than 500 oil wells are drilled every week in the US.

• If all the barrels of oil produced worldwide in one day were laid end to end, they would stretch twice around the Equator.

HOW THE WORLD OBTAINS ITS ENERGY

This diagram shows the percentage of each energy source currently used worldwide.

Oil 37.9%

Gas 20%

Hydro 6.8%

Nuclear 5.3%

Coal 30%

INDUSTRY

INDUSTRY IS AN organized economic activity. It deals with the extraction and use of raw materials, with manufacturing and construction, and with putting the products of these activities to profitable use.

CLASSIFICATION OF INDUSTRIES

There are three basic types of industry.

PRIMARY
These industries are concerned with the extraction of basic raw materials. Examples include agriculture, forestry, fishing, and mining.

Forestry industry

SECONDARY
These industries convert raw materials into other products. They can be further divided into heavy industry, e.g., shipbuilding, and light industry, e.g., textiles and clothing.

Clothing industry

TERTIARY
Tertiary (third-tier) industries offer a service rather than a product, e.g., banking and tourism. Today, this type of industry is expanding.

Cashier at work in a building society.

MAJOR INDUSTRIAL PRODUCERS

All total figures given are in millions, except where indicated. Where a country has a large share of the market, producer and figure are given in parentheses.

Industry	Top producers	Total (in millions)	World total (in millions)
Transportation Cars, buses, and trucks	Europe Asia North America	15 (Germany: 4.5) 14 (Japan: 9.7) 12	45
Commercial aircraft	North America Europe	2203* 814*	3,207*
Ships	Asia Europe	814 (Japan: 535)* 546*	1,452*
Bicycles	Asia Europe	59 (China: 36) 10	84
Communications TV and radio	Asia Europe	172 (China: 42) 32	253
Telephones	Asia North America	66 18.7	107
Electronic components	Japan North America	78,000 480	81,000
Fuel Coal	Asia North America Europe	1,566 tons (China 1,213) 962 tons 579 tons	3,806 tons
Crude oil	Asia North America	1,206 tons Saudi Arabia (445) 658 tons	3,275 tons
Construction and engineering Cement	Asia Europe	648 tons (China 269) 256 tons	1,265 tons
Pig iron for steel making	Asia Europe	238 tons 136 tons	580 tons
Timber	Asia North America	1,404.8 cubic yards 937.8 cubic yards	4,512.6 cubic yards

* Figures for commercial aircraft and ships are not in millions.

DISTRIBUTION OF MAJOR INDUSTRIES

Cars, buses, and trucks

Commercial aircraft

Ships

Bicycles

TV and radio sets

Telephones

Transistors and semiconductors

Coal

Crude oil

Cement

Pig iron for steel making

Timber

INDUSTRY FACTS

• Japan, which lacks most of the important industrial minerals, depends heavily on imports, importing about 95% of its iron ore, tin, copper, zinc, and lead. It is the world's largest importer of coal, natural gas, and oil.

• Mexico produces one-fifth of the world's silver.

• British Columbia produces about one-quarter of the marketable timber in North America. It also supplies the world with chopsticks.

• Wind power from approximately 1,100 windmills in Denmark supplies 3% of its energy needs.

• Gold provides between 40% and 46% of South Africa's export earnings.

OIL INDUSTRY

Oil is found under the ocean floor or in places that were once covered by the sea. Complex technology is used to drill deep wells and extract oil from the seabed. Despite concerns about pollution and oil wells running dry, there is no sign of decline in the demand for oil for fuel and for making chemicals.

TYPES OF OIL RIG

Shallow water
A jack-up rig is used. Its legs extend to the seabed.

Deep water
A tension-leg rig is used. It floats but is chained to the ocean floor.

Very deep water
Ships are used. The oil drill comes out through a hole in the hull.

COAL INDUSTRY

Coal is valuable as an industrial fuel and for making chemicals. It is formed from the remains of decaying plant life, which solidified into coal over millions of years.

TYPES OF COAL MINE

Shaft mine

Drift mine

Open-cast mine

Shaft mine
Miners tunnel vertically when coal is deep under the ground.

Drift mine
Miners tunnel horizontally if a coal seam emerges near the surface of the ground.

Strip mine
If the coal is near the surface, the covering layers of ground are stripped away to reveal the coal.

FOOD INDUSTRY

The food industry processes much of our food so that it is safe to eat, looks appealing, and will remain fresh for a longer period of time. Food can be processed in many different ways.

MILK INTO CHEESE

There are many types of cheese, but most of them share the same basic stages of production.

A tank truck will transport milk to the dairy.

The milk is pasteurized to destroy bacteria.

Another type of bacteria is added to the milk to produce lactic acid. The acid thickens the milk and makes it sour.

The milk is warmed, and rennet, which comes from a calf's stomach, is added. This makes the milk lumpy.

The watery part of the milk (the whey) is drained away and made into food for farm animals, leaving solid lumps, called curds.

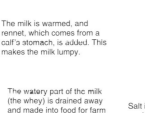

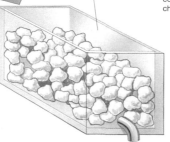

Salt is added to the curds, which are pressed to get rid of any remaining whey. The curds are shaped into molds. They are left in a cool place to ripen into cheese.

WAYS OF PROCESSING FOOD

Canning
Foods are boiled, put in cans, then heated to kill any remaining bacteria. The cans are then sealed to prevent air from bringing oxygen and bacteria to the food.

Cans on an assembly line

Freeze-drying
Food is frozen, and the water is removed. This kills all the bacteria, which cannot live without water.

Astronauts in space use freeze-dried food.

Pasteurizing
Liquids such as milk are heated to 158°F (70°C) for 15 seconds and then cooled quickly. This preserves the flavour while killing the bacteria.

Freezing
In fluidized freezing, small food items, such as peas, pass over very cold air (-29°F/-34°C) on a conveyer belt. The food freezes in minutes.

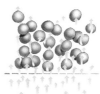

The cold air makes the peas rise.

ADDITIVES

Additives are natural or synthetic chemicals that are added to food to prevent it from going bad too quickly and to make food look appetizing.

Beta carotene, a natural coloring from carrots, may be added to orange juice to strengthen color.

Synthetic chemicals are added to cola to improve flavor.

Emulsifiers ensure that fat and water remain combined. They are used in such foods as yogurt.

The synthetic chemical – butylated hydroxytoluene (BHT) – stops the fat in corn chips from decaying.

Colorings and flavorings
Natural color pigments may break up, so artificial or natural colorings are used as a replacement. Synthetic flavorings, which copy natural flavorings, may also be used.

In cookies, bases such as sodium and ammonium hydrogen carbonate improve flavor and prevent changes in acidity and color.

The preservative sodium nitrite is added to salami and hot dogs.

In rolls, a natural chemical, such as vitamin C, stops oxygen from reacting with fat in the bread.

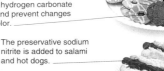

PAPER INDUSTRY

Paper is made in large factories called paper mills. Wood is ground up, mixed with water, and turned into wood pulp. The pulp is then pressed and rolled by machine into a layer of paper.

Most paper comes from softwood trees, such as spruce and pine.

Trees are cut into logs and transported to a paper mill.

The logs are broken down into chips.

Wood chips are heated to a pulp to release fibers.

Fibers are mixed with fillers and dyes.

Water is removed from the pulp by suction.

Rollers remove any remaining water and compress the paper.

A large roll of paper is finally produced.

Wastepaper is added and the fibers are reused to make recycled paper.

Wastepaper is taken back for recycling.

Tissue is made from fibers that are lifted by a knife from the paper as it rolls off the machine.

PAPER PRODUCTS

Other paper products, such as tissue and cardboard, are made in a similar way to paper. The color, strength, and texture of paper can be changed by dyeing, printing, and mixing it with other materials, such as wax or plastic.

MOTOR INDUSTRY

In the motor industry, computer-controlled robots are programmed to carry out repetitive jobs previously performed by people. Robots are used to weld, paint, or drill engine parts. This has helped improve efficiency in car factories.

Cars being spray-painted by robots.

CERAMIC INDUSTRY

Ceramics may be divided into two groups: materials that are molded into shape before being heated, such as pottery and bricks, and materials that are shaped after being treated by heat, such as cement.

Building bricks

Ceramic head made from cement mixture.

POTTERY INDUSTRY

Pottery clay is a mixture of two clays: kaolin (china clay), which gives clay its smooth texture, and ball clay, which adds strength. The moist clay is molded, then placed in a kiln and heated until it hardens.

Detailed decorative work is still done by hand.

ELECTRICITY FACTS

• The amount of electricity a country produces is closely related to its industrial activity.

• Electricity production is measured in units, or kilowatt-hours. One unit is equivalent to leaving a hundred-watt light bulb on for ten hours.

• A typical household uses 6,000 units in a year.

• The world production exceeds 12 trillion units.

• About 60% of production is used in industry, commerce, and transportation and for public lighting.

MAJOR ELECTRICITY PRODUCERS

Producer	Units produced
North America	3.774 trillion
Asia (mostly Japan and the Pacific Coast)	2.7 trillion
Europe	2.0 trillion

GLASS INDUSTRY

Glass has many advantages. It is easily shaped, rustproof, and cheap to make, and it can be recycled.

Sodium carbonate

Limestone (calcium carbonate)

Glass

Sand

Limestone, waste glass (for recycling), sand, and sodium carbonate are put into a furnace.

Molds are used to make glass bottles: a lump of hot, molten glass (a gob) is placed in a bottle-shaped mold.

Air is blown into the mold to make the glass inflate into a bubble, which expands to fit the shape of the mold.

Once hardened, the glass bottle is removed from the mold.

To make sheets of glass for windows, the molten glass is poured onto a pool of molten tin: this makes the glass spread out, until it is as smooth as the molten tin.

The glass is cooled slowly on rollers.

When the glass has cooled and hardened, it is cut with a diamond-tipped cutter.

INDUSTRIAL WORDS

Automation Repetitive work carried out by machines that need little human control.

Component One part of a finished product.

Consumerism Economic system based on the continued increase of goods produced to satisfy increased human need.

Depression A period of low output in trade and industry.

Economy The administration of a country's trade, industry, and money supply.

GNP Gross National Product. The total value of a country's industrial production.

Mass production Manufacture of goods repeating the same processes on a large scale.

Nationalize To make an industry operate under state control.

Production line The assembling, in several stages, of a product by the workforce.

Robotics Use of computer-controlled machines that carry out jobs previously done by humans.

Staple industry A country's most important industry.

ROADS

THE FIRST MAJOR road builders were the Romans, who built roads for their armies and messengers. Today, networks of roads and superhighways cover most countries, linking cities, towns, and rural areas. More and more cars, buses, trains, and trucks use the roads to transport people and goods.

COUNTRIES WITH THE BUSIEST ROADS

Country	Distance traveled by a vehicle per km road	
	x 1,000km	x 1,000 miles
Portugal	1,716	1,066
UK	1,140	708
Italy	1,138	707
Netherlands	896	557
Germany	866	538
Spain	687	427
Switzerland	628	390
Finland	513	319
US	510	317
Sweden	435	270

COUNTRIES WITH THE MOST ROADS

Country	x 1,000km of road	x 1,000 miles of road
US	6,328	3,932
Russia	1,588	987
Japan	1,120	696
France	811	504
Germany	549	341
UK	380	236

ANCIENT ROADS

The Romans created a system of roads to serve their empire in Europe from about 400 B.C. to A.D. 400. The straight, wide roads were made up of several layers. Many of these roads are still in use today.

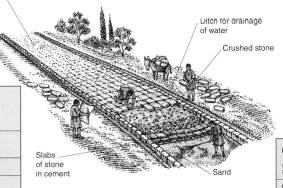

Large paving stones

Ditch for drainage of water

Crushed stone

Slabs of stone in cement

Sand

MODERN ROADS

Today's roads are built to withstand heavy traffic. First, the ground is leveled and trenches are dug. Drains are laid to carry water away. The road is composed of several layers of crushed stone and soil, with a top layer of concrete or asphalt and stone chips.

Macadam, cement, or concrete

Sand, gravel, or stone

COUNTRIES WITH THE DENSEST ROAD NETWORK

Country	km (per 1,000 sq km)	miles (per 1,000 sq km)
Belgium	4,205	6,768
Japan	3,002	4,830
Netherlands	2,478	3,989
Luxembourg	1,970	3,170
Germany	1,900	3,059
Switzerland	1,722	2,771
Denmark	1,643	2,644
UK	1,553	2,499

COUNTRIES WITH THE MOST SUPERHIGHWAYS

Country	x 1,000km of highway	x 1,000 miles of highway
US	84.9	52.8
Canada	15.0	9.3
Germany	10.8	6.7
France	7.6	4.7
Italy	6.8	4.2
Japan	4.9	3.0

ROAD NETWORK

Different types of road have different uses. Superhighways and two-lane highways link towns and cities. Smaller roads intersect towns and cities to connect neighborhoods and homes. In most countries people drive on the right-hand side of the road. In some countries, such as Australia, Britain, and Japan, people drive on the left-hand side.

SUPERHIGHWAY
A wide road, usually consisting of three lanes in each direction, a superhighway is specially designed for fast-moving traffic traveling long distances.

BYPASS
This type of road carries traffic around the edges of cities, avoiding city centers.

Bypass

TRAFFIC CIRCLE
This allows traffic to change direction without crossing other lines of traffic.

Traffic circle

Crossroads

CROSSROADS
When roads meet at a crossroads, traffic on one road is stopped by traffic lights to give way to traffic on the other road.

ROAD RECORDS

EARLIEST LONG-DISTANCE road, the Persian Royal Road, was 1,775 miles (2,857km) long.

LONGEST ROAD is the Pan-American Highway. It runs from Alaska to Brasilia, Brazil, and is more than 15,000 miles (24,140km) in length.

LONGEST NATIONAL HIGHWAY is the Trans-Canada, at 4,860 miles (7,821km).

HIGHEST ROAD lies between Tibet and Xinjiang, China. In places, it is 18,480ft (5,633m) above sea level.

LOWEST ROAD is by the Dead Sea in Israel, at 1,290ft (392m) below sea level.

CONSTRUCTION

FROM EARLY TIMES, people have built all kinds of structures: tunnels and bridges to cross natural barriers; canals for transporting goods and for irrigation. Today, engineers are constantly improving construction methods and materials to produce canals that link oceans, and skyscrapers that are more than a hundred floors high.

BRIDGES APPLYING?

The first bridges were made by placing tree trunks across rivers and by laying flat stones on rocks in the middle of streams. Today, bridges made of concrete and steel span lakes, rivers, deep valleys, roads, and railroad lines.

Early clapper bridge, England

TYPES OF BRIDGE

Suspension
The deck, or roadway, is suspended from long steel cables attached to tall towers standing near each end of the bridge. The cables are made of thousands of steel wires bound tightly together.

Suspension bridge

Arch bridge

Arch
This type of bridge is supported by an arch, propped up by abutments. The deck is usually straight and does not follow the curve of the arch. It is sometimes built below, as well as above, the arch.

Cantilever bridge

Cable-stayed bridge

Bascule
This is a type of drawbridge. Its two sections can be raised at an angle to allow ships to pass through.

Bascule bridge

Beam
Most bridges with a short span are beam bridges. Each end of the bridge rests on the ground or on piers.

Beam bridge

Cantilever
This is a type of beam bridge. Each half of the bridge balances on a supporting pier that is embedded in the river.

Cable-stayed
The deck is supported by steel cables connected to towers. Early cable-stayed bridges had pairs of towers, but today, single towers are also built in the center of the deck. Its style is midway between a beam bridge and a suspension bridge. It requires fewer piers than a beam bridge and does not need the heavy anchorages of a suspension bridge.

Swing
This type of bridge can be swung to one side to allow ships to pass through.

This swing bridge, in the foreground of the picture, is in Newcastle-upon-Tyne, England.

Pontoon
This type of bridge floats on the water. The deck rests on hollow concrete blocks, called pontoons, which lie on the water. Each pontoon is anchored to concrete blocks, which are buried in the bed of the lake.

Pontoon bridge, Istanbul, Turkey

BRIDGES HOLDING WORLD RECORD FOR LONGEST MAIN SPAN

Bridge	Country	Date built	Type	Length m	ft
Ponte D'Augusto	Italy	220 B.C.	stone arch	30	98
Martorell	Spain	218 B.C.	stone arch	37	121
Chaochow	China	A.D. 617	stone arch	37	121
Bern	Switzerland	1204	stone arch	46	151
Scaligero	Italy	1356	stone arch	49	161
Trezzo over R. Adda (destroyed in 1416)	Italy	1377	stone arch	72	236
Schaffhausen	Switzerland	1755	wooden arch	59	193
Reichenau	Switzerland	1758	wooden arch	73	239
Union Bridge	Scotland	1820	suspension	137	449
Menai Straits	Wales	1826	suspension	177	581
Fribourg	Switzerland	1834	suspension	265	869
Cincinnati	US	1867	suspension	323	1,060
Brooklyn	US	1883	suspension	487	1,598
Forth Rail	Scotland	1889	cantilever	521	1,709
Quebec	Canada	1917	cantilever	549	1,801
Ambassador	Canada/US	1929	suspension	565	1,854
George Washington	US	1931	suspension	1,067	3,501
Golden Gate	US	1937	suspension	1,280	4,199
Verrazano	US	1964	suspension	1,298	4,258
Humber	England	1981	suspension	1,410	4,626
Great Belt East	Denmark	1997*	suspension	1,624	5,328
Akashi Kaikyo	Japan	1998*	suspension	1,990	6,529

SUSPENSION BRIDGES WITH LONGEST MAIN SPAN

Bridge	Country	Date built	Length m	ft
Akashi Kaikyo, Hyogo	Japan	1998*	1,990	6,529
Great Belt East	Denmark	1997*	1,624	5,328
Humber	England	1981	1,410	4,626
Tsing Ma	Hong Kong	1997*	1,377	4,518
Verrazano Narrows	US	1964	1,298	4,258
Golden Gate	US	1937	1,280	4,199
Höga Kusten	Sweden	2000*	1,210	3,970
Mackinac Straits	US	1957	1,158	3,799
Minami Bisan Seto	Japan	1988	1,100	3,609
Bosporus 2	Turkey	1988	1,090	3,576
Bosporus 1	Turkey	1973	1,074	3,524
George Washington	US	1931	1,067	3,501
Kurushima 3, Ehime	Japan	1999*	1,030	3,379
Kurushima 2, Ehime	Japan	1999*	1,020	3,346
April 25	Portugal	1966	1,013	3,323
Forth Road	Scotland	1964	1,006	3,300
Kita Bisan Seto, Kagawa	Japan	1988	990	3,248
Severn	England	1966	988	3,241
Shimotsui	Japan	1988	940	3,084
Ohnaruto	Japan	1985	876	2,874

* Planned completion date

BRIDGE FACTS

- The first bridge made of iron was built in 1779 in Shropshire, England.

Ironbridge, England

- The longest bridge in the world is the Second Lake Pontchartrain Causeway, in Louisiana. Each of its concrete spans measures 56ft (17m). The total length of the bridge is nearly 24 miles (38km). Land cannot be seen from its center.

- The Tay Bridge in Scotland had been standing for just over two years when it collapsed during a stormy night in 1879. A train was crossing the wrought-iron bridge at the time, and 75 people were killed.

BRIDGE WORDS

Pier

Abutment End support for an arch.
Aqueduct Water-carrying bridge.
Box-girder Hollow girder, or beam, built in the shape of a box for strength.
Caisson Watertight structure used for preventing water and mud from flowing into foundation excavations.

Box-girder

Clapper A type of bridge made of large slabs of stone placed over boulders.

Clapper bridge

Cofferdam Temporary dam used to keep out water while people work on a riverbed.
Creep Gradual change in shape of materials under pressure.
Form Structure built to form, or shape, concrete on a bridge and to hold it while it hardens.
Hangers The wires or bars that connect the cables to the deck in a suspension bridge.
Lift bridge A bridge with a deck that rises in the air, like an elevator.
Pier A support for the middle spans of a beam or arch bridge. The foundation of the tower on a suspension or cantilever bridge.
Reinforced concrete Concrete that contains steel rods, bars, wires, or mesh.
Viaduct A bridge carrying a road or railroad.

Lift bridge

Wrought iron Iron that is hammered into shape.

CANALS

Canals are manmade waterways. Most canals are used by boats to transport cargo and people; others are used to take water to dry land or drain water from marshy ground. Some canals, such as the Suez Canal in the Middle East and the Panama Canal in Central America, link seas and oceans.

HOW A LOCK WORKS

A canal lock is used to change the water level. A lock is a section of canal, large enough to take one or more boats, that has large, watertight gates at each end. By opening and closing paddles, or valves, in one pair of gates, water is allowed to run into or out of the lock, and so raise or lower the water level to the same height as that in the next section of canal.

The narrowboat passes through the open gate into the lock.

Open gates

Closed gates

Upper water level

Lower water level

The paddles, or valves, in the lower gates are opened to let water out and the narrowboat is carried down with the dropping water level.

Gates are now closed.

The narrowboat is fully inside the lock.

Paddles are opened, and water rushes out.

The lower gates can now be opened for the boat to pass through.

Lower water level

Gates are opened.

Upper water level

DAMS

People need a constant supply of water to live. Efficient collection and storage of water is essential, especially in countries where there is little rainfall. Dams are built either to divert or to store water.

DAM RECORDS

OLDEST KNOWN DAM in the world is the Sadd el-Kafara in Egypt. It was built out of earth and rock in about 3000 B.C.

LARGEST DAM in the world is the Syncrude Tailings dam in Canada, at 706,000,000 cu ft (540,000,000cu m).

LONGEST SEA DAM in the world is the Afsluitdijk in the Netherlands. Built in two sections, its total length is 38.8 miles (62.5km).

LONGEST SHIP CANALS

Canal	Location	Date built	Length km	Length miles
Suez	Links the Red Sea with the Mediterranean Sea	1869	174	108
Kiel	Links the North Sea with the Baltic Sea, Germany	1895	99	62
Panama	Links the Atlantic Ocean and the Caribbean Sea with the Pacific Ocean	1914	81	50
Manchester	England	1894	57	35

CANAL FACTS

- The Chinese were the first people to build canal locks along the Great Canal of China, which ran from Peking to Hangzhou. The canal was built during the 1200s and is still used today.

- Leonardo da Vinci (1452–1519), Italian artist and engineer, designed locks for the Languedoc Canal, France, which was completed in 1681. It linked the Mediterranean Sea with the Atlantic Ocean.

- The largest lock in the world is the Berendrecht lock in Antwerp, Belgium. It is 1,640ft (500m) long and 223ft (68m) wide. It has four sliding lock gates.

- The Netherlands has more than 4,971 miles (8,000km) of canals.

TYPES OF DAM

Arch dam
This has a curved shape, with the inside of the curve facing downstream.

Arch dam

Buttress dam
This has a series of props, or buttresses, which are on the side of the dam facing downstream.

Buttress dam

Embankment dam
This is made of a huge pile of soil or rocks. Like the massive dam, the embankment dam relies on its sheer bulk to hold back water.

Embankment dam

Massive dam
This is built of concrete and relies on its size and weight to withstand the pressure of a huge amount of stored water.

Massive dam

TALLEST DAMS

Dam	Location	Date built	Height m	Height ft
Rogun	Tajikistan	1989	325	1,066
Nourek	Tajikistan	1979	317	1,040
Grande Dixence	Switzerland	1962	285	935
Inguri	Georgia	1979	271	889
Vaiont	Italy	1961	265	869
Mica	British Columbia, Canada	1973	244	801

TUNNELS

Tunnels have a variety of uses. Many are built for transportation purposes: to pass through or under obstacles such as mountains, rivers, and busy roads. They are also used to carry sewage, water from reservoirs, and power and communication cables, and in mining.

TYPES OF TUNNELS
Road tunnels
These are built to allow traffic to pass through mountains, and under rivers and busy crossroads.

LONGEST ROAD TUNNELS

Tunnel	Country	Date built	Length km	miles
St. Gotthard	Switzerland	1980	16.3	10.1
Frejus	France/Italy	1978	12.7	7.9
Mont Blanc	France/Italy	1965	11.6	7.2
Mersey	England	1934	4.2	2.6
Kanmon	Japan	1958	3.5	2.2

TUNNEL FACTS

• The Channel Tunnel, which links England and France, was completed in 1994. Trains carry people, cars, and goods through the tunnel. It is 32.2 miles (51.8km) long.

• The longest water tunnel in the world is the Delaware Aqueduct, built in 1944. It is 104.9 miles (168.9km) long, more than twice the length of the second longest, the Orange-Fish in South Africa.

• The fastest rate of tunnel-driving in soft ground, using a tunneling shield, is 1,644ft (501m) in five days, on the London Ring Main Tunnel in 1992.

Pedestrian tunnel

Pedestrian tunnels
These allow people to cross busy streets safely.

Train tunnels
Underground train systems exist in many of the major cities of the world. They offer a fast form of transportation, and save valuable space above ground.

Train tunnel

Road tunnel

Water tunnel

Water tunnels
These are built just below the surface. Some carry freshwater, others carry sewage.

HOW A TUNNEL IS BUILT
Tunneling shields are used to drive a tunnel through soft ground. As the shield moves forward, the front cutting edge bores through rock and earth. Tunnel lining, fitted behind the shield, prevents the walls and roof of the tunnel from collapsing. In hard ground, huge drilling machines, called moles, are often used.

SKYSCRAPERS

From early times, people have built tall buildings. The Romans built apartment buildings 15 floors high. Today, advances in construction methods have resulted in many high-rise buildings, such as the 110-floor Sears Tower in Chicago.

A tunneling shield breaking through earth

BUILDING A SKYSCRAPER
A skyscraper has an inner frame made of steel or concrete. The frame holds the floors and walls (often made of glass) together. The building is supported by a foundation – usually a pit containing reinforced concrete.

LONGEST RAILROAD TUNNELS

Tunnel	Country	Date built	Length km	miles
AlpTransit Link	Switzerland	2007*	57	35.4
Seikan	Japan	1985	53.9	33.5
Channel	France/England	1994	51.8	32.2
Northern line	England	1939	27.8	17.3
Daishimizu	Japan	1982	22.2	13.8
Simplon 2	Switerland/Italy	1922	19.8	12.3
Simplon 1	Swizerland/Italy	1906	19.8	12.3
Shin Kanmon	Japan	1973	18.7	11.6
Appenines	Italy	1931	18.6	11.5
Rokko	Japan	1971	16.2	10
Henderson	US	1975	15.8	9.8
Haruna	Japan	1982	15.4	9.6
St. Gotthard	Switzerland	1882	15	9.3
Nakayama	Japan	1982	14.8	9.2
Lötschberg	Switzerland	1913	14.5	9

* Planned completion date

TALLEST TOWERS

Tower	Location	Date built	Height m	ft
KTHI-TV Mast	North Dakota	1963	629	2,064
KSLA-TV Mast	Louisiana	1982	579	1,900
CN Tower	Toronto, Canada	1975	555	1,821
Ostankino TV Tower	Moscow Russia	1967	537	1,762
WTVM & WRBL TV Mast	Georgia (US)	1962	533	1,749
WBIR TV Mast	Tennessee	1963	533	1,749
KFVS TV Mast	Cape Girardeau (US)	1960	511	1,676

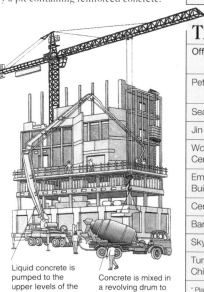

Liquid concrete is pumped to the upper levels of the building.

Concrete is mixed in a revolving drum to stop it from setting.

TALLEST OFFICE BUILDINGS

Office building	Location	Date built	Height m	ft
Petronas Tower	Kuala Lumpur, Malaysia	1995*	450	1,476
Sears Tower	Chicago	1974	443	1,453
Jin Mao Building	Shanghai, China	1998*	418	1,371
World Trade Center	New York	1973	417	1,368
Empire State Building	New York	1931	381	1,250
Central Plaza	Hong Kong	1992	374	1,227
Bank of China	Hong Kong	1989	368	1,207
Sky Central Plaza	Guangzhou, China	1995*	364	1,194
Tuntex and Chien-Tai	Kaoshiung, China	1996*	347	1,138

* Planned completion date

INTERNATIONAL WORLD

In this section, the latest computer-generated maps show all the countries of the world in amazing detail. Data boxes provide up-to-date statistics, and lifestyle facts, prepared in association with embassies worldwide, give authoritative information about how people live today.

The Physical World • The Political World • How To Use The Map Pages
All the Countries and Continents of the World • Flags • Mapping
Raw Materials • Farming and Fisheries • Population
Living Standards • Debt and Wealth

THE PHYSICAL WORLD

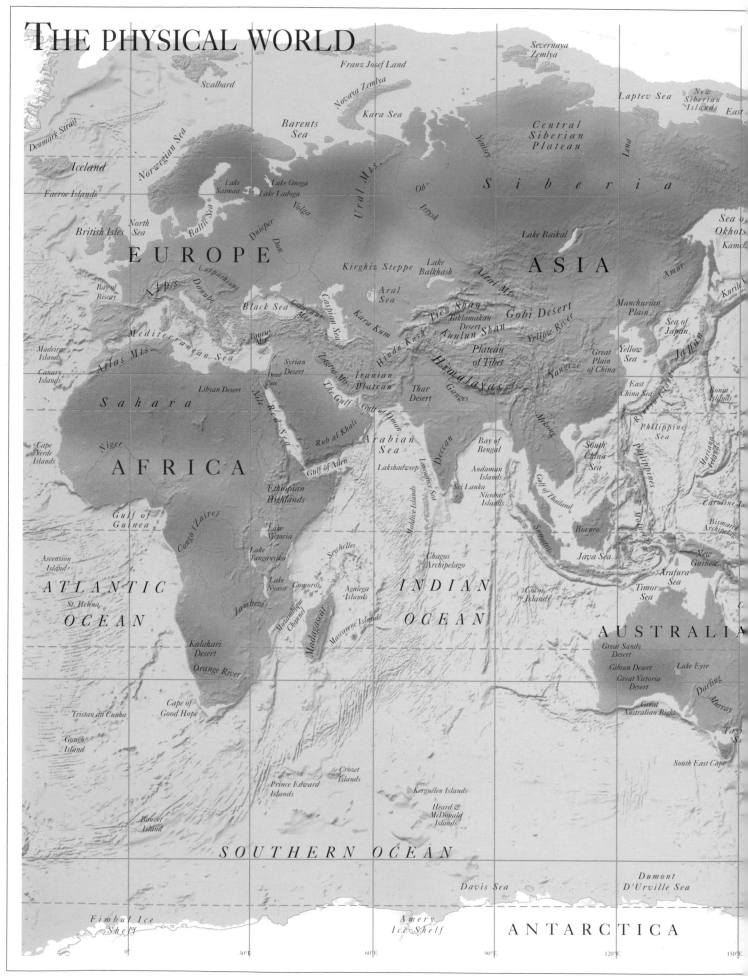

Denmark Strait

Iceland

Faeroe Islands

British Isles

EUROPE

Bay of
Biscay

Alps

Madeira
Islands

Canary
Islands

Atlas Mts.

Sahara

Cape
Verde
Islands

Niger

AFRICA

Gulf of
Guinea

Ascension
Island

ATLANTIC
OCEAN

St. Helena

Tristan da Cunha

Gough
Island

Cape of
Good Hope

Svalbard

Franz Josef Land

Novaya Zemlya

Norwegian Sea

Barents
Sea

Kara Sea

Lake
Saimaa

Lake Onega
Lake Ladoga

North
Sea

Baltic Sea

Volga

Dnieper

Don

Carpathians

Danube

Black Sea

Caucasus
Mts.

Caspian Sea

Taurus
Mts.

Mediterranean Sea

Libyan Desert

Dead
Sea

Syrian
Desert

Nile

Red Sea

Gulf of Aden

Ethiopian
Highlands

Lake
Victoria

Lake
Tanganyika

Congo (Zaire)

Lake
Nyasa

Zambezi

Comoros

Mozambique Channel

Madagascar

Kalahari
Desert

Orange River

Severnaya
Zemlya

Laptev Sea

New
Siberian
Islands

East

Central
Siberian
Plateau

Siberia

Lena

Ob'

Yenisey

Irtysh

Ural Mts.

Kirghiz Steppe

Aral
Sea

Lake
Balkhash

Lake Baikal

Altai Mts.

ASIA

Amur

Sea of
Okhotsk

Kamch

Kara Kum

Kunlun Shan

Tien Shan

Taklamakan
Desert

Gobi Desert

Yellow River

Manchurian
Plain

Kurile

Sea of
Japan

Japan

Hindu Kush

Plateau
of Tibet

Himalayas

Yangtze

Great
Plain
of China

Yellow
Sea

Iranian
Plateau

The Gulf

Zagros Mts.

Thar
Desert

Ganges

Mekong

East
China Sea

Bonin
Islands

Gulf of Oman

Arabian
Sea

Rub al Khali

Deccan

Bay of
Bengal

South
China
Sea

Philippine
Sea

Philippines

Mariana
Islands

Lakshadweep

Laccadive Sea

Maldive Islands

Andaman
Islands

Sri Lanka

Nicobar
Islands

Gulf of Thailand

Caroline Is.

Seychelles

Chagos
Archipelago

INDIAN

OCEAN

Cocos
Islands

Borneo

Java Sea

Bismarck
Archipelago

New
Guinea

Agalega
Islands

Mascarene Islands

Sumatra

Timor
Sea

Arafura
Sea

AUSTRALIA

Great Sandy
Desert

Gibson Desert

Great Victoria
Desert

Lake Eyre

Darling

Murray

Great
Australian Bight

Tas
S

South East Cape

Crozet
Islands

Prince Edward
Islands

Kerguélen Islands

Heard &
McDonald
Islands

Bouvet
Island

SOUTHERN OCEAN

Davis Sea

Dumont
D'Urville Sea

Fimbul Ice
Shelf

Amery
Ice Shelf

ANTARCTICA

0°   30°E   60°E   90°E   120°E   150°E

ARCTIC OCEAN

Chukchi
Sea

Beaufort
Sea

Queen Elizabeth Islands

Baffin
Bay

Greenland

Greenland Sea

Davis Strait

Arctic Circle

60°N

Bering
Strait

Yukon

Mackenzie

Great Bear
Lake

Great Slave
Lake

Hudson
Bay

Labrador
Sea

Bering
Sea

Gulf of
Alaska

Coast Mts.

Rocky Mountains

NORTH

Newfoundland

Aleutian Islands

Coast Ranges

Missouri

AMERICA

ATLANTIC

Azores

Sonoran
Desert

Rio Grande

Sierra Madre

Mississippi

Great Lakes

Appalachian Mts.

OCEAN

30°N

Midway Islands

Gulf of
Mexico

Bermuda
Islands

Tropic of Cancer

Hawaiian Islands

PACIFIC

CENTRAL

Bahamas

Greater Antilles

Leeward
Islands

Windward Islands

Islands

OCEAN

AMERICA

Caribbean Sea

Galápagos
Islands

Andes

Llanos

Equator

0

Phoenix Islands

Line Islands

Amazon

Amazonia

SOUTH

São Francisco

Marquesas Islands

AMERICA

Samoa

Tahiti

Tuamotu

Lake Titicaca

Fiji

Society Islands

Cook Islands

Tubuai
Islands

Plateau of
Mato Grosso

Tropic of Capricorn

Pitcairn Islands

Sala y Gómez

Easter Island

Atacama Desert

Paraná

Andes

Pampas

30°S

Juan Fernández
Islands

New
Zealand

Chatham Islands

Patagonia

ATLANTIC

Bounty Islands

Antipodes
Islands

Falkland
Islands

OCEAN

Cape Horn

South
Sandwich
Islands

Scotia Sea

60°S

Drake Passage

South Orkney
Islands

South Shetland
Islands

Antarctic Circle

Bellingshausen
Sea

Ross Sea

Amundsen Sea

ANTARCTICA

Weddell Sea

180

150°W

120°W

90°W

60°W

30°W

THE POLITICAL WORLD

THE COUNTRIES OF the world, which number 192, are spread over seven continents and vary greatly in size. The Russian Federation, for example, is almost 39 million times bigger than the Vatican City.

INTERNATIONAL TIME ZONES

The world is made up of 24 different time-zones, as shown on the map below. In each zone, the clocks are set to a different time of day. Time zones ensure that noon in each country is fixed at about midday, and that midnight falls in the middle of the night.

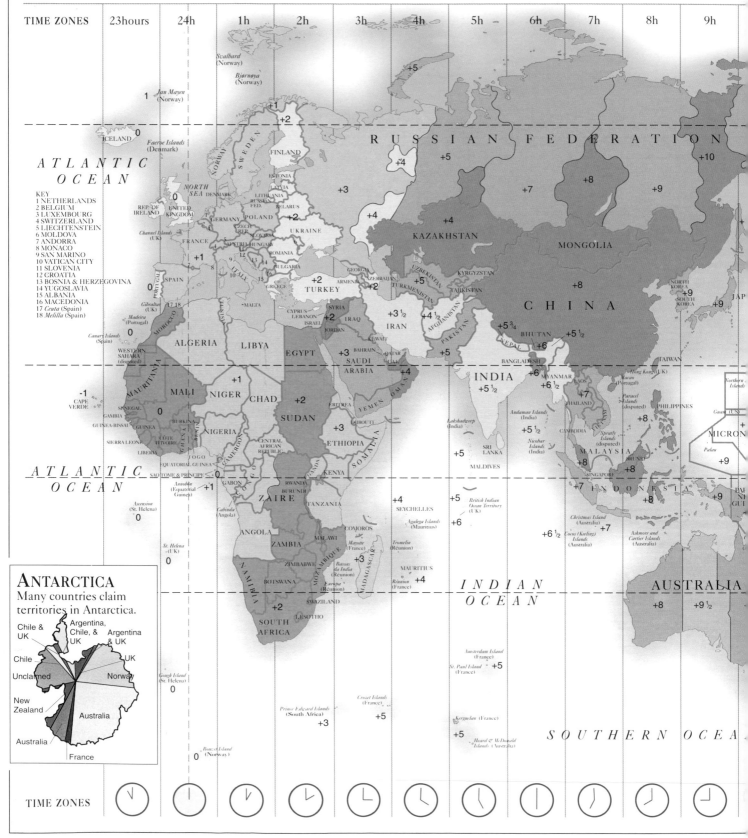

TIME ZONES	23hours	24h	1h	2h	3h	4h	5h	6h	7h	8h	9h

KEY
1 NETHERLANDS
2 BELGIUM
3 LUXEMBOURG
4 SWITZERLAND
5 LIECHTENSTEIN
6 MOLDOVA
7 ANDORRA
8 MONACO
9 SAN MARINO
10 VATICAN CITY
11 SLOVENIA
12 CROATIA
13 BOSNIA & HERZEGOVINA
14 YUGOSLAVIA
15 ALBANIA
16 MACEDONIA
17 *Ceuta* (Spain)
18 *Melilla* (Spain)

ANTARCTICA

Many countries claim territories in Antarctica.

Chile & UK
Argentina, Chile, & UK
Argentina & UK
Chile
UK
Unclaimed
Norway
New Zealand
Australia
Australia
France

TIME ZONES

RECORDS

CONTINENT WITH MOST COUNTRIES
is Africa, with 54 countries.

ONLY CONTINENT THAT IS ALSO
a country is Australia.

LARGEST ISLAND
is Greenland, at 839,852sq miles (2,175,219sq km).

LARGEST COUNTRY
is the Russian Federation, with an area of
6,592,846sq miles (17,075,400sq km).

SMALLEST COUNTRY
is the Vatican City, with an area of just
0.17sq miles (0.44sq km).

INTERNATIONAL DATE LINE

When you cross this imaginary line from east to west, the date changes. The western side is a day ahead of the eastern side.

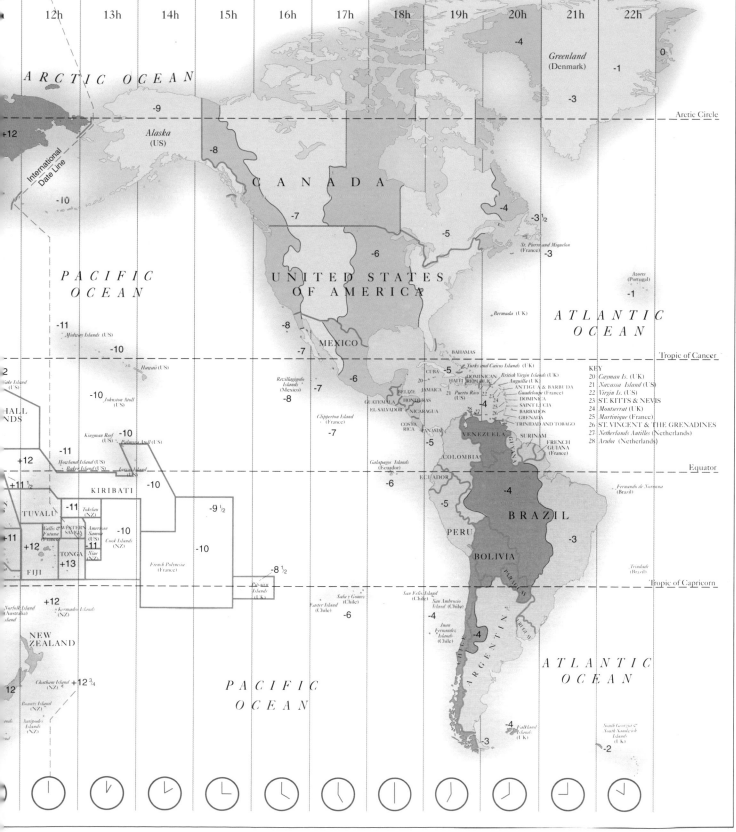

KEY
20 *Cayman Is.* (UK)
21 *Navassa Island* (US)
22 *Virgin Is.* (US)
23 ST. KITTS & NEVIS
24 *Montserrat* (UK)
25 *Martinique* (France)
26 ST. VINCENT & THE GRENADINES
27 *Netherlands Antilles* (Netherlands)
28 *Aruba* (Netherlands)

285

How to Use the Map Pages

The maps in International World are organized into sections, based on continents. There is a section for North America, South America, Europe, Africa, Asia, and Australia. At the start of each section there is a map showing the whole continent, followed by maps of the countries located on that continent. This page explains the information and symbols that appear on and around these country maps.

Data boxes

Every country in this section has a box with important statistics about that country. Some of the main countries contain more detailed information than others.

Flag

The national flag for each country or territory is shown at the top of the data box.

Area

The figure shown is the total area of the country, and includes all inland water (e.g., lakes, reservoirs, and rivers).

Government

The type of government ruling the country at the time this book went to press is described. Some governments, however, are fairly unstable and may change at short notice.

Independence

This is the date when a country broke free from the control of another power and became independent. The date when a republic was formed, or a state was declared, may also be given.

Currency

The paper or metal money used as the system of exchange, and in current use in that country, is named.

Population

This figure is the number of people registered in the most recent census as living in the country. Most countries round up their estimated population to the nearest thousand. Migration and famine will affect these figures.

Density

The average number of people occupying each square mile or square kilometer of the country is given. The figure is based on land area only, not on the total area.

Official Language

This language, or languages, is used by the government, and is not necessarily the most widely spoken language.

✝ Major Religions

The percentage breakdown of religions currently practiced by the population is shown. A religious symbol, such as this cross for Christianity, appears when a religion is followed by 75% or more of the population.

LOCATOR MAPS

The red area on the globe shows the location of the countries on the page, or spread, in relation to the continent.

LANGUAGE

This spells out a traditional greeting in the main language of the country.

INTERNATIONAL WORLD

ICELAND

ICELAND, EUROPE'S second-largest island, has the lowest population density in Europe. The remote interior can be reached only by special vehicle, pony, or small plane.

Area 39,769sq miles (103,000sq km)
Government Presidential republic
Independence 1944, from British and US control during World War II
Currency Icelandic króna
Population 300,000
Density 7.8 per sq mile (3 per sq km)
Official Language Icelandic
✝ **Major Religions** Evangelical Lutheran Church of Iceland 96%, other Protestant and Roman Catholic 3%, nonreligious 1%

WEATHER FACTS
86°F (30°C) 33.9in (860mm) -32.8°F (-36°C)
51.8°F (10.6°C) 32.4°F (0.2°C)

LAND PROFILE

LIFESTYLE FACTS
- The Althing, the Icelandic parliament, has been in existence since the 13th century and is one of the oldest surviving assemblies in the world.
- Iceland has the most solfataras (volcanic vents) and hot springs in the world. Many of its towns are heated by underground hot water.
- Iceland produces more than a third of the world's cod-liver oil, and is the biggest consumer of it.

HOT SPRINGS
Deildartunguhver hot springs blow out 66 gallons (250 liters) of hot water every second. Over a 24-hour period, they produce enough water to fill 105,600 baths.

LANGUAGE
A traditional greeting in Icelandic is *góðan daginn*.

100 krónur

Siglufjördur
Akureyri
ICELAND Vatnajökull
Deildartunguhver
Reykjavik
Hafnarfjördhur Kópavogur
954ft

NORWAY

NORWAY MEANS "the way to the north." It is a land of beautiful fjords (valleys flooded by rising levels): the longest is Sogne Fj at 126 miles (203 kilometers).

Area 125,058sq miles (323,900sq km)
Government Constitutional monar
Independence from Sweden, 1
Territories Svalbard archipelago, J Mayen Island
Currency Norwegian krone
Population 4,247,546
Density 36 per sq mile (14 per sq k
Official Language Nynorsk (new Norwegian) and Bokmaal (older)
✝ **Major Religions** Evangelical Lutheran and other Protestant 87.9 Roman Catholic 0.8%, other 11.3%

WEATHER FACTS
93°F (34°C) 28.7in (730mm) -15
61.3°F (16.3°C) 25.7°F (-3.5

LAND PROFILE

DENMARK

DENMARK, WHICH IS divided into numerous islands, has a 4,500-mile (7,300km) coastline. It is the only Scandinavian country belonging to the European Community (EC).

Area 16,629sq miles (43,070sq km)
Government Constitutional monarchy
State founded c. 950
Territories Faeroe Islands, Greenland
Currency Danish krone
Population 5,143,000
Density 319 per sq mile (123 per sq km)
Official Language Danish
✝ **Major Religions** Evangelical Lutheran Church 91%; Roman Catholic 2%, other and nonreligious 7%

WEATHER FACTS
95°F (35°C) 27.7in (704mm) -11.2°F (-24°C)
61.3°F (16.3°C) 34.3°F (1.3°C)

LAND PROFILE
Almost two-thirds of the land is farmed.

LANGUAGE
A traditional greeting in Danish is *goddag*.

100 kroner

LIFESTYLE FACTS
- Lego was created by a Danish carpenter in the 1930s. Legoland Park is a miniature, working village created from 35 million plastic bricks.
- Denmark has one of the lowest private ownerships of cars in Europe. Cyclists are encouraged with special lanes, and Copenhagen was the first city to create a pedestrian street.
- Denmark has over twice as many pigs as humans, and Danish bacon is a successful export product. Danish farmers produce three times more food than is needed to feed the population.

LITTLE MERMAID
Situated by Copenhagen harbor, this statue of the mermaid from Hans C. Andersen's fairy tale was sculpted in 1913 by Edvard Eriksen (1876–1959). In 1964, her head was sawed off, but was soon replaced.

308

WEATHER FACTS

Country's hottest recorded temperature
95°F (35°C)

Average annual rainfall in capital city
27.7in (704mm)

Country's coldest recorded temperature
-11.2°F (24°C)

61.3°F (16.3°C)
Average summer temperature in capital city

34.3°F (1.3°C)
Average winter temperature in capital city

LANDMARK

This is the country's most recognizable building or statue and has been chosen by the embassy or consulate of the featured country. The map shows location of the landmark, with an illustration similar to the photogra[ph]

LAND PROFILE

This artwork shows how the land in a country divides into areas such as forest or desert, how much is built on (urban), and how much is available for farming (agriculture). Barren land indicates areas such as the bare rocks of mountain tops, or salt flats.

KEY

- Urban
- Forest
- Grassland
- Tundra
- Agriculture
- Wetland
- Desert
- Barren

SCANDINAVIA

KEY TO MAPS

The maps in this section have been created to give an accurate representation of the landscape.

COLORS

The different physical features and climate zones are listed below.

- Snow/ice
- Tundra
- Coniferous forest
- Temperate forest
- Temperate rainforest
- Mediterranean vegetation
- Temperate grassland
- Cold desert
- Hot desert
- Tropical forest
- Tropical rainforest
- Tropical grassland
- Mountains
- Wetland
- Neighboring countries

SYMBOLS

The symbols below appear on the map to represent places and physical features.

- NORWAY — Country
- Oslo — Capital city
- Bergen • — Major city
- Sami (Lapps) — Subject talked about in text
- ☀ — Hottest place
- ❄ — Coldest place
- Highest point
- Borders
- Disputed borders
- State borders
- Lakes (largest)
- Rivers (longest)

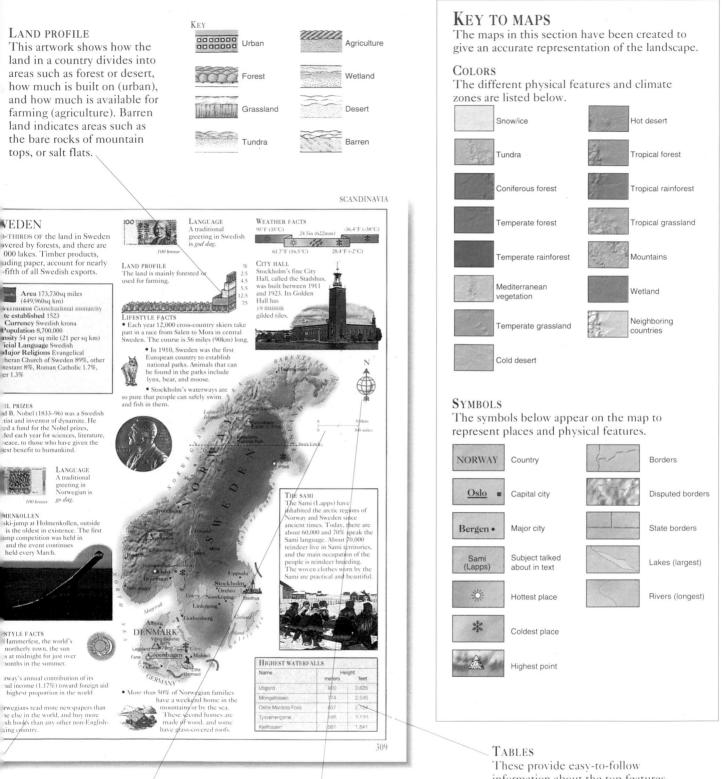

SWEDEN

TWO-THIRDS of the land in Sweden is covered by forests, and there are 100,000 lakes. Timber products, including paper, account for nearly one-fifth of all Swedish exports.

Area 173,730sq miles (449,960sq km)
Government Constitutional monarchy
State established 1523
Currency Swedish krona
Population 8,700,000
Density 54 per sq mile (21 per sq km)
Official Language Swedish
Major Religions Evangelical Lutheran Church of Sweden 89%, other Protestant 8%, Roman Catholic 1.7%, other 1.3%

NOBEL PRIZES
Alfred B. Nobel (1833–96) was a Swedish chemist and inventor of dynamite. He created a fund for the Nobel prizes, awarded each year for sciences, literature, and peace, to those who have given the greatest benefit to humankind.

LANGUAGE
A traditional greeting in Norwegian is *go dag*.
100 kroner

HOLMENKOLLEN
The ski-jump at Holmenkollen, outside Oslo, is the oldest in existence. The first jump competition was held in 1892 and the event continues to be held every March.

LIFESTYLE FACTS
• In Hammerfest, the world's most northerly town, the sun stays at midnight for just over two months in the summer.
• Norway's annual contribution of its national income (1.17%) toward foreign aid is the highest proportion in the world.
• Norwegians read more newspapers than anyone else in the world, and buy more English books than any other non-English-speaking country.

LANGUAGE
A traditional greeting in Swedish is *god dag*.
100 kronor

LAND PROFILE
The land is mainly forested or used for farming.

	%
	2.5
	4.5
	5.5
	12.5
	75

LIFESTYLE FACTS
• Each year 12,000 cross-country skiers take part in a race from Salen to Mora in central Sweden. The course is 56 miles (90km) long.
• In 1910, Sweden was the first European country to establish national parks. Animals that can be found in the parks include lynx, bear, and moose.
• Stockholm's waterways are so pure that people can safely swim and fish in them.

WEATHER FACTS
95°F (35°C)   24.5in (622mm)   -36.4°F (-38°C)
61.7°F (16.5°C)   28.4°F (-2°C)

CITY HALL
Stockholm's fine City Hall, called the Stadshus, was built between 1911 and 1923. Its Golden Hall has 19 million gilded tiles.

THE SAMI
The Sami (Lapps) have inhabited the arctic regions of Norway and Sweden since ancient times. Today, there are about 60,000 and 70% speak the Sami language. About 70,000 reindeer live in Sami territories, and the main occupation of the people is reindeer breeding. The woven clothes worn by the Sami are practical and beautiful.

• More than 50% of Norwegian families have a weekend home in the mountains or by the sea. These second homes are made of wood, and some have grass-covered roofs.

HIGHEST WATERFALLS		
Name	Height meters	feet
Utigord	800	2,625
Mongefossen	774	2,540
Ostre Mardola Foss	657	2,154
Tyssetrengane	646	2,120
Kjelfossen	561	1,841

LIFESTYLE FACTS
These facts give details about food, sports, industry, or events that are unique to the country. They have been chosen from information supplied by the country itself to realistically reflect life in the country.

SCALE
This shows how distance on the map relates to miles and kilometers, and can be used to see how big a country is. Not all maps are drawn to the same scale.

COMPASS POINT
This fixes the direction of North (N), and gives the position of the country in relation to North.

TABLES
These provide easy-to-follow information about the top features of a country. They may list the highest waterfalls, as shown here, or the most cars manufactured, or chief exports.

NORTH AND CENTRAL AMERICA

CANADA AND THE United States of America cover most of the continent of North America. To the south lie Mexico and the seven small countries of Central America. The western side of the continent is dominated by the Rocky Mountains, which run from Canada to Mexico.

Area 9,358,340sq miles (24,238,000sq km)
Countries 24
Largest Canada
Smallest Grenada
🏛 **Population** 429,862,000
Density 52 per sq mile (20 per sq km)
Major Languages English, Spanish, French, Amerindian and Inuit languages, Nahuatl (Aztec)

▲ **Highest point** Mount Denali, Alaska 20,322ft (6,194m)
▼ **Lowest point** Death Valley, California 282ft (86m) below sea level
☼ **Highest temperature** 135°F (57°C) Death Valley, California
❄ **Lowest temperature** -87°F (-66°C) Northice, Greenland

COUNTRIES, TERRITORIES, AND CAPITALS

Name	Capital	Name	Capital
Antigua and Barbuda	St. John's	Guatemala	Guatemala City
Bahamas	Nassau	Haiti	Port-au-Prince
Barbados	Bridgetown	Honduras	Tegucigalpa
Belize	Belmopan	Jamaica	Kingston
Canada	Ottawa	Mexico	Mexico City
Costa Rica	San José	Nicaragua	Managua
Cuba	Havana	Panama	Panama City
Dominica	Roseau	St. Kitts and Nevis	Basseterre
Dominican Republic	Santo Domingo	St. Lucia	Castries
El Salvador	San Salvador	St. Vincent and the Grenadines	Kingstown
Greenland	Godthåb	Trinidad and Tobago	Port of Spain
Grenada	St. George's	US	Washington, DC

TIME ZONES

4:00 Vancouver 6:00 Mexico City 9:00 Godthåb 12:00 Greenwich

TOP CITY POPULATIONS

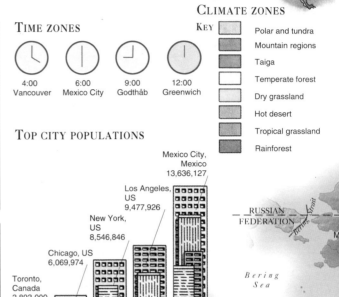

Mexico City, Mexico 13,636,127
Los Angeles, US 9,477,926
New York, US 8,546,846
Chicago, US 6,069,974
Toronto, Canada 3,893,000

CLIMATE ZONES

KEY
Polar and tundra
Mountain regions
Taiga
Temperate forest
Dry grassland
Hot desert
Tropical grassland
Rainforest

RUSSIAN FEDERATION
Bering Sea
ALAS (U.
Mount Der 20,32 (6,194
Aleutian Islands

Midway Islands (US)
Hawaiian Islands
PACIFIC OCEAN

CONTINENT FACTS
• British Columbia produces 25% of the timber sold in North America. It also supplies the world with chopsticks.

• Grenada is the only country in the Western world where spices such as nutmeg, cinnamon, and cloves grow in abundance.

• Surfing as a competitive sport began on the island of Oahu in Hawaii. Surfing waves can reach about 26ft (8m) high.

GRAND CANYON
The Grand Canyon was gouged out of rock by the Colorado River. The canyon is 217 miles (349km) long, up to 19 miles (30km) wide, and 1 mile (1.6km) deep. At its deepest point it cuts through rock 2,000 million years old.

LONGEST ROADS (see map on pages 292-3)

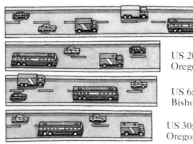

Trans-Canada Highway: St. John's, Newfoundland to Victoria, B.C. 4,860 miles (7,821km)

US 20: Boston, Massachusetts to Newport, Oregon 3,365 miles (5,415km)

US 6: Provincetown, Massachusetts to Bishop, California 3,249 miles (5,229km)

US 30: Atlantic City, New Jersey to Astoria, Oregon 3,119 miles (5,019km)

AGE BREAKDOWN

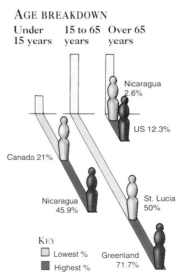

| Under 15 years | 15 to 65 years | Over 65 years |

Nicaragua 2.6%
US 12.3%
Canada 21%
Nicaragua 45.9%
St. Lucia 50%
Greenland 71.7%

KEY
☐ Lowest %
☐ Highest %

FEWEST DOCTORS

Haiti	1 to 7,050 people
Jamaica	1 to 6,687 people
Guatemala	1 to 3,999 people
St. Vincent and the Grenadines	1 to 3,800 people
St. Lucia	1 to 3,400 people

LONGEST LIFE SPAN

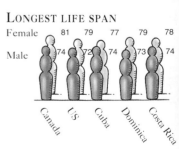

	Canada	US	Cuba	Dominica	Costa Rica
Female	81	79	77	79	78
Male	74	72	74	73	74

CROSS SECTION

Coast Range
Great Basin
Mississippi
Lake Michigan
Lake Erie
Rocky Mts.
Appalachian Mts.
Pacific Ocean
Atlantic Ocean

9,843ft
(3,000m)

0 Sea level

-14,764ft
-(4,500m)

Length: 3,600 miles (5,800km)

LARGEST LAKES

The largest lakes, except for Lake Michigan (US), lie partly or completely in Canada.

Lake Superior
31,700sq miles
(82,103sq km)

Lake Huron
23,000sq miles
(59,570sq km)

Lake Michigan
22,300sq miles
(57,757sq km)

Great Bear Lake
12,096sq miles
(31,328sq km)

Great Slave Lake
11,031sq miles
(28,570sq km)

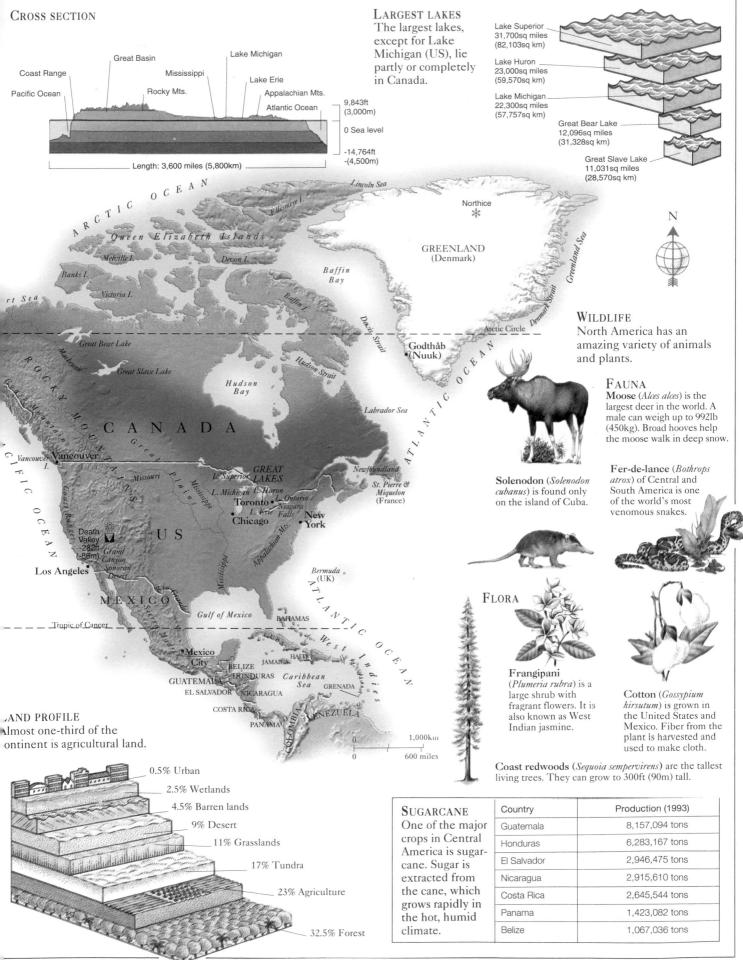

WILDLIFE

North America has an amazing variety of animals and plants.

FAUNA

Moose (*Alces alces*) is the largest deer in the world. A male can weigh up to 992lb (450kg). Broad hooves help the moose walk in deep snow.

Fer-de-lance (*Bothrops atrox*) of Central and South America is one of the world's most venomous snakes.

Solenodon (*Solenodon cubanus*) is found only on the island of Cuba.

FLORA

Frangipani (*Plumeria rubra*) is a large shrub with fragrant flowers. It is also known as West Indian jasmine.

Cotton (*Gossypium hirsutum*) is grown in the United States and Mexico. Fiber from the plant is harvested and used to make cloth.

Coast redwoods (*Sequoia sempervirens*) are the tallest living trees. They can grow to 300ft (90m) tall.

LAND PROFILE

Almost one-third of the continent is agricultural land.

0.5% Urban
2.5% Wetlands
4.5% Barren lands
9% Desert
11% Grasslands
17% Tundra
23% Agriculture
32.5% Forest

SUGARCANE

One of the major crops in Central America is sugarcane. Sugar is extracted from the cane, which grows rapidly in the hot, humid climate.

Country	Production (1993)
Guatemala	8,157,094 tons
Honduras	6,283,167 tons
El Salvador	2,946,475 tons
Nicaragua	2,915,610 tons
Costa Rica	2,645,544 tons
Panama	1,423,082 tons
Belize	1,067,036 tons

CANADA

CANADA IS THE second largest country in the world. Across the center of the country lie the Prairies, a flat plain used for growing wheat and grazing cattle. Most Canadians live around the Great Lakes and the St. Lawrence River.

Area 3,851,808sq miles (9,976,140sq km)
Government Federal democracy, with British sovereign as constitutional monarch
Independence 1931, from Britain
Currency Canadian dollar
Population 27,400,000
Density 8 per sq mile (3 per sq km)
Official Languages English, French
✝ **Major Religions** Roman Catholic 46.5%, Protestant 41.2%, other 12.3%

WEATHER FACTS

113°F (45°C)   34in (872mm)   -81.4°F (-63°C)

66.6°F (19.2°C)   12°F (-11°C)

10 Canadian dollars

LAND PROFILE
More than half the land in Canada is covered by forest.

%
0.5
1
2
5
5.5
27
59

THE CN TOWER
The Canadian National (CN) Tower in Toronto is the tallest free-standing structure in the world at 1,821ft (555m) high. It was built as a TV transmitter and was completed in 1975.

TORONTO SKYDOME
• SkyDome is the world's first stadium with a moving roof. Seating is on four levels and can hold 50,000 people.

• The field is covered with 106 rolls of Astroturf, joined together with 8 miles (12.8km) of zippers.

WOOD AND PAPER EXPORTS (1992)
Canada is the world's largest exporter of forest products. These include lumber for building, as well as wood pulp for paper.

Destination	Amount (in tons)
United States	10,481,595
Europe	5,376,939
Asia	1,905,778
South America	724,393
Central America	233,258

LIFESTYLE FACTS

• Canada is such a vast country that it takes 3 days and 3 nights to travel by train from Toronto to Vancouver – a distance of 2,776 miles (4,467km).

• Dinosaur Provincial Park, on the banks of the Red Deer River in Alberta, is one of the greatest sites for dinosaur remains in the world. The *Albertosaurus* is one of the large dinosaurs that once roamed around this area.

• Canada produces 75% of the world's maple syrup. Each March, sap is collected from sugar maple trees and boiled down into syrup. A maple leaf is the symbol of Canada.

• Some places in Canada are freezing cold for months on end. A family can flood their yard and use it as a hockey rink.

CANADIAN PEOPLE
Many people have settled in Canada. The largest ethnic groups, after the British and French, are Italian and German.

Languages spoken	% of population
English	66.3
French	23.2
Italian	5.9
German	1.1
Chinese	0.4
Other	3.1

CITY OF MONTREAL
This square in Montreal was named after Jacques Cartier (1491–1557), the explorer who claimed Canada for the French in 1535. Today, Canada is a bilingual country, and two-thirds of the people in Montreal still speak French.

GREENLAND

THE WORLD'S LARGEST island, Greenland is part of Denmark. Almost all of Greenland lies within the Arctic Circle, and the land is permanently covered with ice. Most of the island is uninhabited.

Area 840,004sq miles (2,175,600sq km)
Government Constitutional monarchy, as part of kingdom of Denmark
Currency Danish krone
Population 55,558
Density 0.4 per sq mile (0.16 per sq km)
Official Language Greenlandic, Danish
✝ Major Religions Evangelical Lutheran 99%, Roman Catholic 1%

LIFESTYLE FACTS

- Greenland's 55,000-plus inhabitants live in the capital, Godthåb, 16 small towns, and 66 other settlements. There are no roads or rail links between areas, so travel is by air or sea.

- In winter the skidoo, a kind of motorcycle on skis, is used to travel across the snow.

- More than 85% of Greenland is a massive ice sheet with an average thickness of 5,000ft (1,524m). Icebreaker ships are used to keep the sea channels open.

- Only low-growing plants with shallow roots, such as the Arctic rhododendron, Arctic poppy, saxifrage, and bilberry, can survive the harsh climate.

Arctic rhododendron (Rhododendron lapponicum)

Arctic poppy (Papaver lapponicum)

Saxifrage (Saxifraga sp.)

This fishing community lies near Cape Farvel on the southernmost tip of Greenland.

ALONG THE COAST

Greenland has more than 24,430 miles (39,315km) of jagged coastline. Most people live along the coast and work in the fishing industry. In the south, the Gulf Stream current helps keep the sea free of ice.

FISH EXPORTS

Greenland's fishing rights cover more than 772,204,000sq miles (2,000,000sq km) of sea. Shrimp accounts for 80% of the country's exports. Cod, salmon, haddock, and other fish make up the remaining 20%.

WILDLIFE

Conditions within the Arctic Circle are harsh, but the animals that live there are well adapted to the ice and snow.

Hooded seal *(Cystophora cristata)* lives in the seas around the polar ice cap.

Caribou *(Rangifer tarandus)* has broad hooves to walk in snow.

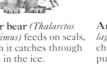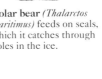

Walrus *(Odobenus rosmarus)* has long tusks which it uses to haul itself up on to the ice.

Polar bear *(Thalarctos maritimus)* feeds on seals, which it catches through holes in the ice.

Arctic fox *(Alopex lagopus)* has fur that changes from brown to pure white in winter.

INUIT ART

Kenojuak, a famous Inuit painter, is shown with her work. Inuit art also includes fine carvings in ivory and bone.

Lincoln Sea
Wandel Sea
GREENLAND
(Denmark)
Greenland Sea
Disko I.
• Ilulissat
Gunnbjørn Fjeld
12,146ft (3,702m)
Denmark Strait
Davis Strait
• Sisimrut
Arctic Circle
• Godthåb
(Nuuk)
N
Cape Farvel
Labrador Sea
ATLANTIC OCEAN
0   700 km
0   400 miles
Newfoundland
wick
Edward   • St. John's
St. Pierre &
lottetown *Miquelon*
ton   (France)
ifax
tia
le

Inuit child from Hudson Bay, Canada

INUIT FACTS

- Large areas of Canada and Greenland are still inhabited by the original settlers of these lands. They are called the Inuit, which means "people."

- Inuit build temporary snowhouses (correctly called *illuviga*) when they go hunting. Igloo is their word for any other kind of house.

- The main food source for the Inuit is the animals they hunt. Hunting is vital to their survival and provides food and clothing. Inuit hunt caribou, seal, walrus, and fish.

- Some words we use, such as kayak and anorak, are taken from the Inuit language.

THE NUNAVUT AGREEMENT

This agreement was reached in 1992 and is the largest land claim in Canadian history. Its terms include:

- The Inuit receive title to 135,136sq miles (350,000sq km) of land in 1999.

- They also have 13,999sq miles (36,257sq km) of underground mineral rights.

- The Inuit are granted $1.15 billion by Canada in compensation to be paid over 14 years (this sum based on value with interest by end of 14-year period).

UNITED STATES OF AMERICA

THE UNITED STATES OF AMERICA (US) is made up of 50 states plus the District of Columbia. Two of the states, Alaska and Hawaii, are separate from the others. The US is the world's wealthiest country, with vast areas of rich farmland and supplies of coal, oil, and minerals.

 Area 3,618,784sq miles (9,372,610sq km)
Government Federal democracy
Independence 1776, from Britain
Territories Northern Mariana Islands, Puerto Rico, American Samoa, Guam, United States Virgin Islands, Marshall Islands, Federated States of Micronesia, Johnston Atoll, Line Islands, Midway Islands, Wake Island, Baker and Howland Islands, Jarvis Island, Kingman Reef, Navassa Island, Palau, Palmyra Atoll
Currency United States dollar
Population 255,200,000
Density 73 per sq mile (28 per sq km)
Official Language English
Major Religions Protestant 61%, Roman Catholic 25%, Jewish 2%, other 12%

WEATHER FACTS

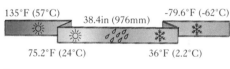

135°F (57°C)   38.4in (976mm)   -79.6°F (-62°C)

75.2°F (24°C)   36°F (2.2°C)

LAND PROFILE
More than one-third of the country is covered in forest.

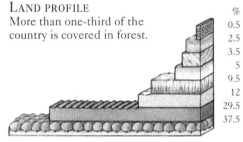

%
0.5
2.5
3.5
5
9.5
12
29.5
37.5

MAJOR AREAS OF WILD LANDS (1994)
Large areas of wild land have been set aside as parks and nature reserves.

State	% of state	Key animal
Alaska	15.03	Moose
Idaho	6.98	Cougar
Washington	5.91	Grizzly bear
California	5.81	Mountain lion
Wyoming	4.91	American buffalo
Florida	3.78	Manatee

10 US dollars

LIFESTYLE FACTS
• Alaska was bought from Russia in 1867 for 2 cents an acre. Today the state is rich in oil and other natural resources.

• Inland storms called tornadoes, or twisters, suck up dust as they swirl across the landscape.

 • The average American eats 110lb (50kg) of meat each year; more than twice as much as the average European.

• The US is the major producer of household waste. Every day, the average person produces about 4lb (1.8kg) of garbage.

• There is one television for every 1.2 people living in the United States.

HOLLYWOOD
Hollywood is the film capital of America. The fine weather and varied landscape attracted film directors from the East Coast to a small town called Hollywood in about 1910.

THE FIRST AMERICANS
The first people to live in North America arrived from Asia more than 20,000 years ago. This Native American, Chief Looking Horse (above), is a member of the Sioux from a reservation at Wounded Knee in South Dakota.

NATIVE AMERICAN FACTS
• Today 544 tribes of about 1.5 million Native Americans live on reservations, which they govern themselves.

• The Navajo of Arizona, New Mexico, and Utah is the biggest tribe. People still practice traditional pottery and weaving: Navajo rugs are woven into geometric patterns and are colored with natural dyes.

HAWAIIAN ISLANDS
Hawaii is a group of 20 volcanic islands in the Pacific Ocean. One of the largest active volcanoes in the world, Mauna Loa, is located on the main island of Hawaii. It last erupted in 1984. Two types of lava, *Aa* and *pahoehoe*, get their names from Hawaiian words.

WHEATFIELDS OF NEBRASKA
The United States is the largest exporter of wheat and produces more than half the world's corn. This supply of food is grown on the open plains, or prairies, which stretch across the Midwest.

WASHINGTON, DISTRICT OF COLUMBIA
Washington is the capital city of the US. It is home to the Capitol Building, which is the center of government and houses the Senate and the House of Representatives.

BASEBALL
Baseball is America's national sport. The first game between two organized teams was played in New Jersey in 1846.

THE CAR INDUSTRY
The US has more cars on the road than any other country (see page 277 for longest roads). It also has the highest ratio of cars, with 570 for every 1,000 persons.

see page 277 for longest roads

BEST-SELLING CARS (1993)

Model	Number sold
Ford F-series pickup	565,089
Chevrolet C/K pickup	544,373
Ford Taurus	360,448
Ford Ranger	340,184
Honda Accord	330,030
Ford Explorer	302,201
Toyota Camry	299,737
Chevrolet Cavalier	273,617
Ford Escort	269,034
Dodge Caravan	262,838

AMISH
The Amish are a Protestant group who came to America from Switzerland in the 18th century. Members do not conform to modern ways of life: they reject the use of electric lights and telephones and drive horses and buggies rather than cars.

STATUE OF LIBERTY, NEW YORK
• The statue was given to the US by France in 1884. It was designed by Auguste Bartholdi (1834–1904) and shipped across the Atlantic, packed in 210 crates.

• The statue is 306ft 8in (93.5m) high, including the pedestal she stands on.

• Visitors can climb 171 steps up to the viewing gallery in the head of the statue for a spectacular view of the New York skyline.

MISSISSIPPI RIVER
The Mississippi is one of the world's busiest waterways. Ships can travel for nearly 1,802 miles (2,900km) from Minneapolis to New Orleans. The first steamboat appeared on the Mississippi in 1811.

EVERGLADES FACTS
• Southern Florida has a vast area of cypress swamp called the Everglades. It is home to many rare animals and plants.

• The green tree frog has sticky suction pads on its toes that help it grip the slippery branches.

Tree frog

• The American alligator grows up to 12ft (3.6m) long and may live for 50 years. It propels itself through the water with its tail.

ARCHITECTURE
The many different styles of American architecture reflect the diverse climate and conditions of the US.

Plantation homes
People who grew rich on the profits of the plantations in the 19th century built grand mansions in European styles.

Clapboard
Houses in the eastern states are often built of overlapping wooden boards, known as clapboard, to keep out rain.

Art deco style
The Chrysler building was designed by William van Alen (b.1914) in the 1920s.

Major American architect
Frank Lloyd Wright (1867–1959) designed houses that blend with the landscape.

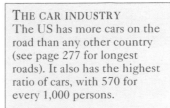

Map labels
North Dakota, Bismarck, Minnesota, South Dakota, Pierre, St Paul, Minneapolis, Nebraska, Lincoln, Madison, Wisconsin, Iowa, Des Moines, Lake Superior, Lake Michigan, Lake Huron, GREAT LAKES, Michigan, Lansing, Lake Ontario, Lake Erie, Niagara Falls, Maine, Augusta, Montpelier, Vermont, Concord, New Hampshire, Albany, New York, Boston, Massachusetts, Providence, Cape Cod, Provincetown, Rhode Island, Hartford, Connecticut, Long I., Chicago, Illinois, Indiana, Columbus, Ohio, Springfield, Indianapolis, Pennsylvania, Harrisburg, Philadelphia, New York, Trenton, New Jersey, Atlantic City, Annapolis, Dover, Delaware, Maryland, Washington D.C., Charleston, West Virginia, Frankfort, Kentucky, Virginia, Richmond, St. Lawrence, Topeka, Jefferson City, Missouri, Nashville, Tennessee, Raleigh, North Carolina, Kansas, Oklahoma City, Oklahoma, Little Rock, Arkansas, Columbia, South Carolina, AMERICA, Texas, Louisiana, Jackson, Mississippi, Alabama, Montgomery, Atlanta, Georgia, Austin, Houston, Baton Rouge, New Orleans, Tallahassee, Mississippi Delta, Florida, Gulf of Mexico, ATLANTIC OCEAN, N

0   500km
0   300 miles

UNITED STATES OF AMERICA: STATES OF THE UNION

THE UNITED STATES of America originally consisted of 13 colonies on the East Coast, all of them ruled by Britain until independence in 1776. Today there are 50 states, governed by the federal government in Washington, D.C., each with its own set of laws. For example, the age for holding a driving licence varies, as does the number of states that uphold the death sentence for murder.

The bald eagle is the national symbol of the US.

ALABAMA

Area 51,705sq miles (133,916sq km)
Capital Montgomery
Population 4,118,000
Entry into Union December 14, 1819
✿ **State flower** Camellia

ALASKA

Area 591,000sq miles (1,530,690sq km)
Capital Juneau
Population 527,000
Entry into Union January 3, 1959
✿ **State flower** Forget-me-not

ARIZONA

Area 114,000sq miles (295,260sq km)
Capital Phoenix
Population 3,556,000
Entry into Union February 14, 1912
✿ **State flower** Saguaro blossom

ARKANSAS

Area 53,187sq miles (137,754sq km)
Capital Little Rock
Population 2,406,000
Entry into Union June 15, 1836
✿ **State flower** Apple blossom

Stretch limo

CALIFORNIA

Area 158,707sq miles (411,049sq km)
Capital Sacramento
Population 29,063,000
Entry into Union September 9, 1850
✿ **State flower** California poppy

COLORADO

Area 104,091sq miles (269,596sq km)
Capital Denver
Population 3,317,000
Entry into Union August 1, 1876
✿ **State flower** Columbine

CONNECTICUT

Area 5,018sq miles (12,997sq km)
Capital Hartford
Population 3,239,000
Entry into Union January 9, 1788
✿ **State flower** Mountain laurel

DELAWARE

Area 2,045sq miles (5,297sq km)
Capital Dover
Population 673,000
Entry into Union December 7, 1787
✿ **State flower** Peach blossom

FLORIDA

Area 58,664sq miles (151,940sq km)
Capital Tallahassee
Population 12,671,000
Entry into Union March 3, 1845
✿ **State flower** Orange blossom

Baseball game

GEORGIA

Area 58,910sq miles (152,577sq km)
Capital Atlanta
Population 6,435,000
Entry into Union January 2, 1788
✿ **State flower** Cherokee rose

Surfer

HAWAII

Area 6,471sq miles (16,760sq km)
Capital Honolulu
Population 1,112,000
Entry into Union August 21, 1959
✿ **State flower** Yellow hibiscus

IDAHO

Area 89,564sq miles (231,971sq km)
Capital Boise
Population 1,014,000
Entry into Union July 3, 1890
✿ **State flower** Mock orange

ILLINOIS

Area 56,345sq miles (145,933sq km)
Capital Springfield
Population 11,658,000
Entry into Union December 3, 1818
✿ **State flower** Native violet

Appaloosa horse

INDIANA

Area 36,185sq miles (93,719sq km)
Capital Indianapolis
Population 5,593,000
Entry into Union December 11, 1816
✿ **State flower** Peony

IOWA

Area 56,275sq miles (145,752sq km)
Capital Des Moines
Population 2,840,000
Entry into Union December 28, 1846
✿ **State flower** Wild rose

THE WHITE HOUSE
The White House in Washington, D.C., is the official residence of the president and his family. The 3-story, 100-room mansion was designed by Irish-born architect James Hoban (1762–1831) and completed in 1800. The building is made of white limestone, which is how it got its name.

KANSAS

Area 82,277sq miles (213,097sq km)
Capital Topeka
Population 2,513,000
Entry into Union January 29, 1861
✿ **State flower** Native sunflower

Cowboy hat

KENTUCKY

Area 40,410sq miles (104,662sq km)
Capital Frankfort
Population 3,727,000
Entry into Union June 1, 1792
✿ **State flower** Goldenrod

LOUISIANA

Area 47,752sq miles (123,678sq km)
Capital Baton Rouge
Population 4,382,000
Entry into Union April 30, 1812
✿ **State flower** Southern magnolia

MAINE

Blueberries

Area 33,265sq miles (86,156sq km)
Capital Augusta
Population 1,222,000
Entry into Union March 15, 1820
✿ **State flower** White pine cone

MARYLAND

Area 10,460sq miles (27,091sq km)
Capital Annapolis
Population 4,694,000
Entry into Union April 28, 1788
✿ **State flower** Black-eyed susan

MASSACHUSETTS

Area 8,284sq miles (21,456sq km)
Capital Boston
Population 5,913,000
Entry into Union February 6, 1788
✿ **State flower** Mayflower

MICHIGAN

Area 58,527sq miles (151,585sq km)
Capital Lansing
Population 9,273,000
Entry into Union January 26, 1837
✿ **State flower** Apple blossom

KANSAS

American beaver

MINNESOTA

Area 84,402sq miles (218,601sq km)
Capital St. Paul
Population 4,353,000
Entry into Union May 11, 1858
✿ **State flower** Showy lady's slipper

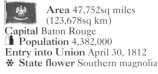
Dixieland jazz band

MISSISSIPPI

Area 47,689sq miles (123,515sq km)
Capital Jackson
Population 2,621,000
Entry into Union December 10, 1817
✿ **State flower** Magnolia

MISSOURI
Area 69,697sq miles
(180,515sq km)
Capital Jefferson City
Population 5,159,000
Entry into Union August 10, 1821
✼ State flower Hawthorn

MONTANA
Area 147,046sq miles
(380,849sq km)
Capital Helena
Population 806,000
Entry into Union November 8, 1889
✼ State flower Bitterroot

American football

NEBRASKA
Area 77,355sq miles
(200,349sq km)
Capital Lincoln
Population 1,611,000
Entry into Union March 1, 1867
✼ State flower Golden rod

NEVADA
Area 110,561sq miles
(110,561sq miles)
Capital Carson City
Population 1,111,000
Entry into Union October 31, 1864
✼ State flower Sagebrush

NEW HAMPSHIRE
Area 9,279sq miles
(24,033sq km)
Capital Concord
Population 1,107,000
Entry into Union June 21, 1788
✼ State flower Lilac

Yellow taxicab

NEW JERSEY
Area 7,787sq miles
(20,168sq km)
Capital Trenton
Population 7,736,000
Entry into Union December 18, 1787
✼ State flower Purple violet

Roadrunner

NEW MEXICO
Area 121,593sq miles
(314,926sq km)
Capital Sante Fe
Population 1,528,000
Entry into Union January 6, 1912
✼ State flower Yucca

New York skyline

NEW YORK
Area 49,108sq miles
(127,190sq km)
Capital Albany
Population 17,950,000
Entry into Union July 26, 1788
✼ State flower Rose

NORTH CAROLINA
Area 52,699sq miles
(136,490sq km)
Capital Raleigh
Population 6,571,000
Entry into Union November 21, 1789
✼ State flower Flowering dogwood

NORTH DAKOTA
Area 70,702sq miles
(183,118sq km)
Capital Bismarck
Population 660,000
Entry into Union November 2, 1889
✼ State flower Wild prairie rose

OHIO
Area 41,330sq miles
(107,045sq km)
Capital Columbus
Population 10,907,000
Entry into Union March 1, 1803
✼ State flower Scarlet carnation

OKLAHOMA
Area 69,919sq miles
(181,090sq km)
Capital Oklahoma City
Population 3,224,000
Entry into Union November 16, 1907
✼ State flower Mistletoe

OREGON
Area 97,073sq miles
(251,419sq km)
Capital Salem
Population 2,820,000
Entry into Union February 14, 1859
✼ State flower Oregon grape

PENNSYLVANIA
Area 45,308sq miles
(117,348sq km)
Capital Harrisburg
Population 12,040,000
Entry into Union December 12, 1787
✼ State flower Mountain laurel

RHODE ISLAND
Area 1,212sq miles
(3,139sq km)
Capital Providence
Population 998,000
Entry into Union May 29, 1790
✼ State flower Violet

Chopper bike

SOUTH CAROLINA
Area 77,116sq miles
(199,730sq km)
Capital Columbia
Population 3,512,000
Entry into Union May 23, 1788
✼ State flower Yellow jessamine

*Mount Rushmore
National Monument*

SOUTH DAKOTA
Area 77,116sq miles
(199,730sq km)
Capital Pierre
Population 715,000
Entry into Union November 2, 1889
✼ State flower Pasqueflower

TENNESSEE
Area 42,144sq miles
(109,152sq km)
Capital Nashville
Population 4,940,000
Entry into Union June 1, 1796
✼ State flower Iris

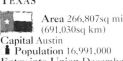
Cowboys roping cattle

TEXAS
Area 266,807sq miles
(691,030sq km)
Capital Austin
Population 16,991,000
Entry into Union December 29, 1845
✼ State flower Bluebonnet

UTAH
Area 84,899sq miles
(219,888sq km)
Capital Salt Lake City
Population 1,707,000
Entry into Union January 4, 1896
✼ State flower Sego lily

Halloween lantern

VERMONT
Area 9,614sq miles
(24,900sq km)
Capital Montpelier
Population 567,000
Entry into Union March 4, 1791
✼ State flower Red clover

VIRGINIA
Area 40,767sq miles
(105,586sq km)
Capital Richmond
Population 6,098,000
Entry into Union June 25, 1788
✼ State flower Flowering dogwood

WASHINGTON
Area 68,139sq miles
(176,480sq km)
Capital Olympia
Population 4,761,000
Entry into Union November 11, 1889
✼ State flower Coast rhododendron

WEST VIRGINIA
Area 24,232sq miles
(62,761sq km)
Capital Charleston
Population 1,857,000
Entry into Union June 20, 1863
✼ State flower Rhododendron

WISCONSIN
Area 56,153sq miles
(145,436sq km)
Capital Madison
Population 4,867,000
Entry into Union May 29, 1848
✼ State flower Wood violet

WYOMING
Area 97,809sq miles
(253,325sq km)
Capital Cheyenne
Population 475,000
Entry into Union July 10, 1890
✼ State flower Indian paintbrush

STATE FACTS

• Only about 800 grizzly bears are left in the US; many of them roam wild in the mountain forests of Idaho and Wyoming.

• Georgia grows nearly one-half the US's total crop of peanuts. Over half the crop is used for making peanut butter, the rest for edible oil and animal feed.

• Rhode Island is the smallest state. It gave its name to a chicken, the Rhode Island Red, first bred in 1857.

• There are more engineers and scientists in New Jersey than in any other state.

• The Stock Exchange on Wall Street, New York, is the largest in the world, handling more than 100 million shares a day.

• Silicon Valley, south of San Francisco, has one of the world's largest concentrations of high-technology industry.

• One-third of the world's cherry crop is grown along the shores of Lake Michigan.

• The US's top tourist destinations include Disney World in Florida, with more than 20 million visitors a year.

MEXICO

THIS IS A land of contrasts, with snow-capped mountains, a high central plateau, and tropical rainforests. It is the world's leading producer of silver. The capital, Mexico City, is the largest city in the world. Southern Mexico is often affected by earthquakes.

10 Mexican pesos

Area 756,065sq miles (1,958,200sq km)
Government Federal republic
Independence 1821, from Spain
Currency Mexican peso
Population 88,200,000
Density 119 per sq mile (46 per sq km)
Official Language Spanish
† Major Religions Roman Catholic 94.7%, Protestant 1%, other 4.3%

WEATHER FACTS

117°F (47°C)   25°F (-4°C)
36in (929mm)
73°F (22.8°C)   64°F (17.8°C)

LAND PROFILE

More than one-third of Mexico is desert.

%
0.5
0.5
15.5
20.5
26
37

LIFESTYLE FACTS

• There are more Spanish speakers in Mexico than in any other country.

• Beekeeping is an important activity, especially in the south. Mexico is one of the world's main exporters of natural honey.

• Mexicans eat a variety of spicy foods using chilies. Pancakes, called *tortillas*, are made from corn flour and filled with meat, vegetables, and cheese.

• Many familiar garden plants, such as poinsettias, marigolds, and dahlias, originated in Mexico.

• Mexico has more than 6,000 miles (9,650km) of coastline, and fishing for shrimp is an important industry. Natural bath sponges are harvested off the Gulf of Mexico.

FEAST DAY

Day of the Dead (November 1) is a feast day when food and drink are offered to dead relatives. Bakers sell sweets in the shapes of skulls and coffins.

DESERT FACTS

• The largest of all cacti is the giant saguaro from the Sonoran Desert. It can grow to 60ft (18m) high.

• The tiny elf owl hides from the heat of the day in the cool branches of the saguaro.

Elf owl

LANGUAGE

A traditional greeting in Spanish is *buenos días*.

JAGUAR

The jaguar (*Panthera onca*) lives in the jungles of Central America. Its spotted coat acts as camouflage.

SILVER

Mexico is rich in minerals and supplies one-fifth of the world's silver. Some of the silver is made into jewelry; it is also used as a coating for photographic film.

Silver and turquoise jewelry

ACAPULCO BEACH

Tourism is a vital part of Mexico's economy. The busy resort of Acapulco, on the Pacific Coast, has more than 1,900,000 visitors every year.

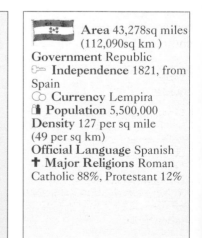

GUATEMALA

HIGH MOUNTAINS AND volcanoes, tropical forests, and lakes cover Guatemala. More than half the population are Mayas.

NATIONAL BIRD

The quetzal (*Pharomachrus mocinno*) is found in Guatemala. The male's long tail feathers help him attract a mate.

Area 42,043sq miles (108,890sq km)
Government Presidential republic
Independence 1821, from Spain
Currency Quetzal
Population 9,700,000
Density 230 per sq mile (89 per sq km)
Official Language Spanish
Major Religions Roman Catholic 65%, Protestant 33%, other 2%

WEAVING

Traditional textiles from Guatemala are made in more than 325 variations of style and color. Every Maya village has its unique style of dress made from handwoven textiles.

EL SALVADOR

A LINE OF volcanoes dominates El Salvador. The layers of volcanic ash and lava make fertile soil for growing coffee.

Area 8,124sq miles (21,040sq km)
Government Presidential republic
Independence 1821, from Spain
Currency Salvadorean colon
Population 5,400,000
Density 676 per sq mile (261 per sq km)
Official Language Spanish
† Major Religions Roman Catholic 82%, Evangelical 18%

HONDURAS

MOST PEOPLE WORK on small farms growing rice, beans, and corn for themselves. Cattle are raised for beef exports.

Area 43,278sq miles (112,090sq km)
Government Republic
Independence 1821, from Spain
Currency Lempira
Population 5,500,000
Density 127 per sq mile (49 per sq km)
Official Language Spanish
† Major Religions Roman Catholic 88%, Protestant 12%

BELIZE

BELIZE IS A land of tropical jungles, mountains, and swamps. The climate is ideal for growing citrus fruits and sugar cane.

PEOPLE OF BELIZE
More than half the population of Belize are Creole. All Creoles are of African descent and speak the English-Creole dialect.

Area 8,865sq miles (22,960sq km)
Government Parliamentary democracy
☞ **Independence** 1981, from Britain
∞ **Currency** Belizean dollar
📊 **Population** 194,000
Density 23 per sq mile (9 per sq km)
Official Language English
✝ **Major Religions** Roman Catholic 62%, Anglican 12%, Methodist 6%, other 20%

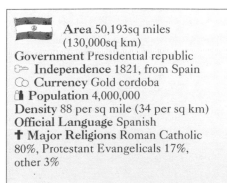

PALENQUE, CITY OF THE MAYA
For many years, Mexico was home to a series of native American peoples. One of the most important groups, the Maya, built the city of Palenque in about 500 A.D.

LAKE NICARAGUA
Lake Nicaragua is the only freshwater lake to contain ocean animals such as the bullshark. The lake was once part of an ocean bay that was cut off by volcanic activity.

ANCIENT SITES IN CENTRAL AMERICA		
Site	Culture	Country
Tula	Toltec	Mexico
Tenochtitlán	Aztec	Mexico
Copán	Maya	Honduras
Tikal	Maya	Guatemala
Cerros	Maya	Belize

CACAO PLANT FACTS
• Central America is a major exporter of cacao, from which cocoa and chocolate are made.
• The cacao tree is a tropical plant. It sprouts long, thin pods, called cherelles, which grow to about 10in (25cm) long.
• Each pod contains 30 to 40 beans. In the 16th century, cacao beans were considered so valuable the Aztecs used them as money.

PANAMA

PANAMA FORMS A land link between the North and South American continents. The Panama Canal cuts through the country, linking the Caribbean Sea with the Pacific Ocean.

Area (29,761sq miles) 77,080sq km
Government Presidential republic
☞ **Independence** 1903, from Colombia
∞ **Currency** Balboa
📊 **Population** 2,500,000
Density 85 per sq mile (33 per sq km)
Official Language Spanish
✝ **Major Religions** Roman Catholic 86.2%, Protestant 6%, Jewish 4%, others 3.8%

PANAMA CANAL FACTS
• The canal opened in 1914 and cut the sailing distance from New York to San Francisco by 8,000 miles (13,000km).
• More than 200 million cubic yards (153 million cubic meters) of rubble were dug up when the 50-mile (80-km) canal was built.

NICARAGUA

THE LARGEST COUNTRY in Central America, Nicaragua has large tropical forests and a swampy Caribbean shore, called the Mosquito Coast.

Area 50,193sq miles (130,000sq km)
Government Presidential republic
☞ **Independence** 1821, from Spain
∞ **Currency** Gold cordoba
📊 **Population** 4,000,000
Density 88 per sq mile (34 per sq km)
Official Language Spanish
✝ **Major Religions** Roman Catholic 80%, Protestant Evangelicals 17%, other 3%

COSTA RICA

ONE-THIRD OF Costa Rica, which means "rich coast," is covered with forests that include mahogany and tropical cedar trees.

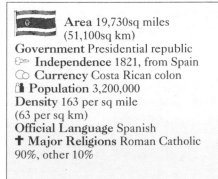

Area 19,730sq miles (51,100sq km)
Government Presidential republic
☞ **Independence** 1821, from Spain
∞ **Currency** Costa Rican colon
📊 **Population** 3,200,000
Density 163 per sq mile (63 per sq km)
Official Language Spanish
✝ **Major Religions** Roman Catholic 90%, other 10%

THE CARIBBEAN

THESE ISLANDS, ALSO known as the West Indies, form a 2,000-mile (3,200-km) chain stretching from the coast of Florida almost to Venezuela. Tourists flock to the beautiful beaches: 1.5 million people each year to the Bahamas alone.

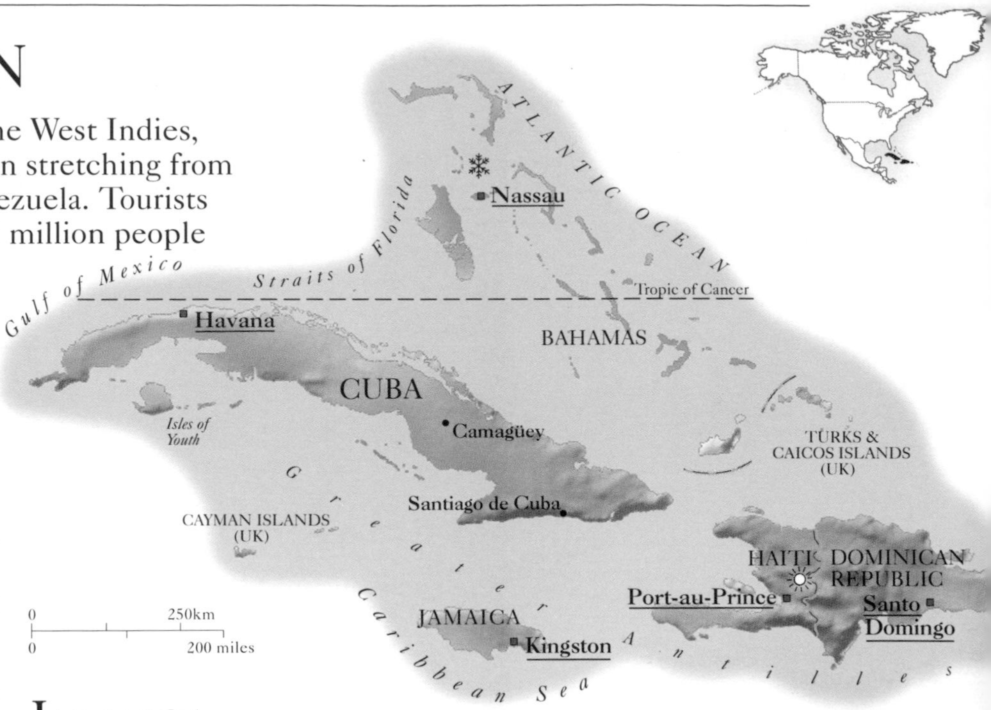

CUBA

CUBA IS THE only communist state in the Western Hemisphere, and Fidel Castro has been its leader since January 1959. World-famous Cuban cigars are a major export.

Area 42,803sq miles (110,860sq km)
Government Communist state
Independence 1898, from Spain. US troops withdrew in 1902
Currency Cuban peso
Population 10,800,000
Density 251 per sq mile (97 per sq km)
Official Language Spanish
Major Religions Roman Catholic 40%, Protestant 1.4%, other 3.5%, nonreligious 55.1%

THE SMALLEST BIRD
Cuba is the home of the world's smallest bird. The bee hummingbird, known in Cuba as the *zunzuncito*, is just 2.4in (6cm) long: roughly the same size as a red admiral butterfly.

Bee Hummingbird

Red Admiral

JAMAICA

JAMAICA, THE HOME of reggae music, is the third largest of the Caribbean islands. Most of its income is derived from mining bauxite, the chief source of aluminum, and the tourist industry.

Area 4,244sq miles (10,991sq km)
Government Parliamentary democracy, member of the British Commonwealth
Independence 1962, from Britain
Currency Jamaican dollar
Population 2,440,000
Density 598 per sq mile (231 per sq km)
Official Language English
Major Religions Protestant 56%, Roman Catholic 5%, other and nonreligious 39%

NATIONAL HERO
Marcus Garvey (1887-1940) is one of Jamaica's national heroes. He founded the Universal Negro Improvement Association in 1914.

MAJOR TOURIST DESTINATIONS
(Figures show visitors per year)

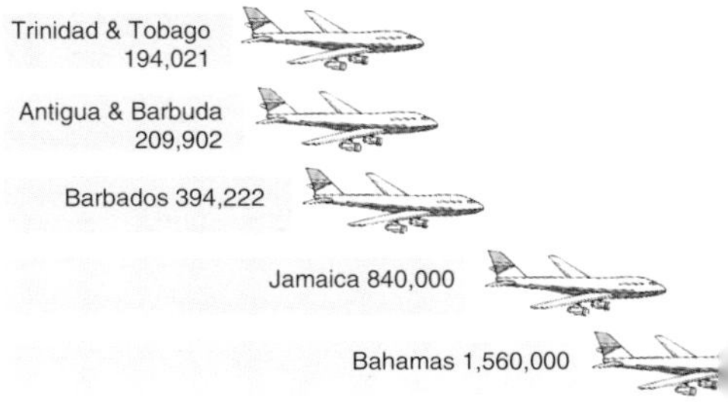

Trinidad & Tobago 194,021

Antigua & Barbuda 209,902

Barbados 394,222

Jamaica 840,000

Bahamas 1,560,000

Map labels: ATLANTIC OCEAN · Gulf of Mexico · Straits of Florida · Tropic of Cancer · Nassau · Havana · BAHAMAS · CUBA · Isles of Youth · Camagüey · Santiago de Cuba · TURKS & CAICOS ISLANDS (UK) · CAYMAN ISLANDS (UK) · Greater · HAITI · DOMINICAN REPUBLIC · Port-au-Prince · Santo Domingo · JAMAICA · Kingston · Antilles · Caribbean Sea · ARUBA (Neth.) · NETHER. ANTI. (Ne... · Les...

Scale: 0 — 250km · 0 — 200 miles

BAHAMAS

THE BAHAMAS are made up of more than 700 islands and cays (small islands). Only about 30 of these are inhabited.

Area 5,359sq miles (13,880sq km)
Independence 1973, from Britain
Currency Bahamian dollar
Population 300,000
Official Language English

HAITI

THE PEOPLE of this mountainous country are French-speaking, and many practice the folk religion called voodoo.

Area 10,714sq miles (27,750sq km)
Independence 1804, from France
Currency Gourde
Population 6,800,000
Official Languages French, Haitian, Creole

DOMINICA

THE IMPERIAL parrot, shown on the Dominican flag, is found only in the dense tropical forests of the northern mountains.

Area 290sq miles (750sq km)
Independence 1978, from Britain
Currency East Caribbean dollar
Population 83,000
Official Language English

ST. LUCIA

THE PITONS, twin volcanic peaks that rise about 2,600ft (800m) above the lush forests, are St. Lucia's best-known landmarks.

Area 239sq miles (620sq km)
Independence 1979, from Britain
Currency East Caribbean dollar
Population 153,000
Official Language English

BEST-KNOWN CARIBBEAN FRUIT

Guava
The guava is a pear-shaped fruit with cream or pink flesh.

Papaya
The flesh of the pawpaw is orange, like an apricot's.

Mango
The juicy mango is green, red, or orange-pink in color.

REGIONAL WEATHER

Records

41°F (5°C)

100.4°F (38°C)

Averages

60in (1,529mm)

80.6°F (27°C)   76°F (24.5°C)

DOMINICAN REPUBLIC

THE DOMINICAN REPUBLIC is called *Quisqueya* in native Arawak Indian. It is the second largest country in the Caribbean.

Area 18,815sq miles (48,730sq km)
Independence 1865, from Spain
Currency Dominican Republic peso
Population 7,500,000
Official Language Spanish

CARIBBEAN MUSIC AND DANCE FACTS

• The biggest and most famous carnival in the Caribbean takes place in Trinidad and Tobago every year. People spend months creating the costumes.

• Calypso music originated in Trinidad, although it is popular throughout the Caribbean. Steel bands are musicians who play calypso and their drums, called pans, are made out of oil drums. The rhythms of calypso music show a strong African influence.

• Reggae music emerged in Jamaica in the 1970s and developed from earlier Jamaican musical styles. Reggae has achieved worldwide popularity through the songs of musicians such as Bob Marley.

• Bob Marley (1945–81) was the most famous Jamaican reggae singer, who had hit records around the world in the 1970s. He believed in world peace and equality among people, and his songs were a powerful means of spreading this message.

ANTIGUA AND BARBUDA

SUGAR WAS once the main export from these islands. Today tourism is more important, and Barbuda is also an animal reserve.

Area 170sq miles (440sq km)
Independence 1981, from Britain
Currency East Caribbean dollar
Population 63,880
Official Language English

BARBADOS

TOURISM IS the leading industry in Barbados, employing almost 40% of the workforce. Sugar is an important export, and a traditional local dish is the famous flying fish.

Area 166sq miles (430sq km)
Independence 1966, from Britain
Currency Barbados dollar
Population 300,000
Official Language English

GRENADA

ON GRENADA, the "spice island," nutmeg, cloves, cinnamon, and saffron grow abundantly. Cacao is also an important export.

Area 131sq miles (340sq km)
Independence 1974, from Britain
Currency East Caribbean dollar
Population 84,000
Official Language English

GREATEST WEST INDIES BATSMEN (1994)		
Cricketer	Tests	Runs
I.V.A. Richards	121	8,540
G.S. Sobers	93	8,032
C.G. Greenidge	108	7,558
C.H. Lloyd	110	7,515
D.L. Haynes	103	7,487

ST. KITTS AND NEVIS

ST. CHRISTOPHER is commonly known as St. Kitts. It is separated from its sister island, Nevis, by a 2-mile-wide (3 km) sea channel.

Area 139sq miles (360sq km)
Independence 1983, from Britain
Currency East Caribbean dollar
Population 44,000
Official Language English

ST. VINCENT AND THE GRENADINES

ST. VINCENT, the largest of the islands of this nation, has black volcanic beaches. The Grenadines group consists of 32 smaller islands.

Area 131sq miles (340sq km)
Independence 1979, from Britain
Currency East Caribbean dollar
Population 117,000
Official Language English

TRINIDAD AND TOBAGO

TRINIDAD, the larger of these two islands, is rich in oil and natural gas. Tobago has fine beaches and an 18-hole championship golf course.

Area 1,981sq miles (5,130sq km)
Independence 1962, from Britain
Currency Trinidad & Tobago dollar
Population 1,300,000
Official Language English

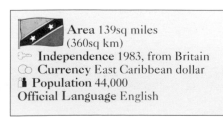

Map labels: Leeward Islands, BRITISH VIRGIN ISLANDS (UK), San Juan, ANGUILLA (UK), VIRGIN ISLANDS (US), ANTIGUA & BARBUDA, ST. KITTS & NEVIS, MONTSERRAT (UK), Caribbean Sea, GUADELOUPE (France), DOMINICA, MARTINIQUE (France), ST. LUCIA, BARBADOS, Windward Islands, ST. VINCENT & THE GRENADINES, GRENADA, Spanish Main, Antilles, TRINIDAD & TOBAGO, Port of Spain, ATLANTIC OCEAN, N

SOUTH AMERICA

THE CONTINENT OF South America is dominated by the Andes, the world's longest mountain chain, passing through seven countries. Brazil is the largest country, occupying almost half the continent.

CLIMATE ZONES
KEY

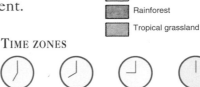

	Polar and tundra
	Mountain region
	Mediterranean
	Dry grassland
	Hot desert
	Rainforest
	Tropical grassland

Area 6,840,388sq miles (17,716,530sq km)
Countries 12
Largest Brazil 3,286,489sq miles (8,511,970sq km)
Smallest Surinam 63,039sq miles (163,270sq km)
Population 304,325,000
Density 44 per sq mile (17 per sq km)
Major Languages Spanish, Portuguese, Quechua, Guarani, Aymara
▲ **Highest point** Mount Aconcagua 22,836ft (6,960m)
▼ **Lowest point** Valdés Peninsula 131ft (40m) below sea level
☀ **Highest temperature** 120°F (49°C) Rivadavia, Argentina
❄ **Lowest temperature** -27°F (-33°C) Sarmiento, Argentina

TIME ZONES

7:00 Lima	8:00 Caracas	9:00 Buenos Aires	12:00 Greenwich

FEWEST DOCTORS

Guyana	1 per 6,200 people
Chile	1 per 2,383 people
Bolivia	1 per 1,540 people
Surinam	1 per 1,300 people

CONTINENT FACTS
• At 13,000ft (4,000m) above sea level, Lake Titicaca is the world's highest lake. It lies across the borders of Peru and Bolivia.
• The continent of South America experiences extremes of weather. In parts of Colombia, more than 460in (11,700mm) of rain falls per year, while the Atacama Desert, Chile, is the world's driest place.
• Both the tomato and the potato originated in South America. Andean farmers grow potatoes at altitudes of more than 6,550ft (2,000m).

COUNTRIES AND CAPITALS

Name	Capital
Argentina	Buenos Aires
Bolivia	La Paz
Brazil	Brasilia
Chile	Santiago
Colombia	Santa Fe de Bogotá
Ecuador	Quito
Guyana	Georgetown
Paraguay	Asunción
Peru	Lima
Surinam	Paramaribo
Uruguay	Montevideo
Venezuela	Caracas

AGE BREAKDOWN

Under 15 years	15 to 65 years	Over 65 years

3.4% Paraguay
11.4% Uruguay
25.8% Uruguay
42.5% Bolivia
54.1% Bolivia
63.6% Chile

KEY
☐ Lowest %
☐ Highest %

LONGEST LIFE SPAN

Female 77 76 75 73 72
Male 70 68 68 67 66
Uruguay Chile Argentina Venezuela Colombia

NATIVE PEOPLE
The homes of the Quechua Indians of Ecuador and Peru are some of the highest settlements in the world. These Andean peoples have adapted physically to the low-oxygen atmosphere.

Quechua children outside their school

TOP CITY POPULATIONS
(Metropolitan Area)

Santiago Chile 4,545,784
Lima Peru 6,404,500
Rio de Janeiro Brazil 9,600,528
Buenos Aires Argentina 12,600,000
São Paulo Brazil 15,199,423

RAINFOREST AREA
The Amazonian rainforest is 12.8 times bigger than France.

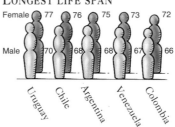

Amazon area 2.7 million sq miles (7 million sq km)

France area 210,669sq miles (545,630sq km)

HIGHEST WATERFALLS

Angel Falls 3,212ft (979m)

Cuquenan 2,000ft (610m)

WORLD'S LONGEST MOUNTAIN RANGES

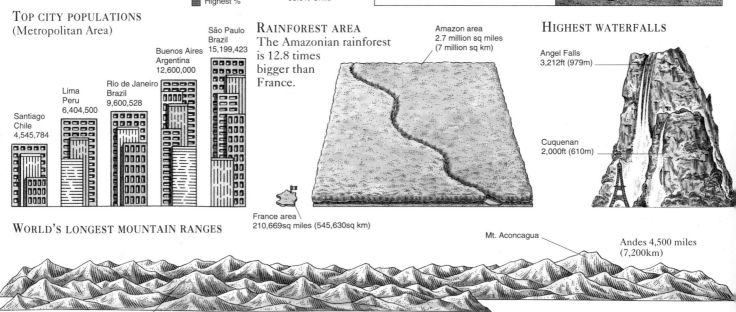

Mt. Aconcagua
Andes 4,500 miles (7,200km)

Mt. McKinley
Rocky Mountains, US 3,600 miles (4,800km)

COFFEE TREE

Coffee is the fruit of the coffee tree, an evergreen that reaches a height of 6–9ft (2–3m). After or while flowering, the branches bear green "cherries" that ripen to red. The cherries split open to reveal two seeds – the coffee beans – which are then washed, dried, and roasted.

TOP COFFEE EXPORTERS (1993)

Country	Bags	Tons
Brazil	18,501,000	1,223,630
Colombia	13,570,000	897,501
Ecuador	1,508,000	99,737
Peru	1,031,0001	68,189

WILDLIFE

Rainforests and mountains are home to a huge variety of animals and plants.

FAUNA

Giant armadillo (*Priodontes maximus*) has the biggest claws of any living animal.

Toco toucan (*Ramphastos toco*) has the largest bill of all the toucans.

Llama (*Lama glama*) is most important for transport in the Andes.

FLORA

Opuntia (*Cactaceae*) bear pear-shaped fruits known as prickly pears.

Puya (*Puya raimondii*) is an herbaceous plant that has 8,000 flowers.

Monkey puzzle (*Araucaria araucana*), the Chile Pine, is native to the Andes.

CROSS-SECTION

Pacific Ocean
Andes
Amazon Basin
Guiana Highlands
Atlantic Ocean

14,764ft (4,500m)
0 Sea level
-19,685ft (6,000m)
Peru–Chile trench

Length: 2,730 miles (4,400km)

LAND PROFILE

Urban 0.5%
Wetlands 1%
Barren land 4%
Desert 4%
Agriculture 5%
Grassland 19%
Forest 66.5%

COLOMBIA

COLOMBIA IS FAMOUS for producing high-quality coffee – its major cash crop. Some of the finest emeralds are mined here and account for 90 percent of world output.

Area 401,050sq miles (1,038,700sq km)
Government Presidential republic
Independence 1819, from Spain
Territories San Andres, Providencia, San Bernado, Islas del Rosario, Isla Fuerte and Gorgona, Gorgonilla, and Malpelo
Currency Colombian peso
Population 33,400,000
Density 83 per sq mile (32 per sq km)
Official Language Spanish
✝ **Major Religions** Roman Catholic 95%, other 5%

WEATHER FACTS

120°F (49°C)   17.4in (444mm)   14°F (-10°C)
73°F (23°C)   42°F (6°C)

10,000 pesos

LAND PROFILE

Almost half of Colombia is covered with dense forest.

%
0.5
1
1
16
33
48.5

LIFESTYLE FACTS

• Many great writers have come from Colombia, including world-famous novelist Gabriel García Márquez (born 1928), who won the Nobel Prize for literature in 1982.

• Colombia is one of the world's biggest exporters of quality coffee.

• Colombians are great music lovers. The *tiple*, a small guitar, is the national instrument.

• Ninety-six percent of Colombians live on less than half the land area. Almost all live in the west of the country.

ORCHID

Colombia's national symbol is the orchid.

THE WALLED CITY

Cartagena, in northern Colombia, became famous in the 16th century. Spanish ships stopped off there to collect South American gold.

ECUADOR

ECUADOR'S NAME COMES from its position on the equator. It is a country of very varied landscape, from low coastal regions to high Andean peaks and dense jungle.

Area 109,480sq miles (283,560sq km)
Government Presidential republic
Independence 1830, from Spain
Currency Sucre
Population 11,100,000
Density 104 per sq mile (40 per sq km)
Official Language Spanish
✝ **Major Religions** Roman Catholic 93%, Protestant and Jewish 7%

LAND PROFILE

More than 90% of Ecuador is forested or used for farming.

%
.5
5
41.5
53

GALAPAGOS ISLANDS

The Galapagos islands lie 603 miles (970km) off the coast of Ecuador. Many of the animals there are not found anywhere else. British scientist Charles Darwin (1809–82) made important discoveries there concerning his theory of natural selection (see p.68).

Galapagos tortoise

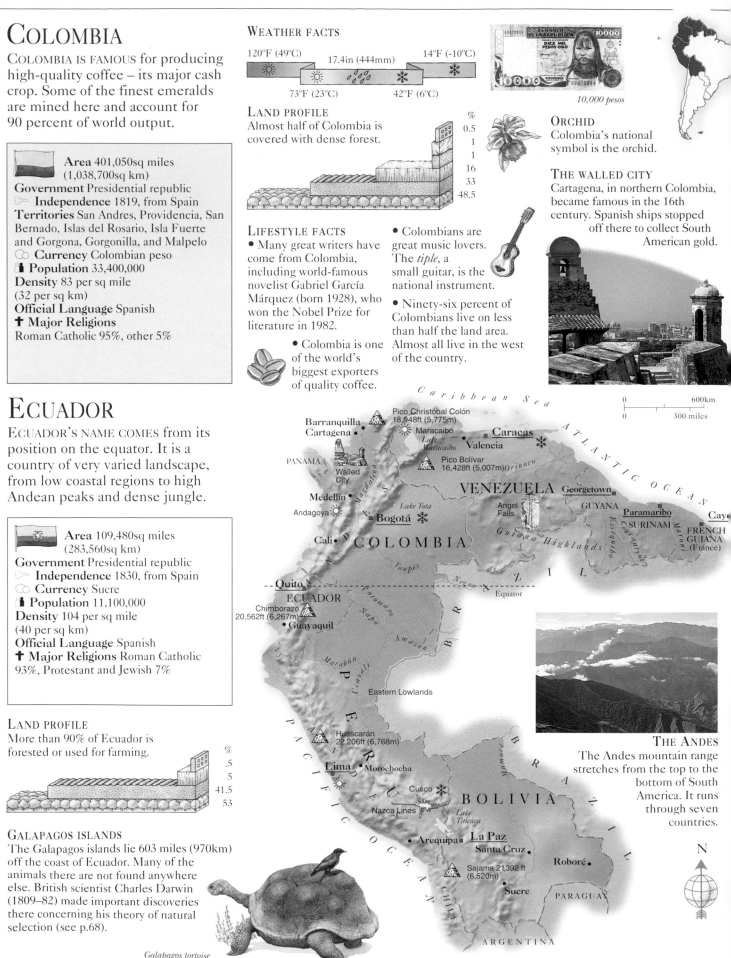

THE ANDES

The Andes mountain range stretches from the top to the bottom of South America. It runs through seven countries.

VENEZUELA

VENEZUELA IS THE world's third greatest oil producer. Oil provides 80 percent of export earnings and has made Venezuela one of the richest countries in South America.

Area 352,140sq miles (912,050sq km)
Government Presidential republic
Independence 1821, from Spain
Currency Bolivar
Population 20,200,000
Density 60 per sq mile (23 per sq km)
Official Language Spanish
Major Religions Roman Catholic 89%, other 11%

PERU

PERU CONTAINS many spectacular ruins. They were built during the time of the Inca empire (see p.389), which was destroyed by Spanish invaders in the 16th century.

Area 496,230sq miles (1,285,220sq km)
Government Presidential republic
Independence 1824, from Spain
Currency Nuevo sol
Population 22,500,000
Density 47 per sq mile (18 per sq km)
Official Languages Spanish and Quechua
Major Religions Roman Catholic 95%, other 5%

WEATHER FACTS

120°F (49°C)   17.4in (444mm)   14°F (-10°C)
73°F (23°C)   42°F (6°C)

LAND PROFILE

More than half of Venezuela is densely forested.

%
1
2
5
34
58

ANGEL FALLS

The Angel Falls, in southeastern Venezuela, is the highest waterfall in the world, with a drop of 3,212ft (979m) The falls are named after American pilot Jimmy Angel (died 1956), who found them in 1935.

WEATHER FACTS

120°F (49°C)   17.4in (444mm)   14°F (-10°C)
73°F (23°C)   42°F (6°C)

NAZCA LINES

Huge animal figures and strange shapes were cut into the ground in southern Peru thousands of years ago. The whole design can be seen only from the air.

Nazca hummingbird figure

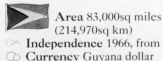

Andean condor

ANDEAN CONDOR

The Andean condor is the heaviest bird of prey in the world, with a wingspan of more than 10ft (3m). It lives in the highest parts of the Andes mountains and feeds on dead animals.

BOLIVIA

BOLIVIA IS A mountainous country with no coastline. Farmers make up half of its population; many of them are very poor, and grow just enough food for their families to live on.

Area 424,160sq miles (1,098,580sq km)
Government Presidential republic
Independence 1825, from Spain
Currency Boliviano
Population 7,500,000
Density 18 per sq mile (7 per sq km)
Official Languages Aymara, Quechua, and Spanish
Major Religions Roman Catholic 93%, other 7%

LAND PROFILE

Two-thirds of Peru is jungle.

%
0.5
7
13
13
66.5

HIGHEST TRACK

The highest section of railroad track in the world, in Peru, lies at an altitude of 15,688ft (4,782m). The track passes through a tunnel on the Morochocha branch of Peruvian State Railways.

Highest railroad in the world

GUYANA

A FERTILE COASTAL strip of land just 10 miles (16km) wide is where 90 percent of the population lives. Much of the rest of Guyana is covered with dense rainforest.

Area 83,000sq miles (214,970sq km)
Independence 1966, from Britian
Currency Guyana dollar
Population 800,000
Official Language English

SURINAM

SURINAM'S CLIMATE is humid and tropical. Its rich wildlife includes jaguars, pumas, and ocelots, plus a variety of reptiles such as iguanas, rattlesnakes, and boa constrictors.

Area 63,040sq miles (163,270sq km)
Independence 1975, from Netherlands
Currency Surinam guilder
Population 425,000
Official Language Dutch

FRENCH GUIANA

FRENCH GUIANA IS the only European colony in South America. It is a part of France, and sends two members to the French National Assembly (parliament).

Area 34,750sq miles (90,000sq km)
Currency French franc
Population 118,000
Official Language French

ARGENTINA

CENTRAL ARGENTINA is covered with lush grasslands called the *pampas*, where crops are grown and cattle and sheep are reared. This area produces three-quarters of Argentina's income.

Area 1,056,641sq miles (2,736,690sq km)
Government Federal republic
⚷ **Independence** 1816, from Spain
⚭ **Currency** Argentinian peso
🛉 **Population** 32,370,298
Density 30 per sq mile (11.6 per sq km)
Official Language Spanish
✝ **Major Religions** Roman Catholic 90%, Protestant 2%, others 8%

WEATHER FACTS

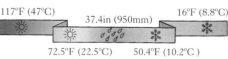

117°F (47°C)   37.4in (950mm)   16°F (8.8°C)
72.5°F (22.5°C)   50.4°F (10.2°C)

LIFESTYLE FACTS

• Soccer is the national sport. Argentina hosted and won the World Cup in 1978, then won again in Mexico City in 1986.

• The Argentinian daily drink is a tea called *maté*. It is made from a tree used since ancient times by native South Americans.

• *Gauchos*, cowboys who work on the huge Argentinian cattle ranches, are folklore heroes. They also created dances which feature fast, complex footwork.

PATAGONIA

The region of Patagonia in southern Argentina is home to unique wildlife such as the pudu, the smallest known deer.

Pudu

THE CEIBO FLOWER

The ceibo is Argentina's national flower.

PALACIO DEL CONGRESO

The Argentinian government meets in the magnificent *Palacio del Congreso* (Congress building) in the *centro* (city center) area of the capital, Buenos Aires.

WELSH TEAS

Welsh immigrants settled in Patagonia more than 100 years ago. Their descendants still follow Welsh traditions, such as eating porridge for breakfast, drinking tea, and singing Welsh songs.

CHILE

CHILE RETURNED to being a democracy in 1989: elections were held for the first time in nearly 20 years.

Area 292,260sq miles (756,950sq km)
Government Republic
⚷ **Independence** 1818, from Spain
⚭ **Currency** Chilean peso
🛉 **Population** 13,200,000
Density 45.1 per sq mile (17.4 per sq km)
Official Language Spanish
✝ **Major Religions** Roman Catholic 80%, others 20%

WEATHER FACTS

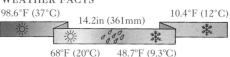

98.6°F (37°C)   14.2in (361mm)   10.4°F (12°C)
68°F (20°C)   48.7°F (9.3°C)

LIFESTYLE FACTS

• Soccer is the sport with the largest following in Chile. Skiing is popular in winter; the world speed ski record of 106mph (171km/h) was set there.

• More copper is produced in Chile than any other country in the world.

• Chileans are very well educated: 94% of the population can read and write.

• Chile is famous for its fine wines. Chilean grapes are also used to make *pisco*, a brandy.

PARAGUAY

NINETY PERCENT of Paraguayans are *Mestizo* – a mixture of native Guarani Indian and Spanish blood. Half of the working population is employed in agriculture.

Area 157,047sq miles (406,750sq km)
⚷ **Independence** 1811, from Spain
⚭ **Currency** Guarani
🛉 **Population** 4,300,000
Official Language Spanish

URUGUAY

ALMOST HALF of Uruguay's population lives in the capital city, Montevideo. Much of the city's electricity is provided by hydroelectric dams.

Area 68,498sq miles (177,410sq km)
⚷ **Independence** 1825, from Spain
⚭ **Currency** Uruguayan peso
🛉 **Population** 3,100,000
Official Language Spanish

Map labels: PERU, BOLIVIA, PARAGUAY, BRAZIL, Atacama Desert, Gran Chaco, Asunción, Lake Ypoá, San Miguel de Tucumán, Ojos del Salado 22,573ft (6,880m), Santiago del Estero, Córdoba, Salado, Paraná, Uruguay, Aconcagua 22,836ft (6,960m), Rosario, Mendoza, Negro, Lake Mirim, URUGUAY, Santiago, Buenos Aires, La Plata, Montevideo, Plate, Victorica, Concepción, Colorado, Congress Hall, Pampa, Chiloé Island, ARGENTINA, ANDES, Lake General Carrera, Baker, PACIFIC OCEAN, ATLANTIC OCEAN, Patagonia, Lake Argentino, Punta Arenas, Tierra del Fuego, Cape Horn, CHILE

N

0   500km
0   300 miles

BRAZIL

BRAZIL OCCUPIES NEARLY half the continent of South America and is the fifth largest country in the world. The country supplies 85 percent of the world's orange juice and is the largest producer of coffee. Around 70 percent of the population is under 30 years of age.

Area 3,286,489sq miles (8,511,970sq km)
Government Federal Republic
Independence 1822, from Portugal
Currency Real, formerly cruzeiro
Population 153,164,000
Density 47 per sq mile (18 per sq km)
Official Language Portuguese
Major Religions Roman Catholic 89%, Protestant 6%, Afro-American Spiritist 2%, other 3%

WEATHER FACTS

105.8°F (41°C)   63.1 in (1,603mm)   24.8°F (-4°C)
72°F (22.3°C)   68°F (19.8°C)

LAND PROFILE

Tropical rainforests cover almost 60% of Brazil.

%
0.3
0.5
10
29.7
59.5

LIFESTYLE FACTS

• More than 1.5 million of Rio de Janeiro's 5 million plus population live in shanty towns known as *favelas*.

• Soccer is Brazil's favorite sport, and the country has more than 20,000 soccer teams. The brilliant Brazilian player, Pele, is known throughout the world.

• Brasilia, the capital city since 1960, was built on the Central Plains to help develop inland areas of Brazil. The modern cathedral is the city's main landmark.

1,000 cruzeiros

LANGUAGE

A traditional greeting in Portuguese is *bom dia*.

BRAZILIAN COFFEE EXPORTS (1992/93)

Destination	No. of 132lb (60kg) bags
US	3,744,946
Italy	1,944,648
Germany	1,451,188
Japan	1,415,307
Belgium/Luxembourg	680,349

AMAZON RAINFOREST FACTS

• The Amazon Basin lies across the equator. This hot, wet, region contains the world's largest tropical rainforest, which is 12 times the size of France.

• The Amazon River and its tributaries make up 20% of the world's supply of freshwater. This powerful river delivers an average of 204 billion gallons (773 billion liters) of water an hour into the Atlantic Ocean.

MAJOR RAINFOREST PEOPLES

Name of tribe and territory	Estimated population
Tikuna	25,000
Yanomani	7,500
Guajajara	7,000
Xavante	5,000
Sateré Maué	4,700

The Yanomani live in vine- and leaf-thatched homes in the forests of northern Brazil and southern Venezuela.

CHRIST THE REDEEMER

The statue of Christ the Redeemer overlooks Rio de Janeiro from Mount Corcovado. It was designed by French sculptor Paul Landowsky, and was completed in 1931.

RIO CARNIVAL

The carnival in Rio de Janeiro is the biggest in the world and takes place every year before Lent. The highlight of the carnival is the parade of the Samba schools.

RAINFOREST WILDLIFE FACTS

• The rainforest is home to 250 varieties of mammals, 1,800 species of birds, and more than 10,000 species of trees.

• Hummingbirds beat their wings 55 times per second – 200 times per second during courtship flights. They can also hover in one place, or even fly backward.

• The two-toed sloth is the world's slowest animal. It takes 6.5 hours to cover just 1 mile (1.6km). The sloth also spends 21.5 hours asleep each day.

• The anaconda is the world's heaviest snake, and can weigh up to 507 lb (230 kg).

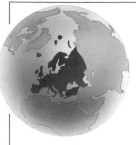

EUROPE

EUROPE IS THE second smallest continent and has a varied landscape and climate. Southern Europe is mostly hilly or mountainous and generally warm and dry. The north is wetter and cooler, with flat plains and thick forests. Europe includes the western third of the Russian Federation.

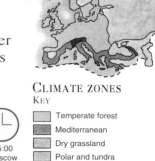

Area 9,246,339sq miles (23,947,919sq km)
Countries 48
Largest Russian Federation 6,592,846sq miles (17,075,400sq km): European Russia 1,527,349sq miles (3,955,818sq km)
Smallest Vatican City 0.17sq miles (0.44sq km)
🏛 **Population** 747,041,279
Density 80 per sq mile (31 per sq km)

Major Languages Russian, German, Turkish, Italian, English
▲ **Highest point** Mount El'brus, Russian Federation 18,510 ft (5,642m)
☑ **Lowest point** Caspian Sea 92ft (28m) below sea level
☀ **Highest temperature** 122°F (50°C), Seville, Spain
❄ **Lowest temperature** -67°F (-55°C), Ust 'Shchugor, Russian Federation

TIME ZONES

12:00 Greenwich   13:00 Berlin   14:00 Athens   15:00 Moscow

CLIMATE ZONES
KEY

- Temperate forest
- Mediterranean
- Dry grassland
- Polar and tundra
- Taiga
- Mountain regions

LONGEST RIVERS

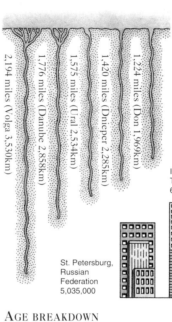

2,194 miles (Volga 3,530km)
1,776 miles (Danube 2,858km)
1,575 miles (Ural 2,534km)
1,420 miles (Dnieper 2,285km)
1,224 miles (Don 1,969km)

MOST POPULAR CITIES

The cities of Europe are popular with tourists from all over the world. The most visited cities in 1993 were, in order, London, Paris, Rome, Vienna, and Madrid.

TOP CITY POPULATIONS

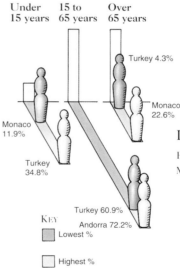

St. Petersburg, Russian Federation 5,035,000
Istanbul, Turkey 6,407,000
London, UK 6,803,100
Paris, France 8,252,877
Moscow, Russian Federation 9,000,000

COUNTRIES, TERRITORIES, AND CAPITALS

Name	Capital	Name	Capital
Albania	Tirana	Liechtenstein	Vaduz
Andorra	Andorra la Vella	Lithuania	Vilnius
Armenia	Yerevan	Luxembourg	Luxembourg
Austria	Vienna	Macedonia	Skopje
Azerbaijan	Baku	Malta	Valetta
Belgium	Brussels	Moldova	Kishinev or Chisinau
Belarus	Minsk	Monaco	Monaco
Bosnia & Herzegovina	Sarajevo	Netherlands	Amsterdam
Bulgaria	Sofia	Norway	Oslo
Croatia	Zagreb	Poland	Warsaw
Cyprus	Nicosia	Portugal	Lisbon
Czech Republic	Prague	Romania	Bucharest
Denmark	Copenhagen	Russian Federation	Moscow
Estonia	Tallinn	San Marino	San Marino
Finland	Helsinki	Slovakia	Bratislava
France	Paris	Slovenia	Ljubljana
Georgia	Tbilisi	Spain	Madrid
Germany	Berlin	Sweden	Stockholm
Greece	Athens	Switzerland	Berne
Hungary	Budapest	Turkey	Ankara
Iceland	Reykjavik	Ukraine	Kiev
Ireland, Republic of	Dublin	United Kingdom	London
Italy	Rome	Vatican City	Vatican City
Latvia	Riga	Yugoslavia	Belgrade

AGE BREAKDOWN

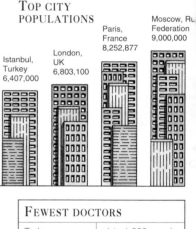

Under 15 years   15 to 65 years   Over 65 years

Monaco 11.9%
Turkey 34.8%
Turkey 60.9%
Andorra 72.2%
Turkey 4.3%
Monaco 22.6%

KEY
- Lowest %
- Highest %

FEWEST DOCTORS

Turkey	1 to 1,260 people
Liechtenstein	1 to 948 people
Malta	1 to 900 people
United Kingdom	1 to 879 people
Ireland	1 to 700 people

LONGEST LIFE SPAN

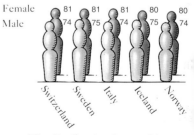

Female / Male

Switzerland 81/74   Sweden 81/75   Italy 81/74   Iceland 80/75   Norway 80/74

CONTINENT FACTS

- Most of the world's amber is found along the Baltic coast of Lithuania. Amber, the fossilized sap of ancient trees, is a precious stone. It is used in the treatment of arthritis.

- The French are the world's greatest snail eaters. They eat about 27,558 tons each year. Snails, *Helix pomatia* and *Helix aspersa*, are gathered from the wild.

- Germany is Europe's leading producer of chemicals; these are used in industry to make paint, cosmetics, and medicines.

- The Vatican City is the only place in the world where Latin is the official language.

- The St. Gotthard tunnel in Switzerland is the world's longest road tunnel. It is 10.1 miles (16.3km) long.

- The largest cotton mill in Europe is in Estonia. Cotton is grown in the Baltic States.

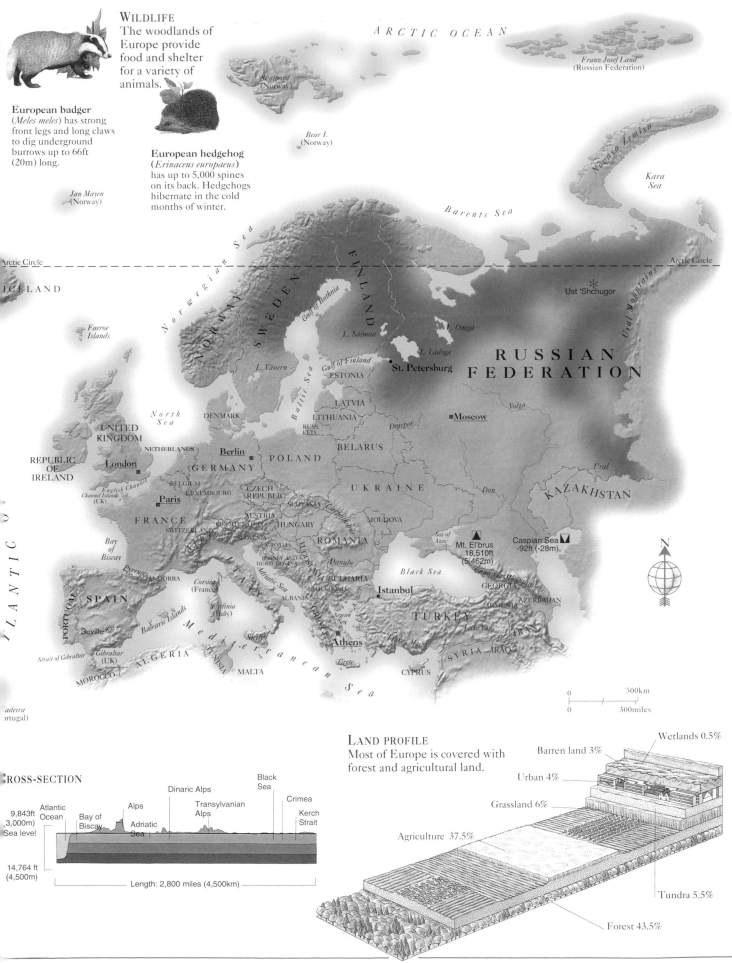

ARCTIC OCEAN

Franz Josef Land
(Russian Federation)

WILDLIFE
The woodlands of
Europe provide
food and shelter
for a variety of
animals.

European badger
(*Meles meles*) has strong
front legs and long claws
to dig underground
burrows up to 66ft
(20m) long.

European hedgehog
(*Erinaceus europaeus*)
has up to 5,000 spines
on its back. Hedgehogs
hibernate in the cold
months of winter.

Svalbard
(Norway)

Bear I.
(Norway)

Jan Mayen
(Norway)

Novaya Zemlya

Kara Sea

Barents Sea

Arctic Circle — Arctic Circle

ICELAND

Faeroe Islands

Norwegian Sea

NORWAY

SWEDEN

FINLAND

Gulf of Bothnia

L. Saimoa

L. Onega

Ust 'Shchugor

Ural Mountains

L. Ladoga

**RUSSIAN
FEDERATION**

North Sea

UNITED
KINGDOM

London

REPUBLIC
OF
IRELAND

English Channel

Channel Islands
(UK)

DENMARK

NETHERLANDS

BELGIUM
LUXEMBOURG

Berlin

GERMANY

POLAND

Baltic Sea

Gulf of Finland

St. Petersburg

ESTONIA

LATVIA

LITHUANIA

RUSS.
FED.

BELARUS

Dnieper

Moscow

Volga

CZECH
REPUBLIC

Paris

FRANCE

SWITZERLAND

LIECHTENSTEIN

AUSTRIA

SLOVAKIA

HUNGARY

SLOVENIA
CROATIA

UKRAINE

Don

Ural

KAZAKHSTAN

MOLDOVA

ROMANIA

Carpathians

Sea of Azov

Mt. El'brus
18,510ft
(5,462m)

Caucasus Mountains

Caspian Sea
-92ft (-28m)

N

Bay of Biscay

Pyrenees

ANDORRA

Corsica
(France)

BOSNIA AND
HERZEGOVINA

Adriatic Sea

Danube

BULGARIA

Black Sea

GEORGIA

ARMENIA
AZERBAIJAN

SPAIN

PORTUGAL

Seville

Balearic Islands

Sardinia
(Italy)

ITALY

MACEDONIA

ALBANIA

GREECE

Aegean Sea

Istanbul

TURKEY

Lake Van

IRAN

Gibraltar
(UK)

Strait of Gibraltar

MOROCCO

ALGERIA

TUNISIA

Sicily

MALTA

Mediterranean Sea

Athens

Crete

Ionian Sea

CYPRUS

SYRIA
IRAQ

ATLANTIC OCEAN

Madeira
(Portugal)

0 — 500km
0 — 300miles

CROSS-SECTION

9,843ft
(3,000m)
Sea level

Atlantic
Ocean

Bay of
Biscay

Alps

Adriatic
Sea

Dinaric Alps

Transylvanian
Alps

Black
Sea

Crimea

Kerch
Strait

14,764 ft
(4,500m)

Length: 2,800 miles (4,500km)

LAND PROFILE
Most of Europe is covered with
forest and agricultural land.

Wetlands 0.5%

Barren land 3%

Urban 4%

Grassland 6%

Agriculture 37.5%

Tundra 5.5%

Forest 43.5%

ICELAND

ICELAND, EUROPE'S second largest island, has the lowest population density in Europe. The remote interior can be reached only by special vehicle, pony, or small plane.

Area 39,769sq miles (103,000sq km)
Government Presidential republic
Independence 1944, from British and US control during World War II
Currency Icelandic króna
Population 300,000
Density 8 per sq mile (3 per sq km)
Official Language Icelandic
Major Religions Evangelical Lutheran Church of Iceland 96%, other Protestant and Roman Catholic 3%, nonreligious 1%

WEATHER FACTS
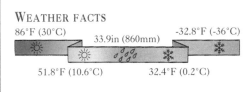
86°F (30°C)   -32.8°F (-36°C)
33.9in (860mm)
51.8°F (10.6°C)   32.4°F (0.2°C)

LAND PROFILE

%
0.5
24
75.5

LIFESTYLE FACTS
• The Althing, the Icelandic parliament, has been in existence since the 13th century and is one of the oldest surviving assemblies in the world.

• Iceland has the most solfataras (volcanic vents) and hot springs in the world. Many of its towns are heated by underground hot water.

• Iceland produces more than a third of the world's cod-liver oil, and is the biggest consumer of it.

HOT SPRINGS

Deildartunguhver hot springs blow out 66 gallons (250 liters) of hot water every second. Over a 24-hour period, they produce enough water to fill 105,600 baths.

100 krónur

LANGUAGE
A traditional greeting in Icelandic is *godan daginn*.

Arctic Circle
Siglufjördur
Akureyri
ICELAND
Vatnajökull
Teiga
Deildartunguhver
Reykjavik   Thingvallavatn
Hafnarfjördhur   Kópavogur   Hvannadalshnúkur
6,954ft (2,119m)

N

0   500km
0   300 miles

DENMARK

DENMARK, WHICH IS divided into numerous islands, has a 4,500-mile (7,300km) coastline. It is the only Scandinavian country belonging to the European Community (EC).

Area 16,629sq miles (43,070sq km)
Government Constitutional monarchy
State founded c. 950
Territories Faeroe Islands, Greenland
Currency Danish krone
Population 5,200,000
Density 319 per sq mile (123 per sq km)
Official Language Danish
Major Religions Evangelical Lutheran Church 91%, Roman Catholic 2%, other and nonreligious 7%

WEATHER FACTS

95°F (35°C)   -11.2°F (-24°C)
27.7in (704mm)
61.3°F (16.3°C)   34.3°F (1.3°C)

LAND PROFILE
Almost two-thirds of the land is farmed.
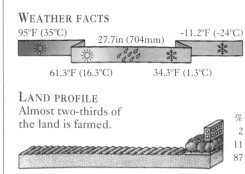
%
2
11
87

100 kroner

LANGUAGE
A traditional greeting in Danish is *goddag*.

LIFESTYLE FACTS
• Lego was created by a Danish carpenter in the 1930s. Legoland Park is a miniature, working village created from 35 million plastic bricks.

• Denmark has one of the lowest private ownerships of cars in Europe. Cyclists are encouraged with special lanes, and Copenhagen was the first city to create a pedestrian street.

• Denmark has over twice as many pigs as humans, and Danish bacon is a successful export product. Danish farmers produce three times more food than is needed to feed the population.

LITTLE MERMAID
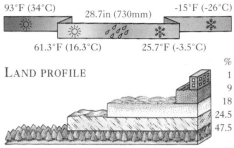
Situated by Copenhagen harbor, this statue of the mermaid from Hans C. Andersen's fairy tale was sculpted in 1913 by Edvard Eriksen (1876–1959). In 1964, her head was sawed off but was soon replaced.

NORWAY

NORWAY MEANS "the way to the north." It is a land of beautiful fjords (valleys flooded by rising sea levels): the longest is Sogne Fjord, at 126 miles (203 kilometers).

Area 125,058sq miles (323,900sq km)
Government Constitutional monarchy
Independence from Sweden, 1905
Territories Svalbard archipelago, Jan Mayen Island
Currency Norwegian krone
Population 4,000,000
Density 36 per sq mile (14 per sq km)
Official Language Nynorsk (new Norwegian) and Bokmaal (older)
Major Religions Evangelical Lutheran and other Protestant 87.9%, Roman Catholic 0.8%, other 11.3%

WEATHER FACTS
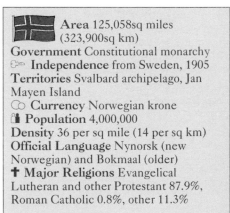
93°F (34°C)   -15°F (-26°C)
28.7in (730mm)
61.3°F (16.3°C)   25.7°F (-3.5°C)

LAND PROFILE

%
1
9
18
24.5
47.5

SWEDEN

TWO-THIRDS OF the land in Sweden is covered by forests, and there are 100,000 lakes. Timber products, including paper, account for nearly one-fifth of all Swedish exports.

100 kronor

Area 173,730sq miles (449,960sq km)
Government Constitutional monarchy
State established 1523
Currency Swedish krona
Population 8,700,000
Density 54 per sq mile (21 per sq km)
Official Language Swedish
✝ Major Religions Evangelical Lutheran Church of Sweden 89%, other Protestant 8%, Roman Catholic 1.7%, other 1.3%

NOBEL PRIZES
Alfred B. Nobel (1833–96) was a Swedish scientist and inventor of dynamite. He created a fund for the Nobel prizes, awarded each year for sciences, literature, and peace, to those who have given the greatest benefit to humankind.

100 kroner

LANGUAGE
A traditional greeting in Norwegian is *go dag*.

HOLMENKOLLEN
The ski jump at Holmenkollen, outside Oslo, is the oldest in existence. The first ski-jump competition was held in 1892, and the event continues to be held every March.

LIFESTYLE
• In Hammerfest, the world's northernmost town, the sun shines at midnight for just over two months in the summer

• Norway's annual contribution of its national income (1.17%) toward foreign aid is the highest proportion in the world.

• Norwegians read more newspapers than anyone else in the world, and buy more English books than any other non-English-speaking country.

LANGUAGE
A traditional greeting in Swedish is *goddag*.

LAND PROFILE
The land is mainly forested or used for farming.

%
2.5
4.5
5.5
12.5
75

LIFESTYLE FACTS
• Each year 12,000 cross-country skiers take part in a race from Salen to Mora in central Sweden. The course is 56 miles (90km) long.

• In 1910, Sweden was the first European country to establish national parks. Animals that can be found in the parks include lynx, bear, and moose.

• Stockholm's waterways are so pure that people can safely swim and fish in them.

WEATHER FACTS
95°F (35°C)   24.5in (622mm)   -36.4°F (-38°C)
61.7°F (16.5°C)   28.4°F (-2°C)

CITY HALL
Stockholm's fine City Hall, called the Stadshus, was built between 1911 and 1923. Its Golden Hall has 19 million gilded tiles.

THE SAMI
The Sami (Lapps) have inhabited the arctic regions of Norway and Sweden since ancient times. Today, there are about 60,000 and 70% speak the Sami language. About 70,000 reindeer live in Sami territories, and the main occupation of the people is reindeer breeding. The woven clothes worn by the Sami are practical and beautiful.

• More than 50% of Norwegian families have a weekend home in the mountains or by the sea. These second homes are made of wood, and some have grass-covered roofs.

HIGHEST WATERFALLS

Name	Height	
	m	ft
Utigord	800	2,625
Mongefossen	774	2,540
Ostre Mardola Foss	657	2,154
Tyssetrengane	646	2,120
Kjellfossen	561	1,841

UNITED KINGDOM

THE UNITED KINGDOM, also known as Britain, is made up of England, Wales, Scotland, and Northern Ireland. London, the capital, has a population of almost 7 million, and is the political and financial center.

Area 94,549sq miles (244,880sq km)
Government Constitutional monarchy
Unification 1707, between England/Wales and Scotland; 1801, between Britain and Ireland.
Territories Anguilla, Bermuda, British Antarctic Territory, British India Ocean Territory, British Virgin Islands, Cayman Islands, Falkland Islands, Gibraltar, Hong Kong, Montserrat, Pitcairn Islands, St. Helena and dependencies, South Georgia and the South Sandwich Islands, Turks and Caicos Islands
Currency Pound sterling
Population 55,487,000
Density 616 per sq mile (238 per sq km)
Official Language English
Major Religions Protestant 52.1%, Roman Catholic 9.2%, Muslim 2.6%, Sikh 0.9%, Jewish 0.7%, Hindu 0.5%, other 34%

WEATHER FACTS

93°F (34°C)   23in (593mm)   43.7°F (6.5°C)
58.3°F (14.6°C)   1.4°F (-17°C)

LAND PROFILE

Almost three-quarters of the land is farmed.

%
4
11
14
71

LIFESTYLE FACTS

• There are more than 25,000 different names for the public houses (pubs) where people in Britain meet to talk and drink. The most popular name is *The Red Lion*.

• The Eisteddfod is a Welsh arts festival held every August. The festival dates back to 1176 when competitions were held for poet-musicians. The winner was awarded a "chair," or position, in the royal court.

HOUSES OF PARLIAMENT

This palace is the headquarters of the British Government. Its famous clock tower has a huge bell called Big Ben.

LANGUAGE

A national greeting in English is hello.

0   150km
0   100 miles

SCOTTISH TARTAN

Members of a Scottish clan have their own tartan. This cloth, often worn as a kilt, is woven with a crisscross pattern. There are more than 2,000 varieties of tartan.

Shetland Is.

Orkney Is.

Outer Hebrides
Lewis
North Uist
Skye
South Uist
Murray Firth
North West Highlands
Ben Nevis 4,406ft (1,343m)
SCOTLAND
Glasgow   Edinburgh
Islay
Southern Uplands
Newcastle upon Tyne
NORTHERN IRELAND
Donegal Bay
Belfast
Lough Neagh
UNITED KINGDOM
North Sea
REPUBLIC OF IRELAND
Isle of Man
Irish Sea
Mullingar
Galway
Trinity College
Dublin
Dun Laoghaire
Liverpool   Manchester
Anglesey
Shannon
The Wash
Limerick
Wicklow Mts.
Cardigan Bay
Cambrian Mts.
Birmingham
Carantuohill 3,416ft (1,041m)
Waterford
St. George's Channel
Severn
ENGLAND
Cork
WALES
Brecon Beacons
Thames
N
Cardiff
London
Bristol Channel
Houses of Parliament
Stonehenge
Strait of Dover
Plymouth
Isle of Wight
Isles of Scilly
English Channel
Guernsey
Channel Islands   *Jersey (U.K.)*
ATLANTIC OCEAN

10 pounds sterling

SYMBOLS

England, rose; Wales, leek; Scotland, thistle; and Ireland, shamrock.

STONEHENGE

This prehistoric stone circle in southern England was completed in about 1600 B.C.

REPUBLIC OF IRELAND

IRELAND IS A mainly rural country with a wet and mild climate and rich grass for dairy farming. Tourists come to fish in the rivers and lakes.

Area 27,135sq miles (70,280sq km)
Government Parliamentary republic
Independence 1921 Irish Free State granted to 26 counties in southern Ireland.
Currency Punt
Population 3,523,401
Density 132 per sq mile (51 per sq km)
Official Language Irish
Major Religions Roman Catholic 93%, Anglican 3%, other 4%

1 Irish punt

WEATHER FACTS

86°F (30°C)   30in (762mm)   10°F (-12°C)
54.7°F (12.6°C)   43.5°F (6.4°C)

LAND PROFILE

Almost all of Ireland is farmland.

%
0.5
1
3.5
14.5
80.5

BOOK OF KELLS

This page is from the *Book of Kells*, the four gospels set down by an 8th-century Irish monk. It is displayed in the Trinity College Library, Dublin, where a page is turned each day.

SPAIN

SPAIN IS THE SECOND largest country in Europe, and one of the most mountainous. Madrid, the capital, is Europe's highest city. Spain's warm climate and fine beaches attract 50 million visitors a year.

Area 192,874sq miles (499,542sq km)
Government Constitutional monarchy
Independence 1469 Reunification of Spain against Moorish invaders
Territories Canary Islands, Balearic Islands, Ceuta, Mellila, Islas Chafarinas; Peñón de Vélez de la Gomera; Peñón de Alhucemas
Currency Peseta
Population 39,100,000
Density 202 per sq mile (78 per sq km)
Official Language Castilian Spanish
✝ **Major Religions** Roman Catholic 96%, other 4%

ALHAMBRA PALACE
This beautiful palace of the Moorish (Muslim) rulers of 14th-century Spain sits high above the city of Granada. Also a fortress with huge towers, Alhambra means "red castle."

PORTUGAL

IN THE 15TH CENTURY Portugal was a great seafaring nation with many famous explorers. Today, Portuguese is the seventh most spoken language in the world.

LANGUAGE
A traditional greeting in Portuguese is *bom dia*.

Area 35,502sq miles (91,949sq km)
Government Parliamentary republic
Independence 1910, Republic declared
Territories Azores, Madeiras, Macao
Currency Escudo
Population 9,900,000
Density 280 per sq mile (108 per sq km)
Official Language Portuguese
✝ **Major Religions** Roman Catholic 97%, Protestant 1%, other 2%.

WEATHER FACTS
120°F (49°C) 17.5in (444mm) -4°F (-20°C)
66.7°F (19.3°C) 47.3°F (8.5°C)

LAND PROFILE
Almost half of Spain's land is farmed.

%
0.5
0.5
1
20
28.5
49.5

LIFESTYLE FACTS
• Spain is the world's third largest wine producer. Famous Spanish wines include sherry, first produced in the town of Jerez.

• During the "running of the bulls" in Pamplona, men test their courage by running in front of a herd of bulls.

WEATHER FACTS
120°F (49°C) 27.9in (708mm) 10°F (-12°C)
70.7°F (21.5°C) 52.7°F (11.5°C)

LAND PROFILE
Two-thirds of Portugal is farmland and forest.

%
1
15
39
45

CORK FACTS
• Cork is made from the bark of the cork oak tree.

• Portugal supplies more than half the world's cork.

• The main product made from cork is the bottle stopper.

LANGUAGE
A traditional greeting in Castilian Spanish is *buenos días*.

FLOWER
The red carnation is the Spanish national flower.

AMAZING OLIVES
Spain is the world's top producer of olives and olive products. In one year, enough olives are grown to supply every person in the world with 70 each.

The cockerel is Portugal's national symbol.

ANDORRA

ANDORRA IS TUCKED away in the high valleys of the Pyrenees and its perpetual snow attracts many skiers. It is the fourth smallest independent state in Europe.

Area 181sq miles (468sq km)
Government Co-principality (France and Spain)
Independence 1278, established as a state
Currencies French Franc and Spanish Peseta
Population 58,000
Density 324 per sq mile (125 per sq km)
Official language Catalan

NETHERLANDS

THE DUTCH PEOPLE made their fortunes from the sea in the 17th century with a worldwide trading network. Today, Rotterdam is the world's largest and busiest port.

Area 14,413sq miles (37,330sq km)
Government Constitutional monarchy
Kingdom established 1830
Territories Aruba, Netherlands Antilles
Currency Guilder
Population 15,200,000
Density 1,160 per sq mile (448 per sq km)
Official Language Dutch
Major Religions Roman Catholic 36%, Protestant 30%, Muslim 2.2%, other and nonreligious 31.8%

DUTCH WATER FACTS

• Without protective dunes and dykes, half the land area of the Netherlands would be flooded by the sea twice a day.

• Almost 20% of the Netherlands is made up of inland water. Windmills once pumped out water; now, the pumps are electric.

BELGIUM

BELGIUM COMBINES two cultures: the French-speaking Walloons and the Flemings, who speak a form of Dutch. Brussels, the capital, is host to the European Community (EC).

Area 11,783sq miles (30,518 sq km)
Currency Belgian franc
Government Constitutional monarchy
Independence 1830, from the Netherlands
Population 10,000,000
Density 790 per sq mile (305 per sq km)
Official Languages French, Dutch, and German
Major Religions Roman Catholic 89.5%, Muslim 2.5%, Protestant 0.5%, Jewish 0.4%, other and nonreligious 7.1%

ATOMIUM

Erected in 1958 in Brussels, this amazing space-age structure represents an iron crystal. The Atomium houses a permanent scientific exhibition on the history of medicine.

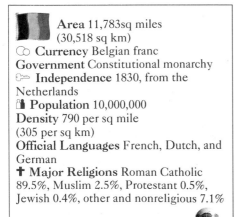

LAND PROFILE

The Netherlands is intensely farmed.

%
3.5
12
84.5

LIFESTYLE FACTS

• There are 14 million bicycles between 15 million people in the Netherlands. This is the highest proportion in the world.

• If the canals freeze over, the Dutch take part in a *tocht*, a long skating tour. Official tour routes between villages are announced on TV and radio.

• More Dutch cheese is exported than any other cheese in the world. Half of all milk produced is made into cheese.

FLOWER POWER

The Netherlands is the world's largest exporter of flowers and bulbs. In spring, fields packed with brightly colored tulips attract thousands of visitors.

0	75km
0	40 miles

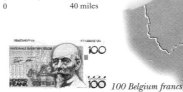

100 Belgium francs

WEATHER FACTS

98.6°F (37°C)   32in (825mm)   0°F (-18°C)

62.6°F (17°C)   36.7°F (2.6°C)

LAND PROFILE

%
7
35
58

LIFESTYLE FACTS

• Belgium is the third-biggest producer of chocolates in the world.

• Belgians spend more on food and drink than their European neighbors. Brussels has 25 restaurants holding a prized Michelin rosette – more than twice as many as London, which is eight times bigger.

• Bruges is the center of European lacemaking; women have made exquisite lace here for centuries.

• Belgium has the world's densest railroad system: there are 5,224 miles (8,408km) of tracks.

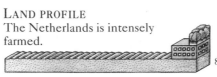
25 guilders

WEATHER FACTS

98.6°F (37°C)   23in (580mm)   -13°F (-25°C)

61.7°F (16.5°C)   36.1°F (2.3°C)

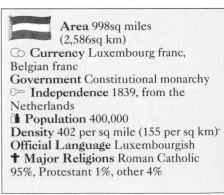

LUXEMBOURG

LUXEMBOURG IS A Grand Duchy, with a Grand Duke as Head of State. Luxembourg City is a major international banking center.

Area 998sq miles (2,586sq km)
Currency Luxembourg franc, Belgian franc
Government Constitutional monarchy
Independence 1839, from the Netherlands
Population 400,000
Density 402 per sq mile (155 per sq km)
Official Language Luxembourgish
Major Religions Roman Catholic 95%, Protestant 1%, other 4%

FRANCE

FRANCE IS THE LARGEST of the twelve countries in the European Community (EC), and its leading agricultural power. Ninety percent of the land is farmed, and one in five French people lives and works in the countryside.

Area 210,669sq miles (545,630sq km)
Government Republic
🗝 **Independence** 1789
Territories Corsica, French Guiana, Guadeloupe, Martinique, Reunion, Mayotte, St. Pierre & Miquelon, Bassas da India, Clipperton Island, Europa Island, French Polynesia, French Southern and Antarctic Lands, Juan de Nova Island, New Caledonia, Glorioso Islands, Tromelin Island, Wallis, Futuna
🪙 **Currency** Franc
Population 57,200,000
Density 269 per sq mile (104 per sq km)
Official Language French
✝ **Major Religions** Roman Catholic 80%, Muslim 4.5%, Protestant and other 15.5%

EIFFEL TOWER
A.G. Eiffel (1823–1923) designed this famous tower. It is 984ft (300m) high and was built for the Paris World Exposition of 1889.

WEATHER FACTS
102°F (39°C)   17.4in (44.4cm)   1°F (-17°C)

73°F (23°C)   42°F (6°C)

LAND PROFILE
The majority of land is farmed and there are extensive forests.

%
1
3
36
60

LIFESTYLE FACTS
• France is the world's second biggest producer of cheese and curd. There is a different cheese for every single day of the year.

• Bicycle races are a top spectator sport in France. The Tour de France is the world's longest bicycle race. It covers 2,312 miles (3,720km) and takes three weeks. The first race was held in 1903.

FASTEST TRAIN
France holds the record for the fastest train, the TGV. It reached 320.1mph (515.3km/h) in 1990. The fastest recorded journey is between Paris and Mâcon, covered at an average speed of 135mph (217km/h).

100 French francs

LANGUAGE
A traditional greeting in French is *bonjour*.

PARIS, CITY OF CULTURE
Paris is a very successful mix of different architectural styles, from world-famous historic monuments to ultra-modern glass-and-steel structures.

The *Grand Louvre* museum, France's second most visited monument, houses the world-famous *Mona Lisa*. The glass pyramid over the entrance was built in 1989.

The *Centre Georges Pompidou*, which contains France's National Museum of Modern Art, is the most visited public building in the country. The center was opened in 1977.

BEST CELLAR
France, along with Italy, is the world's leading wine producer. In 1990, wine production totalled 4,875,000,000 bottles: enough for a bottle taller than the Statue of Liberty.

MONACO

THE TINY COUNTRY of Monaco, which has an orchestra larger than its army, is the most densely populated country in Europe.

Area 0.75sq miles 1.95sq km
Government Constitutional monarchy
🗝 **Independence** 1861, state established
🪙 **Currency** French franc
Population 28,000
Density 37,190 per sq mile (14,359 per sq km)
Official Language French
✝ **Major Religions** Roman Catholic 95%, other 5%

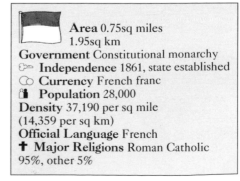

Map labels:
English Channel
BELGIUM
LUXEMBOURG
GERMANY
Lille
Lens
Valenciennes
Le Havre
Rouen
Reims
Channel Islands (UK)
Brest
Paris
Eiffel Tower
Strasbourg
Nancy
Seine
Rennes
Le Mans
Orléans
Loire
Mulhouse
Dijon
SWITZERLAND
Nantes
Tours
F R A N C E
Poiters
Lake Geneva
Mont Blanc 15,782ft (4810m)
Clermont-Ferrand
Mâcon
Lyon
ITALY
Angoulême
St. Étienne
Grenoble
Massif Central
Bordeaux
Les Landes
Garonne
Rhône
MONACO
Toulouse
Montpellier
Nice
Marseille
Toulon
ATLANTIC OCEAN
Pyrenees
SPAIN
ANDORRA
MEDITERRANEAN SEA
Ligurian Sea
Corsica
Ajaccio
Mediterranean Sea

N

0   100km
0   100 miles

GERMANY

THE FEDERAL REPUBLIC of Germany holds a key position in Central Europe. A divided country for 41 years, reunification with the German Democratic Republic took place on October 3, 1990.

Area 134,950sq miles (349,520sq km)
Government Federal republic
Reunification October 3, 1990
Territories Ruegen
Currency Mark
Population 80,300,000
Density 596 per sq mile (230 per sq km)
Official Language German
Major Religions Protestant 36%, Roman Catholic 35%, Muslim 2%, others 1%, nonreligious 27%

WEATHER FACTS

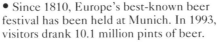

101°F (39°C)   24.4in (619mm)   -21°F (-30°C)
57.7°F (14.3°C)   37.4°F (3°C)

LAND PROFILE

%
0.5
5.5
45.5
48.5

BRANDENBURG GATE

From 1961, this last town gateway was blocked, separating East Berlin from West Berlin. On December 22, 1989, the gate was reopened.

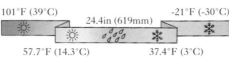

10 Deutschmark

LANGUAGE

A traditional greeting in German is *Guten Tag*.

LIFESTYLE FACTS

• West Germany's soccer team won the World Cup championship three times: Berne in 1954, Munich in 1974, and Rome in 1990.

• 40 million Germans travel abroad for their vacations every year: this represents 51% of the population.

• The Federal Republic is the third largest producer of cars in the world, after Japan and the United States. In 1991, 4.6 million cars were produced, and 2.2 million of these were exported.

• Wurst (sausage) is a traditional and popular German food. There are about 1,500 varieties.

FAIRS AND FESTIVALS

• Since 1810, Europe's best-known beer festival has been held at Munich. In 1993, visitors drank 10.1 million pints of beer.

• Each spring, the world's biggest trade fair is held in Hanover. Exhibitors from 50 countries display the latest industrial technology.

• Cologne carnival is a five-day festival held seven weeks before Easter. The most important day is Rose Monday, when chocolates and gifts are thrown to the crowd from carnival processions.

• Frankfurt Book Fair, held every October, attracts publishers and booksellers from all over the world. In 1993, there were 252,000 visitors and 8,463 exhibitors.

FAIRYTALE CASTLE

Neuschwanstein Castle, one of the most fantastic, fairytale castles in the world, was dreamed up by King Ludwig II of Bavaria (1845–86). Sadly, Ludwig, who had a two-story room built for his gold and ivory throne, died before the castle was completed.

BAYREUTH

Each year, the Bavarian city of Bayreuth hosts a festival in honor of the famous composer Richard Wagner (1813–83). His operas are staged in the specially built *Festspielhaus* (Festival Theater).

Wagner's Opera Lohengrin

TOP GERMAN CAR MANUFACTURERS (1992)

Manufacturer	Number of cars produced
Volkswagen	1,549,503
Opel	1,071,544
BMW	580,295
Daimler-Benz	531,457
Audi	492,085
Porsche	16,559

Source: German Chamber of Industry & Commerce

DENMARK
NORTH SEA
North Frisian Is.
East Frisian Is.
BALTIC SEA
Oderhaff
NETHERLANDS
Hamburg
Bremen
Elbe
Oder
POLAND
Berlin
Brandenburg Gate
Hanover
GERMANY
Brocken 3,747ft (1,142m)
Harz Mts.
Leipzig
Essen   Dortmund
Duisburg
Düsseldorf
Thuringian Forest
Cologne
Grosser Beerberg 3,222ft (982m)
Ore Mts.
BELGIUM
Bonn
Wasser Kuppe 3,117ft (950m)
CZECH. REP.
Frankfurt
Bayreuth
Main
Nuremberg
Franconian Jura
Bohemian Forest
Rhine
Stuttgart
Black Forest
Swabian Jura
Danube
FRANCE
Munich
Freiburg im Breisgau
Lake Constance
Neuschwanstein
Bavarian Alps
AUSTRIA
Rhine
SWITZERLAND
Zugspitze 9,271ft (2,963m)

0   150km
0   100 miles
N

SWITZERLAND

JUST ONE-QUARTER of Switzerland is habitable: the remaining land consists of high mountains, forests, and ice. Every minute, 215 to 325 square feet of Swiss land are built on.

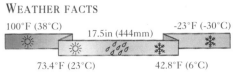

WEATHER FACTS

100°F (38°C) 17.5in (444mm) -23°F (-30°C)
73.4°F (23°C) 42.8°F (6°C)

LAND PROFILE

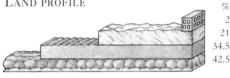

	%
	2
	21
	34.5
	42.5

LIFESTYLE FACTS

• The Swiss are famous bankers, and their banks attract money from investors all over the world. There is a bank for every 1,600 Swiss people.

• Watches are Switzerland's best-known export. The watchmaking center in Neuchâtel developed both the quartz watch and the atomic clock.

• The surplus of home produced milk led to two important Swiss inventions, baby formula and condensed milk. Other Swiss milk products are cheese and fine chocolate.

50 Swiss francs

LANGUAGE

A traditional greeting in French is *bonjour*; in German *Guten Tag*; in Italian *buongiorno*.

TOP CHOCOLATE EATERS

Country	Amount per person	
	kg	lb
Switzerland	11.3	25.0
Norway	7.9	17.4
Belgium	7.8	17.2

N

Area 15,355sq miles (39,770sq km)
Government Federal republic
Independence 1648, from the Holy Roman Empire
Currency Swiss Franc
Population 6,800,000
Density 443 per sq mile (171 per sq km)
Official Languages German, French, Italian
✝ **Major Religions** Roman Catholic 47.6%, Protestant 44.3%, Jewish 0.3%, others and nonreligious 7.8%

JET D'EAU

The water from the jet d'eau, the famous fountain situated in the center of Geneva's harbor, gushes 460ft (140 meters) in the air.

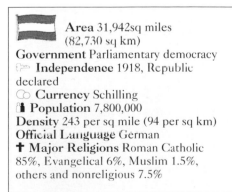

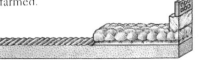

TOP SKI RESORTS

Swiss   Austria

0   100km
0   60 miles

LANDMARK

St. Stephan's Cathedral, more than 600 years old, is one of Vienna's most famous buildings.

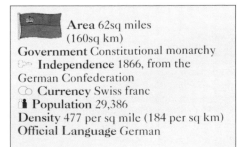

AUSTRIA

AUSTRIA'S FINE CITIES and beautiful mountainous landscape – 40 percent of the land lies at an altitude of more than 3,500 feet – attract about 18 million visitors a year.

Area 31,942sq miles (82,730 sq km)
Government Parliamentary democracy
Independence 1918, Republic declared
Currency Schilling
Population 7,800,000
Density 243 per sq mile (94 per sq km)
Official Language German
✝ **Major Religions** Roman Catholic 85%, Evangelical 6%, Muslim 1.5%, others and nonreligious 7.5%

LANGUAGE

A traditional greeting in German is *Guten Tag*

100 Austrian schillings

WEATHER FACTS

100.4°F (38°C) 25.2in (640mm) -16.6°F (-27°C)
66.7°F (19.3°C) 32°F (0°C)

LAND PROFILE

Almost two-thirds of the land is farmed.

	%
	1
	4
	30
	65

LIFESTYLE FACTS

• Many great composers were Austrian; they include Mozart (1756–91), Haydn (1732–1809), Schubert (1797–1828), and Johann Strauss (1825–99), who composed the famous Viennese waltz, *The Blue Danube*.

• Skiing is Austria's national sport. The first ski school was set up at St. Anton am Arlberg, and Austrian Annemarie Moser-Proll (b. 1953) is a celebrated woman skier.

LIECHTENSTEIN

THIS TINY COUNTRY is ruled by a prince. Liechtenstein is famous for its royal art collection and its postage stamps. One of the principal exports is false teeth.

Area 62sq miles (160sq km)
Government Constitutional monarchy
Independence 1866, from the German Confederation
Currency Swiss franc
Population 29,386
Density 477 per sq mile (184 per sq km)
Official Language German

ITALY

THIS IMPORTANT INDUSTRIAL nation has most of its factories as well as rich farmland concentrated in the north. The south is mountainous and farmers grow olives, and grapes for making wine. Italy includes the large islands of Sicily and Sardinia.

Area 116,321sq miles (301,270sq km)
Government Parliamentary republic
Republic Declared in 1948
Currency Lira
Population 57,719,000
Density 510 per sq mile (197 per sq km)
Official Language Italian
† Major Religions Roman Catholic 83.2%, Protestant 0.3%, Jewish 0.1%, nonreligious and atheist 16.4%

WEATHER FACTS

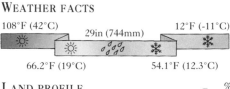

108°F (42°C)   29in (744mm)   12°F (-11°C)
66.2°F (19°C)   54.1°F (12.3°C)

LAND PROFILE

More than 68% of Italy is agricultural land.

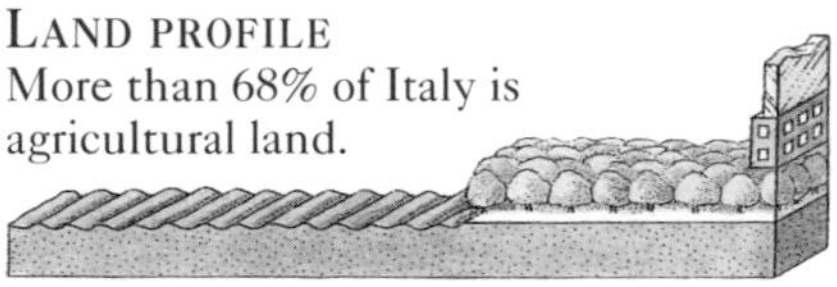

%
1.5
2.5
27.5
68.5

LIFESTYLE FACTS

- The Palio of Siena is a twice-yearly bareback horse race round the city's main square. The palio is the silk banner awarded to the winner.

- The most popular resort is Venice, with more than 7.5 million tourists a year. The city has 118 islands, 177 canals, and 400 bridges.

VATICAN CITY

- The Vatican City in Rome is the world's smallest independent state. It is the world center for the Roman Catholic religion, and its ruler is the pope.

- There has been a pope for more than 1,900 years – since the time of St. Peter, who was the first pope.

- St. Peter's is the largest and most important cathedral in the Christian world, first built by the Roman Emperor Constantine in about A.D.330

TOWER OF PISA

The leaning tower of Pisa is made of white marble and was built between 1174 and 1350. The tower is 177ft (54m) tall and leans at an angle of 11.3 degrees from the vertical.

1,000 lira

LANGUAGE

A traditional greeting in Italian is *buon giorno*.

MAJOR TOURIST ATTRACTIONS (1992)

Location	People
Excavations, Pompeii	1,296,633
Uffizi Gallery, Florence	1,020,972
Franciscan Abbey, Cassino	956,200
Pantheon, Rome	857,585
Galleria dell"Accademia, Florence	687,428
The Forum, Rome	651,183

FOOD FACTS

- There are more than 600 different types of pasta.

- More than 4.4 million tons of tomatoes are grown in Italy every year. Many are used to make sauces for pasta dishes.

- Genuine mozzarella cheese is made from the milk of the water buffalo. It is made fresh daily in many parts of Italy.

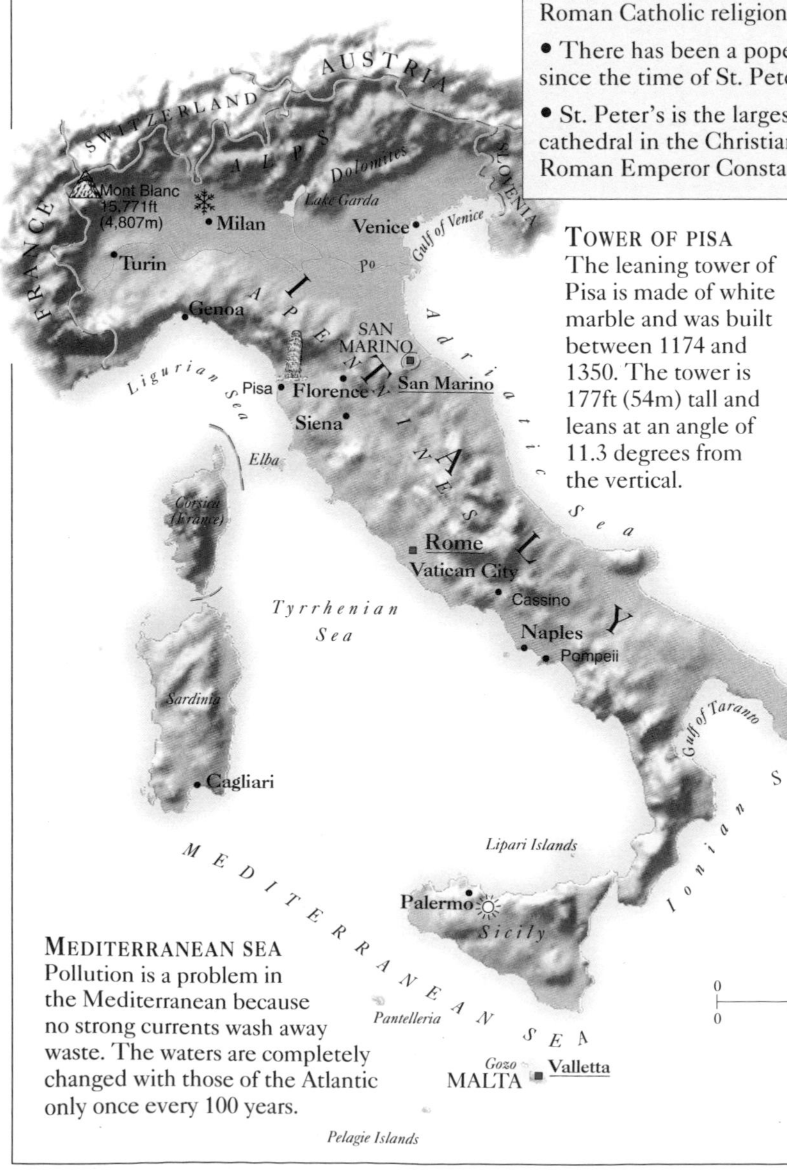

SAN MARINO

THE TINY REPUBLIC of San Marino is located in the mountains of central Italy. Tourism accounts for 60 percent of the country's income.

Area 24 sq miles (61sq km)
Independence 1631, recognition as a city state
Currency Italian lira
Population 20,000
Official Language Italian

MALTA

MALTA'S SEVERAL ISLANDS are in the Mediterranean. The climate is warm but there are no rivers and little rain to provide water for crops.

Area 124sq miles (320sq km)
Independence 1964, from Britain
Currency Maltese lira
Population 356,000
Official Languages English, Maltese

MEDITERRANEAN SEA

Pollution is a problem in the Mediterranean because no strong currents wash away waste. The waters are completely changed with those of the Atlantic only once every 100 years.

Map labels: FRANCE, SWITZERLAND, AUSTRIA, SLOVENIA, Mont Blanc 15,771ft (4,807m), Milan, Lake Garda, Dolomites, Venice, Gulf of Venice, Turin, Po, Genoa, ALPS, APENNINES, Ligurian Sea, SAN MARINO, Pisa, Florence, San Marino, Siena, Adriatic Sea, Elba, Corsica (France), ITALY, Rome, Vatican City, Tyrrhenian Sea, Cassino, Naples, Pompeii, Gulf of Taranto, Sardinia, Ionian Sea, Cagliari, Lipari Islands, MEDITERRANEAN SEA, Palermo, Sicily, Pantelleria, Gozo, Valletta, MALTA, Pelagie Islands, N, 0 200km, 0 120 miles

FINLAND

A COUNTRY WITH 187,888 lakes, Finland also has vast forests of pine and spruce. Timber, used to make paper and furniture, provides most of the wealth of the country. Finland also includes part of Lapland.

Area 130,533sq miles (338,130sq km)
Government Parliamentary republic
Independence 1917, from Soviet Union
Territories Åland Islands
Currency Markka
Population 4,998,478
Density 41 per sq mile (16 per sq km)
Official Languages Finnish, Swedish
✝ **Major Religions** Lutheran 88.7%, Finnish Orthodox 1.1%, Roman Catholic 0.7%, other 9.5%

LIFESTYLE FACTS

• Finnish women were the first in Europe to get the vote, in 1906.

• The world's longest cross-country ski race is held in March each year. Skiers race from Kuusamo on the Russian border to Tornio on the Swedish border, across southern Lapland.

• Savonlinna Opera Festival is the most successful cultural event in Finland. It was founded in 1912 by opera singer Aino Ackte and is held in the courtyard of the

ESTONIA

MUCH OF ESTONIA is flat countryside with fields and forests, marshes and lakes. The main industries include engineering and textiles.

Area 17,422sq miles (45,125sq km)
Government Presidential republic
Independence 1991, from Soviet Union
Currency Kroon
Population 1,591,000
Density 93 per sq mile (36 per sq km)
Official Language Estonian
Major Religions No figures available. Most people Evangelical Lutheran, some are Russian Orthodox

HELPING HANDS

In 1989, the Estonians formed a chain across their land, and into Latvia and Lithuania. The 400-mile (644-km) link symbolized their bid for freedom from the Soviet Union.

WEATHER FACTS

91.4°F (33°C) 27in (688mm) -43°F (-41°C)
68.5°F (20.3°C) 27.3°F (-2.6°C)

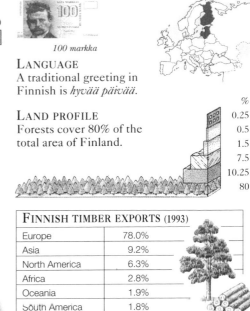
100 markka

LANGUAGE
A traditional greeting in Finnish is *hyvää päivää*.

LAND PROFILE
Forests cover 80% of the total area of Finland.

%
0.25
0.5
1.5
7.5
10.25
80

FINNISH TIMBER EXPORTS (1993)	
Europe	78.0%
Asia	9.2%
North America	6.3%
Africa	2.8%
Oceania	1.9%
South America	1.8%

HELSINKI CATHEDRAL
This great cathedral was designed in the 19th century by architect Carl Engel. It was laid out in its present form of a Greek cross with a central tower.

SAUNA CABIN
The sauna is a national tradition and Finns have at least one a week. There are about 1.4 million saunas in Finland: one for every 3.5 people.

LATVIA

A MIXTURE OF forested hills and plains, Latvia is often called Amberland because so much amber can be found on its Baltic shore.

Area 24,938sq miles (64,589sq km)
Government Parliamentary republic
Independence 1991, from Soviet Union
Currency Lats
Population 2,693,000
Density 109 per sq mile (42 per sq km)
Official Language Latvian
Major Religions No figures available. Predominantly Lutheran, also Roman Catholic and Russian Orthodox

LITHUANIA

MOST OF LITHUANIA is a low-lying plain with many small lakes formed by glaciers. Winter temperatures can fall below freezing for four months.

Area 25,174sq miles (65,200sq km)
Government Parliamentary republic
Independence 1991, from Soviet Union
Currency Litas
Population 3,765,000
Density 150 per sq mile (58 per sq km)
Official Language Lithuanian
Major Religions No figures available. Predominantly Roman Catholic, also Evangelical Lutheran and Reformist

POLAND

AN INDUSTRIAL COUNTRY rich in coal and copper, Poland has large textile, iron, steel, and shipbuilding industries. Much of the landscape is flat, and about one-third of the people work on the land.

Area 120,726sq miles (312,680sq km)
Government Parliamentary democracy
Republic declared 1947
Currency Zloty
Population 38,400,000
Density 326 per sq mile (126 per sq km)
Official Language Polish
✝ Major Religions Roman Catholic 95%, Protestant 0.3%, Muslim 0.01%, other 4.69%

CZECH REPUBLIC

THE HOMELAND OF the Czechs was originally called Bohemia. Much of the country is flat farmland. Prague, the capital, has many churches with gilded roofs, which gave the city the name *zlata Praha*, or golden Prague.

Area 30,450sq miles (78,864sq km)
Government Republic
Independence 1992, from former Czechoslovakia
Currency Czech koruna
Population 10,302,215
Density 339 per sq mile (131 per sq km)
Official Language Czech
Major Religions No figures available

SLOVAKIA

FORMERLY PART OF the kingdom of Hungary, Slovakia is a hilly country of thick forests dominated by the Carpathian Mountains. Bratislava, on the Danube, is the capital city and main export point.

Area 18,932sq miles (49,035sq km)
Government Republic
Independence 1992, from former Czechoslovakia
Currency Slovak koruna
Population 5,289,600
Density 282 per sq mile (108 per sq km)
Official Language Slovak
Major Religions No figures available

WEATHER FACTS

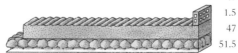

101°F (39°C) 22in (550mm) -18°F (-28°C)
66°F (18.9°C) 25°F (-3.9°C)

LAND PROFILE

%
1.5
47
51.5

LIFESTYLE FACTS

• Poland has Europe's oldest operating salt mine at Wieliczka, near Kraków. The layers of salt go down to 1,073ft (327m).

• Education is compulsory between the ages of 7 and 18, and 98 percent of Poles can read and write.

• Open-air museums, known as *skansens*, exhibit a selection of typical, old wooden buildings such as barns, churches, and windmills.

PRAGUE'S CLOCK

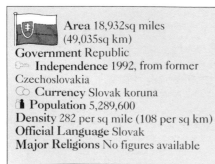

The astronomical clock in the Old Town Hall, Prague, was installed in 1410. The clock's interlocking circles show phases of the Sun and Moon. It has run nonstop since 1572.

100,000 zloty

LANGUAGE

A traditional greeting in Polish is *dzień dobry*.

WAWEL CASTLE

Wawel Castle is built on a rocky embankment of the Vistula River in the old capital of Kraków. Many Polish kings are buried in the castle's underground crypts.

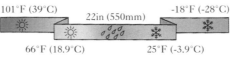

TRADITIONAL POLISH FOOD

Poland can be extremely cold, so many dishes are planned to be warm and filling.
Krupnik A thick soup made with barley or buckwheat. Also the name of a strong drink.
Pierozki Dumplings filled with meat, mushrooms, cooked cabbage, or cheese.
Bigos A meat stew using wild boar, hare, or venison and *wiejska*, a Polish sausage.

Polish dumplings

UKRAINE

MUCH OF THE Ukraine consists of vast flat plains called steppes. Chief crops include winter wheat, corn, barley, sugar beets, and potatoes.

Area 233,098sq miles (603,700sq km)
Government Presidential republic
Independence 1991, from Soviet Union
Currency Karbovanets (temporary)
Population 52,158,000
Density 233 per sq mile (86 per sq km)
Official Language Ukrainian
Major Religions No figures available

UKRAINE CROPS (1992)
(In thousand tons)

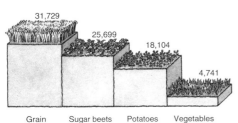

31,729 — Grain
25,699 — Sugar beets
18,104 — Potatoes
4,741 — Vegetables

BISON
The Bialowieza Forest is the largest ancient forest in Europe. It is home to the last 500 or so remaining European bison. The bison is the biggest European mammal and can measure 6.6ft (2m).

Hand-carved wooden cross from Romania

Kharkiv
Dnipropetrovs'k
Donets'k
Zaporizhzhya
ka Reservoir
Sea of Azov
SEA

BELARUS

AGRICULTURE IS THE main occupation in Belarus, despite poor soil. The capital city, Minsk, produces agricultural machinery.

Area 80,154sq miles (207,600sq km)
Government Parliamentary republic
Independence 1991, from Soviet Union
Currency Rouble
Population 10,295,000
Density 129 per sq mile (50 per sq km)
Official Language Belorussian
Major Religions No figures available

ROMANIA

FORESTS COVER ABOUT one-quarter of Romania, and lumber is an important product. The Danube River is used for transportation and as a source of hydroelectric power.

Area 91,699sq miles (237,500sq km)
Government Presidential republic
Independence 1881, from Ottoman Empire
Currency Leu
Population 23,300,000
Density 262 per sq mile (101 per sq km)
Official Language Romanian
✝ Major Religions Roman Orthodox 70%, Roman Catholic 6%, Catholic Eastern Rite 3%, Protestant 6%, other 15%

FACTS ABOUT ROMANIA AND HUNGARY
• There are about 410,000 gypsies (or Romanies) in Romania. The gypsies are thought to have arrived from India (via the Middle East) in about the 5th century A.D.

• Transylvania, which means "beyond the forest," is an area of Romania where music and folk art remain untouched. This wayside cross shows the skill of the woodcarver.

• Sunflowers are grown in Hungary for the oil that is extracted from their seeds. The stems of sunflowers turn so that the flowers can always face toward the sun.

• Peppers are cultivated in Hungary and ground into the spice paprika. The rose paprika of Hungary has a special sweet flavor and is used in stews such as *gulyas*, or goulash. Paprika is made from the pods of the pepper *Capsicum annuum*.

MOLDOVA

WARM SUMMERS AND mild winters make Moldova ideal for growing fruit, especially grapes. Moldovan people are Romanian in origin.

Area 13,012sq miles (33,700sq km)
Government Presidential republic
Independence 1991, from Soviet Union
Currency Rouble
Population 4,362,000
Density 337 per sq mile (130 per sq km)
Official Language Romanian
Major Religions No figures available

HUNGARY

HUNGARY HAS FERTILE soil and farmers grow wheat, sugar beets, and tobacco. The capital, Budapest, was originally two towns, Buda and Pest, on either side of the Danube River.

Area 35,919sq miles (93,030sq km)
Government Parliamentary republic
Independence 1918, after collapse of Austro-Hungarian monarchy
Currency Forint
Population 10,500,000
Density 295 per sq mile (114 per sq km)
Official Language Hungarian
✝ Major Religions Roman Catholic 65%, Calvinist 19%, Lutheran 4%, Greek Orthodox 2.9%, Eastern Orthodox 2.6%, other 6.5%

The Gellert Baths in Budapest

• Hungary is famous for its medicinal waters, and Budapest has at least 120 hot springs. Every day 18 million gallons (70 million liters) of water well up to the surface, allowing thousands of people to enjoy the healing baths.

• The Danube River rises in the Alps of Germany and flows through eight countries on its journey to the Black Sea. The Danube is also called the Donau, Danuj, Duna, Dunav, Dunarea, and Dunay.

BULGARIA

BULGARIA HAS HIGH mountains and more than 600 natural springs. Grapes grow abundantly on the fertile plains, making Bulgaria the world's fourth largest wine exporter.

Area 42,823sq miles (110,910sq km)
Government Parliamentary republic
Republic declared 1946
Currency Leva
Population 9,000,000
Density 207 per sq mile (80 per sq km)
Official Language Bulgarian
Major Religions Bulgarian Orthodox 85%, Muslim 10%, Jewish 0.8%, other or nonreligious 4.2%

LANDMARK
St. Alexander Nevsky Cathedral, Sofia, completed in 1912, was built in honor of the Russian soldiers who died in the 1877–78 Russo–Turkish War.

GREECE

MORE THAN 1,400 islands surround Greece's heavily indented coastline; only 154 are inhabited. Greece has the second largest fleet of merchant ships in the world.

Area 50,962sq miles (131,990sq km)
Government Parliamentary democracy
Independence 1829, from Ottoman Empire
Currency Drachma
Population 10,200,000
Density 199 per sq mile (77 per sq km)
Official Language Greek
Major Religions Greek Orthodox 98%, Muslim 1.5%, Roman Catholic and Protestant, and Jewish 0.5%

LAND PROFILE
Even though 80% of Greece is mountainous, almost two-thirds of the land is used for farming and grazing.

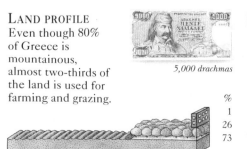

5,000 drachmas

%
1
26
73

WEATHER FACTS
104°F (40.6°C)   25in (635mm)   -13°F (-25°C)
69°F (20°C)   28°F (-2.2°C)

LIFESTYLE FACTS

• Rose oil is one of the most precious ingredients of perfume. Bulgaria is the major supplier of rose oil and has the world's largest rose gardens at Kazanluk.

• Bulgarians nod their heads when they mean "no" and shake them when they mean "yes."

• In Gabrovo, Bulgaria, there is a national museum devoted entirely to humor called The House of Humor and Satire.

OLIVE
The national symbol of Greece is the olive branch.

LANGUAGE
A traditional greeting in Greek is *kalimera*. καΛημερα

WEATHER FACTS
111°F (44°C)   16.3in (414mm)   10°F (-12°C)
82.8°F (28.2°C)   47°F (8.6°C)

GREEK MUSIC
One of the most important instruments in traditional Greek music is the bouzouki, which has metal strings. Traditional music is played at religious festivals and special occasions such as weddings.

LANGUAGE
A traditional greeting in Bulgarian is *dobró útro*.

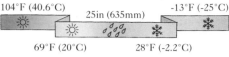

LAND PROFILE
Bulgaria has extensive forests, and the land is mainly used for farming.

%
2
39
59

LION
The lion is the national symbol of Bulgaria; it is depicted on the coat of arms.

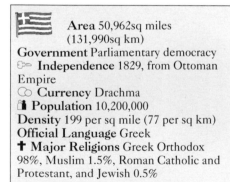

ROMANIA
Danube
Ruse
YUGOSLAVIA
BULGARIA
Varna
Iskur
Gabrovo
Sofia
Alexander Nevsky Cathedral
Kazanluk
Burgas
Lake Scutari
Drin
Korab 9,026ft (2,751m)
Musala 9,597ft (2,925m)
Stara Zagora
Plovdiv
ALBANIA
MACEDONIA
Bla
Po
Tirana
Bosphorus
Istanbul
Kavala
Sea of Marmara
Hereke
Lake Prespa
Thessaloniki
Bursa
Bithynia
Ankara
Olympus 9,570ft (2,917m)
Limnos
Eskisehir
TURK
Corfu
Trikkala
Larisa
Aegean Sea
Lesvos
Phrygia
Cappado
Ionian Islands
GREECE
Izmir
Kay
Parthenon
Chios
Patrai
Peloponnese
Athens
Euboea
Pamukkale
Konya
Ionian Sea
Samos
Cyclades
Dodecanese
Antalya
Adar
Kos
Taurus Mountains
M
Rhodes
Sea of Crete
Nicosia
Crete
Iráklion
Olympus 6,406ft (1,951m)
CYPRUS
MEDITERRANEAN SEA

PARTHENON
The Parthenon is a world-famous classical Greek temple dedicated to the goddess of Athens, Athena. It sits on a hill in Athens called the Acropolis, and was constructed between 447 and 432 B.C.

TURKEY

TURKEY LIES IN both Europe and Asia. The two continents are separated by the Bosphorus, site of the capital city, Istanbul, and one of the world's busiest waterways.

Area 300,947sq miles (779,450sq km)
Government Parliamentary republic
Republic declared 1923
Currency Turkish lira
Population 58,400,000
Density 192 per sq mile (74 per sq km)
Official Language Turkish
Major Religions Muslim 99%, Orthodox Christian, Roman Catholic, Protestant, Jewish 1%

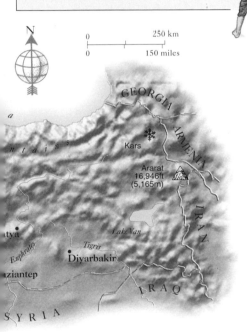

N
0   250 km
0   150 miles

GEORGIA
ARMENIA
Kars
Ararat 16,946ft (5,165m)
IRAN
Lake Van
Tigris
Euphrates
Diyarbakir
ziantep
IRAQ
SYRIA

LIFESTYLE FACTS

• Greece, with its many mountains, has the greatest number of hill-farms in Europe. Goats are ideally suited to the terrain.

• In summer the flat roofs of houses on Greek islands are used for drying fruit and, in winter, for collecting rainwater.

• 8.2 million tourists visit Greece every year, drawn there by its ancient sites and sunny beaches.

TOP GREEK TOURIST RESORTS (1993)

Resort	Visitors
Crete	6,573,000
Rhodes	5,650,000
Athens	2,500,000
Corfu	2,020,000

Source: Greek National Tourism Organization

WEATHER FACTS

109°F (43°C)   14.4in (367mm)   -33°F (-36°C)
73°F (23°C)   32.5°F (0.3°C)

LAND PROFILE

Land use in Turkey is predominantly agricultural.

%
0.75
4.25
23.5
28.0
43.5

LIFESTYLE FACTS

• Grapes, one of the world's oldest crops, were first grown in Anatolia. From here they spread to other parts of the world.

• Turkey's national sport is wrestling. *Kirkpinar*, the feast of wrestling, has been held each spring for 626 years.

PAMUKKALE

Pamukkale, meaning "cotton castle," is a brilliant-white hillside of cascading thermal pools fringed with stalactites. People have bathed in the warm, healing waters since Roman times.

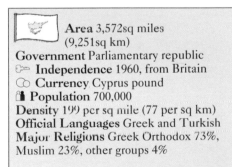

ALBANIA

MOST ALBANIANS live in remote mountain villages in this tiny, mountainous country. Albania's main crops are wheat, barley, tobacco, potatoes, and fruit.

Area 11,100sq miles (28,750sq km)
Government Presidential republic
Independence 1912, from Turkey
Currency Lek
Population 3,300,000
Density 313 per sq mile (121 per sq km)
Official Language Albanian
Major Religions Muslim 70%, Orthodox Christian 20%, Roman Catholic 10%

LIFESTYLE FACTS

• Since World War II, Albania has had the fastest-growing population in Europe. Good health care services for mother and child receive the highest priority from the government.

• More than half of the Albanian people earn their living from farming.

• In 1992, there were only about 6,000 telephones in the whole of Albania – one for every 550 people.

LANGUAGE

A traditional greeting in Turkish is *iyi günler.*

TURKISH CARPETS

Turkey produces about 474 million sq ft (44 million sq m) of carpets each year. There are about 400 types of carpet, produced in centers such as Hereke, Malatya, Konya, and Kayseri.

• Turkey is the world's leading grower and exporter of figs, producing 56,000–67,000 tons of the fruit every year. Fresh, ripe figs are picked for eating from mid-July, or left to dry first on the tree branches, and then for a further two to four days in the hot sun.

TULIP

Turkey's national symbol is the tulip.

CYPRUS

CYPRUS IS THE LARGEST island in the eastern Mediterranean. It is home to both Greek and Turkish communities and, since 1974, has been split into two parts.

Area 3,572sq miles (9,251sq km)
Government Parliamentary republic
Independence 1960, from Britain
Currency Cyprus pound
Population 700,000
Density 199 per sq mile (77 per sq km)
Official Languages Greek and Turkish
Major Religions Greek Orthodox 73%, Muslim 23%, other groups 4%

LIFESTYLE FACTS

• The ancient monuments of Cyprus are so important that some have been added to the UNESCO World Cultural Heritage list.

• Clothing, footwear, potatoes, grapes, and citrus fruit are Cyprus' main exports.

• The mouflon (*Ovis musimon*), a reddish brown wild sheep, is native to Cyprus. It is the smallest wild sheep, reaching a height of just 29in (74cm).

CROATIA

PART OF CROATIA runs along the coast of the Adriatic Sea and was once a popular tourist destination. Supplies of limestone around Split help support the concrete industry.

Area 21,830sq miles (56,540sq km)
Government Presidential democracy
Currency Kruna
Population 4,600,000
Density 210 per sq mile (81 per sq km)
Official Language Croatian
Major Religions Roman Catholic 76.5%, Orthodox 11%, Muslim 1.2%, other 11.3%

SLOVENIA

SLOVENIA IS AN industrialized country with supplies of iron and steel. It is also a major producer of mercury, which is used in thermometers.

Area 7,818sq miles (20,250sq km)
Government Presidential democracy
Currency Tolar
Population 1,900,000
Density 243 per sq mile (94 per sq km)
Official Language Slovene
Major Religions No figures available. Most people are Roman Catholic

LANGUAGE
A traditional greeting in Serbo-Croat is *dobró útro*.

REGIONAL LIFESTYLE FACTS

- The Dalmatian dog is named after the coastal region of Dalmatia in Croatia, which was its first known home.

- Walnuts grow well in the warm summers and well-drained soils of Yugoslavia.

- The Dubrovnik region of Bosnia and Herzegovina is famous for its traditional costumes of white dresses, embroidered blouses, and vests.

- The picturesque city of Ljubljana is surrounded by mountains. Dominated by a medieval fortress, the city has an opera house, an art gallery, and a museum.

Traditional costume from Dubrovnik

YUGOSLAVIA

MADE UP OF the republics of Serbia and Montenegro, Yugoslavia is mountainous in the south, while the north is flat farmland. The capital, Belgrade, lies on the River Danube.

Area 39,449sq miles (102,173sq km)
Government Presidential republic
Currency new Yugoslav dinar
Population 10,580,892
Density 269 per sq mile (104 per sq km)
Official Language Serbo-Croat
Major Religions No figures available

MACEDONIA

ONCE PART OF GREECE, Macedonia is a mountainous region. Farmers grow wheat, millet, and barley in the upland valleys. Tobacco is the main crop grown for export.

Area 9,287sq miles (25,715sq km)
Government Parliamentary republic
Currency Denar
Population 1,900,000
Density 192 per sq mile (74 per sq km)
Official Language Macedonian
Major Religions Christian 64.5%, Muslim 21%, other 14.5%

BOSNIA AND HERZEGOVINA

MINING FOR MINERALS, such as iron, copper, and silver, is an important part of the country's economy. Farmers grow olives, pomegranates, figs, rice, and tobacco.

Area 19,741sq miles (51,130sq km)
Government Parliamentary republic
Currency Bosnian dinar
Population 4,200,000
Density 212 per sq mile (82 per sq km)
Official Language Serbo-Croat
Major Religions Islam is the dominant single religion, while 50% are Christian divided between Serbian Orthodox and Roman Catholic

CIVIL WAR
1n 1990, Yugoslavia began to break up into independent countries. Serbia resisted this process, and in 1991 fighting broke out in both Croatia and Bosnia and Herzegovina. When this book went to press, the borders in this region were still under dispute.

The war-torn city of Sarajevo

GEORGIA

MOST OF GEORGIA is mountainous. The Black Sea coast is popular with tourists. The country has a humid climate that is ideal for growing tea and citrus fruits.

 **Area** 26,911sq miles (69,700sq km)
Government Parliamentary republic
Independence 1991, from Soviet Union
Currency Rouble
Population 5,471,000
Official Language Georgian
Major Religions Christian 97%, Muslim 2%, other 1%

LIFESTYLE FACTS
• Vines thrive on the warm, sunny hills of eastern Georgia, where wine and brandy are produced.
• Visitors are attracted to Georgia's health spas, waterfalls, and natural caves.

THE BLACK SEA
Tourism is a major part of the Georgian economy. Many resorts and spas, with beaches and forests, attract tourists to the coast of the Black Sea.

The Black Sea resort of Bat'umi

• Sweet tea, served black and strong, is a popular drink throughout the countries that lie around the Caucasus Mountains. Crops for both green and black teas are grown on large plantations in Georgia.

LANGUAGE
A traditional greeting in Georgian is *garmardzobat*.

TEXTILES
Georgia is famous for its silk and textiles. Brightly patterned cloth is woven with gold and silver thread. The cloth is often worn as a headscarf.

ARMENIA

ARMENIA IS A mainly mountainous country, and most people live in the foothills or around the Ararat Plain. Crops include orchard fruits such as peaches, apricots, and cherries.

 Area 11,506sq miles (29,800sq km)
Government Parliamentary republic
Independence 1991, from Soviet Union
Currency Armenian dram
Population 3,489,000
Official Language Armenian
Major Religions Armenian Orthodox (Christian) 94%, other 6%

LIFESTYLE FACTS

• Armenia grows rare plants used in perfumery and medicine, including geranium, rose, peppermint, cinchona bark, and basma.

• Lake Sevan is a major recreation area and offers windsurfing, sailing, swimming, and water skiing.

MAIN AGRICULTURAL PRODUCTS

Product	Amount (thousand tons)
Vegetables	511.8
Potatoes	353.8
Wheat	347.2
Grapes	224.0
Meat	158.0
Berries	134.5

Map labels

RUSSIAN FEDERATION
Caucasus Mountains
Black Sea
Shkara 17,068ft (5,202m)
GEORGIA
Kura
Tbilisi
L. Paravani
Bat'umi
Bazar-Dyuzi 14,699ft (4,480m)
L. Adzhinour
Caspian Sea
Baku
TURKEY
Aragats 13,419ft (4,090m)
L. Sevan
Kura
AZERBAIJAN
Yerevan
Razdan
ARMENIA
Ararat Plain
AZERBAIJAN
Naxçivan
Aras
Länkäran
IRAN

AZERBAIJAN

OIL AND NATURAL gas are the most important products in Azerbaijan and Baku, the capital, is the major industrial center. Fruit, walnuts, and hazelnuts are valuable export crops.

 Area 33,436sq miles (86,600sq km)
Government Presidential republic
Independence 1991, from Soviet Union
Currency Rouble
Population 7,283,000
Official Language Azerbaijani
Major Religions Shi'ite Muslims 70%, Sunni Muslims 29%, other 1%

LIFESTYLE FACTS
• In the warm climate around Länkäran, farmers grow oranges, lemons, and figs.

• Light industry in Azerbaijan includes cotton and woolen goods, footwear, traditional household items, and souvenirs.

WILDLIFE FACTS
• The mountains and forests of Azerbaijan are home to a variety of wildlife, including wild boar, brown bears, European bison, chamois, and leopards, although the leopard is now very rare.

Chamois

• The mild winters attract birds to the coast of the Caspian Sea. A wildlife preserve provides a seasonal resting place for flamingoes, swans, pelicans, herons, and hawks.

Pelican

• Musical tradition is strong in Azerbaijan. The music of the *ashugs*, who improvise songs to their own accompaniment on a stringed instrument called a *kobuz*, is extremely popular.

• Almost 90% of Azerbaijan's electricity is produced at hydroelectric power stations throughout the country.

RUSSIAN FEDERATION

THE LARGEST COUNTRY in the world, the Russian Federation stretches across two continents – Europe and Asia – that are separated by the Ural Mountains. Most people live in the western third of the country.

Area 6,592,846sq miles (17,075,400sq km)
Government Presidential republic
Independence 1991, from the former Soviet Union
Currency Rouble
Population 149,003,000
Density 23 per sq mile (9 per sq km)
Official Language Russian
Major Religions No figures available. Most people are Russian Orthodox. There is a small community of Jews; also Muslims and Buddhists

WEATHER FACTS

102°F (39°C) 22.6in (575mm) -90°F (-68°C)
66°F (18.9°C) 16°F (-9°C)

LAND PROFILE
Half the land in the Russian Federation is forest land.

%
0.5
2
6
10
13
18.5
50

ST. BASIL'S CATHEDRAL
The 16th-century St. Basil's Cathedral in Moscow is a magnificent example of old Russian architecture. It is situated within the Kremlin, the original fortress at the historic heart of the city. The cathedral was completed in 1560 and has nine great domes. It is now open as a museum.

St. Basil's was built on the orders of Czar Ivan IV the Terrible in gratitude for his military victories.

LANGUAGE
A traditional greeting in Russian is *zdravstvuyitye*.
Здравствуйте

NATIONAL ANIMAL
The brown bear (*Ursus arctos*) is the national symbol of Russia. In folklore it is linked with kindness and wisdom. Bears eat fruits, berries, and bulbs that they dig up with their claws.

LIFESTYLE FACTS
• Ballet is a popular form of entertainment in Russia. The dance company that became the Bolshoi Ballet was founded in 1773. It is famous for classical ballets such as *Swan Lake*.

• From October to March, Moscow receives an average of 15 minutes sunshine per day. Snow can lie on the ground for up to five months every year.

• Russians love to eat ice cream, which can be bought from places marked *morozhenoe*.

ST. PETERSBURG
St. Petersburg, formerly called Leningrad, is a major industrial center. The center of the city is the Nevsky Prospekt, a street lined with shops, cafés, and theaters.

PASTIMES
• One of the most famous circuses in the world is in Russia. The acrobats of the New Moscow Circus are highly skilled.

• Chess is a popular game; many people practice in Gorky Park, Moscow.

TOLSTOY
Leo Tolstoy (1828–1910) is one of the world's greatest novelists. His most famous book, *War and Peace*, is set in Russia during the Napoleonic Wars. It examines the feelings of the Russians as the French invade their country in 1812.

FAMOUS RUSSIAN WRITERS

Name	Date	Key work
Alexander Pushkin	1799–1837	Eugene Onegin
Feyodor Dostoyevsky	1821–81	Crime and Punishment
Boris Pasternak	1890–1960	Dr. Zhivago
Vladimir Nabokov	1899–1977	Lolita
Alexander Solzhenitsyn	b.1918–	The Gulag Archipelago

• The former Soviet Union had more than half of all movie theaters in the world, with 80 million ticket sales a week. Sergei Eisenstein, a famous Russian film-maker from the 1920s, made *Battleship Potemkin*.

• Reading is popular in Russia. Men spend one-eighth of their free time reading a book or newspaper. Women spend one-sixth of their free time reading.

POPULAR RUSSIAN FOOD
Russians have a fattening diet that includes potatoes, fats, and sugar. Their caloric intake is 70% higher than that in the US.
Borscht This pinkish red soup is made from beets. It can be eaten hot or cold, and is often served with sour cream.
Blinis These pancakes are made using buckwheat, filled with meat or cheese, and then browned.
Charlotte Russe This special pudding was created for Russian royalty. It is made in a mold lined with sponge, and filled with both ice cream and whipped cream.

A plate of blinis served with red caviar.

SIBERIAN WEALTH
Beneath its icy surface, western Siberia has vast reserves of coal, gas, and oil. The area provides fuel for the industries of western Russia, and gas is piped to western Europe.

SIBERIA FACTS
• The region of Siberia covers 4.8 million sq miles (12.5 million sq km) of the eastern, or Asiatic, part of Russia. Its name comes from the word *sibi* which means "sleeping land."

• In the north lies the tundra, where the ground is frozen for much of the year. This is known as permafrost.

• The snowy owl (*Nyctea scandiaca*) glides over the tundra hunting for small mammals.

• South of the tundra, vast expanses of conifers make up the largest forest in the world. The cones of the larch, fir, and spruce trees provide food for animals during the long winter.

• The Chukchi people live on the Kamchatka peninsula and survive by hunting, herding reindeer, and fishing. The Siberian husky was first raised by the Chukchi, who used the dogs as companions and to pull their sleds.

GOLD AND DIAMONDS
During the 1840s, prospectors found gold in the area around the Lena River, in northern Siberia. Today the area has four major gold fields, as well as 800 diamond mines.

Heavy-duty machinery digs for minerals in northern Siberia.

Map labels
Severnaya Zemlya
ARCTIC OCEAN
Laptev Sea
New Siberian Islands
East Siberian Sea
Bear Islands
Wrangel I.
Chukchi Sea
Bering Strait
Arctic Circle
Central Siberian Plateau
Lena
❄ Verkhoyansk
• Anadyr'
N FEDERATION
Siberia
Kamchatka
▲ Klyuchevskaya Sopka 15,584ft (4,750m)
Commander Islands
Bering Sea
Sea of Okhotsk
Sakhalin I.
• Novosibirsk
• Irkutsk
L. Baikal
• Chita
MONGOLIA
CHINA
Sea of Okhotsk
N
Kurile Islands
PACIFIC OCEAN
• Vladivostok
Sea of Japan

URAL MOUNTAIN FACTS
• The Ural Mountains stretch for 1,300 miles (2,100km) from the Kara Sea in the north to Kazakhstan in the south.

• Only 25–125 miles (40–200km) wide, the mountains left Russia open to attack in its early history.

RUSSIAN ICONS
Beautiful icons, religious images painted on wood, adorn Russian churches and homes. For many years Christians were persecuted in the old Soviet Union.

This icon shows the Madonna and Child.

TIME DIFFERENCE
The Russian Federation covers 10 time zones. This means that when it is morning in the west, it is already early evening in the east.

Time to get up in St. Petersburg

At school in Irkutsk

Getting ready for bed in Anadyr'

TRANS-SIBERIAN EXPRESS
The longest railroad line in the world crosses the Russian Federation. Started in 1881, the railroad was vital for the mining and transport of Siberia's minerals. The journey from Moscow to Vladivostock takes about 165 hours.

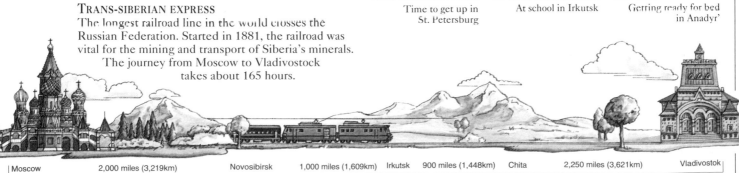

| Moscow | 2,000 miles (3,219km) | Novosibirsk | 1,000 miles (1,609km) | Irkutsk | 900 miles (1,448km) | Chita | 2,250 miles (3,621km) | Vladivostok |

AFRICA

AFRICA IS THE second largest and warmest of the continents. It is also the only continent through which the equator and both tropics pass. Landscape and vegetation include rainforest, grassy savanna, and hot desert.

Area 11,633,846sq miles (30,131,536sq km)
Countries 54
Largest Sudan 967,498sq miles (2,505,810sq km)
Smallest Seychelles 108sq miles (280sq km)
Population 637,271,000
Density 54 per sq mile (21 per sq km)
Major Languages Arabic, Swahili, Hausa, Somali, Amharic

▲ **Highest point** Kilimanjaro, Tanzania 19,341ft (5,895m)
▼ **Lowest point** Lake Assal, Djibouti 512ft (156m) below sea level
☀ **Highest temperature** 136°F (58°C) Al' Aziziyah, Libya
❊ **Lowest temperature** -11°F (-24°C) Ilfrane, Morocco

CLIMATE ZONES

KEY
- Mediterranean
- Dry grassland
- Hot desert
- Rainforest
- Tropical grassland

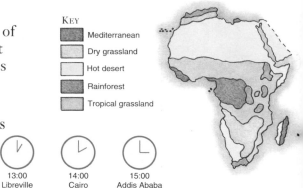

TIME ZONES

12:00	13:00	14:00	15:00
Greenwich	Libreville	Cairo	Addis Ababa

CONTINENT FACTS

- The world's largest desert is the African Sahara, with an area of 3,320,000sq miles (8,600,000sq km). It is bigger than all of Australia.

- Half of all Africans are under 15, making Africa the continent with the world's highest percentage of young people. Only 3 out of 100 can expect to live to 65 years of age.

- Western Sahara, with only 2.6 people per sq mile (1 per sq km), is the world's least densely populated country.

- The earliest evidence of humans – the oldest known human footprints – were found in the Olduvai Gorge, Tanzania.

- Africa has more countries than any other continent: 54 in total.

COUNTRIES, TERRITORIES, AND CAPITALS

Name	Capital	Name	Capital
Algeria	Algiers	Madagascar	Antananarivo
Angola	Luanda	Malawi	Lilongwe
Benin	Porto-Novo	Mali	Bamako
Botswana	Gaborone	Mauritania	Nouakchott
Burkina	Ouagadougou	Mauritius	Port Louis
Burundi	Bujumbura	Morocco	Rabat
Cameroon	Yaoundé	Mozambique	Maputo
Cape Verde	Praia	Namibia	Windhoek
Central African Republic	Bangui	Niger	Niamey
Chad	N'Djamena	Nigeria	Abuja
Comoros	Moroni	Rwanda	Kigali
Congo	Brazzaville	Sao Tome and Principe	São Tomé
Côte d'Ivoire	Yamoussoukro	Senegal	Dakar
Djibouti	Djibouti	Seychelles	Victoria
Egypt	Cairo	Sierra Leone	Freetown
Equatorial Guinea	Malabo	Somalia	Mogadishu
Eritrea	Asmara	South Africa	Pretoria
Ethiopia	Addis Ababa	Sudan	Khartoum
Gabon	Libreville	Swaziland	Mbabane
Gambia	Banjul	Tanzania	Dodoma
Ghana	Accra	Togo	Lomé
Guinea	Conakry	Tunisia	Tunis
Guinea-Bissau	Bissau	Uganda	Kampala
Kenya	Nairobi	Western Sahara	Laâyoune
Lesotho	Maseru	Zaire	Kinshasa
Liberia	Monrovia	Zambia	Lusaka
Libya	Tripoli	Zimbabwe	Harare

AGE BREAKDOWN

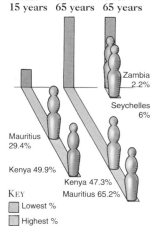

Under 15 years | 15 to 65 years | Over 65 years

Mauritius 29.4%
Kenya 49.9%
Kenya 47.3%
Mauritius 65.2%
Zambia 2.2%
Seychelles 6%

KEY
- Lowest %
- Highest %

FEWEST DOCTORS

Rwanda	1 to 72,990 people
Equatorial Guinea	1 to 62,000 people
Burkina	1 to 57,320 people
Malawi	1 to 45,740 people
Mozambique	1 to 39,500 people

LONGEST LIFE SPAN

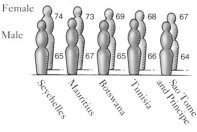

Female: 74, 73, 69, 68, 67
Male: 65, 67, 65, 66, 64

Seychelles, Mauritius, Botswana, Tunisia, Sao Tome and Principe

GREAT RIFT VALLEY

This valley, the longest crack in the Earth's crust, stretches for 5,400 miles (8,700km). In East Africa, the sides of the valley are 4,100ft (1,250m) high.

LONGEST RIVERS

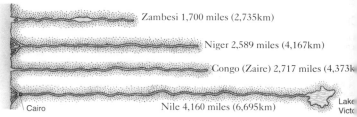

Zambesi 1,700 miles (2,735km)
Niger 2,589 miles (4,167km)
Congo (Zaire) 2,717 miles (4,373km)
Nile 4,160 miles (6,695km)
Cairo
Lake Victo...

TOP CITY POPULATIONS

Cairo, Egypt 6,452,000
Kinshasa, Zaire 3,741,000
Alexandria, Egypt 3,170,000
Abidjan, Ivory Coast 2,700,000
Casablanca, Morocco 2,600,000

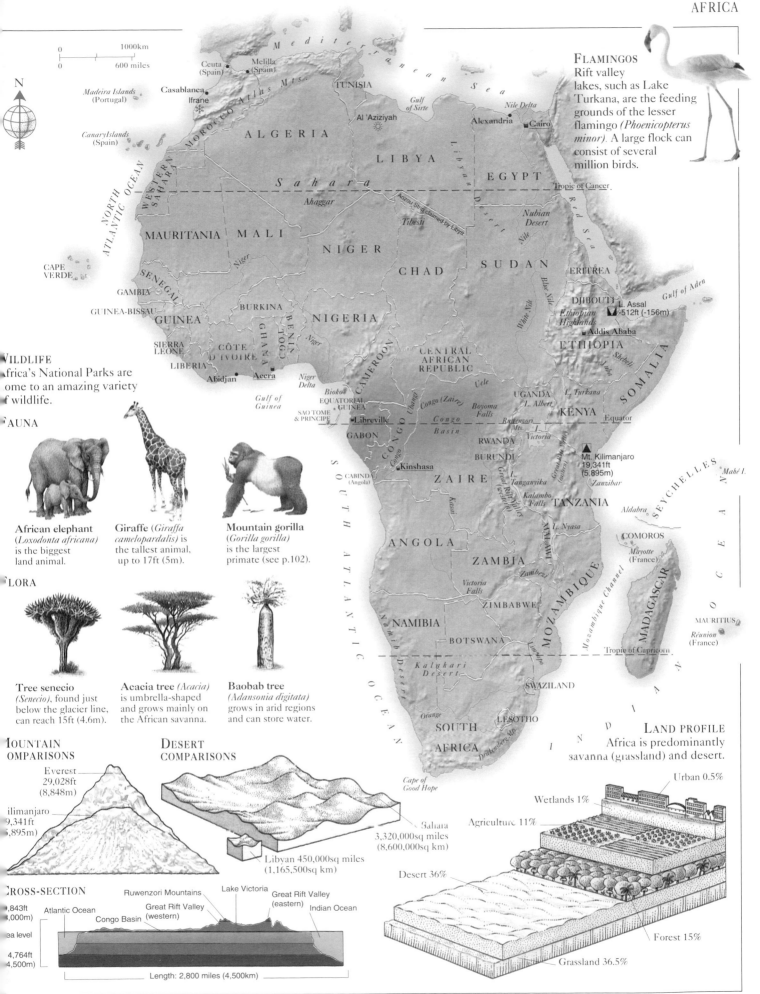

FLAMINGOS
Rift valley lakes, such as Lake Turkana, are the feeding grounds of the lesser flamingo *(Phoenicopterus minor)*. A large flock can consist of several million birds.

N

0 ——— 1000km
0 ——— 600 miles

WILDLIFE
Africa's National Parks are home to an amazing variety of wildlife.

FAUNA

African elephant *(Loxodonta africana)* is the biggest land animal.

Giraffe *(Giraffa camelopardalis)* is the tallest animal, up to 17ft (5m).

Mountain gorilla *(Gorilla gorilla)* is the largest primate (see p.102).

FLORA

Tree senecio *(Senecio)*, found just below the glacier line, can reach 15ft (4.6m).

Acacia tree *(Acacia)* is umbrella-shaped and grows mainly on the African savanna.

Baobab tree *(Adansonia digitata)* grows in arid regions and can store water.

MOUNTAIN COMPARISONS

Everest
29,028ft
(8,848m)

Kilimanjaro
19,341ft
(5,895m)

DESERT COMPARISONS

Sahara
3,320,000sq miles
(8,600,000sq km)

Libyan 450,000sq miles
(1,165,500sq km)

LAND PROFILE
Africa is predominantly savanna (grassland) and desert.

Urban 0.5%

Wetlands 1%

Agriculture 11%

Desert 36%

Forest 15%

Grassland 36.5%

CROSS-SECTION

13,843ft
(4,000m)

Sea level

14,764ft
(4,500m)

Atlantic Ocean
Congo Basin
Great Rift Valley (western)
Ruwenzori Mountains
Lake Victoria
Great Rift Valley (eastern)
Indian Ocean

Length: 2,800 miles (4,500km)

327

EGYPT

MOST OF EGYPT is barren desert, with 99 percent of the population living by the Nile River. Farmers, called *fellahin*, grow cotton, wheat, rice, and vegetables. The Great Pyramid at Giza is one of the seven wonders of the ancient world.

Area 386,662sq miles (1,001,450sq km)
Government Presidential republic
Independence 1936, from Britain
Currency Egyptian pound
Population 54,800,000
Density 142 per sq mile (55 per sq km)
Official Language Arabic
Major Religions Muslim 86%, Christian 13%, other 1%

WEATHER FACTS

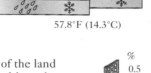

124°F (51°C) 1.1in (29mm) 34°F (1°C)
82.8°F (28.2°C) 57.8°F (14.3°C)

LAND PROFILE

Only 4.5 percent of the land in Egypt can be cultivated.

%
0.5
0.5
4.5
6.5
88.0

LIFESTYLE FACTS

• Overpopulation is a problem in Egypt. The estimated birth rate is one baby born every 24 seconds.

• Egypt is the world's leading producer of dates, and the fourth largest producer of watermelons.

• Tolls from the Suez Canal, completed in 1869, now bring the Egyptian government more than $500 million each year.

One Egyptian pound

LANGUAGE

A traditional greeting in Arabic is *ahlan wasahlan*. أهلاً وسهلاً

GREAT PYRAMIDS

The pyramids at Giza were built in about 2600 B.C. to house the mummified bodies of Egyptian kings, or pharaohs. The largest pyramid contains more than 2 million stone blocks and took 100,000 men more than 20 years to build.

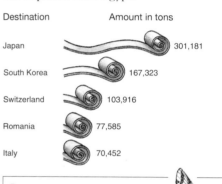

MAJOR COTTON IMPORTERS (1992)

One-third of the world's cotton is grown in and exported from Egypt.

Destination	Amount in tons
Japan	301,181
South Korea	167,323
Switzerland	103,916
Romania	77,585
Italy	70,452

SUDAN

THE LARGEST COUNTRY in Africa, Sudan includes both swamps and deserts. Sudan exports gum arabic, used in watercolor painting.

Area 967,498sq miles (2,505,810sq km)
Independence 1956, from Anglo-Egyptian agreement
Currency Sudanese pound
Population 26,700,000
Official Language Arabic
Major Religions Muslim 70%, Christian 9%, traditional beliefs 20%, other 1%

ETHIOPIA

FOUR OUT OF five Ethiopians work on the land, with coffee as the main cash crop. The Blue Nile flows from Lake Tana in the north.

Area 471,778sq miles (1,221,900sq km)
Foundation More than 2,000 years; never colonized
Currency Birr
Population 53,000,000
Official Language Amharic
Major Religions Muslim 40%, Ethiopian Orthodox 40%, traditional beliefs 15%, other 5%

LOCUST ATTACK

Massive swarms of locusts sometimes sweep across the African continent, destroying huge areas of crops in just minutes. Large swarms can weigh up to 50,000 tons.

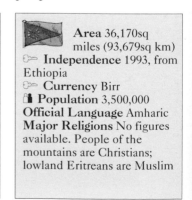

SOMALIA

SOMALIA'S ECONOMY is based on rearing animals for use or profit. Bananas, a major export, are grown on riverside plantations.

Area 246,202sq miles (637,660sq km)
Independence 1960, formation of Somali Republic
Currency Somali shilling
Population 8,041,000
Official Languages Arabic, Somali
Major Religions Muslim 100%

WATER FACTS

• Two billion people in the world lack access to safe water.

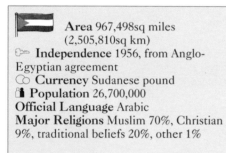

• A family of six needs about 20 gallons (91 liters) of water a day for basic needs, such as drinking and keeping clean.

• In Ethiopia 39.5 million people have no access to a safe supply of water. In Sudan the figure is 14.7 million, in Somalia, 4.8 million.

• In the Sudan it takes at least 2 hours, or a journey of 5 miles (8km), every day to fetch water. This work is usually done by women and children.

DJIBOUTI

THIS IMPORTANT TRADING port for Ethiopia occupies a prime site between the Indian Ocean and the Red Sea.

Area 8,958sq miles (23,200sq km)
Independence 1977, from France
Currency Djibouti franc
Population 500,000
Official Language Arabic, French
Major Religions Muslim 94%, other 6%

ERITREA

FARMING IS DIFFICULT in Eritrea, a hot country with very little rainfall and locust plagues. Many people live as nomads.

Area 36,170sq miles (93,679sq km)
Independence 1993, from Ethiopia
Currency Birr
Population 3,500,000
Official Language Amharic
Major Religions No figures available. People of the mountains are Christians; lowland Eritreans are Muslim

TANZANIA

THE MAIN EXPORT crops of Tanzania include sisal, which is used to make rope. Most of the world's cloves grow on the islands of Zanzibar.

Area 364,901sq miles (945,090sq km)
Independence 1961, from Britain
Currency Tanzanian shilling
Population 27,800,000
Official Languages Swahili, English
Major Religions Christian 33%, Muslim 33%, traditional beliefs 30%, other 4%

KENYA

KENYA LIES ON the equator. It consists of dry grasslands, which are home to wildlife such as elephants, lions, and zebras. Most people live in the highlands of the southwest, where there is enough rain to grow crops and graze cattle and sheep.

Area 224,082sq miles (580,370sq km)
Government Presidential republic
Independence 1963, from Britain
Currency Kenya shilling
Population 25,200,000
Density 114 per sq mile (44 per sq km)
Official Language Swahili
Major Religions Protestant 38%, Roman Catholic 28%, traditional beliefs 26%, Muslim 6%, other 2%

WEATHER FACTS

98.6°F (37°C)   37.8in (959mm)   41°F (5°C)

65.5°F (18.6°C)   61.7°F (16.5°C)

LIFESTYLE FACTS

• Kenya has the world's youngest population with about 50% of the people under 15 years of age.

• There are two rainy seasons in Kenya. The "long" rains are between March and May and "short" rains between October and November.

• Kenya produces 80% of the world's pyrethrum. This is a type of chrysanthemum: the flowers are used for making insecticide.

LAND PROFILE

Almost two-thirds of Kenya is covered in arid grassland.

%
0.5
2.6
8.6
10.7
14.9
62.7

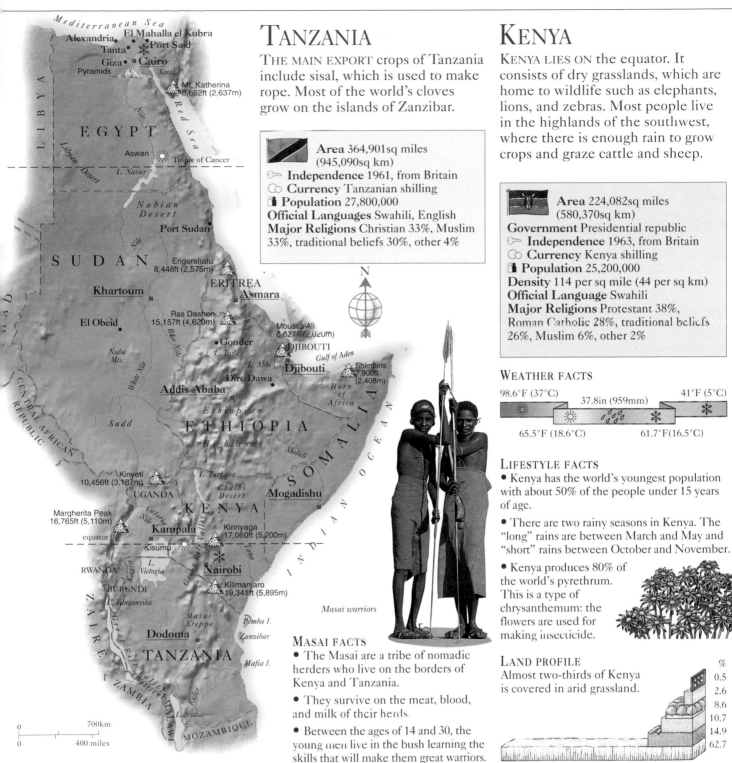

Masai warriors

MASAI FACTS

• The Masai are a tribe of nomadic herders who live on the borders of Kenya and Tanzania.

• They survive on the meat, blood, and milk of their herds.

• Between the ages of 14 and 30, the young men live in the bush learning the skills that will make them great warriors.

UGANDA

ONE-FIFTH OF Uganda consists of large lakes and swamps. Most farmers grow their own food, such as sweet potatoes, corn, and beans, although coffee is grown for export.

Area 91,074sq miles (235,880sq km)
Independence 1962, from Britain
Currency Uganda shilling
Population 16,876,000
Official Languages English, Swahili
Major Religions Roman Catholic 38%, Protestant 33%, traditional beliefs 13%, Muslim 5%, Hindu and other 11%

MAJOR NATIONAL PARKS AND GAME RESERVES

Name	Size	Key animal
Selous Tanzania, Tanzania	17,375sq miles (45,000sq km)	
Tsavo National Park, Kenya	8,036sq miles (20,812sq km)	
Serengeti National Park, Tanzania	5,700sq miles (14,76 sq km)	
Ruaha National Park, Tanzania	5,000sq miles (12,950sq km)	
Ngorongoro Conservation Area, Tanzania	3,202sq miles (8,292sq km)	

MOROCCO

MOROCCO HAS MILD winters and hot, dry summers. On the fertile coastal plains farmers grow fruits and vegetables that are canned for export. Most people are Berbers, a name given to them by their Arab conquerors in the 7th century.

Area 172,414sq miles (446,550sq km)
Government Constitutional monarchy
Independence 1956, from France
Currency Moroccan dirham
Population 26,300,000
Density 153 per sq mile (59 per sq km)
Official Language Arabic
Major Religions Sunni Muslim 99%, Christian, Jewish, and other 1%

WEATHER FACTS

120°F (49°C)   20in (503mm)   27°F (-3°C)

72°F (22.2°C)   55.4°F (13°C)

LAND PROFILE

Almost 40% of Morocco is grassland.

| % |
| 0.2 |
| 2.3 |
| 11.1 |
| 23 |
| 24.5 |
| 38.9 |

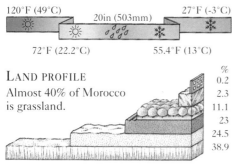

FLOWER FACTS

• In Morocco, roses, gladioli, carnations, irises, and marigolds are grown for export. In 1991, production exceeded 2,700 tons.

• Saffron, used to flavor rice, is produced in the eastern region of Morocco. Saffron comes from the crocus flower, and it takes about 400,000 stamens to make 2.2lb (1kg).

CAPE VERDE

THE VOLCANIC Cape Verde islands are divided into the Windward and Leeward groups. Most of the people are Creole, and the main crops include bananas and sugarcane.

Area 1,556sq miles (4,030sq km)
Independence 1975, from Portugal
Currency Cape Verde escudo
Population 400,000
Official Language Portuguese
Major Religions Roman Catholic 97%, Protestant and other 3%

LIFESTYLE FACTS

• A covered market, called a souk, is where Moroccan traders sell spices, fruits, and textiles.

• Skilled craftworkers make beautiful pictures using wood from lemon, cedar, and sandalwood trees.

• The Moroccan leather industry produces shoes, bags, and clothes. Tanning, the process of turning animal skins into leather, is also an important industry.

FANTASIA

Every year in Morocco there is an event called the Fantasia. Two groups of horsemen in traditional dress charge the length of the arena, firing rifles. The spectacle dates back to the ancient warfare tactics of Berber horsemen.

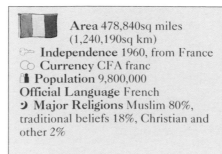

WESTERN SAHARA

WESTERN SAHARA IS the emptiest country in the world with just 2.6 persons per sq mile (one person per sq km). Few crops are grown, but farmers raise goats and sheep.

Area 97,344sq miles (252,120sq km)
Independence 1976, from Spain; currently occupied by Morocco
Currency Moroccan dirham
Population 200,000
Official Language none; most people speak different Arabic dialects
Major Religion Muslim 100%

MALI

ONLY ABOUT 2 percent of Mali is arable land. Cotton and peanuts are the main crops. The Malinke and Songhai tribes have a reputation for fine music and dancing.

Area 478,840sq miles (1,240,190sq km)
Independence 1960, from France
Currency CFA franc
Population 9,800,000
Official Language French
Major Religions Muslim 80%, traditional beliefs 18%, Christian and other 2%

LANGUAGE

A traditional greeting in Arabic is *ahlan wasahlan*.

أَهْلاً وَسَهْلاً

MARRAKESH MOSQUE

The Koutoubia Mosque, Marrakesh, was built during the 11th century on the orders of Yacoub El Mansour. Its minaret stands 230ft (70m) tall. It is known as the booksellers' mosque because traders used to gather outside to sell their books.

MAJOR CANNED EXPORTS (1992)	
Product	Value US$
Sardines	99,176,059
Olives	41,317,852
Apricots	13,159,900
Tomatoes	11,994,936
Green beans	4,364,106

MAURITANIA

SAND DUNES COVER half this hot, dry country. Antelopes, lions, and elephants live in the southern grasslands. Fish from the Atlantic are exported.

Area 395,955sq miles (1,025,520sq km)
Independence 1960, from France
Currency Ouguiya
Population 2,100,000
Official Language Arabic
Major Religions Sunni Muslim 99%, other 1%

NIGER

NORTHERN NIGER IS almost empty; most people live in the south. One-sixth of the population still lives as nomads. Niger is one of the world's top producers of uranium.

Area 48,919sq miles (126,700 sq km)
Independence 1960, from France
Currency CFA franc
Population 8,300,000
Official Language French
Major Religions Sunni Muslim 85%, traditional beliefs 14.5%, Christian 0.5%

ALGERIA

MORE THAN 80 percent of
Algeria lies within the
Sahara desert. The
discovery of oil and
natural gas in the desert
has made these the
country's main exports.

Area 919,595sq miles
(2,381,740sq km)
Independence 1962, from France
Currency Dinar
Population 26,300,000
Official Language Arabic
Major Religions Sunni Muslim 99%,
Christian, Jewish, and other 1%

ROCK ART
This rock painting from
Tassili N'Ajjer, dated
about 6000 B.C., shows
nomadic herders. Until
about 4500 B.C., the
Sahara was not a desert.
There was enough rain to
support animals, such as
gazelles and buffaloes.

SAHARA FACTS
• The Sahara (the word means desert) is
the world's largest desert and covers
3,320,000sq miles (8,600,000sq km):
larger than the US.

• The dromedary camel is adapted to
life in the desert. It can travel 100
miles (160km) a day for eight days
without drinking any water.

• Despite its popular image,
only about 20% of the
Sahara is continuous sand.
The sand often forms into pyramid-shaped
dunes which can be up to 750ft (230m) tall.

PIPED WATER
Beneath the Sahara there are vast
underground supplies of water. The
Libyans are building a series of
pipelines to carry water to the coastal
areas for increased crop production.

DESERT TRIBES
The Tuareg, who are
of Berber origin,
are nomadic
tribes who live
on the edge
of the Sahara.
Long scarves
protect them
from the heat
and dust.

TUNISIA

GENERALLY TUNISIA HAS poor soil
and relies on tourism for most of its
income. Esparto grass, which grows
on the plains, is used to make
quality paper.

Area 63,170sq miles
(163,610sq km)
Independence 1956, from France
Currency Tunisian dinar
Population 8,400,000
Official Language Arabic
Major Religions Muslim 99%,
Christian, Jewish, and other 1%

FALCONRY
In Tunisia, falcons
are used to hunt quail,
hare, and partridge
during the summer.

MEDITERRANEAN SEA

Tunis
Algiers
Strait of Gibraltar
Melilla (Spain)
Ceuta (Spain)
Rabat
Chambi 5,066ft (1,544m)
Tripoli
Gulf of Sirte

Koutoubia Mosque (Marrakesh)

ATLANTIC OCEAN
WESTERN SAHARA
MOROCCO
ATLAS MOUNTAINS
TUNISIA

Laâyoune

ALGERIA
LIBYA
EGYPT
SAHARA
Libyan Desert

Kediet Ijill 3,002ft (915m)
Tahat 9,573ft (2,918m)
Ahaggar
Bette 7,500ft (2,286m)

MAURITANIA
Nouakchott
L. Rkiz

MALI
Tassili N'Ajjer
Tibesti

Emi Koussi 11,205ft (3,415m)

L. Faguibine
Bagzane 6,634ft (2,022m)

CAPE VERDE
São Tiago Praia

Senegal
NIGER
CHAD

GUINEA
Bamako
2,510ft (765m)
BURKINA
Niamey
N'Djamena
L. Chad
SUDAN

CÔTE D'IVOIRE
NIGERIA
CAMEROON
Charr
CENTRAL AFRICAN REPUBLIC

75km
40 miles

LIBYA

LIBYA IS ONE of the world's leading
producers of oil. Although the
country is mainly desert, citrus
fruits, figs, and dates are grown in
the southern oases.

Area 679,362sq miles
(1,759,540sq km)
Independence 1951, from Italy
Currency Libyan dinar
Population 4,900,000
Official Language Arabic
Major Religions Sunni Muslim 97%,
other 3%

CHAD

CHAD HAS A landscape of grassland,
desert, and tropical forests. Cotton
is grown in the south of the country.
Sodium bicarbonate (baking soda) is
mined near Lake Chad.

Area 495,755sq miles
(1,284,000sq km)
Independence 1960, from France
Currency CFA franc
Population 5,800,000
Official Languages Arabic, French
Major Religions Muslim 50%,
traditional beliefs 43%, Christian 7%

NIGERIA

NIGERIA IS AFRICA'S most heavily populated country, and two-thirds of the people live in farming villages. The most valuable crops are cacao, palm products, and rubber, with oil as the main export.

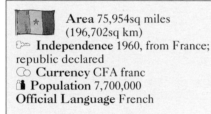

Area 356,669sq miles (923,770sq km)
Government Transitional government
Independence 1960, from Britain
Currency Naira
Population 115,700,000
Density 329 per sq mile (127 per sq km)
Official Language English

LAND PROFILE
More than half of Nigeria is grassland.

%
0.2
3.5
4.5
25.5
66.3

LIFESTYLE FACTS
• Although no school attendance is required, Nigeria has 33 universities with more than 243,000 students.

• All twins in Nigeria, boys and girls, are given the same names. The firstborn is called Taiwo, the second is Kehinde.

• The main ethnic groups in Nigeria are the Hausa (north), the Ibo (east), and the Yoruba (south and west).

10 Naira

LANGUAGE
A traditional greeting in Hausa is *ina-kwna*.

MARKETS
This scene in Benin City shows a woman buying chilies for a hot sauce used in cooking. She wears a length of patterned cloth, called a *pagne*, around her waist.

SENEGAL

IN THIS FLAT COUNTRY, peanuts are grown to make oil for export. The capital, Dakar, is West Africa's most important port.

Area 75,954sq miles (196,702sq km)
Independence 1960, from France; republic declared
Currency CFA franc
Population 7,700,000
Official Language French

THE GAMBIA

GAMBIA IS AFRICA'S smallest country, and stretches for 200 miles (320km) on either side of the Gambia River. The main cash crop is peanuts.

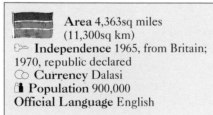

Area 4,363sq miles (11,300sq km)
Independence 1965, from Britain; 1970, republic declared
Currency Dalasi
Population 900,000
Official Language English

PEANUT FACTS
• Peanuts (or groundnuts) are a major crop in West Africa. Despite the name, it is not a true nut.

• The peanut pod has the unusual habit of ripening underground.

• There are about 300 by-products of peanuts, including flour, soap, and plastics.

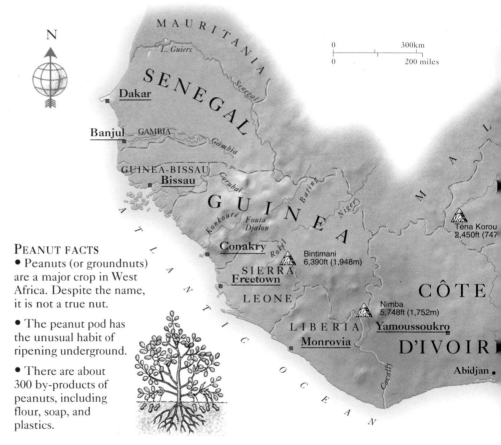

GUINEA-BISSAU

THE COAST HAS A monsoon climate with heavy rainfall between May and October. Waterbirds include pelicans and flamingos.

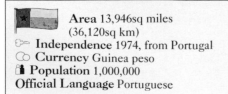

Area 13,946sq miles (36,120sq km)
Independence 1974, from Portugal
Currency Guinea peso
Population 1,000,000
Official Language Portuguese

GUINEA

GUINEA IS THE world's second biggest producer of the mineral bauxite. Iron ore, gold, and diamonds are also mined here.

Area 94,927sq miles (245,860sq km)
Independence 1958, from France
Currency Guinean franc
Population 6,100,000
Official Language French

SIERRA LEONE

PORTUGUESE EXPLORERS in the 15th century named this country, which means "lion mountain." Diamonds and bauxite are the main exports.

Area 27,653sq miles (71,620sq km)
Independence 1961, from Britain
Currency Leone
Population 4,400,000
Official Language English

LANGUAGE RHYTHMS

The Ashanti language of West Africa is a tonal language, and a special drum can be played to reproduce the tonal pattern of a word. Drum language, which has its own vocabulary, can be used to send messages from one village to another.

TALKING DRUMS

animal skin

"waist"

leather thongs

The *kalungu*, or talking drum, is held together with thongs that link the two skins. When the "waist" is squeezed, the sound can be changed.

LIBERIA

LIBERIA WAS FOUNDED as a home for freed slaves from the US. High-quality iron ore has replaced rubber as the country's most valuable product.

Area 43,000sq miles (111,370sq km)
Independence 1847, independent state founded
Currency Liberian dollar
Population 2,800,000
Official Language English

CÔTE D'IVOIRE

THERE ARE 66 different tribes living in the Ivory Coast. The Dan tribe carve beautiful masks for use in their traditional ceremonies.

Area 124,504sq miles (322,463sq km)
Independence 1960, from France
Currency CFA franc
Population 12,900,000
Official Language French

BURKINA

BURKINA IS AN inland country on the southern edge of the Sahara Desert. Infertile soils mean that less than 10 percent of the land can be farmed.

Area 105,869sq miles 274,200sq km)
Independence 1960, from France
Currency CFA franc
Population 9,500,000
Official Language French

NIGERIA WEATHER FACTS

114°F (46°C)   72in (1,838mm)   43°F (6°C)

81.7°F (27.6°C)   78.8°F (26°C)

ANCIENT KINGDOM OF BENIN

The kingdom of Benin, founded in the forests of what is now Nigeria, rose to power during the 14th century. Its skilled craftworkers made spectacular bronze heads and figures.

WEST AFRICAN RELIGIONS
Percentages of population

	Muslim	Christian	Traditional
Benin	15	18	67
Burkina	35	10	55
Côte d'Ivoire	23	12	65
Gambia	90	9	1
Ghana	12	43	45
Guinea	95	1.5	3.5
Guinea-Bissau	38	8	54
Liberia	14	68	18
Nigeria	50	40	10
Senegal	90	5	5
Sierra Leone	30	10	60
Togo	15	35	50

GHANA

GHANA WAS THE first African country to win its independence. Ghana exports more cacao than any other country in the world.

Area 92,101sq miles (238,540sq km)
Independence 1957, from Britain
Currency Cedi
Population 16,000,000
Official Language English

TOGO

THE POPULATION OF Togo has about 30 ethnic groups, many from other parts of West Africa. Nearly half the people are under 15 years of age.

Area 21,927sq miles (56,790sq km)
Independence 1960, from France
Currency CFA franc
Population 3,800,000
Official Language French

BENIN

BENIN HAS A coastline fringed with saltwater lakes. Lake villages and old palaces make Benin popular with tourists.

Area 43,483sq miles (112,620sq km)
Independence 1960, from France
Currency CFA franc
Population 4,900,000
Official Language French

GABON

GABON LIES ACROSS the equator and is hot and rainy. About 75 percent of the country is rainforest. Gabon is the world's fourth largest producer of manganese.

Area 103,348sq miles (267,670sq km)
Independence 1960, from France
Currency CFA franc
Population 1,200,000
Official Language French
Major Religions Christian 60%, traditional beliefs 39%, Muslim, Hindu, and other 1%

TRADITIONAL BELIEFS

• Many Africans follow religious systems that existed before the introduction of the major faiths, such as Islam and Christianity.

• Many of these traditions suggest that natural objects, such as mountains and rivers, have a spirit. Spirits can be good or evil.

• Fetishes are figures thought to be inhabited by a spirit. A good spirit can be activated by rubbing the figure's nose or forehead and offering a prayer.

EQUATORIAL GUINEA

RIO MUNI, on the mainland, and the island of Bioko, make up Equatorial Guinea. Most people belong to the Fang, a group known for their storytelling and music.

Area 10,830sq miles (28,050sq km)
Independence 1968, from Spain
Currency CFA franc
Population 400,000
Official Language Spanish
Major Religions Roman Catholic 90%, other 10%

TURTLE BEACH
Thousands of turtles come to the south shore of the island of Bioko, in January and February each year, to lay their eggs. Only one in every 100 will survive.

Green turtle

CAMEROON

TROPICAL RAINFORESTS COVER much of the Republic of Cameroon. The country's main export is cacao, which is used to make cocoa and chocolate.

Area 183,568sq miles (475,440sq km)
Independence 1960, from France
Currency CFA franc
Population 12,200,000
Official Languages English, French
Major Religions Christian 53%, traditional beliefs 25%, Muslim 22%

LIVING IN THE RAINFOREST

• Large areas of Central Africa are covered in rainforest. The forest is warm and damp and home to wildlife such as chimpanzees, leopards, and a wealth of birdlife.

• In the rainforests, there are groups of people commonly known as pygmies (a name they dislike). They survive by hunting animals and gathering wild plants, nuts, and honey.

• Forest homes are made from a framework of poles tied together and thatched with large leaves. No crops are planted, so there is no need to cut down this forest retreat.

• The main forest people are the Twa, the BaKa, and the Mbuti, who live in an area that covers parts of Gabon, Congo, Central African Republic, Cameroon, and Zaire.

SAO TOME AND PRINCIPE

THESE VOLCANIC ISLANDS lie in the Gulf of Guinea. About 40 percent of the land is planted with cacao trees. Most people live in São Tomé.

Area 372sq miles (964sq km)
Independence 1975, from Portugal
Currency Dobra
Population 124,000
Official Language Portuguese
Major Religions Roman Catholic 84%, Protestant 15%, other 1%

YAOUNDÉ
Yaoundé is the capital city and business center of Cameroon. It also has many schools and research institutes.

CENTRAL AFRICAN REPUBLIC

TIMBER, COFFEE, and cotton are the main exports here. Along the rivers, used for access to the sea, are hippopotamuses and crocodiles.

Area 240,534sq miles (622,980sq km)
Independence 1960, from France
Currency CFA franc
Population 3,200,000
Official Languages French, Sango
Major Religions Traditional beliefs 60%, Christian 35%, Muslim 5%

CONGO

ALMOST TWO-THIRDS of the Congo is covered with tropical rainforest. The coast and swamps contain coconut palms and mangroves.

Area 132,047sq miles (342,000sq km)
Independence 1960, from France
Currency CFA franc
Population 2,400,000
Official Language French
Major Religions Traditional beliefs 50%, Roman Catholic 25%, Protestant 23%, Muslim 2%

ANGOLA

THE MAIN PRODUCTS of Angola are oil and diamonds. The long coastline also provides good fishing for sardines and mackerel.

Area 481,353sq miles (1,246,700sq km)
Independence 1975, from Portugal
Currency New kwanza
Population 9,900,000
Official Language Portuguese
Major Religions Christian 90%, traditional beliefs 10%

N

CHAD

NIGERIA

CAMEROON

CENTRAL
AFRICAN
REPUBLIC

Mt. Toussoro
4,364ft (1,330m)

Kotto

SUDAN

Bangui

Bomu

Uele

Cameroon Mountain
13,436ft (4,095m)

Sanaga

Yaoundé

Malabo
Bioko

EQUATORIAL GUINEA
Gulf of Guinea

SAO TOME &
PRINCIPE
São Tomé

Rio
Muni

Mont Tembo
3,937ft (1,200m)

Libreville

GABON

L. Onangué

Ogooué

CONGO

Ubangi

Congo (Zaire)

Aruwimi

Margherita Peak
16,765ft (5,110m)

UGANDA

Equator

Karisimbi
14,787ft (4,507m)

Kigali
RWANDA

L. Kivu

Bujumbura
BURUNDI

Lukuga

Lualaba

Lomami

Malagarasi R.

TANZANIA

Brazzaville
Monts de la Lékéti
3,412ft (1,040m)

Kinshasa

CABINDA
(Angola)
Cabinda

ZAIRE

Luanda

Cuanza

ATLANTIC OCEAN

ANGOLA

Serra do Môco
8,596ft (2,620m)

6,782ft
(2,067m)

L. Tanganyika

ZAMBIA

Muchinga Mts.

Lusaka

L. Kariba

MOZAMBIQUE

Zambezi

Victoria
Falls

ZIMBABWE

NAMIBIA

BOTSWANA

0 ___ 75 km
0 ___ 40 miles

FISHING METHODS
The coasts of Angola are dotted with fishing villages. Some fish are caught by using conical traps that hang from specially built scaffolding.

RWANDA

RWANDA IS ONE of Africa's most densely populated countries. Chief exports include coffee, tungsten, tea, and pyrethrum.

R   **Area** 10,170sq miles (26,340sq km)
Independence 1962, from Belgium
Currency Rwanda franc
Population 7,500,000
Official Languages French, Rwanda
Major Religions Traditional beliefs 50%, Roman Catholics 45%, Protestants, Muslims, and other 5%

GORILLAS OF RWANDA
One of the last remaining sanctuaries of the mountain gorilla is in Rwanda. The largest of all primates, gorillas live in female groups with one male.

BURUNDI

A TINY, DENSELY populated country, Burundi is only 165 miles (265km) wide. Nickel, copper, and cobalt are mined in the southeast.

Area 10,745sq miles (27,830sq km)
Independence 1962, from Belgium
Currency Burundi franc
Population 5,800,000
Official Languages French, Kirundi
Major Religions Christian 60%, traditional beliefs 39%, Muslim 1%

REGIONAL LIFESTYLE FACTS
• Sao Tome has the highest literacy rate in Central Africa (63%) and the third highest life expectancy in all of Africa.
• The wooden masks of Central Africa inspired the Spanish artist Picasso (see p.163).

Mask from Zaire

• A vegetarian dish from the Central African Republic consists of spinach or greens mixed with peanut butter to make a thick stew. It is served with rice or cornmeal.
• Makossa, the music of Cameroon, is popular all over Africa. Musicians use a thumb piano (sanza), flute, and percussion.

Thumb piano

• In parts of Zambia, areas of dense forest are burned to clear the land for farming. The ash acts as a fertilizer.

ZAIRE

THIS COUNTRY IS the world's largest producer of industrial diamonds. Minerals, mainly copper, make up 80 percent of total exports.

Area 905,567sq miles (2,345,410sq km)
Independence 1960, from Belgium
Currency Zaire
Population 39,900,000
Official Language French
Major Religions Traditional beliefs 50%, Roman Catholic 38%, Protestant 12%

VICTORIA FALLS
Victoria Falls lies on the border of Zambia and Zimbabwe. Water falls 354ft (108m), and has twice the drop of Niagara Falls. The spray can be seen from 40 miles (65km) away.

ZAMBIA

ZAMBIA IS A large, landlocked country. The economy relies on road and rail transportation through the port of Dar-es-Salaam in Tanzania.

Area 290,584sq miles (752,610sq km)
Independence 1964, from Britain
Currency Zambian kwacha
Population 8,600,000
Official Language English
Major Religions Christian 70%, traditional beliefs 28%, other 2%

SOUTH AFRICA

MOST OF South Africa lies on a plateau, or tableland, about 2,953 feet (900 meters) above sea level. Land is used for grazing and wool is an important export. Minerals, such as gold, platinum, diamonds, and coal, provide most of the wealth.

Area 471,446sq miles (1,221,040sq km)
Government Presidential republic
Foundation 1961, declaration of Republic of South Africa
Territories Transkei, Bophuthatswana, Ciskei, and Venda
Currency Rand
Population 39,800,000
Density 85 per sq mile (33 per sq km)
Official Languages Afrikaans, English
Major Religions Christian 66%, Hindu and Muslim 20%, other 14%

CENTER OF GOVERNMENT

The Parliament Building in Cape Town was used for the first time in 1885. The building provided chambers for the two Houses of the Cape Parliament, as well as a large library. Nelson Mandela took office here as the first black president of South Africa in May 1994.

MAJOR SOUTH AFRICAN LANGUAGES	
Language	Number of speakers
Zulu	8,541,173
Xhosa	6,891,358
Afrikaans	6,188,981
Tswana	3,601,609
North Sotho	3,437,971
English	3,432,042

NAMIBIA

THIS HOT, DRY country includes the barren Namib Desert and part of the Kalahari. Namibia's main exports are diamonds and minerals.

Area 318,260sq miles (824,290sq km)
Independence 1990, from South Africa
Currency Rand
Population 1,500,000
Official Language English
Major Religions Christian 90%, traditional beliefs 10%

WEATHER FACTS

108°F (42°C) 31in (784mm) 16°F (-9°C)

70.7°F (21.5°C) 57°F (13.9°C)

LAND PROFILE

In South Africa 27% of the land is used for agriculture.

%
0.5
10
12.5
27
50

LIFESTYLE FACTS

- In April 1994, the first free elections were held. These followed years of apartheid, which denied black South Africans any voting power.
- Every year Zulus celebrate Shaka Day. Between 1818 and 1828, a great warrior called Shaka created the Zulu nation from many black clans in South Africa.
- South Africa has the fourth largest Indian community in the world.
- South Africa has the world's deepest gold mine. It is 12,392ft (3,777m) deep.

SWAZILAND

THIS SMALL COUNTRY lies within South Africa. It is well watered from four rivers that provide irrigation for citrus fruits and sugarcane.

Area 6,703sq miles (17,360sq km)
Independence 1968, from Britain
Currency Lilangeni
Population 800,000
Official Languages English, Swazi
Major Religions Christian 60%, traditional beliefs 40%

SAVANNA FACTS

- The springbok, a small antelope, lives on the grasslands. If alarmed, it can leap 11.5ft (3.5m) in the air with its back arched. This is called "pronking."
- The trees in the African savanna include several species of acacia. The sweet-thorn acacia sends tap roots down 213ft (65m) to seek out water.

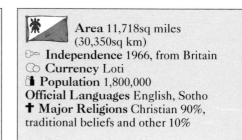

- The oldest surviving tribes of southern Africa are the San. These people now live in the semi-desert regions of Botswana and Namibia.

10 rand

LANGUAGE

A traditional greeting in Zulu is *kunjani*.

NATIONAL BIRD

The blue crane is the national bird; it lives in protected areas throughout South Africa.

PRECIOUS MINERALS

South Africa is the world's leading supplier of gold and platinum. The country produces 40% of the world's gold, and 72% of its platinum.

MAJOR PLATINUM MARKETS (1992)	
Destination	Amount in ounces (grams)
Japan	1,860,000oz (52,731,000g)
Western Europe	840,000oz (23,814,000g)
North America	715,000oz (20,270,250g)
Other	385,000oz (10,914,750g)

LESOTHO

LESOTHO IS AN independent nation within South Africa. The mountain slopes provide good pasture for cattle and sheep.

Area 11,718sq miles (30,350sq km)
Independence 1966, from Britain
Currency Loti
Population 1,800,000
Official Languages English, Sotho
Major Religions Christian 90%, traditional beliefs and other 10%

BOTSWANA

THE KALAHARI, a semidesert with grass and thorn bushes, covers much of Botswana. Most of its income comes from mining diamonds.

Area 224,607sq miles (581,730sq km)
Independence 1966, from Britain
Currency Pula
Population 1,300,000
Official Language English
Major Religions Traditional beliefs 50%, Christian 30%, Muslim and other 10%

ZIMBABWE

MOST PEOPLE IN the landlocked country of Zimbabwe belong to the Shona or Matabele tribes. Main cash crops are tobacco, cotton, and sugar.

Area 150,804sq miles (390,580sq km)
Independence 1980, from Britain
Currency Zimbabwe dollar
Population 10,600,000
Official Language English
Major Religions Syncretic (part Christian, part traditional beliefs) 50%, Christian 25%, traditional beliefs 24%, Muslim 1%

CAPITAL OF ZIMBABWE
Harare, named after the African chief Neharawe, is the capital of Zimbabwe. It is a modern city with wide, tree-lined streets.

MATABELE HOMES
Matabele women decorate their homes with bright geometric patterns.

COMOROS

THE THREE MAIN islands of Comoros lie between mainland Africa and Madagascar. More than half of its food has to be imported.

Area 861sq miles (2,230sq km)
Independence 1975, from France
Currency CFA franc
Population 600,000
Official Languages Arabic, French
Major Religions Muslim 99%, Roman Catholic 0.5%, other 0.5%

MADAGASCAR

THE MAIN EXPORTS of Madagascar are coffee, cloves, and vanilla. The fourth largest island in the world, Madagascar has a varied climate and a wide range of wildlife.

Area 226,657sq miles (587,040sq km)
Independence 1960, from France
Currency Malagasy franc
Population 12,800,000
Official Languages French, Malagasy
Major Religions Traditional beliefs 50%, Christian 43%, Muslim 7%

MADAGASCAR WILDLIFE FACTS
• Many unique animals evolved on Madagascar, which is isolated from mainland Africa.
• Two-thirds of the world's chameleons live on the island. These animals can change color when threatened.
• Madagascar is also home to the Indri, the largest of the world's lemurs.

PEOPLE OF MADAGASCAR
The fertility rate of women here is one of the highest in the world. More than two-fifths of the population is under 15 years of age.

MOZAMBIQUE

MOZAMBIQUE IS ONE of the poorest countries in the world. Most farms are state owned and exports include coconuts, cotton, tea, and sugar.

Area 309,496sq miles (801,590sq km)
Independence 1975, from Portugal
Currency Metical
Population 16,142,000
Official Language Portuguese
Major Religions Traditional beliefs 60%, Christian 30%, Muslim 10%

COCONUT
Copra, the dried flesh of the coconut, is used to make soap, shampoo, and margarine.

MALAWI

THIS NARROW COUNTRY is only 100 miles (160km) wide. Tobacco has recently overtaken tea as Malawi's major cash crop.

Area 45,884sq miles (118,840sq km)
Independence 1964, from Britain
Currency Malawi kwacha
Population 10,400,000
Official Languages English, Chewa
Major Religions Christian 75%, Muslim 10%, other 15%

ASIA

ASIA IS THE world's largest continent and includes hot, dry deserts, icy tundra, and tropical rainforests. Asia also has the largest population of any continent, with 60 percent of the world's people.

Area 17,251,315sq miles (44,680,718sq km)
Countries 44
Largest Russian Federation 6,592,846sq miles (17,075,400sq km)
Smallest Maldives 116sq miles (300sq km)
Population 3,280,232,000
Density 189 per sq mile (73 per sq km)
Major Languages Chinese, Hindi, Japanese, Bengali, Punjabi

▲ **Highest point** Mount Everest, Nepal/China 29,029ft (8,848m)
◹ **Lowest point** Dead Sea, Israel/Jordan 1,312ft (400m) below sea level
☀ **Highest temperature** 129°F (54°C), Tirat Tsvi, Israel
❄ **Lowest temperature** -90°F (-68°C) Verkhoyansk and Oimekon, Russian Federation

CLIMATE ZONES

KEY

- Mountain regions
- Polar and tundra
- Taiga
- Dry grassland
- Mediterranean
- Temperate forest
- Rainforest
- Tropical grassland
- Hot desert

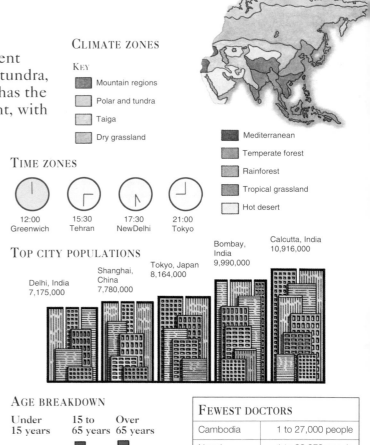

TIME ZONES

| 12:00 Greenwich | 15:30 Tehran | 17:30 NewDelhi | 21:00 Tokyo |

TOP CITY POPULATIONS

Delhi, India 7,175,000
Shanghai, China 7,780,000
Tokyo, Japan 8,164,000
Bombay, India 9,990,000
Calcutta, India 10,916,000

COUNTRIES, TERRITORIES, AND CAPITALS

Name	Capital	Name	Capital
Afghanistan	Kabul	Myanmar	Rangoon
Bahrain	Al Manama	Nepal	Kathmandu
Bangladesh	Dhaka	North Korea	Pyongyang
Bhutan	Thimphu	Oman	Muscat
Brunei	Bandar Seri Begawan	Pakistan	Islamabad
Cambodia	Phnom Penh	Philippines	Manila
China	Beijing	Qatar	Doha
Hong Kong	Victoria	Russian Federation	Moscow
India	New Delhi	Saudi Arabia	Riyadh
Indonesia	Jakarta	Singapore	Singapore
Iran	Tehran	South Korea	Seoul
Iraq	Baghdad	Sri Lanka	Colombo
Israel	Jerusalem	Syria	Damascus
Japan	Tokyo	Taiwan	Taipei
Jordan	Amman	Tajikistan	Dushanbe
Kazakhstan	Alma Ata	Thailand	Bangkok
Kuwait	Kuwait	Turkmenistan	Ashkhabad
Kyrgyzstan	Bishkek	United Arab Emirates	Abu Dhabi
Laos	Vientiane	Uzbekistan	Tashkent
Lebanon	Beirut	Vietnam	Hanoi
Malaysia	Kuala Lumpur	Yemen	Sana
Maldives	Male		
Mongolia	Ulan Bator		

AGE BREAKDOWN

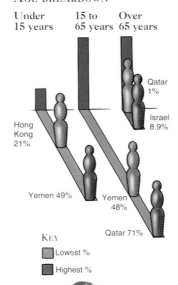

Under 15 years
15 to 65 years
Over 65 years

Hong Kong 21%
Qatar 1%
Israel 8.9%

Yemen 49%
Yemen 48%
Qatar 71%

KEY
- Lowest %
- Highest %

FEWEST DOCTORS

Cambodia	1 to 27,000 people
Nepal	1 to 20,978 people
Bhutan	1 to 9,700 people
Indonesia	1 to 7,372 people
Sri Lanka	1 to 7,255 people

LONGEST LIFESPAN

Female   82   78   77   77   76
Male   76   74   74   71   72

Japan   Israel   Brunei   Singapore   Kuwait

GROWING RICE

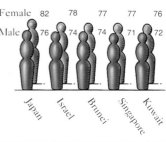

About 90 percent of the world's rice is grown in Asia. Rice, along with wheat and corn, supplies the basic food needs for more than half the population of the world.

CONTINENT FACTS

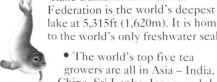

- Lake Baikal in the Russian Federation is the world's deepest lake at 5,315ft (1,620m). It is home to the world's only freshwater seal.

- The world's top five tea growers are all in Asia – India, China, Sri Lanka, Japan, and the Russian Federation.

Baikal seal

- All the world's major religions originated in Asia. They include Christianity, Islam, Judaism, Hinduism, Buddhism, and Sikhism.

- The highest city in the world is Lhasa, in Tibet, which lies at 11,975ft (3,650m) above sea level.

TALLEST MOUNTAINS

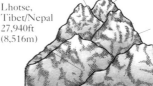

K2 (Mount Godwin Austen), Kashmir/China, 28,251ft (8,611m)

Mount Everest, Nepal/China, 29,030ft (8,848m)

Lhotse, Tibet/Nepal 27,940ft (8,516m)

Kangchenjunga, India/Nepal, 28,169ft (8,586m)

Makalu, Tibet/Nepal 27,766ft (8,463m)

CROSS-SECTION (SOUTH AND EAST)

Arctic Ocean
Kara Sea
Ural Mountains
Kirghiz Steppe
Kara Kum
Aral Sea
Iranian Plateau
Arabian Sea

4,921ft (1,500m)
0 Sea level
-9,843ft (3,000m)

Length: 5,000 miles (8,000km)

CROSS-SECTION (NORTH AND WEST)

29,029ft (8,848m)
Himalayas
Plateau of Tibet
Daxue Shan
Great Plain of China
Yellow Sea
Korea
Sea of Japan
Thar Desert
Red Basin
Honshu

Sea level
0
-14,764ft (4,500m)

Length: 5,000 miles (8,000km)

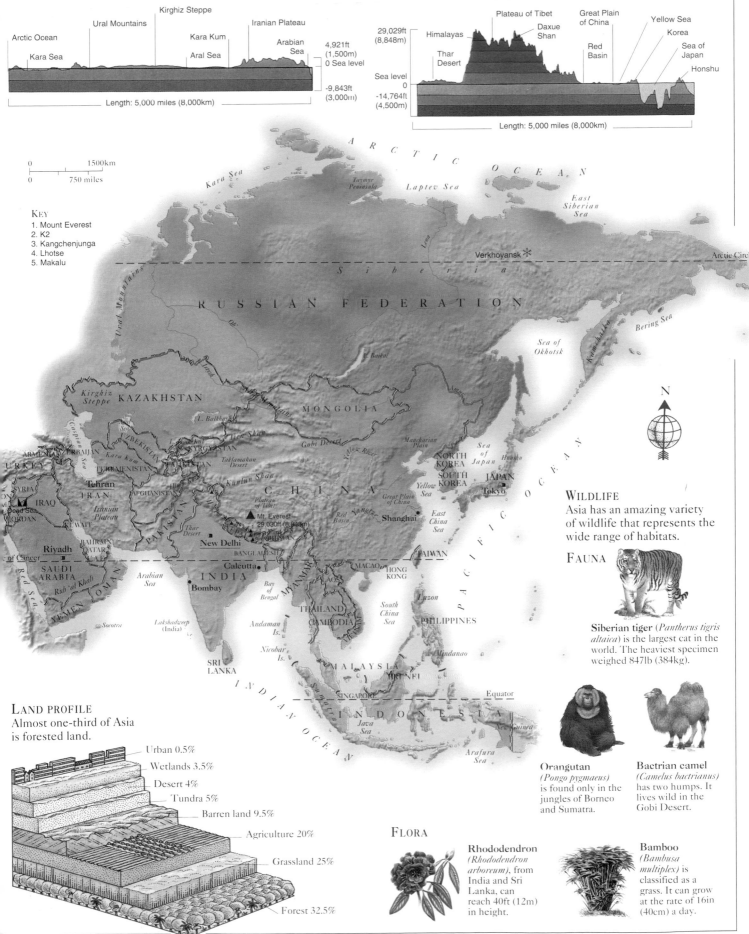

0   1500km
0   750 miles

KEY
1. Mount Everest
2. K2
3. Kangchenjunga
4. Lhotse
5. Makalu

ARCTIC OCEAN

Kara Sea
Taymyr Peninsula
Laptev Sea
East Siberian Sea

Verkhoyansk ❄

Arctic Circle

Siberia

RUSSIAN FEDERATION

Ob'
Irtysh
L. Baikal
Bering Sea
Sea of Okhotsk
Kamchatka

Kirghiz Steppe
KAZAKHSTAN
L. Balkhash
MONGOLIA
Manchurian Plain
NORTH KOREA
Sea of Japan
Honshu

Caspian Sea
Sea of Aral
UZBEKISTAN
KYRGYZSTAN
Tien Shan
Gobi Desert
Yellow River
SOUTH KOREA
JAPAN
Tokyo

ARMENIA
AZERBAIJAN
TURKMENISTAN
TAJIKISTAN
Taklamakan Desert
Kunlun Shan
CHINA
Yellow Sea
Shanghai
East China Sea

TURKEY
Kara Kum
Tehran
AFGHANISTAN
Plateau of Tibet
Mt. Everest 29,030ft (8,848m)
Yangtze
Red Basin
Great Plain of China

SYRIA
IRAQ
IRAN
Iranian Plateau
PAKISTAN
Thar Desert
TAIWAN

Dead Sea
JORDAN
KUWAIT
New Delhi
BANGLADESH
MACAO
HONG KONG

Tropic of Cancer
BAHRAIN
QATAR
Riyadh
U.A.E.
INDIA
Calcutta
MYANMAR
LAOS
South China Sea
Luzon

SAUDI ARABIA
OMAN
Rub 'al Khali
Arabian Sea
Bombay
Bay of Bengal
THAILAND
CAMBODIA
PHILIPPINES

Red Sea
YEMEN
Socotra
Lakshadweep (India)
Andaman Is.
Mindanao

SRI LANKA
Nicobar Is.
MALAYSIA
BRUNEI

INDIAN OCEAN
Sumatra
SINGAPORE
Equator
INDONESIA
New Guinea

PACIFIC OCEAN

N

Java Sea
Arafura Sea

LAND PROFILE
Almost one-third of Asia is forested land.

Urban 0.5%
Wetlands 3.5%
Desert 4%
Tundra 5%
Barren land 9.5%
Agriculture 20%
Grassland 25%
Forest 32.5%

WILDLIFE
Asia has an amazing variety of wildlife that represents the wide range of habitats.

FAUNA

Siberian tiger (*Pantherus tigris altaica*) is the largest cat in the world. The heaviest specimen weighed 847lb (384kg).

Orangutan (*Pongo pygmaeus*) is found only in the jungles of Borneo and Sumatra.

Bactrian camel (*Camelus bactrianus*) has two humps. It lives wild in the Gobi Desert.

FLORA

Rhododendron (*Rhododendron arboreum*), from India and Sri Lanka, can reach 40ft (12m) in height.

Bamboo (*Bambusa multiplex*) is classified as a grass. It can grow at the rate of 16in (40cm) a day.

ISRAEL

ABOUT FOUR-FIFTHS of Israelis are Jewish, and many Jews all over the world consider the State of Israel their homeland. The average age in Israel is very young: 25.6 years.

Area 7,992sq miles (20,700sq km)
Government Parliamentary democracy
Independence 1948, from Britain
Territories Disputes over land with Jordan and Syria
Currency New Shekel
Population 5,100,000
Density 650 per sq mile (251 per sq km)
Official Languages Hebrew and Arabic
Major Religions Jewish 82%, Muslim 14%, Christian 2%, Druze and other 2%

LAND PROFILE
Almost half of Israel is desert.

%
1.5
5.0
20.5
29.5
43.5

50 New shekels

LIFESTYLE FACTS
• Israel produces 95% of its own food, including delicious oranges, bananas, and avocados.

WESTERN WALL
Also called the Wailing Wall, this is a most sacred Jewish place of prayer and pilgrimage. It is all that remains of the Second Temple of Solomon, built about 200 B.C.

• 3% of Israelis live on 270 *kibbutzim*. These are communities, often farms, where families live together, sharing decisions, work, and property.

DEAD SEA
This inland sea lies 1,300ft (400m) below sea level, and is the lowest point on Earth. Its water is the saltiest known, and this allows people to float easily.

LEBANON

UNTIL THE outbreak of civil war in 1975, Lebanon was the trading and financial center of the Middle East. Its fertile inland plain yields fruits, vegetables, grains, and tobacco.

Area 4,015sq miles (10,400sq km)
Government Parliamentary democracy
Independence 1941, from France
Currency Lebanese Pound
Population 2,800,000
Official Language Arabic
Major Religions Muslim 57%, Christian 43%

SYRIA

THIS LAND OF rocky deserts and ancient cities has been called the cradle of civilization: the world's first alphabet was found in Ugarit.

Area 71,498sq miles (185,180sq km)
Government Republic
Independence 1946, from France
Currency Syrian Pound
Population 13,300,000
Official Language Arabic
Major Religions Muslim 74%, Alawite, Druze, and other Muslim sects 16%, Christian 10%

DAMASCUS
The capital of Syria, Damascus is the world's most ancient inhabited city. It is famous for its souqs (markets).

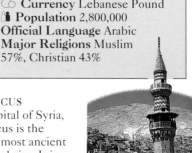

PALMYRA
Palmyra (city of palms) now lies in ruins. It was once a major stopping place for traveling merchants taking the shortest route to the Mediterranean.

REGIONAL WEATHER FACTS
Records

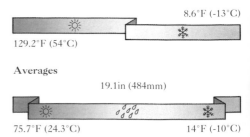

8.6°F (-13°C)

129.2°F (54°C)

Averages

19.1in (484mm)

75.7°F (24.3°C)   14°F (-10°C)

JORDAN

THE ARABIAN desert covers almost two-thirds of Jordan. Nomadic bedouin herders were the first desert-dwellers; now their numbers are dwindling.

Area 55,433sq miles (89,210sq km)
Government Constitutional monarchy
Independence 1946, from Britain
Currency Jordanian dinar
Population 4,300,000
Official Language Arabic
Major Religions Muslim 93%, other (mostly Christian) 7%

PETRA
This beautiful, rose-red city was carved from solid rock more than 2,000 years ago.

Map labels

N

TURKEY

Aleppo
Jabbul Salt Marsh
Lake Asad
Euphrates
Jabal 'Abd al 'Aziz
Tigris

IRAQ

SYRIA

Orontes

Homs

Tripoli
Qornet es Saouda 10,132ft (3,087m)
Palmyra

Beirut
LEBANON

Syrian Desert

Litani

Damascus

MEDITERRANEAN SEA

Mt. Hermon 9,236ft (2,814m)
Har Meron 3,965ft (1,208m)
Tirat Zevi
Haifa
Petah Tiqwa
Tel Aviv-Jaffa
Holon
West Bank
Jordan
Amman
Jerusalem
Western Wall
Gaza Strip
Dead Sea

ISRAEL

JORDAN

Negev
Petra
Ma'an

Ardh es Suwwan

SAUDI ARABIA

EGYPT

Eilat
Jabal Ram 5,757ft (1,754m)
Gulf of Aqaba

0   150km
0   100 miles

IRAQ

IRAQ'S STATE religion is Islam, and its followers are called Muslims. From 1980 to 1988, Iraq was at war with Iran.

- **Area** 169,236sq miles (438,320sq km)
- **Independence** 1932, from Britain
- **Currency** Iraqi dinar
- **Population** 19,300,000

SAUDI ARABIA

THIS KINGDOM is the world's leading producer and exporter of oil, and holds 25 percent of world oil reserves.

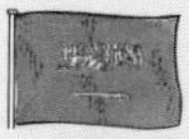

- **Area** 830,000sq miles (2,149,690sq km)
- **Independence and Unification** 1932
- **Currency** Saudi riyal
- **Population** 15,900,000

ARABIC
Arabic is the religious language of Muslims all over the world, whether they are Arabs or not.

LANGUAGE
A traditional greeting in Arabic is *ahlan wasahlan*.

أهلا و سهلا

ARAB HOUSES
Most Arabs are of the Muslim faith, which says that women must cover themselves from everyone except their families. Muslim houses have a screened balcony that shields women from the outside, and also keeps the house cool.

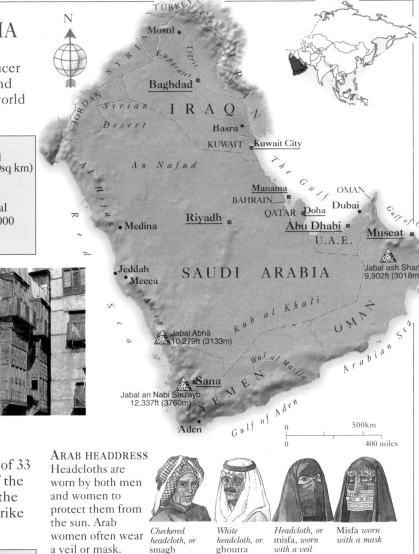

KUWAIT

IRAQ INVADED oil-rich Kuwait in 1990. The Iraqis were driven out seven months later during the Gulf War.

- **Area** 6,880sq miles (17,820sq km)
- **Independence** 1961, from Britain
- **Currency** Kuwaiti dinar
- **Population** 2,000,000

BAHRAIN

BAHRAIN IS MADE up of 33 islands in the west of the Arabian Gulf. It was the first Arab nation to strike oil, in 1932.

- **Area** 263sq miles (680sq km)
- **Independence** 1971, from Britain
- **Currency** Bahrain dinar
- **Population** 500,000

ARAB HEADDRESS
Headcloths are worn by both men and women to protect them from the sun. Arab women often wear a veil or mask.

Checkered headcloth, or smagh

White headcloth, or ghoutra

Headcloth, or misfa, worn with a veil

Misfa worn with a mask

MAJOR OIL PRODUCERS	Country	Barrels per day (1993)
The countries in the table are members of OPEC (Organization of Petroleum Exporting Countries), which was formed in 1960.	Saudi Arabia	8,378,000
	Iran	3,439,000
	United Arab Emirates	2,283,000
	Kuwait	1,822,000
	Data supplied by OPEC Data Services, Vienna	

YEMEN

NORTH AND South Yemen were united in 1990 to form the Republic of Yemen. Oil finds are small compared to wealthy neighboring countries.

- **Area** 203,850sq miles (527,970sq km)
- **Unification** 1990
- **Currency** Northern riyal and southern dinar
- **Population** 12,500,000

OMAN

SINCE 1970, when Sultan Qaboos took power, Oman's oil wealth has been used to develop industry, education, and health care.

- **Area** 82,031sq miles (212,460sq km)
- **Independence** 1951, from Britain
- **Currency** Omani rial
- **Population** 1,600,000

QATAR

UP TO 70 percent of Qatar's people were attracted there by jobs in the oil industry. Qatar has one of the lowest death rates in the world.

- **Area** 4,247sq miles (11,000sq km)
- **Independence** 1971, from Britain
- **Currency** Qatar riyal
- **Population** 500,000

UNITED ARAB EMIRATES

THE UAE HAS some of the richest oil deposits in the world. Money from oil is used to turn the desert into farmland.

- **Area** 32,278sq miles (83,600sq km)
- **Independence** 1971, from Britain
- **Currency** UAE dirham
- **Population** 1,700,000

Map labels: TURKEY, Mosul, N, SYRIA, Euphrates, Tigris, IRAN, Baghdad, JORDAN, Syrian Desert, I R A Q, Basra, KUWAIT, Kuwait City, An Nafud, Al Hijaz, The Gulf, Manama, OMAN, BAHRAIN, QATAR, Doha, Dubai, Gulf of Oman, Riyadh, Abu Dhabi, Muscat, U.A.E., Medina, Red Sea, SAUDI ARABIA, Jabal ash Sham 9,902ft (3018m), Asir, Jeddah, Mecca, Rub al Khali, OMAN, Jabal Abha 10,279ft (3133m), Wal al Masila, Arabian Sea, Sana, Jabal an Nabi Shu'ayb 12,337ft (3760m), Y E M E N, Aden, Gulf of Aden

500km / 400 miles

IRAN

ORIGINALLY CALLED PERSIA, Iran is a flat, mainly barren land surrounded by mountains. The only fertile areas are near the Caspian Sea and the foothills of the mountains. The country has large reserves of oil, natural gas, and minerals.

Area 636,296sq miles (1,648,000sq km)
Government Islamic republic
Independence 1925, from Britain
Currency Iranian rial
Population 61,600,000
Density 98 per sq mile (38 per sq km)
Official Language Farsi (Persian)
Major Religions Shi'ite Muslim 95%, Sunni Muslim 4%, Baha'i, Christian, Jewish, and Zoroastrian 1%

ARCHITECTURE
The Imam Mosque is in the traditional Islamic architectural style. The mosque, built in 1020, is decorated with fine tile work.

Imam Mosque, Isfahan

The modern Shayad Monument was built to commemorate King Cyrus's birth, 2,500 years ago. He united the Persian Empire.

Shayad Monument, Tehran

WEATHER FACTS
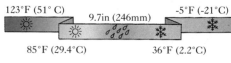

123°F (51° C)   9.7in (246mm)   -5°F (-21°C)
85°F (29.4°C)   36°F (2.2°C)

LAND PROFILE
Only 6.5% of Iran is agricultural land.

%
0.5
0.5
6.5
11.5
22
59

LIFESTYLE FACTS
• All Iranian men have to join the armed forces at the age of 16. The only reasons for exemption are poor health or the death of a brother in military service since 1979.

• Wrestling and horseracing are traditional sports, although rugby and volleyball are the most popular modern games.

• Iran is the world's second largest oil producer. Oil accounts for 80% of revenue and 95% of foreign exchange earnings.

• Most towns get their water supply from a series of long irrigation tunnels, called *qanat*, which bring water from the mountains.

MUSLIM FACTS
• Muslims believe that the last and greatest of the prophets was Muhammad, who was born in Arabia in A.D. 570. Islam is the name that the prophet Muhammad gave to the religion of the Muslims.

• All women in Iran, even tourists, must cover their bodies. Only hands, feet, and face may show. Records are kept of anyone breaking this law.

Iranian woman in traditional headcloth

LANGUAGE
A traditional greeting in Farsi is *salam*.

سلام

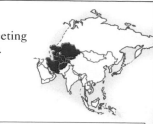

MAJOR OIL MARKETS (1992)

Importer	Thousand barrels per day
Western Europe	1,195
Asia and Far East	938
Eastern Europe	185
Latin America	125
Africa	45
Middle East	30

PERSIAN CARPETS
Hand-woven carpets are Iran's second largest export. Persian carpets have different patterns according to their region of origin. These include Isfahan, Kashan, Kerman, Qom, Shiraz, and Tabriz.

• After Muhammad's death, there was a dispute among his followers about who should lead the Muslims. The Sunnis followed the Caliphs while the Shi'ites decided to follow Muhammad's cousin, Ali.

• Under Islam it is possible for a man to have four wives, but he must treat them all equally.

• The Koran is the Holy Book of the Muslims. It is the basis for Muslim law on all important aspects of life, and is treated with great respect.

TURKMENISTAN

TURKMENISTAN IS AN extremely dry land, with large supplies of natural gas beneath the Kara Kum desert. In irrigated areas, farmers grow cotton, wheat, grapes, and melons.

Area 188,456sq miles (488,100sq km)
Government Presidential republic
Independence 1991, from Soviet Union
Currency Manat
Population 3,861,000
Density 21 per sq mile (8 per sq km)
Official Language Turkmen
Major Religions No figures available. Most are Sunni Muslim; some Russian Orthodox

AFGHANISTAN

THIS AGRICULTURAL COUNTRY is divided by the Hindu Kush Mountains, where many people still live as nomads. In villages, farmers raise sheep to export the lambskins.

Area 251,773sq miles (652,090sq km)
Government Islamic republic
Independence 1919, from Britain
Currency Afghani
Population 19,100,000
Density 75 per sq mile (29 per sq km)
Official Languages Dari (Persian) and Pashtu
Major Religions Sunni Muslim 80%, Shi'ite Muslim 19%, Hindu, Jewish, and Sikh 1%

TAJIKISTAN

THE PAMIR MOUNTAINS of Tajikistan have one of the world's longest mountain glaciers – 45 miles (72km) long. In the valleys, farmers grow fruit, rice, and cotton.

Area 55,251sq miles (143,100sq km)
Government Parliamentary republic
Independence 1991, from Soviet Union
Currency Rouble
Population 5,587,000
Density 101 per sq mile (39 per sq km)
Official Language Tajik
Major Religions No figures available. Most are Sunni Muslim; some Shi'ites, Russian Orthodox, and Jewish

Map labels:
RUSSIAN FEDERATION
Petropavlovsk
Semipalatinsk
Karaganda
Kirghiz Steppe
Kazakh Uplands
Belukha 14,784ft (4,506m)
KAZAKHSTAN
Atyrau
Aral Sea
Lake Balkhash
UZBEKISTAN
Syr Darya
Alma-Ata
Bishkek
Shymkent
KYRGYZSTAN
Tashkent
Naryn
Pobedy Peak 24,407ft (7,439m)
CASPIAN SEA
Amu Darya
TURKMENISTAN
Samarkand
Tien Shan
CHINA
Kara Kum
11,61ft (4,424m)
TAJIKISTAN
Lake Karakul
Commuism Peak 24,591ft (7,495m)
AZERBAIJAN
Ashgabat
10,292ft (3,137m)
Dushanbe
Tabriz
Pamirs
Mashhad
Damavand 18,607ft (5,671m)
Noshaq 24,558ft (7,485m)
Tehran
Dasht-e Kavir
Hindu Kush
Qom
Kabul
Bakhtaran
Kashan
AFGHANISTAN
Isfahan
Imam Mosque
Ahvaz
Abadan
IRAN
Helmand
Dasht-e Lut
PAKISTAN
The Gulf
Strait of Hormuz
Gulf of Oman
0 — 600km
0 — 300 miles

N

KAZAKHSTAN

MOST OF KAZAKHSTAN is a
dry plain, with mountains
to the southeast. The
main crop is wheat, which
is grown in the north.
Industries include mining
for copper, lead, gold, and
silver.

Area 1,049,155sq
miles (2,717,300sqkm)
Government Parliamentary
republic
Independence 1991, from
Soviet Union
Currency Tenge
Population 17,048,000
Density 15.5 per sq mile
(6 per sq km)
Official Language Kazakh
Major Religions No
figures available. Most are
Sunni Muslim, with a small
Russian Orthodox community

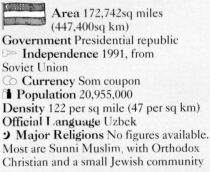

YURTS
Yurts, traditional homes of the
Kazakhs, can be 5ft (1.5m)
high and 20ft (6m) across.
Their collapsible frameworks
of wood are held tight by
leather thongs. Felt is then
stretched over the frame and
lashed into position.

leather thong
felt covering

UZBEKISTAN

MUCH OF UZBEKISTAN is desert. In
the east, mountain streams irrigate
the land, and farmers can grow
cotton, rice, and mulberry trees for
feeding silkworms.

Area 172,742sq miles
(447,400sq km)
Government Presidential republic
Independence 1991, from
Soviet Union
Currency Som coupon
Population 20,955,000
Density 122 per sq mile (47 per sq km)
Official Language Uzbek
Major Religions No figures available.
Most are Sunni Muslim, with Orthodox
Christian and a small Jewish community

KYRGYZSTAN

MANY OF THE Kyrgyz people are
nomads who tend their flocks on the
slopes of the Tien Shan Mountains.
In Bishkek, there are factories for
processing leather and soap.

Area 76,641sq miles
(198,500sq km)
Government Presidential republic
Independence 1991, from
Soviet Union
Currency Soms
Population 4,518,000
Density 60 per sq mile (23 per sq km)
Official Language Kyrgyz
Major Religion No figures
available. Most are Sunni Muslim

CASPIAN SEA
• The Caspian Sea is the largest inland
lake in the world and covers an area of
143,205sq miles (371,000sq km).

• Sturgeon are found in the Caspian Sea.
These fish can grow up to 23ft (7m) long,
and their eggs, called caviar, are an
expensive delicacy.
Caviar is a major
export from Iran.

• Salmon, bream, mullet, carp, catfish, and
perch are also caught for export.

MAKING SILK
Silk is produced
by the white moth
caterpillar, or
silkworm. After
caterpillars have
spun a silken
cocoon, they are
put into boiling
water. The silk is
removed and spun
into threads.

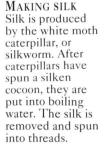

mulberry
leaves
silkworm

INDIA

INDIA HAS THE world's second largest population, and a wide variety of peoples, religions, and languages. The mountainous north contrasts with the low-lying south.

Area 1,269,345sq miles (3,287,590sq km)
Government Federal parliamentary democracy
Independence 1947, from Britain
Currency Indian rupee
Population 879,500,000
Density 767 per sq mile (296 per sq km)
Official Languages Hindi, English, Konkani, Manipuri, Nepali; 19 languages recognized constitutionally
Major Religions Hindu 83%, Muslim 11%, Christian 2%, Sikh 2%, Buddhist 1%, Jain 0.5%, Parsee and Jewish 0.43%, other 0.07%

WEATHER FACTS

114.8°F (46°C)   25.3in (642mm)   6.8°F (-14°C)

88.9°F (31.6°C)   57.2°F (14°C)

100 Indian rupees

LAND PROFILE

Forest, rainforest, and crops, such as rice, flourish in India.

%
1
1.5
4
11.5
40
42

LANGUAGE

A traditional greeting in Hindi is *namaskar*. नमस्कार

Traditional seven-stringed sitar

LIFESTYLE FACTS

• Each Indian region has its own unique range of dishes. There are at least a hundred different ways of preparing curry sauces, and up to 30 spices to choose from.

• Kabaddi is an ancient sport, popular all over India. Two teams (women or men) play on a field, raiding each other's territory, while chanting.

• In classical Indian music, rhythms are very complicated, and the ability to sing is very highly regarded. The tabla (twin drums) and stringed instruments, such as the tambura and sitar, accompany the voice.

• India produces more films than any other country in the world: more than 800 every year. Bombay is the center of the Indian film industry.

NATIONAL SYMBOL

India's national symbol is the Royal Bengal tiger, which is a protected species.

TAJ MAHAL

The Taj Mahal, situated just outside Agra, was built by Mughal emperor Shah Jahan (1592–1666) as a tomb and monument to his favorite wife, Mumtaz Mahal. Her body lies beneath it. The Taj Mahal took 22 years to build and is one of the most visited buildings in the world.

INDIAN TEA PRODUCTION, (1992)

Area	Tons
Assam, Bengal, Bihar, and Tripura	598,946
Punjab, Uttar Pradesh, and Himachal Pradesh	2,166
South India	174,838
Total	775,950
Source: International Tea Committee	

TEXTILES

Textiles and clothing together make up India's second biggest export sector, after gems and jewelry. Textiles and clothes are produced in factories, but many people still work at home to produce beautiful, and often ancient, designs.

K2 8,611m (28,251ft)

Controlled by China, claimed by India

Peshawar
Islamabad Rawalpindi Srinagar
Gujranwala
Lahore
Faisalabad
Minar-e-Pakistan
Multan
Jacobabad
Nanda Devi 7,817m (25,646ft)
Kula Kangri 7,554m (24,783ft)
New Delhi
Kathmandu Thimphu
Jaipur Agra Lucknow Pashupatinath Mt. Everest 8,848m (29,029ft) BHUTAN
Taj Mahal Kanpur Ghaghra Patna Cherrapunji
Karachi Hyderabad Ganges Range Dhaka
Tropic of Cancer
Ahmadabad Vindhya Range Narmada Calcutta BANGLADESH
Surat Satpura Range Nagpur
I N D I A
Bombay Godavari Chilika Lake
Pune
Hyderabad
Bangalore Madras
Indus
Sulaiman Range
Thar Desert
AFGHANISTAN
PAKISTAN
IRAN
NEPAL
Himalayan Range
Brahmaputra
BURMA
Jamuna
Western Ghats
Eastern Ghats
Arabian Sea
Bay of Bengal
INDIAN OCEAN

N

0   500km
0   300 miles

RAINFALL

The rainiest town in the world is Cherrapunji, northeastern India, with an average 450in (11,437mm) of rainfall per year. This amount of rain would almost cover six adults standing on each other's shoulders.

PAKISTAN

IN 1988, BENAZIR BHUTTO became the only woman to lead a Muslim country when she was first elected prime minister of Pakistan.

Area 307,376sq miles (796,100sq km)
Government Federal parliamentary democracy
Independence 1947, from British India
Currency Pakistani rupee
Population 115,588,000
Density 419.6 per sq mile (162 per sq km)
Official Language Urdu
Major Religions Muslim 97%, Hindu 1.7%, Christian 1.3%

WEATHER FACTS

127.4°F (53°C) 35.4in (900mm) 24.8°F (-4°C)
87.1°F (30.6°C) 52.3°F (11.3°C)

LAND PROFILE

Pakistan is mostly covered in grassland and desert.

%
1
1.5
4
11.5
40
42

LIFESTYLE FACTS

• Pakistan's population, with one of the world's highest growth rates, is set to reach 150 million by the 21st century. Half the population is less than 15 years old.

• Pakistan has one of the world's best cricket teams. They won the cricket world cup in 1992 under captain Imran Khan

LANGUAGE

A traditional greeting in Nepali is *namaste*.

100 Pakistani rupees

MINAR-E

The Minar-e-Pakistan is a fine tower in Lahore. It was built on a historic spot in 1940 to commemorate Pakistan Day.

• Pakistan's male squash players are the best in the world. Jahangir Khan (b.1963) remained unbeaten for 5 years, 7 months, and one day: an all-time world record.

LANGUAGE

A traditional greeting in Urdu is *assalm-u-alaikum.* السلام علیکم

NEPAL

NEPAL IS A mountainous country, lying mostly in the Himalayas. About 250,000 people visit each year, mainly for mountain climbing.

LIFESTYLE FACTS

• In Nepal the traditional greeting is to press the palms together in a prayerlike gesture.

• The Nepalese celebrate 50 religious festivals each year, involving 120 days of celebrations. They are so frequent that they often overlap.

LANGUAGE

A traditional greeting in Nepali is *namaste*.

HINDU STATE

Nepal is the world's only Hindu state. Its many superb temples include gold-roofed Pashupatinath, the holiest of all the Nepalese temples dedicated to the god Shiva. Non-Hindus are not allowed to enter the temple.

Area 54,363sq miles (140,800sq km)
Government Constitutional monarchy
State established 1869
Currency Nepalese rupee
Population 20,600,000
Density 391 per sq miles (151 per sq km)
Official Language Nepali
Major Religions Hindu 90%, Buddhist 5.3%, Muslim 2.7%, Christian 0.21%, other 1.79%

BHUTAN

BHUTAN IS A Buddhist state, ruled by a king who allows only 2,250 tourists per year. Nine out of ten Bhutanese are farmers and herders.

Area 18,147sq miles (47,000sq km)
Government Monarchy, advised by parliament and priests
Independence 1949, from Britain
Currency Ngultrum
Population 1,600,000
Density 88 per sq mile (34 per sq km)
Official Language Dzongkha
Major Religions Mahayana Buddhist 70%, Hindu 24%, other 6%

VEGETATION

m
7,500
Bare rock; nothing can survive
Shrubs and dry alpine scrub 4,600
4,000
Coniferous forest
Evergreen and broadleaf forest 3,000
2,000
Tropical forest 1,000
0

LIFESTYLE FACTS

• Bhutanese food is hot and spicy. The national dish is *emadatsi*, made of chili peppers in cheese sauce.

• Rare blue sheep and snow leopards live on high ground.

• Archery is the Bhutanese national sport. Competitors may distract each other by jumping in front of the targets.

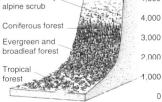

BANGLADESH

BANGLADESH IS A low, flat land, and hundreds of square miles are flooded every year. It is the world's most densely populated country.

Area 55,598sq miles (143,998sq km)
Government Parliamentary democracy
Independence 1971, from Pakistan
Currency Taka
Population 119,300,000
Density 2,308 per sq mile (891 per sq km)
Official Language Bengali
Major Religions Muslim 86.6%, Hindu 12.1%, Buddhist and Christian 1.3%

FLOOD PLAIN

Bangladesh, located on a low-lying delta, is flooded by monsoon rainfall from June to the end of September.

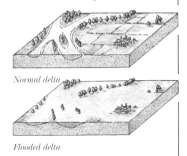

Normal delta

Flooded delta

LIFESTYLE FACTS

• Bangladesh's economy is based mainly on agriculture; the main export is jute, a plant used like cotton.

• Rivers form a huge transportation network: there are about 5,200 miles of waterways in Bangladesh.

SRI LANKA

FORMERLY CALLED CEYLON,
Sri Lanka is an island country off
the southeast coast of India. It has a
warm, tropical climate with two
monsoon seasons each year. Tea and
rubber plantations cover much of
the land. Gemstones and spices are
important exports.

Area 25,332sq miles
(65,610sq km)
Government Presidential democracy
Currency Sri Lanka rupee
Population 17,700,000
Density 707 per sq mile (273 per sq km)
Official Languages Sinhala, Tamil
Major Religions Buddhist 69%, Hindu
15%, Christian 8%, Muslim 8%

WEATHER FACTS

104°F (40°C)   27°F (-3°C)
99.5in (2,527mm)
81°F (27.2°C)   80°F (26.7°C)

LANGUAGE
A traditional greeting
in Sinhalese is
aubowan.

NATIONAL LANDMARK
The city of Kandy is home to
the 16th-century Buddhist Temple
of the Tooth (*Dalada Maligawa*).
This is where a sacred tooth, said
to be one of Buddha's, is kept in a
special casket.

INDIAN ELEPHANT
The Indian elephant
(*Elephas maximus*) is
similar to its African
relative, but it has
smaller ears and four
nails on each back
foot instead of three.

LIFESTYLE FACTS
• Most Sri Lankans make their own curry
powder by grinding a mixture of local spices
and herbs with a mortar and pestle.

• Every summer, during the *Perahera*
festival, elephants wearing embroidered
cloth parade through the city of Kandy.

• Sri Lanka has 242 species of
butterfly. During March and
April, the seasonal migration is a
spectacular sight.

TEA GROWING
Sri Lanka is one of the world's
top tea growers. Each year,
more than 401 million lb (182
million kg) of tea is exported
worldwide. Expert tasters will
check the quality and value
before making a purchase.

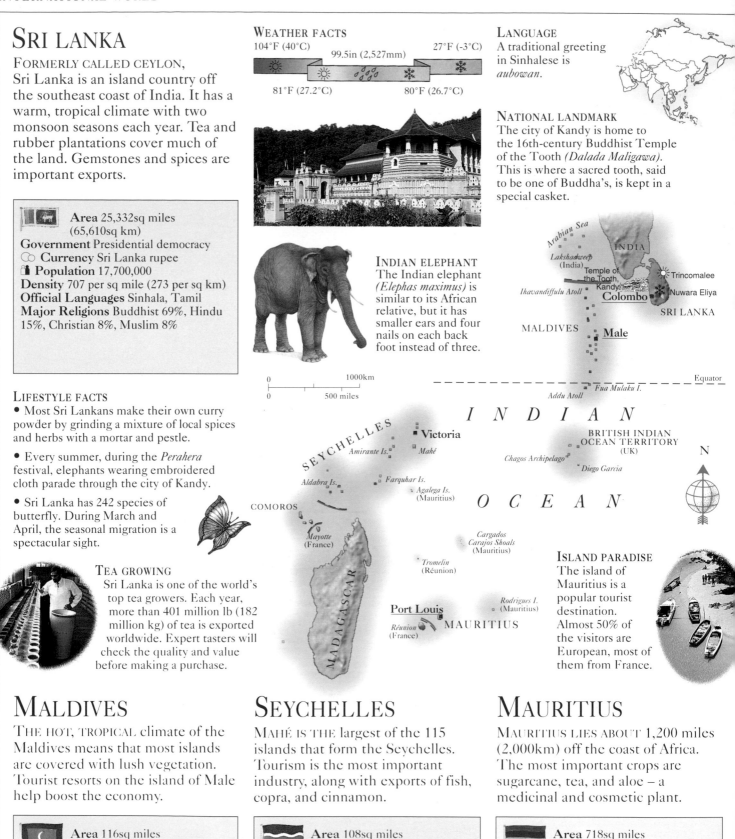

ISLAND PARADISE
The island of
Mauritius is a
popular tourist
destination.
Almost 50% of
the visitors are
European, most of
them from France.

MALDIVES

THE HOT, TROPICAL climate of the
Maldives means that most islands
are covered with lush vegetation.
Tourist resorts on the island of Male
help boost the economy.

Area 116sq miles
(300sq km)
Government Islamic presidential system
Currency Rufiyaa
Population 200,000
Official Language Dhivehi (Maldivian)
Major Religions Sunni Muslim 99%,
other 1%

SEYCHELLES

MAHÉ IS THE largest of the 115
islands that form the Seychelles.
Tourism is the most important
industry, along with exports of fish,
copra, and cinnamon.

Area 108sq miles
(280sq km)
Government Presidential republic
Currency Seychelles rupee
Population 68,000
Official Language Seselwa (French
Creole)
Major Religions Christian 98%,
other 2%

MAURITIUS

MAURITIUS LIES ABOUT 1,200 miles
(2,000km) off the coast of Africa.
The most important crops are
sugarcane, tea, and aloe – a
medicinal and cosmetic plant.

Area 718sq miles
(1,860sq km)
Government Presidential republic
Currency Mauritian rupee
Population 1,100,000
Official Language English
Major Religions Hindu 52%, Christian
28%, Muslim 17%, other 3%

THAILAND

THAILAND IS THE world's leading exporter of rice, and paddy fields cover much of the land. Most Thais are Buddhists, and the country has more than 30,000 Buddhist temples.

Area 198,117sq miles (513,120sq km)
Government Constitutional monarchy
Unification 1782, Thailand never colonized
Currency Baht
Population 56,100,000
Density 285 per sq mile (110 per sq km)
Official Language Thai
Major Religions Buddhist 95%, Muslim 3.8%, Christian 0.5%, Hindu 0.1%, other 0.6%

MYANMAR

THE NORTH OF Myanmar is flat, and farmers grow peanuts, millet, and cotton. Teak forests cover the south. The timber is hauled to rivers by elephants, and floated to sawmills.

Area 261,217sq miles (676,550sq km)
Government Military dictatorship
Independence 1948, from Britain
Currency Kyat
Population 43,700,000
Density 171 per sq mile (66 per sq km)
Official Language Burmese
Major Religions Buddhist 87.2%, Christian 5.6%, Muslim 3.6%, Hindu 1%, other 2.6%

CAMBODIA

MOST PEOPLE IN Cambodia are descendants of the Khmers who arrived in Southeast Asia in about 2000 B.C. Today, farmers grow rice, bananas, coconuts, and cotton.

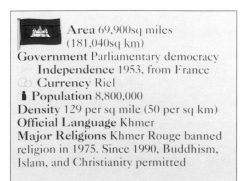

Area 69,900sq miles (181,040sq km)
Government Parliamentary democracy
Independence 1953, from France
Currency Riel
Population 8,800,000
Density 129 per sq mile (50 per sq km)
Official Language Khmer
Major Religions Khmer Rouge banned religion in 1975. Since 1990, Buddhism, Islam, and Christianity permitted

REGIONAL WEATHER FACTS

68.7in (1744mm)

80.6°F (27°C)   77.7°F (25.4°C)

MONSOON

Most of Southeast Asia is affected by the monsoon winds, which bring heavy rainfall every year from May to October. "Monsoon" comes from the Arabic word meaning season. Although the rains are vital for crops, such as rice, they can also cause disastrous floods.

LIFESTYLE FACTS

• Myanmar's rubies are considered the finest in the world. In the East, a ruby is thought to protect the wearer from harm.

• All young men in Thailand are expected to become monks for at least three months of their lives and reject all material wealth.

ANGKOR WAT

The magnificent temple city of Angkor Wat in Cambodia was built by the Khmers in the 12th century A.D.

LAOS

LAOS HAS MANY mountains and forests, and most people live in the Mekong River valley. Only about 4 percent of the land is suitable for agriculture. Tin is mined for export.

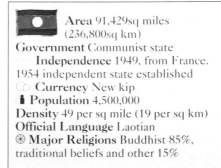

Area 91,429sq miles (236,800sq km)
Government Communist state
Independence 1949, from France. 1954 independent state established
Currency New kip
Population 4,500,000
Density 49 per sq mile (19 per sq km)
Official Language Laotian
Major Religions Buddhist 85%, traditional beliefs and other 15%

LANGUAGE

A traditional greeting in Thai is *sawatdee.* สวัสดี

THAI BOXING

Thai boxers use their feet, knees, elbows, and fists to fight.

Hkakabo Razi 19,296ft (5,881m)

Kumon Range

L. Indawgyi

Chin Hills

BANGLADESH

INDIA

CHINA

Mandalay

Irrawaddy

MYANMAR

Bay of Bengal

Salween

Inthanon 8,514ft (2,595m)

Rangoon

Mekong

Luang Prabang Range

Fan Si Pan 10,312ft (3,143m)

Hanoi

Gulf of Tongking

LAOS

Bia 9,252ft (2,820m)

Vientiane

VIETNAM

Mae Nam Ping

THAILAND

Gulf of Martaban

Andaman Sea

Bangkok

Batdambang

Tonle Sap

Angkor Wat

CAMBODIA

Gulf of Thailand

Aoral 5,948ft (1,813m)

Phnom Penh

Ho Chi Minh City

Isthmus of Kra

Samui I.

Phuket I.

Luang Lagoon

SOUTH CHINA SEA

Songkhla

MALAYSIA

N

0   500km
0   300 miles

VIETNAM

VIETNAM IS A warm, monsoon land with heavy rainfall and thick forests. Many forests were destroyed during the Vietnam War. Rice, corn, and sweet potatoes are the main crops.

Area 127,244sq miles (329,560sq km)
Government Communist state
Unification 1976, proclamation of Socialist Republic of Vietnam
Currency New dong
Population 69,500,000
Density 554 per sq mile (214 per sq km)
Official Language Vietnamese
Major Religions Buddhist 55%, Christian 7%, other 38%

CHINA

THE THIRD LARGEST country in the world, China contains almost one-quarter of the world's people. The landscape varies enormously. In the north there are dry deserts, while the south is warm and humid. Rice grows well in the warm, moist soil.

Area 3,705,405sq miles (9,596,960sq km)
Government Communist state
Unification 221 B.C., separate states united under First Emperor
Currency Renminbi (also called the yuan)
Population 1,188,000,000
Density 329 per sq mile (127 per sq km)
Official Language Mandarin Chinese
Major Religions Buddhist 6%, Muslim 2%, nonreligious 59%, traditional beliefs 20%, other 13%

WEATHER FACTS

111°F (44°C)   24in (623mm)   -30°F (-34°C)
79°F (26°C)   24°F (-4.4°C)

GREAT WALL OF CHINA
The Great Wall of China is the longest manmade structure in the world. In 214 B.C. the First Emperor ordered one wall over 1,460 miles (2,350km) long to guard the northern frontier.

MONGOLIA

THE CLIMATE IN Mongolia is severe and it is one of the least populated countries in the world. Most people were nomadic herders but land is now organized into state farms.

Area 604,250sq miles (1,565,000sq km)
Government Parliamentary democracy
Republic Mongolian People's Republic declared, 1924
Currency Tugrik
Population 2,300,000
Density 3 per sq mile (1 per sq km)
Official Language Khalka Mongol
Major Religions Limited religious practice due to former communist regime. Principal religion is Tibetan Buddhist, with 4% Muslim

LAND PROFILE
Most Chinese live in just 15% of the total land area.

%
1.5
2
6.5
9
21
24
36

LIFESTYLE FACTS
• The population in China increases by about 17 million people a year. To try to limit the expansion, one-child families are given priority for housing and medical care.

• One in five Chinese live in large cities; the rest live in the countryside. Most people travel by bicycle and there are 17,500,000 made in China every year.

REGIONAL CHINESE FOOD
• Peking (now Beijing) dishes often include duck and sweet and sour sauces.

• Food from the region of Sichuan is usually spicy, with garlic, chilis, and ginger.

• Cantonese cooking often features shellfish and other seafoods.

• Shangainese dishes can include steamed dumplings, as well as bird's nest soup made from the nests of cave swiftlets in southeast China.

TIBET FACTS
• Tibet lies in the highlands of southwest China at an average height of 14,800ft (4,500m). This is higher than most European mountains.

• Prayer flags are a Tibetan tradition symbolizing the Buddhist faith. Before the Chinese occupation, they flew from every home as a symbol of good luck.

Tibetan prayer flags

MONGOLIAN LIFESTYLE FACTS
• One-third of Mongolia is covered by the vast Gobi Desert. Gobi is the Mongolian word for "waterless place."

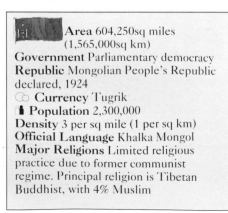

• Mongols are expert horsemen. The Three Games of Men festival takes place every July and includes a 20-mile (32-km) horse race for children aged seven to 12, wrestling, and archery.

• Mongolia has resources of coal, oil, and gold. The main coal mines are found near the capital city of Ulan Bator.

10 yuan

LANGUAGE
A traditional greeting in Mandarin is *nin hao*. 你好

IMPERIAL PALACE, BEIJING
The Imperial Palace in Beijing was built for the Emperor Zhu Di during the Ming Dynasty (1368–1644). The palace complex contains nearly 1,000 buildings. Only the emperor's family and people doing business were allowed into the central palace, which became known as the Forbidden City.

MAIN CHINESE OCCUPATIONS (1992)

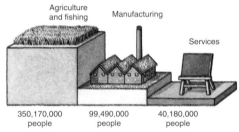

Agriculture and fishing   Manufacturing   Services

350,170,000 people   99,490,000 people   40,180,000 people

• The Dalai Lama is the head of the Tibetan Buddhists. He went into exile in India after Tibet was invaded by China in 1950. Dalai Lama is a Mongolian word meaning "great ocean."

• Tibetans consider it bad luck if it snows during a marriage procession. But it is good luck to meet a funeral procession or a passer-by carrying a pitcher of water.

• Because of the cool, dry air of Tibet, grain can be stored for up to 60 years.

MACAO

THIS SMALL TERRITORY lies on the south coast of China. Textiles, incense, and fireworks are Macao's major exports.

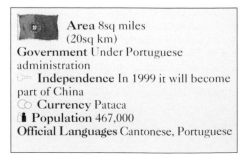

Area 8sq miles (20sq km)
Government Under Portuguese administration
Independence In 1999 it will become part of China
Currency Pataca
Population 467,000
Official Languages Cantonese, Portuguese

SOUTH KOREA

FORESTS COVER 70 percent of South Korea. Chief crops are rice and tobacco, and fishing is an important industry.

Area 38,232sq miles (99,020sq km)
Government Presidential democracy
Republic Republic of Korea declared, 1948
Currency Won
Population 44,200,000
Density 1,160 per sq mile (448 per sq km)
Official Language Korean
Major Religions Mahayana Buddhist 47%, Protestant 38%, Roman Catholic 11%, Confucian 3%, other 1%

NORTH KOREA

MOST PEOPLE LIVE on the coastal plains in the east of this mountainous country. Minerals such as copper and zinc are mined.

Area 46,541sq miles (120,540sq km)
Government Communist state
Republic Democratic People's Republic of Korea founded in 1948
Currency Won
Population 22,600,000
Density 487 per sq mile (188 per sq km)
Official Language Korean
Major Religions Organized religion not encouraged by the state

NORTH AND SOUTH KOREA FACTS

- Korean ginseng is a plant that is highly valued for its ability to improve memory and restore energy. The plant takes about seven years to mature.

- For centuries women divers, called *haenyo*, have collected seaweed and sea cucumbers from the coast off Cheju Island. A *haenyo* can dive to 60ft (18m) and hold her breath for four minutes.

- The remains of the oldest observatory in the world are in eastern South Korea. It was built in about A.D. 634.

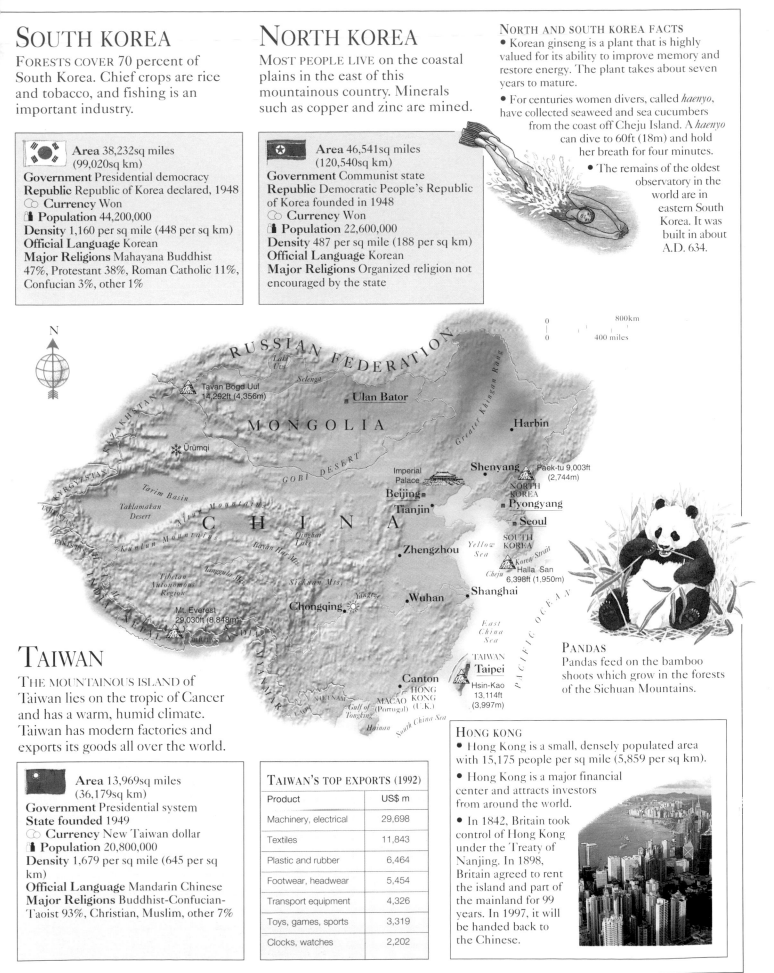

TAIWAN

THE MOUNTAINOUS ISLAND of Taiwan lies on the tropic of Cancer and has a warm, humid climate. Taiwan has modern factories and exports its goods all over the world.

Area 13,969sq miles (36,179sq km)
Government Presidential system
State founded 1949
Currency New Taiwan dollar
Population 20,800,000
Density 1,679 per sq mile (645 per sq km)
Official Language Mandarin Chinese
Major Religions Buddhist-Confucian-Taoist 93%, Christian, Muslim, other 7%

PANDAS

Pandas feed on the bamboo shoots which grow in the forests of the Sichuan Mountains.

TAIWAN'S TOP EXPORTS (1992)

Product	US$ m
Machinery, electrical	29,698
Textiles	11,843
Plastic and rubber	6,464
Footwear, headwear	5,454
Transport equipment	4,326
Toys, games, sports	3,319
Clocks, watches	2,202

HONG KONG

- Hong Kong is a small, densely populated area with 15,175 people per sq mile (5,859 per sq km).

- Hong Kong is a major financial center and attracts investors from around the world.

- In 1842, Britain took control of Hong Kong under the Treaty of Nanjing. In 1898, Britain agreed to rent the island and part of the mainland for 99 years. In 1997, it will be handed back to the Chinese.

JAPAN

JAPAN IS MADE up of a chain of about 3,900 volcanic islands. The four main islands are Hokkaido, Honshu, Shikoku, and Kyushu. Tokyo, the capital, is one of the most densely populated cities in the world.

Area 145,869sq miles (377,800sq km)
Government Parliamentary democracy
Independence Restored, 1952, after World War II occupation
Territories Ogasawara Islands
Currency Yen
Population 124,500,000
Density 857 per sq mile (331 per sq km)
Official Language Japanese
Major Religions Shintoist 92%, Buddhist 76%, other 11%. Many Japanese follow both Shintoism and Buddhism

WEATHER FACTS

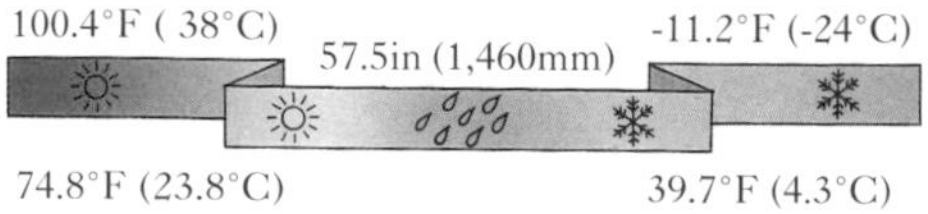

100.4°F (38°C)   57.5in (1,460mm)   -11.2°F (-24°C)
74.8°F (23.8°C)   39.7°F (4.3°C)

LANGUAGE
A traditional greeting in Japanese is *konnichiwa*. こんにちは

1,000 Japanese yen

BLOSSOM
The cherry blossom is the national flower of Japan and is celebrated with festivals in spring.

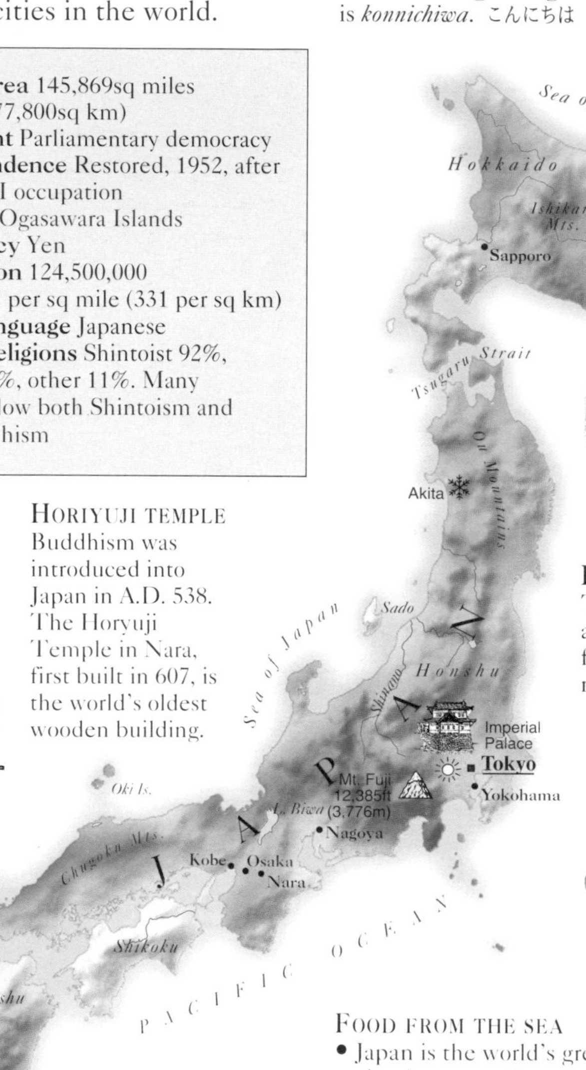

HORIYUJI TEMPLE
Buddhism was introduced into Japan in A.D. 538. The Horyuji Temple in Nara, first built in 607, is the world's oldest wooden building.

PHEASANT
The pheasant often appears in Japanese folklore and is the national bird.

LIFESTYLE FACTS
• A Japanese employee works longer hours (2,100 hours per year) than a worker in the United States (1,900 hours) or in Germany or France (1,600 hours).

• Japan has more golf courses per sq mile than any other country. Owing to lack of suitable space, there are multistory driving ranges.

• The Ainu, the aboriginal people of Japan, have their own culture, language, and religion. They live on Hokkaido.

• In Japan, traditional flower arranging is called *ikebana*. The display is based on three main lines that symbolize heaven, earth, and humankind.

IMPERIAL PALACE
The Imperial Palace was built on the grounds of Tokyo Castle. It is the official residence of the Japanese royal family. The present emperor, Akihito, is a direct descendant of the legendary first emperor Jimmu (660–585 B.C.).

FOOD FROM THE SEA
• Japan is the world's greatest fishing nation in terms of volume of catch. More than 10 million tons of fish are caught each year.

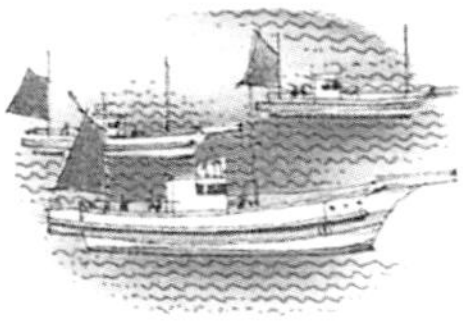

• Fish is the major source of protein, and each person in Japan eats an average of 66lb (30kg) of fish a year.

• Life expectancy in Japan is the highest in the world: 81.8 years for women and 75.9 years for men.

SUMO WRESTLERS
Sumo wrestlers may weigh up to 617lb (280kg). To maintain this colossal weight, a wrestler eats a daily stew of seafood, meat, vegetables, and tofu, called *chanko-nabe*.

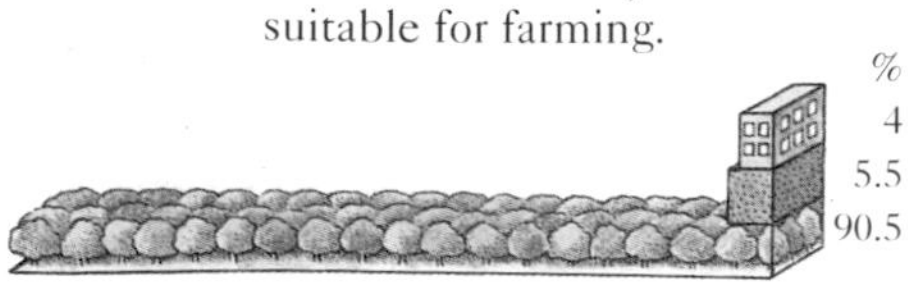

MOUNT FUJI FACTS
• Mount Fuji is one of Japan's 60 active volcanoes. It has not erupted since 1707.

• Mount Fuji is sacred to the Japanese, and in summer people climb to the shrine on the summit.

LAND PROFILE
Most of Japan is mountainous. Only 15% is suitable for farming.

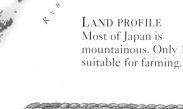

%
4
5.5
90.5

TOP ELECTRONIC EXPORTS (1991)
(Value in US $1,000's)

Export	Value	Quantity
TV cameras	6,089,207	10,584,747
Video recorders	5,749,019	22,738,529
Radios	3,117,454	26,180,047
Televisions	2,187,811	7,482,983
Tape recorders	1,438,636	25,681,470

Map labels: Sea of Okhotsk, Kurile Islands, Iturup, Kunashir, Shikotan, Hokkaido, Ishikari Mts., Sapporo, Tsugaru Strait, Ou Mountains, Akita, Sea of Japan, Sado, Shinano, Honshu, Oki Is., L. Biwa, Mt. Fuji 12,385ft (3,776m), Imperial Palace, Tokyo, Yokohama, Nagoya, Kobe, Osaka, Nara, Chugoku Mts., Tsushima, Shikoku, Kyushu, PACIFIC OCEAN, East China Sea, Osumi Is., Amami Is., Ryukyu Islands, Okinawa, JAPAN, N

0   250km
0   150 miles

INDONESIA

INDONESIA IS THE world's biggest island chain. It has more than 17,000 islands and covers three time zones. The weather is hot, wet, and humid. Rice is the most important food crop.

Area 735,358sq miles (1,904,570sq km)
Government Military regime
Independence 1949, declared Republic of the United States of Indonesia.
Currency Rupiah
Population 191,200,000
Density 259 per sq mile (100 per sq km)
Official Language Bahasa Indonesia
Major Religions Muslim 86.9%, Christian 9.6%, Hindu 1.9%, Buddhist 1%, traditional beliefs 0.6%

REGIONAL WEATHER FACTS

94.6in (2,403mm)

80.2°F (26.8°C)   80.1°F (26.7°C)

REGIONAL FACTS

• In Malaysia, workers collect latex from rubber trees. They make a diagonal cut in the tree and then collect the white latex, or rubber, that oozes from the cut.

• Java produces the world's finest batik: traditional cloth decorated using wax and dyes.

• Indonesia is the largest Islamic country in the world.

LANGUAGE

A traditional greeting in Bahasa is *selamat pagi*.

PHILIPPINES

THE PHILIPPINES IS a collection of more than 7,000 islands. Rainfall can be heavy, and typhoons sweep through the northern islands.

Area 115,830sq miles (300,000sq km)
Government Federal democracy
Independence 1946, from United States
Currency Philippine peso
Population 65,200,000
Density 544 per sq mile (210 per sq km)
Official Languages English, Pilipino
Major Religions Roman Catholic 84%, Protestant 10%, Muslim 5%, Buddhist and other 1%

KOMODO DRAGON
The world's largest lizard is found on the island of Komodo. It eats anything it can catch, even people.

MALAYSIA

THE COUNTRY OF Malaysia covers the Malay Peninsula and northern Borneo. Malaysia is the world's leading producer of natural rubber.

Area 127,317sq miles (329,750sq km)
Government Parliamentary monarchy
Independence 1957, from Britain
Currency Ringgit
Population 1,880,000
Density 148 per sq mile (57 per sq km)
Official Languages Bahasa Malay, English
Major Religions Muslim 53%, Buddhist 19%, Chinese faiths 11.6%, Christian 7%, Hindu 6.9%, traditional beliefs 2%, Sikh and other 0.5%

SINGAPORE

SINGAPORE IS A small and successful country. Most people work in industries making electrical goods, clothes, and transportation items.

Area 240sq miles (620sq km)
Government Parliamentary republic
Independence 1965, breaks away from Malaysia
Currency Singapore dollar
Population 2,800,000
Density 12,968 per sq mile (5,007 per sq km)
Official Languages Bahasa Malay, English, Mandarin, Tamil
Major Religions Buddhist-Taoist 53%, Muslim 16%, Hindu 4%, Christian 1%, other (including Sikh) and none 26%

BRUNEI

BRUNEI IS A tiny, but extremely rich, country on the island of Borneo. The wealth comes from local oil, and the people of Brunei pay no taxes.

Area 2,228sq miles (5,770sq km)
Government Absolute monarchy
Independence 1984, from British control
Currency Brunei dollar
Population 300,000
Density 148 per sq mile (57 per sq km)
Official Languages Malay, English
Major Religions Muslim 66% (mainly Sunni), Buddhist 14%, Christian 10%, other 10%

AUSTRALASIA AND OCEANIA

THIS AREA COVERS the continent of Australia, as well as New Zealand and numerous island groups in the Pacific Ocean. Climate zones vary greatly across the region; they include the wet, tropical conditions of the Pacific Islands as well as the hot, dry deserts of central Australia.

Area 3,285,048sq miles (8,508,238sq km)
Countries 13
Largest Australia 2,967,908sq miles (7,686,850sq km)
Smallest Nauru 8sq miles (21sq km)
🏢 **Population** 27,229,000
Density 8 per sq mile (3 per sq km)
Major Languages English, Italian (Australia), Fijian (Fiji), Hindi (Fiji), Greek (Australia)

▲ **Highest point** Mt. Wilhelm, Papua New Guinea 14,793ft (4,509m)
🔽 **Lowest point** Lake Eyre, Australia -49ft (-15m)
☀ **Highest temperature** 128°F (53°C), Bourke, Australia
❄ **Lowest temperature** -8°F (-22°C), Canberra, Australia

CLIMATE ZONES

KEY
- Mountains
- Hot desert
- Dry grassland
- Mediterranean
- Temperate forest
- Tropical grassland
- Rainforest

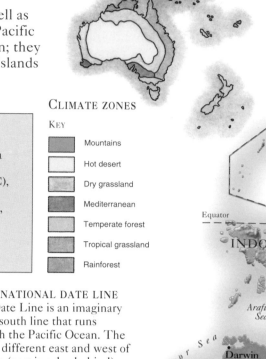

COUNTRIES, TERRITORIES, AND CAPITALS

Name	Capital
Australia	Canberra
Fiji	Suva
Kiribati	Bairiki
Marshall Islands	Majuro
Micronesia (Federated States of)	Kolonia
Nauru	No capital
New Zealand	Wellington
Papua New Guinea	Port Moresby
Solomon Islands	Honiara
Tonga	Nuku'alofa
Tuvalu	Funafuti
Vanuatu	Port Vila
Western Samoa	Apia

TIME ZONES

Greenwich 12:00
Perth 20:00
Sydney 22:00
Majuro 24:00 (midnight)

INTERNATIONAL DATE LINE
The Date Line is an imaginary north–south line that runs through the Pacific Ocean. The date is different east and west of the line (east is a day behind).

TOP CITY POPULATIONS

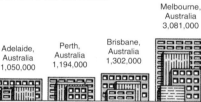

Adelaide, Australia 1,050,000
Perth, Australia 1,194,000
Brisbane, Australia 1,302,000
Melbourne, Australia 3,081,000
Sydney, Australia 3,657,000

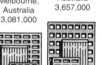

MILFORD SOUND
Milford Sound in New Zealand is a spectacular fjord that was created when the sea flooded a glaciated valley.

CONTINENT FACTS
• In Australia, the Royal Flying Doctor Service provides emergency medical treatment for people who live vast distances from the nearest source of medical help.

• New Zealand's North Island is a volcanic region, with three active volcanoes, hot springs, geysers, and boiling mud pools.
• There are about 25,000 islands in the Pacific Ocean, but only a few thousand are inhabited. The islands stretch across an area that is larger than the entire continent of Asia.

LARGEST DESERTS

Great Victoria 260,000sq miles (647,000sq km)

Great Sandy 157,000sq miles (407,000sq km)

Gibson 120,000sq miles (310,800sq km)

Simpson 40,000sq miles (103,600sq km)

AGE BREAKDOWN

Under 15 years
15 to 65 years
Over 65 years

Papua New Guinea 2.7%
Australia 11.2%
Tuvalu 31.8%
Marshall Islands 48.8%
Marshall Islands 48%
Australia 66.9%

KEY
- Lowest %
- Highest %

FEWEST DOCTORS

Papua New Guinea	1 to 10,083 people
Solomon Islands	1 to 8,812 people
Vanuatu	1 to 8,344 people
Western Samoa	1 to 4,075 people
Tonga	1 to 3,625 people

LONGEST LIFE SPAN

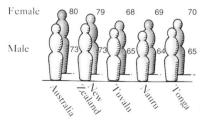

| Female | 80 | 79 | 68 | 69 | 70 |
| Male | 73 | 73 | 65 | 64 | 65 |

Australia, New Zealand, Tuvalu, Nauru, Tonga

P A C I F I C   O C E A N

Northern Mariana Islands

Wake I. (US)

MARSHALL ISLANDS

Majuro

Caroline Islands

MICRONESIA

Palmyra I. (US)

International Date Line

Gilbert Islands

Line Islands

N

K I R I B A T I

NAURU

Phoenix Islands

ismarck Sea

a

PAPUA NEW GUINEA

TUVALU

Tokelau (New Zealand)

Marquesas Islands

SOLOMON ISLANDS

Wallis & Futuna (France)

WESTERN SAMOA

American Samoa (US)

Coral Sea Islands (Australia)

VANUATU

FIJI

TONGA

Cook Islands (New Zealand)

French Polynesia (France)

New Caledonia (France)

Niue (NZ)

Tropic of Capricorn

Great Barrier Reef

Pitcairn Islands (UK)

•Brisbane

Norfolk I. (Australia)

Kermadec Islands (New Zealand)

•Sydney

NEW ZEALAND

■ **Canberra**

Tasman Sea

North Island

elbourne

Tasmania

■ **Wellington**

•Hobart

South Island

Chatham Islands

Milford Sound

Stewart I.

Bounty Islands

Antipodes Islands

Auckland Islands

Cambell I.

CROSS-SECTION

Indian Ocean | Mt. Bruce | Great Victoria Desert | Great Dividing Range | Tasman Sea | Pacific Ocean | New Zealand

9,843ft (3,000m)
0 Sea level
-14,764ft (-4,500m)

Length: 4,500 miles (7,250km)

0   1000km
0   600 miles

LAND PROFILE
Almost half the continent is covered in desert.

Barren land 0.25%   Urban 0.25%

Wetlands 3%

Agriculture 10.5%

Grassland 36%

Forest 5%

Desert 45%

FLORA

WILDLIFE
Many of these animals and plants are unique to Australasia and Oceania.

FAUNA

Tasmanian devil (*Sarcophilus harrisi*) is found only in Tasmania. It eats all of its prey – bones, fur, and feathers – until nothing is left.

Queen Alexandra's butterfly (*Ornithoptera alexandrae*) is the world's largest butterfly, with a wingspan that can measure up to 11in (28cm) across.

Red kangaroo (*Macropus rufus*) is the biggest marsupial in the world. A large male kangaroo can clear more than 26ft (8m) in one leap.

Spinning gum (*Eucalyptus perriniana*), from Australia, is so-called because some leaves form spinning disks.

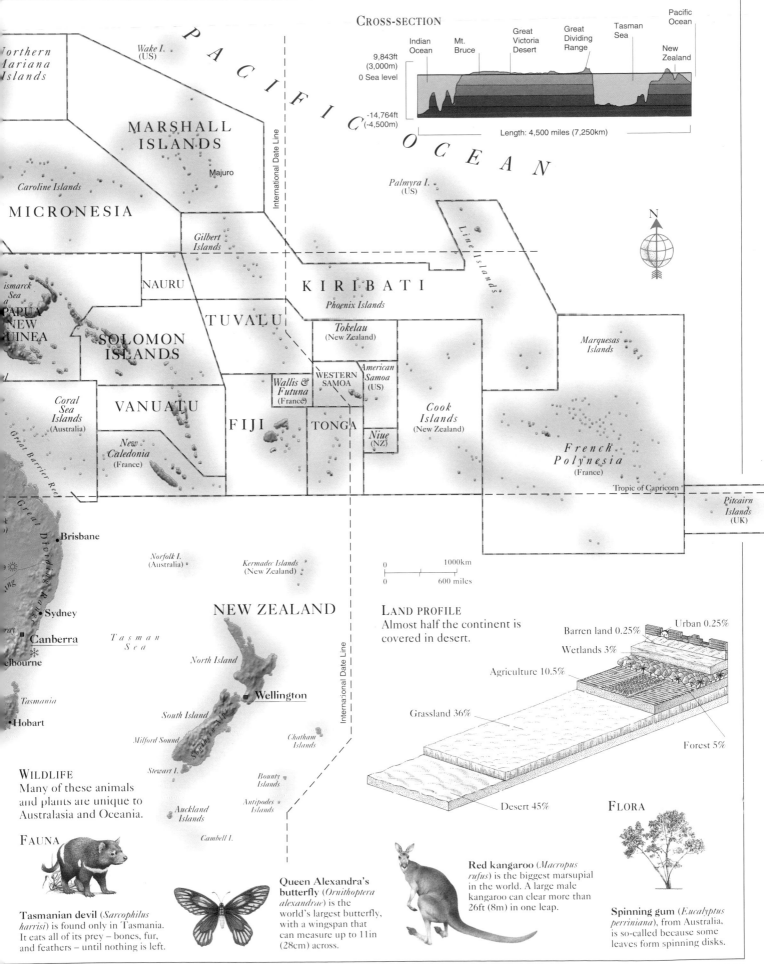

353

NEW ZEALAND

TWO MAIN ISLANDS and a number of smaller islands make up New Zealand. Its rich pastureland makes it one of the world's main producers of meat, dairy products, and wool. New Zealand is in an earthquake zone, and tremors are felt every year.

Area 103,807sq miles (268,860sq km)
Government Unitarian parliamentary democracy, with British sovereign as constitutional monarch
⌐ **Independence** 1947, from Britain
Territories Cook Islands, Niue, Tokelau
◯ **Currency** New Zealand dollar
Population 3,500,000
Density 34 per sq mile (13 per sq km)
Official Languages English, Maori
✝ **Major Religions** Anglican 24%, Presbyterian 18%, Roman Catholic 15%, Methodist 5%, other 38%

BEEHIVE BUILDING

This circular building, in the capital city of Wellington, is one of three parliament buildings. It was designed by British architect Sir Basil Spence (1907–76) and was opened in 1977.

SHEEP FARMING

The mild climate of New Zealand provides permanent pasture for the country's 56.2 million sheep. About 335,000 tons of wool are shorn a year, most of it used to supply top-quality knitting yarns for export.

MAORI FACTS

• New Zealand's first settlers were the Maori – Polynesians who arrived in about A.D. 950. They called the country Aotearoa, which means "the land of the long white cloud."

• At the 1991 census, the Maori population of New Zealand stood at 434,847, with 89% living on North Island. Almost one-third of Maoris are under 10 years of age.

• *Maoritanga* is the word for Maori culture; traditional Maori art is preserved through woodcarving and stone sculpture.

Maori woodcarver

WEATHER FACTS

95°F (35°C)   47.4in (1,205mm)   21.2°F (-6°C)
61.3°F (16.3°C)   49.1°F (9.5°C)

LIFESTYLE FACTS

• Sports are important to the people of New Zealand. The most popular sports for people over 15 years of age are swimming, diving, waterpolo, cycling, snooker and pool, tennis, and aerobics.

• In 1893, New Zealand became the first country where women could vote in national elections.

• Orchards produce a wide range of fruits ranging from apples to tamarillos, avocadoes, and kiwi fruit.

kiwi fruit

• Hiking is a popular pastime in New Zealand, where 13% of the land is turned over to National Parks.

NEW ZEALAND

Auckland, Bay of Plenty, Hamilton, NORTH ISLAND, L. Taupo, Hastings, Tasman Sea, Cook Strait, Wellington, Mt. Cook 12,317ft (3,754m), Christchurch, Chatham Islands, Southern Alps, SOUTH ISLAND, Dunedin, Stewart I., Bounty Islands, Snares Islands, Antipodes Islands, Auckland Islands, Campbell I., PACIFIC OCEAN

0 — 1750km
0 — 1000 miles

PAPUA NEW GUINEA

PAPUA NEW GUINEA occupies the eastern half of a large island. The land is mountainous, and there are deposits of gold, oil, and copper.

Area 178,703sq miles (462,840sq km)
Government Parliamentary democracy, with British monarch as head of state
⌐ **Independence** 1975, from Australian administration
◯ **Currency** Kina
Population 4,100,000
Density 23 per sq mile (9 per sq km)
Official Language English

10 New Zealand dollars

LAND PROFILE

More than two-thirds of the land is used for grazing.

%
1.5
5
20
32
41.4

MICRONESIA

MORE THAN 600 islands and islets make up the Federated States of Micronesia. Plants include black pepper, which is grown for export.

Area 1,120sq miles (2,900sq km)
⌐ **Independence** 1986, from the United States
◯ **Currency** United States dollar
Population 101,000
Density 373 per sq mile (144 per sq km)
Official Language English

NAURU

THE SMALL ISLAND of Nauru is surrounded by a coral reef. Agriculture is limited because of the infertile soil.

Area 8sq miles (21sq km)
⌐ **Independence** 1968, from UN supervision
◯ **Currency** Australian dollar
Population 9,000
Density 1,111 per sq mile (429 per sq km)
Official Language Nauruan

SOLOMON ISLANDS

MOST OF THE eight main islands in the Solomon Islands are thickly forested and have a hot, wet climate. Islanders catch tuna for export.

Area 11,158sq miles (28,900sq km)
⌐ **Independence** 1978, from Britain
◯ **Currency** Solomon Islands dollar
Population 300,000
Density 29 per sq mile (11 per sq km)
Official Language English

MARSHALL ISLANDS

THE MARSHALL ISLANDS consist of two parallel chains of coral atolls. Farming and fishing, as well as raising pigs, are the main activities.

Area 70sq miles
(181sq km)
Independence 1986, from UN supervision
Currency United States dollar
Population 48,000
Density 686 per sq mile (265 per sq km)
Official Language Marshallese

WESTERN SAMOA

THE PEOPLE OF Western Samoa are mainly Polynesians, descendants of the Maori. Frequent typhoons cause widespread damage to the islands.

Area 1,097sq miles
(2,840sq km)
Independence 1962, from UN supervision
Currency Tala
Population 169,000
Density 155 per sq mile (60 per sq km)
Official Languages English, Samoan

KIRIBATI

THE ISLANDS OF Kiribati have poor soil, so people rely on fishing. They use leaves from the pandanus tree to thatch their traditional homes.

Area 274sq miles
(710sq km)
Republic Declared 1979
Currency English
Population 66,000
Density 241 per sq mile (93 per sq km)
Official Language English

KIRIBATI CANOE
Fishing from canoes is traditional for the Pacific Ocean islanders. This fisherman from Kiribati has an outrigger, or float, on his canoe, for balance in rough seas.

TUVALU

FORMERLY THE ELLICE ISLANDS, Tuvalu is made up of nine small coral atolls. The sale of postage stamps is an important source of income.

Area 10sq miles
(26sq km)
Independence 1978, from Britain
Currency Australian dollar and Tuvaluan dollar
Population 9,450
Density 896 per sq mile (346 per sq km)
Official Language English

FIJI

MADE UP OF 322 islands, more than half of Fiji's land area is covered with forests. Coconuts are grown on plantations around the coasts.

Area 7,054sq miles
(18,270sq km)
Independence 1970, from Britain
Currency Fiji dollar
Population 715,375
Density 98 per sq mile (38 per sq km)
Official Language English

SUGARCANE
Sugar is the main cash crop in Fiji. Women cut the cane using machetes.

VANUATU

THE VANUATU ISLANDS form a chain about 497 miles (800km) long. Bananas, oranges, and pineapples are grown in the fertile volcanic soil.

Area 4,707sq miles
(12,190sq km)
Independence 1980, from France and Britain
Currency Vatu
Population 163,000
Density 34 per sq mile (13 per sq km)
Official Languages Bislama, English, French

TONGA

THERE ARE 169 islands in Tonga, some made of coral and some that are volcanic. Tonga is the last remaining Polynesian kingdom.

Area 290sq miles
(750sq km)
Independence 1970, from Britain
Currency Pa'anga
Population 94,000
Density 339 per sq mile (131 per sq km)
Official Languages English, Tongan

AUSTRALIA

THIS COUNTRY-CONTINENT is one of the oldest and flattest landmasses. Much of the country is hot and dry and farmers graze sheep and cattle, growing crops in places where irrigation is possible. Most people live in cooler coastal cities.

Area 2,967,908sq miles (7,686,850sq km)
Government Federal democracy with British monarch as head of state
Independence 1901, Commonwealth of Australia created
Territories Australian Antarctic Territory, Christmas Island, Cocos (Keeling) Islands, Norfolk Island, Heard and McDonald Islands, Ashmore and Cartier Islands, Coral Sea Islands.
Currency Australian dollar
Population 17,746,600
Density 5 per sq mile (2 per sq km)
Official Language English
Major Religions Roman Catholic 26%, Anglican 40%, Uniting Church and Methodist 8%, Presbyterian 4%, other Protestant 6%, other 16%

WEATHER FACTS

126°F (52°C)   24.8in (629mm)   -7.6°F (-22°C)

68.4°F (20.2°C)   44.1°F (6.7°C)

LAND PROFILE
Forests cover 5.5% of the land in Australia.

%
0.5
1
5.5
7.5
38.5
47

LIFESTYLE FACTS
• Voting is compulsory in Australia. Failure to vote is punishable by a fine.

• Australia is the world's leading producer of wool (30%). There are about 7 sheep for every person in Australia.

• Melbourne, the state capital of Victoria, has the fifth largest Greek population in the world.

20 Australian dollars

GREAT BARRIER REEF
This reef, the largest structure built by living creatures, stretches for 1,243 miles (2,000km) off the Queensland coast. There are more than 400 types of coral and 1,500 species of fish.

AUSTRALIAN FLOWER
The national flower is the golden wattle.

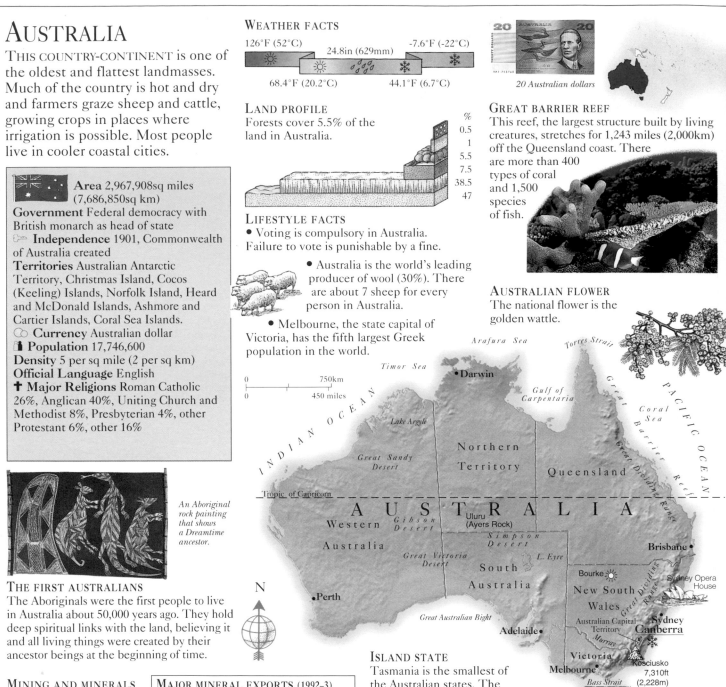

An Aboriginal rock painting that shows a Dreamtime ancestor.

Arafura Sea
Torres Strait
Timor Sea
•Darwin
Gulf of Carpentaria
Lake Argyle
Great Sandy Desert
Northern Territory
Queensland
INDIAN OCEAN
PACIFIC OCEAN
Coral Sea
Great Barrier Reef
Great Dividing Range
Tropic of Capricorn
A U S T R A L I A
Western Australia
Gibson Desert
Uluru (Ayers Rock)
Simpson Desert
Great Victoria Desert
South Australia
L. Eyre
Brisbane •
Bourke
New South Wales
Sydney Opera House
•Perth
Great Australian Bight
Adelaide •
Australian Capital Territory
• Sydney
Canberra
Murray
Victoria
Kosciusko 7,310ft (2,228m)
Melbourne •
Bass Strait
Tasman Sea
Tasmania
• Hobart

0   750km
0   450 miles

N

THE FIRST AUSTRALIANS
The Aboriginals were the first people to live in Australia about 50,000 years ago. They hold deep spiritual links with the land, believing it and all living things were created by their ancestor beings at the beginning of time.

MINING AND MINERALS
Australia is a major source of minerals. It is the world's largest exporter of coal, and has the world's most productive diamond mine near Lake Argyle in Western Australia.

MAJOR MINERAL EXPORTS (1992–3)

Mineral	Value in Aus $
Coal	7,529,000,000
Gold	4,302,000,000
Iron	4,045,000,000
Alumina	2,340,000,000
Zinc	1,020,000,000

AUSTRALIAN MARSUPIAL FACTS
• Marsupials are animals that carry and suckle their young in a pouch in the front of their body.

• The koala feeds on the leaves of eucalyptus trees found in eastern Australia.

• The gray kangaroo has powerful hind legs and can jump at least 26ft (8m).

• The striped possum eats ants, bees, and termites in the rainforests of Queensland.

Koala

ISLAND STATE
Tasmania is the smallest of the Australian states. The southwest of the island is a natural wilderness and has been made a World Heritage Site.

MOST POPULAR SPORTS (1992)
Australians love to play sports, and will host the Olympic Games in the year 2000.

Sport	Club members
Tennis	560,000
Cricket	559,600
Golf	487,765
Bowls	408,367
Netball	350,552
Australian football	342,745
Soccer	272,520

SYDNEY OPERA HOUSE
Sydney Opera House, designed by Danish architect Jörn Utzon (born 1918), was completed in 1973. The shell-shaped roofs are covered with more than one million Swedish ceramic tiles.

ANTARCTICA

ANTARCTICA IS THE coldest, windiest place on Earth. The harsh conditions mean there are no permanent human inhabitants – only visiting scientists working in research stations. The land is rich in oil and minerals, but mining is prohibited under the terms of the Antarctic Treaty.

WEATHER FACTS

59°F (15°C)   12in (303mm)   -128.2°F (-89°C)

N

Area 5,366,818sq miles (13,900,000sq km)
Government None
Currency Not applicable
Population Staff of scientific stations – in winter about 1,000 people, in summer about 4,000
Density Not applicable
Official Language Not applicable
Major Religions Not applicable

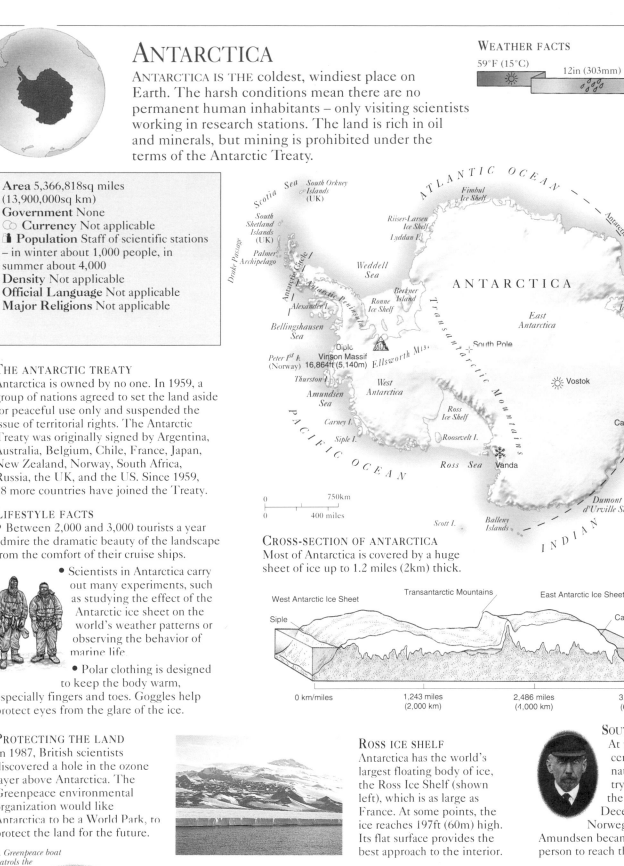

THE ANTARCTIC TREATY
Antarctica is owned by no one. In 1959, a group of nations agreed to set the land aside for peaceful use only and suspended the issue of territorial rights. The Antarctic Treaty was originally signed by Argentina, Australia, Belgium, Chile, France, Japan, New Zealand, Norway, South Africa, Russia, the UK, and the US. Since 1959, 28 more countries have joined the Treaty.

LIFESTYLE FACTS
● Between 2,000 and 3,000 tourists a year admire the dramatic beauty of the landscape from the comfort of their cruise ships.

● Scientists in Antarctica carry out many experiments, such as studying the effect of the Antarctic ice sheet on the world's weather patterns or observing the behavior of marine life.

● Polar clothing is designed to keep the body warm, especially fingers and toes. Goggles help protect eyes from the glare of the ice.

CROSS-SECTION OF ANTARCTICA
Most of Antarctica is covered by a huge sheet of ice up to 1.2 miles (2km) thick.

West Antarctic Ice Sheet   Transantarctic Mountains   East Antarctic Ice Sheet

Siple   Casey

9,843ft (3,000m)
0 Sea level
-6,562ft (-2,000m)

0 km/miles   1,243 miles (2,000 km)   2,486 miles (4,000 km)   3,729 miles (6,000 km)

PROTECTING THE LAND
In 1987, British scientists discovered a hole in the ozone layer above Antarctica. The Greenpeace environmental organization would like Antarctica to be a World Park, to protect the land for the future.

A Greenpeace boat patrols the icy seas.

ROSS ICE SHELF
Antarctica has the world's largest floating body of ice, the Ross Ice Shelf (shown left), which is as large as France. At some points, the ice reaches 197ft (60m) high. Its flat surface provides the best approach to the interior.

SOUTH POLE

At the turn of the century, many nations were trying to reach the South Pole. December 14, 1911, Norwegian Roald Amundsen became the first person to reach the South Pole.

WILDLIFE
Antarctica is too cold for any land animals except the smallest insects. But the sea is rich in food, and many seabirds and sea mammals live on and around the nearby islands.

Blue whale *(Balaenoptera musculus)* is the largest animal ever to have lived, reaching up to 98ft (30m) in length. It spends summers in Antarctic waters.

Emperor penguin *(Aptenodytes forsteri)* is the world's largest penguin; it can grow up to 4ft (1.2m) tall. The female lays one egg, which the male carries on his feet until the egg hatches.

FLAGS

THESE NATIONAL FLAGS represent the 198 main countries and territories of the world. The designs usually reflect the country's culture or religion.

Guatemala Honduras Belize

Barbados Bahamas Antigua & Barbuda

SOUTH AMERICA
The three-striped flag, or tricolor, is often used here.

Surinam Brazil

EUROPE
Many of the European flags use a variation of the cross.

England Wales Northern Ireland Republic of Ireland Spain Portugal Andorra Netherlands

Belgium Luxembourg France Monaco Germany Austria Switzerland Liechtenstein

Italy Vatican City Malta San Marino Finland Lithuania Latvia Estonia

Ukraine Poland Czech Republic Hungary Romania Moldova Belarus Slovakia

Turkey Greece Bulgaria Albania Cyprus Yugoslavia Croatia Bosnia and Herzegovina

Slovenia Macedonia Armenia Azerbaijan Georgia Russian Federation

AFRICA
Many African flags include the colors green, yellow, and red.

Egypt Ethiopia Kenya Tanzania

Uganda Somalia Sudan Eritrea Djibouti Algeria

NORTH AND CENTRAL AMERICA
Blue appears in many flags here.

Canada Greenland US

Mexico Nicaragua Panama El Salvador Costa Rica

Cuba Haiti Jamaica Trinidad & Tobago Dominican Republic

Dominica Grenada St. Kitts & Nevis St. Lucia St. Vincent & The Grenadines

Colombia Peru Venezuela Bolivia Ecuador Guyana

Argentina Chile Uruguay Paraguay

Sweden Denmark Norway Iceland United Kingdom Scotland

FLAG FACTS
• Vexillology is the word for the study of flags. The name comes from the Latin *vexillum*, a banner carried by Roman soldiers.
• Throughout the world, a white flag is flown to indicate a truce.
• At sea, lowering the ship's flag, or ensign, is a sign of surrender.
• The continent of Antarctica has no flags. The land belongs to no one and can be used only for peaceful research.

AFRICA
(Flags of Africa continued)

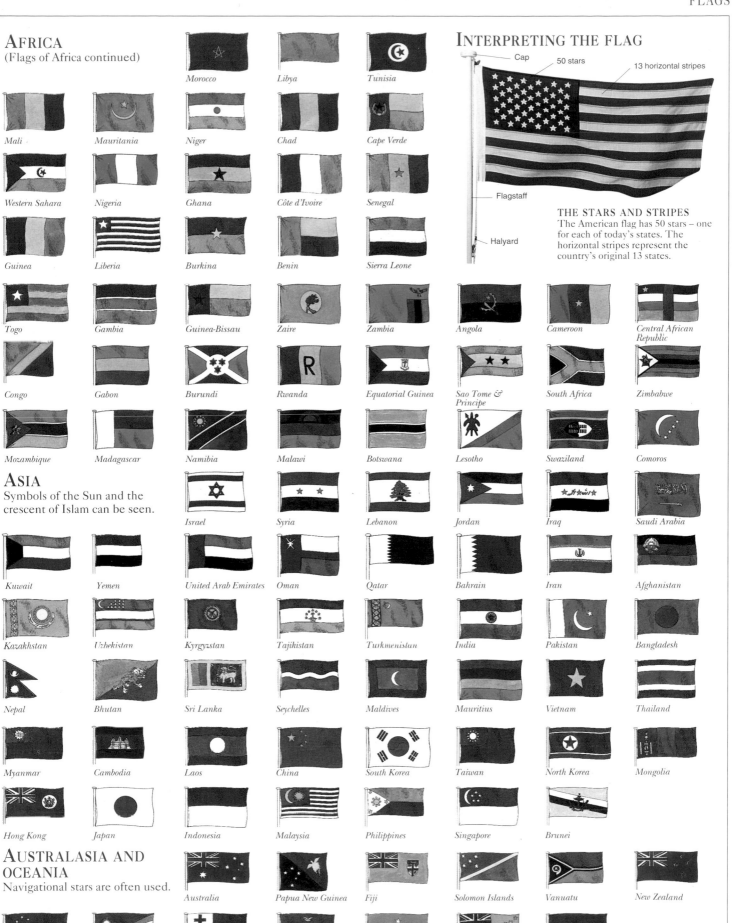

Morocco *Libya* *Tunisia*

Mali *Mauritania* *Niger* *Chad* *Cape Verde*

Western Sahara *Nigeria* *Ghana* *Côte d'Ivoire* *Senegal*

Guinea *Liberia* *Burkina* *Benin* *Sierra Leone*

Togo *Gambia* *Guinea-Bissau* *Zaire* *Zambia* *Angola* *Cameroon* *Central African Republic*

Congo *Gabon* *Burundi* *Rwanda* *Equatorial Guinea* *Sao Tome & Principe* *South Africa* *Zimbabwe*

Mozambique *Madagascar* *Namibia* *Malawi* *Botswana* *Lesotho* *Swaziland* *Comoros*

INTERPRETING THE FLAG

Cap   50 stars   13 horizontal stripes

Flagstaff

Halyard

THE STARS AND STRIPES
The American flag has 50 stars – one for each of today's states. The horizontal stripes represent the country's original 13 states.

ASIA
Symbols of the Sun and the crescent of Islam can be seen.

Israel *Syria* *Lebanon* *Jordan* *Iraq* *Saudi Arabia*

Kuwait *Yemen* *United Arab Emirates* *Oman* *Qatar* *Bahrain* *Iran* *Afghanistan*

Kazakhstan *Uzbekistan* *Kyrgyzstan* *Tajikistan* *Turkmenistan* *India* *Pakistan* *Bangladesh*

Nepal *Bhutan* *Sri Lanka* *Seychelles* *Maldives* *Mauritius* *Vietnam* *Thailand*

Myanmar *Cambodia* *Laos* *China* *South Korea* *Taiwan* *North Korea* *Mongolia*

Hong Kong *Japan* *Indonesia* *Malaysia* *Philippines* *Singapore* *Brunei*

AUSTRALASIA AND OCEANIA
Navigational stars are often used.

Australia *Papua New Guinea* *Fiji* *Solomon Islands* *Vanuatu* *New Zealand*

Western Somoa *Marshall Islands* *Tonga* *Kiribati* *Micronesia* *Tuvalu* *Nauru*

MAPPING

TODAY, MOST PLACES in the world have been visited and mapped; photographs taken from space have given us an accurate picture of the Earth's surface. Over the years, mapmakers, known as cartographers, have created maps for different purposes. People can use an atlas to find a particular place or a smaller-scale map to drive or walk from one place to another.

EARLY MAPPING

Before the world was mapped out as it is today, people understood only the world that they knew. This clay tablet shows the earliest map of the world, which was made in Babylon (now Iraq) in about 1000 B.C. The outer circle is marked as the ocean with the known world depicted in the center.

READING A MAP

A map is like an aerial photograph of the landscape and is designed to show a detailed part of the Earth's surface. To make good use of a map you must know how to "read" it.

The map (right) shows the landscape that appears in the photograph below.

Tree symbols show that an area is wooded.

Contour lines are imaginary lines joining places of the same height above sea level.

The church on the map is shown by a circle and a cross.

Legend

Dotted green lines on the map show the route of footpaths between fields.

The bigger a place is, the bigger its name appears on the map.

The steeper the hill, the closer together the contour lines.

SCALE
A graduated line shows the real distance that 1 inch or 1 centimeter represents on the map.

1,000m　Meters　Kilometers　1km

1,000yd　Yards　0　Miles

LEGEND
Modern maps have a panel called a legend, or key, explaining what the symbols mean. These symbols are designed to save space, so that the mapmakers can include more information and place names on the map.

USING A COMPASS
A compass is an instrument used to find directions. The needle of a compass is magnetized and always pulls the needle so that it points north. However, it points to magnetic north, which is not true north. Markers within the compass also show south, west, east, and the angles in between.

North

Northwest　Northeast

West　East

Southwest　Southeast

South

LONGITUDE AND LATITUDE
Lines of longitude are vertical lines that run through the poles, while lines of latitude are horizontal lines that run parallel to the equator. These imaginary lines on the Earth's surface help map readers locate places on a map.

North Pole 90°　Greenwich meridian

60°　60°

30°　30°

0° West　0° East

Equator

30°　Tropic of Cancer

Tropic of Capricorn

60°　60°

90° South Pole

Lines of latitude run parallel to the equator.

Lines of longitude run north to south between the poles.

PROJECTIONS
To show the Earth on a flat sheet of paper, mapmakers use a projection. Imagine a glass globe with a light at its center. This light projects shadows onto a sheet of paper, which forms the basis of the map.

CONICAL
In this projection, the imaginary sheet of paper forms a cone, touching the Earth along a particular line of latitude. This system shows the least distortion to areas.

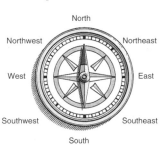

Conical projection

CYLINDRICAL
The paper is rolled around the Earth, touching it at the equator. This shows north at the top, but the areas are distorted.

Cylindrical projection

ZENITHAL
The paper touches the globe at one point. If this point is the pole, the lines of longitude show their correct angles.

Zenithal projection

MERCATOR
Gerard Kremer (1512–94) was a Flemish geographer who found a way to show the globe on a flat map. He was called Mercator, or merchant, because he made maps for ocean-going traders.

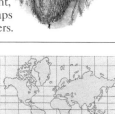

WORLD MAPS
Mercator's world map was made in 1569. His projection shows the correct shapes of the continents but distorts their areas. Arno Peters's projection, made in 1977, distorts the shapes of countries but shows their true size.

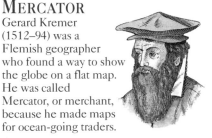

Mercator projection

Peters projection

MAP FACTS
• Amerigo Vespucci (1454–1512) made maps of the New World based on the reports of his sea captains. His maps were referred to as Amerigo's land, or America.

• In 1884, when Britain was a great sea power, Greenwich was chosen as the place from which all measurements of longitude were to be made.

SATELLITE MAPS
With space technology, we can now compile maps from satellite photographs. This view of the Earth from space was made using thousands of separate images.

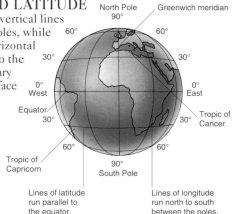

RAW MATERIALS

NATURAL SUBSTANCES THAT are extracted from the ground, from water, or from the air are called raw materials. These substances can be changed by chemical processes into many different types of material that can be put to everyday use.

DISTRIBUTION OF RAW MATERIALS

Bauxite (aluminum oxide) Copper Kaolin (clay) Oil Sulfur

Coal Iron ore Natural gas Cement Wood

RAW MATERIAL FACTS

• Copper is a good conductor of heat and electricity. It lasts a long time because it does not rust easily and is ideal for making wires and hot-water pipes.

• Aluminum, extracted from bauxite ore, is lightweight, easy to work and shape, yet durable. It is ideal for making bicycle frames, aircraft, and motor vehicle parts.

OIL

Crude oil, from which thousands of products are made, is found under the ground or sea. The oil is separated into various parts by a process called fractional distillation: it is heated to form different gases, then each gas condenses back into a liquid at a different temperature.

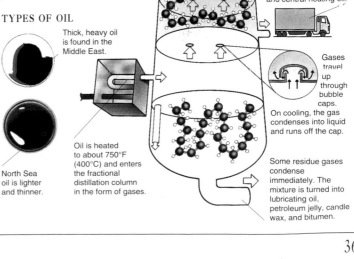

Gasoline is created at 70°–160°F (20°–70°C). It provides fuel for motor cars, and can be made into plastics and detergents.

Kerosene condenses at 320°–480°F (160°–250°C). It provides fuel for jet engines, is used for heating and lighting, and in solvents for paints.

Propane and butane gases are used as fuel for camping stoves, lights, and cigarette lighters.

Naphtha can be made into car fuel, plastics, drugs, pesticides, and fertilizers.

Gas oil is made at 480°–660°F (250°–350°C). It is used for diesel fuel and central heating oil.

Gases travel up through bubble caps. On cooling, the gas condenses into liquid and runs off the cap.

Some residue gases condense immediately. The mixture is turned into lubricating oil, petroleum jelly, candle wax, and bitumen.

TYPES OF OIL

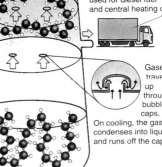

Thick, heavy oil is found in the Middle East.

North Sea oil is lighter and thinner.

Oil is heated to about 750°F (400°C) and enters the fractional distillation column in the form of gases.

LEADING PRODUCERS OF RAW MATERIALS

Material	Top producers	Total* (in millions)	World total* (in millions)
Bauxite (aluminum oxide)	Australia	41.2	
	Guinea	18.2	1,173
Coal	China	1,162	
	US	980	6,484
Copper	Chile	1.8	
	US	1.7	10.1
Natural Gas	CIS	28,110 cu ft	
	US	17,260 cu ft	74,160,870 cu ft
Iron ore	CIS	266	
	China	182	1,085
Kaolin (clay)	CIS	2.2	
	Republic of Korea	1.4	25.5
Oil	CIS	669	
	US	411	
	Saudi Arabia	283	3,293
Salt	US	39.1	
	China	31.2	208
Sulfur	US	12.8	
	China	8.2	66.5
Wood	US	39,164 cu ft	
	CIS	30,441 cu ft	252,394 cu ft

*All figures in tonnes apart from cu ft= cubic feet.

FARMING AND FISHERIES

In 9000 B.C., people in the Middle East began to grow crops. They were the first farmers. Since then, people have tried many different ways of producing crops, rearing animals, and catching fish. Today, farming and fishing are major international industries.

MAJOR WORLD CROPS AND LIVESTOCK

The map shows the top producer of each crop or livestock.

Cattle	Corn	Soybeans
Coffee	Oats	Tea
Cotton	Potatoes	Tobacco
Cow's milk	Rice	Wheat
Hen's eggs	Rubber	Wood
Hogs	Sheep	Wool

TOP AGRICULTURAL PRODUCERS

Product	Top Producer	Second	Third
Cattle	Australia	Brazil	US
Coffee	Brazil	Colombia	Indonesia
Corn	US	China	Brazil
Cotton	China	US	Former USSR
Cow's milk	US	Germany	Russia
Hen's eggs	China	US	Russia
Hogs	China	US	Russia
Oats	Former USSR	US	Canada
Potatoes	Russia	Poland	China
Rice	China	India	Indonesia
Rubber	Malaysia	Indonesia	Thailand
Sheep	Australia	China	New Zealand
Soybeans	US	Brazil	China
Tea	India	China	Sri Lanka
Tobacco	China	US	India
Wheat	China	Former USSR	US
Wood	US	Russia	China
Wool	Australia	Former USSR	New Zealand

CROP FACTS

• More than half the world's population relies on three grains – wheat, corn, and rice – for their basic food needs.

• Asia produces more than nine-tenths of the world's rice and could not feed itself on any other crop.

• More than 500 varieties of grape are grown along the Black Sea coast in Georgia.

• Eighty-five percent of the world's orange juice is supplied by Brazil.

• Malaysia's rubber trees are descended from about 11 seedlings, sent to Malaysia from Kew Gardens, England, in 1877.

SHEEP JAM

In New Zealand, sheep outnumber people by 20 to 1 and have the right of way on the roads.

SELECTING AND CULTIVATING CROPS

Only the strongest plants are selected and cultivated. This has caused the size, shape, and flavor of many crops to change over the years.

Wild tomatoes

Though smaller, wild tomatoes are sweeter and more strongly flavored than cultivated tomatoes.

Cultivated tomato

Cultivated corncob

Wild carrot

Cultivated carrot

Early corncob

A wild cabbage has bitter-tasting, leathery leaves.

A cultivated cabbage has tightly packed leaves.

FROM GRAIN TO FOOD

The wide variety of grain grown can be made into many different types of food.

Bread wheat

Bread wheat's large grains have a high gluten content – this makes bread dough elastic.

Whole-wheat flour

White bread, from bleached flour

Brown bread, from unbleached flour

Long grain rice

Rice plant

Durum wheat has a low gluten content and is used to make pasta and cookies.

Types of pasta

Pasta comes in a variety of shapes and sizes.

Ruotedi carro, or "cartwheels"

Spaghetti

FARMING PROCESSES

SUBSISTENCE FARMING
When farmers grow enough food to support themselves and their families, but leave little or nothing to be sold, this is known as subsistence farming. Subsistence farming is more common in developing countries, such as Kenya, Africa.

Subsistence farming in Sudan

INTENSIVE FARMING
In this type of farming, production of crops and livestock is maximized by the use of machinery and chemicals. Up to ten people can be fed from land that once fed one person.

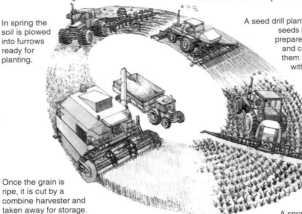

In spring the soil is plowed into furrows ready for planting.

A seed drill plants the seeds in the prepared soil and covers them again with soil.

Once the grain is ripe, it is cut by a combine harvester and taken away for storage.

A sprayer is used to spray crops with pesticides to kill any insects that may harm the young plants.

Battery hens
One disadvantage of intensive farming is that it can lead to unnatural treatment of animals. Egg-laying hens are often kept in coops in buildings called batteries, where they do not have enough space to flap their wings or turn around. Because of concern for animal welfare and a preference for naturally grown food, more people are returning to natural, or organic, farming methods.

Battery hens, Texas, US

FISHING INDUSTRY

Most fish are caught in the seas near the coast, above the continental shelf. Different fishing methods are used, largely depending on whether the fish swim near the surface of the sea (pelagic fish) or on or near the seabed (demersal fish).

WAYS OF CATCHING FISH

Deep-water trawling
Cone-shaped nets, about 100ft (30m) wide, are pulled along the seabed by a trawler. Used to catch demersal fish, such as cod.

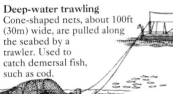

Midwater trawling
Trawling nets are towed by either one or two trawlers. Used to catch pelagic fish, such as herring.

Trawler

Drift nets
Long nets, up to 60 miles (95km) in length, are left to drift in the water and used to catch pelagic fish.

Drift nets are attached to a boat.

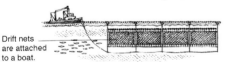

Purse-seining
Pelagic fish are surrounded by a huge net and the net lines are drawn together, like purse strings, until the fish are completely enclosed in the net.

Lining
Long lines with baited hooks are laid, either on the seabed, to catch demersal fish, or near the surface, to catch tuna and mackerel.

Baskets or netting pots
These are used to catch shellfish, such as crabs and lobsters. The openings are designed so the fish can easily swim in but find it difficult to get out.

FISHING GROUNDS
The continental shelf (shown in blue on the map) is the land surrounding each continent, covered by shallow seawater. It is rich in nutrients, and is an excellent feeding ground for fish.

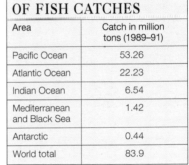

FISHING FACTS

- At least 25% of the world's diet of animal protein is derived from fish and other seafood.

- Japan catches about 11 million tons of fish each year, more than any other country in the world.

- Fish and fish products account for about 70% of Iceland's export earnings. They consume more cod-liver oil than any other nation, and produce more than one-third of the world's supply.

- In Vietnam, bomb craters remaining after the Indochinese conflicts (1946–75) have since been turned into pools for farming fish.

WORLD DISTRIBUTION OF FISH CATCHES

Area	Catch in million tons (1989–91)
Pacific Ocean	53.26
Atlantic Ocean	22.23
Indian Ocean	6.54
Mediterranean and Black Sea	1.42
Antarctic	0.44
World total	83.9

FISH PRODUCTS

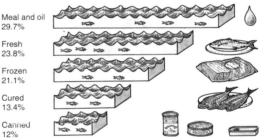

Meal and oil 29.7%
Fresh 23.8%
Frozen 21.1%
Cured 13.4%
Canned 12%

FISH FARMING
Some types of fish, such as trout and carp, are kept on fish farms. Enclosures are built on lakes, ponds, or estuaries. Most fish farming occurs in freshwater, but in some countries, such as Japan, fish farms have been built along sheltered coastal waters.

Salmon farm, Norway

AGRICULTURAL WORDS

Agroforestry System of growing trees and crops together.
Biotechnology To scientifically change plants and animals for the benefit of humans.
Cash crops Crops grown for trade.
Hydroponics Growing plants without soil using water and nutrients.

Irrigation To water dried-up land by using water channels, pipes, or sprinklers.
Nomadic Moving from place to place to find new grazing land, food, and water.
Rainforest A forest that grows in hot, tropical areas that have high rainfall.
Subsoil Layer of soil underneath topsoil.
Topsoil The uppermost, fertile layer of soil.

POPULATION

THE TOTAL POPULATION of the world now stands at 5.7 billion. Some continents are experiencing a population explosion, others are beginning to stabilize their growth. Many people think that an increasing population is the greatest problem facing the world.

WORLD POPULATION

Europe:
747,042,000
13.8% of world population

North/Central America:
429,862,000
7.9% of world population

South America:
304,325,000
5.6% of world population

Africa:
637,271,000
11% of world population

Asia:
3,280,232,000
60.5% of world population

Oceania:
27,229,000
0.5% of world population

MOST POPULATED COUNTRIES

Country	Total population (in millions)
China	1,192.0
India	911.6
United States	260.8
Indonesia	199.7
Brazil	155.3
Russia	147.8
Pakistan	126.4
Japan	125.0
Bangladesh	116.6
Nigeria	98.1
Mexico	91.8
Germany	81.2
Vietnam	73.1
Philippines	68.7

Source: Population Concern

FERTILITY RATES

The fertility rate corresponds to the average number of children born to a woman in her lifetime. Even if every couple had only two children starting tomorrow, the world's population would still grow to at least 8 billion.

Rwanda 8.5
Malawi 7.6
Saudi Arabia 6.4
Nicaragua 5.1
Cambodia 4.5
India 3.9
China 2.2
Germany 1.5

POPULATION GROWTH RATES

This table shows the current rate of population increase and the time it will take each region to double in size.

Region	Increase (annual %)	Doubling Time (years)
Africa	2.9	24
Latin America	2.0	35
Asia	1.7	41
Oceania	1.2	57
North America	0.7	98
Europe	0.1	1,025

Source: Population Concern

GROWTH FACT

• About 97% of global population growth between now and 2050 is projected to occur in Africa, Asia, and Latin America – the countries least able to absorb such increases.

POPULATION MOMENTUM

Three people are born every second, nearly 11,000 every hour, and more than 255,000 every day.

POPULATION FACTS

• One-third of the world's people are under the age of 15.

• By 2025, the total number of people aged 60 and over will be about 1.2 billion (14% of the world's population). The majority of them, almost 71%, will be living in the developed countries.

• 75% of the world's population cannot be expected to reach their sixtieth birthday.

AGING POPULATION

Aging populations occur in more developed countries. Here, people choose not to have many children because infant mortality is low and the cost of living high. Advanced medicines help increase life expectancy and enable the existing population to live longer.

YOUNG POPULATION

People in developing countries have more children. Health care is poor, many babies die at birth, and people do not have long lives. In such countries, numbers of young people have increased dramatically: in Africa almost half the population is under the age of 15.

LEAST DENSELY POPULATED COUNTRIES

Country	Population per sq km	per sq mile
Western Sahara	1	2.6
Mongolia	1	2.6
Namibia	2	5.2
Australia	2	5.2

URBANIZATION

Modern technology has enabled more people to live in a smaller space. Today, nearly 50% of the world's population, about 2.6 billion people, live in cities. Of these urban dwellers, half live in cities of more than 500,000 people.

Sprawling suburbs of Mexico City

WORLD URBAN GROWTH

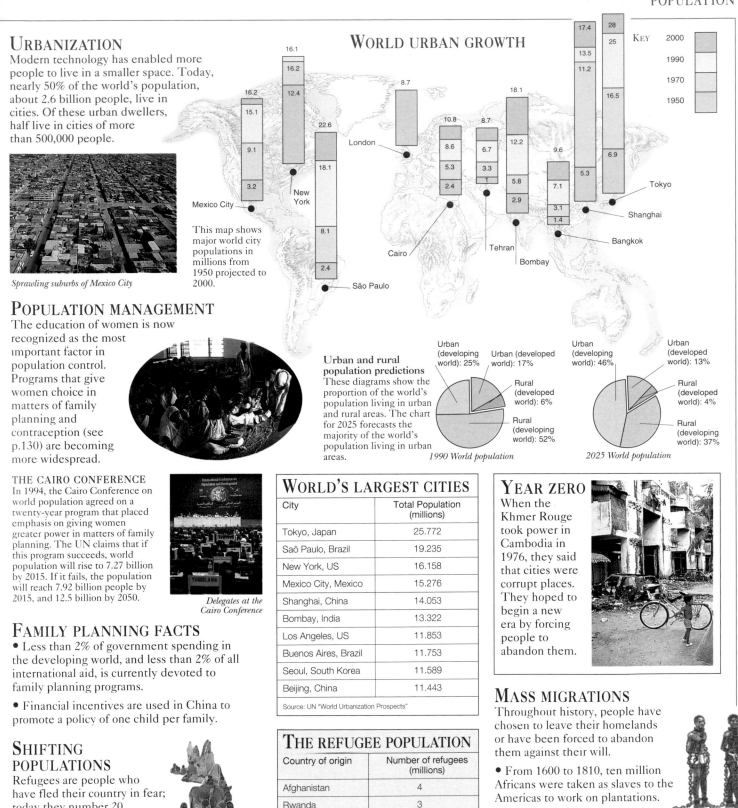

This map shows major world city populations in millions from 1950 projected to 2000.

KEY
2000
1990
1970
1950

POPULATION MANAGEMENT

The education of women is now recognized as the most important factor in population control. Programs that give women choice in matters of family planning and contraception (see p.130) are becoming more widespread.

Urban and rural population predictions
These diagrams show the proportion of the world's population living in urban and rural areas. The chart for 2025 forecasts the majority of the world's population living in urban areas.

Urban (developing world): 25%
Urban (developed world): 17%
Rural (developed world): 6%
Rural (developing world): 52%
1990 World population

Urban (developing world): 46%
Urban (developed world): 13%
Rural (developed world): 4%
Rural (developing world): 37%
2025 World population

THE CAIRO CONFERENCE
In 1994, the Cairo Conference on world population agreed on a twenty-year program that placed emphasis on giving women greater power in matters of family planning. The UN claims that if this program succeeds, world population will rise to 7.27 billion by 2015. If it fails, the population will reach 7.92 billion people by 2015, and 12.5 billion by 2050.

Delegates at the Cairo Conference

FAMILY PLANNING FACTS
• Less than 2% of government spending in the developing world, and less than 2% of all international aid, is currently devoted to family planning programs.

• Financial incentives are used in China to promote a policy of one child per family.

SHIFTING POPULATIONS
Refugees are people who have fled their country in fear; today they number 20 million. People become refugees for many reasons, such as war, politics, and religious and racial discrimination. Some refugees, like the Vietnamese boat people, have undertaken difficult and dangerous journeys to safety.

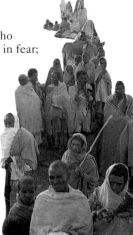

WORLD'S LARGEST CITIES

City	Total Population (millions)
Tokyo, Japan	25.772
São Paulo, Brazil	19.235
New York, US	16.158
Mexico City, Mexico	15.276
Shanghai, China	14.053
Bombay, India	13.322
Los Angeles, US	11.853
Buenos Aires, Brazil	11.753
Seoul, South Korea	11.589
Beijing, China	11.443

Source: UN "World Urbanization Prospects"

THE REFUGEE POPULATION

Country of origin	Number of refugees (millions)
Afghanistan	4
Rwanda	3
Palestine	2.8
Former Yugoslavia	1.3
Burundi	0.8
Mozambique	0.7
Liberia	0.7
Angola	0.5
Sri Lanka	0.5
Sudan	0.4
Azerbaijan	0.3

YEAR ZERO
When the Khmer Rouge took power in Cambodia in 1976, they said that cities were corrupt places. They hoped to begin a new era by forcing people to abandon them.

MASS MIGRATIONS
Throughout history, people have chosen to leave their homelands or have been forced to abandon them against their will.

• From 1600 to 1810, ten million Africans were taken as slaves to the Americas to work on plantations.

• Expansion in North America came via mass immigration: from 1860 to 1910, the population rose from 31 to 92 million.

SPACE POPULATIONS
Scientists explore ways to enable people to live on other planets. An experiment in Texas to create an artificial atmosphere was called Biosphere II. Although it failed, there is still hope that one day people may live in artificial atmospheres on the Moon.

LIVING STANDARDS

HIGH STANDARDS IN health, nutrition, and education are considered fundamental to the well-being of a nation. Generally, if a country is wealthy, its population will enjoy a high standard of living. If it is poor, people may not get enough to eat and may also lack social services such as hospitals and schools. Poverty also exists in developed countries, where a high standard of living for a few people can mean that others struggle to afford necessities.

World Health Organization

CHILD MORTALITY RATES

This table shows how many children under 5 die each year per 1,000 children.

Country	Infant deaths
Niger	320
Angola	292
Mozambique	287
Afghanistan	257
Sierra Leone	249
Finland	7
Singapore	7
Sweden	7
Japan	6
Source: UNICEF (1992)	

BIRTH AND DEATH RATES

Region	Births (millions per year)	Deaths (millions per year)
Asia	84.8	27.1
Africa	29.4	9.1
South America	12.7	3.3
Europe	8.7	8.0
North America	4.6	2.6
Oceania	0.6	0.2

LIFE EXPECTANCY

The graph below shows the average age to which men and women are expected to live.

Women
Men

41, 42, 45, 49, 68, 71, 55, 56, 74, 80, 72, 79

Afghanistan, Burkina, China, India, Australia, US

DISEASE

In tropical countries, infections are spread by organisms that carry disease from person to person. Developing countries also tend to suffer from diseases carried by contaminated food and water. In these countries, children are most at risk: life expectancy is low and disease cripples many. Diseases linked with industrialization and wealth, such as cancer and heart disease, have brought new health problems to developed countries.

DISEASE FACTS

• Measles, diarrhea, and pneumonia kill an estimated 7 million children a year.

• Tetanus kills 600,000 babies each year even though immunization exists.

• Every year polio cripples 140,000 children.

• Following WWI, a global influenza epidemic killed nearly 22 million people between 1918 and 1920.

• Infectious diseases account for 25% of all deaths in the developing world, compared with just 1.4% of total deaths in the developed world.

SAFE WATER

UNICEF (United Nations Children's Fund) defines safe water as "20 liters per person per day, at a source within one kilometer from the user's dwelling." Most diseases are spread through water contaminated by waste. Dehydration also causes many deaths. WHO aims to provide as many people as possible with clean water and proper sanitation.

WATER FACTS

• 22% of Mozambique's population has safe water.

• Two-thirds of the world's families do not have running water in their homes.

• If clean, safe water were made available for the entire world's population, 80% of sickness and disease would be prevented.

• Almost 2 billion people, most of them in the developing world, do not have access to the minimum level of safe drinking water.

SALAAM BOMBAY

Every year, an estimated 13 million children die, the equivalent of the entire population of Bombay, India.

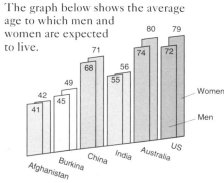

HEALTH AND SICKNESS

The World Health Organization (WHO) defines "health" as a state of physical, mental, and social well-being. The absence of adequate food and sanitation causes much sickness around the world. The availability of doctors and hospitals also contributes to maintaining a nation's health.

Malaria has killed more than any other disease in recorded history. It kills at least 2 million people every year, most of them children in Africa, and infects 10 million with the disease. Mosquitoes carry the parasite, which is becoming increasingly resistant to western medicines.

AIDS stands for Acquired Immune Deficiency Syndrome. In 1990, it was estimated that more than 80% of the estimated 8.8 million people infected with HIV (see p.125) live in developing countries. More than 1.8 million people will have died as a result of AIDS by the year 2000.

Children collecting water in Africa.

DOCTORS PER POPULATION

The graph below shows how many people there are per doctor in each country.

Nepal 20,000
Laos 4,380
United Arab Emirates 1,000
Latvia 200
Rwanda 72,990

FOOD AND NUTRITION

Food production has been increased to deal with the growing world population. Nutrition is not just a matter of good food; immunization, safe water supply, and a basic education would all reduce child malnutrition. Millions of people, most of them in the developing world, still suffer from malnutrition.

Undernourished child

FOOD PRODUCTION

The Food and Agriculture Organization (FAO) was set up in 1945, as part of the United Nations. It aims to reduce malnutrition, to improve efficiency in food production and distribution, and to improve life in rural areas.

Food and Agriculture Organization

EDUCATION

Education remains the single most important factor in creating a better world. Educating women has been shown to improve health care, reduce infant mortality, and lead to greater control over population growth.

Family planning in Africa

EDUCATION FACTS

• In 1993, almost 130 million children, two-thirds of them girls, were denied primary education.

• About one billion adults cannot read or write.

FOOD SUPPLY

The "Dietary energy supply" (DES) is the amount of food available per person per day, and is measured in calories. The table below compares the DES in some developed and developing countries.

Ireland — 3,837
Greece — 3,816
— 3,732
US — 3,664
— 1,989
Denmark — 1,680
Chad
Mozambique

ADULT LITERACY RATES

This table shows the percentage of each region's male and female population aged over 15 years who can read and write.

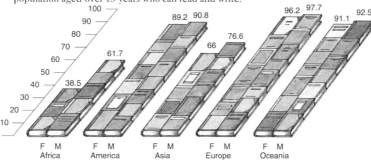

Africa: F 38.5 M 61.7
America: F 89.2 M 90.8
Asia: F 66 M 76.6
Europe: F 96.2 M 97.7
Oceania: F 91.1 M 92.5

HIGHEST SPENDERS ON EDUCATION

This table shows % of income (GNP) spent on education.

Country	% of GNP
Liechtenstein	11.8
Surinam	9.7
Libya	9.6
Algeria	9.1
Seychelles	9.1

LOWEST SPENDERS ON EDUCATION

This table shows % of income (GNP) spent on education.

Country	% of GNP
Somalia	0.4
Indonesia	0.9
Zaire	0.9
Paraguay	1.0
Laos	1.2

NORTH–SOUTH DIVIDE

Economic differences between developed and developing countries are also seen as a physical divide. The developed countries mainly occupy the northern part of the planet and the developing countries the south. This is known as the "North–South divide."

ECONOMIC FACTS

• A person from a developed nation consumes 20 to 30 times more of the world's resources than a person from the developing world.

• The average Ghanaian spends $5 a year in the shops compared to $9,000 for the average Japanese.

THE HUMAN INDEX

Many people now consider GNP (see p.368) to be an unreliable reflection of a nation's development. The United Nations publishes "The Human Development Index," which is an alternative way of measuring the well-being and economic progress of a nation. Different indicators of living standards are recorded (e.g. education, life expectancy, nutrition, access to water), to help establish an accurate world ranking for development. This index also recognizes poor living standards in the developed world.

NUTRITION FACTS

• About one-third of the developing world's children are underweight.

• 80% of the food for home consumption in Africa is grown by women.

SCHOOL'S OUT

Almost 80 million children in developing countries do not attend primary school.

BEST PUPIL/ TEACHER RATIO

Country	Pupils per teacher
San Marino	6
Sweden	6
Austria	11
Qatar	11

WORST PUPIL/ TEACHER RATIO

Country	Pupils per teacher
Central African Republic	90
Equatorial Guinea	68
Chad	67
Burundi	67

HIGHEST LIVING STANDARDS

Country	Rank	Assessment
Japan	1	High income and savings by individuals
Canada	2	Among the highest figures of GNP per person
Norway	3	High standards of health and social services
Switzerland	4	High income per person

Source: United Nations (1993)

LOWEST LIVING STANDARDS

Country	Rank	Assessment
Guinea	173	Just 32% of population has access to safe water
Sierra Leone	172	Daily energy supply is only 79% of requirements
Afghanistan	171	Average life expectancy is about 40 years
Burkina	170	69% of population have access to safe water

Source: United Nations (1993)

DEBT AND WEALTH

LEVELS OF PROSPERITY around the world differ from country to country. Although the wealth of a nation is not simply a matter of money, what a country has or owes can indicate its prosperity.

WEALTH AND TRADE
A country's wealth depends on factors of production such as natural resources, capital, and labor. Some countries are rich in large amounts of mineral deposits like coal, oil, gold, and copper. Others may have a large amount of capital in the form of money from business or a highly skilled workforce. These resources are traded within a country, as well as on the world market.

IMPORTS AND EXPORTS
Imports are what one country buys from another; exports are what it sells to another. By trading internationally, a country can sell what it produces to pay for things it is unable to produce itself. When a country does not produce enough wealth, it must borrow money from another country to pay for its imports.

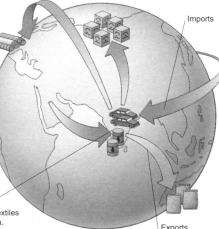

Imports

India imports cars from Japan and oil from the Arabian peninsula. It exports tea and textiles to Europe, and rice to Australia.

Exports

Out of sight, out of mind: a South American shantytown situated on the fringe of the city.

THE UNEQUAL WORLD
The world has experienced an exceptional growth in wealth since the 1950s with technology making the means of production more efficient. Many countries, particularly those situated in the southern hemisphere of the planet, have not benefited from this growth and are known as "developing" countries. The resulting inequality is known as the "North–South" divide.

THE DEBT CRISIS
Some developing countries borrow money for development from banking organizations like the World Bank. These institutions charge interest on the money borrowed. The longer a country takes to pay back the loan, the more interest they are charged. Some countries have to use much of the money they earn from trade to repay this interest instead of using it for development. Developed countries have been criticized for controlling developing countries through debt.

Economic inequalities
Economic alliances between developed countries have widened the gap between rich and poor nations.

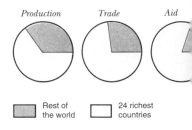

Production   Trade   Aid

Rest of the world   24 richest countries

Chart of debt in comparison with GNP

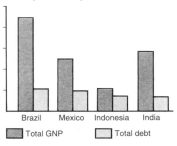

Brazil   Mexico   Indonesia   India

Total GNP   Total debt

RICHEST AND POOREST
Economists judge a nation's wealth by looking at its Gross National Product, or GNP (the income generated per year). GNP per capita shows the average income of each person. Although useful, many believe that this does not reflect the true prosperity of a country.

Country	GNP per capita (US$)	Country	GNP per capita (US$)
Switzerland	36,230	Mozambique	60
Luxembourg	35,260	Eritrea	110
Japan	28,220	Ethiopia	110
Sweden	26,780	Tanzania	110
Denmark	25,930	Nepal	170
Norway	25,800	Sierra Leone	170
Iceland	23,670	Uganda	170
Germany	23,030	Bhutan	180
Finland	22,980	Cambodia	200

IMF AND WORLD BANK
The International Monetary Fund (IMF) and World Bank were set up after World War II to help Europe redevelop. When developing countries became independent they also turned to these banks for aid.

International Monetary Fund

The World Bank

NOT-SO-GOLDEN HANDSHAKE
Ten countries are home to three-quarters of the world's poor, and yet they receive only 26% of total global aid.

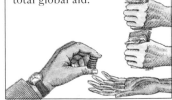

OIL WEALTH
Producers of particular goods have formed alliances to protect their mutual economic interests. OPEC, the Organization of Petroleum Exporting Countries, was set up to represent the interests of petroleum-exporting, developing countries. The price of oil has a greater effect on the international economy than any other product.

Representatives at an OPEC conference

OIL CRISIS
In 1973, OPEC restricted the amount of oil it was exporting, which in turn increased the price of oil around the world. This affected the wealth of many countries, especially the US with its high consumption of oil by industry. To save gasoline, the American authorities had to introduce a 30mph (50km/h) speed limit.

Cars lining up for gasoline during the oil crisis.

TOP AID DONORS

Aid supplier	Aid as % of GNP (1992)
Norway	1.11
Sweden	1.05
Denmark	1.04
Netherlands	0.88
France	0.61
Finland	0.55

Source: UNICEF "The Progress of Nations"

HISTORY

Spanning the period from 40,000 B.C. to the present day, this extensive and absorbing section includes all the key dates and events in world history. Comparative timelines provide a global overview of events in each continent at any given time, and detailed tables list key personalities for every historical era.

Early Toolmakers and Artists • Early Farmers and Towns • Egypt and Mesopotamia
Expanding Empires and Mediterranean Trade • Ancient Greece and the Rise of Rome
Imperial Rome and Christianity • Islam and the Vikings • Mongols and Crusaders
Marco Polo and the Black Death • Renaissance and the Americas
Religious Conflict and Akbar • Manchu China, Supreme Rulers, and Slavery
Enlightenment, Revolution, and Napoleon • Europe in Turmoil and the British Empire
American Civil War and the Scramble for Africa • World War I and the Russian Revolution
Interwar Years and Communists in China • World War II • Cold War and the Middle East
African Independence • Middle East and the End of the Cold War • Great Civilizations
Rulers and Leaders • Presidents and Prime Ministers • Explorers • Battles and Wars
Revolutions and Rights • Archaeology and History

40,000 B.C.

AFRICA			30,000 Disappearance of the Neanderthals
ASIA	40,000 Cro-Magnon humans living at Skhūl and Kafzel (Israel)		27,000–19,000 Female statuettes made at various sites, including locations in Russia
EUROPE	40,000 Neanderthals active in France at La Chapelle-Aux-Saints, La Ferassie, and La Quina. Cro-Magnons start to spread to Europe	35,000 Start of Upper Paleolithic Period (flaked stone tools, bone and horn implements)	30,000 Probable date of earliest figurative art in Fra (Dordogne). Disappearance of Neanderthals 27,000–19,000 Female statuettes at various sites in France and Italy
AMERICAS		35,000 First humans arrive in North America from Asia	
OCEANIA	40,000 Probable arrival of Aboriginals in Australia		

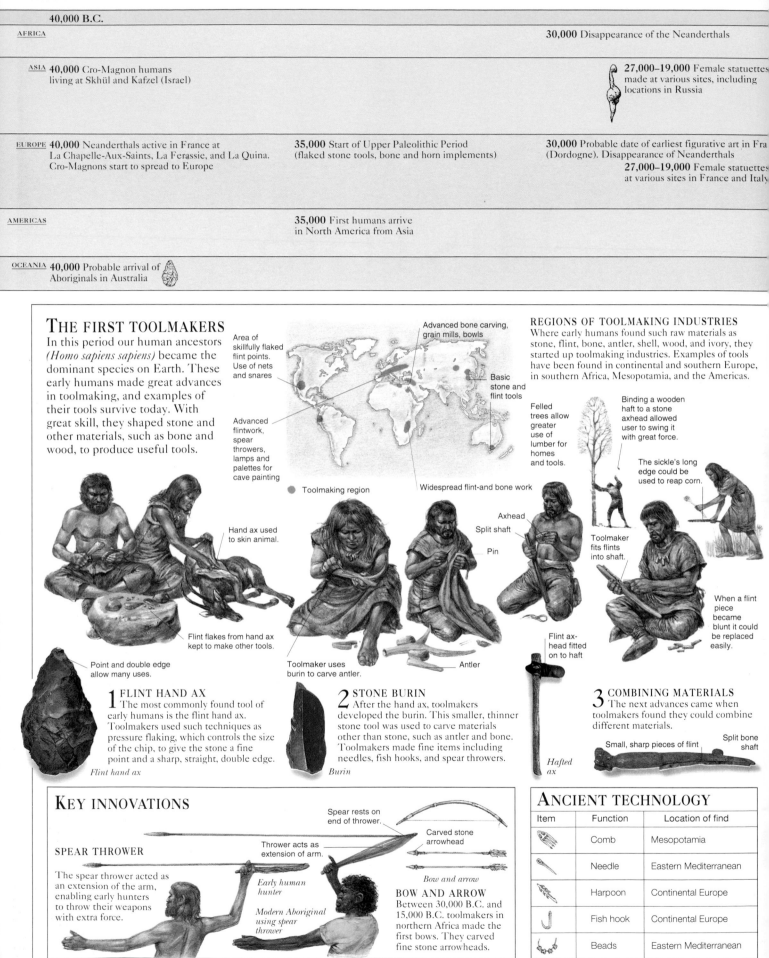

THE FIRST TOOLMAKERS

In this period our human ancestors *(Homo sapiens sapiens)* became the dominant species on Earth. These early humans made great advances in toolmaking, and examples of their tools survive today. With great skill, they shaped stone and other materials, such as bone and wood, to produce useful tools.

Area of skillfully flaked flint points. Use of nets and snares

Advanced flintwork, spear throwers, lamps and palettes for cave painting

Advanced bone carving, grain mills, bowls

Basic stone and flint tools

● Toolmaking region

Widespread flint-and-bone work

REGIONS OF TOOLMAKING INDUSTRIES

Where early humans found such raw materials as stone, flint, bone, antler, shell, wood, and ivory, they started up toolmaking industries. Examples of tools have been found in continental and southern Europe, in southern Africa, Mesopotamia, and the Americas.

Felled trees allow greater use of lumber for homes and tools.

Binding a wooden haft to a stone axhead allowed user to swing it with great force.

The sickle's long edge could be used to reap corn.

Hand ax used to skin animal.

Axhead
Split shaft
Pin

Toolmaker fits flints into shaft.

Flint flakes from hand ax kept to make other tools.

Toolmaker uses burin to carve antler.

Antler

Flint ax-head fitted on to haft

When a flint piece became blunt it could be replaced easily.

Point and double edge allow many uses.

1 FLINT HAND AX
The most commonly found tool of early humans is the flint hand ax. Toolmakers used such techniques as pressure flaking, which controls the size of the chip, to give the stone a fine point and a sharp, straight, double edge.

Flint hand ax

2 STONE BURIN
After the hand ax, toolmakers developed the burin. This smaller, thinner stone tool was used to carve materials other than stone, such as antler and bone. Toolmakers made fine items including needles, fish hooks, and spear throwers.

Burin

Hafted ax

3 COMBINING MATERIALS
The next advances came when toolmakers found they could combine different materials.

Small, sharp pieces of flint
Split bone shaft

KEY INNOVATIONS

SPEAR THROWER

The spear thrower acted as an extension of the arm, enabling early hunters to throw their weapons with extra force.

Spear rests on end of thrower.

Thrower acts as extension of arm.

Carved stone arrowhead

Early human hunter

Modern Aboriginal using spear thrower

Bow and arrow

BOW AND ARROW
Between 30,000 B.C. and 15,000 B.C. toolmakers in northern Africa made the first bows. They carved fine stone arrowheads.

ANCIENT TECHNOLOGY

Item	Function	Location of find
	Comb	Mesopotamia
	Needle	Eastern Mediterranean
	Harpoon	Continental Europe
	Fish hook	Continental Europe
	Beads	Eastern Mediterranean

15,000 Last rainy period in northern Africa

16,000 Coldest point
in glaciation

12,500 Rise of Magdalenian toolmakers
(bone and antler harpoons, fishing spears)

14,000–11,000 El-Kebareh
culture (Israel), with free-
standing round huts

11,000 Rise of Natufian culture

10,500 Earliest pottery:
Fukui cave, Japan

15,000 Cave paintings,
Lascaux, France

12,500 Rise of Magdalenian toolmakers
(bone and antler harpoons, fishing spears)

15,000–10,000 Magdalenian culture,
high point of mural and portable art

11,000 Cave paintings,
Altimira, Spain

) Cave dwellers present in Brazil

15,000 Cave art begins in
Brazil (shelter of Toca do
Boqueirao de Pedra Furada)

24,000 Earliest known cremation, Lake
Mungo, New South Wales, Australia

16,000 Cave art,
north coast of Australia

THE FIRST ARTISTS

Creating art is an activity that distinguishes humans from other animals. Early artists used the walls of caves to paint animals and images, but they rarely painted people, and never landscapes. They did, though, carve small statues of people.

LASCAUX ART
This painted horse of about 15,000 B.C. was found in the Lascaux caves, France. The feathered dots may have been magical hunting symbols.

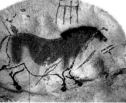

Brown powder sprayed on

ARTISTS' METHODS
Early artists used natural materials for different colored paints. They applied paint with brushes of hair or sticks, or pads made from moss or animal skin. They drew lines with sharp stones.

Charcoal, for black

Clay, for brown

Green clay, for green

Altimira
EUROPE
Lascaux
Günnersdorf •
Pech Merle
• Petersfels
Mas d'Azil
Dolni Věstonice •
Willendorf •

• Cave and
portable art site

• Portable
art site

CAVE ART FACTS
● In cave art, pictures of rarer animals (bears, big cats, rhinoceroses) often appear in more remote parts of the cave; common ones (aurochs, deer, mammoths) often appear at the entrance.

● The Lascaux paintings have suffered more in the last 50 years from human perspiration, body heat, and microorganisms than in the 15,000-year period during which they lay undisturbed.

● Artists may have applied some colors by blowing paint through hollow reeds onto the cave wall.

LOCATIONS OF ANCIENT ART
The best-preserved paintings are on the walls of caves in France and Spain that remained undiscovered until this century. Objects carved in wood, stone, or bone are known as portable art objects.

"VENUS" FIGURINES
Several small female statues, called "Venus" figurines, have been found across Europe, and may represent goddesses; their large size may symbolize pregnancy (for fertility worship) or obesity (for abundant food).

A CAVE DISCOVERED
In 1940 Marcel Ravidat led three friends to a hole he had spied while walking his dog at Lascaux, France. He dropped down through the hole into a cave. By matchlight he saw beautiful paintings, made thousands of years earlier.

ICE AGE LIFE

For at least the last two million years the world's climate has regularly swung between cold and warm periods. When cold struck, landscapes, rivers, lakes, and vegetation changed greatly. Humans had to adapt to the new environment to survive.

Ice Age hunters trap a mammoth

ICE AGE HUNTERS
Ice Age people used many parts of the animals that they hunted: they made warm clothes from the fur and skin, and some used mammoth bones to support the animal-skin walls of their huts.

Mammoth
bone hut

Harpoon

ICE AGE SPREAD
At the peak of the last Ice Age, ice sheets covered huge areas of the world, and sea levels dropped. Emerging land formed bridges between continents separated today.

Ice Age coast
Present-day coast
Ice sheet
c.18,000 B.C.

TROPICAL THAMES
The world experienced warm periods as well as ice ages. Bones found underneath Trafalgar Square, London, prove that hippopotamuses swam in the River Thames during one of these warmer spells.

NATUFIAN CULTURE
In 11,000 B.C. the Natufians of Palestine became probably the first people to abandon a hunter-based, nomadic lifestyle and settle down. They began to live permanently in caves, or in circular huts.

Grain store

Huts of mud,
reed, and lumber

Natufians gathered wild
grain and stored it in huts.

House

Headdress of
shell beads

Wild grain made coarse bread
that wore down Natufians' teeth.

Burial customs
Natufians often buried their dead with personal items: necklaces and bracelets of bone or beads.

Natufian woman

10,000 B.C.

AFRICA	**10,000** Hunting camps established in Sahara region after Ice Age ends	**8500** First rock paintings, Sahara region	**8000** Pottery made in Sahara region
ASIA	**10,000** Ice cap retreats	**9000–8000** Cereals (wheat and barley) grown in Jordan and Syria. Pottery made at Mureybet, Syria. Domestication of goats and sheep in Iran and Jordan	**8000** Jericho, the first town, appears. Ice Age ends in Far East **7500** Domestication of pigs, Crimea
EUROPE	**10,000** Ice cap retreats	**8300** Retreat of glaciers	
AMERICAS		**9,000** First people reach southern tip of South America **8500** Cultivation of wild grasses and beans, Peru	**8000** Semipermanent settlements, North America
OCEANIA			

THE FIRST FARMERS

In 8000 B.C., people in the Middle East cultivated crops for the first time. They grew mainly varieties of wheat and barley. The new strains of wheat they developed slowly spread around the Mediterranean, then farther afield.

EARLY CROPS

Wild species of wheat were not ideal as food crops because their seed heads would shatter when ripe. Farmers solved this by hybridization (combining different wheat strains) to create new types of wheat.

Wild einkorn   Einkorn   Wild emmer   Emmer

Wild and hybridized species of grain

Wheat
Early cereal grain, used for bread

Barley
Milled for bread, also used for beer

Lentil
Pulse, dried or eaten fresh

Yam
Large tuber, high in starch

Millet
Asian cereal high in protein

Rice
High-protein cereal

Corn
Grows in cobs (heads)

Tapioca
From root of manioc plant

THE SPREAD OF AGRICULTURE

In western Asia and Europe knowledge of farming spread from the central area of Syria, Palestine, Iran, Iraq, and Turkey. Farmers in the Far East developed their crops independently, while in the Americas farmers appeared later, in about 7000 B.C.

DOMESTICATED ANIMALS

When they began to grow crops, farmers also domesticated wild animals. Domestication often changed a species' appearance.

Wild Animal   Domesticated Animal

Asiatic moufflon   Sheep
Near East 8000 B.C.

Wild Animal   Domesticated Animal

Wolf   Dog
Near East 11,000 B.C.

Wild boar   Pig
Near East 7500 B.C.

Bezoar goat   Goat
Near East 8900 B.C.

Aurochs   Cow
Near East 7000 B.C.

GREEN SAHARA

The Sahara Desert was once a fertile region with organized communities. 8,000-year-old paintings on cliff walls at Tassili-n-Ajjer, Libya, show many species of animal, hunters, a woman pounding flour, wedding ceremonies, and a family with a pet dog.

DOLMENS

Chûn Quoit, Cornwall, U.K.

Dolmens are the first great stone monuments of Europe and date from about 4500 B.C. They are the remains of ancient chamber tombs, and consist of a large, flat stone, supported by upright stones. Their existence shows a great knowledge of engineering.

EARLY BREADMAKING

Early humans collected the seed heads of wild wheats and ground them using a stone quern (hand-mill). After separating the husks from the coarse flour, they mixed the flour with water and baked unleavened (unrisen) bread.

Clay oven
Baked bread
Sealed opening
Smooth pestle
Wheat seed heads
Stone quern

CROPS FOR TEXTILES

By 5000 B.C. the Egyptians were growing flax to make linen fabric. They harvested the flax at different times to produce various linen goods: young green stems were used for fine cloth and the tougher fibers of ripe flax could be made into ropes or mats.

Spindle on which flax fibers were spun

Coarse Egyptian linen sheet

| 00 B.C. | | | | 4000 B.C. |

6500 Cattle domesticated

6500–5700 Çatal Hüyük, Turkey, important early town

5000 Irrigation in Mesopotamia. Rice farming in China. Ubaid culture in Mesopotamia

4500 Farming around River Ganges, India

00–6500 Domestication of .en, eastern Mediterranean

6500 Date of earliest surviving textile, Çatal Hüyük

6200 Copper smelted, central Turkey

4400 Horse domesticated in Russia

6500 Britain separated from mainland as ice melts

6500 First farming communities, southeast Europe

5000 Farming begins, western Europe. Gold and copper used in Balkans

4500 First megalithic tombs, Brittany and Portugal

6500 Cultivation of potato, Peru

5000 First settlements in Anåhuac, Mexico. Corn grown, Mexico. Beginnings of domestication of llama and alpaca in Andes

5000 New Guinea and Tasmania separated from Australia as sea level rises

THE FIRST TOWNS

Towns and trade began to develop at the same time as agriculture and in the same parts of the world. The first townspeople were craft workers, priests, and traders. They depended on nearby farmers for food and on areas further afield for trade.

JERICHO
Jericho in the Near East was probably the first town, built in about 8000 B.C. It had a strong stone wall, a tower and defensive ditch, and a large and well-organized population.

Stone tower at Jericho

Reconstruction of Çatal Huyuk

Sometimes a courtyard was used as a rubbish dump by surrounding houses.

Mud-brick walls

Ladder

Staircase

Doorway

Cross-section of Jericho Tower, 32ft (10m) wide

Ditch

ÇATAL HÜYÜK
Çatal Hüyük is the site of a well-preserved town in Turkey from 6500 B.C. Its mud-brick houses had shared walls; there were no streets. Its people went about by climbing over the rooftops.

TRADERS
Goods from distant lands were found in the ruins of Çatal Hüyük: obsidian (volcanic glass), cowrie shells from the Mediterranean, and turquoise from Sinai.

Entrance through rooftop

Lumber and reeds support roofs

Lack of streets made town easy to defend.

Turkish obsidian

Turquoise

Cowrie shells

SMALL WORLD
In 10,000 B.C. the entire population of the world was about 12 million. This is two-thirds of the current population of New York State.

EVIDENCE OF RELIGION

Human skulls
Jericho's dead were sometimes buried beneath the floors of the houses with their skulls (though not the jaw) removed and decorated.

Cowrie shells   Plaster

Shrine paintings
Some rooms in Çatal Hüyük were decorated with religious images. Here vultures with human legs (perhaps priests in costume) attack a headless figure.

Early clay stamps

• From about 6000 B.C. town dwellers in the Middle East began using clay stamps to mark their personal property. Traders may also have used them to mark their goods.

TOWN FACTS
• Early towns were sited in places with reliable springs; with mountains nearby where wild crops could grow; and with enough rainfall for the crops.

• In Çatal Hüyük, the average man lived to the age of 34, the average woman to the age of 30.

• Excavations at Jarmo revealed eleven towns, each one built on top of the other at different times.

KEY EARLY TOWNS

Town	Area	Date	Industry/Craft
Jericho	Eastern Mediterranean	8000 B.C.	Pottery
Çatal Hüyük	Turkey	7000 B.C.	Obsidian toolmaking
Jarmo	Iraq	c.7000 B.C.	Textile weaving
Khirokitia	Cyprus	c.6000 B.C.	Stone and wood articles

FIRST POTTERY
The earliest pottery is more than 12,000 years old and comes from Japan. African and Near Eastern people each discovered it about 3,000 years later.

Pinching method

Potter hollows out solid lump of clay.

Potter coils single stretched piece of clay.

Coiling method

Decorated pot from Nasunahara, Japan: one of the earliest-known pottery vessels

FIRST METALWORKERS
In 7000–6000 B.C. people discovered that certain rocks, called ores, would release pure metal when heated. The metal could then be beaten into shape to make useful objects, or melted and poured directly into molds.

Copper spearhead

Furnace at c.2200°F (c.1200°C)

Molten metal is poured into mold.

Bag bellows

Clay nozzle

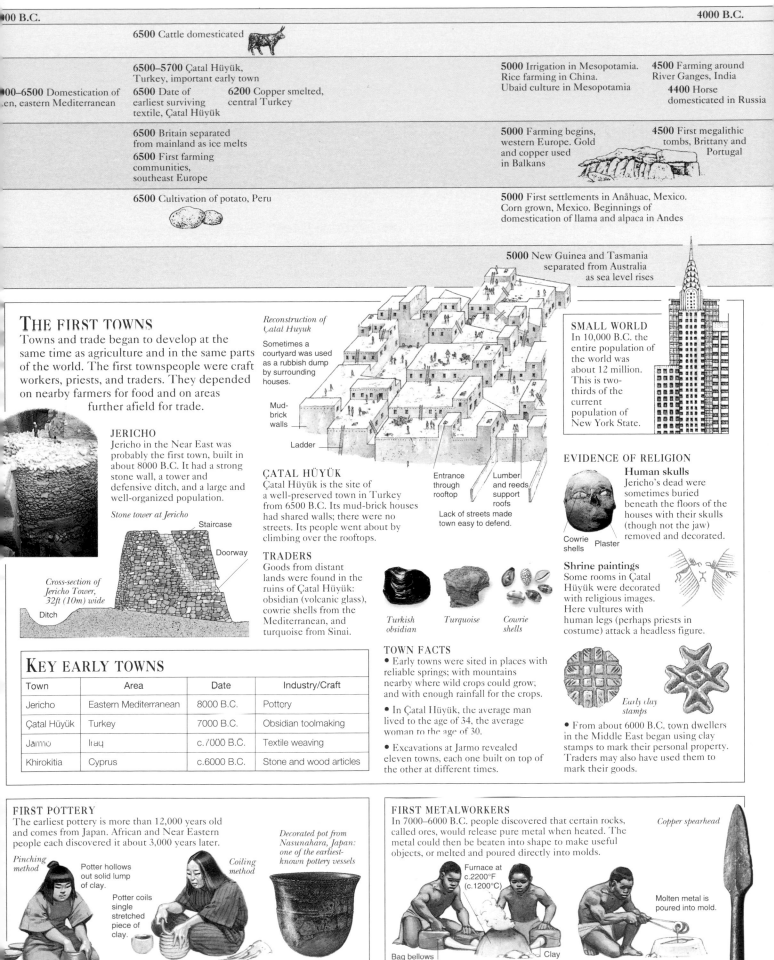

4000 B.C.

AFRICA	**3750** First bronze alloy (also used by Sumerians)	**3500** First sailing vessels, Egypt	**3000** Development of hieroglyphic writing	**2590** Building of Gre Pyramid of Khufu at
			3100 Menes the Fighter unites Upper and Lower Egypt	**2686** Beginning of Egyptian Old Kingdom
				2646 Pyramid of Zoser at Saq
ASIA **4000** Beginning of bronze casting, Middle East		**3500** Earliest Chinese city, Liang-ch'eng chen. Mesopotamians invent wheel and plow	**3000** Development of Sumerian cities	
		3250 Earliest pictographic writing, Mesopotamia	**2850** Legendary Golden Age in China	
			2750 Gilgamesh, legendary king of Uru	
EUROPE		**3200** Beginnings of early Cycladic civilization in Aegean islands	**3000** Spread of copper use	
			2900 Danubian culture, central Europe	
AMERICAS		**3200** Corn farmed in South America	**3000** First pottery in Americas	
OCEANIA			**3000** Probable introduction of dogs in Australia	

ANCIENT EGYPT

In about 3500 B.C. Egyptians established one of the world's longest-lasting civilizations along the fertile banks of the Nile. Ruled by pharaohs (kings) and serviced by a large priesthood, Egyptians were famous for their stone building skills, their hieroglyphic writing, and their elaborate cult of the dead.

PYRAMID BUILDERS

Egyptians had a ready supply of stone, a good transport system on the Nile, and a large labor force. This enabled them to become the first people to build with stone on a large scale. The details of their building methods, however, have been lost.

Mummy · Cartonnage (papier-mâché) mummy-case · Coptic jar for internal organs

BURIAL FACTS

• Any important Egyptian was carefully mummified after death. Internal organs were placed in jars, and the body preserved with natron (salts) and wrapped in linen bandages.

• Egyptians placed mummies in a series of decorated cases, often painted with a portrait of the dead person. The nest of cases was then placed in a stone coffin, called a sarcophagus.

Saqqara Earliest pyramid (stepped) and first known stone building

Dahshur Bent pyramid of King Snefru, about 330ft (100m) high

Giza Khufu's tomb and world's largest stone structure

Probable method of pyramid construction

Slave team

Temporary ramp

Stones dragged up on rollers

HIEROGLYPHIC WRITING

Egyptians used hieroglyphs for temple inscriptions and religious texts. A hieroglyph can stand for an object, an idea, or a sound. Scribes and priests, who alone understood hieroglyphs, grew more powerful when their writing skills were needed for administration.

Tutankhamun's cartouche (name inscription)

• City   Ancient coastline

• Heliopolis
• Memphis

Thebes

LANDMARKS IN STONE

From the Nile delta as far south as modern-day Sudan, Egyptians built pyramid tombs in various styles, and temples to their gods. Many of these monuments are still standing.

Abu Simbel Temple of Rameses II, cut into solid rock face

Sphinx Khafre's guard, 240ft (73m) long

KEY INNOVATIONS

SAIL

Egyptians constructed sailing ships from about 3500 B.C. Ships were first built from the Nile's reeds, and later from foreign lumber.

POTTERY KILN

Kilns, invented in both Egypt and Mesopotamia, produced better-quality pots.

KEY PHARAOHS

Zoser (c.2700 B.C.) – first pyramid builder.

Hatshepsut (c.1473–58 B.C.) – first female ruler in history.

Thutmose III (1479–25 B.C.) expanded empire's territories.

Akhenaton (1370–52 B.C.) started a new religion.

Tutankhamun (1353–35 B.C.), a boy-king, revived old gods.

Rameses II (1290–24 B.C.) - last great military pharaoh.

STONEHENGE

Stonehenge is a circle of stones on Salisbury Plain, England. Construction began in about 2200 B.C. Some of the huge stones had to be transported more than 134 miles (216km), from Wales. On the summer solstice, the sun rises directly over the axis of the monument.

Foundation pit

Lintel stone

Sarsen stone

Wooden platform used to raise lintel

Builders drag stones into place using rollers.

Probable method of construction of Stonehenge

INDUS VALLEY CIVILIZATION

In 1921 archaeologists discovered the remains of a unknown civilization from about 2500 B.C. Based in the Indian cities of Harappa and Mohenjo-Daro, its people lived in mud-brick houses and had baths, vast granaries, and drainage systems. Their writing appears on seals, but it has never been deciphered.

Mohenjo-Daro sculpture (c.2100 B.C.), probably of a priest or divine king

Great Bath, Mohenjo-Daro

Ritual baths

The size of the Great Bath at Mohenjo-Daro and the footbath at its entrance suggest that it was used for purifying rituals, perhaps by priests.

B.C.				1500 B.C.

Beginnings of desiccation
ng out) of Sahara region

2133 Beginning of
Egyptian Middle Kingdom

1786 End of Egyptian
Middle Kingdom

1652 War between Egypt
and Hyksos people from Asia

2182 End of Egyptian
Old Kingdom

1567 Beginning of
Egyptian New Kingdom

Beginnings of Indus civilization.
e domesticated, Central Asia

2371 Semites under Sargon of Akkad
begin to occupy entire plain of Shinar –
greatest Mesopotamian empire established

2000 Hittites begin
invasions of Anatolia

1800 Beginnings of
Assyrian empire

1900 Decline of Indus civilization

1792 Birth of Hammurabi,
founder of Babylonian empire

1500 Chinese
ideographic
script in use

Earliest barrow burials in Britain.
nings of Dolmen period of
dinavian Neolithic age

2200 The first Stonehenge built.
End of Scandinavian Dolmen period

1600 Beginnings of
Mycenean civilization, Greece

1500 Linear B
script in use
on Crete

2000 Beginnings of
Minoan civilization, Crete

Earliest large settlements in
s area, with temple mounds

2000 First metalworking, Peru.
Inuits reach northern Greenland

2000 Beginnings of settlement
of Melanesia, South Pacific

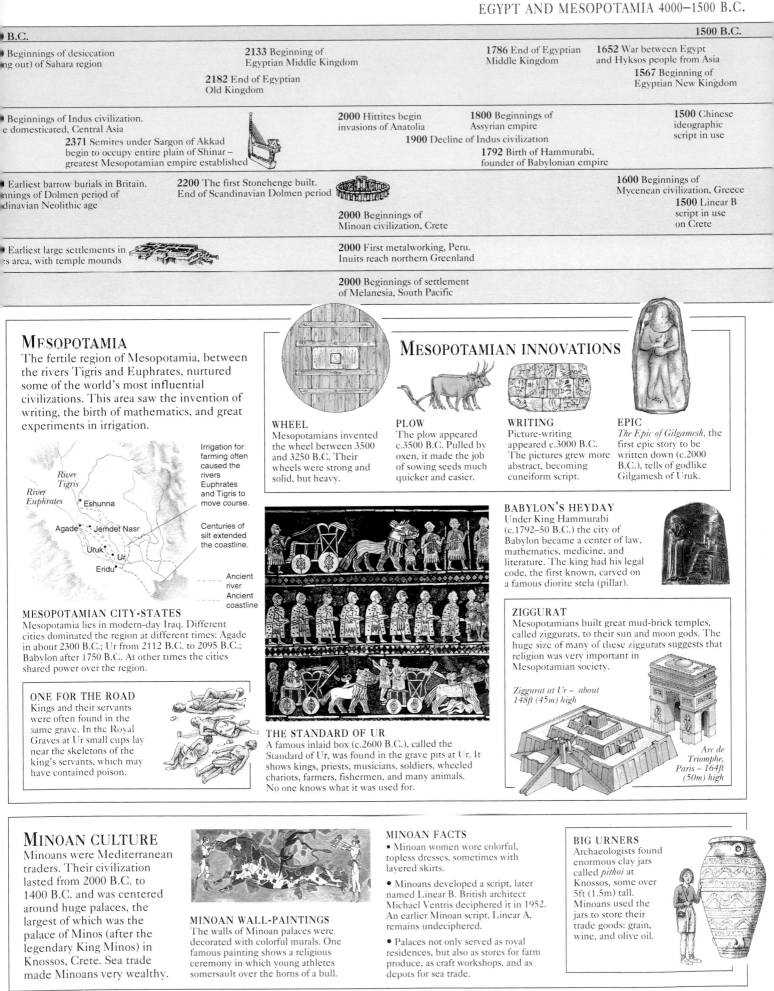

MESOPOTAMIA

The fertile region of Mesopotamia, between the rivers Tigris and Euphrates, nurtured some of the world's most influential civilizations. This area saw the invention of writing, the birth of mathematics, and great experiments in irrigation.

River Tigris
River Euphrates
Eshunna
Agade • Jemdet Nasr
Uruk • Ur
Eridu •

Irrigation for farming often caused the rivers Euphrates and Tigris to move course.

Centuries of silt extended the coastline.

Ancient river
Ancient coastline

MESOPOTAMIAN CITY-STATES
Mesopotamia lies in modern-day Iraq. Different cities dominated the region at different times: Agade in about 2300 B.C.; Ur from 2112 B.C. to 2095 B.C.; Babylon after 1750 B.C. At other times the cities shared power over the region.

ONE FOR THE ROAD
Kings and their servants were often found in the same grave. In the Royal Graves at Ur small cups lay near the skeletons of the king's servants, which may have contained poison.

MESOPOTAMIAN INNOVATIONS

WHEEL
Mesopotamians invented the wheel between 3500 and 3250 B.C. Their wheels were strong and solid, but heavy.

PLOW
The plow appeared c.3500 B.C. Pulled by oxen, it made the job of sowing seeds much quicker and easier.

WRITING
Picture-writing appeared c.3000 B.C. The pictures grew more abstract, becoming cuneiform script.

EPIC
The Epic of Gilgamesh, the first epic story to be written down (c.2000 B.C.), tells of godlike Gilgamesh of Uruk.

BABYLON'S HEYDAY
Under King Hammurabi (c.1792–50 B.C.) the city of Babylon became a center of law, mathematics, medicine, and literature. The king had his legal code, the first known, carved on a famous diorite stela (pillar).

ZIGGURAT
Mesopotamians built great mud-brick temples, called ziggurats, to their sun and moon gods. The huge size of many of these ziggurats suggests that religion was very important in Mesopotamian society.

Ziggurat at Ur – about 148ft (45m) high

Arc de Triomphe, Paris – 164ft (50m) high

THE STANDARD OF UR
A famous inlaid box (c.2600 B.C.), called the Standard of Ur, was found in the grave pits at Ur. It shows kings, priests, musicians, soldiers, wheeled chariots, farmers, fishermen, and many animals. No one knows what it was used for.

MINOAN CULTURE
Minoans were Mediterranean traders. Their civilization lasted from 2000 B.C. to 1400 B.C. and was centered around huge palaces, the largest of which was the palace of Minos (after the legendary King Minos) in Knossos, Crete. Sea trade made Minoans very wealthy.

MINOAN WALL-PAINTINGS
The walls of Minoan palaces were decorated with colorful murals. One famous painting shows a religious ceremony in which young athletes somersault over the horns of a bull.

MINOAN FACTS
• Minoan women wore colorful, topless dresses, sometimes with layered skirts.

• Minoans developed a script, later named Linear B. British architect Michael Ventris deciphered it in 1952. An earlier Minoan script, Linear A, remains undeciphered.

• Palaces not only served as royal residences, but also as stores for farm produce, as craft workshops, and as depots for sea trade.

BIG URNERS
Archaeologists found enormous clay jars called *pithoi* at Knossos, some over 5ft (1.5m) tall. Minoans used the jars to store their trade goods: grain, wine, and olive oil.

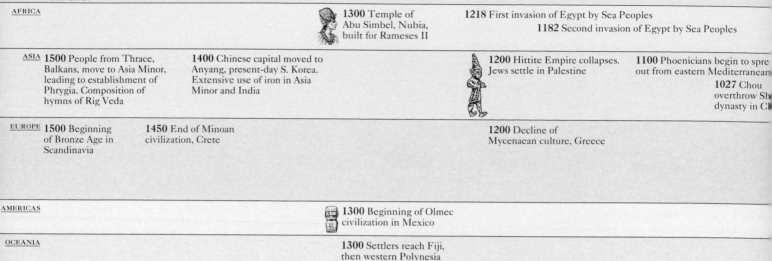

1500 B.C.

AFRICA

1300 Temple of Abu Simbel, Nubia, built for Rameses II

1218 First invasion of Egypt by Sea Peoples

1182 Second invasion of Egypt by Sea Peoples

ASIA **1500** People from Thrace, Balkans, move to Asia Minor, leading to establishment of Phrygia. Composition of hymns of Rig Veda

1400 Chinese capital moved to Anyang, present-day S. Korea. Extensive use of iron in Asia Minor and India

1200 Hittite Empire collapses. Jews settle in Palestine

1100 Phoenicians begin to spread out from eastern Mediterranean

1027 Chou overthrow Sh dynasty in Cl

EUROPE **1500** Beginning of Bronze Age in Scandinavia

1450 End of Minoan civilization, Crete

1200 Decline of Mycenaean culture, Greece

AMERICAS

1300 Beginning of Olmec civilization in Mexico

OCEANIA

1300 Settlers reach Fiji, then western Polynesia

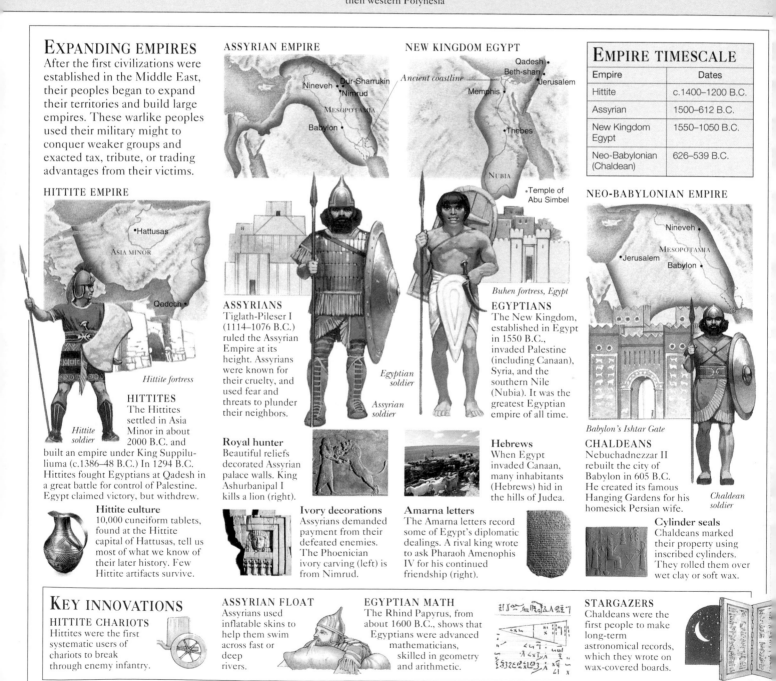

EXPANDING EMPIRES

After the first civilizations were established in the Middle East, their peoples began to expand their territories and build large empires. These warlike peoples used their military might to conquer weaker groups and exacted tax, tribute, or trading advantages from their victims.

HITTITE EMPIRE

Hittite fortress

HITTITES
The Hittites settled in Asia Minor in about 2000 B.C. and built an empire under King Suppilu-liuma (c.1386–48 B.C.) In 1294 B.C. Hittites fought Egyptians at Qadesh in a great battle for control of Palestine. Egypt claimed victory, but withdrew.

Hittite soldier

Hittite culture
10,000 cuneiform tablets, found at the Hittite capital of Hattusas, tell us most of what we know of their later history. Few Hittite artifacts survive.

ASSYRIAN EMPIRE

ASSYRIANS
Tiglath-Pileser I (1114–1076 B.C.) ruled the Assyrian Empire at its height. Assyrians were known for their cruelty, and used fear and threats to plunder their neighbors.

Assyrian soldier

Royal hunter
Beautiful reliefs decorated Assyrian palace walls. King Ashurbanipal I kills a lion (right).

Ivory decorations
Assyrians demanded payment from their defeated enemies. The Phoenician ivory carving (left) is from Nimrud.

NEW KINGDOM EGYPT

Ancient coastline

Buhen fortress, Egypt

Egyptian soldier

EGYPTIANS
The New Kingdom, established in Egypt in 1550 B.C., invaded Palestine (including Canaan), Syria, and the southern Nile (Nubia). It was the greatest Egyptian empire of all time.

Amarna letters
The Amarna letters record some of Egypt's diplomatic dealings. A rival king wrote to ask Pharaoh Amenophis IV for his continued friendship (right).

Hebrews
When Egypt invaded Canaan, many inhabitants (Hebrews) hid in the hills of Judea.

EMPIRE TIMESCALE

Empire	Dates
Hittite	c.1400–1200 B.C.
Assyrian	1500–612 B.C.
New Kingdom Egypt	1550–1050 B.C.
Neo-Babylonian (Chaldean)	626–539 B.C.

NEO-BABYLONIAN EMPIRE

Babylon's Ishtar Gate

CHALDEANS
Nebuchadnezzar II rebuilt the city of Babylon in 605 B.C. He created its famous Hanging Gardens for his homesick Persian wife.

Chaldean soldier

Cylinder seals
Chaldeans marked their property using inscribed cylinders. They rolled them over wet clay or soft wax.

KEY INNOVATIONS

HITTITE CHARIOTS
Hittites were the first systematic users of chariots to break through enemy infantry.

ASSYRIAN FLOAT
Assyrians used inflatable skins to help them swim across fast or deep rivers.

EGYPTIAN MATH
The Rhind Papyrus, from about 1600 B.C., shows that Egyptians were advanced mathematicians, skilled in geometry and arithmetic.

STARGAZERS
Chaldeans were the first people to make long-term astronomical records, which they wrote on wax-covered boards.

B.C.   **600 B.C.**

900 Foundation of kingdom of Kush in Nubia

814 Phoenicians found their colony at Carthage

600 Phoenicians sail around Africa

Kingdom of Israel – King David

800 Aryans from present-day Iran expand into southern India

771 Chou state collapses in China

721–05 Assyrian Empire at its greatest extent

660 Jimmu, legendary first Japanese emperor

650 Chinese begin to use iron

612 Decline of Assyrian power after Medes and Scythians destroy Nineveh

604 Nebuchadnezzar II is ruler of Babylonian Empire

Etruscans in Italy

776 First recorded Olympic Games, Greece

753 Traditional date of foundation of Rome

750 Greek city-states establish settlements around Mediterranean

700 Beginning of Halstatt culture (Iron Age) in central and western Europe

650 Earliest surviving Latin inscriptions

621 First written laws of Athens (Laws of Dracon)

900 Height of Chavin civilization in Andes

800 Zapotec civilization of Central America produces first writing in Americas

Most of Polynesian Islands settled

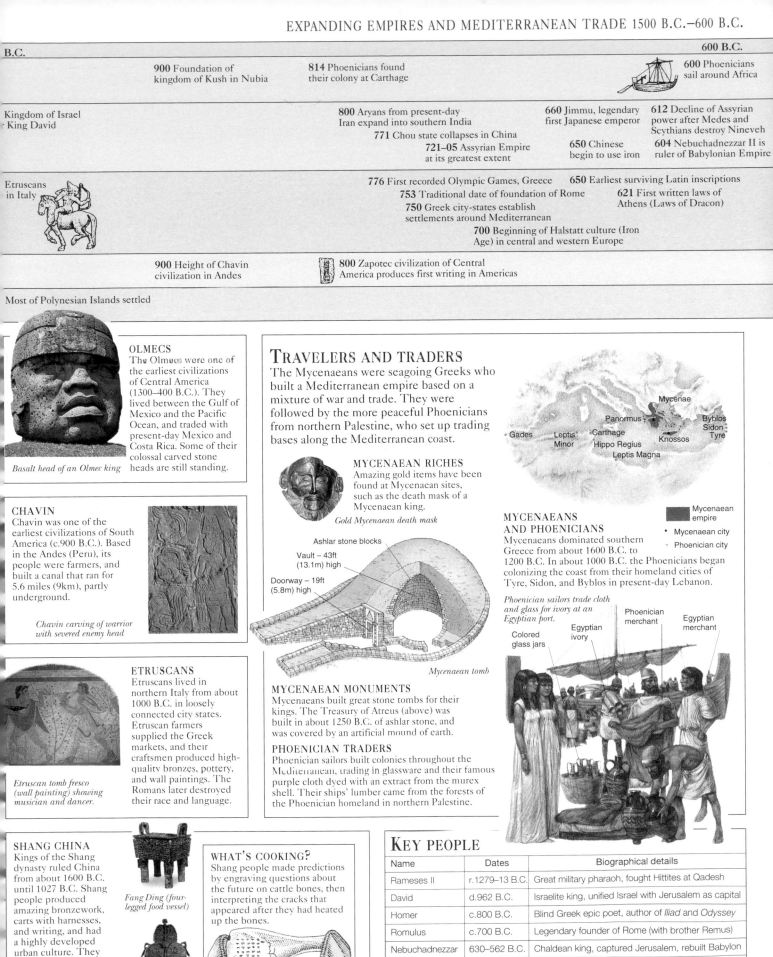

OLMECS
The Olmecs were one of the earliest civilizations of Central America (1300–400 B.C.). They lived between the Gulf of Mexico and the Pacific Ocean, and traded with present-day Mexico and Costa Rica. Some of their colossal carved stone heads are still standing.

Basalt head of an Olmec king

CHAVIN
Chavin was one of the earliest civilizations of South America (c.900 B.C.). Based in the Andes (Peru), its people were farmers, and built a canal that ran for 5.6 miles (9km), partly underground.

Chavin carving of warrior with severed enemy head

ETRUSCANS
Etruscans lived in northern Italy from about 1000 B.C. in loosely connected city states. Etruscan farmers supplied the Greek markets, and their craftsmen produced high-quality bronzes, pottery, and wall paintings. The Romans later destroyed their race and language.

Etruscan tomb fresco (wall painting) showing musician and dancer.

SHANG CHINA
Kings of the Shang dynasty ruled China from about 1600 B.C. until 1027 B.C. Shang people produced amazing bronzework, carts with harnesses, and writing, and had a highly developed urban culture. They used cowrie shells for money, and traded far and wide in beautiful jade carvings.

Fang Ding (four-legged food vessel)

Wine vessel

WHAT'S COOKING?
Shang people made predictions by engraving questions about the future on cattle bones, then interpreting the cracks that appeared after they had heated up the bones.

TRAVELERS AND TRADERS
The Mycenaeans were seagoing Greeks who built a Mediterranean empire based on a mixture of war and trade. They were followed by the more peaceful Phoenicians from northern Palestine, who set up trading bases along the Mediterranean coast.

MYCENAEAN RICHES
Amazing gold items have been found at Mycenaean sites, such as the death mask of a Mycenaean king.

Gold Mycenaean death mask

Ashlar stone blocks

Vault – 43ft (13.1m) high

Doorway – 19ft (5.8m) high

Mycenaean tomb

MYCENAEAN MONUMENTS
Mycenaeans built great stone tombs for their kings. The Treasury of Atreus (above) was built in about 1250 B.C. of ashlar stone, and was covered by an artificial mound of earth.

PHOENICIAN TRADERS
Phoenician sailors built colonies throughout the Mediterranean, trading in glassware and their famous purple cloth dyed with an extract from the murex shell. Their ships' lumber came from the forests of the Phoenician homeland in northern Palestine.

Mycenae · Panormus · Byblos · Sidon · Gades · Leptis Minor · Carthage · Knossos · Tyre · Hippo Regius · Leptis Magna

■ Mycenaean empire
• Mycenaean city
· Phoenician city

MYCENAEANS AND PHOENICIANS
Mycenaeans dominated southern Greece from about 1600 B.C. to 1200 B.C. In about 1000 B.C. the Phoenicians began colonizing the coast from their homeland cities of Tyre, Sidon, and Byblos in present-day Lebanon.

Phoenician sailors trade cloth and glass for ivory at an Egyptian port.

Colored glass jars · Egyptian ivory · Phoenician merchant · Egyptian merchant

KEY PEOPLE

Name	Dates	Biographical details
Rameses II	r.1279–13 B.C.	Great military pharaoh, fought Hittites at Qadesh
David	d.962 B.C.	Israelite king, unified Israel with Jerusalem as capital
Homer	c.800 B.C.	Blind Greek epic poet, author of *Iliad* and *Odyssey*
Romulus	c.700 B.C.	Legendary founder of Rome (with brother Remus)
Nebuchadnezzar	630–562 B.C.	Chaldean king, captured Jerusalem, rebuilt Babylon
Ashurbanipal	d.627 B.C.	Last great Assyrian king, founded first catalogued library of ancient Middle East at Nineveh
Sappho	c.600 B.C.	Greek lyric poetess from island of Lesbos

600 B.C.

AFRICA	**600** Building of temple of the Sun at Meroë, Sudan	**500** Iron Age in sub-Saharan Africa. Beginning of Nok culture in northern Nigeria	**304** Egypt independent under Ptole

ASIA
560 *Tao Te Ching* appears, Taoist philosophical work by Lao-Tzu
550 Cyrus II of Persia defeats Medes and founds Persian Empire
539 Persians conquer Neo-Babylonian Empire
521 Height of the Persian Empire under Darius I
500 Caste system established in India
479 Death of Confucius (b.551)
486 Death of Buddha
403 Start of "Warring States" period in China
334–26 Alexander the Great (b.356) con Asia Minor, Persia, and parts of India
323 Death of Alexander the Great and division of his empire
322 Chandragupta founds Mauryan Empire in India

EUROPE
510 Foundation of Roman Republic
505 Establishment of democracy in Athens
478 Confederacy of Delos (Athenian League) founded
480 Greeks defeat Persians at Battle of Salamis
490 Greeks defeat Persians at Battle of Marathon
450 La Tène (Iron Age) culture in central and western Europe
431–04 Peloponnesian Wars: Sparta defeats Athens
338 Macedonians gain control of Greece at Battle of Chaeronea

AMERICAS
400 Decline of Olmec civilization

OCEANIA
500 Trading contacts established in South Pacific islands

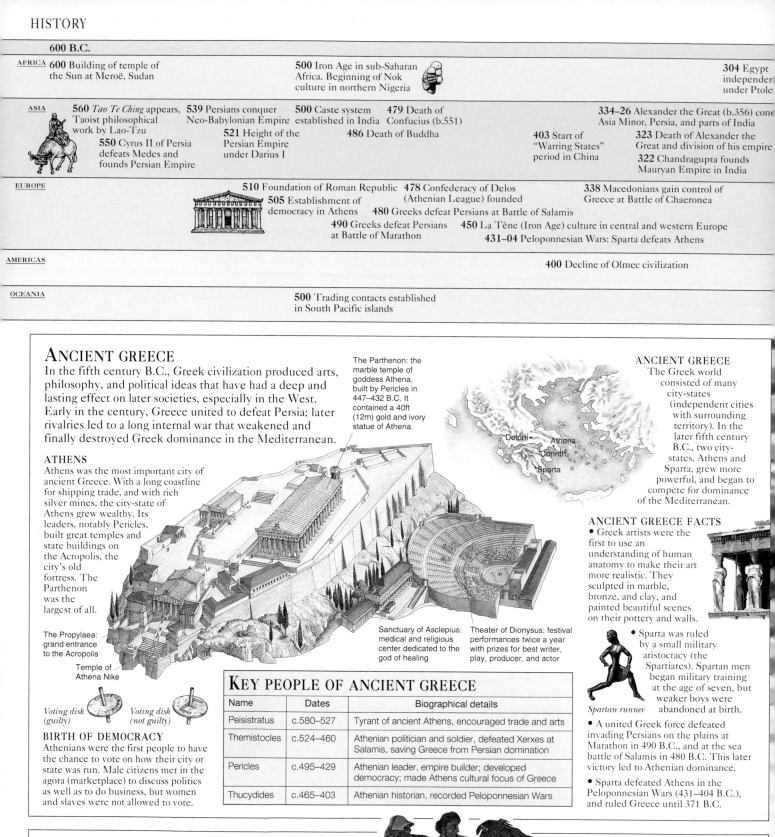

ANCIENT GREECE

In the fifth century B.C., Greek civilization produced arts, philosophy, and political ideas that have had a deep and lasting effect on later societies, especially in the West. Early in the century, Greece united to defeat Persia; later rivalries led to a long internal war that weakened and finally destroyed Greek dominance in the Mediterranean.

ATHENS

Athens was the most important city of ancient Greece. With a long coastline for shipping trade, and with rich silver mines, the city-state of Athens grew wealthy. Its leaders, notably Pericles, built great temples and state buildings on the Acropolis, the city's old fortress. The Parthenon was the largest of all.

The Propylaea: grand entrance to the Acropolis

Temple of Athena Nike

Voting disk (guilty) *Voting disk (not guilty)*

BIRTH OF DEMOCRACY

Athenians were the first people to have the chance to vote on how their city or state was run. Male citizens met in the agora (marketplace) to discuss politics as well as to do business, but women and slaves were not allowed to vote.

The Parthenon: the marble temple of goddess Athena, built by Pericles in 447–432 B.C. It contained a 40ft (12m) gold and ivory statue of Athena.

Delphi • Athens • Corinth • Sparta

Sanctuary of Asclepius: medical and religious center dedicated to the god of healing

Theater of Dionysus: festival performances twice a year with prizes for best writer, play, producer, and actor

ANCIENT GREECE

The Greek world consisted of many city-states (independent cities with surrounding territory). In the later fifth century B.C., two city-states, Athens and Sparta, grew more powerful, and began to compete for dominance of the Mediterranean.

ANCIENT GREECE FACTS

• Greek artists were the first to use an understanding of human anatomy to make their art more realistic. They sculpted in marble, bronze, and clay, and painted beautiful scenes on their pottery and walls.

• Sparta was ruled by a small military aristocracy (the Spartiates). Spartan men began military training at the age of seven, but weaker boys were abandoned at birth.

Spartan runner

• A united Greek force defeated invading Persians on the plains at Marathon in 490 B.C., and at the sea battle of Salamis in 480 B.C. This later victory led to Athenian dominance.

• Sparta defeated Athens in the Peloponnesian Wars (431–404 B.C.), and ruled Greece until 371 B.C.

KEY PEOPLE OF ANCIENT GREECE

Name	Dates	Biographical details
Peisistratus	c.580–527	Tyrant of ancient Athens, encouraged trade and arts
Themistocles	c.524–460	Athenian politician and soldier, defeated Xerxes at Salamis, saving Greece from Persian domination
Pericles	c.495–429	Athenian leader, empire builder; developed democracy; made Athens cultural focus of Greece
Thucydides	c.465–403	Athenian historian, recorded Peloponnesian Wars

ALEXANDER

In just eight years Alexander the Great (356–323 B.C.) built the largest empire the world had ever seen. He helped spread Greek, or Hellenistic, culture all over Asia, but his early death, at the age of 33, left his empire leaderless and divided.

Gaugamela
Pella
Issus
Alexandria
Babylon
Persepolis
Kabul

→ Alexander's route
■ Alexander's empire

ALEXANDER'S CONQUESTS

Alexander led his forces to victory from Greece as far as the Indus valley. He took with him not only soldiers, but engineers, artists, and philosophers. He founded some 70 cities, notably Alexandria in Egypt.

Alexander at Issus

BATTLE OF ISSUS

Outnumbered six to one, Alexander defeated the Persian Emperor, Darius, at Issus in 333 B.C.

BRIDE BRIBE

After conquering Darius, Alexander encouraged the Hellenistic and Persian cultures to mix. He offered money to the first 10,000 Macedonian soldiers who wished to marry Persian women.

290 Foundation of library at Alexandria, Egypt

149–6 Rome destroys Carthage in Third Punic War, founding province of Africa

100 Camel introduced into Sahara region

30 Egypt becomes Roman province on death of Mark Antony (b.82) and Cleopatra (b.69)

262 Mauryan Emperor Asoka converts to Buddhism

221 Ch'in Shih Huang-ti (c.259–210), the first emperor, unites China

185 Bactrians from present-day Afghanistan conquer northwest India

112 "Silk Road" opens up, giving West some access to China

240 Beginning of Parthian dynasty in northern Persia

207 Chinese unity disintegrates

64 Roman general Pompey (106–28) conquers Syria

202 China reunited under Han dynasty

53 Parthia halts Roman eastward expansion

290 Rome gains control of central Italy

49 Julius Caesar invades Gaul

31 Battle of Actium gives Octavian (later Emperor Augustus) power over Rome

264–41 First Punic War (Rome versus Carthage): Rome wins control of Sicily

218–01 Second Punic War: Roman general Scipio defeats Hannibal

46 Julius Caesar reforms calendar

27 Roman Empire replaces Republic

45 Julius Caesar becomes sole ruler of Rome after civil war

Height of North American mound-building cultures. Beginning of Early Maya Period, Central America

200 Height of Nazca civilization, Peru

100 Anasazi, Hohokam, and Mogollon peoples begin farming in southwestern North America. Okvik hunters settle in northern Alaska

THE RISE OF ROME

From a shepherds' village in central Italy, Rome grew to be the focus of an empire that controlled most of western Europe. Its rise to power was based on discipline, virtue, and military prowess, but it took centuries of warfare for Romans to secure their empire. They exported Rome's lifestyle and technology to all their provinces.

■ 201 B.C.
■ 44 B.C.
■ A.D.14
□ A.D.117

Patricians   *Soldier and slave*   *Plebeians*

ROME'S EXPANSION AND EMPIRE
Rome secured the Mediterranean only after three long wars, the Punic Wars, in which it defeated the sea-based empire of Carthage. Julius Caesar later conquered Gaul.

Londinium
Trier
GAUL
Byzantium
Rome
Antioch
Carthage
Alexandria

ROMAN SOCIETY
Roman society was divided into several levels: patricians (aristocrats), plebeians (citizens), subjects (in the provinces), and slaves. Women were expected to be mothers, but rich females had some freedom.

KEY INNOVATIONS

HEATED BATHS
Roman baths were heated by external fires, stoked by slaves. The fire's hot air circulated underneath a raised floor and heated the water above.

AQUEDUCTS
Roman engineers built great aqueducts. Water in this one at Nîmes dropped only 56ft (17m) over 31 miles (50km).

Nîmes aqueduct

THE ROMAN ARMY

Legate (general)

Centurion   *Aquilifer (standard bearer)*   *Trumpeter*   *Auxiliary*

Army structure and command
The Roman army was divided into about 28 legions of about 5,000 infantry soldiers each; a legion contained 10 cohorts; a cohort contained 6 centuries of 80 men each. Officers called centurions commanded each century, and wore crests on their helmets so that they could easily be seen in battle.

Military technology
The Roman catapult, or *ballista*, could launch boulders or arrows over an enemy's defenses. Covered siege towers and battering rams protected soldiers inside.

Foreign legions
When their empire began to expand, Romans had to recruit soldiers, called auxiliaries, from the countries they had conquered. After 25 years auxiliaries could become Roman citizens.

Boulders placed here.

Protected battering ram

Frame built to withstand high tension.

Twisted cord

Siege tower

Soldiers collect ammunition.

Testula

Roman tactics
Soldiers advancing under attack would form a *testula* (tortoise), a formation of upheld shields that protected them from arrows, missiles, or burning oil.

MAURYAN EMPIRE
Mauryan emperor Asoka conquered and unified India. In 262 B.C. he became a Buddhist and set up thousands of stupas (monuments) to Buddha around the empire. Each is said to contain a part of Buddha's body.

Buddhist stupa at Sanchi, India, c.150 B.C.

CH'IN DYNASTY OF CHINA
In 221 B.C. China was unified under its first emperor, Ch'in Shih Huang-ti (c.259–210 B.C.). He centralized the government, standardized money, weights, and measures, and built grand monuments in his own honor.

The Great Wall: a 1,860-mile defense against northern Huns

Terra-cotta army
Ch'in Shih Huang-ti built himself a great underground tomb.

Tomb had 7,000 statues of fully armed warriors, some with horses.

ADENA AND HOPEWELL
From 700 B.C. to A.D. 400 the Adena, and later the Hopewell, farming societies flourished in North America. They built huge, mysterious earth mounds, and filled their graves with beautifully carved objects.

Serpent mound, Ohio; 1,310ft (400m) uncoiled

A.D. 1

AFRICA	**50** Kingdom of Axum (Ethiopia) begins to expand	**150** Berbers and Mandingos start to dominate Sudan area	**250** Axum controls trade in Red Sea

ASIA
9 Han dynasty overthrown in China **70** Romans seize Jerusalem and destroy Jewish temple **200** Completion of Mishnah (Jewish law).
25 Han dynasty restored **105** Paper first used in China Composition of Ramayana, Mahabharata (Indian epics), and Bhagavad Gita (Hindu scripture)
30 Jesus Christ crucified in Jerusalem **132** Jewish revolt against Rome, leading to dispersal of Jews **220** Han dynasty ends; China divided into three states
46–57 St. Paul's missionary journeys **224** Sassanian dynasty founded in Persia **245** China and Funan (first Southeast Asian state) in con
60 Beginning of Kushan Empire in India

EUROPE
43 Romans invade Great Britain **79** Eruption of Vesuvius, southern Italy **117** Roman Empire reaches its maximum extent **238** Goths begin to encroach on Roman Empire **293** Empe Diocletian reorganize Roman Er

AMERICAS **1** Beginning of Moche civilization in northern Peru

OCEANIA **1–100** Hindu-Buddhists from Southeast Asia colonize Sumatra and Java

IMPERIAL ROME

The Roman Republic was shaken by a series of civil wars that began in 49 B.C. In 27 B.C. the general and adopted son of Julius Caesar, Octavian, defeated his rival Mark Antony and, as Augustus, became the first emperor. His reforms brought peace and prosperity to the Empire and created a power structure that lasted until the last emperor, Romulus Augustulus, was deposed in A.D. 476.

AUGUSTUS

Though he preserved many of the Republic's old institutions, Augustus (previously Octavian) had overall power; he even encouraged a cult of Augustus, in which he was worshipped as a god. He passed his title and powers on to his son Tiberius in A.D. 14.

Emperor Augustus

IMPERIAL TRIUMPH

Emperors used military triumphs to reinforce their power. They paraded defeated enemies through Rome to the cheers of onlookers.

ROMAN CHARIOT RACES

Rome's *Circus Maximus* was a great stadium in which chariot races were held. Races were often dangerous and the teams (reds, blues, greens, whites) inspired fans throughout the empire.

KEY PEOPLE OF ANCIENT ROME

Name	Dates	Biographical details
Julius Caesar	100–44 B.C.	Conquered Gaul, won civil war, dictator of Rome (46–44), murdered 44 BC
Augustus	63 B.C.–A.D.19	Julius Caesar's adopted son, defeated Mark Antony to become first emperor
Trajan	A.D. 53–117	Popular emperor, extended Empire eastward, began vast building program
Hadrian	A.D. 76–138	Emperor, secured boundaries of Empire, built Hadrian's Wall as defense
Diocletian	A.D. 245–316	Emperor, restored order after near anarchy. Last persecutor of Christians

DECLINE OF THE ROMAN EMPIRE
Reliance on army

The emperor Septimius Severus ended a civil war in A.D. 193, but his reliance on the army to restore order showed that no future emperor could enjoy total power: he would need the support of the army.

Collaboration with barbarians

In the third century A.D., hostile barbarians from northern Europe stepped up pressure on the Empire's borders. Rome increasingly relied on local forces in their provinces and many locals rose to important government positions. Later, these leaders took more power into their own hands.

Shifting center

In the fourth and fifth centuries A.D. the Empire gradually fragmented; there were capitals at different times at Ravenna, Milan, Trier, Sirmium, and Constantinople.

Visigoth

DIVISION OF EMPIRE

In A.D. 293 Emperor Diocletian changed the structure of the Empire. He divided it into two parts (east and west), each with an emperor and a deputy. He ruled the east, and gave the west to Maximian. He called the new system a tetrarchy, and it helped him deal with the growing problem of civil unrest.

The four tetrarchs

PAVING THE WAY

By the early 4th century A.D., Romans had built a road network of 52,800 miles (85,000km). It took six days to go from Londinium (London) to Rome. In the 1800s the journey took just as long.

Imperial border ---- Division of the Empire

Londinium • Trier • Rome • Byzantium • Carthage

→Visigoths →Vandals →Burgundians
→Ostrogoths →Franks →Angles

ROME UNDER SIEGE

Rome devoted much of its resources to defending its long borders. From the 4th century A.D., economic problems forced a weakening in defense. Visigoths under Alaric captured and sacked Rome in A.D. 410, and Attila the Hun invaded Gaul in A.D. 451.

325 Axum destroys
kingdom of Meroë

400 Christianity adopted in Axum
439 Vandals establish kingdom in northern Africa

533 Emperor Justinian wins
back northern Africa for Rome

04 Invasion of Huns
rther splits up China

480 End of
Gupta Empire

520 Rise of mathematics in India;
decimal number system invented

320 Chandragupta I founds
Gupta Empire in northern India

531 Height of Sassanian Empire

550 Buddhism introduced into Japan

589 China reunified
under Sui dynasty

313 Toleration of Christians in Roman
Empire as result of Edict of Milan

410 Visigoths invade Italy and Spain, sack Rome

450 Angles, Jutes, and Saxons settle in Great Britain

552 Emperor Justinian restores
Italy to Roman control

330 Emperor Constantine moves capital
of Roman Empire to Constantinople

476 Last western
Roman emperor,
Romulus Augustulus,
overthrown

486 Clovis establishes Frankish kingdom
in present-day northern France, Belgium,
and parts of western Germany

568 Lombards take
over northern Italy

370 Huns appear in Europe

493 Ostrogoths take over in Italy

590 Pope Gregory the Great
(c.540–604) expands papal power

Great civilized states in Mexico
te Alban, Teotihuacán)

600 Height of Mayan
civilization, central America

Eastern Polynesia settled

THE COMING OF CHRISTIANITY

Mainly Christian
by A.D. 600

* Christian center

Christianity began as a minor sect in a remote corner of the Roman Empire. A series of events brought it wider fame, until the Emperor Constantine was himself converted. In A.D. 391, Emperor Theodosius I made it Rome's official religion and banned all other religions.

Cantauri
Augusta Treverorum
Turones
Arelate · Roma
Toletum Byzantium
Ephesus Edessa Artashat
Antioch
Carthage Damascus
Jerusalem
Alexandria

JESUS OF NAZARETH
In about A.D. 30 the Jewish teacher Jesus of Nazareth, who was seen by the Roman and Jewish authorities as a revolutionary, was crucified. His apostles, or followers, spread his message.

SPREAD OF CHRISTIANITY
After Jesus' death, his apostles took his message abroad. Christianity spread rapidly within the Roman Empire. The centers of Antioch and Edessa carried it eastward into Persia. Later it reached China and India.

ST. PAUL'S JOURNEYS
Paul of Tarsus, one of Jesus' apostles, made four journeys around the Mediterranean coast, preaching Christianity. This new faith excluded no one, offering salvation to rich and poor alike, and Christian martyrs inspired many people to convert.

St. Paul, in a mosaic from St. Peter's, Rome

EARLY CHRISTIANITY FACTS

Christian fish symbol

• The fish was an early Christian symbol. In Greek, the letters of the word for fish stand for "Jesus Christ, God's Son, Savior."

Captive lion

• Christians were persecuted in the Roman Empire. Emperor Nero had Christians thrown to the lions, and Diocletian had priests tortured.

Fragment of Gospel text

• Key books of the New Testament – the gospels of disciples Matthew, Mark, and Luke – were written in A.D. 65–70.

CONSTANTINE
In A.D. 313 Emperor Constantine became a Christian and gave Christians freedom to worship with the Edict of Milan. The church could then flourish.

SASSANIAN EMPIRE
The Sassanian Empire lasted from A.D. 224 to 641 and was centered around the city of Ctesiphon (Baghdad). At its height under King Khosrow (A.D. 531–79), it stretched from the River Indus to the Euphrates. Sassanians were great architects and followed the Zoroastrian religion (see p.143).

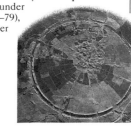

Ramparts form perfect circle 1.2 miles (2km) in diameter
Circular city at Firuzabad

MAYAN CIVILIZATION
The Mayan civilization of Central America flourished between A.D. 300 and 900. Mayans built great pyramidal temples; they also developed writing and advanced mathematics. Mayan astronomers had calculated the exact length of the solar year and lunar month and could predict eclipses. They played a form of basketball that was half religious ceremony, half sport. Anyone who scored had the right to demand the property of any spectator they managed to catch.

Players could only use hips, elbows, and ankles to control the ball.

ROME AND JUDAISM
From A.D. 66 to 70 Jews in Palestine, led by important priests and Pharisees, revolted against Roman rule. Emperor Vespasian, with his son Titus, brutally suppressed the revolt. A second Jewish rebellion of A.D. 132 to 135 was put down by Emperor Hadrian.

Capture of Jerusalem
In A.D. 70 Titus captured Jerusalem, plundering and destroying its great Jewish temple. The resulting diaspora (dispersal) of Jews carried Judaism as far as Spain and Africa.

Sacking of the temple of Jerusalem

Masada
In A.D. 73, the last Jewish stronghold, at Masada on the shores of the Dead Sea, fell to the Romans. When the Romans broke into the fortress, they found that all 960 Jews inside had killed themselves rather than be captured.

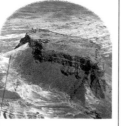

Remains of siege ramp

Fortress at Masada

AXUM
In the 4th century A.D., Axum in northeastern Africa overthrew the rule of the city of Meroë and became an important power. Its exports of African ivory and sea trade brought great wealth. Axumites built great granite towers, or stelas, as monuments to their civilization. The tallest surviving stela stands at 75.5ft (23m) high – as high as 16 people standing on each other's shoulders.

Great Stela at Axum

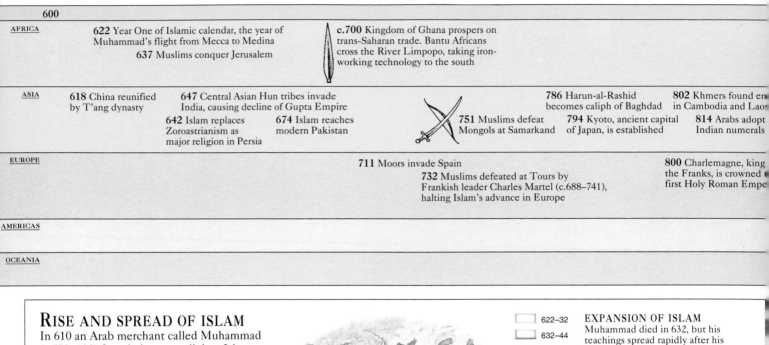

600

AFRICA
622 Year One of Islamic calendar, the year of Muhammad's flight from Mecca to Medina
637 Muslims conquer Jerusalem

c.700 Kingdom of Ghana prospers on trans-Saharan trade. Bantu Africans cross the River Limpopo, taking iron-working technology to the south

ASIA
618 China reunified by T'ang dynasty
647 Central Asian Hun tribes invade India, causing decline of Gupta Empire
642 Islam replaces Zoroastrianism as major religion in Persia
674 Islam reaches modern Pakistan
751 Muslims defeat Mongols at Samarkand
786 Harun-al-Rashid becomes caliph of Baghdad
794 Kyoto, ancient capital of Japan, is established
802 Khmers found em in Cambodia and Lao
814 Arabs adopt Indian numerals

EUROPE
711 Moors invade Spain
732 Muslims defeated at Tours by Frankish leader Charles Martel (c.688–741), halting Islam's advance in Europe
800 Charlemagne, king the Franks, is crowned first Holy Roman Empe

AMERICAS

OCEANIA

RISE AND SPREAD OF ISLAM

In 610 an Arab merchant called Muhammad (c.570–632) founded a new religion: Islam. His teachings were an inspiration to the Arab peoples, and by 750, Muslims (the followers of Islam) had gained control of a massive area stretching from Spain to Afghanistan. The Muslim advance spread trade, culture, and science, as well as Islam.

622–32	
632–44	
644–750	
750–850	

EXPANSION OF ISLAM
Muhammad died in 632, but his teachings spread rapidly after his death. By 850 Muslims had made Islam the most important civilization after China.

El Cid

EL CID
Rodrigo Diaz de Vivar (c.1043–99) was the real name of "El Cid," a Spanish knight and outlaw who fought against Muslim colonists. His greatest achievement was the capture of the Spanish city of Valencia in 1094, which made him a national hero.

Great Mosque at Córdoba

CÓRDOBA'S GREAT MOSQUE
Arab colonists built the Great Mosque at Córdoba, southern Spain, between 784 and 990. One of the largest and most complex Islamic mosques, it has 850 marble columns supporting arches on two levels.

Muslim at prayer

Prayer rug

MUHAMMAD'S JOURNEY
Muhammad's religious ideas were initially unpopular. In 622, established merchants forced him to flee Mecca for Medina, but in 630 Muhammad returned to the city in triumph. Since then, Muslims at prayer have always faced Mecca.

HARUN-AL-RASHID
Harun-al-Rashid (766–809) ruled the Islamic world at its height. The wealth and culture of his court at Baghdad inspired the tales of *The Thousand and One Nights*. His wife would drink only from gold and silver gem-studded vessels.

Harun-al-Rashid

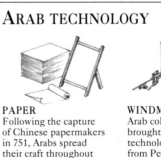

ARAB TECHNOLOGY

PAPER
Following the capture of Chinese papermakers in 751, Arabs spread their craft throughout the Islamic world.

WINDMILL
Arab colonists brought windmill technology to Spain from Persia in the 10th century.

OPTICS
Arabic scholar Alhazen (c.965–1039) wrote the first accurate account of vision. He gave us the term "lens."

CHARLEMAGNE
King Charlemagne of the Franks (742–814) conquered most of the Christian lands of Western Europe and founded the Holy Roman Empire in 800. He encouraged learning with a new, clear script called Carolingian miniscule.

KEY PEOPLE

Name	Dates	Biographical details
Muhammad	c.570–632	Arab merchant and religious teacher, founder of Islam
Rabiah-al-Adawiyah	712–801	Female Arab mystic and religious teacher
Charlemagne	742–814	King of the Franks (people of northwestern Europe), conquered Western Europe, spread Christianity
Harun-al-Rashid	766–809	Caliph of Baghdad, ruled Islamic world at its height
Leif Eriksson	c.1000	Viking explorer, reached North American coast in 1000
William of Normandy	c.1028–87	Duke of Normandy, conquered England in 1066
El Cid	c.1043–99	Spanish knight and outlaw, fought Muslims in Spain

POPE SYLVESTER
Pope Sylvester II (940–1003) introduced Arabic numerals (0-9) and the astrolabe (an aid to navigation) to Europe from Muslim Spain.

Astrolabe

900 Hausa kingdom of Daura founded in northern Nigeria

920 Ghana's Golden Age begins

980 Arab traders settle on East African coast

1054 Ghana conquered by Muslim Almoravid dynasty

888 Chola dynasty of Tamil kings replaces the Pallavas in southern India and Sri Lanka

935–41 Civil war in Japan

960 Sung Dynasty takes over China

861 The Vikings discover Iceland

4 Kenneth MacAlpine (d. 858) feats the Picts and unites Scotland

911 The Viking Rollo is granted Normandy

930 Cordoba becomes seat of Arab learning in Spain

966 Poles converted to Christianity

982 Erik the Red settles in Greenland

997 Stephen I (977–1038) becomes first King of Hungary

1000 Leif Eriksson, son of Erik the Red, sails down North American coast. He names it "Vinland"

1066 William of Normandy invades England

1096 First Crusade begins

900 Mixtec civilization begins in Mexico

980 Toltecs set up capital at Tula (Mexico)

1000 Chimu civilization of Peru founded

950 Polynesian navigator Kupe discovers New Zealand, and first Maori settlers arrive

TRADERS AND RAIDERS

Late in the eighth century people from present-day Denmark, Norway, and Sweden, called Vikings, began to leave their overcrowded homelands in search of treasure to plunder or new land to settle. Their golden age of trade, exploration, and colonization lasted until 1100.

Carved figurehead

ROUTES OF VIKING TRAVEL

Vikings were great traders. They dealt in many goods, exchanging slaves, fur, wood, honey, walrus tusks, whale oil, feathers, and down for silver, silk, spices, and wine.

Viking homeland
Settlement
Sea route
River route

York
Dublin
Novgorod
Birka
Byzantium (Istanbul)
Baghdad
L'Anse aux Meadows

Viking trading post

Viking traders carried their goods in knorrs – small, stable ships.

VIKING LONGSHIPS

The key to Viking success was their skill in building and sailing ships. Their longships were the fastest ships of the time; they had both sail and oar, and their flat bottoms enabled them to navigate both inland rivers and seas.

VIKING TRADING POSTS

Many great cities such as York, England, and Dublin, Ireland, started as places where Vikings met with locals to exchange goods.

Novgorod

VIKING FACTS

• Viking graffiti can still be seen in a gallery of Istanbul's great mosque, Hagia Sophia.

• Vikings reached the Americas in 1000, 500 years before Christopher Columbus.

• After a battle, Viking women would feed those with belly wounds a strong-smelling soup of onions and herbs. If, later, they smelled this mix at the wound, they knew that the intestine had been pierced and that the victim would soon die.

Battle helmet   Hand ax

BERSERKERS

Some warriors were called "berserkers" – from *bare sark*, meaning shirtless. A berserker with battle-fever was said to have the strength of a bull and would fight without shirt or armor. Our word "berserk" comes from the name for these Viking madmen.

ROLLO OF NORMANDY

In 911 Rollo, a Norseman chief, was granted land in northern France by the King of France, in return for his promise to defend it. William the Conqueror was Rollo's descendant.

VIKING SUPERMEN

The Emperor of Byzantium was so impressed by the courage, strength, and size of the Viking warriors he had seen that he recruited them for his personal bodyguard. It was called the Varangian guard.

Broadsword

Varangian guard

Rollo of Normandy

NORMANDY

BIRTH OF RUSSIA

According to the 12th-century Russian Chronicle, Novgorod Slavs invited Vikings to rule over them. Vikings were also called "Rus," so when they took over the area it was called the Land of Rus, and later, Russia.

KING WENCESLAS

Wenceslas (907–29) was the first ruler of Bohemia, central Europe. He became a Christian and helped spread Christianity in Bohemia. Murdered outside his church by his own brother, Wenceslas was later made the patron saint of Hungary, Poland, and Bohemia.

KEY INVENTIONS

GUNPOWDER

In 1044 Chinese chemist Wu Ching Tsao Yao published the first known recipe for gunpowder. The explosive mix was first used for fireworks.

FIRST PRINTED BOOKS

The Diamond Sutra, dated 868, is the world's oldest printed book. It is a Buddhist scripture printed from blocks of wood onto sheets of paper and joined into a scroll.

FIRST NOVEL

In 1001 a Japanese noblewoman called Murasaki Shikibu wrote the first novel. Over 600,000 words long, *The Tale of Genji* tells of a prince's quest for true love and wisdom.

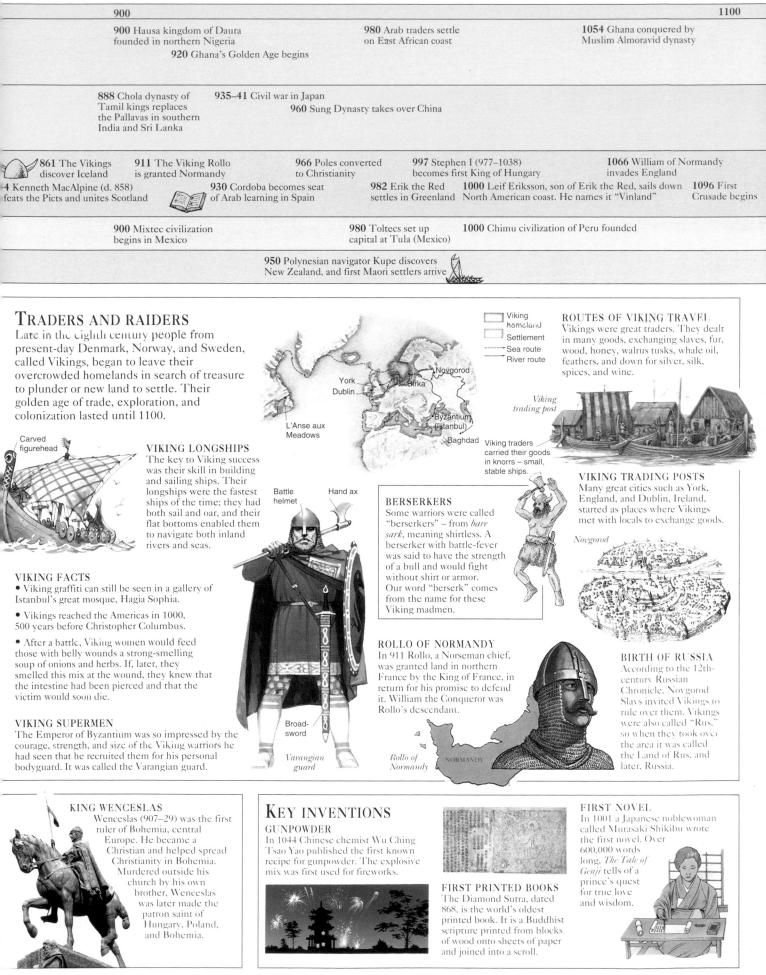

1100

AFRICA c.1100 First Iron Age settlement in Zimbabwe

1104 Crusaders capture Acre

1169 Saladin (1137–93) becomes ruler of Egypt

ASIA

1156 Civil war between rival clans in Japan leads to domination by samurai warlords

EUROPE

1115 French philosopher Peter Abelard (1079–1142) begins teaching in Paris. St. Bernard (1090–1153) founds important monastery at Clairvaux

1143 Alfonso Henriques (c.1109–85) becomes first King of Portugal

1170 Murder of Thomas Becket (1118–70), Archbishop of Canterbury, England

1119 Bologna University, one of Europe's oldest, founded in Italy

AMERICAS

1151 Fall of the Toltec Empire in Mexico

OCEANIA 1100s Giant statues first erected on Easter Island, South Pacific

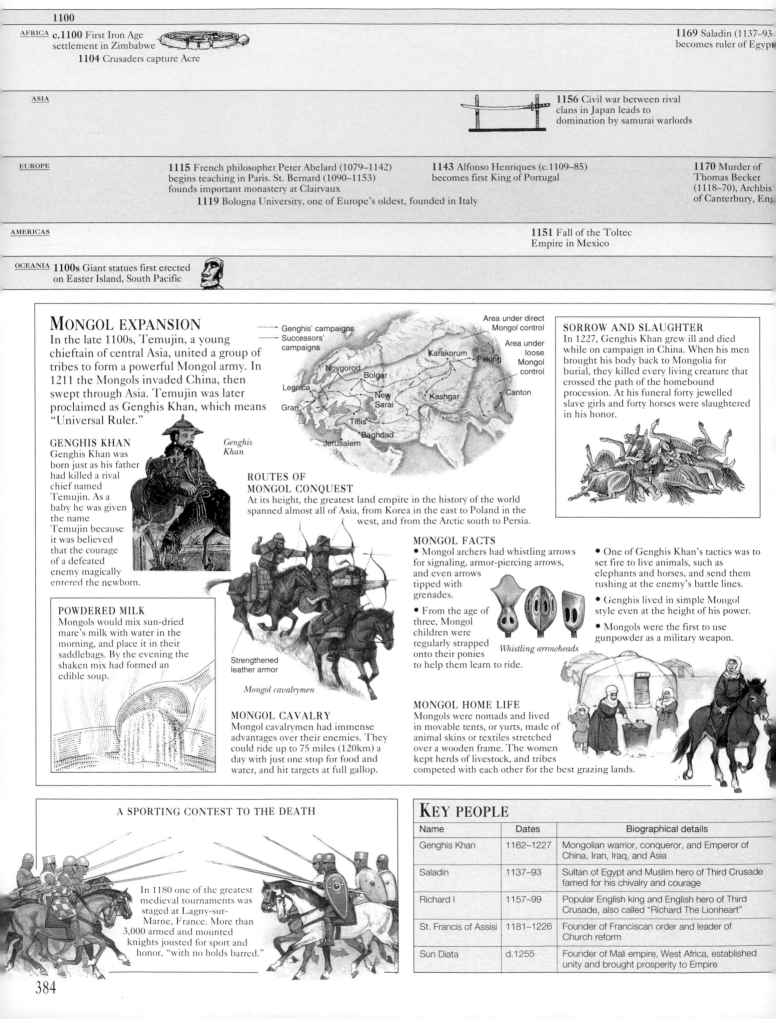

MONGOL EXPANSION

In the late 1100s, Temujin, a young chieftain of central Asia, united a group of tribes to form a powerful Mongol army. In 1211 the Mongols invaded China, then swept through Asia. Temujin was later proclaimed as Genghis Khan, which means "Universal Ruler."

- - - - - Genghis' campaigns
—— Successors' campaigns

Area under direct Mongol control
Area under loose Mongol control

Karakorum • Peking
Novgorod
Bolgar
Legnica
New Sarai • Kashgar
Gran • Canton
Tiflis
Baghdad
Jerusalem

Genghis Khan

GENGHIS KHAN
Genghis Khan was born just as his father had killed a rival chief named Temujin. As a baby he was given the name Temujin because it was believed that the courage of a defeated enemy magically entered the newborn.

ROUTES OF MONGOL CONQUEST
At its height, the greatest land empire in the history of the world spanned almost all of Asia, from Korea in the east to Poland in the west, and from the Arctic south to Persia.

SORROW AND SLAUGHTER
In 1227, Genghis Khan grew ill and died while on campaign in China. When his men brought his body back to Mongolia for burial, they killed every living creature that crossed the path of the homebound procession. At his funeral forty jewelled slave girls and forty horses were slaughtered in his honor.

POWDERED MILK
Mongols would mix sun-dried mare's milk with water in the morning, and place it in their saddlebags. By the evening the shaken mix had formed an edible soup.

Strengthened leather armor

Mongol cavalrymen

MONGOL CAVALRY
Mongol cavalrymen had immense advantages over their enemies. They could ride up to 75 miles (120km) a day with just one stop for food and water, and hit targets at full gallop.

MONGOL FACTS
- Mongol archers had whistling arrows for signaling, armor-piercing arrows, and even arrows tipped with grenades.
- From the age of three, Mongol children were regularly strapped onto their ponies to help them learn to ride.

Whistling arrowheads

- One of Genghis Khan's tactics was to set fire to live animals, such as elephants and horses, and send them rushing at the enemy's battle lines.
- Genghis lived in simple Mongol style even at the height of his power.
- Mongols were the first to use gunpowder as a military weapon.

MONGOL HOME LIFE
Mongols were nomads and lived in movable tents, or yurts, made of animal skins or textiles stretched over a wooden frame. The women kept herds of livestock, and tribes competed with each other for the best grazing lands.

A SPORTING CONTEST TO THE DEATH

In 1180 one of the greatest medieval tournaments was staged at Lagny-sur-Marne, France. More than 3,000 armed and mounted knights jousted for sport and honor, "with no holds barred."

KEY PEOPLE

Name	Dates	Biographical details
Genghis Khan	1162–1227	Mongolian warrior, conqueror, and Emperor of China, Iran, Iraq, and Asia
Saladin	1137–93	Sultan of Egypt and Muslim hero of Third Crusade famed for his chivalry and courage
Richard I	1157–99	Popular English king and English hero of Third Crusade, also called "Richard The Lionheart"
St. Francis of Assisi	1181–1226	Founder of Franciscan order and leader of Church reform
Sun Diata	d.1255	Founder of Mali empire, West Africa, established unity and brought prosperity to Empire

1187 Saladin captures Jerusalem from Crusaders

1190 Lalibela becomes Emperor of Ethiopia

1229 Sixth Crusaders recapture Jerusalem

1244 Egyptians retake Jerusalem

1235 Sun Diata (d.1255) founds empire of Mali, West Africa

1191 Zen Buddhism first introduced to Japan

1206 Genghis Khan (1162–1227) founds Mongol Empire. Islam takes root in new Kingdom of Delhi, India, founded by Aibak, a former slave

1232 Explosive rockets used in war between Chinese and conquering Mongols

1237 Mongol army begins to conquer Russia

5 Work begins on ...ndon Bridge, ...n Bridge, and "Leaning Tower"

1204 Fourth Crusaders sack and loot Constantinople. King John of England (1167–1216) loses French lands

1209 St. Francis (1181–1226) founds Franciscan order

1215 St. Dominic (1170–1221) founds Dominican Order. King John of England seals Magna Carta

1240s German towns begin regional trades, later forming powerful and protective trading alliance, the Hanseatic League

c.1200 Cuzco, Peru, becomes an Inca center. First corn farmers settle along banks of Mississippi

1200 First settlers from Indonesia and Philippines arrive in Fiji and spread throughout Polynesia

ZEN BUDDHISM

In 1191 Zen Buddhism was introduced to Japan by a monk named Eisai (1141–1215). Zen Buddhism stressed personal instruction by a master (rather than the study of scriptures) as the path to self-knowledge.

MAGNA CARTA

In 1215 King John of England was forced to seal the Magna Carta, or Great Charter. It gave political rights to his most powerful subjects and made the king subject to law.

Royal seal

THIRTEENTH-CENTURY BUILDINGS

Chartres Cathedral, the finest example of French Gothic architecture, took 31 years to build in the mid-13th century. At the same time, the Maya of Central America began building the massive temples of their new capital at Mayapan, in modern-day Mexico.

North spire (burned down 1194, rebuilt by 1510)

South spire (1160)

Maya Temple

Only priests were allowed to go to the top of the steps

Chartres Cathedral

THE CRUSADES

By 1095 the Saracens (Muslims) had gained control of the holy lands in the Middle East. European Christians, urged on by Pope Urban II, organized armed expeditions, or crusades, to recapture the lands. The First Crusade was a triumph. Others were less successful, and the last ended in 1291.

— 1st Crusade
--- 2nd Crusade
→ 3rd Crusade

Paris · Bruges · Vienna · Genoa · Toulouse · Marseilles · Rome · Constantinople · Damascus · Acre · Jerusalem

CRUSADE ROUTES

The first two crusader armies assembled at meeting points in Europe, and fought their way overland across Asia Minor. Later, European control of the Mediterranean allowed crusaders to take a sea route to the Holy Land.

Helmet
Surcoat
Hauberk (chain-mail shirt)

CRUSADER

Crusaders took their name from the cross (Latin *crux*) that was sewn on to their clothing. Crusader knights wore suits of armor and vowed to follow strict codes of chivalry.

Chausses (chain-mail leggings)

Typical Crusader of the order of Knights Templar

Conical helmet
Nasal (nose-guard)
Shield
Scimitar

Saracen warrior

CHILDREN'S CRUSADE

In 1212 thousands of unarmed children believing in the power of innocence set off from Europe for the Holy Land. Most died on the way, or were sold as slaves in Africa.

SARACEN WARRIOR

The term Saracen was used to describe any Arab, Turk, or other follower of Islam. They used a shield of Persian design and a long, curved sword called a scimitar.

DOME OF THE ROCK

The magnificent Dome of the Rock mosque in Jerusalem was built by an Arab caliph between 685 and 691 on a Jewish temple site. When the crusaders controlled Jerusalem, however, they turned it into a Christian church.

Shield of the order of Knights Hospitaller

Shield of the order of Teutonic Knights

KRAK DES CHEVALIERS

Begun in 1142, and now in modern-day Syria, this is the most impressive crusader fortress. Its storerooms could provide hundreds of people with food for five years.

MAJOR CRUSADES

Crusade	Dates	Result
First Crusade	1096–99	Crusaders take Antioch, then Jerusalem in July 1099
Second Crusade	1147–49	Incompetence leads to Crusader defeat in Anatolia
Third Crusade	1189–92	Crusaders win coast from Tyre to Jaffa but Jerusalem remains uncaptured
Fourth Crusade	1202–04	Crusaders loot Constantinople
Children's Crusade	1212	Thousands of innocent children march to death and slavery in North Africa
5th–8th	1218–91	Partial and short–lived Crusader victories

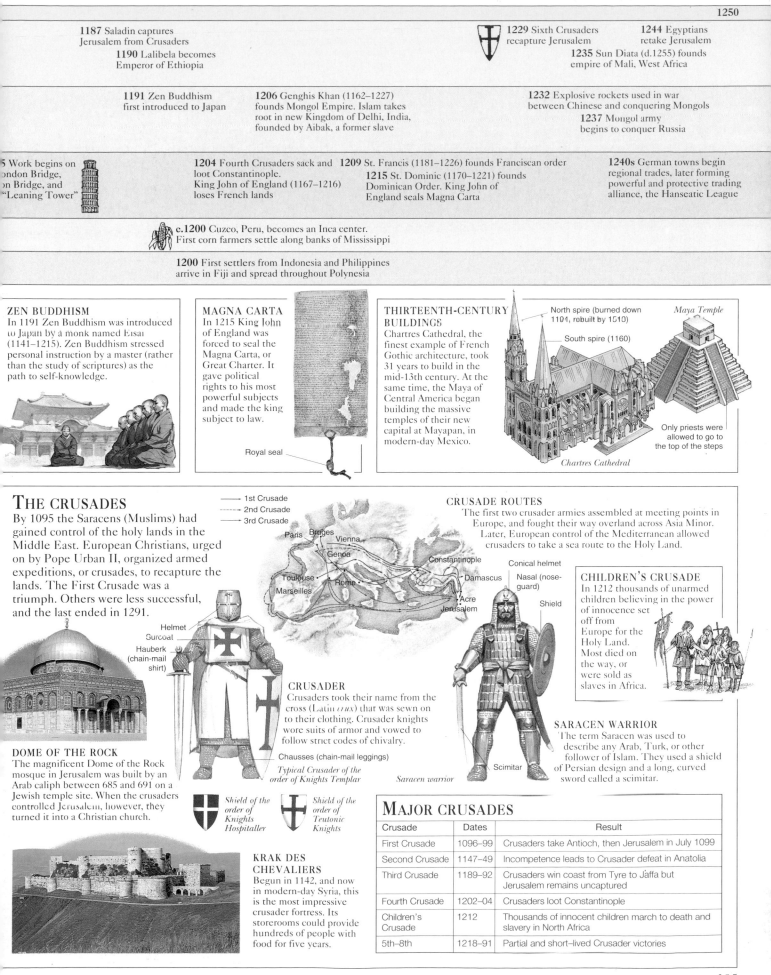

1250

AFRICA	**1250** Mamelukes, rebel slave-soldiers, become rulers of Egypt	**1300** Foundation of Benin kingdom in Nigeria	**1324** Mansa Musa (d.1332), emperor of Mali, makes pilgrimage to Mecca	**1348** Plague devastates Egypt
	1260 Mamelukes halt Mongol advance at Battle of Ain Jalut in Palestine	**1291** Saracens capture Acre, ending the Crusades		

ASIA	**1250** A Japanese monk, Nicherin (1222–82), proclaims *Lotus Sutra* the supreme Buddhist scripture	**1281** The *Kamikaze* (Divine Wind) drives Mongol invaders from Japan	**1340** Hindu empire of Vijayanagar in India becomes center of resistance to Islam
		c.1294 Persians convert to Islam	

EUROPE	**1273** Rudolf Habsburg (1218–91) becomes ruler of Germany, founding the powerful Habsburg dynasty	**1309** Pope moves to Avignon, leading to great rift in Western Church (1378)	**1346** Battle of Crécy begins Hundred Years War between England and France
			1347 Plague (Black Death) reaches Europe

AMERICAS	**c.1250** Mayans restore empire and build new capital at Mayapan. Incas expand their capital at Chan-chan in northern Peru	**c.1300** Incas begin major expansion through Andes	**1325** Aztecs found their capital at Tenochtitlán (now Mexico City)

OCEANIA	**c.1250** Religious assembly platforms built throughout Polynesian Islands

MARCO POLO'S EPIC JOURNEY

In 1271, brothers Niccolo and Maffeo Polo, merchants of Venice, Italy, took Niccolo's 16-year-old son Marco on their second trading journey to the East. Marco had many amazing experiences in the depths of China, and when he returned to Europe 24 years later, he was able to give the first detailed account of daily life in the East.

POLO'S FOOTSTEPS
On their second journey the Polos travelled the ancient Silk Route of Central Asia, which, before the Mongol Empire, could only be used by Arab traders. They took three-and-a-half years to reach the palace of the Mongol emperor, including a year's rest for Marco to recover from illness.

Polo's journey (1271–95)

VENICE
In the 13th century, Venice was the busiest port in the world. Venetian traders supplied Europe's markets with the precious products of the East: silk, spices, and porcelain.

Polos leave Venice

PASTA AND ICE CREAM
The Chinese invented two of modern Italy's most famous dishes: pasta and ice cream. Italian merchants returning from the East brought back the recipes.

The court of Kublai Khan

KUBLAI KHAN
Mongol Emperor, Kublai Khan, was eager to learn about European society and welcomed the Polos at his palace in Shangtu, China.

HUMAN KITE-RIDERS
Marco Polo told terrifying tales of wicker kites. These hoisted live prisoners into the sky, both to test the wind and to bring good luck before ships sailed. Few of the prisoners survived.

POLO TELLS HIS STORY
In 1298 Marco Polo was locked up in Genoa, Italy. There he dictated the story of his journey to a fellow prisoner called Rustichello. The tale amazed Europeans and was translated into several languages.

POLO'S TRUE STORIES
• Polo described Eastern springs that gushed oil. Europeans had doubts, but Polo had not lied: he had seen the Baku oilfields in modern-day Azerbaijan.

• Polo spoke of rocks that could be ground up and spun into a fireproof cloth: they were asbestos rocks, well known in China, but unheard-of in 13th-century Europe.

• The Chinese were the first people to use paper money as currency. Venetian merchants, who still used gold and silver coins as currency, could not believe this.

Early Chinese paper money

KAMIKAZE – DIVINE WIND OF JAPAN
In 1281 the Mongols attacked Japan by sea, hoping to enlarge their vast empire. A timely typhoon destroyed their fleet and put to flight those Mongols already on land. The Japanese named this typhoon the "Divine Wind" or *Kamikaze*.

The Mongol fleet breaks up on Japan's coast

KEY INNOVATIONS

EYEGLASSES
By the early 14th century, reading glasses with curved lenses were being made in a Venice factory.

ACCOUNTANCY
From the 1340s, European merchants began using double-entry book-keeping to record their business.

JOAN OF ARC
In 1431 Joan of Arc (1412–31) was tried by her English enemies and burned as a witch. Inspired by divine visions, the young French shepherdess had led the armies of King Charles VII to a great victory that proved the turning point of the Hundred Years War. Since that time she has been honored as a saint.

2 Moroccan scholar Battuta (1304–68) kes his great journey ss Sahara to Mali

c.1400 Kingdom of Zimbabwe thrives on gold trade

1432 Portuguese explorers reach the Azores

lajapahit Empire d in Java

1368 Tai Tsu (1328–98), founder of Ming dynasty, drives Mongols from China

1398 Mongol leader Tamerlane (1336–1405) sacks Delhi

1405 Death of Tamerlane and fall of Mongol Empire

1448 Major reforms in Thailand under King Traillok (1431–88)

1404–33 Chinese navigator Cheng Ho (1371–1435) explores India and East Africa

1411 Ahmad Shah founds Ahmadabad, important commercial city in India

1358 The *Jacquerie*: French peasants revolt against raised taxes. Rebel peasants defeated and killed

1380 Russians halt Tatar Mongols at Battle of Kulikovo

1389 Ottoman Turks crush Serbs and neighbors at Battle of Kossovo

1429 Siege of Orléans lifted by French soldier-saint Joan of Arc's forces

1381 Peasants' Revolt in England led by Wat Tyler and John Ball

camapitzin becomes Aztec ruler, ng Aztec power

1400 Viracocha (d.1438): first Inca overlord to establish permanent rule over conquered tribes

1438 Inca overlord Pachacuti (d.1471) greatly enlarges Inca Empire

laoris create rock ew Zealand

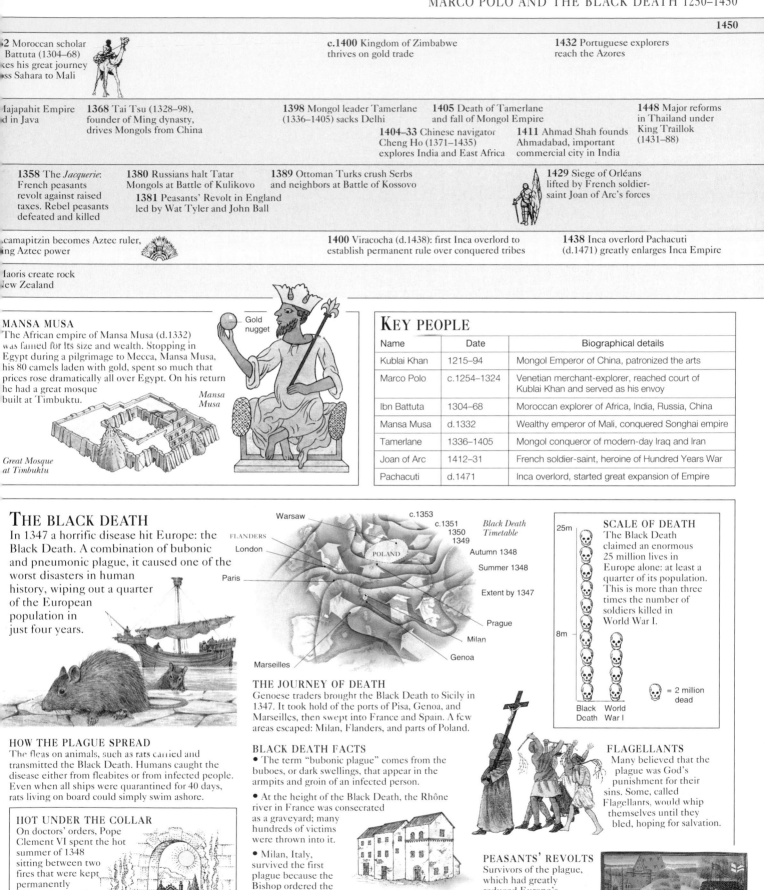

MANSA MUSA

The African empire of Mansa Musa (d.1332) was famed for its size and wealth. Stopping in Egypt during a pilgrimage to Mecca, Mansa Musa, his 80 camels laden with gold, spent so much that prices rose dramatically all over Egypt. On his return he had a great mosque built at Timbuktu.

Gold nugget

Mansa Musa

Great Mosque at Timbuktu

KEY PEOPLE

Name	Date	Biographical details
Kublai Khan	1215–94	Mongol Emperor of China, patronized the arts
Marco Polo	c.1254–1324	Venetian merchant-explorer, reached court of Kublai Khan and served as his envoy
Ibn Battuta	1304–68	Moroccan explorer of Africa, India, Russia, China
Mansa Musa	d.1332	Wealthy emperor of Mali, conquered Songhai empire
Tamerlane	1336–1405	Mongol conqueror of modern-day Iraq and Iran
Joan of Arc	1412–31	French soldier-saint, heroine of Hundred Years War
Pachacuti	d.1471	Inca overlord, started great expansion of Empire

THE BLACK DEATH

In 1347 a horrific disease hit Europe: the Black Death. A combination of bubonic and pneumonic plague, it caused one of the worst disasters in human history, wiping out a quarter of the European population in just four years.

Warsaw
FLANDERS
London
POLAND
Paris
Marseilles
Genoa
Milan
Prague

c.1353
c.1351
1350
1349

Black Death Timetable

Autumn 1348
Summer 1348
Extent by 1347

25m
8m

SCALE OF DEATH
The Black Death claimed an enormous 25 million lives in Europe alone: at least a quarter of its population. This is more than three times the number of soldiers killed in World War I.

Black Death
World War I

💀 = 2 million dead

THE JOURNEY OF DEATH
Genoese traders brought the Black Death to Sicily in 1347. It took hold of the ports of Pisa, Genoa, and Marseilles, then swept into France and Spain. A few areas escaped: Milan, Flanders, and parts of Poland.

HOW THE PLAGUE SPREAD
The fleas on animals, such as rats carried and transmitted the Black Death. Humans caught the disease either from fleabites or from infected people. Even when all ships were quarantined for 40 days, rats living on board could simply swim ashore.

BLACK DEATH FACTS
• The term "bubonic plague" comes from the buboes, or dark swellings, that appear in the armpits and groin of an infected person.

• At the height of the Black Death, the Rhône river in France was consecrated as a graveyard; many hundreds of victims were thrown into it.

• Milan, Italy, survived the first plague because the Bishop ordered the first three houses that it struck to be walled up. The dead, sick, and healthy were all trapped inside.

Condemned homes

• In 1348 the Black Death killed the great Italian historian Giovanni Villani (b.1275). His writings end in mid-sentence, with, "And this plague lasted until....."

HOT UNDER THE COLLAR
On doctors' orders, Pope Clement VI spent the hot summer of 1348 sitting between two fires that were kept permanently stoked. Although he didn't know it, the heat probably kept the fleas at bay, and he survived.

FLAGELLANTS
Many believed that the plague was God's punishment for their sins. Some, called Flagellants, would whip themselves until they bled, hoping for salvation.

PEASANTS' REVOLTS
Survivors of the plague, which had greatly reduced Europe's workforce, demanded higher pay and better conditions. French peasants revolted in 1358; English peasants in 1381. Both revolts were crushed and their leaders killed.

Rebel leader Wat Tyler is murdered.

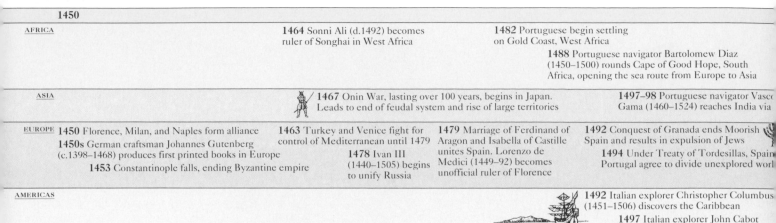

AFRICA

1464 Sonni Ali (d.1492) becomes ruler of Songhai in West Africa

1482 Portuguese begin settling on Gold Coast, West Africa

1488 Portuguese navigator Bartolomew Diaz (1450–1500) rounds Cape of Good Hope, South Africa, opening the sea route from Europe to Asia

ASIA

1467 Onin War, lasting over 100 years, begins in Japan. Leads to end of feudal system and rise of large territories

1497–98 Portuguese navigator Vasco Gama (1460–1524) reaches India via

EUROPE

1450 Florence, Milan, and Naples form alliance
1450s German craftsman Johannes Gutenberg (c.1398–1468) produces first printed books in Europe
1453 Constantinople falls, ending Byzantine empire

1463 Turkey and Venice fight for control of Mediterranean until 1479
1478 Ivan III (1440–1505) begins to unify Russia

1479 Marriage of Ferdinand of Aragon and Isabella of Castille unites Spain. Lorenzo de Medici (1449–92) becomes unofficial ruler of Florence

1492 Conquest of Granada ends Moorish Spain and results in expulsion of Jews
1494 Under Treaty of Tordesillas, Spain Portugal agree to divide unexplored worl

AMERICAS

1492 Italian explorer Christopher Columbus (1451–1506) discovers the Caribbean
1497 Italian explorer John Cabot (c.1450–c.1498) discovers Newfound

OCEANIA

FALL OF BYZANTIUM
In 1453 Constantinople, capital of the centuries-old Byzantine Empire, fell to the Ottoman sultan Muhammad II. He had dragged 70 ships overland to avoid a huge iron chain protecting the waterway into the city.

PRINCE DRACULA (THE IMPALER)
The cruelties of the sadistic Romanian prince Vlad Dracul or "Vlad the Impaler" inspired the Dracula legend. He reigned for less than ten years, yet caused at least 50,000 deaths. After his own violent death in 1476, his severed head was impaled on a stake for public display.

FERDINAND AND ISABELLA
In 1479, Ferdinand of Aragon and Isabella of Castille married and formed a larger, Christian Spanish kingdom. In 1492 their forces captured Granada, the last Muslim outpost in Spain. The new rulers were intolerant of other religions: 165,000 Jews were told to convert to Christianity or leave Spain.

THE RENAISSANCE
15th-century Europe experienced a great cultural movement called the Renaissance (meaning "rebirth"). It began in the prosperous cities of Italy and was inspired by the rediscovery of ancient Greek and Roman ideas on art, literature, and science.

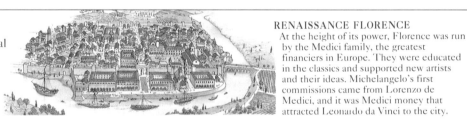

RENAISSANCE FLORENCE
At the height of its power, Florence was run by the Medici family, the greatest financiers in Europe. They were educated in the classics and supported new artists and their ideas. Michelangelo's first commissions came from Lorenzo de Medici, and it was Medici money that attracted Leonardo da Vinci to the city.

RENAISSANCE INNOVATIONS

COAL MINING
In the 1520s the first coal mines were opened in Newcastle, England, and Liège, Belgium.

FLIGHT DESIGNS
Leonardo da Vinci made detailed designs for a flying machine, a parachute, and a helicopter.

PRINTING PRESS
German printer Johannes Gutenberg (d.1468) made the first European movable-type printing press in Mainz, Germany.

LUCREZIA BORGIA
Lucrezia Borgia (1480–1519) was the daughter of Rodrigo Borgia (Pope Alexander VI). She was famed for her charity and great learning – she wrote poetry in three languages. Exhausted by eleven pregnancies, she died in childbirth.

ENIGMATIC SMILE
Leonardo da Vinci's greatest painting, the *Mona Lisa*, was sold to Francis I of France. He kept it in his bathroom.

MICHELANGELO
By studying Greek and Roman art, Renaissance artists learned how to draw "in perspective" – to show depth on a flat canvas – and how to depict the proportions of the body. Michelangelo's huge statue of the biblical hero David, completed in Florence in 1504, is the most famous example of classical Renaissance sculpture.

David – *height 18ft (5.49m)*

RENAISSANCE FIGURES

Name	Dates	Biographical details
Lorenzo de Medici	1449–92	Florentine patron of the arts, poet, classical scholar, banker, ruler of Florence
Leonardo da Vinci	1452–1519	Italian artist, sculptor, architect, engineer, inventor, anatomist
Desiderius Erasmus	1466–1536	Influential Dutch Renaissance thinker and priest, critical of the church
Niccolo Machiavelli	1469–1527	Florentine statesman, author of political masterpiece *The Prince*
Albrecht Dürer	1471–1528	German artist of the Northern Renaissance; painter and printmaker
Michelangelo	1475–1564	Italian painter, sculptor, and architect; painted ceiling of Sistine Chapel, Vatican
Andreas Vesalius	1514–64	Anatomist and physician; wrote first complete description of the human body

Bantus in southern trade with Europeans. states develop in Africa

1517 Egypt and Syria conquered by Ottomans

1542 Portuguese traders reach Japan

1502 Safayid dynasty begins in Persia

1520–21 Portuguese traders reach China
1526 Babur becomes first Mogul Emperor of India

1546 Burma united under King Tabin Shweti

c.1503 Leonardo da Vinci (1452–1519) paints *Mona Lisa*

1512 Italian artist Michelangelo (1475–1564) completes ceiling of Sistine Chapel

1520 Suleiman I (1494–1566) begins greatest reign of Ottoman empire
1517 German monk Martin Luther (1483–1546) sets off the Reformation

1533 Ivan the Terrible comes to the throne in Russia
1529 Ottoman Turks besiege Vienna

1545 Council of Trent starts Catholic Counter-Reformation
1541 French Protestant reformer Jean Calvin (1509–64) sets up Puritan state in Geneva

1501–02 Amerigo Vespucci (1454–1512) explores coast of Brazil. African slaves taken to the West Indies

1519 Portuguese explorer Ferdinand Magellan (1480–1521) sails across Pacific Ocean. Spaniard Hernan Cortès (1485–1547) overthrows Aztec empire

1532 Spaniard Francisco Pizarro (1475–1541) brings down Inca empire, South America
1534 French explorer Jacques Cartier (1491–1557) sails St. Lawrence River, Canada

1526 Portuguese landings in Polynesia

1550 Maoris settle on South Island, New Zealand

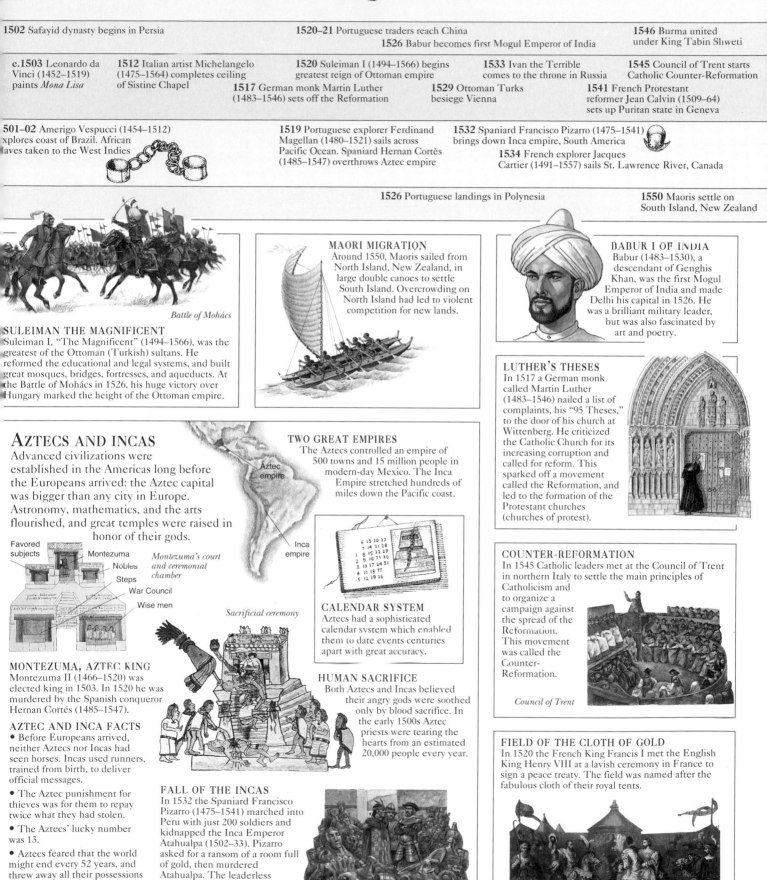

Battle of Mohács

SULEIMAN THE MAGNIFICENT
Suleiman I, "The Magnificent" (1494–1566), was the greatest of the Ottoman (Turkish) sultans. He reformed the educational and legal systems, and built great mosques, bridges, fortresses, and aqueducts. At the Battle of Mohács in 1526, his huge victory over Hungary marked the height of the Ottoman empire.

MAORI MIGRATION
Around 1550, Maoris sailed from North Island, New Zealand, in large double canoes to settle South Island. Overcrowding on North Island had led to violent competition for new lands.

BABUR I OF INDIA
Babur (1483–1530), a descendant of Genghis Khan, was the first Mogul Emperor of India and made Delhi his capital in 1526. He was a brilliant military leader, but was also fascinated by art and poetry.

LUTHER'S THESES
In 1517 a German monk called Martin Luther (1483–1546) nailed a list of complaints, his "95 Theses," to the door of his church at Wittenberg. He criticized the Catholic Church for its increasing corruption and called for reform. This sparked off a movement called the Reformation, and led to the formation of the Protestant churches (churches of protest).

AZTECS AND INCAS
Advanced civilizations were established in the Americas long before the Europeans arrived: the Aztec capital was bigger than any city in Europe. Astronomy, mathematics, and the arts flourished, and great temples were raised in honor of their gods.

Aztec empire

Inca empire

Favored subjects
Montezuma
Nobles
Steps
War Council
Wise men

Montezuma's court and ceremonial chamber

Sacrificial ceremony

TWO GREAT EMPIRES
The Aztecs controlled an empire of 500 towns and 15 million people in modern-day Mexico. The Inca Empire stretched hundreds of miles down the Pacific coast.

CALENDAR SYSTEM
Aztecs had a sophisticated calendar system which enabled them to date events centuries apart with great accuracy.

MONTEZUMA, AZTEC KING
Montezuma II (1466–1520) was elected king in 1503. In 1520 he was murdered by the Spanish conqueror Hernan Cortés (1485–1547).

AZTEC AND INCA FACTS
• Before Europeans arrived, neither Aztecs nor Incas had seen horses. Incas used runners, trained from birth, to deliver official messages.

• The Aztec punishment for thieves was for them to repay twice what they had stolen.

• The Aztecs' lucky number was 13.

• Aztecs feared that the world might end every 52 years, and threw away all their possessions in preparation.

HUMAN SACRIFICE
Both Aztecs and Incas believed their angry gods were soothed only by blood sacrifice. In the early 1500s Aztec priests were tearing the hearts from an estimated 20,000 people every year.

FALL OF THE INCAS
In 1532 the Spaniard Francisco Pizarro (1475–1541) marched into Peru with just 200 soldiers and kidnapped the Inca Emperor Atahualpa (1502–33). Pizarro asked for a ransom of a room full of gold, then murdered Atahualpa. The leaderless empire crumbled.

COUNTER-REFORMATION
In 1545 Catholic leaders met at the Council of Trent in northern Italy to settle the main principles of Catholicism and to organize a campaign against the spread of the Reformation. This movement was called the Counter-Reformation.

Council of Trent

FIELD OF THE CLOTH OF GOLD
In 1520 the French King Francis I met the English King Henry VIII at a lavish ceremony in France to sign a peace treaty. The field was named after the fabulous cloth of their royal tents.

Timeline 1550–

	1550					
AFRICA						**1591** Moroccans and European mercenaries destroy Songhai e[mpire]
ASIA		**1566** Death of Suleiman I: Ottoman empire at greatest extent	**1577** Akbar the Great (1542–1605) completes unification of northern India		**1590** Shah Abbas of Persia (1557– makes peace with Ottoman Turke **1592** Japan invades Korea commander Hideyoshi	
EUROPE	**1555** Peace of Augsburg permits each German ruler to decide religion of subjects	**1564** Death of Michelangelo. Shakespeare born	**1571** Battle of Lepanto: Christian European alliance defeats Ottoman Turkish fleet **1572** St. Bartholomew's Day Massacre of Protestants in France	**1588** England defeats Spanish Armada **1582** Gregorian calendar reform introduced in Catholic countries	**1598** Edict of Na[ntes] ends civil war in F[rance] giving Catholics a[nd] Huguenots equal	
AMERICAS		**1567** Portuguese establish Rio de Janeiro, Brazil	**1579** Francis Drake (c.1540–96) establishes British claim to west coast of North America			
OCEANIA		**1567** Spanish explorer Mendaña (1541–95) becomes first European to reach Solomon Islands			**1595** Mendaña lands on Ma[rquesas] Islands, central South Pacific	

RELIGION DIVIDES EUROPE

Luther's protests led to the formation of Protestant churches and split Christians in Europe into violent rival groups. War often broke out as each country struggled with the new religious alliances.

Battle of Lepanto

BATTLE OF LEPANTO
In 1571 an alliance of European sea powers led by the Pope defeated the Ottoman fleet at the Battle of Lepanto, Greece. The battle ended Turkish threats to Europe by sea, and allowed Catholics to turn to their struggles with European Protestants.

DIVINE DICTATION
St. Mary-Magdalen dei Pazzi (1566–1607) was famed for the length of her religious trances, during which she was thought to speak sacred truths. Six secretaries would record her words for hours, and sometimes days, at a time.

ELIZABETH I OF ENGLAND

The Protestant Elizabeth I ruled England from 1558 to 1603 and showed tolerance towards other religions. She never married and so avoided sharing her power with a foreign king.

The Spanish had 130 ships. The English had less than 100.

Battle of the Spanish Armada

SPANISH ARMADA
In August 1588 the English fleet defeated Philip's massive invasion fleet, the Spanish Armada. The victory was a triumph for Protestantism.

PHILIP OF SPAIN

Philip II of Spain was the most powerful Catholic monarch in Europe. When Queen Elizabeth I executed the Catholic Mary Queen of Scots, he organized a fleet (the Spanish Armada) to invade England and restore Catholic rule. It set sail in July 1588.

RETRACTABLE BLADE
Witch-hunters claimed that witches felt no pain when stabbed. When the witch-hunters wanted to condemn a person of a different religion from their own, they used a retractable blade.
Spring
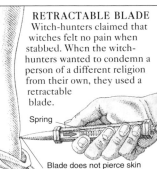
Blade does not pierce skin

LANDMARKS OF A RELIGIOUS AGE

St. Bartholomew's Day Massacre

Catherine de Medici with Huguenots

St. Bartholomew's Day Massacre
On August 24, 1572, the Catholic queen regent of France, Catherine de Medici, secretly ordered the massacre of thousands of French Protestants (Huguenots). This St. Bartholomew's Day Massacre was meant to destroy the Huguenots; instead it re-opened hostilities between Huguenots and Catholics.

Edict of Nantes (1598)
In 1593 the Protestant Henry of Navarre became a Catholic in order to be confirmed as Henry IV of France. His law, the Edict of Nantes, ended France's religious wars by allowing Protestants to worship.

Gunpowder Plot
In 1605 a Catholic plot to murder James I of England was discovered. Guy Fawkes was planning to light gunpowder in the cellars of Parliament while James was giving an address; he was caught and executed after torture. The discovery of the Gunpowder Plot led to greater persecution of English Catholics.

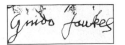
Guy Fawkes's signature before his torture

Guy Fawkes's signature after his torture

Jesuit missionaries
Spanish nobleman Ignatius de Loyola founded the Society of Jesus, or the Jesuits, as the missionaries of the Catholic Counter-Reformation. From 1550 Jesuits were in action all over Europe, and soon they began converting the peoples of the Americas to Christianity. Wherever traders went, Jesuits followed.

Persecuted Puritans
Rival groups of Protestants sometimes persecuted each other. In 1620 a group of Puritans, also known as Pilgrims, set sail from Plymouth, England, to North America in search of religious freedom.

The Mayflower

All major European powers
~~ish~~ trading posts on African coast

1620s Queen Nzinga of Mbundu
defeats the Portuguese

~~B~~eginning of Tokugawa period in Japan.
~~h~~ East India Company founded
~~6~~02 Dutch East India Company founded

1604 Russians settle in Siberia

1605 Failure of Gunpowder Plot
and arrest of Guy Fawkes

1610 Assassination of French
King Henry IV (b.1553)

1613 Michael Romanov (r.1613–45)
becomes first Russian Romanov czar

1618 Beginning of
Thirty Years' War

1631 Sacking of
Magdeburg, Germany:
worst atrocity of
Thirty Years' War

1607 John Smith (1580–1631) founds
colony of Virginia at Jamestown

1608 Quebec founded

1609 Henry Hudson (c.1565–1611)
sails up Hudson River

1620 Mayflower
sets sail for
North America

1625 French begin
to settle West Indies

1626 Dutch found New
Amsterdam (now New York)

1630 Dutch East India
Company seizes part of
Brazil for its sugar and silver

1629 Massachusetts colony founded

1606 Portuguese navigator De Quiros arrives at Tahiti, and Spanish
navigator Luis Vaez de Torres sails between Australia and New Guinea

AKBAR THE GREAT

The Mogul Emperor Akbar (1542–1605) gave
his expanding empire a superb structure of
government. Although he was a Muslim, he
also won the support of non-Muslims by
his tolerance of other religions. He even
tried to start a new religion – Din Illahl –
and supported many Hindu practices.

HINDU MARRIAGES

In 1562 and 1570 Akbar married
Hindu Rajput princesses, despite
his Islamic beliefs. The marriages
demonstrated his respect for his
Hindu subjects.

*Muslim Emperor Akbar
with his Hindu bride*

*Festivities at
the birth of
Akbar's son*

AKBAR'S ART

The arts blossomed
under Akbar. A
series of beautiful
paintings, called *The
Annals of Akbar*, were
prepared in the late
1590s and show
scenes from his life.

Extent of
Mogul Empire

AKBAR'S MOGUL EMPIRE

At his death Akbar's empire stretched from
Afghanistan in the north, to Bengal in the east,
and Gujarat in the west.

AKBAR'S FAVORITE

Akbar, a keen hunter, trained
cheetahs to catch and kill his prey.
His favorite once jumped a
ravine to kill a blackbuck deer.
From then it was carried into the
hunt on a cushioned litter.

INABAT-KHANA

In 1575 Akbar built
the Inabat-Khana
(house of worship) in
which Muslims of
many traditions,
Zoroastrians, Hindu
pandits, and yogis
came to discuss their
religious beliefs.

*Akbar in religious
discussion*

TOKUGAWA JAPAN

In 1603 Ieyasu (1543–1616) of the
Tokugawa clan became *shogun* (ruler) of
Japan after defeating his rivals at the Battle
of Sekigahara (1600). He placed the
government in Edo (now Tokyo) and
forced his remaining rivals to move there.

Sloping roof gives
view of enemy.

Decorative
gable

Fireproof and
bulletproof plaster

Windows
could be
used as
gunports.

*Gatehouse of
Edo Castle,
Tokyo*

Stone
rampart

DISTRACTING HIS RIVALS

From 1604 to 1614, Ieyasu forced his rival *daimyo*
(samurai warlords) to build and enlarge a castle at
Edo. By the time he died he had built
the world's biggest castle.

Dutch trading post

JAPAN IN ISOLATION

In 1636 the Tokugawa regime prevented all Japanese
from traveling abroad, and in 1641 expelled all
foreigners. A Dutch trading post in Nagasaki Bay was
the only contact with the outside world until 1854.

KEY PEOPLE

Name	Dates	Biographical details
Ignatius de Loyola	1491–1556	Spanish ex-soldier and priest, founded Society of Jesus (Jesuits) in 1534
Philip II	1527–98	King of Spain and Portugal, champion of the Catholic Counter-Reformation
Elizabeth I	1533–1603	Queen of England during period of naval supremacy, artistic excellence, and international trade
Akbar	1542–1605	Mogul emperor, famous for religious tolerance and support of the arts
Tokugawa Ieyasu	1543–1616	Shogun (ruler) of Japan, ended wars, unified country, banned Christianity
Henry IV	1553–1610	King of France, converted to Catholicism from Protestantism to re-unify France
William Shakespeare	1564–1616	English dramatist and poet; plays include *Hamlet* and *King Lear*

KEY INNOVATIONS

PENCILS

Pencils were first produced
in England in 1565.

MERCATOR'S MAP

In 1569 Flemish
geographer Gerhard
Mercator (1512–94)
published a map on his
new projection, which
is still in use today.

1640

| AFRICA | | **1652** Dutch found Cape colony in southern Africa | **1663** Death of Queen Nzinga of Mbundu | **1670s** French settle in Senegal | | **1690s** Ashanti kingdom established on Gold Coas |

ASIA **1644** Manchu dynasty replaces Ming dynasty in China **1657** Edo (Tokyo) is destroyed by a great fire **1661** English East India Company acquires Bombay **1662** K'ang Hsi begins reign in China **1669** Mogul emperor Aurangzeb prohibits Hinduism **1683** K'ang Hsi conquers Formosa (Taiwan) **1688** Genroku Period, rise of merchant class in Japan (until

EUROPE **1642** Civil War in England **1643** Louis XIV begins reign **1649** Charles I of England executed. Commonwealth set up under Oliver Cromwell **1648** End of the Thirty Years War **1660** English monarchy restored **1661** Bank of Sweden issues first European bank notes **1672** Third Anglo-Dutch trade war begins **1677** Ottomans at war with Russia **1682** Peter the Great begins reign **1683** Siege of Vienna by Ottoman forces fails **1688** England's "Glorious Revolution" **1690** Battle of the Boy Protestant William of C defeats Catholic James

AMERICAS **1642** De Maisonneuve founds Ville-Marie (now Montreal) **1664** England seizes New Amsterdam (now New York) from Dutch **1670** Colony of South Carolina founded. English Hudson's Bay Company founded **1675** War between colonists and Native Americans devastates New England **1680** French explorer Robert Cavalier de la Salle claims Mississippi valley for France **1683** William Penn signs treaty with Native Americans **1692** Sale witch trial New Eng

OCEANIA **1642** Abel Tasman becomes first European to reach Van Dieman's Land (Tasmania) **1680** The dodo becomes extinct

---

MANCHU CHINA

In 1644 the Manchus invaded China at the request of an unhappy Ming (Chinese) general. After the conquest, however, the Manchu leader Fu-lin (r.1638–61) made himself emperor. The *Ch'ing*, or Pure, dynasty that he founded ruled China for more than 250 years until 1912.

Under Manchu control by:
◻ 1644
◻ 1660
◻ 1760

MANCHURIAN EMPIRE
Manchuria lies in the northeastern region of modern-day China.

MING MANDARINS
Mandarins were the top officials of Ming China and were famed for their organizing skills. When the Manchus conquered China the mandarins were left to carry on with their work.

Manchus forced the Chinese to braid their hair, as they did, into a queue, or pigtail, as a sign of inferiority.

Manchu lord with Ming Chinese

Art of Manchu period

ART AND LEARNING
The second emperor, K'ang Hsi (1654–1722), like Fu-lin, saw the value of Ming culture. He requested scholars to write a Ming history, as well as dictionaries, encyclopedias, and technical works.

SUPREME RULERS

Kings and queens held massive political power in seventeenth-century Europe. Louis XIV of France (1638–1715), the most powerful of all, made decisions without regard to parliament or leading aristocrats.

THE AGE OF LOUIS XIV
• Louis ruled France for 62 years – during this time it became the most powerful country in Europe.

• Louis forced the nobles to live at his Versailles palace so that he could watch them closely.

• Louis' keen support of the arts earned him the nickname "The Sun King," after Apollo, Greek god of the arts.

Hall of Mirrors at Versailles

• In 1685 Louis abolished a law called the Edict of Nantes, which had protected the rights of French Protestants (Huguenots). Many went to England, where their businesses and crafts were successful.

CHARLES I
In 1649 the unpopular Charles I (1600–49) was beheaded by his English subjects, an event that shocked Europe. Parliament limited his successors' powers.

Execution of Charles I

A boyar (Russian noble)

Peter the Great forces the old-fashioned boyars, or nobles, to shave their beards in modern European style.

King Louis XIV of France in classical costume

SUICIDAL CHEF
In 1676 Le Grand Vatel, the famous chef to the Prince de Condé, committed suicide because a meal he had prepared for Louis XIV did not meet with the king's full approval.

PETER THE GREAT
In 1682 Peter the Great (1672–1725) became Czar of Russia. He was a leader of great energy and reorganized the army, founded the navy, and built a new capital at St. Petersburg.

KEY PEOPLE

Name	Dates	Biographical details
Nzinga of Mbundu	1582–1663	Queen of Mbundu, West Africa, fought Portuguese slave traders, offered shelter to runaway slaves from neighboring states
Oliver Cromwell	1599–1658	Victorious commander of English Parliamentary forces in civil war of 1642–48, Lord Protector (ruler) of England, 1653–58
Charles I	1600–49	British king executed after losing civil war against Parliamentary armies
Fu-lin	r.1638–61	First Manchu Emperor of China, increased number of Chinese in government
Louis XIV	1638–1715	Absolute ruler during period when France led in politics, arts, and culture
Peter the Great	1672–1725	Czar of Russia, imported Western Europe's ideas and technology

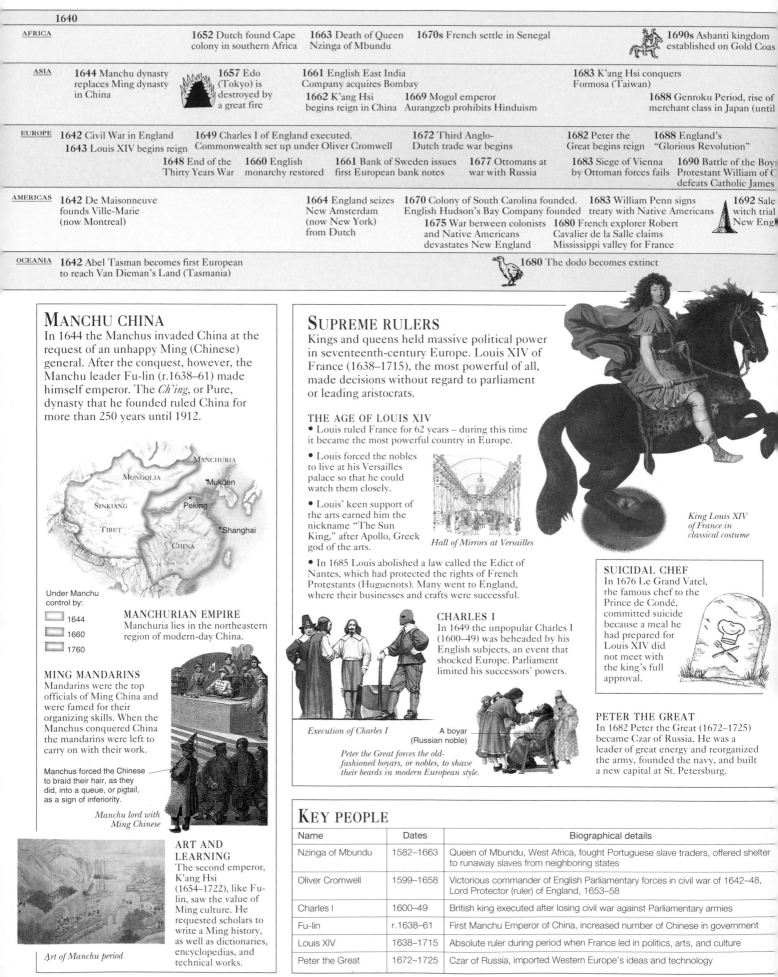

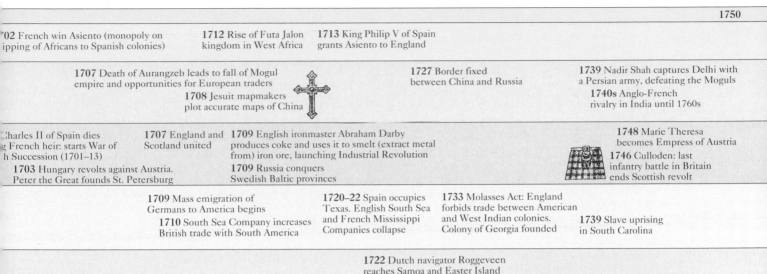

'02 French win Asiento (monopoly on shipping of Africans to Spanish colonies)

1712 Rise of Futa Jalon kingdom in West Africa

1713 King Philip V of Spain grants Asiento to England

1707 Death of Aurangzeb leads to fall of Mogul empire and opportunities for European traders

1708 Jesuit mapmakers plot accurate maps of China

1727 Border fixed between China and Russia

1739 Nadir Shah captures Delhi with a Persian army, defeating the Moguls

1740s Anglo-French rivalry in India until 1760s

Charles II of Spain dies French heir: starts War of Succession (1701–13)

1703 Hungary revolts against Austria. Peter the Great founds St. Petersburg

1707 England and Scotland united

1709 English ironmaster Abraham Darby produces coke and uses it to smelt (extract metal from) iron ore, launching Industrial Revolution

1709 Russia conquers Swedish Baltic provinces

1748 Marie Theresa becomes Empress of Austria

1746 Culloden: last infantry battle in Britain ends Scottish revolt

1709 Mass emigration of Germans to America begins

1710 South Sea Company increases British trade with South America

1720–22 Spain occupies Texas. English South Sea and French Mississippi Companies collapse

1733 Molasses Act: England forbids trade between American and West Indian colonies. Colony of Georgia founded

1739 Slave uprising in South Carolina

1722 Dutch navigator Roggeveen reaches Samoa and Easter Island

THE SLAVE TRADE

When Europeans settled in the Americas, they transported Africans to work as slaves on the cotton, sugar, and tobacco plantations and in the silver mines. Slaves were forced to travel in horrific conditions, and were often worked to death once they had arrived.

Sugar, cotton, and rum

English-owned and French-owned slaves

Arab-owned slaves

Portuguese-owned slaves

Slaves packed in as tightly as possible

Plan of slave ship owned by Brookes of Liverpool, England

THE MIDDLE PASSAGE

The slave ship shown was designed to carry more than 400 people on the journey from Africa to America, called the Middle Passage. The supersonic jet *Concorde* would require three trips to transport 400 people over the Atlantic, yet *Concorde* is three times this ship's length.

Queen Nzinga seated on her attendant's back meets with the Portuguese at Luanda.

THE TRIANGULAR SLAVE ROUTE

Slave ships took a triangular route. They sailed from Europe to Africa to get slaves, over to the Americas to exchange slaves for sugar, cotton, and rum, then returned to Europe to sell those goods.

Size comparison of slave ship and Concorde

QUEEN NZINGA

Queen Nzinga of Mbundu, West Africa, opposed European slave traders. Her army was swelled by runaway slaves who had fled to her lands.

TRADER PORTS PROSPER

Atlantic ports such as Bristol, England, and Bordeaux, France, grew rich due to their strategic position between Europe, Africa, and the West Indies.

Bristol docks

SLAVE TRADE FACTS

• Between 1500 and 1800, European ships transported about 12 million people from their homes in Africa to the colonies of the Americas – more than the entire population of 15th-century North America.

• By 1800, the total African slave population of South America was just 1.2 million; most slaves died of overwork within a few years of arriving.

• The slave trade was more profitable than the trade in ebony, ivory, or gold.

• The Portuguese called their slave ships *tumbeiros*, meaning coffins, because they lost more than 30% of their human cargo during the voyage.

• In 1781 the captain of the *Zong* threw 132 slaves overboard to collect the insurance.

Branding mark burned into skin

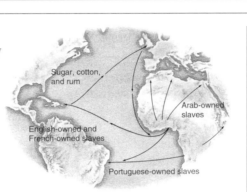

KING AGAJA

King Agaja (1673–1740) of Dahomey raided and enslaved his weaker neighbors. European and Arab traders bought his captives as slaves.

MARKETS FOR PEOPLE

Once slaves reached the Caribbean, South America, or the colonies of North America, they were sold to the highest bidder. If different traders had used the same ship they had their own slaves branded with hot irons to identify them after the journey.

European slave traders assemble their captured slaves for sale.

COFFEE AND CROISSANTS

In 1683 the Ottomans ended their siege of Vienna, Austria, and gave up their invasion of Europe. Viennese survivors tasted strange beans found in the Ottomans' camp: coffee beans. Viennese bakers made crescent-shaped pastries called croissants to celebrate the end of the siege.

KEY INNOVATIONS

18th-century orrery shows planetary motion

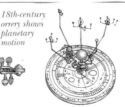

STRADIVARIUS'S VIOLIN

Italian craftsman Antonio Stradivarius (c.1644–1737) perfected the art of violin-making. The secret of his varnish has never been discovered.

NEWTON'S LAWS

English scientist Isaac Newton (1642–1727) first formulated the laws of gravity in his book *Principia* (1687).

IRON SMELTING

In 1709 Englishman Abraham Darby (c.1678–1717) made the first industrial iron by smelting pig iron with coke, not charcoal.

1750

AFRICA	

1768 Ali Bey becomes
ruler of independent Egypt

ASIA **1750** China conquers Tibet   **1757** Battle of Plassey:
British conquer Bengal   **1761** Battle of Panipat:
Marathas defeated by Afghans

EUROPE   **1755** Earthquake at Lisbon, Portugal
1756–63 Seven Years War
between Britain and France   **1762** Catherine the Great
begins reign over Russia   **1772** First Partition of Poland
between Prussia, Russia, and Austria   **1789** Storming of the Ba
French Revolution begi

1757 First English canal built   **1769** Richard Arkwright builds first cotton factory   **1781** Joseph II abolishes
serfdom (a form of peasant
slavery) in Austrian Empire

1771 Russia conquers Crimea

AMERICAS   **1759** English forces defeat French
on Plains of Abraham, Quebec   **1773** Boston Tea Party:
protest against British tea tax   **1780** Tupac Amara leads Inca
of Peru in revolt against Spain

1763 Pontiac (1720–69)
leads Native American
uprising against British in North America   **1775–83** American Revolution   **1787–9** US Constitution an
Bill of Rights written and ra

1776 US Declaration of
Independence signed

OCEANIA   **1768–71** Captain Cook's first voyage on *Endeavour*   **1788** British colony of Ne
South Wales, Australia, fo

THE ENLIGHTENMENT

Followers of the 18th-century movement
called the Enlightenment believed that
reason and science could help to free people
from rigid governments and organized
religions. Enlightenment ideas about justice,
equality, and freedom for all inspired the
American and French revolutions.

L'Encyclopédie

THE ENCYCLOPEDIA

French philosophers Denis Diderot and Jean Le Rond
d'Alembert collected and published the ideas of the
Enlightenment in the multivolume *L'Encyclopédie*
between 1751 and 1786. It included
contributions by thinkers
such as Voltaire and Rousseau.

VOLTAIRE

The French thinker Voltaire
(1694–1778) was a key figure in
the Enlightenment. His witty
writings criticized religious
intolerance and backward
governments and rulers.

*Marble sculpture
of Voltaire*

BENJAMIN FRANKLIN

American Benjamin
Franklin (1706–90) was a
typical Enlightenment
figure – scientist,
philosopher, and
statesman. In 1776 he
went to France to raise
support for the
American struggle
against British rule.

*Benjamin
Franklin*

Ship's
cloth   Lobster

CAPTAIN COOK

English navigator James Cook
(1728–79) explored the
South Pacific. He sensibly
kept his ships clean and
well ventilated; he gave his
crews fresh vegetables and
lime juice which saved
them from scurvy.

Cook trades with Islanders

COWPOX FOR SMALLPOX

Catherine the Great of Russia,
who used to write to
Voltaire, set an
example to her
fearful subjects
when she had
herself and her
heir vaccinated
by cowpox
against smallpox.

REVOLUTION AND UNREST

*Washington
crosses the
Delaware River
before battle*

American Revolution 1775–83

Americans disliked paying taxes to a government in
which they had no representation. Led by George
Washington, they had won independence by 1783.

French Revolution, 1789

In return for funding the bankrupt Louis XVI, the
French lords, clergy, and commons demanded more
power. On July 14, 1789, their supporters in Paris
stormed the Bastille prison, an ancient symbol of
royal authority, and launched the French Revolution.

Reign of Terror

In 1792 France chose a
new form of government:
a republic. Louis XVI was
executed in January 1793,
and from mid-1793 to July
1794 anti-republicans
were executed, often
without trial. The period
was called "The Terror."

Guillotine

Execution of Louis XVI

Toussaint L'Ouverture

In 1791 slaves in the French colony
of Sainte Domingue (Haiti) rose
up to fight for their freedom.
Their leader Toussaint
L'Ouverture (1743–1803)
was himself a former slave. In
spite of his successes he was
captured by Napoleon and
died a prisoner in France.

KEY PEOPLE

Name	Dates	Biographical details
Voltaire	1694–1778	Key French intellectual of the Enlightenment, wrote novel, *Candide* (1759)
Benjamin Franklin	1706–90	American author, publisher, inventor, scientist, and diplomat, helped frame the US Declaration of Independence, inspired French revolutionaries
Jean–Jacques Rousseau	1712–78	French philosopher and political writer, inspired leaders of revolution
George Washington	1732–99	American commander-in-chief (1775–83) and first US President (1789–97)
Catherine the Great	1729–96	Empress of Russia, brought Russia fully into Western European cultural life
Napoleon Bonaparte	1769–1821	French general, later emperor, established the principles of the French Revolution in law and government and spread them by military conquest

EUROPE COLONIZES OCEANIA

In 1788 the first 750 European settlers in
Australia set up camp on the shores of Sydney
Harbor. They were convicts who had been
shipped from the overcrowded prisons of
repressive 18th-century Britain.

Convicts disembark at Sydney Cove.

1830

1804 British win control of Cape of Good Hope

1822 Liberia founded for freed slaves

1824–7 First Ashanti War between Britain and the Ashanti of the Gold Coast (Ghana)

1794 Qaja Dynasty of Persia begins; rules until 1925

1819 Singapore founded by Stamford Raffles (1721–1826)

1824 Britain and Burma (Myanmar) at war

793 Louis XVI executed. econd Partition of Poland

1796 Napoleon's Italian campaigns. Jenner introduces smallpox vaccine

1804 Napoleon becomes Emperor of the French

1805 Battle of Trafalgar

1815 Battle of Waterloo

1821–9 Greek War of Independence from Ottoman Turkey

1795 New French government, the Directory, set up

1801 Union of Great Britain and Ireland

1814 Congress of Vienna restores European monarchies

1825 First passenger railroad opened in England

1 Constitutional Act creates Upper Canada (Ontario) Lower Canada (Quebec). Revolution in Haiti by former slave Toussaint L'Ouverture (1743–1803)

793 York (now Toronto) founded

1810 Buenos Aires gains independence

1811 Paraguay and Venezuela gain independence

1812–14 US and Britain at war: Washington, D.C. burned

1818 Chile gains independence

1819 US purchases Florida from Spain

1821 Mexico gains independence

1822 Brazil gains independence

1823 Monroe Doctrine: US declares Americas free from European intervention

1806 First white women arrive in New Zealand

1817 First European emigrants settle Australian grasslands

1825 Van Diemen's Land becomes separate colony

KEY INNOVATIONS

SPINNING JENNY
In 1764 English weaver James Hargreaves invented his "Spinning Jenny." It enabled one worker to spin several threads at once.

Spinning Jenny

COTTON MILLS
In 1769 English businessman Richard Arkwright (1732–92) set up the first cotton mill, or factory.

FIRST TRAINS
In 1829 English engineer George Stephenson built one of the first steam locomotives, *The Rocket*.

HOT AIR BALLOON
The first manned flight took place in 1783 in a hot air balloon made and flown by the French Montgolfier brothers. They sailed over Paris for 25 minutes.

BLACK HOLE OF CALCUTTA
The Black Hole of Calcutta was a suffocatingly small cell in which a local Indian official held 64 British prisoners in 1756. The British publicized the resulting deaths of 43 of the prisoners in its campaign for total control of India.

Cell measured 18ft (5.5m) by 14ft 10in (4.5m)

British prisoners in Calcutta

CHAKA: ZULU WARLORD
The great Zulu warlord Chaka (d.1828) owed his success to a brilliantly organized and highly trained army. For greater speed, his warriors went into battle barefoot. They were not allowed to marry until the age of 40, when they could leave the army.

Assegai (slender iron-tipped spear)

Reinforced shield of strong leather

Chaka in battle dress

NAPOLEON'S IMPACT
By 1812 the brilliant French general Napoleon Bonaparte (1769–1821) had conquered almost all of Europe. He gave himself great power, but also made the French government and army more efficient and open.

Napoleon crowned himself Emperor of the French in 1804.

× Major battle
— French border
--- Campaign route
▢ French empire

Moscow
Borodino 1812
Jena 1806
Waterloo 1815
Leipzig 1813
Austerlitz 1805
Paris
Marengo 1800
Trafalgar 1805
To Egypt

NAPOLEON'S CAMPAIGNS
Napoleon's greatest campaigns were fought in Italy in 1796 and in Austria, Prussia, and the Rhine in 1806–7. His Russian campaign of 1812 was a disaster and he was defeated for good at Waterloo, Belgium, in 1815.

JOSEPHINE
Josephine de Beauharnais (1763–1814), Napoleon's first wife, had political connections that were very useful to him in his early career.

NAPOLEON FACTS
• On October 5, 1795, Napoleon saved the post-revolutionary government when he ordered his artillery to shoot down royalist rebels in Paris.

• Many ancient monuments, including the Sphinx, were excavated on Napoleon's Egyptian campaigns.

• Napoleon owed the success of his own career to talent. So, he made promotion in his army depend on ability, rather than on birth and money.

• In 1812 Napoleon fought his way to Moscow with 450,000 men. Russians burned the city and he was forced to return to France. 440,000 of his men died of cold and hunger.

SIMON BOLIVAR
While Napoleon was conquering Spain, the Spanish colonies of South America, led by Simon Bolivar and José de San Martin, rose up in rebellion. By 1825 they had all gained full independence.

Simon Bolivar

EROICA SYMPHONY
German composer Ludwig van Beethoven (1770–1827) dedicated his Third Symphony to Napoleon, whom he saw as a champion of democracy. After Napoleon made himself Emperor of the French, Beethoven crossed out the dedication on his manuscript copy.

Ludwig van Beethoven

DEADLY DECOR
Napoleon was finally exiled to the Atlantic island of St. Helena. Mold in the green dye (arsenic oxide) of his bedroom wallpaper is now thought to have contributed to his slow death.

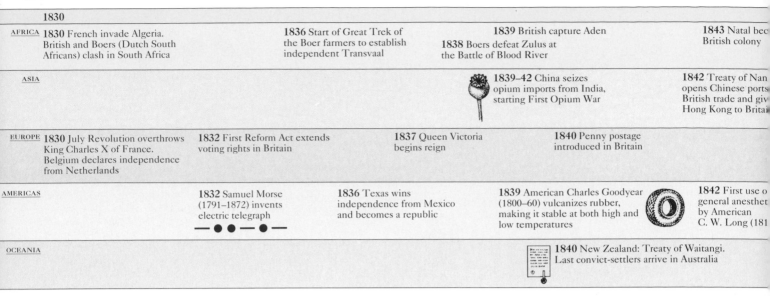

1830

AFRICA	**1830** French invade Algeria. British and Boers (Dutch South Africans) clash in South Africa	**1836** Start of Great Trek of the Boer farmers to establish independent Transvaal	**1839** British capture Aden. **1838** Boers defeat Zulus at the Battle of Blood River	**1843** Natal bec British colony
ASIA			**1839–42** China seizes opium imports from India, starting First Opium War	**1842** Treaty of Nan opens Chinese ports British trade and giv Hong Kong to Britai
EUROPE	**1830** July Revolution overthrows King Charles X of France. Belgium declares independence from Netherlands	**1832** First Reform Act extends voting rights in Britain	**1837** Queen Victoria begins reign	**1840** Penny postage introduced in Britain
AMERICAS		**1832** Samuel Morse (1791–1872) invents electric telegraph	**1836** Texas wins independence from Mexico and becomes a republic	**1839** American Charles Goodyear (1800–60) vulcanizes rubber, making it stable at both high and low temperatures	**1842** First use o general anesthet by American C. W. Long (181
OCEANIA				**1840** New Zealand: Treaty of Waitangi. Last convict-settlers arrive in Australia

EUROPE IN TURMOIL

In 1848, demands for democracy and national independence shook Europe's towns and cities. Industrial growth had made many people rich; now they wanted their fair share of political power. They rose up with students and workers and called for equality and democracy.

Karl Marx

KARL MARX
In 1848 German thinkers Karl Marx (1818–83) and Friedrich Engels (1820–95) published the *Communist Manifesto*. It described a just society, without classes of people or private property: a communist society.

GARIBALDI AND RISORGIMENTO
The Italian revolts of 1848–9 failed, but the 1860 *Risorgimento* (Reawakening) was a triumph. Patriot and leader of the "Redshirts," Giuseppe Garibaldi used guerilla war tactics in the struggle for Italian unification. He captured Sicily and southern Italy to form a new Italian state.

Garibaldi

MONARCHIES IN CRISIS
The last king of France
In 1848 the unpopular King Louis Philippe of France abdicated. Louis Napoleon became president of the new republic; monarchy was over in France.

Frankfurt parliament
In 1848 Germans in Frankfurt set up their first national parliament. Though it soon failed, this parliament fueled hopes of a unified German nation.

Boy emperor
In 1848, 18-year-old Franz Joseph became emperor of the troubled Hapsburg realms of central Europe. His uncle, Ferdinand I, had abdicated in the Vienna revolution.

Emperor Franz Joseph

FLASHPOINTS OF REVOLUTION
In the first four months of 1848 Europe was rocked by almost 50 separate revolutions in France, Prussia, Austria, and almost all the minor German and Italian states.

Berlin
Frankfurt
Paris
Vienna
Prague
Budapest
Milan
Venice
Rome
Palermo

▼ Center of revolution

CONCENTRATION OF POWER
In no European nation of 1830 did voters exceed more than 5% of the population. This meant only one in twenty had a say in their government.

CHOLERA
Cholera, caused by drinking contaminated water, spread easily in the overcrowded cities of industrial Europe. Public panic about the disease encouraged revolution.

FAMINE AND EMIGRATION
In the 1840s, sometimes called "The Hungry Forties," famine struck much of Europe – it killed more than one million people in Ireland alone. As a result many Europeans emigrated, chiefly to the Americas.

KEY INNOVATIONS

FARADAY'S COIL
English scientist Michael Faraday's copper coil (see p.229) demonstrated the connection between electricity and magnetism.

PHOTOGRAPHY
In 1839 French artist and physicist Louis Jacques Daguerre developed his superior photographic process, the Daguerreotype.

POSTAGE STAMPS
Postage stamps were first issued in Britain in 1840, and in the US in 1847. The first stamp was the "penny black."

RAIL NETWORK
By 1847 steam-powered trains served all parts of Britain. The rest of the world soon built rail networks.

THE LURE OF GOLD
American carpenter John Marshall discovered flakes of gold on land in California in 1848. Despite his efforts to keep the discovery secret, the news soon broke out and people rushed from Europe and from the eastern US in the hope of finding their fortunes. A similar gold rush occurred in New South Wales, Australia, in 1851.

Gold nugget

1847 Bantus defeated by British in southern Africa

1854 Independent Orange Free State set up, South Africa
1855 Livingstone discovers Victoria Falls, sparking off European exploration of the African interior

–49 British and Sikhs : Sikh defeat leads to h rule over their land, the Punjab

1848 Nasir ad-Din begins reign as Shah (ruler) of Persia

1850–64 Taiping revolt in China
1852–53 Second war between England and Burma

1853–54 US forces Japan to open up to Western trade

1856 Persia's seizure of Herat, Afghanistan, leads to war with Britain, until 1857

1857 Britain governs India directly after "Indian Mutiny"
1858 Treaty of Tientsin forces China to trade with West

–46 Failure of o crop in Ireland to severe famine

1848 Year of Revolution in Europe
1849 Collapse of revolutionary movements
1851 Great Exhibition held in London

1852 Louis Napoleon Bonaparte becomes Napoleon III
1853–56 Crimean War between Russia, Britain and France

1856 Bessemer invents industrial steel-making process

1858 S.S. Great Eastern, largest ship of its time, launched
1859–61 War of Italian unification

Texas and Florida ne US states
1846 US and Mexico at war over Texas

1848 California Gold Rush helps open up US west. First US women's rights convention in New York State

1851 I. S. Singer makes first pedal-powered sewing machine
1850 California becomes a US state

1853 Completion of railroad from New York to Chicago

1850 Australian Colonies Act enables New South Wales, Tasmania, and South Australia to have virtual self-government
1851 Australian Gold Rush begins

THE BRITISH EMPIRE

Between 1830 and 1860, Western powers forced isolated countries to open their ports to western goods: Turkey, Egypt, Persia, China, then Japan. The British, with the strongest navy and the most advanced industries in the world, took control of these rich eastern markets by diplomacy or force, and built a vast trading empire.

QUEEN VICTORIA
Queen Victoria (r.1837–1901) had the longest reign of any British monarch. She presided over the peak of the British Industrial Revolution and over the development of an enormous colonial empire.

NORTH AMERICA · CARIBBEAN · Ascension Is. · St. Helena · Mauritius · India · Hong Kong · Singapore · Australia · New Zealand

☐ British empire ☐ Under British influence

THE BRITISH EMPIRE
In 1860 the British had either direct control or great influence over territories throughout the world. Important groups of islands gave them control of the major sea routes and trading advantages.

Chinese opium smokers

THE FIRST OPIUM WAR
Opium grown in India was bought by the British and sold in China for silks, spices, and tea. In 1839 Britain crushed a Manchu attempt to stop the drug trade at Canton. They forced the Chinese to grant trade and land rights to Western powers.

TREATY OF WAITANGI
In 1840 Britain and the Maori leaders of North Island, New Zealand, made an agreement which gave Britain formal possession in return for recognizing ancient Maori land rights.

Ceremonial dress of Maori leader

British and Maoris at Waitangi

LADY WITH THE LAMP
In 1854 Florence Nightingale (1820–1910) pioneered modern nursing by organizing the care of British soldiers during the Crimean War. Every night she walked 4 miles (6km) on her ward rounds.

GREAT EXHIBITION FACTS

Visitors at the Great Exhibition

• In 1851 London hosted the first international exhibition. The Great Exhibition showed 14,000 objects in celebration of the industrial age.

• Victoria's adored husband Prince Albert (1819–61) made the exhibition his pet project and much of its success was due to him. He died of typhoid, ironically caused by inferior, old-fashioned sanitation.

• The exhibition was housed in a glass and cast-iron building called the Crystal Palace. It was built in five months in Hyde Park and covered 19 acres.

INDIAN UPRISING
The "Indian Mutiny" of 1857 began when Indian soldiers refused to bite open cartridges greased with animal fats, forbidden to Hindus and Muslims. The rebellion became a massive protest against British rule.

US OPENS JAPAN TO TRADE
In 1853 Commodore Perry of the US Navy steamed into Tokyo Bay to demand that Japan open its ports to trade. His "black ships" forced the Japanese to give in.

KEY PEOPLE

Name	Dates	Biographical details
Michael Faraday	1791–1867	English scientist, discovered relationship between electricity and magnetism
Samuel Morse	1791–1872	American inventor of electric telegraph and developer of Morse code (1838)
Giuseppe Garibaldi	1807–82	Italian leader of *Risorgimento* "Redshirts," refused hono rs for service
David Livingstone	1813–73	Scottish missionary and explorer, influenced Western attitudes toward Africa
Karl Marx	1818–83	Philosopher and economist, wrote *The Communist Manifesto* and *Das Kapital*
Victoria	1819–1901	Queen of Great Britain and Ireland, Empress of India from 1876, revived popularity of monarchy in Britain over her long and stable reign
Florence Nightingale	1820–1910	English nurse, pioneered nursing as a profession during Crimean War of 1853–6

1860

| AFRICA | **1860s** Britain, France, Belgium, Germany, and Portugal begin to explore and colonize inner Africa | **1869** Suez Canal opens | **1879** Zulu War: British defeat Zul[u] Cetewayo at Ulundi in South Afric[a] |

| ASIA | **1861** Empress Tze Hsi begins 47-year rule of China | **1870s** Japan industrializes | **1872** Samurai's feudal control of Japan ends. Compulsory education introduced |

| EUROPE | **1864** International Red Cross founded by Swiss Henri Dunant. Otto von Bismarck leads Prussia to victory against Denmark | **1866** Dynamite invented by Swedish chemist Alfred Nobel. Prussia, led by Bismarck, defeats Austria | **1870s** Most Western European countries industrialize. **1871** Bismarck invades and defeats France. Britain legalizes trade unions | **1876** French build refrigerated cargo ships |

| AMERICAS | **1861** US Civil War begins. **1862** Billy Barker strikes gold in Williams Creek, British Columbia | **1865** Union wins Civil War. Lincoln assassinated. **1867** Mexicans force French withdrawal from Mexico. British North America Act brings Dominion of Canada into being, with Sir John A. Macdonald as first prime minister. US buys Alaska from Russia. **1869** First transcontinental railroad completed across US | **1876** Sioux and Cheyenne tribes defeat Custer at the Battle of Little Bighorn. **1877–1911** Rule of Porfirio Diaz in Me[xico]. **1879** Chile defeats Peru and Boliv[ia] in war over nitrates (ends 1883). Electric light bulb invented |

| OCEANIA | **1860–70** Maori Wars in New Zealand: Maoris fight white settlers | | **1876** New Zealand–Australia cable laid |

AMERICAN CIVIL WAR

In 1861, deep divisions between northern and southern American states plunged the country into open warfare. The agricultural South, with its work force of black slaves, feared the industrial North's economic power and resented its efforts to ban the spread of slavery. In 1865 the North won, but more than 600,000 had died in the fight.

NORTH AGAINST SOUTH

The 11 southern states of the Confederacy made Richmond, Virginia, their capital, while the 23 Union states were based at Washington. In 1861, the Confederates won the first major battle of the war at Bull Run, Virginia, and almost overran Washington. But the great Union victory at Gettysburg (1863) foreshadowed the end of Confederate resistance.

Union general *Confederate general*

Union states
Slave states remaining in the Union
Confederate states

Washington
Richmond

CIVIL WAR FACTS

• More than 200,000 black soldiers fought for the Union.

• Twice as many men died of disease as died in battle.

• The 1860 election of the anti-slavery president Abraham Lincoln was the immediate cause of war. His leadership brought victory to the Union and an end to slavery, but he was shot dead at a theater by a Confederate just five days after their surrender.

FORCES OF WAR

The northern, or Union, states had more soldiers, industry, and money than the southern, or Confederate, states. The Union also controlled the navy, and used it to block supplies reaching the South, but the Confederacy had excellent generals.

WHITE ELEPHANTS

The King of Siam, southeast Asia, offered Abraham Lincoln the use of a troop of his war elephants in the fight to preserve the Union. The President declined the offer.

KEY BATTLES

Battle	Date	Victor	Details
Bull Run	July 1861	Confederacy	5,000 dead
Antietam	Sep 1862	Union	21,000 dead in one day
Gettysburg	July 1863	Union	40,000 dead

LEVI'S JEANS

In the 1860s, American tailor Levi Strauss made the first pair of denim jeans. The tough cotton fabric, woven only in Nîmes, France, was ideal for miners of the Gold Rush. Later, workers, farmers, and cowboys began wearing jeans.

WOMEN VOTERS

In 1893, New Zealand became the first country to give women the right to vote in national elections. Almost a quarter of the female population had signed petitions demanding votes.

BOXER REBELS

In the late 19th century, economic and natural disasters weakened China's government. Western powers there grew stronger, until in 1899, an officially supported peasant rebellion, the Boxer Rebellion, tried to rid China of all foreigners. It was soon crushed by Western forces.

BISMARCK

Otto von Bismarck (1815–98) was the chief minister of Prussia, Germany. He led Prussia to victory against Denmark (1864), Austria (1866), and France (1871). He then founded the German Empire with Prussian King William I (1797–1888) as emperor.

Otto von Bismarck

GERMANY FACTS

• Before 1867, Germany consisted of more than 38 states. After 1871, Bismarck proclaimed all Germany an empire.

• After political unification, Germany rapidly built up its industries and armies. By 1914, the German army was twice the size of France's, and 12 times the size of Britain's.

• Bismarck was known as the "Iron Chancellor." In reality, he was prone to nervous attacks.

KEY PEOPLE

Name	Dates	Biographical details
Abraham Lincoln	1809–65	US President, preserved Union in US Civil War, emancipated slaves. Shot dead at Ford's theater
Otto von Bismarck	1815–98	Founder and first Chancellor of German Empire
Susan B. Anthony	1820–1906	Crusader for US women's right to vote
Harriet Tubman	1820–1913	Escaped US slave, helped 300 slaves flee to North
Alfred Nobel	1833–96	Swedish chemist, invented dynamite in 1866
Karl Benz	1844–1929	German engineer, built first practical car
Sigmund Freud	1856–1939	Austrian doctor, founder of psychoanalysis

1881 First Boer War: white Dutch settlers (Boers) rebel against British rule
1882 British begin rule in Egypt   **1886** Gold discovered in South Africa

1895–96 Italy and Ethiopia at war: Ethiopia wins
1899 Second Boer War

s Britain and France
e into Burma and Vietnam   **1885** Indian National
Congress Party formed

1899 Boxer Rebellion
of Chinese peasants

1884 Berlin conference decides
colonial divisions in Africa.
First deep subway built in London
1885 Karl Benz builds first
car driven by internal
combustion engine

1888 Scottish surgeon John
Dunlop (1840–1921) patents
pneumatic (air-filled) tire
1889 English chemist Frederick
Abel invents cordite (explosive)

1896 Modern Olympic
Games introduced in Greece

1897 Greece and Turkey at war

1882 Thomas Edison designs
first hydroelectric power station
1884 First skyscraper built in Chicago.
Scheme for standard time devised by
Canadian Sir Sandford Fleming (1827-1915)

1889 Pedro II abdicates and
Brazil declared a republic
1890 Battle of Wounded Knee: last
massacre of Native Americans in US.
First moving picture (film) shows
appear in New York

1895 Cuban revolt against Spanish rule
1896 Gold struck in Klondike, Canada
1898 US wins Spanish-
American War and takes over
the Philippines. Cuba obtains
independence from Spain

1883 Volcano erupts on island of Krakatau
1885 Britain and Germany divide up New Guinea

1893 Women granted the vote in New Zealand. New Zealand
Prime Minister Richard Seddon introduces advanced social reforms

INDUSTRY AND INNOVATION

The later 19th century saw a dramatic growth in technology and industry. Factories multiplied and cities expanded, aided by better transportation, such as railroads, and new inventions.

SOCIALISM

Many people who worked in the new factories lived in bad conditions. They began to demand rights through trade unions and socialist organizations.

INDUSTRY FACTS

● With industrial growth came an explosion in the size and population of cities. Germany in 1871 consisted mainly of small towns. By 1914 it had 30 cities of more than 100,000 people.

● After 1870, new industries – the chemical and electrical industries – joined the older coal, iron, and textile industries as a result of scientific discoveries.

KEY INNOVATIONS

SKYSCRAPERS

The large-scale production of steel made it possible for architects to construct buildings around steel "skeletons." The first skyscraper, the Chicago Home Insurance Building, was built in 1884.

LIGHTBULB

Englishman Joseph Swan and American Thomas Edison invented light-bulbs in the late 1870s.

CAR

In 1885, German engineer Karl Benz built the first car driven by an internal combustion engine. He fitted the engine onto a two-seat tricycle and patented the invention in 1886.

TELEPHONE

Scottish-born speech therapist Alexander Graham Bell invented the telephone in 1876.

SCRAMBLE FOR AFRICA

Before 1870, European interest in Africa was confined to coastal towns that were important for sea trade. In the 1870s European armies followed missionaries and explorers into the interior, and by 1914 nearly all of Africa had been colonized.

CARVING UP AFRICA

France and Britain held the greatest proportion of African territories. Germany, Italy, Portugal, and Belgium also held territories. Most of today's borders come from the lines drawn by Europeans at an 1884 conference in Berlin. No native Africans were invited to attend.

ICE CREAM TO EMPIRE

Cecil Rhodes, the empire-builder of British South Africa, began his career selling ice cream to diamond-mine workers. He later gained control of 90 percent of the world's production of diamonds.

The British wanted to unite their southern and northern territories in Africa; the French, their western and eastern lands.

King Menelik of Ethiopia

Stanley's hat

Livingstone's hat

Zulu shield

French
British
Portuguese
German
Belgian
Spanish
Italian
Independent

No African group accepted colonization without resistance.

1. Independent Liberia
Liberia was the first African country to become independent, in 1847. It was founded by freed American slaves.

2. Menelik's victory
Though Europeans had guns, African resistance to the European advance was often fierce. In 1896, Emperor Menelik of Ethiopia defeated the Italians at a famous battle at Adowa and secured Ethiopia's independence.

3. Intrepid explorers
From 1850, several Europeans, including Richard Burton, Henry Speke, Mary Kingsley, David Livingstone, and Henry Stanley, explored Central Africa.

4. Fight for South Africa
In South Africa, Africans had to fight both British and Boers (white Dutch settlers). Zulus, led by King Cetewayo, held out, but were finally defeated by Britain in 1879.

5. The Boers
In 1899, a major war broke out between the British and the Boers. By 1902, Britain had defeated the Boers, who were mostly farmers. Within ten years, however, Britain gave Boers the power to rule South Africa.

1900

AFRICA	**1902** Ovimbundu people of Angola revolt against Portuguese rule **1905** Maji Maji rebellion in Tanzania against German rule leaves 75,000 dead. Union of South Africa, independent of Britain, formed
ASIA	**1901** Peace of Peking ends Boxer Rebellion in China **1905** Japan wins Russo-Japanese War **1907** British company finds oil in Persia (now Iran) **1909** China attac[k] Tibet
EUROPE	**1900** German navy law calls for increases in sea power. Britain responds with similar increases; arms race begins **1903** Women's Union formed in Britain by suffragette Emmeline Pankhurst. First Tour de France cycle race **1904** Entente Cordiale (friendly understanding) between Britain and France **1905** October Manifesto: Czar of Russia forced to grant democratic rights. Einstein formulates his Special Theory of Relativity **1908** First steel and glass buil[d] AEG Turbine factory, Berlin
AMERICAS	**1900** Coca Cola first produced **1901** Theodore Roosevelt becomes youngest-ever US president after assassination of President McKinley **1902** British and German fleets seize Venezuelan navy. Plastic invented in US **1903** US bicyclemakers Orville and Wilbur Wright build first airplane and make first successful powered flight **1906** US forces occupy Cuba. Earthquake in San Francisco, US **1907** First comic strips appear in US **1909** US explore[r] Robert Peary (1856–1920) clai[m] to have reached North Pole
OCEANIA	**1901** Commonwealth of Australia proclaimed. New Zealand takes over Cook Islands **1907** New Zealand becomes a dominion. Federal basic wage set in Australia

WORLD WAR I

In the early 1900s, Europe was kept at peace by a complex system of alliances. When the heir to the Austro-Hungarian Empire, Archduke Ferdinand, was shot dead in 1914, the system collapsed, and war broke out. A combination of new weapons with old tactics resulted in war on a huge scale and a vast death toll: more than 20 million dead.

KEY BATTLES

Battle	Date	Outcome
Tannenberg	Aug 1914	Germans halt Russian advance
The Marne	Sep 1914	Last mobile action of western war; Germans pushed back to trench front
Passchendaele	July 1917	British defeated in sea of mud
Cambrai	Nov 1917	First successes with British tanks

BATTLE OF THE SOMME

More people – 1,265,000 – died in the Battle of the Somme in 1916 than in any other World War I battle. Artillery gunfire from the battle could be heard in England.

Somme death toll

650,000 German

420,000 British

195,000 French

WAR ON TWO FRONTS

World War I involved so many countries that it became known as the Great War. Although it was fought mainly in Europe, other nations, notably Japan and the US, were also involved. In western Europe, French and British forces fought Germans around Belgium and France.

Soldiers lived, slept, ate, fought, and often died in trenches. Heavy guns would pound an enemy's trenches before an attack.

British trench

TRENCH WARFARE

Much fighting took place between lines of trenches dug by soldiers. When one army charged at another, many died, since both sides had machine guns. The area between trenches, called No Man's Land, was often a muddy wasteland full of dead bodies and craters. Conditions were terrible and disease was rife.

Allied powers
Central powers
Neutral states

Front lines
1914
1915
1918

German trench

FIRST WARPLANES

Aircraft were first used to spy on enemy trenches, but later were fitted with bombs and machine guns. The most successful fighter pilots, such as the German Baron von Richthofen who was credited with shooting down 80 enemy planes, were called aces.

WORLD WAR I FACTS

• World War I was the first to make use of entire adult populations. Men were conscripted (called up) into the armed forces, and women worked in armaments factories and on farms. It changed the way wars were fought forever.

• Poison gas, in this case chlorine, was first used in war by Germans at the Battle of Ypres (1915).

• Governments concealed the extent of the slaughter from the public by publishing false statistics.

• The Germans surrendered at 11:00 a.m. on the 11th of November 1918. On every anniversary of this day, the war dead are remembered in religious services around the world.

SINKING OF THE LUSITANIA

On May 7, 1915, the British passenger liner *Lusitania* was sunk by a German submarine. It went down with 1,198 civilians, including 198 Americans. The attack hastened US entry into the war.

Victims from the Lusitania

KEY INNOVATIONS

MACHINE GUN
Machine guns turned the western front from a mobile war into a static trench war. A few could kill thousands.

TANKS
The first practical tank, *Big Willie*, was built by the British in 1916. Tanks proved slow but effective.

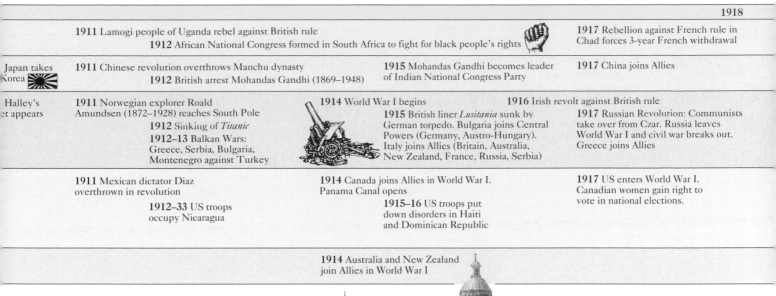

1911 Lamogi people of Uganda rebel against British rule
1912 African National Congress formed in South Africa to fight for black people's rights

1917 Rebellion against French rule in Chad forces 3-year French withdrawal

Japan takes Korea

1911 Chinese revolution overthrows Manchu dynasty
1912 British arrest Mohandas Gandhi (1869–1948)

1915 Mohandas Gandhi becomes leader of Indian National Congress Party

1917 China joins Allies

Halley's et appears

1911 Norwegian explorer Roald Amundsen (1872–1928) reaches South Pole
1912 Sinking of *Titanic*
1912–13 Balkan Wars: Greece, Serbia, Bulgaria, Montenegro against Turkey

1914 World War I begins
1915 British liner *Lusitania* sunk by German torpedo. Bulgaria joins Central Powers (Germany, Austro-Hungary). Italy joins Allies (Britain, Australia, New Zealand, France, Russia, Serbia)

1916 Irish revolt against British rule
1917 Russian Revolution: Communists take over from Czar. Russia leaves World War I and civil war breaks out. Greece joins Allies

1911 Mexican dictator Diaz overthrown in revolution
1912–33 US troops occupy Nicaragua

1914 Canada joins Allies in World War I. Panama Canal opens
1915–16 US troops put down disorders in Haiti and Dominican Republic

1917 US enters World War I. Canadian women gain right to vote in national elections.

1914 Australia and New Zealand join Allies in World War I

RUSSIAN REVOLUTION

In the early 20th century, rapid industrialization threatened the rule of the tyrannical Czar Nicholas II, since workers began to demand their rights. In 1917, Vladimir Lenin, leader of the Bolshevik Party, led a revolution that overthrew czarist rule. In its place he set up the world's first Communist regime and pulled Russia out of World War I.

RUSSIAN REVOLUTION FACTS

• In March 1917, food and fuel were in short supply in the cities. Angry citizens in St. Petersburg began strikes and riots. Troops ordered to break up the riots joined the rioters instead. The Czar abdicated, and a temporary government was set up.

• In November 1917, the war was going badly for Russia and the temporary government had failed to ease the food and fuel shortages. The Bolsheviks were able to seize power after besieging the government in the Winter Palace in St. Petersburg.

• In July 1918, Czar Nicholas II and his family were shot by the Bolsheviks.

• The "October Revolution" actually happened in November, because at that time Russians used a different calendar from the rest of the world. Lenin brought it into line in 1918.

• Lenin's Communists, called the Red Army, were led by Trotsky.

Aurora

Winter Palace, St. Petersburg

The Bolsheviks had supporters in the Navy. During the October Revolution, the cruiser *Aurora* steamed upriver toward St. Petersburg. It fired blanks over the roof of the Winter Palace during the siege of the temporary government.

• Lenin gave land from old estates to the peasants, gave workers the power to run their factories, and confiscated the property of the Church. He faced armed opposition from "White" Russians, who wanted the Czar restored. A civil war began, ending in 1921 with the Red Army triumphant.

REVOLUTION EXPRESS

Until April 1917, Lenin had been in exile in Switzerland. When Russian Communists gained permission for him to return, the German government agreed, on condition that he remain on a sealed train until his destination.

KEY PEOPLE OF THE REVOLUTION

Czar Nicholas II (1868–1918) became unpopular after his 1905 promises of democracy proved empty. When he became personally involved in the war, he also took the blame for the army's successive defeats.

Vladimir Lenin (1870–1924) formed the Social Democratic Party in 1898, which had to meet in secret, since the czarist government immediately banned it. When the time came, Lenin's followers, the Bolsheviks, were ready.

Leon Trotsky (1879–1940) was a brilliant writer and speaker, and the most popular leader after Lenin. He created the Red Army, led it to victory in the Civil War, and defeated a Polish invasion.

Josef Stalin (1879–1953) was a key administrator in the Bolshevik party. When Lenin died in 1924, Stalin struggled with Trotsky for power. Stalin succeeded and ruled the country until 1953.

RUSSO–JAPANESE WAR 1904-05

In 1904, Japan, hoping to capture Manchuria, launched a surprise attack on Russian forces there. Japan won a series of victories ending in 1905 with the total destruction of the Russian fleet. It was the first time in modern history that an Asian power had defeated a European power.

Battle of Liao Yang, 1904

SINKING OF THE TITANIC

At midnight on April 15, 1912, the *Titanic*, the world's largest ocean liner, struck an iceberg on its maiden voyage. It sank, and 1,513 lives were lost.

IRELAND AND THE EASTER RISING

In 1912, Britain agreed to give Ireland home rule, but when World War I began, the plan was postponed. In 1916, those Irish who wanted independence organized armies, took control of Dublin, and declared a republic. Britain put down this "Easter Rising," but it led to greater support for a republic.

Dublin barricades

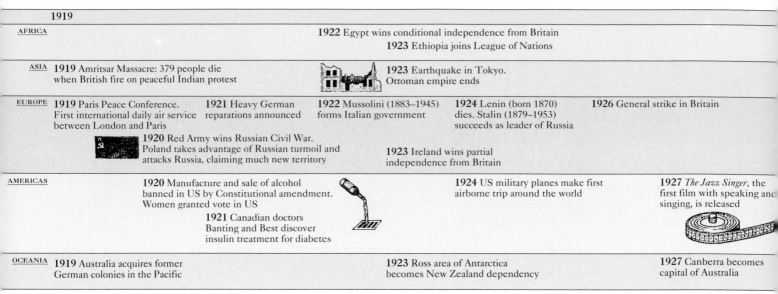

1919

AFRICA
1922 Egypt wins conditional independence from Britain
1923 Ethiopia joins League of Nations

ASIA
1919 Amritsar Massacre: 379 people die when British fire on peaceful Indian protest
1923 Earthquake in Tokyo. Ottoman empire ends

EUROPE
1919 Paris Peace Conference. First international daily air service between London and Paris
1921 Heavy German reparations announced
1922 Mussolini (1883–1945) forms Italian government
1924 Lenin (born 1870) dies. Stalin (1879–1953) succeeds as leader of Russia
1926 General strike in Britain
1920 Red Army wins Russian Civil War. Poland takes advantage of Russian turmoil and attacks Russia, claiming much new territory
1923 Ireland wins partial independence from Britain

AMERICAS
1920 Manufacture and sale of alcohol banned in US by Constitutional amendment. Women granted vote in US
1924 US military planes make first airborne trip around the world
1927 *The Jazz Singer*, the first film with speaking and singing, is released
1921 Canadian doctors Banting and Best discover insulin treatment for diabetes

OCEANIA
1919 Australia acquires former German colonies in the Pacific
1923 Ross area of Antarctica becomes New Zealand dependency
1927 Canberra becomes capital of Australia

AFTERMATH OF WAR
After World War I, various plans were laid to make sure such a war could never happen again. Germany was blamed and severely punished, while the Allies drew together and formed a pact to protect themselves from further attacks. The victors thought they had secured lasting peace.

PARIS PEACE CONFERENCE
In 1919, the victors organized a conference at which Germany lost much of its territory, including its African colonies. It was forced to disarm and make huge reparations (compensation). Many felt that the Allies had treated Germany harshly and unfairly.

The signing of the peace treaty between the Allies and Germany in the Hall of Mirrors at Versailles in 1919

THE WORLD BETWEEN THE WARS

Soviet (Russian) worker

• The victors joined together to form the League of Nations and promised to seek peaceful solutions to problems. Defeated countries were not allowed to join and the US preferred to stay out of world affairs.

• Hitler's economic policies eased Germany's crisis, and few stood against his 1934 seizure of power.

• In the late 1920s Stalin forced Russia to industrialize very quickly; millions died of starvation. Later he enforced his rule by intimidating and murdering millions of Soviet citizens.

German Empire 1914
Russian Empire 1914
Austro-Hungarian Empire 1914
Postwar borders

THE POSTWAR SETTLEMENT
The defeat of Germany, the destruction of the Austro-Hungarian empire, and the Bolshevik Revolution completely changed the map of Europe. Several states, such as Poland and the Baltic and Yugoslavian states, gained independence.

REPARATIONS
The reparations the Allies forced on the Germans gave their economy no chance to recover, and they had to borrow again to keep paying. In 1923, it took a whole wheelbarrow of German marks to buy a loaf of bread.

Amount borrowed: 33 million marks

Reparation payments: 36.1 million marks

1918–1931

THE GREAT DEPRESSION
In October 1929, stockbrokers in New York, having pushed share prices above their real value, panicked and sold 13 million shares in one day. This event, referred to as the stockmarket crash, was a major cause of the worldwide economic crisis that followed. Millions of people lost jobs, businesses, savings, and homes.

THE DUST BOWL
Drought struck the midwestern and western US at the time of the Crash, and the soil of the farmlands was blown away in strong winds. Their land now a desert, many farmers lost everything and went west. The region was called the Dust Bowl.

Homeless victims of the Great Depression

GREAT DEPRESSION FACTS
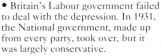

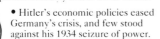

• By 1933 the US had 14 million unemployed. Franklin D. Roosevelt, elected president in 1932, devised his "New Deal" programs to create jobs and ease the depression.

• German factory production levels halved between 1929 and 1932. Germans blamed their system of government, a view that the Nazis later used to take absolute power.

• Britain's Labour government failed to deal with the depression. In 1931, the National government, made up from every party, took over, but it was largely conservative.

• Japan's rice and textile markets suffered greatly and the military used widespread economic misery to seize power from the elected rulers.

A FISTFUL OF WOOD
In 1932, a shortage of ready cash led the authorities of Tenino, Washington, to issue "notes" made of wood. There were notes worth $10, $5, $1, 50¢, and 25¢.

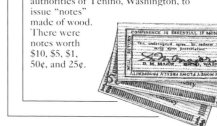

KEY PEOPLE

Name	Dates	Biographical details
Mohandas Gandhi	1869–1948	Crusader for Indian independence, founder of modern Indian state
Adolf Hitler	1889–1945	*Führer* (leader) of the German Nazi Party, dictator from August 1934
Francisco Franco	1892–1975	Spanish general and dictator 1939–75
Haile Selassie	1892–1975	Progressive emperor of Ethiopia
Al Capone	1899–1947	Notorious gangster in Chicago
Jesse Owens	1913–80	Black US Olympic athlete, challenged Hitler's belief in white superiority

GANGSTERS
The sale of alcohol was banned in the US in 1920. An illegal trade in alcohol immediately sprang up in major cities, backed by gangs of criminals. Gang leaders, such as Al "Scarface" Capone, grew very powerful. Capone was eventually jailed in 1930 for tax evasion.

Al Capone (center)

1930 Ras (Prince) Tafari crowned as Haile Selassie I in Ethiopia

1934 Lagos Youth Movement formed, demanding self-government for Nigeria

1935 Italy invades Ethiopia

1930s Gandhi leads nonviolent opposition to British rule in India

1934–35 Long March in China

1936 Japan signs alliance with Germany

1937 Japan and China at war. Japan occupies much of Chinese coast

1933 Adolf Hitler, (1889–1945), *führer* (leader) of Nazi Party, becomes German Chancellor

1936 Germany hosts Olympic Games in Berlin

1936–39 Spanish Civil War between Communists and Fascists: Fascist victory

1937 Jet engine invented in Britain

1938 Hitler takes over Czechoslovakia

US stockmarket crash: s of shares on American exchange fall rapidly

1931 British Parliament gives Canada final independence

1933 Franklin D. Roosevelt becomes US President. Ban on sale and manufacture of alcohol lifted

1937 Airmail service from Australia to Britain introduced

1937 Royal New Zealand Air Force formed

REVOLUTION IN CHINA

Between the wars, Communism rose to be the major force in China. From 1927, Communists led by Mao Tse-tung tried to overthrow Chiang Kai-shek's corrupt Nationalist government in a bloody civil war. In 1937, Japan took advantage of China's domestic turmoil by invading the north, further damaging Chiang's power. Mao and Communism triumphed in 1949.

KEY LEADERS

Chiang Kai-shek (1887–1975), although at first allied with the Communists who helped him take power in 1925, broke with them soon after. His rule was harsh and corrupt, and the fortunes he amassed while his people starved made him unpopular.

Mao Tse-tung (1893–1976) drew support from peasants, but early in the Civil War was outfought by Chiang's armies. On the Long March, he became leader of the party and wrote the *Red Book*, which described life under Communism.

CHINA FACTS

• Mao Tse-tung was born a peasant and educated himself. He became involved in peasant affairs in 1921.

• In April 1927, Chiang Kai-shek had several hundred Communists and union organizers shot in Shanghai. The ensuing chaos in the Communist Party enabled him to seize power.

• In 1929, Mao established a strong Communist base in Kiangsi. Communist troops from all over China fled there after Chiang Kai-shek broke his alliance with the Communists.

• Mao was forced to leave behind his two children on the Long March. He never located them after the war.

TURMOIL IN THE EAST

Chiang Kai-shek's forces, called the Kuomintang (Nationalists), drove the Communists into the southern hills of Jiangxi. Although the Kuomintang ruled most of China, Communists held many remote, agricultural areas.

Peking
Yenan
Nanking
Shanghai

O   Area of early Communist rule

→   Route of the Long March

   Under Japanese rule by 1938

   Under Communist rule by 1945

   Communist base

During the 6,000-mile Long March, more than three-quarters of the original 100,000 died of cold, hunger, or from attacks by Chiang's forces or local warlords.

THE LONG MARCH

In October 1934, 100,000 Communists, mainly peasants, marched for a year across swamps, mountains, and large rivers, to escape Chiang Kai-shek's armies. Survivors set up a base at Yenan in a deep gorge, where they lived in cliff caves.

THE RISE OF JAPAN

• In the late 1930s, Japan's military seized power and were anxious to show Japan's strength in war and empire-building. They invaded China in 1937 and occupied much territory.

• Japan withdrew after defeat in World War II, but its occupation had weakened Chiang's armies and helped bring Mao to power.

HEN HORNS Hens in crates on boats on the crowded Shanghai River acted as horns, warning other craft at night.

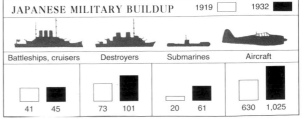

JAPANESE MILITARY BUILDUP		1919 □	1932 ■
Battleships, cruisers	Destroyers	Submarines	Aircraft
41 45	73 101	20 61	630 1,025

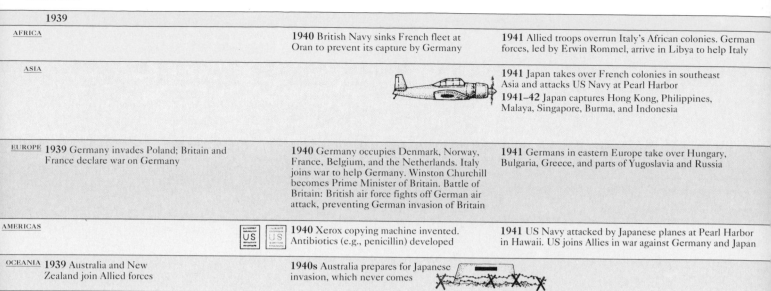

1939

AFRICA
1940 British Navy sinks French fleet at Oran to prevent its capture by Germany

1941 Allied troops overrun Italy's African colonies. German forces, led by Erwin Rommel, arrive in Libya to help Italy

ASIA
1941 Japan takes over French colonies in southeast Asia and attacks US Navy at Pearl Harbor
1941–42 Japan captures Hong Kong, Philippines, Malaya, Singapore, Burma, and Indonesia

EUROPE **1939** Germany invades Poland; Britain and France declare war on Germany

1940 Germany occupies Denmark, Norway, France, Belgium, and the Netherlands. Italy joins war to help Germany. Winston Churchill becomes Prime Minister of Britain. Battle of Britain: British air force fights off German air attack, preventing German invasion of Britain

1941 Germans in eastern Europe take over Hungary, Bulgaria, Greece, and parts of Yugoslavia and Russia

AMERICAS
1940 Xerox copying machine invented. Antibiotics (e.g., penicillin) developed

1941 US Navy attacked by Japanese planes at Pearl Harbor in Hawaii. US joins Allies in war against Germany and Japan

OCEANIA **1939** Australia and New Zealand join Allied forces

1940s Australia prepares for Japanese invasion, which never comes

WORLD WAR II

Militaristic and nationalistic governments rose to power in Germany, Italy, and Japan, as a result of the Great Depression of the 1930s and the Versailles Treaty of World War I. All were intent on expanding their power and territory. Global war broke out with Germany's invasion of Poland in 1939, eventually costing over 50 million lives.

LEADERS OF THE AXIS POWERS

Adolf Hitler (1889–1945) founded the Nazi Party in the 1920s. He seized power in 1933, and quickly destroyed all opposition. His dreams of empire ended with the failure of his Russian invasion. At the war's end he shot himself.

Benito Mussolini (1883–1945) founded the Fascist movement in Italy in 1919. In 1922, he gained power and ruled as a dictator. He took Italy into the war in 1940 on the Axis side and, after their defeat, was captured and executed by Italian rebels in April 1945.

Emperor Hirohito (1901–89), though seen as a god in Japan, had little power. Japanese pilots thought it an honor to die for the Emperor. They went on *kamikaze* missions in which they flew into Allied ships in planes packed with explosives.

WORLD WAR II FACTS
• Germany brutally put down any resistance to its rule. Those suspected of opposing German occupation were often tortured or killed by the feared Nazi police, the Gestapo. In occupied countries many joined secret resistance groups.

• In August 1939, the USSR signed a pact with Germany, called the Nazi–Soviet pact, which carved up Poland and the Baltic states between the two. In June 1941, Germany's invasion of Russia, called "Operation Barbarossa," broke the pact.

• The Nazis passed laws to discriminate against Jews. During the war they built camps around Europe, called concentration camps, where they killed six million Jews, along with Slavs, Gypsies, homosexuals, and political prisoners.

Belsen concentration camp

German soldier   *Italian soldier*   *Japanese soldier*

The 1940 "Blitz" of London was the first long, large-scale bombing campaign from the air.

THE OCCUPATION OF EUROPE
By 1942, Germany had conquered most of Europe and a great area of Russia. Its *blitzkreig* (lightning campaign) tactics devastated the Allies and it was not until 1943, with US entry into the war and the Allies' huge rearmament programs, that the tide turned against Germany. In June 1944, the Allies landed in Normandy, France. Russia matched their successes, and by May 1945 the war in Europe was over.

Leningrad
·Moscow
London Berlin
Paris· ·Stalingrad
Rome

■ Maximum extent of Axis empire (1942)
□ Allied states
□ Neutral states
→ British and US advances (1943–5)
→ Russian advances (1943–5)

BOMBING AND THE BLITZ
World War II marked the first use of large-scale bombing raids, or blitzes, to try to destroy civilian morale and industrial efficiency. In 1945, a single British raid on the German city of Dresden killed more people than either of the atomic bombs dropped on Japan.

KEY GENERALS

Name	Dates	Biographical details
D. MacArthur	1880–1964	US general, recaptured much of South Pacific from Japanese, received Japanese surrender aboard USS *Missouri*
B. L. Montgomery	1887–1976	British general, defeated Rommel, led Allied invasion of France
Erwin Rommel	1891–1944	German tank commander, won huge victories in North Africa
G. K. Zhukov	1896–1974	Red Army (Russian) commander, recaptured Russian lands; his troops were first to enter Berlin at end of war

Allied troops land in Morocco and force
~~nel's~~ troops to retreat from El Alamein

US Navy defeats Japan in Coral Sea
~~ew~~ Guinea and at Midway Island.

1943–44 Series of island-hopping
victories by US pushes Japanese back

1944 Japan attacks India
but is defeated at Kohima

1945 US drops first atomic bombs on Japanese
cities of Hiroshima and Nagasaki. Emperor
Hirohito authorizes Japanese surrender

1943 Allies invade Italy
1943–44 Germans driven out of Russia

1944 Allies invade France
and drive back Germans

1945 German forces surrender

Enrico Fermi builds first nuclear
~~r~~ in US. Canadian raid on Dieppe

1943 Argentine Revolution brings
Juan Perón to power as virtual dictator

1945 Canadian forces liberate Holland.
Total Canadian losses in WWII: 42,222

Japanese bomb Darwin, Australia,
~~nvade~~ New Guinea and part of Papua

1944 Japanese prisoners of war in
Australia stage mass breakout

1945 Australia recovers New Guinea
and Papua territory from Japan

LEADERS OF THE ALLIED POWERS

Josef Stalin
(1879–1953) was taken
by surprise when
Germany invaded.
Hitler's troops
came very close to
Moscow, but were
pushed back by
cold, hunger, and
the bravery of Soviet
troops: millions of them
died on the eastern front.

Winston Churchill
(1874–1965), a veteran
of World War I, had
warned against the
rise of Hitler and
Nazism during the
1930s. Britain
turned to him for
leadership in the war,
and his many rousing
speeches on the radio
inspired the Allies to victory.

**Franklin D.
Roosevelt**
(1882–1945), US
President, urged
America into the
war despite its
initial reluctance.
He supported the
Allies with large
amounts of arms and
food. He died just
before the Allied victory.

KEY INNOVATIONS

RADAR
Britain developed the first
radar powerful enough to
detect approaching enemy
aircraft. It gave Britain a
huge advantage in the air.

NYLON
In 1942, nylon was first
produced in the US,
initially used for hosiery
and parachutes.

WORLD WAR II IN ASIA AND THE PACIFIC
In December 1941, Japan made a surprise attack on the US Navy
at Pearl Harbor, Hawaii, sinking or damaging 18 ships, and
destroying 200 aircraft. The US immediately declared
war, but within six months Japan had conquered the
US, British, and Dutch colonies in the Indian and
Pacific Oceans. Japan could not, however, defend
such a vast empire, and by 1943 the US had begun
a series of bitterly fought, island-hopping, victories.

Maximum extent of
Japanese occupation,
August 1942

US, British, Common-
wealth advances (1943–5)

Soviet advances (1943–5)

Russian soldier   *British soldier*   *American soldier*

WORLD WAR II LIFESTYLE FACTS
• In cities throughout Europe,
children were evacuated to safer
homes in the countryside. Those
left often slept in underground
train stations, or air-raid shelters.

• At night, the smallest amount of light was
visible from the air, so cities introduced
blackouts to make it hard for enemy pilots
to find targets. Curtains had to be closed
and the use of car headlights minimized.

• Some foods, such as
meat, eggs, and
sweets, were scarce
during the war, so
families had "ration
books" showing their
weekly allowance.

• The army floated huge balloons over
London. Enemy planes had to avoid the
steel cables that tied them to the ground,
and so could not get close to their targets.

THE ATOMIC BOMB
On August 6, 1945, President Harry
Truman ordered an atomic bomb to be
dropped on Hiroshima, Japan. It instantly
killed about 80,000 people. A second was
dropped on Nagasaki three days later and
led to Japan's surrender. The war was
over, but people were still dying from
radiation sickness decades later.
Mushroom cloud following bombing of Nagasaki

KEY BATTLES

Battle	Date	Victor
Crossing of the Meuse	1940	Germany pierces French "Maginot Line" defenses
Battle of Britain	1941	Britain's air defense prevents German seaborne invasion
Midway	1942	US cripples Japanese Navy
El Alamein	1942	British push back Rommel
Normandy (D-Day)	1944	Largest seaborne attack ever: Allies force German retreat

THE HUMAN COST OF WORLD WAR II
Estimates of total deaths in World War II vary
between 40 and 60 million, because the mass
dispersal of armies and huge migrations at the
war's end made it impossible to compile
statistics. More civilians died than soldiers,
largely from famine, disease, air raids, and
executions by occupying forces. Poland lost
20 percent of its prewar population.

Italy: 395,000
Britain: 357,000
US: 298,000
Japan: 1,972,000   Germany: 4,200,000   USSR: 18,000,000

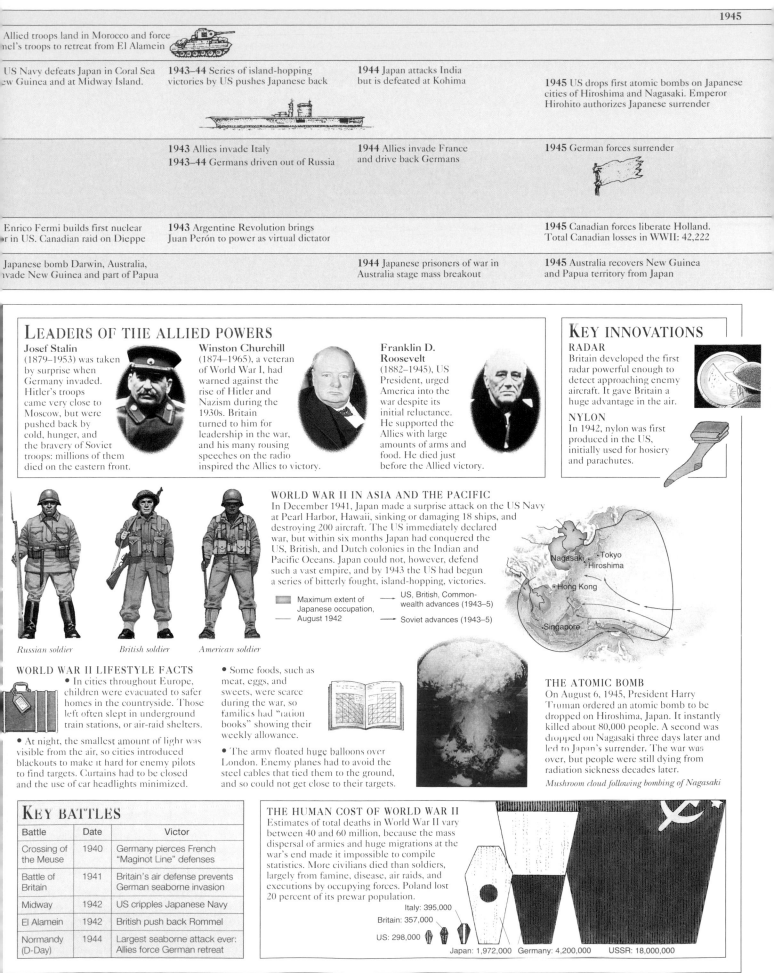

	1946		
AFRICA			**1950** Group Areas Act, South Africa orders segregation of races (apartheid) **1951** Libyan independence from Italy sanctioned by UN
ASIA	**1947** India wins independence from Great Britain amid riots that kill half a million	**1948** Gandhi assassinated in India; Nehru takes over. State of Israel created	**1950** China occupies Tibet. Korean War begins between North Korea (supported by China) and South Korea (supported by UN); ends 1953 **1949** Mao Tse-tung proclaims new Communist Republic of China. Vietnam, with aid from China, fights French rule
EUROPE	**1947** Marshall Plan offers US aid to European countries to help rebuild their economies after World War II	**1948** Berlin Airlift overcomes USSR's blockade of West Berlin. Communist coup in Czechoslovakia	**1949** Germany split into East and West. NATO formed **1952** Greece and Turkey join NATO
AMERICAS		**1948** Harry Truman (1884–1972) wins presidential election	**1950** US Senator Joseph McCarthy begins anticommunist "witch-hunts"
OCEANIA	**1947** South Pacific Commission formed to discuss economic and health issues of South Pacific islands		**1951** Australia, New Zealand, and US sign ANZUS Pact defense alliance

THE COLD WAR

After World War II, Europe was split by an "iron curtain" dividing USSR-backed East from US-backed West. This rivalry was known as the Cold War, with each side distrusting the other and expecting an attack at any time. The US and the USSR began stockpiling nuclear weapons, and the arms race was born. In 1945, there were only three nuclear weapons in the world; in 1962, there were 2,000. Later, each side had enough to destroy the world many times over.

THE TWO GERMANIES
Germany was carved up by its conquerors at the end of World War II. The US, France, and Great Britain controlled the West and the USSR controlled the East. The old capital, Berlin, was in East Germany, but was also divided between the two sides, by a wall erected in August 1961.
The Berlin Wall

NATO FACTS
• The North Atlantic Treaty Organization, NATO, was founded in 1949 by the Western countries to protect themselves against attack from the USSR and its allies.

• The US provided over $25 billion of military aid in NATO's first 20 years, a third of its total funds.

• By 1959, the US had more than 1,400 military bases, including 275 bases for nuclear bombers, in 31 countries around the world.

• The first hydrogen bomb, tested in 1952, was as powerful as the total of all bombs dropped on Germany and Japan during World War II, including the atomic bombs dropped on Hiroshima and Nagasaki.

• Between 1950 and 1954, Senator Joe McCarthy led a "witch-hunt" to identify Communist sympathizers in the US. In some areas of society people were encouraged to betray friends and colleagues. Many were wrongly accused and lost their jobs; some were imprisoned.

USSR and aligned Communist countries

NATO countries and allies

THE WEST
In response to the growing threat of Communism in the East, the countries of Western Europe formed a military alliance with North America. The US, via the Marshall Plan, sent money to these countries to help them rebuild their economies after World War II.

THE EAST
Immediately after World War II, Stalin closed the borders of Eastern Europe and placed the countries bordering Russia under the control of the USSR. Opponents of Communism were imprisoned and more than a million were killed.

WARSAW PACT FACTS
• The Warsaw Pact was founded in 1955. It allowed Soviet troops to be stationed in any Communist Eastern European country.

• Between 1949 and 1958, three million people escaped from East to West Berlin. In 1961, East Germany erected the Berlin Wall to close off access between the two sectors.

• The USSR's intercontinental ballistic missiles (ICBMs), first developed in 1957, had a range of 7,000 miles (11,300km).

HUNGARIAN UPRISING
In 1956, many Hungarians rebelled against Soviet domination and Communist rule of their country, and Hungary tried to leave the Warsaw Pact. However, tanks and troops from the USSR quickly ended their revolt and killed the leaders.

Hungarian rebel

THE THIRD WAY
The US and the USSR encouraged many countries to take sides in the Cold War. Some, like India, Egypt, and Yugoslavia, chose the "Third Way" and stayed out of the conflict.
Nasser (Egypt), Nehru (India), and Tito (Yugoslavia)

AERIAL ASSISTANCE
In 1948, the USSR blockaded Berlin, forcing the West to deliver supplies by air. For five months, planes landed at Tempelhof airport, Berlin, every four minutes. There was only one accident.

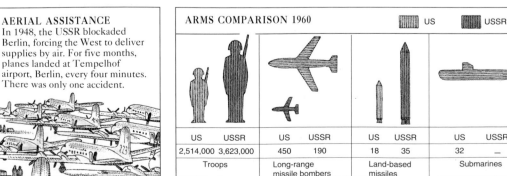

ARMS COMPARISON 1960

	US	USSR

US	USSR	US	USSR	US	USSR	US	USSR
2,514,000	3,623,000	450	190	18	35	32	—
Troops		Long-range missile bombers		Land-based missiles		Submarines	

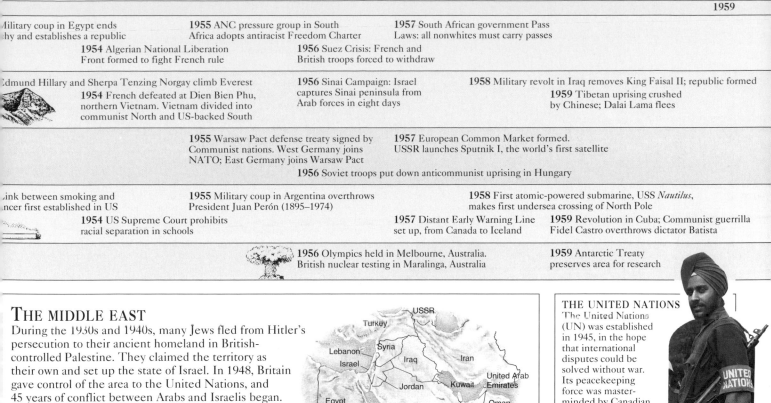

Military coup in Egypt ends [...]hy and establishes a republic

1954 Algerian National Liberation Front formed to fight French rule

[...]dmund Hillary and Sherpa Tenzing Norgay climb Everest

1954 French defeated at Dien Bien Phu, northern Vietnam. Vietnam divided into communist North and US-backed South

1955 ANC pressure group in South Africa adopts antiracist Freedom Charter

1956 Suez Crisis: French and British troops forced to withdraw

1956 Sinai Campaign: Israel captures Sinai peninsula from Arab forces in eight days

1957 South African government Pass Laws: all nonwhites must carry passes

1958 Military revolt in Iraq removes King Faisal II; republic formed

1959 Tibetan uprising crushed by Chinese; Dalai Lama flees

1955 Warsaw Pact defense treaty signed by Communist nations. West Germany joins NATO; East Germany joins Warsaw Pact

1956 Soviet troops put down anticommunist uprising in Hungary

1957 European Common Market formed. USSR launches Sputnik I, the world's first satellite

[...]ink between smoking and [...]ncer first established in US

1954 US Supreme Court prohibits racial separation in schools

1955 Military coup in Argentina overthrows President Juan Perón (1895–1974)

1957 Distant Early Warning Line set up, from Canada to Iceland

1958 First atomic-powered submarine, USS *Nautilus*, makes first undersea crossing of North Pole

1959 Revolution in Cuba; Communist guerrilla Fidel Castro overthrows dictator Batista

1956 Olympics held in Melbourne, Australia. British nuclear testing in Maralinga, Australia

1959 Antarctic Treaty preserves area for research

THE MIDDLE EAST

During the 1930s and 1940s, many Jews fled from Hitler's persecution to their ancient homeland in British-controlled Palestine. They claimed the territory as their own and set up the state of Israel. In 1948, Britain gave control of the area to the United Nations, and 45 years of conflict between Arabs and Israelis began.

NASSER
Egyptian leader Gamal A. Nasser (1918–70) planned to unite the Arab countries against Israel. In 1956, he took over the important Suez Canal Company, owned by Britain and France, and became even more popular.

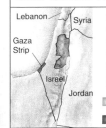

Arab woman during failed Anglo-French attempt to recapture Suez Canal

ALGERIAN WAR
Civil war broke out in Algeria in 1954, with Ahmed Ben Bella's National Liberation Front seeking Algerian independence from France. A guerrilla war between the NLF and colonists ended in a French withdrawal in 1962.

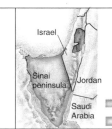

French soldiers check Algerian identity papers

MIDDLE EAST MAP
The Middle East was governed by Great Britain and France between the two World Wars. In 1917, Britain had promised to create a Jewish homeland, and in 1948, Palestine was divided between Jordan and the new Jewish settlers. Israel was created in place of Palestine.

THE UNITED NATIONS
The United Nations (UN) was established in 1945, in the hope that international disputes could be solved without war. Its peacekeeping force was masterminded by Canadian Lester B. Pearson.

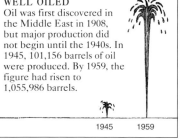

UN peacekeeper

WELL OILED
Oil was first discovered in the Middle East in 1908, but major production did not begin until the 1940s. In 1945, 101,156 barrels of oil were produced. By 1959, the figure had risen to 1,055,986 barrels.

1945   1959

ARAB-ISRAELI CONFLICT

War of Independence, 1948
When Israel became independent in 1948, the surrounding Arab countries immediately invaded. After 15 months of fighting, Jordan had occupied much of east Israel and Egypt – the Gaza Strip.

Under Jordanian rule
Under Egyptian rule

Sinai Campaign, 1956
Owing to increased Arab trade blockades, Israel invaded the Sinai peninsula in October 1956 and captured the entire area in eight days. Following a UN peace-keeping mission, Israel withdrew.

Area captured (1956) and returned (1957) by Israel
Under Jordanian rule

THE DALAI LAMA

Tibet's spiritual leader, the Dalai Lama, was forced to flee the country with 100,000 followers in 1959 after an unsuccessful Tibetan revolt against Chinese occupation. He has lived in exile ever since, traveling worldwide and gaining support for the Tibetan cause. He won the Nobel Peace Prize in 1989 for this work.

KEY PEOPLE

Name	Dates	Biographical details
Ho Chi Minh	1890–1969	Leader of North Vietnam, 1945–69. Led fight against French colonial rule
Nikita Khrushchev	1894–1971	Soviet leader during Cold War years 1958–64
Edmund Hillary	born 1919	New Zealand explorer and first, with Nepalese Sherpa Tenzing Norgay, to climb Everest (1953)
Dalai Lama	born 1935	Spiritual ruler of Tibet, fled to India after failed 1959 revolt against Chinese occupation. Lives in exile
Charles de Gaulle	1890–1970	President of French Fifth Republic 1958–69. Offered independence to African colonies

KEY INNOVATIONS

HEART PACEMAKER
In 1951, the first heart pacemaker was invented. It used electric shocks to stabilize the heartbeat.

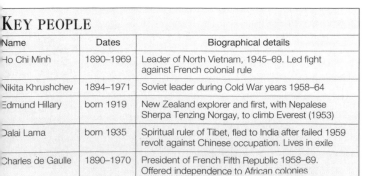

Heart pacemaker

NONSTICK FRYING PAN
The first nonstick frying pan, lined with a low-friction plastic, appeared in 1956.

SATELLITE
In 1957, the USSR launched Sputnik 1, the world's first space satellite. It stayed in orbit until early 1958, when it burned up in Earth's atmosphere.

Sputnik 1

1960

AFRICA	**1960** 17 African colonies gain independence. Peaceful demonstration at Sharpeville against white rule in South Africa; 69 protestors killed and ANC banned **1961** Patrice Lumumba, first Prime Minister of Congo, assassinated **1962** UN imposes sanctions on South Africa in protest of apartheid **1964** ANC leader Nelson Mandela jailed in South Africa **1965** White-ruled Rhodesia declares independence from Britain
ASIA	**1963** Diem, leader of South Vietnam, assassinated in military coup **1964–65** War between Indonesia and Malaysia **1965** US starts bombing North Vietnam **1966** Cultural Revolut[ion] begins in China; Red Guard formed
EUROPE	**1961** Berlin Wall built. Russian cosmonaut Yuri Gagarin is first man in space **1963** Russian Valentina Tereshkova is first woman in space **1964** Fighting between Greeks and Turks in Cyprus
AMERICAS	**1961** John F. Kennedy (1917–63) becomes youngest elected US President **1962** Cuban Missile Crisis **1963** President Kennedy assassinated. Lester B. Pearson becomes Prime Minister of Canada **1965** Civil rights leader Malcolm X assassinated. Riots in Chicago and Los Angeles
OCEANIA	**1960** Aboriginals become Australian citizens and gain full voting rights two years later **1965** Ferdinand E. Marcos (1917–89) elected President of the Philippines

AFRICAN INDEPENDENCE

Weakened by World War II, France and Britain found it hard to maintain their overseas colonies. During the 1950s and 1960s, many African countries gained independence. These new states faced great financial problems and were dependent on aid donated by richer countries. Many also suffered civil wars as military leaders seized control.

NELSON MANDELA
The African National Congress (ANC), a political party and black rights group, was banned in South Africa in 1960. In 1964, its leader, Nelson Mandela, was captured and imprisoned. He was finally released in 1989, and the ban lifted in 1990.

Ian Smith

RHODESIA
In 1965, the white government of Rhodesia, led by Ian Smith, declared independence from Britain. After a long guerrilla war, the black majority finally won power in 1980, and Rhodesia was renamed Zimbabwe.

TRUNK ROAD
In 1971, an East German woman was smuggled from East to West by her French fiancé. She spent a 70-minute train journey hidden inside two adjacent suitcases. Her fiancé had removed two of the side panels before the train's inspectors arrived.

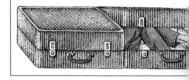

KEY INNOVATIONS

LASER
In 1960, American physicist T.H. Maiman made the first laser, using a synthetic ruby crystal. Lasers are used in industry and medicine.

CONCORDE
In 1969, the first supersonic airliner, *Concorde*, crossed the Atlantic in three hours, flying at 1,000mph (1,600km/h).

POCKET CALCULATOR
From 1972, many companies made pocket calculators. These small computers were made possible by the production of tiny electronic circuits, called silicon chips.

AFRICAN INDEPENDENCE TABLE

	Country	Independence	Details
	Ghana	1957, from Great Britain	First leader, Kwame Nkrumah (1909–72), became one of Africa's most powerful politicians, but corruption led to his defeat in 1966
	Congo	1960, from France	Independence led to immediate civil war. The country's first leader, Patrice Lumumba (born 1925), was assassinated in 1961
	Senegal	1960, from France	Able leader and distinguished poet, Léopold Senghor (b.1906), ruled for two decades following independence
	Nigeria	1960, from Great Britain	Military coups have left the army in control of the country for 25 of the 34 years since independence
	Mauritania	1960, from France	Mokhtar Ould Daddah (b.1924), first Mauritanian lawyer, led the country from independence until the military overthrew him in 1978
	Uganda	1962, from Great Britain	Following independence, the government changed seven times, four of them resulting in violence, and there were two civil wars
	Kenya	1963, from Great Britain	Jomo Kenyatta (c.1894–1978), who had fought against British rule in the 1950s, became the country's first leader
	Mozambique	1975, from Portugal	Independence leader, Samora Machel (1933–86), set out to provide education and health care for all, despite his country's debts
	Angola	1975, from Portugal	Independence led to a civil war that is still being fought

KEY PEOPLE

Name	Dates	Biographical details
Antonio Salazar	1889–1970	Dictator of Portugal, 1932–68. Kept Portugal's African colonies while other countries decolonized
Kwame Nkrumah	1909–72	Independence leader and first President of Ghana
Richard Nixon	1913–94	US President 1969–74. Began bombing of Cambodia. Resigned over Watergate scandal
Andrei Sakharov	1921–	Russian nuclear physicist and human rights advocate; first Russian to gain Nobel Peace Prize
Yuri Gagarin	1934–68	Russian cosmonaut. First man in space, aboard spacecraft Vostok 1. Orbited Earth in 89 minutes

CASTRO AND CUBA
In 1962, the Cuban dictator Fidel Castro (born 1927) allowed the USSR to build missile bases in Cuba, which threatened the US. President Kennedy ordered the US Navy to blockade Cuba and the Russians agreed to withdraw.

Fidel Castro

MOON LANDING
In July 1969, 600 million television viewers saw US astronaut Neil Armstrong become the first person to set foot on the moon. He and two other astronauts arrived there after a four-day journey aboard the spacecraft Apollo 11.

Neil Armstrong

Civil War in Nigeria. Biafra region away from Nigerian Federation. Christiaan Barnard completes first transplant in South Africa

1970 Biafra defeated by Federal Nigerian Government in Civil War

1975 Portugal grants independence to its African colonies

Six-Day War between Israelis and Arabs
1968 US troops kill hundreds of unarmed civilians in Vietnamese village of My Lai

1971 Indian troops defeat West Pakistan in Kashmir. Newly independent East Pakistan becomes Bangladesh

1970 US bombs Cambodia

1973 October War: Arab states attack Israel. Arab states restrict oil supplies and start world economic crisis

1972 Ceylon becomes republic, as Sri Lanka

Military coup in Greece
1969 Britain sends troops to Northern Ireland
1968 Riots in Paris by students and workers. Anticommunist uprising in Prague

1971 Women granted the right to vote in Switzerland

1973 Britain, Ireland and Denmark join the Common Market

1975 Spanish dictator Franco dies; Juan Carlos becomes king

1968 Pierre Trudeau becomes Prime Minister of Canada
1969 American Neil Armstrong the first person on the moon

1970 Quebec MP Pierre Laporte is murdered by Quebec separatists, precipitating October Crisis

1973 Military coup in Chile removes Marxist President Salvador Allende
1974 US President Richard Nixon resigns over Watergate scandal

New Zealand vote ed to 20-year-olds

1972 Sydney Opera House opens

1974 Papua New Guinea becomes independent

SOCIAL REVOLUTION

During the 1960s and 1970s, people all over the world began to demand greater rights. Some protested against sexual and racial discrimination and against war. Others used the new freedom to express themselves through music, films, and literature. During this period people questioned many old traditions and chose different lifestyles.

CIVIL RIGHTS

Following independence movements in Africa, many black Americans sought more rights. Leaders, such as Martin Luther King, Jr. and Malcolm X, staged protests demanding equality.

WOMEN'S MOVEMENT

Women all over the world began to demand equality with men and more recognition. The contraceptive pill and legalized abortion gave many women much greater freedom.

ANTIGOVERNMENT PROTESTS

Protests against governments broke out in countries on both sides in the Cold War. In 1968, students rioted in Paris and took over the universities. In the same year, Soviet troops invaded Prague to crush the reforms of Czech leader Alexander Dubcek, which they feared would weaken the Warsaw Pact. In the US, huge demonstrations against involvement in the Vietnam War took place across the country.

MUSIC

Popular music became a way of criticizing war. In 1969, 400,000 people attended a concert near Woodstock, New York, to hear singers such as Joan Baez and Jimi Hendrix. Meanwhile, the Beatles and the Rolling Stones (left) were selling millions of records a year.

CIVIL RIGHTS FACTS

• Until the Civil Rights Act (1964), shops, movie theaters, and libraries could be divided into separate areas for blacks and whites.

• In August 1965, civil unrest led to five days of rioting on the streets of Los Angeles; 35 people were killed, $175 million of damage was caused, and 14,000 National Guardsmen were called in to control rioters and looters.

HIPPIES

Hippies felt that the West was dominated by big business, so they "dropped out" of society. Some lived in communes and grew their own food. They were also associated with the use of narcotics (drugs).

VIETNAM WAR

In 1965, the US, with Australia and New Zealand, sent troops to help South Vietnam fight the communist North. By 1973, public protest led all allied troops to withdraw and Vietnam became a communist country.

CIVILIAN SUFFERING

Intensive bombing left hundreds of thousands of civilians dead or injured and countless others as homeless refugees.

VIETNAM WAR FACTS

• Money: the US spent $150 billion on the war.

• Deaths: two million Vietnamese and 58,000 allied soldiers and nurses died in Vietnam.

• Trees: chemicals such as Agent Orange destroyed large parts of Vietnam's jungle; much is still deforested today.

KEY ASSASSINATIONS

John F. Kennedy (1917–63) became the youngest elected US President in 1961. He was shot in a motorcade in Dallas, Texas. Controversy surrounds his death.

Malcolm X (1925–65) was a militant Muslim black rights leader. After hostility with a rival Muslim group, he was shot at a rally in Harlem, New York City.

Martin Luther King, Jr. (1929–68), a black Baptist minister, was a brilliant speaker for the Civil Rights movement. He was shot in Memphis, Tennessee.

Robert Kennedy (1925–68), US Attorney General, Senator, and John Kennedy's brother, was shot while campaigning for the US Presidential nomination.

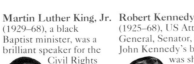

THE CULTURAL REVOLUTION IN CHINA

In China, Mao Tse-tung began his own social revolution. From 1966 to 1977, he brought industry and agriculture under state control. He closed schools and colleges and forced teachers and students to work on the land. Any opposition was brutally put down by the Red Guards, or Communist Party police.

Children recite phrases from the Red Book during the Cultural Revolution.

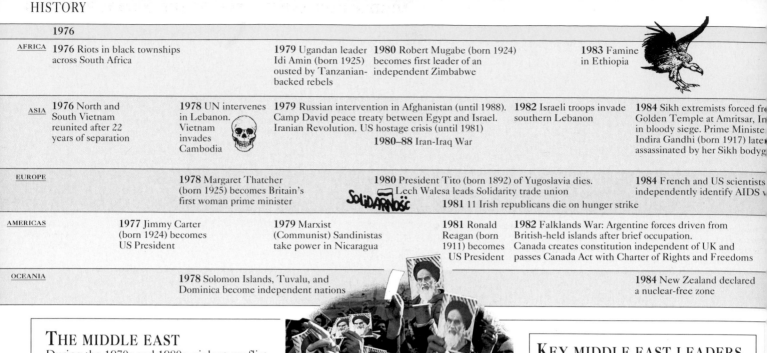

AFRICA **1976** Riots in black townships across South Africa

1979 Ugandan leader Idi Amin (born 1925) ousted by Tanzanian-backed rebels

1980 Robert Mugabe (born 1924) becomes first leader of an independent Zimbabwe

1983 Famine in Ethiopia

ASIA **1976** North and South Vietnam reunited after 22 years of separation

1978 UN intervenes in Lebanon. Vietnam invades Cambodia

1979 Russian intervention in Afghanistan (until 1988). Camp David peace treaty between Egypt and Israel. Iranian Revolution. US hostage crisis (until 1981)

1980–88 Iran-Iraq War

1982 Israeli troops invade southern Lebanon

1984 Sikh extremists forced fr[om] Golden Temple at Amritsar, In[dia] in bloody siege. Prime Ministe[r] Indira Gandhi (born 1917) late[r] assassinated by her Sikh bodyg[uard]

EUROPE **1978** Margaret Thatcher (born 1925) becomes Britain's first woman prime minister

SOLIDARNOŚĆ Lech Walesa leads Solidarity trade union

1980 President Tito (born 1892) of Yugoslavia dies.

1981 11 Irish republicans die on hunger strike

1984 French and US scientists independently identify AIDS v[irus]

AMERICAS **1977** Jimmy Carter (born 1924) becomes US President

1979 Marxist (Communist) Sandinistas take power in Nicaragua

1981 Ronald Reagan (born 1911) becomes US President

1982 Falklands War: Argentine forces driven from British-held islands after brief occupation. Canada creates constitution independent of UK and passes Canada Act with Charter of Rights and Freedoms

OCEANIA **1978** Solomon Islands, Tuvalu, and Dominica become independent nations

1984 New Zealand declared a nuclear-free zone

THE MIDDLE EAST

During the 1970s and 1980s, violent conflict continued to break out in the Middle East. The main causes of war and unrest were religious differences and territorial disputes. Oil brought great wealth to the region.

Oil fields in Libya

PLO members

Iranian supporters of the Ayatollah Khomeini

IRANIAN REVOLUTION

In 1979, a revolution overthrew the Shah (King) of Iran and brought the Ayatollah Khomeini to power. The Ayatollah, a fundamentalist (strict) Muslim, was hostile to the West. When the Shah entered the US, Iranian students stormed the US embassy in Tehran and held 53 Americans hostage for more than a year.

OIL

In 1973, Arab states raised their oil prices, causing economic disaster in many countries that depended on their oil. In 1990, Saddam Hussein, the Iraqi leader, invaded oil-rich Kuwait. He was expelled by a United Nations coalition force.

PLO AND ISRAEL

The Palestine Liberation Organization (PLO) represents Palestinians living in exile or under Israeli rule. It was responsible for bombings, hijackings, and attacks on Israelis. In 1993, the PLO and Israel agreed to make peace. A year later, PLO leader Yasir Arafat returned from exile in Tunis and Palestinians in the Gaza Strip became self-governing.

KEY MIDDLE EAST LEADERS

Anwar Sadat (1918–81), president of Egypt from 1970, unsuccessfully invaded Israeli-held territory in 1973. He signed first major Arab peace treaty with Israel and was assassinated by Muslim fundamentalists.

Saddam Hussein (born 1937), president of Iraq since coup in 1968, put down opposition using secret police, warred with Iran (1980–88), and unsuccessfully invaded Kuwait in 1990.

Muammar Qaddafi (born 1942), leader of Libya since coup in 1969, made Libya strictly Muslim, nationalized the oil industry, promoted Arab unity, and funded terrorist groups worldwide.

Ayatollah Khomeini (1900–89), political and religious leader of Iran after revolution of 1979, declared Iran a strictly Islamic republic.

Yasir Arafat (born 1929), leader of Palestinians-in-exile and chairman of PLO from 1968, eventually secured Palestinian independence from Israel in the Gaza Strip in 1993.

KEY CONFLICTS OF THE MIDDLE EAST

Region/conflict	Year	Details
Mecca, Saudi Arabia	1979	Muslim extremists seize Grand Mosque. Saudis recapture it after bloody battle
Iran–Iraq War	1980–88	War begins when Iraqi forces attack the world's largest oil refinery at Abadan, Iran. Iraq gains minimal territory. More than a million lives are lost
Lebanon	1982	Israel invades Lebanon, destroys PLO power base, and forces PLO to evacuate
West Bank, Gaza Strip (see p.340)	1987–8	Intifada (Palestinian uprising) leads to rioting and unrest in Israeli-held territories. Severely suppressed by Israeli military: 300 killed, thousands wounded
Gulf War	1990–91	Iraq invades oil-rich Kuwait. US-led UN forces expel Sadam Hussein's troops

KEY INNOVATIONS

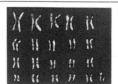

TESTTUBE BABY
In 1978, the first human conceived outside the mother's body – an English girl named Lesley Brown – was born.

VIDEO RECORDER
In 1975, the first home videotape system – the *Betamax* system – was launched by the Japanese company Sony.

PERSONAL COMPUTER
In 1981, the American company IBM produced the first desktop computer, the IBM-PC.

GENOME PROJECT
Since 1991, scientists have been trying to map all the genetic material in human chromosomes – the human genome.

RISE OF ASIAN ECONOMIES

Since the 1960s, the economies of many East Asian countries have expanded and prospered. With stable governments, advanced factories, and plentiful, cheap labor, living standards have risen dramatically in Japan, Hong Kong, Singapore, South Korea, and Taiwan.

Japanese executives at a business training camp

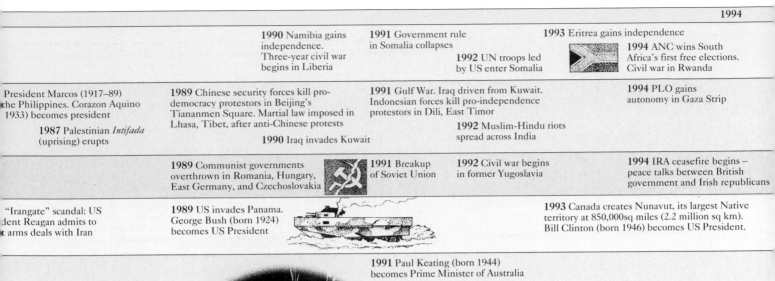

1990 Namibia gains independence. Three-year civil war begins in Liberia

1991 Government rule in Somalia collapses

1992 UN troops led by US enter Somalia

1993 Eritrea gains independence

1994 ANC wins South Africa's first free elections. Civil war in Rwanda

President Marcos (1917–89) the Philippines. Corazon Aquino 1933) becomes president

1987 Palestinian *Intifada* (uprising) erupts

1989 Chinese security forces kill pro-democracy protestors in Beijing's Tiananmen Square. Martial law imposed in Lhasa, Tibet, after anti-Chinese protests

1990 Iraq invades Kuwait

1991 Gulf War. Iraq driven from Kuwait. Indonesian forces kill pro-independence protestors in Dili, East Timor

1992 Muslim-Hindu riots spread across India

1994 PLO gains autonomy in Gaza Strip

1989 Communist governments overthrown in Romania, Hungary, East Germany, and Czechoslovakia

1991 Breakup of Soviet Union

1992 Civil war begins in former Yugoslavia

1994 IRA ceasefire begins – peace talks between British government and Irish republicans

"Irangate" scandal: US dent Reagan admits to arms deals with Iran

1989 US invades Panama. George Bush (born 1924) becomes US President

1993 Canada creates Nunavut, its largest Native territory at 850,000sq miles (2.2 million sq km). Bill Clinton (born 1946) becomes US President.

1991 Paul Keating (born 1944) becomes Prime Minister of Australia

THE COLD WAR ENDS
Communist leader Mikhail Gorbachev launched a new era of freedom in the USSR. The failure of his economic plans made him and his party unpopular, and in 1991 democrat Boris Yeltsin gained power in the country's first free elections.

GLASNOST AND PERESTROIKA
When Mikhail Gorbachev came to power, he pressed for economic reform. His policy of *glasnost* (openness) revealed how weak the Soviet Union had become, but his *perestroika* (remodeling) policy failed to solve his country's problems.

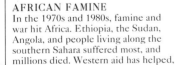

Food lines in Soviet Russia

THAWING OF THE COLD WAR
Relations between the superpowers – the US and USSR – improved greatly after Gorbachev came to power. In 1987, Gorbachev and US President Ronald Reagan agreed to reduce the number of nuclear weapons in their countries.

Gorbachev and Reagan meet.

Anticommunists remove statue of Felix Dzerzhinsky, founder of USSR's secret service.

AUGUST COUP
In August 1991, a powerful group of Communists who wished to halt the progress of reform took Gorbachev prisoner and, with the support of the army, seized power. The radical reformer Boris Yeltsin and the people of Moscow gathered in defiance around the Russian Parliament building, and the coup soon failed. A few days later, Yeltsin and Gorbachev banned the Communist party. Communist rule in the Soviet Union was over.

SOVIET SPLIT
The USSR was home to more than 140 different national groups. When Communism weakened, many of these called for, and were given, self-rule. On December 21, 1991, the Soviet Union ceased to exist.

THE FALL OF COMMUNISM
Glasnost encouraged open demands for independence from republics and allies of the USSR. When economic hardship caused unrest in some of these states, Gorbachev was unwilling to intervene using force. In December 1989, the Berlin Wall came down. Within two years, people in the USSR's allied states had toppled their Communist leaders.

Yeltsin outside Russian Parliament during 1991 coup.

GLOBAL AWARENESS
Today, aided by campaigning environmental groups, people have become more aware of the terrible damage inflicted on the Earth by industrial pollution, overuse of natural resources, overpopulation, and widespread deforestation.

Hole in ozone layer

False-color satellite image of Earth's atmosphere above South Pole

ENVIRONMENTAL FACTS
• In 1987, 33 countries agreed to phase out the use of CFCs, the industrial gases responsible for damage to the ozone layer.

• In 1984, the leakage of poisonous gas from an American-owned pesticide company caused the death of more than 2,500 people in Bhopal, India.

• In 1986, the world's worst nuclear accident occurred at Chernobyl, Ukraine. Clouds of radiation spread over Europe and beyond.

• In 1992, the Earth Summit in Rio de Janeiro, Brazil, brought together representatives from more than 170 countries to discuss global environmental issues.

AFRICAN FAMINE
In the 1970s and 1980s, famine and war hit Africa. Ethiopia, the Sudan, Angola, and people living along the southern Sahara suffered most, and millions died. Western aid has helped, but has not cured, these countries' problems.

Live Aid benefit concert for African famine

KEY PEOPLE

Name	Dates	Biographical details
Nelson Mandela	born 1918	Leader of ANC, jailed for 26 years elected president in South Africa's first free elections (1994)
Margaret Thatcher	born 1925	Britain's first woman prime minister, developed a rigid (strict) style of politics called Thatcherism
Mikhail Gorbachev	born 1931	Reformist Soviet leader, initiated nuclear disarmament, and presided over end of Cold War
Boris Yeltsin	born 1931	First elected president of Russian Federation
Lech Walesa	born 1943	Polish trade union leader, led anticommunist Solidarity movement. Elected president in 1990

WAR IN FORMER YUGOSLAVIA
Following the collapse of Communism, Yugoslavia split into different states. Different national identities and religious divisions sparked off a bloody war that has continued, despite international peace efforts, since 1992.

Woman in Sarajevo mourns child, shot by sniper.

GREAT CIVILIZATIONS

7000–1580 B.C.
Jericho
Region Jordan
Major cities Jericho
Features of civilization First true urban settlement; fortifications (including ramps); plastered skulls

1600–1027 B.C.
Shang China
Region China
Major cities Zhengzhou, Anyang
Features of civilization Ideographic script; development of bronze casting; bone oracles

c.3400 B.C.
Sumerian
Region Lower Mesopotamia
Major cities Ur, Eridu, Lagash, Uruk
Features of civilization Early cities; advances in architecture (ziggurats), and sculpture; invention of writing (cuneiform); legal codes; money economy; division of labor

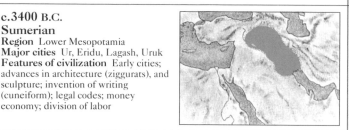

c.1500–1300 B.C.
Mycenean
Region Mainland southern Greece, Crete
Major cities Mycenae, Tiryns, Pylos
Features of civilization Architecture (fortified cities, megaron houses, and tholos tombs); ivory, gold, and bronzework; linear B script

3050–322 B.C.
Egyptian
Region Nile Valley
Major cities Saqqara, Giza, Luxor, Thebes
Features of civilization Stone building; hieroglyphic writing (also demotic and hieratic writing); funerary art; sailing boats; agriculture

1027–256 B.C.
Chou China
Region China (for some time divided into eastern and western sections)
Major cities Loyang
Features of civilization Jadework and cast ironworking; composite bow; Confucianism, Taoism

c.2500–1400 B.C.
Minoan
Region Crete
Major cities Knossos, Mallia, Phaistos
Features of civilization Palace architecture and interior decoration; linear scripts; decorated pottery; bronzework and goldwork

c.1000–574 B.C.
Phoenician
Region Coastal plane of Lebanon and Syria; then trading posts or colonies around Mediterranean
Major cities Tyre, Sidon, Byblos, Carthage
Features of civilization Ships and trading; purple dye from murex shells; alphabet

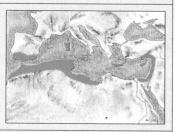

c.2600–2000 B.C.
Indus
Region Indus Valley, Pakistan
Major cities Mohenjo-daro, Harappa
Features of civilization Town planning (grid plans and drains, granaries); seal stones with indecipherable script; copper-bronze technology; standardized weights and measures

1000–600 B.C.
Olmec
Region Mexico
Major cities San Lorenzo, Tenochtitlán
Features of civilization Stone carvings (masks); jade carvings

c.1750–1200 B.C.
Hittite
Region Anatolia (Turkey), and outposts in northern Syria
Major cities Boghazköy
Features of civilization Fortifications; iron smelting; use of chariot in warfare

c.1000–200 B.C.
Chavin
Region Peru, Andes
Major cities Chavin de Huantár
Features of civilization Pottery; metalwork; sculpture (human and jaguar heads)

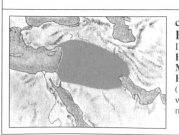

c.1792–c.1595 B.C.
Babylonian
Later Neo-Babylonian, 626–539 B.C.
Region Mesopotamia
Major cities Babylon
Features of civilization Fortifications (Ishtar Gate and great fortified city walls); astronomy and mathematics; law-making; famous for "Hanging Gardens"

c.900–100 B.C.
Etruscan
Region Northern Italy
Major cities Populonia, Tarquinia, Caere (modern Tuscany)
Features of civilization Bronzeworking; sculpture

883–612 B.C. (at height)
Assyrian
Region Mesopotamia, Iran, Turkey, Syria
Major cities Assur, Nineveh, Nimrud, Khorsabad
Features of civilization Palace and temple complexes; sculpture, especially carved reliefs; military conquests

A.D. 330–1453
Byzantine
Region Eastern Roman Empire
Major cities Constantinople
Features of civilization Mosaic art and wall-painting; jewelry and metalwork; fortifications; legal codes; philosophy; history; literature

750 B.C.–A.D. 350
Meroë
Region Sudan (Nubia)
Major cities Meroë
Features of civilization Ironworking; trade in gold, ivory, and raw materials; temple architecture

A.D. 600–794
Nara
Region Japan
Major cities Nara
Features of civilization Buddhist culture including pagoda-type temples

c.800–300 B.C.
Classical Greek
Region Greece, Aegean Sea
Major cities Athens, Sparta, Delphi
Features of civilization Classical architecture; flourishing of literature (drama, poetry, philosophy, history); pottery (vase painting), and sculpture; politics (democracy)

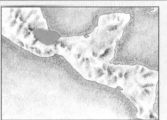

A.D. 900–1168
Toltec
Region Central Mexico
Major cities Tula, Chichen Itza
Features of civilization Continuation of Maya culture; use of metals

509 B.C.–A.D. 410
Roman
Region Mediterranean, Middle East, Italy, Spain, France, Britain
Major cities Rome
Features of civilization Building and civil engineering using vaults, arches, concrete (temples, walls, roads, aqueducts, ampitheaters); military organization and technology

A.D. c. 900–1400
Khmer
Region Cambodia
Major cities Angkor
Features of civilization Temple architecture; relief sculpture; agricultural irrigation program

221–206 B.C.
Ch'in China
Region China
Major cities Hsienyang, Loyang, Chiuyuan, Lingling
Features of civilization Great Wall; imperial tombs; standardization of script, weights and measures, and currency; unification of China

A.D. 1100–1350
Ife
Region Southwest Nigeria
Major cities Ife
Features of civilization Sculpture (human heads) in terra-cotta, or cast in copper or brass

321–187 B.C.
Mauryan
Region India
Major cities Pataliputra (Patna), Sanchi
Features of civilization Adoption of Buddhism, stupas; road network; unification of India

A.D. 1200–1572
Inca
Region Peru
Major cities Cuzco, Machu Picchu
Features of civilization Stone building: roads, palaces, fortifications, and temples; quipus (form of writing using knots); textiles

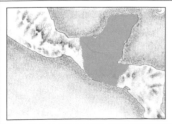

A.D. 300–900
Maya (Classic)
Region Mexico, Guatemala
Major cities Tikal, Copan, Chichen Itza
Features of civilization Pictorial writing; astronomy, mathematics, and calendar system; stone temples on stepped pyramids; decorative art

A.D. 1345–1521
Aztec
Region Mexico
Major cities Tenochtitlán
Features of civilization Jewelry and featherwork; codex-form books; military organization; religious architecture

RULERS AND LEADERS

EGYPTIAN PERIODS AND DYNASTIES

Period	Dynasty	Dates	Main pharaohs
Early dynastic	1-2	c.3100–c.2686 B.C.	Narmer (Menes)
Old Kingdom	3-6	c.2686–c.2160 B.C.	Zoser
			Khufu
First Intermediate Period	7-10	c.2160–c.2130 B.C.	
Middle Kingdom	11-12	c.2130–c.1786 B.C.	Mentuhotep II
Second Intermediate Period	13-17	c:1786–c.1550 B.C.	Hyksos rule
New Kingdom	18-20	c.1550–c.1050 B.C.	Amenhotep I
			Queen Hatshepsut
			Thutmose III
			Akhenaton
			Tutankhamun
			Rameses II
Third Intermediate Period	21-25	c.1085–667 B.C.	Nubian rule
Late Period	26-31	c.664–333 B.C.	Darius III
Foreign rulers		333–30 B.C.	Alexander the Great
			Ptolemy I Soter
			Queen Cleopatra VII

(Note: Hatshepsut and Cleopatra strictly queen regents)

ANCIENT EMPIRES FACTS

• Under the Roman Emperor Augustus, the empire, arts, and literature flourished, and the era was called the Golden Age. Augustus came to be regarded as a god, and from then on all successful emperors were worshiped as gods after their deaths.

• The Roman Emperor Caligula was thought to have had his father, mother, and two elder brothers murdered in order to become emperor. Nero had his mother and his first wife murdered. Both emperors were so hated that their reigns were erased from the official Roman records.

• China got its name in the 3rd century B.C. It comes from the ruling name of the first emperor, Ch'in Shi Huangti (221–202 B.C.).

• When the daughter of the T'ang dynasty Emperor Yizong fell ill, twenty leading doctors were called to the capital to cure her. All failed, and all were beheaded.

• The Egyptian Emperor Rameses II (c.1250–1213 B.C.) was a captain in the army and had his own harem by the time he was ten years old. By the end of his reign, at the age of 90, he had fathered 111 sons and 67 daughters.

CHINESE DYNASTIES AND REPUBLICS

Dynasty	Dates	Main rulers
Hsia	c.2200–c.1600 B.C.	
Shang	c.1600–c.1027 B.C.	Wu-ting
Chou	c.1027–c.256 B.C.	Wen-wang
Qin (Ch'in)	221–206 B.C.	Ch'in Shih huang-ti
Early Han	206 B.C.–A.D. 9	Wu-ti
Hsin	A.D. 9–25	Wang Mang
Later Han	25–220	Kuang-wuti
Three Kingdoms	220–265	
Western Chin	265–317	Liu Yüan
Eastern Chin	317–420	
Southern	420–589	Wu-ti
Sui	581–618	Wen-ti
T'ang	618–690	T'ai-tsung
Chou	690–705	Wu-hou
T'ang	705–907	Hsüan-tsung
Northern Five, Southern Ten	907–960	
Song (Sung)	960–1279	T'ai-tsu
Yuan (Mongol)	1279–1368	Kublai Khan
Ming	1368–1644	Ch'eng Tsu
Qing (Manchu)	1644–1911	Ch'ien-lung
Republic (Nationalist)	1911–1949	Sun Yat-sen, Chiang Kai-shek
People's Republic (Communist)	1949–	Mao Tse-Tung

Emperor Wu-ti

KEY ROMAN RULERS

ROMAN REPUBLIC

Ruler	Reign
Lucius Cornelius Sulla	82–78 B.C.
Pompey, Crassus, Caesar (First Triumvirate)	60–53 B.C.
Pompey	52–47 B.C.
Julius Caesar	46–44 B.C.
Mark Antony, Octavian, Lepidus (Second Triumvirate)	43–31 B.C.

ROMAN EMPIRE

Emperor	Reign
Augustus (Octavian)	27 B.C.–A.D. 14
Tiberius	14–37
Caligula	37–41
Claudius	41–54
Nero	54–68
Vespasian	69–79
Titus	79–81
Domitian	81–96
Trajan	98–117
Hadrian	117–138
Antoninus Pius	138–161
Marcus Aurelius	161–180
Commodus	180–192
Septimius Severus	193–211
Alexander Severus	222–235
Valerian	253–259
Diocletian (in the east)	284–305
Maximian (in the west)	286–305
Constantine the Great	311–337
Valentinian I (west)	364–375
Valens (east)	364–378
Theodosius the Great (east; and, after 394, west)	379–395
Honorius (west)	395–423
Theodosius II (east)	408–450
Valentinian III (west)	425–455
Zeno (east)	474–491
Romulus Augustulus (west)	475–476

JAPANESE PERIODS

Periods	Dates
Yamato	250–710
Nara	710–794
Heian	794–1192
Kamakura	1192–1333
Muromachi	1333–1573
Momoyama	1573–1603
Edo	1603–1867
Meiji	1867–1912
Taisho	1912–1926
Showa	1926–1989
Heisei	1989–

• Few Japanese emperors have wielded true power. Aristocrats and, later, military dictatorship, or shogunates, ruled in the emperor's name. The last shoguns were the Tokugawa clan, a clan that held power throughout the Edo Period.

• The Japanese people saw their emperors as gods. After Japan's defeat in World War II, Emperor Hirohito (Showa) renounced his divinity.

KEY HOLY ROMAN EMPERORS

Emperor	Reign
Charlemagne	800–814
Otto I, the Great	936–973
Henry IV	1056–1106
Frederick I, Barbarossa	1152–90
Frederick II	1212–50
Rudolf I	1273–92
Adolf of Nassau	1292–98
Albert I, King of Germany	1298–1308
Albert II	1437–39
Frederick III	1440–93
Maximilian I	1493–1519
Charles V (Charles I of Spain)	1519–56
Ferdinand I	1556–64
Maximilian II	1564–76
Rudolf II	1576–1612
Matthias	1612–19
Ferdinand II	1619–37
Ferdinand III	1637–57
Leopold I	1658–1705
Joseph I	1705–11
Charles VI	1711–40
(War of Austrian Succession	1740–48)
Charles VII of Bavaria	1742–45
Francis I of Lorraine	1745–65
Joseph II	1765–90
Leopold II	1790–92
Francis II	1792–1806
(Last Holy Roman Emperor)	

• From 1437 to 1806, all the Holy Roman Emperors came from the Habsburg dynasty.

RUSSIAN RULERS

Czars and Czarinas	Reign
Ivan III, the Great	1462–1505
Basil III	1505–33
Ivan IV, the Terrible	1533–84
Fyodor I	1584–98
Boris Godunov	1598–1605
Fyodor II	1605
Demetrius	1605–06
Basil (IV) Shuiski	1606–10
Interregnum	1610–13
Michael Romanov	1613–45
Alexis	1645–76
Fyodor III	1676–82
Ivan V and Peter the Great	1682–89
Peter I	1689–1725
Catherine I	1725–27
Peter II	1727–30
Anna	1730–40
Ivan VI	1740–41
Elizabeth	1741–1762
Peter III	1762
Catherine II, the Great	1762–96
Paul I	1796–1801
Alexander I	1801–25
Nicholas I	1825–55
Alexander II	1855–81
Alexander III	1881–94
Nicholas II	1894–1917

KEY POPES

Pope	Reign
St. Peter	c.42–67
St. Clement I	c.88–97
St. Stephen I	254–257
St. Leo I, the Great	440–461
St. Gregory I, the Great	590–604
St. Leo IX	1049–54
St. Gregory VII	1073–85
Urban II	1088–99
Innocent III	1198–1216
Alexander VI	1492–1503
Paul III	1534–49
Gregory XIII	1572–85
Pius IX	1846–78
John XXIII	1958–63
John Paul II	1978–

POPE FACTS

• The pope is the chief bishop of the Roman Catholic Church. He is considered the successor to St. Peter, the first pope.

• New popes are elected by the College of Cardinals in the Vatican, Rome, at a secret meeting. The Cardinals may not leave the Vatican until a new pope has been chosen.

• There have been more than 30 antipopes, rivals to the officially elected popes.

• Pope John XXI served for 9 months, but was killed in 1277 when a ceiling collapsed on him.

• The shortest-serving pope was Urban VII, who reigned for just 12 days in 1590.

• The longest-serving pope, Pius IX, had 31 years in office and died at the age of 85.

FRENCH RULERS

Name	Reign	Name	Reign
Carolingians		Charles VII	1422–61
Louis IV	936–954	Louis XI	1461–83
Lothair	954–986	Charles VIII	1483–98
Louis V	986–987	Louis XII	1498–1515
		Francis I	1515–47
Capets		Henry II	1547–59
Hugh Capet	987–996	Francis II	1559–60
Robert II, the Pious	996–1031	Charles IX	1560–74
Henry I	1031–60	Henry III	1574–89
Philip I	1060–1108		
Louis VI	1108–37	**Bourbon**	
Louis VII	1137–80	Henry IV, of Navarre	1589–1610
Philip II	1180–1223	Louis XIII	1610–43
Louis VIII	1223–26	Louis XIV	1643–1715
Louis IX	1226–70	Louis XV	1715–74
Philip III	1270–85	Louis XVI	1774–93
Philip IV	1285–1314		
Louis X	1314–16	**First Republic and Empire**	
Philip V	1316–22	Napoleon Bonaparte	1799–1814
Charles IV	1322–28	(After 1804, as Emperor Napoleon I)	
Valois		**Restoration of monarchy**	
Philip VI	1328–50	Louis XVIII	1814–24
John II	1350–64	Charles X	1824–30
Charles V	1364–80	Louis Philippe	1830–48
Charles VI	1380–1422	**Second to Fifth Republics**	1848–

Francis I

SPANISH RULERS

Name	Reign	Name	Reign
Ferdinand II of Aragon	1479–1516	Ferdinand VII	1808
and Isabella I of Castille	1474–1504	(Joseph Bonaparte	1808–13)
Habsburgs		Ferdinand VII (2nd time)	1814–33
Charles I	1516–56	Isabella II	1833–68
Philip II	1556–98	Amadeus of Savoy	1870–73
Philip III	1598–1621	**First Republic**	1873–74
Philip IV	1621–65		
Charles II	1665–1700	**Bourbons (restored)**	
Bourbons		Alfonso XII	1874–85
Philip V (abdicated)	1700–24	Maria Cristina (Regent)	1885–86
Louis I	1724	Alfonso XIII	1886–1931
Philip V (restored)	1724–46	**Second Republic**	1931–39
Ferdinand VI	1746–59	Francisco Franco (Dictator)	1939–75
Charles III	1759–88	**Bourbons (restored)**	
Charles IV	1788–1808	Juan Carlos I	1975–

KINGS AND QUEENS OF GREAT BRITAIN

ENGLAND

Monarch	Reign
Saxons	
Egbert	827–839
Ethelwulf	839–858
Ethelbald	858–860
Ethelbert	860–865
Ethelred I	865–871
Alfred the Great	871–899
Edward the Elder	899–924
Athelstan	924–939
Edmund	939–946
Edred	946–955
Edwy	955–959
Edgar	959–975
Edward the Martyr	975–978
Ethelred II, the Unready	978–1016
Edmund Ironside	1016
Danes	
Canute	1016–35
Harold I Harefoot	1035–40
Hardicanute	1040–42
Saxons	
Edward the Confessor	1042–66
Harold II	1066
Normans	
William I, the Conqueror	1066–87
William II	1087–1100
Henry I	1100–35
Stephen	1135–54
Plantagenets	
Henry II	1154–89
Richard I	1189–99
John	1199–1216
Henry III	1216–72
Edward I	1272–1307
Edward II	1307–27
Edward III	1327–77
Richard II	1377–99
Lancaster	
Henry IV	1399–1413
Henry V	1413–22
Henry VI	1422–61

Alfred the Great

Monarch	Reign
York	
Edward IV	1461–83
Edward V	1483
Richard III	1483–85
Tudors	
Henry VII	1485–1509
Henry VIII	1509–47
Edward VI	1547–53
Mary I	1553–58
Elizabeth I	1558–1603

Henry VIII

BRITAIN

Monarch	Reign
Stuarts	
James I, VI of Scotland	1603–25
Charles I	1625–49
Commonwealth	1649–60
Stuarts (restoration)	
Charles II	1660–85
James II	1685–88
William III, jointly with	1689–1702
Mary II	1689–94
Anne	1702–14
House of Hanover	
George I	1714–27
George II	1727–60
George III	1760–1820
George IV	1820–30
William IV	1830–37
Victoria	1837–1901
House of Saxe-Coburg	
Edward VII	1901–10
House of Windsor	
George V	1910–36
Edward VIII	1936
George VI	1936–52
Elizabeth II	1952–

Elizabeth II

SCOTLAND

Monarch	Reign
Malcolm II	1005–34
Duncan I	1034–40
Macbeth	1040–57
Malcolm III Canmore	1058–93
Donald Bane	1093–94
Duncan II	1094
Donald Bane (restored)	1094–97
Edgar	1097–1107
Alexander I	1107–24
David I	1124–53
Malcolm IV	1153–65
William the Lion	1165–1214
Alexander II	1214–49
Alexander III	1249–86
Margaret of Norway	1286–90
Interregnum	1290–92
John Balliol	1292–96
Interregnum	1296–1306
Robert I, the Bruce	1306–29
David II	1329–71
Stuarts	
Robert II	1371–90
Robert III	1390–1406
James I	1406–37
James II	1437–60
James III	1460–88
James IV	1488–1513
James V	1513–42
Mary, Queen of Scots	1542–67
James VI, I of England	1567–1625

Mary, Queen of Scots

SAFE RAVEN

Legend has it that when ravens leave the Tower of London, the throne of England will fall. So, a family of ravens is kept at the tower with their wings clipped.

PRESIDENTS OF THE UNITED STATES

President	Term of office	President	Term of office	President	Term of office
George Washington	1789–97	Abraham Lincoln	1861–65	Herbert C. Hoover	1929–33
John Adams	1797–1801	Andrew Johnson	1865–69	Franklin D. Roosevelt	1933–45
Thomas Jefferson	1801–09	Ulysses S. Grant	1869–77	Harry S Truman	1945–53
James Madison	1809–17	Rutherford B. Hayes	1877–81	Dwight D. Eisenhower	1953–61
James Monroe	1817–25	James A. Garfield	Mar–Sept 1881	John F. Kennedy	1961–63
John Quincy Adams	1825–29	Chester A. Arthur	1881–85	Lyndon B. Johnson	1963–69
Andrew Jackson	1829–37	Grover S. Cleveland	1885–89	Richard M. Nixon	1969–74
Martin van Buren	1837–41	Benjamin Harrison	1889–93	Gerald R. Ford	1974–77
William H. Harrison	Mar–April 1841	Grover S. Cleveland	1893–97	James E. Carter	1977–81
John Tyler	1841–45	William McKinley	1897–1901	Ronald W. Reagan	1981–89
James K. Polk	1845–49	Theodore Roosevelt	1901–09	George Bush	1989–93
Zachary Taylor	1849–50	William H. Taft	1909–13	William J. Clinton	1993–
Millard Fillmore	1850–53	Woodrow Wilson	1913–21		
Franklin Pierce	1853–57	Warren G. Harding	1921–23		
James Buchanan	1857–61	Calvin Coolidge	1923–29		

F.D. Roosevelt

BRITISH PRIME MINISTERS

Prime Minister	Term of office	Prime Minister	Term of office
Sir Robert Walpole	1721–42	Earl Russell	1865–66
Earl of Wilmington	1742–43	Earl of Derby	1866–68
Henry Pelham	1743–54	Benjamin Disraeli	1868
Duke of Newcastle	1754–56	William Gladstone	1868–74
Duke of Devonshire	1756–57	Benjamin Disraeli	1874–80
Duke of Newcastle	1757–62	William Gladstone	1880–85
Earl of Bute	1762–63	Marquess of Salisbury	1885–86
George Grenville	1763–65	William Gladstone	1886
Marquess of Rockingham	1765–66	Marquess of Salisbury	1886–92
Earl of Chatham (Pitt the Elder)	1766–67	William Gladstone	1892–94
Duke of Grafton	1767–70	Earl of Rosebery	1894–95
Lord North	1770–82	Marquess of Salisbury	1895–1902
Marquess of Rockingham	1782	Arthur Balfour	1902–05
Earl of Shelburne	1782–1783	Sir Henry Campbell-Bannerman	1905–08
Duke of Portland	1783	Herbert Asquith	1908–16
William Pitt, the Younger	1783–1801	David Lloyd-George	1916–22
Henry Addington	1801–04	Andrew Bonar Law	1922–23
William Pitt	1804–06	Stanley Baldwin	1923–24
Lord Grenville	1806–07	James Ramsay-MacDonald	1924
Duke of Portland	1807–09	Stanley Baldwin	1924–29
Spencer Perceval	1809–12	James Ramsay-MacDonald	1929–35
Earl of Liverpool	1812–27	Stanley Baldwin	1935–37
George Canning	1827	Neville Chamberlain	1937–40
Viscount Goderich	1827–28	Winston Churchill	1940–45
Duke of Wellington	1828–30	Clement Attlee	1945–51
Earl Grey	1830–34	Sir Winston Churchill	1951–55
Viscount Melbourne	1834	Sir Anthony Eden	1955–57
Sir Robert Peel	1834–35	Harold Macmillan	1957–63
Viscount Melbourne	1835–41	Sir Alec Douglas-Home	1963–64
Sir Robert Peel	1841–46	Harold Wilson	1964–70
Lord John Russell	1846–52	Edward Heath	1970–74
Earl of Derby	1852	Harold Wilson	1974–76
Earl of Aberdeen	1852–55	James Callaghan	1976–79
Viscount Palmerston	1855–58	Margaret Thatcher	1979–90
Earl of Derby	1858–59	John Major	1990–
Viscount Palmerston	1859–65		

Robert Walpole

Pitt the Younger

Winston Churchill

AUSTRALIAN PRIME MINISTERS

Prime Minister	Term of office
Edmund Barton	1901–03
Alfred Deakin	1903–04
John C. Watson	1904
George Houston Reid	1904–05
Alfred Deakin	1905–08
Andrew Fisher	1908–09
Alfred Deakin	1909–10
Andrew Fisher	1910–13
Joseph Cook	1913–14
Andrew Fisher	1914–15
William M. Hughes	1915–23
Stanley M. Bruce	1923–29
James H. Scullin	1929–32
Joseph A. Lyons	1932–39
Robert Gordon Menzies	1939–41
Arthur William Fadden	1941
John Curtin	1941–45
Joseph Benedict Chifley	1945–49
Robert Gordon Menzies	1949–66
Harold Edward Holt	1966–67
John Grey Gorton	1968–71
William McMahon	1971–72
Edward Gough Whitlam	1972–75
John Malcolm Fraser	1975–83
Robert James Hawke	1983–91
Paul J. Keating	1991–

Stanley M. Bruce

CANADIAN PRIME MINISTERS

Prime Minister	Term of office
John MacDonald	1867–73
Alexander Mackenzie	1873–78
John MacDonald	1878–91
John Abott	1891–92
John Thompson	1892–94
Mackenzie Bowell	1894–96
Charles Tupper	1896
Wilfred Laurier	1896–1911
Robert L. Borden	1911–20
Arthur Meighen	1920–21
W.L. Mackenzie King	1921–26
Arthur Meighen	1926
W.L. Mackenzie King	1926–30
R.B. Bennett	1930–35
W.L. Mackenzie King	1935–48
Louis St Laurent	1948–57
John G. Diefenbaker	1957–63
Lester B. Pearson	1963–68
Pierre Elliott Trudeau	1968–79
Joe Clark	1979–80
Pierre Elliott Trudeau	1980–84
John Turner	1984
Brian Mulroney	1984–93
Kim Campbell	1993
Jean Chrétien	1993–

RUSSIAN LEADERS

General secretaries	Term of office
Vladimir Illich Lenin	1917–22
Joseph Stalin	1922–53
Nikita Krushchev	1953–64
Leonid Brezhnev	1964–82
Yuri Andropov	1982–84
Konstantin Chernenko	1984–85
Mikhail Gorbachev	1985–92
Russian presidents	
Boris Yeltsin	1992–

INDIAN PRIME MINISTERS

Prime Ministers	Term of office
Jawaharlal Nehru	1947–64
Lal Bahadur Shastri	1964–66
Indira Gandhi	1966–77
Morarji Desai	1977–79
Indira Gandhi	1980–84
Rajiv Gandhi	1984–89
V.P. Singh	1989–90
Chandra Shekhar	1990–91
P.V. Narasima Rao	1991–

Indira Gandhi

WORLD LEADER FACTS

• In 1803, Thomas Jefferson wanted to buy part of the French colony of Louisiana for the US and was prepared to pay up to $10 million. France, however, threatened by war in Europe, agreed to sell much more land. Jefferson was able to double the size of the US for just $15 million.

• William Pitt the Younger, prime minister of Britain at the end of the 18th century, took office at the very young age of 24.

• In 1809, George Canning, Britain's foreign minister, who later became prime minister, fought a duel with Lord Castlereagh, the war minister. Canning was wounded in the leg, and both Ministers resigned afterward.

• The White House, the US president's official home, is built from sandstone that is naturally gray. Only after it was burned in 1814 was it painted white to hide the resulting smoke stains.

READY TEDDY

Teddy bears get their name from US President Theodore "Teddy" Roosevelt, who, when on a hunting trip in Mississippi, refused to shoot a bear cub.

EXPLORERS

PEOPLE HAVE ALWAYS WANTED to travel to distant regions that are unknown to them, for various reasons. Trade, conquest, and settlement were common motives in the past; scientific research or sheer adventure often inspire today's explorers. Some explorers, such as the Polynesians who sailed across the Pacific Ocean, are little known to us, since they left no written records of their journeys.

NORTHERN PASSAGES
NORTHWEST PASSAGE (NWP)

1497 John Cabot, Italian, backed by British merchants, reached Newfoundland in Canada in search of NWP. He believed he had found Asia. A second voyage in 1498 ended in mystery, since Cabot was never seen again.

Cabot's men could scoop up cod from the Grand Banks.

1576 Martin Frobisher, British, reached Baffin Island in search of NWP. Found Frobisher Bay.

1610–11 Henry Hudson, British, backed by Dutch, reached Hudson Bay in search of NWP. Abandoned to die after his crew mutinied.

1845–47 John Franklin, British, died west of King William Island in search of NWP. Ship stuck in ice.

NORTHEAST PASSAGE (NEP)

1596–98 Willem Barents, Dutch, reached Kara Sea in search of NEP.

1878–79 Nils Nordenskjold, Norwegian, first explorer to complete the NEP. Also a scientific expedition.

NORTH ATLANTIC OCEAN AND NORTH AMERICA

c.330 B.C. Pytheas, Greek, sails into North Atlantic, around Britain and "Thule" (Iceland or Norway).

800–1100 Viking travelers (Leif Eriksson, Erik the Red) cross North Atlantic, starting settlements in Newfoundland and Greenland; they discover "Vinland" (modern US).

1527–28 Pánfilo de Narváez, Spanish, reached Florida.

1534–42 Jacques Cartier, French, sailed through the Gulf of St. Lawrence into the St. Lawrence River, in Canada. Huron Indian villages that he found became Quebec and Montreal.

1615–16 Samuel de Champlain, French, founder of French Canada, helped establish the fur trade.

NORTH AND CENTRAL AMERICA

1492–93 Christopher Columbus, Italian, backed by the Spanish, sailed the Atlantic to the West Indies and, on later voyages, the coasts of Central and South America. Columbus died believing that he had been the first European to find a westerly route to Asia, not the first European in Central America.

1519–21 Hernán Cortés, Spanish, captured Mexico for Spain. He conquered the massive Aztec empire of Mexico with the help of thousands of local rebels.

1528–36 Álvar Núñez Cabeza de Vaca, Spanish, traveled to Florida with Spanish *conquistador* (conqueror) Pánfilo de Narváez. Starvation, disease, and hostility killed most of the company. De Vaca was saved by Yaqui tribesmen and journeyed into Mexico.

1678–80 Robert Cavelier de la Salle, French, explored the Great Lakes and sailed down the Mississippi River to the Gulf of Mexico. In 1687, his expedition to find the Mississippi delta from the sea ended in failure and his death.

BURNING BOATS

When Cortés decided to invade the Aztec empire with a force of just 508 soldiers and 100 sailors, he burned his ships, so that his men would see victory or death.

1804–06 Meriwether Lewis and William Clark, Americans, were sent by US President Thomas Jefferson to search for a route to the Pacific Ocean from St. Louis. Their journeys took them along the Missouri, Yellowstone, and Columbia rivers by canoe, meeting with local peoples on the way.

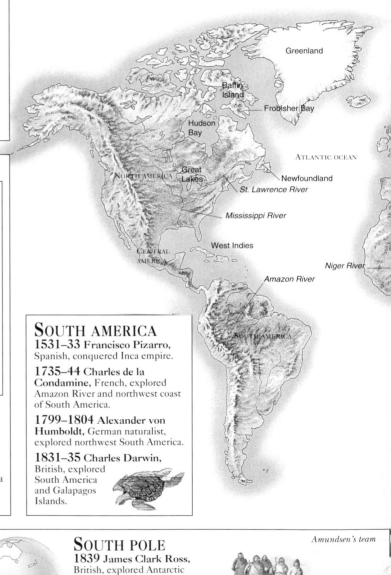

Greenland
Baffin Island
Frobisher Bay
Hudson Bay
ATLANTIC OCEAN
NORTH AMERICA
Great Lakes
Newfoundland
St. Lawrence River
Mississippi River
West Indies
CENTRAL AMERICA
Niger River
Amazon River
SOUTH AMERICA

SOUTH AMERICA

1531–33 Francisco Pizarro, Spanish, conquered Inca empire.

1735–44 Charles de la Condamine, French, explored Amazon River and northwest coast of South America.

1799–1804 Alexander von Humboldt, German naturalist, explored northwest South America.

1831–35 Charles Darwin, British, explored South America and Galapagos Islands.

CIRCUMNAVIGATIONS

1519–22 Ferdinand Magellan, Portuguese, set off to circumnavigate the globe. Just one of his 5 ships and 18 of his 260-man crew survived. In 1521, Magellan himself was killed by locals in the Philippines. Sebastián de Elcano took command.

1577–80 Francis Drake, English, circumnavigated the globe in the *Golden Hind*, plundering Spanish ships and lands on the way.

Ferdinand Magellan

SOUTH POLE

Antarctic region

1839 James Clark Ross, British, explored Antarctic coast and ice sheet in his ships *Erebus* and *Terror*.

1910–12 Roald Amundsen, Norwegian, was first to reach South Pole. He used sleds pulled by dogs.

1910–13 Robert Falcon Scott, British, was just beaten to Pole by Amundsen. He used both ponies and dogs, but difficult conditions killed all the animals. The four-man team died on the return journey.

Amundsen's team

NORTH POLE

1871 Charles Hall, American, made three expeditions, came close to North Pole. Died three weeks after third and last expedition.

1893–96 Fridtjof Nansen, Norwegian, attempted and failed to reach North Pole by ship and sled. Nansen was picked up by a British ship on Franz Joseph Land.

1908–09 Robert Peary, American, after last of eight expeditions, claimed to have reached Pole; there is still doubt about his claim.

Nansen's ship Fram *was designed to move with ice floes, without being crushed.*

EURASIA

138–116 B.C. Chang Ch'ien, Chinese, traveled westward across Asia to Samarkand and beyond, to find allies for emperor Wu-Ti.

Chang Ch'ien at the court of Wu-Ti

A.D. 399–414 Fa Hsien, Chinese, traveled across Asia on the Silk Road to Khotan, then down into India, before crossing the sea to Sri Lanka. He was a Buddhist monk, and wanted to learn more about the origins and texts of Buddhism.

629–649 Hsüan Tsang, Chinese, followed Fa Hsien's route to India, and traveled extensively there.

800–1100 Viking travelers and traders sailed along Dnieper and Volga Rivers, and reached Constantinople and Baghdad.

1260–71 Polo brothers Niccolo and Maffeo, and Niccolo's son Marco, from Venice, traveled across Asia to China. Marco stayed for 20 years, working for Kublai Khan.

1541–52 Francis Xavier, Spanish Jesuit, sailed to Japan. First European to visit Japan.

1602–07 Bento de Goes, Portuguese, joined Jesuits in India and went from Agra across Asia as far as Suchow.

1661–64 John Grueber and Albert d'Orville, German and Belgian, were the first Europeans to reach Lhasa, Tibet, from China.

1725–29 and 1734–41 Vitus Bering, Danish, appointed by Czar of Russia, crossed Asia by land before going out to find out whether Russia and America were joined.

AUSTRALIA

1828–30 and 1844–45 Charles Sturt, British, mapped Murray and Darling Rivers, then explored central Australia.

1840–41 Edward Eyre, British, found land route along south coast from Adelaide to Albany.

1860–61 Robert Burke, William Wills, Irish and English, make south–north journey across Australia from Melbourne.

1861–62 John Stuart, Scottish, crossed Australia from Adelaide to Darwin (south to north).

Burke and Wills, who died on their return journey to Melbourne

PACIFIC

1567–1607 Mendaña, Quirós, Torres, Spanish, made various voyages across Pacific from South America past Pacific islands and, on one journey, as far as Manila.

1642–43 Abel Janszoon Tasman, Dutch, sailed from Mauritius to Tasmania, New Zealand, Fiji, New Guinea, Java.

1766–69 Louis Bougainville, French, sailed from Falklands, across Pacific to Great Barrier Reef, then to New Guinea and Java.

1768–79 James Cook, British, made three voyages around Pacific, visiting New Zealand and Australia. Extensive mapping of southern Pacific and its islands.

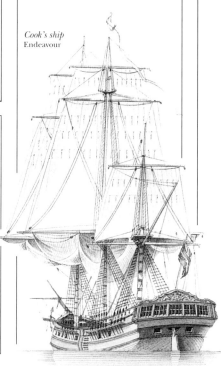

Cook's ship Endeavour

AFRICA

c.1500 B.C. Queen Hatshepsut, Egyptian, sent explorers to the land of Punt (possibly East Africa).

c.500 B.C. Hanno, Phoenician, sailed from Carthage, down the West African coast, and up the Senegal River, looking for sites for Phoenician colonies.

1324–53 Ibn Battuta, from Tangier, North Africa, traveled through Sahara to Mali and Timbuktu, also traveled extensively in Middle East and Arabia.

1795–97, 1805–06 Mungo Park, Scottish, reached Niger River in West Africa, later followed it upstream.

1827–28 René Caillié, French, traveled from West Africa across Sahara to Tangier. First European in Timbuktu.

Livingstone on the Zambezi River, Africa

1841–73 David Livingstone, Scottish, four expeditions, crossed southern Africa and traveled south to Cape Town and Port Elizabeth.

1844–45, 1850–55 Heinrich Barth, German, traveled across Sahara and in West Africa.

1857–63 Richard Burton and John Hanning Speke, British, made three expeditions to Africa.

1871–89 Henry Morton Stanley, American, made three expeditions, across Africa and up Congo River.

SOUTH ATLANTIC OCEAN AND AFRICA

1485–86 Diogo Cão, Portuguese, first of the professional explorers, sailed down the West African coast as far as Cape Cross.

1487–88 Bartolemeu Días, Portuguese, sailed down the West African coast, past the southernmost point, the Cape of Good Hope. He then entered the Indian Ocean, before turning back.

1497–98 Vasco da Gama, Portuguese, sailed down the West African coast, around the Cape of Good Hope, up the East African coast and across the Indian Ocean to Calicut, India. He was the first European to reach India by sea.

BATTLES AND WARS

MAJOR WARS

B.C. **c.3100**	First recorded war in history, between Upper and Lower Egypt. Pharaoh Narmer (Menes) unified Egypt.
c.1600–600	Continual warring between the three great powers of the Middle East: Egypt, Babylon, and Assyria.
c.1200 **Trojan War**	Legendary war between Greeks and Trojans, described in Homer's *Iliad*. However, legend was probably based on a real war between Greeks and people of Troy.
490–479 **Persian Wars**	Fought between Persia and anti-Persian alliance of Sparta and Athens. Persia ultimately defeated.
431–404 **Peloponnesian War**	Fought between Athens and Sparta, two long-standing rivals. Sparta was the land power, Athens the sea power. Sparta was victorious.
264–146 **Punic Wars**	Prolonged struggle between Rome and Carthage. Ended in Rome's victory and total destruction of Carthage.
A.D. **c.1096–1291** **Crusades**	Series of warring pilgrimages undertaken by European Christians to recapture Jerusalem from Turkish Muslims. In 1099, Crusaders captured Jerusalem but in 1187 Saladin recaptured the city. In 1291 the Crusaders were finally thrown out.
1137–1453 **Hundred Years War**	Irregular succession of wars between France and England. Ended in victory for France.
1455–85 **Wars of the Roses**	English war between Houses of Lancaster and York. House of Lancaster was victorious.
1618–48 **Thirty Years War**	Complex European war fought mainly on German soil. Began as a struggle of German Protestants against Habsburgs, Catholics, and the Holy Roman Empire. War gradually involved most European powers, and ended with Protestant victory.
1642–49 **English Civil War**	Fought between Parliament (Roundheads) and Royalists (Cavaliers). Parliament victorious. War ended with execution of King Charles I. Monarchy later restored.
1700–21 **Great Northern War**	Fought between Russia and Sweden. Sweden defeated.
1701–13 **War of the Spanish Succession**	Struggle between France and Austria over who was to rule Spain. France defeated.
1756–63 **Seven Years War**	Fought between Austria, France, Russia, and Sweden on one side; Britain, Hanover, and Prussia on the other. Britain and the German states victorious.
1775–83 **American Revolution**	Fought between British-ruled American colonies and Britain. Colonies gained independence and formed United States of America.
1792–1815 **Napoleonic Wars**	Fought between France and an alliance between Austria, Britain, Russia, Prussia, and Sweden. France defeated.
1812–14 **War of 1812**	Fought between United States and Britain. US victorious.
1821–29 **Greek War of Independence**	Greece fought for and gained independence from Turkey.
1839–42 **First Opium War**	Trade war between Britain and China. China forced to open trade ports to western countries.
1846–48 **Mexican-American War**	Fought between US and Mexico. Mexico was defeated.
1853–56 **Crimean War**	Britain, France, Sardinia, and Turkey fought against Russia, and won.
1861–65 **American Civil War**	Fought between Union (northern states) and Confederacy (southern states). Union victorious. First war to be photographed extensively.
1866 **Austro-Prussian War**	Fought between Austria and Prussia. Austria defeated.
1870–71 **Franco-Prussian War**	Prussia and other German states fought France, and won.
1894–95 **Chinese-Japanese War**	Fought between China and Japan. Japan victorious.
1898–99 **Spanish-American War**	Fought between US and Spain. US victorious.
1899–1902 **Second Boer War**	Britain and Commonwealth countries fought Boers and won control of South Africa.
1904–05 **Russo-Japanese War**	Fought between Russia and Japan. Japan victorious.
1914–18 **World War I (The Great War)**	Fought between Germany, Austria-Hungary, and Turkey on one side; British Commonwealth, Belgium, France, Italy, Russia, and US on the other. Germany defeated.
1918–21 **Russian Civil War**	Fought between Reds (Bolsheviks) and anti-Communists, known as Whites. Bolsheviks victorious.
1931–1933 **Chinese-Japanese War**	Fought between Japan and China. Japan victorious.
1936–39 **Spanish Civil War**	Anarchist uprising that became a struggle between Nationalists (Fascists) and Republicans. Nationalists won.
1937–45 **Chinese-Japanese War**	Fought between China and Japan. China victorious.
1939–45 **World War II**	Global conflict involving every major world power. Fought between Axis powers of Nazi Germany, Italy, and Japan on one side; Allied powers of British Commonwealth, USSR, and US on the other. Germany and the Axis powers defeated. US and USSR emerged as world's "superpowers."

1950–53 Korean War	Fought between North (Communist) Korea and South Korea (aided by US and allies). North Korea defeated.	1971 Pakistan Civil War	Fought between Bangladesh (east Pakistan) and west Pakistan. Bangladesh victorious.
1965–75 Vietnam War	Fought between North (Communist) Vietnam and South Vietnam (aided by US and allies). US withdrew in 1973. In 1975, North Vietnam won the war.	1973 October War	Arabs and Israelis fought. United Nations (UN) called a ceasefire.
1967 Six-Day War	Fought between Israel and Arab forces led by Egypt. Israel won.	1980–88 Iran-Iraq War	Iran and Iraq fought. Ceasefire was negotiated.
1967–70 Nigerian Civil War	Fought between Biafra and Federal Government. Biafra was defeated.	1991 Gulf War	Iraq fought UN forces, headed by US. Iraq defeated.
1968– Civil War, Northern Ireland	Prolonged conflict between Protestants and Catholics. Peace talks begin, 1994.	1991– Civil War, former Yugoslavia	Prolonged ethnic, territorial, and religious conflict between Serbian, Croatian, and Muslim forces, fought in former Yugoslavia.

MAJOR BATTLES

B.C. 490 Marathon (Greece)	10,000 Athenians and allies defeated 50,000 Persian troops. After battle, Pheidippides, a runner, ran to Athens to report victory. Exhausted, he delivered message and died. The modern marathon is named after his achievement.	732 Tours (France)	The Franks, led by Charles Martel, defeated Muslim invaders from Spain, securing Western European independence.
480 Salamis (Greece)	Combined Greek fleet, led by Athenian Themistocles and Spartan Eurybiades, defeated larger invading Persian fleet under King Xerxes. Secured Greek independence in the Mediterranean.	1260 Ain Jalut (Palestine)	Muslim general Kutuz defeated combined Mongol and Christian mounted forces. First major victory against massive Mongol empire, also ended Crusaders' hopes of recovering Holy Land.
415–413 Siege of Syracuse (Sicily)	40,000-strong Athenian force massacred in failed invasion of Syracuse. Ended Athenian military supremacy over Greek world.	1066 Hastings (Britain)	Norman (French) soldiers, led by William the Conqueror, crossed English Channel and defeated Saxon forces, led by Harold II. Norman conquest brought England into realm of Western Europe and created a unified, centralized state.
405 Aegispotamoi (Turkey)	Spartan fleet under Lysander defeated last Athenian fleet, ending Peloponnesian War.	1415 Agincourt (France)	10,000 English under Henry V defeated 30,000 French, and recaptured Normandy. Demonstrated superiority of English longbowmen over French knights.
331 Gaugamela (Persia)	Alexander the Great's supreme victory. He defeated Persian King Darius, and opened up the East to Greek ideas and culture.	1429 Siege of Orléans (France)	English siege of Orléans lifted by French forces. England's hopes of total conquest of France destroyed by Joan of Arc, who revived French unity and courage. Decisive moment of Hundred Years War.
202 Zama (Tunisia)	Roman force under Scipio ended Punic Wars against Carthage with a massive victory over Hannibal. End of 400-year-old Carthaginian empire.	1453 Siege of Constantinople (Turkey)	Ottoman Turks, led by Sultan Mehmed II, besieged and captured Constantinople (Istanbul). Marked end of the Byzantine Empire.
31 Actium (Greece)	Octavian (later Augustus) defeated Mark Antony and Cleopatra at sea, ending decades of civil war. Marked end of Roman Republic and beginning of Imperial Rome.	1521 Siege of Tenochtitlán (Mexico)	Landing with a small force, Spanish explorer Hernán Cortés won allies from enemies of Aztecs, and attacked Aztec capital, Tenochtitlán. Siege ended in total defeat of Aztecs, who had the greatest empire in Americas. Started European colonization.
A.D. 378 Adrianople (Turkey)	Goths (Germanic tribes) inflicted a crippling defeat on Roman army, sending panic throughout Roman Empire. Emperor Valens was killed in the battle, and Roman tactics shown to be outdated.		
636 Yarmuk (Israel)	Arab leader Khalid ibn-al Walid, with 25,000 men, defeated and killed 50,000-strong Byzantine force in a desert sandstorm. Brought Jerusalem under Arab control, and opened the way to Arab expansion in Egypt, North Africa, and Spain.	1571 Lepanto (Greece)	Christian fleet of more than 200 galleys, led by Don John of Austria, defeated Turkish fleet of more than 200 galleys, led by Ali Pasha. More than 30,000 men drowned in one afternoon. Last major naval battle to use oar-powered galleys.
718 Siege of Constantinople (Turkey)	Leo the Isaurian, Emperor of Byzantium, defeated Saracen Arabs using "greek fire," an inflammable substance that ignited on contact with water. Halted Arab advance into Western Europe.	1588 Spanish Armada (Britain)	Spanish fleet of 130 ships, led by Duke of Medina Sidonia, defeated by 97 English ships and by heavy storms. 86 Spanish ships survived. Major blow to Counter-Reformation.

Date / Battle	Description	Date / Battle	Description
1645 Naseby (Britain)	14,000 British Parliamentary troops, under Fairfax, defeated 10,000 Royalist troops under Prince Rupert. Spelled the end of Charles I's power and beginning of Republican rule.	**1876** Little Bighorn (United States)	About 3,000 Sioux and Cheyenne warriors, led by Sitting Bull and Crazy Horse, destroyed part of the 7th US Cavalry, led by Colonel George Custer. The only survivor from Custer's force was a horse.
1704 Blenheim (Germany)	British-Austrian army, under Duke of Marlborough, defeated a French-Bavarian force, under Marshal Tallard. Ended Stuart claims to throne of England, and prevented French domination in Europe.	**1905** Tsushima (West of Japan)	Japanese fleet under Admiral Togo destroyed Russian fleet, under Rozhdestvenski. Decisive battle of Russo-Japanese War.
1709 Poltava (Ukraine)	Russian Czar, Peter the Great, defeated Sweden for control of Baltic Sea. Ended 80 years of Swedish military domination and began Russian empire's expansion.	**1914** The Marne (France)	Strategic victory for French and British Commonwealth forces that halted the German advance. Last mobile battle in the west in World War I. Long trench battles followed.
1757 Plassey (India)	Robert Clive's 3,200-strong British force defeated 50,000-strong Bengali army to install a puppet nawab (king) and to seize power for British East India Company. First step on road to British domination of India.	**1916** The Somme (France)	The Somme was the bloodiest battle of World War I, taking 1,265,000 lives. British Coomonwealth and French forces captured just 125sq miles (320sq km) of ground.
1759 Quebec (Canada)	British general James Wolfe defeated French forces under the Marquis de Montcalm in a night attack on the Plains of Abraham outside Quebec. Gave Britain control of Canada. Both generals died in battle.	**1917** Passchendaele (Belgium)	5-month battle of trench warfare. British Commonwealth forces advanced 5 miles (8km) and lost more than 400,000 men. 57,000 were killed in just a few hours on July 1.
1777 Saratoga (United States)	Decisive American victory in American Revolution. British troops, led by Burgoyne, surrendered to Americans.	**1940** Britain	German air force of 2,500 planes launched attack on Britain. Smaller Royal Air Force defeated them and prevented planned seaborne invasion.
1781 Yorktown (United States)	General Cornwallis, with 8,000 British troops, was hemmed in, and surrendered to a larger American force under George Washington. End of American Revolution.	**1942** Midway (Pacific)	Japanese attempt to capture Midway Island defeated by US Navy. First naval battle in which opposing ships never saw each other. Marked the new dominance of the aircraft carrier.
1805 Trafalgar (South of Spain)	Nelson destroyed French-Spanish fleet south of Cadiz, Spain, and with it Napoleon's plans to invade England.	**1942** El Alamein (Egypt)	Allied forces, led by General Montgomery (British), drove German Afrika Korps, under Erwin Rommel, out of Egypt, deep into Libya. Britain's greatest victory of WW II.
1805 Austerlitz (Czech Republic)	65,000 French troops, led by Napoleon Bonaparte, defeated 83,000 Austrian and Russian forces. Napoleon's greatest victory.	**1942–43** Stalingrad (Russia)	German forces surrendered to Soviet Russians after long siege of Stalingrad (Volgograd). One of the bloodiest battles in history: more than 600,000 Soviet soldiers killed and more than 1 million dead in total.
1815 Waterloo (Belgium)	Napoleon was defeated by combined British, Dutch, Belgian, and Prussian forces. This finally ended Napoleonic Wars.	**1944** Normandy (France) D-Day	Allied forces, led by General Eisenhower (American), invaded German-occupied northern France. Largest-ever seaborne attack: 38 convoys of 745 ships, with more than 4,000 landing craft, 156,000 men, and 300 minesweepers.
1854 Balaclava (Crimea)	British defeat of a Russian attack in the Crimean War. Famous for charge of Lord Cardigan's Light Brigade, which only one-third of his men survived.		
1863 Gettysburg (United States)	Decisive battle of American Civil War. Federal forces under George Meade defeated Confederates under Robert E. Lee. Heavy losses on both sides: approximately 40,000 Union and Confederate troops killed.	**1954** Dien Bien Phu (Vietnam)	Vietnamese defeated French forces, ending French control of Vietnam. Led to establishment of North and South Vietnam: one Communist, the other US-aided.
1870 Sedan (France)	Prussia, led by Moltke, inflicted crushing defeat on France. This ended Second Empire and forced abdication of Emperor Napoleon III.	**1991** Operation Desert Storm (Iraq)	Airborne attack on Iraq by United Nations Coalition forces. Broke Iraqi resistance and led to swift end of Gulf War.

WAR FACTS

• The Geneva Convention of 1949 separates civilians from the military in four major ways: the military wear clothes that show they are soldiers, openly carry weapons, are under the control of a commander, and obey the laws and customs of war.

• Germ warfare's use was first recorded in the 14th century. Tartars, besieging a Crimean city, catapulted plague-infected corpses over the walls, spreading disease among the inhabitants.

• War has killed more than 100 million people in this century, 20 million since 1945.

• In 1905, Russia's Baltic fleet took seven months to reach its enemy, Japan. Japanese Navy destroyed it in 36 hours.

• In World War I, about 19 million died: 95% soldiers, 5% civilians. In World War II, more than 50 million died: 50% soldiers, 50% civilians.

WAR RECORDS

MOST WARLIKE LEADER was Sargon of Akkad (c.2370 B.C.), who waged 34 wars in 55 years.

SHORTEST WAR lasted just 38 minutes, between Britain and Zanzibar (East Africa) in 1896.

REVOLUTIONS AND RIGHTS

FRENCH REVOLUTION

1788 France bankrupt
King Louis XVI, nobles, and Church hold power. Louis summons Estates-General (ancient parliament) to raise extra taxes.

1789 Meeting of Estates-General at Versailles, May 5. Third Estate (middle-class representatives) demands democratic reforms.

National Assembly set up by Third Estate rebels to rule France, June 10. Louis sends troops to Versailles.

Storming of the Bastille (royal fortress and hated symbol of tyranny) by people of Paris, July 14. Revolution spreads around France. Peasants burn chateaus and manors.

Declaration of the Rights of Man adopted by Assembly, August 27.

1790 Nobility abolished.

1791 Royal family flee Paris, but are captured, June.

1792 Revolutionary War begins, as Austria and Prussia attack France. Monarchy abolished; France declared a republic.

1793 Louis XVI executed (Jan 21).

Jacobins (extreme revolutionary group) take power in July.

Reign of Terror, from September 1793 to July 1794. 300,000 people arrested and about 17,000 guillotined.

1795 The Directory (a five-man executive body) takes power.

1799 Napoleon Bonaparte overthrows Directory and takes power.

KEY PEOPLE

Name	Dates	Biographical details
Louis XVI	1754–93	King of France, opposed to reform. Tried for treason and guillotined
Georges Danton	1759–94	Jacobin leader and Minister of Justice. Voted for execution of King but opposed Reign of Terror. Arrested and guillotined
Maximilien Robespierre	1758–94	Lawyer and Jacobin revolutionary. Head of Committee of Public Safety. Key figure in Reign of Terror. Arrested and guillotined
Olympes de Gouges	1748–94	Revolutionary. Wrote *Declaration of the Rights of Women and Citizens*. Arrested and guillotined

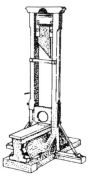

Guillotine of the French Revolution, invented as a humane method of execution.

RUSSIAN REVOLUTION

1917 Petrograd bread riots (March 8). Army joins with workers. Soviets (councils) of soldiers, peasants, and workers set up all over Russia.

Czar abdicates (March 15). Moderate provisional (temporary) government set up. Power struggles begin between government and soviets, and between Mensheviks (moderates) and Bolsheviks (Communists).

Lenin returns to Russia (April). His "April Theses" declare independence of Bolsheviks, and call for revolution.

Bolsheviks take over Petrograd, led by Trotsky (November 7–8).

 **Bolsheviks seize control of Moscow and European Russia.** Lenin passes law giving land to peasants. Creates Cheka (secret police force) to enforce party's decisions. Abolishes ranks in society and army. Nationalizes all factories and banks. Takes schools from Church and gives to state (November–December).

1918 Russia leaves World War I after Treaty of Brest-Litovsk between Russia and Germany, March 3.

Czar and royal family executed, in Yekaterinburg (now Sverdlovsk), July.

KEY PEOPLE

Name	Dates	Biographical details
Nicholas II	1868–1918	Last czar of Russia, overthrown in revolution
Vladimir Illich Lenin	1870–1924	Founder of Bolshevik Party and leader of revolution. Ruled Soviet Union 1917–24
Leon Trotsky	1879–1940	Bolshevik and head of Red Army. Organized revolution with Lenin; murdered by Stalin
Josef Stalin	1879–1953	Succeeded Lenin. Forced intense industrialization and collectivization of land

1918–21 Civil War between Reds (Bolsheviks) and Whites (anti-Bolsheviks) results in Red victory. More than 20 million die.

1918–22 Socialist reforms

1922 Soviet Union established, the world's first Communist state.

AMERICAN REVOLUTION

1773 Parliament passes the Stamp Act, which is protested in the 13 colonies; the tax is repealed in 1776.

"Boston Tea Party" (December): Patriot colonists protest tea tax by dumping tea into Boston Harbor. British troops occupy Boston.

1774 Delegates from the 13 colonies form a Continental Congress to persuade the British government to recognize their rights.

1775 Fighting between Patriot and British forces begins (April) with clashes at Lexington and Concord, Massachusetts.

George Washington appointed commander-in-chief of the Continental Army (May), the main Patriot fighting force.

1776 Continental Congress adopts Declaration of Independence (July 4), written primarily by Thomas Jefferson.

British capture New York City (November), forcing Washington to retreat into Pennsylvania.

1777 After a major Patriot victory at Saratoga, New York, France enters the war on the Patriots' side (October).

KEY PEOPLE

Name	Dates	Biographical details
George Washington	1732–99	Patriot commander. Presided over Constitutional Convention (1787) First president of the United States (1789–97)
John Adams	1735–1826	Massachusetts lawyer. Helped draft Declaration. Second president (1797–1801)
Thomas Jefferson	1743–1826	Virginia plantation owner, lawyer, and diplomat. Third president (1801–09)

1781 British army under Lord Cornwallis surrenders (October 17–19) to Patriot and French forces at Yorktown, Virginia, in the last major battle of the war.

1783 Treaty of Paris negotiated by Benjamin Franklin and John Adams and signed: Britain recognizes the independence of the United States of America.

BLACK RIGHTS

1600–1810 Ten million Africans are taken to the Americas as slaves.

1823–33 Antislavery society set up in Britain to end slavery in colonies.

1909 W.E.B. Du Bois (1889–1963) helps found National Association for the Advancement of Colored People to end racial inequality in the US.

1912 African National Congress (ANC) founded in South Africa to secure racial equality and black representation in parliament.

1914 Marcus Garvey (1887–1940) founds Universal Negro Improvement Association in Harlem, New York.

1925 A. Philip Randolph (1889–1979) organizes and leads the first successful black trade union.

1950–59 Apartheid laws set up in South Africa. These discriminate against blacks and "coloreds."

1954 US Supreme Court rules that segregated education (by color) is "inherently unequal."

1955 Martin Luther King, Jr. (1929–1968) organizes campaign to desegregate bus service in Montgomery, Alabama. This becomes a mass protest across southern US.

1960 Sharpeville Massacre. 69 die and 200 injured in protest against South Africa's racist "Pass Laws."

1964 Nelson Mandela (born 1918), leader of military wing of ANC, jailed for life in South Africa.

1965–68 US Congress outlaws discrimination. Martin Luther King assassinated.

1989 F.W. De Klerk, president of South Africa, lifts ban on ANC and releases Nelson Mandela (1990).

1994 First all-party elections in South Africa. ANC wins 62% of vote; Nelson Mandela becomes president.

ARCHAEOLOGY AND HISTORY

ARCHAEOLOGISTS HELP US understand the past by digging up ancient sites and studying what they find there. In the past, they often looked only for treasure. Today, archaeologists use science to piece together a full picture of an ancient society.

At every stage of an excavation, archaeologists take photographs, make drawings, and write detailed notes on everything they find, and where they find it.

EXCAVATION

When archaeologists discover a site that they wish to investigate, they organize an excavation, or "dig." They work in teams, and each person has a different skill, such as surveying, excavation, drawing, or photography. Most archaeologists today work on "rescue" digs, where construction work, such as city center redevelopment, threatens to disturb or destroy ancient remains.

The site's finds are later processed. This includes recording, labeling, bagging, examining, drawing, conserving, and documenting.

ANALYSIS METHODS

Human skull

Comparisons of skulls can also show where they fit into an evolutionary pattern.

• Looking at bone finds can tell scientists about the diet and health of ancient peoples, as well as their burial customs.

• Analysis of materials such as seeds, pollen, and animal remains builds up a picture of the ancient environment. It can show which crops were grown for food, and how people lived.

• Dendrochronology is the study of tree rings to date wooden objects. In a good year, trees grow more and have larger rings than in a bad year. Rings on the object can be identified with those of other logs that have already been dated.

AD 1344
AD 1338 AD 1338
AD 1329 AD 1329
AD 1322

Tree sections show ring matches.

• Many sites have had different inhabitants at different times. Archaeologists dig a vertical cross-section through the earth of a site. This reveals the "layers" of time, the most recent occurring at the top.

• Radiocarbon dating is a very accurate scientific method of dating. All living things contain some radioactive carbon (C-14). After a living thing dies, this C-14 decays (its atoms break down) at a known rate. If the amount of C-14 in an organic find (wood, antler, etc.) is known, its age can be estimated.

DETECTION METHODS

• Using geophysics, we can show what lies underground without excavating. One technique, called resistivity, uses two electrical probes driven into the ground at different places. The resistance of the ground to the current can indicate underground remains.

• X-rays can reveal details of objects that are too brittle to be handled, or encrusted with rock.

AERIAL PHOTOGRAPHY

Sun at noon

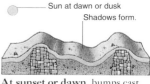

During the daytime, the slight bumps made by buried remains cannot be seen clearly.

Sun at dawn or dusk
Shadows form.

At sunset or dawn, bumps cast shadows easily seen from the air.

Crop growth can be affected by old earthworks or stoneworks, and this can be seen easily from the air.

PHASES OF HISTORY

Phase		Historian	Characteristics
Ancient Near Eastern:		Egyptian/Mesopotamian chroniclers	Recorded and praised the deeds of kings and emperors with little concern for accuracy
Classical:	Greece	Herodotus (c.484–c.425 B.C.)	His histories tell of famous military and political activities
		Thucydides (455–400 B.C.)	Closely examined military events of his time and their political consequences
	Rome	Livy (c.60 B.C.–A.D. 17)	Interested in historical figures and morality. He tried to be unbiased
		Tacitus (c.A.D. 56–120)	Wrote vivid, detailed accounts with some accuracy
Medieval:	Europe	Orosius (c.417)	First Christian historian. Promoted Christian world view over Paganism
		Bede (c.672–735)	"The Father of English History," who carefully researched the reliability of his sources
		Villehardouin (c.1150–c.1213)	His histories included eyewitness accounts of military activity
		Froissart (c.1333–1401)	His closely researched accounts emphasized the lives and battles of knights
	Muslim World	Al-Tabari (c.923)	Produced a religious history of the conflicts and customs of Muslims
		Ibn Khaldun (1332–1406)	Wrote political, economic, and social history
Renaissance:		Biondo (1392–1463)	Used many accurate sources in his chronological history of Italy
		Guicciardini (1483–1540)	Described historical events in a clear and methodical manner
Enlightenment:	18th Century	Gibbon (1737–94)	His writings examined the movement and patterns of historical events
	19th Century	Ranke (1795–1886)	Attempted to understand the past through scientific research methods
	20th Century	Febvre (1878–1956) Braudel (1902–85)	They broadened the subject matter by emphasizing social and economic matters, as well as describing military, political, and geographical affairs

INDEX AND CREDITS

INDEX

Page numbers in **bold** type refer to main entries

O

PICTURE SOURCES

The publisher would like to thank the following for their kind permission to reproduce the photographs:

ABBREVIATIONS

t-top	cra-center right above	c-center
b-bottom	cl-center left	ca-center above
l-left	cr-center right	cb-center below
r-right	clb-center left below	bc-bottom center
tl-top left	crb-center right below	tc-top center
tr-top right	bl-bottom left	
cla-center left above	br-bottom right	

A

© Aardman Animations 186c. **Action Plus** 199clb/Chris Barry 213c; R.Francis 197cb, 199bl; Tony Henshaw 193c, 199c, 215cr; Mike Hewitt 212br; Glyn Kirk 212crb, 215tc; Robert Lewis 190br. **Lorna Ainger** 162b, 178tc. **AKG, London** 132cb, 133crb, 144cb, 145c, 172bl, 188tr, l, 242crb. **Allsport**/David Klutho 201bc. **Alton Telegraph Photo**/Robert Graul 129car. **Ampex** 187bl. **Ancient Art and Architecture Collection** 32cl, 135bc, 142cr, 166tl, cal, 382cl, 384tl, 385cl/Ronald Sheridan 373br. **Animals Unlimited** 105cl. **Directed and Produced by Animation City/AC Live** 184bc. **Archiv fur Kunst und Geschicte, Berlin** 182tc, 184tr, 380c, 381c, bl, 390bl. **Ardea**/Liz Bomford 97tc. **Art Directors/Carl Young** 152c. **Aviation Photographers International** 265cb.

B

B&U International Picture Service 279c. **BFI Stills, Posters & Designs** 164cra, 186tr. **Barnaby's Picture Library**/Georg Sturm 142c. **Michael Barrett Levy** 182bl, 187cr. **Norman Barratt** 190. **Basketball Hall of Fame, Springfield, Massachusetts** 190crb. © **Bayreuther Festspiele GmbH**/Wilhelm Rauh 314bc. **Bibliotheque de L'Assemblée Nationale,Paris** 190cra. **Biofotos**/Heather Angel 92crb. © **1993 Boeing Commercial Airplane Group** 265br. **Bridgeman Art Library**/ Bodleian Library, Oxford 386tl; British Museum, London 160cr; Christie's, London 162cr; City of Bristol Museum & Art Gallery 393cr; British Library, London 350ca, 392bl; Department of the Environment, London 385tc; Egyptian National Museum, Cairo 374ca; Fervers Gallery, London 169cr; Giraudon 69cr, 161cl; Greater London Council 132cl; Hermitage, St.Petersburg 160cl; Historiches Museum Der Stadt,Vienna 169cr; Institute of Directors, London 397c; Sir Godfrey Kneller 145cra; Louvre, Paris 374bc; Musée de L'Armée, Paris/Giraudon 395c; Museum of Mankind 138tc; Nationalgalerie, Berlin, Hornform, 1924, Wassily Kandinsky © ADAGP, Paris & DACS, London 1995, 161cb; Prado, Madrid 390cl; Private Collection 133clb, 190ca, 390tl, 397tl; Salvator Rosa 145tl; Royal College of Physicians, London 133cra; Tretyakov Gallery, Moscow 324c; Trinity College, Dublin 310br; by courtesy of the Board of Trustees of the V&A, London 391cl, 169c. **British Library** 141cra. **British Red Cross** 132crb. **Brothers Quay** 186cl. **Bureau International des Poids et Mesure Sevres** 240clb.

C

Camera Press/Curtis/RBO 409bcl; Karsh of Ottawa 409bl; Herbie Knott 410c; Ian Stone 409br; Eli Weinberg 408tl. **California Institute of Technology** 44bl. **J.Allan Cash Ltd.** 140bc, 340br, 342cl, 348cb, 379bl, 390br. **Casio Electronics Co.Ltd.** 182cb, bc. **Jean-Loup Charmet** 166cbr, 173br, 239br. **Lester Cheeseman** 143cl. **Chicago Historical Institute** 157cl. **Christies Colour Library** 47br. **Bruce Coleman Ltd.**/Fred Bruemmer 291cr; Jane Burton 86cr, 93cbr; Alain Compost 95cb; Gerald Cubitt 336cl, 354bl; Peter Davey 101cb; Andrew Davies 272bl; Jack Dermid 93crb; Keith Gunnar 43ct; David C.Houston 288clb; Stephen J.Krasemann 63crb, 106bl; S.Nielsen 23cr; Dieter & Mary Plage 335cr; Dr. Eckart Pott 108bc, 101bc, 291tr; Andy Price 354bl, Jens Rydell 235c; John Shaw 50clb; Austin James Steven 93tr, 95tl; Kim Taylor 95tr, 236crb; Barrie Wilkins 106c; Gunter Ziesler 112cl; Christian Zuber 329c. **Colorsport** 194bc, 196cr, 197c, cr, 199bc, 200cl, 210bl, bc, 213cr, 214c, cr, 215bl/ © duomo-David Madison 191cra, William R.Sallaz 214cl/Olympia, Roberto Bettini 217cb/Sipa Sport, Pascal Huit 216cb, Lacombe 217c, R.Martin 215bc. **Comstock** 379br, 381tr. **Michael Copsey** 46cb, 53cr & cra, 56cla, cl, 75tl, 138cr, 141tl, 242c, 326br, 344cl, 352c.

D

Daihatsu 253cr. **James Davis Travel Photography** 142bl, 143cr, 171bl, 303ca, 350bc. **Dessau**/Peter Kuhn 156cb. © **The Walt Disney Company** 186tl, cl, cb. **C.M.Dixon** 161tc, tr, 373cra, 377tc, 378bc. Courtesy **Anthony d'Offray Gallery, London** 161bl. **Dominic Photography**/Catherine Ashmore 174c. **Dr. Peter Dorrell** 373tl. **Dulciana**/J.D.Sharp 184cl.

E

E.T.Archive 139cb, 169tr, 374br, 377cl, 395bc, 398br, 401bl, 402tl/Biblioteca Marciana, Venice 190cla; Metropolitan Museum of Art 176br; Plymouth City Art Gallery 176bc. **Mary Evans Picture Library** 18cla, 18cra, 32tr, tl, cla, c, cra & clb, 68cr, 69cl, 71tr, cla, 132cra, 133tr, 140cra, 143tr, bl, 144cr, cra, crb, 145ca, cra, 152tc, cr, 167cl, cr, 169cla, 176cb, 178ca, cl, clb, 190c, cr, 239cr, cb, 247tr, cra, cl, clb, 248tc, 249tl, cr, cb, 264ca, 265cra, cl, cr, 357crb, 380cl, 386c, 388tc, 389br, 393cl, 394cra, 396clb, c, 397ca, 398bl, 399tr, cr, 402tr, 415cr, 416, 417tl, cl, c, Elenore Plaisted Abbott 178cr; Carrey, Le Petit Parisien 264cra; A.W.Diggelmann in La Conquete du Ciel 264cr; Explorer 133cla, 169ca; G.W.Lambert 419c; Alexander Meledin Collection 402bl, 420br; J.K.Stieler 395crb; Steve Rumney 169cl; N.C.Wyeth 138tr.

F

Werner Forman Archive/Anthropology Museum, Veracruz University, Jalapa 377tl; British Museum, London 190tr; J.Paul Getty Museum, Malibu, USA 190cal; Private Collection, Prague 354cl; Tanzania National Museum, Dar es Salaam 169tc. **Fotomas Index** 395bl. **John Frost Historical Newspaper Service** 188cla, cl, c, cb. **Fuji** 164bc.

G

Genesis 34bl. **Geoscience Features** 51clb. **courtesy of Andy Goldsworthy** 161bc. **Ronald Grant Archive** 169crb, 184ca, clb, 185bl. **Greenpeace**/Gleizes 153tc; Morgan 357bl.

H

Sonia Halliday Photographs 135tc, 157ca, 160tc, 188tc, 381tl, l, Laura Lushington 381bc; James Wellard 331tr. **Robert Harding Picture Library** 42cl, 71tl, 171cr, 290bl, 309br, 330tr, 331bl, 340tc, crb, 345tr, 366bc, 371tl, 374, cra, cb, crb, 377clb, 385bl, 392tr, Mohamed Amin 31bc; Bildagentur Schuster/Kim Hart 309bl/Layda 348cra; C.Bowman 293bl; Cordier/Explorer 336bc; K.Gillham 317cr; Ian Griffiths 334c; Kosel 51cl; J.Desmarteau 394tc; FPG International 398clb, 400bl; Robert Francis 46c; Robert Frerck/Odyssey/Chicago 278bc; David Hughes 157cla; F.Jackson 342cr, 343bl; Krafft 43tc; Robert McLeod 62bl, 410br; Geoff Renner 55bl; Christopher Rennie 383bl; Rolf Richardson 320cl, 379bc; Paul van Riel 411cl; Sackim 315cr; Andy Williams 279tl; JHC Wilson 184cra; Adam Woolfitt 319br, 342cla; Earl Young 152tr, 293tc. **The Hindu Newspaper** 188clb. **Michael Holford** 89clb, 154tl, 160tl, 374cr, 375c, cra, 376clb, cb, cl, cbr, crb, 377bl, 380cb, 394cl, 378cr. **Rebecca Hossack Gallery** 146tr. **Hulton-Deutsch Collection** 18ca, 34tr, 45c, 132br, 144clb, 145clb, 151c, 153c, 156crb, 160crb, bl, 165c, 166bar, 169bl, 170clb, crb, 174cra, cr, 176bl, 178br, bc, 181c, tr, tl, ca, 182tl, 188cr, 190c, bl, 193crb, 194crb, 245cla, 261bl, 264cl, c, clb, crb, 396tl, 398cra, 400crb, 401br, 406tc, cl, br, 407tr, 408tc, 417tr, bc, 422crb/ Bettmann Archive 182cra; Terry Fincher 407tl. **Robert Hunt Library** 404tc. **Henry E.Huntington Library & Art Gallery** 18clb. **Hutchison Library** 171c, 337br/H.R.Dorig 377cla; Sarah Errington 148ca, 363tl; Melanie Friend 141bl; Julia Highet 171cra; Michael McIntyre 139cr, 146cb, 171lc, 347c; Christine Pemberton 141tr; Pern 146bc; Bernard Regent 143tl; John Ryle 148cl; Liba Taylor 142cra; Anna Tully 171tl.

I

The Image Bank/Charles S.Allen 272cl; Alan Becker 314c; A.Boccaccio 274tl; Lionel F.Brown 236cr; Gary Cralle 53crb; Fotoworld 308bc; Chris Hackett 294cr; G.Heisler 276tr; Lionel Isy-Schwart 171t, 354cra; Ronald Johnson 272clb; Tadao Kimura 379cra;Kim Keitt/Stockphotos,Inc. 169bc; Romilly Lockyer 310bl; Michael Melford 109clb; Arthur Meyerson 363tr; Alfred Pasieka 268tr; Co.Rentmeester 274cla; Guido Alberto Rossi 53br, 320br, 346cr, 363crb; Steve Satushek 321c; Michael Skott 367bl; Harold Sund 293tl, 324ca; A.T.Willett 245br; Trevor Wood 43cl. **Image Select** 129tr, 132clb, 172bc, br, bl, 178cb, crb, 392cl. © **Imax Corporation** 184br. **Impact Photos**/Steve Benbow 297tc; John Cole 293bc. A.J.Deane 319clb; Paul Forster 354cl; Alan Keohane 147bc; Peter Menzel 149tc; Tony Page

156cra. **Institut Pasteur** 133cl. **International Coffee Organization** 301tr. **By courtesy of the Israel Antiquities Authority** 371br.

JKL

Japan Archive 169cra. **Robert Jones** 355bl. **A.F.Kersting** 378cra. **Keymed Ltd.**127tc, clb. **David King Collection** 144crb, 152bc, 166bal. **Kobal Collection** 31cr, 184cla, bl, 236c. **Konica** 164c. **Frank Lane Picture Agency** 79cl/ Silvestris 62clb, 63br, 87tc; T&P Gardner 109bl; R.Wilmshurst 106cr. **Leica** 164cl. **Eleni Leoussi** 169br. **Mike Linley** 93clb.

M

Magnum Photos Ltd. 165cb, 334tr/ Abbas 342c, 365tl; Collection Astier 401crb; Bruno Barbey 143br; Ian Berry 18crb; Cagnoni 408bc; Bruce Davidson 409tl; Stuart Franklin 365clb; Ernst Haas 364bl; Philippe Halsman 169cb; David Hurn 148cr, 365br; S.Meiselas 152tl; Wayne Miller 403tl; Michael K.Nichols 364bc; Pinkhassov 411tc; Raghu Rai 365cl; Marc Riboud 409c; David Scherman 165cr; Nicolas Tikhomiroff 407c. **Mander & Mitcheson** 166c, cr, bl, 168cl, 169clb, 170cla, c. © **Moroccan Embassy**/Philippe Ploquin 330ca.

N

NASA 21tr, 27bl, 29cr, 34cra, c, cr, cb, 35c, cr, br, 36cb, br, 45br, 60br, 182c, cr, 245bl, 275c, 408br, 411cr/ JPL 35ca, cra. **NHPA**/Stephen Dalton 95clb; Manfred Danegger 101br; Douglas Dickens 109 c, cb; George Gainsburgh 75cla; Peter Parks 87tl; John Shaw 79tr; Martin Wendler 95tc, 109tl, cl. **Edmund Nagele, FRPS** 296cra. **National Film Board of Canada** 186cla. **National Maritime Museum** 390tc. **National Motor Museum, Beaulieu** 253tl, cla, cl.ca, c, cr, br, 255. **Nationwide Building Society** 274cl. **Natural History Museum Publications** 105clb. **Nature Photographers Ltd.**/ J.F.Reynolds 101crb. **Network Photographers**/Roger Hutchings 322bc. © **Nobel Foundation**/Svensk Reportaget Janst 309c. **Northern Ireland Tourist Board** 46cla. **Novosti** 34tl, 35tl, 323ca, 383cr.

OP

The Open University 32bc. **Oxford Scientific Films**/Animals,Animals/ Raymond A.Mendex 95ca/ Breck P.Kent 85c; Fred Bavendam 87tr & cra; G.I.Bernard 91cl; Fredrik Ehrenstrom 85br; Michael

Fogden 92ca, cra; Rudie Kuiter 97tl; London Scientific Films 85cla; Root Okapia 102crb; Kjell Sandved 86cra. **Panos Pictures**/Rob Cousins 367cl; Jean-Leo Dugast 346cl; Ron Giling 367tr; Trevor Page 367tl; Nick Robinson 366cr; Liba Taylor 337tc; Penny Tweedie 146bl. **Ann & Bury Peerless** 139cl, bl, br, 140tr, 141cr, 142tr, tc. **Chris Pellant** 46bc. **Planet Earth Pictures**/Peter David 97bl; Robert Hessler 43tl; A.Kerstitch 87cla; Ken Lucas 97ca, cal; Paulo de Oliveira 97tcr. **Philips** 187ca. **Photostage**/Donald Cooper 166cbl, br, 174crb, br. **Pictor International** 340cra, 345c, 346tc/Leo Aarons 376cr. **Pictorial Press Ltd.** 409tc. **Richard Platt** 368tc. **Polish Cultural Institute** 318cra. **Popperfoto** 190cl, 247bl, 298cr, 401ca, cb, cra, 402bc, 404c, 405tl, tc, tr, crb, 407crb, 409cl, bc, bcr, 411cb, br. **The Post Office** 268bl. **Press Association** 152cb. **Q&A Pictures** 280c.

R

Range 145crb, 160br/Bettmann 132bc, 133cr, 159bl, 244ca, tr, 248clb, 253tc, 255crb, 265bc/Bettmann/ UPI 165crb, 188crb, 245cra, 246bc. **Redferns**/David Redfern 173bc. **Retna Pictures Ltd.**/Adrian Boot 299ca. **Reuters**/Visnews Library 365cr. **Rex Features Ltd.** 152ca, 265cb, crb, 273cb, 409tr, 411bl/Collection Privee/Sipa 292c, 404tr; D.Turner Givens 350cr; Dave Hogan 305bl; Peter Lomas 120bl; Mark Sherman 368bc; Sipa Press 292c, 403bl, 409cr, 410tl, tctr, cr/Cheryl Hatch 410cb/F.Mitri 410cl/Robert 411clb/ Setboun 410crb; Ian Waldie 149br; Markus Zeffler 153cl. **Michael Roaf** 156ca. **Roger-Viollet** 245tc. **Ann Ronan at Image Select** 32tc, 115cl, cr, 132tl, cla, ca, cr, c, 133tc, 135clb, 144tc, c, cla, cl, 145cla, tr, 164bc, 172bcl, 173bcl, 224cra, 242br, 243clb, 244tc, cla, 248tr, c, 249tc, 259crb, 396cr, 418bl/ WHO Jean Mohr 132bl **Royal Britannic Gardens, Kew** 77br.

S

© **Fotograf H.J.Schuffenhauer** 314cl. **The Science Museum/Science and Society Picture Library** 239bc. **Science Photo Library** 123cla, 128crb, 249c/Bill van Aken/CSIRO 65cr; Argonne National Laboratory 248bc; Alex Bartel 245cr; Biofoto Associates 117tc; Martin Bond 65bc, 272crb, 273cl; Dr. Goran Bredberg 119c; Dr. Jeremy Burgess 120crb, 248ca; CNRI 83crb, 115ca, cra,cb,120br,127cb, br, 237cr/ Prof.C.Ferlaud 121 / Secchi, Lecaque, Roussel, Uclaf 115cr; Jean-Loup Charmet 32ca; Martin Dohrn 366tr; Ralph Eagle 118cl;

Prof. Harold Edgerton 164cr; Fred Espenak 24tr; Simon Fraser 272c; Stevie Grand 227cra; Hale Observatories 24crb; Adam Hart-Davis 118bl; Anthony Howarth 247br, 64br; Dr. William Hsin-Min Ku 19cb; Manfred Kage 123tl; John Mead 272ca; Astrid & Hans-Frieder Michler 115tr, 129cl; Laurence Migdale 366cra; Hank Morgan 128bc; Prof. P. Motta,Dept. of Anatomy, University "La Sapienza," Rome 122tc; NASA 34crb, 35cla, cl, crb, 36cr, 51cr; NIBSC 125cl; National Library of Medicine 117bc; Novosti Press Agency 31crb, 34cl, 35tc, tr; Omikron 121 ; David Parker 45bl; Pekka Parviainen 30br; Alfred Pasieka 126clb; Petit Format/CSI 84crb; Petit Format,Institut Pasteur,Charles Dauguet 125br; Phillipe Plailly 225bl; Chris Priest & Mark Clarke 125cb; J.C.Revy 133bl; Royal Observatory, Edinburgh 30ca; Gregory Sams 238br, 249br; John Sanford 31cl; Tom van Sant/ Geosphere Project, Santa Monica 368br; Francoise Sauze 135cr; Dr. Klaus Schiller 121, 127cl; Science Source 123cl; Sinclair Stammers 85cl, crb; James Stevenson 126cb, 131cr; Prof. Yoshiaki Sofoe 19clb; Andrew Syred 85bc; Gianni Tortoli 227tr; Alexander Tsiaras 240cl; U.S. Dept. of Energy 272br; Dr. E.Walker 128cb; M.I.Walker 247ca; John Walsh 84cb, 115c SPL/ 186br/ Scala/Biblioteca Nazionale, Firenze 389bl. **Mark Shearman** 195cr. **Harry Smith**/Polunin Collection 75c. **Sony UK Ltd.** 187tl, c, bc. **Sotheby's** 242bl. **South American Pictures**/Marion Morrison 302br; Tony Morrison 303cb, crb **Frank SpoonerPictures**/Gamma/ Novosti 324tr/Daniel Simon 368bl. **Sporting Pictures(UK)Ltd.**183tl, 191c, 192br, 193cl, 195crb, 201bl, 208cl, bl, 211cr, 213br, bl, 217br. **Stadelsches Kunstinstitut, Frankfurt a.m.**/Ursula Edelmann, Frankfurt a.m. 160cb. **Starland Picture Library**/AT&T Bell Laboratories 32bl. **Dr. F.Richard Stephenson** 22bl. **Still Pictures** 332tr/ Andy Crump 355tr; Mark Edwards 147cb, 305cr; Julio Etchart/ Reportage 300cr; John Maier 368tr. **Tony Stone Images** 296bl, 296cr, 297cl/Doug Armand 299cb; Oliver Benn 315cl; 382cla; Jon Bradley 157c; Julian Calder 312c; John Callahan 349br; Tony Craddock 51cr, 312bl; John Edwards 290tr; David H.Endersbee 278bl; Robert Everts 309tr; Robert Frerck 311cl; Jon Gray 56tl; Michael Harris 141c; David Hiser 291bl; John Lamb315cra; Ian Murphy171tc; Hugh Sitton 338cb; Nabeel Turner 139tl, 140bl, 341c. **Sygma** 114cb/David Gomle 146clb; Bill Nation 147tc.

Syndication International/Macdonald, Aldus Archive 182clb,390bc.

T

Telegraph Colour Library 365bl/ Colorific!/Jaakko Avikainen 324bl; John de Visser/Black Star 324tl. **Telesat, Canada** 182cl. **Time UK** 243bl. **Toyota** 253clb. **TRH Pictures/** DOD 262c; U.S.A.F. 266br.

UWZ

UPI, Bettmann 18cb, 32cb & crb. **Vireo**/Academy of Natural Sciences, Philadelphia 99tr. **Wedgwood** 276cr. **Straker Welds** 181bl. **Wellcome Institute Library, London** 133cra. **West Africa** 166bc. **Wiedenfeld & Nicolson Archives**/British Museum 393tl. **Rodney Wilson** 156c, clb, 318c, 372r. © **The Wimbledon Lawn Tennis Museum** 190cb.**ZEFA** 135cb, 147br, 148tr, 151tl, cl, 271cb, 275cra, 357cb/ Damm 171cl; W.F.Davidson 278tc; J.Distler 302 cra; A.Edgeworth 146br; Goebel 305cra; Hackenberg 157cb; Harlicek 331cl; K.Lehnartz 147c; G.Mebbs 243crb; Resea 150br; S.Velberg 149tr. **ZEON** 181bc. **Zoological Society of London** 95c. **Sam Zwemmer** 340bc.

Other photography by Max Alexander; Sue Barnes; Geoff Brightling; Peter Chadwick; Andy Crawford; Geoff Dann; Richard Davies (Oxford Scientific Film); Philip Dowell © pp 80, 81, 83, 96, 321, 372; Mike Dunning; Neil Fletcher; Jo Foord; Philip Gatward; Frank Greenaway; Steve Gorton; Peter Hayman; Stephen Hayward; John Heseltine; Chas Howson; Colin Keates; Dave King; Bob Langrish; C. Laubscher; Mike Linley; Andrew McRobb; E.Meacher; Stephen Oliver; Roger Phillips; Martin Phomer; Steve Ridley; Tim Ridley; Kim Sayer; Karl Shone; James Stephenson; Harry Taylor; Kim Taylor; Andreas Von Einsiedel; Matthew Ward; Jerry Young © pp84, 89, 91, 93, 94, 95, 104, 106

With thanks to: British Museum, British Library, Museum of London, Natural History Museum, National Maritime Museum, Naturmuseum, Senkenberg Frankfurt, Beaulieu National Motor Museum, National Maritime Museum, National Gallery, Science Museum,

ILLUSTRATORS

ACKNOWLEDGMENTS

Additional editorial and research assistance
Laaren Brown, Céline Carez, Carolyn Clark, Kitty Hauser, Connie Mersel, Ray Rogers, Francesca Stich, Kirstin Ward

Additional design assistance
Duncan Brown, Diane Clouting, Sharon Grant, Chetan Joshi, Jill Planck

Indexer Hilary Bird

Proofreader Jill Somerscales

In addition, Dorling Kindersley would like to thank the following people and organizations for their assistance in the production of this book:

All embassies, consulates, and high commissions for supplying information; Alpine Club Library; American Society of Plastic and Reconstructive Surgeons; Amstrad; Anglo-American Corporation; Dr. Louis Arrington, University of Wisconsin; *Automotive News*; Baha'i Faith National Centre; BBC Engineering Department; BBC Radio; BBC TV; Bernafron UK Ltd; Julee Binder; Ian Blatchford; Blockbuster Entertainment; Craig Bohnert, US Canoe and Kayak Team; British Film Institute; British Geological Survey; British Humanities Library; British Library Environmental Information Service; British Meteorological Office; British Olympic Association; British Olympic Federation; British Paralympic Association; British Science Library; British Telecom; British Trust for Ornithology; Broadcasters' Audience Research Board Ltd; Buddhist Society; Carluccio's; Centre for Global Energy Studies; Dr. Gerry Cherry, University of Georgia; Christie's International Fine Art Auctioneers; Church of Scientology; Charles B. Clayman, MD; Confederation of European Paper Industries; Rev. Heather Cook; Cousins' Properties; Mick Czaky, Antelope Films; Camela Decaire; Far East Trading Service Inc; First Interstate World Center; Food and Agriculture Organization; Stephanie Giordano; Kim H. Gottshall; Great British

China Centre; Greenpeace; Gordon C. Hamilton; Linda Hoyt, Maguire Thomas Partners; Independent Television Library; Institute for African Alternatives; International Coffee Organisation; International Olympic Committee; John Oliver Jones; Jefferey Kaufman; Kenya Wildlife Service; Julie Kusminska, London Video Access; Language of Dance Centre; Bernard Lavery; Sharon Ralls Lemon; London Contemporary Dance Theatre; Mary Anne Lynch; Mac Warehouse; Magnetic Trading Company; Margarita Publications Ltd; Sir Robert Menzies Centre for Australian Studies; Ministry of Agriculture, Fisheries and Food; *Motor Trend* Magazine; MTV International; Museum of Mankind; National Agricultural Centre; National Earthquake Information Center, US Geological Survey; National Motor Museum, Beaulieu; National Society's Religious Education Centre; Natural History Museum; OPEC; Overseas Development Administration; OXFAM; Oxford Museum of the History of Science; Philips Corporation; Pilkington Research Laboratories; Population Concern, Fiona Barr; Refugee Council; Jill Rutter; Andy Roor, US Department of Agriculture; Royal Air Force Museum; Royal Botanic Gardens, Kew; Royal Institute of the Blind; Royal National Institute for the Deaf; Ann Rumsey, New York Botanical Garden; Scout Association; *Screen Digest*; Dr. Kanwaljit Singh; Smithsonian Institution; Sony; STC Submarine Systems Ltd; Survival International, London; Swiss Bank Corporation, Leslie Prescott;

Tea Board of India; Theatre Museum; UNESCO; UNICEF, Anne Luzeekyi; United Airlines; United Nations; US National Archery Association; US Olympic Shooring Association; Virtual Vision; Voluntary Services Overseas, Tom Crick; Wales Green Party; Professor David A. Warrell, John Radcliffe Hospital, Oxford University; Water Aid; Chuck Weiss, American Canoe Association; Wellcome Foundation Ltd; Dr. Andrew Wilkins, MRC, The Gambia; Andrew Wilson, Department of Anthropology Oxford University; Woodlands Heritage Museum; World Bank; World Conservation Monitoring Centre; World Health Organization

Logos and Insignias
The Major League Baseball Club insignias depicted in this book are reproduced with the permission of Major League Baseball Properties and are the exclusive property of the respective Major League Clubs and may not be reproduced without their written consent.

The helmet logos on page 205 are registered trademarks of the Teams indicated.

The Silver Fern Device and the New Zealand Rugby Union logo on page 203 are trademarked and owned by the New Zealand Rugby Football Union and used with their permission.

Model of dinosaur page 70, Roby Braun